UNITED NATIONS CONFERENCE ON TRADE AND DEVELOPMENT
CONFERENCE DES NATIONS UNIES SUR LE COMMERCE ET LE DÉVELOPPEMENT

CNUCED

UNCTAD

UNCTAD
HANDBOOK
OF STATISTICS

MANUEL
DE STATISTIQUES
DE LA CNUCED

2012

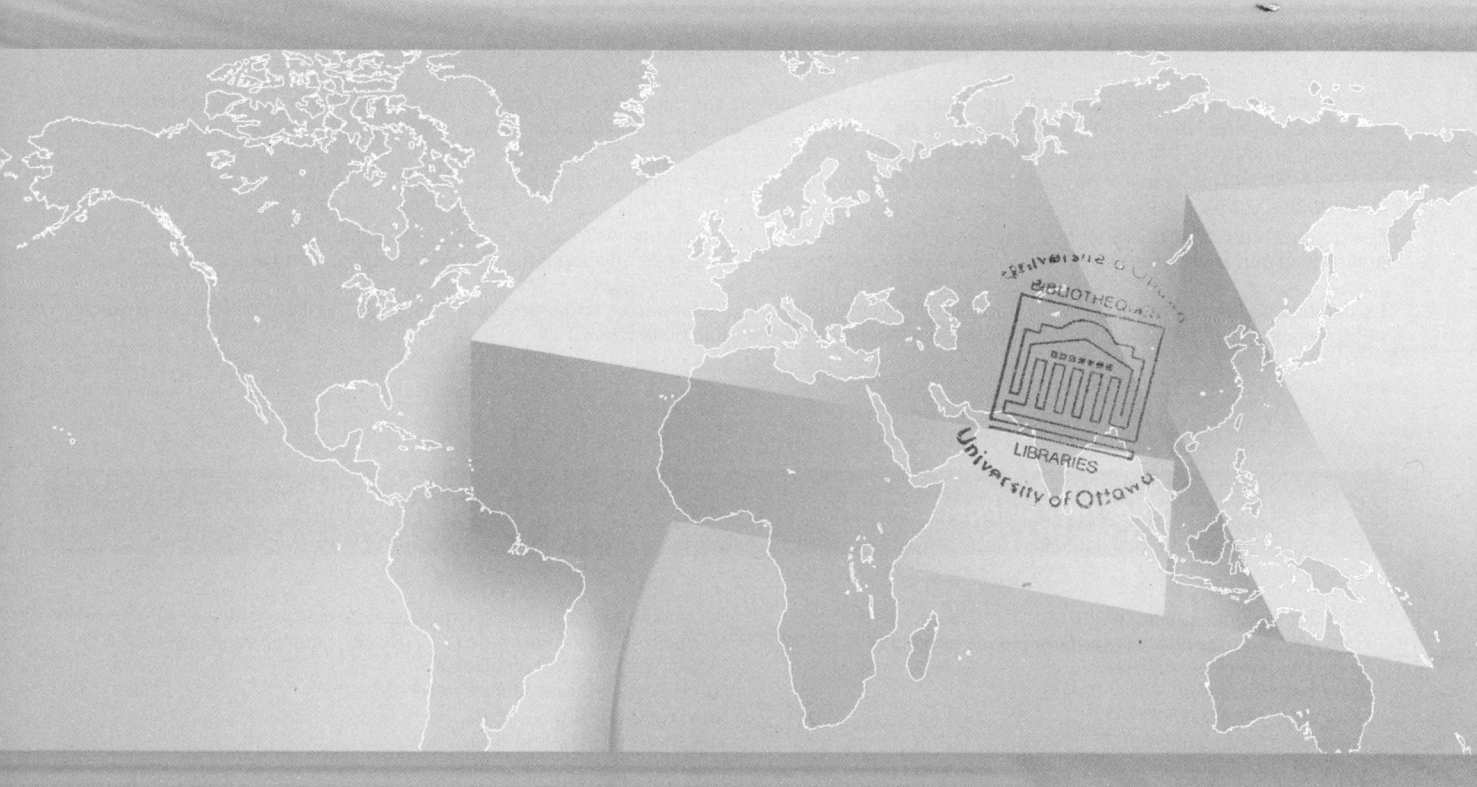

UNITED NATIONS
New York and Geneva

2012

NATIONS UNIES
New York et Genève

How to order the *Handbook*   Comment commander le *Manuel*

To order the print version of the
UNCTAD Handbook of Statistics, please contact:
United Nations Publications
300 East 42nd Street, Room IN-919
New York, NY 10017, USA
Telephone: 1-212-963-8302
Toll free: 1-800-253-9646
Fax: 1-212-963-3489
Internet: https://unp.un.org

Pour commander la version imprimée du
Manuel de Statistiques de la CNUCED, veuillez vous adresser à :
Publications des Nations Unies
300 East 42nd Street, Bureau IN-919
New York, NY 10017, USA
Téléphone : 1-212-963-8302
Numéro vert : 1-800-253-9646
Fax : 1-212-963-3489
Internet : https://unp.un.org

TD/STAT. 37
UNITED NATIONS PUBLICATION – PUBLICATION DES NATIONS UNIES

Sales number / Numéro de vente : B.12.II.D.1
ISBN 978-92-1-112836-9
e-ISBN 978-92-1-055688-0
ISSN 0251-9461

© Copyright United Nations 2012
All rights reserved

ii

The *UNCTAD Handbook of Statistics* provides essential data for analysing and measuring world trade, investment, international financial flows and development. Reliable statistical information is often considered as the first step during the preparation of making recommendations or taking decisions that countries will commit for many years as they strive to integrate into the world economy and improve the living standards of their citizens. Whether it is for research, consultation or technical cooperation, UNCTAD requires comparable, often detailed economic, demographic and social data, over several decades and for as many countries as possible.

In addition to facilitating the work of the secretariat's economists, the *UNCTAD Handbook of Statistics* also enables other users, such as policymakers, research specialists, academics, officials from national governments or international organizations, executive managers or members of non-governmental organizations (NGOs) from developing, transition or developed countries to have access to this rich statistical information. The *Handbook* further offers journalists comprehensive information in a presentation that meets their needs.

This publication is available in printed copy and DVD. Moreover, the underlying data of the *Handbook* are available online at *UNCTADstat* (http://unctadstat.unctad.org). Unlike the *Handbook*, which captures statistics at one point of time, *UNCTADstat* is continuously updated, enriched and providing users with the latest available data. In this regard, users should use caution when comparing data between the *Handbook* and *UNCTADstat,* as the date of update may differ.

In this edition of the *Handbook*, the presentation of data for trade in services by service category has changed. Table 5.2 now includes statistics for selected country groups, in addition to those on main exporters and importers among individual economies, by service category.

To provide better and more relevant statistics to users, you are invited to fill up the feedback questionnaire on the last page or you can send your comments directly to **statistics@unctad.org**.

Le but du *Manuel de statistiques de la CNUCED* est de fournir les données statistiques essentielles à l'analyse du commerce mondial, de l'investissement, des flux financiers internationaux et du développement. Une information statistique fiable est souvent le préalable à la formulation de recommandations et à la prise de décisions qui engageront les pays pour de longues années dans leur processus d'intégration dans l'économie mondiale et l'amélioration des conditions de leurs peuples. Que ce soit pour la recherche, la concertation ou la coopération technique, la CNUCED a besoin de données économiques, démographiques et sociales comparables et souvent détaillées, disponibles si possible sur plusieurs décennies et pour un maximum de pays.

Au-delà de la mobilisation et de la vérification des données, du calcul d'indicateurs dérivés qui alimentent les travaux des économistes du secrétariat, le *Manuel de statistiques de la CNUCED* est l'occasion de partager une base statistique riche avec les décideurs et les chercheurs, qu'ils soient universitaires, fonctionnaires d'administrations nationales ou d'organisations internationales, cadres d'entreprises ou membres d'organisations non gouvernementales de pays en développement, en transition ou développés. Les journalistes trouvent aussi dans ce manuel une information synthétique dans une présentation bien adaptée à leurs préoccupations.

Le *Manuel* est disponible en version imprimée et DVD. Les données présentées dans le *Manuel* sont disponibles en ligne, dans *UNCTADstat* (http://unctadstat.unctad.org). À la différence du *Manuel* qui présente des statistiques figées à un moment donné, *UNCTADstat* est actualisé et enrichi régulièrement pour mettre à la disposition des utilisateurs les données les plus récentes. À cet égard, il est important de signaler que les données d'*UNCTADstat* et du *Manuel* ne pourront être comparées systématiquement en raison de la différence de date de leur mise à jour et de publication.

Dans cette édition du *Manuel*, la présentation des données sur le commerce des services par catégories de services à été modifiée. Désormais, le tableau 5.2 comprend les statistiques d'une sélection de groupements de pays en plus des données des principales économies exportatrices et importatrices pour chacune des catégories de services.

Pour mieux nous adapter aux besoins de nos utilisateurs et mettre à leur disposition des statistiques pertinentes, nous vous invitons à remplir le questionnaire qui se trouve en fin de publication. Vous pouvez également nous faire part de vos commentaires en nous écrivant à **statistics@unctad.org**.

TABLE OF CONTENTS	TABLE DES MATIÈRES

Note ii	Note ii
How to order the *Handbook* ii	Comment commander le *manuel* ii
Foreword iii	Introduction iii
Table of contents.. iv	Table des matières.. iv
Explanation of symbols vii	Signification des symboles vii
General notes viii	Notes générales xxii
Distribution of countries and territories..................... xi	Répartition des pays et territoires............................. xxv
Distribution by geographical region	Répartition par régions géographiques
- Developing economies.. xii	- Économies en développement xxvi
- Transition economies xiv	- Économies en transition xxviii
- Developed economies... xiv	- Économies développées xxviii
Distribution of developing economies by economic grouping xv	Répartition des économies en développement par groupements économiques xxix
Distribution of economies by trade group xviii	Répartition des économies par groupements commerciaux xxxii
Distribution of economies by interregional grouping xx	Répartition des économies par groupements interrégionaux xxxiv
Abbreviations and acronyms xxi	Abréviations et acronymes xxxv
Product classification for international trade.............. xxxvi	Classification des produits pour le commerce international xxxvi

PART ONE International merchandise trade	PREMIÈRE PARTIE Commerce international des marchandises

1.1.1 Exports and imports of countries and geographical regions - Value .... 2 - Share 10	1.1.1 Exportations et importations des pays et des régions géographiques - Valeur .... 2 - Part.. 10
1.1.2 Exports and imports of economic groupings - Value .... 20 - Share 22	1.1.2 Exportations et importations des groupements économiques - Valeur .... 20 - Part.. 22
1.1.3 Exports and imports of trade groups - Value .... 24 - Share 26	1.1.3 Exportations et importations des groupements commerciaux - Valeur .... 24 - Part.. 26
1.2.1 Annual average growth rates of exports and imports of countries and geographical regions................. 28	1.2.1 Taux d'évolution annuels moyens des exportations et importations des pays et des régions géographiques 28
1.2.2 Annual average growth rates of exports and imports of economic groupings.. 38	1.2.2 Taux d'évolution annuels moyens des exportations et importations des groupements économiques..................... 38
1.2.3 Annual average growth rates of exports and imports of trade groups.. 40	1.2.3 Taux d'évolution annuels moyens des exportations et importations des groupements commerciaux..................... 40
1.3.1 Value of trade balance, and as percentage of imports of countries and geographical regions.................. 42	1.3.1 Valeur de la balance commerciale et sa part dans les importations des pays et des régions géographiques 42
1.3.2 Value of trade balance, and as percentage of imports of economic groupings.. 52	1.3.2 Valeur de la balance commerciale et sa part dans les importations des groupements économiques..................... 52
1.4 Intra-trade of trade groups 54	1.4 Commerce interne des groupements commerciaux........... 54

TABLE OF CONTENTS | TABLE DES MATIÈRES

PART TWO
International merchandise trade by region

2.1 Country trade structure by partner
- Exports by main region of destination 58
- Imports by main region of origin 70

2.2 Export and import structure by partner and product group
- **A.** World.. 82
- **B.** Developing economies 86
- **C.** Developing economies: Africa 90
- **D.** Developing economies: America 94
- **E.** Developing economies: Asia 98
- **F** Developing economies: Eastern, Southern and South-Eastern Asia 102
- **G.** Developing economies: Western Asia 106
- **H.** Developing economies: Oceania 110
- **I.** Developing economies: Major petroleum and gas exporters 114
- **J.** Developing economies: Major manufactured goods exporters 118
- **K.** Transition economies.. 122
- **L.** Developed economies 126

PART THREE
International merchandise trade by product

3.1 Country trade structure by product group
- Exports 132
- Imports 145

3.2 Export structure by product
- **A.** World.. 158
- **B.** Developing economies 163
- **C.** Developed economies 168
- **D.** Individual countries and territories 173
- **E.** Major exporters for leading products among developing economies 195

3.3 Concentration and structural change indices of product markets
- Exports 204
- Imports.. 208

PART FOUR
International merchandise trade indicators

4.1.1 Export and import concentration and diversification indices of countries and geographical regions 214

4.1.2 Export and import concentration and diversification indices of economic groupings 224

4.2.1 International merchandise trade indices of countries and geographical regions
- Volume indices of exports and imports 226
- Unit value indices of exports and imports 234
- Terms of trade indices and purchasing power indices of exports 242

4.2.2 International merchandise trade indices of economic groupings
- Volume indices of exports and imports 250
- Unit value indices of exports and imports 252
- Terms of trade indices and purchasing power indices of exports 254

4.3 Average applied import MFN tariff rates on non-agricultural and non-fuel products 256

DEUXIÈME PARTIE
Commerce international des marchandises par régions

2.1 Structure du commerce des pays par partenaires
- Exportations par principales régions de destination.........58
- Importations par principales régions d'origine................70

2.2 Structure des exportations et importations par partenaires et groupes de produits
- **A.** Monde.. 82
- **B.** Économies en développement 86
- **C.** Économies en développement : Afrique...................... 90
- **D.** Économies en développement : Amérique................... 94
- **E.** Économies en développement : Asie 98
- **F.** Économies en développement : Asie orientale méridionale et du Sud-Est 102
- **G.** Économies en développement : Asie occidentale 106
- **H.** Économies en développement : Océanie.................... 110
- **I.** Économies en développement : principaux exportateurs de pétrole et de gaz............................. 114
- **J.** Économies en développement : principaux exportateurs d'articles manufacturés....................... 118
- **K.** Économies en transition.. 122
- **L.** Économies développées.. 126

TROISIÈME PARTIE
Commerce international des marchandises par produits

3.1 Structure du commerce des pays par groupes de produits
- Exportations 132
- Importations... 145

3.2 Structure des exportations par produits
- **A.** Monde.. 158
- **B.** Économies en développement 163
- **C.** Économies développées 168
- **D.** Pays et territoires individuels..................................... 173
- **E.** Principaux exportateurs de produits majeurs parmi les économies en développement 195

3.3 Indices de concentration et de changement structurel des marchés de produits
- Exportations 204
- Importations... 208

QUATRIÈME PARTIE
Indicateurs du commerce international des marchandises

4.1.1 Indices de concentration et de diversification des exportations et importations des pays et des régions géographiques.. 214

4.1.2 Indices de concentration et de diversification des exportations et importations des groupements économiques 224

4.2.1 Indices du commerce international des marchandises des pays et des régions géographiques
- Indices du volume des exportations et importations 226
- Indices de la valeur unitaire des exportations et importations.. 234
- Indices des termes de l'échange et du pouvoir d'achat des exportations 242

4.2.2 Indices du commerce international des marchandises des groupements économiques
- Indices du volume des exportations et importations 250
- Indices de la valeur unitaire des exportations et importations.. 252
- Indices des termes de l'échange et du pouvoir d'achat des exportations 254

4.3 Droits de douane moyens NPF appliqués à l'importation des produits non-agricoles et non-pétroliers 256

v

TABLE OF CONTENTS	TABLE DES MATIÈRES

PART FIVE
International trade in services

5.1.1 Value of exports and imports of services of countries and geographical regions...................................274

5.1.2 Value of exports and imports of services of economic groupings.................................282

5.1.3 Value of exports and imports of services of trade groups..284

5.2 Exports and imports of services by service category
- Transport 286
- Travel..288
- Communications.................................290
- Construction 292
- Computer and information 294
- Insurance..296
- Financial services...............................298
- Royalties and license fees.................300
- Other business services 302
- Personal, cultural and recreational services..................304

5.3 World merchant fleet by flag of registration and type of ship of countries and geographical regions 307

PART SIX
Commodities

6.1 Annual and quarterly indices of free-market prices of selected primary commodities..........................322

6.2 Instability indices and trends in free market prices for selected primary commodities 328

PART SEVEN
International finance

7.1.1 Balance of payments: Current account net of countries and geographical regions 332

7.1.2 Balance of payments: Current account net of economic groupings 340

7.1.3 Balance of payments: Current account net of trade groups..342

7.2.1 Foreign direct investment: Inward and outward flows of countries and geographical regions 344

7.2.2 Foreign direct investment: Inward and outward flows of economic groupings 352

7.2.3 Foreign direct investment: Inward and outward flows of trade groups 354

7.3.1 Migrants' remittances: Receipts of countries and geographical regions 356

7.3.2 Migrants' remittances: Receipts of economic groupings 364

7.4.1 Migrants' remittances: Payments of countries and geographical regions 366

7.4.2 Migrants' remittances: Payments of economic groupings 374

7.5.1 International reserves of developing economies by country and geographical region 376

7.5.2 International reserves of developing economies by economic grouping................................382

CINQUIÈME PARTIE
Commerce international des services

5.1.1 Valeur des exportations et importations de services des pays et des régions géographiques........................274

5.1.2 Valeur des exportations et importations de services des groupements économiques 282

5.1.3 Valeur des exportations et importations de services des groupements commerciaux 284

5.2 Exportations et importations des services par catégories de services
- Transports..286
- Voyages...288
- Communications 290
- Bâtiment et travaux publics 292
- Informatique et information 294
- Services d'assurance.........................296
- Services financiers.............................298
- Redevances et droits de licence........300
- Autres services aux entreprises.........302
- Services personnels, culturels et relatifs aux loisirs........304

5.3 Flotte marchande mondiale par pavillons d'immatriculation et par types de navires des pays et des régions géographiques......................................307

SIXIÈME PARTIE
Produits de base

6.1 Indices annuels et trimestriels des prix d'une sélection de produits de base sur le marché libre............322

6.2 Indices d'instabilité et tendances des prix d'une sélection de produits de base sur le marché libre............328

SEPTIÈME PARTIE
Finance internationale

7.1.1 Balance des paiements : compte courant net des pays et des régions géographiques.........................332

7.1.2 Balance des paiements : compte courant net des groupements économiques................................340

7.1.3 Balance des paiements : compte courant net des groupements commerciaux..............................342

7.2.1 Investissement étranger direct : flux entrants et sortants des pays et des régions géographiques..............344

7.2.2 Investissement étranger direct : flux entrants et sortants des groupements économiques 352

7.2.3 Investissement étranger direct : flux entrants et sortants des groupements commerciaux 354

7.3.1 Envois de fonds des migrants : recettes des pays et des régions géographiques...........................356

7.3.2 Envois de fonds des migrants : recettes des groupements économiques................................364

7.4.1 Envois de fonds des migrants : paiements des pays et des régions géographiques...........................366

7.4.2 Envois de fonds des migrants : paiements des groupements économiques................................374

7.5.1 Réserves internationales des économies en développement par pays et régions géographiques 376

7.5.2 Réserves internationales des économies en développement par groupements économiques 382

TABLE OF CONTENTS

7.6.1 Official financial flows from bilateral and multilateral sources by country and geographical region 384

7.6.2 Official financial flows from bilateral and multilateral sources to developing economies by economic grouping 398

7.7 External long-term debt by lending source
    A. Developing economies 402
    B. Developing economies: Africa 403
    C. Developing economies: America 404
    D. Developing economies: Asia 405
    E. Developing economies: Oceania 406
    F. Developing economies: Major petroleum and gas exporters 407
    G. Developing economies: Major manufactured goods exporters 408

PART EIGHT
Development indicators

8.1.1 Nominal gross domestic product: Total and per capita of countries and geographical regions 412

8.1.2 Nominal gross domestic product: Total and per capita of economic groupings 420

8.2.1 Annual average growth rates of total and per capita real gross domestic product of countries and geographical regions 422

8.2.2 Annual average growth rates of total and per capita real gross domestic product of economic groupings 430

8.3.1 Nominal gross domestic product by type of expenditure and by kind of economic activity of countries and geographical regions 432

8.3.2 Nominal gross domestic product by type of expenditure and by kind of economic activity of economic groupings 450

8.4.1 Population and labour force of countries and geographical regions 454

8.4.2 Population and labour force of economic groupings 472

TABLE DES MATIÈRES

7.6.1. Flux financiers publics bilatéraux et multilatéraux par pays et régions géographiques 384

7.6.2 Flux financiers publics bilatéraux et multilatéraux à destination des économies en développement par groupements économiques 398

7.7 Dette extérieure à long terme par catégories de prêts
    A. Économies en développement 402
    B. Économies en développement : Afrique 403
    C. Économies en développement : Amérique ... 404
    D. Économies en développement : Asie 405
    E. Économies en développement : Océanie 406
    F. Économies en développement : principaux exportateurs de pétrole et de gaz 407
    G. Économies en développement : principaux exportateurs d'articles manufacturés 408

HUITIÈME PARTIE
Indicateurs du développement

8.1.1 Produit intérieur brut nominal : total et par habitant des pays et des régions géographiques 412

8.1.2 Produit intérieur brut nominal : total et par habitant des groupements économiques 420

8.2.1 Taux de croissance annuels moyens du produit intérieur brut réel total et par habitant des pays et des régions géographiques 422

8.2.2 Taux de croissance annuels moyens du produit intérieur brut réel total et par habitant des groupements économiques 430

8.3.1 Produit intérieur brut nominal par catégories de dépenses et par branches d'activité économique des pays et des régions géographiques 432

8.3.2 Produit intérieur brut nominal par catégories de dépenses et par branches d'activité économique des groupements économiques 450

8.4.1 Population et main-d'œuvre des pays et des régions géographiques 454

8.4.2 Population et main-d'œuvre des groupements économiques 472

EXPLANATION OF SYMBOLS

0   Zero means that the amount is nil or negligible.

_   The symbol underscore indicates that the item is not applicable

..   Two dots indicate that the data are not available or are not separately reported.

-   The use of a hyphen on data area means that data is estimated and included in the aggregation but not to be shown. A hyphen between years (e.g. 1985-1990) signifies the full period involved, including the initial and final years.

(b)   Break in the series

(e)   Estimate

(f)   Forecast

(p)   Provisional data

(r)   Revised data

Some exceptions are indicated in footnotes.

SIGNIFICATION DES SYMBOLES

0   Un zéro signifie que le montant est nul ou négligeable.

_   Un tiret signifie que la rubrique est sans objet.

..   Deux points signifient que les données ne sont pas disponibles ou ne sont pas communiquées séparément.

-   Le trait d'union dans le champ des données indique que le chiffre est estimé et inclus dans l'agrégation mais n'est pas publié. Le trait d'union entre deux millésimes (par exemple 1985-1990) indique qu'il s'agit de la période tout entière, y compris la première et la dernière année mentionnées.

(b)   Interruption de la série

(e)   Estimation

(f)   Prévision

(p)   Donnée provisoire

(r)   Donnée révisée

Les exceptions sont indiquées dans les notes en bas de page.

These notes summarize the content of each part of the *Handbook* according to the revised Table of Contents of the present issue of the *Handbook of Statistics*.

The tables included in this book represent analytical summaries of the full time series contained in the *UNCTAD Handbook of Statistics 2012* on DVD.

PART ONE
International merchandise trade

Table **1.1** shows the value of total exports (f.o.b.) and imports (c.i.f.), expressed in millions of dollars and percentages of the world total, of individual countries and geographical regions (1.1.1), economic groupings (1.1.2), and trade groups (1.1.3). The trade flows shown in table 1.1.1 refer to the General Trade System except for the countries which employ the Special Trade System and which are marked with an asterisk. The General Trade System is used when the statistical territory of a compiling country coincides with its economic territory. Consequently, imports include all goods entering the economic territory of a compiling country and exports include all goods leaving the economic territory of the compiling country. The Special Trade System is used when the statistical territory comprises only a particular part of the economic territory within which "goods may be disposed of without customs restriction". In such a case, imports include all goods entering the free circulation area of the compiling country, which means cleared through customs for home use, and exports include all goods leaving the free circulation area of a compiling country.

Average annual growth rates of international trade derived from table 1.1 are presented in table **1.2**.

Table **1.3** contains trade balances (exports f.o.b. minus imports c.i.f.) and these balances, as a percentage of imports of individual countries, geographical regions and economic groupings.

Table **1.4** shows the relative importance of trade among group members as compared to the regional or total trade of that group.

PART TWO
International merchandise trade by region

Table **2.1** shows the export and import structure of individual countries by main regions of destination and origin. Data are presented for as many individual countries as possible, while trade partners are grouped in 14 major clusters.

Table **2.2 (A to L)** presents the structure of exports by destination and imports by origin by major commodity groups for 12 selected country groups. The table provides detailed information on the world trade network for 19 regions of origin and destination and six commodity groups.

Totals of international merchandise trade presented in the tables found in parts one and two are not strictly comparable due to complementary but different sources and remaining unallocated trade flows, despite efforts to distribute trade flows by destination, origin and commodity group.

Exports by destination may differ considerably in some cases from data on imports as reported by countries of destination for a variety of factors, among which the following may be of particular importance:
- Most import data are reported on a c.i.f. rather than an f.o.b. basis;
- There is a time lag between the date on which goods are recorded as exports and their arrival at their destination;
- There may be considerable differences between the recorded destination of exports and the actual destination as shown in import statistics.

PART THREE
International merchandise trade by product

Table **3.1** shows the export and import structure of individual economies by commodity groups for selected years for nine commodity groups (total, all food items, agricultural raw materials, fuels, ores and metals, manufactured goods, including chemical products, machinery and transport equipment and other manufactured goods).

Table **3.2 (A, B and C**, respectively) presents the structure of exports for the world, for developing and developed economies, by product, at the SITC group (Revision 3, 3-digit) level. Each product share of world exports is calculated for each economic grouping as well as the average annual growth rate and the latter's deviation in relation to the world growth rate.

Table **3.2D** establishes for each economy the list of main products exported (SITC group, Revision 3, 3-digit level). Each product's share of total exports of individual countries, geographical regions and the world is also indicated.

Table **3.2E** lists major exporters of 70 leading products among developing economies at the SITC group (Revision 3, 3-digit) level as well as corresponding shares in world trade.

Table **3.3** provides concentration indices and structural change indices for exports and imports by product group at SITC (Revision 3, 3-digit) level. The first indicator shows how a product market is concentrated in a few countries or homogeneously distributed among several countries. The structural change indicator shows whether the market share for a given product among export countries has changed significantly when compared with a reference year.

Totals of international merchandise trade presented in the tables of this third part may also differ from the data contained in the first part for the above reasons, to which must be added margins of exports and imports not distributed by commodity group or the use of different product nomenclatures by the exporting and importing countries.

PART FOUR
International merchandise trade indicators

Table **4.1** includes calculation results of concentration and diversification indices for individual countries, geographical regions and economic groupings. This concentration index specifically shows how exports and imports of individual countries or country groupings are concentrated on several products or otherwise distributed in a more homogeneous manner among a series of products. The diversification indicator signals whether the structure of exports or imports by product of a given country or country grouping differs from the structure by product shown for the world.

Table **4.2** contains volume indices of exports and imports, rounding out trade value available in tables 1.1 and 1.2, unit value indices of exports and imports and derived terms of trade and purchasing power of exports presented at the level of individual countries and geographical regions (4.2.1) and economic groupings (4.2.2).

To improve data coverage, especially for the latest periods, the following procedure was used in the calculation of unit value indices:
- A set of average prices indices at SITC (Revision 3, 3-digit) group level was constructed using *UNCTADstat* Commodity Price Statistics, international and national sources and UNCTAD secretariat estimates;
- At the country level, unit value indices were calculated using current year's trade values as weights at the SITC (Revision 3, 3-digit) level. Trade values are available in table 3.2.
In some instances these indices may differ from the estimates published in official sources, since the main aim is to provide tentative estimates for most developing countries on a comparable basis.

Table **4.3** presents average applied import MFN tariff rates for major categories of non-agricultural and non-fuel products by individual markets.

PART FIVE
International trade in services

Tables **5.1.1**, **5.1.2** and **5.1.3** present exports and imports of total trade in services by individual country, geographical region, economic grouping and trade group. The statistics shown are a result of the common work of UNCTAD and World Trade Organization (WTO) and they correspond to the definitions of the IMF *Balance of Payments Manual (BPM5, 1993)*. The aggregate data from tables 5.1 include estimates of missing values that are not shown separately. Services are defined as the economic output of intangible commodities that may be produced, transferred and consumed at the same time. However, services cover a heterogeneous range of intangible products and activities that are difficult to capture within a single definition and are sometimes hard to separate from goods. Services are outputs produced to order, and they typically include changes in the condition of the consumers realized through the activities of the producers at the demand of customers. By the time production of a service is completed, it must have been provided to a consumer.

Table **5.2** presents statistics on international trade in services by category of service for selected country groups and for major individual economy exporters and importers among developing and transition economies, as well as among developed countries. The data shown are a result of the common work of UNCTAD and WTO and they correspond to the definitions of the IMF *Balance of Payments Manual (BPM5, 1993)*. The following services categories are included: transport, travel, communication, construction, computer and information services, insurance, financial services, royalties and licence fees, other business services, and personal, cultural and recreational services.

To the extent possible, the inter-agency Task Force on Statistics of International Trade in Services aims to explain and reduce the divergences noticed in statistics for trade in services published by different international organizations. An overview of existing databases covering statistics on international trade in services is described at http://unstats.un.org/unsd/tradeserv/TFSITS/matrix.htm.

Table **5.3** concerns international maritime transport. It contains data on the world merchant fleet by flag of registration and by type of ship by region and economy, highlighting the group of major open-registry countries. A ship owner who registers his or her vessel in an open-registry country does not need to have any connection with a country of registry. The number of open-registry countries has varied over the years. The group in this table includes 10 countries. Table 5.3 contains consolidated time series from various issues of the UNCTAD *Review of Maritime Transport*. The Review reports on the worldwide evolution of shipping, ports and multimodal transport related to the major traffics of liquid bulk, dry bulk and containers.

PART SIX
Commodities

Table **6.1** includes aggregated price indices for primary commodity groups such as food, tropical beverages, vegetable oilseeds and oils, agricultural raw materials and minerals, ores and metals, as well as an all groups price index in current United States dollars. Also included are the annual and quarterly free-market price indices for selected commodities exported by developing economies. The weight of price indices for the above mentioned commodity groups (2000=100) are based on the value of exports of developing countries from 1999 to 2001.

Table **6.2** presents instability indices and trends in free-market prices for selected primary commodities that are of particular interest to developing economies.

PART SEVEN
International finance

Tables **7.1.1**, **7.1.2** and **7.1.3** present values of the current account net in millions of dollars and as percentages of GDP for individual countries, geographical regions, and trade and economic groupings. Balance-of-payments current account data cover all transactions between residents and non-residents of a reporting economy. In general, the current account balance describes the difference between current receipts and expenditures for internationally traded goods, services and income payments. At the same time, from a national perspective, the current account balance would equal the gap between national savings and domestic investment.

Tables **7.2.1**, **7.2.2** and **7.2.3** contain information on foreign direct investment (FDI) inflows and outflows by individual country, geographical region, economic grouping and trade group. These figures correspond to the Statistical Annexes of the UNCTAD *World Investment Report 2012*. FDI is defined as an investment involving a long-term relationship and reflecting a lasting interest in and control by a resident entity in one economy (foreign direct investor or parent enterprise) of an enterprise resident in a different economy (FDI enterprise or affiliate enterprise or foreign affiliate). Such investment involves both the initial transaction between the two entities and all subsequent transactions between them and among foreign affiliates. A direct investment enterprise is defined as an incorporated or unincorporated enterprise in which the direct investor, resident in another economy, owns 10 percent or more of the ordinary shares or voting power (or the equivalent).

Tables **7.3.1** and **7.3.2** present values of receipts (credits) of total migrants' remittances, in millions of dollars, for individual economies and regional and economic groupings. They also show total remittances receipts as percentage of GDP and international trade. The *Balance of Payments Manual* (*BPM5, 1993*) classifies workers' remittances, compensation of employees and migrants' transfers separately. In this table, their sum is given in order to present a clearer picture of the flows that enter economies via transactions by migrants and temporary or cross-border workers. *BPM5* defines workers' remittances as goods and financial instruments transferred by migrants living and working (being residents) in a new economy to residents of the economy in which the migrants formerly resided. A migrant must live and work in the new economy for more than one year to be considered a resident there. Compensation of employees includes wages, salaries and other benefits, in cash or in kind, earned by individuals – in economies where they are not residents – for work performed for residents of those economies. It covers seasonal and other short-term workers and border workers. Migrants' transfers cover flows of goods and changes in financial items that arise from migration (change of residence for at least one year).

Tables **7.4.1** and **7.4.2** include data on payments (debits) of total migrants' remittances, based on the same approach used for tables 7.3.1 and 7.3.2.

Tables **7.5.1** and **7.5.2** present statistics on total international reserves (including gold) of developing countries by country, region and economic grouping, in millions of dollars. Other calculations included show months of imports that these reserves could finance at current import levels, as well as the annual change in total reserves. According to the IMF definition, international reserves consist of the sum of the country's foreign exchange, its reserve position in the IMF, the monetary gold reserves, and the United States dollar value of SDR holdings by its monetary authorities.

Tables **7.6** give a summary of official financial flows by type of flow, country, region and economic grouping. Flows from bilateral and multilateral sources are shown, as recorded by the Organization for Economic Cooperation and Development (OECD) Development Assistance Committee (DAC).

Tables **7.7** present time series on the external long-term indebtedness of developing economies. They also provide a detailed breakdown of public and publicly guaranteed debt by source of lending. External debt data in this table are based on the Debtor Reporting System (DRS) maintained by the World Bank.

PART EIGHT
Development indicators

Table 8.1 provides information on total and per capita nominal gross domestic product (GDP) (in United States dollars) by individual country, geographical region and economic grouping. The GDP figures in dollars are derived from GDP data provided in national currencies. The prevailing annual average market exchange rates, as reported by IMF, have been used for the conversion from national currencies to dollars.

Table 8.2 contains annual average growth rates of total and per capita real GDP by individual country, geographical region and economic grouping. The growth rates are based on GDP in United States dollars at constant 2005 prices.

Table 8.3 provides data on GDP by type of expenditure and kind of economic activity by country, geographical region and economic grouping.

Tables 8.4.1 and 8.4.2 provide some estimates on population and labour force: total population, urban population (as a percentage of total population), total labour force, female labour force (as a percentage of total labour force), total agriculture labour force and female labour force (as a percentage of total agriculture labour force). The figures for certain groups may be different from those published by the sources cited when the UNCTAD definitions for those groups are different.

OTHER NOTES

Unless otherwise specified, country aggregates are the sums of the relevant country data by group. Calculations of aggregates may in some cases include data estimated by the UNCTAD secretariat that are not necessarily all reported separately.

Because of rounding, details and percentages in tables do not necessarily add up to totals.

Data were collected and checked to ensure that they matched the geographical coverage of the countries, as described at the beginning of the *Handbook*. However, some gaps could not be avoided due to data unavailability and are described in the notes at the end tables.

Unless otherwise stated, dollars ($) refer to United States dollars and data in dollars are expressed in current United States dollars of the year to which they refer.

Average annual growth rates are defined as the coefficient b in the exponential trend function $y = ae^{bt}$ where t stands for time. This method takes all observations in a period into account. Therefore, the resulting growth rates reflect trends that are not unduly influenced by exceptional values.

The country distributions presented are for statistical convenience only and follow those used by the Statistics Division, Department of Economic and Social Affairs (DESA), of the United Nations. They are grouped by economic criteria or by adhesion to commercial agreements for the purpose of statistical analysis and research.

The term "economies", as used in this publication, refers to regions, countries and territories. In case of change in the statistical coverage of a country, it is identified by adding an end year after the country name. For example, Indonesia (...2002) indicates that the statistical coverage of Indonesia, including Timor-Leste, was valid until 2002.

The composition of country groupings is evolving in order to provide relevant statistics for research and analysis. In this regard, UNCTAD reviews and updates the definition and composition of groups every year. User should be aware that the changes may impact significantly the figures from one given release to the other. The detailed changes in the groups are thoroughly outlined in the section Methodology & Classifications at *UNCTADstat* website.

1. Geographical regions

There is no established convention for the designation of "developed" and "developing" countries or areas in the United Nations system. In common practice, Israel and Japan in Asia, Bermuda, Canada, Greenland, Saint Pierre et Miquelon, and the United States in North America, Australia and New Zealand in Oceania, and Europe are considered "developed" regions or areas. This section includes all countries and territories divided into three major categories: developing countries, transition economies and developed economies. Each category is further divided by geographical regions.

1) Developing economies
This category includes countries and territories in America, Africa, Asia and Oceania not specified below. The geographical regions are further subdivided into subregions in order to present more detailed statistics. Exceptions are specified in table footnotes.

2) Transition economies
This group includes countries in transition from centrally planned to market economies.

3) Developed economies
This category is subdivided into four geographical regions: America, Asia, Europe and Oceania.

World' total represents the sum of the figures of the three above-mentioned groups plus the figures of a group of territories and partners not elsewhere classified, whose composition is detailed below. Data of these territories are included in the world total if they have been reported but are not presented individually or in any group, either by geography, economy or trade.
The composition of the group "not elsewhere classified" is as follows:
- Territories: Antarctica, Bouvet Island, British Antarctic Territory, British Indian Ocean Territory, Christmas Island, Cocos (Keeling) Islands, French Southern Territories, Heard and McDonald Islands, Norfolk Island, Pitcairn, Saint Barthélemy, Saint Martin (French part), South Georgia and South Sandwich Islands, United States Minor Outlying Islands, and United States Miscellaneous Pacific Islands.
- Partners: "Confidential information and differences", "Neutral zone", "Free zones", "Bunkers", and "ship stores". These specific partners are only used in the merchandise trade tables.

The total of each group presented in the *Handbook* is also completed, should the case arise, with data that have not been allocated to the different elements composing the group.

2. Economic groupings of developing countries

The *Handbook* provides numerous and varied groups of countries and territories in order to provide easy access to the statistics necessary for socio-economic analysis and development research.

Developing economies are presented at three levels of aggregation: the total group, the group excluding China (referring to continental China) and the group excluding the least developed countries.

The category of heavily indebted poor countries includes those economies benefiting from the HIPC debt reduction initiative of the World Bank and the International Monetary Fund.

LDCs and landlocked developing countries (LLDCs) are recognized by the United Nations as categories that require special attention from the international community.

Since 1994, the United Nations has recognized the particular problems of the Small Island Developing States (SIDS), even though the criteria for drawing up an official list of SIDS have not yet been determined. The unofficial list is used by UNCTAD for analytical purposes only.

The developing economies are also categorized into three subgroups according to their average 2004-2006 per capita GDP: high-income (above \$4,500), middle-income (between \$1,000 and \$4,500) and low-income (below \$1,000).

The group of major petroleum and gas exporters consists of countries whose share of petroleum and gas (SITC code 33 plus 34) was not less than 50 per cent of their total exports, and whose exports of these products amounted to at least 1 per cent of petroleum and gas world share for the period 2004–2006. This group is divided into three geographical zones: Africa, America and Asia.

The group of major manufactured goods exporters consists of economies whose share of manufactured products (SITC 5 to 8, excluding 667 and 68) was not less than 50 per cent of their total exports, and whose exports of these products amounted to at least 1 per cent of manufactured goods world share for the period 2004–2006. The group comprises countries in America and Asia.

The composition of the groups of emerging economies (in America and Asia) and newly industrialized Asian economies (composed of first and second tier) corresponds to UNCTAD's *Trade and Development Report*.

The different geographical regions are also presented at various levels of aggregation:

- Africa: Northern Africa excluding Sudan, sub-Saharan Africa, including Sudan, including and excluding South Africa.

- America: Central America and Greater Caribbean Islands excluding Puerto Rico, including and excluding Mexico, South America and Central America, and South America excluding Brazil.

- Asia: Eastern and South-Eastern Asia excluding China, and Southern Asia excluding India.

3. Trade groups and interregional groupings

Statistics of trade groups with special analytic interest are presented according to their pertinence. These groupings include all relevant economies and are sub-classified by geographical regions, with the exception of following interregional groups: African, Caribbean and Pacific Group of States; Asia–Pacific Economic Cooperation; Black Sea Economic Cooperation; and Commonwealth of Independent States.

DISTRIBUTION BY GEOGRAPHICAL REGION

DEVELOPING ECONOMIES

AFRICA

Eastern Africa

Burundi	Malawi	Uganda
Comoros	Mauritius	United Republic of Tanzania
Djibouti	Mayotte	Zambia
Eritrea	Mozambique	Zimbabwe
Ethiopia	Rwanda	
Kenya	Seychelles	
Madagascar	Somalia	

Middle Africa

Angola	Congo	Sao Tome and Principe
Cameroon	Democratic Republic of the Congo	
Central African Republic	Equatorial Guinea	
Chad	Gabon	

Northern Africa

Algeria	Morocco	Western Sahara
Egypt	Sudan	
Libya	Tunisia	

Southern Africa

Botswana	Namibia	Swaziland
Lesotho	South Africa	

Western Africa

Benin	Guinea	Nigeria
Burkina Faso	Guinea-Bissau	Saint Helena
Cape Verde	Liberia	Senegal
Côte d'Ivoire	Mali	Sierra Leone
Gambia	Mauritania	Togo
Ghana	Niger	

AMERICA

Caribbean islands

Greater Caribbean	**Small Caribbean islands**	
Cuba	Anguilla	Dominica
Dominican Republic	Antigua and Barbuda	Grenada
Haiti	Aruba	Montserrat
Jamaica	Bahamas	Saint Kitts and Nevis
	Barbados	Saint Lucia
	Bonaire, Saint Eustatius and Saba*	Saint Vincent and the Grenadines
	British Virgin Islands	Sint Maarten (dutch part)*
	Cayman Islands	Trinidad and Tobago
	Curaçao*	Turks and Caicos Islands

* Netherlands Antilles were dissolved on 10 October 2010. The composition of all groupings has been modified accordingly.

Central America

Belize	Guatemala	Nicaragua
Costa Rica	Honduras	Panama
El Salvador	Mexico	

DISTRIBUTION BY GEOGRAPHICAL REGION

DEVELOPING ECONOMIES (concluded)

AMERICA (concluded)

South America

Argentina	Ecuador	Suriname
Bolivia (Plurinational State of)	Falkland Islands (Malvinas)	Uruguay
Brazil	Guyana	Venezuela (Bolivarian Republic of)
Chile	Paraguay	
Colombia	Peru	

ASIA

Eastern Asia

China	Macao, Special Administrative
Democratic People's Republic	Region of China
of Korea	Mongolia
Hong Kong, Special Administrative	Republic of Korea
Region of China	Taiwan Province of China

Southern Asia

Afghanistan	India	Nepal
Bangladesh	Iran (Islamic Republic of)	Pakistan
Bhutan	Maldives	Sri Lanka

South-Eastern Asia

Brunei Darussalam	Malaysia	Thailand
Cambodia	Myanmar	Timor-Leste
Indonesia	Philippines	Viet Nam
Lao People's Democratic Republic	Singapore	

Western Asia

Bahrain	Occupied Palestinian territory	Turkey
Iraq	Oman	United Arab Emirates
Jordan	Qatar	Yemen
Kuwait	Saudi Arabia	
Lebanon	Syrian Arab Republic	

OCEANIA

American Samoa	Micronesia (Federated States of)	Samoa
Cook Islands	Nauru	Solomon Islands
Fiji	New Caledonia	Tokelau
French Polynesia	Niue	Tonga
Guam	Northern Mariana Islands	Tuvalu
Kiribati	Palau	Vanuatu
Marshall Islands	Papua New Guinea	Wallis and Futuna Islands

DISTRIBUTION BY GEOGRAPHICAL REGION

TRANSITION ECONOMIES

Albania
Armenia
Azerbaijan
Belarus
Bosnia and Herzegovina
Croatia
Georgia
Kazakhstan

Kyrgyzstan
Montenegro
Republic of Moldova
Russian Federation
Serbia
Tajikistan
The former Yugoslav Republic
   of Macedonia

Turkmenistan
Ukraine
Uzbekistan

DEVELOPED ECONOMIES

AMERICA

Bermuda
Canada
Greenland
Saint Pierre and Miquelon

United States of America
   including Puerto Rico and
   United States Virgin Islands

ASIA

Israel
Japan

EUROPE

Andorra
Austria
Belgium
Bulgaria
Cyprus
Czech Republic
Denmark
Estonia
Faeroe Islands
Finland including Åland Islands
France including French Guyana,
   Guadeloupe, Martinique,
   Monaco and Réunion
Germany

Gibraltar
Greece
Holy See
Hungary
Iceland
Ireland
Italy
Latvia
Lithuania
Luxembourg
Malta
Netherlands
Norway including Svalbard
   and Jan Mayen

Poland
Portugal
Romania
San Marino
Slovakia
Slovenia
Spain
Sweden
Switzerland including Liechtenstein
United Kingdom of Great Britain and
   Northern Ireland including Channel
   Islands and Isle of Man

OCEANIA

Australia
New Zealand

DISTRIBUTION OF DEVELOPING ECONOMIES BY ECONOMIC GROUPING

Heavily indebted poor countries (40)

Afghanistan	Gambia	Nicaragua
Benin	Ghana	Niger
Bolivia (Plurinational State of)	Guinea	Rwanda
Burkina Faso	Guinea-Bissau	Sao Tome and Principe
Burundi	Guyana	Senegal
Cameroon	Haiti	Sierra Leone
Central African Republic	Honduras	Somalia
Chad	Kyrgyzstan	Sudan
Comoros	Liberia	Togo
Congo	Madagascar	Uganda
Côte d'Ivoire	Malawi	United Republic of Tanzania
Democratic Republic of the Congo	Mali	Zambia
Eritrea	Mauritania	
Ethiopia	Mozambique	

Landlocked developing countries (31)

Afghanistan	Kazakhstan*	Rwanda
Armenia*	Kyrgyzstan*	Swaziland
Azerbaijan*	Lao People's Democratic Republic	Tajikistan*
Bhutan	Lesotho	The former Yugoslav Republic
Bolivia (Plurinational State of)	Malawi	of Macedonia*
Botswana	Mali	Turkmenistan*
Burkina Faso	Mongolia	Uganda
Burundi	Nepal	Uzbekistan*
Central African Republic	Niger	Zambia
Chad	Paraguay	Zimbabwe
Ethiopia	Republic of Moldova*	

* These countries are classified as economies in transition (neither developed nor developing).
However, as they are landlocked States, they are also members of this group.

Small island developing States (29)

Antigua and Barbuda	Maldives	Samoa
Bahamas	Marshall Islands	Sao Tome and Principe
Barbados	Mauritius	Seychelles
Cape Verde	Micronesia (Federated States of)	Solomon Islands
Comoros	Nauru	Timor-Leste
Dominica	Palau	Tonga
Fiji	Papua New Guinea	Trinidad and Tobago
Grenada	Saint Kitts and Nevis	Tuvalu
Jamaica	Saint Lucia	Vanuatu
Kiribati	Saint Vincent and the Grenadines	

Least developed countries (48)

Africa and Haiti	*Year of inclusion in the group*		*Year of inclusion in the group*	*Asia*	*Year of inclusion in the group*
Angola	1994	Malawi	1971	Afghanistan	1971
Benin	1971	Mali	1971	Bangladesh	1975
Burkina Faso	1971	Mauritania	1986	Bhutan	1971
Burundi	1971	Mozambique	1988	Cambodia	1991
Central African Republic	1975	Niger	1971	Lao People's Democratic Republic	1971
Chad	1971	Rwanda	1971	Myanmar	1987
Democratic Republic of the Congo	1991	Senegal	2000	Nepal	1971
Djibouti	1982	Sierra Leone	1982	Yemen	1971
Equatorial Guinea	1982	Somalia	1971		
Eritrea	1994	Sudan	1971	*Islands*	
Ethiopia	1971	Togo	1982	Comoros	1977
Gambia	1975	Uganda	1971	Kiribati	1986
Guinea	1971	United Republic of Tanzania	1971	Samoa	1971
Guinea-Bissau	1981	Zambia	1991	Sao Tome and Principe	1982
Haiti	1971			Solomon Islands	1991
Lesotho	1971			Timor-Leste	2003
Liberia	1990			Tuvalu	1986
Madagascar	1991			Vanuatu	1985

DISTRIBUTION OF DEVELOPING ECONOMIES BY ECONOMIC GROUPING

UNCTAD ECONOMIC GROUPINGS

2004-2006 average per capita current GDP above $4,500: High-income (48)

American Samoa
Anguilla
Antigua and Barbuda
Argentina
Aruba
Bahamas
Bahrain
Barbados
Bonaire, Saint Eustatius and Saba
British Virgin Islands
Brunei Darussalam
Cayman Islands
Chile
Cook Islands
Costa Rica
Curaçao
Equatorial Guinea
Falkland Islands (Malvinas)

French Polynesia
Guam
Hong Kong, Special Administrative
   Region of China
Kuwait
Lebanon
Libya
Macao, Special Administrative
   Region of China
Malaysia
Mexico
Montserrat
New Caledonia
Niue
Northern Mariana Islands
Oman
Palau
Qatar

Republic of Korea
Saint Kitts and Nevis
Saint Lucia
Saudi Arabia
Seychelles
Singapore
Sint Maarten (dutch part)
Taiwan Province of China
Trinidad and Tobago
Turkey
Turks and Caicos Islands
United Arab Emirates
Uruguay
Venezuela (Bolivarian Republic of)

2004-2006 average per capita current GDP between $1,000 and $4,500: Middle-income (50)

Algeria
Belize
Bolivia (Plurinational State of)
Botswana
Brazil
Cape Verde
China
Colombia
Congo
Cuba
Dominica
Dominican Republic
Ecuador
Egypt
El Salvador
Fiji
Gabon

Grenada
Guatemala
Honduras
Iran (Islamic Republic of)
Jamaica
Jordan
Maldives
Marshall Islands
Mauritius
Micronesia (Federated States of)
Morocco
Namibia
Nauru
Occupied Palestinian territory
Panama
Paraguay
Peru

Philippines
Saint Helena
Saint Vincent and the Grenadines
Samoa
South Africa
Sri Lanka
Suriname
Swaziland
Syrian Arab Republic
Thailand
Tokelau
Tonga
Tunisia
Tuvalu
Vanuatu
Wallis and Futuna Islands

2004-2006 average per capita current GDP below $1,000: Low-income (60)

Afghanistan
Angola
Bangladesh
Benin
Bhutan
Burkina Faso
Burundi
Cambodia
Cameroon
Central African Republic
Chad
Comoros
Côte d'Ivoire
Democratic People's Republic of Korea
Democratic Republic of the Congo
Djibouti
Eritrea
Ethiopia
Gambia
Ghana
Guinea

Guinea-Bissau
Guyana
Haiti
India
Indonesia
Iraq
Kenya
Kiribati
Lao People's Democratic Republic
Lesotho
Liberia
Madagascar
Malawi
Mali
Mauritania
Mongolia
Mozambique
Myanmar
Nepal
Nicaragua
Niger

Nigeria
Pakistan
Papua New Guinea
Rwanda
Sao Tome and Principe
Senegal
Sierra Leone
Solomon Islands
Somalia
Sudan
Timor-Leste
Togo
Uganda
United Republic of Tanzania
Viet Nam
Yemen
Zambia
Zimbabwe

DISTRIBUTION OF DEVELOPING ECONOMIES BY ECONOMIC GROUPING

Major petroleum and gas exporters (12)

Africa	*America*	*Asia*
Algeria	Venezuela (Bolivarian Republic of)	Iran (Islamic Republic of)
Angola		Iraq
Libya		Kuwait
Nigeria		Oman
		Qatar
		Saudi Arabia
		United Arab Emirates

Major manufactured goods exporters (8)

America	*Asia*
Mexico	China
	Hong Kong, Special Administrative Region of China
	Malaysia
	Republic of Korea
	Singapore
	Taiwan Province of China
	Thailand

Emerging economies (10)

America	*Asia*
Argentina	Malaysia
Brazil	Republic of Korea
Chile	Singapore
Mexico	Taiwan Province of China
Peru	Thailand

Newly industrialized Asian economies (8)

First tier	*Second tier*
Hong Kong, Special Administrative Region of China	Indonesia
Republic of Korea	Malaysia
Singapore	Philippines
Taiwan Province of China	Thailand

DISTRIBUTION OF ECONOMIES BY TRADE GROUP

AFRICA

Arab Maghreb Union – UMA (5) *Year of accession*

Algeria	1989
Libya	1989
Mauritania	1989
Morocco	1989
Tunisia	1989

Common Market for Eastern and Southern Africa (19) - COMESA

Burundi	1994
Comoros	1994
Democratic Republic of the Congo	1994
Djibouti	1994
Egypt	1994
Eritrea	1994
Ethiopia	1994
Kenya	1994
Libya	2005
Madagascar	1994
Malawi	1994
Mauritius	1994
Rwanda	1994
Seychelles	1994
Sudan	1994
Swaziland	1994
Uganda	1994
Zambia	1994
Zimbabwe	1994

East African Community (5) - EAC

Burundi	2007
Kenya	2001
Rwanda	2007
Uganda	2001
United Republic of Tanzania	2001

Economic Community of Central African States (10) - ECCAS *Year of accession*

Angola	1999
Burundi	1983
Cameroon	1983
Central African Republic	1983
Chad	1983
Congo	1983
Democratic Republic of The Congo	1983
Equatorial Guinea	1983
Gabon	1983
Sao Tome and Principe	1983

Economic Community of the Great Lakes Countries (3) - CEPGL

Burundi	1976
Democratic Republic of the Congo	1976
Rwanda	1976

Economic Community of West African States (15) - ECOWAS

Benin	1975
Burkina Faso	1975
Cape Verde	1977
Côte d'Ivoire	1975
Gambia	1975
Ghana	1975
Guinea	1975
Guinea-Bissau	1975
Liberia	1975
Mali	1975
Niger	1975
Nigeria	1975
Senegal	1975
Sierra Leone	1975
Togo	1975

Economic and Monetary Community of Central Africa (6) - CEMAC *Year of accession*

Cameroon	1994
Central African Republic	1994
Chad	1994
Congo	1994
Equatorial Guinea	1994
Gabon	1994

Mano River Union (4) - MRU

Côte d'Ivoire	2008
Guinea	1980
Liberia	1973
Sierra Leone	1973

Southern African Development Community (15) - SADC

Angola	1992
Botswana	1992
Democratic Republic of the Congo	1992
Lesotho	1992
Madagascar	2005
Malawi	1992
Mauritius	1992
Mozambique	1992
Namibia	1992
Seychelles	2007
South Africa	1994
Swaziland	1992
United Republic of Tanzania	1992
Zambia	1992
Zimbabwe	1992

West African Economic and Monetary Union (8) - UEMOA

Benin	1994
Burkina Faso	1994
Côte d'Ivoire	1994
Guinea-Bissau	1997
Mali	1994
Niger	1994
Senegal	1994
Togo	1994

AMERICA

Andean Community (4) - ANCOM *Year of accession*

Bolivia (Plurinational State of)	1996
Colombia	1996
Ecuador	1996
Peru	1996

Caribbean Community (15) - CARICOM

Antigua and Barbuda	1974
Bahamas	1983
Barbados	1973
Belize	1974
Dominica	1974
Grenada	1974
Guyana	1973
Haiti	2002
Jamaica	1973
Montserrat	1974
Saint Kitts and Nevis	1974
Saint Lucia	1974
Saint Vincent and the Grenadines	1974
Suriname	1995
Trinidad and Tobago	1973

Central American Common Market (5) - CACM *Year of accession*

Costa Rica	1962
El Salvador	1961
Guatemala	1961
Honduras	1961
Nicaragua	1961

Free Trade Area of the Americas (34) - FTAA

Antigua and Barbuda	1994
Argentina	1994
Bahamas	1994
Barbados	1994
Belize	1994
Bolivia (Plurinational State of)	1994
Brazil	1994
Canada	1994
Chile	1994
Colombia	1994
Costa Rica	1994
Dominica	1994

Year of accession

Dominican Republic	1994
Ecuador	1994
El Salvador	1994
Grenada	1994
Guatemala	1994
Guyana	1994
Haiti	1994
Honduras	1994
Jamaica	1994
Mexico	1994
Nicaragua	1994
Panama	1994
Paraguay	1994
Peru	1994
Saint Kitts and Nevis	1994
Saint Lucia	1994
Saint Vincent and the Grenadines	1994
Suriname	1994
Trinidad and Tobago	1994
United States of America	1994
Uruguay	1994
Venezuela (Bolivarian Republic of)	1994

AMERICA (concluded)

Latin American Integration Association (12) - LAIA

	Year of accession
Argentina	1980
Bolivia (Plurinational State of)	1980
Brazil	1980
Chile	1980
Colombia	1980
Cuba	1999
Ecuador	1980
Mexico	1980
Paraguay	1980
Peru	1980
Uruguay	1980
Venezuela (Bolivarian Republic of)	1980

Mercado Común del Sur (4) - MERCOSUR

	Year of accession
Argentina	1994
Brazil	1994
Paraguay	1994
Uruguay	1994

North American Free Trade Agreement (3) - NAFTA

	Year of accession
Canada	1994
Mexico	1994
United States of America	1994

Organization of American States (35) - OAS

	Year of accession
Antigua and Barbuda	1981
Argentina	1948
Bahamas	1982
Barbados	1967
Belize	1991
Bolivia (Plurinational State of)	1948
Brazil	1948
Canada	1990
Chile	1948
Colombia	1948
Costa Rica	1948
Cuba	2009
Dominica	1979
Dominican Republic	1948
Ecuador	1948
El Salvador	1948
Grenada	1975
Guatemala	1948
Guyana	1948
Haiti	1948
Honduras	1948
Jamaica	1969
Mexico	1948
Nicaragua	1948
Panama	1948
Paraguay	1948
Peru	1951
Saint Kitts and Nevis	1984
Saint Lucia	1979
Saint Vincent and the Grenadines	1981
Suriname	1977
Trinidad and Tobago	1967
United States of America	1951
Uruguay	1951
Venezuela (Bolivarian Republic of)	1951

Organization of Eastern Caribbean States (9) - OECS

	Year of accession
Anguilla	1995
Antigua and Barbuda	1981
British Virgin Islands	1984
Dominica	1981
Grenada	1981
Montserrat	1981
Saint Kitts and Nevis	1981
Saint Lucia	1981
Saint Vincent and the Grenadines	1981

ASIA

Asia–Pacific Trade Agreement (6) - APTA

	Year of accession
Bangladesh	1975
China	2001
India	1975
Lao People's Democratic Republic	1975
Republic of Korea	1975
Sri Lanka	1975

Association of South-East Asian Nations (10) - ASEAN

	Year of accession
Brunei Darussalam	1984
Cambodia	1999
Indonesia	1967
Lao People's Democratic Republic	1997
Malaysia	1967
Myanmar	1997
Philippines	1967
Singapore	1967
Thailand	1967
Viet Nam	1995

Economic Cooperation Organization (10) - ECO

	Year of accession
Afghanistan	1992
Azerbaijan	1992
Iran (Islamic Republic of)	1985
Kazakhstan	1992
Kyrgyzstan	1992
Pakistan	1985
Tajikistan	1992
Turkey	1985
Turkmenistan	1992
Uzbekistan	1992

Gulf Cooperation Council (6) - GCC

	Year of accession
Bahrain	1981
Kuwait	1981
Oman	1981
Qatar	1981
Saudi Arabia	1981
United Arab Emirates	1981

South Asian Association for Regional Cooperation (8) - SAARC

	Year of accession
Afghanistan	2007
Bangladesh	1985
Bhutan	1985
India	1985
Maldives	1985
Nepal	1985
Pakistan	1985
Sri Lanka	1985

EUROPE

European Free Trade Association (3) - EFTA

	Year of accession
Iceland	1970
Norway	1960
Switzerland	1960

European Union (27) - EU

	Year of accession
Austria	1995
Belgium	1957
Bulgaria	2008
Cyprus	2004
Czech Republic	2004
Denmark	1973
Estonia	2004
Finland	1995
France	1957
Germany	1957
Greece	1981
Hungary	2004
Ireland	1973
Italy	1957
Latvia	2004
Lithuania	2004
Luxembourg	1957
Malta	2004
Netherlands	1957
Poland	2004
Portugal	1986
Romania	2008
Slovakia	2004
Slovenia	2004
Spain	1986
Sweden	1995
United Kingdom	1973

Euro area (17)

	Year of accession
Austria	2002
Belgium	2002
Cyprus	2008
Estonia	2011
Finland	2002
France	2002
Germany	2002
Greece	2002
Ireland	2002
Italy	2002
Luxembourg	2002
Malta	2008
Netherlands	2002
Portugal	2002
Slovakia	2009
Slovenia	2007
Spain	2002

DISTRIBUTION OF ECONOMIES BY TRADE GROUP

OCEANIA

Year of accession

Melanesia Spearhead Group (4) - MSG

Fiji	1998
Papua New Guinea	1993
Solomon Islands	1993
Vanuatu	1993

DISTRIBUTION OF ECONOMIES BY INTERREGIONAL GROUPING

African, Caribbean and Pacific Group of States (79) - ACP

Angola	Gambia	Rwanda
Antigua and Barbuda	Ghana	Saint Kitts and Nevis
Bahamas	Grenada	Saint Lucia
Barbados	Guinea	Saint Vincent and the Grenadines
Belize	Guinea-Bissau	Samoa
Benin	Guyana	Sao Tome and Principe
Botswana	Haiti	Senegal
Burkina Faso	Jamaica	Seychelles
Burundi	Kenya	Sierra Leone
Cameroon	Kiribati	Solomon Islands
Cape Verde	Lesotho	Somalia
Central African Republic	Liberia	South Africa
Chad	Madagascar	Sudan
Comoros	Malawi	Suriname
Congo	Mali	Swaziland
Cook Islands	Marshall Islands	Timor-Leste
Côte d'Ivoire	Mauritania	Togo
Cuba	Mauritius	Tonga
Democratic Republic of the Congo	Micronesia (Federated States of)	Trinidad and Tobago
Djibouti	Mozambique	Tuvalu
Dominica	Namibia	Uganda
Dominican Republic	Nauru	United Republic of Tanzania
Equatorial Guinea	Niger	Vanuatu
Eritrea	Nigeria	Zambia
Ethiopia	Niue	Zimbabwe
Fiji	Palau	
Gabon	Papua New Guinea	

Asia-Pacific Economic Cooperation (21) - APEC	*Year of accession*	Black Sea Economic Cooperation (12) - BSEC	*Year of accession*	Commonwealth of Independent States (11) - CIS	*Year of accession*
Australia	1989	Albania	1992	Armenia	1991
Brunei Darussalam	1989	Armenia	1992	Azerbaijan	1991
Canada	1989	Azerbaijan	1992	Belarus	1991
Chile	1994	Bulgaria	1992	Kazakhstan	1991
China	1991	Georgia	1992	Kyrgyzstan	1991
Hong Kong, Special Administrative Region of China	1991	Greece	1992	Republic of Moldova	1991
Indonesia	1989	Republic of Moldova	1992	Russian Federation	1991
Japan	1989	Romania	1992	Tajikistan	1991
Malaysia	1989	Russian Federation	1992	Turkmenistan	1991
Mexico	1993	Serbia	2004	Ukraine	1991
New Zealand	1989	Turkey	1992	Uzbekistan	1991
Papua New Guinea	1993	Ukraine	1992		
Peru	1998				
Philippines	1989				
Republic of Korea	1989				
Russian Federation	1998				
Singapore	1989				
Taiwan Province of China	1991				
Thailand	1989				
United States of America	1989				
Viet Nam	1998				

ACP	African, Caribbean and Pacific Group of States
ANCOM	Andean Community
APEC	Asia–Pacific Economic Cooperation
APTA	Asia-Pacific Trade Agreement (former Bangkok Agreement)
ASEAN	Association of South-East Asian Nations
BPM	*Balance of Payments Manual* (IMF)
BSEC	Black Sea Economic Cooperation
CACM	Central American Common Market
CARICOM	Caribbean Community
CCSA	Committee for the Coordination of Statistical Activities
CEMAC	Economic and Monetary Community of Central Africa
CEPGL	Economic Community of the Great Lakes Countries
c.i.f.	cost, insurance and freight
CIS	Commonwealth of Independent States
COMESA	Common Market for Eastern and Southern Africa
DAC	Development Assistance Committee (of OECD)
DRS	Debtor Reporting System
EAC	East African Community
ECCAS	Economic Community of Central African States
ECE	Economic Commission for Europe
ECLAC	Economic Commission for Latin America and the Caribbean
ECO	Economic Cooperation Organization
ECOWAS	Economic Community of West African States
EFTA	European Free Trade Association
EIU	Economic Intelligence Unit
ESCAP	Economic and Social Commission for Asia and the Pacific
ESCWA	Economic and Social Commission for Western Asia
EU	European Union
excl.	excluding
FAO	Food and Agriculture Organization of the United Nations
FDI	foreign direct investment
f.o.b.	free on board
FTAA	Free Trade Area of the Americas
GATS	General Agreement on Trade in Services
GCC	Gulf Cooperation Council
GDP	gross domestic product
GFCF	gross fixed capital formation
GNP	gross national product
HIPC	heavily indebted poor countries
HS	Harmonized System
ILO	International Labour Organization
IMF	International Monetary Fund
LAIA	Latin American Integration Association
LDC	least developed country
MERCOSUR	Mercado Común del Sur
MFN	most favoured nation
MRU	Mano River Union
MSG	Melanesia Spearhead Group
NAFTA	North American Free Trade Agreement
n.e.s.	not elsewhere specified
NIE	newly industrialized economies
n.i.e.	not included elsewhere
NPISHs	non-profit institutions serving households
OA	official aid
OAS	Organization of American States
ODA	official development assistance
OECD	Organization for Economic Cooperation and Development
OECS	Organization of Eastern Caribbean States
OOF	other official flows
OPEC	Organization of the Petroleum Exporting Countries
SAARC	South Asian Association for Regional Cooperation
SADC	Southern African Development Community
SAR	Special Administrative Region
SDR	special drawing right
SFR	Socialist Federative Republic of Yugoslavia (former)
SIDS	Small Island Developing States
SITC	Standard International Trade Classification
TFYR	The former Yugoslav Republic of Macedonia
TNC	transnational corporation
TRAINS	Trade Analysis and Information System
UMA	Arab Maghreb Union
UN/DESA/SD	United Nations Department of Economic and Social Affairs, Statistics Division
UNDP	United Nations Development Programme
UNESCO	United Nations Educational, Scientific and Cultural Organization
UNICEF	United Nations Children's Fund
USSR	Union of Soviet Socialist Republics
WAEMU	West African Economic and Monetary Union
WITS	World Integrated Trade Solution
WTO	World Trade Organization

Ces notes générales présentent le contenu de chaque tableau du *Manuel de statistiques* ainsi que les modifications introduites dans cette nouvelle édition, s'il y a lieu.

Les tableaux inclus dans cette publication constituent un résumé analytique des séries chronologiques complètes publiées dans le *Manuel de statistiques 2012 de la CNUCED* sur DVD.

PREMIÈRE PARTIE
Commerce international des marchandises

Les tableaux **1.1** donnent la valeur des exportations (f.a.b.) et des importations (c.a.f.) totales de marchandises, exprimée en millions de dollars et en pourcentage du monde, des pays et régions géographiques (1.1.1), groupements économiques (1.1.2) et groupements commerciaux (1.1.3). Les flux du commerce présentés dans le tableau 1.1.1 se réfèrent au Système du Commerce Général, à l'exception des pays et territoires qui utilisent le Système du Commerce Spécial et qui sont munis d'un astérisque. Le Système du Commerce Général est utilisé lorsque le territoire statistique d'un pays coïncide avec son territoire économique, et en conséquence, les importations comprennent tous les biens admis sur le territoire du pays déclarant et les exportations tous les biens qui le quittent. Le Système du Commerce Spécial est utilisé lorsque le territoire statistique ne comprend qu'une partie du territoire économique à l'intérieur de laquelle « les biens peuvent être écoulés librement sans restriction douanière ». Dans ce cas, les importations comprennent tous les biens qui entrent dans la zone de libre circulation du pays déclarant, c'est-à-dire qui ont été dédouanés pour mise à la consommation et les exportations comprennent tous les biens qui quittent la zone de libre circulation du pays déclarant.

Les taux d'évolution annuels moyens du commerce international des marchandises, calculés à partir des valeurs des tableaux 1.1, figurent dans les tableaux **1. 2**.

Les tableaux **1.3** présentent les balances commerciales (exportations f.a.b. moins importations c.a.f.), ainsi que ces mêmes balances en pourcentage des importations des pays, régions géographiques et groupements économiques.

Le tableau **1.4** indique l'importance des échanges entre pays membres de groupements commerciaux par rapport aux exportations régionales et totales de ces groupements.

DEUXIÈME PARTIE
Commerce international des marchandises par régions

Le tableau **2.1** présente la structure des exportations et des importations des pays par régions de destination et d'origine. Le plus grand nombre possible de pays en développement sont inclus tandis que les partenaires commerciaux sont regroupés en 14 groupes considérés comme particulièrement importants pour l'analyse du commerce international.

Les tableaux **2.2** (**A** à **L**) indiquent la structure des exportations par destination ainsi que des importations par origine et par groupes de produits pour le monde et une sélection de 12 groupements de pays. Le tableau fournit une information détaillée sur le réseau du commerce international avec le monde, 19 régions d'origine et de destination, et pour six différents groupes de produits.

Les totaux du commerce international des marchandises présentés dans les tableaux des première et deuxième parties ne sont pas strictement comparables en raison de sources complémentaires mais différentes et d'une marge d'exportations et d'importations non distribuées, en dépit des efforts déployés pour répartir les flux commerciaux par destinations et origines.

Les exportations ventilées par destinations peuvent accuser un écart parfois considérable par rapport aux importations déclarées par les pays destinataires en raison de divers facteurs dont les plus importants sont les suivants :

- Les importations sont déclarées en principe "valeur c.a.f." plutôt que "valeur f.a.b.";

- Les importations de marchandises peuvent arriver à destination et être enregistrées longtemps après la date de leur enregistrement à l'exportation ;

- D'importantes différences peuvent exister entre la destination des exportations déclarée par les pays exportateurs et la destination réelle telle qu'indiquée dans les statistiques d'importation.

TROISIÈME PARTIE
Commerce international des marchandises par produits

Le tableau **3.1** fournit la structure des exportations et des importations des pays par produits classés en 9 groupes (total, produits alimentaires, matières premières d'origine agricole, combustibles, minerais et métaux, produits manufacturés, dont produits chimiques, machines et matériel de transport, articles manufacturés divers) pour plusieurs années.

Les tableaux **3.2A**, **B** et **C** présentent respectivement les exportations par produits du monde, des économies en développement et développées, à niveau très détaillé (CTCI révision 3, position à trois chiffres). Les parts que représente chaque produit dans les exportations du monde et de la région, sont calculées pour chaque groupe d'économies, ainsi que le taux annuel de croissance et l'écart de ce dernier par rapport au taux de croissance mondial.

Le tableau **3.2D** établit, pour chaque économie, la liste des principaux produits qu'elle exporte (CTCI révision 3, position à trois chiffres). La part de chaque produit dans le total des exportations du pays, de la région et du monde est également indiquée.

Le tableau **3.2E** liste les plus gros exportateurs de 70 produits parmi les produits les plus exportés par les économies en développement (CTCI révision 3, position à trois chiffres), ainsi que les parts correspondantes dans le commerce mondial.

Le tableau **3.3** fournit les indices de concentration et de changements structurels des exportations et des importations des produits au niveau de la CTCI (révision 3, position à trois chiffres). Le premier indicateur a vocation à montrer comment le marché d'un produit est concentré sur quelques pays ou réparti de façon plus homogène entre les pays. L'indicateur de changement structurel indique si la répartition du commerce d'un produit entre les pays exportateurs ou importateurs a connu une évolution importante par rapport à une année de référence.

Les totaux du commerce international des marchandises présentés dans les tableaux de cette troisième partie peuvent aussi être différents des données de la première partie pour les raisons précédemment citées, auxquelles il convient d'ajouter des marges d'exportations et d'importations non distribuées par groupes de produits ou l'utilisation de nomenclatures différentes de produits par le pays exportateur et le pays importateur.

QUATRIÈME PARTIE
Indicateurs du commerce international des marchandises

Les tableaux **4.1** contiennent les résultats du calcul des indices de concentration et de diversification des pays, régions géographiques et groupements économiques. Cet indice de concentration a vocation à montrer comment les exportations et importations d'un pays ou groupe de pays sont concentrées sur quelques produits ou réparties de façon plus homogène sur une gamme de produits. L'indicateur de diversification indique si la structure par produits des exportations ou importations d'un pays ou groupe de pays diverge de la structure par produits observée au niveau du monde.

Les tableaux **4.2** fournissent les indices de volume des exportations et des importations complétant ainsi l'information en valeur disponible dans les tableaux 1.1 et 1.2, les indices de la valeur unitaire des exportations et importations ainsi que les indices de termes de l'échange et le pouvoir d'achat des exportations dérivés des indices de valeur unitaire. Ces indices sont calculés au niveau des pays et régions géographiques (4.2.1) et des groupements économiques (4.2.2).

Afin d'améliorer la couverture des données et spécialement pour les années récentes, la méthode suivante a été utilisée pour le calcul des valeurs unitaires :

- Un ensemble d'indices de prix moyens au niveau des groupes de la CTCI (révision 3, position à 3 chiffres) a été construit en utilisant des données provenant de *UNCTADstat* Statistiques des produits de base, des sources internationales et nationales ainsi que des estimations du secrétariat de la CNUCED.
- Au niveau des pays individuels, les indices de la valeur unitaire ont été calculés en utilisant comme pondération les valeurs des exportations et des importations de l'année courante disponibles dans la table 3.2 au niveau de la CTCI (révision 3, position à 3 chiffres).

Dans certains cas ces indices peuvent différer des estimations publiées dans les sources officielles, le but principal étant de fournir des estimations approximatives et comparables pour la plupart des pays en développement.

Le tableau **4.3** contient les données sur les droits de douane NPF moyens appliqués à l'importation des principales catégories de produits non-agricoles et non-pétroliers, par marchés individuels.

CINQUIÈME PARTIE
Commerce international des services

Les tableaux **5.1.1**, **5.1.2** et **5.1.3** présentent les exportations et les importations totales des services par pays, par régions géographiques, groupements économiques et groupements commerciaux. Les statistiques comprises sont le résultat d'un travail commun entre la CNUCED et l'Organisation mondiale du commerce (OMC) et elles correspondent aux définitions du *Manuel de la balance des paiements* du FMI (*MBP5, 1993*). Les agrégats inclus dans le tableau 5.1 comprennent les valeurs estimées qui ne sont pas présentées séparément. Les services sont définis comme rendements économiques de produits intangibles qui peuvent être produits, transférés et consommés au même moment. Cependant, les services recouvrent un groupe large et hétérogène de produits et d'activités que l'on peut difficilement englober dans une définition. Parfois, la démarcation entre services et marchandises n'est pas aisée. Les services sont produits sur commande et ont généralement pour résultat un changement des conditions des consommateurs qui ont demandé ces services. Pour que la production d'un service soit terminée, il doit être fourni au consommateur.

Le tableau **5.2** présente les statistiques sur le commerce international des services par catégories de services pour une sélection de groupements de pays, ainsi que pour les principaux exportateurs et importateurs parmi les économies en développement et en transition, et parmi les pays développés. Ces statistiques sont le résultat d'un travail commun entre la CNUCED et l'OMC et elles correspondent aux définitions du *Manuel de la balance des paiements* du FMI (*MBP5, 1993*). Le tableau présente des données pour les catégories de services suivantes: les transports; les voyages; les services de communications; les services du bâtiment et des travaux publics; les services d'assurance; les services financiers; les services informatiques et d'information; les redevances et droits de licence; les autres services aux entreprises; et les services personnels, culturels et relatifs aux loisirs.

Dans la mesure du possible, le but du groupe de travail inter-agences sur les statistiques du commerce international de services est d'expliquer et réduire les divergences relevées dans les statistiques sur les services publiées par différentes organisations internationales. Un aperçu des bases de données couvrant les statistiques du commerce international des services est disponible sur

http://unstats.un.org/unsd/tradeserv/TFSITS/matrix.htm.

Le tableau **5.3** concerne le transport maritime international. Il contient des données sur la flotte marchande mondiale par pavillons d'immatriculation et par types de navires et fait spécialement ressortir le groupe des principaux pays de libre immatriculation. Un propriétaire qui enregistre son navire dans un pays "libre d'immatriculation" ne doit avoir aucune relation avec ce pays. Le nombre de pays de libre immatriculation a changé au cours des années.

Dans le tableau 5.3, le groupe comprend 10 pays. Le tableau incorpore les informations consolidées provenant des différentes éditions de la publication *Review of Maritime Transport*.

Elle rend compte de l'évolution mondiale du transport multimodal, portuaire et maritime concernant les principaux trafics de vracs liquides, de vracs secs et de conteneurs.

SIXIÈME PARTIE
Produits de base

Le tableau **6.1** donne les indices annuels et trimestriels de prix en dollars courants sur le marché libre d'une sélection de produits de base exportés par les économies en développement. Ces indices sont aussi disponibles au niveau des groupes de produits de base suivants : produits alimentaires, boissons tropicales, huiles et graines oléagineuses, matières premières d'origine agricole, minéraux, minerais et métaux ainsi qu'un indice de l'ensemble. Les pondérations ont été calculées à partir de la valeur des exportations des pays en développement de 1999 à 2001 et les indices en utilisant 2000=100 comme année de base.

Le tableau **6.2** complète l'information sur les prix des produits de base par les indices d'instabilité et les tendances de prix sur le marché libre d'une sélection de produits de base ayant une importance particulière pour les économies en développement.

SEPTIÈME PARTIE
Finance internationale

Les tableaux **7.1.1**, **7.1.2** et **7.1.3** fournissent les valeurs de compte courant net par pays, par régions et par groupements économiques et commerciaux. Les chiffres sont présentés en millions de dollars, ainsi qu'en pourcentage du produit intérieur brut. Le compte des transactions courantes de la balance des paiements recouvre toutes les transactions entre entités résidentes et non-résidentes de l'économie déclarante. En général, la balance du compte courant indique la différence entre les recettes et les paiements pour les biens, les services et les revenus faisant partie des transactions internationales. De même, de la perspective nationale, la balance du compte courant représente l'écart entre les épargnes nationales et l'investissement intérieur.

Les tableaux **7.2.1**, **7.2.2** et **7.2.3** sont consacrés aux investissements directs en provenance de l'étranger (IED). Ils représentent les flux entrants et sortants de l'IED par pays et régions géographiques, groupements économiques et groupements commerciaux. Les chiffres correspondent aux données contenues dans l'Annexe statistique du *World Investment Report 2012* de la CNUCED. L'investissement étranger direct (IED) est un investissement impliquant une relation à long terme et témoignant de l'intérêt durable d'une entité résidant dans un pays (investisseur étranger direct ou société mère) à l'égard d'une entreprise résidant dans un autre pays (entreprise bénéficiaire, entreprise affiliée, ou encore filiale étrangère). Cet investissement englobe à la fois la transaction initiale entre les deux entités et toutes les transactions ultérieures entre elles et entre filiales étrangères, qu'elles soient constituées ou non en sociétés. L'entreprise d'investissement direct est définie comme une entreprise dotée ou non de la personnalité morale, dans laquelle un investisseur direct qui est résident d'une autre économie détient au moins 10% des actions ordinaires ou des droits de vote (ou l'équivalent).

Les tableaux **7.3.1** et **7.3.2** fournissent les informations sur les recettes (crédits) des envois de fonds des travailleurs et migrants - en millions de dollars - par pays, par régions et par groupements économiques. Ces données sont également communiquées en pourcentage du PIB et du commerce international. Le *Manuel de la balance des paiements* du FMI (*MBP5, 1993*) classe séparément les envois de fonds des travailleurs, la rémunération des salariés et les transferts des migrants. Dans ce tableau leur somme est présentée afin de mieux cerner les flux entrant une économie à travers les transferts liés aux travailleurs migrants ou autres travailleurs employés à l'étranger à court-terme. Selon la définition du *MBP5* les envois de fonds des travailleurs sont les transferts de biens ou d'actifs financiers effectués par les migrants qui vivent et travaillent (considérés comme résidents) dans une économie en faveur des résidents de leur ancien pays de résidence.

Un migrant doit vivre et travailler dans une nouvelle économie durant plus d'une année pour y être considéré résident. La rémunération des salariés comprend les salaires, traitements et autres prestations, en numéraire ou nature, gagnés par les particuliers, dans une économie où ils ne sont pas résidents, pour un travail exécuté au profit d'un résident de cette économie.

Les salariés peuvent être des travailleurs saisonniers ou d'autres travailleurs à temps limité ou encore des travailleurs frontaliers. Les transferts des migrants couvrent les flux de biens et les variations des actifs financiers qui résultent de la migration (changement de résidence pour une durée d'un an au moins).

Les tableaux 7.4.1 et 7.4.2 font apparaître les statistiques sur les paiements (débits) des envois des travailleurs et migrants, suivant la même approche utilisée dans les tableaux 7.3.1 et 7.3.2.

Les tableaux 7.5.1 et 7.5.2 incluent les données relatives aux réserves internationales (y compris l'or) des économies en développement par pays, par régions et par groupements économiques. Les mois d'importation que ces réserves peuvent financer, dans la situation actuelle du commerce international du pays, sont également indiqués, ainsi que la variation annuelle des réserves totales. Selon la définition du FMI, les réserves totales représentent la somme des avoirs du pays en devises, la position de ses réserves au FMI, les réserves de l'or monétaire, et la valeur en dollars des États-Unis des avoirs en DTS de ses autorités monétaires.

Les flux financiers publics sont présentés dans les tableaux 7.6 par catégories de flux, pays, régions géographiques et groupements économiques. La définition des flux bilatéraux et multilatéraux est conforme aux publications du Comité d'aide au développement (CAD) de l'OCDE.

Les tableaux 7.7 contiennent les données sur la dette extérieure à long terme des principaux groupes d'économies en développement, en particulier la ventilation détaillée de la dette publique ou garantie par l'État par sources d'emprunt. Les données de la dette extérieure présentées dans ces tableaux se basent sur le Système de notification des pays débiteurs (SNPD), géré par la Banque mondiale.

HUITIÈME PARTIE
Indicateurs du développement

Les tableaux 8.1 fournissent le produit intérieur brut (PIB) nominal total et par habitant des pays, régions géographiques et groupements économiques. Les données de PIB en dollars ont été obtenues à partir des valeurs de PIB exprimées à l'origine en monnaies nationales. Les taux de change moyens annuels sur le marché libre, obtenus des séries statistiques du FMI, ont été utilisés pour la plupart des pays lors de la conversion en dollars.

Les taux annuels moyens de variation du PIB réel total et du PIB réel par habitant des pays, régions géographiques et groupements économiques sont disponibles dans les tableaux 8.2. Les taux de croissance se basent sur le PIB aux prix constants en dollars de l'année 2005.

Le PIB total est décomposé par catégories de dépenses et la valeur ajoutée totale par branches d'activité économique dans les tableaux 8.3 pour les pays, régions géographiques et groupements économiques.

Les tableaux 8.4.1 et 8.4.2 présentent des estimations sur la population et la main-d'œuvre : population totale, population urbaine (en pourcentage de la population totale), main-d'œuvre totale, main-d'œuvre féminine (en pourcentage de la main-d'œuvre totale), main-d'œuvre dans l'agriculture, main-d'œuvre féminine (en pourcentage de la main-d'œuvre totale dans l'agriculture). Les chiffres pour certains groupes peuvent être différents de ceux publiés par la Division de la population lorsque les définitions de la CNUCED de ces groupes sont différentes.

AUTRES NOTES

Sauf indication contraire, les agrégats de pays sont obtenus en sommant les données des pays composant le groupe. Les calculs d'agrégats peuvent dans certains cas inclure des données estimées par le secrétariat de la CNUCED qui ne sont pas nécessairement toutes rapportées séparément.

Par ailleurs, la somme des chiffres et des pourcentages indiqués dans les tableaux ne correspond pas nécessairement aux totaux en raison des arrondis.

Les données ont été collectées et vérifiées pour qu'elles correspondent à la couverture géographique des pays, telle qu'elle est décrite en début de *Manuel*. Toutefois certains écarts n'ont pu être évités en fonction de la disponibilité des données. Ils sont alors décrits dans les notes de fin de tableau.

Sauf indication contraire, le terme «dollar» s'entend du dollar des États-Unis d'Amérique et les données en dollars sont exprimées en dollars courants de l'année à laquelle elles se réfèrent.

Les taux moyens d'évolution annuelle sont définis par le coefficient b de la fonction exponentielle de tendance $y = ae^{bt}$, où t représente le temps. Cette méthode permet de prendre en compte toutes les observations concernant une période donnée sans que le taux de croissance obtenu ne soit trop affecté par des valeurs exceptionnelles.

Les pays et territoires sont présentés suivant des critères géographiques conformes à ceux de la Division de statistique, Département des affaires économiques et sociales (DAES) de l'ONU. Les pays et territoires sont aussi regroupés suivant des critères économiques ou d'adhésion à des accords commerciaux à des fins d'analyse statistique et de recherche.

Dans cette publication, le terme «économie» couvre les régions, les pays et les territoires. Une année ajoutée au nom d'un pays indique un changement de la couverture statistique de ce pays. Par exemple, Indonésie (...2002) indique que la couverture statistique de l'Indonésie incluant le Timor-Leste était valide jusqu'à la fin 2002.

La composition des groupements de pays évolue constamment pour mettre des statistiques pertinentes à la disposition de la recherche et de l'analyse. C'est pourquoi la CNUCED révise et met à jour la définition et la composition des groupes chaque année. Ces changements peuvent affecter de manière significative les chiffres d'une année de publication à l'autre. Le détail des changements est disponible dans la section Méthodologie & Nomenclatures sur le site web de *UNCTADstat*.

1. Régions géographiques

La distinction entre pays ou régions "développés" et "en développement" ne correspond à aucune nomenclature officielle à l'échelle du système des Nations Unies. Dans la pratique, on considère généralement comme développés Israël et Japon pour l'Asie, Bermudes, Canada, États-Unis, Groenland et Saint-Pierre-et-Miquelon pour l'Amérique septentrionale, Australie et Nouvelle-Zélande pour l'Océanie et l'Europe. Les pays et territoires sont répartis en trois grandes catégories, les économies en développement, les économies en transition et les économies développées, elles-mêmes subdivisées suivant des critères géographiques.

1) Économies en développement
Ces économies sont réparties entre quatre grandes régions géographiques : Afrique, Amérique, Asie et Océanie elles-mêmes subdivisées en sous-régions pour permettre la présentation de statistiques plus détaillées. Les exceptions à ce classement que l'on retrouve dans certains tableaux sont indiquées dans des notes.

2) Économies en transition
Il s'agit des pays opérant la transition d'une économie planifiée à une économie de marché.

3) Économies développées
Ces économies sont réparties entre quatre grandes régions géographiques : Amérique, Asie, Europe et Océanie.

Le total 'Monde' inclut la somme des données de ces trois groupes à laquelle s'ajoutent les données d'un groupement 'Autres territoires' (territoires ou partenaires non classés ailleurs), dont la composition est détaillée ci-dessous. Lorsqu'elles sont rapportées, les données relatives à ces territoires ne sont pas présentées individuellement.

La composition du groupement 'Autres territoires' est la suivante:
-Territoires non-classés ailleurs : Antarctique, île Bouvet, Territoire britannique de l'Antarctique, Territoire britannique de l'océan Indien, île Christmas, îles des Cocos (Keeling), Terres australes et antarctiques françaises, îles Heard et McDonald, île Norfolk, Pitcairn, Saint-Barthélemy, Saint-Martin (partie française), Géorgie du Sud et îles Sandwich méridionales, îles mineures éloignées des États-Unis et îles du Pacifique sous administration des États-Unis.

- Partenaires non classés ailleurs : 'combustibles de soute et provisions de bord', 'informations confidentielles et différences', 'zone neutre', 'zones franches' qui sont utilisés exclusivement dans les tableaux du commerce de marchandises.

Les statistiques présentées au niveau de chacun des groupements précédemment décrits sont calculées à partir des valeurs des pays qui entrent dans la composition du groupement et complétées le cas échéant par un reliquat qu'il n'a pas été possible de répartir entre les éléments du groupement.

2. Groupements économiques des économies en développement

Dans le *Manuel de statistiques de la CNUCED*, les regroupements des pays et territoires en développement sont nombreux et variés afin de disposer facilement des données statistiques nécessaires à l'analyse socio-économique et aux recherches sur le développement.

Les économies en développement sont présentées à trois niveaux d'agrégation : le groupe dans son intégralité, puis sans la Chine continentale et enfin sans les pays les moins avancés.

Le groupe des pays pauvres très endettés inclut les pays bénéficiant de l'initiative de désendettement de la Banque mondiale et du Fonds monétaire international.

Les PMA et les pays en développement sans littoral sont des groupes de pays qui requièrent une attention particulière de la communauté internationale. Les PMA sont présentés aux niveaux d'agrégation suivants : Afrique et Haïti, Asie et les îles. Depuis 1994, les Nations Unies ont également pris en compte les problèmes particuliers des petits États insulaires en développement mais n'ont pas établi de liste officielle de ces États. La liste présentée dans le *Manuel de statistiques* est utilisée par la CNUCED à des fins analytiques uniquement.

Les économies en développement sont également réparties en trois groupes de revenu en fonction du PIB par habitant pour la moyenne des années de 2004 à 2006 : revenu élevé (supérieur à 4 500 dollars), revenu intermédiaire (compris entre 1 000 et 4 500 dollars) et revenu faible (inférieur à 1 000 dollars).

Le groupement des principaux exportateurs de pétrole et de gaz comprend les pays, dont la part de pétrole et de gaz (CTCI codes 33 plus 34), ne représentait 1) pas moins de 50 % de leurs exportations totales, et les exportations de ces produits s'élevaient à 2) au moins 1% de la part mondiale pour la période 2004-2006. Les pays composant ce groupement sont répartis en trois zones géographiques : Afrique, Amérique et Asie.

Le groupement des principaux exportateurs d'articles manufacturés (CTCI 5 à 8 moins 667 et 68), répartis entre Amérique et Asie, comprend les économies dont la part d'articles manufacturés ne représentait 1) pas moins de 50 % de leurs exportations totales, et 2) leurs exportations d'articles manufacturés représentait au moins 1% de la part mondiale pour la période 2004-2006.

La composition des groupements des économies émergentes (réparties entre Amérique et Asie) et des économies nouvellement industrialisées d'Asie (première et deuxième génération) correspond à celle utilisée dans le *Rapport sur le commerce et le développement* de la CNUCED.

Les différentes régions géographiques sont également présentées à différents niveaux d'agrégation :
- Afrique : Afrique septentrionale sans le Soudan, Afrique subsaharienne, Soudan compris, avec et sans l'Afrique du Sud.
- Amérique : Amérique centrale et Grandes Antilles sans Porto Rico, avec et sans le Mexique, Amérique du Sud et centrale, Amérique du Sud sans le Brésil.
- Asie : Asie orientale et du Sud-Est sans la Chine et Asie méridionale sans l'Inde.

3. Groupements commerciaux et interrégionaux

Les statistiques des groupements régionaux et commerciaux sont présentées dès lors qu'elles sont pertinentes et présentent un intérêt analytique. Ces groupements englobent toutes les économies concernées et sont classés selon les grandes régions géographiques utilisées précédemment, à l'exception des groupements interrégionaux suivants : le groupe des États d'Afrique, des Caraïbes et du Pacifique, le groupe de Coopération économique de l'Asie et du Pacifique, le groupe de Coopération économique de la mer Noire et la Communauté des États indépendants.

RÉPARTITION PAR RÉGIONS GÉOGRAPHIQUES

ÉCONOMIES EN DÉVELOPPEMENT

AFRIQUE

Afrique orientale

Burundi	Malawi	Seychelles
Comores	Maurice	Somalie
Djibouti	Mayotte	Zambie
Érythrée	Mozambique	Zimbabwe
Éthiopie	Ouganda	
Kenya	République-Unie de Tanzanie	
Madagascar	Rwanda	

Afrique centrale

Angola	Gabon	République démocratique du Congo
Cameroun	Guinée équatoriale	Sao Tomé-et-Principe
Congo	République centrafricaine	Tchad

Afrique septentrionale

Algérie	Maroc	Tunisie
Égypte	Sahara occidental	
Libye	Soudan	

Afrique australe

Afrique du Sud	Lesotho	Swaziland
Botswana	Namibie	

Afrique occidentale

Bénin	Guinée	Nigéria
Burkina Faso	Guinée-Bissau	Sainte-Hélène
Cap-Vert	Libéria	Sénégal
Côte d'Ivoire	Mali	Sierra Leone
Gambie	Mauritanie	Togo
Ghana	Niger	

AMÉRIQUE

Amérique centrale

Belize	Guatemala	Nicaragua
Costa Rica	Honduras	Panama
El Salvador	Mexique	

Amérique du Sud

Argentine	Équateur	Suriname
Bolivie (État plurinational de)	Guyana	Uruguay
Brésil	Îles Falkland (Malvinas)	Venezuela (République bolivarienne du)
Chili	Paraguay	
Colombie	Pérou	

ÉCONOMIES EN DÉVELOPPEMENT (fin)

AMÉRIQUE (fin)

Caraïbes

Grandes Antilles

Cuba
Haïti
Jamaïque
République dominicaine

Petites Antilles

Anguilla	Îles Caïmanes
Antigua-et-Barbuda	Îles Turques et Caïques
Aruba	Îles Vierges britanniques
Bahamas	Montserrat
Barbade	Sainte-Lucie
Bonaire, Saint-Eustache et Saba*	Saint-Kitts-et-Nevis
Curaçao*	Saint-Martin (partie néerlandaise)*
Dominique	Saint-Vincent-et-les Grenadines
Grenade	Trinité-et-Tobago

* Les Antilles néerlandaises ont été dissoutes le 10 Octobre 1010. La composition des groupements auxquels elles appartiennent a été révisée en accord avec ces changements.

ASIE

Asie orientale

Chine
Hong Kong, région administrative
   spéciale de Chine
Macao, région administrative
   spéciale de Chine

Mongolie
Province chinoise de Taiwan
République de Corée
République populaire démocratique
   de Corée

Asie méridionale

Afghanistan	Inde	Népal
Bangladesh	Iran (République islamique d')	Pakistan
Bhoutan	Maldives	Sri Lanka

Asie du Sud-Est

Brunéi Darussalam	Myanmar	Thaïlande
Cambodge	Philippines	Timor-Leste
Indonésie	République démocratique populaire lao	Viet Nam
Malaisie	Singapour	

Asie occidentale

Arabie saoudite	Koweït	Territoire palestinien occupé
Bahreïn	Liban	Turquie
Émirats arabes unis	Oman	Yémen
Iraq	Qatar	
Jordanie	République arabe syrienne	

OCÉANIE

Fidji	Kiribati	Polynésie française
Guam	Micronésie (États fédérés de)	Samoa
Îles Cook	Nauru	Samoa américaines
Îles Mariannes septentrionales	Nioué	Tokélaou
Îles Marshall	Nouvelle-Calédonie	Tonga
Îles Salomon	Palaos	Tuvalu
Îles Wallis-et-Futuna	Papouasie-Nouvelle-Guinée	Vanuatu

RÉPARTITION PAR RÉGIONS GÉOGRAPHIQUES

ÉCONOMIES EN TRANSITION

Albanie
Arménie
Azerbaïdjan
Bélarus
Bosnie-Herzégovine
Croatie
ex-République yougoslave
   de Macédoine

Fédération de Russie
Géorgie
Kazakhstan
Kirghizistan
Monténégro
Ouzbékistan
République de Moldova
Serbie

Tadjikistan
Turkménistan
Ukraine

ÉCONOMIES DÉVELOPÉES

AMÉRIQUE

Bermudes
Canada

États-Unis d'Amérique, y compris
   Porto Rico et les îles Vierges
   américaines

Groenland
Saint-Pierre-et-Miquelon

ASIE

Israël
Japon

EUROPE

Allemagne
Andorre
Autriche
Belgique
Bulgarie
Chypre
Danemark
Espagne
Estonie
Finlande, y compris les îles d'Åland
France, y compris la Guadeloupe,
   la Guyane française, la Martinique,
   Monaco et la Réunion
Gibraltar

Grèce
Hongrie
Îles Féroé
Irlande
Islande
Italie
Lettonie
Lituanie
Luxembourg
Malte
Norvège, y compris les îles Svalbard
   et Jan Mayen
Pays-Bas
Pologne

Portugal
République tchèque
Roumanie
Royaume-Uni de Grande-Bretagne
   et d'Irlande du Nord, y compris les îles
   Anglo-Normandes et l'île de Man
Saint-Marin
Saint-Siège
Slovaquie
Slovénie
Suède
Suisse, y compris le Liechtenstein

OCÉANIE

Australie
Nouvelle-Zélande

RÉPARTITION DES ÉCONOMIES EN DÉVELOPPEMENT PAR GROUPEMENTS ÉCONOMIQUES

Pays pauvres très endettés (40)

Afghanistan	Guinée-Bissau	République centrafricaine
Bénin	Guyana	République démocratique du Congo
Bolivie (État plurinational de)	Haïti	République-Unie de Tanzanie
Burkina Faso	Honduras	Rwanda
Burundi	Kirghizistan	Sao Tomé-et-Principe
Cameroun	Libéria	Sénégal
Comores	Madagascar	Sierra Leone
Congo	Malawi	Somalie
Côte d'Ivoire	Mali	Soudan
Érythrée	Mauritanie	Tchad
Éthiopie	Mozambique	Togo
Gambie	Nicaragua	Zambie
Ghana	Niger	
Guinée	Ouganda	

Pays en développement sans littoral (31)

Afghanistan	Kirghizistan*	République de Moldova*
Arménie*	Lesotho	Rwanda
Azerbaïdjan*	Malawi	Swaziland
Bhoutan	Mali	Tadjikistan*
Bolivie (État plurinational de)	Mongolie	Tchad
Botswana	Népal	Turkménistan*
Burkina Faso	Niger	Zambie
Burundi	Ouganda	Zimbabwe
Éthiopie	Ouzbékistan*	
ex-République yougoslave	Paraguay	
de Macédoine*	République centrafricaine	
Kazakhstan*	République démocratique populaire lao	

* Ces pays font partie du groupement des économies en transition (ni développées ni en développement).
Cependant, comme ce sont des pays sans littoral, ils appartiennent aussi à ce groupement.

Petits États insulaires en développement (29)

Antigua-et-Barbuda	Jamaïque	Saint-Vincent-et-les Grenadines
Bahamas	Kiribati	Samoa
Barbade	Maldives	Sao Tomé-et-Principe
Cap-Vert	Maurice	Seychelles
Comores	Micronésie (États fédérés de)	Timor-Leste
Dominique	Nauru	Tonga
Fidji	Palaos	Trinité-et-Tobago
Grenade	Papouasie-Nouvelle-Guinée	Tuvalu
Îles Marshall	Sainte-Lucie	Vanuatu
Îles Salomon	Saint-Kitts-et-Nevis	

Pays les moins avancés (48)

Afrique et Haïti	Année d'inclusion dans le groupe		Année d'inclusion dans le groupe	*Asie*	Année d'inclusion dans le groupe
Angola	1994	Mozambique	1988	Afghanistan	1971
Bénin	1971	Niger	1971	Bangladesh	1975
Burkina Faso	1971	Ouganda	1971	Bhoutan	1971
Burundi	1971	République centrafricaine	1975	Cambodge	1991
Djibouti	1982	République démocratique du Congo	1991	Myanmar	1987
Érythrée	1994	République-Unie de Tanzanie	1971	Népal	1971
Éthiopie	1971	Rwanda	1971	République démocratique populaire lao	1971
Gambie	1975	Sénégal	2000	Yémen	1971
Guinée	1971	Sierra Leone	1982	*Îles*	
Guinée-Bissau	1981	Somalie	1971	Comores	1977
Guinée Équatoriale	1982	Soudan	1971	Îles Salomon	1991
Haïti	1971	Tchad	1971	Kiribati	1986
Lesotho	1971	Togo	1982	Samoa	1971
Libéria	1990	Zambie	1991	Sao Tomé-et-Principe	1982
Madagascar	1991			Timor-Leste	2003
Malawi	1971			Tuvalu	1986
Mali	1971			Vanuatu	1985
Mauritanie	1986				

RÉPARTITION DES ÉCONOMIES EN DÉVELOPPEMENT PAR GROUPEMENTS ÉCONOMIQUES

GROUPEMENTS ÉCONOMIQUES DE LA CNUCED

PIB courant par habitant supérieur à 4 500 dollars pour la moyenne 2004-2006 : Revenu élevé (48)

Anguilla
Antigua-et-Barbuda
Arabie saoudite
Argentine
Aruba
Bahamas
Bahreïn
Barbade
Bonaire, Saint-Eustache et Saba
Brunéi Darussalam
Chili
Costa Rica
Curaçao
Émirats arabes unis
Guam
Guinée équatoriale
Hong-Kong, région administrative
   spéciale de Chine

Îles Caïmanes
Îles Cook
Îles Falkland (Malvinas)
Îles Mariannes du Nord
Îles Turques et Caïques
Îles Vierges britanniques
Koweït
Liban
Libye
Macao, région administrative
   spéciale de Chine
Malaisie
Mexique
Montserrat
Nioué
Nouvelle-Calédonie
Oman
Palaos

Polynésie française
Province chinoise de Taiwan
Qatar
République de Corée
Sainte-Lucie
Saint-Kitts-et-Nevis
Saint-Martin (partie néerlandaise)
Samoa américaines
Seychelles
Singapour
Trinité-et-Tobago
Turquie
Uruguay
Venezuela (République bolivarienne du)

PIB courant par habitant compris entre 1 000 et 4 500 dollars pour la moyenne 2004-2006 : Revenu intermédiaire (50)

Afrique du Sud
Algérie
Belize
Bolivie (État plurinational de)
Botswana
Brésil
Cap-Vert
Chine
Colombie
Congo
Cuba
Dominique
Égypte
El Salvador
Équateur
Fidji
Gabon

Grenade
Guatemala
Honduras
Îles Marshall
Îles Wallis-et-Futuna
Iran (République islamique d')
Jamaïque
Jordanie
Maldives
Maroc
Maurice
Micronésie (États fédérés de)
Namibie
Nauru
Panama
Paraguay
Pérou

Philippines
République arabe syrienne
République dominicaine
Sainte-Hélène
Saint-Vincent-et-les Grenadines
Samoa
Sri Lanka
Suriname
Swaziland
Territoire palestinien occupé
Thaïlande
Tokélaou
Tonga
Tunisie
Tuvalu
Vanuatu

PIB courant par habitant inférieur à 1 000 dollars pour la moyenne 2004-2006 : Revenu faible (60)

Afghanistan
Angola
Bangladesh
Bénin
Bhoutan
Burkina Faso
Burundi
Cambodge
Cameroun
Comores
Côte d'Ivoire
Djibouti
Érythrée
Éthiopie
Gambie
Ghana
Guinée
Guinée-Bissau
Guyana
Haïti
Îles Salomon

Inde
Indonésie
Iraq
Kenya
Kiribati
Lesotho
Libéria
Madagascar
Malawi
Mali
Mauritanie
Mongolie
Mozambique
Myanmar
Népal
Nicaragua
Niger
Nigéria
Ouganda
Pakistan
Papouasie-Nouvelle-Guinée

République centrafricaine
République démocratique du Congo
République populaire démocratique
   de Corée
République démocratique populaire lao
République-Unie de Tanzanie
Rwanda
Sao Tomé-et-Principe
Sénégal
Sierra Leone
Somalie
Soudan
Tchad
Timor-Leste
Togo
Viet Nam
Yémen
Zambie
Zimbabwe

RÉPARTITION DES ÉCONOMIES EN DÉVELOPPEMENT PAR GROUPEMENTS ÉCONOMIQUES

Principaux pays exportateurs de pétrole et de gaz (12)

Afrique
Algérie
Angola
Libye
Nigéria

Amérique
Venezuela
  (République bolivarienne du)

Asie
Arabie saoudite
Émirats arabes unis
Iran (République islamique d')
Iraq
Koweït
Oman
Qatar

Principaux pays exportateurs d'articles manufacturés (8)

Amérique
Mexique

Asie
Chine
Hong Kong, région administrative
  spéciale de Chine
Malaisie
Province chinoise de Taiwan
République de Corée
Singapour
Thaïlande

Économies émergentes (10)

Amérique
Argentine
Brésil
Chili
Mexique
Pérou

Asie
Malaisie
Province chinoise de Taiwan
République de Corée
Singapour
Thaïlande

Économies nouvellement industrialisées d'Asie (8)

Première génération
Hong Kong, région administrative
  spéciale de Chine
Province chinoise de Taiwan
République de Corée
Singapour

Deuxième génération
Indonésie
Malaisie
Philippines
Thaïlande

RÉPARTITION DES ÉCONOMIES PAR GROUPEMENTS COMMERCIAUX

AFRIQUE

	Année d'adhésion
Communauté de l'Afrique de l'Est (5) – CAE	
Burundi	2007
Kenya	2001
Ouganda	2001
République-Unie de Tanzanie	2001
Rwanda	2007
Communauté de développement de l'Afrique australe (15) – CDAA	
Afrique du Sud	1994
Angola	1992
Botswana	1992
Lesotho	1992
Madagascar	2005
Malawi	1992
Maurice	1992
Mozambique	1992
Namibie	1992
République démocratique du Congo	1992
République-Unie de Tanzanie	1992
Seychelles	2007
Swaziland	1992
Zambie	1992
Zimbabwe	1994
Communauté économique des États de l'Afrique centrale (10) – CEEAC	
Angola	1999
Burundi	1983
Cameroun	1983
Congo	1983
Gabon	1983
Guinée équatoriale	1983
République centrafricaine	1983
République démocratique du Congo	1983
Sao Tomé-et-Principe	1983
Tchad	1983

	Année d'adhésion
Communauté économique et monétaire de l'Afrique centrale (6) – CEMAC	
Cameroun	1994
Congo	1994
Gabon	1994
Guinée équatoriale	1994
République centrafricaine	1994
Tchad	1994
Communauté économique des États de l'Afrique de l'Ouest (15) – CEDEAO	
Bénin	1975
Burkina Faso	1975
Cap-Vert	1977
Côte d'Ivoire	1975
Gambie	1975
Ghana	1975
Guinée	1975
Guinée-Bissau	1975
Libéria	1975
Mali	1975
Niger	1975
Nigéria	1975
Sénégal	1975
Sierra Leone	1975
Togo	1975
Communauté économique des pays des Grands Lacs (3) – CEPGL	
Burundi	1976
République démocratique du Congo	1976
Rwanda	1976
Marché commun des États de l'Afrique de l'Est et du Sud (19) – COMESA	
Burundi	1994
Comores	1994
Djibouti	1994
Égypte	1994
Érythrée	1994
Éthiopie	1994
Kenya	1994
Libye	2005

	Année d'adhésion
Madagascar	1994
Malawi	1994
Maurice	1994
Ouganda	1994
République démocratique du Congo	1994
Rwanda	1994
Seychelles	1994
Soudan	1994
Swaziland	1994
Zambie	1994
Zimbabwe	1994
Union du fleuve Mano (4) – UFM	
Côte d'Ivoire	2008
Guinée	1980
Libéria	1973
Sierra Leone	1973
Union du Maghreb arabe (5) – UMA	
Algérie	1989
Libye	1989
Maroc	1989
Mauritanie	1989
Tunisie	1989
Union économique et monétaire Ouest-africaine (8) – UEMOA	
Bénin	1994
Burkina Faso	1994
Côte d'Ivoire	1994
Guinée-Bissau	1997
Mali	1994
Niger	1994
Sénégal	1994
Togo	1994

AMÉRIQUE

	Année d'adhésion
Accord de libre-échange nord-américain (3) - ALENA	
Canada	1994
États-Unis d'Amérique	1994
Mexique	1994
Association latino-américaine d'intégration (12) - ALADI	
Argentine	1980
Bolivie (État plurinational de)	1980
Brésil	1980
Chili	1980
Colombie	1980
Cuba	1999
Équateur	1980
Mexique	1980
Paraguay	1980
Pérou	1980
Uruguay	1980
Venezuela (République bolivarienne du)	1980

	Année d'adhésion
Communauté andine (4) - ANCOM	
Bolivie (État plurinational de)	1996
Colombie	1996
Équateur	1996
Pérou	1996
Communauté des Caraïbes (15) - CARICOM	
Antigua-et-Barbuda	1974
Bahamas	1983
Barbade	1973
Belize	1974
Dominique	1974
Grenade	1974
Guyana	1973
Haïti	2002
Jamaïque	1973
Montserrat	1974
Sainte Lucie	1974
Saint-Kitts-et-Nevis	1974
Saint-Vincent-et-les- Grenadines	1974
Suriname	1995
Trinité-et-Tobago	1973

	Année d'adhésion
Marché commun d'Amérique centrale (5) - MCAC	
Costa Rica	1962
El Salvador	1961
Guatemala	1961
Honduras	1961
Nicaragua	1961
Marché commun sud-américain (4) - MERCOSUR	
Argentine	1994
Brésil	1994
Paraguay	1994
Uruguay	1994

RÉPARTITION DES ÉCONOMIES PAR GROUPEMENTS COMMERCIAUX

AMÉRIQUE (fin)

	Année d'adhésion		Année d'adhésion		Année d'adhésion
Organisation des États américains (35) - OEA		République dominicaine	1948	Brésil	1994
		Sainte-Lucie	1979	Canada	1994
Antigua-et-Barbuda	1981	Saint-Kitts-et-Nevis	1984	Chili	1994
Argentine	1948	Saint-Vincent-et-les Grenadines	1981	Colombie	1994
Bahamas	1982	Suriname	1977	Costa Rica	1994
Barbade	1967	Trinité-et-Tobago	1967	Dominique	1994
Belize	1991	Uruguay	1948	El Salvador	1994
Bolivie (État plurinational de)	1948	Venezuela (Rép. Bolivarienne du)	1948	Équateur	1994
Brésil	1948			États-Unis d'Amérique	1994
Canada	1990	**Organisation des États des Caraïbes orientales (9) - OECO**		Grenade	1994
Chili	1948			Guatemala	1994
Colombie	1948	Anguilla	1995	Guyana	1994
Costa Rica	1948	Antigua-et-Barbuda	1981	Haïti	1994
Cuba	2009	Dominique	1981	Honduras	1994
Dominique	1979	Grenade	1981	Jamaïque	1994
El Salvador	1948	Îles Vierges britanniques	1984	Mexique	1994
Équateur	1948	Montserrat	1981	Nicaragua	1994
États-Unis d'Amérique	1948	Sainte-Lucie	1981	Panama	1994
Grenade	1975	Saint-Kitts-et-Nevis	1981	Paraguay	1994
Guatemala	1948	Saint-Vincent-et-les Grenadines	1981	Pérou	1994
Guyana	1948			République dominicaine	1994
Haïti	1948	**Zone de libre-échange des Amériques (34) - ZLEA**		Sainte-Lucie	1994
Honduras	1948	Antigua-et-Barbuda	1994	Saint-Kitts-et-Nevis	1994
Jamaïque	1969	Argentine	1994	Saint-Vincent-et-les Grenadines	1994
Mexique	1948	Bahamas	1994	Suriname	1994
Nicaragua	1948	Barbade	1994	Trinité-et-Tobago	1994
Panama	1948	Belize	1994	Uruguay	1994
Paraguay	1948	Bolivie (État plurinational de)	1994	Venezuela (République bolivarienne du)	1994
Pérou	1948				

ASIE

	Année d'adhésion		Année d'adhésion		Année d'adhésion
Accord commercial de l'Asie et du Pacifique (6) - ACAP		**Association des nations de l'Asie du Sud-Est (10) - ANASE**		Oman	1981
				Qatar	1981
Bangladesh	1975	Brunéi Darussalam	1984		
Chine	2001	Cambodge	1999	**Organisation de coopération économique (10) - ECO**	
Inde	1975	Indonésie	1967	Afghanistan	1992
République de Corée	1975	Malaisie	1967	Azerbaïdjan	1992
République démocratique populaire lao	1975	Myanmar	1997	Iran (République islamique d')	1985
Sri Lanka	1975	Philippines	1967	Kazakhstan	1992
		République démocratique populaire lao	1997	Kirghizistan	1992
Association de l'Asie du Sud pour la coopération régionale (8) - SAARC		Singapour	1967	Ouzbékistan	1992
		Thaïlande	1967	Pakistan	1985
Afghanistan	2007	Viet Nam	1995	Tadjikistan	1992
Bangladesh	1985			Turkménistan	1992
Bhoutan	1985	**Conseil de coopération du Golfe (6) - CCG**		Turquie	1985
Inde	1985				
Maldives	1985	Arabie saoudite	1981		
Népal	1985	Bahreïn	1981		
Pakistan	1985	Émirats arabes unis	1981		
Sri Lanka	1985	Koweït	1981		

EUROPE

	Année d'adhésion		Année d'adhésion		Année d'adhésion
Association européenne de libre-échange (3) - AELE		Hongrie	2004	**Zone euro (17)**	
		Irlande	1973	Allemagne	2002
Islande	1970	Italie	1957	Autriche	2002
Norvège	1960	Lettonie	2004	Belgique	2002
Suisse	1960	Lituanie	2004	Chypre	2008
		Luxembourg	1957	Espagne	2002
Union européenne (27) - EU		Malte	2004	Estonie	2011
Allemagne	1957	Pays-Bas	1957	Finlande	2002
Autriche	1995	Pologne	2004	France	2002
Belgique	1957	Portugal	1986	Grèce	2002
Bulgarie	2008	République tchèque	2004	Irlande	2002
Chypre	2004	Roumanie	2008	Italie	2002
Danemark	1973	Royaume-Uni	1973	Luxembourg	2002
Espagne	1986	Slovaquie	2004	Malte	2008
Estonie	2004	Slovénie	2004	Pays-Bas	2002
Finlande	1995	Suède	1995	Portugal	2002
France	1957			Slovaquie	2009
Grèce	1981			Slovénie	2007

RÉPARTITION DES ÉCONOMIES PAR GROUPEMENTS COMMERCIAUX

OCÉANIE

Année d'adhésion

Groupe Fer de lance mélanésien (4)

Fidji	1998
Îles Salomon	1993
Papouasie-Nouvelle-Guinée	1993
Vanuatu	1993

RÉPARTITION DES ÉCONOMIES PAR GROUPEMENTS INTERRÉGIONAUX

Groupe des États d'Afrique, des Caraïbes et du Pacifique (79) - ACP

Afrique du Sud	Guinée équatoriale	République démocratique du Congo
Angola	Guyana	République dominicaine
Antigua-et-Barbuda	Haïti	République-Unie de Tanzanie
Bahamas	Îles Cook	Rwanda
Barbade	Îles Marshall	Sainte-Lucie
Belize	Îles Salomon	Saint-Kitts-et-Nevis
Bénin	Jamaïque	Saint-Vincent-et-les Grenadines
Botswana	Kenya	Samoa
Burkina Faso	Kiribati	Sao Tomé-et-Principe
Burundi	Lesotho	Sénégal
Cameroun	Libéria	Seychelles
Cap-Vert	Madagascar	Sierra Leone
Comores	Malawi	Somalie
Congo	Mali	Soudan
Côte d'Ivoire	Maurice	Suriname
Cuba	Mauritanie	Swaziland
Djibouti	Micronésie (États fédérés de)	Tchad
Dominique	Mozambique	Timor-Leste
Érythrée	Namibie	Togo
Éthiopie	Nauru	Tonga
Fidji	Niger	Trinité-et-Tobago
Gabon	Nigéria	Tuvalu
Gambie	Nioué	Vanuatu
Ghana	Ouganda	Zambie
Grenade	Palaos	Zimbabwe
Guinée	Papouasie-Nouvelle-Guinée	
Guinée-Bissau	République centrafricaine	

Année d'adhésion

Coopération économique de l'Asie et du Pacifique (21) - CEAP

Australie	1989
Brunéi Darussalam	1989
Canada	1989
Chili	1994
Chine	1991
États-Unis d'Amérique	1989
Fédération de Russie	1998
Hong Kong, région administrative spéciale de Chine	1991
Indonésie	1989
Japon	1989
Malaisie	1989
Mexique	1993
Nouvelle-Zélande	1989
Papouasie-Nouvelle-Guinée	1993
Pérou	1998
Philippines	1989
Province chinoise de Taiwan	1991
République de Corée	1989
Singapour	1989
Thaïlande	1989
Viet Nam	1998

Année d'adhésion

Coopération économique de la mer Noire (12) - CEMN

Albanie	1992
Arménie	1992
Azerbaïdjan	1992
Bulgarie	1992
Fédération de Russie	1992
Géorgie	1992
Grèce	1992
République de Moldova	1992
Roumanie	1992
Serbie	2004
Turquie	1992
Ukraine	1992

Année d'adhésion

Communauté des États indépendants (11) - CEI

Arménie	1991
Azerbaïdjan	1991
Bélarus	1991
Fédération de Russie	1991
Kazakhstan	1991
Kirghizistan	1991
Ouzbékistan	1991
République de Moldova	1991
Tadjikistan	1991
Turkménistan	1991
Ukraine	1991

ABRÉVIATIONS ET ACRONYMES

AASP	autres apports du secteur public
ACAP	Accord commercial de l'Asie et du Pacifique (ex-Accord de Bangkok)
ACP	Groupe des États d'Afrique, des Caraïbes et du Pacifique
AELE	Association européenne de libre-échange
AGCS	Accord général sur le commerce des services
ALADI	Association latino-américaine d'intégration
ALENA	Accord de libre-échange nord-américain
ANASE	Association des nations de l'Asie du Sud-Est
ANCOM	Communauté andine
anc.	ancien, ancienne, anciennement
AP	aide publique
APD	aide publique au développement
CAD	Comité d'aide au développement (OCDE)
CARICOM	Communauté des Caraïbes
CCG	Conseil de coopération du Golfe
CCSA	Comité de coordination des activités statistiques
CAE	Communauté de l'Afrique de l'Est
CDAA	Communauté de développement de l'Afrique australe
CEAP	Coopération économique de l'Asie et du Pacifique
CEDEAO	Communauté économique des États de l'Afrique de l'Ouest
CEE	Commission économique pour l'Europe
CEEAC	Communauté économique des États de l'Afrique centrale
CEI	Communauté des États indépendants
CEMAC	Communauté économique et monétaire de l'Afrique centrale
CEMN	Coopération économique de la mer Noire
CEPALC	Commission économique pour l'Amérique Latine et les Caraïbes
CEPGL	Communauté économique des pays des Grands Lacs
CESAP	Commission économique et sociale pour l'Asie et le Pacifique
CESAO	Commission économique et sociale pour l'Asie occidentale
c.a.f.	coût, assurance, fret
COMESA	Marché commun d'Afrique de l'Est et du Sud
CTCI	Classification type pour le commerce international
DTS	droit de tirage spécial
EIU	Economic Intelligence Unit
f.a.b.	franco à bord
FAO	Organisation des Nations Unies pour l'alimentation et l'agriculture
FBCF	formation brute de capital fixe
FMI	Fonds monétaire international
IED	Investissement étranger direct
ISBLM	institutions sans but lucratif au service des ménages
LERY	L'ex-République yougoslave de Macédoine
MBP	Manuel de la balance des paiements (FMI)
MCAC	Marché commun d'Amérique centrale
MERCOSUR	Marché commun sud-américain
MSG	Groupe Fer de lance mélanésien
n.c.a.	non classé ailleurs
n.d.a.	non dénommé ailleurs
NEI	nouvelles économies industrialisées
NPF	nation la plus favorisée
OCDE	Organisation de coopération et de développement économiques
OCE	Organisation de coopération économique
OEA	Organisation des États américains
OECO	Organisation des États des Caraïbes orientales
OIT	Organisation internationale du travail
OMC	Organisation mondiale du commerce
ONU/DAES/DS	Organisation des Nations Unies, Département des affaires économiques et sociales, Division de statistique
OPEP	Organisation des pays exportateurs de pétrole
PIB	produit intérieur brut
PMA	pays les moins avancés
PNB	produit national brut
PNUD	Programme des Nations Unies pour le développement
PPTE	pays pauvres très endettés
RAS	région administrative spéciale
RSF	République socialiste fédérative de Yougoslavie (anc.)
SAARC	Association de l'Asie du Sud pour la coopération régionale
SH	Système harmonisé
SNPD	Système de notification des pays débiteurs
STN	société transnationale
UE	Union européenne
UEMOA	Union économique et monétaire des États de l'Afrique de l'Ouest
UFM	Union du fleuve Mano
UMA	Union du Maghreb arabe
UNESCO	Organisation des Nations Unies pour l'éducation, la science et la culture
UNICEF	Fonds des Nations Unies pour l'enfance
URSS	Union des Républiques socialistes soviétiques
ZLEA	Zone de libre échange des Amériques

The *Handbook of Statistics* refers to the Standard International Trade Classification (SITC) Revision 3 detailed below.

Depending on the table, nomenclature of statistics is detailed at the 3-digit level or by broad product groupings as follows:

Le *Manuel de statistiques* se réfère à la Classification type pour le commerce international (CTCI) révision 3 détaillée ci-dessous.

Selon les tableaux, les statistiques sont présentées, au niveau détaillé de la nomenclature (position à trois chiffres) ou par groupements de produits dont la composition est la suivante :

SITC Codes – Codes CTCI	Product groupings	Groupements de produits
0 to 9 – 0 à 9	All products	Total tous produits
0 + 1 + 22 + 4	All food items	Produits alimentaires
2 - (22 + 27 + 28)	Agricultural raw materials	Matières premières d'origine agricole
27 + 28 + 68 + 667 + 971	Ores, metals, precious stones and non-monetary gold	Minerais, métaux, pierres précieuses et or à usage non monétaire
3	Fuels	Combustibles
5 + 6 + 7 + 8 - (667 + 68)	Manufactured goods:	Articles manufacturés :
5	- Chemical products	- Produits chimiques
7	- Machinery and transport equipment	- Machines et matériel de transport
6 + 8 - (667 + 68)	- Other manufactured goods	- Articles manufacturés divers

Codes	Standard International Trade Classification (SITC) Revision 3 (1 to 3 digits)	Classification type pour le commerce international (CTCI) Révision 3 (positions de un à trois chiffres)
0	**Food and live animals**	**Produits alimentaires et animaux vivants**
00	**Live animals other than animals of division 03**	**Animaux vivants autres que ceux figurant dans la division 03**
001	Live animals other than animals of division 03	Animaux vivants autres que ceux figurant dans la division 03
01	**Meat and meat preparations**	**Viandes et préparations de viande**
011	Meat of bovine animals, fresh, chilled or frozen	Viande des animaux de l'espèce bovine, fraîche, réfrigérée/congel.
012	Other meat and edible meat offal	Autres viandes et abats comestibles
016	Meat, edible meat offal, salted, dried; flours, meals	Viandes et abats comestibles salés, fumés; farines et poudres
017	Meat, edible meat offal, prepared, preserved, n.e.s.	Préparations de viandes et d'abats, n.d.a.
02	**Dairy products and birds' eggs**	**Produits laitiers et oeufs d'oiseaux**
022	Milk, cream and milk products (excluding butter, cheese)	Lait et produits laitiers (sauf beurre, fromages)
023	Butter and other fats and oils derived from milk	Beurre et autres matières grasses du lait
024	Cheese and curd	Fromages et caillebotte
025	Birds' eggs, and eggs' yolks; egg albumin	Oeufs d'oiseaux et jaunes d'oeufs frais, blanc d'oeuf
03	**Fish (not marine mammals), crustaceans, molluscs and aquatic invertebrates and preparations thereof**	**Poissons (sauf mammifères marins), crustacés, mollusques et autres invertébrés aquatiques et préparations**
034	Fish, fresh (live or dead), chilled or frozen	Poissons frais, vivants ou morts, réfrigérés ou congelés
035	Fish, dried, salted or in brine; smoked fish	Poissons séchés, salés, fumés
036	Crustaceans, molluscs and aquatic invertebrates	Crustacés, mollusques et invertébrés aquatiques
037	Fish, aqua. invertebrates, prepared, preserved, n.e.s.	Poissons, crustacés, mollusques, préparés ou conservés, n.d.a.
04	**Cereals and cereal preparations**	**Céréales et préparations à base de céréales**
041	Wheat (including spelt) and meslin, unmilled	Froment (dont épeautre) et méteil non moulus
042	Rice	Riz
043	Barley, unmilled	Orge non mondée
044	Maize (not including sweet corn), unmilled	Maïs non moulu
045	Cereals, unmilled (excluding wheat, rice, barley, maize)	Céréales non moulues (sauf froment, riz, orge, maïs)
046	Meal and flour of wheat and flour of meslin	Semoules et farines de froment et farines de méteil
047	Other cereal meals and flour	Autres semoules et farines de céréales
048	Cereal preparations, flour of fruits or vegetables	Préparations à base de céréales, de farines, de fécules
05	**Vegetables and fruit**	**Légumes et fruits**
054	Vegetables, fresh, chilled, frozen or simply preserved; roots tubers and other edible vegetable products, n.e.s. fresh, dried	Légumes et plantes potagères, frais, réfrigérés, congelés ou simplement conservés; autres produits végétaux n.d.a. frais, séchés
056	Vegetables, roots, tubers, prepared, preserved, n.e.s.	Préparations ou conserves de légumes, n.d.a.
057	Fruits and nuts (excluding oil nuts), fresh or dried	Fruits (sauf oléagineux), frais ou secs
058	Fruit, preserved, and fruit preparations (no juice)	Préparations et conserves de fruits (sauf jus)
059	Fruit and vegetable juices, unfermented, no spirit	Jus de fruits, non fermentés, sans alcool
06	**Sugars, sugar preparations and honey**	**Sucres, préparations à base de sucre et miel**
061	Sugars, molasses and honey	Sucres, mélasses et miel
062	Sugar confectionery	Sucreries
07	**Coffee, tea, cocoa, spices and manufactures thereof**	**Café, thé, cacao, épices, et produits dérivés**
071	Coffee and coffee substitutes	Café et succédanés du café
072	Cocoa	Cacao
073	Chocolate, food preparations with cocoa, n.e.s.	Chocolat et autres préparations du cacao, n.d.a.
074	Tea and mate	Thé et maté
075	Spices	Épices

08	**Feeding stuff for animals (excluding unmilled cereals)**	**Nourriture destinée aux animaux (sauf céréales non moulues)**
081	Feeding stuff for animals (excluding unmilled cereals)	Nourriture destinée aux animaux (sauf céréales non moulues)
09	**Miscellaneous edible products and preparations**	**Produits et préparations alimentaires divers**
091	Margarine and shortening	Margarine et graisses culinaires
098	Edible products and preparations, n.e.s.	Produits et préparations alimentaires, n.d.a.
1	**Beverages and tobacco**	**Boissons et tabacs**
11	**Beverages**	**Boissons**
111	Non-alcoholic beverages, n.e.s.	Boissons non alcooliques, n.d.a.
112	Alcoholic beverages	Boissons alcooliques
12	**Tobacco and tobacco manufactures**	**Tabacs bruts et fabriqués**
121	Tobacco, unmanufactured; tobacco refuse	Tabacs bruts ou non fabriqués; déchets de tabac
122	Tobacco, manufactured (whether or not containing tobacco substitutes)	Tabacs fabriqués (même contenant des succédanés de tabac)
2	**Crude materials, inedible, except fuels**	**Matières brutes non comestibles, sauf carburants**
21	**Hides, skins and furskins, raw**	**Cuirs, peaux et pelleteries, bruts**
211	Hides and skins (except furskins), raw	Cuirs et peaux (sauf pelleteries), bruts
212	Furskins, raw, other than hides and skins of group 211	Pelleteries brutes autres que ceux du groupe 211
22	**Oil seeds and oleaginous fruits**	**Graines et fruits oléagineux**
222	Oil seeds and oleaginous fruits (excluding flour) of a kind used for the extraction of soft' oils	Graines et fruits oléagineux (sauf farines) servant normalement à l'extraction d'huiles végétales fixes douces
223	Oil seeds and oleaginous fruits (incl. flour, n.e.s.) of a kind used for the extraction of other fixed vegetable oils	Graines et fruits oléagineux (y compris les farines) servant normalement à l'extraction d'autres huiles végétales fixes
23	**Crude rubber (including synthetic and reclaimed)**	**Caoutchouc brut (y compris synthétique et régénéré)**
231	Natural rubber, balata, gutta percha, guayule, chicle and similar natural gums, in primary forms	Caoutchouc naturel, balata, gutta-percha, guayule, chicle et gommes naturelles analogues sous formes primaires
232	Synthetic rubber; reclaimed rubber; waste and scrap	Caoutchouc synthétique; caoutchouc régénéré; déchets et débris
24	**Cork and wood**	**Liège et bois**
244	Cork, natural, raw and waste (incl. blocks, sheets)	Liège naturel brut et déchets (dont blocs, feuilles)
245	Fuel wood (excluding wood waste) and wood charcoal	Bois de chauffage (sauf déchets), charbon de bois
246	Wood in chips or particles and wood waste	Bois en plaquettes, particules, déchets de bois
247	Wood in the rough or roughly squared	Bois bruts ou équarris
248	Wood, simply worked, and railway sleepers of wood	Bois simplement travaillés, traverses de bois pour voies ferrées
25	**Pulp and waste paper**	**Pâtes à papier et déchets de papier**
251	Pulp and waste paper	Pâtes à papier et déchets de papier
26	**Textiles fibres and their wastes**	**Fibres textiles et leurs déchets**
261	Silk	Soie
263	Cotton	Coton
264	Jute and other textile bast fibre, n.e.s., not spun; tow, waste	Jute et autres fibres textiles libériennes, n.d.a.; déchets
265	Vegetable textile fibres, not spun; waste of them	Fibres textiles végétales (sauf coton, jute); déchets
266	Synthetic fibres suitable for spinning	Fibres synthétiques discontinues, pour filature
267	Other man-made fibres suitable for spinning and waste	Autres fibres synthétiques/artificielles pouvant être filées; déchets
268	Wool and other animal hair (including wool tops)	Laines et autres poils (dont rubans de laine)
269	Worn clothing and other worn textile articles, rags	Friperie, drilles et chiffons
27	**Crude fertilizers, other than those of division 56, & crude minerals (excluding coal, petroleum & precious stones)**	**Engrais bruts, autres que ceux de la division 56 et minéraux bruts (à l'exclusion du charbon, pétrole et pierres précieuses)**
272	Crude fertilizers (excluding those of division 56)	Engrais bruts (sauf ceux de la division 56)
273	Stone, sand and gravel	Pierres, sables et graviers
274	Sulphur and unroasted iron pyrites	Soufre et pyrites de fer non grillées
277	Natural abrasives, n.e.s. (including industrial diamonds)	Abrasifs naturels, n.d.a. (dont diamants industriels)
278	Other crude minerals	Autre minéraux bruts
28	**Metalliferous ores and metal scrap**	**Minerais métallifères et déchets de métaux**
281	Iron ore and concentrates	Minerais de fer et leurs concentrés
282	Ferrous waste and scrap; remelting ingots, iron, steel	Déchets et débris de fer, fonte, acier; lingots
283	Copper ores and concentrates; copper mattes, cement copper	Minerais de cuivre, concentrés; mattes de cuivre; cuivre de cément
284	Nickel ores and concentrates; nickel mattes, etc.	Minerais de nickel et concentrés; mattes, etc.
285	Aluminium ores and concentrates (including alumina)	Minerais d'aluminium et concentrés (dont alumine)
286	Ores and concentrates of uranium or thorium	Minerais d'uranium ou de thorium et concentrés
287	Ores and concentrates of base metals, n.e.s.	Minerais de métaux communs et concentrés, n.d.a.
288	Non-ferrous base metal waste and scrap, n.e.s.	Déchets et débris de métaux communs non ferreux, n.d.a.

	PRODUCT CLASSIFICATION FOR INTERNATIONAL TRADE	CLASSIFICATION DES PRODUITS POUR LE COMMERCE INTERNATIONAL
289	Ores and concentrates of precious metals; waste, scrap	Minerais de métaux précieux et concentrés; débris et déchets
29	**Crude animal and vegetable materials, n.e.s.**	**Matières brutes d'origine animale ou végétale, n.d.a.**
291	Crude animal materials, n.e.s.	Matières brutes d'origine animale, n.d.a.
292	Crude vegetable materials, n.e.s.	Matières brutes d'origine végétale, n.d.a.
3	**Mineral fuels, lubricants and related materials**	**Combustibles minéraux, lubrifiants et produits connexes**
32	**Coal, coke and briquettes**	**Houilles, cokes et briquettes**
321	Coal, whether or not pulverized, not agglomerated	Houilles, même pulvérisées, mais non agglomérées
322	Briquettes, lignites and peat	Briquettes, lignite et tourbe
325	Coke and semi-cokes of coal, lignite or peat; retort carbon	Cokes, semi-cokes de houille, lignite ou tourbe; charbon de cornue
33	**Petroleum, petroleum products and related materials**	**Pétrole et produits dérivés du pétrole et produits connexes**
333	Petroleum oils, oils from bituminous materials, crude	Huiles brutes de pétrole ou de minéraux bitumineux
334	Petroleum oils or bituminous minerals > 70 % oil	Huiles de pétrole ou minéraux bitumineux > 70% huile
335	Residual petroleum products, n.e.s., related materials	Produits résiduels du pétrole, n.d.a.; produits connexes
34	**Gas, natural and manufactured**	**Gaz naturel et gaz manufacturé**
342	Liquefied propane and butane	Propane et butane liquéfiés
343	Natural gas, whether or not liquefied	Gaz naturel, même liquéfié
344	Petroleum gases, other gaseous hydrocarbons, n.e.s.	Gaz de pétrole et autres hydrocarbures gazeux, n.d.a.
345	Coal gas, water gas and similar gases (excl. hydrocarbons)	Gaz de houille, pauvre et similaires (sauf hydrocarbures)
35	**Electric current**	**Énergie électrique**
351	Electric current	Énergie électrique
4	**Animal and vegetable oils, fats and waxes**	**Huiles, graisses et cires d'origine animale ou végétale**
41	**Animal oils and fats**	**Huiles et graisses d'origine animale**
411	Animal oils and fats	Huiles et graisses d'origine animale
42	**Fixed vegetable fats and oils, crude, refined or fractionated**	**Graisses et huiles végétales fixes, brutes, raffinées ou fractionnées**
421	Fixed vegetable oils & fats, 'soft', crude, refined or fractionated	Huiles végétales fixes, douces, brutes, épurées ou raffinées
422	Fixed vegetable fats and oils, crude, refined, fractionated, other than 'soft'	Huiles végétales fixes, brutes, épurées ou raffinés, autres que douces
43	**Animal and vegetable fats and oils, processed; waxes of animal or vegetable origin; inedible mixtures**	**Huiles et graisses animales ou végétales, préparées ; cires d'origine animale et végétale; mélanges non alimentaires**
431	Animal or veg. oils and fats, processed, n.e.s.; waxes, mixt.	Huiles et graisses animales ou végétales, préparées, n.d.a.; cires
5	**Chemicals and related products, n.e.s.**	**Produits chimiques et produits connexes, n.d.a.**
51	**Organic chemicals**	**Produits chimiques organiques**
511	Hydrocarbons, n.e.s., and halogenated, nitr. derivatives	Hydrocarbures, n.d.a., dérivés halogènes, nitrosés, sulfonés, nitrés
512	Alcohols, phenols, and their derivatives	Alcools, phénols, et leurs dérivés halogénés
513	Carboxylic acids, anhydrides, halides, peroxides; derivatives	Acides carboxyliques, anhydrides, halogénures, péroxydes; dérivés
514	Nitrogen-function compounds	Composés à fonctions azotées
515	Organo-inorganic, heterocyclic compounds, nucl. acids	Composés organo-inorganiques et composés hétérocycliques; sels
516	Other organic chemicals	Autres produits chimiques organiques
52	**Inorganic chemicals**	**Produits chimiques inorganiques**
522	Inorganic chemical elements, oxides and halogen salts	Produits chimiques inorganiques : éléments, oxydes, sels
523	Metallic salts and peroxysalts, of inorganic acids	Sels et persels métalliques des acides inorganiques
524	Other inorganic chemicals; organic and inorganic compounds of precious metals	Autres produits chimiques inorganiques, composés organiques ou inorganiques de métaux précieux
525	Radioactive and associated materials	Matières radioactives et produits associés
53	**Dyeing, tanning and colouring materials**	**Produits pour teinture et tannage et colorants**
531	Synthetic organic colouring matter and colouring lakes	Matières colorantes organiques synthétiques; préparations, laques
532	Dyeing and tanning extracts, synthetic tanning materials	Extraits pour teinture et tannage
533	Pigments, paints, varnishes and related materials	Pigments, peintures, vernis et produits connexes
54	**Medical and pharmaceutical products**	**Produits médicinaux et pharmaceutiques**
541	Medicinal and pharmaceutical products, excluding 542	Produits médicinaux et pharmaceutiques (sauf 542)
542	Medicaments (including veterinary medicaments)	Médicaments pour médecine humaine ou vétérinaire
55	**Essential oils and resinoids and perfume materials; toilet, polishing and cleaning preparations**	**Huiles essentielles, résinoïdes et produits de parfumerie; préparations pour la toilette; produits d'entretien et détersifs**
551	Essential oils, perfume and flavour materials	Huiles essentielles, produits utilisés en parfumerie et en confiserie
553	Perfumery, cosmetics or toilet preparations (exclusing soaps)	Produits de parfumerie ou de toilette préparés et préparations cosmétiques (à l'exclusion des savons)
554	Soaps, cleansing and polishing preparations	Savons, produits d'entretien et détersifs
56	**Fertilizers (other than those of group 272)**	**Engrais (autres que ceux du groupe 272)**

562	Fertilizers (other than those of group 272)	Engrais (autres que ceux du groupe 272)
57	**Plastics in primary forms**	**Matières plastiques sous formes primaires**
571	Polymers of ethylene, in primary forms	Polymères de l'éthylène, sous formes primaires
572	Polymers of styrene, in primary forms	Polymères du styrène, sous formes primaires
573	Polymers of vinyl chloride or of halogenated olefins	Polymères du chlorure de vinyle ou d'autres oléfines halogènes
574	Polyeacetals, other polyethers and epoxide resins, polyesters	Polyacetals, autres polyéthers et résines époxydes, polyesters
575	Other plastics, in primary forms	Autres matières plastiques, sous formes primaires
579	Waste, parings and scrap, of plastics	Déchets, rognures et débris de matières plastiques
58	**Plastics in non-primary forms**	**Matières plastiques sous formes autres que primaires**
581	Tubes, pipes and hoses of plastics	Tubes et tuyaux en matières plastiques
582	Plates, sheets, films, foil and strip, of plastics	Plaques, feuilles, rubans en matières plastiques
583	Monofilament, cross-sectional dimension > 1 mm, rods, sticks, profile shapes, of plastics	Monofilaments, coupe transversale > 1mm (monofils), joncs, bâtons et profiles, en matières plastiques
59	**Chemical materials and products, n.e.s.**	**Matières et produits chimiques, n.d.a.**
591	Insecticides and similar products, for retail sale	Insecticides, produits similaires, pour la vente au détail
592	Starches, wheat gluten; albuminoidal substances; glues	Amidons, fécules, gluten de froment; matières albuminoïdes; colles
593	Explosives and pyrotechnic products	Explosifs et articles de pyrotechnie
597	Prepared additives for mineral oils; lubricating preparations;	Additifs pour huiles minérales
598	Miscellaneous chemical products, n.e.s.	Produits chimiques divers, n.d.a.
6	**Manufactured goods classified chiefly by material**	**Articles manufacturés classés principalement d'après la matière première**
61	**Leather, leather manufactures, n.e.s. and dressed furskins**	**Cuirs et peaux, préparés et ouvrages en cuir, n.d.a.; et pelleteries apprêtées**
611	Leather	Cuirs et peaux préparés
612	Manufactures of leather, n.e.s.; saddlery and harness	Ouvrages en cuir, n.d.a.; articles de bourrellerie ou de sellerie
613	Furskins, tanned or dressed, excluding those of 8483	Pelleteries tannées ou apprêtées (sauf 8483)
62	**Rubber manufactures, n.e.s.**	**Caoutchouc manufacturé, n.d.a.**
621	Materials of rubber (e.g. pastes, plates, sheets, bods, etc.)	Produits en caoutchouc (pâtes, plaques, feuilles, fils, tubes, etc.)
625	Rubber tyres, interchangeable tyre treads, tyre flaps and inner tubes for wheels of all kinds	Pneumatiques, en caoutchouc; bandes de roulement amoviles pour pneumatiques, "flaps" et chambres à air pour tous types de roues
629	Articles of rubber, n.e.s.	Ouvrages en caoutchouc, n.d.a.
63	**Cork and wood manufactures (excluding furniture)**	**Ouvrages en liège et en bois (à l'exclusion des meubles)**
633	Cork manufactures	Ouvrages en liège
634	Veneers, plywood, and other wood, worked, n.e.s.	Placage, contre-plaqué et autres bois travaillés, n.d.a.
635	Wood manufacture, n.e.s.	Ouvrages en bois, n.d.a.
64	**Paper, paperboard, aricles of paper pulp, of paper, or of paperboard**	**Papiers, cartons et ouvrages en pâte de cellulose, en papier ou en carton**
641	Paper and paperboard	Papiers et cartons
642	Paper and paperboard, cut to shape or size, and articles of paper or paperboard	Papiers et cartons découpés en vue d'un usage déterminé; ouvrages en papier ou carton
65	**Textile yarn, fabrics, made-up articles, n.e.s., and related products**	**Fils, tissus, articles textiles façonnés, n.d.a. et produits connexes**
651	Textile yarn	Fils textiles
652	Cotton fabrics, woven (excluded narrow or special fabrics)	Tissus de coton (sauf petites largeurs ou spéciaux)
653	Fabrics, woven, of man-made fabrics	Tissus en matières textiles synthétiques ou artificielles
654	Other textile fabrics, woven	Autres tissus
655	Knitted or crocheted fabrics, n.e.s.	Étoffes de bonneterie (dont velours), n.d.a.
656	Tulles, trimmings, lace, ribbons and other small wares	Tulles, dentelles et autres articles de mercerie
657	Special yarn, special textile fabrics and related	Fils spéciaux, tissus spéciaux et produits connexes
658	Made-up articles, wholly or chiefly of textile materials, n.e.s	Articles confectionnés entièrement ou principalement en matières textiles, n.d.a.
659	Floor coverings, etc.	Revêtements de sols, etc.
66	**Non metallic mineral manufactures, n.e.s.**	**Articles minéraux non métalliques manufacturés, n.d.a.**
661	Lime, cement and fabricated construction materials (excluding glass and clay materials)	Chaux, ciments et matériaux de construction fabriqués (sauf argile et verre)
662	Clay construction and refractory construction materials	Matériaux de construction réfractaires, en argile
663	Mineral manufactures, n.e.s.	Articles minéraux manufacturés, n.d.a.
664	Glass	Verre
665	Glassware	Ouvrages en verre
666	Pottery	Poterie

667	Pearls, precious and semi-precious stones	Perles fines ou de culture, pierres gemmes et similaires
67	**Iron and steel**	**Fer et acier**
671	Pig iron and spiegeleisen, sponge iron, powder and granules	Fonte, fer spongieux, poudres de fer et d'acier
672	Ingots, primary forms, of iron or steel; semi-finished products	Lingots et autres formes primaires en fer ou acier;
673	Flat-rolled prod., iron, non-alloy steel, not coated	Produits laminés plats, en fer ou aciers non alliés
674	Flat-rolled prod., iron, non-alloy steel, coated, clad	Produits laminés plats, fer, aciers non alliés, zingués
675	Flat-rolled products of alloy steel	Produits laminés plats, en aciers alliés
676	Iron and steel bars, rods, angles, shapes and sections	Barres et profilés en fer ou acier (y compris les palplanches)
677	Rails and railway track construction mat., iron, steel	Rails et autres éléments de voies ferrées, en fonte, fer ou acier
678	Wire of iron or steel	Fils de fer ou d'acier
679	Tubes, pipes and hollow profiles, fittings, iron, steel	Tubes, profilés creux et accessoires, fer ou acier
68	**Non-ferrous metals**	**Métaux non ferreux**
681	Silver, platinum, other metals of the platinum group	Argent, platine et métaux de la mine du platine
682	Copper	Cuivre
683	Nickel	Nickel
684	Aluminium	Aluminium
685	Lead	Plomb
686	Zinc	Zinc
687	Tin	Étain
689	Miscellaneous non-ferrous base metals for metallurgy	Autres métaux communs non ferreux utilisés en métallurgie
69	**Manufactures of metal, n.e.s.**	**Articles manufacturés en métal, n.d.a.**
691	Structures and parts, n.e.s., of iron, steel, aluminium	Constructions et parties, n.d.a. en fonte, fer, acier ou aluminium
692	Metal containers for storage or transport	Récipients métalliques pour le stockage ou le transport
693	Wire products (excluding electrical) and fencing grills	Ouvrages en fils métalliques (sauf électriques), grillages
694	Nails, screws, nuts, bolts, rivets and the like, of iron, steel, copper or aluminium	Pointes, clous, vis, écrous, boulons, rondelles, rivets et aricles similaires, en fer, en acier, en cuivre ou en aluminium
695	Tools for use in the hand or in machine	Outils à main et outils pour machines
696	Cutlery	Coutellerie
697	Household equipment of base metal, n.e.s.	Articles d'économie domestique en métaux communs, n.d.a.
699	Manufactures of base metal, n.e.s.	Articles manufacturés en métaux communs, n.d.a.
7	**Machinery and transport equipment**	**Machines et matériel de transport**
71	**Power generating machinery and equipment**	**Machines génératrices, moteurs et leur équipement**
711	Steam or other vapour generating boilers, super-heated water boilers and auxiliary plant for use therewith; parts	Chaudières à vapeur, chaudières dites "à eau surchauffée", et leurs appareils auxiliaires, leurs parties et pièces détachées
712	Steam turbines and other vapour turbines, parts thereof, n.e.s.	Turbines à vapeur, leurs parties et pièces détachées, n.d.a.
713	Internal combustion piston engines and parts thereof, n.e.s.	Moteurs à explosion ou à combustion interne, n.d.a.
714	Engines and motors, non-electric; parts, n.e.s.	Moteurs et machines motrices, non électrique; leurs parties n.d.a.
716	Rotating electric plant and parts thereof, n.e.s.	Appareils électriques rotatifs, leurs pièces détachées, n.d.a.
718	Other power generating machinery and parts thereof, n.e.s.	Moteurs et machines motrices, leurs parties et pièces, n.d.a.
72	**Machinery specialized for particular industries**	**Machines et appareils spécialisés pour industries particulières**
721	Agricultural machinery (excluding tractors) and parts	Machines agricoles (sauf tracteurs), parties, pièces
722	Tractors (excluding those of 71414 and 74415)	Tracteurs (sauf 74414 et 74415)
723	Civil ingineering and contractors' plant and equipment	Appareils et matériel de génie civil et de construction; parties
724	Textile and leather machinery, and parts thereof, n.e.s.	Machines pour l'industrie textile, cuir et peaux, n.d.a.
725	Paper mill and pulp mill machinery; paper cutting machines and other machinery; parts thereof	Machines et appareils pour la fabrication de la pâte à papier et du papier; coupeuses et autres appareils; leurs parties et pièces
726	Printing and bookbinding machinery, and parts thereof	Machines pour imprimerie, brochage, reliure; parties
727	Food-processing machines (excluding domestic)	Machines pour industrie alimentaire (appareils ménagers exclus)
728	Other machinery and equipment specialized for particular industries, and parts thereof, n.e.s.	Autres machines et appareils spécialisées pour industries particulières, et leurs parties et pièces détachées, n.d.a.
73	**Metal working machinery**	**Machines et appareils pour le travail des métaux**
731	Machine-tools working by removing metal or other material	Machines-outils travaillant par enlèvement de métal/autres matières
733	Machine-tools for working metal (without removing material)	Machines pour travail des métaux (sans enlèvement de matière)
735	Parts, n.e.s., and accessories for machines of 731, 733	Pièces et accessoires, n.d.a., des machines des groupes 731, 733
737	Metalworking machinery (excluding machine tools) and parts	Machines pour travail des métaux, n.d.a.; pièces détachées
74	**General industrial machinery and equipment, n.e.s. and machine parts, n.e.s.**	**Machines et appareils industriels d'application générale, n.d.a.; parties et pièces détachées de machines, d'appareils, d'engins**
741	Heating and cooling equipment and parts thereof, n.e.s.	Appareils de chauffage et de réfrigération, n.d.a.; pièces détachées
742	Pumps for liquids; liquid elevators; parts for such pumps	Pompes pour liquides; élévateurs à liquides; parties et pièces

Code	English	Français
743	Pumps (excluding liquid), air and gas compressors, and fans; centrifuges; filtering or purifying apparatus; parts	Pompes (sauf pour liquides), compresseurs; ventilateurs; hottes aspirantes; centrifugeuses; appareils pour la filration, l'épuration
744	Mechanical handling equipment, and parts, n.e.s.	Équipement mécanique de manutention, pièces, n.d.a.
745	Other non-electrical machinery, tools and mechanical apparatus, and parts thereof, n.e.s.	Machines, appareils et outils non électriques et leurs parties et pièces détachées, n.d.a.
746	Ball or roller bearings	Roulements à billes, à galets, à rouleaux ou à aiguilles
747	Taps, cocks, valves and similar appliances, for pipes, boiler shells, tanks, vats and the like	Articles de robinetterie, oragnes similaires pour tuyauteries, chaudières, réservoirs, cubes ou contenants similaires
748	Transmission shafts and cranks; bearings housings; gears and gearing; flywheels and pulleys; clutches, shaft couplings	Arbres de transmission et manivelles; engrenages et roues de friction; volants et poulies; embrayages, organes d'accouplement
749	Non-electric parts and accessories. of machinery, n.e.s.	Parties, non électriques d'appareils mécaniques, n.d.a.
75	**Office machines and automatic data processing machines**	**Machines et appareils de bureau ou pour le traitement automatique de l'information**
751	Office machines	Machines et appareils de bureau
752	Automatic data processing machines and units thereof; magnetic or optical readers	Machines automatiques de traitement de l'information et leurs unités; lecteurs magnétiques ou optiques
759	Parts, accessories for machines of groups 751, 752	Parties et pièces détachées pour groupes 751, 752
76	**Telecommunications and sound recording apparatus and reproducing apparatus and equipment**	**Appareils et équipements de télécommunication et pour l'enregistrement et la reproduction du son**
761	Television receivers, whether or not combined	Téléviseurs, même combinés à d'autres appareils
762	Radio-broadcast receivers, whether or not combined	Appareils de radiodiffusion, même combinés à d'autres appareils
763	Sound recorders or reproducers; television image and sound recorders or reproducers, prepared unrecorded media	Appareils d'enregistrement ou de reproduction du son; appareils d'enregistrement/reproduction de l'image et du son en télévision
764	Telecommunication equipment, n.e.s.; and parts, n.e.s.	Équipements de télécommunication, n.d.a. et parties
77	**Electrical machinery, apparatus and appliances, n.e.s. and electrical parts thereof**	**Machines et appareils électriques, n.d.a.; et leurs parties et pièces détachées électriques**
771	Electric power machinery, and parts thereof	Appareils pour production, transformation de l'électricité
772	Apparatus for switching or protecting electrical circuits or for making connections; switchboard, control panels	Appareils pour la coupure, la protection, le branchement la connexion des circuits électriques; tableaux de commande
773	Equipment for distributing electricity, n.e.s.	Équipement pour la distribution d'électricité, n.d.a.
774	Electro-diagnostic apparatus for medical or veterinary sciences and radiological apparatus	Appareils d'électrodiagnostic à usage médical ou vétérinaire et appareils de radiologie
775	Household type, electrical and non-electrical equipment, n.e.s.	Machines et appareils, électriques ou non, à usage domestique, n.d.a.
776	Thermionic, cold cathode or photo-cathode valves and tubes; diodes, transistors and similar;	Lampes, tubes, valves électroniques à cathode chaude, froide ou à photocathode; diodes, transistors et dispositifs similaires
778	Electrical machinery and apparatus, n.e.s.	Machines et appareils électriques, n.d.a.
78	**Road vehicles (including air-cushion vehicles)**	**Véhicules routiers (y compris les véhicules à coussin d'air)**
781	Motor cars and other motor vehicles principally designed for the transport of persons	Véhicules de tourisme et autres véhicules automobiles principalement conçus pour le transport de personnes
782	Motor vehicles for the transport of goods and special purposes	Véhicules automobiles pour le transport de marchandises et pour usages spéciaux
783	Road motor vehicles, n.e.s.	Véhicules routiers, n.d.a.
784	Parts and accessories of the motor vehicles of groups 722, 781, 782, and 783	Parties, pièces détachées et accessoires des véhicules automobiles des groupes 722, 781, 782 et 783
785	Motorcycles and cycles, motorized or not; invalid carriages	Motocycles et cycles, avec ou sans moteur; fauteuils roulants
786	Trailers and semi-trailers; other vehicles, not mechanically propelled; specially designed & equiped transport containers	Remorques et semi-remorques; autres véhicules non automobiles; cadres et conteneurs conçus et équipés pour le transport
79	**Other transport equipment**	**Autres matériels de transport**
791	Railway vehicles and associated equipment	Véhicules et matériel pour chemin de fer
792	Aircraft and associated equipment; spacecraft and spacecraft launch vehicles, parts thereof	Aéronefs et matériels connexes; véhicules spatiaux et leurs véhicules lanceurs; leurs parties et pièces détachées
793	Ships, boats (including hovercrafts) and floating structures	Navires, bateaux (y compris les aéroglisseurs) et engins flottants
8	**Miscellaneous manufactured articles**	**Articles manufacturés divers**
81	**Prefabricated buildings, sanitary plumbing, heating and lighting fixtures and fittings, n.e.s.**	**Constructions préfabriquées, appareils sanitaires et appareillage de plomberie, de chauffage et d'éclairage, n.d.a.**
811	Prefabricated buildings	Constructions préfabriquées
812	Sanitary, plumbing and heating fixtures, and fittings, n.e.s.	Appareils sanitaires et appareillage de plomberie, chauffage, n.d.a.
813	Lighting fixtures and fittings, n.e.s.	Appareillages d'éclairage, n.d.a.
82	**Furniture and parts thereof; bedding, mattresses, mattress supports, cushions and similar stuffed furnishings**	**Meubles et leurs parties; articles de literie; matelas, sommiers coussins, articles similaires rembourrés/garnis intérieurement**

821	Furniture and parts thereof; bedding, mattresses, mattress supports, cushions and similar stuffed furnishings	Meubles et leurs parties; articles de literie; matelas, sommiers, coussins et articles similaires rembourrés ou garnis intérieurement
83	**Travel goods, handbags and similar containers**	**Articles de voyage, sacs à mains et contenants similaires**
831	Travel goods, handbags and similar containers	Articles de voyage, sacs à mains et contenants similaires
84	**Articles of apparel, and clothing accessories**	**Vêtements et accessoires du vêtement**
841	Men's or boy's clothing of textile fabrics, not knitted or crocheted	Articles d'habillement en matières textiles pour hommes et garçonnets, autres que de bonneterie
842	Women's and girl's clothing, of textile fabrics, not knitted or crocheted	Articles d'habillement en matières textiles pour femmes ou fillettes, autres que de bonneterie
843	Men's or boy's clothing, of textile, knitted, crocheted	Articles d'habillement, en bonneterie pour hommes et garçonnets
844	Women's and girl's clothing,of textile, knitted or crocheted	Articles d'habillement, en bonneterie pour femmes ou fillettes
845	Articles of apparel, of textile fabrics, n.e.s.	Vêtements en matières textiles, même en bonneterie, n.d.a.
846	Clothing accessories, of textile fabrics	Accessoires du vêtement en matières textiles
848	Articles of apparel, clothing access., excluding textile	Vêtements et accessoires en matières non textiles
85	**Footwear**	**Chaussures**
851	Footwear	Chaussures
87	**Professional, scientific, and controlling instruments and apparatus, n.e.s.**	**Instruments et appareils professionnels, scientifiques et de contrôle, n.d.a.**
871	Optical instruments and apparatus, n.e.s.	Appareils et instruments d'optique, n.d.a.
872	Instruments and appliances, n.e.s., for medical, surgical, dental or veterinary purposes	Instruments et appareils, n.d.a. pour la médecine, la chirurgie, l'art dentaire ou l'art vétérinaire
873	Meters and counters, n.e.s.	Compteurs et instruments de mesure, n.d.a.
874	Measuring, checking, analysing and controlling instruements and apparatus, n.e.s.	Appareils et instruments de mesure, de vérification, d'analyse et de contrôle, n.d.a.
88	**Photographic apparatus, equipment and supplies and optical goods, n.e.s.; watches and clocks**	**Appareils et fournitures de photographie et d'optique, n.d.a.; montres et horloges**
881	Photographic apparatus and equipment, n.e.s.	Appareils et équipement photographiques, n.d.a.
882	Cinematographic and photographic supplies	Fournitures cinématographiques et photographiques
883	Cinematograph films, exposed and developed, whether or not incorporating sound track	Films cinématographiques, impressionnés, développés, comportant ou non l'enregistrement du son
884	Optical goods, n.e.s.	Éléments d'optique et articles de lunetterie, n.d.a.
885	Watches and clocks	Horlogerie
89	**Miscellaneous manufactured articles, n.e.s.**	**Articles manufacturés divers, n.d.a.**
891	Arms and ammunition	Armes et munitions
892	Printed matter	Imprimés
893	Articles, n.e.s., of plastics	Ouvrages, n.d.a. en matières plastiques
894	Baby carriages, toys, games and sporting goods	Voitures pour le transport des enfants, jouets, jeux et articles pour divertissements et pour sports
895	Office and stationery supplies, n.e.s.	Articles de papeterie et fournitures de bureau, n.d.a.
896	Works of art, collectors' pieces and antiques	Objets d'art, de collection et d'antiquité
897	Jewellery and articles of precious material., n.e.s.	Articles de bijouterie et d'orfèvrerie, n.d.a.
898	Musical instruments, parts and accessories therof; records, tapes and other sound or similar recordings	Instruments de musique et leurs parties; disques, bandes et autres supports pour l'enregistrement du son
899	Miscellaneous manufactured articles, n.e.s.	Autres articles manufacturés divers
9	**Commodities and transactions, not classified elsewhere in the SITC**	**Articles et transactions, non classés ailleurs dans la CTCI**
91	**Postal packages not classified according to kind**	**Colis postaux non classés par catégorie**
911	Postal packages not classified according to kind	Colis postaux non classés par catégorie
93	**Special transactions and commodities not classified according to kind**	**Transactions spéciales et articles spéciaux non classés par catégorie**
931	Special transactions and commodities not classified according to kind	Transactions spéciales et articles spéciaux non classés par catégorie
96	**Coin (other than gold coin), not being legal tender**	**Monnaies (autres que les pièces d'or) n'ayant pas cours légal**
961	Coin (other than gold coin), not being legal tender	Monnaies (autres que les pièces d'or) n'ayant pas cours légal
97	**Gold, non-monetary (excluding ores and concentrates)**	**Or, à usage non monétaire (sauf minerais et concentrés d'or)**
971	Gold, non-monetary (excluding gold ores and concentrates)	Or, à usage non monétaire (sauf minerais et concentrés d'or)

1

INTERNATIONAL **MERCHANDISE** TRADE

COMMERCE INTERNATIONAL DES **MARCHANDISES**

Region, country or territory	Exports (f.o.b.) - Exportations (f.a.b.) Millions of dollars							
	1980	1990	2000	2005	2008	2009	2010	2011
WORLD	2 035 542	3 478 778	6 444 189	10 513 383	16 137 233	12 518 117	15 257 877	18 211 356
DEVELOPING ECONOMIES	599 757	840 994	2 052 172	3 815 605	6 293 307	4 988 924	6 407 121	7 785 920
TRANSITION ECONOMIES	85 426	118 715	153 995	362 603	738 737	477 263	620 064	827 542
DEVELOPED ECONOMIES	1 350 359	2 519 070	4 238 022	6 335 175	9 105 190	7 051 930	8 230 692	9 597 894
Developing economies: Africa	121 876	105 101	149 161	318 303	561 559	394 888	508 201	590 766
Eastern Africa	7 012	7 321	9 905	16 665	28 112	26 148	32 361	39 374
Burundi*(1)	65	75	50	56	54	62	100	122
Comoros*	11	18	14	12	7	15	21	(e)25
Djibouti (2)	13	25	32	40	69	77	85	(e)95
Eritrea (3)			19	11	(e)11	(e)11	(e)12	(e)415
Ethiopia (...1991)	425	298	–	–	–	–	–	–
Ethiopia	–	–	486	926	1 602	1 618	2 330	2 615
Kenya	1 245	1 032	1 734	3 293	4 972	4 463	5 151	5 754
Madagascar*	401	318	824	855	1 310	1 052	1 080	(e)1 590
Malawi	295	417	379	508	879	1 188	1 066	1 425
Mauritius	435	1 194	1 552	2 138	2 384	1 939	2 261	2 647
Mayotte	..	..	3	6	8	7	-	-
Mozambique	281	126	364	1 745	2 653	2 147	2 243	3 604
Rwanda	121	109	53	125	268	193	297	417
Seychelles	21	57	194	340	430	395	400	478
Somalia	141	(e)150	(e)193	(e)251	(e)415	(e)422	(e)450	(e)518
Uganda	345	152	460	1 016	2 712	2 995	3 107	2 409
United Republic of Tanzania	511	331	734	1 684	3 040	2 982	4 051	4 735
Zambia (4)	1 305	1 309	892	1 810	5 099	4 312	7 200	9 018
Zimbabwe	1 396	1 711	1 923	1 850	2 200	2 269	(e)2 500	(e)3 500
Middle Africa	8 856	11 818	17 112	49 527	109 704	71 304	91 205	117 375
Angola (5)	1 902	3 884	7 921	24 109	63 914	40 828	50 595	65 689
Cameroon*(6)	1 384	2 002	1 833	2 861	4 300	3 370	3 878	(e)4 600
Central African Republic*(6)	116	120	161	129	150	124	(e)139	(e)156
Chad*(5)	71	234	183	3 144	4 169	2 795	(e)3 534	(e)4 114
Congo*(6)	911	981	2 489	4 745	8 324	6 072	(e)9 309	(e)10 800
Dem. Rep. of the Congo*	2 269	2 326	824	2 403	4 400	3 500	(e)5 400	(e)6 003
Equatorial Guinea (5)	14	62	1 097	7 064	14 930	9 108	(e)9 964	(e)13 500
Gabon*(7)	2 173	2 204	2 602	5 065	9 506	5 499	8 374	(e)12 500
Sao Tome and Principe	17	4	3	7	11	8	11	(e)13
Northern Africa	44 042	36 856	54 273	114 519	218 828	142 072	178 019	169 486
Algeria*	13 871	12 880	22 031	46 002	79 298	45 194	57 051	73 436
Egypt	3 046	2 585	4 675	10 652	26 246	23 062	26 438	30 528
Libya	21 910	13 225	12 725	31 358	61 950	37 055	48 935	16 463
Morocco*	2 441	4 265	7 185	11 190	20 345	14 054	17 765	21 519
Sudan (...2011) (8)	543	374	1 807	4 824	11 671	8 257	11 404	9 694
Tunisia (9)	2 231	3 527	5 850	10 494	19 319	14 449	16 427	17 847
Southern Africa	28 433	27 242	37 168	65 181	96 874	75 485	97 084	116 127
Botswana*	504	1 785	2 763	4 425	4 951	3 456	4 716	5 848
Lesotho	58	62	221	651	894	726	852	(e)1 010
Namibia	1 459	1 086	1 320	2 070	3 188	3 101	4 011	4 362
South Africa	(b)26 039	23 753	31 950	56 261	86 118	66 542	85 700	102 858
Swaziland	373	557	914	1 774	1 723	1 660	1 805	(e)2 049
Western Africa	33 532	21 862	30 704	72 410	108 040	79 880	109 532	148 404
Benin*	63	288	392	578	1 282	1 225	(e)1 388	(e)1 849
Burkina Faso	90	152	206	468	693	900	1 288	(e)1 800
Cape Verde (10)	4	6	11	18	32	35	45	73
Côte d'Ivoire*	3 135	3 072	3 888	7 697	10 301	10 518	10 532	11 049
Gambia (11)	31	31	15	8	14	66	35	95
Ghana	1 258	897	1 671	2 802	5 270	5 840	7 960	(e)12 700
Guinea*	401	671	666	846	1 342	1 050	1 471	1 433
Guinea-Bissau	11	19	62	89	128	122	(e)120	(e)245
Liberia*	600	(e)868	(e)329	131	234	155	241	358
Mali*	205	359	545	1 101	2 097	1 774	2 056	(e)2 460
Mauritania*	194	447	355	625	1 811	1 357	2 085	2 768
Niger*	566	283	283	489	912	997	1 040	(e)1 250
Nigeria	25 934	13 596	20 975	55 145	80 615	52 657	77 844	108 296
Saint Helena	(e)1	(e)7	(e)9	(e)20	(e)34	(e)31	(e)31	(e)37
Senegal (12)	477	762	920	1 575	2 206	2 017	2 161	2 542
Sierra Leone*	224	138	13	158	216	233	341	350
Togo*	338	268	364	659	853	903	(e)893	(e)1 100

For sources and notes, see end of table 1.1.1.

Imports (c.i.f.) - Importations (c.a.f.) Millions de dollars								Régions, pays ou territoires
1980	1990	2000	2005	2008	2009	2010	2011	
2 078 123	3 588 121	6 658 904	10 800 749	16 486 891	12 701 471	15 426 006	18 379 265	**MONDE**
496 880	797 036	1 916 379	3 425 789	5 746 496	4 661 229	6 020 648	7 321 081	ÉCONOMIES EN DÉVELOPPEMENT
83 598	139 945	104 129	271 242	610 769	410 289	497 240	640 648	ÉCONOMIES EN TRANSITION
1 497 645	2 651 139	4 638 396	7 103 718	10 129 625	7 629 954	8 908 119	10 417 537	ÉCONOMIES DÉVELOPPÉES
96 856	94 406	129 897	257 115	470 082	411 053	469 777	568 317	**Économies en développement : Afrique**
10 706	*12 734*	*16 983*	*32 148*	*59 738*	*53 322*	*60 457*	*74 448*	*Afrique orientale*
168	231	148	267	402	402	509	752	Burundi*(1)
29	52	43	99	180	210	227	277	Comores*
213	215	207	277	574	451	364	(e)416	Djibouti (2)
		471	(e)495	(e)602	(e)587	(e)690	(e)901	Érythrée (3)
722	1 081	–	–	–	–	–	–	Éthiopie (...1991)
–	–	1 262	4 095	8 680	7 974	8 602	8 896	Éthiopie
2 125	2 223	3 105	6 149	11 074	10 207	12 090	14 814	Kenya
764	566	997	1 706	3 781	3 201	2 500	(e)2 850	Madagascar*
439	575	532	1 164	2 204	2 022	2 173	2 428	Malawi
614	1 618	2 207	3 157	4 651	3 733	4 386	5 158	Maurice
..	..	139	309	606	502	-	-	Mayotte
800	878	1 162	2 408	4 008	3 764	3 564	6 306	Mozambique
262	287	213	471	1 174	1 308	1 431	(e)1 730	Rwanda
99	187	342	675	1 053	794	733	876	Seychelles
435	(e)81	(e)343	(e)626	(e)1 131	(e)931	(e)955	(e)1 175	Somalie
293	288	1 538	2 054	4 526	4 247	4 697	4 593	Ouganda
1 258	1 364	1 524	3 287	7 081	6 296	8 013	11 184	République-Unie de Tanzanie
1 088	1 255	888	2 558	5 060	3 793	5 321	7 191	Zambie (4)
1 396	1 833	1 861	2 350	2 950	2 900	(e)3 700	(e)4 400	Zimbabwe
5 884	*6 992*	*7 619*	*19 073*	*42 506*	*43 979*	*41 040*	*51 053*	*Afrique centrale*
1 328	1 578	3 040	8 353	20 982	22 660	16 667	21 736	Angola (5)
1 602	1 400	1 484	2 735	5 400	4 442	5 133	(e)6 500	Cameroun*(6)
81	154	117	173	300	271	(e)305	(e)380	République centrafricaine*(6)
74	499	317	949	2 020	2 002	(e)2 100	(e)2 100	Tchad*(5)
562	621	479	1 343	3 053	2 896	(e)4 051	(e)5 100	Congo*(6)
1 519	1 739	697	2 690	4 300	3 900	(e)4 500	(e)5 306	Rép. dém. du Congo*
26	61	504	1 310	3 746	5 205	(e)5 680	(e)6 000	Guinée équatoriale (5)
674	918	952	1 471	2 591	2 501	2 492	(e)3 800	Gabon*(7)
19	21	30	50	114	103	112	132	Sao Tomé-et-Principe
31 553	*37 374*	*48 472*	*86 954*	*173 705*	*156 054*	*172 076*	*188 605*	*Afrique septentrionale*
10 559	9 770	9 152	20 357	39 475	39 258	41 000	47 220	Algérie*
4 860	9 216	13 963	19 816	48 775	44 946	52 923	58 903	Égypte
6 777	5 336	3 703	6 058	9 116	10 037	10 506	(e)5 000	Libye
4 255	6 922	11 534	20 790	42 366	32 881	35 385	44 293	Maroc*
1 576	619	1 553	6 757	9 352	9 691	10 045	9 231	Soudan (...2011) (8)
3 526	5 513	8 567	13 177	24 622	19 241	22 218	23 958	Tunisie (9)
22 807	*23 053*	*35 704*	*73 316*	*110 009*	*89 133*	*111 531*	*140 668*	*Afrique australe*
693	1 947	2 082	3 232	5 211	4 728	5 657	7 272	Botswana*
427	673	809	1 410	2 032	1 978	2 203	(e)2 525	Lesotho
1 156	1 163	1 550	2 577	4 340	4 980	5 360	(e)6 453	Namibie
(e,b)19 906	(e)18 606	(e)30 211	(e)64 192	(e)96 704	(e)75 647	(e)96 249	(e)122 418	Afrique du Sud
625	664	1 052	1 904	1 723	(e)1 800	(e)2 062	(e)2 000	Swaziland
25 906	*14 253*	*21 119*	*45 623*	*84 123*	*68 565*	*84 672*	*113 542*	*Afrique occidentale*
331	265	613	1 018	2 289	2 064	(e)2 161	(e)2 700	Bénin*
359	536	611	1 251	2 211	1 870	2 048	(e)2 600	Burkina Faso
68	136	230	438	825	709	742	947	Cap-Vert (10)
2 991	2 098	2 482	5 865	7 884	6 960	7 849	6 720	Côte d'Ivoire*
165	188	187	260	322	304	285	344	Gambie (11)
1 129	1 205	2 976	5 347	10 269	8 046	10 922	(e)15 300	Ghana
270	723	612	820	1 366	1 060	1 405	2 106	Guinée*
55	86	60	123	227	235	(e)229	(e)328	Guinée-Bissau
535	210	(e)668	324	849	563	719	1 044	Libéria*
439	602	806	1 544	3 339	2 431	2 855	(e)3 250	Mali*
286	220	454	1 424	1 966	1 422	1 928	2 473	Mauritanie*
594	389	395	943	1 575	2 364	2 290	(e)2 400	Niger*
16 643	5 627	8 721	21 314	42 378	33 747	44 129	63 949	Nigéria
(e)13	(e)19	(e)39	(e)56	(e)54	(e)46	(e)61	56	Sainte-Hélène
1 052	1 220	1 553	3 498	6 528	4 713	4 782	5 909	Sénégal (12)
427	149	149	345	533	521	770	1 717	Sierra Leone*
551	581	562	1 054	1 509	1 509	(e)1 496	(e)1 700	Togo*

Pour les sources et les notes, se reporter à la fin du tableau 1.1.1.

Region, country or territory	Exports (f.o.b.) - Exportations (f.a.b.) Millions of dollars							
	1980	1990	2000	2005	2008	2009	2010	2011
Developing economies: America	111 352	143 940	366 518	583 963	911 550	698 511	886 947	1 103 231
Caribbean	*22 368*	*11 670*	*19 003*	*26 689*	*40 681*	*23 876*	*27 264*	*38 433*
Anguilla	..	..	4	15	12	23	13	16
Antigua and Barbuda	26	21	81	83	65	51	45	43
Aruba (13)	..	155	2 524	4 416	5 456	1 952	264	5 179
Bahamas (14)	5 009	238	576	549	956	711	702	835
Barbados	228	215	272	359	445	369	429	465
Cayman Islands	..	..	..	60	17	19	13	22
Cuba*	5 577	4 910	1 676	2 319	3 957	3 092	4 966	(e)6 300
Curaçao	–	–	–	–	–	–	–	928
Dominica*	10	55	54	41	40	36	37	31
Dominican Republic (15)	962	735	5 737	6 145	6 748	5 483	6 754	8 536
Grenada	17	26	48	28	31	29	24	28
Haiti	226	160	318	470	480	576	579	767
Jamaica	963	1 158	1 295	1 500	2 439	1 316	1 328	1 603
Montserrat*	1	2	1	1	4	3	1	1
Netherlands Antilles*(16)	5 162	1 790	2 009	608	1 088	810	811	–
Saint Kitts and Nevis*	24	28	33	34	51	48	45	55
Saint Lucia	70	134	43	64	164	163	215	161
Saint Vincent and the Grenadines*	15	83	51	40	52	49	42	(e)42
Sint Maarten (Dutch part)	–	–	–	–	–	–	–	127
Trinidad and Tobago*	4 077	1 960	4 274	9 941	18 650	9 126	10 982	(e)13 272
Turks and Caicos Islands	..	..	9	15	25	21	16	-
Central America	*23 379*	*45 703*	*182 934*	*243 223*	*331 578*	*266 668*	*339 321*	*400 008*
Belize	111	133	218	208	310	260	304	376
Costa Rica*	1 002	1 448	5 850	7 026	9 575	8 711	9 343	10 238
El Salvador (17)	1 075	644	2 941	3 436	4 641	3 866	4 499	5 309
Guatemala (18)	1 520	1 163	2 711	5 381	7 737	7 214	8 463	10 463
Honduras (19)	829	934	3 343	5 048	6 199	4 825	5 742	7 204
Mexico	18 031	40 711	166 368	213 891	291 827	229 683	298 138	349 569
Nicaragua (20)	451	331	643	858	1 473	1 393	1 845	2 294
Panama, excl. Canal Zone	361	–	–	–	–	–	–	–
Panama*(21)	–	340	859	7 375	9 817	10 717	10 987	14 555
South America	*65 605*	*86 566*	*164 581*	*314 051*	*539 292*	*407 967*	*520 363*	*664 790*
Argentina*	8 021	12 353	26 341	40 351	70 588	56 065	68 500	84 269
Bolivia (Plurinational State of)	942	926	1 230	2 791	7 058	4 918	6 290	8 332
Brazil	20 132	31 414	55 119	118 529	197 942	152 995	201 915	256 040
Chile*	4 705	8 373	19 210	41 267	66 456	51 963	70 897	81 411
Colombia	3 924	6 721	13 043	21 146	38 265	32 784	39 710	56 507
Ecuador	2 481	2 714	4 927	10 100	18 818	13 863	17 415	22 345
Falkland Islands (Malvinas)	(e)8	(e)17	(e)93	(e)173	(e)192	(e)143	(e)179	(e)190
Guyana*	389	251	502	553	795	763	880	1 116
Paraguay	310	959	869	1 655	4 463	3 167	4 534	5 517
Peru*	3 898	3 231	7 028	17 368	31 529	26 885	35 565	46 118
Suriname	514	472	396	997	1 743	1 402	2 026	2 345
Uruguay	1 059	1 693	2 295	3 405	6 421	5 417	6 707	7 997
Venezuela (Bolivarian Rep. of)	19 221	17 444	33 529	55 716	95 021	57 603	65 745	92 602
Developing economies: Asia	364 287	589 244	1 531 395	2 906 673	4 810 726	3 888 444	5 002 915	6 081 187
Eastern Asia	*76 165*	*280 556*	*774 891*	*1 538 367*	*2 475 001*	*2 090 464*	*2 715 762*	*3 202 121*
China	18 099	62 091	249 203	761 953	1 428 660	1 201 790	1 578 270	1 899 180
China, Hong Kong SAR	19 752	82 151	201 860	289 337	362 675	318 510	390 143	428 732
China, Macao SAR	613	1 701	2 539	2 476	1 997	961	870	869
China, Taiwan Province of	19 786	67 079	147 777	197 779	255 062	203 691	274 641	308 257
Korea, Dem. People's Rep. of	..	1 857	708	1 338	2 060	1 995	2 555	(e)3 700
Korea, Republic of (22)	17 512	65 016	172 268	284 419	422 007	361 614	466 384	556 602
Mongolia	403	661	536	1 065	2 539	1 903	2 899	4 780
Southern Asia	*26 127*	*47 005*	*92 725*	*197 506*	*354 368*	*285 323*	*379 363*	*495 342*
Afghanistan	670	235	137	384	540	403	388	(e)350
Bangladesh	759	1 671	6 389	9 297	15 380	15 073	19 243	24 564
Bhutan	17	70	103	258	519	496	641	(e)620
India (23)	8 586	17 969	42 379	99 620	194 531	164 921	226 392	302 644
Iran (Islamic Rep. of)*	12 328	19 305	28 345	64 525	113 668	78 830	101 950	130 544
Maldives	8	78	109	162	331	169	198	346
Nepal	80	175	804	863	939	823	834	918
Pakistan	2 618	5 589	9 028	16 051	20 323	17 523	21 410	25 344
Sri Lanka	1 062	1 912	5 430	6 347	8 137	7 085	8 307	10 011

For sources and notes, see end of table 1.1.1.

Imports (c.i.f.) - Importations (c.a.f.) Millions de dollars								Régions, pays ou territoires
1980	1990	2000	2005	2008	2009	2010	2011	
123 594	126 632	391 887	540 302	933 419	695 168	900 678	1 100 165	**Économies en développement : Amérique**
27 362	18 701	32 412	43 580	70 687	48 956	53 806	67 692	*Caraïbes*
..	..	95	130	272	169	158	153	Anguilla
88	255	407	526	806	534	501	471	Antigua-et-Barbuda
..	581	2 582	4 288	6 011	2 449	1 378	5 891	Aruba (13)
7 546	1 112	2 074	2 567	3 230	2 699	2 862	3 410	Bahamas (14)
525	704	1 156	1 604	1 879	1 471	1 562	1 805	Barbade
..	..	..	1 191	1 078	893	828	914	Îles Caïmanes
6 505	6 745	4 843	8 084	15 373	9 619	11 499	(e)14 300	Cuba*
							2 130	Curaçao
48	118	148	165	247	233	222	219	Dominique*
1 964	3 006	9 479	9 869	15 993	12 296	15 299	17 423	République dominicaine (15)
50	105	239	334	363	282	317	329	Grenade
375	332	1 036	1 454	2 315	2 124	3 146	3 020	Haïti
1 171	1 928	3 301	4 460	8 465	5 064	5 225	6 489	Jamaïque
12	48	22	30	38	30	29	29	Montserrat*
5 676	2 141	2 862	1 950	3 079	2 607	2 687	–	Antilles néerlandaises*(16)
45	110	196	210	325	285	268	(e)271	Saint-Kitts-et-Nevis*
124	271	355	479	657	539	662	700	Sainte-Lucie
57	136	162	240	373	333	379	(e)348	Saint-Vincent-et-les Grenadines*
–	–	–	–	–	–	–	734	Saint-Martin (partie néerlandaise)
3 178	1 109	3 308	5 694	9 591	6 955	6 480	(e)8 699	Trinité-et-Tobago*
..	..	149	304	591	375	302	-	Îles Turques et Caïques
29 743	51 774	208 906	278 273	396 213	301 685	382 651	449 495	*Amérique centrale*
150	211	524	593	837	669	699	831	Belize
1 540	1 990	6 389	9 812	15 366	11 460	13 557	16 218	Costa Rica*
966	1 263	4 948	6 809	9 818	7 306	8 485	10 118	El Salvador (17)
1 598	1 649	5 171	10 499	14 547	11 531	13 838	16 610	Guatemala (18)
1 009	938	3 988	6 545	10 453	7 299	8 550	10 338	Honduras (19)
22 144	43 548	182 702	231 821	325 157	246 104	316 556	368 399	Mexique
887	637	1 805	2 595	4 300	3 438	4 229	5 180	Nicaragua (20)
1 449								Panama, sans la zone du canal
–	1 539	3 379	9 600	15 737	13 877	16 737	21 802	Panama*(21)
66 489	56 157	150 569	218 449	466 518	344 528	464 222	582 978	*Amérique du Sud*
10 545	4 078	25 154	28 693	57 413	39 105	56 443	73 922	Argentine*
665	687	1 830	2 341	5 081	4 434	5 384	7 664	Bolivie (État plurinational de)
24 961	22 522	58 643	77 628	182 377	133 673	191 537	236 960	Brésil
5 797	7 940	18 507	32 735	61 903	41 364	59 388	74 908	Chili*
4 739	5 589	11 539	21 204	39 320	32 898	40 683	54 675	Colombie
2 253	1 862	3 721	10 287	18 852	15 090	20 591	24 286	Équateur
(e)6	(e)32	(e)61	(e)59	(e)55	(e)51	(e)99	(e)193	Îles Falkland (Malvinas)
396	311	582	788	1 312	1 161	1 397	1 763	Guyana*
615	1 352	2 260	3 274	9 033	6 940	10 040	12 316	Paraguay
2 499	2 634	7 415	12 502	29 953	21 870	30 030	37 558	Pérou*
504	472	526	1 050	1 304	1 390	1 397	1 667	Suriname
1 680	1 343	3 466	3 879	8 943	6 907	8 619	10 623	Uruguay
11 827	7 335	16 865	24 008	50 971	39 646	38 613	46 441	Venezuela (Rép. bolivarienne du)
272 880	570 904	1 388 271	2 618 650	4 328 441	3 543 149	4 636 227	5 636 885	**Économies en développement : Asie**
85 536	265 898	742 792	1 411 364	2 208 651	1 858 754	2 518 342	3 051 382	*Asie orientale*
19 941	53 345	225 024	660 206	1 131 620	1 004 170	1 396 200	1 742 850	Chine
22 447	82 492	212 805	299 533	388 505	347 311	433 111	483 633	Chine (RAS de Hong Kong)
543	1 533	2 255	3 913	5 365	4 622	5 513	7 769	Chine (RAS de Macao)
19 764	54 831	139 927	182 571	240 690	174 582	251 498	281 438	Province chinoise de Taiwan
..	2 930	1 686	2 718	3 580	3 095	3 530	(e)4 800	Corée, Rép. populaire dém. de
22 292	69 844	160 481	261 238	435 275	322 843	425 212	524 366	Corée, République de (22)
548	924	615	1 184	3 616	2 131	3 278	6 527	Mongolie
39 540	57 368	95 211	236 847	466 845	380 721	507 183	646 050	*Asie méridionale*
841	936	1 176	2 470	3 020	3 336	5 154	(e)6 300	Afghanistan
2 599	3 618	8 883	13 889	23 840	21 851	27 794	36 187	Bangladesh
50	81	175	386	540	530	855	(e)950	Bhoutan
14 864	23 580	51 523	142 842	320 785	257 187	350 098	463 781	Inde (23)
13 427	18 330	14 347	40 041	57 401	50 768	65 769	68 319	Iran (Rép. islamique d')*
29	137	389	745	1 388	967	1 091	1 465	Maldives
342	624	1 573	2 283	3 590	4 384	5 128	5 773	Népal
5 350	7 376	10 864	25 357	42 329	31 648	37 783	43 578	Pakistan
2 037	2 685	6 281	8 834	13 953	10 049	13 512	19 696	Sri Lanka

Pour les sources et les notes, se reporter à la fin du tableau 1.1.1.

Region, country or territory	Exports (f.o.b.) - Exportations (f.a.b.) Millions of dollars							
	1980	1990	2000	2005	2008	2009	2010	2011
South-Eastern Asia	**73 957**	**144 148**	**429 846**	**654 886**	**998 961**	**813 492**	**1 052 365**	**1 240 727**
Brunei Darussalam*	4 581	2 213	3 903	6 249	10 721	7 200	8 908	12 428
Cambodia (5)	16	86	1 389	2 910	4 708	4 196	5 143	(e)6 950
Indonesia (...2002)	23 950	25 674	65 404		–	–	–	–
Indonesia	–	–	–	86 995	139 606	119 646	158 074	200 587
Lao People's Dem. Rep.*	28	79	330	553	1 092	1 005	1 746	(e)2 400
Malaysia (24)	12 945	29 452	98 229	140 870	209 719	157 516	198 800	228 259
Myanmar	477	325	1 620	3 776	6 882	6 662	8 661	9 238
Philippines	5 741	8 117	37 757	41 255	49 462	38 421	51 541	48 042
Singapore (25)	19 375	52 730	137 804	229 649	338 176	269 832	351 867	409 503
Thailand	6 505	23 068	68 963	110 178	175 897	151 910	195 371	226 402
Timor-Leste (26)	–	–	–	8	13	8	17	12
Viet Nam	339	2 404	14 447	32 442	62 685	57 096	72 237	96 906
Western Asia	**188 038**	**117 536**	**233 934**	**515 914**	**982 397**	**699 166**	**855 425**	**1 142 998**
Bahrain (5)	3 606	3 761	6 194	10 242	17 316	11 874	13 647	19 650
Iraq*	26 349	10 314	18 743	23 697	63 726	42 405	54 599	85 635
Jordan	574	1 064	1 899	4 302	7 788	6 531	7 023	7 964
Kuwait*	19 842	7 042	19 436	44 868	87 446	53 962	67 080	103 462
Lebanon (27)	955	494	715	2 337	4 454	4 187	5 021	5 664
Occupied Palestinian territory	..	..	401	335	558	518	576	759
Oman	2 387	5 508	11 319	18 692	37 719	28 053	36 601	47 092
Qatar*	5 680	3 529	11 425	25 339	55 727	48 306	72 790	107 095
Saudi Arabia*(28)	101 577	44 416	77 481	180 572	313 462	192 296	251 143	360 092
Syrian Arab Republic*	2 108	4 212	4 633	9 174	15 410	10 855	12 304	(e)8 500
Turkey*	2 910	12 959	27 775	73 476	132 027	102 143	113 883	134 907
United Arab Emirates	21 967	23 544	49 835	117 271	239 180	191 776	212 262	252 556
Yemen, Arab Republic	23							
Yemen, Democratic	60							
Yemen*	–	692	4 079	5 608	7 584	6 259	8 497	(e)9 622
Developing economies: Oceania	**2 242**	**2 710**	**5 098**	**6 667**	**9 471**	**7 080**	**9 057**	**10 735**
American Samoa*(29)	127	311	346	374	(e)570	(e)470	(e)300	(e)310
Cook Islands	4	5	9	5	4	3	5	3
Fiji	377	398	539	704	923	629	847	(e)902
French Polynesia*	30	111	244	210	195	148	153	150
Guam	61	82	74	52	105	51	46	43
Kiribati	3	3	4	4	15	20	(e)15	(e)20
Marshall Islands	–	3	9	25	20	21	32	(e)35
Micronesia (Federated States of)	–	4	22	19	27	25	(e)25	(e)25
Nauru	65	60	28	4	121	25	55	69
New Caledonia*	409	480	606	1 090	1 300	993	1 483	1 717
Niue	..	0	0	0	0	(e)0	(e)0	(e)0
Northern Mariana Islands	–	..	1 017	651	(e)115	(e)9	(e)5	(e)3
Palau	–	..	12	14	13	8	7	7
Papua New Guinea	1 031	1 144	2 070	3 276	5 714	4 404	5 745	6 915
Samoa (27)	17	9	14	87	72	46	60	54
Solomon Islands*	74	70	69	103	210	163	221	404
Tokelau	..	..	..	(e)0	-	-	-	-
Tonga	7	11	9	10	9	8	8	(e)11
Tuvalu	..	0	0	0	(e)0	(e)0	(e)0	(e)0
Vanuatu	36	19	26	38	57	57	49	67
Wallis and Futuna Islands	..	..	-	(e)0	-	-	-	-
Transition economies	**85 426**	**118 715**	**153 995**	**362 603**	**738 737**	**477 263**	**620 064**	**827 542**
Albania	..	230	261	658	1 355	1 091	1 545	1 951
Armenia*	–	–	294	950	1 057	698	1 011	1 316
Azerbaijan (30)	–	–	1 745	7 649	30 586	21 097	26 476	34 495
Belarus	–	–	7 326	15 979	32 571	21 304	25 284	41 192
Bosnia and Herzegovina*(31)	–	–	1 069	2 406	5 029	3 954	4 803	5 850
Croatia*	–	–	4 432	8 773	14 112	10 474	11 806	13 375
Georgia (32)	–	–	323	865	1 507	1 140	1 581	2 188
Kazakhstan*(33)	–	–	8 812	27 849	71 172	43 196	59 544	88 273
Kyrgyzstan	–	–	511	672	1 856	1 673	1 760	1 972
Montenegro	–	–	–	–	659	403	437	632
Republic of Moldova	–	–	472	1 091	1 597	1 283	1 542	2 217
Russian Federation (34)	–	–	105 036	243 799	471 765	303 388	400 420	521 968
Serbia and Montenegro*	–	–	1 711	5 058	–	–	–	–
Serbia	–	–	–	–	10 972	8 345	9 795	11 775
SFR of Yugoslavia	8 978	14 308	–	–	–	–	–	–
Tajikistan (32)	–	–	784	891	1 406	1 010	1 206	1 257
TFYR of Macedonia*	–	–	1 323	2 041	3 920	2 692	3 291	4 433

For sources and notes, see end of table 1.1.1.

1980	1990	2000	2005	2008	2009	2010	2011	Régions, pays ou territoires
65 641	*162 346*	*380 121*	*602 900*	*947 071*	*728 141*	*954 652*	*1 151 071*	*Asie du Sud-Est*
572	1 001	1 107	1 491	2 543	2 449	2 460	2 937	Brunéi Darussalam*
180	164	1 936	3 918	6 508	5 830	6 791	(e)9 300	Cambodge (5)
10 834	21 768	43 075						Indonésie (...2002)
–	–	–	75 725	127 538	93 786	135 323	176 881	Indonésie
92	185	535	882	1 405	1 414	2 060	(e)2 650	Rép. dém. populaire lao*
10 779	29 258	81 963	114 410	164 406	123 695	164 736	187 592	Malaisie (24)
357	270	2 371	1 908	4 256	4 348	4 760	9 019	Myanmar
8 291	13 004	37 027	49 487	60 485	45 857	58 533	63 693	Philippines
24 007	60 899	134 545	200 047	319 780	245 785	310 791	365 770	Singapour (25)
9 214	33 045	61 923	118 158	179 168	134 734	185 121	228 848	Thaïlande
–	–	–	112	269	295	298	340	Timor-Leste (26)
1 314	2 752	15 638	36 761	80 714	69 949	83 779	104 041	Viet Nam
82 164	*85 291*	*170 148*	*367 539*	*705 874*	*575 533*	*656 050*	*788 382*	*Asie occidentale*
3 483	3 712	4 633	9 393	14 246	9 613	11 190	12 106	Bahreïn (5)
8 707	6 526	11 009	23 532	32 888	36 858	39 275	50 581	Iraq*
2 402	2 600	4 597	10 506	16 764	14 534	15 085	18 463	Jordanie
6 533	3 972	7 156	15 801	24 872	20 340	22 413	25 261	Koweït*
3 650	2 525	6 230	9 633	16 754	16 574	18 460	20 750	Liban (27)
..	..	2 383	2 667	3 569	3 601	3 959	4 492	Territoire palestinien occupé
1 732	2 681	5 040	8 827	22 925	17 865	19 775	23 620	Oman
1 447	1 695	3 252	10 061	27 900	24 922	23 240	25 672	Qatar*
30 165	24 107	30 197	59 463	115 134	95 544	106 863	129 017	Arabie saoudite*(28)
4 124	2 400	3 815	10 862	18 105	15 443	17 562	(e)16 600	République arabe syrienne*
7 910	22 303	54 503	116 774	201 964	140 928	185 544	240 842	Turquie*
8 631	11 199	35 009	84 642	200 300	170 127	183 430	210 945	Émirats arabes unis
1 853	–	–	–	–	–	–	–	Yémen, République arabe du
1 527	–	–	–	–	–	–	–	Yémen, Démocratique
–	1 571	2 324	5 378	10 452	9 185	9 255	10 034	Yémen*
3 550	*5 095*	*6 324*	*9 722*	*14 554*	*11 858*	*13 966*	*15 714*	*Économies en développement : Océanie*
95	360	506	506	680	600	(e)550	(e)690	Samoa américaines*(29)
23	52	51	81	108	70	81	83	Îles Cook
562	754	856	1 607	2 259	1 437	1 821	(e)2 300	Fidji
547	928	1 072	1 702	2 169	1 717	1 726	1 628	Polynésie française*
400	461	421	533	649	635	698	708	Guam
17	27	40	76	74	68	73	(e)110	Kiribati
–	56	55	94	(e)100	(e)105	(e)135	(e)140	Îles Marshall
–	84	107	130	155	172	(e)170	(e)170	Micronésie (États fédérés de)
12	34	27	26	90	102	22	32	Nauru
456	883	922	1 774	3 233	2 574	3 313	3 699	Nouvelle-Calédonie*
..	4	2	8	8	(e)5	(e)5	(e)7	Nioué
–	..	-	-	-	-	-	-	Îles Mariannes du Nord
–	..	127	108	130	93	101	124	Palaos
1 176	1 118	1 151	1 728	3 560	3 200	(e)3 950	(e)4 550	Papouasie-Nouvelle-Guinée
63	81	90	239	288	231	310	346	Samoa (27)
89	91	92	185	328	268	405	466	Îles Salomon*
..	..	1	(e)0	-	-	-	-	Tokélaou
38	62	69	120	166	145	159	(e)184	Tonga
..	5	5	13	26	(e)14	(e)16	(e)25	Tuvalu
73	96	87	149	314	294	285	304	Vanuatu
..	..	37	51	-	-	-	-	Îles Wallis-et-Futuna
83 598	*139 945*	*104 129*	*271 242*	*610 769*	*410 289*	*497 240*	*640 648*	*Économies en transition*
..	423	1 091	2 618	5 251	4 550	4 406	5 395	Albanie
–	–	882	1 768	4 427	3 303	3 783	4 196	Arménie*
–	–	1 172	4 211	7 575	6 514	6 746	9 733	Azerbaïdjan (30)
–	–	8 646	16 708	39 381	28 569	34 884	45 743	Bélarus
–	–	3 101	7 109	12 202	8 776	9 223	11 051	Bosnie-Herzégovine*(31)
–	–	7 887	18 560	30 728	21 203	20 051	22 708	Croatie*
–	–	709	2 490	6 066	4 386	5 097	6 948	Géorgie (32)
–	–	5 040	17 333	37 815	28 409	30 438	38 039	Kazakhstan*(33)
–	–	558	1 189	4 072	3 040	3 223	4 261	Kirghizistan
–	–	–	–	3 731	2 313	2 182	2 544	Monténégro
–	–	776	2 292	4 899	3 278	3 855	5 191	République de Moldova
–	–	49 348	137 977	321 170	210 984	273 614	354 549	Fédération de Russie (34)
–	–	3 711	11 679	–	–	–	–	Serbie-et-Monténégro*
–	–	–	–	22 875	16 047	16 734	20 139	Serbie
15 076	18 871	–	–	–	–	–	–	RSF de Yougoslavie
–	–	675	1 330	3 270	2 569	2 658	3 186	Tadjikistan (32)
–	–	2 094	3 228	6 843	5 038	5 449	7 003	LERY de Macédoine*

Pour les sources et les notes, se reporter à la fin du tableau 1.1.1.

Region, country or territory	Exports (f.o.b.) - Exportations (f.a.b.) Millions of dollars							
	1980	1990	2000	2005	2008	2009	2010	2011
Turkmenistan (32)	–	–	2 506	4 944	11 920	(e)5 000	(e)6 500	(e)13 000
Ukraine (32)	–	–	14 573	34 228	66 954	39 782	51 478	68 394
USSR	76 449	104 177	–	–	–	–	–	–
Uzbekistan (32)	–	–	2 817	4 749	10 298	10 735	11 587	13 254
Developed economies: America	**293 549**	**521 758**	**1 058 872**	**1 267 050**	**1 753 795**	**1 371 158**	**1 664 016**	**1 932 623**
Bermuda (5)	37	60	51	49	24	29	15	13
Canada	67 734	127 629	276 617	359 430	452 162	314 003	386 026	451 722
Greenland	211	452	271	402	488	371	390	473
Saint Pierre and Miquelon	1	26	(e)14	(e)10	(e)11	(e)6	(e)5	(e)5
United States (35)	225 566	393 592	781 918	907 158	1 301 110	1 056 750	1 277 580	1 480 410
Developed economies: Asia	**135 979**	**299 156**	**510 700**	**637 630**	**842 874**	**628 653**	**828 165**	**890 212**
Israel*	5 538	11 576	31 404	42 770	60 825	47 934	58 392	67 648
Japan	130 441	287 580	479 296	594 860	782 049	580 719	769 773	822 564
Developed economies: Europe	**893 466**	**1 649 010**	**2 590 701**	**4 302 737**	**6 290 651**	**4 873 375**	**5 493 861**	**6 465 880**
Andorra*	..	..	45	142	96	63	54	77
Austria*	17 489	41 135	67 543	125 131	180 553	136 438	152 413	177 190
Belgium*	-	-	187 906	334 265	469 924	368 637	408 352	477 784
Bulgaria*	10 372	4 822	4 809	11 739	22 271	16 253	20 610	28 118
Cyprus*	532	957	951	1 464	1 626	1 252	1 401	1 823
Czechoslovakia (36)	14 891	11 906						
Czech Republic*(37)	–	–	28 996	78 079	146 203	112 501	132 854	162 043
Denmark*(38)	16 749	37 037	51 166	85 086	116 448	93 606	97 299	113 181
Estonia*(32)	–	–	3 830	7 713	12 407	9 012	11 582	16 712
Faeroe Islands	187	400	477	602	852	762	825	998
Finland*	14 150	26 571	45 989	65 471	96 064	62 602	69 451	78 893
France*	116 409	217 265	326 802	463 240	613 737	482 832	522 957	595 269
Germany, Democratic Republic of	17 312							
Germany, Federal Republic of	192 860							
Germany*	–	410 104	550 447	970 521	1 440 297	1 115 537	1 257 712	1 470 307
Gibraltar (39)	10	83	127	200	283	264	258	246
Greece*	5 153	8 105	11 722	17 271	26 275	20 387	21 692	31 640
Hungary*(40)	8 671	9 598	28 016	62 911	108 063	82 674	95 391	112 067
Iceland	918	1 592	1 892	3 091	5 355	4 057	4 604	5 348
Ireland*	8 398	23 747	77 222	109 613	125 209	115 462	116 384	126 594
Italy	78 104	170 486	239 924	372 983	540 544	405 273	446 871	522 481
Latvia	–	–	1 865	5 159	10 103	7 671	9 523	13 113
Lithuania*(32)	–	–	3 548	11 802	23 550	16 388	20 728	28 012
Luxembourg*	3 005	6 305	8 357	18 790	25 590	21 253	19 729	21 749
Malta	483	1 130	2 443	2 398	3 467	2 846	3 582	4 380
Netherlands*	84 948	131 775	232 554	406 208	635 327	495 889	573 699	666 207
Norway	18 543	34 047	60 058	103 751	171 764	116 778	130 669	159 253
Poland*	14 191	13 627	31 651	89 401	169 766	135 954	159 570	187 154
Portugal*	4 640	16 422	24 303	38 134	56 905	44 033	48 689	58 838
Romania	11 209	5 775	10 367	27 730	49 334	40 404	49 451	62 603
Slovakia*	–	–	11 889	31 876	70 853	55 856	64 601	79 202
Slovenia*	–	–	8 732	19 240	33 989	26 072	29 172	34 709
Spain	20 720	55 521	114 966	192 566	280 350	226 424	254 173	306 017
Sweden*	30 906	57 538	86 917	130 909	182 583	130 255	158 397	186 982
Switzerland*	29 634	63 794	80 467	130 930	200 615	172 474	195 609	234 426
United Kingdom	110 137	185 107	284 720	384 321	470 250	353 466	415 559	502 465
Developed economies: Oceania	**27 365**	**49 146**	**77 749**	**127 759**	**217 870**	**178 744**	**244 650**	**309 180**
Australia	21 944	39 752	63 870	105 832	186 965	153 884	212 362	271 696
New Zealand	5 421	9 394	13 879	21 927	30 905	24 860	32 288	37 484

For sources and notes, see end of table 1.1.1.

Imports (c.i.f.) - Importations (c.a.f.) Millions de dollars								Régions, pays ou territoires
1980	1990	2000	2005	2008	2009	2010	2011	
–	–	1 786	2 947	5 650	(e)6 800	(e)5 600	(e)7 400	Turkménistan (32)
–	–	13 956	36 136	85 535	45 487	60 911	82 608	Ukraine (32)
68 522	120 651	–	–	–	–	–	–	URSS
–	–	2 697	3 666	9 277	9 023	8 386	9 953	Ouzbékistan (32)
320 210	**641 358**	**1 505 269**	**2 068 241**	**2 588 993**	**1 937 111**	**2 363 195**	**2 720 060**	**Économies développées : Amérique**
343	595	719	985	1 159	1 064	988	910	Bermudes (5)
62 544	123 244	244 778	331 553	417 364	329 907	392 109	452 228	Canada
328	445	364	593	922	764	853	965	Groenland
10	86	(e)108	(e)50	(e)58	(e)76	(e)66	(e)66	Saint-Pierre-et-Miquelon
256 985	516 987	1 259 300	1 735 060	2 169 490	1 605 300	1 969 180	2 265 890	États-Unis (35)
151 080	**252 162**	**417 196**	**562 073**	**830 287**	**599 808**	**753 635**	**929 903**	**Économies développées : Asie**
9 784	16 794	37 686	47 142	67 656	49 278	61 209	75 830	Israël*
141 296	235 368	379 510	514 931	762 631	550 530	692 426	854 073	Japon
998 484	**1 706 134**	**2 630 167**	**4 321 269**	**6 476 036**	**4 902 304**	**5 557 832**	**6 486 526**	**Économies développées : Europe**
..	..	1 019	1 802	1 932	1 581	1 514	1 597	Andorre*
24 444	49 088	72 215	127 275	183 545	142 488	158 856	191 161	Autriche*
-	-	177 073	318 571	464 413	351 943	392 896	464 600	Belgique*
9 650	4 710	6 505	18 163	36 758	23 444	25 489	32 455	Bulgarie*
1 202	2 568	3 846	6 313	10 600	7 803	8 561	8 596	Chypre*
12 774	13 106							Tchécoslovaquie (36)
–	–	33 852	76 481	141 461	104 626	126 530	151 356	République tchèque*(37)
19 340	33 248	45 445	75 551	108 918	82 799	84 797	97 772	Danemark*(38)
–	–	5 052	10 234	15 961	10 099	12 254	17 559	Estonie*(32)
219	333	533	747	988	783	776	978	Îles Féroé
15 635	27 001	34 358	58 742	91 409	60 645	68 737	84 121	Finlande*
137 554	240 753	338 103	503 920	713 883	558 618	609 064	712 902	France*
19 082	–	–	–	–	–	–	–	Allemagne, Rép. dém. d'
188 002	–	–	–	–	–	–	–	Allemagne, Rép. fédérale d'
	346 153	495 970	776 758	1 180 253	922 622	1 053 799	1 252 261	Allemagne*
110	362	482	551	827	747	746	867	Gibraltar (39)
10 548	19 777	33 397	54 414	92 204	69 169	63 732	60 786	Grèce*
9 245	8 671	31 955	66 525	108 498	77 448	88 093	102 452	Hongrie*(40)
999	1 680	2 591	4 557	6 166	3 604	3 920	4 841	Islande
11 153	20 682	50 915	68 537	83 624	62 452	60 218	66 433	Irlande*
100 741	181 968	238 167	384 634	559 637	413 436	486 580	556 720	Italie
–	–	3 184	8 694	16 077	9 772	11 680	16 268	Lettonie
–	–	5 219	15 542	30 972	18 230	23 380	31 731	Lituanie*(32)
3 612	7 596	11 250	21 884	32 026	25 228	25 068	28 684	Luxembourg*
938	1 961	3 400	3 679	5 279	4 460	5 057	6 284	Malte
88 419	126 475	217 728	363 675	578 577	441 371	515 912	598 232	Pays-Bas*
16 926	27 231	34 391	55 481	90 293	68 970	77 326	90 853	Norvège
16 690	8 413	48 940	101 598	207 956	148 858	177 878	207 393	Pologne*
9 309	25 264	39 854	61 159	94 033	71 375	75 563	80 252	Portugal*
13 843	9 843	13 055	40 463	83 712	54 106	62 068	76 200	Roumanie
–	–	13 412	34 635	73 611	55 426	64 966	77 202	Slovaquie*
–	–	10 116	20 328	36 884	26 401	30 065	35 480	Slovénie*
34 078	87 554	155 757	288 669	419 094	292 039	326 701	373 278	Espagne
33 438	54 245	72 700	111 652	167 818	119 394	148 802	175 768	Suède*
36 356	69 691	82 487	126 574	183 516	155 378	176 281	208 280	Suisse*
115 545	224 416	347 198	513 464	655 111	516 991	590 526	673 164	Royaume-Uni
27 871	**51 486**	**85 763**	**152 135**	**234 309**	**190 730**	**233 457**	**281 048**	**Économies développées : Océanie**
22 399	41 985	71 529	125 281	200 273	165 471	201 639	243 701	Australie
5 472	9 501	14 235	26 854	34 036	25 259	31 818	37 347	Nouvelle-Zélande

Pour les sources et les notes, se reporter à la fin du tableau 1.1.1.

1.1.1 Exports and imports of countries
and geographical regions
Share

Region, country or territory	Exports (f.o.b.) - Exportations (f.a.b.) Percentage - En pourcentage										
	1980	1990	1995	2000	2005	2006	2007	2008	2009	2010	2011
WORLD	**100**	**100**	**100**	**100**	**100**	**100**	**100**	**100**	**100**	**100**	**100**
DEVELOPING ECONOMIES	29.464	24.175	27.704	31.845	36.293	37.480	37.744	38.999	39.854	41.992	42.753
TRANSITION ECONOMIES	4.197	3.413	2.354	2.390	3.449	3.754	3.925	4.578	3.813	4.064	4.544
DEVELOPED ECONOMIES	66.339	72.412	69.942	65.765	60.258	58.766	58.331	56.423	56.334	53.944	52.703
Developing economies: Africa	**5.987**	**3.021**	**2.188**	**2.315**	**3.028**	**3.076**	**3.132**	**3.480**	**3.155**	**3.331**	**3.244**
Eastern Africa	*0.344*	*0.210*	*0.187*	*0.154*	*0.159*	*0.170*	*0.174*	*0.174*	*0.209*	*0.212*	*0.216*
Burundi*(1)	0.003	0.002	0.002	0.001	0.001	0.000	0.000	0.000	0.000	0.001	0.001
Comoros*	0.001	0.001	0.000	0.000	0.000	0.000	0.000	0.000	0.000	0.000	(e)0.000
Djibouti (2)	0.001	0.001	0.000	0.000	0.000	0.000	0.000	0.000	0.001	0.001	(e)0.001
Eritrea (3)	_	_	0.002	0.000	0.000	0.000	0.000	(e)0.000	(e)0.000	(e)0.000	(e)0.002
Ethiopia (...1991)	0.021	0.009	_	_	_	_	_	_	_	_	_
Ethiopia	_	_	0.008	0.008	0.009	0.009	0.009	0.010	0.013	0.015	0.014
Kenya	0.061	0.030	0.036	0.027	0.031	0.028	0.029	0.031	0.036	0.034	0.032
Madagascar*	0.020	0.009	0.010	0.013	0.008	0.008	0.009	0.008	0.008	0.007	(e)0.009
Malawi	0.015	0.012	0.008	0.006	0.005	0.005	0.006	0.005	0.009	0.007	0.008
Mauritius	0.021	0.034	0.030	0.024	0.020	0.019	0.016	0.015	0.015	0.015	0.015
Mayotte	..	..	..	0.000	0.000	0.000	0.000	0.000	0.000	-	-
Mozambique	0.014	0.004	0.003	0.006	0.017	0.020	0.017	0.016	0.017	0.015	0.020
Rwanda	0.006	0.003	0.001	0.001	0.001	0.001	0.001	0.002	0.002	0.002	0.002
Seychelles	0.001	0.002	0.001	0.003	0.003	0.003	0.003	0.003	0.003	0.003	0.003
Somalia	0.007	(e)0.004	(e)0.003	(e)0.003	(e)0.002	(e)0.002	(e)0.002	(e)0.003	(e)0.003	(e)0.003	(e)0.003
Uganda	0.017	0.004	0.009	0.007	0.010	0.010	0.014	0.017	0.024	0.020	0.013
United Republic of Tanzania	0.025	0.010	0.013	0.011	0.016	0.016	0.016	0.019	0.024	0.027	0.026
Zambia (4)	0.064	0.038	0.020	0.014	0.017	0.031	0.033	0.032	0.034	0.047	0.050
Zimbabwe	0.069	0.049	0.041	0.030	0.018	0.016	0.017	0.014	0.018	(e)0.016	(e)0.019
Middle Africa	*0.435*	*0.340*	*0.220*	*0.266*	*0.471*	*0.506*	*0.550*	*0.680*	*0.570*	*0.598*	*0.645*
Angola (5)	0.093	0.112	0.072	0.123	0.229	0.263	0.317	0.396	0.326	0.332	0.361
Cameroon*(6)	0.068	0.058	0.031	0.028	0.027	0.029	0.026	0.027	0.027	0.025	(e)0.025
Central African Republic*(6)	0.006	0.003	0.003	0.002	0.001	0.001	0.001	0.001	0.001	(e)0.001	(e)0.001
Chad*(5)	0.003	0.007	0.005	0.003	0.030	0.028	0.026	0.026	0.022	(e)0.023	(e)0.023
Congo*(6)	0.045	0.028	0.023	0.039	0.045	0.050	0.040	0.052	0.049	(e)0.061	(e)0.059
Dem. Rep. of the Congo*	0.111	0.067	0.032	0.013	0.023	0.022	0.022	0.027	0.028	(e)0.035	(e)0.033
Equatorial Guinea (5)	0.001	0.002	0.002	0.017	0.067	0.068	0.073	0.093	0.073	(e)0.065	(e)0.074
Gabon*(7)	0.107	0.063	0.052	0.040	0.048	0.045	0.045	0.059	0.044	0.055	(e)0.069
Sao Tome and Principe	0.001	0.000	0.000	0.000	0.000	0.000	0.000	0.000	0.000	0.000	(e)0.000
Northern Africa	*2.164*	*1.059*	*0.678*	*0.842*	*1.089*	*1.134*	*1.161*	*1.356*	*1.135*	*1.167*	*0.931*
Algeria*	0.681	0.370	0.198	0.342	0.438	0.450	0.429	0.491	0.361	0.374	0.403
Egypt	0.150	0.074	0.066	0.073	0.101	0.113	0.116	0.163	0.184	0.173	0.168
Libya	1.076	0.380	0.164	0.197	0.298	0.323	0.335	0.384	0.296	0.321	0.090
Morocco*	0.120	0.123	0.133	0.111	0.106	0.105	0.109	0.126	0.112	0.116	0.118
Sudan (...2011) (8)	0.027	0.011	0.011	0.028	0.046	0.047	0.063	0.072	0.066	0.075	0.053
Tunisia (9)	0.110	0.101	0.106	0.091	0.100	0.096	0.108	0.120	0.115	0.108	0.098
Southern Africa	*1.397*	*0.783*	*0.664*	*0.577*	*0.620*	*0.622*	*0.622*	*0.600*	*0.603*	*0.636*	*0.638*
Botswana*	0.025	0.051	0.041	0.043	0.042	0.037	0.037	0.031	0.028	0.031	0.032
Lesotho	0.003	0.002	0.003	0.003	0.006	0.006	0.005	0.006	0.006	0.006	(e)0.006
Namibia	0.072	0.031	0.027	0.020	0.020	0.022	0.021	0.020	0.025	0.026	0.024
South Africa	(b)1.279	0.683	0.575	0.496	0.535	0.542	0.545	0.534	0.532	0.562	0.565
Swaziland	0.018	0.016	0.017	0.014	0.017	0.015	0.013	0.011	0.013	0.012	(e)0.011
Western Africa	*1.647*	*0.628*	*0.439*	*0.476*	*0.689*	*0.644*	*0.625*	*0.670*	*0.638*	*0.718*	*0.815*
Benin*	0.003	0.008	0.008	0.006	0.005	0.006	0.007	0.008	0.010	(e)0.009	(e)0.010
Burkina Faso	0.004	0.004	0.005	0.003	0.004	0.005	0.004	0.004	0.007	0.008	(e)0.010
Cape Verde (10)	0.000	0.000	0.000	0.000	0.000	0.000	0.000	0.000	0.000	0.000	0.000
Côte d'Ivoire*	0.154	0.088	0.072	0.060	0.073	0.070	0.062	0.064	0.084	0.069	0.061
Gambia (11)	0.002	0.001	0.000	0.000	0.000	0.000	0.000	0.000	0.001	0.000	0.001
Ghana	0.062	0.026	0.033	0.026	0.027	0.031	0.031	0.033	0.047	0.052	(e)0.070
Guinea*	0.020	0.019	0.014	0.010	0.008	0.009	0.009	0.008	0.008	0.010	0.008
Guinea-Bissau	0.001	0.001	0.000	0.001	0.001	0.001	0.001	0.001	0.001	(e)0.001	(e)0.001
Liberia*	0.029	(e)0.025	(e)0.016	(e)0.005	0.001	0.001	0.001	0.001	0.001	0.002	0.002
Mali*	0.010	0.010	0.009	0.008	0.010	0.013	0.011	0.013	0.014	0.013	(e)0.014
Mauritania*	0.010	0.013	0.009	0.006	0.006	0.011	0.010	0.011	0.011	0.014	0.015
Niger*	0.028	0.008	0.006	0.004	0.005	0.004	0.005	0.006	0.008	0.007	(e)0.007
Nigeria	1.274	0.391	0.238	0.325	0.525	0.473	0.465	0.500	0.421	0.510	0.595
Saint Helena	(e)0.000	(e)0.000	(e)0.000	(e)0.000	(e)0.000	(e)0.000	(e)0.000	(e)0.000	(e)0.000	(e)0.000	(e)0.000
Senegal (12)	0.023	0.022	0.019	0.014	0.015	0.013	0.012	0.014	0.016	0.014	0.014
Sierra Leone*	0.011	0.004	0.001	0.000	0.002	0.002	0.002	0.001	0.002	0.002	0.002
Togo*	0.017	0.008	0.007	0.006	0.006	0.005	0.005	0.005	0.007	(e)0.006	(e)0.006

For sources and notes, see end of table.

1980	1990	1995	2000	2005	2006	2007	2008	2009	2010	2011	Régions, pays ou territoires
				Imports (c.i.f.) - Importations (c.a.f.) Percentage - En pourcentage							
100	100	100	100	100	100	100	100	100	100	100	MONDE
23.910	22.213	28.639	28.779	31.718	32.320	33.172	34.855	36.698	39.029	39.833	ÉCONOMIES EN DÉVELOPPEMENT
4.023	3.900	2.204	1.564	2.511	2.807	3.279	3.705	3.230	3.223	3.486	ÉCONOMIES EN TRANSITION
72.067	73.887	69.157	69.657	65.771	64.873	63.550	61.440	60.071	57.747	56.681	ÉCONOMIES DÉVELOPPÉES
4.661	2.631	2.371	1.951	2.381	2.422	2.591	2.851	3.236	3.045	3.092	Économies en développement : Afrique
0.515	0.355	0.299	0.255	0.298	0.308	0.319	0.362	0.420	0.392	0.405	Afrique orientale
0.008	0.006	0.004	0.002	0.002	0.003	0.002	0.002	0.003	0.003	0.004	Burundi*(1)
0.001	0.001	0.001	0.001	0.001	0.001	0.001	0.001	0.002	0.001	0.002	Comores*
0.010	0.006	0.003	0.003	0.003	0.003	0.003	0.003	0.004	0.002	(e)0.002	Djibouti (2)
		0.009	0.007	(e)0.005	(e)0.004	(e)0.004	(e)0.004	(e)0.005	(e)0.004	(e)0.005	Érythrée (3)
0.035	0.030	–	–	–	–	–	–	–	–	–	Éthiopie (...1991)
–	–	0.022	0.019	0.038	0.042	0.041	0.053	0.063	0.056	0.048	Éthiopie
0.102	0.062	0.057	0.047	0.057	0.059	0.063	0.067	0.080	0.078	0.081	Kenya
0.037	0.016	0.012	0.015	0.016	0.015	0.018	0.023	0.025	0.016	0.016	Madagascar*
0.021	0.016	0.009	0.008	0.011	0.010	0.010	0.013	0.016	0.014	0.013	Malawi
0.030	0.045	0.038	0.033	0.029	0.029	0.027	0.028	0.029	0.028	0.028	Maurice
..	..	..	0.002	0.003	0.003	0.003	0.004	0.004	-	-	Mayotte
0.038	0.024	0.013	0.017	0.022	0.023	0.021	0.024	0.030	0.023	0.034	Mozambique
0.013	0.008	0.005	0.003	0.004	0.005	0.005	0.007	0.010	0.009	(e)0.009	Rwanda
0.005	0.005	0.004	0.005	0.006	0.006	0.006	0.006	0.006	0.005	0.005	Seychelles
0.021	(e)0.002	(e)0.005	(e)0.005	(e)0.006	(e)0.006	(e)0.006	(e)0.007	(e)0.007	(e)0.006	(e)0.006	Somalie
0.014	0.008	0.020	0.023	0.019	0.021	0.024	0.027	0.033	0.030	0.025	Ouganda
0.061	0.038	0.032	0.023	0.030	0.034	0.037	0.043	0.050	0.052	0.061	République-Unie de Tanzanie
0.052	0.035	0.013	0.013	0.024	0.025	0.028	0.031	0.030	0.034	0.039	Zambie (4)
0.067	0.051	0.051	0.028	0.022	0.019	0.018	0.018	0.023	(e)0.024	(e)0.024	Zimbabwe
0.283	0.195	0.114	0.114	0.177	0.179	0.216	0.258	0.346	0.266	0.278	Afrique centrale
0.064	0.044	0.028	0.046	0.077	0.071	0.096	0.127	0.178	0.108	0.118	Angola (5)
0.077	0.039	0.021	0.022	0.025	0.025	0.029	0.033	0.035	0.033	(e)0.035	Cameroun*(6)
0.004	0.004	0.003	0.002	0.002	0.002	0.002	0.002	0.002	(e)0.002	(e)0.002	République centrafricaine*(6)
0.004	0.014	0.009	0.005	0.009	0.011	0.012	0.012	0.016	(e)0.014	(e)0.011	Tchad*(5)
0.027	0.017	0.013	0.007	0.012	0.016	0.018	0.019	0.023	(e)0.026	(e)0.028	Congo*(6)
0.073	0.048	0.020	0.010	0.025	0.023	0.024	0.026	0.031	(e)0.029	(e)0.029	Rép. dém. du Congo*
0.001	0.002	0.002	0.008	0.012	0.016	0.019	0.023	0.041	(e)0.037	(e)0.033	Guinée équatoriale (5)
0.032	0.026	0.017	0.014	0.014	0.014	0.015	0.016	0.020	0.016	(e)0.021	Gabon*(7)
0.001	0.001	0.001	0.000	0.000	0.001	0.001	0.001	0.001	0.001	0.001	Sao Tomé-et-Principe
1.518	1.042	0.879	0.728	0.805	0.771	0.850	1.054	1.229	1.115	1.026	Afrique septentrionale
0.508	0.272	0.193	0.137	0.188	0.173	0.194	0.239	0.309	0.266	0.257	Algérie*
0.234	0.257	0.224	0.210	0.183	0.168	0.190	0.296	0.354	0.343	0.320	Égypte
0.326	0.149	0.096	0.056	0.056	0.049	0.047	0.055	0.079	0.068	(e)0.027	Libye
0.205	0.193	0.191	0.173	0.192	0.194	0.224	0.257	0.259	0.229	0.241	Maroc*
0.076	0.017	0.023	0.023	0.063	0.065	0.061	0.057	0.076	0.065	0.050	Soudan (...2011) (8)
0.170	0.154	0.151	0.129	0.122	0.122	0.134	0.149	0.151	0.144	0.130	Tunisie (9)
1.097	0.642	0.699	0.536	0.679	0.730	0.713	0.667	0.702	0.723	0.765	Afrique australe
0.033	0.054	0.036	0.031	0.030	0.025	0.028	0.032	0.037	0.037	0.040	Botswana*
0.021	0.019	0.021	0.012	0.013	0.012	0.012	0.012	0.016	0.014	(e)0.014	Lesotho
0.056	0.032	0.031	0.023	0.024	0.023	0.025	0.026	0.039	0.035	(e)0.035	Namibie
(e,b)0.958	(e)0.519	(e)0.591	(e)0.454	(e)0.594	(e)0.654	(e)0.634	(e)0.587	(e)0.596	(e)0.624	(e)0.666	Afrique du Sud
0.030	0.018	0.019	0.016	0.018	0.016	0.013	0.010	(e)0.014	(e)0.013	(e)0.011	Swaziland
1.247	0.397	0.380	0.317	0.422	0.433	0.494	0.510	0.540	0.549	0.618	Afrique occidentale
0.016	0.007	0.014	0.009	0.009	0.010	0.014	0.014	0.016	(e)0.014	(e)0.015	Bénin*
0.017	0.015	0.009	0.009	0.012	0.012	0.012	0.013	0.015	0.013	(e)0.014	Burkina Faso
0.003	0.004	0.005	0.003	0.004	0.004	0.005	0.005	0.006	0.005	0.005	Cap-Vert (10)
0.144	0.058	0.056	0.037	0.054	0.047	0.047	0.048	0.055	0.051	0.037	Côte d'Ivoire*
0.008	0.005	0.003	0.003	0.002	0.002	0.002	0.002	0.002	0.002	0.002	Gambie (11)
0.054	0.034	0.036	0.045	0.050	0.055	0.056	0.062	0.063	0.071	(e)0.083	Ghana
0.013	0.020	0.016	0.009	0.008	0.008	0.009	0.008	0.008	0.009	0.011	Guinée*
0.003	0.002	0.003	0.001	0.001	0.001	0.001	0.001	0.001	(e)0.001	0.002	Guinée-Bissau
0.026	0.006	(e)0.010	(e)0.010	0.003	0.004	0.004	0.005	0.004	0.005	0.006	Libéria*
0.021	0.017	0.015	0.012	0.014	0.015	0.015	0.020	0.019	0.019	(e)0.018	Mali*
0.014	0.006	0.008	0.007	0.013	0.009	0.010	0.012	0.011	0.012	0.013	Mauritanie*
0.029	0.011	0.007	0.006	0.009	0.008	0.008	0.010	0.019	0.015	(e)0.013	Niger*
0.801	0.157	0.157	0.131	0.197	0.216	0.263	0.257	0.266	0.286	0.348	Nigéria
(e)0.001	(e)0.001	(e)0.000	(e)0.001	(e)0.001	(e)0.001	(e)0.001	(e)0.000	(e)0.000	(e)0.000	0.000	Sainte-Hélène
0.051	0.034	0.027	0.023	0.032	0.030	0.034	0.040	0.037	0.031	0.032	Sénégal (12)
0.021	0.004	0.003	0.002	0.003	0.003	0.003	0.003	0.004	0.005	0.009	Sierra Leone*
0.026	0.016	0.011	0.008	0.010	0.009	0.009	0.009	0.012	(e)0.010	(e)0.009	Togo*

Pour les sources et les notes, se reporter à la fin du tableau.

Region, country or territory	Exports (f.o.b.) - Exportations (f.a.b.) Percentage - En pourcentage										
	1980	1990	1995	2000	2005	2006	2007	2008	2009	2010	2011
Developing economies: America	**5.470**	**4.138**	**4.442**	**5.688**	**5.554**	**5.746**	**5.585**	**5.649**	**5.580**	**5.813**	**6.058**
Caribbean	*1.099*	*0.335*	*0.250*	*0.295*	*0.254*	*0.272*	*0.249*	*0.252*	*0.191*	*0.179*	*0.211*
Anguilla	..	..	0.000	0.000	0.000	0.000	0.000	0.000	0.000	0.000	0.000
Antigua and Barbuda	0.001	0.001	0.001	0.001	0.001	0.001	0.000	0.000	0.000	0.000	0.000
Aruba (13)	..	0.004	0.026	0.039	0.042	0.039	0.037	0.034	0.016	0.002	0.028
Bahamas (14)	0.246	0.007	0.003	0.009	0.005	0.006	0.006	0.006	0.006	0.005	0.005
Barbados	0.011	0.006	0.005	0.004	0.003	0.004	0.004	0.003	0.003	0.003	0.003
Cayman Islands	..	..	..	..	0.001	0.000	0.000	0.000	0.000	0.000	0.000
Cuba*	0.274	0.141	0.031	0.026	0.022	0.025	0.028	0.025	0.025	0.033	(e)0.035
Curaçao	–	–	–	–	–	–	–	–	–	–	0.005
Dominica*	0.000	0.002	0.001	0.001	0.000	0.000	0.000	0.000	0.000	0.000	0.000
Dominican Republic (15)	0.047	0.021	0.073	0.089	0.058	0.054	0.051	0.042	0.044	0.044	0.047
Grenada	0.001	0.001	0.000	0.001	0.000	0.000	0.000	0.000	0.000	0.000	0.000
Haiti	0.011	0.005	0.002	0.005	0.004	0.004	0.004	0.003	0.005	0.004	0.004
Jamaica	0.047	0.033	0.028	0.020	0.014	0.015	0.016	0.015	0.011	0.009	0.009
Montserrat*	0.000	0.000	0.000	0.000	0.000	0.000	0.000	0.000	0.000	0.000	0.000
Netherlands Antilles*(16)	0.254	0.051	0.029	0.031	0.006	0.006	0.005	0.007	0.006	0.005	–
Saint Kitts and Nevis*	0.001	0.001	0.000	0.001	0.000	0.000	0.000	0.000	0.000	0.000	0.000
Saint Lucia	0.003	0.004	0.002	0.001	0.001	0.001	0.001	0.001	0.001	0.001	0.001
Saint Vincent and the Grenadines*	0.001	0.002	0.001	0.001	0.000	0.000	0.000	0.000	0.000	0.000	(e)0.000
Sint Maarten (Dutch part)	–	–	–	–	–	–	–	–	–	–	0.001
Trinidad and Tobago*	0.200	0.056	0.047	0.066	0.095	0.117	0.096	0.116	0.073	0.072	(e)0.073
Turks and Caicos Islands	..	..	..	0.000	0.000	0.000	0.000	0.000	0.000	0.000	-
Central America	*1.149*	*1.314*	*1.732*	*2.839*	*2.313*	*2.332*	*2.200*	*2.055*	*2.130*	*2.224*	*2.196*
Belize	0.005	0.004	0.003	0.003	0.002	0.002	0.002	0.002	0.002	0.002	0.002
Costa Rica*	0.049	0.042	0.067	0.091	0.067	0.068	0.067	0.059	0.070	0.061	0.056
El Salvador (17)	0.053	0.019	0.032	0.046	0.033	0.031	0.029	0.029	0.031	0.029	0.029
Guatemala (18)	0.075	0.033	0.038	0.042	0.051	0.050	0.049	0.048	0.058	0.055	0.057
Honduras (19)	0.041	0.027	0.034	0.052	0.048	0.043	0.041	0.038	0.039	0.038	0.040
Mexico	0.886	1.170	1.536	2.582	2.034	2.064	1.941	1.808	1.835	1.954	1.920
Nicaragua (20)	0.022	0.010	0.009	0.010	0.008	0.008	0.009	0.009	0.011	0.012	0.013
Panama, excl. Canal Zone	0.018	–	–	–	–	–	–	–	–	–	–
Panama*(21)	–	0.010	0.012	0.013	0.070	0.066	0.063	0.061	0.086	0.072	0.080
South America	*3.223*	*2.488*	*2.460*	*2.554*	*2.987*	*3.141*	*3.136*	*3.342*	*3.259*	*3.410*	*3.650*
Argentina*	0.394	0.355	0.405	0.409	0.384	0.384	0.398	0.437	0.448	0.449	0.463
Bolivia (Plurinational State of)	0.046	0.027	0.021	0.019	0.027	0.032	0.032	0.044	0.039	0.041	0.046
Brazil	0.989	0.903	0.898	0.855	1.127	1.136	1.146	1.227	1.222	1.323	1.406
Chile*	0.231	0.241	0.310	0.298	0.393	0.484	0.483	0.412	0.415	0.465	0.447
Colombia	0.193	0.193	0.196	0.202	0.201	0.201	0.213	0.237	0.262	0.260	0.310
Ecuador	0.122	0.078	0.083	0.076	0.096	0.105	0.099	0.117	0.111	0.114	0.123
Falkland Islands (Malvinas)	(e)0.000	(e)0.000	(e)0.001	(e)0.001	(e)0.002	(e)0.001	(e)0.001	(e)0.001	(e)0.001	(e)0.001	(e)0.001
Guyana*	0.019	0.007	0.009	0.008	0.005	0.005	0.005	0.005	0.006	0.006	0.006
Paraguay	0.015	0.028	0.018	0.013	0.016	0.015	0.020	0.028	0.025	0.030	0.030
Peru*	0.192	0.093	0.106	0.109	0.165	0.196	0.199	0.195	0.215	0.233	0.253
Suriname	0.025	0.014	0.009	0.006	0.009	0.010	0.010	0.011	0.011	0.013	0.013
Uruguay	0.052	0.049	0.041	0.036	0.032	0.033	0.032	0.040	0.043	0.044	0.044
Venezuela (Bolivarian Rep. of)	0.944	0.501	0.364	0.520	0.530	0.540	0.499	0.589	0.460	0.431	0.508
Developing economies: Asia	**17.896**	**16.938**	**20.986**	**23.764**	**27.647**	**28.595**	**28.963**	**29.811**	**31.063**	**32.789**	**33.392**
Eastern Asia	*3.742*	*8.065*	*10.867*	*12.025*	*14.632*	*15.170*	*15.599*	*15.337*	*16.700*	*17.799*	*17.583*
China	0.889	1.785	2.874	3.867	7.247	7.988	8.689	8.853	9.600	10.344	10.429
China, Hong Kong SAR	0.970	2.361	3.356	3.132	2.752	2.611	2.458	2.247	2.544	2.557	2.354
China, Macao SAR	0.030	0.049	0.039	0.039	0.024	0.021	0.018	0.012	0.008	0.006	0.005
China, Taiwan Province of	0.972	1.928	2.155	2.293	1.881	1.843	1.758	1.581	1.627	1.800	1.693
Korea, Dem. People's Rep. of	..	0.053	0.019	0.011	0.013	0.012	0.012	0.013	0.016	0.017	(e)0.020
Korea, Republic of (22)	0.860	1.869	2.415	2.673	2.705	2.682	2.651	2.615	2.889	3.057	3.056
Mongolia	0.020	0.019	0.009	0.008	0.010	0.013	0.013	0.016	0.015	0.019	0.026
Southern Asia	*1.284*	*1.351*	*1.255*	*1.439*	*1.879*	*1.947*	*1.990*	*2.196*	*2.279*	*2.486*	*2.720*
Afghanistan	0.033	0.007	0.003	0.002	0.004	0.003	0.004	0.003	0.003	0.003	(e)0.002
Bangladesh	0.037	0.048	0.068	0.099	0.088	0.097	0.089	0.095	0.120	0.126	0.135
Bhutan	0.001	0.002	0.002	0.002	0.002	0.003	0.005	0.003	0.004	0.004	(e)0.003
India (23)	0.422	0.517	0.592	0.658	0.948	1.004	1.070	1.205	1.317	1.484	1.662
Iran (Islamic Rep. of)*	0.606	0.555	0.355	0.440	0.614	0.635	0.633	0.704	0.630	0.668	0.717
Maldives	0.000	0.002	0.002	0.002	0.002	0.002	0.002	0.002	0.001	0.001	0.002
Nepal	0.004	0.005	0.007	0.012	0.008	0.007	0.006	0.006	0.007	0.005	0.005
Pakistan	0.129	0.161	0.154	0.140	0.153	0.140	0.127	0.126	0.140	0.140	0.139
Sri Lanka	0.052	0.055	0.073	0.084	0.060	0.057	0.055	0.050	0.057	0.054	0.055

For sources and notes, see end of table.

			Imports (c.i.f.) - Importations (c.a.f.) Percentage - En pourcentage								Régions, pays ou territoires
1980	1990	1995	2000	2005	2006	2007	2008	2009	2010	2011	
5.947	**3.529**	**4.744**	**5.885**	**5.002**	**5.192**	**5.362**	**5.662**	**5.473**	**5.839**	**5.986**	**Économies en développement : Amérique**
1.317	*0.521*	*0.383*	*0.487*	*0.403*	*0.416*	*0.403*	*0.429*	*0.385*	*0.349*	*0.368*	*Caraïbes*
..	..	0.001	0.001	0.001	0.002	0.002	0.002	0.001	0.001	0.001	Anguilla
0.004	0.007	0.007	0.006	0.005	0.005	0.005	0.005	0.004	0.003	0.003	Antigua-et-Barbuda
..	0.016	0.034	0.039	0.040	0.038	0.036	0.036	0.019	0.009	0.032	Aruba (13)
0.363	0.031	0.024	0.031	0.024	0.024	0.022	0.020	0.021	0.019	0.019	Bahamas (14)
0.025	0.020	0.015	0.017	0.015	0.013	0.012	0.011	0.012	0.010	0.010	Barbade
..	..	..	..	0.011	0.008	0.007	0.007	0.007	0.005	0.005	Îles Caïmanes
0.313	0.188	0.054	0.073	0.075	0.082	0.076	0.093	0.076	0.075	(e)0.078	Cuba*
										0.012	Curaçao
0.002	0.003	0.002	0.002	0.002	0.001	0.001	0.001	0.002	0.001	0.001	Dominique*
0.095	0.084	0.099	0.142	0.091	0.098	0.095	0.097	0.097	0.099	0.095	République dominicaine (15)
0.002	0.003	0.002	0.004	0.003	0.002	0.003	0.002	0.002	0.002	0.002	Grenade
0.018	0.009	0.012	0.016	0.013	0.014	0.012	0.014	0.017	0.020	0.016	Haïti
0.056	0.054	0.054	0.050	0.041	0.043	0.047	0.051	0.040	0.034	0.035	Jamaïque
0.001	0.001	0.001	0.000	0.000	0.000	0.000	0.000	0.000	0.000	0.000	Montserrat*
0.273	0.060	0.035	0.043	0.018	0.018	0.018	0.019	0.021	0.017	_	Antilles néerlandaises*(16)
0.002	0.003	0.003	0.003	0.002	0.002	0.002	0.002	0.002	0.002	(e)0.001	Saint-Kitts-et-Nevis*
0.006	0.008	0.006	0.005	0.004	0.005	0.004	0.004	0.004	0.004	0.004	Sainte-Lucie
0.003	0.004	0.003	0.002	0.002	0.002	0.002	0.002	0.003	0.002	(e)0.002	Saint-Vincent-et-les Grenadines*
										0.004	Saint-Martin (partie néerlandaise)
0.153	0.031	0.033	0.050	0.053	0.052	0.054	0.058	0.055	0.042	(e)0.047	Trinité-et-Tobago*
..	..	..	0.002	0.003	0.004	0.004	0.004	0.003	0.002	-	Îles Turques et Caïques
1.431	*1.443*	*1.760*	*3.137*	*2.576*	*2.596*	*2.511*	*2.403*	*2.375*	*2.481*	*2.446*	*Amérique centrale*
0.007	0.006	0.005	0.008	0.005	0.005	0.005	0.005	0.005	0.005	0.005	Belize
0.074	0.055	0.078	0.096	0.091	0.093	0.091	0.093	0.090	0.088	0.088	Costa Rica*
0.046	0.035	0.064	0.074	0.063	0.063	0.062	0.060	0.058	0.055	0.055	El Salvador (17)
0.077	0.046	0.063	0.078	0.097	0.096	0.095	0.088	0.091	0.090	0.090	Guatemala (18)
0.049	0.026	0.036	0.060	0.061	0.059	0.062	0.063	0.057	0.055	0.056	Honduras (19)
1.066	1.214	1.448	2.744	2.146	2.168	2.078	1.972	1.938	2.052	2.004	Mexique
0.043	0.018	0.019	0.027	0.024	0.024	0.025	0.026	0.027	0.027	0.028	Nicaragua (20)
0.070											Panama, sans la zone du canal
	0.043	0.048	0.051	0.089	0.087	0.093	0.095	0.109	0.108	0.119	Panama*(21)
3.199	*1.565*	*2.601*	*2.261*	*2.023*	*2.181*	*2.449*	*2.830*	*2.713*	*3.009*	*3.172*	*Amérique du Sud*
0.507	0.114	0.382	0.378	0.266	0.276	0.313	0.348	0.308	0.366	0.402	Argentine*
0.032	0.019	0.027	0.027	0.022	0.023	0.024	0.031	0.035	0.035	0.042	Bolivie (État plurinational de)
1.201	0.628	1.034	0.801	0.710	0.775	0.887	1.106	1.052	1.242	1.289	Brésil
0.279	0.221	0.304	0.278	0.303	0.310	0.330	0.375	0.326	0.385	0.408	Chili*
0.228	0.156	0.264	0.173	0.196	0.211	0.232	0.238	0.259	0.264	0.297	Colombie
0.108	0.052	0.080	0.056	0.095	0.098	0.095	0.114	0.119	0.133	0.132	Équateur
(e)0.000	(e)0.001	(e)0.001	(e)0.001	(e)0.001	(e)0.001	(e)0.001	(e)0.000	(e)0.000	(e)0.001	(e)0.001	Îles Falkland (Malvinas)
0.019	0.009	0.010	0.009	0.007	0.007	0.007	0.008	0.009	0.009	0.010	Guyana*
0.030	0.038	0.060	0.034	0.030	0.038	0.041	0.055	0.055	0.065	0.067	Paraguay
0.120	0.073	0.145	0.111	0.116	0.124	0.143	0.182	0.172	0.195	0.204	Pérou*
0.024	0.013	0.011	0.008	0.010	0.008	0.007	0.008	0.011	0.009	0.009	Suriname
0.081	0.037	0.055	0.052	0.036	0.038	0.040	0.054	0.054	0.056	0.058	Uruguay
0.569	0.204	0.228	0.253	0.222	0.271	0.327	0.309	0.312	0.250	0.253	Venezuela (Rép. bolivarienne du)
13.131	**15.911**	**21.412**	**20.848**	**24.245**	**24.618**	**25.129**	**26.254**	**27.896**	**30.055**	**30.670**	**Économies en développement : Asie**
4.116	*7.411*	*10.834*	*11.155*	*13.067*	*13.321*	*13.388*	*13.396*	*14.634*	*16.325*	*16.602*	*Asie orientale*
0.960	1.487	2.522	3.379	6.113	6.401	6.700	6.864	7.906	9.051	9.483	Chine
1.080	2.299	3.680	3.196	2.773	2.705	2.576	2.356	2.734	2.808	2.631	Chine (RAS de Hong Kong)
0.026	0.043	0.039	0.034	0.036	0.037	0.038	0.033	0.036	0.036	0.042	Chine (RAS de Macao)
0.951	1.528	1.980	2.101	1.690	1.641	1.539	1.460	1.375	1.630	1.531	Province chinoise de Taiwan
..	0.082	0.026	0.025	0.025	0.024	0.021	0.022	0.024	0.023	(e)0.026	Corée, Rép. populaire dém. de
1.073	1.947	2.580	2.410	2.419	2.501	2.500	2.640	2.542	2.756	2.853	Corée, République de (22)
0.026	0.026	0.008	0.009	0.011	0.012	0.015	0.022	0.017	0.021	0.036	Mongolie
1.903	*1.599*	*1.392*	*1.430*	*2.193*	*2.278*	*2.408*	*2.832*	*2.997*	*3.288*	*3.515*	*Asie méridionale*
0.040	0.026	0.007	0.018	0.023	0.021	0.020	0.018	0.026	0.033	(e)0.034	Afghanistan
0.125	0.101	0.128	0.133	0.129	0.130	0.130	0.145	0.172	0.180	0.197	Bangladesh
0.002	0.002	0.002	0.003	0.004	0.003	0.004	0.003	0.004	0.006	(e)0.005	Bhoutan
0.715	0.657	0.663	0.774	1.323	1.443	1.602	1.946	2.025	2.270	2.523	Inde (23)
0.646	0.511	0.244	0.215	0.371	0.330	0.315	0.348	0.400	0.426	0.372	Iran (Rép. islamique d')*
0.001	0.004	0.005	0.006	0.007	0.007	0.008	0.008	0.008	0.007	0.008	Maldives
0.016	0.017	0.025	0.024	0.021	0.020	0.022	0.022	0.035	0.033	0.031	Népal
0.257	0.206	0.219	0.163	0.235	0.241	0.228	0.257	0.249	0.245	0.237	Pakistan
0.098	0.075	0.099	0.094	0.082	0.083	0.079	0.085	0.079	0.088	0.107	Sri Lanka

Pour les sources et les notes, se reporter à la fin du tableau.

1.1.1 Exports and imports of countries
and geographical regions
Share

Region, country or territory	Exports (f.o.b.) - Exportations (f.a.b.) Percentage - En pourcentage										
	1980	1990	1995	2000	2005	2006	2007	2008	2009	2010	2011
South-Eastern Asia	*3.633*	*4.144*	*6.208*	*6.670*	*6.229*	*6.351*	*6.173*	*6.190*	*6.499*	*6.897*	*6.813*
Brunei Darussalam*	0.225	0.064	0.046	0.061	0.059	0.063	0.055	0.066	0.058	0.058	0.068
Cambodia (5)	0.001	0.002	0.017	0.022	0.028	0.030	0.029	0.029	0.034	0.034	(e)0.038
Indonesia (...2002)	1.177	0.738	0.877	1.015	–	–	–	–	–	–	–
Indonesia					0.827	0.853	0.842	0.865	0.956	1.036	1.101
Lao People's Dem. Rep.*	0.001	0.002	0.006	0.005	0.005	0.007	0.007	0.007	0.008	0.011	(e)0.013
Malaysia (24)	0.636	0.847	1.428	1.524	1.340	1.323	1.256	1.300	1.258	1.303	1.253
Myanmar	0.023	0.009	0.016	0.025	0.036	0.037	0.045	0.043	0.053	0.057	0.051
Philippines	0.282	0.233	0.338	0.586	0.392	0.391	0.360	0.307	0.307	0.338	0.264
Singapore (25)	0.952	1.516	2.284	2.138	2.184	2.240	2.135	2.096	2.156	2.306	2.249
Thailand	0.320	0.663	1.090	1.070	1.048	1.078	1.098	1.090	1.214	1.280	1.243
Timor-Leste (26)	–	–	–	–	0.000	0.000	0.000	0.000	0.000	0.000	0.000
Viet Nam	0.017	0.069	0.105	0.224	0.309	0.328	0.346	0.388	0.456	0.473	0.532
Western Asia	*9.238*	*3.379*	*2.657*	*3.630*	*4.907*	*5.126*	*5.201*	*6.088*	*5.585*	*5.606*	*6.276*
Bahrain (5)	0.177	0.108	0.079	0.096	0.097	0.101	0.097	0.107	0.095	0.089	0.108
Iraq*	1.294	0.296	0.038	0.291	0.225	0.252	0.289	0.395	0.339	0.358	0.470
Jordan	0.028	0.031	0.034	0.029	0.041	0.043	0.041	0.048	0.052	0.046	0.044
Kuwait*	0.975	0.202	0.247	0.302	0.427	0.461	0.446	0.542	0.431	0.440	0.568
Lebanon (27)	0.047	0.014	0.013	0.011	0.022	0.023	0.026	0.028	0.033	0.033	0.031
Occupied Palestinian territory	..	..	0.008	0.006	0.003	0.003	0.004	0.003	0.004	0.004	0.004
Oman	0.117	0.158	0.117	0.176	0.178	0.178	0.172	0.234	0.224	0.240	0.259
Qatar*	0.279	0.101	0.067	0.177	0.241	0.277	0.296	0.345	0.386	0.477	0.588
Saudi Arabia*(28)	4.990	1.277	0.967	1.202	1.718	1.739	1.664	1.942	1.536	1.646	1.977
Syrian Arab Republic*	0.104	0.121	0.069	0.072	0.087	0.090	0.082	0.095	0.087	0.081	(e)0.047
Turkey*	0.143	0.373	0.417	0.431	0.699	0.705	0.765	0.818	0.816	0.746	0.741
United Arab Emirates	1.079	0.677	0.564	0.773	1.115	1.200	1.274	1.482	1.532	1.391	1.387
Yemen, Arab Republic	0.001	–	–	–	–	–	–	–	–	–	–
Yemen, Democratic	0.003	–	–	–	–	–	–	–	–	–	–
Yemen*	–	0.020	0.038	0.063	0.053	0.055	0.045	0.047	0.050	0.056	(e)0.053
Developing economies: Oceania	**0.110**	**0.078**	**0.088**	**0.079**	**0.063**	**0.063**	**0.064**	**0.059**	**0.057**	**0.059**	**0.059**
American Samoa*(29)	0.006	0.009	0.005	0.005	0.004	0.004	(e)0.003	(e)0.004	(e)0.004	(e)0.002	(e)0.002
Cook Islands	0.000	0.000	0.000	0.000	0.000	0.000	0.000	0.000	0.000	0.000	0.000
Fiji	0.019	0.011	0.011	0.008	0.007	0.006	0.005	0.006	0.005	0.006	(e)0.005
French Polynesia*	0.001	0.003	0.004	0.004	0.002	0.002	0.001	0.001	0.001	0.001	0.001
Guam	0.003	0.002	0.002	0.001	0.000	0.000	0.001	0.001	0.000	0.000	0.000
Kiribati	0.000	0.000	0.000	0.000	0.000	0.000	0.000	0.000	0.000	(e)0.000	(e)0.000
Marshall Islands	–	0.000	0.000	0.000	0.000	0.000	0.000	0.000	0.000	(e)0.000	(e)0.000
Micronesia (Federated States of)	–	0.000	0.000	0.000	0.000	0.000	0.000	0.000	0.000	(e)0.000	(e)0.000
Nauru	0.003	0.002	0.001	0.000	0.000	0.000	0.000	0.001	0.000	0.000	0.000
New Caledonia*	0.020	0.014	0.009	0.009	0.010	0.011	0.015	0.008	0.008	0.010	0.009
Niue	..	0.000	0.000	0.000	0.000	0.000	0.000	0.000	(e)0.000	(e)0.000	(e)0.000
Northern Mariana Islands	–	..	..	0.016	0.006	0.004	0.002	(e)0.001	(e)0.000	(e)0.000	(e)0.000
Palau	–	0.000	0.000	0.000	0.000	0.000	0.000	0.000	0.000	0.000	0.000
Papua New Guinea	0.051	0.033	0.051	0.032	0.031	0.034	0.033	0.035	0.035	0.038	0.038
Samoa (27)	0.001	0.000	0.000	0.000	0.001	0.001	0.001	0.000	0.000	0.000	0.000
Solomon Islands*	0.004	0.002	0.003	0.001	0.001	0.001	0.001	0.001	0.001	0.001	0.002
Tokelau	..	..	..	..	(e)0.000	(e)0.000	(e)0.000	-	-	-	-
Tonga	0.000	0.000	0.000	0.000	0.000	0.000	0.000	0.000	0.000	0.000	(e)0.000
Tuvalu	..	0.000	0.000	0.000	0.000	0.000	0.000	(e)0.000	(e)0.000	(e)0.000	(e)0.000
Vanuatu	0.002	0.001	0.001	0.000	0.000	0.000	0.000	0.000	0.000	0.000	0.000
Wallis and Futuna Islands	..	..	..	-	(e)0.000	(e)0.000		-	-	-	-
Transition economies	**4.197**	**3.413**	**2.354**	**2.390**	**3.449**	**3.754**	**3.925**	**4.578**	**3.813**	**4.064**	**4.544**
Albania	..	0.007	0.004	0.004	0.006	0.007	0.008	0.008	0.009	0.010	0.011
Armenia*	–	–	0.005	0.005	0.009	0.008	0.009	0.007	0.006	0.007	0.007
Azerbaijan (30)	–	–	0.011	0.027	0.073	0.107	0.152	0.190	0.169	0.174	0.189
Belarus	–	–	0.093	0.114	0.152	0.163	0.173	0.202	0.170	0.166	0.226
Bosnia and Herzegovina*(31)	–	–	0.003	0.017	0.023	0.027	0.030	0.031	0.032	0.031	0.032
Croatia*	–	–	0.087	0.069	0.083	0.086	0.088	0.087	0.084	0.077	0.073
Georgia (32)	–	–	0.003	0.005	0.008	0.008	0.009	0.009	0.009	0.010	0.012
Kazakhstan*(33)	–	–	0.101	0.137	0.265	0.315	0.341	0.441	0.345	0.390	0.485
Kyrgyzstan	–	–	0.008	0.008	0.006	0.007	0.009	0.011	0.013	0.012	0.011
Montenegro	–	–	–	–	–	–	–	0.004	0.003	0.003	0.003
Republic of Moldova	–	–	0.014	0.007	0.010	0.009	0.010	0.010	0.010	0.010	0.012
Russian Federation (34)	–	–	1.601	1.630	2.319	2.505	2.529	2.923	2.424	2.624	2.866
Serbia and Montenegro*	–	–	0.030	0.027	0.048	0.059	0.069	–	–	–	–
Serbia	–	–	–	–	–	–	–	0.068	0.067	0.064	0.065
SFR of Yugoslavia	0.441	0.411	–	–	–	–	–	–	–	–	–
Tajikistan (32)	–	–	0.014	0.012	0.008	0.012	0.010	0.009	0.008	0.008	0.007
TFYR of Macedonia*	–	–	0.023	0.021	0.019	0.020	0.024	0.024	0.022	0.022	0.024

For sources and notes, see end of table.

				Imports (c.i.f.) - Importations (c.a.f.) Percentage - En pourcentage							Régions, pays ou territoires
1980	1990	1995	2000	2005	2006	2007	2008	2009	2010	2011	
3.159	*4.525*	*6.784*	*5.708*	*5.582*	*5.565*	*5.442*	*5.744*	*5.733*	*6.189*	*6.263*	*Asie du Sud-Est*
0.028	0.028	0.040	0.017	0.014	0.013	0.015	0.015	0.019	0.016	0.016	Brunéi Darussalam*
0.009	0.005	0.023	0.029	0.036	0.039	0.038	0.039	0.046	0.044	(e)0.051	Cambodge (5)
0.521	0.607	0.776	0.647	–	–	–	–	–	–	–	Indonésie (...2002)
–	–	–	–	0.701	0.652	0.652	0.774	0.738	0.877	0.962	Indonésie
0.004	0.005	0.011	0.008	0.008	0.009	0.007	0.009	0.011	0.013	(e)0.014	Rép. dém. populaire lao*
0.519	0.815	1.483	1.231	1.059	1.060	1.028	0.997	0.974	1.068	1.021	Malaisie (24)
0.017	0.008	0.025	0.036	0.018	0.021	0.023	0.026	0.034	0.031	0.049	Myanmar
0.399	0.362	0.541	0.556	0.458	0.437	0.404	0.367	0.361	0.379	0.347	Philippines
1.155	1.697	2.377	2.021	1.852	1.930	1.844	1.940	1.935	2.015	1.990	Singapour (25)
0.443	0.921	1.351	0.930	1.094	1.041	0.990	1.087	1.061	1.200	1.245	Thaïlande
–	–	–	–	0.001	0.001	0.001	0.002	0.002	0.002	0.002	Timor-Leste (26)
0.063	0.077	0.156	0.235	0.340	0.364	0.439	0.490	0.551	0.543	0.566	Viet Nam
3.954	*2.377*	*2.401*	*2.555*	*3.403*	*3.454*	*3.891*	*4.281*	*4.531*	*4.253*	*4.290*	*Asie occidentale*
0.168	0.103	0.071	0.070	0.087	0.080	0.077	0.086	0.076	0.073	0.066	Bahreïn (5)
0.419	0.182	0.055	0.165	0.218	0.178	0.149	0.199	0.290	0.255	0.275	Iraq*
0.116	0.072	0.071	0.069	0.097	0.093	0.095	0.102	0.114	0.098	0.100	Jordanie
0.314	0.111	0.149	0.107	0.146	0.139	0.149	0.151	0.160	0.145	0.137	Koweït*
0.176	0.070	0.139	0.094	0.089	0.078	0.086	0.102	0.130	0.120	0.113	Liban (27)
..	..	0.032	0.036	0.025	0.022	0.022	0.022	0.028	0.026	0.024	Territoire palestinien occupé
0.083	0.075	0.081	0.076	0.082	0.088	0.112	0.139	0.141	0.128	0.129	Oman
0.070	0.047	0.065	0.049	0.093	0.133	0.164	0.169	0.196	0.151	0.140	Qatar*
1.452	0.672	0.536	0.453	0.551	0.563	0.632	0.698	0.752	0.693	0.702	Arabie saoudite*(28)
0.198	0.067	0.090	0.057	0.101	0.093	0.103	0.110	0.122	0.114	(e)0.090	République arabe syrienne*
0.381	0.622	0.682	0.818	1.081	1.128	1.192	1.225	1.110	1.203	1.310	Turquie*
0.415	0.312	0.401	0.526	0.784	0.809	1.052	1.215	1.339	1.189	1.148	Émirats arabes unis
0.089	–	–	–	–	–	–	–	–	–	–	Yémen, République arabe du
0.073	–	–	–	–	–	–	–	–	–	–	Yémen, Démocratique
–	0.044	0.030	0.035	0.050	0.049	0.060	0.063	0.072	0.060	0.055	Yémen*
0.171	**0.142**	**0.113**	**0.095**	**0.090**	**0.088**	**0.089**	**0.088**	**0.093**	**0.091**	**0.085**	**Économies en développement : Océanie**
0.005	0.010	0.008	0.008	0.005	0.005	0.005	0.004	0.005	(e)0.004	(e)0.004	Samoa américaines*(29)
0.001	0.001	0.001	0.001	0.001	0.001	0.001	0.001	0.001	0.001	0.000	Îles Cook
0.027	0.021	0.017	0.013	0.015	0.015	0.013	0.014	0.011	0.012	(e)0.013	Fidji
0.026	0.026	0.019	0.016	0.016	0.013	0.013	0.013	0.014	0.011	0.009	Polynésie française*
0.019	0.013	0.008	0.006	0.005	0.004	0.005	0.004	0.005	0.005	0.004	Guam
0.001	0.001	0.001	0.001	0.001	0.001	0.000	0.000	0.001	0.000	(e)0.001	Kiribati
–	0.002	0.001	0.001	0.001	0.001	0.001	(e)0.001	(e)0.001	(e)0.001	(e)0.001	Îles Marshall
–	0.002	0.002	0.002	0.001	0.001	0.001	0.001	0.001	(e)0.001	(e)0.001	Micronésie (États fédérés de)
0.001	0.001	0.001	0.000	0.000	0.000	0.000	0.001	0.001	0.000	0.000	Nauru
0.022	0.025	0.018	0.014	0.016	0.017	0.020	0.020	0.020	0.021	0.020	Nouvelle-Calédonie*
..	0.000	0.000	0.000	0.000	0.000	0.000	0.000	(e)0.000	(e)0.000	(e)0.000	Nioué
–	..	–	-	-	-	-	-	-	-	-	Îles Mariannes du Nord
–	..	0.001	0.002	0.001	0.001	0.001	0.001	0.001	0.001	0.001	Palaos
0.057	0.031	0.028	0.017	0.016	0.019	0.021	0.022	0.025	(e)0.026	(e)0.025	Papouasie-Nouvelle-Guinée
0.003	0.002	0.002	0.001	0.002	0.002	0.002	0.002	0.002	0.002	0.002	Samoa (27)
0.004	0.003	0.003	0.001	0.002	0.002	0.002	0.002	0.002	0.003	0.003	Îles Salomon*
..	..	..	0.000	(e)0.000	(e)0.000	(e)0.000	-	-	-	-	Tokélaou
0.002	0.002	0.001	0.001	0.001	0.001	0.001	0.001	0.001	0.001	(e)0.001	Tonga
..	0.000	0.000	0.000	0.000	0.000	0.000	0.000	(e)0.000	(e)0.000	(e)0.000	Tuvalu
0.003	0.003	0.002	0.001	0.001	0.002	0.002	0.002	0.002	0.002	0.002	Vanuatu
..	..	..	0.001	0.000	0.000	-	-	-	-	-	Îles Wallis-et-Futuna
4.023	**3.900**	**2.204**	**1.564**	**2.511**	**2.807**	**3.279**	**3.705**	**3.230**	**3.223**	**3.486**	**Économies en transition**
..	0.012	0.014	0.016	0.024	0.025	0.029	0.032	0.036	0.029	0.029	Albanie
–	–	0.013	0.013	0.016	0.018	0.023	0.027	0.026	0.025	0.023	Arménie*
–	–	0.013	0.018	0.039	0.043	0.042	0.046	0.051	0.044	0.053	Azerbaïdjan (30)
–	–	0.106	0.130	0.155	0.181	0.201	0.239	0.225	0.226	0.249	Bélarus
–	–	0.021	0.047	0.066	0.059	0.068	0.074	0.069	0.060	0.060	Bosnie-Herzégovine*(31)
–	–	0.140	0.118	0.172	0.174	0.181	0.186	0.167	0.130	0.124	Croatie*
–	–	0.009	0.011	0.023	0.030	0.037	0.037	0.035	0.033	0.038	Géorgie (32)
–	–	0.073	0.076	0.160	0.191	0.229	0.229	0.224	0.197	0.207	Kazakhstan*(33)
–	–	0.010	0.008	0.011	0.016	0.020	0.025	0.024	0.021	0.023	Kirghizistan
–	–						0.023	0.018	0.014	0.014	Monténégro
–	–	0.016	0.012	0.021	0.022	0.026	0.030	0.026	0.025	0.028	République de Moldova
–	–	1.317	0.741	1.277	1.464	1.722	1.948	1.661	1.774	1.929	Fédération de Russie (34)
–	–	0.051	0.056	0.108	0.121	0.152	–	–	–	–	Serbie-et-Monténégro*
–	–	–	–	–	–	–	0.139	0.126	0.108	0.110	Serbie
0.725	0.526	–	–	–	–	–	–	–	–	–	RSF de Yougoslavie
–	–	0.015	0.010	0.012	0.014	0.017	0.020	0.020	0.017	0.017	Tadjikistan (32)
–	–	0.033	0.031	0.030	0.030	0.037	0.042	0.040	0.035	0.038	LERY de Macédoine*

Pour les sources et les notes, se reporter à la fin du tableau.

Region, country or territory	Exports (f.o.b.) - Exportations (f.a.b.) Percentage - En pourcentage										
	1980	1990	1995	2000	2005	2006	2007	2008	2009	2010	2011
Turkmenistan (32)	–	–	0.036	0.039	0.047	0.059	0.057	0.074	(e)0.040	(e)0.043	(e)0.071
Ukraine (32)	–	–	0.254	0.226	0.326	0.316	0.352	0.415	0.318	0.337	0.376
USSR	3.756	2.995	–	–	–	–	–	–	–	–	–
Uzbekistan (32)	–	–	0.066	0.044	0.045	0.046	0.057	0.064	0.086	0.076	0.073
Developed economies: America	**14.421**	**14.998**	**15.015**	**16.431**	**12.052**	**11.770**	**11.274**	**10.868**	**10.953**	**10.906**	**10.612**
Bermuda (5)	0.002	0.002	0.001	0.001	0.000	0.000	0.000	0.000	0.000	0.000	0.000
Canada	3.328	3.669	3.712	4.293	3.419	3.210	2.973	2.802	2.508	2.530	2.480
Greenland	0.010	0.013	0.007	0.004	0.004	0.003	0.003	0.003	0.003	0.003	0.003
Saint Pierre and Miquelon	0.000	0.001	0.000	(e)0.000	(e)0.000	(e)0.000	(e)0.000	(e)0.000	(e)0.000	(e)0.000	(e)0.000
United States (35)	11.081	11.314	11.294	12.134	8.629	8.556	8.298	8.063	8.442	8.373	8.129
Developed economies: Asia	**6.680**	**8.599**	**8.926**	**7.925**	**6.065**	**5.715**	**5.482**	**5.223**	**5.022**	**5.428**	**4.888**
Israel*	0.272	0.333	0.368	0.487	0.407	0.386	0.386	0.377	0.383	0.383	0.371
Japan	6.408	8.267	8.559	7.438	5.658	5.330	5.096	4.846	4.639	5.045	4.517
Developed economies: Europe	**43.893**	**47.402**	**44.711**	**40.202**	**40.926**	**40.076**	**40.368**	**38.982**	**38.931**	**36.007**	**35.505**
Andorra*	..	..	0.001	0.001	0.001	0.001	0.001	0.001	0.001	0.000	0.000
Austria*	0.859	1.182	1.115	1.048	1.190	1.126	1.166	1.119	1.090	0.999	0.973
Belgium*	-	-	3.443	2.916	3.179	3.020	3.071	2.912	2.945	2.676	2.624
Bulgaria*	0.510	0.139	0.104	0.075	0.112	0.124	0.132	0.138	0.130	0.135	0.154
Cyprus*	0.026	0.028	0.024	0.015	0.014	0.011	0.010	0.010	0.010	0.009	0.010
Czechoslovakia (36)	0.732	0.342	–	–	–	–	–	–	–	–	–
Czech Republic*(37)	–	–	0.419	0.450	0.743	0.782	0.873	0.906	0.899	0.871	0.890
Denmark*(38)	0.823	1.065	0.983	0.794	0.809	0.762	0.735	0.722	0.748	0.638	0.621
Estonia*(32)	–	–	0.036	0.059	0.073	0.080	0.078	0.077	0.072	0.076	0.092
Faeroe Islands	0.009	0.011	0.007	0.007	0.006	0.005	0.005	0.005	0.006	0.005	0.005
Finland*	0.695	0.764	0.782	0.714	0.623	0.636	0.641	0.595	0.500	0.455	0.433
France*	5.719	6.245	5.831	5.071	4.406	4.083	3.987	3.803	3.857	3.427	3.269
Germany, Democratic Republic of	0.850	–	–	–	–	–	–	–	–	–	–
Germany, Federal Republic of	9.475	–	–	–	–	–	–	–	–	–	–
Germany*	–	11.789	10.111	8.542	9.231	9.124	9.414	8.925	8.911	8.243	8.074
Gibraltar (39)	0.000	0.002	0.002	0.002	0.002	0.002	0.002	0.002	0.002	0.002	0.001
Greece*	0.253	0.233	0.213	0.182	0.164	0.171	0.168	0.163	0.163	0.142	0.174
Hungary*(40)	0.426	0.276	0.247	0.435	0.598	0.620	0.680	0.670	0.660	0.625	0.615
Iceland	0.045	0.046	0.035	0.029	0.029	0.028	0.034	0.033	0.032	0.030	0.029
Ireland*	0.413	0.683	0.864	1.198	1.043	0.895	0.866	0.776	0.922	0.763	0.695
Italy	3.837	4.901	4.515	3.723	3.548	3.432	3.562	3.350	3.237	2.929	2.869
Latvia	–	–	0.025	0.029	0.049	0.051	0.059	0.063	0.061	0.062	0.072
Lithuania*(32)	–	–	0.052	0.055	0.112	0.116	0.122	0.146	0.131	0.136	0.154
Luxembourg*	0.148	0.181	0.150	0.130	0.179	0.189	0.163	0.159	0.170	0.129	0.119
Malta	0.024	0.032	0.037	0.038	0.023	0.023	0.024	0.021	0.023	0.023	0.024
Netherlands*	4.173	3.788	3.924	3.609	3.864	3.817	3.924	3.937	3.961	3.760	3.658
Norway	0.911	0.979	0.811	0.932	0.987	1.006	0.973	1.064	0.933	0.856	0.874
Poland*	0.697	0.392	0.442	0.491	0.850	0.912	0.999	1.052	1.086	1.046	1.028
Portugal*	0.228	0.472	0.440	0.377	0.363	0.368	0.374	0.353	0.352	0.319	0.323
Romania	0.551	0.166	0.153	0.161	0.264	0.267	0.288	0.306	0.323	0.324	0.344
Slovakia*	–	–	0.166	0.184	0.303	0.345	0.417	0.439	0.446	0.423	0.435
Slovenia*	–	–	0.161	0.136	0.183	0.191	0.214	0.211	0.208	0.191	0.191
Spain	1.018	1.596	1.890	1.784	1.832	1.760	1.805	1.737	1.809	1.666	1.680
Sweden*	1.518	1.654	1.554	1.349	1.245	1.217	1.203	1.131	1.041	1.038	1.027
Switzerland*	1.456	1.834	1.577	1.249	1.245	1.218	1.228	1.243	1.378	1.282	1.287
United Kingdom	5.411	5.321	4.596	4.418	3.656	3.694	3.148	2.914	2.824	2.724	2.759
Developed economies: Oceania	**1.344**	**1.413**	**1.289**	**1.206**	**1.215**	**1.204**	**1.207**	**1.350**	**1.428**	**1.603**	**1.698**
Australia	1.078	1.143	1.026	0.991	1.007	1.016	1.007	1.159	1.229	1.392	1.492
New Zealand	0.266	0.270	0.264	0.215	0.209	0.188	0.201	0.192	0.199	0.212	0.206

For sources and notes, see next page.

1980	1990	1995	2000	2005	2006	2007	2008	2009	2010	2011	Régions, pays ou territoires
					Imports (c.i.f.) - Importations (c.a.f.) Percentage - En pourcentage						
–	–	0.026	0.027	0.027	0.021	0.025	0.034	(e)0.054	(e)0.036	(e)0.040	Turkménistan (32)
–	–	0.296	0.210	0.335	0.364	0.425	0.519	0.358	0.395	0.449	Ukraine (32)
3.297	3.363										URSS
–	–	0.053	0.041	0.034	0.035	0.044	0.056	0.071	0.054	0.054	Ouzbékistan (32)
15.409	**17.874**	**17.945**	**22.605**	**19.149**	**18.411**	**16.897**	**15.703**	**15.251**	**15.320**	**14.800**	**Économies développées : Amérique**
0.016	0.017	0.011	0.011	0.009	0.009	0.008	0.007	0.008	0.006	0.005	Bermudes (5)
3.010	3.435	3.208	3.676	3.070	2.891	2.728	2.531	2.597	2.542	2.461	Canada
0.016	0.012	0.008	0.005	0.005	0.006	0.005	0.006	0.006	0.006	0.005	Groenland
0.000	0.002	0.001	(e)0.002	(e)0.000	(e)0.001	(e)0.000	(e)0.000	(e)0.001	(e)0.000	(e)0.000	Saint-Pierre-et-Miquelon
12.366	14.408	14.717	18.912	16.064	15.505	14.155	13.159	12.639	12.765	12.329	États-Unis (35)
7.270	**7.028**	**6.978**	**6.265**	**5.204**	**5.092**	**4.756**	**5.036**	**4.722**	**4.885**	**5.060**	**Économies développées : Asie**
0.471	0.468	0.565	0.566	0.436	0.407	0.414	0.410	0.388	0.397	0.413	Israël*
6.799	6.560	6.413	5.699	4.768	4.685	4.342	4.626	4.334	4.489	4.647	Japon
48.047	**47.550**	**42.798**	**39.498**	**40.009**	**40.028**	**40.518**	**39.280**	**38.596**	**36.029**	**35.293**	**Économies développées : Europe**
..	..	0.020	0.015	0.017	0.014	0.013	0.012	0.012	0.010	0.009	Andorre*
1.176	1.368	1.265	1.084	1.178	1.108	1.141	1.113	1.122	1.030	1.040	Autriche*
–	–	3.149	2.659	2.950	2.840	2.880	2.817	2.771	2.547	2.528	Belgique*
0.464	0.131	0.108	0.098	0.168	0.188	0.210	0.223	0.185	0.165	0.177	Bulgarie*
0.058	0.072	0.071	0.058	0.058	0.056	0.060	0.064	0.061	0.055	0.047	Chypre*
0.615	0.365										Tchécoslovaquie (36)
–	–	0.504	0.508	0.708	0.753	0.827	0.858	0.824	0.820	0.824	République tchèque*(37)
0.931	0.927	0.877	0.682	0.699	0.691	0.686	0.661	0.652	0.550	0.532	Danemark*(38)
–	–	0.049	0.076	0.095	0.109	0.110	0.097	0.080	0.079	0.096	Estonie*(32)
0.011	0.009	0.006	0.008	0.007	0.006	0.007	0.006	0.006	0.005	0.005	Îles Féroé
0.752	0.753	0.563	0.516	0.544	0.560	0.572	0.554	0.477	0.446	0.458	Finlande*
6.619	6.710	5.663	5.077	4.666	4.377	4.414	4.330	4.398	3.948	3.879	France*
0.918	–	–	–	–	–	–	–	–	–	–	Allemagne, Rép. dém. d'
9.047											Allemagne, Rép. fédérale d'
–	9.647	8.857	7.448	7.192	7.323	7.382	7.159	7.264	6.831	6.813	Allemagne*
0.005	0.010	0.008	0.007	0.005	0.005	0.006	0.005	0.006	0.005	0.005	Gibraltar (39)
0.508	0.551	0.495	0.502	0.504	0.514	0.549	0.559	0.545	0.413	0.331	Grèce*
0.445	0.242	0.294	0.480	0.616	0.632	0.669	0.658	0.610	0.571	0.557	Hongrie*(40)
0.048	0.047	0.034	0.039	0.042	0.048	0.047	0.037	0.028	0.025	0.026	Islande
0.537	0.576	0.617	0.765	0.635	0.591	0.586	0.507	0.492	0.390	0.361	Irlande*
4.848	5.071	3.933	3.577	3.561	3.574	3.580	3.394	3.255	3.154	3.029	Italie
–	–	0.035	0.048	0.080	0.093	0.107	0.098	0.077	0.076	0.089	Lettonie
–	–	0.070	0.078	0.144	0.156	0.171	0.188	0.144	0.152	0.173	Lituanie*(32)
0.174	0.212	0.186	0.169	0.203	0.215	0.196	0.194	0.199	0.163	0.156	Luxembourg*
0.045	0.055	0.056	0.051	0.034	0.035	0.034	0.032	0.035	0.033	0.034	Malte
4.255	3.525	3.537	3.270	3.367	3.367	3.447	3.509	3.475	3.344	3.255	Pays-Bas*
0.814	0.759	0.629	0.516	0.514	0.520	0.563	0.548	0.543	0.501	0.494	Norvège
0.803	0.234	0.555	0.735	0.941	1.026	1.159	1.261	1.172	1.153	1.128	Pologne*
0.448	0.704	0.623	0.599	0.566	0.571	0.575	0.570	0.562	0.490	0.437	Portugal*
0.666	0.274	0.196	0.196	0.375	0.413	0.492	0.508	0.426	0.402	0.415	Roumanie
–	–	0.176	0.201	0.321	0.363	0.424	0.446	0.436	0.421	0.420	Slovaquie*
–	–	0.181	0.152	0.188	0.195	0.221	0.224	0.208	0.195	0.193	Slovénie*
1.640	2.440	2.168	2.339	2.673	2.655	2.724	2.542	2.299	2.118	2.031	Espagne
1.609	1.512	1.242	1.092	1.034	1.030	1.072	1.018	0.940	0.965	0.956	Suède*
1.749	1.942	1.530	1.239	1.172	1.143	1.129	1.113	1.223	1.143	1.133	Suisse*
5.560	6.254	5.103	5.214	4.754	4.857	4.466	3.974	4.070	3.828	3.663	Royaume-Uni
1.341	**1.435**	**1.437**	**1.288**	**1.409**	**1.341**	**1.379**	**1.421**	**1.502**	**1.513**	**1.529**	**Économies développées : Océanie**
1.078	1.170	1.170	1.074	1.160	1.126	1.158	1.215	1.303	1.307	1.326	Australie
0.263	0.265	0.266	0.214	0.249	0.216	0.221	0.206	0.199	0.206	0.203	Nouvelle-Zélande

Pour les sources et les notes, se reporter à la page suivante.

1.1.1 Exports and imports of countries and geographical regions

Sources:
UNCTAD secretariat calculations, based on:
- UN DESA Statistics Division, *Yearbook of International Trade Statistics*
- UN DESA Statistics Division, *Monthly Bulletin of Statistics*
- UN DESA Statistics Division, *UN COMTRADE*
- IMF, *International Financial Statistics*
- IMF, *Direction of Trade Statistics*
- IMF, *Balance of Payments Statistics*
- WTO, *Statistics database*
- Eurostat, *Comext*
- World Bank, *World Development Indicators*
- OECD, *OECD.Stat Extracts*
- OPEC, *Annual Statistical Bulletin*
- Economist Intelligence Unit, *Country Data*
- Other international and national sources

Notes:
(*)	Special Trade System.
(1)	Excluding exports of gold.
(2)	From 1996 onward, imports f.o.b.
(3)	From 2011 onwards, commercial mining is included.
(4)	Prior to 2008, special trade.
(5)	Imports f.o.b.
(6)	Trade with other member countries of CEMAC is excluded. Imports f.o.b.
(7)	Trade with other member countries of CEMAC is excluded.
(8)	Prior to 1995, data refer to fiscal year ending June.
(9)	Prior to 1974, special trade.
(10)	Excluding re-exports (oil for bunkering).
(11)	Prior to 2009, re-exports is excluded
(12)	Prior to 2005, special trade.
(13)	Prior to 1986, included in Netherlands Antilles. Including exports and imports of crude oil and oil products. Prior to 2000, free zone trade is excluded. Imports f.o.b.
(14)	From 1990 onwards, trade statistics exclude certain oil and chemical products. Imports f.o.b.
(15)	Prior to 1993, excluding free trade processing zones. Imports f.o.b.
(16)	Prior to 1986, including Aruba.
(17)	Prior to 1992, excluding free trade processing zones.
(18)	Prior to 2002, special trade.
(19)	From 1990 onward, including goods for processing. Imports f.o.b.
(20)	Excluding free trade processing zones.
(21)	Prior to 2005, excluding customs free zones.
(22)	Excluding imports of goods financed through foreign aid.
(23)	Excluding military goods, fissionable materials, bunkers, ships and aircraft.
(24)	Inter-trade between the States of Malaysia included. From 1965 onwards, excluding military imports and offshore installations of petroleum industry.
(25)	Including trans-shipments to and from peninsular Malaysia.
(26)	Excluding exports of oil and gas.
(27)	Prior to 2001, special trade.
(28)	Excluding defense imports.
(29)	Data refer to fiscal year ending September.
(30)	Excluding military goods, precious metals and goods procured in foreign ports.
(31)	Prior to 1998, data refer to the Federation of Bosnia and Herzegovina only. The other entity of Bosnia and Herzegovina, Republika Srpska, is not included.
(32)	Prior to 1994, covers only trade with countries outside the CIS.
(33)	Prior to 1994, covers only trade with countries outside the CIS. As of 2011 adjusted to include bilateral trade with Russia.
(34)	Prior to 1994, excluding trade with independent states resulting from the former USSR.
(35)	Prior to 1975, excluding non-monetary gold.
(36)	From 1985 onwards, data are not comparable to those shown for prior periods due to revisions of the koruna-to-US dollar exchange rate.
(37)	From 1995 onward, including goods for processing.
(38)	Prior to 1988, excluding ships.
(39)	Excluding petroleum products.
(40)	Prior to 1996, excluding customs free zones.

Sources :
Calculs du secrétariat de la CNUCED, basés sur :
- ONU DAES Division de statistique, *Annuaire statistique du commerce international*
- ONU DAES Division de statistique, *Bulletin mensuel de statistique*
- ONU DAES Division de statistique, *ONU COMTRADE*
- FMI, *Statistiques financières internationales*
- FMI, *Direction of Trade Statistics*
- FMI, *Statistiques de la balance des paiements*
- OMC, *Base de données statistiques*
- Eurostat, *Comext*
- Banque mondiale, *Indicateurs du développement dans le monde*
- OCDE, *OECD.Stat Extracts*
- OPEP, *Bulletin statistique annuel*
- Economist Intelligence Unit, *Country Data*
- Autres sources internationales et nationales

Notes :
(*)   Système du commerce spécial.
(1)   Non-compris les exportations d'or.
(2)   À partir de 1996, importations f.a.b.
(3)   À partir de 2011, l'exploitation minière commerciale est incluse.
(4)   Avant 2008, commerce spécial.
(5)   Importations f.a.b.
(6)   Non-compris le commerce avec les autres pays membres de la CEMAC. Importations f.a.b.
(7)   Non-compris le commerce avec les autres pays membres de la CEMAC.
(8)   Avant 1995, les données se rapportent à l'exercice budgétaire finissant en juin.
(9)   Avant 1974, commerce spécial.
(10)   Non-compris les réexportations (huile pour mise en soute).
(11)   Avant 2009, non-compris les réexportations.
(12)   Avant 2005, commerce spécial.
(13)   Avant 1986, compris dans Antilles néerlandaises. Les données comprennent les exportations et importations de pétrole brut et produits dérivés. Avant 2000, non-compris les zones franches douanières. Importations f.a.b.
(14)   À partir de 1990, certains produits pétroliers et chimiques ne sont plus inclus dans les statistiques du commerce. Importations f.a.b.
(15)   Avant 1993, non-compris les zones franches douanières. Importations f.a.b.
(16)   Avant 1986, y compris Aruba.
(17)   Avant 1992, non-compris les zones franches douanières.
(18)   Avant 2002, commerce spécial.
(19)   À partir de 1990, y compris les biens destinés à subir des transformations. Importations f.a.b.
(20)   Non-compris les zones franches douanières.
(21)   Avant 2005, non-compris les zones franches douanières.
(22)   Non-compris les biens d'importation financés par l'aide à l'étranger.
(23)   Non-compris les biens à usage militaire, le matériel fissile, le combustible de soute et l'avitaillement des navires et aéronefs.
(24)   Y compris le commerce entre les États de la Malaisie. Non-compris les importations militaires et l'installation près des côtes de l'industrie pétrolière.
(25)   Y compris les transbordements vers et en provenance de la Malaisie péninsulaire.
(26)   Non-compris les exportations de pétrole et le gaz.
(27)   Avant 2001, commerce spécial.
(28)   Non-compris les importations de la défense.
(29)   Les données se rapportent à l'exercice budgétaire finissant en septembre.
(30)   Non-compris les biens à usage militaire, les métaux précieux et les biens fournis dans les ports étrangers.
(31)   Avant 1998, les données se réfèrent uniquement à la Fédération de la Bosnie-Herzégovine. L'autre entité de la Bosnie-Herzégovine, Republika Srpska, n'est pas incluse.
(32)   Avant 1994, concerne seulement le commerce avec les pays extérieurs à la CEI.
(33)   Avant 1994, concerne seulement le commerce avec les pays extérieurs à la CEI. À partir de 2011, y compris le commerce bilatéral avec la Russie.
(34)   Avant 1994, non-compris le commerce avec les républiques indépendantes de l'ancienne URSS.
(35)   Avant 1975, non-compris l'or industriel.
(36)   À partir de 1985, les chiffres ne sont pas comparables à ceux des années antérieures à cause des révisions du taux de change de la couronne par rapport au dollar des États-Unis.
(37)   À partir de 1995, y compris les biens destinés à subir des transformations.
(38)   Avant 1988, non-compris les navires.
(39)   Non-compris les produits pétroliers.
(40)   Avant 1996, non-compris les zones franches douanières.

1.1.2 Exports and imports of economic groupings
Value

Economic grouping	Exports (f.o.b.) - Exportations (f.a.b.) Millions of dollars							
	1980	1990	2000	2005	2008	2009	2010	2011
DEVELOPING ECONOMIES	599 757	840 994	2 052 172	3 815 605	6 293 307	4 988 924	6 407 121	7 785 920
Developing economies excluding China	581 658	778 903	1 802 969	3 053 652	4 864 647	3 787 134	4 828 851	5 886 740
Developing economies excluding LDCs	585 168	822 720	2 016 024	3 733 147	6 124 772	4 859 916	6 243 965	7 586 517
High-income developing economies	342 709	502 510	1 248 395	2 042 710	3 134 314	2 423 041	3 058 383	3 655 246
Middle-income developing economies	144 058	231 797	582 281	1 358 077	2 404 399	1 954 913	2 541 146	3 069 065
Low-income developing economies	112 990	106 687	221 493	414 811	754 586	610 963	807 584	1 061 602
Heavily indebted poor countries (IMF)	20 313	20 434	28 159	55 116	96 831	82 831	104 730	124 308
Landlocked developing countries	8 386	10 726	32 791	76 877	179 366	125 165	162 280	221 326
Small island developing States	12 546	6 996	11 409	19 608	33 284	19 872	23 865	28 637
Least developed countries	*14 588*	*18 274*	*36 148*	*82 458*	*168 535*	*129 007*	*163 156*	*199 403*
Africa and Haiti	12 301	14 817	21 166	58 548	130 506	93 773	117 608	144 145
Asia	2 129	3 334	14 852	23 650	37 644	34 917	45 154	54 662
Islands	158	123	129	259	385	317	394	596
Major petroleum and gas exporters	*272 968*	*174 688*	*313 764*	*687 294*	*1 291 726*	*868 966*	*1 096 594*	*1 442 963*
Africa	63 617	43 585	63 652	156 614	285 777	175 734	234 425	263 885
America	19 221	17 444	33 529	55 716	95 021	57 603	65 745	92 602
Asia	190 130	113 658	216 583	474 964	910 929	635 629	796 424	1 086 476
Major exporters of manufactured goods	*132 006*	*422 299*	*1 242 471*	*2 228 076*	*3 484 023*	*2 894 546*	*3 753 614*	*4 406 504*
America	18 031	40 711	166 368	213 891	291 827	229 683	298 138	349 569
Asia	113 975	381 588	1 076 103	2 014 185	3 192 196	2 664 863	3 455 476	4 056 935
Emerging economies	*130 912*	*333 426*	*899 106*	*1 394 301*	*2 059 203*	*1 662 154*	*2 162 077*	*2 546 430*
America	54 788	96 081	274 066	431 406	658 342	517 591	675 014	817 407
Asia	76 124	237 346	625 040	962 895	1 400 861	1 144 563	1 487 063	1 729 023
Newly industrialized Asian economies	*125 567*	*353 287*	*930 061*	*1 380 483*	*1 952 604*	*1 621 140*	*2 086 821*	*2 406 384*
First tier	76 425	266 976	659 709	1 001 184	1 377 920	1 153 647	1 483 035	1 703 094
Second tier	49 141	86 311	270 352	379 299	574 684	467 493	603 786	703 290
Developing economies: Africa	121 876	105 101	149 161	318 303	561 559	394 888	508 201	590 766
Northern Africa excluding Sudan	43 500	36 482	52 466	109 695	207 158	133 815	166 615	159 792
Sub-Saharan Africa	78 376	68 618	96 695	208 608	354 401	261 074	341 586	430 974
Sub-Saharan Africa excluding South Africa	52 337	44 865	64 745	152 347	268 283	194 532	255 886	328 116
Developing economies: America	111 352	143 940	366 518	583 963	911 550	698 511	886 947	1 103 231
Central America and Greater Caribbean Islands excluding Puerto Rico	31 107	52 666	191 959	253 656	345 201	277 135	352 947	417 213
Central America and Greater Caribbean Islands excluding Mexico and Puerto Rico	13 076	11 955	25 591	39 765	53 374	47 452	54 809	67 644
South America and Central America	88 984	132 269	347 515	557 274	870 870	674 634	859 683	1 064 798
South America excluding Brazil	45 473	55 152	109 463	195 522	341 350	254 972	318 448	408 750
Developing economies: Asia	364 287	589 244	1 531 395	2 906 673	4 810 726	3 888 444	5 002 915	6 081 187
Eastern and South-Eastern Asia excluding China	132 023	362 613	955 534	1 431 300	2 045 302	1 702 166	2 189 857	2 543 668
Southern Asia excluding India	17 542	29 035	50 345	97 887	159 837	120 402	152 971	192 698

Source:
Data in this table are based on trade figures in table 1.1.1.

Imports (c.i.f.) - Importations (c.a.f.) Millions de dollars								Groupements économiques
1980	1990	2000	2005	2008	2009	2010	2011	
496 880	**797 036**	**1 916 379**	**3 425 789**	**5 746 496**	**4 661 229**	**6 020 648**	**7 321 081**	**ÉCONOMIES EN DÉVELOPPEMENT**
476 939	743 691	1 691 355	2 765 583	4 614 876	3 657 059	4 624 448	5 578 231	Économies en développement sans la Chine
471 838	771 569	1 872 991	3 338 642	5 584 308	4 507 004	5 852 692	7 113 581	Économies en développement sans les PMA
243 111	452 919	1 153 707	1 741 122	2 749 077	2 142 642	2 698 712	3 176 891	Économies en développement à revenu élevé
158 925	236 585	561 254	1 241 930	2 138 423	1 800 849	2 413 303	2 969 496	Économies en développement à revenu intermédiaire
94 844	107 532	201 279	442 427	858 390	717 236	908 131	1 174 192	Économies en développement à revenu faible
25 048	24 024	36 902	75 124	134 788	116 937	135 750	164 146	Pays pauvres très endettés (FMI)
10 813	15 805	36 476	75 150	153 520	131 233	147 989	183 660	Pays en développement sans littoral
15 717	10 405	17 293	26 031	41 907	31 336	33 515	40 689	Petits États insulaires en développement
25 042	*25 468*	*43 388*	*87 147*	*162 188*	*154 225*	*167 955*	*207 500*	*Pays les moins avancés*
16 912	17 645	24 029	55 109	106 985	101 863	104 432	125 288	Afrique et Haïti
7 841	7 450	18 973	31 115	53 612	50 878	61 796	80 212	Asie
289	373	387	922	1 592	1 484	1 726	2 000	Îles
117 776	*98 156*	*147 491*	*322 456*	*644 342*	*561 772*	*611 679*	*717 760*	*Principaux exportateurs de pétrole et de gaz*
35 307	22 311	24 617	56 081	111 951	105 702	112 302	137 905	Afrique
11 827	7 335	16 865	24 008	50 971	39 646	38 613	46 441	Amérique
70 642	68 510	106 010	242 367	481 420	416 424	460 764	533 415	Asie
150 588	*427 262*	*1 199 370*	*2 067 984*	*3 184 601*	*2 599 224*	*3 483 225*	*4 182 896*	*Principaux exportateurs d'articles manufacturés*
22 144	43 548	182 702	231 821	325 157	246 104	316 556	368 399	Amérique
128 445	383 714	1 016 668	1 836 163	2 859 444	2 353 120	3 166 669	3 814 497	Asie
152 003	*328 599*	*871 261*	*1 259 803*	*1 996 122*	*1 483 754*	*1 991 313*	*2 379 762*	*Économies émergentes*
65 947	80 722	292 421	383 379	656 803	482 115	653 955	791 748	Amérique
86 056	247 877	578 839	876 424	1 339 319	1 001 639	1 337 358	1 588 014	Asie
127 629	*365 140*	*871 747*	*1 301 169*	*1 915 847*	*1 488 592*	*1 964 325*	*2 312 221*	*Économies nouvellement industrialisées d'Asie*
88 511	268 066	647 758	943 389	1 384 250	1 090 521	1 420 612	1 655 207	Première génération
39 118	97 075	223 989	357 780	531 597	398 071	543 713	657 014	Deuxième génération
96 856	**94 406**	**129 897**	**257 115**	**470 082**	**411 053**	**469 777**	**568 317**	**Économies en développement : Afrique**
29 977	36 756	46 919	80 197	164 354	146 363	162 031	179 374	Afrique septentrionale sans le Soudan
66 879	57 650	82 978	176 918	305 729	264 690	307 745	388 943	Afrique subsaharienne
46 973	39 044	52 767	112 725	209 025	189 044	211 496	266 525	Afrique subsaharienne sans l'Afrique du Sud
123 594	**126 632**	**391 887**	**540 302**	**933 419**	**695 168**	**900 678**	**1 100 165**	**Économies en développement : Amérique**
39 759	63 785	227 565	302 141	438 360	330 787	417 820	490 726	Amérique centrale et Grandes Antilles sans Porto Rico
17 615	20 237	44 863	70 320	113 203	84 683	101 264	122 327	Amérique centrale et Grandes Antilles sans le Mexique et Porto Rico
96 232	107 931	359 474	496 722	862 732	646 212	846 873	1 032 473	Amérique du Sud et Amérique centrale
41 528	33 635	91 925	140 821	284 141	210 855	272 685	346 018	Amérique du Sud sans le Brésil
272 880	**570 904**	**1 388 271**	**2 618 650**	**4 328 441**	**3 543 149**	**4 636 227**	**5 636 885**	**Économies en développement : Asie**
131 235	374 899	897 889	1 354 057	2 024 102	1 582 725	2 076 794	2 459 603	Asie orientale et Asie du Sud-Est sans la Chine
24 675	33 788	43 688	94 005	146 060	123 534	157 085	182 269	Asie méridionale sans l'Inde

Source :
Les données dans ce tableau ont été calculées d'après les chiffres du tableau 1.1.1.

1.1.2 Exports and imports of economic groupings
Share

Economic grouping	Exports (f.o.b.) - Exportations (f.a.b.) Percentage										
	1980	1990	1995	2000	2005	2006	2007	2008	2009	2010	2011
DEVELOPING ECONOMIES	**29.46**	**24.17**	**27.70**	**31.85**	**36.29**	**37.48**	**37.74**	**39.00**	**39.85**	**41.99**	**42.75**
Developing economies excluding China	28.58	22.39	24.83	27.98	29.05	29.49	29.06	30.15	30.25	31.65	32.32
Developing economies excluding LDCs	28.75	23.65	27.24	31.28	35.51	36.63	36.83	37.95	38.82	40.92	41.66
High-income developing economies	16.84	14.45	17.22	19.37	19.43	19.63	19.07	19.42	19.36	20.04	20.07
Middle-income developing economies	7.08	6.66	7.71	9.04	12.92	13.77	14.45	14.90	15.62	16.65	16.85
Low income developing economies	5.55	3.07	2.78	3.44	3.95	4.08	4.22	4.68	4.88	5.29	5.83
Heavily indebted poor countries (IMF)	1.00	0.59	0.47	0.44	0.52	0.55	0.55	0.60	0.66	0.69	0.68
Landlocked developing countries	0.41	0.31	0.52	0.51	0.73	0.85	0.94	1.11	1.00	1.06	1.22
Small island developing States	0.62	0.20	0.19	0.18	0.19	0.21	0.19	0.21	0.16	0.16	0.16
Least developed countries	*0.72*	*0.53*	*0.46*	*0.56*	*0.78*	*0.85*	*0.92*	*1.04*	*1.03*	*1.07*	*1.09*
Africa and Haiti	0.60	0.43	0.30	0.33	0.56	0.61	0.69	0.81	0.75	0.77	0.79
Asia	0.10	0.10	0.16	0.23	0.22	0.24	0.23	0.23	0.28	0.30	0.30
Islands	0.01	0.00	0.00	0.00	0.00	0.00	0.00	0.00	0.00	0.00	0.00
Major petroleum and gas exporters	*13.41*	*5.02*	*3.39*	*4.87*	*6.54*	*6.79*	*6.82*	*8.00*	*6.94*	*7.19*	*7.92*
Africa	3.13	1.25	0.67	0.99	1.49	1.51	1.55	1.77	1.40	1.54	1.45
America	0.94	0.50	0.36	0.52	0.53	0.54	0.50	0.59	0.46	0.43	0.51
Asia	9.34	3.27	2.35	3.36	4.52	4.74	4.77	5.64	5.08	5.22	5.97
Major exporters of manufactured goods	*6.49*	*12.14*	*17.14*	*19.28*	*21.19*	*21.83*	*21.99*	*21.59*	*23.12*	*24.60*	*24.20*
America	0.89	1.17	1.54	2.58	2.03	2.06	1.94	1.81	1.83	1.95	1.92
Asia	5.60	10.97	15.60	16.70	19.16	19.77	20.04	19.78	21.29	22.65	22.28
Emerging economies	*6.43*	*9.58*	*12.63*	*13.95*	*13.26*	*13.43*	*13.06*	*12.76*	*13.28*	*14.17*	*13.98*
America	2.69	2.76	3.26	4.25	4.10	4.26	4.17	4.08	4.13	4.42	4.49
Asia	3.74	6.82	9.37	9.70	9.16	9.17	8.90	8.68	9.14	9.75	9.49
Newly industrialized Asian economies	*6.17*	*10.16*	*13.94*	*14.43*	*13.13*	*13.02*	*12.56*	*12.10*	*12.95*	*13.68*	*13.21*
First tier	3.75	7.67	10.21	10.24	9.52	9.38	9.00	8.54	9.22	9.72	9.35
Second tier	2.41	2.48	3.73	4.20	3.61	3.65	3.56	3.56	3.73	3.96	3.86
Developing economies: Africa	**5.99**	**3.02**	**2.19**	**2.31**	**3.03**	**3.08**	**3.13**	**3.48**	**3.15**	**3.33**	**3.24**
Northern Africa excluding Sudan	2.14	1.05	0.67	0.81	1.04	1.09	1.10	1.28	1.07	1.09	0.88
Sub-Saharan Africa	3.85	1.97	1.52	1.50	1.98	1.99	2.03	2.20	2.09	2.24	2.37
Sub-Saharan Africa excluding South Africa	2.57	1.29	0.95	1.00	1.45	1.45	1.49	1.66	1.55	1.68	1.80
Developing economies: America	**5.47**	**4.14**	**4.44**	**5.69**	**5.55**	**5.75**	**5.59**	**5.65**	**5.58**	**5.81**	**6.06**
Central America and Greater Caribbean Islands excluding Puerto Rico	1.53	1.51	1.87	2.98	2.41	2.43	2.30	2.14	2.21	2.31	2.29
Central America and Greater Caribbean Islands excluding Mexico and Puerto Rico	0.64	0.34	0.33	0.40	0.38	0.37	0.36	0.33	0.38	0.36	0.37
South America and Central America	4.37	3.80	4.19	5.39	5.30	5.47	5.34	5.40	5.39	5.63	5.85
South America excluding Brazil	2.23	1.59	1.56	1.70	1.86	2.01	1.99	2.12	2.04	2.09	2.24
Developing economies: Asia	**17.90**	**16.94**	**20.99**	**23.76**	**27.65**	**28.59**	**28.96**	**29.81**	**31.06**	**32.79**	**33.39**
Eastern and South-Eastern Asia excluding China	6.49	10.42	14.20	14.83	13.61	13.53	13.08	12.67	13.60	14.35	13.97
Southern Asia excluding India	0.86	0.83	0.66	0.78	0.93	0.94	0.92	0.99	0.96	1.00	1.06

Source:
Data in this table are based on trade figures in table 1.1.1.

Imports (c.i.f.) - Importations (c.a.f.) En pourcentage											Groupements économiques
1980	1990	1995	2000	2005	2006	2007	2008	2009	2010	2011	
23.91	**22.21**	**28.64**	**28.78**	**31.72**	**32.32**	**33.17**	**34.85**	**36.70**	**39.03**	**39.83**	**ÉCONOMIES EN DÉVELOPPEMENT**
22.95	20.73	26.12	25.40	25.61	25.92	26.47	27.99	28.79	29.98	30.35	Économies en développement sans la Chine
22.70	21.50	27.98	28.13	30.91	31.50	32.30	33.87	35.48	37.94	38.70	Économies en développement sans les PMA
11.70	12.62	17.11	17.33	16.12	16.35	16.47	16.67	16.87	17.49	17.29	Économies en développement à revenu élevé
7.65	6.59	8.54	8.43	11.50	11.78	12.21	12.97	14.18	15.64	16.16	Économies en développement à revenu intermédiaire
4.56	3.00	2.99	3.02	4.10	4.18	4.49	5.21	5.65	5.89	6.39	Économies en développement à revenu faible
1.21	0.67	0.58	0.55	0.70	0.71	0.74	0.82	0.92	0.88	0.89	Pays pauvres très endettés (FMI)
0.52	0.44	0.64	0.55	0.70	0.74	0.83	0.93	1.03	0.96	1.00	Pays en développement sans littoral
0.76	0.29	0.26	0.26	0.24	0.24	0.24	0.25	0.25	0.22	0.22	Petits États insulaires en développement
1.21	*0.71*	*0.65*	*0.65*	*0.81*	*0.82*	*0.87*	*0.98*	*1.21*	*1.09*	*1.13*	*Pays les moins avancés*
0.81	0.49	0.39	0.36	0.51	0.52	0.56	0.65	0.80	0.68	0.68	Afrique et Haïti
0.38	0.21	0.25	0.28	0.29	0.29	0.30	0.33	0.40	0.40	0.44	Asie
0.01	0.01	0.01	0.01	0.01	0.01	0.01	0.01	0.01	0.01	0.01	Îles
5.67	*2.74*	*2.23*	*2.21*	*2.99*	*3.02*	*3.50*	*3.91*	*4.42*	*3.97*	*3.91*	*Principaux exportateurs de pétrole et de gaz*
1.70	0.62	0.47	0.37	0.52	0.51	0.60	0.68	0.83	0.73	0.75	Afrique
0.57	0.20	0.23	0.25	0.22	0.27	0.33	0.31	0.31	0.25	0.25	Amérique
3.40	1.91	1.53	1.59	2.24	2.24	2.57	2.92	3.28	2.99	2.90	Asie
7.25	*11.91*	*17.42*	*18.01*	*19.15*	*19.45*	*19.25*	*19.32*	*20.46*	*22.58*	*22.76*	*Principaux exportateurs d'articles manufacturés*
1.07	1.21	1.45	2.74	2.15	2.17	2.08	1.97	1.94	2.05	2.00	Amérique
6.18	10.69	15.97	15.27	17.00	17.28	17.18	17.34	18.53	20.53	20.75	Asie
7.31	*9.16*	*13.08*	*13.08*	*11.66*	*11.82*	*11.65*	*12.11*	*11.68*	*12.91*	*12.95*	*Économies émergentes*
3.17	2.25	3.31	4.39	3.55	3.65	3.75	3.98	3.80	4.24	4.31	Amérique
4.14	6.91	9.77	8.69	8.11	8.17	7.90	8.12	7.89	8.67	8.64	Asie
6.14	*10.18*	*14.77*	*13.09*	*12.05*	*11.97*	*11.53*	*11.62*	*11.72*	*12.73*	*12.58*	*Économies nouvellement industrialisées d'Asie*
4.26	7.47	10.62	9.73	8.73	8.78	8.46	8.40	8.59	9.21	9.01	Première génération
1.88	2.71	4.15	3.36	3.31	3.19	3.07	3.22	3.13	3.52	3.57	Deuxième génération
4.66	**2.63**	**2.37**	**1.95**	**2.38**	**2.42**	**2.59**	**2.85**	**3.24**	**3.05**	**3.09**	**Économies en développement : Afrique**
1.44	1.02	0.86	0.70	0.74	0.71	0.79	1.00	1.15	1.05	0.98	Afrique septentrionale sans le Soudan
3.22	1.61	1.52	1.25	1.64	1.72	1.80	1.85	2.08	1.99	2.12	Afrique subsaharienne
2.26	1.09	0.92	0.79	1.04	1.06	1.17	1.27	1.49	1.37	1.45	Afrique subsaharienne sans l'Afrique du Sud
5.95	**3.53**	**4.74**	**5.89**	**5.00**	**5.19**	**5.36**	**5.66**	**5.47**	**5.84**	**5.99**	**Économies en développement : Amérique**
1.91	1.78	1.98	3.42	2.80	2.83	2.74	2.66	2.60	2.71	2.67	Amérique centrale et Grandes Antilles sans Porto Rico
0.85	0.56	0.53	0.67	0.65	0.67	0.66	0.69	0.67	0.66	0.67	Amérique centrale et Grandes Antilles sans le Mexique et Porto Rico
4.63	3.01	4.36	5.40	4.60	4.78	4.96	5.23	5.09	5.49	5.62	Amérique du Sud et Amérique centrale
2.00	0.94	1.57	1.38	1.30	1.41	1.56	1.72	1.66	1.77	1.88	Amérique du Sud sans le Brésil
13.13	**15.91**	**21.41**	**20.85**	**24.25**	**24.62**	**25.13**	**26.25**	**27.90**	**30.05**	**30.67**	**Économies en développement : Asie**
6.32	10.45	15.10	13.48	12.54	12.49	12.13	12.28	12.46	13.46	13.38	Asie orientale et Asie du Sud-Est sans la Chine
1.19	0.94	0.73	0.66	0.87	0.84	0.81	0.89	0.97	1.02	0.99	Asie méridionale sans l'Inde

Source :
Les données dans ce tableau ont été calculées d'après les chiffres du tableau 1.1.1.

Trade group	Exports (f.o.b) - Exportations (f.a.b.) Millions of dollars							
	1980	1990	2000	2005	2008	2009	2010	2011
AFRICA								
CEMAC	4 668	5 604	8 365	23 008	41 380	26 968	35 199	45 670
CEPGL	2 455	2 510	927	2 583	4 722	3 755	5 798	6 543
COMESA	34 219	25 781	29 556	63 990	127 986	94 123	119 593	95 248
EAC	2 287	1 699	3 031	6 173	11 046	10 696	12 706	13 438
ECCAS	9 042	12 002	17 215	49 708	110 026	71 559	91 602	117 915
ECOWAS	33 337	21 408	30 340	71 765	106 195	78 492	107 416	145 599
MRU	4 360	4 749	4 896	8 834	12 092	11 956	12 586	13 190
SADC	36 849	38 597	51 950	101 768	181 874	135 045	172 801	213 226
UMA	40 648	34 344	48 146	99 668	182 723	112 110	142 262	132 033
WAEMU	4 884	5 202	6 661	12 657	18 473	18 456	19 478	22 294
AMERICA								
ANCOM	11 246	13 592	26 227	51 405	95 671	78 449	98 980	133 302
CACM	4 877	4 519	15 488	21 750	29 624	26 008	29 892	35 508
CARICOM	11 681	4 936	8 161	14 869	26 226	14 901	17 638	21 139
FTAA	393 904	658 287	1 418 738	1 842 944	2 654 070	2 063 201	2 544 291	3 022 577
LAIA	88 302	131 447	331 634	528 537	832 346	638 434	820 381	1 017 008
MERCOSUR	29 522	46 418	84 624	163 940	279 414	217 644	281 656	353 824
NAFTA	311 331	561 932	1 224 903	1 480 479	2 045 099	1 600 436	1 961 744	2 281 701
OAS	399 481	663 197	1 420 414	1 845 262	2 658 028	2 066 293	2 549 256	3 028 877
OECS	164	349	314	307	419	402	421	378
ASIA								
APTA	46 045	148 738	476 000	1 162 188	2 069 806	1 751 488	2 300 342	2 795 402
ASEAN	73 957	144 148	429 846	654 878	998 948	813 484	1 052 348	1 240 715
ECO	18 527	38 088	82 461	201 190	393 796	281 610	344 703	443 395
GCC	155 060	87 800	175 690	396 984	750 850	526 267	653 523	889 947
SAARC	13 799	27 700	64 380	132 981	240 700	206 493	277 413	364 798
EUROPE								
EFTA	49 095	99 433	142 417	237 771	377 734	293 309	330 883	399 027
EU	844 175	1 549 094	2 447 635	4 064 021	5 911 686	4 578 977	5 161 841	6 065 531
Euro area	627 049	1 223 684	1 915 580	3 176 885	4 613 115	3 589 804	4 002 459	4 669 795
OCEANIA								
MSG	1 518	1 631	2 704	4 121	6 904	5 253	6 862	8 288
INTERREGIONAL								
ACP	98 208	80 916	115 066	236 210	398 484	289 926	377 991	475 428
APEC	627 358	1 331 401	3 112 906	4 689 933	7 075 152	5 633 765	7 235 029	8 484 755
BSEC	29 644	31 892	177 376	419 458	815 701	556 010	699 483	901 573
CIS	–	–	144 876	342 802	701 183	449 165	586 807	787 337

For sources and notes, see end of table 1.1.3.

24

Imports (c.i.f.) - Importations (c.a.f.) Millions de dollars								Groupements commerciaux
1980	1990	2000	2005	2008	2009	2010	2011	
								AFRIQUE
3 018	3 653	3 852	7 980	17 110	17 316	19 761	23 880	CEMAC
1 949	2 256	1 058	3 429	5 876	5 611	6 440	7 788	CEPGL
23 570	27 984	34 784	62 742	120 177	112 203	127 459	135 722	COMESA
4 106	4 392	6 528	12 229	24 258	22 461	26 741	33 074	CAE
6 314	7 509	7 980	19 812	44 083	45 690	42 980	53 535	CEEAC
25 607	14 013	20 626	44 143	82 103	67 097	82 683	111 014	CEDEAO
4 222	3 179	3 912	7 354	10 632	9 104	10 743	11 586	UFM
31 347	34 080	47 958	99 959	162 299	138 994	160 588	205 252	SADC
25 402	27 761	33 410	61 806	117 545	102 839	111 037	122 944	UMA
6 371	5 777	7 082	15 296	25 561	22 146	23 710	25 607	UEMOA
								AMÉRIQUE
10 157	10 772	24 504	46 334	93 206	74 292	96 688	124 184	ANCOM
6 001	6 476	22 301	36 259	54 483	41 035	48 659	58 464	MCAC
14 268	7 222	14 036	20 195	31 744	23 768	25 148	30 052	CARICOM
430 925	757 316	1 885 352	2 590 879	3 493 776	2 614 183	3 244 986	3 793 581	ZLEA
94 231	105 635	336 945	456 456	804 377	597 648	789 383	962 053	ALADI
37 801	29 295	89 523	113 474	257 766	186 624	266 639	333 821	MERCOSUR
341 673	683 779	1 686 780	2 298 434	2 912 011	2 181 311	2 677 845	3 086 517	ALENA
437 430	764 061	1 890 196	2 598 963	3 509 149	2 623 802	3 256 485	3 807 881	OEA
423	1 043	1 623	2 115	3 081	2 405	2 538	2 521	OECO
								ASIE
61 826	153 257	452 727	1 087 891	1 926 877	1 617 514	2 214 876	2 789 531	ACAP
65 641	162 346	380 121	602 788	946 802	727 846	954 354	1 150 731	ANASE
27 528	48 945	92 818	215 318	372 373	283 035	351 300	431 611	ECO
51 991	47 366	85 287	188 187	405 377	338 411	366 910	426 620	CCG
26 113	39 038	80 864	196 806	409 444	329 953	441 414	577 731	SAARC
								EUROPE
54 281	98 602	119 468	186 611	279 974	227 952	257 526	303 974	AELE
943 874	1 606 837	2 508 665	4 131 559	6 192 315	4 671 241	5 297 271	6 179 110	UE
713 349	1 250 184	1 900 613	3 103 428	4 635 034	3 515 574	3 958 028	4 614 551	Zone euro
								OCÉANIE
1 900	2 059	2 186	3 669	6 461	5 199	6 461	7 621	MSG
								INTERRÉGIONAUX
91 643	77 018	113 895	219 348	376 016	316 295	366 929	459 312	ACP
669 769	1 404 563	3 341 991	5 150 069	7 456 260	5 765 149	7 417 475	8 855 252	CEAP
41 951	57 057	175 394	417 306	872 436	582 197	711 979	899 043	CEMN
–	–	85 537	225 557	523 072	347 976	434 097	564 860	CEI

Pour les sources et les notes, se reporter à la fin du tableau 1.1.3.

1.1.3 Exports and imports of trade groups
Share

Trade group	Exports (f.o.b) - Exportations (f.a.b.) Percentage										
	1980	1990	1995	2000	2005	2006	2007	2008	2009	2010	2011
AFRICA											
CEMAC	0.23	0.16	0.12	0.13	0.22	0.22	0.21	0.26	0.22	0.23	0.25
CEPGL	0.12	0.07	0.03	0.01	0.02	0.02	0.02	0.03	0.03	0.04	0.04
COMESA	1.68	0.74	0.46	0.46	0.61	0.65	0.69	0.79	0.75	0.78	0.52
EAC	0.11	0.05	0.06	0.05	0.06	0.06	0.06	0.07	0.09	0.08	0.07
ECCAS	0.44	0.35	0.22	0.27	0.47	0.51	0.55	0.68	0.57	0.60	0.65
ECOWAS	1.64	0.62	0.43	0.47	0.68	0.63	0.61	0.66	0.63	0.70	0.80
MRU	0.21	0.14	0.10	0.08	0.08	0.08	0.07	0.07	0.10	0.08	0.07
SADC	1.81	1.11	0.88	0.81	0.97	1.02	1.07	1.13	1.08	1.13	1.17
UMA	2.00	0.99	0.61	0.75	0.95	0.99	0.99	1.13	0.90	0.93	0.73
WAEMU	0.24	0.15	0.13	0.10	0.12	0.12	0.11	0.11	0.15	0.13	0.12
AMERICA											
ANCOM	0.55	0.39	0.41	0.41	0.49	0.53	0.54	0.59	0.63	0.65	0.73
CACM	0.24	0.13	0.18	0.24	0.21	0.20	0.19	0.18	0.21	0.20	0.19
CARICOM	0.57	0.14	0.11	0.13	0.14	0.17	0.14	0.16	0.12	0.12	0.12
FTAA	19.35	18.92	19.36	22.02	17.53	17.44	16.78	16.45	16.48	16.68	16.60
LAIA	4.34	3.78	4.01	5.15	5.03	5.21	5.09	5.16	5.10	5.38	5.58
MERCOSUR	1.45	1.33	1.36	1.31	1.56	1.57	1.60	1.73	1.74	1.85	1.94
NAFTA	15.29	16.15	16.54	19.01	14.08	13.83	13.21	12.67	12.78	12.86	12.53
OAS	19.63	19.06	19.39	22.04	17.55	17.47	16.81	16.47	16.51	16.71	16.63
OECS	0.01	0.01	0.01	0.00	0.00	0.00	0.00	0.00	0.00	0.00	0.00
ASIA											
APTA	2.26	4.28	6.03	7.39	11.05	11.84	12.56	12.83	13.99	15.08	15.35
ASEAN	3.63	4.14	6.21	6.67	6.23	6.35	6.17	6.19	6.50	6.90	6.81
ECO	0.91	1.09	1.17	1.28	1.91	2.03	2.16	2.44	2.25	2.26	2.43
GCC	7.62	2.52	2.04	2.73	3.78	3.96	3.95	4.65	4.20	4.28	4.89
SAARC	0.68	0.80	0.90	1.00	1.26	1.31	1.36	1.49	1.65	1.82	2.00
EUROPE											
EFTA	2.41	2.86	2.42	2.21	2.26	2.25	2.23	2.34	2.34	2.17	2.19
EU	41.47	44.53	42.28	37.98	38.66	37.81	38.13	36.63	36.58	33.83	33.31
Euro area	30.80	35.18	33.70	29.73	30.22	29.27	29.89	28.59	28.68	26.23	25.64
OCEANIA											
MSG	0.07	0.05	0.07	0.04	0.04	0.04	0.04	0.04	0.04	0.04	0.05
INTERREGIONAL											
ACP	4.82	2.33	1.80	1.79	2.25	2.28	2.30	2.47	2.32	2.48	2.61
APEC	30.82	38.27	45.43	48.31	44.61	44.98	44.41	43.84	45.00	47.42	46.59
BSEC	1.46	0.92	2.78	2.75	3.99	4.23	4.42	5.05	4.44	4.58	4.95
CIS	–	–	2.20	2.25	3.26	3.55	3.70	4.35	3.59	3.85	4.32

Sources:
UNCTAD secretariat calculations, based on:
- UN DESA Statistics Division, *Yearbook of International Trade Statistics*
- UN DESA Statistics Division, *Monthly Bulletin of Statistics*
- UN DESA Statistics Division, *UN COMTRADE*
- IMF, *International Financial Statistics*
- IMF, *Direction of Trade Statistics*
- IMF, *Balance of Payments Statistics*
- WTO, *Statistics database*
- Eurostat, *Comext*
- World Bank, *World Development Indicators*
- OECD, *OECD.Stat Extracts*
- OPEC, *Annual Statistical Bulletin*
- Economist Intelligence Unit, *Country Data*
- Other international and national sources

Imports (c.i.f.) - Importations (c.a.f.) En pourcentage											Groupements commerciaux
1980	1990	1995	2000	2005	2006	2007	2008	2009	2010	2011	
											AFRIQUE
0.15	0.10	0.07	0.06	0.07	0.08	0.10	0.10	0.14	0.13	0.13	CEMAC
0.09	0.06	0.03	0.02	0.03	0.03	0.03	0.04	0.04	0.04	0.04	CEPGL
1.13	0.78	0.63	0.52	0.58	0.56	0.59	0.73	0.88	0.83	0.74	COMESA
0.20	0.12	0.12	0.10	0.11	0.12	0.13	0.15	0.18	0.17	0.18	CAE
0.30	0.21	0.12	0.12	0.18	0.19	0.22	0.27	0.36	0.28	0.29	CEEAC
1.23	0.39	0.37	0.31	0.41	0.42	0.48	0.50	0.53	0.54	0.60	CEDEAO
0.20	0.09	0.08	0.06	0.07	0.06	0.06	0.06	0.07	0.07	0.06	UFM
1.51	0.95	0.91	0.72	0.93	0.97	0.98	0.98	1.09	1.04	1.12	SADC
1.22	0.77	0.64	0.50	0.57	0.55	0.61	0.71	0.81	0.72	0.67	UMA
0.31	0.16	0.14	0.11	0.14	0.13	0.14	0.16	0.17	0.15	0.14	UEMOA
											AMÉRIQUE
0.49	0.30	0.52	0.37	0.43	0.45	0.49	0.57	0.58	0.63	0.68	ANCOM
0.29	0.18	0.26	0.33	0.34	0.34	0.34	0.33	0.32	0.32	0.32	MCAC
0.69	0.20	0.19	0.21	0.19	0.19	0.18	0.19	0.19	0.16	0.16	CARICOM
20.74	21.11	22.54	28.31	23.99	23.44	22.10	21.19	20.58	21.04	20.64	ZLEA
4.53	2.94	4.08	5.06	4.23	4.41	4.59	4.88	4.71	5.12	5.23	ALADI
1.82	0.82	1.53	1.34	1.05	1.13	1.28	1.56	1.47	1.73	1.82	MERCOSUR
16.44	19.06	19.37	25.33	21.28	20.56	18.96	17.66	17.17	17.36	16.79	ALENA
21.05	21.29	22.60	28.39	24.06	23.52	22.18	21.28	20.66	21.11	20.72	OEA
0.02	0.03	0.02	0.02	0.02	0.02	0.02	0.02	0.02	0.02	0.01	OECO
											ASIE
2.98	4.27	6.00	6.80	10.07	10.57	11.02	11.69	12.73	14.36	15.18	ACAP
3.16	4.52	6.78	5.71	5.58	5.56	5.44	5.74	5.73	6.19	6.26	ANASE
1.32	1.36	1.34	1.39	1.99	2.04	2.13	2.26	2.23	2.28	2.35	ECO
2.50	1.32	1.30	1.28	1.74	1.81	2.19	2.46	2.66	2.38	2.32	CCG
1.26	1.09	1.15	1.21	1.82	1.95	2.09	2.48	2.60	2.86	3.14	SAARC
											EUROPE
2.61	2.75	2.19	1.79	1.73	1.71	1.74	1.70	1.79	1.67	1.65	AELE
45.42	44.78	40.57	37.67	38.25	38.29	38.75	37.56	36.78	34.34	33.62	UE
34.33	34.84	31.59	28.54	28.73	28.45	28.89	28.11	27.68	25.66	25.11	Zone euro
											OCÉANIE
0.09	0.06	0.05	0.03	0.03	0.04	0.04	0.04	0.04	0.04	0.04	MSG
											INTERRÉGIONAUX
4.41	2.15	1.91	1.71	2.03	2.12	2.20	2.28	2.49	2.38	2.50	ACP
32.23	39.14	46.50	50.19	47.68	47.25	45.59	45.23	45.39	48.08	48.18	CEAP
2.02	1.59	3.16	2.63	3.86	4.21	4.75	5.29	4.58	4.62	4.89	CEMN
–	–	1.94	1.28	2.09	2.37	2.77	3.17	2.74	2.81	3.07	CEI

Sources :
Calculs du secrétariat de la CNUCED, basés sur :
- ONU DAES Division de statistique, *Annuaire statistique du commerce international*
- ONU DAES Division de statistique, *Bulletin mensuel de statistique*
- ONU DAES Division de statistique, *ONU COMTRADE*
- FMI, *Statistiques financières internationales*
- FMI, *Direction of Trade Statistics*
- FMI, *Statistiques de la balance des paiements*
- OMC, *Base de données statistiques*
- Eurostat, *Comext*
- Banque mondiale, *Indicateurs du développement dans le monde*
- OCDE, *OECD.Stat Extracts*
- OPEP, *Bulletin statistique annuel*
- Economist Intelligence Unit, *Country Data*
- Autres sources internationales et nationales

Region, country or territory	Exports (f.o.b) - Exportations (f.a.b.) Percentage										
	80-00	90-00	00-10	05-08	05-09	05-11	2005	2008	2009	2010	2011
WORLD	7.1	6.7	10.9	15.4	6.5	7.4	14.4	15.1	-22.4	21.9	19.4
DEVELOPING ECONOMIES	7.7	9.1	14.4	18.0	9.0	10.4	22.9	19.0	-20.7	28.4	21.5
TRANSITION ECONOMIES	1.4	6.4	18.3	26.2	10.9	11.1	28.4	34.3	-35.4	29.9	33.5
DEVELOPED ECONOMIES	7.2	5.9	8.5	13.0	4.7	5.1	9.2	11.4	-22.6	16.7	16.6
Developing economies: Africa	1.9	3.3	16.4	20.5	8.8	8.8	37.2	27.9	-29.7	28.7	16.2
Eastern Africa	3.3	4.7	13.7	18.9	12.8	13.5	13.2	15.3	-7.0	23.8	21.7
Burundi*(1)	-2.1	-4.3	7.9	-0.3	1.3	13.0	19.2	-13.3	14.6	62.0	21.3
Comoros*	-3.1	-10.9	-2.9	-11.8	0.7	(e)14.0	-35.5	-47.8	107.3	37.8	(e)22.1
Djibouti (2)	4.2	7.1	11.3	18.6	16.8	(e)14.4	4.0	18.5	12.4	10.0	(e)11.6
Eritrea (3)	–	–	(e)-6.7	(e)0.4	(e)-1.7	(e)45.9	0.1	(e)-15.3	(e)-2.7	(e)10.1	(e)3 361.7
Ethiopia	–	–	18.7	20.3	16.7	19.4	36.5	25.4	1.0	44.0	12.2
Kenya	3.8	6.3	12.2	15.1	10.3	9.6	22.7	21.9	-10.2	15.4	11.7
Madagascar*	3.8	9.0	5.2	16.3	7.3	(e)7.0	-13.8	5.8	-19.7	2.7	(e)47.2
Malawi	3.4	0.9	12.2	21.1	21.9	16.8	5.1	1.2	35.1	-10.2	33.7
Mauritius	9.4	3.6	3.6	2.9	-1.7	1.6	7.3	6.5	-18.7	16.7	17.0
Mayotte	..	..	–	6.3	1.5	–	31.3	-0.9	-12.4	–	–
Mozambique	2.7	10.3	19.1	13.5	5.4	7.2	16.1	10.0	-19.1	4.5	60.7
Rwanda	-5.2	-3.8	18.3	28.0	15.8	20.0	27.1	51.4	-28.0	54.3	40.4
Seychelles	12.6	15.5	8.3	6.8	4.4	4.5	16.8	19.5	-8.1	1.2	19.4
Somalia	(e)3.8	(e)6.5	(e)7.7	(e)18.6	(e)15.2	(e)12.4	(e)35.7	(e)19.9	(e)1.7	(e)6.6	(e)15.0
Uganda	2.0	15.4	25.8	41.4	34.8	19.2	34.0	35.6	10.4	3.7	-22.5
United Republic of Tanzania	3.3	7.8	18.2	21.1	17.4	19.1	14.1	37.0	-1.9	35.8	16.9
Zambia (4)	0.3	-0.8	25.9	39.2	22.6	24.1	14.9	10.4	-15.4	67.0	25.2
Zimbabwe	3.0	3.4	(e)4.5	7.3	5.2	(e)8.6	-2.0	-8.3	3.1	(e)10.2	(e)40.0
Middle Africa	3.4	3.4	23.1	29.9	14.0	12.5	54.9	42.3	-35.0	27.9	28.7
Angola (5)	6.6	6.1	27.4	38.5	19.1	14.7	78.9	44.0	-36.1	23.9	29.8
Cameroon*(6)	3.7	-1.3	9.8	13.1	5.3	(e)5.6	15.5	19.3	-21.6	15.1	(e)18.6
Central African Republic*(6)	3.4	3.6	(e)-0.4	6.0	-1.3	(e)-0.2	-3.7	-15.7	-17.6	(e)12.3	(e)12.1
Chad*(5)	7.1	0.3	(e)42.5	9.7	-0.2	(e)2.4	43.0	14.9	-33.0	(e)26.4	(e)16.4
Congo*(6)	3.7	7.5	(e)16.6	17.5	8.4	(e)12.9	38.2	47.7	-27.1	(e)53.3	(e)16.0
Dem. Rep. of the Congo*	-3.2	-6.1	(e)20.9	21.5	13.2	(e)16.4	25.3	41.9	-20.5	(e)54.3	(e)11.2
Equatorial Guinea (5)	23.6	41.2	(e)27.5	27.9	11.7	(e)8.2	53.6	46.2	-39.0	(e)9.4	(e)35.5
Gabon*(7)	1.9	1.6	14.5	22.6	7.5	(e)13.0	35.9	50.7	-42.2	52.3	(e)49.3
Sao Tome and Principe	-6.1	-6.2	13.8	12.8	7.0	(e)10.7	25.9	58.0	-23.7	35.5	(e)18.2
Northern Africa	0.8	2.9	16.6	23.5	9.4	5.7	38.9	34.5	-35.1	25.3	-4.8
Algeria*	0.3	3.0	14.4	18.9	3.4	4.4	43.4	31.8	-43.0	26.2	28.7
Egypt	0.5	3.8	23.5	33.3	24.5	18.8	38.6	62.0	-12.1	14.6	15.5
Libya	-2.7	-2.3	20.1	24.9	8.2	-6.0	62.4	31.9	-40.2	32.1	-66.4
Morocco*	7.5	7.8	11.0	21.9	9.7	9.5	12.7	32.6	-30.9	26.4	21.1
Sudan (...2011) (8)	2.1	14.0	24.2	36.4	19.7	13.0	27.7	31.4	-29.2	38.1	-15.0
Tunisia (9)	7.1	6.0	12.4	23.3	12.1	8.3	8.4	27.4	-25.2	13.7	8.6
Southern Africa	3.1	3.3	11.8	14.3	5.6	7.8	15.9	11.1	-22.1	28.6	19.6
Botswana*	9.5	5.0	7.1	4.8	-4.0	1.9	26.0	-4.3	-30.2	36.5	24.0
Lesotho	11.5	12.4	13.8	11.1	4.8	(e)6.1	-8.1	16.1	-18.8	17.3	(e)18.6
Namibia	2.0	0.9	14.3	15.0	10.5	11.8	13.3	9.2	-2.7	29.3	8.8
South Africa	(b)2.7	3.1	12.2	15.3	6.2	8.2	16.6	12.7	-22.7	28.8	20.0
Swaziland	7.6	6.0	6.2	-0.4	-1.8	(e)1.1	-9.2	-8.4	-3.6	8.8	(e)13.5
Western Africa	1.2	3.5	17.0	14.0	5.3	10.3	55.2	23.4	-26.1	37.1	35.5
Benin*	14.1	3.3	(e)15.5	31.5	22.8	(e)19.2	1.7	22.5	-4.5	(e)13.4	(e)33.2
Burkina Faso	7.2	12.6	19.3	13.2	15.9	(e)23.8	-2.4	11.3	29.9	43.0	(e)39.7
Cape Verde (10)	6.8	11.0	16.4	19.0	20.2	25.8	16.0	66.4	10.1	26.4	63.4
Côte d'Ivoire*	2.6	5.4	11.4	9.4	8.5	6.3	11.2	18.8	2.1	0.1	4.9
Gambia (11)	-5.3	-12.6	12.8	18.5	55.2	49.8	-20.2	9.2	383.0	-47.0	170.8
Ghana	3.9	9.0	17.2	22.7	19.9	(e)25.5	14.4	22.0	10.8	36.3	(e)59.5
Guinea*	2.7	0.6	8.5	16.6	7.2	8.0	11.4	11.5	-21.8	40.1	-2.6
Guinea-Bissau	8.5	13.6	(e)9.0	15.6	12.3	(e)15.8	18.1	19.8	-5.2	(e)-1.0	(e)103.3
Liberia*	(e)0.4	(e)-8.8	(e)1.4	21.3	7.9	14.3	26.5	25.1	-33.6	55.4	48.4
Mali*	8.1	6.1	13.9	21.4	13.4	(e)11.7	12.7	34.8	-15.4	15.9	(e)19.7
Mauritania*	2.9	-2.0	23.7	37.9	20.1	20.7	42.2	29.2	-25.0	53.6	32.8
Niger*	-1.4	0.0	16.4	23.8	22.3	(e)18.1	11.9	37.5	9.3	4.3	(e)20.2
Nigeria	0.4	3.2	18.9	13.5	2.5	9.0	77.0	23.8	-34.7	47.8	39.1
Saint Helena	(e)15.2	(e)2.6	(e)11.9	(e)19.3	(e)14.3	(e)10.6	(e)-5.4	(e)40.0	(e)-10.8	(e)0.5	(e)19.7
Senegal (12)	3.6	4.0	9.3	11.3	8.8	8.5	4.4	33.5	-8.6	7.1	17.6
Sierra Leone*	-12.8	-29.5	33.3	10.3	7.3	11.7	14.3	-11.8	8.0	46.5	2.5
Togo*	3.8	6.7	(e)10.1	9.2	9.8	(e)9.3	9.6	21.8	5.9	(e)-1.1	(e)23.1

For sources and notes, see end of table.

Imports (c.i.f.) - Importations (c.a.f.) En pourcentage											Régions, pays ou territoires
80-00	90-00	00-10	05-08	05-09	05-11	2005	2008	2009	2010	2011	
7.0	6.7	10.6	15.2	6.3	7.1	13.9	15.5	-23.0	21.5	19.1	**MONDE**
8.1	8.6	14.1	18.8	10.3	11.6	18.0	21.4	-18.9	29.2	21.6	ÉCONOMIES EN DÉVELOPPEMENT
0.9	3.3	19.7	31.4	14.9	12.0	22.0	30.5	-32.8	21.2	28.8	ÉCONOMIES EN TRANSITION
6.9	6.2	8.6	12.6	3.8	4.3	11.7	11.7	-24.7	16.8	16.9	ÉCONOMIES DÉVELOPPÉES
2.2	4.4	16.2	22.4	14.9	12.9	21.6	27.1	-12.6	14.3	21.0	**Économies en développement : Afrique**
4.0	4.4	15.9	22.6	15.7	13.7	22.1	31.1	-10.7	13.4	23.1	*Afrique orientale*
-1.3	-6.9	15.8	9.7	7.8	14.0	51.6	26.1	0.0	26.6	47.7	Burundi*(1)
3.0	-1.7	19.2	21.9	21.6	19.0	15.3	29.9	17.2	7.8	22.0	Comores*
-0.8	-1.3	10.5	28.7	16.3	(e)4.8	6.1	21.3	-21.5	-19.3	(e)14.2	Djibouti (2)
_	_	(e)3.6	(e)6.3	(e)5.5	(e)9.7	(e)3.1	(e)17.9	(e)-2.3	(e)17.5	(e)30.6	Érythrée (3)
_	_	23.0	26.7	20.2	13.9	42.5	49.4	-8.1	7.9	3.4	Éthiopie
3.6	6.0	17.1	21.8	15.4	14.4	35.1	23.2	-7.8	18.5	22.5	Kenya
3.3	6.3	15.3	31.9	22.1	(e)8.9	1.6	43.5	-15.3	-21.9	(e)14.0	Madagascar*
4.2	-0.6	16.6	22.7	18.6	14.4	24.8	59.7	-8.3	7.5	11.7	Malawi
9.6	4.1	9.0	13.1	6.0	6.7	13.9	19.5	-19.8	17.5	17.6	Maurice
..	..	-	26.2	15.9	-	9.9	21.4	-17.2	-	-	Mayotte
2.1	1.2	14.6	17.2	13.1	13.4	18.4	31.4	-6.1	-5.3	76.9	Mozambique
-1.1	-1.6	23.4	34.4	31.4	(e)25.0	66.1	59.2	11.5	9.4	(e)20.9	Rwanda
8.8	9.6	10.0	15.7	6.8	2.3	35.9	22.6	-24.6	-7.6	19.5	Seychelles
(e)-2.7	(e)26.6	(e)11.6	(e)20.8	(e)12.2	(e)8.6	(e)2.6	(e)27.5	(e)-17.7	(e)2.6	(e)23.0	Somalie
8.5	21.0	15.7	30.8	22.4	14.6	19.4	29.6	-6.2	10.6	-2.2	Ouganda
3.0	0.1	20.1	28.8	19.9	20.0	20.6	32.7	-11.1	27.3	39.6	République-Unie de Tanzanie
0.2	-1.0	20.8	26.0	13.7	15.9	18.9	26.3	-25.1	40.3	35.1	Zambie (4)
4.7	2.3	(e)7.5	8.2	6.9	(e)11.2	6.6	15.7	-1.7	(e)27.6	(e)18.9	Zimbabwe
1.5	3.1	21.0	31.4	26.1	17.6	28.2	38.1	3.5	-6.7	24.4	*Afrique centrale*
4.0	7.8	24.3	37.8	33.2	18.1	43.2	53.6	8.0	-26.4	30.4	Angola (5)
-0.2	2.0	14.1	26.2	16.3	(e)13.8	13.7	28.6	-17.7	15.6	(e)26.6	Cameroun*(6)
2.0	0.2	(e)12.5	20.5	13.8	(e)12.4	13.9	20.7	-9.8	(e)12.6	(e)24.6	République centrafricaine*(6)
9.0	-1.3	(e)16.0	28.7	20.9	(e)12.9	-0.5	15.8	-0.9	(e)4.9	(e)0.0	Tchad*(5)
1.0	2.9	(e)24.0	30.9	21.6	(e)21.9	34.5	20.6	-5.1	(e)39.9	(e)25.9	Congo*(6)
-3.7	-5.7	(e)21.9	17.0	12.1	(e)11.5	31.1	26.5	-9.3	(e)15.4	(e)17.9	Rép. dém. du Congo*
16.5	29.7	(e)29.5	41.4	40.2	(e)29.6	20.0	35.7	39.0	(e)9.1	(e)5.6	Guinée équatoriale (5)
1.3	2.2	11.9	21.2	15.8	(e)14.3	9.2	20.1	-3.5	-0.4	(e)52.5	Gabon*(7)
4.3	-0.7	17.3	29.7	21.4	15.8	20.3	44.2	-9.4	8.6	17.3	Sao Tomé-et-Principe
1.9	4.1	16.0	26.1	19.4	14.4	20.5	43.2	-10.2	10.3	9.6	*Afrique septentrionale*
-0.8	0.8	17.9	25.1	21.2	16.1	11.2	42.9	-0.5	4.4	15.2	Algérie*
2.4	7.7	17.9	34.6	28.3	22.4	54.4	80.2	-7.8	17.7	11.3	Égypte
-2.3	-3.0	11.1	14.3	15.2	(e)3.4	-4.4	35.0	10.1	4.7	(e)-52.4	Libye
6.3	5.5	15.3	27.4	16.0	11.6	16.7	32.4	-22.4	7.6	25.2	Maroc*
(e)1.0	9.8	22.9	11.2	9.1	5.4	65.8	6.6	3.6	3.7	-8.1	Soudan (…2011) (8)
6.3	5.2	11.2	23.5	13.3	9.7	2.8	28.9	-21.9	15.5	7.8	Tunisie (9)
3.8	5.6	14.3	14.3	6.1	8.3	14.5	8.2	-19.0	25.1	26.1	*Afrique australe*
7.0	1.9	12.4	18.6	13.7	14.5	-0.1	28.1	-9.3	19.6	28.6	Botswana*
5.6	2.0	12.0	13.3	10.3	(e)9.9	-2.8	16.8	-2.7	11.4	(e)14.6	Lesotho
3.3	3.9	15.1	19.3	18.8	(e)16.8	7.6	23.3	14.7	7.6	(e)20.4	Namibie
(e,b)3.6	(e)6.2	(e)14.6	(e)14.4	(e)5.2	(e)7.8	(e)16.6	(e)6.8	(e)-21.8	(e)27.2	(e)27.2	Afrique du Sud
5.1	5.1	(e)7.1	-3.4	(e)-2.3	(e)0.9	-1.4	-6.7	(e)4.5	(e)14.5	(e)-3.0	Swaziland
0.1	3.8	17.5	23.5	13.5	13.8	34.0	19.4	-18.5	23.5	34.1	*Afrique occidentale*
4.0	9.7	(e)16.2	34.1	22.6	(e)15.6	13.7	12.4	-9.8	(e)4.7	(e)25.0	Bénin*
4.0	3.6	14.5	20.0	12.7	(e)11.0	-1.5	31.7	-15.4	9.5	(e)26.9	Burkina Faso
7.9	6.0	15.0	24.9	14.9	10.9	1.4	10.1	-14.1	4.7	27.6	Cap-Vert (10)
1.5	3.5	14.3	10.8	6.7	3.8	24.4	18.0	-11.7	12.8	-14.4	Côte d'Ivoire*
4.3	0.2	8.7	9.0	5.5	3.6	13.4	0.4	-5.7	-6.2	20.6	Gambie (11)
7.1	9.1	16.3	23.8	13.2	(e)15.8	31.2	24.7	-21.6	35.7	(e)40.1	Ghana
4.8	-3.0	9.6	19.4	9.1	13.2	5.1	12.2	-22.4	32.5	49.9	Guinée*
2.4	-4.1	(e)18.6	23.5	19.0	(e)15.6	28.3	18.4	3.8	(e)-2.9	(e)43.4	Guinée-Bissau
(e)1.8	(e)11.1	(e)10.9	35.2	18.6	17.2	9.9	60.3	-33.7	27.7	45.2	Libéria*
5.2	4.7	14.8	28.4	16.4	(e)12.3	13.1	52.8	-27.2	17.4	(e)13.8	Mali*
3.9	3.1	18.3	12.5	5.3	9.9	54.3	36.3	-27.7	35.5	28.2	Mauritanie*
-0.2	0.8	20.9	18.9	26.4	(e)20.8	25.8	37.1	50.2	-3.1	(e)4.8	Niger*
-2.5	3.1	20.7	27.1	14.8	16.1	50.5	12.8	-20.4	30.8	44.9	Nigéria
(e)5.2	(e)8.8	(e)7.3	(e)1.7	(e)-7.5	(e)-4.7	(e)40.6	(e)-49.4	(e)-14.1	(e)33.3	(e)-8.6	Sainte-Hélène
2.3	3.9	14.4	24.0	12.4	7.7	23.2	34.0	-27.8	1.5	23.6	Sénégal (12)
-4.4	-4.2	15.2	15.6	12.1	25.4	20.5	19.5	-2.3	47.8	122.9	Sierra Leone*
2.2	5.5	(e)12.4	12.8	11.0	(e)8.5	19.5	22.0	-0.1	(e)-0.9	(e)13.7	Togo*

Pour les sources et les notes, se reporter à la fin du tableau.

Region, country or territory	Exports (f.o.b) - Exportations (f.a.b.) Percentage										
	80-00	90-00	00-10	05-08	05-09	05-11	2005	2008	2009	2010	2011
Developing economies: America	6.4	10.7	11.3	15.6	6.5	8.5	21.6	16.4	-23.4	27.0	24.4
Caribbean	*-2.1*	*6.8*	*6.9*	*14.1*	*-0.1*	*1.2*	*23.6*	*16.7*	*-41.3*	*14.2*	*41.0*
Anguilla	-	(e)26.6	18.6	-10.3	8.3	4.6	149.2	24.8	100.6	-45.1	29.5
Antigua and Barbuda	5.5	2.8	-3.3	-8.8	-10.4	-10.4	44.8	10.3	-22.4	-10.8	-4.1
Aruba (13)	(e)35.0	16.8	-5.4	7.6	-13.8	-20.1	28.6	4.8	-64.2	-86.5	1859.7
Bahamas (14)	-17.3	8.5	6.6	19.6	8.6	4.1	15.1	19.2	-25.6	-1.2	18.9
Barbados	-0.2	3.9	7.0	8.5	0.6	1.3	29.2	-15.4	-17.2	16.4	8.3
Cayman Islands	..	..	(e)-22.8	-31.2	-23.9	-15.6	..	-37.0	11.8	-31.6	69.2
Cuba*	-9.1	-1.7	12.5	20.8	9.0	(e)14.4	-0.6	-0.6	-21.9	60.6	(e)26.9
Dominica*	6.1	0.6	-2.9	-2.2	-3.2	-4.1	0.1	5.8	-9.4	1.6	-15.1
Dominican Republic (15)	11.7	26.6	2.2	3.7	-2.1	2.8	3.5	-5.8	-18.7	23.2	26.4
Grenada	2.5	6.3	-5.4	5.9	3.0	-0.9	-12.4	-8.6	-4.4	-17.2	14.2
Haiti	0.4	12.2	8.2	1.2	3.8	7.0	20.2	-8.1	20.1	0.5	32.4
Jamaica	3.6	2.1	4.0	17.7	0.0	-3.6	7.9	9.7	-46.0	0.9	20.7
Montserrat*	-0.5	0.3	8.2	46.7	30.9	-2.2	-66.0	50.3	-22.5	-65.1	14.3
Netherlands Antilles*(16)	-5.4	-0.4	-9.4	18.8	10.8	_	16.6	60.9	-25.6	0.1	_
Saint Kitts and Nevis*	2.4	0.5	3.5	11.0	9.5	7.3	-14.8	50.1	-7.0	-5.5	21.3
Saint Lucia	0.8	-11.1	18.1	34.2	27.4	18.9	-19.5	53.9	-0.8	31.8	-24.7
Saint Vincent and the Grenadines*	2.5	-4.9	0.7	10.9	7.6	(e)1.3	8.9	9.4	-6.0	-15.4	(e)1.1
Trinidad and Tobago*	-0.1	6.8	14.8	20.1	1.0	(e)-0.1	52.5	39.2	-51.1	20.3	(e)20.9
Turks and Caicos Islands	-	-	11.2	16.0	10.8	-	20.5	52.4	-16.2	-22.9	-
Central America	*10.5*	*16.0*	*7.5*	*10.7*	*3.5*	*6.3*	*15.7*	*7.5*	*-19.6*	*27.2*	*17.9*
Belize	4.3	5.0	5.6	12.5	5.9	7.3	-2.6	16.3	-16.1	17.0	23.5
Costa Rica*	11.2	17.0	7.0	11.2	6.0	4.8	11.5	2.1	-9.0	7.3	9.6
El Salvador (17)	7.1	18.8	4.9	10.2	4.6	6.0	4.0	15.6	-16.7	16.4	18.0
Guatemala (18)	4.5	10.2	12.4	13.1	8.7	10.2	6.8	12.2	-6.8	17.3	23.6
Honduras (19)	8.2	15.3	6.2	7.3	0.7	3.8	11.3	7.2	-22.2	19.0	25.5
Mexico	11.0	16.1	7.0	10.7	3.0	6.1	13.1	7.3	-21.3	29.8	17.3
Nicaragua (20)	1.7	10.3	12.8	19.4	14.2	16.5	13.5	23.4	-5.4	32.5	24.3
Panama*(21)	_	9.4	39.7	10.0	9.9	10.8	681.5	11.3	9.2	2.5	32.5
South America	*5.5*	*7.2*	*14.9*	*19.3*	*9.1*	*10.5*	*26.4*	*22.7*	*-24.4*	*27.6*	*27.8*
Argentina*	7.6	10.1	11.9	20.4	11.3	11.3	16.7	26.5	-20.6	22.2	23.0
Bolivia (Plurinational State of)	2.3	4.3	21.3	34.0	18.9	16.8	30.1	58.3	-30.3	27.9	32.5
Brazil	5.4	5.9	15.5	18.4	9.1	11.4	22.6	23.2	-22.7	32.0	26.8
Chile*	10.0	9.4	17.2	17.0	6.0	8.0	26.9	-1.8	-21.8	36.4	14.8
Colombia	8.1	7.4	14.7	21.9	14.2	15.4	30.3	28.5	-14.3	21.1	42.3
Ecuador	4.3	6.8	16.4	21.5	10.8	11.3	30.3	35.8	-26.3	25.6	28.3
Falkland Islands (Malvinas)	(e)15.4	(e)27.5	(e)7.6	(e)5.0	(e)-1.4	(e)1.4	(e)22.4	(e)7.7	(e)-25.8	(e)25.6	(e)5.8
Guyana*	4.7	8.7	6.1	13.1	9.9	11.4	-6.8	17.1	-4.0	15.4	26.9
Paraguay	7.7	1.7	19.1	40.5	24.4	21.8	6.5	58.4	-29.0	43.2	21.7
Peru*	4.2	9.0	20.6	21.5	12.2	14.1	35.6	13.1	-14.7	32.3	29.7
Suriname	-0.1	0.4	19.1	20.0	11.4	14.1	23.5	28.3	-19.6	44.5	15.8
Uruguay	5.5	5.2	14.3	22.5	15.2	14.6	16.2	43.2	-15.6	23.8	19.2
Venezuela (Bolivarian Rep. of)	2.3	6.3	12.2	18.1	4.5	4.9	40.5	35.8	-39.4	14.1	40.9
Developing economies: Asia	9.0	9.5	14.9	18.2	9.5	10.9	21.8	18.5	-19.2	28.7	21.6
Eastern Asia	*13.1*	*10.0*	*15.3*	*17.3*	*9.5*	*11.0*	*19.7*	*13.2*	*-15.5*	*29.9*	*17.9*
China	14.7	14.5	22.4	23.5	13.9	14.1	28.4	17.3	-15.9	31.3	20.3
China, Hong Kong SAR	14.5	8.3	7.8	7.9	3.3	5.6	11.6	5.3	-12.2	22.5	9.9
China, Macao SAR	7.2	3.9	-8.2	-6.3	-19.3	-20.1	-11.9	-21.4	-51.9	-9.5	0.0
China, Taiwan Province of	10.8	7.2	8.0	9.0	1.9	5.7	13.7	3.5	-20.1	34.8	12.2
Korea, Dem. People's Rep. of	(e)-9.2	-9.2	12.7	15.4	12.1	(e)16.7	4.7	22.3	-3.2	28.1	(e)44.8
Korea, Republic of (22)	12.2	10.1	12.4	14.1	7.7	10.1	12.0	13.6	-14.3	29.0	19.3
Mongolia	-1.7	0.7	21.2	32.4	18.0	22.9	22.4	34.4	-25.1	52.4	64.9
Southern Asia	*6.4*	*6.5*	*17.5*	*21.2*	*12.1*	*14.2*	*32.2*	*27.0*	*-19.5*	*33.0*	*30.6*
Afghanistan	-9.8	-2.0	20.1	13.0	3.9	(e)-2.1	25.9	8.7	-25.3	-3.7	(e)-9.9
Bangladesh	12.5	15.7	13.0	16.9	13.1	15.7	11.9	23.5	-2.0	27.7	27.7
Bhutan	11.5	7.0	24.3	29.5	16.6	(e)12.1	41.0	-22.9	-4.5	29.4	(e)-3.3
India (23)	9.4	9.5	20.1	24.8	15.9	18.1	30.0	29.7	-15.2	37.3	33.7
Iran (Islamic Rep. of)*	2.4	1.2	17.6	20.2	8.2	9.6	47.1	28.1	-30.6	29.3	28.0
Maldives	13.9	4.4	8.0	24.2	4.9	6.4	-10.7	45.2	-49.0	16.9	75.4
Nepal	10.7	13.1	2.5	2.9	0.2	0.4	11.8	8.1	-12.4	1.4	10.1
Pakistan	7.9	4.3	9.6	7.9	3.6	6.7	20.0	13.9	-13.8	22.2	18.4
Sri Lanka	9.6	11.3	5.9	9.0	3.9	6.1	10.2	5.1	-12.9	17.3	20.5
South-Eastern Asia	*11.1*	*11.1*	*11.2*	*14.8*	*7.2*	*9.3*	*15.3*	*15.5*	*-18.6*	*29.4*	*17.9*
Brunei Darussalam*	-1.7	2.4	11.1	17.7	6.5	8.6	23.6	39.8	-32.8	23.7	39.5
Cambodia (5)	32.1	26.8	14.5	16.7	10.2	(e)12.5	4.0	15.2	-10.9	22.6	(e)35.1

For sources and notes, see end of table.

Imports (c.i.f.) - Importations (c.a.f.) En pourcentage											Régions, pays ou territoires
80-00	90-00	00-10	05-08	05-09	05-11	2005	2008	2009	2010	2011	
7.8	12.0	10.7	19.9	9.2	10.2	19.6	22.0	-25.5	29.6	22.1	**Économies en développement : Amérique**
0.2	7.1	8.0	16.9	5.7	4.6	27.5	23.0	-30.7	9.9	25.8	*Caraïbes*
-	(e)13.0	12.4	26.1	7.5	-2.1	26.7	9.6	-37.8	-6.5	-2.9	Anguilla
7.8	4.4	5.6	14.6	2.2	-4.3	15.8	10.8	-33.7	-6.1	-5.9	Antigua-et-Barbuda
(e)18.8	9.4	1.9	11.6	-8.4	-7.7	19.5	17.3	-59.3	-43.7	327.4	Aruba (13)
-8.0	7.7	6.0	7.6	1.8	2.3	29.9	4.1	-16.5	6.1	19.2	Bahamas (14)
3.3	7.2	5.0	5.4	-0.3	0.4	13.6	9.9	-21.7	6.2	15.6	Barbade
..	..	(e)-6.2	-3.0	-5.3	-4.9	..	3.6	-17.2	-7.3	10.4	Îles Caïmanes
-4.8	2.5	12.5	22.1	7.9	(e)6.8	44.1	41.2	-37.4	19.5	(e)24.4	Cuba*
6.5	3.5	7.1	14.6	11.4	5.8	13.9	26.2	-5.5	-4.8	-1.5	Dominique*
9.5	12.0	6.7	16.9	7.4	7.6	25.1	17.6	-23.1	24.4	13.9	République dominicaine (15)
7.8	8.7	4.9	4.6	-1.4	-0.7	33.4	-0.5	-22.4	12.4	4.0	Grenade
3.7	14.4	11.2	14.7	11.1	13.8	11.3	37.7	-8.3	48.1	-4.0	Haïti
5.8	7.1	7.7	24.1	7.5	2.9	18.2	25.5	-40.2	3.2	24.2	Jamaïque
3.9	-6.3	4.2	7.4	2.2	-0.3	3.6	28.5	-22.2	-0.9	0.3	Montserrat*
-3.6	1.3	0.4	16.3	9.6	_	13.2	20.8	-15.3	3.1	_	Antilles néerlandaises*(16)
7.8	5.7	5.2	14.9	9.1	(e)3.4	15.2	19.6	-12.2	-6.0	(e)1.0	Saint-Kitts-et-Nevis*
6.6	2.3	7.8	10.7	3.5	4.4	9.6	3.5	-18.1	23.0	5.7	Sainte-Lucie
6.1	3.8	9.5	16.2	10.2	(e)6.6	6.7	14.2	-10.6	13.8	(e)-8.3	Saint-Vincent-et-les Grenadines*
0.0	12.1	10.1	18.9	8.2	(e)4.3	17.2	25.2	-27.5	-6.8	(e)34.2	Trinité-et-Tobago*
-	-	13.5	24.0	6.1	-	37.7	1.8	-36.5	-19.6	-	Îles Turques et Caïques
12.2	14.0	7.5	12.4	3.8	5.9	14.6	10.6	-23.9	26.8	17.5	*Amérique centrale*
6.3	5.9	4.2	11.0	4.6	3.8	14.1	22.3	-20.1	4.6	18.8	Belize
10.9	13.9	9.2	15.8	6.2	6.3	18.7	18.6	-25.4	18.3	19.6	Costa Rica*
9.9	14.0	6.7	13.0	3.8	4.3	7.6	11.3	-25.6	16.1	19.3	El Salvador (17)
7.6	11.6	10.5	11.7	3.9	5.5	10.8	7.2	-20.7	20.0	20.0	Guatemala (18)
8.0	16.8	9.7	17.4	5.9	5.5	12.3	17.6	-30.2	17.1	20.9	Honduras (19)
13.4	14.2	6.8	11.8	3.2	5.6	12.2	9.6	-24.3	28.6	16.4	Mexique
3.1	11.6	10.7	18.4	9.7	10.2	17.3	20.1	-20.0	23.0	22.5	Nicaragua (20)
_	8.7	23.5	18.4	11.8	12.9	167.1	18.6	-11.8	20.6	30.3	Panama*(21)
7.1	11.1	15.0	28.9	15.7	15.4	24.9	33.5	-26.1	34.7	25.6	*Amérique du Sud*
10.3	16.9	14.6	26.5	12.1	14.2	27.8	28.4	-31.9	44.3	31.0	Argentine*
6.8	9.7	13.9	28.8	20.5	20.0	27.0	47.0	-12.7	21.4	42.4	Bolivie (État plurinational de)
7.2	12.6	14.9	32.9	18.9	18.6	16.9	44.0	-26.7	43.3	23.7	Brésil
9.9	10.2	15.0	23.6	9.9	12.2	32.0	31.3	-33.2	43.6	26.1	Chili*
6.9	9.6	15.3	23.3	13.8	14.2	26.6	18.6	-16.3	23.7	34.4	Colombie
5.0	7.7	17.5	21.3	12.8	14.3	25.0	39.0	-20.0	36.5	17.9	Équateur
(e)12.2	(e)8.2	(e)2.2	(e)1.5	(e)-4.1	(e)14.9	(e)-27.7	(e)-39.8	(e)-6.6	(e)93.4	(e)94.4	Îles Falkland (Malvinas)
5.0	7.3	10.7	18.6	12.3	12.9	21.0	23.9	-11.5	20.4	26.2	Guyana*
10.7	7.0	19.9	38.4	23.9	22.3	22.5	54.2	-23.2	44.7	22.7	Paraguay
6.8	12.2	17.5	33.7	19.6	18.4	23.8	47.1	-27.0	37.3	25.1	Pérou*
1.5	0.9	12.9	7.0	8.5	8.6	41.9	24.9	6.6	0.5	19.3	Suriname
7.9	10.1	14.3	30.9	19.5	17.0	24.6	56.2	-22.8	24.8	23.3	Uruguay
2.3	5.8	14.3	29.5	15.3	7.8	41.0	9.2	-22.2	-2.6	20.3	Venezuela (Rép. bolivarienne du)
9.4	8.3	14.7	18.2	10.0	11.8	17.5	20.7	-18.1	30.9	21.6	**Économies en développement : Asie**
12.7	9.3	14.5	16.1	8.8	11.8	14.6	15.6	-15.8	35.5	21.2	*Asie orientale*
13.0	13.0	20.9	19.8	12.7	15.8	17.6	18.3	-11.3	39.0	24.8	Chine
14.4	8.8	8.3	9.1	4.6	7.0	10.5	5.7	-10.6	24.7	11.7	Chine (RAS de Hong Kong)
7.5	2.2	10.5	11.7	5.1	8.5	12.5	0.0	-13.9	19.3	40.9	Chine (RAS de Macao)
11.8	8.5	8.0	9.5	0.8	5.5	8.6	9.6	-27.5	44.1	11.9	Province chinoise de Taiwan
(e)-7.0	-7.0	8.3	8.8	4.4	(e)7.5	19.3	17.2	-13.5	14.1	(e)36.0	Corée, Rép. populaire dém. de
11.1	7.1	12.6	18.2	7.9	9.8	16.4	22.0	-25.8	31.7	23.3	Corée, République de (22)
-4.2	0.5	20.5	44.8	22.9	27.1	16.0	70.8	-41.1	53.8	99.1	Mongolie
4.8	5.1	20.5	25.0	15.7	16.6	32.8	35.8	-18.4	33.2	27.4	*Asie méridionale*
-3.2	5.5	11.0	7.2	7.9	(e)16.8	13.5	7:1	10.5	54.5	(e)22.2	Afghanistan
7.3	11.3	13.3	19.4	13.9	15.9	15.4	28.2	-8.3	27.2	30.2	Bangladesh
4.8	7.9	16.2	13.1	9.2	(e)15.9	-6.0	2.7	-1.9	61.3	(e)11.1	Bhoutan
6.9	10.1	24.6	30.7	19.3	19.5	43.2	40.3	-19.8	36.1	32.5	Inde (23)
0.2	-5.2	15.5	12.5	8.5	10.0	13.1	27.7	-11.6	29.5	3.9	Iran (Rép. islamique d')*
15.1	11.8	14.2	22.6	9.7	8.3	16.1	26.6	-30.3	12.8	34.3	Maldives
8.5	10.7	14.0	17.2	18.2	17.7	17.8	15.0	22.1	16.9	12.6	Népal
4.5	3.1	16.8	17.7	8.3	7.7	41.3	29.9	-25.2	19.4	15.3	Pakistan
7.8	8.9	9.2	15.8	5.8	10.7	10.8	23.5	-28.0	34.5	45.8	Sri Lanka
11.0	8.3	11.5	15.9	7.2	9.5	17.3	21.9	-23.1	31.1	20.6	*Asie du Sud-Est*
6.9	1.6	9.1	20.1	15.2	11.2	4.9	21.1	-3.7	0.5	19.4	Brunéi Darussalam*
14.8	25.2	14.8	18.0	11.7	(e)12.8	19.8	19.8	-10.4	16.5	(e)37.0	Cambodge (5)

Pour les sources et les notes, se reporter à la fin du tableau.

Region, country or territory	Exports (f.o.b) - Exportations (f.a.b.) Percentage										
	80-00	90-00	00-10	05-08	05-09	05-11	2005	2008	2009	2010	2011
Indonesia (…2002)	6.3	8.7	–								
Indonesia	–	–	–	16.8	9.8	12.8	22.9	18.3	-14.3	32.1	26.9
Lao People's Dem. Rep.*	16.1	15.4	19.6	23.2	15.1	(e)23.3	52.2	18.3	-7.9	73.7	(e)37.4
Malaysia (24)	12.7	12.2	9.2	13.7	5.0	6.5	12.0	19.1	-24.9	26.2	14.8
Myanmar	7.3	14.4	17.3	23.6	16.8	15.5	60.3	10.1	-3.2	30.0	6.7
Philippines	11.4	18.6	3.8	6.3	-1.0	1.3	4.0	-2.1	-22.3	34.1	-6.8
Singapore (25)	12.2	9.9	12.0	13.4	5.6	8.0	15.6	13.0	-20.2	30.4	16.4
Thailand	15.2	10.5	12.6	16.9	9.8	11.1	14.5	14.3	-13.6	28.6	15.9
Timor-Leste (26)	–	–	–	11.9	3.5	9.8	0.0	95.5	-38.5	112.5	-29.4
Viet Nam	21.0	22.7	19.4	24.3	17.2	18.0	22.5	29.1	-8.9	26.5	34.2
Western Asia	**2.0**	**6.5**	**17.6**	**23.3**	**11.2**	**11.2**	**34.4**	**34.8**	**-28.8**	**22.3**	**33.6**
Bahrain (5)	2.0	3.5	11.7	18.4	6.7	7.6	35.5	27.0	-31.4	14.9	44.0
Iraq*	-6.4	34.1	17.6	38.4	20.9	19.8	33.1	57.5	-33.5	28.8	56.8
Jordan	6.5	6.6	15.0	20.7	13.2	9.7	9.7	36.0	-16.1	7.5	13.4
Kuwait*	-0.1	16.5	19.0	23.5	8.5	10.2	56.9	39.9	-38.3	24.3	54.2
Lebanon (27)	-0.3	4.1	20.6	24.3	17.7	15.2	6.3	24.6	-6.0	19.9	12.8
Occupied Palestinian territory	-	(e)1.1	7.6	20.5	13.8	12.8	7.3	8.9	-7.2	11.0	31.9
Oman	6.7	5.7	14.8	24.8	14.7	15.3	40.1	56.3	-25.6	30.5	28.7
Qatar*	1.9	10.1	23.4	29.4	19.7	24.0	37.3	34.3	-13.3	50.7	47.1
Saudi Arabia*(28)	-0.1	3.1	16.5	19.2	5.4	8.3	43.3	34.4	-38.7	30.6	43.4
Syrian Arab Republic*	4.8	0.9	11.8	17.5	7.0	(e)-0.2	22.6	33.5	-29.6	13.3	(e)-30.9
Turkey*	10.8	9.1	17.4	22.0	11.5	8.7	16.3	23.1	-22.6	11.5	18.5
United Arab Emirates	5.1	6.5	19.7	26.4	16.0	11.8	29.0	33.9	-19.8	10.7	19.0
Yemen*	–	20.6	9.7	8.9	3.6	(e)7.8	37.7	20.4	-17.5	35.8	(e)13.2
Developing economies: Oceania	**5.6**	**4.4**	**7.8**	**12.8**	**3.3**	**5.6**	**9.3**	**5.6**	**-25.2**	**27.9**	**18.5**
American Samoa*(29)	4.3	1.4	(e)1.8	(e)13.8	(e)7.5	(e)-4.5	-16.1	(e)26.7	(e)-17.5	(e)-36.2	(e)3.3
Cook Islands	0.2	0.0	-7.8	-3.2	-10.7	-5.6	-26.7	-20.1	-33.6	82.0	-40.0
Fiji	4.5	5.6	4.5	9.4	0.6	(e)3.5	1.2	22.3	-31.9	34.7	(e)6.5
French Polynesia*	14.0	9.6	-2.3	-3.2	-6.3	-5.3	13.5	17.0	-24.2	3.3	-2.2
Guam	3.8	-0.5	0.6	30.4	6.7	-5.0	-1.8	14.8	-51.4	-9.8	-6.5
Kiribati	2.7	6.1	(e)20.9	51.9	48.3	(e)28.7	74.5	53.4	33.3	(e)-25.0	(e)33.3
Marshall Islands	–	4.1	9.1	-6.4	-2.7	(e)8.5	28.2	10.4	3.0	55.3	(e)8.4
Micronesia (Federated States of)	–	9.8	(e)0.0	14.7	10.9	(e)6.5	5.7	27.0	-8.8	(e)0.4	(e)0.0
Nauru	-6.3	-5.3	11.2	225.5	103.2	65.4	-73.8	572.2	-79.3	120.0	25.4
New Caledonia*	4.1	1.7	12.4	10.2	-2.2	2.9	5.2	-38.2	-23.6	49.3	15.8
Niue	(e)9.9	9.9	(e)-13.2	-46.0	(e)-58.1	(e)-51.0	14.1	-99.3	(e)5.4	(e)0.0	(e)0.0
Northern Mariana Islands	–	..	(e)-38.5	(e)-43.2	(e)-63.2	(e)-64.3	-21.2	(e)-62.6	(e)-92.2	(e)-44.4	(e)-40.0
Palau	–	(e)-8.9	-4.5	-5.1	-10.9	-12.8	137.3	12.4	-34.6	-13.3	-5.6
Papua New Guinea	6.2	3.6	14.0	19.6	9.5	10.6	28.2	22.0	-22.9	30.5	20.4
Samoa (27)	-1.6	12.0	5.5	-1.7	-11.1	-8.0	2.3	-26.1	-36.1	29.4	-8.6
Solomon Islands*	4.1	2.3	16.2	27.6	15.8	20.8	6.3	27.9	-22.4	35.5	82.2
Tokelau	..	..	-	-	-	-	(e)36.4	-	-	-	-
Tonga	3.3	-3.8	-2.6	-3.7	-5.2	(e)-0.3	-34.1	2.7	-13.1	5.9	(e)33.2
Tuvalu	(e)-6.7	-15.3	(e)28.9	(e)37.7	(e)52.4	(e)40.1	-53.1	(e)64.5	(e)100.0	(e)0.0	(e)0.0
Vanuatu	-0.1	4.8	11.4	13.3	10.1	6.8	1.2	12.8	0.0	-14.0	38.1
Wallis and Futuna Islands	..	..	-	-	-	-	(e)-19.1	-	-	-	-
Transition economies	**1.4**	**6.4**	**18.3**	**26.2**	**10.9**	**11.1**	**28.4**	**34.3**	**-35.4**	**29.9**	**33.5**
Albania	(e)1.4	7.9	20.2	28.0	16.6	17.8	8.8	25.7	-19.5	41.6	26.3
Armenia*	–	–	12.3	5.3	-5.5	1.6	32.9	-13.3	-34.0	45.0	30.1
Azerbaijan (30)	–	–	38.6	59.2	33.4	23.6	111.6	43.8	-31.0	25.5	30.3
Belarus	–	–	16.4	26.4	11.4	12.1	16.0	34.2	-34.6	18.7	62.9
Bosnia and Herzegovina*(31)	–	–	20.4	27.6	15.2	12.7	25.8	21.0	-21.4	21.5	21.8
Croatia*	–	–	12.5	17.4	6.8	5.0	9.3	14.1	-25.8	12.7	13.3
Georgia (32)	–	–	19.8	20.8	10.2	13.8	33.8	21.5	-24.3	38.7	38.4
Kazakhstan*(33)	–	–	25.4	35.5	16.2	16.4	35.2	49.0	-39.3	37.8	48.2
Kyrgyzstan	–	–	16.8	41.1	29.1	18.8	-6.8	40.5	-9.8	5.2	12.1
Montenegro	–	–	–	–	–	–	–	–	-38.8	8.4	44.6
Republic of Moldova	–	–	12.6	14.9	7.7	10.7	11.3	19.2	-19.7	20.1	43.8
Russian Federation (34)	–	–	17.7	23.8	9.2	10.0	33.1	33.1	-35.7	32.0	30.4
Serbia and Montenegro*	–	–	–	–	–	–	23.9	–	–	–	–
Serbia	–	–	–	–	–	–	–	–	-23.9	17.4	20.2
Tajikistan (32)	–	–	7.0	15.2	2.6	1.3	-2.6	-4.2	-28.2	19.4	4.2
TFYR of Macedonia*	–	–	13.4	25.8	11.0	10.3	21.8	16.8	-31.3	22.3	34.7
Turkmenistan (32)	–	–	(e)13.3	31.5	(e)5.5	(e)8.4	27.8	50.5	(e)-58.1	(e)30.0	(e)100.0
Ukraine (32)	–	–	15.1	25.4	9.0	9.1	4.8	35.8	-40.6	29.4	32.9
Uzbekistan (32)	–	–	18.8	30.7	25.1	18.8	11.0	28.3	4.2	7.9	14.4
Developed economies: America	**7.5**	**7.5**	**6.2**	**11.4**	**3.7**	**5.2**	**12.8**	**11.0**	**-21.8**	**21.4**	**16.1**
Bermuda (5)	3.9	-0.7	-10.2	-19.3	-11.0	-16.6	-32.9	-11.1	20.8	-48.3	-13.3
Canada	7.2	8.3	4.9	7.9	-1.2	1.4	18.0	8.5	-30.6	22.9	17.0

For sources and notes, see end of table.

Imports (c.i.f.) - Importations (c.a.f.) En pourcentage											Régions, pays ou territoires
80-00	90-00	00-10	05-08	05-09	05-11	2005	2008	2009	2010	2011	
7.9	6.2	–						–	–	–	Indonésie (…2002)
–	–	–	18.6	9.3	13.7	37.7	37.0	-26.5	44.3	30.7	Indonésie
10.3	12.7	16.0	15.1	13.0	(e)19.2	23.7	31.7	0.6	45.8	(e)28.6	Rép. dém. populaire lao*
12.9	9.5	8.6	12.8	3.9	6.5	8.7	12.0	-24.8	33.2	13.9	Malaisie (24)
12.8	22.6	7.6	30.4	24.2	24.8	-12.2	31.1	2.1	9.5	89.5	Myanmar
10.5	12.5	4.9	6.9	-0.4	2.5	7.3	4.8	-24.2	27.6	8.8	Philippines
10.6	7.8	11.4	16.2	7.3	8.4	15.2	21.5	-23.1	26.4	17.7	Singapour (25)
12.9	5.0	12.7	14.4	6.1	10.0	25.2	26.8	-24.8	37.4	23.6	Thaïlande
			37.4	33.9	24.0	-8.2	52.6	9.9	1.0	14.1	Timor-Leste (26)
13.6	22.9	20.6	30.9	20.6	17.3	15.0	28.8	-13.3	19.8	24.2	Viet Nam
3.2	*7.0*	*17.8*	*24.9*	*15.0*	*12.0*	*20.3*	*27.1*	*-18.5*	*14.0*	*20.2*	*Asie occidentale*
1.2	0.3	11.9	14.4	4.1	3.1	27.2	30.4	-32.5	16.4	8.2	Bahreïn (5)
-8.5	27.7	16.0	10.2	13.9	15.4	10.5	54.2	12.1	6.6	28.8	Iraq*
2.4	5.1	15.6	17.0	10.9	8.6	29.3	24.1	-13.3	3.8	22.4	Jordanie
0.9	5.5	13.8	17.0	9.1	7.0	25.1	16.7	-18.2	10.2	12.7	Koweït*
5.5	8.7	12.1	20.9	17.8	15.0	0.2	36.8	-1.1	11.4	12.4	Liban (27)
-	(e)9.2	8.2	10.6	9.0	9.0	12.4	13.6	0.9	9.9	13.5	Territoire palestinien occupé
5.1	6.1	17.1	38.3	24.0	16.4	-0.4	43.5	-22.1	10.7	19.4	Oman
5.2	7.4	28.2	40.7	26.4	13.6	67.6	19.1	-10.7	-6.7	10.5	Qatar*
-0.5	0.8	16.5	25.1	15.6	12.3	25.5	27.7	-17.0	11.8	20.7	Arable saoudile*(28)
0.4	3.6	18.8	19.4	12.3	(e)8.1	29.1	23.5	-14.7	13.7	(e)-5.5	République arabe syrienne*
10.7	10.3	17.0	20.2	7.7	9.5	19.7	18.8	-30.2	31.7	29.8	Turquie*
8.8	10.7	21.5	34.8	23.2	15.7	17.6	33.4	-15.1	7.8	15.0	Émirats arabes unis
–	0.6	17.9	26.2	17.5	10.5	34.8	22.8	-12.1	0.8	8.4	Yémen*
3.9	*1.6*	*9.2*	*14.6*	*7.1*	*6.9*	*6.4*	*15.1*	*-18.5*	*17.8*	*12.5*	*Économies en développement : Océanie*
5.9	3.0	(e)1.8	10.5	5.1	(e)2.7	-16.2	4.6	-11.8	(e)-8.3	(e)25.5	Samoa américaines*(29)
4.9	-3.8	7.1	9.7	-2.0	-2.7	7.0	1.6	-35.0	14.6	3.7	Îles Cook
3.8	3.0	9.0	10.7	0.0	(e)3.1	11.2	25.5	-36.4	26.7	(e)26.3	Fidji
3.9	1.6	6.0	8.8	2.9	-0.5	15.0	16.4	-20.8	0.5	-5.7	Polynésie française*
3.5	-0.8	4.6	9.5	6.3	5.3	5.8	-5.7	-2.1	9.9	1.4	Guam
6.1	4.1	6.5	-0.1	-0.8	(e)4.9	28.7	5.1	-7.6	7.2	(e)50.7	Kiribati
–	0.9	(e)8.4	(e)2.8	(e)3.2	(e)7.5	12.1	(e)0.0	(e)5.0	(e)28.6	(e)3.7	Îles Marshall
–	1.3	(e)5.2	5.8	7.0	(e)5.1	-1.9	8.8	10.8	(e)-1.2	(e)0.0	Micronésie (États fédérés de)
2.6	-11.0	11.0	53.5	45.4	1.3	43.6	57.1	13.8	-78.6	46.3	Nauru
6.2	1.1	15.0	23.2	12.4	11.4	8.1	15.1	-20.4	28.7	11.7	Nouvelle-Calédonie*
(e)-6.6	-6.6	(e)14.1	4.1	(e)-2.5	(e)-0.6	5.6	14.1	(e)-35.1	(e)0.0	(e)40.0	Nioué
–	..	–	–	–	–	–	–	–	–	–	Îles Mariannes du Nord
–	(e)17.0	-0.1	5.0	-1.8	0.0	0.7	21.1	-28.6	8.2	23.6	Palaos
1.2	-0.8	(e)15.2	27.4	18.2	(e)15.7	2.8	20.7	-10.1	(e)23.4	(e)15.2	Papouasie-Nouvelle-Guinée
4.3	0.9	11.6	5.4	-0.2	4.4	13.7	8.4	-19.9	34.4	11.6	Samoa (27)
3.1	0.7	19.3	22.1	12.2	15.2	52.3	14.3	-18.3	51.2	15.0	Îles Salomon*
-	-	-	-	-	-	(e)-39.5	-	-	-	-	Tokélaou
4.0	1.9	9.2	12.4	7.5	(e)7.0	14.9	16.2	-12.8	9.8	(e)15.8	Tonga
(e)4.4	4.2	(e)14.9	26.4	(e)9.4	(e)8.8	13.0	72.9	(e)-47.1	(e)14.3	(e)56.2	Tuvalu
2.5	0.9	16.2	25.7	18.8	11.0	16.4	36.0	-6.2	-3.1	6.7	Vanuatu
..	..	-	-	-	-	-3.5	-	-	-	-	Îles Wallis-et-Futuna
0.9	*3.3*	*19.7*	*31.4*	*14.9*	*12.0*	*22.0*	*30.5*	*-32.8*	*21.2*	*28.8*	*Économies en transition*
(e)10.0	9.4	17.3	27.1	17.9	11.2	13.4	25.4	-13.3	-3.2	22.5	Albanie
–	–	19.4	37.1	21.6	14.1	30.9	34.9	-25.4	14.5	10.9	Arménie*
–	–	21.5	20.9	13.1	11.6	19.8	25.3	-14.0	3.6	44.3	Azerbaïdjan (30)
–	–	18.3	32.6	17.8	15.0	1.3	37.3	-27.5	22.1	31.1	Bélarus
–	–	14.4	21.0	9.8	6.2	18.8	25.5	-28.1	5.1	19.8	Bosnie-Herzégovine*(31)
–	–	12.2	18.5	6.4	1.0	11.9	19.0	-31.0	-5.4	13.3	Croatie*
–	–	27.5	35.3	17.7	13.5	34.9	16.3	-27.7	16.2	36.3	Géorgie (32)
–	–	23.9	30.5	15.7	10.2	35.7	15.7	-24.9	7.1	25.0	Kazakhstan*(33)
–	–	26.0	50.1	30.0	19.3	25.5	46.0	-25.3	6.0	32.2	Kirghizistan
–	–	–	–	–	–	–	–	-38.0	-5.7	16.6	Monténégro
–	–	20.2	29.6	14.0	11.5	29.3	32.8	-33.1	17.6	34.7	République de Moldova
–	–	21.1	32.8	15.3	13.3	28.8	30.6	-34.3	29.7	29.6	Fédération de Russie (34)
–	–	–	–	–	–	-1.2	–	–	–	–	Serbie-et-Monténégro*
–	–	–	–	–	–	–	–	-29.8	4.3	20.3	Serbie
–	–	18.9	35.7	21.6	13.5	11.7	33.2	-21.4	3.5	19.9	Tadjikistan (32)
–	–	14.3	29.4	16.0	11.4	10.1	31.2	-26.4	8.2	28.5	LERY de Macédoine*
–	–	(e)13.1	25.8	(e)27.9	(e)19.4	-11.2	56.1	(e)20.4	(e)-17.6	(e)32.1	Turkménistan (32)
–	–	18.7	33.4	11.6	10.5	24.6	41.1	-46.8	33.9	35.6	Ukraine (32)
–	–	16.0	37.1	29.1	18.1	8.1	46.4	-2.7	-7.1	18.7	Ouzbékistan (32)
7.9	*9.1*	*6.0*	*7.6*	*0.0*	*2.4*	*14.5*	*7.4*	*-25.2*	*22.0*	*15.1*	*Économies développées : Amérique*
3.3	2.7	4.9	5.7	2.1	-1.9	-0.3	-0.7	-8.2	-7.1	-7.9	Bermudes (5)
7.3	7.5	6.4	8.1	1.5	3.4	18.4	7.2	-21.0	18.9	15.3	Canada

Pour les sources et les notes, se reporter à la fin du tableau.

Region, country or territory	Exports (f.o.b) - Exportations (f.a.b.) Percentage										
	80-00	90-00	00-10	05-08	05-09	05-11	2005	2008	2009	2010	2011
Greenland	2.7	-3.6	4.7	6.5	0.1	0.9	5.8	13.5	-24.0	5.3	21.3
Saint Pierre and Miquelon	(e)12.9	(e)-3.4	(e)-2.3	(e)-8.4	(e)-22.0	(e)-23.3	(e)50.2	(e)-24.3	(e)-47.6	(e)-7.1	(e)-14.4
United States (35)	7.6	7.2	6.6	12.7	5.5	6.6	10.8	11.9	-18.8	20.9	15.9
Developed economies: Asia	**7.1**	**4.4**	**6.4**	**9.9**	**1.7**	**4.2**	**5.5**	**9.7**	**-25.4**	**31.7**	**7.5**
Israel*	9.8	11.1	8.1	12.8	5.0	6.3	10.8	12.5	-21.2	21.8	15.9
Japan	7.0	4.1	6.3	9.6	1.4	4.1	5.2	9.5	-25.7	32.6	6.9
Developed economies: Europe	**7.1**	**5.6**	**9.5**	**13.8**	**5.2**	**4.8**	**8.5**	**11.2**	**-22.5**	**12.7**	**17.7**
Andorra*	-	(e)1.2	3.6	-12.7	-18.7	-15.1	17.4	-24.4	-34.0	-14.6	42.7
Austria*	8.9	6.1	9.9	13.6	4.6	3.9	5.9	10.5	-24.4	11.7	16.3
Belgium*	-	-	9.6	12.6	4.5	4.1	9.1	9.2	-21.6	10.8	17.0
Bulgaria*	-6.7	2.2	18.0	23.7	11.0	11.8	18.2	20.4	-27.0	26.8	36.4
Cyprus*	5.0	1.3	5.6	3.7	-1.1	2.4	54.8	16.8	-23.0	11.9	30.2
Czech Republic*(36)	–	–	18.5	23.8	12.3	10.4	13.4	19.5	-23.1	18.1	22.0
Denmark*(37)	7.5	3.7	8.3	11.1	4.3	3.1	10.6	13.0	-19.6	3.9	16.3
Estonia*(32)	–	–	13.3	16.8	5.8	9.3	30.3	12.8	-27.4	28.5	44.3
Faeroe Islands	6.0	1.6	5.7	12.5	7.7	7.5	-3.0	14.2	-10.6	8.3	21.0
Finland*	7.4	8.0	6.7	13.9	1.3	0.0	6.6	6.9	-34.8	10.9	13.6
France*	7.4	5.0	6.2	10.1	3.0	2.6	2.6	9.8	-21.3	8.3	13.8
Germany*	–	3.9	10.2	14.6	5.6	4.9	6.9	9.2	-22.5	12.7	16.9
Gibraltar (38)	16.5	10.0	9.8	13.5	7.4	2.2	1.5	-6.8	-6.7	-2.2	-4.6
Greece*	6.0	3.6	9.2	14.9	5.9	6.5	13.0	11.6	-22.4	6.4	45.9
Hungary*(39)	5.4	12.7	15.1	20.4	9.5	7.7	13.4	13.4	-23.5	15.4	17.5
Iceland	5.5	3.2	10.9	21.8	10.3	7.6	6.7	12.2	-24.3	13.5	16.1
Ireland*	13.2	13.8	4.7	5.2	2.5	1.9	4.8	3.2	-7.8	0.8	8.8
Italy	7.7	4.6	8.1	13.8	4.4	3.4	5.6	8.3	-25.0	10.3	16.9
Latvia	–	–	20.5	26.1	13.8	13.7	28.9	21.8	-24.1	24.1	37.7
Lithuania*(32)	–	–	21.0	25.4	12.4	12.6	27.1	37.5	-30.4	26.5	35.1
Luxembourg*	7.4	3.3	11.1	9.7	3.6	0.2	15.8	11.7	-16.9	-7.2	10.2
Malta	10.6	6.3	5.1	14.0	5.7	7.9	-4.6	1.0	-17.9	25.9	22.3
Netherlands*	6.7	7.0	11.5	16.3	7.4	6.7	13.9	15.5	-21.9	15.7	16.1
Norway	6.4	5.2	11.1	17.6	5.9	4.6	25.7	26.0	-32.0	11.9	21.9
Poland*	5.2	9.9	19.9	24.1	13.5	11.0	19.3	21.3	-19.9	17.4	17.3
Portugal*	11.1	5.3	9.0	14.6	5.4	4.7	6.8	8.6	-22.6	10.6	20.8
Romania	-2.7	8.5	18.5	21.5	12.4	12.5	18.1	22.0	-18.1	22.4	26.6
Slovakia*	–	–	21.6	31.4	17.9	13.5	15.1	21.2	-21.2	15.7	22.6
Slovenia*	–	–	15.5	21.7	10.4	7.7	17.8	13.1	-23.3	11.9	19.0
Spain*	11.0	8.3	9.7	13.8	6.1	6.0	5.6	10.8	-19.2	12.3	20.4
Sweden*	6.8	6.0	8.3	12.0	2.0	3.5	6.4	8.3	-28.7	21.6	18.0
Switzerland*	7.1	3.0	10.4	15.4	8.9	8.6	6.4	16.6	-14.0	13.4	19.8
United Kingdom*	6.6	5.5	5.1	6.1	-1.2	1.6	10.8	6.6	-24.8	17.6	20.9
Developed economies: Oceania	**6.6**	**4.8**	**13.3**	**19.1**	**11.3**	**14.3**	**19.4**	**28.7**	**-18.0**	**36.9**	**26.4**
Australia	6.7	5.0	14.0	20.2	12.4	15.4	22.5	32.5	-17.7	38.0	27.9
New Zealand	5.9	4.2	9.6	13.2	5.7	8.1	6.5	9.9	-19.6	29.9	16.1

For sources and notes, see next page.

Imports (c.i.f.) - Importations (c.a.f.) En pourcentage											Régions, pays ou territoires
80-00	90-00	00-10	05-08	05-09	05-11	2005	2008	2009	2010	2011	
1.7	-1.0	11.1	15.6	8.4	7.0	8.4	19.5	-17.1	11.6	13.2	Groenland
(e)14.4	(e)2.5	(e)0.3	(e)3.5	(e)7.3	(e)4.0	(e)-27.8	(e)-5.4	(e)31.7	(e)-13.3	(e)1.0	Saint-Pierre-et-Miquelon
8.1	9.5	5.9	7.5	-0.3	2.3	13.7	7.4	-26.0	22.7	15.1	États-Unis (35)
6.2	**4.9**	**7.9**	**13.3**	**4.1**	**6.4**	**13.0**	**22.3**	**-27.8**	**25.6**	**23.4**	**Économies développées : Asie**
7.9	8.6	6.4	13.2	3.9	6.0	10.0	14.6	-27.2	24.2	23.9	Israël*
6.1	4.6	8.0	13.3	4.2	6.5	13.3	23.1	-27.8	25.8	23.3	Japon
6.6	**5.0**	**9.8**	**14.7**	**5.3**	**4.7**	**10.2**	**12.0**	**-24.3**	**13.4**	**16.7**	**Économies développées : Europe**
-	(e)3.1	5.2	2.9	-1.7	-3.0	3.4	1.0	-18.2	-4.2	5.5	Andorre*
8.0	4.5	9.7	13.5	5.3	5.1	6.3	12.7	-22.4	11.5	20.3	Autriche*
-	-	10.1	13.7	4.9	4.4	11.7	13.0	-24.2	11.6	18.3	Belgique*
-5.6	5.3	18.4	26.7	10.2	6.2	25.5	22.9	-36.2	8.7	27.3	Bulgarie*
7.6	4.3	10.9	19.4	8.9	4.6	15.0	23.2	-26.4	9.7	0.4	Chypre*
_	_	15.7	23.1	11.0	9.5	9.5	19.9	-26.0	20.9	19.6	République tchèque*(36)
6.2	4.2	8.7	13.1	4.4	2.1	11.0	11.3	-24.0	2.4	15.3	Danemark*(37)
_	_	11.4	16.0	1.5	3.6	23.0	1.9	-36.7	21.3	43.3	Estonie*(32)
3.0	5.5	6.2	11.6	3.3	1.9	18.8	-2.7	-20.7	-0.9	26.1	Îles Féroé
5.3	5.1	10.0	16.1	3.5	2.8	14.4	12.0	-33.7	13.3	22.4	Finlande*
6.3	3.8	8.0	12.7	4.9	4.2	7.2	13.3	-21.7	9.0	17.0	France*
_	3.5	9.9	15.1	6.3	5.9	8.7	12.0	-21.8	14.2	18.8	Allemagne*
11.5	1.7	7.6	15.6	8.4	5.2	3.8	-2.9	-9.7	-0.2	16.3	Gibraltar (38)
7.5	5.1	10.4	19.6	8.9	0.8	3.9	17.6	-25.0	-7.9	-4.6	Grèce*
6.5	13.5	12.8	18.1	6.5	4.8	10.1	13.7	-28.6	13.7	16.3	Hongrie*(39)
5.5	5.5	8.7	10.7	-4.3	-4.5	28.2	-7.8	-41.6	8.8	23.5	Islande
9.4	10.7	3.9	7.6	-0.5	-2.7	11.1	-0.1	-25.3	-3.6	10.3	Irlande*
5.8	3.2	9.1	13.5	3.9	4.0	8.5	9.5	-26.1	17.7	14.4	Italie
_	_	17.1	23.7	5.8	5.3	22.7	5.1	-39.2	19.5	39.3	Lettonie
_	_	18.3	25.9	8.2	8.3	25.7	27.0	-41.1	28.2	35.7	Lituanie*(32)
8.2	4.2	10.6	12.7	4.8	2.1	9.4	14.4	-21.2	-0.6	14.4	Luxembourg*
8.7	4.4	6.3	12.7	6.1	6.9	1.2	10.1	-15.5	13.4	24.3	Malte
6.4	6.7	11.3	16.9	7.4	6.7	14.0	17.6	-23.7	16.9	16.0	Pays-Bas*
5.2	4.1	11.1	18.3	8.1	6.2	14.3	12.3	-23.6	12.1	17.5	Norvège
8.1	18.3	16.6	27.3	13.4	10.2	13.5	25.7	-28.4	19.5	16.6	Pologne*
9.8	5.3	9.0	15.5	6.1	2.9	11.5	14.6	-24.1	5.9	6.2	Portugal*
-0.7	6.8	19.9	28.4	11.3	7.5	23.9	19.2	-35.4	14.7	22.8	Roumanie
_	_	19.5	29.2	15.4	11.5	16.2	21.6	-24.7	17.2	18.8	Slovaquie*
_	_	14.5	22.8	9.9	7.2	14.7	17.0	-28.4	13.9	18.0	Slovénie*
9.7	6.0	10.1	13.7	2.7	1.7	11.9	7.8	-30.3	11.9	14.3	Espagne*
5.5	4.4	9.9	15.1	4.2	5.2	11.4	9.7	-28.9	24.6	18.1	Suède*
6.1	2.5	9.1	13.3	6.9	7.0	9.1	13.9	-15.3	13.5	18.2	Suisse*
7.1	5.6	6.8	8.2	1.0	2.1	9.3	2.8	-21.1	14.2	14.0	Royaume-Uni*
6.5	**6.3**	**12.5**	**15.8**	**8.3**	**9.3**	**14.4**	**19.1**	**-18.6**	**22.4**	**20.4**	**Économies développées : Océanie**
6.7	6.4	13.1	17.1	9.6	10.3	14.5	21.1	-17.4	21.9	20.9	Australie
6.0	5.9	9.7	9.2	1.2	4.1	14.0	8.1	-25.8	26.0	17.4	Nouvelle-Zélande

Pour les sources et les notes, se reporter à la page suivante.

Sources:

UNCTAD secretariat calculations, based on:
- UN DESA Statistics Division, *Yearbook of International Trade Statistics*
- UN DESA Statistics Division, *Monthly Bulletin of Statistics*
- UN DESA Statistics Division, *UN COMTRADE*
- IMF, *International Financial Statistics*
- IMF, *Direction of Trade Statistics*
- IMF, *Balance of Payments Statistics*
- WTO, *Statistics database*
- Eurostat, *Comext*
- World Bank, W*orld Development Indicators*
- OECD, *OECD.Stat Extracts*
- OPEC, *Annual Statistical Bulletin*
- Economist Intelligence Unit, *Country Data*
- Other international and national sources

Notes:
(*)	Special Trade System.
(1)	Excluding exports of gold.
(2)	From 1996 onward, imports f.o.b.
(3)	From 2011 onwards, commercial mining is included.
(4)	Prior to 2008, special trade.
(5)	Imports f.o.b.
(6)	Trade with other member countries of CEMAC is excluded. Imports f.o.b.
(7)	Trade with other member countries of CEMAC is excluded.
(8)	Prior to 1995, data refer to fiscal year ending June.
(9)	Prior to 1974, special trade.
(10)	Excluding re-exports (oil for bunkering).
(11)	Prior to 2009, re-exports is excluded
(12)	Prior to 2005, special trade.
(13)	Prior to 1986, included in Netherlands Antilles. Including exports and imports of crude oil and oil products. Prior to 2000, free zone trade is excluded. Imports f.o.b.
(14)	From 1990 onwards, trade statistics exclude certain oil and chemical products. Imports f.o.b.
(15)	Prior to 1993, excluding free trade processing zones. Imports f.o.b.
(16)	Prior to 1986, including Aruba.
(17)	Prior to 1992, excluding free trade processing zones.
(18)	Prior to 2002, special trade.
(19)	From 1990 onward, including goods for processing. Imports f.o.b.
(20)	Excluding free trade processing zones.
(21)	Prior to 2005, excluding customs free zones.
(22)	Excluding imports of goods financed through foreign aid.
(23)	Excluding military goods, fissionable materials, bunkers, ships and aircraft.
(24)	Inter-trade between the States of Malaysia included. From 1965 onwards, excluding military imports and offshore installations of petroleum industry.
(25)	Including trans-shipments to and from peninsular Malaysia.
(26)	Excluding exports of oil and gas.
(27)	Prior to 2001, special trade.
(28)	Excluding defense imports.
(29)	Data refer to fiscal year ending September.
(30)	Excluding military goods, precious metals and goods procured in foreign ports.
(31)	Prior to 1998, data refer to the Federation of Bosnia and Herzegovina only. The other entity of Bosnia and Herzegovina, Republika Srpska, is not included.
(32)	Prior to 1994, covers only trade with countries outside the CIS.
(33)	Prior to 1994, covers only trade with countries outside the CIS. As of 2011adjusted to include bilateral trade with Russia.
(34)	Prior to 1994, excluding trade with independent states resulting from the former USSR.
(35)	Prior to 1975, excluding non-monetary gold.
(36)	From 1995 onward, including goods for processing.
(37)	Prior to 1988, excluding ships.
(38)	Excluding petroleum products.
(39)	Prior to 1996, excluding customs free zones.

Sources :
Calculs du secrétariat de la CNUCED, basés sur :
- ONU DAES Division de statistique, *Annuaire statistique du commerce international*
- ONU DAES Division de statistique, *Bulletin mensuel de statistique*
- ONU DAES Division de statistique, *ONU COMTRADE*
- FMI, *Statistiques financières internationales*
- FMI, *Direction of Trade Statistics*
- FMI, *Statistiques de la balance des paiements*
- OMC, *Base de données statistiques*
- Eurostat, *Comext*
- Banque mondiale, *Indicateurs du développement dans le monde*
- OCDE, *OECD.Stat Extracts*
- OPEP, *Bulletin statistique annuel*
- Economist Intelligence Unit, *Country Data*
- Autres sources internationales et nationales

Notes :
(*)   Système du commerce spécial.
(1)   Non-compris les exportations d'or.
(2)   À partir de 1996, importations f.a.b.
(3)   À partir de 2011, l'exploitation minière commerciale est incluse.
(4)   Avant 2008, commerce spécial.
(5)   Importations f.a.b.
(6)   Non-compris le commerce avec les autres pays membres de la CEMAC. Importations f.a.b.
(7)   Non-compris le commerce avec les autres pays membres de la CEMAC.
(8)   Avant 1995, les données se rapportent à l'exercice budgétaire finissant en juin.
(9)   Avant 1974, commerce spécial.
(10)   Non-compris les réexportations (huile pour mise en soute).
(11)   Avant 2009, non-compris les réexportations.
(12)   Avant 2005, commerce spécial.
(13)   Avant 1986, compris dans Antilles néerlandaises. Les données comprennent les exportations et importations de pétrole brut et produits dérivés. Avant 2000, non-compris les zones franches douanières. Importations f.a.b.
(14)   À partir de 1990, certains produits pétroliers et chimiques ne sont plus inclus dans les statistiques du commerce. Importations f.a.b.
(15)   Avant 1993, non-compris les zones franches douanières. Importations f.a.b.
(16)   Avant 1986, y compris Aruba.
(17)   Avant 1992, non-compris les zones franches douanières.
(18)   Avant 2002, commerce spécial.
(19)   À partir de 1990, y compris les biens destinés à subir des transformations. Importations f.a.b.
(20)   Non-compris les zones franches douanières.
(21)   Avant 2005, non-compris les zones franches douanières.
(22)   Non-compris les biens d'importation financés par l'aide à l'étranger.
(23)   Non-compris les biens à usage militaire, le matériel fissile, le combustible de soute et l'avitaillement des navires et aéronefs.
(24)   Y compris le commerce entre les États de la Malaisie. Non-compris les importations militaires et l'installation près des côtes de l'industrie pétrolière.
(25)   Y compris les transbordements vers et en provenance de la Malaisie péninsulaire.
(26)   Non-compris les exportations de pétrole et le gaz.
(27)   Avant 2001, commerce spécial.
(28)   Non-compris les importations de la défense.
(29)   Les données se rapportent à l'exercice budgétaire finissant en septembre.
(30)   Non-compris les biens à usage militaire, les métaux précieux et les biens fournis dans les ports étrangers.
(31)   Avant 1998, les données se réfèrent uniquement à la Fédération de la Bosnie-Herzégovine. L'autre entité de la Bosnie-Herzégovine, Republika Srpska, n'est pas incluse.
(32)   Avant 1994, concerne seulement le commerce avec les pays extérieurs à la CEI.
(33)   Avant 1994, concerne seulement le commerce avec les pays extérieurs à la CEI. À partir de 2011, y compris le commerce bilatéral avec la Russie.
(34)   Avant 1994, non-compris le commerce avec les républiques indépendantes de l'ancienne URSS.
(35)   Avant 1975, non-compris l'or industriel.
(36)   À partir de 1995, y compris les biens destinés à subir des transformations.
(37)   Avant 1988, non-compris les navires.
(38)   Non-compris les produits pétroliers.
(39)   Avant 1996, non-compris les zones franches douanières.

1.2.2 Annual average growth rates of exports and imports of economic groupings

Economic grouping	Exports (f.o.b.) - Exportations (f.a.b.) Percentage										
	80-00	90-00	00-10	05-08	05-09	05-11	2005	2008	2009	2010	2011
DEVELOPING ECONOMIES	**7.7**	**9.1**	**14.4**	**18.0**	**9.0**	**10.4**	**22.9**	**19.0**	**-20.7**	**28.4**	**21.5**
Developing economies excluding China	7.1	8.5	12.6	16.5	7.7	9.3	21.6	19.5	-22.1	27.5	21.9
Developing economies excluding LDCs	7.7	9.1	14.3	17.8	8.9	10.3	22.6	18.7	-20.7	28.5	21.5
High-income developing economies	8.1	9.1	11.6	15.0	6.4	8.0	19.3	17.2	-22.7	26.2	19.5
Middle-income developing economies	8.0	9.6	18.1	21.0	11.5	12.3	26.0	18.7	-18.7	30.0	20.8
Low-income developing economies	4.9	8.1	16.4	21.8	12.7	14.7	31.9	27.6	-19.0	32.2	31.5
Heavily indebted poor countries (IMF)	2.6	4.7	15.7	20.1	12.5	12.9	18.1	25.6	-14.5	26.4	18.7
Landlocked developing countries	9.2	11.3	21.0	32.2	16.6	15.5	29.2	36.2	-30.2	29.7	36.4
Small island developing States	-0.3	4.4	11.0	17.4	2.9	2.6	30.6	28.1	-40.3	20.1	20.0
Least developed countries	*5.0*	*7.6*	*19.5*	*26.6*	*14.8*	*13.6*	*36.2*	*30.9*	*-23.5*	*26.5*	*22.2*
Africa and Haiti	3.0	4.2	22.7	30.6	16.3	13.7	42.3	35.4	-28.1	25.4	22.6
Asia	11.0	16.4	13.0	16.0	10.9	13.2	23.5	17.4	-7.2	29.3	21.1
Islands	1.8	2.0	11.2	15.6	7.9	11.9	2.0	10.3	-17.6	24.0	51.4
Major petroleum and gas exporters	*0.9*	*4.7*	*17.8*	*22.6*	*9.6*	*10.1*	*44.8*	*35.2*	*-32.7*	*26.2*	*31.6*
Africa	-0.1	2.1	19.2	21.8	7.0	6.8	63.1	31.9	-38.5	33.4	12.6
America	2.3	6.3	12.2	18.1	4.5	4.9	40.5	35.8	-39.4	14.1	40.9
Asia	1.1	5.3	18.1	23.4	11.0	11.6	40.1	36.1	-30.2	25.3	36.4
Major exporters of manufactured goods	*12.8*	*10.9*	*13.6*	*16.1*	*8.3*	*10.0*	*17.9*	*13.1*	*-16.9*	*29.7*	*17.4*
America	11.0	16.1	7.0	10.7	3.0	6.1	13.1	7.3	-21.3	29.8	17.3
Asia	13.1	10.3	14.3	16.6	8.8	10.4	18.4	13.6	-16.5	29.7	17.4
Emerging economies	*10.9*	*10.3*	*11.0*	*13.7*	*6.0*	*8.5*	*14.8*	*12.5*	*-19.3*	*30.1*	*17.8*
America	8.5	11.8	11.0	14.9	6.2	8.7	18.0	12.7	-21.4	30.4	21.1
Asia	12.2	9.7	10.9	13.2	5.9	8.4	13.5	12.3	-18.3	29.9	16.3
Newly industrialized Asian economies	*11.9*	*9.5*	*10.0*	*12.2*	*5.5*	*7.9*	*13.3*	*10.9*	*-17.0*	*28.7*	*15.3*
First tier	12.5	8.8	10.1	11.2	4.9	7.5	13.0	9.2	-16.3	28.6	14.8
Second tier	10.8	11.5	10.0	14.6	7.0	9.0	14.1	15.3	-18.7	29.2	16.5
Developing economies: Africa	1.9	3.3	16.4	20.5	8.8	8.8	37.2	27.9	-29.7	28.7	16.2
Northern Africa excluding Sudan	0.8	2.7	16.3	22.9	8.9	5.3	39.4	34.7	-35.4	24.5	-4.1
Sub-Saharan Africa	2.5	3.6	16.4	19.2	8.7	10.5	36.0	24.3	-26.3	30.8	26.2
Sub-Saharan Africa excluding South Africa	2.4	3.9	18.2	20.6	9.6	11.3	44.9	28.6	-27.5	31.5	28.2
Developing economies: America	6.4	10.7	11.3	15.6	6.5	8.5	21.6	16.4	-23.4	27.0	24.4
Central America and Greater Caribbean Islands excluding Puerto Rico	9.1	15.4	7.4	10.7	3.4	6.3	15.2	7.1	-19.7	27.4	18.2
Central America and Greater Caribbean Islands excluding Mexico and Puerto Rico	3.4	12.0	9.8	10.6	5.5	7.2	27.7	6.2	-11.1	15.5	23.4
South America and Central America	7.4	10.9	11.5	15.7	6.7	8.8	21.5	16.4	-22.5	27.4	23.9
South America excluding Brazil	5.6	8.0	14.6	19.8	9.1	10.0	28.9	22.4	-25.3	24.9	28.4
Developing economies: Asia	9.0	9.5	14.9	18.2	9.5	10.9	21.8	18.5	-19.2	28.7	21.6
Eastern and South-Eastern Asia excluding China	11.8	9.6	10.3	12.5	5.8	8.3	13.6	11.5	-16.8	28.7	16.2
Southern Asia excluding India	4.6	4.3	14.6	17.2	7.8	9.5	34.6	23.9	-24.7	27.1	26.0

Source:
Data in this table are based on trade figures in table 1.1.1.

Imports (c.i.f.) - Importations (c.a.f.) En pourcentage											Groupements économiques
80-00	90-00	00-10	05-08	05-09	05-11	2005	2008	2009	2010	2011	
8.1	**8.6**	**14.1**	**18.8**	**10.3**	**11.6**	**18.0**	**21.4**	**-18.9**	**29.2**	**21.6**	**ÉCONOMIES EN DÉVELOPPEMENT**
7.8	8.2	12.8	18.5	9.7	10.5	18.1	22.1	-20.8	26.5	20.6	Économies en développement sans la Chine
8.3	8.7	14.0	18.7	10.1	11.5	17.9	21.1	-19.3	29.9	21.5	Économies en développement sans les PMA
9.7	8.8	11.1	16.4	7.5	8.5	14.6	17.0	-22.1	26.0	17.7	Économies en développement à revenu élevé
7.4	8.8	17.0	19.8	11.9	13.9	18.6	22.7	-15.8	34.0	23.0	Économies en développement à revenu intermédiaire
4.0	7.4	19.0	24.6	15.9	16.1	31.9	34.0	-16.4	26.6	29.3	Économies en développement à revenu faible
3.0	5.7	15.8	21.4	14.1	12.6	23.6	27.6	-13.2	16.1	20.9	Pays pauvres très endettés (FMI)
8.3	9.3	17.7	27.1	17.7	14.3	18.5	30.1	-14.5	12.8	24.1	Pays en développement sans littoral
1.1	6.0	9.3	17.0	7.2	5.3	16.2	20.1	-25.2	7.0	21.4	Petits États insulaires en développement
3.5	*6.4*	*16.6*	*23.1*	*17.6*	*14.7*	*22.8*	*30.2*	*-4.9*	*8.9*	*23.5*	*Pays les moins avancés*
2.7	4.3	18.5	24.8	19.1	14.1	26.8	33.8	-4.8	2.5	20.0	Afrique et Haïti
4.8	10.4	13.5	19.9	14.8	15.7	16.5	23.8	-5.1	21.5	29.8	Asie
3.5	0.7	17.7	19.7	14.4	13.1	18.4	26.1	-6.8	16.4	15.8	Îles
0.7	*3.2*	*18.2*	*26.7*	*18.0*	*13.3*	*21.6*	*29.0*	*-12.8*	*8.9*	*17.3*	*Principaux exportateurs de pétrole et de gaz*
-1.5	1.3	19.0	26.9	20.2	15.6	25.7	30.7	-5.6	6.2	22.8	Afrique
2.3	5.8	14.3	29.5	15.3	7.8	41.0	9.2	-22.2	-2.6	20.3	Amérique
1.2	3.4	18.5	26.4	17.8	13.4	19.1	31.1	-13.5	10.6	15.8	Asie
12.5	*9.5*	*12.8*	*15.4*	*7.7*	*10.5*	*14.6*	*15.9*	*-18.4*	*34.0*	*20.1*	*Principaux exportateurs d'articles manufacturés*
13.4	14.2	6.8	11.8	3.2	5.6	12.2	9.6	-24.3	28.6	16.4	Amérique
12.4	8.9	13.6	15.8	8.2	11.1	14.9	16.6	-17.7	34.6	20.5	Asie
11.2	*9.5*	*10.6*	*16.3*	*6.6*	*9.0*	*14.9*	*20.0*	*-25.7*	*34.2*	*19.5*	*Économies émergentes*
10.6	13.7	10.2	19.5	8.7	10.6	16.0	22.7	-26.6	35.6	21.1	Amérique
11.6	7.7	10.8	14.8	5.6	8.3	14.4	18.8	-25.2	33.5	18.7	Asie
11.9	*8.1*	*10.2*	*13.5*	*5.4*	*8.1*	*14.3*	*16.4*	*-22.3*	*32.0*	*17.7*	*Économies nouvellement industrialisées d'Asie*
12.1	8.1	10.1	13.4	5.5	7.9	12.7	14.7	-21.2	30.3	16.5	Première génération
11.2	7.9	10.6	13.8	5.2	8.8	18.9	21.1	-25.1	36.6	20.8	Deuxième génération
2.2	**4.4**	**16.2**	**22.4**	**14.9**	**12.9**	**21.6**	**27.1**	**-12.6**	**14.3**	**21.0**	**Économies en développement : Afrique**
1.9	4.0	15.6	27.2	20.2	15.0	17.8	46.0	-10.9	10.7	10.7	Afrique septentrionale sans le Soudan
2.4	4.7	16.5	20.1	12.4	11.8	23.4	18.8	-13.4	16.3	26.4	Afrique subsaharienne
1.8	3.9	17.4	23.3	16.2	14.0	27.6	25.3	-9.6	11.9	26.0	Afrique subsaharienne sans l'Afrique du Sud
7.8	**12.0**	**10.7**	**19.9**	**9.2**	**10.2**	**19.6**	**22.0**	**-25.5**	**29.6**	**22.1**	**Économies en développement : Amérique**
10.3	13.1	7.6	13.0	4.1	6.0	15.6	12.0	-24.5	26.3	17.4	Amérique centrale et Grandes Antilles sans Porto Rico
4.7	10.0	10.5	17.0	7.1	7.3	28.3	19.6	-25.2	19.6	20.8	Amérique centrale et Grandes Antilles sans le Mexique et Porto Rico
9.2	12.6	10.9	20.2	9.5	10.6	18.9	21.9	-25.1	31.1	21.9	Amérique du Sud et Amérique centrale
7.0	10.4	15.1	26.5	13.9	13.5	29.9	27.5	-25.8	29.3	26.9	Amérique du Sud sans le Brésil
9.4	**8.3**	**14.7**	**18.2**	**10.0**	**11.8**	**17.5**	**20.7**	**-18.1**	**30.9**	**21.6**	**Économies en développement : Asie**
11.8	8.2	10.5	14.1	6.0	8.5	14.3	16.9	-21.8	31.2	18.4	Asie orientale et Asie du Sud-Est sans la Chine
3.2	1.3	14.5	15.4	9.3	10.9	19.7	27.0	-15.4	27.2	16.0	Asie méridionale sans l'Inde

Source :
Les données dans ce tableau ont été calculées d'après les chiffres du tableau 1.1.1.

1.2.3 Annual average growth rates of exports and imports of trade groups

Trade group	Exports (f.o.b) - Exportations (f.a.b.) Percentage										
	80-00	90-00	00-10	05-08	05-09	05-11	2005	2008	2009	2010	2011
AFRICA											
CEMAC	3.5	3.4	18.7	20.4	7.8	9.4	38.9	40.0	-34.8	30.5	29.7
CEPGL	-3.3	-5.9	20.3	21.5	13.1	16.5	25.3	41.4	-20.5	54.4	12.8
COMESA	-0.3	1.2	18.9	25.6	13.3	7.4	38.5	32.7	-26.5	27.1	-20.4
EAC	2.8	7.0	16.4	21.9	17.3	14.6	21.9	29.4	-3.2	18.8	5.8
ECCAS	3.3	3.3	23.1	29.8	14.0	12.5	54.8	42.3	-35.0	28.0	28.7
ECOWAS	1.2	3.6	16.9	13.8	5.2	10.1	55.4	23.3	-26.1	36.8	35.5
MRU	2.1	2.4	11.0	10.3	8.4	6.8	11.5	17.4	-1.1	5.3	4.8
SADC	3.2	3.3	15.5	21.3	10.0	10.5	25.9	21.4	-25.7	28.0	23.4
UMA	0.9	2.5	15.4	21.8	6.8	3.5	39.5	31.4	-38.6	26.9	-7.2
WAEMU	3.3	5.1	12.1	12.7	10.8	9.5	9.4	23.0	-0.1	5.5	14.5
AMERICA											
ANCOM	5.7	7.5	17.2	22.4	13.1	14.3	32.0	25.9	-18.0	26.2	34.7
CACM	7.6	15.1	7.9	11.0	5.7	6.8	9.1	8.7	-12.2	14.9	18.8
CARICOM	-2.7	5.1	12.0	18.6	2.8	1.8	35.7	30.5	-43.2	18.4	19.9
FTAA	7.4	8.3	7.7	12.7	4.6	6.3	15.4	12.8	-22.3	23.3	18.8
LAIA	7.0	10.6	11.5	16.0	6.7	8.8	20.6	16.7	-23.3	28.5	24.0
MERCOSUR	6.0	7.0	14.5	19.3	10.0	11.6	20.8	24.9	-22.1	29.4	25.6
NAFTA	7.8	8.3	6.3	11.3	3.6	5.4	12.8	10.4	-21.7	22.6	16.3
OAS	7.3	8.2	7.7	12.8	4.6	6.4	15.4	12.8	-22.3	23.4	18.8
OECS	2.9	-2.8	4.2	9.9	8.2	4.9	3.3	26.6	-4.1	4.8	-10.2
ASIA											
APTA	12.9	12.2	19.3	21.3	12.6	13.6	23.9	17.6	-15.4	31.3	21.5
ASEAN	11.1	11.1	11.2	14.8	7.2	9.3	15.3	15.5	-18.6	29.4	17.9
ECO	7.3	7.0	18.6	24.8	12.1	11.2	30.0	30.4	-28.5	22.4	28.6
GCC	1.5	5.3	18.1	22.8	10.6	11.3	39.3	35.6	-29.9	24.2	36.2
SAARC	9.0	9.1	17.4	21.6	13.8	16.3	26.0	26.5	-14.2	34.3	31.5
EUROPE											
EFTA	6.8	3.8	10.7	16.5	7.7	6.9	14.1	20.6	-22.4	12.8	20.6
EU	7.1	5.7	9.4	13.6	5.0	4.7	8.2	10.6	-22.5	12.7	17.5
Euro area	7.5	5.6	9.3	13.7	5.2	4.5	7.2	10.1	-22.2	11.5	16.7
OCEANIA											
MSG	5.6	3.9	12.4	18.1	8.3	9.9	21.7	22.1	-23.9	30.6	20.8
INTERREGIONAL											
ACP	1.8	4.0	15.5	18.8	8.1	9.8	34.1	23.7	-27.2	30.4	25.8
APEC	9.3	8.5	10.6	14.6	6.5	8.3	15.5	13.7	-20.4	28.4	17.3
BSEC	10.4	17.4	17.6	24.4	10.8	10.5	25.5	31.7	-31.8	25.8	28.9
CIS	–	–	18.4	26.3	10.8	11.2	29.2	35.3	-35.9	30.6	34.2

Source:
Data in this table are based on trade figures in table 1.1.1.

40

Imports (c.i.f.) - Importations (c.a.f.) En pourcentage											Groupements commerciaux
80-00	90-00	00-10	05-08	05-09	05-11	2005	2008	2009	2010	2011	
											AFRIQUE
1.7	3.1	18.0	29.1	22.6	18.7	14.8	25.4	1.2	14.1	20.8	CEMAC
-2.9	-5.2	21.5	19.1	14.9	14.1	36.5	31.9	-4.5	14.8	20.9	CEPGL
1.8	4.4	16.4	23.8	18.7	14.6	31.0	43.7	-6.6	13.6	6.5	COMESA
3.7	5.2	17.8	25.6	18.4	16.6	29.3	28.5	-7.4	19.1	23.7	CAE
1.3	2.7	21.0	31.2	26.0	17.7	29.2	38.5	3.6	-5.9	24.6	CEEAC
0.0	3.8	17.5	23.8	13.7	13.9	33.5	19.1	-18.3	23.2	34.3	CEDEAO
1.6	2.8	13.2	13.4	7.9	7.7	21.0	19.8	-14.4	18.0	7.8	UFM
3.7	4.6	15.4	17.4	10.1	10.3	17.2	16.1	-14.4	15.5	27.8	SADC
2.0	2.6	14.8	24.3	17.0	12.2	10.0	35.2	-12.5	8.0	10.7	UMA
2.3	3.9	15.0	19.1	12.7	9.0	19.4	27.6	-13.4	7.1	8.0	UEMOA
											AMÉRIQUE
6.5	10.0	16.2	26.1	15.6	15.7	25.5	32.1	-20.3	30.1	28.4	ANCOM
8.4	13.6	9.2	14.6	5.3	5.9	12.9	13.9	-24.7	18.6	20.2	MCAC
0.0	7.8	8.4	16.1	6.7	4.7	19.1	21.0	-25.1	5.8	19.5	CARICOM
8.0	9.7	7.1	10.3	2.1	4.3	15.4	10.8	-25.2	24.1	16.9	ZLEA
8.7	12.4	10.9	20.7	9.7	10.8	18.4	22.8	-25.7	32.1	21.9	ALADI
8.1	13.1	14.9	31.4	17.5	17.7	19.9	40.9	-27.6	42.9	25.2	MERCOSUR
8.3	9.6	6.1	8.0	0.3	2.8	14.2	7.6	-25.1	22.8	15.3	ALENA
7.9	9.7	7.1	10.4	2.1	4.3	15.4	10.9	-25.2	24.1	16.9	OEA
7.3	4.9	7.0	13.2	4.8	1.4	15.8	10.1	-21.9	5.5	-0.6	OECO
											ASIE
11.0	10.1	18.9	20.9	12.5	15.0	20.1	22.5	-16.1	36.9	25.9	ACAP
11.0	8.3	11.5	15.9	7.2	9.5	17.3	21.9	-23.1	31.1	20.6	ANASE
6.8	5.6	17.2	20.1	9.8	10.0	20.8	22.4	-24.0	24.1	22.9	ECO
2.5	4.8	19.0	30.1	19.3	13.4	22.0	30.0	-16.5	8.4	16.3	CCG
6.4	8.8	21.5	27.3	16.9	17.6	37.7	37.1	-19.4	33.8	30.9	SAARC
											EUROPE
5.8	3.1	9.7	14.8	7.0	6.5	11.0	12.8	-18.6	13.0	18.0	AELE
6.7	5.1	9.8	14.7	5.3	4.6	10.1	12.0	-24.6	13.4	16.6	UE
6.8	4.7	9.7	14.6	5.4	4.6	9.8	12.4	-24.2	12.6	16.6	Zone euro
											OCÉANIE
2.2	0.6	13.2	20.3	11.1	10.9	8.7	22.6	-19.5	24.3	17.9	MSG
											INTERRÉGIONAUX
1.9	5.1	14.9	19.7	11.5	10.9	23.4	19.8	-15.9	16.0	25.2	ACP
9.1	8.7	9.8	12.9	4.8	7.3	15.1	14.6	-22.7	28.7	19.4	CEAP
9.6	12.3	18.3	28.1	12.5	10.4	21.2	28.8	-33.3	22.3	26.3	CEMN
_	_	20.4	32.6	15.6	13.0	24.7	32.1	-33.5	24.7	30.1	CEI

Source :
Les données dans ce tableau ont été calculées d'après les chiffres du tableau 1.1.1.

Region, country or territory	Trade balance (1) - Balance commerciale (1) Millions of dollars - Millions de dollars								
	1989-91	1994-96	1999-01	2004-06	2005-07	2006-08	2007-09	2008-10	2009-11
WORLD	-107 861	-68 212	-197 148	-273 220	-260 102	-280 866	-263 388	-233 713	-173 131
DEVELOPING ECONOMIES	18 691	-54 926	99 240	380 887	498 439	550 770	476 683	420 326	393 002
TRANSITION ECONOMIES	-8 813	5 101	35 665	86 507	93 920	106 122	92 374	105 922	125 564
DEVELOPED ECONOMIES	-117 739	-18 387	-332 054	-740 613	-852 461	-937 759	-832 445	-759 962	-691 697
Developing economies: Africa	4 026	-5 340	4 261	51 828	67 986	78 082	48 120	37 912	14 903
Eastern Africa	*-4 774*	*-5 989*	*-7 356*	*-14 831*	*-18 025*	*-23 406*	*-26 660*	*-28 965*	*-30 115*
Burundi*(2)	-143	-106	-87	-238	-280	-326	-315	-366	-460
Comoros*	-30	-48	-37	-86	-105	-134	-164	-191	-218
Djibouti (3)	-186	-164	-169	-247	-311	-400	-431	-386	-324
Eritrea (4)	–	-416	-449	-478	-488	-523	-555	-615	-580
Ethiopia (...1991)	-526								
Ethiopia	–	-789	-1 067	-3 176	-3 955	-5 258	-5 989	-6 569	-6 303
Kenya	-1 080	-832	-1 235	-2 866	-3 880	-4 962	-5 585	-6 262	-7 248
Madagascar*	-119	-112	-174	-786	-1 023	-1 562	-2 006	-2 013	-1 610
Malawi	-211	-121	-165	-549	-570	-793	-890	-1 088	-981
Mauritius	-376	-503	-558	-1 031	-1 324	-1 740	-1 906	-2 062	-2 143
Mayotte	..	..	-146	-313	-384	-483	-528	-547	-495
Mozambique	-731	-646	-671	-561	-596	-827	-1 203	-1 431	-1 880
Rwanda	-209	-158	-183	-325	-450	-637	-861	-1 052	-1 187
Seychelles	-128	-191	-233	-306	-404	-500	-507	-451	-377
Somalia	36	-36	-154	-436	-475	-588	-589	-577	-557
Uganda	-94	-555	-1 012	-1 123	-1 300	-1 559	-1 520	-1 552	-1 676
United Republic of Tanzania	-954	-861	-888	-1 727	-2 349	-3 162	-3 491	-3 772	-4 575
Zambia (5)	209	309	50	-210	186	448	389	812	1 409
Zimbabwe	-231	-761	-228	-372	-317	-400	-510	-860	-910
Middle Africa	*4 209*	*5 094*	*7 050*	*28 913*	*38 643*	*50 891*	*46 936*	*48 229*	*47 937*
Angola (6)	2 028	2 291	3 474	15 495	23 192	32 250	30 611	31 676	32 016
Cameroon*(7)	425	452	178	206	-16	-424	-922	-1 142	-1 409
Central African Republic*(7)	-6	5	31	-35	-53	-89	-123	-154	-179
Chad*(6)	-193	-232	-292	1 814	2 027	2 011	1 608	1 459	1 414
Congo*(7)	338	208	1 359	3 301	3 523	4 146	3 850	4 569	4 712
Dem. Rep. of the Congo*	475	550	154	-203	-258	-129	-200	200	399
Equatorial Guinea (6)	-14	-42	601	5 149	6 464	8 274	7 513	6 457	5 229
Gabon*(8)	1 175	1 884	1 574	3 233	3 824	4 931	4 688	5 265	5 860
Sao Tome and Principe	-18	-22	-30	-47	-59	-80	-90	-100	-105
Northern Africa	*-3 311*	*-8 398*	*-1 771*	*26 702*	*37 069*	*42 922*	*24 174*	*12 362*	*-9 052*
Algeria*	2 844	1 352	8 482	24 192	30 445	35 171	26 097	20 603	16 068
Egypt	-7 614	-8 170	-10 125	-7 113	-9 018	-13 473	-18 425	-23 633	-25 582
Libya	5 624	4 264	6 596	23 805	32 884	42 062	40 023	39 427	25 637
Morocco*	-2 467	-2 894	-3 768	-9 578	-12 502	-16 642	-19 173	-19 489	-19 740
Sudan (...2011) (9)	-415	-772	-213	-1 549	-1 415	2	330	748	130
Tunisia (10)	-1 644	-2 179	-2 742	-3 055	-3 323	-4 197	-4 677	-5 295	-5 565
Southern Africa	*3 638*	*-518*	*1 307*	*-10 268*	*-12 503*	*-14 169*	*-13 767*	*-13 743*	*-17 545*
Botswana*	-112	417	610	971	1 248	764	-141	-824	-1 212
Lesotho	-627	-864	-583	-768	-843	-969	-1 120	-1 247	-1 373
Namibia	-50	-188	-324	-438	-449	-663	-1 211	-1 460	-1 773
South Africa	4 533	248	1 669	-9 955	-12 383	-13 268	-11 261	-10 080	-13 071
Swaziland	-105	-133	-64	-79	-75	-32	-35	-132	-116
Western Africa	*4 263*	*4 472*	*5 031*	*21 313*	*22 801*	*21 844*	*17 438*	*20 030*	*23 679*
Benin*	41	-162	-266	-420	-641	-830	-946	-873	-821
Burkina Faso	-369	-278	-420	-829	-917	-1 162	-1 181	-1 082	-843
Cape Verde (11)	-125	-223	-226	-453	-558	-682	-733	-722	-749
Côte d'Ivoire*	751	1 059	1 405	2 231	2 158	2 353	2 654	2 886	3 523
Gambia (12)	-146	-193	-159	-239	-269	-288	-285	-265	-246
Ghana	-334	-435	-1 503	-2 398	-3 103	-3 921	-3 648	-3 389	-2 590
Guinea*	-45	-35	88	28	30	13	-16	11	-206
Guinea-Bissau	-62	-82	1	-42	-63	-84	-99	-107	-102
Liberia*	435	225	-164	-233	-283	-424	-455	-500	-524
Mali*	-162	-308	-259	-367	-447	-713	-843	-899	-749
Mauritania*	161	61	-79	-361	-213	1	-87	-21	129
Niger*	-91	-104	-125	-403	-460	-530	-838	-1 093	-1 256
Nigeria	4 977	5 546	7 732	27 166	30 691	32 159	28 235	30 288	32 324
Saint Helena	-12	-26	-31	-38	-59	-53	-39	-22	-22
Senegal (13)	-486	-366	-644	-1 789	-2 419	-3 219	-3 412	-3 213	-2 895
Sierra Leone*	-25	-97	-121	-164	-182	-226	-269	-345	-695
Togo*	-244	-111	-200	-377	-462	-549	-600	-622	-603

For sources and notes, see end of table.

Percentage of imports (1) Part dans les importations en pourcentage (1)									Régions, pays ou territoires
1989-91	1994-96	1999-01	2004-06	2005-07	2006-08	2007-09	2008-10	2009-11	
-3.11	-1.35	-3.10	-2.56	-2.12	-1.94	-1.79	-1.55	-1.15	**MONDE**
2.46	-3.82	5.50	10.71	12.29	11.67	9.43	7.65	6.60	ÉCONOMIES EN DÉVELOPPEMENT
-5.89	4.78	33.88	30.60	27.47	23.23	18.28	20.66	23.40	ÉCONOMIES EN TRANSITION
-4.62	-0.53	-7.45	-10.25	-10.61	-10.37	-9.18	-8.43	-7.68	ÉCONOMIES DÉVELOPPÉES
4.37	**-4.63**	**3.21**	**19.38**	**22.36**	**20.91**	**11.40**	**7.90**	**2.73**	**Économies en développement : Afrique**
-40.16	*-38.11*	*-42.49*	*-45.98*	*-46.78*	*-48.38*	*-50.13*	*-50.13*	*-48.18*	*Afrique orientale*
-63.42	-56.56	-64.18	-79.63	-81.99	-84.48	-83.86	-83.80	-82.88	Burundi*(2)
-59.86	-83.23	-73.07	-85.67	-89.59	-92.32	-92.96	-93.26	-91.57	Comores*
-89.20	-89.76	-84.75	-84.85	-85.60	-86.35	-86.19	-82.48	-78.86	Djibouti (3)
–	-83.37	-95.82	-97.62	-97.55	-97.69	-97.90	-98.18	-83.43	Érythrée (4)
-62.06									Éthiopie (...1991)
–	-65.75	-68.65	-77.92	-78.46	-79.84	-79.76	-78.06	-74.41	Éthiopie
-50.86	-30.39	-40.52	-46.83	-51.35	-54.24	-55.33	-56.26	-58.28	Kenya
-22.78	-18.63	-18.56	-45.42	-49.44	-54.59	-61.84	-63.10	-56.05	Madagascar*
-36.05	-22.64	-27.50	-49.82	-46.11	-47.36	-46.14	-50.76	-44.49	Malawi
-25.06	-24.56	-25.69	-32.04	-36.86	-42.35	-46.45	-48.42	-48.40	Maurice
..	..	-97.91	-98.05	-98.11	-98.38	-98.60	-98.69	-98.65	Mayotte
-84.86	-77.18	-59.21	-23.54	-21.82	-23.91	-32.55	-37.94	-40.96	Mozambique
-67.65	-76.99	-73.52	-71.34	-74.88	-76.10	-79.50	-80.57	-80.13	Rwanda
-73.45	-71.71	-54.87	-46.98	-52.53	-55.69	-55.81	-51.59	-47.03	Seychelles
52.07	61.54	-41.37	-64.54	-61.65	-62.79	-59.66	-56.95	-54.50	Somalie
-26.87	-53.45	-67.58	-53.33	-48.94	-45.46	-37.44	-34.48	-36.97	Ouganda
-72.25	-56.09	-55.75	-49.82	-53.99	-56.75	-56.04	-53.05	-53.25	République-Unie de Tanzanie
22.30	43.72	7.02	-11.13	2.88	12.88	9.90	16.59	24.81	Zambie (5)
-11.76	-24.17	-12.49	-16.23	-13.40	-14.78	-17.69	-26.54	-24.88	Zimbabwe
64.80	*81.68*	*87.50*	*150.37*	*162.19*	*161.66*	*123.53*	*114.15*	*104.76*	*Afrique centrale*
142.46	136.93	113.78	194.22	225.52	230.85	169.92	162.79	161.99	Angola (6)
33.43	40.57	13.29	6.99	1.28	-7.04	-19.56	-22.98	-25.93	Cameroun*(7)
1.00	3.52	27.14	-19.68	-25.29	-33.52	-44.21	-52.87	-55.87	République centrafricaine*(7)
-45.99	-51.01	-55.15	170.07	162.57	120.91	84.65	71.42	67.94	Tchad*(6)
50.78	37.94	232.27	233.10	192.64	165.73	134.98	137.38	117.08	Congo*(7)
28.59	62.67	24.07	-7.90	-8.66	-4.32	-5.58	4.02	7.63	Rép. dém. du Congo*
-22.67	-0.42	99.72	355.62	338.51	291.61	214.51	149.66	91.80	Guinée équatoriale (6)
139.04	217.08	169.93	212.32	217.59	225.11	193.09	207.60	194.96	Gabon*(8)
-77.52	-80.44	-92.00	-87.47	-88.98	-90.43	-91.44	-91.00	-90.82	Sao Tomé-et-Principe
-7.40	*-19.31*	*-3.53*	*30.09*	*36.71*	*34.80*	*17.04*	*6.82*	*-5.21*	*Afrique septentrionale*
33.29	14.82	89.99	118.59	132.75	124.38	77.91	51.72	36.60	Algérie*
-63.12	-69.86	-70.64	-40.09	-40.10	-40.08	-45.01	-48.31	-48.97	Égypte
106.84	94.23	164.90	390.00	520.19	574.16	481.43	404.85	288.07	Libye
-38.43	-31.09	-34.48	-45.78	-48.37	-50.30	-53.77	-53.01	-52.82	Maroc*
-52.63	-57.79	-13.92	-21.94	-19.12	-1.32	3.73	7.85	1.25	Soudan (...2011) (9)
-32.65	-29.44	-30.98	-22.36	-21.08	-21.47	-22.35	-24.17	-25.49	Tunisie (10)
15.77	*-0.97*	*3.78*	*-13.25*	*-13.94*	*-14.22*	*-13.84*	*-13.40*	*-15.24*	*Afrique australe*
-5.78	23.98	30.54	30.74	36.97	23.01	-1.55	-16.17	-21.04	Botswana*
-90.45	-84.01	-71.80	-52.86	-54.38	-55.09	-58.34	-60.21	-61.55	Lesotho
-3.97	-11.75	-20.65	-17.22	-15.00	-17.28	-27.11	-29.81	-31.77	Namibie
24.37	1.58	5.77	-14.47	-15.54	-15.07	-12.85	-11.32	-12.99	Afrique du Sud
-16.01	-13.19	-6.09	-4.12	-3.91	-1.62	-1.96	-6.74	-5.92	Swaziland
30.05	*24.49*	*23.07*	*47.19*	*42.91*	*32.82*	*23.06*	*24.76*	*25.52*	*Afrique occidentale*
16.86	-23.57	-39.90	-39.96	-43.99	-44.24	-44.42	-40.14	-35.98	Bénin*
-75.87	-57.55	-64.89	-61.89	-62.10	-64.11	-61.12	-52.54	-39.91	Burkina Faso
-95.18	-96.22	-95.48	-96.23	-96.55	-96.59	-96.20	-95.05	-93.78	Cap-Vert (11)
35.72	42.48	53.46	41.22	35.53	35.34	37.17	38.65	49.91	Côte d'Ivoire*
-79.04	-88.72	-92.76	-96.04	-96.20	-95.81	-90.04	-87.25	-79.48	Gambie (12)
-29.06	-20.91	-46.70	-44.08	-46.26	-46.63	-40.83	-34.41	-23.84	Ghana
-6.13	-3.89	14.93	2.87	3.35	1.69	-1.31	0.66	-9.41	Guinée*
-77.43	-65.67	2.44	-32.41	-40.08	-45.44	-45.28	-46.37	-40.34	Guinée-Bissau
184.10	53.85	-34.88	-63.85	-63.82	-68.15	-69.89	-70.46	-68.20	Libéria*
-33.34	-43.31	-29.90	-23.97	-24.09	-26.92	-31.00	-30.74	-26.45	Mali*
69.89	14.37	-17.58	-30.46	-13.94	2.13	-5.11	-1.45	5.18	Mauritanie*
-24.60	-27.22	-30.80	-45.46	-45.64	-43.60	-47.38	-51.50	-53.45	Niger*
88.70	81.13	83.61	131.10	115.57	92.74	73.20	74.22	67.26	Nigéria
-66.06	-83.55	-75.39	-61.31	-71.43	-62.04	-48.65	-39.62	-39.07	Sainte-Hélène
-40.35	-27.83	-39.53	-53.15	-59.56	-63.31	-63.16	-59.40	-56.33	Sénégal (13)
-14.34	-56.45	-89.19	-48.72	-46.63	-48.47	-53.37	-56.85	-63.54	Sierra Leone*
-48.31	-7.35	-35.04	-37.09	-40.94	-42.94	-42.36	-41.31	-38.57	Togo*

Pour les sources et les notes, se reporter à la fin du tableau.

Region, country or territory	Trade balance (1) - Balance commerciale (1) Millions of dollars - Millions de dollars								
	1989-91	1994-96	1999-01	2004-06	2005-07	2006-08	2007-09	2008-10	2009-11
Developing economies: America	10 510	-23 510	-30 108	42 270	38 684	16 841	-342	-10 753	-2 441
Caribbean	*-7 886*	*-7 306*	*-13 119*	*-15 966*	*-19 306*	*-23 678*	*-25 900*	*-27 209*	*-26 960*
Anguilla	..	-55	-85	-141	-188	-237	-215	-184	-143
Antigua and Barbuda	-219	-305	-337	-479	-569	-668	-630	-560	-456
Aruba (14)	-413	-348	-204	-11	67	-161	-324	-722	-774
Bahamas (15)	-796	-1 047	-1 427	-1 932	-2 200	-2 285	-2 188	-2 141	-2 241
Barbados	-490	-506	-846	-1 189	-1 205	-1 268	-1 239	-1 223	-1 192
Cayman Islands	..	..	..	-1 074	-1 054	-1 030	-983	-917	-860
Cuba*	-2 397	-1 151	-3 216	-5 412	-6 621	-8 505	-8 283	-8 159	-7 020
Curaçao							—	—	—
Dominica*	-60	-66	-88	-117	-135	-163	-187	-197	-190
Dominican Republic (16)	-2 320	-1 505	-3 383	-3 747	-5 242	-7 082	-7 498	-8 201	-8 082
Grenada	-83	-110	-179	-266	-304	-313	-306	-293	-282
Haiti	-184	-429	-716	-1 042	-1 124	-1 408	-1 514	-1 983	-2 122
Jamaica	-747	-1 328	-1 935	-2 927	-3 641	-4 663	-4 766	-4 557	-4 177
Montserrat*	-38	-27	20	-27	-28	-30	-29	-30	-28
Netherlands Antilles*(17)	-349	-650	-525	-1 353	-1 576	-1 793	-1 887	-1 888	—
Saint Kitts and Nevis*	-80	-114	-149	-176	-208	-240	-250	-245	-226
Saint Lucia	-157	-206	-307	-423	-480	-507	-466	-439	-454
Saint Vincent and the Grenadines*	-60	-86	-135	-207	-238	-278	-295	-314	-310
Sint Maarten (Dutch part)	—	—	—	—	—	—	—	—	—
Trinidad and Tobago*	509	609	576	4 527	5 885	7 489	5 654	5 244	3 749
Turks and Caicos Islands	..	..	-143	-326	-444	-537	-495	-402	-320
Central America	*-7 809*	*-11 575*	*-25 100*	*-35 279*	*-41 035*	*-50 896*	*-49 866*	*-47 661*	*-42 611*
Belize	-111	-97	-279	-365	-402	-449	-451	-444	-419
Costa Rica*	-374	-698	-593	-2 686	-3 224	-4 226	-4 041	-4 252	-4 315
El Salvador (18)	-717	-1 478	-1 910	-3 477	-4 070	-4 672	-4 474	-4 201	-4 078
Guatemala (19)	-560	-1 208	-2 556	-5 154	-5 899	-6 463	-5 935	-5 501	-5 280
Honduras (20)	-50	-169	-709	-1 606	-2 209	-3 128	-3 278	-3 179	-2 805
Mexico	-4 565	-5 395	-15 410	-17 732	-20 060	-25 194	-24 758	-22 723	-17 890
Nicaragua (21)	-363	-576	-1 221	-1 722	-2 032	-2 395	-2 419	-2 419	-2 438
Panama*(22)	-1 068	-1 954	-2 422	-2 539	-3 138	-4 370	-4 509	-4 943	-5 386
South America	*26 205*	*-4 629*	*8 112*	*93 515*	*99 025*	*91 415*	*75 424*	*64 118*	*67 131*
Argentina*	5 837	-1 578	1 737	12 066	11 713	12 219	13 736	14 064	13 122
Bolivia (Plurinational State of)	110	-333	-576	604	837	1 346	1 154	1 122	686
Brazil	10 688	-3 171	-2 458	37 705	38 958	30 513	22 964	15 088	16 260
Chile*	683	-887	907	12 178	16 436	15 110	11 884	8 887	9 537
Colombia	1 333	-3 409	626	-746	-1 698	-2 031	-1 516	-714	249
Ecuador	602	403	652	-15	238	289	-324	-1 479	-2 114
Falkland Islands (Malvinas)	-16	-4	43	87	96	104	105	103	56
Guyana*	-50	-48	-90	-198	-306	-400	-432	-478	-521
Paraguay	-290	-1 962	-1 249	-1 884	-2 525	-3 509	-3 795	-4 616	-5 359
Peru*	617	-1 788	-471	5 364	6 966	5 869	4 702	4 042	6 369
Suriname	-17	-75	-109	59	141	305	255	360	439
Uruguay	238	-853	-1 097	-487	-840	-1 523	-1 751	-1 975	-2 009
Venezuela (Bolivarian Rep. of)	6 471	9 076	10 197	28 783	29 008	33 122	28 442	29 713	30 417
Developing economies: Asia	6 383	-24 694	126 658	289 882	395 079	459 833	433 420	398 089	385 428
Eastern Asia	*10 823*	*-7 172*	*41 451*	*124 556*	*198 458*	*244 906*	*257 809*	*231 826*	*193 289*
China	3 421	11 392	25 289	103 809	180 296	245 393	252 072	225 577	178 673
China, Hong Kong SAR	-347	-15 748	-9 254	-13 292	-17 066	-22 278	-25 923	-32 533	-42 223
China, Macao SAR	62	-37	119	-1 370	-2 089	-2 733	-3 284	-3 891	-5 068
China, Taiwan Province of	13 007	9 892	11 207	13 908	20 877	20 599	23 403	22 208	26 357
Korea, Dem. People's Rep. of	-937	-353	-846	-1 309	-1 432	-1 478	-1 330	-1 198	-1 058
Korea, Republic of (23)	-4 524	-12 340	15 020	22 882	17 969	5 819	13 382	22 225	37 393
Mongolia	-173	21	-85	-71	-97	-416	-511	-561	-785
Southern Asia	*-12 217*	*-5 057*	*-7 308*	*-37 903*	*-49 832*	*-74 211*	*-90 857*	*-111 899*	*-124 642*
Afghanistan	-514	-326	-1 171	-2 044	-2 194	-2 325	-2 578	-3 393	-4 550
Bangladesh	-2 005	-2 639	-2 755	-4 185	-4 989	-6 278	-7 127	-7 930	-8 984
Bhutan	-17	-21	-74	-121	5	41	31	-89	-193
India (24)	-4 336	-3 578	-9 162	-41 006	-59 542	-87 219	-99 085	-114 075	-125 703
Iran (Islamic Rep. of)*	-1 974	6 602	9 541	23 062	34 838	45 433	42 707	40 170	42 156
Maldives	-64	-184	-291	-582	-718	-875	-908	-916	-937
Nepal	-434	-885	-775	-1 413	-1 776	-2 186	-2 822	-3 502	-4 237
Pakistan	-2 044	-2 601	-1 524	-8 924	-12 318	-16 551	-16 961	-17 501	-16 244
Sri Lanka	-828	-1 425	-1 095	-2 692	-3 140	-4 250	-4 114	-4 662	-5 952

For sources and notes, see end of table.

Percentage of imports (1) Part dans les importations en pourcentage (1)									Régions, pays ou territoires
1989-91	1994-96	1999-01	2004-06	2005-07	2006-08	2007-09	2008-10	2009-11	
8.76	-9.74	-8.20	7.63	6.30	2.83	0.14	-1.13	-0.26	**Économies en développement : Amérique**
-41.93	*-36.32*	*-43.06*	*-37.13*	*-37.96*	*-39.19*	*-44.34*	*-47.67*	*-47.93*	*Caraïbes*
..	-97.39	-96.15	-92.36	-93.08	-95.52	-92.80	-91.36	-89.21	Anguilla
-88.95	-86.99	-84.24	-86.88	-88.35	-90.89	-91.40	-91.10	-90.74	Antigua-et-Barbuda
-61.18	-19.46	-10.13	-0.48	1.47	-2.61	-9.32	-36.78	-37.73	Aruba (14)
-59.56	-85.62	-74.60	-76.96	-76.40	-73.66	-72.74	-73.18	-74.88	Bahamas (15)
-70.68	-68.60	-76.12	-76.94	-73.23	-72.80	-73.47	-74.58	-73.90	Barbade
..	..	..	-96.23	-96.62	-97.78	-97.90	-98.24	-97.97	Îles Caïmanes
-43.99	-41.55	-66.54	-66.82	-68.49	-69.47	-68.51	-66.31	-60.20	Cuba*
									Curaçao
-53.91	-57.43	-63.53	-73.66	-76.73	-79.68	-82.99	-83.91	-84.54	Dominique*
-75.09	-28.57	-38.50	-36.06	-43.59	-50.28	-53.52	-56.36	-54.09	République dominicaine (16)
-75.48	-83.07	-80.92	-90.21	-91.36	-91.32	-90.70	-91.20	-91.21	Grenade
-53.54	-78.96	-69.89	-69.67	-69.32	-73.19	-73.71	-77.91	-76.35	Haïti
-40.56	-49.40	-60.56	-64.75	-66.05	-67.65	-70.75	-73.27	-74.63	Jamaïque
-96.01	-90.11	-95.12	-92.02	-93.90	-91.96	-89.86	-91.65	-93.78	Montserrat*
-17.11	-29.56	-20.60	-69.04	-70.28	-68.89	-69.01	-67.80	_	Antilles néerlandaises*(17)
-74.55	-83.30	-82.93	-81.92	-85.08	-85.26	-85.00	-83.59	-82.12	Saint-Kitts-et-Nevis*
-56.14	-66.78	-86.49	-84.17	-84.66	-80.81	-76.02	-70.82	-71.45	Sainte-Lucie
-44.22	-64.88	-73.39	-84.37	-84.92	-85.79	-85.56	-86.79	-87.43	Saint-Vincent-et-les Grenadines*
_	_	_	_	_	_	_	_	_	Saint-Martin (partie néerlandaise)
41.69	41.48	17.01	75.71	89.26	95.88	66.83	65.05	51.09	Trinité-et-Tobago*
..	..	-94.73	-95.36	-96.27	-96.49	-95.83	-94.99	-94.59	Îles Turques et Caïques
-14.20	*-11.78*	*-12.83*	*-12.64*	*-12.80*	*-14.04*	*-13.95*	*-13.08*	*-11.31*	*Amérique centrale*
-48.62	-37.82	-58.48	-61.14	-61.81	-61.14	-61.71	-60.19	-57.45	Belize
-19.90	-17.39	-9.05	-26.95	-28.24	-31.34	-29.77	-30.92	-30.65	Costa Rica*
-54.10	-48.77	-40.56	-49.76	-51.99	-53.05	-51.43	-48.93	-47.20	El Salvador (18)
-32.51	-39.48	-49.65	-48.38	-49.16	-48.51	-44.48	-41.03	-37.77	Guatemala (19)
-5.16	-9.35	-18.35	-24.27	-28.51	-34.46	-36.51	-35.81	-32.35	Honduras (20)
-9.43	-6.46	-9.07	-7.61	-7.54	-8.38	-8.40	-7.58	-5.87	Mexique
-53.79	-57.73	-67.29	-66.18	-66.45	-66.05	-63.96	-60.53	-57.19	Nicaragua (21)
-74.84	-76.14	-73.48	-40.79	-27.38	-32.19	-31.30	-31.58	-30.12	Panama*(22)
46.41	*-3.27*	*5.42*	*42.37*	*36.94*	*27.56*	*19.93*	*15.37*	*14.85*	*Amérique du Sud*
126.11	-7.21	8.91	43.67	33.91	28.01	30.36	29.23	26.24	Argentine*
18.94	-22.58	-32.56	24.42	28.62	35.18	26.25	22.21	12.15	Bolivie (État plurinational de)
50.06	-3.33	-4.47	47.34	41.11	26.39	16.61	9.47	9.31	Brésil
8.85	-4.81	5.33	36.67	40.77	34.54	25.48	17.45	17.89	Chili*
25.98	-26.06	5.80	-3.25	-5.61	-6.41	-4.40	-1.81	0.20	Colombie
30.54	10.26	22.38	-0.83	1.79	2.34	-2.06	-7.91	-10.51	Équateur
-46.55	-10.04	92.18	134.88	142.78	162.40	174.64	169.66	85.77	Îles Falkland (Malvinas)
-16.76	-9.11	-15.18	-24.23	-33.23	-36.43	-36.57	-36.93	-36.00	Guyana*
-15.40	-67.79	-59.09	-50.85	-54.21	-54.59	-52.29	-53.27	-54.80	Paraguay
22.62	-25.00	-6.66	40.46	43.81	32.60	21.69	15.54	21.38	Pérou*
-2.37	-15.82	-21.95	6.70	13.69	26.58	21.55	26.48	28.80	Suriname
19.01	-28.57	-33.28	-11.67	-16.94	-22.26	-23.82	-23.99	-22.82	Uruguay
80.79	89.88	60.76	120.13	92.44	77.22	60.56	67.33	71.65	Venezuela (Rép. bolivarienne du)
1.26	-2.21	9.96	10.66	12.71	12.75	11.36	9.60	8.51	**Économies en développement : Asie**
3.98	*-1.29*	*6.41*	*8.36*	*11.71*	*12.73*	*12.98*	*10.79*	*8.42*	*Asie orientale*
5.99	8.67	12.53	14.52	21.73	25.34	24.43	19.66	13.90	Chine
-0.24	-8.42	-4.61	-4.37	-5.01	-6.09	-7.08	-8.29	-9.86	Chine (RAS de Hong Kong)
4.75	-1.67	5.62	-33.29	-44.44	-53.12	-64.86	-75.40	-84.08	Chine (RAS de Macao)
23.05	10.15	9.77	7.33	10.23	9.45	11.60	10.62	11.80	Province chinoise de Taiwan
-32.80	-26.53	-53.06	-48.67	-48.98	-46.21	-40.95	-35.21	-28.69	Corée, Rép. populaire dém. de
-5.76	-9.12	11.32	9.05	6.06	2.08	4.35	6.21	9.28	Corée, République de (23)
-19.05	5.47	-14.16	-7.02	-5.67	-12.23	-17.10	-17.35	-16.35	Mongolie
-21.89	*-6.80*	*-7.98*	*-16.32*	*-17.19*	*-19.68*	*-22.66*	*-24.78*	*-24.53*	*Asie méridionale*
-67.91	-64.91	-89.29	-84.88	-83.67	-82.89	-84.13	-87.50	-91.60	Afghanistan
-56.19	-43.15	-31.56	-30.15	-30.83	-31.64	-33.18	-32.42	-31.30	Bangladesh
-20.30	-19.02	-40.68	-29.98	-2.12	7.67	5.93	-11.76	-22.06	Bhoutan
-19.96	-10.43	-18.59	-28.40	-32.15	-35.18	-36.55	-36.86	-35.32	Inde (24)
-7.78	49.05	66.33	57.98	82.49	94.78	83.58	69.44	67.12	Iran (Rép. islamique d')*
-46.46	-69.26	-73.76	-75.27	-77.73	-77.01	-79.29	-80.19	-80.26	Maldives
-71.05	-69.72	-52.17	-62.91	-66.92	-70.80	-75.76	-79.61	-83.02	Népal
-26.98	-23.52	-14.58	-35.13	-41.73	-46.83	-47.30	-46.65	-43.27	Pakistan
-31.04	-27.99	-18.22	-29.61	-30.84	-35.36	-34.23	-36.57	-39.06	Sri Lanka

Pour les sources et les notes, se reporter à la fin du tableau.

Region, country or territory	Trade balance (1) - Balance commerciale (1) Millions of dollars - Millions de dollars								
	1989-91	1994-96	1999-01	2004-06	2005-07	2006-08	2007-09	2008-10	2009-11
South-Eastern Asia	*-14 042*	*-29 392*	*47 008*	*62 781*	*74 247*	*74 215*	*75 234*	*78 318*	*90 907*
Brunei Darussalam*	1 237	218	2 171	4 777	5 421	6 561	6 166	6 459	6 897
Cambodia (6)	-67	-338	-534	-853	-1 143	-1 408	-1 593	-1 694	-1 877
Indonesia (...2002)	4 412	6 571	19 728						
Indonesia	–	–	–	16 636	19 687	19 953	20 947	20 226	24 106
Lao People's Dem. Rep.*	-103	-303	-203	-285	-217	-211	-288	-345	-324
Malaysia (25)	154	-1 541	16 546	25 464	28 402	34 687	36 132	37 733	36 184
Myanmar	-51	-394	-806	1 350	2 292	2 544	2 649	2 947	2 145
Philippines	-4 117	-11 298	660	-7 105	-7 358	-8 288	-8 549	-8 484	-10 026
Singapore (26)	-6 830	-6 136	4 210	29 252	32 939	29 203	26 187	27 840	36 285
Thailand	-8 270	-13 385	6 040	-1 354	2 221	3 791	8 823	8 052	8 327
Timor-Leste (27)	–	–	–	-103	-122	-172	-237	-275	-299
Viet Nam	-406	-2 786	-804	-4 997	-7 876	-12 446	-15 001	-14 141	-10 510
Western Asia	*21 819*	*16 927*	*45 507*	*140 448*	*172 207*	*214 923*	*191 233*	*199 844*	*225 874*
Bahrain (6)	-286	229	1 166	1 090	1 935	2 675	2 680	2 596	4 087
Iraq*	2 042	-384	5 160	1 731	9 267	19 492	18 501	17 236	18 642
Jordan	-1 311	-2 121	-2 387	-5 561	-6 754	-7 678	-8 255	-8 347	-8 855
Kuwait*	1 524	5 360	8 404	27 935	36 340	47 509	45 794	46 954	52 163
Lebanon (28)	-2 328	-6 296	-5 778	-7 180	-7 602	-9 270	-11 122	-12 709	-13 638
Occupied Palestinian territory	..	-1 470	-2 120	-2 261	-2 451	-2 677	-2 907	-3 159	-3 399
Oman*	2 106	2 073	4 706	8 337	9 564	11 208	11 047	13 937	16 829
Qatar*	1 507	729	6 561	14 970	16 842	21 025	23 091	33 587	51 452
Saudi Arabia*(29)	15 378	24 727	35 590	113 683	135 148	160 887	146 032	146 453	157 369
Syrian Arab Republic*	1 127	-1 649	247	-1 061	-1 789	-2 124	-3 464	-4 180	-5 982
Turkey*	-6 988	-13 219	-16 811	-43 904	-53 377	-62 256	-57 171	-60 128	-72 127
United Arab Emirates	10 207	8 511	9 736	32 372	35 552	37 636	29 677	29 787	30 698
Yemen, Arab Republic	–	–	–	–	–	–	–	–	–
Yemen, Democratic	–								
Yemen*	–	-51	1 032	298	-469	-1 501	-2 670	-2 184	-1 365
Developing economies: Oceania	*-2 228*	*-1 381*	*-1 571*	*-3 094*	*-3 311*	*-3 987*	*-4 515*	*-4 923*	*-4 888*
American Samoa*(30)	-55	-183	-155	-144	-158	-150	-147	-163	-253
Cook Islands	-46	-55	-39	-80	-91	-100	-91	-82	-75
Fiji	-280	-321	-328	-921	-1 020	-1 164	-1 064	-1 040	-1 060
French Polynesia*	-768	-742	-796	-1 418	-1 552	-1 713	-1 746	-1 705	-1 540
Guam	-321	-298	-346	-460	-508	-529	-575	-593	-634
Kiribati	-22	-27	-35	-62	-63	-59	-56	-55	-65
Marshall Islands	-47	-51	-50	-69	-74	-78	-82	-89	-97
Micronesia (Federated States of)	-76	-79	-84	-116	-118	-123	-132	-140	-146
Nauru	33	6	5	-18	-30	-13	-29	-5	-3
New Caledonia*	-305	-414	-448	-686	-719	-1 136	-1 407	-1 781	-1 797
Niue	-4	-4	-2	-6	-5	-5	-6	-6	-6
Northern Mariana Islands	..	..	..	162		..	..	..	..
Palau	..	-36	-92	-99	-97	-105	-100	-99	-99
Papua New Guinea	-121	1 030	794	1 433	1 720	1 922	1 697	1 718	1 788
Samoa (28)	-74	-85	-81	-162	-177	-198	-190	-217	-242
Solomon Islands*	-29	9	-17	-67	-100	-112	-115	-135	-117
Tokelau	..	..	..	0	0	0	0	..	..
Tonga	-47	-61	-62	-102	-117	-133	-143	-148	-153
Tuvalu	-5	-6	-6	-12	-14	-18	-18	-19	-18
Vanuatu	-64	-66	-68	-124	-153	-202	-225	-244	-237
Wallis and Futuna Islands	..	..	-33	-53	-54	-57	..	..	..
Transition economies	*-8 813*	*5 101*	*35 665*	*86 507*	*93 920*	*106 122*	*92 374*	*105 922*	*125 564*
Albania	-224	-536	-910	-1 975	-2 444	-3 089	-3 488	-3 406	-3 255
Armenia*	–	-382	-562	-881	-1 357	-2 208	-2 679	-2 916	-2 753
Azerbaijan (31)	–	-197	482	3 761	8 802	15 327	17 606	19 108	19 692
Belarus	–	-868	-973	-2 021	-2 588	-4 615	-6 164	-7 892	-7 139
Bosnia and Herzegovina*(32)	–	-1 093	-1 980	-4 255	-4 756	-5 579	-5 856	-5 472	-4 814
Croatia*	–	-2 367	-3 811	-9 822	-11 455	-13 731	-13 604	-11 863	-9 435
Georgia (33)	–	-355	-425	-1 836	-2 762	-3 740	-3 927	-3 774	-3 841
Kazakhstan*(34)	–	928	2 879	10 978	13 391	21 005	21 071	25 750	31 376
Kyrgyzstan	–	-141	-63	-594	-1 008	-1 575	-1 684	-1 682	-1 706
Montenegro	–	–	–	–	–	–	–	-2 242	-1 856
Republic of Moldova	–	-165	-247	-1 212	-1 731	-2 431	-2 549	-2 537	-2 428
Russian Federation (35)	–	13 932	43 498	101 558	112 384	127 309	117 188	123 268	128 876
Serbia and Montenegro*	–	-1 700	-2 244	-7 393	-8 838	–	–	–	
Serbia						–	–	-8 848	-7 669
SFR of Yugoslavia	-2 239	–	–	–	–	–	–	–	–
Tajikistan (33)	–	-55	33	-346	-583	-1 058	-1 470	-1 625	-1 647
TFYR of Macedonia*	–	-464	-631	-1 268	-1 470	-2 048	-2 376	-2 476	-2 358
Turkmenistan (33)	–	523	293	2 381	3 631	5 055	2 923	1 790	1 567

For sources and notes, see end of table.

Percentage of imports (1) Part dans les importations en pourcentage (1)									Régions, pays ou territoires
1989-91	1994-96	1999-01	2004-06	2005-07	2006-08	2007-09	2008-10	2009-11	
-8.49	-8.56	13.72	10.36	10.66	9.61	9.53	9.15	9.92	*Asie du Sud-Est*
120.77	11.18	186.27	310.19	313.33	314.15	260.21	259.24	259.76	Brunéi Darussalam*
-42.68	-34.01	-28.54	-20.92	-24.36	-25.00	-26.81	-26.65	-25.85	Cambodge (6)
22.32	17.65	51.63	–				–	–	Indonésie (…2002)
–	–	–	23.97	23.34	21.53	21.27	17.95	19.26	Indonésie
-56.00	-49.03	-38.82	-34.35	-22.52	-17.51	-21.55	-22.13	-17.85	Rép. dém. populaire lao*
1.94	-2.08	22.80	21.68	21.85	23.33	24.95	25.19	23.23	Malaisie (25)
-1.57	-30.37	-33.34	61.70	89.78	77.71	69.17	65.63	45.87	Myanmar
-33.21	-39.89	2.13	-14.29	-13.80	-14.33	-15.63	-15.46	-17.58	Philippines
-11.51	-5.17	3.55	14.37	14.13	11.11	9.75	9.58	11.65	Singapour (26)
-25.54	-20.04	10.76	-1.06	1.25	2.89	6.60	5.49	5.74	Thaïlande
			-92.38	-93.31	-94.07	-96.22	-95.58	-96.02	Timor-Leste (27)
-15.85	-32.80	-5.12	-13.48	-15.27	-18.80	-21.08	-18.16	-13.00	Viet Nam
25.95	13.99	27.68	37.18	39.06	38.66	30.63	30.35	32.28	*Asie occidentale*
-7.67	5.67	27.08	11.32	18.80	22.97	23.28	22.34	35.93	Bahreïn (6)
23.75	-15.79	49.25	7.67	43.01	74.03	66.14	49.28	41.12	Iraq*
-53.99	-55.91	-54.10	-55.20	-57.16	-55.32	-55.41	-54.02	-55.12	Jordanie
27.42	70.07	112.81	178.47	200.74	223.28	203.37	205.39	224.72	Koweït*
-81.44	-91.10	-87.61	-74.56	-72.47	-71.69	-72.99	-73.65	-73.41	Liban (28)
..	-79.70	-85.51	-86.98	-85.93	-84.91	-84.54	-85.14	-84.72	Territoire palestinien occupé
79.41	48.32	90.15	86.67	86.86	71.12	57.54	68.89	80.50	Oman
96.00	32.17	206.24	154.56	111.16	93.78	90.22	135.59	208.07	Qatar*
60.78	93.13	118.55	190.78	188.34	177.87	144.05	136.18	138.46	Arabie saoudite*(29)
47.57	-31.42	5.98	-10.50	-13.90	-13.68	-21.94	-24.84	-36.15	République arabe syrienne*
-34.56	-36.14	-35.75	-37.01	-37.57	-36.76	-33.02	-33.59	-36.71	Turquie*
87.93	39.27	27.33	36.80	34.35	27.97	17.04	15.95	16.06	Émirats arabes unis
–	–	–	–	–	–	–	–	–	Yémen, République arabe du
–	–	–	–	–	–	–	–	–	Yémen, Démocratique
–	-0.34	44.64	5.30	-4.07	-14.64	-28.44	-22.50	-14.72	Yémen*
-43.17	-23.03	-25.99	-31.33	-29.97	-31.13	-34.78	-36.79	-35.71	**Économies en développement : Océanie**
-14.74	-39.20	-31.24	-25.54	-27.06	-23.74	-22.87	-27.77	-40.73	Samoa américaines*(30)
-91.39	-92.82	-86.36	-93.53	-95.05	-95.92	-95.80	-95.35	-95.43	Îles Cook
-41.85	-36.18	-36.81	-56.51	-58.60	-59.59	-57.83	-56.30	-56.85	Fidji
-87.60	-76.76	-77.70	-87.96	-89.14	-90.26	-91.13	-91.16	-91.09	Polynésie française*
-80.42	-77.93	-82.30	-89.73	-88.80	-86.65	-87.50	-89.74	-93.10	Guam
-85.36	-82.14	-86.44	-93.42	-90.16	-85.26	-78.78	-76.57	-77.30	Kiribati
-90.19	-70.64	-83.14	-76.59	-78.35	-80.61	-80.56	-78.69	-77.09	Îles Marshall
-93.55	-82.34	-79.29	-86.62	-85.99	-84.86	-84.29	-84.41	-85.37	Micronésie (États fédérés de)
190.92	24.09	47.51	-63.79	-80.33	-40.50	-36.64	36.46	63.31	Nauru
-35.38	-43.96	-46.81	-37.25	-33.32	-40.40	-48.77	-58.81	-56.74	Nouvelle-Calédonie*
-98.75	-93.22	-90.32	-87.82	-74.62	-75.34	-85.85	-99.65	-99.64	Nioué
..	..	..	24.40	..	..	..	..	..	Îles Mariannes du Nord
..	-69.99	-88.54	-89.74	-88.08	-89.15	-90.28	-91.39	-92.82	Palaos
-7.39	66.85	69.94	74.52	76.78	67.10	52.30	47.86	45.02	Papouasie-Nouvelle-Guinée
-88.35	-92.08	-73.49	-66.40	-67.70	-71.54	-72.79	-78.61	-81.71	Samoa (28)
-27.56	6.09	-19.60	-36.03	-43.61	-40.85	-39.20	-40.09	-32.61	Îles Salomon*
..	..	..	42.70	83.19	149.22	44.14	..	..	Tokélaou
-80.72	-82.21	-87.15	-89.76	-92.49	-93.42	-94.36	-94.67	-94.48	Tonga
-95.37	-97.67	-99.31	-99.31	-99.51	-99.48	-98.90	-98.47	-98.26	Tuvalu
-75.88	-70.39	-73.84	-74.37	-76.82	-79.23	-80.28	-81.84	-80.50	Vanuatu
..	..	-99.87	-99.93	-99.94	-99.94	..	..	..	Îles Wallis-et-Futuna
-5.89	4.78	33.88	30.60	27.47	23.23	18.28	20.66	23.40	**Économies en transition**
-48.88	-74.63	-76.66	-74.19	-74.35	-74.13	-74.83	-71.72	-68.27	Albanie
–	-57.05	-66.13	-49.19	-54.45	-64.41	-72.62	-76.09	-73.60	Arménie*
–	-23.47	36.53	77.15	160.16	234.21	259.84	273.39	256.93	Azerbaïdjan (31)
–	-16.79	-12.27	-10.85	-10.49	-14.80	-19.37	-23.41	-20.97	Bélarus
–	-85.97	-67.77	-62.95	-59.37	-56.91	-57.01	-53.89	-49.98	Bosnie-Herzégovine*(32)
–	-33.09	-45.88	-52.03	-52.19	-52.64	-52.27	-48.60	-44.27	Croatie*
–	-65.02	-59.27	-67.73	-71.49	-74.80	-75.13	-72.71	-70.50	Géorgie (33)
–	22.67	59.22	61.21	56.14	65.32	62.12	78.63	93.25	Kazakhstan*(34)
–	-17.92	-10.41	-40.39	-49.98	-53.64	-50.68	-48.27	-48.03	Kirghizistan
							-81.63	-79.24	Monténégro
–	-18.62	-31.58	-52.71	-59.03	-64.02	-63.98	-62.76	-59.39	République de Moldova
–	21.03	86.28	71.83	62.87	52.94	44.95	45.68	45.79	Fédération de Russie (35)
–	-47.27	-56.37	-58.06	-54.76			–	–	Serbie-et-Monténégro*
							-47.17	-43.67	Serbie
-12.91	–	–	–	–	–	–	–	–	RSF de Yougoslavie
–	-8.43	4.92	-24.99	-30.67	-38.66	-52.63	-57.43	-58.62	Tadjikistan (33)
–	-28.74	-33.81	-38.60	-36.21	-38.19	-41.65	-42.96	-40.96	LERY de Macédoine*
–	37.51	13.54	87.94	122.01	136.42	67.76	33.52	21.76	Turkménistan (33)

Pour les sources et les notes, se reporter à la fin du tableau.

1.3.1 Value of trade balance, and as percentage of imports of countries and geographical regions

Region, country or territory	Trade balance (1) - Balance commerciale (1) Millions of dollars - Millions de dollars								
	1989-91	1994-96	1999-01	2004-06	2005-07	2006-08	2007-09	2008-10	2009-11
Ukraine (33)	–	-2 000	281	-1 636	-6 633	-12 191	-11 869	-11 240	-9 784
USSR	-6 351	–	–	–	–	–	–	–	–
Uzbekistan (33)	–	42	46	1 069	1 337	1 316	1 475	1 978	2 738
Developed economies: America	**-110 673**	**-166 799**	**-403 671**	**-777 961**	**-827 365**	**-838 701**	**-744 253**	**-700 110**	**-684 189**
Bermuda (6)	-494	-505	-671	-973	-1 048	-1 114	-1 103	-1 048	-968
Canada	2 935	20 383	27 555	28 119	29 033	31 340	15 411	4 270	-7 498
Greenland	-14	-80	-90	-210	-269	-350	-390	-430	-449
Saint Pierre and Miquelon	-55	-48	-97	-43	-37	-40	-55	-59	-64
United States (36)	-113 046	-186 550	-430 368	-804 854	-855 044	-868 537	-758 117	-702 843	-675 210
Developed economies: Asia	**59 553**	**87 050**	**80 670**	**82 016**	**76 221**	**55 231**	**43 644**	**38 654**	**21 228**
Israel*	-5 188	-9 965	-6 674	-4 054	-4 296	-5 116	-4 383	-3 664	-4 114
Japan	64 741	97 015	87 343	86 070	80 518	60 347	48 027	42 318	25 342
Developed economies: Europe	**-63 748**	**67 895**	**-1 411**	**-21 317**	**-77 409**	**-133 026**	**-113 164**	**-92 762**	**-37 849**
Andorra*	..	-941	-1 005	-1 634	-1 689	-1 747	-1 713	-1 604	-1 499
Austria*	-8 020	-9 661	-4 605	-1 377	-674	-957	-2 820	-5 162	-8 822
Belgium*	..	12 326	12 288	17 333	16 719	13 325	13 857	12 553	15 111
Bulgaria*	580	-291	-1 778	-6 376	-8 673	-11 361	-11 035	-8 852	-5 469
Cyprus*	-1 587	-2 368	-2 822	-4 995	-5 883	-7 258	-7 579	-7 562	-6 828
Czechoslovakia (37)	-16								
Czech Republic*(38)	–	-4 726	-4 335	785	2 552	3 601	5 647	6 314	8 295
Denmark*(39)	3 127	5 576	5 549	8 496	7 239	6 571	7 825	10 280	12 906
Estonia*(33)	–	-728	-1 182	-2 893	-3 646	-3 990	-3 101	-1 771	-869
Faeroe Islands	66	61	-11	-95	-183	-180	-142	-36	16
Finland*	-99	9 036	10 786	8 204	7 621	6 930	4 974	2 442	-852
France*	-20 505	5 091	-2 246	-35 165	-52 615	-72 437	-82 362	-87 346	-93 176
Germany, Federal Republic of	–								
Germany*	–	56 854	69 830	196 268	220 294	242 388	239 611	218 957	204 958
Gibraltar (40)	-281	-308	-345	-374	-445	-509	-525	-505	-530
Greece*	-11 062	-14 481	-20 598	-39 120	-44 951	-54 547	-56 531	-52 250	-39 989
Hungary*(41)	355	-2 946	-3 369	-3 860	-2 261	-1 201	1 542	4 030	7 380
Iceland	-105	22	-476	-1 554	-1 974	-1 755	-758	109	548
Ireland*	3 267	11 584	27 684	39 850	38 108	38 277	44 089	50 254	56 446
Italy	-12 382	31 308	8 320	-12 941	-16 357	-18 838	-13 007	-22 322	-27 370
Latvia	–	-550	-1 348	-3 999	-5 307	-6 120	-5 026	-3 410	-2 471
Lithuania*(33)	–	-824	-1 775	-4 016	-5 409	-6 636	-5 508	-3 972	-2 738
Luxembourg*	-1 291	-2 094	-2 827	-3 517	-3 950	-5 064	-5 167	-5 250	-5 416
Malta	-776	-988	-863	-1 304	-1 385	-1 561	-1 596	-1 633	-1 664
Netherlands*	5 106	15 488	16 485	42 323	49 117	53 855	56 443	56 351	60 093
Norway	6 261	10 135	21 073	46 702	54 036	65 103	61 757	60 874	56 517
Poland*	2 389	-7 731	-16 659	-14 338	-17 973	-26 638	-25 541	-23 134	-17 151
Portugal*	-8 402	-9 818	-15 456	-22 687	-26 181	-30 882	-31 359	-30 448	-25 210
Romania	-1 410	-2 225	-2 915	-13 533	-20 402	-27 617	-25 955	-20 232	-13 305
Slovakia*	–	-1 123	-2 015	-2 664	-2 659	-2 659	-1 475	-898	688
Slovenia*	–	-921	-1 272	-1 131	-1 151	-1 753	-1 560	-1 372	-664
Spain	-31 291	-13 931	-36 564	-95 517	-115 601	-129 814	-113 393	-92 296	-68 468
Sweden*	3 697	14 299	14 326	20 759	18 352	16 854	13 732	11 740	10 556
Switzerland*	-5 846	1 785	-1 194	5 951	7 237	11 485	15 031	17 841	20 857
United Kingdom	-36 654	-29 017	-62 090	-134 899	-159 316	-177 888	-181 518	-174 451	-169 731
Developed economies: Oceania	**-2 871**	**-6 533**	**-7 642**	**-23 351**	**-23 909**	**-21 263**	**-18 672**	**-5 744**	**9 113**
Australia	-3 278	-6 398	-7 079	-19 458	-19 882	-17 835	-16 377	-4 724	9 044
New Zealand	408	-134	-563	-3 894	-4 027	-3 428	-2 295	-1 020	69

For sources and notes, see next page.

Percentage of imports (1) Part dans les importations en pourcentage (1)									Régions, pays ou territoires
1989-91	1994-96	1999-01	2004-06	2005-07	2006-08	2007-09	2008-10	2009-11	
—	-12.51	1.76	-2.48	-12.92	-18.40	-17.65	-16.58	-15.08	Ukraine (33)
-3.96	—	—	—	—	—	—	—	—	URSS
—	4.00	1.57	27.98	28.15	21.98	18.89	22.71	30.10	Ouzbékistan (33)
-17.60	**-18.06**	**-28.80**	**-37.95**	**-36.84**	**-34.68**	**-31.99**	**-30.35**	**-29.25**	**Économies développées : Amérique**
-90.31	-90.68	-93.58	-95.06	-96.75	-97.72	-97.63	-97.90	-98.11	Bermudes (6)
2.39	12.09	11.88	8.70	8.11	8.09	3.51	0.66	-2.16	Canada
-3.41	-18.72	-24.03	-34.22	-38.87	-43.88	-47.66	-50.95	-52.24	Groenland
-65.76	-83.90	-84.81	-69.69	-65.17	-65.77	-83.46	-88.60	-92.59	Saint-Pierre-et-Miquelon
-22.37	-24.57	-36.80	-46.64	-45.34	-42.78	-38.88	-36.44	-34.65	États-Unis (36)
24.49	**25.88**	**21.36**	**15.01**	**12.24**	**8.27**	**6.50**	**5.40**	**3.48**	**Économies développées : Asie**
-30.78	-34.51	-18.95	-8.74	-8.25	-8.52	-7.08	-5.81	-6.04	Israël*
28.54	31.32	25.51	17.19	14.12	9.79	7.76	6.40	4.32	Japon
-3.84	**3.12**	**-0.03**	**-0.37**	**-1.46**	**-2.27**	**-1.87**	**-1.53**	**-0.69**	**Économies développées : Europe**
..	-95.19	-95.56	-92.22	-92.33	-93.31	-94.80	-95.82	-95.87	Andorre*
-17.26	-15.44	-6.35	-1.10	-0.55	-0.54	-1.84	-3.31	-5.20	Autriche*
..	8.29	7.12	5.55	4.65	3.40	3.55	3.29	3.84	Belgique*
10.74	-5.49	-27.65	-33.94	-36.22	-37.57	-36.09	-29.74	-21.06	Bulgarie*
-63.79	-66.55	-74.30	-80.11	-80.46	-83.08	-84.14	-84.08	-82.13	Chypre*
0.56	—	—	—	—	—	—	—	—	Tchécoslovaquie (37)
—	-18.10	-12.72	0.85	2.54	2.96	4.85	5.29	6.53	République tchèque*(38)
9.66	13.24	12.20	11.32	8.71	6.80	8.40	11.57	14.52	Danemark*(39)
—	-27.83	-24.78	-27.14	-27.45	-26.66	-20.94	-12.84	-7.03	Estonie*(33)
21.08	21.29	-2.02	-12.58	-20.98	-19.10	-14.36	-3.41	1.85	Îles Féroé
-0.14	31.89	32.62	14.11	10.98	8.85	6.17	3.12	-0.65	Finlande*
-9.09	1.71	-0.61	-6.86	-9.29	-11.27	-12.96	-13.91	-14.73	France*
—	—	—	—	—	—	—	—	—	Allemagne, Rép. fédérale d'
—	13.02	14.41	24.76	24.13	23.16	22.73	20.76	19.22	Allemagne*
-81.93	-72.17	-73.72	-63.61	-64.10	-64.79	-64.91	-65.25	-67.19	Gibraltar (40)
-57.37	-57.37	-64.39	-68.88	-68.54	-69.62	-70.67	-69.33	-61.48	Grèce*
5.20	-19.02	-10.82	-5.83	-3.15	-1.47	2.06	4.88	8.14	Hongrie*(41)
-6.11	2.13	-19.04	-31.01	-34.40	-28.06	-9.75	5.63	13.50	Islande
16.76	37.29	55.95	59.38	51.21	47.81	59.87	75.96	89.57	Irlande*
-7.23	15.92	3.67	-3.09	-3.71	-3.84	-2.56	-4.52	-5.43	Italie
—	-28.92	-41.94	-43.61	-44.37	-43.20	-34.81	-25.71	-19.79	Lettonie
—	-22.02	-33.96	-25.33	-26.95	-26.91	-21.28	-15.14	-11.06	Lituanie*(33)
-17.35	-22.56	-24.48	-15.63	-15.38	-17.36	-18.01	-19.05	-20.41	Luxembourg*
-42.04	-36.23	-28.88	-33.59	-32.78	-32.61	-32.97	-33.22	-31.88	Malte
4.23	8.83	7.83	11.58	11.57	10.95	11.32	11.12	11.64	Pays-Bas*
24.30	31.19	62.46	82.34	82.22	83.29	76.40	76.18	71.20	Norvège
27.63	-25.23	-34.62	-13.70	-13.40	-15.52	-14.15	-12.44	-9.57	Pologne*
-35.36	-31.24	-38.86	-36.40	-36.81	-37.42	-37.96	-37.79	-33.52	Portugal*
-17.58	-21.94	-21.85	-32.04	-36.81	-40.01	-36.27	-28.91	-21.17	Roumanie
—	-10.51	-14.59	-7.33	-6.13	-4.72	-2.15	-1.18	0.94	Slovaquie*
—	-10.23	-12.58	-5.67	-4.58	-5.41	-4.57	-4.02	-2.13	Slovénie*
-37.43	-13.01	-24.53	-32.53	-34.40	-34.34	-30.17	-25.92	-20.90	Espagne
7.26	22.99	21.01	18.62	14.43	11.62	9.36	8.11	7.31	Suède*
-9.13	2.42	-1.43	4.69	4.92	6.88	9.03	10.43	11.51	Suisse*
-17.45	-11.13	-18.30	-25.57	-27.11	-28.13	-30.21	-29.83	-28.87	Royaume-Uni
-5.34	**-8.91**	**-9.04**	**-15.81**	**-13.98**	**-10.98**	**-9.11**	**-2.84**	**2.84**	**Économies développées : Océanie**
-7.40	-10.74	-10.13	-15.99	-13.88	-10.92	-9.44	-2.78	3.27	Australie
4.90	-0.81	-3.76	-15.05	-14.42	-11.37	-7.14	-3.10	0.09	Nouvelle-Zélande

Pour les sources et les notes, se reporter à la page suivante.

Sources:
UNCTAD secretariat calculations, based on:
- UN DESA Statistics Division, *Yearbook of International Trade Statistics*
- UN DESA Statistics Division, *Monthly Bulletin of Statistics*
- UN DESA Statistics Division, *UN COMTRADE*
- IMF, *International Financial Statistics*
- IMF, *Direction of Trade Statistics*
- IMF, *Balance of Payments Statistics*
- WTO, *Statistics database*
- Eurostat, *Comext*
- World Bank, W*orld Development Indicators*
- OECD, *OECD.Stat Extracts*
- OPEC, *Annual Statistical Bulletin*
- Economist Intelligence Unit, *Country Data*
- Other international and national sources

Notes:
(*)   Special Trade System.
(1)   Average of three continuous years.
(2)   Excluding exports of gold.
(3)   From 1996 onward, imports f.o.b.
(4)   From 2011 onwards, commercial mining is included.
(5)   Prior to 2008, special trade.
(6)   Imports f.o.b.
(7)   Trade with other member countries of CEMAC is excluded. Imports f.o.b.
(8)   Trade with other member countries of CEMAC is excluded.
(9)   Prior to 1995, data refer to fiscal year ending June.
(10)   Prior to 1974, special trade.
(11)   Excluding re-exports (oil for bunkering).
(12)   Prior to 2009, re-exports is excluded
(13)   Prior to 2005, special trade.
(14)   Prior to 1986, included in Netherlands Antilles. Including exports and imports of crude oil and oil products. Prior to 2000, free zone trade is excluded. Imports f.o.b.

(15)   From 1990 onwards, trade statistics exclude certain oil and chemical products. Imports f.o.b.
(16)   Prior to 1993, excluding free trade processing zones. Imports f.o.b.
(17)   Prior to 1986, including Aruba.
(18)   Prior to 1992, excluding free trade processing zones.
(19)   Prior to 2002, special trade.
(20)   From 1990 onward, including goods for processing. Imports f.o.b.
(21)   Excluding free trade processing zones.
(22)   Prior to 2005, excluding customs free zones.
(23)   Excluding imports of goods financed through foreign aid.
(24)   Excluding military goods, fissionable materials, bunkers, ships and aircraft.
(25)   Inter-trade between the States of Malaysia included. From 1965 onwards, excluding military imports and offshore installations of petroleum industry.
(26)   Including trans-shipments to and from peninsular Malaysia.
(27)   Excluding exports of oil and gas.
(28)   Prior to 2001, special trade.
(29)   Excluding defense imports.
(30)   Data refer to fiscal year ending September.
(31)   Excluding military goods, precious metals and goods procured in foreign ports.
(32)   Prior to 1998, data refer to the Federation of Bosnia and Herzegovina only. The other entity of Bosnia and Herzegovina, Republika Srpska, is not included.
(33)   Prior to 1994, covers only trade with countries outside the CIS.
(34)   Prior to 1994, covers only trade with countries outside the CIS. As of 2011adjusted to include bilateral trade with Russia.
(35)   Prior to 1994, excluding trade with independent states resulting from the former USSR.
(36)   Prior to 1975, excluding non-monetary gold.
(37)   From 1985 onwards, data are not comparable to those shown for prior periods due to revisions of the koruna-to-US dollar exchange rate.
(38)   From 1995 onward, including goods for processing.
(39)   Prior to 1988, excluding ships.
(40)   Excluding petroleum products.
(41)   Prior to 1996, excluding customs free zones.

Sources :
Calculs du secrétariat de la CNUCED, basés sur :
- ONU DAES Division de statistique, *Annuaire statistique du commerce international*
- ONU DAES Division de statistique, *Bulletin mensuel de statistique*
- ONU DAES Division de statistique, *ONU COMTRADE*
- FMI, *Statistiques financières internationales*
- FMI, *Direction of Trade Statistics*
- FMI, *Statistiques de la balance des paiements*
- OMC, *Base de données statistiques*
- Eurostat, *Comext*
- Banque mondiale, *Indicateurs du développement dans le monde*
- OCDE, *OECD.Stat Extracts*
- OPEP, *Bulletin statistique annuel*
- Economist Intelligence Unit, *Country Data*
- Autres sources internationales et nationales

Notes :
(*)   Système du commerce spécial.
(1)   Moyenne de trois années consécutives.
(2)   Non-compris les exportations d'or.
(3)   À partir de 1996, importations f.a.b.
(4)   À partir de 2011, l'exploitation minière commerciale est incluse.
(5)   Avant 2008, commerce spécial.
(6)   Importations f.a.b.
(7)   Non-compris le commerce avec les autres pays membres de la CEMAC. Importations f.a.b.
(8)   Non-compris le commerce avec les autres pays membres de la CEMAC.
(9)   Avant 1995, les données se rapportent à l'exercice budgétaire finissant en juin.
(10)   Avant 1974, commerce spécial.
(11)   Non-compris les réexportations (huile pour mise en soute).
(12)   Avant 2009, non-compris les réexportations.
(13)   Avant 2005, commerce spécial.
(14)   Avant 1986 compris dans Antilles néerlandaises. Les données comprennent les exportations et importations de pétrole brut et produits dérivés. Avant 2000, non-compris les zones franches douanières. Importations f.a.b.
(15)   À partir de 1990, certains produits pétroliers et chimiques ne sont plus inclus dans les statistiques du commerce. Importations f.a.b.
(16)   Avant 1993, non-compris les zones franches douanières. Importations f.a.b.
(17)   Avant 1986, y compris Aruba.
(18)   Avant 1992, non-compris les zones franches douanières.
(19)   Avant 2002, commerce spécial.
(20)   À partir de 1990, y compris les biens destinés à subir des transformations. Importations f.a.b.
(21)   Non-compris les zones franches douanières.
(22)   Avant 2005, non-compris les zones franches douanières.
(23)   Non-compris les biens d'importation financés par l'aide à l'étranger.
(24)   Non-compris les biens à usage militaire, le matériel fissile, le combustible de soute et l'avitaillement des navires et aéronefs.
(25)   Y compris le commerce entre les États de la Malaisie. Non-compris les importations militaires et l'installation près des côtes de l'industrie pétrolière.
(26)   Y compris les transbordements vers et en provenance de la Malaisie péninsulaire.
(27)   Non-compris les exportations de pétrole et le gaz.
(28)   Avant 2001, commerce spécial.
(29)   Non-compris les importations de la défense.
(30)   Les données se rapportent à l'exercice budgétaire finissant en septembre.
(31)   Non-compris les biens à usage militaire, les métaux précieux et les biens fournis dans les ports étrangers.
(32)   Avant 1998, les données se réfèrent uniquement à la Fédération de la Bosnie-Herzégovine. L'autre entité de la Bosnie-Herzégovine, Republika Srpska, n'est pas incluse.
(33)   Avant 1994, concerne seulement le commerce avec les pays extérieurs à la CEI.
(34)   Avant 1994, concerne seulement le commerce avec les pays extérieurs à la CEI. À partir de 2011, y compris le commerce bilatéral avec la Russie.
(35)   Avant 1994, non-compris le commerce avec les républiques indépendantes de l'ancienne URSS.
(36)   Avant 1975, non-compris l'or industriel.
(37)   À partir de 1985, les chiffres ne sont pas comparables à ceux des années antérieures à cause des révisions du taux de change de la couronne par rapport au dollar des États-Unis.
(38)   À partir de 1995, y compris les biens destinés à subir des transformations.
(39)   Avant 1988, non-compris les navires.
(40)   Non-compris les produits pétroliers.
(41)   Avant 1996, non-compris les zones franches douanières.

Economic grouping	Trade balance (1) - Balance commerciale (1) Millions of dollars - Millions de dollars								
	1989-91	1994-96	1999-01	2004-06	2005-07	2006-08	2007-09	2008-10	2009-11
DEVELOPING ECONOMIES	**18 691**	**-54 926**	**99 240**	**380 887**	**498 439**	**550 770**	**476 683**	**420 326**	**393 002**
Developing economies excluding China	15 270	-66 317	73 951	277 078	318 143	305 377	224 611	194 750	214 329
Developing economies excluding LDCs	25 781	-45 128	109 661	384 995	497 673	546 326	481 562	428 216	405 707
High-income developing economies	34 103	-4 249	81 262	284 713	327 817	355 700	329 583	341 769	372 808
Middle-income developing economies	-11 324	-43 403	10 644	119 905	203 755	253 698	233 959	182 628	127 159
Low-income developing economies	-4 089	-7 274	7 432	-23 419	-32 749	-58 146	-86 331	-103 541	-106 470
Heavily indebted poor countries (IMF)	-3 433	-6 194	-10 641	-18 174	-22 965	-28 948	-33 517	-34 361	-34 988
Landlocked developing countries	-4 292	-7 397	-5 698	2 984	8 838	16 878	11 139	11 356	15 296
Small island developing States	-3 658	-4 016	-6 224	-6 119	-6 629	-7 362	-9 672	-9 912	-11 055
Least developed countries	*-7 090*	*-9 798*	*-10 420*	*-4 108*	*765*	*4 444*	*-4 879*	*-7 890*	*-12 705*
Africa and Haiti	-2 496	-4 597	-4 861	3 809	10 049	16 743	10 615	9 536	7 981
Asia	-4 352	-4 956	-5 287	-7 253	-8 491	-11 325	-14 398	-16 190	-19 385
Islands	-242	-245	-272	-664	-793	-974	-1 095	-1 235	-1 301
Major petroleum and gas exporters	*52 735*	*70 145*	*116 179*	*341 531*	*423 769*	*517 951*	*470 257*	*479 831*	*505 770*
Africa	15 473	13 452	26 284	90 658	117 210	141 642	124 966	121 994	106 045
America	6 471	9 076	10 197	28 783	29 008	33 122	28 442	29 713	30 417
Asia	30 791	47 617	79 698	222 090	277 551	343 188	316 849	328 125	369 309
Major exporters of manufactured goods	*-7 953*	*-33 261*	*53 649*	*162 936*	*245 577*	*292 021*	*309 318*	*288 378*	*263 106*
America	-4 565	-5 395	-15 410	-17 732	-20 060	-25 194	-24 758	-22 723	-17 890
Asia	-3 388	-27 866	69 058	180 668	265 638	317 214	334 076	311 101	280 996
Emerging economies	*6 797*	*-36 329*	*37 329*	*139 732*	*156 421*	*132 616*	*136 454*	*137 415*	*171 944*
America	13 260	-12 819	-15 694	49 581	54 013	38 517	28 528	19 358	27 398
Asia	-6 462	-23 510	53 023	90 151	102 408	94 099	107 926	118 057	144 546
Newly industrialized Asian economies	*-6 514*	*-43 985*	*64 156*	*86 390*	*97 672*	*83 486*	*94 401*	*97 267*	*116 402*
First tier	1 306	-24 331	21 183	52 749	54 718	33 343	37 049	39 740	57 812
Second tier	-7 820	-19 654	42 973	33 641	42 953	50 143	57 352	57 527	58 590
Developing economies: Africa	**4 026**	**-5 340**	**4 261**	**51 828**	**67 986**	**78 082**	**48 120**	**37 912**	**14 903**
Northern Africa excluding Sudan	-3 258	-7 626	-1 557	28 251	38 485	42 920	23 845	11 613	-9 182
Sub-Saharan Africa	7 284	2 286	5 819	23 578	29 502	35 162	24 275	26 299	24 085
Sub-Saharan Africa excluding South Africa	2 752	2 038	4 149	33 532	41 885	48 431	35 536	36 379	37 156
Developing economies: America	**10 510**	**-23 510**	**-30 108**	**42 270**	**38 684**	**16 841**	**-342**	**-10 753**	**-2 441**
Central America and Greater Caribbean Islands excluding Puerto Rico	-13 458	-15 988	-34 351	-48 408	-57 663	-72 554	-71 927	-70 562	-64 013
Central America and Greater Caribbean Islands excluding Mexico and Puerto Rico	-8 893	-10 594	-18 941	-30 675	-37 603	-47 361	-47 169	-47 839	-46 123
South America and Central America	18 396	-16 204	-16 988	58 236	57 990	40 519	25 558	16 457	24 519
South America excluding Brazil	15 517	-1 458	10 570	55 810	60 067	60 903	52 460	49 029	50 871
Developing economies: Asia	**6 383**	**-24 694**	**126 658**	**289 882**	**395 079**	**459 833**	**433 420**	**398 089**	**385 428**
Eastern and South-Eastern Asia excluding China	-6 640	-47 956	63 169	83 529	92 409	73 728	80 971	84 568	105 523
Southern Asia excluding India	-7 880	-1 479	1 855	3 102	9 709	13 008	8 228	2 177	1 061

Source:
Data in this table are based on trade figures in table 1.1.1.

Notes:
(1)   Average of three continuous years.

Percentage of imports (1) Part dans les importations en pourcentage (1)									Groupements économiques
1989-91	1994-96	1999-01	2004-06	2005-07	2006-08	2007-09	2008-10	2009-11	
2.46	-3.82	5.50	10.71	12.29	11.67	9.43	7.65	6.60	**ÉCONOMIES EN DÉVELOPPEMENT**
2.27	-5.03	4.61	9.78	9.94	8.27	5.58	4.46	4.50	Économies en développement sans la Chine
3.46	-3.21	6.25	11.13	12.61	11.89	9.82	8.06	7.05	Économies en développement sans les PMA
7.85	-0.62	7.69	15.94	16.27	15.17	13.62	13.48	13.82	Économies en développement à revenu élevé
-4.76	-9.97	2.03	8.96	13.38	14.41	12.39	8.76	5.74	Économies en développement à revenu intermédiaire
-4.01	-4.72	3.65	-5.56	-6.03	-7.98	-11.52	-12.66	-11.83	Économies en développement à revenu faible
-15.07	-20.68	-27.86	-24.38	-25.63	-26.14	-28.10	-26.73	-25.43	Pays pauvres très endettés (FMI)
-29.22	-21.81	-15.53	2.77	8.68	13.52	7.92	7.29	8.51	Pays en développement sans littoral
-32.62	-29.37	-36.87	-24.24	-21.76	-20.39	-27.58	-28.65	-31.66	Petits États insulaires en développement
-29.21	*-29.68*	*-23.77*	*-5.76*	*0.25*	*3.35*	*-3.01*	*-5.10*	*-7.70*	*Pays les moins avancés*
-15.08	-22.93	-19.70	5.69	14.30	19.55	11.52	8.89	6.58	Afrique et Haïti
-57.44	-39.58	-28.17	-23.67	-22.91	-24.84	-29.05	-29.36	-30.05	Asie
-64.17	-53.46	-63.52	-71.38	-73.03	-74.35	-75.58	-77.20	-75.34	Îles
52.78	*62.71*	*77.60*	*104.20*	*108.31*	*104.09*	*82.16*	*78.14*	*78.33*	*Principaux exportateurs de pétrole et de gaz*
69.84	59.74	101.34	161.60	174.24	166.25	124.86	110.09	88.78	Afrique
80.79	89.88	60.76	120.13	92.44	77.22	60.56	67.33	71.65	Amérique
44.41	60.59	74.64	90.04	95.26	93.01	74.68	71.57	76.39	Asie
-1.65	*-3.88*	*5.11*	*7.53*	*10.00*	*10.55*	*10.96*	*9.51*	*8.16*	*Principaux exportateurs d'articles manufacturés*
-9.43	-6.46	-9.07	-7.61	-7.54	-8.38	-8.40	-7.58	-5.87	Amérique
-0.76	-3.45	7.72	9.45	12.17	12.82	13.16	11.34	9.57	Asie
2.66	*-5.56*	*4.87*	*10.94*	*10.73*	*8.22*	*8.43*	*7.92*	*9.20*	*Économies émergentes*
17.39	-7.49	-5.78	12.56	12.03	7.93	5.55	3.60	4.61	Amérique
-2.19	-4.77	10.59	10.23	10.16	8.40	9.81	10.02	11.45	Asie
-1.41	*-5.86*	*8.36*	*6.62*	*6.59*	*5.19*	*5.91*	*5.69*	*6.40*	*Économies nouvellement industrialisées d'Asie*
0.76	-4.51	3.82	5.57	5.14	2.94	3.28	3.24	4.36	Première génération
-7.54	-9.37	21.25	9.55	10.57	11.26	13.04	12.20	11.84	Deuxième génération
4.37	-4.63	3.21	19.38	22.36	20.91	11.40	7.90	2.73	**Économies en développement : Afrique**
-7.08	-18.07	-3.17	34.50	41.55	37.97	18.05	6.77	-5.55	Afrique septentrionale sans le Soudan
12.85	3.02	6.93	12.86	14.13	13.46	8.45	8.52	6.81	Afrique subsaharienne
7.23	3.98	7.77	29.27	31.29	29.03	18.78	17.41	15.67	Afrique subsaharienne sans l'Afrique du Sud
8.76	-9.74	-8.20	7.63	6.30	2.83	0.14	-1.13	-0.26	**Économies en développement : Amérique**
-20.78	-14.64	-16.11	-15.88	-16.51	-18.24	-18.37	-17.67	-15.58	Amérique centrale et Grandes Antilles sans Porto Rico
-45.73	-39.14	-43.43	-44.18	-45.44	-48.57	-47.92	-47.56	-44.85	Amérique centrale et Grandes Antilles sans le Mexique et Porto Rico
17.77	-7.41	-5.07	11.46	10.09	6.34	3.67	2.28	3.01	Amérique du Sud et Amérique centrale
44.63	-2.28	11.68	39.56	34.64	28.41	22.07	19.28	18.61	Amérique du Sud sans le Brésil
1.26	-2.21	9.96	10.66	12.71	12.75	11.36	9.60	8.51	**Économies en développement : Asie**
-1.40	-6.25	7.98	6.14	5.98	4.43	4.83	4.68	5.47	Asie orientale et Asie du Sud-Est sans la Chine
-22.53	-3.66	4.34	2.54	9.06	10.83	6.37	1.43	0.19	Asie méridionale sans l'Inde

Source :
Les données dans ce tableau ont été calculées d'après les chiffres du tableau 1.1.1.

Notes :
(1) Moyenne de trois années consécutives.

Trade group	Value of intra-trade (exports in millions of dollars) Valeur du commerce interne au groupement (exportations en millions de dollars)						Intra-trade of groups regional exports Commerce interne des exportations régionales		
	1995	2000	2005	2009	2010	2011	1995	2000	2005
AFRICA									
CEMAC	84	101	305	719	881	772	33.8	34.0	38.3
CEPGL	5	4	26	45	54	91	3.6	15.9	9.6
COMESA	1 366	1 409	3 339	7 538	9 538	7 776	41.7	45.2	53.5
EAC	539	496	1 165	2 133	2 621	2 607	61.2	59.7	55.1
ECCAS	123	157	394	1 153	1 461	1 075	30.2	46.1	28.0
ECOWAS	2 167	2 732	6 330	7 673	8 874	11 928	79.9	74.2	66.9
MRU	103	111	238	191	165	339	11.4	8.8	10.9
SADC	..	6 428	9 484	16 266	19 393	20 121	..	83.6	75.0
UMA	1 232	1 095	1 906	3 245	3 840	4 704	71.0	71.8	60.0
WAEMU	1 054	972	1 723	2 286	2 547	2 792	57.9	49.3	43.8
AMERICA									
ANCOM	1 804	2 039	4 574	5 977	7 932	9 378	14.5	11.2	12.5
CACM	1 470	2 413	3 727	4 932	5 549	6 105	22.6	20.1	22.1
CARICOM	842	1 250	1 982	1 948	2 481	2 973	22.8	21.5	16.9
FTAA	528 392	866 024	1 114 457	1 120 341	1 392 748	1 653 736	99.3	99.1	98.7
LAIA	36 118	44 481	74 149	102 136	130 289	161 267	25.5	17.3	19.6
MERCOSUR	14 451	17 724	21 118	32 724	43 782	53 663	42.9	38.4	26.6
NAFTA	392 902	681 263	824 515	768 105	955 315	1 101 189	87.2	90.8	90.4
OAS	529 614	867 936	1 118 430	1 125 787	1 399 771	1 662 675	99.4	99.3	99.0
OECS	31	29	35	51	58	49	20.2	20.6	27.6
ASIA									
APTA	21 988	37 785	128 116	205 059	278 579	325 708	12.8	15.8	22.2
ASEAN	80 081	98 189	165 401	198 923	263 024	311 033	41.9	39.1	39.4
ECO	4 892	4 624	14 624	24 953	33 929	42 302	24.5	16.0	20.5
GCC	7 027	8 327	19 416	32 306	32 838	44 130	9.6	6.6	6.9
SAARC	2 436	2 935	9 111	11 668	16 602	20 123	13.7	13.7	15.8
EUROPE									
EFTA	927	842	1 220	2 108	2 088	2 945	1.0	0.8	0.7
EU	1 412 159	1 607 617	2 725 265	3 026 693	3 329 971	3 869 925	91.0	92.4	91.0
Euro area	883 483	956 746	1 619 978	1 791 332	1 945 733	2 243 062	70.4	69.8	68.8
OCEANIA									
MSG	..	18	43	62	78	94	0.0	1.6	2.2
INTERREGIONAL									
ACP	..	14 073	27 478	44 664	53 360	57 330	..	..	..
APEC	1 679 827	2 268 116	3 313 934	3 746 109	4 874 714	5 680 394	..	..	..
BSEC	24 698	24 667	66 213	87 916	119 506	128 413	..	..	..
CIS	29 305	29 271	61 306	87 107	107 179	96 645	..	..	..

Source:
UNCTAD secretariat calculations, based on UNCTAD, *UNCTADstat* Merchandise Trade Matrix

as percentage of of each group du groupement en pourcentage de chaque groupement			Intra-trade of groups as percentage of total exports of each group Commerce interne du groupement en pourcentage des exportations totales de chaque groupement						Groupements commerciaux
2009	2010	2011	1995	2000	2005	2009	2010	2011	
									AFRIQUE
52.2	49.8	44.9	1.4	1.2	1.3	2.7	2.5	1.7	CEMAC
5.2	3.5	..	0.3	0.4	1.0	1.2	0.9	1.4	CEPGL
60.7	61.1	52.0	5.6	4.8	5.2	7.9	7.9	8.1	COMESA
52.9	52.3	50.2	17.2	17.8	18.5	19.9	20.6	19.4	CAE
29.2	26.1	29.2	1.1	0.9	0.8	1.6	1.6	0.9	CEEAC
56.4	54.7	60.4	9.7	9.1	8.8	10.2	8.3	8.2	CEDEAO
6.0	4.9	9.9	1.9	2.4	2.9	1.6	1.3	2.6	UFM
75.1	75.9	78.8	..	12.4	9.3	12.1	11.2	9.9	SADC
61.8	59.5	63.5	3.9	2.3	1.9	2.9	2.7	3.6	UMA
35.9	37.1	37.5	16.1	15.3	14.3	12.6	13.3	12.6	UEMOA
									AMÉRIQUE
12.1	12.8	11.2	8.5	7.8	9.0	7.6	8.0	7.0	ANCOM
25.4	24.7	23.2	15.7	16.0	17.0	18.9	18.8	17.4	MCAC
19.1	18.8	19.2	14.5	15.3	13.6	13.1	14.0	14.1	CARICOM
99.0	99.1	99.0	52.8	61.3	60.5	54.2	54.8	54.7	ZLEA
25.4	25.7	26.0	17.4	13.6	14.0	15.9	15.9	15.9	ALADI
38.2	40.0	39.8	20.5	20.9	12.9	15.1	15.8	15.2	MERCOSUR
85.6	85.2	84.4	46.0	55.7	55.7	48.0	48.7	48.3	ALENA
99.4	99.4	99.4	52.9	61.3	60.7	54.4	55.0	54.9	OEA
27.8	27.1	25.2	10.1	8.9	11.3	12.7	13.8	13.1	OECO
									ASIE
23.4	24.5	23.2	7.0	7.9	11.0	11.6	12.1	11.7	ACAP
37.0	36.8	36.3	24.9	23.0	25.3	24.5	25.0	25.0	ANASE
21.1	21.4	21.2	8.1	5.6	7.4	8.9	9.9	9.6	ECO
7.9	6.3	6.5	6.8	4.8	4.9	6.4	5.1	5.0	CCG
11.2	12.2	11.8	5.1	4.6	6.8	5.3	6.1	5.5	SAARC
									EUROPE
1.0	0.9	1.1	0.7	0.6	0.5	0.7	0.6	0.7	AELE
90.0	89.6	88.9	65.9	67.5	67.6	66.3	64.8	64.4	UE
68.1	67.6	66.8	51.7	51.6	51.5	50.1	48.7	48.2	Zone euro
									OCÉANIE
2.5	2.5	2.3	..	0.7	1.0	1.1	1.1	1.1	MSG
									INTERRÉGIONAUX
..	..	..	..	12.3	11.6	15.5	14.1	12.3	ACP
..	..	..	71.7	73.0	70.8	66.3	67.4	67.3	CEAP
..	..	..	17.7	14.2	15.9	15.9	17.1	15.0	CEMN
..	..	..	26.7	20.5	18.0	19.5	18.4	13.1	CEI

Source :
Calculs du secrétariat de la CNUCED, basés sur la matrice du commerce de marchandises de *UNCTADstat* de la CNUCED

2

INTERNATIONAL **MERCHANDISE** TRADE BY REGION

COMMERCE INTERNATIONAL DES **MARCHANDISES** PAR RÉGIONS

Destination / Origin / Origine	Year / Année	World (millions of dollars) (1) / Monde (millions de dollars) (1)	Developed economies / Économies développées - Europe Total	Europe EU / UE	USA / États-Unis	Japan / Japon	Other / Autres	Transition economies / Économies en transition	Developing economies / Économies en développement Total	Africa / Afrique	America / Amérique	Eastern, Southern and South-Eastern Asia / Asie orientale, méridionale et du Sud-Est	Western Asia / Asie occidentale	Oceania / Océanie
			Total											
Afghanistan	1995	(e)166	21.7	16.5	14.9	4.1	0.7	0.4	41.9	36.4	0.7	2.5	31.5	1.7	0.0
	2005	(e)384	39.2	14.0	13.8	23.0	1.0	1.2	3.5	57.4	2.1	1.2	47.7	6.3	0.0
	2011	(e)350	8.2	5.5	5.5	2.3	0.1	0.3	9.4	82.4	33.9	0.3	44.3	3.9	0.0
Albania - Albanie	1995	(e)202	90.0	84.8	84.2	3.4	0.9	0.8	6.1	3.9	0.3	0.3	0.3	2.9	..
	2005	(e)658	91.6	87.1	87.0	4.2	0.1	0.2	3.3	5.0	0.3	0.5	1.8	2.4	0.0
	2011	(e)1 948	68.9	67.1	66.6	1.3	0.1	0.4	4.9	26.1	7.2	0.5	11.5	7.0	0.0
Algeria - Algérie	1995	9 357	87.6	67.8	66.5	16.7	0.7	2.4	1.6	10.8	2.5	2.8	2.0	3.5	..
	2005	46 002	84.2	56.2	55.6	23.0	0.0	5.0	0.0	15.7	2.2	7.0	2.6	3.9	..
	2011	73 436	80.1	53.1	50.8	20.6	0.3	6.1	0.1	19.8	3.3	5.8	7.0	3.6	0.1
American Samoa - Samoa américaines	1995	272	..	..	..	..	..	..	..	..	..	..	..	..	..
	2005	(e)374	47.3	15.6	11.2	..	9.3	22.3	0.5	52.3	5.1	0.9	38.1	1.0	7.2
	2011	(e)310	41.8	19.7	4.6	..	0.2	21.9	1.9	56.3	28.2	1.3	25.4	0.1	1.3
Andorra - Andorre	1995	48	99.6	99.6	99.6	..	..	0.0	..	0.3	0.0	0.0	0.2	0.0	..
	2005	143	98.9	98.7	98.4	0.1	0.1	0.0	0.1	1.0	0.7	0.3	0.0	0.0	0.0
	2011	(e)77	55.9	53.8	40.7	1.1	0.0	0.9	2.9	41.2	8.2	4.8	28.0	0.2	0.0
Angola	1995	(e)3 723	86.2	21.2	21.2	64.3	0.4	0.2	0.0	13.7	0.3	3.2	10.1	0.0	..
	2005	(e)24 109	56.1	14.7	14.7	40.0	0.1	1.2	0.0	43.9	1.4	7.0	35.4	0.1	..
	2011	(e)65 689	37.4	11.7	11.7	21.8	0.0	3.9	0.0	62.6	2.5	2.0	58.1	0.0	..
Anguilla	1995	(e)1	4.6	3.1	3.1	0.9	0.5	0.1	46.6	48.8	0.2	40.6	8.0	0.0	..
	2005	(e)15	53.7	24.7	24.5	27.7	0.4	0.9	6.5	39.8	1.0	36.5	2.3	..	0.0
	2011	(e)16	74.9	22.5	16.7	47.1	..	5.3	11.9	13.2	0.0	6.6	6.6	0.0	..
Antigua and Barbuda - Antigua-et-Barbuda	1995	(e)53	42.9	27.4	24.1	5.9	0.3	9.3	0.0	57.1	0.6	52.1	4.1	0.3	..
	2005	(e)83	81.8	79.7	79.6	1.9	0.0	0.2	0.0	18.2	2.9	10.5	4.8	0.0	0.0
	2011	(e)43	4.0	3.6	3.6	0.3	0.0	0.1	0.0	96.0	90.4	4.7	0.8	0.0	0.0
Argentina - Argentine	1995	20 963	34.8	23.1	22.0	8.6	2.2	1.0	0.4	64.7	4.1	47.2	11.8	1.6	0.0
	2005	40 106	31.2	17.5	17.1	11.4	0.7	1.7	1.9	65.1	6.1	40.4	15.7	2.8	0.0
	2011	83 950	27.7	17.6	16.9	5.1	1.0	3.9	1.2	69.0	7.6	40.7	17.7	3.0	0.0
Armenia - Arménie	1995	(e)271	16.3	10.7	9.9	5.6	0.1	0.0	58.9	24.7	2.1	0.6	17.7	4.3	..
	2005	(e)937	70.2	50.6	48.7	7.0	0.1	12.5	18.8	11.1	0.1	5.6	4.0	1.4	0.0
	2011	(e)1 320	58.0	44.3	42.7	7.7	0.1	5.9	24.8	17.2	0.3	1.2	11.4	4.3	..
Aruba	1995	(e)1 347	73.3	4.7	4.7	66.5	..	2.0	0.0	26.7	0.9	25.6	0.1	0.1	..
	2005	(e)4 416	87.6	12.6	12.6	73.8	0.0	1.2	0.0	12.4	0.0	10.2	0.0	2.2	..
	2011	(e)5 179	77.0	2.4	2.4	74.3	0.0	0.4	0.0	23.0	1.9	12.5	3.7	4.8	..
Australia - Australie	1995	53 001	43.4	10.4	9.8	5.0	20.2	7.8	0.1	41.6	1.1	0.9	35.9	1.5	2.2
	2005	105 751	46.1	11.1	10.9	6.7	20.4	7.9	0.3	52.2	2.5	1.7	42.7	3.6	1.7
	2011	245 631	33.9	7.4	7.1	3.7	19.2	3.6	0.4	64.7	1.4	1.5	58.0	2.6	1.3
Austria - Autriche	1995	57 583	85.9	80.6	74.5	2.8	1.2	1.3	2.9	7.1	1.1	0.9	3.9	1.3	0.0
	2005	117 722	86.9	78.4	73.1	5.6	1.1	1.7	4.8	8.1	1.2	0.9	4.2	1.7	0.0
	2011	(e)168 435	83.5	77.6	72.8	4.0	0.8	1.2	5.8	10.7	1.0	1.6	5.8	2.2	0.0
Azerbaijan - Azerbaïdjan	1995	(e)547	17.1	16.8	16.7	0.2	0.1	0.1	50.1	32.7	0.2	0.9	26.8	4.8	..
	2005	(e)7 649	63.1	59.9	59.6	1.0	0.0	2.2	22.3	14.6	0.5	0.0	7.2	6.9	0.0
	2011	(e)34 495	72.8	62.9	61.7	7.8	0.0	2.0	12.7	14.6	0.8	0.0	12.4	1.4	0.0
Bahamas	1995	(e)176	80.9	51.6	40.7	25.8	0.8	2.6	1.0	18.1	4.1	4.8	9.1	0.1	0.0
	2005	(e)549	87.4	57.3	55.0	27.9	0.0	2.1	0.2	12.4	0.2	8.0	4.0	0.2	0.0
	2011	(e)835	45.5	12.7	7.9	31.7	0.0	1.1	0.1	54.3	0.4	22.5	31.4	0.1	..
Bahrain - Bahreïn	1995	(e)4 113	30.0	11.4	10.2	6.1	12.2	0.4	0.0	69.1	0.9	0.1	47.8	20.2	0.0
	2005	(e)10 239	27.3	11.4	10.7	8.4	5.6	1.9	0.0	72.2	19.9	0.1	26.6	25.6	0.0
	2011	(e)19 648	24.3	11.6	10.2	5.0	6.2	1.5	0.2	75.5	13.6	0.8	27.9	33.2	0.0
Bangladesh	1995	(e)3 407	83.0	41.9	41.1	34.9	3.6	2.6	0.8	16.2	2.3	0.7	11.3	1.9	0.0
	2005	(e)9 332	88.7	54.5	53.6	28.4	1.3	4.4	0.3	11.0	0.8	0.5	7.7	2.0	0.0
	2011	(e)25 925	83.4	55.3	54.1	20.9	1.8	5.4	1.4	15.3	0.9	1.2	8.5	4.7	0.0
Barbados - Barbade	1995	238	44.0	20.6	20.4	17.2	0.6	5.6	0.1	41.6	0.4	40.5	0.7	0.0	..
	2005	361	32.1	22.3	22.1	8.2	0.0	1.6	0.0	48.8	0.1	48.1	0.5	0.1	0.0
	2011	508	24.7	13.8	13.6	9.1	0.0	1.8	0.0	52.8	0.1	50.4	2.2	0.1	0.0
Belarus - Bélarus	1995	(e)4 804	33.2	31.5	31.1	1.2	0.3	0.2	63.3	3.3	0.3	0.1	2.4	0.5	..
	2005	15 977	46.6	44.9	44.6	1.6	0.0	0.1	44.6	8.4	0.7	1.4	5.6	0.6	..
	2011	40 294	39.7	39.3	38.9	0.2	0.0	0.1	48.3	11.0	0.8	4.3	5.2	0.7	..

For sources and notes, see end of table.

Pour les sources et les notes, se reporter à la fin du tableau.

58

2.1 Country trade structure by partner — Exports by main region of destination
2.1 Structure du commerce des pays par partenaires — Exportations par principales régions de destination

Destination / Origin	Year / Année	World (millions of dollars) (1) / Monde	Developed economies / Économies développées						Transition economies / Économies en transition	Developing economies / Économies en développement					
			Total	Europe		USA / États-Unis	Japan / Japon	Other / Autres		Total	Africa / Afrique	America / Amérique	Eastern, Southern and South-Eastern Asia / Asie orientale, méridionale et du Sud-Est	Western Asia / Asie occidentale	Oceania / Océanie
				Total	EU / UE										
Belgium - Belgique	1995	(e)177 831	86.4	77.3	74.6	4.7	1.7	2.7	1.1	12.1	2.1	1.5	6.7	1.8	0.0
	2005	334 106	88.0	78.2	76.7	6.4	1.0	2.3	1.2	10.2	1.8	1.1	5.2	2.1	0.0
	2011	477 925	82.2	74.4	72.2	5.1	1.0	1.8	1.9	14.6	2.9	1.7	7.2	2.9	0.0
Belize	1995	162	92.2	51.9	51.3	30.0	6.1	4.2	0.1	7.6	0.0	5.8	1.8	0.0	..
	2005	208	74.4	36.3	36.2	33.8	2.2	2.1	0.3	25.3	4.9	13.6	6.3	0.6	0.0
	2011	(e)348	71.8	32.8	32.7	34.9	2.4	1.8	0.3	27.8	2.5	22.3	2.5	0.6	0.0
Benin - Bénin	1995	420	35.9	30.8	30.2	4.9	0.2	0.0	0.7	61.1	20.0	20.0	21.1	0.1	..
	2005	(e)578	9.0	8.9	8.5	0.1	0.0	0.0	0.0	90.9	35.8	0.4	53.6	1.2	..
	2011	(e)1 849	7.3	6.7	6.6	0.5	0.1	0.0	0.0	92.7	41.6	0.2	43.0	7.9	..
Bermuda - Bermudes	1995	(o)56	75.0	60.1	59.8	12.0	1.1	1.8	0.2	24.8	0.4	23.4	1.0	0.1	..
	2005	(e)49	97.7	89.4	89.3	6.5	0.4	1.5	0.0	2.3	0.4	1.6	0.3	0.0	0.0
	2011	(e)13	79.9	39.1	39.0	23.8	0.0	16.9	0.2	19.9	4.4	3.4	12.1	0.0	..
Bhutan - Bhoutan	1995	(e)103	6.9	3.9	3.8	0.3	2.7	0.0	0.1	93.0	0.5	0.9	91.3	0.4	..
	2005	(e)258	1.1	0.7	0.6	0.3	0.1	0.0	..	98.9	0.1	2.0	96.8	0.0	..
	2011	(e)620	3.5	1.9	1.9	0.2	1.3	0.0	0.0	96.5	1.3	0.1	95.1	0.1	..
Bolivia (Plurinational State of) - Bolivie (État plurinational de)	1995	1 181	55.4	27.4	23.7	26.2	0.4	1.4	0.3	44.3	0.1	36.0	0.9	7.3	..
	2005	2 797	26.0	8.0	6.8	13.2	3.7	1.0	0.2	73.8	0.1	70.4	3.3	0.1	0.0
	2011	9 113	28.6	8.6	7.5	11.4	5.0	3.6	0.2	71.1	0.1	60.9	10.0	0.1	0.0
Bonaire, Sint Eustatius and Saba - Bonaire, Saint-Eustache et Saba	2011	(e)6	..	..	..	..	..	..	..	100.0	..	81.7	18.3	..	..
Bosnia and Herzegovina - Bosnie-Herzégovine	1995	(e)152	25.3	22.9	22.7	1.9	0.0	0.6	72.0	2.7	0.3	0.6	1.7	0.1	..
	2005	(e)2 388	63.8	60.6	60.1	2.7	0.1	0.5	30.9	5.3	0.7	0.1	3.7	0.7	0.0
	2011	(e)5 850	62.1	60.8	59.7	0.9	0.1	0.3	33.1	4.8	1.1	0.3	1.5	1.9	0.0
Botswana	1995	(e)2 142	51.0	49.7	34.0	0.9	0.0	0.4	0.0	48.9	48.8	0.1	0.1	0.0	0.0
	2005	4 431	85.9	81.8	74.0	3.6	0.4	0.1	0.0	14.1	12.0	0.0	2.0	0.0	0.0
	2011	5 882	82.7	76.7	70.6	3.8	0.4	1.8	0.0	17.3	13.6	0.0	3.6	0.1	0.0
Brazil - Brésil	1995	46 505	57.3	29.9	28.8	18.9	6.7	1.9	1.4	40.4	3.4	23.1	11.5	2.4	0.0
	2005	118 529	48.2	23.7	22.9	19.2	2.9	2.3	2.9	47.1	5.0	25.5	13.5	3.1	0.0
	2011	256 039	37.4	21.8	20.7	10.1	3.7	1.8	2.1	58.6	4.8	22.4	27.2	4.3	0.0
British Virgin Islands - Îles Vierges britanniques	1995	(e)11	52.6	39.6	32.4	12.9	0.0	0.1	10.5	36.9	0.9	36.0	0.0	0.0	..
Brunei Darussalam - Brunéi Darussalam	1995	(e)2 379	58.2	1.2	1.2	2.5	53.1	1.4	..	41.8	0.0	0.0	41.7	0.1	..
	2005	(e)6 268	58.3	0.9	0.8	9.6	37.1	10.6	0.0	41.7	0.0	0.0	41.7	0.0	0.0
	2011	(e)12 474	60.6	0.1	0.1	0.2	45.4	14.9	0.0	39.4	0.1	0.0	39.2	0.1	0.0
Bulgaria - Bulgarie	1995	(e)5 353	37.0	32.9	31.9	2.3	0.5	1.3	27.9	20.1	3.4	1.6	4.0	11.2	..
	2005	11 739	65.7	60.8	59.6	3.6	0.2	1.2	11.2	18.8	2.2	1.2	3.4	11.7	0.2
	2011	28 165	68.9	66.3	62.4	1.5	0.2	0.9	11.5	19.5	3.3	0.7	4.3	11.2	0.2
Burkina Faso	1995	(e)276	40.9	38.7	33.8	0.2	1.8	0.2	0.0	59.1	39.6	1.2	18.3	0.0	0.0
	2005	(e)468	28.7	26.7	17.0	0.4	1.6	0.1	0.3	71.0	30.6	0.2	40.1	0.1	0.0
	2011	(e)1 800	45.1	40.0	16.2	0.4	2.7	2.0	0.1	54.9	17.3	0.0	33.0	4.5	0.0
Burundi	1995	(e)106	92.8	86.8	80.7	5.9	0.0	0.1	0.1	7.1	6.0	0.1	1.0	0.1	..
	2005	(e)56	74.4	70.7	48.9	3.0	0.4	0.3	1.0	24.5	10.2	0.6	4.1	9.7	..
	2011	(e)122	55.6	52.4	43.4	3.0	0.1	0.2	1.5	42.9	19.3	0.1	14.0	9.5	..
Cambodia - Cambodge	1995	(e)855	18.8	15.1	14.6	1.5	2.0	0.3	1.5	79.7	3.3	0.1	76.3	0.1	0.0
	2005	(e)3 019	83.8	20.9	20.2	56.3	2.8	3.8	0.2	16.0	0.1	0.3	15.4	0.3	0.0
	2011	(e)7 554	79.3	27.9	26.8	38.7	4.2	8.5	1.2	19.5	0.2	1.1	17.3	0.9	0.0
Cameroon - Cameroun	1995	(e)1 539	81.2	77.2	77.0	2.3	1.3	0.4	0.0	18.8	8.7	0.9	8.6	0.6	0.0
	2005	(e)2 861	71.1	66.2	66.1	4.6	0.2	0.3	0.1	27.6	11.6	1.4	13.5	1.2	0.0
	2011	(e)4 600	60.9	54.3	54.1	6.3	0.1	0.2	0.3	38.9	14.3	2.2	21.0	1.4	0.0
Canada	1995	191 118	91.5	7.0	6.5	79.2	4.6	0.7	0.1	8.4	0.7	2.1	5.2	0.5	0.0
	2005	360 552	92.9	6.4	5.7	83.8	2.1	0.6	0.2	6.9	0.5	1.9	4.0	0.5	0.0
	2011	450 397	86.5	9.9	9.0	73.7	2.4	0.6	0.5	13.0	0.8	3.1	8.1	1.0	0.0
Cape Verde - Cap-Vert	1995	9	80.7	78.5	78.3	2.0	0.1	0.1	0.2	19.0	14.4	3.2	0.5	0.8	0.1
	2005	(e)18	71.6	64.5	64.4	7.0	0.1	0.0	0.0	28.4	23.6	0.9	0.4	3.5	..
	2011	69	91.8	88.8	88.0	1.8	0.0	1.3	0.1	8.1	1.8	0.4	4.4	0.4	0.0
Cayman Islands - Îles Caïmanes	1995	(e)4	51.8	22.2	22.2	18.0	0.8	10.8	0.1	48.1	0.2	47.7	0.1	0.1	..
	2005	(e)60	89.8	82.7	82.7	6.8	0.1	0.2	0.0	10.1	0.1	9.6	0.4	0.0	..
	2011	(e)22	94.2	88.1	78.4	5.3	..	0.8	0.8	5.0	0.1	1.8	3.1	0.0	..

For sources and notes, see end of table.

Pour les sources et les notes, se reporter à la fin du tableau.

59

Destination / Origin / Origine	Year / Année	World (millions of dollars) (1) / Monde (millions de dollars) (1)	Developed economies / Économies développées — Total	Europe — Total	Europe — EU / UE	USA / États-Unis	Japan / Japon	Other / Autres	Transition economies / Économies en transition	Developing economies / Économies en développement — Total	Africa / Afrique	America / Amérique	Eastern, Southern and South-Eastern Asia / Asie orientale, méridionale et du Sud-Est	Western Asia / Asie occidentale	Oceania / Océanie
Central African Republic - République centrafricaine	1995	(e)171	88.4	87.6	87.2	0.2	0.2	0.4	0.0	11.5	9.8	0.1	1.3	0.4	..
	2005	(e)129	73.4	67.2	63.9	3.5	1.3	1.4	0.1	26.5	8.2	0.4	13.1	4.7	0.0
	2011	(e)156	50.8	45.7	45.7	3.7	0.9	0.4	0.0	49.2	15.0	0.2	27.8	6.1	0.0
Chad - Tchad	1995	(e)243	91.1	85.1	84.6	2.9	3.1	0.1	0.0	8.9	4.0	0.0	4.6	0.3	..
	2005	(e)3 144	86.8	12.8	12.8	74.0	0.0	0.0	0.1	13.1	0.5	0.0	12.5	0.0	0.0
	2011	(e)4 114	91.6	8.6	8.6	83.0	0.0	0.0	0.0	8.4	0.7	0.0	7.6	0.0	..
Chile - Chili	1995	15 901	60.6	28.2	27.4	13.4	17.9	1.1	0.7	37.5	0.8	19.4	16.4	0.8	0.1
	2005	41 973	54.6	23.6	23.4	16.0	11.9	3.0	0.4	44.2	0.3	18.2	24.4	1.2	0.0
	2011	81 411	44.0	18.7	17.7	11.2	11.1	3.1	0.5	54.8	0.3	18.0	35.4	1.0	0.0
China - Chine	1995	148 779	52.3	14.1	13.7	16.6	19.1	2.4	1.4	46.3	1.7	2.1	40.6	2.0	0.0
	2005	761 953	55.4	19.6	19.1	21.4	11.0	3.4	2.9	41.7	2.4	3.1	33.3	2.8	0.1
	2011	1 898 388	47.8	19.2	18.8	17.1	7.8	3.7	3.7	48.5	3.8	6.4	34.3	3.9	0.2
China, Hong Kong SAR - Chine (RAS de Hong Kong)	1995	173 871	47.4	16.2	15.4	21.8	6.1	3.3	0.2	52.2	1.4	2.8	46.5	1.4	0.0
	2005	292 119	39.5	15.5	14.7	15.9	5.2	2.9	0.2	60.2	0.6	1.4	57.1	1.1	0.1
	2011	455 573	26.8	11.2	10.2	9.4	3.8	2.4	0.5	72.7	0.6	1.6	69.2	1.3	0.0
China, Macao SAR - Chine (RAS de Macao)	1995	2 025	78.8	31.9	31.4	43.5	1.4	2.0	0.0	21.2	0.2	0.5	20.4	0.1	0.1
	2005	2 474	70.8	18.9	18.5	49.4	1.0	1.5	0.0	29.2	0.1	2.7	26.3	0.1	0.0
	2011	870	24.2	9.9	9.6	9.9	2.7	1.7	0.3	75.6	0.5	3.0	71.9	0.1	0.0
China, Taiwan Province of - Province chinoise de Taiwan	1995	(e)111 343	52.8	13.9	13.5	23.7	11.8	3.3	0.2	46.3	1.5	2.4	40.8	1.6	0.0
	2005	(e)189 393	37.2	11.9	11.7	15.1	7.6	2.6	0.4	61.3	0.9	2.0	56.5	1.8	0.1
	2011	(e)306 998	29.6	9.6	9.3	11.8	5.9	2.4	0.6	68.6	1.0	2.2	63.4	1.9	0.1
Colombia - Colombie	1995	10 201	67.1	25.9	25.1	35.6	3.6	2.1	0.1	32.3	0.3	29.4	2.3	0.2	0.0
	2005	21 190	59.9	14.1	13.4	41.8	1.6	2.4	0.5	37.9	0.2	34.3	2.6	0.7	0.0
	2011	56 954	59.2	17.4	15.6	38.5	0.9	2.3	0.4	40.0	0.6	31.9	6.2	1.2	0.0
Comoros - Comores	1995	11	95.6	69.6	69.5	20.2	1.9	3.9	0.4	4.1	2.0	0.9	1.2	0.0	..
	2005	(e)12	59.9	42.7	42.4	5.8	11.1	0.3	0.9	39.2	12.6	0.2	20.2	6.2	0.1
	2011	(e)25	40.4	37.0	36.9	2.6	0.7	0.2	0.2	59.4	0.8	0.1	17.5	41.0	0.1
Congo	1995	(e)1 090	69.6	47.1	46.4	20.5	1.0	1.0	..	30.4	2.3	0.0	27.9	0.1	..
	2005	(e)5 198	38.9	8.0	7.5	30.6	0.2	0.1	0.0	61.1	2.5	4.2	54.0	0.5	0.0
	2011	(e)10 800	47.5	20.9	20.7	21.6	0.0	4.9	0.0	49.3	2.8	0.5	45.5	0.5	..
Cook Islands - Îles Cook	1995	(e)5	88.2	21.6	21.5	16.5	18.6	31.4	0.9	11.0	0.0	3.8	6.6	..	..
	2005	(e)5	60.3	5.6	5.2	12.1	28.0	14.7	..	39.7	..	..	38.9	0.2	0.6
	2011	(e)3	76.9	15.7	15.7	2.9	55.2	3.0	0.6	22.5	3.6	2.1	9.0	7.8	0.0
Costa Rica	1995	(e)3 476	80.6	30.0	28.6	46.8	1.0	2.7	1.2	18.2	0.3	15.8	2.0	0.2	..
	2005	7 151	64.0	27.7	27.1	32.9	1.4	2.0	0.3	35.7	0.3	20.9	14.0	0.4	0.0
	2011	10 222	56.7	21.7	21.3	32.3	0.7	2.0	0.4	42.8	0.2	20.1	22.2	0.3	0.0
Côte d'Ivoire	1995	3 737	69.0	63.5	63.4	4.4	0.5	0.6	2.2	28.2	22.7	0.6	4.1	0.7	0.0
	2005	7 248	57.6	42.9	42.3	14.1	0.1	0.5	1.6	40.6	29.8	5.2	5.0	0.6	0.0
	2011	11 049	57.1	39.2	37.6	11.9	0.0	5.9	0.2	39.6	30.0	2.0	6.4	1.1	0.0
Croatia - Croatie	1995	4 633	80.0	77.5	76.1	1.9	0.0	0.5	13.8	6.2	3.3	1.0	1.3	0.6	0.0
	2005	8 773	69.3	64.5	63.4	3.5	0.6	0.8	21.8	8.9	4.3	0.3	0.5	3.7	0.0
	2011	12 289	66.6	62.5	59.4	2.7	0.6	0.9	21.6	11.2	4.5	1.6	1.5	3.6	0.0
Cuba	1995	(e)1 625	50.0	30.3	29.7	..	5.3	14.4	21.5	28.5	7.3	5.8	14.7	0.7	0.0
	2005	(e)2 319	65.8	42.9	41.6	0.0	1.3	21.6	4.5	29.7	1.7	16.3	11.4	0.3	0.0
	2011	(e)6 300	46.8	22.9	21.9	0.0	0.4	23.5	4.0	49.2	3.1	17.6	28.1	0.4	0.0
Cyprus - Chypre	1995	1 231	59.5	55.6	53.6	1.2	0.2	2.5	16.4	24.1	5.5	0.3	5.9	12.4	0.0
	2005	1 546	67.6	63.6	62.6	1.4	1.0	1.6	3.1	15.6	3.2	0.4	6.0	6.0	0.0
	2011	1 958	64.9	57.5	56.3	0.7	1.2	5.5	3.5	21.3	2.6	0.2	14.1	4.4	0.0
Czech Republic - République tchèque	1995	21 686	88.6	85.3	83.6	2.0	0.6	0.7	5.5	5.8	1.0	0.7	3.1	1.1	0.0
	2005	78 209	90.6	86.4	84.7	3.0	0.5	0.7	4.1	5.3	0.8	0.7	1.9	1.8	0.0
	2011	162 112	88.2	84.9	82.7	2.1	0.4	0.8	5.2	6.6	1.0	0.8	3.0	1.8	0.0
Dem. Rep. of the Congo - Rép. dém. du Congo	1995	(e)1 649	88.3	62.8	61.4	18.0	5.3	2.2	0.0	11.5	7.7	0.1	3.6	0.1	..
	2005	(e)2 403	77.1	59.3	59.2	17.6	0.2	0.0	0.1	22.8	10.2	0.0	12.5	0.0	0.0
	2011	(e)6 003	25.5	12.3	12.3	13.1	0.0	0.0	0.0	74.5	1.6	2.3	70.2	0.4	0.0
Denmark - Danemark	1995	48 789	77.5	68.9	60.8	3.5	3.4	1.7	1.8	10.0	1.7	1.7	4.9	1.6	0.0
	2005	82 415	81.7	71.9	64.8	5.5	2.0	2.3	1.9	8.5	0.8	1.1	5.0	1.5	0.1
	2011	112 784	76.5	67.3	59.4	5.1	1.4	2.8	2.4	12.2	1.0	1.9	7.3	1.9	0.1

For sources and notes, see end of table.

Pour les sources et les notes, se reporter à la fin du tableau.

Destination / Origin	Year / Année	World (millions of dollars) (1) / Monde (millions de dollars) (1)	Developed economies / Économies développées						Transition economies / Économies en transition	Developing economies / Économies en développement					
			Total	Europe		USA / États-Unis	Japan / Japon	Other / Autres		Total	Africa / Afrique	America / Amérique	Eastern, Southern and South-Eastern Asia / Asie orientale, méridionale et du Sud-Est	Western Asia / Asie occidentale	Oceania / Océanie
				Total	EU / UE										
									Percentage / En pourcentage						
Djibouti	1995	(e)14	18.7	18.1	17.9	0.0	0.3	0.3	0.0	81.3	51.8	..	6.9	22.5	..
	2005	(e)40	8.3	7.0	6.9	1.0	0.2	0.1	0.0	91.7	67.1	0.6	6.0	18.0	..
	2011	(e)95	13.2	9.3	9.3	2.4	1.1	0.4	0.0	86.8	47.7	0.2	7.4	31.5	0.0
Dominica - Dominique	1995	45	54.3	46.2	46.2	8.1	0.0	0.0	..	45.2	..	45.2	..	..	..
	2005	42	32.5	27.8	27.8	4.5	0.0	0.3	..	60.8	0.0	60.7	0.0	..	..
	2011	(e)29	25.8	22.1	22.1	3.6	..	0.0	..	74.2	..	74.2	..	..	..
Dominican Republic - République dominicaine	1995	(e)3 780	97.5	9.3	9.2	85.5	1.2	1.6	0.0	2.5	0.1	1.8	0.5	0.0	0.0
	2005	(e)6 183	90.8	9.7	9.4	78.8	0.8	1.5	0.1	9.2	0.1	6.4	2.6	0.1	0.0
	2011	(e)8 536	66.8	12.5	12.2	51.7	0.4	2.2	0.3	32.9	0.3	26.2	6.1	0.2	0.0
Ecuador - Équateur	1995	4 361	67.0	20.8	20.6	42.5	2.7	1.0	1.5	30.7	0.2	22.2	7.8	0.4	0.0
	2005	9 869	64.6	13.0	12.8	50.1	0.7	0.8	3.2	32.0	0.1	30.8	0.7	0.5	0.0
	2011	22 345	59.2	12.2	11.8	44.9	1.6	0.6	3.9	36.5	0.3	34.0	1.7	0.5	0.0
Egypt - Égypte	1995	3 444	70.5	48.7	48.1	15.2	1.3	5.4	1.7	26.1	5.2	0.4	8.7	11.8	..
	2005	10 646	44.8	34.2	34.1	9.0	1.1	0.4	0.9	35.7	6.8	0.3	11.4	17.2	0.0
	2011	30 782	39.1	32.2	31.3	5.2	1.2	0.5	1.8	55.4	13.7	1.3	14.4	26.0	0.0
El Salvador	1995	(e)1 651	66.6	25.8	25.4	37.8	1.2	1.8	0.1	33.3	0.0	32.6	0.6	0.0	..
	2005	3 436	63.3	6.2	6.1	55.5	0.5	1.0	0.8	35.9	0.1	34.7	1.1	0.1	0.0
	2011	(e)5 309	56.5	7.8	7.6	45.1	1.0	2.7	0.2	43.3	0.1	38.9	4.3	0.0	0.0
Equatorial Guinea - Guinée équatoriale	1995	86	83.2	35.9	35.9	31.8	15.5	0.0	..	16.7	4.8	0.0	11.7	0.2	..
	2005	7 064	65.1	29.6	29.1	25.3	3.4	6.8	0.0	34.9	1.0	4.7	29.1	0.1	..
	2011	(e)13 500	62.8	30.4	29.0	12.5	13.5	6.5	0.0	37.2	0.5	6.0	30.6	0.0	..
Eritrea - Érythrée	1995	(e)86	30.5	24.7	24.5	1.9	3.9	0.0	0.0	69.5	20.9	0.1	..	48.4	..
	2005	(e)11	53.3	41.9	41.3	7.0	0.2	4.2	0.0	46.7	27.4	1.3	8.6	9.5	..
	2011	(e)404	97.5	1.7	1.7	0.0	0.0	95.8	0.0	2.5	0.7	0.0	1.3	0.5	..
Estonia - Estonie	1995	1 840	75.9	72.1	69.6	2.9	0.6	0.3	22.2	1.9	0.3	0.5	0.5	0.6	0.0
	2005	8 247	88.1	81.9	76.3	5.0	0.3	0.8	7.9	4.0	0.6	0.8	1.7	0.9	0.0
	2011	18 158	76.3	69.1	65.4	5.7	0.6	0.9	12.6	9.1	2.7	0.9	3.5	2.1	0.0
Ethiopia - Éthiopie	1995	422	71.4	50.9	50.4	6.4	13.0	1.1	0.1	26.0	11.4	..	4.2	10.3	..
	2005	926	53.3	37.8	31.7	4.7	7.2	3.7	0.3	45.9	17.3	0.2	13.7	14.6	0.0
	2011	2 615	47.7	38.9	33.7	3.7	1.4	3.6	0.4	51.9	22.3	0.4	15.6	13.6	0.0
Faeroe Islands - Îles Féroé	1995	(e)362	94.3	90.1	79.8	2.1	1.3	0.8	0.3	2.1	..	0.1	1.2	..	0.8
	2005	602	91.2	84.5	76.8	0.9	3.5	2.3	4.9	3.7	1.2	0.0	2.5	..	..
	2011	(e)998	81.4	68.2	62.5	12.4	..	0.8	3.6	14.9	12.4	0.0	2.6	0.0	0.0
Falkland Islands (Malvinas) - Îles Falkland (Malvinas)	1995	(e)30	98.9	94.3	92.4	1.7	3.0	0.0	..	1.1	0.8	0.0	0.3	..	..
	2005	(e)173	92.4	85.6	85.4	5.7	1.0	0.1	5.8	1.9	1.3	0.1	0.4	..	..
	2011	(e)190	58.6	37.3	36.8	17.3	3.1	0.9	29.7	11.7	5.2	0.3	6.1	0.1	..
Fiji - Fidji	1995	(e)544	86.7	27.2	27.1	14.5	9.4	35.6	..	13.3	0.1	0.0	11.3	0.0	1.8
	2005	(e)702	73.2	16.5	16.5	23.9	6.9	25.9	0.0	26.6	0.0	0.8	4.8	0.2	20.8
	2011	(e)902	60.1	9.5	9.5	16.6	8.6	25.3	0.0	39.8	0.4	3.5	6.8	0.3	28.8
Finland - Finlande	1995	40 409	77.2	65.5	61.2	6.6	2.5	2.6	5.2	14.6	1.5	2.4	9.0	1.7	0.0
	2005	65 238	69.1	59.6	56.2	5.7	1.4	2.3	12.1	17.2	2.2	2.1	7.2	5.6	0.0
	2011	78 794	66.8	57.7	53.6	4.8	1.3	3.0	10.8	17.1	2.2	2.5	9.5	2.9	0.0
France (3)	1995	277 845	72.3	62.6	58.1	6.0	2.0	1.7	0.9	17.6	5.4	2.0	7.3	2.6	0.3
	2005	434 354	79.8	69.2	65.7	7.2	1.5	1.8	1.6	18.5	5.8	1.9	7.0	3.4	0.3
	2011	581 542	73.7	64.6	60.9	5.6	1.6	2.0	2.4	23.6	6.8	2.6	9.6	4.3	0.3
French Polynesia - Polynésie française	1995	(e)196	81.8	23.9	23.5	9.5	44.2	4.2	0.0	16.0	..	0.0	12.6	..	3.4
	2005	210	63.3	17.5	17.0	13.8	28.3	3.7	0.0	36.7	0.0	0.4	34.0	0.0	2.3
	2011	150	60.3	21.7	21.6	16.1	20.8	1.7	0.0	39.7	0.1	1.3	36.0	0.1	2.2
Gabon	1995	(e)2 718	79.8	12.2	11.0	64.1	2.1	1.5	0.0	14.6	2.2	5.0	6.7	0.7	..
	2005	5 069	77.7	14.7	12.5	60.8	0.2	2.0	1.3	21.0	4.7	3.8	12.1	0.4	0.0
	2011	(e)12 175	60.3	21.4	20.5	36.5	2.3	0.2	1.5	38.2	5.2	5.7	26.9	0.4	..
Gambia - Gambie	1995	(e)16	87.6	76.1	76.0	1.3	10.2	0.1	..	12.4	5.6	0.1	6.6	0.0	..
	2005	(e)8	30.4	25.2	25.0	1.1	2.0	2.0	0.3	69.3	17.3	0.6	50.6	0.9	0.0
	2011	95	16.8	16.6	16.6	0.0	..	0.1	0.1	83.1	21.3	0.4	61.1	0.1	0.1
Georgia - Géorgie	1995	(e)158	19.7	19.0	15.2	0.7	0.0	0.1	64.7	14.6	0.0	..	1.6	13.0	..
	2005	865	32.9	25.4	25.0	3.1	0.2	4.2	47.1	19.8	1.6	0.9	2.7	14.6	0.0
	2011	(e)2 192	33.1	20.8	19.7	5.5	0.1	6.7	45.7	21.2	1.2	2.3	4.5	13.2	..

For sources and notes, see end of table.

Pour les sources et les notes, se reporter à la fin du tableau.

Destination / Origin / Origine	Year / Année	World (millions of dollars) (1) / Monde (millions de dollars) (1)	Developed economies / Économies développées						Transition economies / Économies en transition	Developing economies / Économies en développement					
			Total	Europe		USA États-Unis	Japan Japon	Other Autres		Total	Africa Afrique	America Amérique	Eastern, Southern and South-Eastern Asia / Asie orientale, méridionale et du Sud-Est	Western Asia / Asie occidentale	Oceania Océanie
				Total	EU UE										
			Percentage / En pourcentage												
Germany - Allemagne	1995	523 697	82.1	70.5	64.3	7.3	2.5	1.8	2.4	15.3	2.1	2.4	8.3	2.5	0.1
	2005	977 132	81.2	69.0	64.4	8.8	1.7	1.7	3.6	14.9	1.9	2.2	7.6	3.3	0.0
	2011	1 482 202	73.8	63.5	58.2	7.0	1.4	1.9	5.0	20.4	2.0	2.8	11.7	3.9	0.0
Ghana	1995	(e)1 754	84.3	68.1	59.1	11.0	4.4	0.8	1.2	14.6	6.5	0.3	6.4	1.3	0.0
	2005	(e)3 060	64.2	52.9	50.7	6.9	3.1	1.4	5.0	30.8	13.9	2.3	10.1	4.4	0.1
	2011	(e)12 700	63.2	52.5	50.7	8.0	1.7	0.8	4.6	32.2	14.1	1.1	12.2	4.8	0.0
Gibraltar	1995	117	76.8	73.7	33.1	2.8	0.0	0.3	0.2	15.5	6.5	3.9	4.8	0.3	..
	2005	200	97.1	93.5	78.9	2.1	0.0	1.5	0.8	2.2	1.0	0.1	1.0	0.1	..
	2011	246	95.0	91.1	89.9	0.7	0.0	3.2	2.9	2.1	1.0	0.3	0.7	0.1	..
Greece - Grèce	1995	10 955	80.5	74.6	72.5	3.1	0.8	2.0	6.9	12.2	2.6	1.6	2.4	5.6	0.0
	2005	17 434	70.7	63.1	61.8	5.2	0.3	2.0	9.4	18.9	4.6	1.3	3.5	9.4	0.1
	2011	31 711	60.2	52.4	49.9	5.4	0.1	2.2	9.7	24.2	5.5	1.0	5.3	12.2	0.1
Greenland - Groenland	1995	364	98.2	82.7	80.1	1.1	14.1	0.2	..	1.8	0.0	0.2	1.6	0.0	..
	2005	402	91.4	78.7	76.4	2.8	9.9	0.1	0.3	8.3	0.0	0.0	8.3	0.0	0.0
	2011	(e)473	90.8	74.0	71.9	1.8	10.3	4.7	1.2	8.0	0.0	0.0	8.0	0.0	0.0
Grenada - Grenade	1995	22	68.6	42.2	40.4	24.9	..	1.5	0.1	31.3	0.2	31.0	0.1	0.1	..
	2005	28	51.4	34.2	33.9	15.1	0.2	2.0	0.5	48.0	0.2	46.1	1.6	0.2	..
	2011	(e)28	30.9	17.3	16.9	11.1	1.2	1.3	0.1	69.0	32.6	34.8	1.6	..	..
Guam	1995	85	..	..	..	..	..	..	..	..	..	..	..	..	..
	2005	(e)52	64.0	5.3	5.3	..	58.1	0.6	0.0	36.0	0.2	3.0	28.3	0.2	4.2
	2011	(e)43	44.7	3.9	3.5	..	39.6	1.1	0.5	54.8	0.1	0.6	54.0	0.0	0.1
Guatemala	1995	1 936	62.9	15.9	15.1	42.4	2.7	1.9	0.1	37.1	0.8	31.0	3.8	1.5	..
	2005	5 381	61.7	6.5	5.5	51.7	1.3	2.3	0.1	38.2	0.3	33.5	3.2	1.1	0.0
	2011	10 161	52.9	6.8	6.2	40.3	2.3	3.6	0.6	46.4	0.6	39.5	4.1	2.3	0.0
Guinea - Guinée	1995	(e)702	77.6	56.8	55.1	17.4	1.3	2.1	4.6	16.9	7.6	7.7	1.4	0.1	..
	2005	(e)796	52.6	43.5	43.3	7.0	0.1	2.0	29.0	18.3	3.5	0.0	14.8	0.1	0.0
	2011	(e)1 527	37.6	29.3	28.8	5.5	0.0	2.8	20.7	41.7	4.3	27.2	10.0	0.3	0.0
Guinea-Bissau - Guinée-Bissau	1995	(e)24	55.0	54.5	54.5	0.0	0.4	0.0	..	45.0	2.2	0.0	42.7	0.0	..
	2005	(e)89	1.8	1.6	1.6	0.2	0.1	0.0	0.0	98.1	1.5	0.1	96.6	0.0	..
	2011	(e)245	8.0	1.7	1.7	6.1	0.2	0.0	0.0	92.0	0.8	0.1	91.0	..	..
Guyana	1995	(e)455	80.8	33.2	33.0	26.1	1.6	19.9	0.0	17.7	0.5	15.5	1.3	0.4	0.0
	2005	539	72.3	32.8	32.6	18.7	0.6	20.2	0.1	27.6	1.1	20.5	5.8	0.2	0.0
	2011	1 049	73.4	17.1	17.0	28.2	0.6	27.5	3.4	23.1	0.2	19.6	2.9	0.4	0.0
Haiti - Haïti	1995	(e)110	92.4	19.9	18.5	70.4	0.6	1.4	..	1.2	0.1	0.9	0.2	0.0	..
	2005	(e)473	90.1	4.0	3.7	81.5	0.2	4.3	0.0	9.9	0.7	7.8	1.3	0.1	..
	2011	(e)772	96.8	3.6	3.2	89.1	0.2	3.9	0.0	3.2	0.0	2.3	0.8	0.0	0.0
Honduras	1995	(e)1 769	88.3	21.3	20.8	60.4	5.2	1.4	0.2	11.5	0.0	9.5	1.9	0.0	..
	2005	(e)5 048	82.0	12.3	11.9	67.1	0.6	2.0	0.4	17.6	0.0	15.8	1.6	0.1	0.0
	2011	(e)7 204	76.3	15.0	14.7	58.7	0.6	2.0	0.1	23.5	0.4	20.6	2.5	0.1	0.0
Hungary - Hongrie	1995	12 452	83.9	78.8	77.2	3.6	0.7	0.7	11.2	4.9	0.9	0.6	1.6	1.8	0.0
	2005	62 272	86.1	80.9	79.3	3.7	0.8	0.7	6.0	7.4	1.2	0.6	2.0	3.5	0.0
	2011	111 125	80.5	76.3	75.1	2.5	0.7	1.0	8.6	10.9	1.4	0.8	4.8	4.0	0.0
Iceland - Islande	1995	1 803	95.9	69.0	63.0	12.4	11.3	3.2	0.6	3.5	0.6	0.5	2.3	0.1	..
	2005	3 091	93.2	79.6	74.6	8.9	3.2	1.4	1.5	5.4	1.8	1.7	1.7	0.2	..
	2011	5 349	91.2	84.0	78.3	3.7	2.5	1.0	3.7	5.1	2.1	0.5	1.9	0.5	0.0
India - Inde	1995	31 699	56.6	29.3	28.2	17.4	7.0	3.0	3.6	38.3	5.2	1.1	23.7	8.3	0.0
	2005	100 353	45.2	23.2	22.5	16.5	2.4	3.1	1.2	53.3	6.7	2.8	30.4	13.3	0.1
	2011	301 483	34.1	18.7	18.1	10.9	1.9	2.6	1.1	58.6	7.7	4.4	29.0	17.4	0.1
Indonesia - Indonésie	2005	85 660	48.4	12.3	12.1	11.5	21.1	3.5	0.5	51.1	1.9	1.5	44.5	3.0	0.1
	2011	203 497	38.3	10.2	10.1	8.1	16.6	3.5	0.8	60.9	2.8	1.9	53.2	2.7	0.2
Indonesia (...2002) - Indonésie (...2002)	1995	45 443	59.6	15.5	15.3	13.9	27.0	3.1	0.3	39.8	1.3	1.6	33.9	3.0	0.1
Iran (Islamic Rep. of) - Iran (Rép. islamique d')	1995	(e)18 360	61.8	41.5	40.8	1.2	18.1	0.9	3.6	34.6	8.1	1.5	17.6	7.4	0.0
	2005	(e)60 012	48.5	27.2	27.1	0.3	20.8	0.1	1.2	50.3	5.6	0.1	34.2	10.4	0.0
	2011	(e)130 544	29.1	18.1	18.1	0.0	10.8	0.1	1.2	69.6	3.5	0.1	53.3	12.6	0.0
Iraq	1995	(e)1 963	0.4	0.2	0.2	..	0.2	0.0	1.3	98.3	0.0	0.0	4.5	93.7	..
	2005	(e)23 697	80.4	23.1	23.1	49.9	2.3	5.0	0.0	19.6	0.3	2.9	12.0	4.5	0.0
	2011	(e)84 673	50.5	18.1	18.1	24.6	4.5	3.4	0.0	49.5	1.5	1.6	44.1	2.3	..

For sources and notes, see end of table.

Pour les sources et les notes, se reporter à la fin du tableau.

2.1 Country trade structure by partner — Exports by main region of destination
2.1 Structure du commerce des pays par partenaires — Exportations par principales régions de destination

Destination / Origin / Origine	Year / Année	World (millions of dollars) (1) / Monde (millions de dollars) (1)	Developed economies / Économies développées Total	Europe Total	Europe EU UE	USA États-Unis	Japan Japon	Other Autres	Transition economies / Économies en transition	Developing economies / Économies en développement Total	Africa Afrique	America Amérique	Eastern, Southern and South-Eastern Asia / Asie orientale, méridionale et du Sud-Est	Western Asia / Asie occidentale	Oceania Océanie
								Percentage / En pourcentage							
Ireland - Irlande	1995	43 789	89.3	76.3	73.3	8.3	3.0	1.7	0.9	7.1	1.6	1.0	3.3	1.2	0.0
	2005	110 003	90.8	67.8	63.4	18.7	2.6	1.7	0.4	8.3	0.9	1.2	5.1	1.1	0.0
	2011	129 346	89.3	62.3	57.8	23.1	1.9	2.1	0.8	9.8	1.3	1.3	5.3	1.9	0.0
Israel - Israël	1995	19 047	79.8	38.1	36.1	32.2	7.3	2.2	2.2	18.0	1.6	2.7	12.8	1.0	0.0
	2005	42 771	75.8	32.0	30.1	39.3	2.0	2.6	1.7	22.5	1.5	3.3	15.2	2.4	0.0
	2011	67 796	67.1	29.8	27.9	33.2	1.5	2.5	2.5	30.4	2.2	3.9	21.0	3.4	0.0
Italy - Italie	1995	230 441	78.7	66.4	62.1	7.3	2.3	2.7	2.5	18.6	3.5	3.5	7.7	3.9	0.0
	2005	372 957	76.9	65.2	60.7	8.0	1.5	2.3	4.3	17.5	3.8	2.7	6.4	4.6	0.0
	2011	523 179	71.2	61.6	55.4	6.1	1.3	2.2	5.1	22.2	4.2	3.7	8.0	6.2	0.1
Jamaica - Jamaïque	1995	1 424	86.5	36.6	29.1	36.9	1.9	11.0	2.6	10.8	3.5	6.7	0.6	0.0	0.0
	2005	1 514	77.5	30.9	24.0	25.6	1.0	20.0	1.4	21.0	0.0	11.7	7.6	1.8	0.0
	2011	(e)1 603	82.6	25.5	19.7	37.2	1.2	18.7	1.7	15.7	0.1	11.9	3.7	0.1	0.0
Japan - Japon	1995	442 937	48.2	16.9	16.2	27.5	..	3.7	0.3	51.4	1.7	4.2	43.7	1.8	0.1
	2005	594 941	42.4	15.3	14.8	22.9	..	4.2	0.9	56.7	1.4	3.9	48.7	2.7	0.1
	2011	823 292	32.2	13.0	11.6	15.5	..	3.7	1.7	66.1	1.6	5.1	56.2	2.9	0.3
Jordan - Jordanie	1995	1 769	15.1	9.9	9.8	2.5	1.5	1.1	1.4	76.1	5.3	0.4	27.0	43.3	0.0
	2005	4 279	35.5	5.1	5.0	26.7	1.5	2.2	0.4	56.9	6.0	0.3	14.2	36.5	0.0
	2011	7 963	20.8	5.0	4.6	13.2	0.7	2.0	0.6	70.0	7.3	0.4	23.5	38.9	0.0
Kazakhstan	1995	5 227	32.4	30.7	26.7	0.8	0.9	0.1	55.1	12.5	0.2	1.2	9.7	1.4	0.0
	2005	27 846	68.5	61.3	41.2	2.4	0.5	4.3	14.7	16.8	0.1	2.1	13.9	0.8	0.0
	2011	(e)84 864	64.4	56.2	51.0	1.4	0.9	5.9	12.6	23.0	0.3	0.7	19.6	2.4	..
Kenya	1995	1 826	46.9	40.1	38.8	4.0	1.1	1.7	0.1	52.3	40.3	0.1	9.9	1.9	..
	2005	3 420	42.8	31.2	30.1	9.5	0.9	1.3	1.2	53.3	39.6	0.3	10.9	2.5	0.0
	2011	(e)5 775	37.8	29.5	28.0	6.6	0.8	1.0	2.8	59.4	44.8	0.2	11.2	3.2	0.0
Kiribati	1995	(e)7	34.1	2.1	2.1	12.5	16.8	2.7	..	65.9	0.1	0.3	59.4	0.1	6.0
	2005	(e)4	47.1	15.8	15.8	10.8	12.8	7.7	0.3	37.4	16.3	0.3	15.0	0.2	5.6
	2011	(e)20	27.8	4.7	4.7	1.7	19.3	2.1	0.0	72.2	5.2	8.5	56.7	..	1.9
Korea, Dem. People's Rep. of - Corée, Rép. populaire dém. de	1995	(e)959	45.7	10.9	10.8	..	34.6	0.2	0.1	53.9	2.6	26.5	20.7	4.1	..
	2005	(e)1 338	21.4	11.5	11.4	0.0	9.1	0.9	1.3	77.3	4.4	16.0	51.3	5.4	0.2
	2011	(e)3 700	3.1	2.9	2.9	..	..	0.2	0.8	96.0	2.7	11.7	78.8	2.8	0.0
Korea, Republic of - Corée, République de	1995	125 056	51.4	15.1	14.3	19.5	13.6	3.2	1.5	46.9	2.4	5.7	35.6	3.1	0.1
	2005	284 418	42.3	16.0	15.6	14.6	8.4	3.3	2.0	55.5	2.8	5.0	43.6	3.6	0.5
	2011	555 209	31.0	10.5	10.1	10.2	7.1	3.2	2.7	66.2	3.3	6.9	49.9	4.7	1.4
Kuwait - Koweït	1995	12 944	47.1	13.4	13.4	11.6	21.6	0.4	0.0	52.9	2.6	2.4	43.2	4.6	..
	2005	(e)44 909	42.0	10.1	9.9	11.7	19.4	0.8	0.0	58.0	2.8	0.2	51.8	3.2	..
	2011	(e)99 579	28.8	5.7	5.7	8.4	13.7	1.0	0.0	71.2	3.9	0.4	63.0	3.8	..
Kyrgyzstan - Kirghizistan	1995	(e)412	14.5	12.6	12.6	1.6	0.1	0.2	64.0	21.5	0.0	..	19.5	2.0	..
	2005	(e)672	9.7	5.9	3.9	0.7	0.1	3.1	48.6	41.7	0.1	0.1	15.7	25.8	..
	2011	(e)1 979	11.2	10.8	5.7	0.2	0.1	0.1	66.1	22.7	0.3	0.1	12.8	9.5	..
Lao People's Dem. Rep. - Rép. dém. populaire lao	1995	311	57.7	41.2	38.8	4.3	11.4	0.8	0.0	42.1	0.8	0.5	40.8	0.0	..
	2005	553	37.6	33.5	32.5	0.7	1.3	2.1	0.2	62.2	0.0	0.1	61.9	0.2	0.0
	2011	(e)2 400	14.8	7.7	7.6	2.5	4.0	0.5	0.2	85.1	0.0	0.1	84.8	0.1	0.0
Latvia - Lettonie	1995	1 305	60.4	58.6	56.4	1.3	0.3	0.1	38.3	1.3	0.6	0.0	0.3	0.4	..
	2005	5 303	83.6	78.7	74.0	3.2	1.0	0.6	13.1	2.9	0.9	0.9	0.8	0.2	0.0
	2011	12 015	76.8	74.5	71.8	1.2	0.4	0.4	14.8	7.5	1.4	0.3	3.9	1.9	0.0
Lebanon - Liban	1995	(e)656	31.6	23.5	21.0	6.0	0.6	1.5	1.9	60.1	10.6	0.9	1.9	46.7	..
	2005	(e)2 337	25.2	20.2	12.0	3.9	0.2	0.9	0.8	73.1	11.3	0.4	5.9	55.6	0.0
	2011	(e)5 664	24.5	21.2	13.7	1.9	0.6	0.8	1.1	73.8	18.8	0.4	6.6	48.0	0.0
Lesotho	1995	(e)160	42.8	0.7	0.6	40.7	0.0	1.3	0.0	57.2	56.1	0.0	1.1	0.0	..
	2005	(e)651	90.9	5.9	5.9	83.4	0.1	1.5	..	9.1	8.7	0.0	0.2	0.2	..
	2011	(e)1 010	82.2	22.3	22.3	55.1	0.2	4.6	..	17.8	17.6	0.0	0.1	0.1	..
Liberia - Libéria	1995	(e)820	90.0	88.8	88.3	0.9	0.0	0.3	0.0	9.9	0.4	1.7	7.1	0.7	0.0
	2005	(e)131	82.0	75.0	74.6	6.2	0.0	0.7	0.2	17.8	1.0	0.1	16.1	0.7	0.0
	2011	(e)358	65.8	33.7	30.4	21.8	5.8	4.6	3.9	30.3	9.4	0.6	19.6	0.7	0.0
Libya - Libye	1995	(e)9 364	83.7	83.7	80.3	..	0.0	0.0	3.2	13.1	5.7	0.3	2.1	5.0	..
	2005	(e)31 358	86.6	80.7	77.4	5.4	0.0	0.5	0.6	12.7	2.2	0.2	3.0	7.4	..
	2011	(e)16 463	77.1	72.2	71.0	3.7	0.0	1.3	0.2	22.7	4.6	0.6	12.0	5.5	..

For sources and notes, see end of table.

Pour les sources et les notes, se reporter à la fin du tableau.

Destination / Origin / Origine	Year / Année	World (millions of dollars) (1) / Monde (millions de dollars) (1)	Developed economies / Économies développées — Europe Total	EU / UE	USA / États-Unis	Japan / Japon	Other / Autres	Transition economies / Économies en transition	Developing economies / Économies en développement — Total	Africa / Afrique	America / Amérique	Eastern, Southern and South-Eastern Asia / Asie orientale, méridionale et du Sud-Est	Western Asia / Asie occidentale	Oceania / Océanie
			Total											
Lithuania - Lituanie	1995	2 706	55.2 / 54.2	51.1	0.7	0.1	0.1	42.3	2.5	0.1	0.4	1.0	1.0	..
	2005	12 070	74.7 / 67.0	64.0	4.7	0.1	2.9	19.1	6.1	0.3	0.6	3.7	1.4	0.0
	2011	28 154	67.7 / 63.7	61.4	2.6	0.1	1.3	28.0	4.1	1.2	0.3	1.6	1.0	0.0
Luxembourg	1995	(e)7 244	84.3 / 68.8	65.2	5.5	0.5	9.5	0.7	14.7	2.8	5.6	4.0	2.1	0.1
	2005	(e)18 790	93.6 / 90.0	88.3	2.6	0.3	0.7	0.9	5.5	0.7	0.8	2.5	1.5	0.0
	2011	(e)21 749	90.0 / 85.6	82.5	2.7	0.3	1.4	2.1	7.9	1.1	0.9	3.3	2.6	0.0
Madagascar	1995	(e)507	86.1 / 71.3	70.1	8.1	5.5	1.2	0.1	12.4	7.0	0.1	4.8	0.4	0.0
	2005	836	84.7 / 53.6	53.0	27.6	2.4	1.1	0.1	15.2	3.6	0.2	8.7	2.7	0.0
	2011	(e)1 593	57.0 / 45.9	45.1	5.4	1.3	4.3	0.3	42.7	5.9	0.3	35.0	1.5	0.0
Malawi	1995	433	75.7 / 52.6	49.2	12.0	8.6	2.4	1.2	23.1	19.7	1.0	2.0	0.3	0.2
	2005	495	59.0 / 36.1	34.0	17.1	4.3	1.5	6.7	34.1	27.1	1.4	3.1	2.2	0.3
	2011	1 425	47.6 / 29.3	28.3	5.7	1.7	10.9	6.7	45.7	32.0	0.7	11.0	1.6	0.4
Malaysia - Malaisie	1995	73 778	50.6 / 14.6	14.4	20.7	12.7	2.6	0.2	49.2	1.1	1.5	44.2	2.3	0.1
	2005	141 624	45.4 / 12.0	11.8	19.6	9.4	4.3	0.5	54.1	1.4	1.1	48.9	2.6	0.1
	2011	226 993	34.8 / 10.6	10.4	8.3	11.5	4.4	0.7	64.5	2.6	1.8	56.1	3.6	0.3
Maldives	1995	(e)85	63.6 / 38.7	38.4	19.1	5.7	0.1	0.0	36.2	0.1	0.0	35.7	0.3	..
	2005	154	42.4 / 23.9	23.9	3.0	15.3	0.2	0.1	57.5	2.9	0.0	47.8	6.8	..
	2011	(e)346	52.8 / 48.3	47.4	1.5	2.7	0.3	0.1	47.1	2.5	1.0	43.5	0.1	0.0
Mali	1995	(e)443	20.0 / 19.8	11.6	0.1	0.0	0.0	0.0	78.2	75.8	0.0	2.3	0.0	..
	2005	1 075	31.8 / 29.8	12.5	0.7	0.1	1.1	0.5	67.7	28.8	0.3	36.2	2.3	0.0
	2011	(e)2 389	17.3 / 14.7	9.8	1.8	0.1	0.7	0.0	82.7	48.3	0.4	22.7	11.3	0.0
Malta - Malte	1995	1 913	84.1 / 73.1	71.7	9.6	0.9	0.6	0.3	13.3	3.0	0.3	9.2	0.8	..
	2005	2 431	70.0 / 51.2	50.5	13.5	4.0	1.3	0.6	27.4	7.3	1.2	17.0	1.9	0.0
	2011	(e)4 105	52.7 / 35.5	34.5	10.5	5.6	1.1	0.2	42.0	6.7	1.1	30.6	3.7	..
Marshall Islands - Îles Marshall	1995	23	99.7 / 14.4	14.4	37.9	47.3	0.1	0.1	0.2	0.0	..	0.0	..	0.2
	2005	25	92.5 / 85.7	85.7	3.3	3.5	0.0	0.0	7.5	0.0	0.0	7.3	0.1	0.0
	2011	(e)35	54.2 / 48.4	48.2	3.7	1.9	0.0	0.1	45.7	0.6	2.1	43.0	0.0	..
Mauritania - Mauritanie	1995	(e)509	84.8 / 55.2	54.6	1.2	28.4	0.0	1.0	14.2	13.2	0.2	0.7	0.1	..
	2005	(e)556	72.9 / 60.1	59.1	0.1	12.4	0.4	5.7	21.4	19.8	0.0	1.0	0.5	0.0
	2011	(e)2 768	39.9 / 35.3	34.2	0.0	4.5	0.0	1.4	58.7	11.7	0.0	46.4	0.6	0.0
Mauritius - Maurice	1995	1 538	92.4 / 75.8	74.4	14.8	0.6	1.1	0.1	7.4	4.3	1.2	1.9	0.0	0.0
	2005	2 144	72.7 / 62.5	61.5	9.0	0.8	0.4	0.1	20.2	8.5	0.2	3.0	8.4	0.2
	2011	(e)2 647	65.5 / 55.4	53.7	8.9	0.5	0.7	0.3	19.4	14.8	0.4	3.6	0.7	0.0
Mayotte	2005	6	58.8 / 58.7	58.7	0.0	..	0.0	0.7	40.5	40.3	0.0	..	0.2	..
	2011	(e)7	69.5 / 69.3	69.3	0.2	..	0.0	0.3	30.2	23.3	0.1	1.0	5.2	0.5
Mexico - Mexique	1995	79 541	92.3 / 5.0	4.2	83.4	1.2	2.7	0.0	7.6	0.1	6.2	1.2	0.1	0.0
	2005	214 207	93.1 / 4.4	4.3	85.8	0.7	2.2	0.0	6.9	0.2	5.2	1.4	0.1	0.0
	2011	349 569	88.5 / 5.8	5.5	78.7	0.6	3.4	0.2	11.3	0.2	7.5	3.3	0.2	0.0
Micronesia (Federated States of) - Micronésie (États fédérés de)	1995	21	71.5 / 0.0	0.0	11.1	60.4	0.0	..	28.5	..	..	28.5	..	..
	2005	19	7.0 / 0.2	0.2	3.1	3.6	0.0	0.0	93.0	2.6	0.4	90.0	..	..
	2011	(e)25	28.1 / 1.1	1.1	4.4	22.5	0.2	0.0	71.9	0.0	1.4	70.5	0.0	..
Mongolia - Mongolie	1995	(e)473	14.4 / 13.6	13.6	0.2	0.5	0.1	63.2	21.6	..	0.0	21.6	..	..
	2005	1 064	38.9 / 9.8	9.4	15.0	0.6	13.5	5.0	56.2	0.0	0.5	55.5	0.2	0.0
	2011	(e)4 774	9.3 / 2.3	2.3	0.3	0.4	6.3	2.4	88.3	0.0	0.2	87.9	0.2	..
Montenegro - Monténégro	2011	628	53.4 / 53.0	49.7	0.1	0.3	0.0	36.1	5.1	2.2	0.0	0.2	2.6	..
Montserrat	1995	(e)3	86.4 / 71.0	71.0	15.3	..	0.1	0.0	13.5	10.9	2.6	0.0	0.0	..
	2005	(e)1	68.4 / 16.1	16.1	41.2	..	11.1	..	31.6	..	31.6	..	..	..
	2011	(e)1	33.1 / 12.0	11.8	13.3	..	7.8	0.1	66.8	1.0	47.6	18.0	0.3	..
Morocco - Maroc	1995	(e)6 881	81.1 / 70.3	69.3	3.5	6.1	1.2	0.5	18.0	6.4	1.8	7.3	2.5	0.0
	2005	11 185	78.9 / 73.0	71.8	3.0	1.1	1.8	1.4	19.0	3.5	3.6	9.2	2.7	0.0
	2011	(e)21 518	67.7 / 61.2	59.2	4.8	0.7	1.0	1.3	31.1	7.1	6.8	14.0	3.1	0.0
Mozambique	1995	174	65.7 / 41.8	40.5	9.4	13.7	0.8	0.0	34.3	26.3	0.3	7.4	0.4	..
	2005	1 745	73.2 / 71.3	71.1	1.1	0.7	0.1	0.4	26.4	19.4	0.0	6.4	0.6	0.0
	2011	3 604	51.8 / 50.3	49.3	0.9	0.1	0.5	1.2	46.9	30.7	1.0	13.4	1.9	0.0
Myanmar	1995	(e)860	19.9 / 5.2	4.9	6.5	7.0	1.2	0.0	79.0	1.3	0.1	77.2	0.5	..
	2005	(e)3 950	24.8 / 17.6	17.4	..	5.9	1.3	0.3	72.9	0.4	0.3	72.0	0.2	0.0
	2011	(e)9 238	9.6 / 4.8	4.7	..	4.2	0.6	0.2	89.4	0.3	0.2	88.5	0.4	..

For sources and notes, see end of table.

Pour les sources et les notes, se reporter à la fin du tableau.

64

Origin / Origine	Year / Année	World (millions of dollars) (1) / Monde (millions de dollars) (1)	Developed economies / Économies développées Total	Europe Total	Europe EU / UE	USA États-Unis	Japan Japon	Other Autres	Transition economies / Économies en transition	Developing economies / Économies en développement Total	Africa Afrique	America Amérique	Eastern, Southern and South-Eastern Asia / Asie orientale, méridionale et du Sud-Est	Western Asia / Asie occidentale	Oceania Océanie
			Percentage / En pourcentage												
Namibia - Namibie	1995	(e)1 416	34.6	29.9	26.6	2.4	0.7	1.6	0.1	65.1	63.4	0.6	0.9	0.2	0.0
	2005	(e)2 070	63.7	51.3	50.8	7.8	0.9	3.7	0.6	35.6	27.5	0.4	7.3	0.4	0.0
	2011	(e)4 362	54.8	37.0	35.1	8.0	1.1	8.7	0.2	45.0	32.6	0.1	11.9	0.5	0.0
Nauru	1995	28	62.4	1.8	1.7	0.0	1.1	59.4	0.0	37.4	0.3	24.9	12.0	0.2	0.0
	2005	4	56.6	24.7	24.7	3.5	5.1	23.2	2.0	41.5	4.6	1.9	31.8	2.9	0.2
	2011	69	24.3	2.0	2.0	0.4	2.2	19.7	0.1	75.6	0.3	0.8	73.8	0.5	0.1
Nepal - Népal	1995	(e)359	74.9	44.7	42.1	28.7	0.4	1.1	0.0	21.5	0.0	0.2	21.3	0.0	..
	2005	(e)888	28.4	12.9	12.3	13.4	0.9	1.2	0.0	71.6	0.1	0.1	70.7	0.7	..
	2011	(e)918	21.3	11.8	11.2	6.8	0.9	1.9	0.1	78.6	0.2	0.1	76.8	1.3	0.0
Netherlands - Pays-Bas	1995	(e)203 187	87.8	81.6	78.7	3.8	1.2	1.2	1.4	10.2	1.8	1.5	5.1	1.7	0.0
	2005	(e)406 208	87.9	81.3	78.8	4.6	0.7	1.2	1.7	9.8	1.8	1.3	4.6	2.1	0.0
	2011	(e)666 207	86.8	81.7	79.3	3.3	0.6	1.1	2.2	11.0	2.2	1.6	4.9	2.3	0.0
Netherlands Antilles - Antilles néerlandaises	1995	(e)1 522	61.8	31.5	28.5	24.9	1.0	4.3	0.0	38.2	0.9	34.5	2.7	0.1	..
	2005	(e)608	35.0	5.4	5.4	29.1	0.2	0.4	0.0	65.0	1.9	60.8	2.4	0.0	0.0
New Caledonia - Nouvelle-Calédonie	1995	(e)471	90.7	42.1	42.1	8.3	33.4	6.9	0.0	9.3	0.2	0.1	8.8	0.0	0.2
	2005	(e)1 114	61.1	33.8	33.8	2.5	21.0	3.8	1.6	37.2	4.2	0.0	31.0	0.0	2.1
	2011	(e)1 658	67.8	30.1	30.1	4.9	20.0	12.9	0.0	32.1	2.0	0.1	27.7	0.0	2.4
New Zealand - Nouvelle-Zélande	1995	13 745	63.0	14.7	14.3	10.0	16.2	22.1	0.9	32.8	1.2	3.1	23.2	2.3	3.0
	2005	21 729	63.6	15.6	15.1	14.2	10.6	23.1	0.7	34.0	2.1	3.5	22.3	2.7	3.5
	2011	37 633	50.6	11.0	10.7	8.4	7.2	24.0	0.9	46.7	3.9	3.2	32.7	3.8	3.2
Nicaragua	1995	509	78.0	31.4	29.6	43.3	1.9	1.4	0.0	22.0	0.2	19.9	1.9	0.0	..
	2005	866	66.5	8.8	8.6	53.9	0.8	2.9	1.2	32.3	0.1	30.1	1.9	0.1	0.0
	2011	2 281	73.4	8.8	8.2	55.0	0.7	8.8	1.1	25.5	0.1	22.1	3.2	0.1	0.0
Niger	1995	273	52.9	46.4	46.1	0.4	4.3	1.9	0.0	47.0	44.8	0.0	0.8	1.4	..
	2005	(e)489	70.1	49.6	45.0	15.8	3.4	1.2	0.0	29.9	28.6	0.2	1.1	0.1	0.0
	2011	(e)1 250	68.6	38.3	35.4	29.2	0.5	0.5	5.9	25.5	21.7	0.3	3.3	0.3	0.0
Nigeria - Nigéria	1995	(e)12 342	77.0	34.4	33.1	38.3	1.0	3.2	0.1	22.8	5.8	6.2	10.7	0.1	0.0
	2005	(e)55 995	64.4	15.5	15.1	41.4	4.2	3.2	..	32.6	9.0	8.5	15.1	0.0	..
	2011	(e)108 296	64.0	28.9	28.5	29.3	1.4	4.4	0.1	35.9	9.6	9.4	16.6	0.4	0.0
Niue - Nioué	1995	0	66.5	8.5	8.5	10.2	..	47.8	17.8	15.7	5.8	2.1	7.8	..	..
	2005	0	46.1	22.4	22.3	8.4	..	15.3	2.9	51.1	25.9	0.4	24.5	0.1	0.1
	2011	(e)0	60.2	10.0	9.7	1.4	0.3	48.5	3.3	36.5	10.0	1.2	24.1	1.3	0.1
Northern Mariana Islands - Îles Mariannes du Nord	1995	(e)941	91.3	6.2	6.2	..	82.7	2.4	..	8.7	0.4	..	8.1	0.2	..
	2005	(e)651	41.9	24.6	24.5	..	16.7	0.6	0.1	58.1	0.6	24.7	32.6	0.2	..
	2011	(e)3	13.1	11.3	9.8	..	1.4	0.4	2.6	84.3	24.5	2.4	57.3	0.1	..
Norway - Norvège	1995	41 740	92.4	80.0	78.9	6.2	1.8	4.5	0.7	6.9	0.7	1.7	3.8	0.7	0.0
	2005	103 759	90.2	78.8	78.1	6.4	1.0	4.1	1.1	5.2	0.6	1.1	3.0	0.5	0.0
	2011	159 361	91.2	82.4	81.2	5.6	1.2	2.1	1.2	7.6	0.8	1.1	4.8	0.9	0.0
Occupied Palestinian territory - Territoire palestinien occupé	1995	394	..	..	..	..	..	..	..	..	..	..	..	..	..
	2005	(e)335	92.8	4.1	4.0	1.1	0.0	87.5	0.0	7.2	0.9	0.4	0.7	5.3	..
	2011	(e)759	87.7	6.1	5.9	1.2	0.1	80.3	0.0	12.3	1.3	0.0	0.8	10.2	..
Oman	1995	5 917	37.5	1.7	1.7	4.3	30.6	0.9	0.2	62.4	1.8	0.0	49.8	10.7	..
	2005	18 692	21.3	2.9	2.9	2.8	15.2	0.4	0.2	78.5	1.6	0.0	67.3	9.6	0.0
	2011	(e)47 090	17.6	1.9	1.9	4.6	10.4	0.6	0.1	82.3	2.7	0.2	65.1	14.4	0.0
Pakistan	1995	8 158	57.0	32.0	31.2	15.1	6.8	3.2	0.9	40.6	3.0	1.6	24.8	11.2	0.0
	2005	16 050	55.2	27.2	26.6	24.8	0.9	2.3	0.7	44.0	5.7	1.7	22.5	14.0	0.0
	2011	25 344	42.9	25.3	25.0	15.1	0.8	1.7	1.3	55.8	6.7	2.2	31.7	15.2	0.0
Palau - Palaos	1995	13	54.0	0.9	0.9	15.1	38.0	0.0	0.0	45.9	0.1	1.2	44.6	..	..
	2005	14	95.1	1.5	1.5	2.4	91.2	0.0	0.0	4.9	0.0	0.0	4.4	0.3	0.0
	2011	7	95.2	0.3	0.3	1.2	93.7	0.0	0.0	4.8	0.0	0.9	3.9	0.0	..
Panama	1995	577	42.8	26.8	24.2	12.9	2.4	0.7	0.3	56.6	0.2	32.7	22.1	1.6	..
	2005	(e)7 375	38.2	23.4	21.7	13.1	0.8	0.8	1.0	60.4	1.7	45.9	12.4	0.3	0.0
	2011	14 555	26.5	5.5	4.4	15.5	3.5	2.0	0.4	72.9	0.3	63.2	9.0	0.4	0.0
Papua New Guinea - Papouasie-Nouvelle-Guinée	1995	(e)2 654	81.6	19.7	19.7	1.9	25.9	34.1	0.0	18.4	0.0	0.0	18.3	0.0	0.0
	2005	(e)3 490	76.2	14.9	14.8	2.0	13.1	46.2	0.1	23.5	0.5	0.0	22.4	0.0	0.6
	2011	(e)7 368	74.5	14.9	14.8	2.0	10.8	46.9	0.1	25.2	0.4	0.0	24.3	0.0	0.5

For sources and notes, see end of table.

Pour les sources et les notes, se reporter à la fin du tableau.

2.1 Country trade structure by partner — Exports by main region of destination
2.1 Structure du commerce des pays par partenaires — Exportations par principales régions de destination

Destination / Origin / Origine	Year / Année	World (millions of dollars) (1) / Monde (millions de dollars) (1)	Developed economies / Économies développées						Transition economies / Économies en transition	Developing economies / Économies en développement					
			Total	Europe Total	EU UE	USA États-Unis	Japan Japon	Other Autres		Total	Africa Afrique	America Amérique	Eastern, Southern and South-Eastern Asia / Asie orientale, méridionale et du Sud-Est	Western Asia / Asie occidentale	Oceania Océanie
								Percentage / En pourcentage							
Paraguay	1995	919	26.3	19.8	19.4	4.8	0.1	1.6	0.0	73.6	0.6	65.4	7.5	0.1	..
	2005	1 655	12.4	7.2	6.3	3.2	1.0	1.1	6.3	81.2	1.1	72.3	6.1	1.7	0.0
	2011	5 517	20.0	14.4	9.2	2.7	0.9	2.0	4.2	75.8	2.5	67.0	5.3	1.0	..
Peru - Pérou	1995	5 440	63.5	34.8	31.0	17.2	8.4	3.1	0.4	35.2	0.7	17.5	16.8	0.2	0.0
	2005	17 114	62.6	22.0	17.3	30.7	3.5	6.4	0.2	36.8	0.4	20.7	15.4	0.3	0.0
	2011	45 636	58.7	31.2	18.2	13.3	4.8	9.5	0.2	40.4	1.0	17.5	21.8	0.2	0.0
Philippines	1995	17 447	71.7	17.9	17.7	35.8	15.7	2.2	0.1	28.2	0.2	1.1	25.6	1.2	0.1
	2005	41 255	54.5	17.1	17.0	18.0	17.5	1.9	0.1	45.4	0.2	0.7	43.7	0.6	0.1
	2011	48 042	48.1	13.0	12.4	14.8	18.5	1.9	0.1	51.8	0.5	· 1.5	48.4	1.0	0.4
Poland - Pologne	1995	22 862	82.8	79.4	77.8	2.7	0.2	0.5	10.5	6.7	1.3	1.4	3.2	0.8	0.0
	2005	89 378	84.9	81.7	78.6	2.1	0.2	1.0	9.4	5.5	0.9	0.9	1.9	1.9	0.1
	2011	183 292	83.4	80.2	77.1	2.0	0.3	0.9	9.5	7.0	1.0	0.9	2.6	2.3	0.1
Portugal	1995	23 370	91.2	84.1	80.8	4.8	0.9	1.5	0.3	8.0	3.9	1.6	1.7	0.7	0.0
	2005	38 086	87.7	80.3	78.8	5.9	0.4	1.1	0.4	11.2	5.2	1.6	2.9	1.6	0.0
	2011	58 932	78.4	72.7	70.8	4.0	0.6	1.0	0.8	18.4	10.6	3.4	2.9	1.6	0.0
Qatar	1995	(e)3 557	63.1	1.3	1.3	2.6	55.5	3.6	0.0	36.9	1.5	0.0	27.7	7.7	0.0
	2005	(e)25 762	49.6	4.8	4.7	1.7	41.7	1.4	0.0	50.4	1.3	0.1	43.8	5.2	0.0
	2011	(e)114 298	47.1	16.9	16.7	1.2	27.4	1.6	0.1	52.9	0.9	0.8	49.1	2.1	0.0
Republic of Moldova - République de Moldova	1995	746	33.4	29.8	29.5	2.0	0.0	1.6	62.9	3.4	0.7	0.2	0.8	1.6	..
	2005	1 091	42.7	38.3	37.9	3.6	0.1	0.8	51.2	5.8	1.4	0.3	0.6	3.6	0.0
	2011	2 217	51.8	50.2	49.8	0.8	0.4	0.2	35.2	13.0	0.2	1.4	1.2	10.3	0.0
Romania - Roumanie	1995	7 910	65.3	60.5	59.3	2.5	0.4	1.8	6.8	27.5	7.2	2.2	9.2	8.9	0.0
	2005	27 730	77.1	71.8	70.5	4.1	0.3	0.9	6.2	16.6	2.2	0.6	3.2	10.7	0.0
	2011	62 692	75.7	72.9	71.1	1.8	0.4	0.7	8.6	15.7	2.8	0.7	3.1	9.0	0.0
Russian Federation - Fédération de Russie	1995	(e)78 217	51.0	43.4	38.8	4.3	2.8	0.5	18.0	15.2	0.7	3.3	9.1	2.2	0.0
	2005	241 452	67.1	62.2	57.3	2.6	1.5	0.7	14.1	18.7	1.1	2.0	10.3	5.3	0.0
	2011	478 009	57.8	51.0	48.4	3.4	3.0	0.5	6.0	22.2	1.7	1.6	14.7	4.2	0.0
Rwanda	1995	(e)52	72.6	69.2	68.8	2.9	0.2	0.2	0.0	27.4	21.9	0.0	5.4	0.1	..
	2005	(e)125	50.8	44.4	43.5	5.8	0.1	0.5	2.6	45.8	15.8	1.3	27.9	0.8	0.2
	2011	(e)417	18.8	12.7	11.9	5.5	0.2	0.3	0.7	80.5	43.1	1.5	35.4	0.5	..
Saint Helena - Sainte-Hélène	1995	(e)5	86.6	24.1	16.7	0.8	61.6	0.2	0.6	12.8	5.4	0.3	2.5	4.5	..
	2005	(e)20	61.3	16.4	16.4	23.4	20.7	0.8	0.4	38.3	24.0	9.8	4.2	0.2	0.1
	2011	(e)37	68.1	14.7	8.9	36.5	15.2	1.7	0.2	31.6	4.9	7.2	19.5	0.1	..
Saint Kitts and Nevis - Saint-Kitts-et-Nevis	1995	(e)19	91.2	34.5	34.3	51.9	0.1	4.7	0.2	8.6	0.0	8.4	0.1	0.0	..
	2005	(e)34	92.9	18.0	18.0	67.5	0.1	7.3	0.5	6.6	2.8	3.8	0.0	0.0	..
	2011	(e)55	79.6	8.0	7.5	62.9	0.2	8.5	6.9	13.5	0.3	10.2	1.7	1.3	..
Saint Lucia - Sainte-Lucie	1995	109	84.1	56.8	56.7	26.2	0.3	0.9	..	15.3	0.5	14.7	0.1	..	0.0
	2005	64	63.0	43.8	43.8	18.8	0.0	0.3	0.0	37.0	0.0	19.9	17.1	0.0	0.0
	2011	(e)161	54.3	30.2	30.2	23.8	0.0	0.2	0.0	45.7	0.0	32.7	13.0	0.1	..
Saint Pierre and Miquelon - Saint-Pierre-et-Miquelon	1995	6	94.5	37.1	36.2	54.7	1.5	1.2	..	5.0	1.6	3.1	0.3	..	..
	2005	(e)10	59.4	51.2	47.4	8.0	..	0.2	0.1	40.5	4.5	0.1	35.9	0.0	..
	2011	(e)5	99.8	66.8	66.8	3.2	0.3	29.5	0.0	0.2	0.0	0.1	0.1	0.0	0.0
Saint Vincent and the Grenadines - Saint-Vincent-et-les Grenadines	1995	(e)43	61.2	43.0	43.0	7.9	6.9	3.4	..	38.8	0.3	30.5	7.9	..	..
	2005	40	83.5	77.7	77.5	5.7	0.0	0.1	0.7	15.8	0.4	14.5	0.3	0.7	..
	2011	(e)42	62.7	61.3	60.4	1.2	0.0	0.1	0.0	37.3	2.2	26.9	3.6	4.5	..
Samoa	1995	(e)9	88.0	1.8	1.8	0.9	1.7	83.5	10.6	1.2	0.2	0.1	0.7	0.3	0.0
	2005	87	83.8	0.2	0.2	6.4	0.4	76.8	0.0	16.2	0.0	..	0.2	0.0	16.0
	2011	54	84.3	0.6	0.6	3.2	0.5	80.0	..	15.7	0.0	0.0	4.7	..	11.0
Sao Tome and Principe - Sao Tomé-et-Principe	1995	(e)5	67.6	63.0	57.7	2.0	2.5	0.1	1.0	14.4	3.7	1.5	8.6	0.5	..
	2005	(e)7	77.0	74.1	73.8	1.4	0.8	0.7	0.1	22.9	3.3	6.0	6.1	7.5	..
	2011	(e)13	81.2	69.5	69.0	8.7	0.2	2.7	2.8	16.0	11.7	1.5	2.6	0.3	..
Saudi Arabia - Arabie saoudite	1995	(e)49 030	56.1	19.8	19.5	16.8	17.3	2.2	0.0	43.9	2.8	2.3	29.7	9.1	0.0
	2005	(e)180 737	51.1	16.0	15.9	16.8	16.6	1.6	0.0	48.9	3.8	1.1	36.3	7.7	0.0
	2011	(e)360 093	39.4	10.8	10.7	13.5	14.0	1.1	0.2	60.5	4.3	1.2	48.1	6.8	0.0
Senegal - Sénégal	1995	(e)993	44.1	42.1	41.9	0.8	1.1	0.1	0.0	48.1	25.1	0.5	21.9	0.6	0.1
	2005	(e)1 471	30.9	29.4	29.1	0.6	0.9	0.1	0.0	58.4	39.2	0.3	18.2	0.5	0.2
	2011	(e)2 542	23.0	21.6	19.8	0.2	0.9	0.2	0.1	68.4	46.4	0.1	19.1	2.7	0.1

For sources and notes, see end of table.

Pour les sources et les notes, se reporter à la fin du tableau.

Destination	Year Année	World (millions of dollars) (1) Monde (millions de dollars) (1)	Developed economies — Économies développées						Transition economies — Économies en transition	Developing economies — Économies en développement					
			Total	Europe		USA États-Unis	Japan Japon	Other Autres		Total	Africa Afrique	America Amérique	Eastern, Southern and South-Eastern Asia — Asie orientale, méridionale et du Sud-Est	Western Asia — Asie occidentale	Oceania Océanie
Origin / Origine				Total	EU UE										
			Percentage / En pourcentage												
Serbia - Serbie	2011	11 775	59.4	58.4	57.6	0.7	0.0	0.3	36.4	4.2	0.7	0.1	1.0	2.3	0.0
Serbia and Montenegro - Serbie-et-Monténégro	1995	(e)1 531	38.9	36.4	31.4	1.8	0.0	0.7	42.2	4.8	1.9	0.4	1.4	1.1	0.0
	2005	(e)5 058	54.1	52.3	51.5	1.2	0.0	0.6	30.6	3.4	1.0	0.1	0.5	1.7	0.0
Seychelles	1995	53	58.1	50.2	50.1	3.9	3.3	0.7	..	41.8	2.6	0.0	21.5	17.7	..
	2005	340	79.6	69.9	69.8	1.1	7.7	0.9	0.8	19.6	6.2	0.1	3.3	9.9	0.0
	2011	(e)478	86.2	71.4	70.0	1.8	11.7	1.3	0.4	13.4	7.9	0.2	5.0	0.2	0.0
Sierra Leone	1995	(e)42	90.8	55.0	54.1	28.7	2.8	4.3	1.5	7.6	4.4	0.1	3.0	0.2	..
	2005	(e)159	88.5	79.5	79.5	7.3	0.4	1.3	1.5	10.0	3.2	0.8	4.0	2.1	0.0
	2011	(e)350	76.1	62.4	62.1	8.8	1.2	3.7	2.3	21.6	3.2	1.0	9.8	7.7	0.0
Singapore - Singapour	1995	118 263	43.6	14.3	13.9	18.3	7.8	3.2	0.8	55.3	1.3	1.3	51.1	1.3	0.3
	2005	229 652	33.0	12.5	12.2	10.4	5.5	4.6	0.2	66.6	1.0	2.0	60.5	2.2	0.9
	2011	409 504	25.1	10.1	9.6	5.5	4.5	5.0	0.2	73.6	1.1	4.6	65.0	1.7	1.3
Sint Maarten (Dutch part) - Saint-Martin (partie néerlandaise)	2011	127	94.7	..	..	94.7	..	0.0	..	5.3	..	5.3	..	..	..
Slovakia - Slovaquie	1995	8 374	88.4	86.4	85.2	1.3	0.2	0.4	7.5	4.0	0.7	0.6	1.7	1.1	0.0
	2005	31 852	91.7	87.7	86.5	3.2	0.3	0.5	4.2	3.8	0.5	0.4	1.2	1.7	0.0
	2011	78 487	88.5	86.2	84.7	1.5	0.2	0.6	5.4	6.1	0.4	0.5	3.7	1.5	0.0
Slovenia - Slovénie	1995	8 316	77.7	73.6	72.5	3.1	0.3	0.7	19.0	3.3	0.7	0.5	1.3	0.8	0.0
	2005	17 896	73.8	71.1	69.5	2.0	0.1	0.5	22.0	4.1	0.9	0.4	1.3	1.5	0.0
	2011	(e)34 709	62.4	60.6	59.4	1.3	0.1	0.4	15.3	4.4	0.8	0.5	1.7	1.4	0.0
Solomon Islands - Îles Salomon	1995	(e)168	64.6	10.8	10.8	2.5	49.1	2.2	..	35.4	0.4	0.0	35.0	0.0	0.0
	2005	(e)103	18.7	9.1	9.1	1.0	6.9	1.8	0.0	81.3	0.3	0.0	79.0	0.0	2.0
	2011	(e)389	24.1	11.0	11.0	0.3	2.0	10.8	0.0	75.9	0.0	0.1	74.2	0.0	1.6
Somalia - Somalie	1995	(e)170	18.2	18.1	18.1	0.1	..	0.0	0.2	81.6	1.5	0.0	4.3	75.8	..
	2005	(e)251	1.2	0.8	0.8	0.2	0.2	0.0	0.1	98.7	2.7	0.1	13.1	82.9	0.0
	2011	(e)518	6.1	5.7	5.7	0.2	0.1	0.2	0.1	93.8	0.6	0.6	23.3	69.3	0.0
South Africa - Afrique du Sud	1995	(e)29 784	36.1	20.6	17.6	6.6	6.0	2.8	0.3	61.9	47.8	2.0	11.0	1.1	0.0
	2005	(e)56 261	64.6	39.2	37.0	10.5	10.2	4.7	0.4	34.5	13.5	1.5	16.2	3.3	0.0
	2011	92 976	45.3	26.3	23.7	8.9	7.9	2.2	0.5	53.7	15.0	2.0	33.8	2.9	0.0
Spain - Espagne	1995	89 616	83.8	76.5	74.0	4.2	1.4	1.6	0.6	15.6	3.8	5.6	4.2	1.9	0.0
	2005	192 798	80.8	74.6	71.1	4.1	0.7	1.3	1.1	15.8	4.3	5.2	3.2	3.0	0.1
	2011	(e)296 496	78.9	72.7	69.4	3.5	0.9	1.7	1.8	19.3	5.6	5.3	4.4	4.0	0.1
Sri Lanka	1995	(e)3 798	75.5	30.0	29.0	36.3	6.3	2.9	1.8	15.5	2.0	1.4	9.3	2.7	0.0
	2005	6 160	69.3	31.8	31.0	32.2	2.3	3.1	3.3	25.4	1.4	1.7	16.1	6.3	0.0
	2011	10 011	63.6	36.7	35.5	21.4	2.2	3.3	4.4	31.9	1.9	2.4	18.9	8.6	0.1
Sudan (…2011) - Soudan (…2011)	1995	(e)556	48.8	37.4	35.2	5.2	6.2	0.0	0.3	50.9	3.1	0.1	21.6	26.0	..
	2005	4 506	28.2	3.7	3.7	0.3	22.9	1.3	0.1	71.7	2.3	0.2	63.1	6.1	0.0
	2011	(e)10 660	20.2	1.7	1.7	0.1	15.3	3.1	0.0	79.7	2.0	0.2	67.6	10.0	0.0
Suriname	1995	483	85.5	59.7	34.2	20.0	5.5	0.3	0.8	13.7	0.4	12.5	0.9	0.0	..
	2005	997	81.0	48.0	25.6	14.3	1.0	17.8	0.0	18.9	1.3	11.0	1.5	5.1	0.0
	2011	(e)2 345	77.2	33.4	25.9	23.9	0.4	19.5	0.0	22.8	0.3	11.1	2.6	8.9	..
Swaziland	1995	(e)844	13.6	6.4	6.3	5.5	0.8	0.9	0.8	85.7	75.4	0.7	9.3	0.2	0.0
	2005	(e)1 774	48.6	13.6	13.5	14.3	0.6	20.2	0.3	51.1	27.9	0.4	20.4	2.4	0.0
	2011	(e)2 049	52.7	31.0	30.2	15.8	0.2	5.8	0.4	46.8	19.2	5.0	17.8	4.8	0.0
Sweden - Suède	1995	77 436	86.3	71.8	61.7	8.1	3.0	3.3	1.2	12.5	1.6	2.0	7.2	1.7	0.0
	2005	130 264	83.3	68.5	58.4	10.6	1.5	2.8	2.6	13.6	2.3	2.1	6.8	2.3	0.0
	2011	187 179	74.8	65.2	54.6	5.9	1.2	2.5	3.1	17.7	3.5	2.7	8.3	3.2	0.0
Switzerland - Suisse	1995	81 641	80.7	65.2	64.6	8.7	4.0	2.9	0.8	18.5	1.8	2.5	10.8	3.4	0.0
	2005	130 930	80.7	63.3	62.9	10.9	3.6	2.9	1.6	17.7	1.4	2.4	10.2	3.7	0.0
	2011	234 426	73.9	57.3	56.9	10.3	3.2	3.1	2.4	23.7	1.6	2.9	15.0	4.2	0.0
Syrian Arab Republic - République arabe syrienne	1995	(e)3 563	64.9	62.7	62.6	1.4	0.2	0.6	4.4	30.7	5.0	0.2	2.0	23.5	..
	2005	(e)9 174	44.3	40.2	40.1	3.7	0.2	0.2	1.7	53.8	4.8	0.7	0.8	47.5	0.0
	2011	(e)7 843	34.2	29.8	29.8	2.8	1.3	0.3	1.2	64.5	6.5	0.4	2.5	55.1	0.0
Tajikistan - Tadjikistan	1995	(e)749	47.1	29.7	28.9	11.8	5.6	0.0	27.6	11.7	3.6	0.1	6.0	2.0	..
	2005	(e)874	58.0	58.0	55.0	0.0	0.0	0.0	19.6	22.4	0.0	..	6.6	15.8	..
	2011	(e)1 234	14.6	11.8	8.4	1.2	1.2	0.4	16.6	68.8	0.3	0.0	37.7	30.8	..

For sources and notes, see end of table.

Pour les sources et les notes, se reporter à la fin du tableau.

Destination / Origin / Origine	Year / Année	World (millions of dollars) (1) / Monde (millions de dollars) (1)	Developed economies / Économies développées						Transition economies / Économies en transition	Developing economies / Économies en développement					
			Total	Europe		USA États-Unis	Japan Japon	Other Autres		Total	Africa Afrique	America Amérique	Eastern, Southern and South-Eastern Asia / Asie orientale, méridionale et du Sud-Est	Western Asia / Asie occidentale	Oceania Océanie
				Total	EU UE										
			Percentage / En pourcentage												
TFYR of Macedonia - LERY de Macédoine	1995	1 204	71.0	67.8	64.7	3.0	0.1	0.1	14.7	6.7	1.0	0.0	2.2	3.5	0.0
	2005	2 041	60.2	57.4	57.0	2.2	0.4	0.2	31.6	8.2	0.2	4.3	1.3	2.4	0.0
	2011	4 455	62.3	61.3	60.6	0.8	0.0	0.2	30.8	6.9	0.1	0.2	4.6	2.0	..
Thailand - Thaïlande	1995	56 439	55.1	17.5	16.6	17.9	16.8	3.0	0.8	42.9	2.1	1.0	35.9	3.7	0.1
	2005	110 110	48.3	14.3	13.6	15.5	13.6	4.8	0.4	51.2	2.6	1.9	43.2	3.4	0.2
	2011	228 824	37.8	12.8	10.6	9.6	10.5	4.9	0.7	61.1	3.4	3.0	50.6	3.9	0.2
Timor-Leste	2005	(e)8	44.1	2.6	2.3	1.4	1.0	39.1	0.1	55.8	2.5	0.1	51.3	0.0	1.8
	2011	(e)12	22.3	11.7	11.7	0.0	9.5	1.2	0.0	77.6	0.4	0.0	77.2	..	..
Togo	1995	383	50.3	32.4	27.0	6.0	0.3	11.7	0.0	49.6	19.0	4.7	25.5	0.5	..
	2005	(e)659	19.4	16.7	16.4	1.1	0.0	1.6	0.1	80.1	60.2	1.7	17.7	0.5	0.0
	2011	(e)1 100	24.8	22.7	21.7	1.4	0.0	0.8	0.8	73.3	39.3	0.7	27.0	6.3	..
Tokelau - Tokélaou	1995	(e)1	91.2	0.3	0.3	76.9	..	14.0	..	5.1	0.6	0.6	2.5	1.0	0.4
	2005	(e)0	50.7	11.7	11.7	38.0	1.0	0.0	0.0	49.2	8.1	3.4	37.6	0.1	0.0
	2011	(e)0	28.8	11.3	11.3	17.0	0.3	0.2	0.0	71.2	5.4	58.1	7.6	0.0	0.0
Tonga	1995	(e)15	95.0	4.1	4.1	32.6	49.3	9.0	0.1	4.9	..	0.1	4.5	0.2	..
	2005	(e)10	89.5	3.0	3.0	32.4	44.0	10.1	0.0	10.5	0.0	0.4	2.7	..	7.4
	2011	(e)11	43.6	4.6	4.6	11.9	13.4	13.8	0.0	56.4	0.0	5.7	34.5	2.0	14.1
Trinidad and Tobago - Trinité-et-Tobago	1995	2 467	60.1	16.6	16.5	41.7	0.4	1.4	0.2	38.8	0.7	37.6	0.6	0.0	0.0
	2005	9 611	72.8	5.6	5.5	65.4	0.0	1.8	0.0	27.1	0.1	26.7	0.3	0.0	0.0
	2011	(e)13 272	64.6	15.6	15.5	45.9	0.6	2.5	0.0	35.4	1.1	30.4	3.8	0.1	0.0
Tunisia - Tunisie	1995	5 475	82.3	80.6	79.6	1.3	0.3	0.1	0.0	14.6	8.4	0.8	3.5	1.8	0.0
	2005	10 494	81.9	80.6	80.1	0.9	0.2	0.1	0.2	14.3	9.0	0.7	2.5	2.1	0.0
	2011	(e)17 847	78.2	74.9	74.2	2.0	0.9	0.4	0.7	21.1	13.4	1.0	4.0	2.7	0.0
Turkey - Turquie	1995	21 599	68.4	58.8	57.4	7.0	0.8	1.8	10.3	19.3	4.9	0.7	6.2	7.5	0.0
	2005	73 476	68.4	58.5	57.3	6.7	0.3	2.9	8.1	19.4	4.9	0.9	3.8	9.5	0.2
	2011	134 915	54.9	48.5	47.0	3.4	0.2	2.8	12.0	31.2	7.7	1.8	7.7	13.9	0.1
Turkmenistan - Turkménistan	1995	(e)1 939	16.7	15.8	13.4	0.7	0.2	0.0	65.2	18.1	0.1	0.0	9.7	8.3	..
	2005	(e)4 944	24.7	21.1	21.1	2.7	0.0	0.9	63.3	12.0	0.0	0.1	6.1	5.7	0.0
	2011	(e)13 000	12.9	11.7	11.3	1.2	0.0	0.0	20.0	67.1	0.3	0.0	56.0	10.8	0.0
Turks and Caicos Islands - Îles Turques et Caïques	1995	(e)5	69.6	31.7	31.7	37.7	..	0.1	2.6	27.8	0.4	16.9	10.5	0.1	..
	2005	(e)15	99.4	..	..	78.8	..	20.6	..	0.6	..	0.6	..	..	..
	2011	(e)16	80.6	40.8	40.6	39.0	0.3	0.5	0.8	18.7	8.1	2.4	3.7	4.4	0.0
Tuvalu	1995	(e)0	30.1	28.4	28.4	..	0.4	1.3	8.9	61.0	40.5	0.9	19.3	0.2	0.1
	2005	(e)0	83.6	78.5	78.4	1.5	0.6	3.0	2.3	14.1	6.9	0.1	2.4	..	4.7
	2011	(e)0	83.2	9.5	3.6	0.0	67.0	6.6	2.6	14.2	5.1	0.7	0.0	0.1	8.3
Uganda - Ouganda	1995	(e)461	89.4	84.7	74.9	1.7	1.4	1.7	0.1	10.5	7.5	0.1	2.3	0.6	0.0
	2005	(e)1 016	49.3	44.6	39.7	2.8	0.8	1.1	0.9	49.8	31.9	0.2	7.8	10.0	0.0
	2011	(e)2 409	37.7	33.6	31.8	2.9	0.4	0.8	1.4	60.9	45.8	0.1	6.0	9.0	..
Ukraine	1995	(e)13 317	25.4	21.8	20.9	2.6	0.6	0.5	51.5	20.3	1.4	1.4	11.6	5.9	0.0
	2005	34 228	35.4	31.2	29.9	2.8	0.2	1.2	32.6	32.0	7.0	2.3	11.3	11.4	0.0
	2011	68 393	29.3	26.5	26.3	1.6	0.2	1.0	40.0	30.6	4.9	1.9	11.5	12.2	0.0
United Arab Emirates - Émirats arabes unis	1995	(e)27 753	55.2	4.4	4.4	2.2	46.4	2.2	0.5	44.3	2.1	0.1	32.4	9.7	0.0
	2005	(e)115 453	42.0	12.1	11.5	1.6	27.5	0.7	0.8	57.2	4.2	0.1	44.8	8.1	0.0
	2011	(e)236 017	25.5	5.0	4.6	1.0	17.2	2.3	0.6	73.9	4.3	0.3	60.3	9.0	0.0
United Kingdom - Royaume-Uni	1995	234 372	77.3	60.0	56.9	11.5	2.4	3.4	0.9	16.1	2.9	1.7	8.3	3.2	0.0
	2005	384 365	80.8	60.7	57.0	14.7	1.8	3.6	1.4	17.7	2.7	1.4	8.1	5.4	0.0
	2011	472 096	75.1	56.6	53.4	13.3	1.5	3.8	2.5	21.9	3.7	2.2	10.9	5.0	0.0
United Republic of Tanzania - République-Unie de Tanzanie	1995	(e)685	47.2	37.6	32.6	1.8	6.5	1.2	0.1	40.0	13.6	0.1	24.9	1.4	0.0
	2005	1 672	45.3	30.6	26.4	2.0	4.8	8.0	1.2	53.4	24.8	0.1	23.1	5.4	0.0
	2011	4 735	37.7	27.1	19.3	1.7	8.2	0.7	1.4	60.9	27.5	0.1	28.6	4.7	0.0
United States - États-Unis	1995	582 965	58.9	23.1	21.8	..	11.0	24.8	0.6	40.4	1.7	16.4	19.8	2.4	0.1
	2005	904 339	54.9	22.2	20.7	..	6.1	26.5	0.7	44.4	1.7	21.2	18.5	2.9	0.1
	2011	1 479 730	46.9	20.4	18.2	..	4.5	22.0	0.9	52.2	2.2	24.7	21.3	4.0	0.1
Uruguay	1995	2 106	32.1	21.9	21.2	6.0	0.9	3.2	0.3	66.8	0.7	53.4	11.6	1.1	..
	2005	3 405	46.5	19.1	17.6	23.2	0.9	3.4	1.3	49.1	3.9	34.7	9.4	1.0	0.1
	2011	(e)7 951	26.1	20.1	19.0	3.1	1.0	1.9	3.8	70.0	3.1	44.4	18.9	3.5	0.1

For sources and notes, see end of table.

Pour les sources et les notes, se reporter à la fin du tableau.

Destination / Origin / Origine	Year / Année	World (millions of dollars) (1) / Monde (millions de dollars) (1)	Developed economies / Économies développées						Transition economies / Économies en transition	Developing economies / Économies en développement					
			Total	Europe		USA / États-Unis	Japan / Japon	Other / Autres		Total	Africa / Afrique	America / Amérique	Eastern, Southern and South-Eastern Asia / Asie orientale, méridionale et du Sud-Est	Western Asia / Asie occidentale	Oceania / Océanie
				Total	EU / UE										
									Percentage / En pourcentage						
Uzbekistan - Ouzbékistan	1995	3 430	60.0	52.8	52.4	1.1	5.7	0.3	19.1	20.9	0.0	2.4	14.9	3.5	..
	2005	4 749	25.1	18.0	17.9	2.5	3.3	1.3	44.0	31.0	0.1	0.1	23.8	6.9	0.0
	2011	13 254	11.6	9.5	9.3	1.0	1.0	0.2	50.0	38.4	0.3	0.1	19.5	18.5	0.0
Vanuatu	1995	(e)28	85.9	45.4	40.1	0.3	26.5	13.7	0.5	13.6	0.3	0.3	4.7	7.6	0.6
	2005	(e)38	24.2	13.9	13.9	1.0	6.1	3.2	0.0	75.8	0.2	0.1	64.9	8.4	2.2
	2011	(e)67	37.1	18.1	18.1	0.8	16.5	1.8	0.0	62.9	0.2	1.8	57.4	0.1	3.4
Venezuela (Bolivarian Rep. of) - Venezuela (Rép. bolivarienne du)	1995	19 093	67.8	10.2	10.1	53.5	2.0	2.0	0.2	32.0	0.2	31.0	0.7	0.1	..
	2005	55 413	71.7	8.8	8.6	59.9	0.5	2.4	0.1	28.2	0.3	23.0	4.8	0.2	0.0
	2011	(e)92 602	57.7	6.4	6.3	50.3	0.0	0.9	1.8	40.6	0.1	15.6	24.6	0.2	0.0
Viet Nam	1995	(e)5 449	44.7	19.9	16.1	3.1	18.2	3.5	1.6	48.0	0.4	0.8	45.3	1.3	0.0
	2005	32 447	58.9	17.5	17.1	18.3	13.4	9.7	1.0	39.6	2.0	1.8	34.6	1.1	0.1
	2011	(e)96 906	52.9	19.2	17.8	18.2	11.6	3.9	1.6	45.5	3.0	2.1	38.0	2.3	..
Wallis and Futuna Islands - Îles Wallis-et-Futuna	1995	(e)1	44.2	39.7	39.7	3.4	..	1.1	7.5	48.3	30.8	17.5	..	..	..
	2005	(e)0	41.0	40.1	40.1	0.8	..	0.1	0.1	58.9	52.7	0.1	5.4	..	0.7
	2011	(e)0	20.7	19.9	19.9	0.3	..	0.5	0.1	79.2	72.1	0.3	1.3	..	5.4
Western Sahara - Sahara occidental	1995	(e)8	30.0	6.4	6.4	..	23.6	0.0	3.2	66.8	6.5	59.1	1.2	..	..
Yemen - Yémen	1995	(e)1 917	18.5	2.5	2.5	1.6	14.4	0.0	0.0	81.4	8.2	8.0	61.3	3.9	..
	2005	(e)5 608	17.1	4.1	2.2	4.4	6.6	2.0	0.0	82.3	2.5	0.1	71.0	8.7	0.0
	2011	(e)9 622	17.1	5.5	5.5	5.8	5.8	0.0	0.0	82.7	4.3	1.0	66.3	11.1	0.0
Zambia - Zambie	1995	1 055	38.5	16.5	16.2	5.0	16.8	0.2	0.0	61.5	10.3	0.1	39.4	11.7	..
	2005	1 810	30.0	26.8	15.1	1.0	2.0	0.1	0.1	69.9	47.1	0.1	18.9	3.7	0.0
	2011	(e)9 018	28.5	27.2	8.9	0.5	0.8	0.1	0.2	71.2	23.6	0.0	43.2	4.4	..
Zimbabwe	1995	(e)2 121	60.8	44.2	42.5	5.4	9.1	2.1	0.6	38.7	29.6	0.8	7.7	0.5	0.0
	2005	(e)1 850	36.1	25.4	23.0	5.5	4.9	0.3	1.4	62.5	46.7	0.9	12.4	2.4	0.0
	2011	(e)3 500	27.0	22.2	21.7	2.0	2.2	0.6	1.4	71.6	46.7	0.9	21.5	2.4	0.0

Source:
UNCTAD secretariat calculations, based on UNCTAD, *UNCTADstat* Merchandise Trade Matrix

Notes:
(1) Include unspecified destinations.
(2) Exports data include a considerable amount of re-exports.
(3) Estimates. France including French Guiana, Guadeloupe, Martinique, Monaco and Reunion (and excluding intra trade)

Source :
Calculs du secrétariat de la CNUCED, basés sur la matrice du commerce de marchandises de *UNCTADstat* de la CNUCED

Notes :
(1) Y compris des destinations non-spécifiées.
(2) Les données des exportations comprennent une part importante de réexportations.
(3) Estimation. Les données sont dérivées des déclarations rapportées par la France métropolitaine et les départements d'outre-mer par agrégation diminuée des flux intra.

Origin / Origine (Destination)	Year / Année	World (millions of dollars) (1) / Monde (millions de dollars) (1)	Developed economies / Économies développées — Total	Europe — Total	Europe — EU / UE	USA États-Unis	Japan Japon	Other Autres	Transition economies / Économies en transition	Developing economies / Économies en développement — Total	Africa Afrique	America Amérique	Eastern, Southern and South-Eastern Asia / Asie orientale, méridionale et du Sud-Est	Western Asia / Asie occidentale	Oceania Océanie
Afghanistan	1995	(e)387	43.4	17.1	17.0	1.1	23.3	1.9	13.1	43.5	0.0	0.1	42.4	1.0	..
	2005	(e)2 470	26.5	14.1	13.9	8.6	3.2	0.6	14.5	59.0	1.8	0.1	50.3	6.8	..
	2011	(e)6 300	35.1	10.8	10.7	21.3	2.3	0.6	27.9	36.9	1.2	0.2	31.0	4.6	..
Albania - Albanie	1995	(e)714	74.9	72.2	68.9	2.6	0.1	0.1	7.7	10.5	1.5	0.9	1.1	7.0	..
	2005	2 614	73.1	71.3	70.3	1.1	0.2	0.4	9.9	16.8	0.7	1.5	6.5	8.0	0.0
	2011	5 396	71.8	68.3	66.9	1.1	0.2	2.2	12.0	16.2	0.5	1.7	7.9	6.1	0.0
Algeria - Algérie	1995	10 782	83.9	62.2	61.0	13.2	3.4	5.2	1.1	15.0	2.8	3.4	5.2	3.5	0.0
	2005	20 357	66.9	54.4	53.2	6.7	3.8	2.0	4.9	25.6	2.5	6.6	12.2	4.3	0.0
	2011	47 220	61.7	53.4	52.1	4.6	2.3	1.4	1.3	37.0	3.6	8.9	18.7	5.7	0.0
American Samoa - Samoa américaines	1995	416	..	..	..	..	..	..	..	..	..	..	..	..	..
	2005	(e)506	51.4	8.7	8.7	..	2.6	40.2	0.0	48.6	1.2	0.3	27.2	0.0	20.0
	2011	(e)690	22.5	1.2	1.1	..	0.5	20.9	..	77.5	0.2	0.2	66.5	0.0	10.5
Andorra - Andorre	1995	(e)1 025	97.0	92.3	91.1	2.8	1.8	0.1	0.1	2.9	0.2	0.2	2.5	0.1	..
	2005	(e)1 822	..	..	..	..	..	..	..	..	..	..	..	..	..
	2011	(e)1 615	96.6	95.4	94.0	1.1	0.1	0.0	0.0	3.4	0.1	0.2	3.0	0.1	0.0
Angola	1995	(e)1 468	80.8	63.6	62.5	15.1	1.5	0.5	0.0	19.1	8.9	2.4	7.7	0.1	..
	2005	(e)8 353	49.0	34.9	32.7	11.7	1.5	0.9	0.5	50.5	10.8	8.9	28.7	2.1	..
	2011	(e)21 736	52.9	41.1	39.5	9.8	0.9	1.1	0.4	46.7	6.6	9.1	28.9	2.0	0.0
Anguilla	1995	(e)53	6.3	1.6	1.6	4.3	0.1	0.2	0.3	93.4	0.0	93.4	0.0	0.0	..
	2005	(e)130	62.4	25.3	25.2	33.9	1.8	1.4	0.9	36.7	0.0	35.8	0.4	0.5	0.0
	2011	(e)153	86.0	21.9	21.8	58.0	1.6	4.6	2.4	11.6	0.1	5.0	1.9	4.6	..
Antigua and Barbuda - Antigua-et-Barbuda	1995	(e)346	80.8	40.1	39.3	35.2	3.4	2.1	0.1	19.0	0.4	15.0	3.6	0.0	..
	2005	(e)525	56.5	31.4	30.8	22.0	1.3	1.8	0.0	43.5	0.8	12.1	28.1	2.4	0.1
	2011	(e)471	18.5	7.7	7.4	9.6	0.4	0.8	0.0	81.5	0.9	10.2	70.2	0.2	0.0
Argentina - Argentine	1995	20 122	58.8	32.0	30.5	20.9	3.5	2.4	0.5	39.2	1.3	29.3	8.5	0.1	..
	2005	28 689	38.6	19.9	19.1	15.8	1.9	1.0	0.7	59.5	0.6	47.3	11.4	0.2	0.0
	2011	76 949	31.2	17.0	16.1	10.7	1.9	1.6	1.2	61.6	0.9	38.2	21.7	0.9	0.0
Armenia - Arménie	1995	(e)674	37.2	20.2	18.5	16.5	0.1	0.3	44.1	18.7	0.3	0.6	11.7	6.1	..
	2005	(e)1 692	50.0	36.9	34.5	5.3	0.4	7.3	28.0	22.1	0.1	5.8	10.3	5.9	..
	2011	(e)4 109	37.8	31.4	29.9	3.5	1.0	1.9	34.4	27.9	0.6	2.3	19.4	5.6	0.0
Aruba	1995	(e)1 772	75.5	23.5	22.9	48.3	2.5	1.2	0.0	24.5	..	22.3	2.1	0.0	..
	2005	(e)4 288	47.1	12.8	12.2	33.0	0.8	0.6	0.9	52.0	0.1	50.2	1.7	0.0	0.0
	2011	(e)5 891	52.6	15.4	14.7	36.2	0.5	0.5	0.0	47.4	1.0	42.0	4.4	0.1	0.0
Australia - Australie	1995	57 423	69.9	26.5	25.0	21.3	15.2	6.9	0.1	27.9	0.6	1.2	22.0	2.1	1.9
	2005	118 922	54.7	24.4	23.2	13.9	11.0	5.4	0.1	45.1	1.3	1.4	39.2	1.8	1.5
	2011	234 319	43.4	19.3	17.8	11.4	7.9	4.7	0.5	52.3	2.3	2.0	43.4	2.7	1.9
Austria - Autriche	1995	66 406	89.5	82.2	78.2	4.2	2.5	0.6	1.2	7.1	1.3	0.7	4.2	0.9	0.0
	2005	119 950	85.7	79.9	76.0	3.3	2.0	0.6	4.4	9.8	1.1	1.0	6.5	1.3	0.0
	2011	(e)181 217	86.6	83.8	77.9	1.7	0.7	0.3	4.9	8.5	1.3	0.3	4.9	2.0	0.0
Azerbaijan - Azerbaïdjan	1995	(e)668	25.2	20.2	20.0	3.6	1.1	0.3	35.8	38.6	0.0	..	20.6	18.0	..
	2005	4 211	37.1	31.2	29.9	3.4	1.7	0.8	34.4	28.4	1.3	0.4	18.5	8.3	0.0
	2011	9 733	43.4	34.4	32.3	6.5	1.8	0.8	27.3	29.3	6.6	2.5	5.6	14.6	0.0
Bahamas	1995	(e)1 243	94.3	2.7	2.3	90.4	0.3	1.0	..	5.3	0.0	4.6	0.7	0.0	..
	2005	2 567	90.2	2.5	2.1	85.9	1.2	0.7	0.0	9.7	0.0	9.5	0.2	0.0	0.0
	2011	3 410	91.6	1.6	1.2	88.9	0.6	0.5	0.0	6.7	0.1	6.3	0.4	0.0	0.0
Bahrain - Bahreïn	1995	(e)3 679	38.5	23.2	20.9	8.2	3.9	3.3	0.1	58.9	0.6	1.9	10.1	46.3	0.0
	2005	(e)9 339	39.1	24.6	22.8	5.4	6.8	2.3	0.3	60.6	1.1	2.4	14.5	42.6	0.0
	2011	(e)12 106	34.2	18.6	16.5	9.4	3.8	2.5	0.2	65.6	1.2	6.0	18.0	40.4	0.0
Bangladesh	1995	(e)6 694	27.9	12.1	11.3	5.9	7.2	2.8	0.9	70.7	0.5	2.1	65.9	2.2	0.1
	2005	12 631	20.6	10.8	9.8	2.7	4.6	2.4	3.8	75.6	1.7	2.7	58.4	12.7	0.1
	2011	(e)34 295	17.9	7.7	6.9	2.3	4.2	3.6	3.5	78.6	2.6	3.6	62.8	9.6	0.0
Barbados - Barbade	1995	766	72.6	22.7	21.5	37.5	6.1	6.2	0.1	27.2	0.1	23.5	3.6	0.0	..
	2005	1 672	60.0	15.3	14.0	34.1	5.6	5.0	0.5	39.5	0.2	33.9	5.2	0.1	0.0
	2011	1 775	35.7	9.5	8.7	21.0	1.7	3.6	21.2	43.1	0.1	34.2	8.5	0.2	0.0
Belarus - Bélarus	1995	(e)5 563	34.5	33.4	33.0	0.8	0.1	0.2	64.7	0.6	0.0	0.0	0.5	0.1	..
	2005	16 699	25.0	22.9	21.6	1.4	0.3	0.4	66.7	5.2	0.2	1.3	3.2	0.5	0.0
	2011	45 747	21.8	19.8	18.9	1.2	0.5	0.3	61.2	11.8	0.5	3.8	6.6	0.9	0.0

For sources and notes, see end of table.

Pour les sources et les notes, se reporter à la fin du tableau.

70

Origin / Origine / Destination	Year Année	World (millions of dollars) (1) / Monde (millions de dollars) (1)	Developed economies / Économies développées Total	Europe Total	Europe EU UE	USA États-Unis	Japan Japon	Other Autres	Transition economies Économies en transition	Developing economies / Économies en développement Total	Africa Afrique	America Amérique	Eastern, Southern and South-Eastern Asia / Asie orientale, méridionale et du Sud-Est	Western Asia / Asie occiden-tale	Oceania Océanie
			Percentage / En pourcentage												
Belgium - Belgique	1995	(e)164 590	87.2	76.8	74.5	5.4	2.9	2.1	1.3	10.8	3.6	1.7	4.9	0.5	0.0
	2005	320 130	84.5	74.5	72.1	5.4	2.7	1.9	1.8	13.7	2.7	1.9	7.5	1.6	0.0
	2011	465 216	80.0	70.6	68.1	.5.7	2.0	1.7	2.9	17.1	2.4	2.6	9.4	2.6	0.0
Belize	1995	259	65.5	13.8	13.4	44.6	5.0	2.2	0.0	34.5	0.1	30.7	3.7	0.0	..
	2005	(e)593	51.0	15.7	15.4	32.6	1.6	1.1	9.6	39.4	0.5	32.1	6.7	0.1	0.0
	2011	(e)831	48.7	9.9	9.0	37.0	0.8	0.9	3.4	47.8	0.1	38.6	8.9	0.2	0.0
Benin - Bénin	1995	(e)719	54.6	45.1	44.4	5.1	3.9	0.5	0.0	41.2	16.9	1.3	21.2	1.7	0.2
	2005	(e)1 018	31.7	27.7	26.4	2.5	1.1	0.4	0.3	68.0	17.7	1.4	47.0	1.9	0.0
	2011	(e)2 700	33.8	25.3	24.6	7.5	0.5	0.5	0.5	65.7	8.9	2.1	52.7	2.0	0.0
Bermuda - Bermudes	1995	(e)550	75.0	19.0	16.4	44.9	7.1	4.1	8.1	16.8	0.0	11.0	5.7	0.0	0.0
	2005	(e)988	67.6	34.5	32.0	28.9	1.1	3.0	3.3	29.2	0.1	2.4	26.6	0.0	0.0
	2011	(e)893	35.8	16.1	8.7	17.2	0.1	2.4	2.1	62.1	0.9	1.5	59.7	0.0	0.0
Bhutan - Bhoutan	1995	(e)113	48.3	22.2	20.8	1.3	24.5	0.3	0.0	51.7	0.1	1.0	49.3	1.3	..
	2005	(e)387	16.4	9.2	7.8	1.2	6.0	0.1	0.8	82.8	0.4	0.1	81.0	1.3	..
	2011	(e)949	20.2	13.4	10.1	1.1	5.5	0.2	..	79.8	0.2	..	79.6	0.1	..
Bolivia (Plurinational State of) - Bolivie (État plurinational de)	1995	1 396	40.1	16.4	15.7	15.7	6.7	1.3	0.2	59.7	0.1	49.8	3.2	6.6	0.0
	2005	2 343	24.5	9.2	8.8	10.9	3.7	0.8	0.1	75.3	0.1	69.7	5.5	0.0	0.0
	2011	7 673	23.3	8.6	8.2	10.4	3.8	0.5	0.1	76.6	0.1	66.4	10.0	0.2	0.0
Bonaire, Sint Eustatius and Saba - Bonaire, Saint-Eustache et Saba	2011	(e)55	..	..	..	..	..	..	..	100.0	..	40.2	59.8	..	..
Bosnia and Herzegovina - Bosnie-Herzégovine	1995	(e)1 082	36.7	34.1	33.9	2.6	..	0.0	61.5	1.7	0.8	0.2	0.0	0.6	
	2005	(e)7 054	60.5	59.9	59.1	0.4	0.1	0.1	35.5	4.1	0.1	0.5	1.1	2.3	0.0
	2011	(e)11 051	54.8	54.0	53.3	0.6	0.1	0.2	39.8	5.4	0.1	0.4	1.6	3.2	0.0
Botswana	1995	(e)1 902	11.4	8.6	8.5	1.5	0.2	1.1	0.0	88.6	87.1	0.0	1.4	0.0	0.0
	2005	3 162	8.9	6.0	5.9	1.9	0.4	0.7	0.0	91.1	87.7	0.2	3.1	0.1	..
	2011	7 272	10.8	7.0	6.9	1.2	0.7	1.9	0.0	89.1	77.0	0.0	12.0	0.1	0.0
Brazil - Brésil	1995	53 734	63.0	31.0	28.5	23.7	5.1	3.2	0.5	36.2	2.7	21.1	9.1	3.3	0.0
	2005	73 600	51.9	26.8	24.8	17.5	4.6	2.9	1.5	46.7	9.0	16.4	18.3	2.9	0.0
	2011	226 243	43.6	22.1	20.5	15.1	3.5	2.9	2.3	54.1	6.8	17.0	27.5	2.7	0.0
British Virgin Islands - Îles Vierges britanniques	1995	(e)122	14.3	11.3	8.8	2.7	0.2	0.1	82.7	3.1	0.0	3.0	0.1	..	..
Brunei Darussalam - Brunéi Darussalam	1995	(e)2 078	40.4	16.0	15.4	10.0	11.2	3.3	0.0	56.7	0.0	0.1	55.5	1.1	0.0
	2005	(e)1 497	20.9	8.8	8.5	3.3	7.0	1.8	0.0	79.1	0.4	0.1	78.1	0.5	0.0
	2011	(e)2 950	24.6	12.6	12.2	4.4	6.1	1.5	0.0	75.4	0.1	0.1	74.8	0.4	0.0
Bulgaria - Bulgarie	1995	(e)5 651	37.7	34.0	32.3	2.2	0.7	0.8	38.5	9.7	0.9	3.0	3.6	2.2	0.0
	2005	18 162	61.2	57.4	56.3	2.1	0.7	0.9	20.4	17.6	0.4	4.0	6.2	6.9	0.1
	2011	32 494	64.3	61.9	61.0	0.9	0.3	1.2	22.3	13.4	0.7	1.9	5.2	5.7	0.0
Burkina Faso	1995	484	60.2	49.9	49.3	4.3	5.3	0.6	0.1	39.7	31.3	1.8	6.5	0.1	0.0
	2005	1 161	42.9	36.4	36.2	3.2	1.6	1.7	2.4	54.6	41.2	1.8	9.0	2.6	0.0
	2011	(e)2 600	42.3	36.2	36.0	1.8	0.8	3.5	1.4	56.3	38.2	2.8	14.1	1.2	..
Burundi	1995	(e)234	67.7	57.0	56.0	3.4	6.7	0.6	0.0	32.2	15.9	0.3	11.8	4.2	..
	2005	258	48.2	38.3	36.0	2.8	5.8	1.3	0.6	51.1	33.2	0.3	11.4	6.3	..
	2011	(e)752	32.4	23.2	22.9	7.0	2.0	0.2	0.0	67.6	32.2	0.1	14.9	20.4	..
Cambodia - Cambodge	1995	(e)1 187	15.0	6.0	5.9	2.0	5.7	1.3	0.0	84.9	0.1	0.0	84.8	0.0	..
	2005	(e)3 918	10.7	5.6	5.4	1.7	2.5	0.9	0.1	89.1	0.1	0.2	88.7	0.1	..
	2011	(e)9 300	6.5	2.5	2.3	1.7	1.8	0.4	0.1	93.4	0.0	0.2	93.1	0.1	0.0
Cameroon - Cameroun	1995	1 079	76.2	60.7	59.8	7.7	5.5	2.3	0.6	20.4	11.3	1.8	6.8	0.5	0.0
	2005	2 735	47.4	38.2	37.7	4.9	3.3	1.1	1.5	50.2	30.8	4.1	13.6	1.5	0.1
	2011	(e)6 500	43.4	35.4	34.3	3.6	3.1	1.3	0.6	56.0	29.2	4.0	20.7	2.1	..
Canada	1995	164 371	84.7	11.7	10.3	66.8	5.4	0.8	0.3	13.3	0.8	4.2	8.0	0.3	0.0
	2005	314 444	76.4	14.2	12.1	56.5	3.9	1.8	0.6	23.0	1.8	7.0	13.2	1.0	0.0
	2011	450 537	67.4	13.4	11.7	49.5	2.9	1.6	1.1	31.4	3.2	9.7	16.8	1.7	0.0
Cape Verde - Cap-Vert	1995	(e)252	83.9	78.4	78.0	3.2	1.7	0.7	0.2	14.7	4.4	6.1	3.9	0.3	0.0
	2005	(e)438	75.4	70.4	70.1	2.8	1.8	0.3	0.1	24.5	4.3	12.4	2.9	4.9	..
	2011	(e)961	85.9	83.0	82.5	1.3	1.3	0.3	0.1	14.1	2.1	5.1	6.1	0.7	..
Cayman Islands - Îles Caïmanes	1995	(e)391	48.9	19.0	17.6	27.8	0.7	1.4	1.8	49.3	0.0	48.7	0.6	0.0	..
	2005	(e)1 191	83.2	49.3	44.4	31.0	0.8	2.1	0.0	16.8	0.0	12.2	4.6	0.0	..
	2011	(e)914	66.8	21.5	19.9	21.8	23.1	0.4	2.0	31.2	0.0	15.7	15.0	0.6	..

For sources and notes, see end of table.　　　　　Pour les sources et les notes, se reporter à la fin du tableau.

Origin / Origine	Year Année	World (millions of dollars) (1) Monde (millions de dollars) (1)	Developed economies Économies développées						Transition economies Économies en transition	Developing economies Économies en développement					
			Total	Europe		USA États- Unis	Japan Japon	Other Autres		Total	Africa Afrique	America Amérique	Eastern, Southern and South- Eastern Asia Asie orientale, méridionale et du Sud-Est	Western Asia Asie occiden- tale	Oceania Océanie
				Total	EU UE										
Destination			Percentage / En pourcentage												
Central African Republic - République centrafricaine	1995	(e)174	82.7	55.5	55.2	3.2	23.9	0.2	0.1	17.2	14.5	0.5	1.8	0.4	..
	2005	185	60.4	49.4	48.8	8.6	2.0	0.4	0.0	39.6	26.9	1.6	8.7	2.4	..
	2011	(e)380	54.5	41.7	41.3	10.9	1.2	0.6	0.1	45.4	20.9	4.6	16.9	3.0	..
Chad - Tchad	1995	(e)488	69.6	59.8	59.5	6.6	2.6	0.7	0.5	29.9	21.2	0.2	7.8	0.6	..
	2005	(e)949	70.9	54.4	53.9	15.0	0.2	1.3	2.3	26.9	20.0	0.1	3.9	2.8	..
	2011	(e)2 100	64.0	51.3	50.9	11.5	0.2	1.0	2.4	33.6	22.1	0.2	7.9	3.3	..
Chile - Chili	1995	14 903	58.3	22.5	21.4	25.5	6.8	3.6	0.3	40.6	2.1	27.8	10.5	0.1	0.0
	2005	32 926	38.0	16.4	15.8	15.6	3.9	2.1	0.3	57.4	4.9	35.5	16.9	0.1	0.0
	2011	74 907	40.6	14.4	13.8	20.2	3.9	2.1	0.1	54.2	1.0	28.3	24.0	0.9	0.0
China - Chine	1995	132 083	55.8	17.3	16.5	12.2	22.0	4.3	3.7	38.7	1.1	2.2	33.9	1.4	0.1
	2005	659 953	38.5	12.0	11.2	7.4	15.2	4.0	3.2	58.3	3.2	4.0	47.4	3.6	0.1
	2011	1 743 395	38.6	13.9	12.1	7.1	11.2	6.5	3.8	57.3	5.3	6.8	39.1	6.0	0.1
China, Hong Kong SAR - Chine (RAS de Hong Kong)	1995	196 072	37.1	12.2	10.8	7.9	14.6	2.3	0.3	62.7	0.8	0.6	60.6	0.6	0.0
	2005	300 160	26.7	8.9	7.6	5.2	11.0	1.6	0.2	73.2	0.4	0.7	71.4	0.7	0.0
	2011	510 855	27.9	11.6	7.9	6.2	8.5	1.7	0.2	71.9	0.8	1.0	69.0	1.0	0.0
China, Macao SAR - Chine (RAS de Macao)	1995	2 025	20.1	9.6	9.3	3.5	5.7	1.3	0.1	79.7	0.2	0.1	79.2	0.3	..
	2005	(e)3 913	18.2	8.0	7.5	3.0	6.0	1.2	0.1	81.7	0.3	0.3	80.8	0.3	0.0
	2011	7 927	29.5	19.2	15.2	4.8	4.5	1.0	0.0	70.5	0.2	0.9	69.0	0.4	0.0
China, Taiwan Province of - Province chinoise de Taiwan	1995	(e)103 506	70.1	16.3	14.8	20.1	29.2	4.5	1.8	27.7	1.8	2.3	20.3	3.3	0.0
	2005	(e)181 592	51.5	10.7	9.7	11.6	25.3	4.0	1.3	45.6	2.0	1.9	32.8	8.8	0.1
	2011	(e)281 316	42.5	9.6	8.5	9.3	18.5	5.1	1.3	54.4	3.8	2.6	36.3	11.7	0.1
Colombia - Colombie	1995	13 883	68.1	20.9	19.3	33.9	8.9	4.5	0.6	30.2	0.3	24.8	4.9	0.1	0.0
	2005	21 204	49.1	14.9	13.8	28.5	3.3	2.4	1.0	48.2	0.4	33.1	14.6	0.1	0.0
	2011	54 675	44.5	14.7	13.7	25.0	2.6	2.1	0.7	54.0	0.2	31.0	22.3	0.4	0.0
Comoros - Comores	1995	62	72.5	70.3	70.0	0.5	1.7	0.0	0.0	27.5	16.4	0.1	8.9	2.0	0.1
	2005	(e)99	36.7	35.7	35.6	0.2	0.3	0.5	0.4	62.8	24.2	2.2	17.8	18.6	0.0
	2011	(e)277	31.0	30.0	29.9	0.1	0.6	0.3	0.0	68.9	20.8	1.6	24.7	21.8	0.0
Congo	1995	(e)670	74.3	65.5	64.8	7.1	1.5	0.2	0.0	11.1	6.6	0.2	4.3	0.1	..
	2005	(e)1 343	55.8	47.6	47.0	6.8	0.5	0.9	0.3	43.9	14.4	5.1	23.0	1.4	..
	2011	(e)5 501	43.9	37.1	36.0	5.4	0.3	1.1	0.2	49.8	13.2	6.1	25.6	5.0	0.0
Cook Islands - Îles Cook	1995	(e)49	89.7	24.0	24.0	1.9	2.0	61.8	0.2	10.1	..	0.5	9.6	..	..
	2005	(e)81	92.4	5.8	5.8	1.5	2.7	82.4	0.0	7.6	0.0	0.0	5.9	0.0	1.7
	2011	(e)81	89.6	4.3	4.1	4.4	1.2	79.6	0.0	10.4	0.2	0.5	7.1	2.3	0.2
Costa Rica	1995	(e)4 090	67.3	13.8	13.0	48.6	3.4	1.5	0.3	32.4	0.1	27.0	5.3	0.0	0.0
	2005	9 173	64.5	13.4	12.7	42.8	5.8	2.5	0.6	34.9	0.0	26.2	8.6	0.1	0.0
	2011	(e)16 218	61.4	8.3	7.6	43.9	5.3	4.0	0.4	38.2	0.2	25.7	12.1	0.2	0.0
Côte d'Ivoire	1995	(e)2 946	52.4	43.4	42.5	4.0	4.2	0.8	1.6	29.9	17.8	2.3	9.2	0.6	0.0
	2005	5 865	46.4	42.6	41.4	2.0	1.4	0.4	1.4	51.9	30.3	3.4	16.8	1.4	0.0
	2011	6 720	31.7	26.9	26.1	1.9	2.1	0.8	1.1	62.1	32.8	6.0	20.9	2.4	0.0
Croatia - Croatie	1995	7 509	86.3	82.0	79.1	2.7	1.1	0.5	3.6	10.1	3.5	1.9	3.6	1.0	0.0
	2005	18 560	73.6	69.7	67.9	2.2	1.5	0.3	13.9	12.5	1.0	1.6	7.9	2.0	0.0
	2011	20 397	67.2	63.6	61.4	2.2	1.1	0.4	17.9	14.9	0.5	1.5	10.9	1.9	0.0
Cuba	1995	(e)2 805	48.0	38.4	38.0	0.2	0.8	8.6	13.4	38.5	1.7	27.8	8.8	0.3	..
	2005	(e)8 084	41.3	25.9	25.6	5.8	2.9	6.7	2.6	56.0	2.8	38.4	14.5	0.1	0.1
	2011	(e)14 300	28.2	19.7	19.5	3.3	0.3	5.0	1.8	69.9	4.2	51.4	14.3	0.1	..
Cyprus - Chypre	1995	3 694	77.0	54.8	53.4	13.0	6.7	2.5	4.8	14.9	0.9	1.3	10.5	2.3	0.0
	2005	6 382	79.9	67.8	66.7	1.6	3.1	7.5	3.1	15.4	1.4	2.9	8.2	3.0	0.0
	2011	8 719	82.8	69.8	68.3	1.5	0.8	10.6	2.8	12.9	1.4	1.3	8.2	2.0	0.0
Czech Republic - République tchèque	1995	25 303	85.7	81.5	79.2	2.6	1.2	0.5	9.9	4.4	0.3	0.6	3.2	0.3	0.0
	2005	76 527	83.9	78.8	76.4	2.1	2.6	0.5	7.2	8.8	0.5	0.6	7.1	0.6	0.0
	2011	150 542	78.9	75.8	74.0	1.4	1.5	0.3	6.6	14.4	0.3	0.4	13.0	0.7	0.0
Dem. Rep. of the Congo - Rép. dém. du Congo	1995	(e)1 046	50.1	40.3	39.4	6.4	0.9	2.4	0.0	49.8	27.8	0.8	21.1	0.1	..
	2005	(e)2 690	45.1	39.0	38.1	4.0	1.0	1.1	0.2	54.7	46.8	1.8	5.6	0.4	..
	2011	(e)5 306	37.4	30.7	29.9	4.2	1.7	0.8	0.2	62.4	34.2	3.1	24.2	0.9	..
Denmark - Danemark	1995	43 142	84.7	76.1	68.8	4.5	2.6	1.4	1.1	8.2	0.5	1.5	5.9	0.4	0.0
	2005	74 265	82.9	77.8	71.6	2.7	1.0	1.4	2.2	14.6	0.5	1.6	10.1	2.2	0.1
	2011	97 831	81.0	76.3	70.6	2.7	0.5	1.5	2.4	15.0	0.5	1.6	11.3	1.6	0.0

For sources and notes, see end of table.

Pour les sources et les notes, se reporter à la fin du tableau.

Origin / Origine — Destination	Year Année	World (millions of dollars) (1) Monde (millions de dollars) (1)	Developed economies / Économies développées						Transition economies Économies en transition	Developing economies / Économies en développement					
			Total	Europe Total	EU UE	USA États-Unis	Japan Japon	Other Autres		Total	Africa Afrique	America Amérique	Eastern, Southern and South-Eastern Asia / Asie orientale, méridionale et du Sud-Est	Western Asia / Asie occidentale	Oceania Océanie
Djibouti	1995	(e)177	44.5	35.6	35.0	2.6	5.5	0.8	0.0	55.5	12.0	1.7	36.2	5.6	..
	2005	(e)277	20.3	12.0	12.0	4.0	3.7	0.5	0.9	78.8	6.9	0.6	33.9	37.4	..
	2011	(e)416	15.3	8.7	8.7	4.2	2.1	0.3	4.1	80.6	5.5	0.6	46.0	28.5	..
Dominica - Dominique	1995	117	66.8	26.9	25.8	33.1	4.6	2.2	0.4	32.3	0.1	30.7	1.5	0.1	..
	2005	165	57.7	13.8	13.4	36.6	4.6	2.7	0.0	41.5	0.3	37.6	3.6	0.0	0.0
	2011	(e)221	56.7	9.7	9.5	40.9	4.0	2.0	0.0	43.2	0.0	38.6	4.6	0.1	0.0
Dominican Republic - République dominicaine	1995	(e)5 170	77.3	9.4	9.0	63.8	2.7	1.4	0.0	22.6	0.0	18.2	4.3	0.1	..
	2005	(e)9 869	63.2	10.0	9.5	48.4	3.5	1.3	0.3	36.4	0.1	30.8	5.4	0.1	0.0
	2011	(e)18 156	55.8	9.3	8.7	44.8	0.4	1.2	0.4	43.8	0.2	32.5	10.7	0.3	0.1
Ecuador - Équateur	1995	4 195	58.5	16.8	15.8	30.7	8.6	2.3	0.0	39.3	0.8	32.6	5.6	0.3	0.0
	2005	9 609	36.0	11.6	11.0	19.2	3.6	1.6	1.0	62.7	1.1	46.8	14.0	0.7	0.0
	2011	24 286	36.9	10.5	9.8	21.2	3.7	1.5	0.9	61.5	0.6	37.7	22.6	0.5	0.1
Egypt - Égypte	1995	11 739	68.3	44.7	41.9	18.8	2.7	2.1	4.7	21.5	2.4	3.2	11.5	4.3	0.0
	2005	19 812	38.9	25.0	24.0	8.9	2.3	2.6	8.0	38.9	5.4	6.0	12.9	14.6	0.0
	2011	59 269	46.0	30.9	29.4	10.7	2.2	2.2	7.5	46.3	3.0	6.7	20.3	16.3	0.0
El Salvador	1995	(e)3 329	61.0	10.9	10.3	44.0	5.1	1.0	0.1	36.6	0.2	31.2	5.2	0.0	0.0
	2005	6 809	47.7	8.5	8.0	35.8	2.1	1.4	0.7	51.6	0.2	41.9	9.4	0.0	0.0
	2011	(e)10 118	47.9	6.1	5.9	39.1	1.8	0.9	0.1	52.1	0.6	41.6	9.8	0.0	..
Equatorial Guinea - Guinée équatoriale	1995	121	63.2	55.5	54.0	6.7	0.4	0.6	..	35.2	29.4	1.5	4.3	0.0	..
	2005	1 310	80.9	53.6	52.5	25.2	0.6	1.5	0.3	18.8	13.0	1.0	3.3	1.4	..
	2011	(e)6 000	61.1	41.5	40.9	16.3	0.5	2.9	1.0	37.9	9.3	5.5	18.9	4.2	..
Eritrea - Érythrée	1995	(e)434	73.6	40.5	39.2	12.4	20.7	0.0	1.3	25.1	0.4	..	10.3	14.4	..
	2005	(e)487	61.4	49.3	48.5	11.0	0.3	0.8	7.0	31.6	5.6	3.9	6.5	15.6	..
	2011	(e)849	22.2	19.6	19.0	0.8	0.2	1.6	3.7	74.1	16.6	2.1	37.4	18.0	..
Estonia - Estonie	1995	2 546	78.4	73.1	71.7	3.9	1.1	0.3	18.5	3.1	0.1	1.0	1.8	0.2	0.0
	2005	11 018	73.8	69.2	67.8	1.6	2.7	0.3	17.6	8.6	0.4	0.6	7.0	0.6	0.0
	2011	18 780	74.9	71.7	69.8	1.5	0.9	0.8	13.9	11.3	1.1	0.4	9.0	0.7	0.0
Ethiopia - Éthiopie	1995	1 141	60.6	38.8	37.0	12.9	8.4	0.4	0.2	30.0	6.6	0.2	9.7	13.5	..
	2005	4 095	40.5	25.6	24.8	9.2	3.6	2.1	2.3	57.1	6.2	0.9	24.8	25.2	0.0
	2011	8 896	26.2	15.0	14.3	5.5	5.0	0.7	4.7	69.0	4.8	1.1	38.6	24.5	0.0
Faeroe Islands - Îles Féroé	1995	(e)314	92.1	86.5	65.9	2.3	3.0	0.3	0.9	4.3	0.0	0.6	3.0	0.1	0.5
	2005	747	90.3	79.2	59.4	8.6	1.8	0.7	0.2	9.1	0.1	1.2	4.9	0.5	2.4
	2011	(e)978	98.4	97.4	63.7	0.3	..	0.6	0.2	1.4	0.0	1.1	0.2	0.0	..
Falkland Islands (Malvinas) - Îles Falkland (Malvinas)	1995	(e)44	98.1	97.2	97.1	0.7	0.1	0.1	0.1	1.6	0.4	..	1.2	..	..
	2005	(e)59	99.9	97.3	97.2	2.4	0.0	0.2	..	0.1	0.0	0.0	0.1	0.0	..
	2011	(e)193	98.5	95.3	88.2	2.8	0.0	0.4	0.0	1.5	0.0	0.0	1.4	..	..
Fiji - Fidji	1995	(e)892	77.9	4.5	4.3	4.8	6.4	62.1	..	21.3	0.0	0.2	21.0	0.0	0.0
	2005	1 607	54.2	3.4	3.2	3.8	4.2	42.8	0.0	44.4	0.3	0.3	43.3	0.1	0.4
	2011	(e)2 300	39.7	4.4	4.3	2.3	1.6	31.5	0.0	60.2	0.3	0.1	59.2	0.1	0.6
Finland - Finlande	1995	29 520	82.2	67.1	61.2	7.2	6.4	1.6	7.5	8.4	0.5	1.9	5.8	0.2	0.0
	2005	58 473	70.5	61.7	58.4	4.1	3.3	1.4	14.5	14.5	0.5	2.2	11.1	0.7	0.0
	2011	83 862	68.8	64.5	60.9	2.3	0.6	1.4	19.1	10.8	0.8	2.1	7.3	0.5	0.0
France (3)	1995	275 510	73.1	60.3	56.3	7.8	3.5	1.5	1.5	14.8	3.9	2.1	7.2	1.7	0.1
	2005	475 857	76.8	67.0	62.9	5.9	2.7	1.1	3.0	20.1	4.7	1.8	11.0	2.5	0.0
	2011	700 852	71.1	62.5	58.9	5.6	1.9	1.1	4.7	23.7	5.3	1.9	13.5	2.9	0.1
French Polynesia - Polynésie française	1995	(e)1 019	84.3	52.3	51.9	14.0	3.6	14.5	0.0	10.3	0.3	0.9	8.5	0.1	0.5
	2005	1 702	73.6	49.9	49.5	10.0	2.9	10.8	0.0	26.4	0.3	1.0	24.4	0.2	0.5
	2011	1 628	65.6	41.2	40.7	10.3	2.0	12.1	0.1	34.3	0.3	1.2	32.1	0.3	0.4
Gabon	1995	(e)884	78.6	61.2	60.7	10.4	6.0	1.0	0.1	12.2	5.7	1.3	4.8	0.4	0.0
	2005	1 472	76.9	66.7	65.5	6.7	2.9	0.6	0.1	23.0	11.2	2.8	7.4	1.6	0.0
	2011	(e)3 800	68.5	58.0	57.5	6.4	2.7	1.4	0.2	31.2	11.5	2.6	15.8	1.4	0.0
Gambia - Gambie	1995	(e)182	49.5	43.4	43.0	3.0	3.0	0.2	0.2	50.3	13.0	3.0	33.5	0.8	..
	2005	260	32.3	25.2	25.0	5.4	0.8	0.9	0.6	67.0	23.4	6.0	32.7	5.0	0.0
	2011	344	21.0	17.4	17.2	2.7	0.5	0.3	0.2	78.9	17.1	10.5	44.6	6.7	0.0
Georgia - Géorgie	1995	(e)489	47.0	35.6	35.2	10.1	0.2	1.2	37.8	15.2	0.1	0.3	2.6	12.2	..
	2005	(e)2 490	39.8	31.6	31.0	6.9	0.4	0.9	38.7	21.4	0.2	3.1	4.5	13.7	0.0
	2011	(e)6 946	37.7	28.9	28.3	5.3	2.3	1.2	26.2	36.1	0.8	2.8	13.6	18.8	0.0

For sources and notes, see end of table.

Pour les sources et les notes, se reporter à la fin du tableau.

Origin / Origine / Destination	Year / Année	World (millions of dollars) (1) / Monde (millions de dollars) (1)	Developed economies / Économies développées Total	Europe Total	Europe EU UE	USA États-Unis	Japan Japon	Other Autres	Transition economies / Économies en transition	Developing economies / Économies en développement Total	Africa Afrique	America Amérique	Eastern, Southern and South-Eastern Asia / Asie orientale, méridionale et du Sud-Est	Western Asia / Asie occidentale	Oceania Océanie
			Percentage / En pourcentage												
Germany - Allemagne	1995	464 145	82.3	68.7	62.8	6.8	5.3	1.4	2.6	15.0	2.1	2.3	9.0	1.6	0.1
	2005	779 819	76.3	65.3	59.1	6.7	3.5	0.9	4.5	19.0	2.2	2.2	12.8	1.8	0.1
	2011	1 260 298	69.3	59.9	54.8	5.5	2.8	1.2	4.6	22.2	2.4	2.9	15.3	1.7	0.0
Ghana	1995	(e)1 896	68.8	46.7	45.2	13.1	6.4	2.6	0.3	20.0	5.4	3.6	10.2	0.7	0.0
	2005	4 878	43.9	31.5	30.7	6.5	2.0	3.8	0.9	55.2	25.1	4.8	23.8	1.6	0.0
	2011	(e)15 300	41.4	28.2	27.6	8.3	1.2	3.7	1.3	57.3	16.8	3.6	34.3	2.7	0.0
Gibraltar	1995	411	94.7	86.8	84.3	2.9	4.9	0.1	0.8	4.3	1.1	0.1	2.4	0.7	..
	2005	551	82.4	73.7	73.1	4.5	1.5	2.7	15.1	2.5	0.8	0.1	0.4	1.2	..
	2011	867	89.4	54.7	54.4	31.3	0.6	2.8	2.2	8.4	0.2	0.3	6.3	1.6	..
Greece - Grèce	1995	25 927	82.5	75.7	73.7	3.2	2.6	1.0	3.5	14.0	3.1	1.8	6.8	2.2	0.0
	2005	54 894	66.5	60.3	58.6	3.4	2.1	0.8	10.1	23.2	2.6	1.5	12.6	6.6	0.0
	2011	60 832	56.9	53.6	51.9	1.9	0.7	0.8	13.8	29.1	3.9	1.4	15.9	7.9	0.0
Greenland - Groenland	1995	421	98.4	93.2	85.2	1.8	2.1	1.3	0.1	1.6	0.1	0.2	1.3	0.0	0.0
	2005	593	99.4	96.3	93.5	0.7	0.0	2.4	..	0.6	0.0	0.0	0.5	0.0	..
	2011	(e)965	99.1	96.7	91.6	0.7	0.0	1.7	0.2	0.6	0.0	0.0	0.6	0.0	0.0
Grenada - Grenade	1995	129	65.0	15.9	15.4	41.5	3.2	4.5	0.0	34.6	0.0	31.8	2.7	0.1	0.0
	2005	334	59.1	14.5	14.0	37.5	4.0	3.1	0.0	40.9	0.1	35.0	5.7	0.1	0.0
	2011	(e)329	50.9	11.9	11.3	31.9	3.7	3.4	0.0	49.1	0.1	43.3	5.6	0.2	0.0
Guam	1995	442	..	..	..	..	..	..	..	..	..	..	..	..	..
	2005	(e)533	21.3	5.5	5.5	..	13.4	2.4	0.0	78.7	0.0	0.1	78.5	0.0	0.0
	2011	(e)708	19.5	5.8	4.7	..	11.4	2.3	..	80.5	0.0	0.1	80.2	0.1	0.0
Guatemala	1995	3 292	61.8	11.3	10.7	44.9	3.7	2.0	0.8	37.4	0.1	33.5	3.8	0.0	0.0
	2005	10 500	49.8	9.6	7.9	33.9	3.8	2.6	1.1	48.8	0.1	32.0	16.7	0.1	0.0
	2011	16 611	49.5	7.5	6.6	39.2	1.8	1.0	0.7	48.8	0.1	34.7	13.6	0.4	0.0
Guinea - Guinée	1995	819	62.7	48.3	47.5	8.0	6.0	0.5	1.0	36.3	14.4	5.2	16.0	0.7	0.0
	2005	(e)820	48.4	36.0	35.2	10.2	1.2	1.0	2.5	49.0	20.5	2.1	23.3	3.1	0.0
	2011	(e)2 106	54.3	45.0	44.7	4.7	1.4	3.2	1.6	44.1	11.7	3.0	25.8	3.6	0.0
Guinea-Bissau - Guinée-Bissau	1995	(e)133	56.4	48.5	48.0	0.7	7.1	0.1	0.2	43.4	7.3	0.7	35.4	0.0	..
	2005	(e)112	59.2	57.8	57.0	1.2	0.2	0.0	0.1	40.7	28.0	3.6	8.9	0.1	..
	2011	(e)297	52.6	48.9	48.3	3.3	0.3	0.1	0.1	47.3	25.8	7.5	13.3	0.7	..
Guyana	1995	(e)528	61.0	12.8	12.6	35.6	8.6	3.9	0.0	37.5	0.2	32.0	5.2	0.1	..
	2005	778	43.9	10.5	10.3	27.3	3.2	2.9	0.1	56.0	0.3	46.1	9.3	0.3	0.0
	2011	1 684	36.6	8.6	8.6	21.5	3.1	3.4	0.2	63.2	5.6	43.0	14.0	0.6	0.0
Haiti - Haïti	1995	(e)654	81.0	12.2	11.6	61.7	4.3	2.8	0.0	17.1	0.1	12.5	4.5	0.0	..
	2005	(e)1 466	75.6	8.9	8.4	61.6	3.1	2.0	0.1	23.7	0.1	13.9	9.0	0.8	..
	2011	(e)3 045	75.6	8.7	8.3	61.7	3.2	2.0	0.1	23.8	0.1	13.9	9.0	0.8	..
Honduras	1995	1 728	69.7	12.4	11.5	53.0	3.6	0.8	0.1	30.1	0.1	23.9	6.0	0.0	0.0
	2005	(e)6 545	55.5	7.3	6.9	45.6	1.8	0.8	0.5	44.0	0.2	37.5	6.3	0.1	0.0
	2011	(e)10 338	53.1	5.1	4.8	46.0	1.3	0.7	0.8	46.0	0.1	37.7	8.2	0.1	0.0
Hungary - Hongrie	1995	15 186	78.4	72.5	69.8	3.1	2.2	0.6	14.8	6.7	1.0	1.5	3.9	0.3	0.0
	2005	65 920	76.5	71.0	69.9	1.7	3.4	0.3	9.7	13.8	0.1	0.4	12.6	0.7	0.0
	2011	101 520	74.7	70.3	69.5	1.9	1.6	0.9	11.4	13.8	0.2	0.6	12.6	0.5	0.0
Iceland - Islande	1995	1 751	91.2	73.9	62.3	8.4	4.4	4.5	2.4	6.3	0.2	0.7	5.3	0.1	0.0
	2005	4 979	87.7	71.1	62.1	9.3	5.3	2.0	0.6	11.7	0.4	1.8	8.5	1.0	0.0
	2011	4 846	78.3	64.2	46.0	10.9	1.6	1.6	1.0	20.8	0.6	9.9	9.6	0.7	..
India - Inde	1995	36 592	57.6	35.5	33.2	10.2	7.2	4.6	3.5	38.9	5.4	1.7	19.7	12.1	0.0
	2005	140 862	47.2	28.5	24.5	8.0	3.5	7.1	3.0	49.8	4.0	2.8	31.9	11.0	0.1
	2011	462 403	29.1	16.8	12.6	5.1	2.6	4.7	1.7	69.3	8.2	3.3	31.9	25.7	0.1
Indonesia - Indonésie	2005	(e)75 725	31.1	9.0	8.6	5.0	11.8	5.2	1.0	68.0	2.2	1.7	57.6	6.3	0.1
	2011	177 436	26.1	6.5	6.1	5.0	10.3	4.3	1.9	71.9	2.2	2.4	62.2	5.1	0.1
Indonesia (...2002) - Indonésie (...2002)	1995	(e)40 645	62.0	21.6	20.5	9.4	24.9	6.1	0.5	37.5	0.9	2.1	31.8	2.7	0.0
Iran (Islamic Rep. of) - Iran (Rép. islamique d')	1995	(e)13 882	51.3	36.6	32.8	0.3	6.2	8.2	8.2	30.3	1.0	9.2	12.9	7.2	..
	2005	38 675	47.8	43.4	41.0	0.2	3.2	1.0	7.6	43.8	0.6	2.8	20.7	19.7	..
	2011	(e)68 319	20.1	17.2	16.3	0.3	2.0	0.6	6.0	73.9	0.3	3.1	33.5	37.0	..
Iraq	1995	(e)2 891	22.0	21.4	14.5	0.0	0.0	0.5	0.1	77.9	0.6	0.0	11.5	65.7	..
	2005	(e)23 532	32.9	18.5	18.0	11.0	1.2	2.2	2.5	64.5	0.8	0.7	10.7	52.3	0.0
	2011	(e)50 581	25.8	15.7	15.0	7.3	1.1	1.7	3.0	71.3	1.6	1.3	22.7	45.6	..

For sources and notes, see end of table.

Pour les sources et les notes, se reporter à la fin du tableau.

Origin / Origine	Year Année	World (millions of dollars) (1) Monde (millions de dollars) (1)	Developed economies Économies développées						Transition economies Économies en transition	Developing economies Économies en développement					
			Total	Europe Total	EU UE	USA États-Unis	Japan Japon	Other Autres		Total	Africa Afrique	America Amérique	Eastern, Southern and South-Eastern Asia / Asie orientale, méridionale et du Sud-Est	Western Asia / Asie occidentale	Oceania Océanie
Destination			Percentage / En pourcentage												
Ireland - Irlande	1995	32 321	82.8	58.8	56.7	17.7	5.3	1.0	0.2	12.9	1.2	0.7	10.7	0.3	0.0
	2005	70 284	79.9	61.0	57.4	14.1	3.7	1.0	0.2	17.6	0.7	0.9	15.1	0.8	0.0
	2011	67 076	81.1	66.3	62.3	12.2	1.6	1.0	0.3	13.9	1.3	1.6	10.3	0.7	0.0
Israel - Israël	1995	28 344	86.8	60.5	55.2	21.4	3.8	1.0	1.6	11.6	2.0	1.0	7.6	1.0	0.0
	2005	45 032	71.2	47.1	43.1	19.8	3.1	1.2	4.8	24.0	1.5	2.3	16.6	3.6	0.0
	2011	73 526	66.0	43.2	39.0	18.1	3.7	1.0	2.8	31.2	1.2	2.0	24.1	3.9	0.0
Italy - Italie	1995	200 320	79.4	70.4	65.4	4.9	2.2	1.8	4.0	16.6	5.4	2.5	6.7	2.0	0.0
	2005	384 836	68.3	62.1	58.7	3.4	1.6	1.2	5.1	22.3	6.2	2.5	9.8	3.8	0.0
	2011	557 511	61.9	56.6	53.2	3.3	1.1	1.0	9.3	28.4	6.9	3.0	13.4	5.1	0.0
Jamaica - Jamaïque	1995	2 773	73.8	12.0	11.1	50.7	6.7	4.4	0.1	22.5	0.1	17.5	3.7	1.3	0.0
	2005	4 885	57.5	8.1	7.2	41.6	4.4	3.5	0.1	41.0	0.5	34.4	5.7	0.3	0.0
	2011	(e)6 489	45.7	6.5	5.9	33.6	2.5	3.1	0.0	54.3	0.0	44.6	9.1	0.4	0.1
Japan - Japon	1995	336 094	47.6	16.3	14.7	22.6	..	8.7	1.5	50.9	1.4	3.4	37.5	8.3	0.4
	2005	515 866	32.5	12.6	11.4	12.7	..	7.1	1.3	66.2	1.9	2.8	46.4	14.9	0.2
	2011	854 626	28.1	10.6	9.4	8.9	..	8.6	2.4	69.5	2.0	3.9	46.1	17.3	0.2
Jordan - Jordanie	1995	3 696	49.6	35.0	33.4	9.3	3.5	1.7	2.8	45.0	2.8	2.9	14.9	24.4	..
	2005	10 455	36.9	26.0	24.6	5.6	2.8	2.5	4.2	58.9	4.6	1.8	20.1	32.3	0.0
	2011	18 301	31.4	21.5	20.6	5.9	2.0	2.0	4.4	64.0	4.9	2.8	20.5	35.8	0.0
Kazakhstan	1995	3 805	20.1	17.6	16.6	1.7	0.3	0.5	70.3	9.7	0.0	0.5	5.6	3.5	0.0
	2005	17 333	31.5	25.1	24.5	3.9	1.5	0.9	43.8	24.7	0.2	0.8	20.7	3.0	0.0
	2011	(e)38 039	30.3	25.8	24.5	2.6	1.1	0.9	30.9	38.8	0.2	0.8	34.5	3.3	0.0
Kenya	1995	2 818	56.2	41.2	40.0	3.9	9.4	1.6	0.3	43.5	9.8	1.8	21.2	10.7	..
	2005	5 846	38.2	21.5	20.6	10.4	4.5	1.8	1.2	60.6	13.0	1.7	23.4	22.5	0.0
	2011	(e)14 818	28.6	17.9	17.1	4.0	5.2	1.5	1.7	69.7	13.6	1.1	37.0	18.0	0.0
Kiribati	1995	(e)34	68.4	9.7	9.6	5.5	5.7	47.5	0.1	30.6	..	0.2	10.7	..	19.7
	2005	(e)74	61.1	1.4	1.0	3.1	16.4	40.2	..	38.9	0.0	0.5	12.8	..	25.6
	2011	(e)110	48.0	0.9	0.9	11.7	15.5	19.9	0.0	52.0	0.2	0.1	29.8	0.0	21.9
Korea, Dem. People's Rep. of - Corée, Rép. populaire dém. de	1995	(e)1 380	38.6	17.9	17.5	0.4	20.2	0.1	0.1	60.3	0.1	5.2	54.5	0.6	..
	2005	(e)2 718	12.3	8.8	8.7	0.2	2.5	0.7	9.5	78.2	1.4	7.4	59.5	9.7	0.2
	2011	(e)4 800	2.3	1.4	1.4	0.3	..	0.7	2.8	94.9	1.5	2.1	91.0	0.4	0.0
Korea, Republic of - Corée, République de	1995	135 113	68.0	15.0	13.7	22.5	24.1	6.4	1.7	29.6	1.7	2.9	17.3	7.4	0.2
	2005	261 236	46.8	11.2	10.5	11.8	18.5	5.3	1.7	51.4	1.3	2.6	31.0	16.4	0.1
	2011	524 405	38.3	10.0	9.0	8.5	13.0	6.7	2.4	59.3	1.3	3.8	33.7	20.3	0.1
Kuwait - Koweït	1995	7 790	68.3	40.2	38.9	16.1	9.4	2.7	0.3	31.3	1.4	1.6	15.3	13.0	..
	2005	(e)15 807	62.9	36.5	34.7	14.3	8.5	3.6	0.3	36.8	0.6	1.8	18.3	16.0	0.0
	2011	(e)25 228	44.0	21.6	19.9	12.4	6.2	3.8	0.4	55.6	1.7	2.0	31.2	20.7	0.0
Kyrgyzstan - Kirghizistan	1995	522	14.6	8.4	7.8	3.7	1.4	1.2	67.7	15.4	..	4.4	3.6	7.5	..
	2005	1 108	20.1	11.4	10.9	6.1	1.1	1.6	61.9	18.0	0.2	0.7	13.5	3.6	0.0
	2011	4 261	20.3	10.8	10.4	4.9	3.9	0.7	51.2	28.5	0.3	0.4	24.8	3.0	..
Lao People's Dem. Rep. - Rép. dém. populaire lao	1995	589	18.8	9.9	9.8	0.3	5.0	3.7	..	81.1	0.0	0.0	81.0	0.1	..
	2005	882	8.6	4.3	4.1	0.9	1.7	1.8	1.0	90.4	0.3	0.0	90.1	0.0	..
	2011	(e)2 650	10.4	7.0	7.0	0.7	2.0	0.8	0.3	89.3	0.0	0.1	89.1	0.1	..
Latvia - Lettonie	1995	1 818	69.9	66.0	64.3	1.9	0.6	1.4	28.2	1.8	0.1	0.6	0.9	0.2	..
	2005	8 770	78.1	76.4	74.0	1.1	0.3	0.4	18.0	3.9	0.1	0.3	2.9	0.7	0.0
	2011	15 167	79.6	78.6	76.4	0.7	0.2	0.2	15.0	5.4	0.1	0.2	4.5	0.5	..
Lebanon - Liban	1995	(e)7 278	71.2	57.5	52.9	9.7	2.9	1.1	3.1	25.2	2.3	2.1	11.1	9.8	0.0
	2005	(e)9 327	57.2	48.6	45.3	5.5	2.2	0.8	5.6	37.2	3.9	2.2	12.7	18.4	0.0
	2011	(e)20 163	52.7	40.9	37.6	9.9	1.3	0.7	8.0	39.2	7.0	2.8	14.4	15.1	0.0
Lesotho	1995	(e)1 107	2.7	1.6	1.6	0.3	0.6	0.1	0.0	97.3	76.3	0.1	20.9	0.1	..
	2005	(e)1 386	9.5	7.3	7.3	1.6	0.4	0.2	0.0	90.5	7.4	0.6	82.2	0.3	..
	2011	(e)2 525	5.3	2.8	2.8	1.3	1.2	0.0	..	94.7	74.6	0.0	19.9	0.1	..
Liberia - Libéria	1995	(e)510	68.7	33.0	31.4	0.8	34.8	0.0	2.0	29.3	0.7	1.0	27.4	0.2	..
	2005	(e)324	34.7	12.2	10.7	1.4	20.8	0.2	4.8	60.6	2.4	0.3	56.6	1.3	..
	2011	(e)1 044	25.0	5.2	5.0	1.1	18.6	0.1	1.2	73.8	2.2	0.3	70.8	0.6	..
Libya - Libye	1995	(e)5 033	72.5	64.8	62.6	0.5	5.2	2.1	0.3	27.2	9.2	1.8	9.4	6.9	..
	2005	(e)6 042	63.8	58.2	56.4	1.2	3.2	1.2	3.1	33.1	7.8	3.4	13.3	8.6	..
	2011	(e)4 988	43.0	36.9	35.6	3.3	1.7	1.1	6.1	50.9	18.6	3.0	13.9	15.4	..

For sources and notes, see end of table.

Pour les sources et les notes, se reporter à la fin du tableau.

Origin / Origine / Destination	Year / Année	World (millions of dollars) (1) / Monde (millions de dollars) (1)	Developed economies / Économies développées						Transition economies / Économies en transition	Developing economies / Économies en développement					
			Total	Europe		USA États-Unis	Japan Japon	Other Autres		Total	Africa Afrique	America Amérique	Eastern, Southern and South-Eastern Asia / Asie orientale, méridionale et du Sud-Est	Western Asia / Asie occidentale	Oceania Océanie
				Total	EU UE										
			Percentage / En pourcentage												
Lithuania - Lituanie	1995	3 649	55.6	52.8	50.4	1.9	0.2	0.7	40.3	2.2	0.2	1.1	0.6	0.4	..
	2005	15 704	62.7	59.4	58.1	2.6	0.4	0.3	31.1	6.2	0.3	0.7	4.6	0.7	0.0
	2011	31 469	58.1	56.6	55.8	1.2	0.2	0.2	36.8	4.9	1.0	0.4	2.9	0.6	0.0
Luxembourg	1995	(e)8 983	95.9	72.1	66.9	19.8	3.7	0.2	0.3	3.8	0.5	2.0	1.2	0.1	0.0
	2005	(e)21 884	86.8	82.1	79.8	3.5	0.9	0.3	0.5	12.7	0.2	0.2	11.2	1.1	0.0
	2011	(e)28 684	90.2	83.7	82.0	5.3	0.9	0.3	0.8	8.1	0.3	0.8	6.7	0.3	0.0
Madagascar	1995	(e)628	61.5	52.8	51.7	2.9	5.3	0.5	0.2	35.9	10.9	0.7	22.0	2.2	0.0
	2005	1 686	33.4	28.3	27.8	2.4	2.1	0.6	0.1	66.5	14.7	1.9	33.3	16.7	0.0
	2011	(e)2 902	28.0	23.9	23.6	2.2	0.4	1.6	0.0	71.9	13.8	1.2	41.1	15.7	0.0
Malawi	1995	(e)500	35.8	27.1	26.5	3.3	4.1	1.3	0.0	64.2	52.8	0.5	10.3	0.5	0.0
	2005	(e)1 165	18.6	13.7	13.3	3.4	0.9	0.6	0.3	81.1	65.5	0.5	12.1	3.1	..
	2011	(e)2 428	21.3	13.6	12.6	4.9	1.7	1.1	0.2	78.5	49.6	0.8	23.9	4.2	0.0
Malaysia - Malaisie	1995	77 046	65.1	17.6	15.7	16.3	27.5	3.7	0.3	34.6	0.5	1.2	32.1	0.7	0.1
	2005	114 290	42.9	12.8	11.6	12.9	14.5	2.7	0.5	56.5	0.6	1.6	51.4	3.0	0.1
	2011	187 573	35.5	11.3	10.4	9.7	11.4	3.1	0.4	63.7	1.8	2.8	54.4	4.5	0.1
Maldives	1995	268	23.1	15.6	14.7	0.6	5.1	1.8	0.0	76.6	0.4	0.0	66.5	9.6	..
	2005	745	21.9	15.1	14.2	1.1	1.8	3.8	0.0	78.1	0.5	0.2	58.8	18.6	0.0
	2011	1 412	18.1	9.5	8.6	2.1	2.3	4.1	0.0	81.9	0.6	1.9	55.4	24.1	..
Mali	1995	(e)774	44.0	34.7	34.5	4.6	3.8	0.9	0.1	46.5	33.9	3.5	7.8	1.4	..
	2005	1 544	39.4	34.0	33.8	3.2	0.9	1.3	1.8	58.8	45.9	1.8	9.7	1.4	..
	2011	(e)3 250	38.2	31.3	30.9	4.0	1.4	1.5	1.9	59.9	44.4	0.9	13.3	1.3	..
Malta - Malte	1995	2 942	80.2	73.6	72.0	4.2	1.7	0.6	1.2	18.7	4.0	1.0	10.9	2.8	..
	2005	3 865	70.5	64.0	61.8	4.2	1.6	0.7	3.2	26.2	2.8	0.6	18.3	4.5	0.0
	2011	(e)6 284	86.0	81.0	77.3	3.8	0.9	0.4	0.9	13.0	0.4	0.2	10.5	1.9	0.0
Marshall Islands - Îles Marshall	1995	75	97.4	61.9	61.9	5.4	29.8	0.3	0.0	2.2	..	..	2.2	..	0.0
	2005	94	31.6	20.7	19.4	3.2	7.5	0.3	0.6	67.8	0.0	0.0	63.4	4.3	0.0
	2011	(e)140	17.6	2.7	2.6	1.0	13.3	0.6	0.1	82.3	0.3	0.1	80.9	1.0	0.0
Mauritania - Mauritanie	1995	(e)455	70.4	58.4	58.0	6.9	4.6	0.5	0.3	26.8	10.9	0.5	14.8	0.5	..
	2005	(e)1 342	67.8	56.1	53.9	8.0	2.6	1.1	2.1	30.1	8.7	4.7	13.7	3.0	0.0
	2011	(e)2 453	54.9	43.3	43.0	8.2	1.4	2.0	1.4	43.7	9.9	5.8	21.9	6.0	0.0
Mauritius - Maurice	1995	2 000	48.6	36.5	34.0	2.6	4.7	4.8	0.1	50.9	15.1	2.0	29.7	4.2	0.0
	2005	3 160	41.9	32.0	30.7	2.2	3.6	4.1	0.1	58.0	12.0	1.8	30.8	13.4	0.1
	2011	5 159	33.8	24.7	23.6	1.9	2.5	4.7	0.2	66.0	11.4	2.7	49.3	2.6	0.0
Mayotte	2005	309	59.8	56.5	56.3	1.3	1.7	0.3	1.8	38.4	17.9	3.8	13.0	3.7	0.0
	2011	(e)502	87.1	85.7	85.6	1.3	..	0.2	0.0	12.8	3.8	0.0	8.0	0.9	0.0
Mexico - Mexique	1995	72 453	92.2	10.0	9.4	74.5	5.5	2.2	0.1	7.5	0.2	2.2	5.1	0.0	0.0
	2005	221 819	75.3	12.2	11.7	53.6	5.9	3.5	0.4	24.3	0.3	5.8	17.9	0.3	0.0
	2011	350 842	69.1	11.2	10.8	49.8	4.7	3.3	0.5	30.4	0.5	4.1	25.3	0.5	0.0
Micronesia (Federated States of) - Micronésie (États fédérés de)	1995	89	87.1	7.0	7.0	40.5	28.9	10.7	0.0	12.9	..	0.0	12.9	..	..
	2005	130	65.4	1.2	1.2	40.6	14.3	9.4	..	34.6	0.0	2.6	31.4	..	0.5
	2011	(e)170	61.4	0.7	0.7	42.5	10.6	7.5	..	38.6	0.0	0.4	38.2	..	0.0
Mongolia - Mongolie	1995	(e)415	26.9	12.7	11.4	2.3	11.7	0.2	37.5	24.4	0.0	0.0	24.4	0.0	..
	2005	1 183	23.6	10.3	10.2	3.4	6.4	3.5	41.0	35.4	0.0	0.6	34.5	0.2	..
	2011	(e)6 526	20.9	8.3	8.1	5.0	5.1	2.5	25.6	53.5	0.0	0.3	52.1	1.1	..
Montenegro - Monténégro	2011	2 544	38.5	36.5	35.7	0.8	1.1	0.1	43.9	12.0	0.8	1.9	7.9	1.4	0.0
Montserrat	1995	(e)30	77.8	63.2	63.1	12.9	1.5	0.3	..	22.2	0.1	21.5	0.5	0.0	..
	2005	(e)30	72.2	19.8	19.7	45.5	4.1	2.8	0.0	27.8	0.0	24.5	2.6	0.7	..
	2011	(e)29	80.4	19.7	19.1	54.9	3.2	2.6	..	19.6	1.9	12.0	5.8	0.0	..
Morocco - Maroc	1995	(e)10 023	60.7	52.0	50.8	5.6	1.2	1.9	3.8	20.7	5.0	3.6	6.0	6.1	..
	2005	20 803	61.0	54.6	53.2	3.3	1.7	1.3	8.0	30.8	5.3	4.2	11.3	9.9	0.0
	2011	(e)44 286	58.8	48.2	47.1	8.6	0.9	1.1	6.4	34.8	5.4	4.5	11.4	13.5	0.0
Mozambique	1995	(e)727	34.2	23.9	23.2	5.6	2.8	1.8	0.0	65.8	52.7	1.7	9.1	2.2	..
	2005	(e)2 408	30.9	17.9	17.4	2.6	1.4	8.9	0.2	68.9	48.1	2.6	14.7	3.4	0.0
	2011	(e)6 306	27.5	12.9	12.6	6.7	1.7	6.2	0.8	71.7	38.7	2.4	26.6	4.0	0.0
Myanmar	1995	(e)1 348	14.4	6.7	6.5	0.7	6.3	0.7	0.5	84.3	0.0	0.0	84.2	0.1	..
	2005	(e)1 943	7.3	2.3	2.2	0.4	3.9	0.8	2.1	90.3	0.0	0.1	90.1	0.0	..
	2011	(e)9 019	7.9	1.0	0.8	0.5	4.8	1.5	0.9	91.0	0.0	0.2	90.6	0.2	..

For sources and notes, see end of table.

Pour les sources et les notes, se reporter à la fin du tableau.

Origin / Origine — Destination	Year / Année	World (millions of dollars) (1) / Monde (millions de dollars) (1)	Developed economies / Économies développées — Total	Europe — Total	Europe — EU UE	USA États-Unis	Japan Japon	Other Autres	Transition economies / Économies en transition	Developing economies / Économies en développement — Total	Africa Afrique	America Amérique	Eastern, Southern and South-Eastern Asia / Asie orientale, méridionale et du Sud-Est	Western Asia / Asie occidentale	Oceania Océanie
Namibia - Namibie	1995	(e)1 496	14.8	7.5	6.9	6.1	0.4	0.7	0.2	85.0	80.9	2.4	1.6	0.1	0.0
	2005	2 516	12.2	8.1	7.7	3.2	0.2	0.8	0.1	87.7	82.4	0.7	3.9	0.7	0.0
	2011	(e)6 971	53.6	42.0	41.3	8.7	1.2	1.7	0.3	46.1	4.1	16.8	25.0	0.2	..
Nauru	1995	28	90.9	11.6	11.5	1.9	5.5	71.9	0.1	8.9	0.2	0.2	8.5	..	0.0
	2005	26	48.2	5.6	5.5	6.2	0.6	35.8	..	51.8	1.3	..	49.9	..	0.6
	2011	32	62.7	3.8	3.8	1.7	1.2	56.0	..	37.3	0.0	0.0	37.2	..	0.0
Nepal - Népal	1995	(e)1 292	15.4	7.0	6.7	0.7	5.0	2.8	0.3	83.6	0.0	1.2	77.8	4.6	0.0
	2005	(e)2 243	9.7	4.5	4.3	1.2	1.8	2.2	1.0	89.3	0.1	1.3	84.9	3.0	..
	2011	(e)5 773	10.2	5.2	4.4	1.4	1.8	1.8	0.9	89.0	0.2	1.8	78.8	8.2	..
Netherlands - Pays-Bas	1995	(e)185 240	80.8	66.3	63.0	8.7	4.5	1.3	1.5	17.7	2.2	3.3	10.2	2.0	0.0
	2005	(e)363 675	66.4	54.7	51.2	7.3	3.1	1.3	6.1	27.5	2.8	3.8	17.4	3.5	0.0
	2011	(e)598 232	61.2	50.9	46.8	5.9	2.8	1.6	6.7	32.1	3.5	5.3	19.8	3.5	0.0
Netherlands Antilles - Antilles néerlandaises	1995	(e)1 841	62.9	32.9	26.8	25.8	2.9	1.4	0.0	37.1	2.5	29.0	5.6	0.0	..
	2005	(e)1 950	21.0	8.5	8.1	11.8	0.5	0.3	0.0	79.0	0.1	76.4	2.3	0.1	0.0
New Caledonia - Nouvelle-Calédonie	1995	(e)967	85.1	57.2	56.9	2.7	3.9	21.4	..	11.4	0.1	0.1	10.5	..	0.7
	2005	1 774	70.1	48.1	47.5	3.6	3.5	15.0	0.0	29.7	0.4	0.8	27.8	0.3	0.5
	2011	3 697	60.2	39.0	38.1	4.5	2.0	14.8	0.0	39.5	0.4	0.8	37.6	0.4	0.3
New Zealand - Nouvelle-Zélande	1995	13 958	79.0	22.9	21.7	18.7	13.9	23.5	0.0	20.5	0.6	1.1	15.8	2.2	0.8
	2005	26 232	63.6	19.6	18.7	11.0	10.9	22.1	0.1	35.9	1.7	1.1	28.4	4.3	0.4
	2011	36 111	50.6	16.4	15.5	10.3	6.1	17.8	2.6	46.7	0.7	1.5	36.5	7.8	0.2
Nicaragua	1995	1 009	48.1	11.0	10.3	30.2	5.0	1.9	0.7	51.1	0.1	47.1	3.9	0.0	0.0
	2005	2 536	34.2	7.4	6.8	20.7	4.6	1.4	1.7	64.0	0.0	53.4	10.4	0.1	0.0
	2011	5 047	28.3	5.6	5.2	18.8	2.9	1.0	1.4	70.3	0.1	55.3	14.6	0.2	0.0
Niger	1995	345	60.5	46.8	46.4	8.9	4.2	0.5	0.1	39.4	27.6	0.9	10.5	0.3	0.0
	2005	(e)943	50.2	37.1	35.4	10.2	1.2	1.7	0.3	49.5	27.4	2.1	17.2	2.9	..
	2011	(e)2 400	44.5	37.8	36.4	4.1	1.4	1.1	0.2	55.2	25.1	1.8	25.4	2.9	0.0
Nigeria - Nigéria	1995	(e)8 222	67.8	51.8	49.8	11.7	3.5	0.8	0.5	31.7	4.8	5.1	21.4	0.4	..
	2005	(e)21 314	54.2	33.5	31.5	16.9	3.0	0.8	1.9	38.6	6.3	4.5	24.3	3.5	0.1
	2011	(e)64 103	49.2	34.3	32.3	11.2	2.0	1.7	1.8	48.7	6.1	8.1	30.4	3.8	0.4
Niue - Nioué	1995	4	98.8	2.7	2.7	81.3	1.6	13.2	0.0	1.2	..	0.0	1.1	..	..
	2005	8	97.6	26.5	24.9	3.3	0.6	67.2	..	2.4	0.0	0.2	2.0	0.0	0.2
	2011	(e)7	96.8	1.8	1.8	5.5	0.6	88.9	..	3.2	1.5	1.5	0.2	..	0.0
Northern Mariana Islands - Îles Mariannes du Nord	1995	(e)628	62.5	2.2	2.2	..	58.6	1.7	0.0	37.5	..	0.1	37.4	0.0	..
	2005	(e)591	16.5	4.5	4.5	..	10.7	1.3	..	83.5	0.0	0.1	83.2	0.2	0.0
	2011	(e)90	36.3	11.4	11.4	..	20.9	4.0	..	63.7	4.0	0.0	59.6	..	0.0
Norway - Norvège	1995	32 706	87.9	74.8	73.1	6.7	3.8	2.6	2.0	10.2	0.9	2.5	6.4	0.3	0.0
	2005	55 488	82.0	70.8	69.5	5.1	3.2	2.9	2.8	15.2	1.3	2.7	10.3	0.9	0.0
	2011	90 849	76.2	64.3	62.8	5.4	2.2	4.4	2.6	21.1	1.8	2.8	15.6	0.9	0.0
Occupied Palestinian territory - Territoire palestinien occupé	1995	1 658	..	..	..	..	..	..	..	..	..	..	..	..	..
	2005	(e)2 667	88.9	6.1	5.5	0.6	0.7	81.5	0.3	10.8	1.5	0.6	5.8	2.9	0.0
	2011	(e)4 492	87.5	6.9	6.0	0.4	0.3	79.9	0.2	12.3	2.2	0.2	3.8	6.1	0.0
Oman	1995	4 249	59.0	34.5	33.4	5.9	16.0	2.7	0.1	40.8	0.4	0.9	11.5	28.1	0.0
	2005	8 970	51.3	25.0	24.0	6.8	16.7	2.7	1.3	47.4	0.7	1.5	16.8	28.3	0.0
	2011	(e)23 857	37.3	16.7	15.8	6.1	11.9	2.6	0.3	62.4	1.1	3.8	21.2	36.2	0.0
Pakistan	1995	11 704	50.7	27.9	24.7	9.3	10.7	2.7	1.4	47.5	2.3	1.7	25.1	18.4	0.0
	2005	25 097	35.0	19.6	17.6	6.1	6.5	2.8	2.8	61.4	3.3	1.7	28.2	28.1	0.0
	2011	43 578	22.3	11.2	10.4	4.0	4.3	2.7	0.8	76.8	3.3	0.7	35.4	37.5	0.0
Palau - Palaos	1995	49	60.1	1.2	1.2	25.7	32.4	0.8	0.0	39.9	..	0.1	39.7	..	..
	2005	108	54.3	3.8	3.7	31.3	14.1	5.2	..	45.7	..	0.0	45.5	0.1	0.0
	2011	124	53.8	1.2	1.2	31.7	19.3	1.6	0.3	45.8	0.0	0.0	45.8	..	..
Panama	1995	2 511	59.1	8.1	7.2	12.5	37.9	0.6	0.9	36.1	0.1	7.7	28.2	0.0	0.0
	2005	(e)9 600	46.9	8.4	7.6	11.8	26.2	0.5	1.1	46.9	1.7	15.9	29.1	0.3	0.0
	2011	21 802	40.4	5.0	4.4	13.6	21.5	0.3	0.2	59.4	0.1	8.6	50.2	0.4	0.0
Papua New Guinea - Papouasie-Nouvelle-Guinée	1995	(e)1 452	70.8	5.4	5.3	4.4	10.3	50.6	0.0	28.6	0.0	1.0	27.5	0.0	..
	2005	(e)1 611	69.7	2.3	2.0	3.1	4.4	59.9	0.1	30.3	0.3	0.1	29.3	0.1	0.5
	2011	(e)4 241	64.6	4.0	3.8	5.2	4.5	50.9	0.1	35.3	0.3	0.1	34.3	0.1	0.4

For sources and notes, see end of table.

Pour les sources et les notes, se reporter à la fin du tableau.

Origin / Origine Destination	Year Année	World (millions of dollars) (1) Monde (millions de dollars) (1)	Developed economies / Économies développées Total	Europe Total	Europe EU UE	USA États-Unis	Japan Japon	Other Autres	Transition economies Économies en transition	Developing economies / Économies en développement Total	Africa Afrique	America Amérique	Eastern, Southern and South-Eastern Asia Asie orientale, méridionale et du Sud-Est	Western Asia Asie occidentale	Oceania Océanie
Paraguay	1995	3 136	33.5	11.6	11.1	12.5	8.7	0.7	0.0	66.3	0.9	43.5	21.9	0.0	..
	2005	3 274	20.2	11.0	6.6	5.6	3.0	0.6	0.0	78.9	0.3	53.4	25.1	0.1	..
	2011	12 316	15.8	7.0	6.2	5.3	3.2	0.2	0.4	83.7	0.2	48.6	34.6	0.4	0.0
Peru - Pérou	1995	7 584	54.6	19.3	18.3	25.2	7.0	3.1	0.2	44.5	0.2	34.7	9.4	0.3	0.0
	2005	12 502	36.8	12.9	12.0	17.8	3.6	2.6	1.1	62.1	3.4	42.1	16.1	0.4	0.0
	2011	37 747	36.6	11.3	10.9	19.7	3.5	2.2	1.5	61.8	3.0	31.2	26.4	1.2	0.0
Philippines	1995	28 487	57.5	11.5	10.9	18.9	22.1	5.0	1.7	40.8	0.6	1.7	30.6	7.4	0.4
	2005	49 487	47.1	8.5	7.9	18.9	17.1	2.6	0.9	52.0	0.2	1.4	44.4	5.7	0.3
	2011	63 693	33.5	8.0	7.4	10.9	11.0	3.6	2.5	64.0	0.4	1.5	53.1	8.7	0.4
Poland - Pologne	1995	29 019	80.6	74.3	71.2	3.9	1.6	0.7	9.5	9.9	1.6	1.4	6.5	0.3	0.0
	2005	101 539	73.8	68.9	66.2	2.4	2.0	0.5	11.8	14.2	0.7	1.8	10.1	1.5	0.0
	2011	203 028	65.6	61.1	58.6	2.3	1.7	0.4	15.1	18.9	0.8	1.7	14.9	1.4	0.1
Portugal	1995	33 565	85.5	79.7	76.8	3.0	2.2	0.5	0.7	13.8	4.7	2.9	5.0	1.1	0.0
	2005	61 167	82.2	78.7	76.7	1.9	1.2	0.4	2.2	15.6	6.6	3.1	3.8	2.1	0.0
	2011	80 324	77.2	74.4	72.5	1.7	0.6	0.6	2.8	20.0	7.8	4.2	5.9	2.2	0.0
Qatar	1995	3 398	74.8	50.6	46.9	11.4	11.2	1.6	0.4	23.9	0.6	1.4	10.7	11.2	0.0
	2005	10 061	60.2	35.2	33.7	11.6	11.6	1.8	0.4	39.4	0.9	2.0	20.7	15.7	..
	2011	(e)25 672	46.0	28.4	26.0	10.0	4.9	2.8	0.7	40.3	1.4	2.8	19.4	16.7	0.0
Republic of Moldova - République de Moldova	1995	841	34.5	32.7	31.9	1.1	0.1	0.6	64.3	1.2	0.0	0.1	0.3	0.8	..
	2005	2 292	48.7	46.3	45.6	1.6	0.5	0.4	42.9	8.4	0.2	0.9	3.7	3.5	0.0
	2011	5 191	55.6	53.9	53.1	1.0	0.3	0.4	33.0	11.4	0.1	0.6	5.3	5.4	0.0
Romania - Roumanie	1995	10 278	65.0	58.1	55.9	4.0	0.7	2.1	16.0	17.9	4.7	2.1	8.1	3.0	0.0
	2005	40 463	70.0	64.7	63.4	2.8	1.4	1.1	14.4	15.3	0.5	1.8	7.9	5.0	0.0
	2011	76 365	75.7	73.6	72.6	1.2	0.5	0.5	11.0	13.2	0.6	1.4	7.5	3.7	0.0
Russian Federation - Fédération de Russie	1995	(e)68 955	46.1	38.8	37.8	4.6	1.6	1.1	21.1	11.9	0.5	1.8	7.8	1.7	0.0
	2005	(e)137 977	61.7	52.8	51.2	3.6	4.3	1.0	15.8	22.4	0.7	3.7	16.0	2.0	0.0
	2011	(e)354 549	56.9	48.3	46.6	3.4	3.8	1.4	14.3	28.9	0.8	3.0	22.8	2.3	0.0
Rwanda	1995	(e)241	51.3	27.9	26.6	15.0	6.7	1.8	0.3	48.4	38.1	0.1	5.1	5.0	..
	2005	(e)471	38.4	26.6	26.3	2.8	3.6	5.4	1.5	60.1	43.3	2.5	7.9	6.3	0.2
	2011	(e)1 730	29.2	18.0	17.6	9.6	1.0	0.6	0.2	70.6	46.7	0.5	12.2	11.3	0.0
Saint Helena - Sainte-Hélène	1995	(e)23	83.0	80.7	78.8	1.5	0.5	0.2	0.1	16.7	15.0	0.4	1.3	0.0	..
	2005	(e)56	63.8	57.9	57.9	4.3	0.3	1.3	..	36.2	34.3	0.2	1.7	0.0	..
	2011	56	75.5	70.7	70.6	3.9	0.1	0.9	0.0	24.5	23.2	0.2	1.1	0.0	..
Saint Kitts and Nevis - Saint-Kitts-et-Nevis	1995	132	76.7	13.8	13.3	55.1	5.3	2.5	0.0	22.8	0.0	21.0	1.7	0.0	0.0
	2005	210	73.8	9.6	9.3	57.9	3.8	2.4	0.1	26.2	0.1	24.3	1.8	0.0	0.0
	2011	(e)271	73.7	7.6	7.1	60.4	3.3	2.4	0.0	26.3	0.1	22.9	3.2	0.0	0.0
Saint Lucia - Sainte-Lucie	1995	306	70.6	30.8	30.6	32.0	3.8	4.0	0.0	29.4	0.0	26.0	3.3	0.1	0.0
	2005	486	59.6	28.3	27.7	26.2	3.0	2.1	0.0	40.3	0.1	37.8	2.4	0.1	0.0
	2011	(e)698	17.3	5.5	5.3	9.8	1.1	0.9	0.0	82.7	0.0	81.6	1.1	0.0	..
Saint Pierre and Miquelon - Saint-Pierre-et-Miquelon	1995	47	98.4	54.4	54.0	0.9	0.0	43.1	..	1.2	0.4	0.5	0.3	..	..
	2005	(e)50	93.6	59.6	59.6	2.1	0.2	31.7	..	6.4	..	0.0	6.4	..	..
	2011	(e)66	99.5	62.4	62.1	0.2	0.4	36.5	..	0.5	0.0	..	0.4	0.0	..
Saint Vincent and the Grenadines - Saint-Vincent-et-les Grenadines	1995	134	65.5	22.2	21.9	37.7	2.3	3.3	0.0	33.8	0.1	30.3	3.4	0.0	0.0
	2005	240	57.8	15.5	15.1	33.3	4.2	4.9	0.0	42.2	0.1	35.9	6.1	0.1	0.0
	2011	(e)348	52.5	11.2	11.0	34.1	2.4	4.7	0.0	47.5	0.2	41.0	6.0	0.3	0.0
Samoa	1995	(e)95	89.4	1.8	1.8	6.4	23.0	58.2	..	10.6	0.0	1.5	9.1	..	0.0
	2005	(e)239	66.3	1.4	1.4	10.5	7.6	46.8	0.0	33.6	1.1	1.0	20.3	0.0	11.2
	2011	(e)346	50.1	1.4	1.4	6.8	8.7	33.2	0.2	49.7	0.3	0.6	33.5	0.0	15.2
Sao Tome and Principe - Sao Tomé-et-Principe	1995	(e)29	76.9	70.8	70.7	4.4	1.5	0.3	0.0	12.0	6.4	3.0	2.6	..	..
	2005	50	71.8	64.6	64.5	0.1	7.1	0.0	0.0	27.9	21.7	0.8	4.6	0.8	0.0
	2011	(e)132	83.9	75.8	75.5	6.0	2.0	0.2	0.0	16.1	6.9	1.0	6.4	1.7	..
Saudi Arabia - Arabie saoudite	1995	28 085	71.6	39.0	34.0	21.5	8.9	2.2	0.9	25.4	2.9	2.3	14.7	5.5	0.0
	2005	59 510	62.0	34.0	31.7	14.8	9.0	4.2	1.7	35.4	3.1	3.7	20.9	7.8	0.0
	2011	(e)129 017	50.5	30.1	28.4	12.1	5.7	2.6	1.2	48.3	2.5	3.9	33.0	8.9	0.0
Senegal - Sénégal	1995	(e)1 412	51.0	41.5	41.0	5.0	3.2	1.3	1.2	28.5	10.0	5.4	12.7	0.4	..
	2005	3 498	53.4	46.8	46.3	4.3	1.3	1.1	1.8	44.7	21.2	6.0	14.8	2.7	0.0
	2011	5 909	52.9	46.3	45.7	4.1	1.1	1.5	2.2	44.9	15.1	5.8	20.0	4.0	0.0

For sources and notes, see end of table.

Pour les sources et les notes, se reporter à la fin du tableau.

2.1 Country trade structure by partner — Imports by main region of origin
2.1 Structure du commerce des pays par partenaires — Importations par principales régions d'origine

Origin / Origine — Destination	Year Année	World (millions of dollars) (1) / Monde (millions de dollars) (1)	Developed economies / Économies développées — Total	Europe — Total	Europe — EU UE	USA États-Unis	Japan Japon	Other Autres	Transition economies / Économies en transition	Developing economies / Économies en développement — Total	Africa Afrique	America Amérique	Eastern, Southern and South-Eastern Asia / Asie orientale, méridionale et du Sud-Est	Western Asia / Asie occidentale	Oceania Océanie
			Percentage / En pourcentage												
Serbia - Serbie	2011	20 139	59.5	56.9	55.6	1.5	0.8	0.3	24.8	15.7	0.8	1.3	11.1	2.6	0.0
Serbia and Montenegro - Serbie-et-Monténégro	1995	(e)2 666	53.3	48.2	45.3	2.9	1.4	0.8	18.3	12.7	2.3	5.4	3.8	1.2	0.0
	2005	(e)10 461	53.9	49.7	48.4	2.7	1.0	0.5	27.4	12.4	0.5	1.9	7.9	2.2	0.0
Seychelles	1995	255	43.7	32.9	32.4	3.7	5.7	1.5	0.0	55.9	16.1	0.2	23.0	16.6	..
	2005	675	47.0	43.3	43.0	1.9	0.8	1.1	0.0	52.7	9.4	0.2	15.7	27.4	0.0
	2011	(e)850	36.8	31.6	31.2	1.4	2.1	1.6	0.0	63.2	11.0	0.3	20.1	31.8	0.0
Sierra Leone	1995	(e)134	58.8	48.8	46.7	8.6	1.0	0.4	0.8	31.5	11.9	1.2	17.7	0.7	..
	2005	(e)345	36.4	20.9	20.2	5.1	4.1	6.3	0.5	61.7	40.5	3.0	13.7	4.4	0.0
	2011	(e)1 717	35.4	19.8	19.0	5.1	4.2	6.4	0.5	62.7	41.3	3.1	13.7	4.5	0.0
Singapore - Singapour	1995	124 503	53.7	15.3	13.8	15.1	21.1	2.2	0.3	46.0	0.5	0.9	38.5	6.0	0.0
	2005	200 050	36.6	13.0	11.6	11.7	9.6	2.2	0.5	62.8	0.6	1.0	52.2	9.0	0.0
	2011	365 770	33.8	14.0	12.6	10.8	7.2	1.8	1.2	64.9	0.3	2.9	49.9	11.8	0.0
Sint Maarten (Dutch part) - Saint-Martin (partie néerlandaise)	2011	734	94.1	..	..	94.1	..	0.0	..	5.9	..	5.9	..	..	..
Slovakia - Slovaquie	1995	(e)9 225	70.5	66.2	64.5	2.3	1.4	0.5	12.5	5.0	0.6	1.0	3.1	0.3	0.0
	2005	34 226	67.4	63.9	62.9	1.4	1.9	0.2	13.1	10.4	0.2	0.7	8.9	0.6	0.0
	2011	76 690	56.5	53.7	53.1	1.0	1.5	0.3	13.1	18.0	0.4	0.5	16.4	0.7	0.0
Slovenia - Slovénie	1995	9 492	84.4	78.7	76.2	3.1	1.7	0.9	10.0	5.6	1.2	1.0	3.1	0.3	0.0
	2005	19 626	77.0	72.7	70.9	2.0	1.5	0.8	9.3	9.7	0.9	1.7	5.9	1.2	0.0
	2011	(e)35 480	63.7	60.0	58.5	2.7	0.8	0.3	8.8	11.4	0.9	1.5	7.7	1.3	0.0
Solomon Islands - Îles Salomon	1995	(e)154	71.6	3.3	3.3	2.2	11.7	54.4	0.0	28.4	0.3	0.0	28.1	0.0	0.0
	2005	(e)185	46.0	4.0	4.0	1.6	4.4	36.0	0.0	54.0	0.7	0.1	43.2	0.0	9.9
	2011	(e)462	40.6	1.3	1.1	1.3	3.4	34.6	..	59.4	1.1	0.1	50.1	0.0	8.0
Somalia - Somalie	1995	(e)268	22.7	15.5	15.4	5.8	0.6	0.8	0.0	73.9	24.3	11.5	23.7	14.5	..
	2005	(e)626	5.5	3.3	3.3	1.9	0.1	0.2	0.7	93.8	25.1	9.7	16.5	42.5	0.0
	2011	(e)1 175	8.1	7.1	7.0	0.6	0.1	0.2	0.0	91.9	39.2	0.8	38.5	13.5	..
South Africa - Afrique du Sud	1995	(e)30 979	56.4	35.1	32.9	9.8	8.7	2.9	0.1	43.5	25.8	2.1	13.8	1.8	0.0
	2005	(e)64 192	49.5	33.9	32.7	6.8	5.8	3.0	0.2	35.3	3.9	3.4	21.3	6.6	0.1
	2011	(e)122 418	38.9	26.2	25.0	6.5	3.9	2.4	0.3	42.1	6.3	3.1	26.4	6.3	0.0
Spain - Espagne	1995	113 399	79.7	68.5	66.4	6.6	3.3	1.2	1.5	18.8	5.7	4.3	7.0	1.7	0.0
	2005	289 611	70.6	63.7	61.3	3.2	2.5	1.1	2.9	26.5	7.6	4.9	10.5	3.4	0.1
	2011	(e)360 534	64.1	58.8	57.4	3.4	0.9	1.0	4.0	31.9	8.7	6.1	12.0	5.1	0.1
Sri Lanka	1995	(e)5 185	38.1	18.1	17.0	6.2	9.6	4.2	0.4	55.8	0.7	2.2	51.7	1.3	..
	2005	8 307	28.4	17.4	15.6	2.5	4.6	4.0	0.2	71.3	0.5	1.3	64.2	5.4	0.0
	2011	19 696	24.8	13.3	9.8	1.5	5.2	4.8	0.6	74.4	0.5	0.6	66.1	7.1	0.0
Sudan (...2011) - Soudan (...2011)	1995	1 185	48.8	38.6	36.8	5.4	4.4	0.4	0.3	50.9	19.9	0.3	18.1	12.6	0.0
	2005	7 367	34.4	23.8	22.9	1.6	4.6	4.3	2.2	63.4	7.4	1.8	32.9	21.3	0.0
	2011	(e)9 231	23.5	16.3	16.1	0.9	3.4	2.9	2.1	74.4	8.3	2.3	38.7	25.1	..
Suriname	1995	583	70.1	25.0	24.2	42.4	2.1	0.5	..	29.9	0.6	23.5	5.7	0.0	..
	2005	1 050	46.4	22.1	21.9	18.9	4.5	1.0	0.0	41.9	0.1	32.4	9.2	0.3	..
	2011	(e)1 667	53.8	23.0	22.9	25.6	3.5	1.7	0.0	46.2	0.1	35.1	10.8	0.2	..
Swaziland	1995	(e)1 054	5.1	2.6	2.5	1.3	1.0	0.1	0.0	94.9	89.3	0.2	5.4	0.0	0.0
	2005	(e)1 904	4.0	2.7	2.6	0.7	0.3	0.3	0.0	95.9	87.8	0.3	7.6	0.2	0.0
	2011	(e)2 000	18.7	9.5	8.7	6.9	1.5	0.8	1.6	79.7	11.8	2.3	64.9	0.7	..
Sweden - Suède	1995	61 647	91.7	82.0	72.2	5.7	3.0	1.0	0.8	7.5	0.5	1.3	5.1	0.5	0.0
	2005	111 351	87.0	80.7	71.4	3.4	2.1	0.9	3.2	9.7	0.5	1.3	6.8	1.1	0.0
	2011	176 000	82.9	78.0	68.7	3.0	1.3	0.7	5.9	11.0	0.6	1.4	8.1	0.9	0.0
Switzerland - Suisse	1995	80 152	91.7	81.2	80.8	6.4	3.2	0.9	0.6	7.6	1.3	1.1	4.5	0.7	0.0
	2005	126 574	88.8	80.4	80.2	5.6	1.9	0.9	0.9	10.3	2.3	1.0	5.7	1.2	0.0
	2011	207 263	86.3	78.4	78.2	5.0	2.1	0.9	2.0	11.8	1.5	1.4	7.7	1.0	0.0
Syrian Arab Republic - République arabe syrienne	1995	(e)4 709	43.9	32.3	31.7	6.8	4.4	0.4	9.1	34.4	2.9	3.4	17.4	10.6	0.0
	2005	(e)10 862	31.3	26.7	25.7	1.6	2.3	0.7	10.9	57.6	4.7	3.2	21.6	28.2	0.0
	2011	(e)16 600	26.5	22.3	21.2	2.2	1.3	0.6	10.7	62.7	6.2	4.1	25.2	27.3	..
Tajikistan - Tadjikistan	1995	(e)810	32.3	27.8	24.4	3.9	0.1	0.5	55.7	12.0	..	0.0	10.7	1.3	..
	2005	(e)1 330	15.3	13.4	12.9	1.5	0.3	0.2	63.9	20.8	0.6	2.1	13.5	4.6	..
	2011	(e)3 186	8.7	4.4	4.3	4.1	0.0	0.2	32.0	59.3	0.0	0.9	52.6	5.7	..

For sources and notes, see end of table.

Pour les sources et les notes, se reporter à la fin du tableau.

Origin / Origine Destination	Year Année	World (millions of dollars) (1) Monde (millions de dollars) (1)	Developed economies Économies développées Total	Europe Total	EU UE	USA États-Unis	Japan Japon	Other Autres	Transition economies Économies en transition	Developing economies Économies en développement Total	Africa Afrique	America Amérique	Eastern, Southern and South-Eastern Asia Asie orientale, méridionale et du Sud-Est	Western Asia Asie occiden-tale	Oceania Océanie
								Percentage / En pourcentage							
TFYR of Macedonia - LERY de Macédoine	1995	1 719	72.2	66.8	65.7	3.4	0.8	1.2	15.6	8.3	0.6	1.5	2.5	3.7	0.0
	2005	3 228	59.9	56.8	54.7	1.4	0.7	1.1	27.6	12.5	0.3	1.8	6.7	3.6	0.1
	2011	7 007	59.6	56.9	54.3	1.3	0.7	0.7	23.6	16.9	0.6	2.0	9.3	5.0	0.0
Thailand - Thaïlande	1995	70 781	63.9	18.2	16.4	12.0	30.5	3.2	1.9	33.1	1.2	1.6	27.0	3.2	0.1
	2005	118 164	43.6	10.4	9.1	7.4	22.0	3.8	1.6	54.4	1.4	1.7	38.6	12.5	0.2
	2011	228 483	40.7	11.9	7.8	5.9	18.5	4.5	2.6	56.7	1.1	2.0	40.4	13.0	0.2
Timor-Leste	2005	(e)102	30.8	6.7	6.5	6.7	6.1	11.3	0.1	69.1	1.1	0.0	67.7	0.2	0.1
	2011	(e)308	10.5	1.1	1.0	1.6	1.9	5.9	0.0	89.5	0.4	0.2	88.9	0.0	..
Togo	1995	556	51.0	44.2	43.5	3.3	2.6	0.9	0.0	48.9	18.8	1.9	27.8	0.4	0.0
	2005	(e)1 054	39.2	36.3	35.6	1.3	0.9	0.8	0.9	58.5	13.9	2.1	39.3	3.2	0.0
	2011	(e)1 700	26.1	21.5	21.2	3.4	0.7	0.5	0.5	72.8	29.1	2.5	39.4	1.8	0.0
Tokelau - Tokélaou	1995	(e)1	12.1	1.9	1.9	9.2	1.0	0.0	..	87.9	45.4	4.1	24.0	..	14.5
	2005	(e)0	96.1	44.7	44.7	51.4	0.0	0.0	..	3.9	0.7	0.1	2.4	..	0.8
	2011	(e)0	42.4	24.8	23.7	17.6	0.0	0.0	..	57.6	0.5	0.0	55.9	0.0	1.2
Tonga	1995	(e)77	96.8	8.9	8.8	13.1	5.1	69.6	..	3.2	0.0	0.7	2.4	0.0	..
	2005	(e)120	61.6	4.3	4.2	8.6	2.6	46.2	0.0	38.3	0.1	0.8	11.0	0.0	26.5
	2011	(e)184	48.4	1.6	1.2	11.4	2.8	32.7	0.0	51.6	0.0	0.7	20.9	0.2	29.7
Trinidad and Tobago - Trinité-et-Tobago	1995	1 724	80.6	20.8	19.6	50.6	3.2	6.0	0.1	18.8	0.4	12.6	5.7	0.1	0.0
	2005	5 694	48.4	12.4	11.9	29.2	3.9	2.9	0.4	51.2	12.9	31.6	6.5	0.1	0.0
	2011	(e)8 699	50.8	8.9	8.8	32.8	2.6	6.4	6.5	42.7	9.4	22.9	9.9	0.4	0.0
Tunisia - Tunisie	1995	7 903	82.7	74.8	73.2	5.1	1.8	1.1	3.0	13.7	6.8	1.4	2.7	2.8	0.0
	2005	13 174	75.2	70.8	69.7	2.5	1.6	0.3	4.7	19.3	6.4	2.4	6.3	4.1	0.0
	2011	(e)23 956	68.8	65.4	64.2	2.5	0.4	0.5	6.1	25.1	8.0	2.3	9.6	5.2	0.0
Turkey - Turquie	1995	35 707	69.6	53.0	50.5	10.4	3.9	2.2	9.5	20.1	3.9	2.0	9.1	5.1	0.0
	2005	116 774	57.6	49.0	45.2	4.6	2.7	1.3	15.0	26.6	5.2	1.7	17.0	2.7	0.0
	2011	240 839	50.5	40.3	37.9	6.7	1.8	1.7	14.3	31.2	2.8	2.2	23.9	2.2	0.0
Turkmenistan - Turkménistan	1995	(e)1 365	24.6	18.2	17.1	4.3	0.7	1.5	55.8	19.6	0.0	0.1	7.9	11.5	..
	2005	(e)2 947	30.1	18.2	18.0	9.7	1.1	1.2	36.9	33.0	0.0	0.2	11.3	21.5	..
	2011	(e)7 400	25.2	18.6	18.2	2.6	3.5	0.4	27.3	47.6	0.0	0.1	19.4	28.1	..
Turks and Caicos Islands - Îles Turques et Caïques	1995	(e)51	69.7	8.1	7.8	59.5	1.3	0.9	3.9	25.8	0.1	24.6	1.1	..	..
	2005	304	98.3	..	..	98.3	0.0	0.0	0.0	1.7	0.0	1.7	0.0	0.0	..
	2011	(e)302	94.8	6.6	5.3	86.4	0.7	1.1	0.2	4.9	0.9	3.2	0.8	0.1	..
Tuvalu	1995	(e)6	84.0	15.4	15.3	5.2	3.7	59.7	2.7	13.3	..	8.0	4.1	..	1.2
	2005	(e)13	47.3	18.2	18.1	0.1	14.4	14.7	0.2	52.5	0.4	0.0	24.9	..	27.2
	2011	(e)25	44.5	0.3	0.3	0.9	37.3	6.0	0.0	55.5	0.5	..	27.7	0.1	27.2
Uganda - Ouganda	1995	1 038	43.1	31.9	31.2	2.8	7.2	1.3	0.0	56.8	35.7	0.9	15.8	4.0	0.5
	2005	2 054	32.8	20.7	20.2	3.9	5.8	2.4	0.6	66.6	39.9	1.1	16.9	8.6	0.0
	2011	(e)4 561	29.4	19.6	19.0	3.1	6.0	0.7	2.0	68.6	26.2	1.0	25.2	16.3	..
Ukraine	1995	(e)16 052	28.5	24.1	23.3	3.2	0.6	0.5	63.5	5.2	0.7	1.8	2.1	0.7	0.0
	2005	36 122	39.0	34.8	33.7	2.0	1.5	0.7	47.4	13.7	1.2	1.3	9.3	1.8	0.0
	2011	82 608	37.6	32.5	31.2	3.1	1.2	0.7	45.6	16.8	1.1	1.3	12.2	2.1	0.0
United Arab Emirates - Émirats arabes unis	1995	(e)20 984	45.5	27.2	25.5	8.2	8.7	1.5	0.3	45.9	0.4	0.9	36.5	8.1	..
	2005	80 814	52.2	36.5	34.9	8.6	5.4	1.7	1.6	46.2	1.8	1.4	34.6	8.5	0.0
	2011	(e)207 835	37.3	23.1	21.4	8.2	3.8	2.1	0.8	61.9	2.5	1.5	49.5	8.3	..
United Kingdom - Royaume-Uni	1995	261 456	78.9	59.4	54.8	11.1	5.7	2.7	0.6	15.4	2.0	1.8	10.3	1.2	0.1
	2005	515 782	72.7	59.0	53.6	8.0	3.1	2.5	2.0	21.1	3.0	2.0	13.8	2.3	0.0
	2011	634 412	71.9	58.9	51.3	8.1	2.1	2.7	2.0	25.0	3.4	2.0	16.2	3.4	0.0
United Republic of Tanzania - République-Unie de Tanzanie	1995	1 653	45.0	33.3	32.2	3.9	6.9	1.0	0.1	54.9	22.1	0.7	20.1	11.9	0.0
	2005	3 247	30.4	21.1	20.5	3.1	3.9	2.4	1.6	68.0	24.1	1.4	24.2	18.3	0.0
	2011	11 184	26.8	18.7	15.1	2.7	3.4	2.0	1.3	71.9	14.4	1.4	42.3	13.7	0.2
United States - États-Unis	1995	770 821	56.8	19.6	18.1	..	16.5	20.7	0.7	42.5	2.1	14.0	24.6	1.8	0.0
	2005	1 732 321	46.3	19.7	18.5	..	8.2	18.5	1.2	52.5	3.9	17.5	28.0	3.1	0.0
	2011	2 262 586	39.7	18.1	16.6	..	5.9	15.7	1.9	58.4	4.2	19.6	30.7	3.9	0.0
Uruguay	1995	2 866	36.0	22.4	21.4	9.9	2.6	1.2	0.0	62.7	1.5	52.2	8.1	0.9	..
	2005	3 879	20.1	11.3	10.8	6.7	1.1	1.0	8.1	71.8	8.7	51.9	11.0	0.1	0.0
	2011	(e)10 623	20.6	10.7	10.1	7.5	1.0	1.4	6.3	72.9	0.8	56.5	15.2	0.4	0.0

For sources and notes, see end of table.

Pour les sources et les notes, se reporter à la fin du tableau.

Origin / Origine / Destination	Year / Année	World (millions of dollars) (1) / Monde (millions de dollars) (1)	Developed economies / Économies développées Total	Europe Total	Europe EU / UE	USA États-Unis	Japan Japon	Other Autres	Transition economies / Économies en transition	Developing economies / Économies en développement Total	Africa Afrique	America Amérique	Eastern, Southern and South-Eastern Asia / Asie orientale, méridionale et du Sud-Est	Western Asia / Asie occidentale	Oceania Océanie
Uzbekistan - Ouzbékistan	1995	2 750	53.0	43.3	42.3	4.0	5.1	0.6	14.8	32.0	0.0	0.4	22.7	8.9	..
	2005	3 666	27.7	23.9	23.0	2.2	1.1	0.4	40.4	31.8	0.1	0.2	25.0	6.5	..
	2011	9 953	24.2	19.7	18.5	1.2	2.8	0.4	32.7	43.1	0.0	0.1	38.8	4.2	..
Vanuatu	1995	(e)95	80.7	9.5	7.0	0.9	45.0	25.3	0.3	18.1	1.4	0.3	16.3	0.0	0.1
	2005	(e)149	64.9	5.3	5.3	4.7	16.4	38.4	..	34.6	0.1	0.1	23.4	..	11.0
	2011	(e)304	56.8	1.8	1.8	6.8	8.2	40.1	..	42.9	0.1	0.1	28.9	..	13.8
Venezuela (Bolivarian Rep. of) - Venezuela (Rép. bolivarienne du)	1995	10 791	71.6	20.7	19.7	41.3	4.4	5.3	0.1	28.3	0.3	24.0	3.8	0.2	0.0
	2005	21 848	53.2	16.1	15.2	31.0	3.5	2.7	0.2	46.6	0.2	37.6	8.6	0.3	0.0
	2011	(e)46 441	45.7	14.0	13.0	27.7	1.8	2.3	1.8	52.5	0.2	33.9	18.0	0.3	0.1
Viet Nam	1995	(e)8 155	29.1	11.7	10.4	2.2	13.0	2.2	1.7	63.7	0.1	0.1	62.2	1.3	0.0
	2005	36 761	25.2	9.5	7.1	2.4	11.1	2.2	2.8	71.9	0.6	1.4	68.2	1.7	0.1
	2011	(e)105 356	26.5	9.3	7.4	4.3	10.0	2.9	1.0	72.6	0.5	2.2	67.7	2.1	..
Wallis and Futuna Islands - Îles Wallis-et-Futuna	1995	(e)14	93.9	59.6	59.6	0.6	..	33.8	0.1	5.9	0.1	4.9	0.1	..	0.8
	2005	(e)51	66.1	35.3	35.3	1.2	2.8	26.7	0.0	33.9	0.6	1.1	7.0	0.0	25.1
	2011	(e)57	58.3	35.2	34.3	0.5	..	22.6	..	41.7	0.1	..	2.1	0.0	39.5
Western Sahara - Sahara occidental	1995	(e)14	11.7	..	..	2.0	0.2	9.4	0.3	88.0	47.1	..	40.2	0.7	
Yemen - Yémen	1995	(e)1 582	40.5	27.1	26.8	8.6	3.5	1.3	0.4	59.1	4.3	2.8	20.0	31.9	..
	2005	(e)5 400	30.8	20.2	15.6	4.8	3.2	2.7	3.2	66.0	5.4	5.7	21.0	34.0	0.0
	2011	(e)10 034	24.5	15.0	12.8	4.6	1.9	3.1	2.6	72.8	4.8	6.4	25.0	36.6	0.0
Zambia - Zambie	1995	708	34.9	21.7	20.7	4.3	6.2	2.7	0.0	65.1	48.7	0.3	8.0	8.1	0.0
	2005	2 558	24.4	19.5	18.9	1.7	1.4	1.7	0.0	75.6	62.5	0.5	8.9	3.7	0.0
	2011	(e)7 191	13.7	8.8	8.5	2.1	1.9	0.9	0.0	86.3	62.3	0.1	15.1	8.7	..
Zimbabwe	1995	(e)2 659	37.7	24.7	23.0	5.2	6.5	1.3	0.1	62.1	53.7	1.5	6.4	0.5	0.0
	2005	(e)2 350	11.7	8.1	7.6	1.9	1.1	0.7	0.0	88.2	73.7	0.2	8.6	5.7	0.0
	2011	(e)4 400	10.6	7.2	7.0	2.2	0.7	0.5	0.2	89.2	70.5	0.5	14.0	4.3	0.0

Source:
UNCTAD secretariat calculations, based on UNCTAD, *UNCTADstat* Merchandise Trade Matrix

Notes:
(1) Include unspecified destinations.
(2) Exports data include a considerable amount of re-exports.
(3) Estimates. France including French Guiana, Guadeloupe, Martinique, Monaco and Reunion (and excluding intra trade)

Source :
Calculs du secrétariat de la CNUCED, basés sur la matrice du commerce de marchandises de *UNCTADstat* de la CNUCED

Notes :
(1) Y compris des destinations non-spécifiées.
(2) Les données des exportations comprennent une part importante de réexportations.
(3) Estimation. Les données sont dérivées des déclarations rapportées par la France métropolitaine et les départements d'outre-mer par agrégation diminuée des flux intra.

Product group	Year Année	World (1) Monde (1)	Developed economies - Économies développées								Transition economies Économies en transition
			Total	Europe		Canada	USA États-Unis	Japan Japon	Other developed countries Autres économies développées	
				Total	EU UE					

		Millions of dollars									
All products	1995	5 123 350	3 479 861	2 161 979	2 036 189	165 173	755 332	303 844	93 533	98 397
	2005	10 465 300	6 922 211	4 311 559	4 096 781	306 129	1 634 796	487 713	182 014	260 248
	2011	18 087 096	10 219 013	6 529 675	6 154 524	439 427	2 144 129	783 373	322 409	541 601
		Share by destination (percentage)									
All products	1995	100.0	67.9	42.2	39.7	3.2	14.7	5.9	1.8	1.9
	2005	100.0	66.1	41.2	39.1	2.9	15.6	4.7	1.7	2.5
	2011	100.0	56.5	36.1	34.0	2.4	11.9	4.3	1.8	3.0
All food items	1995	100.0	67.4	47.1	45.5	2.0	7.5	9.6	1.1	4.4
(SITC 0 + 1 + 22 + 4)	2005	100.0	68.6	48.4	46.9	2.6	9.9	6.4	1.4	4.4
	2011	100.0	58.9	42.5	41.1	2.4	7.8	4.8	1.5	4.7
Agricultural raw materials	1995	100.0	67.8	41.2	39.3	2.1	11.5	12.0	1.0	0.8
(SITC 2 - 22 - 27 - 28)	2005	100.0	61.8	39.4	38.0	2.3	12.9	6.3	0.9	1.8
	2011	100.0	48.5	34.0	33.0	1.5	7.4	4.8	0.8	2.2
Ores, metals, precious stones	1995	100.0	69.0	41.9	37.4	2.5	11.7	10.1	2.7	1.2
and non-monetary gold	2005	100.0	60.3	37.5	33.4	2.3	11.4	6.1	3.0	1.4
(SITC 27 + 28 + 68 + 667 + 971)	2011	100.0	50.3	33.5	27.6	2.2	7.6	4.9	2.0	1.0
Fuels (SITC 3)	1995	100.0	68.3	35.2	33.3	1.3	17.0	13.5	1.2	2.9
	2005	100.0	65.6	33.9	32.3	1.6	19.4	9.3	1.3	1.3
	2011	100.0	56.4	31.1	29.8	1.5	14.2	8.1	1.4	1.4
Manufactured goods	1995	100.0	67.7	41.7	39.2	3.7	15.9	4.4	1.9	1.5
(SITC 5 to 8 less 667 and 68)	2005	100.0	65.9	41.6	39.5	3.3	15.8	3.5	1.8	2.5
	2011	100.0	57.6	37.2	35.3	2.7	12.5	3.2	1.9	3.5
		Share by major product group (percentage)									
All products	1995	100.0	100.0	100.0	100.0	100.0	100.0	100.0	100.0	100.0
	2005	100.0	100.0	100.0	100.0	100.0	100.0	100.0	100.0	100.0
	2011	100.0	100.0	100.0	100.0	100.0	100.0	100.0	100.0	100.0
All food items	1995	9.0	8.9	10.0	10.3	5.7	4.6	14.5	5.5	20.3
(SITC 0 + 1 + 22 + 4)	2005	6.5	6.8	7.7	7.8	5.7	4.2	8.9	5.1	11.6
	2011	7.7	8.0	9.0	9.3	7.5	5.0	8.4	6.4	12.0
Agricultural raw materials	1995	2.7	2.7	2.6	2.7	1.7	2.1	5.4	1.5	1.1
(SITC 2 - 22 - 27 - 28)	2005	1.6	1.5	1.5	1.5	1.2	1.3	2.1	0.8	1.1
	2011	1.7	1.4	1.6	1.6	1.0	1.0	1.9	0.8	1.2
Ores, metals, precious stones	1995	4.5	4.6	4.5	4.2	3.5	3.6	7.7	6.8	2.7
and non-monetary gold	2005	4.6	4.2	4.2	4.0	3.7	3.4	6.1	8.0	2.6
(SITC 27 + 28 + 68 + 667 + 971)	2011	6.7	6.0	6.3	5.5	6.2	4.3	7.7	7.5	2.3
Fuels (SITC 3)	1995	7.3	7.4	6.1	6.1	3.0	8.5	16.6	4.9	11.2
	2005	14.1	14.0	11.6	11.6	7.9	17.5	28.3	10.6	7.2
	2011	17.4	17.4	15.0	15.3	11.0	20.8	32.5	14.1	8.4
Manufactured goods	1995	72.7	72.4	71.9	71.8	83.2	78.4	53.9	77.4	56.3
(SITC 5 to 8 less 667 and 68)	2005	70.4	70.2	71.0	71.1	78.6	71.3	52.8	72.1	71.3
	2011	63.5	64.7	65.5	65.8	70.7	67.0	46.8	68.1	74.5

For sources and notes, see end of table 2.2.L.

| | Developing economies - Économies en développement | | | | | | Oceania (2) / Océanie (2) | Major petroleum exporters and gas exporters / Principaux exportateurs de pétrole et de gaz | Major manufactured goods exporters / Principaux exportateurs d'articles manufacturés | Year / Année | Destinations |
| | | | Asia / Asie | | | | | | | | |
Total	Africa / Afrique	America / Amérique	Total	Eastern, Southern and South-Eastern Asia / Asie orientale, méridionale et du Sud-Est	China / Chine	Western Asia / Asie occidentale					Groupes de produits
Millions de dollars											
1 461 681	129 516	245 672	1 081 761	956 367	147 021	125 394	4 732	114 818	856 564	1995	Total tous produits
3 232 866	250 589	497 442	2 473 155	2 129 703	595 089	343 452	11 680	313 214	1 912 104	2005	
7 148 266	545 708	1 071 138	5 500 998	4 774 887	1 562 724	726 111	30 422	675 368	4 000 703	2011	
Parts par destinations (en pourcentage)											
28.5	2.5	4.8	21.1	18.7	2.9	2.4	0.1	2.2	16.7	1995	Total tous produits
30.9	2.4	4.8	23.6	20.4	5.7	3.3	0.1	3.0	18.3	2005	
39.5	3.0	5.9	30.4	26.4	8.6	4.0	0.2	3.7	22.1	2011	
25.8	4.4	4.8	16.5	13.0	2.3	3.4	0.1	3.9	10.3	1995	Produits alimentaires
26.2	4.2	5.0	16.7	12.5	2.8	4.2	0.2	4.8	10.2	2005	(CTCI 0 + 1 + 22 + 4)
36.2	5.9	5.8	24.4	18.8	5.2	5.6	0.2	6.7	13.8	2011	
30.4	2.4	3.7	24.2	22.2	5.4	2.0	0.0	1.3	19.2	1995	Matières premières
35.8	2.2	3.9	29.6	27.0	13.5	2.6	0.1	1.4	23.4	2005	d'origine agricole
49.2	2.5	4.3	42.4	39.1	22.6	3.3	0.0	1.8	33.0	2011	(CTCI 2 - 22 - 27 - 28)
27.7	1.3	2.3	24.1	22.1	2.5	2.0	0.0	1.4	18.5	1995	Minerais, métaux, pierres
37.0	1.4	2.6	32.9	29.2	9.8	3.8	0.0	2.8	23.1	2005	précieuses et or (non monétaire)
47.9	1.6	2.3	43.9	39.1	18.3	4.8	0.0	3.1	32.2	2011	(CTCI 27 + 28 + 68 + 667 + 971)
26.0	1.9	4.8	19.1	16.8	1.5	2.2	0.1	0.5	13.6	1995	Combustibles (CTCI 3)
29.5	2.2	4.3	22.9	20.7	4.2	2.2	0.1	1.0	16.9	2005	
40.8	2.7	4.9	33.1	31.0	8.3	2.1	0.1	1.2	23.6	2011	
29.6	2.5	5.0	22.0	19.6	3.1	2.4	0.1	2.3	18.0	1995	Articles manufacturés
31.2	2.3	5.0	23.8	20.5	5.9	3.3	0.1	3.3	19.0	2005	(CTCI 5 à 8 moins 667 et 68)
38.8	3.0	6.6	29.1	24.8	7.9	4.2	0.2	4.2	21.7	2011	
Parts par principaux groupes de produits (en pourcentage)											
100.0	100.0	100.0	100.0	100.0	100.0	100.0	100.0	100.0	100.0	1995	Total tous produits
100.0	100.0	100.0	100.0	100.0	100.0	100.0	100.0	100.0	100.0	2005	
100.0	100.0	100.0	100.0	100.0	100.0	100.0	100.0	100.0	100.0	2011	
8.1	15.6	8.9	7.0	6.3	7.1	12.6	14.5	15.7	5.5	1995	Produits alimentaires
5.5	11.5	6.9	4.6	4.0	3.2	8.4	10.3	10.4	3.6	2005	(CTCI 0 + 1 + 22 + 4)
7.0	14.9	7.6	6.1	5.5	4.6	10.7	7.4	13.9	4.8	2011	
2.9	2.6	2.1	3.1	3.2	5.1	2.2	1.0	1.6	3.1	1995	Matières premières
1.8	1.5	1.3	2.0	2.1	3.7	1.3	1.0	0.8	2.0	2005	d'origine agricole
2.1	1.4	1.2	2.3	2.5	4.4	1.4	0.3	0.8	2.5	2011	(CTCI 2 - 22 - 27 - 28)
4.4	2.3	2.1	5.2	5.4	3.9	3.6	0.6	2.8	5.0	1995	Minerais, métaux, pierres
5.6	2.8	2.5	6.5	6.7	8.0	5.4	0.5	4.3	5.9	2005	précieuses et or (non monétaire)
8.2	3.7	2.7	9.7	10.0	14.3	8.0	0.4	5.6	9.8	2011	(CTCI 27 + 28 + 68 + 667 + 971)
6.7	5.6	7.4	6.6	6.6	3.9	6.7	8.5	1.5	6.0	1995	Combustibles (CTCI 3)
13.5	12.9	12.6	13.7	14.3	10.5	9.5	18.7	4.6	13.0	2005	
17.9	15.4	14.5	18.9	20.4	16.6	9.1	14.1	5.6	18.6	2011	
75.4	71.4	76.4	75.6	76.2	77.6	71.2	72.3	74.9	78.1	1995	Articles manufacturés
71.1	68.3	73.7	70.9	70.8	72.4	71.4	63.7	76.7	73.3	2005	(CTCI 5 à 8 moins 667 et 68)
62.3	62.5	70.5	60.7	59.7	58.1	66.9	69.3	71.2	62.2	2011	

Pour les sources et les notes, se reporter à la fin du tableau 2.2.L.

Product group	Year / Année	World (1) / Monde (1)	Developed economies - Économies développées			Canada	USA / États-Unis	Japan / Japon	Other developed countries / Autres économies développées	Transition economies / Économies en transition
Origin			Total	Europe Total	Europe EU / UE					
Millions of dollars										
All products	1995	5 192 078	3 544 912	2 143 853	2 004 359	197 463	636 067	479 012	88 518	124 693
	2005	10 716 653	6 229 824	4 074 072	3 818 473	362 242	940 741	667 950	184 818	376 089
	2011	18 285 477	9 307 397	6 134 337	5 680 821	452 375	1 442 871	890 579	387 235	797 331
Share by origin (percentage)										
All products	1995	100.0	68.3	41.3	38.6	3.8	12.3	9.2	1.7	2.4
	2005	100.0	58.1	38.0	35.6	3.4	8.8	6.2	1.7	3.5
	2011	100.0	50.9	33.5	31.1	2.5	7.9	4.9	2.1	4.4
All food items	1995	100.0	64.3	42.6	40.9	3.5	13.8	0.5	4.0	2.0
(SITC 0 + 1 + 22 + 4)	2005	100.0	62.0	43.4	41.7	3.6	10.0	0.4	4.6	2.6
	2011	100.0	56.8	39.2	37.3	3.3	10.1	0.4	3.9	3.0
Agricultural raw materials	1995	100.0	65.7	29.7	28.6	12.3	16.6	1.7	5.4	5.3
(SITC 2 - 22 - 27 - 28)	2005	100.0	62.1	33.2	32.5	10.2	12.5	1.8	4.3	6.4
	2011	100.0	54.8	29.4	28.7	6.1	12.6	2.2	4.5	5.7
Ores, metals, precious stones	1995	100.0	60.4	34.7	29.0	6.4	8.5	2.4	8.3	7.5
and non-monetary gold	2005	100.0	52.7	29.7	25.0	4.6	6.0	2.5	10.0	7.6
(SITC 27 + 28 + 68 + 667 + 971)	2011	100.0	50.1	26.5	20.3	3.8	5.9	2.6	11.3	5.4
Fuels (SITC 3)	1995	100.0	30.4	19.4	13.9	4.4	3.2	0.5	2.9	8.9
	2005	100.0	28.8	19.0	14.2	4.9	2.3	0.3	2.4	12.5
	2011	100.0	26.6	15.8	12.7	3.7	3.9	0.5	2.7	14.4
Manufactured goods	1995	100.0	73.0	43.7	41.3	3.2	13.2	12.2	0.7	1.2
(SITC 5 to 8 less 667 and 68)	2005	100.0	63.3	41.5	39.7	2.7	10.0	8.4	0.7	1.4
	2011	100.0	56.8	38.5	36.5	1.8	8.8	7.0	0.7	1.6
Share by major product group (percentage)										
All products	1995	100.0	100.0	100.0	100.0	100.0	100.0	100.0	100.0	100.0
	2005	100.0	100.0	100.0	100.0	100.0	100.0	100.0	100.0	100.0
	2011	100.0	100.0	100.0	100.0	100.0	100.0	100.0	100.0	100.0
All food items	1995	9.1	8.6	9.4	9.7	8.4	10.3	0.5	21.2	7.6
(SITC 0 + 1 + 22 + 4)	2005	6.7	7.2	7.7	7.9	7.1	7.6	0.5	18.0	5.0
	2011	7.6	8.5	8.9	9.2	10.1	9.8	0.6	14.2	5.3
Agricultural raw materials	1995	2.9	2.8	2.1	2.1	9.3	3.9	0.5	9.1	6.4
(SITC 2 - 22 - 27 - 28)	2005	1.7	1.8	1.4	1.5	5.0	2.4	0.5	4.2	3.0
	2011	1.7	1.8	1.5	1.6	4.1	2.7	0.8	3.6	2.2
Ores, metals, precious stones	1995	5.0	4.4	4.2	3.7	8.3	3.5	1.3	24.2	15.6
and non-monetary gold	2005	4.9	4.4	3.8	3.4	6.7	3.3	1.9	28.3	10.6
(SITC 27 + 28 + 68 + 667 + 971)	2011	6.9	6.8	5.4	4.5	10.6	5.1	3.7	36.8	8.5
Fuels (SITC 3)	1995	7.2	3.2	3.4	2.6	8.3	1.9	0.4	12.2	27.0
	2005	13.4	6.6	6.7	5.4	19.3	3.5	0.6	18.3	47.7
	2011	17.6	9.2	8.3	7.2	26.0	8.6	2.0	22.7	58.1
Manufactured goods	1995	72.2	77.2	76.4	77.3	61.3	77.7	95.4	31.3	34.6
(SITC 5 to 8 less 667 and 68)	2005	70.8	77.1	77.2	78.9	57.3	81.0	95.1	28.7	28.3
	2011	64.0	71.3	73.4	75.3	46.0	71.3	91.9	21.0	23.1

For sources and notes, see end of table 2.2.L.

2.2.A Structure des importations par partenaires et groupes de produits
Monde

			Developing economies - Économies en développement								Origines
				Asia / Asie				Major petroleum exporters and gas exporters	Major manufactured goods exporters	Year	
Total	Africa / Afrique	America / Amérique	Total	Eastern, Southern and South-Eastern Asia / Asie orientale, méridionale et du Sud-Est	China / Chine	Western Asia / Asie occidentale	Oceania (2) / Océanie (2)	Principaux exportateurs de pétrole et de gaz	Principaux exportateurs d'articles manufacturés	Année	Groupes de produits
Millions de dollars											
1 432 598	123 561	245 160	1 059 149	925 920	232 593	133 229	4 727	173 927	852 070	1995	Total tous produits
4 037 111	320 467	625 907	3 083 652	2 606 224	1 074 915	477 428	7 085	616 328	2 398 664	2005	
8 028 699	629 255	1 181 308	6 204 542	5 090 606	2 293 522	1 113 935	13 594	1 394 485	4 520 166	2011	
Parts par origines (en pourcentage)											
27.6	2.4	4.7	20.4	17.8	4.5	2.6	0.1	3.3	16.4	1995	Total tous produits
37.7	3.0	5.8	28.8	24.3	10.0	4.5	0.1	5.8	22.4	2005	
43.9	3.4	6.5	33.9	27.8	12.5	6.1	0.1	7.6	24.7	2011	
32.4	4.5	12.5	15.2	13.5	2.7	1.7	0.3	0.7	10.2	1995	Produits alimentaires
35.3	3.9	15.2	16.0	13.6	3.7	2.4	0.2	1.0	9.9	2005	(CTCI 0 + 1 + 22 + 4)
40.0	3.8	16.6	19.4	16.6	3.6	2.8	0.2	1.4	11.1	2011	
28.2	4.3	6.4	17.0	16.4	2.3	0.6	0.5	0.6	12.4	1995	Matières premières
31.4	4.6	7.9	18.5	17.7	3.1	0.8	0.4	0.5	12.1	2005	d'origine agricole
39.5	4.1	8.1	26.9	26.1	3.7	0.7	0.4	0.6	15.5	2011	(CTCI 2 - 22 - 27 - 28)
29.5	6.3	9.9	12.8	11.0	1.9	1.7	0.6	1.7	7.4	1995	Minerais, métaux, pierres
39.2	7.4	12.1	19.4	16.1	3.4	3.3	0.4	3.3	9.2	2005	précieuses et or (non monétaire)
44.1	7.0	14.7	21.9	17.1	3.3	4.8	0.4	4.5	10.3	2011	(CTCI 27 + 28 + 68 + 667 + 971)
58.1	11.7	8.3	37.8	14.8	1.5	23.0	0.2	37.9	8.8	1995	Combustibles (CTCI 3)
56.8	12.4	8.8	35.5	13.3	1.3	22.2	0.1	36.6	8.8	2005	
57.3	11.0	7.8	38.5	14.8	0.8	23.7	0.1	36.2	8.9	2011	
24.6	0.8	3.1	20.6	19.8	5.4	0.9	0.0	0.5	19.2	1995	Articles manufacturés
35.0	0.8	3.9	30.2	28.7	13.2	1.6	0.0	0.8	27.7	2005	(CTCI 5 à 8 moins 667 et 68)
41.4	0.9	4.1	36.5	34.4	18.4	2.1	0.0	1.2	32.8	2011	
Parts par principaux groupes de produits (en pourcentage)											
100.0	100.0	100.0	100.0	100.0	100.0	100.0	100.0	100.0	100.0	1995	Total tous produits
100.0	100.0	100.0	100.0	100.0	100.0	100.0	100.0	100.0	100.0	2005	
100.0	100.0	100.0	100.0	100.0	100.0	100.0	100.0	100.0	100.0	2011	
10.7	17.4	24.1	6.8	6.9	5.5	6.0	25.9	2.0	5.7	1995	Produits alimentaires
6.3	8.8	17.5	3.7	3.8	2.5	3.6	22.8	1.2	3.0	2005	(CTCI 0 + 1 + 22 + 4)
7.0	8.4	19.6	4.4	4.6	2.2	3.5	21.3	1.4	3.4	2011	
2.9	5.2	3.9	2.4	2.6	1.5	0.7	15.3	0.5	2.2	1995	Matières premières
1.4	2.6	2.2	1.1	1.2	0.5	0.3	9.7	0.1	0.9	2005	d'origine agricole
1.5	2.0	2.1	1.3	1.6	0.5	0.2	9.4	0.1	1.1	2011	(CTCI 2 - 22 - 27 - 28)
5.3	13.0	10.4	3.1	3.1	2.1	3.3	30.0	2.5	2.2	1995	Minerais, métaux, pierres
5.1	12.1	10.2	3.3	3.2	1.7	3.6	26.4	2.8	2.0	2005	précieuses et or (non monétaire)
6.9	14.1	15.6	4.4	4.2	1.8	5.4	39.8	4.0	2.9	2011	(CTCI 27 + 28 + 68 + 667 + 971)
15.3	35.7	12.8	13.4	6.0	2.5	64.9	13.7	82.1	3.9	1995	Combustibles (CTCI 3)
20.2	55.5	20.2	16.5	7.3	1.7	66.7	15.5	85.3	5.2	2005	
23.0	56.2	21.2	20.0	9.4	1.1	68.4	12.0	83.4	6.3	2011	
64.3	25.7	46.8	73.0	80.1	87.6	24.1	14.4	11.3	84.5	1995	Articles manufacturés
65.8	20.0	47.8	74.4	83.4	93.0	24.9	23.5	9.7	87.6	2005	(CTCI 5 à 8 moins 667 et 68)
60.4	16.4	40.1	68.8	79.0	93.7	22.3	16.9	10.1	85.0	2011	

Pour les sources et les notes, se reporter à la fin du tableau 2.2.L.

Product group	Year / Année	World (1) / Monde (1)	Total	Europe Total	EU / UE	Canada	USA / États-Unis	Japan / Japon	Other developed countries / Autres économies développées	Transition economies / Économies en transition
Millions of dollars										
All products	1995	1 433 901	802 102	279 023	267 783	16 253	318 941	165 135	22 750	13 481
	2005	3 805 282	1 991 737	715 034	694 724	47 076	823 823	335 906	69 898	48 265
	2011	7 789 922	3 311 925	1 269 534	1 214 537	96 197	1 230 525	562 609	153 060	135 241
Share by destination (percentage)										
All products	1995	100.0	55.9	19.5	18.7	1.1	22.2	11.5	1.6	0.9
	2005	100.0	52.3	18.8	18.3	1.2	21.6	8.8	1.8	1.3
	2011	100.0	42.5	16.3	15.6	1.2	15.8	7.2	2.0	1.7
All food items	1995	100.0	55.5	26.8	25.9	0.9	12.7	13.9	1.1	2.8
(SITC 0 + 1 + 22 + 4)	2005	100.0	51.9	25.2	24.7	1.2	14.8	9.2	1.5	4.0
	2011	100.0	40.2	19.9	19.5	1.2	11.4	6.2	1.5	3.7
Agricultural raw materials	1995	100.0	50.8	23.4	22.7	0.6	11.8	14.0	0.9	0.3
(SITC 2 - 22 - 27 - 28)	2005	100.0	47.1	21.9	21.3	1.0	14.1	9.2	0.9	0.7
	2011	100.0	37.8	18.0	17.8	0.9	10.7	7.2	0.9	1.1
Ores, metals, precious stones	1995	100.0	58.1	26.6	23.2	1.2	12.1	16.5	1.7	0.9
and non-monetary gold	2005	100.0	48.7	24.0	21.0	2.0	11.2	9.1	2.3	0.6
(SITC 27 + 28 + 68 + 667 + 971)	2011	100.0	38.4	19.3	14.4	2.4	7.9	6.8	2.0	0.4
Fuels (SITC 3)	1995	100.0	62.3	19.7	19.4	0.8	19.4	20.8	1.7	0.3
	2005	100.0	56.3	17.0	16.7	1.1	21.7	14.7	1.8	0.1
	2011	100.0	44.2	13.4	13.2	1.1	15.9	11.8	1.9	0.2
Manufactured goods	1995	100.0	54.5	17.5	16.9	1.3	25.5	8.5	1.7	0.9
(SITC 5 to 8 less 667 and 68)	2005	100.0	51.6	18.4	18.0	1.2	23.4	6.7	1.8	1.5
	2011	100.0	43.1	16.8	16.3	1.2	17.5	5.6	2.1	2.3
Share by major product group (percentage)										
All products	1995	100.0	100.0	100.0	100.0	100.0	100.0	100.0	100.0	100.0
	2005	100.0	100.0	100.0	100.0	100.0	100.0	100.0	100.0	100.0
	2011	100.0	100.0	100.0	100.0	100.0	100.0	100.0	100.0	100.0
All food items	1995	10.0	9.9	13.8	13.9	7.8	5.7	12.1	7.2	30.0
(SITC 0 + 1 + 22 + 4)	2005	6.0	6.0	8.1	8.1	5.7	4.1	6.3	4.9	19.0
	2011	6.9	6.5	8.4	8.6	6.5	5.0	6.0	5.3	14.6
Agricultural raw materials	1995	2.7	2.5	3.3	3.3	1.5	1.5	3.3	1.6	0.8
(SITC 2 - 22 - 27 - 28)	2005	1.3	1.2	1.5	1.5	1.1	0.8	1.4	0.7	0.7
	2011	1.5	1.4	1.7	1.7	1.1	1.0	1.5	0.7	1.0
Ores, metals, precious stones	1995	5.2	5.4	7.1	6.4	5.4	2.8	7.4	5.6	4.8
and non-monetary gold	2005	5.1	4.7	6.5	5.9	8.4	2.6	5.3	6.5	2.5
(SITC 27 + 28 + 68 + 667 + 971)	2011	7.0	6.3	8.2	6.4	13.7	3.5	6.6	7.1	1.7
Fuels (SITC 3)	1995	15.1	16.8	15.3	15.6	10.1	13.1	27.2	15.8	4.0
	2005	22.7	24.4	20.5	20.8	20.7	22.8	37.7	22.4	1.4
	2011	23.9	24.8	19.6	20.1	21.6	24.0	39.1	23.5	2.3
Manufactured goods	1995	65.9	64.2	59.4	59.6	74.5	75.6	48.9	69.0	59.7
(SITC 5 to 8 less 667 and 68)	2005	64.1	63.2	62.8	63.1	63.2	69.2	49.0	64.5	76.1
	2011	59.6	60.4	61.3	62.3	56.1	66.0	46.2	62.8	80.2

For sources and notes, see end of table 2.2.L.

2.2.B Structure des exportations par partenaires et groupes de produits
Économies en développement

Total	Africa / Afrique	America / Amérique	Asia / Asie Total	Eastern, Southern and South-Eastern Asia / Asie orientale, méridionale et du Sud-Est	China / Chine	Western Asia / Asie occidentale	Oceania (2) / Océanie (2)	Major petroleum exporters and gas exporters / Principaux exportateurs de pétrole et de gaz	Major manufactured goods exporters / Principaux exportateurs d'articles manufacturés	Year / Année	Destinations / Groupes de produits
\multicolumn{12}{c}{Developing economies - Économies en développement}											Destinations
\multicolumn{10}{c}{Millions de dollars}										
610 993	48 258	73 534	488 393	445 857	82 730	42 537	807	37 883	374 502	1995	Total tous produits
1 748 984	109 665	185 832	1 448 150	1 309 498	368 069	138 652	5 336	137 677	1 083 975	2005	
4 299 563	287 931	480 633	3 511 612	3 156 684	940 601	354 929	19 386	377 691	2 418 495	2011	
\multicolumn{10}{c}{Parts par destinations (en pourcentage)}										
42.6	3.4	5.1	34.1	31.1	5.8	3.0	0.1	2.6	26.1	1995	Total tous produits
46.0	2.9	4.9	38.1	34.4	9.7	3.6	0.1	3.6	28.5	2005	
55.2	3.7	6.2	45.1	40.5	12.1	4.6	0.2	4.8	31.0	2011	
41.1	6.4	6.5	28.2	23.1	4.6	5.1	0.1	5.7	15.6	1995	Produits alimentaires
43.7	6.6	6.5	30.6	23.2	5.1	7.4	0.1	8.4	15.0	2005	(CTCI 0 + 1 + 22 + 4)
56.0	8.6	7.5	39.7	31.0	8.0	8.7	0.1	11.3	18.8	2011	
48.5	3.8	4.9	39.9	37.7	9.3	2.2	0.0	1.9	31.1	1995	Matières premières
51.9	2.7	4.4	44.8	42.1	19.7	2.7	0.0	1.8	33.2	2005	d'origine agricole
61.0	2.3	4.5	54.2	50.8	26.5	3.3	0.0	2.0	39.6	2011	(CTCI 2 - 22 - 27 - 28)
40.5	2.1	3.8	34.7	32.2	5.1	2.4	0.0	2.4	27.2	1995	Minerais, métaux, pierres
50.6	2.1	3.6	44.8	39.4	13.4	5.4	0.0	5.0	31.1	2005	précieuses et or (non monétaire)
60.9	2.2	3.0	55.7	49.3	23.1	6.4	0.0	5.6	39.0	2011	(CTCI 27 + 28 + 68 + 667 + 971)
36.3	2.6	5.4	28.3	25.3	2.4	3.0	0.1	0.3	19.9	1995	Combustibles (CTCI 3)
43.0	2.9	5.1	34.9	32.3	6.4	2.5	0.2	1.0	25.7	2005	
55.1	3.0	4.4	47.5	45.6	11.4	1.9	0.2	1.2	32.8	2011	
44.3	3.2	5.0	36.1	33.3	6.6	2.7	0.1	2.8	28.9	1995	Articles manufacturés
46.7	2.6	4.7	39.3	35.8	10.8	3.5	0.1	4.0	30.6	2005	(CTCI 5 à 8 moins 667 et 68)
54.4	3.7	7.0	43.4	38.6	11.2	4.8	0.3	5.6	30.8	2011	
\multicolumn{10}{c}{Parts par principaux groupes de produits (en pourcentage)}										
100.0	100.0	100.0	100.0	100.0	100.0	100.0	100.0	100.0	100.0	1995	Total tous produits
100.0	100.0	100.0	100.0	100.0	100.0	100.0	100.0	100.0	100.0	2005	
100.0	100.0	100.0	100.0	100.0	100.0	100.0	100.0	100.0	100.0	2011	
9.6	19.0	12.7	8.3	7.4	7.9	17.1	10.9	21.4	6.0	1995	Produits alimentaires
5.7	13.7	8.0	4.8	4.1	3.2	12.2	5.9	14.0	3.2	2005	(CTCI 0 + 1 + 22 + 4)
7.0	16.0	8.4	6.1	5.3	4.6	13.2	3.7	16.1	4.2	2011	
3.1	3.1	2.6	3.2	3.3	4.4	2.0	0.5	1.9	3.3	1995	Matières premières
1.5	1.2	1.2	1.5	1.6	2.7	1.0	0.2	0.6	1.5	2005	d'origine agricole
1.7	1.0	1.1	1.8	1.9	3.3	1.1	0.1	0.6	1.9	2011	(CTCI 2 - 22 - 27 - 28)
4.9	3.2	3.8	5.3	5.3	4.5	4.2	0.5	4.8	5.4	1995	Minerais, métaux, pierres
5.6	3.7	3.8	6.0	5.8	7.0	7.6	0.3	7.0	5.6	2005	précieuses et or (non monétaire)
7.7	4.1	3.3	8.6	8.5	13.4	9.8	0.2	8.0	8.8	2011	(CTCI 27 + 28 + 68 + 667 + 971)
12.8	11.5	15.7	12.5	12.3	6.4	15.3	15.2	1.5	11.5	1995	Combustibles (CTCI 3)
21.2	22.6	23.6	20.8	21.3	15.0	15.8	31.9	6.3	20.5	2005	
23.8	19.7	16.9	25.1	26.8	22.5	10.1	19.0	5.7	25.2	2011	
68.5	62.6	64.4	69.8	70.6	75.9	60.9	68.5	70.0	72.9	1995	Articles manufacturés
65.1	57.3	62.0	66.2	66.7	71.9	61.1	55.6	70.1	68.9	2005	(CTCI 5 à 8 moins 667 et 68)
58.7	58.9	67.9	57.4	56.7	55.2	63.1	66.7	69.3	59.1	2011	

Pour les sources et les notes, se reporter à la fin du tableau 2.2.L.

Product group	Year / Année	World (1) / Monde (1)	Developed economies - Économies développées							Transition economies / Économies en transition
			Total	Europe Total	EU / UE	Canada	USA / États-Unis	Japan / Japon	Other developed countries / Autres économies développées	
Millions of dollars										
All products	1995	1 501 396	888 082	323 423	300 263	19 486	268 549	242 899	33 725	22 390
	2005	3 398 081	1 519 217	602 112	558 535	31 516	428 248	374 414	82 928	76 766
	2011	7 317 753	2 839 560	1 184 010	1 054 660	71 472	774 532	586 006	223 540	186 964
Share by origin (percentage)										
All products	1995	100.0	59.2	21.5	20.0	1.3	17.9	16.2	2.2	1.5
	2005	100.0	44.7	17.7	16.4	0.9	12.6	11.0	2.4	2.3
	2011	100.0	38.8	16.2	14.4	1.0	10.6	8.0	3.1	2.6
All food items	1995	100.0	53.1	19.6	18.8	3.6	22.4	1.5	6.1	0.8
(SITC 0 + 1 + 22 + 4)	2005	100.0	44.1	15.4	14.6	2.7	17.9	1.2	6.9	2.3
	2011	100.0	40.2	13.6	12.8	2.8	17.1	0.7	6.0	2.6
Agricultural raw materials	1995	100.0	53.0	12.0	11.7	4.5	24.5	4.3	7.7	4.7
(SITC 2 - 22 - 27 - 28)	2005	100.0	51.2	14.7	14.3	4.9	20.9	4.0	6.7	7.4
	2011	100.0	48.1	13.1	12.9	5.7	18.9	3.6	6.8	5.9
Ores, metals, precious stones	1995	100.0	56.0	23.0	17.3	2.8	11.9	6.9	11.4	4.0
and non-monetary gold	2005	100.0	45.4	18.8	13.4	1.6	6.7	5.2	13.0	5.0
(SITC 27 + 28 + 68 + 667 + 971)	2011	100.0	44.1	16.7	9.9	1.5	6.4	4.2	15.3	4.0
Fuels (SITC 3)	1995	100.0	16.6	4.4	4.3	0.7	5.9	1.6	4.0	2.0
	2005	100.0	12.5	3.3	2.9	0.3	4.3	0.7	3.8	4.5
	2011	100.0	15.4	4.2	4.0	0.5	6.1	1.1	3.6	5.8
Manufactured goods	1995	100.0	63.9	23.7	22.1	0.9	18.3	20.2	0.9	1.2
(SITC 5 to 8 less 667 and 68)	2005	100.0	50.1	20.3	19.1	0.7	13.9	14.4	0.8	1.4
	2011	100.0	44.4	19.8	18.5	0.7	11.5	11.7	0.7	1.1
Share by major product group (percentage)										
All products	1995	100.0	100.0	100.0	100.0	100.0	100.0	100.0	100.0	100.0
	2005	100.0	100.0	100.0	100.0	100.0	100.0	100.0	100.0	100.0
	2011	100.0	100.0	100.0	100.0	100.0	100.0	100.0	100.0	100.0
All food items	1995	8.4	7.5	7.6	7.9	23.1	10.5	0.8	22.7	4.4
(SITC 0 + 1 + 22 + 4)	2005	5.9	5.8	5.1	5.2	17.2	8.3	0.6	16.7	5.9
	2011	6.9	7.2	5.8	6.2	19.9	11.2	0.6	13.6	7.0
Agricultural raw materials	1995	3.0	2.7	1.7	1.8	10.5	4.1	0.8	10.3	9.5
(SITC 2 - 22 - 27 - 28)	2005	1.9	2.2	1.6	1.7	10.0	3.2	0.7	5.3	6.3
	2011	2.1	2.6	1.7	1.9	12.0	3.7	0.9	4.6	4.8
Ores, metals, precious stones	1995	4.9	4.7	5.3	4.3	10.6	3.3	2.1	24.9	13.3
and non-monetary gold	2005	6.3	6.4	6.7	5.1	11.0	3.4	3.0	33.6	14.1
(SITC 27 + 28 + 68 + 667 + 971)	2011	9.2	10.5	9.5	6.4	14.3	5.6	4.8	46.2	14.3
Fuels (SITC 3)	1995	6.6	1.8	1.3	1.4	3.6	2.2	0.7	11.7	8.9
	2005	12.3	3.4	2.3	2.2	4.2	4.2	0.7	19.2	24.7
	2011	17.5	6.9	4.5	4.9	8.5	10.0	2.3	20.5	39.9
Manufactured goods	1995	75.1	81.1	82.5	83.1	50.7	76.7	93.7	29.1	61.9
(SITC 5 to 8 less 667 and 68)	2005	72.1	80.8	82.4	84.0	57.2	79.7	94.0	22.7	43.3
	2011	62.0	70.9	76.1	79.7	44.0	67.3	90.4	13.8	26.0

For sources and notes, see end of table 2.2.L.

2.2.B Structure des importations par partenaires et groupes de produits
Économies en développement

	Developing economies - Économies en développement									Year	Origines
Total	Africa / Afrique	America / Amérique	Asia / Asie — Total	Eastern, Southern and South-Eastern Asia / Asie orientale, méridionale et du Sud-Est	China / Chine	Western Asia / Asie occidentale	Oceania (2) / Océanie (2)	Major petroleum exporters and gas exporters / Principaux exportateurs de pétrole et de gaz	Major manufactured goods exporters / Principaux exportateurs d'articles manufacturés	Année	Groupes de produits
Millions de dollars											
572 922	39 516	68 348	464 183	406 170	103 297	58 013	876	64 515	361 732	1995	Total tous produits
1 778 948	98 713	181 028	1 497 120	1 264 837	415 411	232 283	2 087	263 501	1 075 516	2005	
4 232 556	277 529	467 312	3 483 201	2 815 718	1 028 605	667 483	4 515	794 149	2 316 370	2011	
Parts par origines (en pourcentage)											
38.2	2.6	4.6	30.9	27.1	6.9	3.9	0.1	4.3	24.1	1995	Total tous produits
52.4	2.9	5.3	44.1	37.2	12.2	6.8	0.1	7.8	31.7	2005	
57.8	3.8	6.4	47.6	38.5	14.1	9.1	0.1	10.9	31.7	2011	
45.5	6.6	13.5	25.2	21.6	4.1	3.6	0.2	1.6	15.3	1995	Produits alimentaires
53.4	4.6	19.5	28.9	23.6	5.0	5.3	0.3	2.6	13.8	2005	(CTCI 0 + 1 + 22 + 4)
57.2	4.4	20.7	31.9	26.2	4.4	5.7	0.2	3.2	14.5	2011	
41.9	6.0	7.4	27.8	26.9	3.3	1.0	0.6	0.8	20.8	1995	Matières premières
41.3	5.8	7.0	27.7	26.5	2.7	1.2	0.9	0.9	17.4	2005	d'origine agricole
46.0	4.5	7.4	33.2	32.4	3.2	0.8	0.8	0.8	19.2	2011	(CTCI 2 - 22 - 27 - 28)
39.7	6.4	9.8	23.3	19.3	3.3	4.0	0.2	3.0	13.8	1995	Minerais, métaux, pierres
49.4	5.9	12.0	31.3	25.5	4.6	5.9	0.1	5.8	13.3	2005	précieuses et or (non monétaire)
51.7	7.2	14.0	30.4	23.4	3.8	7.0	0.2	7.0	12.1	2011	(CTCI 27 + 28 + 68 + 667 + 971)
80.6	8.4	8.0	64.2	28.0	2.7	36.2	0.1	47.8	17.2	1995	Combustibles (CTCI 3)
82.7	10.7	6.7	65.3	28.2	2.9	37.2	0.0	48.2	16.3	2005	
78.4	10.5	6.8	61.1	26.2	1.7	34.9	0.0	47.2	13.8	2011	
34.0	1.4	2.9	29.7	28.4	8.1	1.3	0.0	1.1	26.8	1995	Articles manufacturés
48.2	1.1	3.4	43.7	41.7	15.5	2.1	0.0	1.6	38.1	2005	(CTCI 5 à 8 moins 667 et 68)
54.3	1.1	3.7	49.5	46.4	20.9	3.1	0.0	2.5	42.6	2011	
Parts par principaux groupes de produits (en pourcentage)											
100.0	100.0	100.0	100.0	100.0	100.0	100.0	100.0	100.0	100.0	1995	Total tous produits
100.0	100.0	100.0	100.0	100.0	100.0	100.0	100.0	100.0	100.0	2005	
100.0	100.0	100.0	100.0	100.0	100.0	100.0	100.0	100.0	100.0	2011	
10.0	20.9	24.9	6.8	6.7	5.0	7.7	27.3	3.2	5.3	1995	Produits alimentaires
6.0	9.4	21.5	3.9	3.7	2.4	4.6	25.5	2.0	2.6	2005	(CTCI 0 + 1 + 22 + 4)
6.9	8.0	22.5	4.7	4.7	2.2	4.3	21.9	2.0	3.2	2011	
3.3	6.9	4.9	2.7	3.0	1.5	0.7	32.4	0.6	2.6	1995	Matières premières
1.5	3.8	2.5	1.2	1.4	0.4	0.3	27.0	0.2	1.1	2005	d'origine agricole
1.7	2.5	2.4	1.5	1.7	0.5	0.2	25.8	0.1	1.3	2011	(CTCI 2 - 22 - 27 - 28)
5.1	11.9	10.6	3.7	3.5	2.4	5.0	19.8	3.4	2.8	1995	Minerais, métaux, pierres
5.9	12.8	14.2	4.5	4.3	2.4	5.4	10.8	4.7	2.7	2005	précieuses et or (non monétaire)
8.3	17.5	20.3	5.9	5.6	2.5	7.1	22.8	5.9	3.5	2011	(CTCI 27 + 28 + 68 + 667 + 971)
13.9	20.9	11.6	13.7	6.8	2.6	61.8	8.2	73.3	4.7	1995	Combustibles (CTCI 3)
19.4	45.3	15.4	18.2	9.3	2.9	66.9	8.2	76.5	6.3	2005	
23.7	48.3	18.6	22.4	11.9	2.1	66.9	5.8	76.0	7.6	2011	
66.9	39.3	47.6	72.1	79.0	88.0	24.5	12.0	19.3	83.5	1995	Articles manufacturés
66.4	26.7	45.6	71.6	80.7	91.6	22.0	27.7	15.3	86.8	2005	(CTCI 5 à 8 moins 667 et 68)
58.2	17.7	35.7	64.5	74.8	92.3	21.4	23.6	14.5	83.4	2011	

Pour les sources et les notes, se reporter à la fin du tableau 2.2.L.

Destination \ Product group	Year / Année	World (1) / Monde (1)	Developed economies - Économies développées							Transition economies / Économies en transition
			Total	Europe Total	EU / UE	Canada	USA / États-Unis	Japan / Japon	Other developed countries / Autres économies développées	
Millions of dollars										
All products	1995	113 116	73 244	52 294	49 696	1 030	15 216	3 610	1 093	805
	2005	318 934	216 500	131 752	127 360	5 900	65 421	10 374	3 054	1 508
	2011	581 846	324 118	198 871	189 003	13 531	91 748	14 872	5 096	3 331
Share by destination (percentage)										
All products	1995	100.0	64.8	46.2	43.9	0.9	13.5	3.2	1.0	0.7
	2005	100.0	67.9	41.3	39.9	1.8	20.5	3.3	1.0	0.5
	2011	100.0	55.7	34.2	32.5	2.3	15.8	2.6	0.9	0.6
All food items	1995	100.0	61.4	51.1	49.5	0.6	3.2	5.8	0.7	1.5
(SITC 0 + 1 + 22 + 4)	2005	100.0	65.5	54.2	53.0	1.0	5.6	3.6	1.2	2.8
	2011	100.0	53.5	44.3	43.4	0.8	5.2	2.5	0.9	3.3
Agricultural raw materials	1995	100.0	55.4	46.1	44.9	0.2	2.9	5.7	0.6	0.1
(SITC 2 - 22 - 27 - 28)	2005	100.0	51.0	40.6	39.2	0.2	3.6	6.3	0.4	0.3
	2011	100.0	40.2	33.3	32.0	0.4	3.7	2.3	0.5	0.9
Ores, metals, precious stones	1995	100.0	74.0	51.3	42.2	1.0	10.4	10.2	1.2	0.5
and non-monetary gold	2005	100.0	69.6	48.0	42.1	1.2	10.4	8.9	1.2	1.2
(SITC 27 + 28 + 68 + 667 + 971)	2011	100.0	49.0	33.3	25.6	1.5	5.9	7.6	0.7	1.0
Fuels (SITC 3)	1995	100.0	79.3	49.7	48.1	1.5	26.6	0.6	0.8	0.8
	2005	100.0	70.6	37.5	36.7	2.5	28.3	1.9	0.3	0.0
	2011	100.0	60.3	31.9	31.2	3.3	22.5	1.7	0.9	0.0
Manufactured goods	1995	100.0	44.9	36.2	35.6	0.4	5.7	1.4	1.2	0.4
(SITC 5 to 8 less 667 and 68)	2005	100.0	62.6	45.6	45.1	0.7	9.2	3.8	3.3	0.6
	2011	100.0	52.4	39.8	39.3	0.9	9.0	1.5	1.2	0.7
Share by major product group (percentage)										
All products	1995	100.0	100.0	100.0	100.0	100.0	100.0	100.0	100.0	100.0
	2005	100.0	100.0	100.0	100.0	100.0	100.0	100.0	100.0	100.0
	2011	100.0	100.0	100.0	100.0	100.0	100.0	100.0	100.0	100.0
All food items	1995	16.2	15.3	17.9	18.2	9.8	3.8	29.3	11.6	33.3
(SITC 0 + 1 + 22 + 4)	2005	7.4	7.1	9.7	9.8	3.9	2.0	8.2	8.9	43.2
	2011	8.6	8.3	11.2	11.6	2.8	2.8	8.4	8.4	50.6
Agricultural raw materials	1995	5.2	4.4	5.2	5.3	0.9	1.1	9.2	3.5	1.0
(SITC 2 - 22 - 27 - 28)	2005	2.4	1.8	2.4	2.4	0.3	0.4	4.7	0.9	1.8
	2011	2.4	1.8	2.4	2.4	0.5	0.6	2.2	1.3	3.9
Ores, metals, precious stones	1995	12.9	14.8	14.3	12.4	13.9	10.0	41.2	16.1	8.3
and non-monetary gold	2005	11.2	11.4	13.0	11.8	7.0	5.7	30.6	13.6	28.4
(SITC 27 + 28 + 68 + 667 + 971)	2011	13.8	12.2	13.5	10.9	9.0	5.2	41.3	10.5	24.6
Fuels (SITC 3)	1995	36.8	45.1	39.6	40.2	61.2	72.8	7.4	31.6	40.4
	2005	60.7	63.1	55.2	55.8	82.1	83.9	36.2	16.7	5.8
	2011	57.4	62.2	53.6	55.1	81.7	82.0	38.1	57.2	0.9
Manufactured goods	1995	28.9	20.0	22.6	23.4	14.1	12.1	12.6	37.3	15.8
(SITC 5 to 8 less 667 and 68)	2005	17.5	16.1	19.3	19.7	6.8	7.8	20.4	59.5	20.9
	2011	16.3	15.3	19.0	19.7	6.0	9.3	9.7	22.3	19.8

For sources and notes, see end of table 2.2.L.

2.2.C Structure des exportations par partenaires et groupes de produits
Économies en développement : Afrique

Total	Africa / Afrique	America / Amérique	Asia — Asie Total	Eastern, Southern and South-Eastern Asia / Asie orientale, méridionale et du Sud-Est	China / Chine	Western Asia / Asie occidentale	Oceania (2) / Océanie (2)	Major petroleum exporters and gas exporters / Principaux exportateurs de pétrole et de gaz	Major manufactured goods exporters / Principaux exportateurs d'articles manufacturés	Year / Année	Destinations / Groupes de produits
Millions de dollars											
37 881	23 878	2 385	11 608	9 121	948	2 487	9	2 292	6 071	1995	Total tous produits
96 020	28 841	12 349	54 802	44 794	20 287	10 008	28	6 945	31 235	2005	
251 507	63 465	22 625	165 339	144 653	75 972	20 686	78	16 796	102 679	2011	
Parts par destinations (en pourcentage)											
33.5	21.1	2.1	10.3	8.1	0.8	2.2	0.0	2.0	5.4	1995	Total tous produits
30.1	9.0	3.9	17.2	14.0	6.4	3.1	0.0	2.2	9.8	2005	
43.2	10.9	3.9	28.4	24.9	13.1	3.6	0.0	2.9	17.6	2011	
36.4	28.2	0.4	7.8	4.3	0.3	3.5	0.0	3.8	2.0	1995	Produits alimentaires
31.1	17.0	0.5	13.6	7.7	1.4	5.8	0.1	6.2	4.0	2005	(CTCI 0 + 1 + 22 + 4)
42.7	21.5	1.6	19.6	10.8	2.3	8.8	0.0	8.9	6.7	2011	
43.7	17.4	2.5	23.8	21.4	4.3	2.4	0.0	1.5	15.4	1995	Matières premières
48.4	9.6	0.5	38.3	35.3	16.9	3.0	0.0	1.3	24.9	2005	d'origine agricole
58.5	9.1	2.2	47.2	43.3	21.1	3.9	0.0	1.8	30.8	2011	(CTCI 2 - 22 - 27 - 28)
24.7	6.4	1.5	16.7	14.6	1.4	2.1	0.0	2.0	11.9	1995	Minerais, métaux, pierres
29.1	6.7	0.7	21.8	17.6	7.2	4.1	0.0	2.6	13.0	2005	précieuses et or (non monétaire)
50.0	7.1	0.8	42.2	36.5	22.1	5.6	0.0	3.5	28.9	2011	(CTCI 27 + 28 + 68 + 667 + 971)
17.7	6.0	3.4	8.3	6.4	0.6	2.0	0.0	0.3	4.1	1995	Combustibles (CTCI 3)
27.8	5.5	5.5	16.8	14.5	7.7	2.3	0.0	0.5	10.3	2005	
39.2	6.1	5.4	27.6	26.2	13.6	1.4	0.0	0.4	17.9	2011	
54.1	43.6	1.6	8.8	7.0	0.6	1.7	0.0	3.4	4.1	1995	Articles manufacturés
36.1	19.4	2.4	14.3	10.0	1.7	4.3	0.0	6.1	6.3	2005	(CTCI 5 à 8 moins 667 et 68)
46.5	26.5	2.9	17.1	10.6	2.7	6.6	0.0	8.3	5.9	2011	
Parts par principaux groupes de produits (en pourcentage)											
100.0	100.0	100.0	100.0	100.0	100.0	100.0	100.0	100.0	100.0	1995	Total tous produits
100.0	100.0	100.0	100.0	100.0	100.0	100.0	100.0	100.0	100.0	2005	
100.0	100.0	100.0	100.0	100.0	100.0	100.0	100.0	100.0	100.0	2011	
17.6	21.6	3.0	12.3	8.7	5.0	25.7	30.9	30.7	6.1	1995	Produits alimentaires
7.6	13.9	0.9	5.8	4.1	1.6	13.8	46.2	21.1	3.1	2005	(CTCI 0 + 1 + 22 + 4)
8.5	17.0	3.6	6.0	3.7	1.5	21.4	17.2	26.5	3.3	2011	
6.8	4.3	6.1	12.0	13.8	26.6	5.7	3.2	3.8	14.9	1995	Matières premières
3.9	2.6	0.3	5.4	6.1	6.5	2.4	6.7	1.4	6.2	2005	d'origine agricole
3.3	2.0	1.4	4.1	4.3	4.0	2.7	0.8	1.6	4.3	2011	(CTCI 2 - 22 - 27 - 28)
9.5	3.9	9.2	21.1	23.4	21.4	12.4	7.3	12.5	28.8	1995	Minerais, métaux, pierres
10.8	8.2	1.9	14.1	14.0	12.7	14.7	1.7	13.3	14.8	2005	précieuses et or (non monétaire)
16.0	9.0	2.7	20.5	20.3	23.4	22.0	1.1	17.0	22.6	2011	(CTCI 27 + 28 + 68 + 667 + 971)
19.4	10.4	59.1	29.9	29.0	27.1	33.4	24.7	4.9	28.1	1995	Combustibles (CTCI 3)
56.1	37.0	85.8	59.4	62.7	73.3	44.8	2.5	14.6	63.8	2005	
52.0	32.4	80.1	55.7	60.5	59.6	22.6	56.7	8.0	58.4	2011	
46.6	59.7	22.5	24.6	25.1	19.9	22.8	33.5	48.1	22.1	1995	Articles manufacturés
21.0	37.6	10.8	14.5	12.5	4.7	23.8	42.7	48.7	11.3	2005	(CTCI 5 à 8 moins 667 et 68)
17.5	39.6	12.1	9.8	6.9	3.4	30.1	22.9	46.8	5.4	2011	

Pour les sources et les notes, se reporter à la fin du tableau 2.2.L.

Product group	Year / Année	World (1) / Monde (1)	Developed economies - Économies développées							Transition economies / Économies en transition
			Total	Europe		Canada	USA / États-Unis	Japan / Japon	Other developed countries / Autres économies développées	
				Total	EU / UE					
Millions of dollars										
All products	**1995**	**124 579**	**75 938**	**56 226**	**54 187**	**1 378**	**10 834**	**6 225**	**1 276**	**1 525**
	2005	**256 546**	**126 407**	**95 888**	**92 885**	**1 670**	**17 004**	**8 433**	**3 412**	**6 536**
	2011	**569 643**	**254 047**	**191 350**	**184 476**	**3 839**	**38 919**	**13 412**	**6 528**	**13 359**
Share by origin (percentage)										
All products	**1995**	**100.0**	**61.0**	**45.1**	**43.5**	**1.1**	**8.7**	**5.0**	**1.0**	**1.2**
	2005	**100.0**	**49.3**	**37.4**	**36.2**	**0.7**	**6.6**	**3.3**	**1.3**	**2.5**
	2011	**100.0**	**44.6**	**33.6**	**32.4**	**0.7**	**6.8**	**2.4**	**1.1**	**2.3**
All food items	1995	100.0	51.8	32.9	31.6	3.2	14.0	0.2	1.5	0.5
(SITC 0 + 1 + 22 + 4)	2005	100.0	45.2	29.1	27.9	1.9	11.4	0.1	2.8	3.9
	2011	100.0	41.8	27.2	26.0	1.7	10.0	0.1	2.7	4.5
Agricultural raw materials	1995	100.0	54.5	41.9	41.5	1.7	7.7	1.5	1.7	6.0
(SITC 2 - 22 - 27 - 28)	2005	100.0	57.3	45.5	44.8	2.6	6.1	1.5	1.6	7.8
	2011	100.0	61.1	45.8	45.0	3.4	7.9	2.7	1.3	6.0
Ores, metals, precious stones	1995	100.0	64.4	46.7	42.1	3.4	3.0	1.8	9.5	2.8
and non-monetary gold	2005	100.0	38.5	23.5	21.9	0.8	3.6	0.3	10.3	4.8
(SITC 27 + 28 + 68 + 667 + 971)	2011	100.0	45.0	34.5	33.2	1.6	3.4	0.4	5.0	4.5
Fuels (SITC 3)	1995	100.0	23.2	17.7	17.5	0.4	3.7	0.1	1.3	1.7
	2005	100.0	17.8	15.4	14.7	0.2	1.4	0.1	0.7	4.1
	2011	100.0	28.7	23.6	22.8	0.2	4.4	0.2	0.4	3.7
Manufactured goods	1995	100.0	68.4	51.9	50.1	0.5	8.2	7.2	0.5	1.1
(SITC 5 to 8 less 667 and 68)	2005	100.0	58.6	45.7	44.3	0.5	7.4	4.2	0.8	2.0
	2011	100.0	50.7	39.1	37.7	0.5	7.1	3.3	0.7	1.5
Share by major product group (percentage)										
All products	**1995**	**100.0**	**100.0**	**100.0**	**100.0**	**100.0**	**100.0**	**100.0**	**100.0**	**100.0**
	2005	**100.0**	**100.0**	**100.0**	**100.0**	**100.0**	**100.0**	**100.0**	**100.0**	**100.0**
	2011	**100.0**	**100.0**	**100.0**	**100.0**	**100.0**	**100.0**	**100.0**	**100.0**	**100.0**
All food items	1995	18.5	15.7	13.5	13.5	53.4	29.8	0.6	27.4	7.2
(SITC 0 + 1 + 22 + 4)	2005	12.8	11.7	9.9	9.9	36.5	22.0	0.4	26.7	19.7
	2011	14.4	13.5	11.7	11.6	35.9	21.2	0.8	34.5	27.4
Agricultural raw materials	1995	3.1	2.8	2.9	2.9	4.8	2.7	0.9	5.1	15.2
(SITC 2 - 22 - 27 - 28)	2005	1.6	1.8	1.9	1.9	6.3	1.5	0.7	1.9	4.8
	2011	1.4	1.9	1.9	2.0	7.0	1.6	1.6	1.6	3.6
Ores, metals, precious stones	1995	2.6	2.7	2.7	2.5	8.0	0.9	0.9	24.1	5.9
and non-monetary gold	2005	2.7	2.1	1.7	1.7	3.4	1.5	0.2	21.1	5.1
(SITC 27 + 28 + 68 + 667 + 971)	2011	3.2	3.2	3.3	3.3	7.6	1.6	0.5	14.0	6.1
Fuels (SITC 3)	1995	6.4	2.4	2.5	2.6	2.1	2.7	0.2	8.1	8.9
	2005	11.8	4.3	4.9	4.8	3.9	2.4	0.5	6.1	19.2
	2011	14.5	9.3	10.2	10.2	3.5	9.2	1.0	5.4	22.6
Manufactured goods	1995	67.2	75.5	77.4	77.5	31.3	63.3	97.3	35.1	62.6
(SITC 5 to 8 less 667 and 68)	2005	63.9	76.0	78.2	78.3	49.3	71.0	82.2	36.6	49.4
	2011	61.1	69.5	71.1	71.1	45.9	63.7	85.3	39.3	40.0

For sources and notes, see end of table 2.2.L.

Total	Africa / Afrique	America / Amérique	Asia / Asie — Total	Eastern, Southern and South-Eastern Asia / Asie orientale, méridionale et du Sud-Est	China / Chine	Western Asia / Asie occidentale	Oceania (2) / Océanie (2)	Major petroleum exporters and gas exporters / Principaux exportateurs de pétrole et de gaz	Major manufactured goods exporters / Principaux exportateurs d'articles manufacturés	Year / Année	Origines / Groupes de produits
— Developing economies - Économies en développement											Origines
Millions de dollars											
43 502	22 054	3 040	18 396	14 431	2 394	3 965	12	5 677	10 088	1995	Total tous produits
109 314	34 037	9 692	65 499	46 352	17 785	19 147	87	23 095	34 468	2005	
278 407	66 638	27 305	184 132	138 693	66 163	45 439	331	49 549	100 955	2011	
Parts par origines (en pourcentage)											
34.9	17.7	2.4	14.8	11.6	1.9	3.2	0.0	4.6	8.1	1995	Total tous produits
42.6	13.3	3.8	25.5	18.1	6.9	7.5	0.0	9.0	13.4	2005	
48.9	11.7	4.8	32.3	24.3	11.6	8.0	0.1	8.7	17.7	2011	
46.8	27.7	7.6	11.5	9.5	1.4	2.0	0.0	0.7	5.7	1995	Produits alimentaires
50.0	15.8	16.2	18.0	15.1	2.1	2.9	0.1	1.4	8.9	2005	(CTCI 0 + 1 + 22 + 4)
53.7	13.8	18.8	21.0	17.8	2.5	3.2	0.0	2.0	10.7	2011	
38.9	26.2	3.2	9.5	6.9	0.3	2.6	0.0	0.7	5.1	1995	Matières premières
34.5	18.0	2.0	14.5	11.5	1.8	3.0	0.0	1.6	7.4	2005	d'origine agricole
32.5	11.4	3.3	17.7	15.7	3.3	2.0	0.0	1.3	10.1	2011	(CTCI 2 - 22 - 27 - 28)
32.7	18.1	4.7	9.9	3.6	0.9	6.2	0.0	5.0	2.7	1995	Minerais, métaux, pierres
52.1	34.7	4.7	12.6	6.5	2.6	6.1	0.0	5.2	4.9	2005	précieuses et or (non monétaire)
49.8	21.9	10.6	17.3	10.5	5.8	6.8	0.0	5.9	7.7	2011	(CTCI 27 + 28 + 68 + 667 + 971)
72.0	32.4	1.5	38.0	19.4	0.2	18.6	..	51.0	0.7	1995	Combustibles (CTCI 3)
77.9	33.1	1.6	43.2	11.6	0.4	31.7	0.0	55.8	1.0	2005	
67.5	25.7	1.3	40.5	14.5	0.3	26.1	0.0	40.8	3.0	2011	
29.1	13.7	1.1	14.3	12.2	2.4	2.1	0.0	1.5	10.0	1995	Articles manufacturés
38.2	9.4	1.9	27.0	22.1	10.1	4.8	0.0	3.2	18.3	2005	(CTCI 5 à 8 moins 667 et 68)
47.5	8.4	2.3	36.7	31.0	17.9	5.7	0.1	3.7	24.9	2011	
Parts par principaux groupes de produits (en pourcentage)											
100.0	100.0	100.0	100.0	100.0	100.0	100.0	100.0	100.0	100.0	1995	Total tous produits
100.0	100.0	100.0	100.0	100.0	100.0	100.0	100.0	100.0	100.0	2005	
100.0	100.0	100.0	100.0	100.0	100.0	100.0	100.0	100.0	100.0	2011	
24.8	28.9	57.6	14.5	15.2	13.5	11.6	18.1	2.7	13.0	1995	Produits alimentaires
15.0	15.2	54.7	9.0	10.6	3.8	5.0	26.3	2.0	8.4	2005	(CTCI 0 + 1 + 22 + 4)
15.8	17.0	56.6	9.4	10.6	3.1	5.7	1.5	3.3	8.7	2011	
3.4	4.6	4.1	2.0	1.8	0.5	2.5	0.2	0.5	1.9	1995	Matières premières
1.3	2.1	0.8	0.9	1.0	0.4	0.6	0.4	0.3	0.9	2005	d'origine agricole
0.9	1.4	1.0	0.8	0.9	0.4	0.4	0.5	0.2	0.8	2011	(CTCI 2 - 22 - 27 - 28)
2.4	2.7	5.0	1.7	0.8	1.2	5.1	1.0	2.8	0.9	1995	Minerais, métaux, pierres
3.3	7.2	3.4	1.4	1.0	1.0	2.2	0.5	1.6	1.0	2005	précieuses et or (non monétaire)
3.2	6.0	7.0	1.7	1.4	1.6	2.7	0.1	2.2	1.4	2011	(CTCI 27 + 28 + 68 + 667 + 971)
13.1	11.7	3.9	16.4	10.7	0.8	37.2	..	71.3	0.6	1995	Combustibles (CTCI 3)
21.6	29.4	5.0	20.0	7.5	0.7	50.1	2.1	73.2	0.9	2005	
20.0	31.8	4.1	18.2	8.6	0.4	47.3	1.6	68.0	2.4	2011	
56.0	52.1	29.3	65.1	71.0	83.7	43.5	79.6	22.6	83.3	1995	Articles manufacturés
57.4	45.1	32.0	67.5	78.2	93.2	41.4	70.6	22.5	87.0	2005	(CTCI 5 à 8 moins 667 et 68)
59.5	43.7	29.8	69.5	77.9	94.4	43.7	95.8	26.2	85.9	2011	

Pour les sources et les notes, se reporter à la fin du tableau 2.2.L.

| Product group | Year Année | World (1) Monde (1) | Developed economies - Économies développées | | | | | | | Transition Economies Économies en transition |
| | | | Total | Europe | | Canada | USA États-Unis | Japan Japon | Other developed countries Autres économies développées | |
				Total	EU UE					
Millions of dollars										
All products	**1995**	**230 261**	**162 762**	**41 238**	**38 930**	**4 166**	**107 180**	**9 185**	**994**	**1 504**
	2005	**583 851**	**403 723**	**77 932**	**74 754**	**12 245**	**299 220**	**12 088**	**2 238**	**5 481**
	2011	**1 102 302**	**649 514**	**154 210**	**140 362**	**27 939**	**435 088**	**26 394**	**5 884**	**11 423**
Share by destination (percentage)										
All products	**1995**	**100.0**	**70.7**	**17.9**	**16.9**	**1.8**	**46.5**	**4.0**	**0.4**	**0.7**
	2005	**100.0**	**69.1**	**13.3**	**12.8**	**2.1**	**51.2**	**2.1**	**0.4**	**0.9**
	2011	**100.0**	**58.9**	**14.0**	**12.7**	**2.5**	**39.5**	**2.4**	**0.5**	**1.0**
All food items	1995	100.0	65.2	34.3	33.4	1.1	23.7	5.4	0.8	2.6
(SITC 0 + 1 + 22 + 4)	2005	100.0	57.4	28.3	27.6	1.3	23.0	4.0	0.8	5.1
	2011	100.0	46.0	22.7	22.0	1.5	17.4	3.5	0.9	3.9
Agricultural raw materials	1995	100.0	66.0	30.4	28.9	0.4	24.9	10.0	0.2	0.1
(SITC 2 - 22 - 27 - 28)	2005	100.0	65.7	26.2	24.9	0.9	32.3	5.7	0.6	0.9
	2011	100.0	50.8	24.9	24.6	0.6	19.5	5.0	0.7	1.6
Ores, metals, precious stones	1995	100.0	73.5	33.8	30.1	2.8	20.5	16.1	0.3	0.4
and non-monetary gold	2005	100.0	60.9	26.1	22.9	5.1	19.3	10.3	0.2	0.3
(SITC 27 + 28 + 68 + 667 + 971)	2011	100.0	53.1	24.0	17.5	6.0	14.3	8.1	0.7	0.1
Fuels (SITC 3)	1995	100.0	73.0	8.8	8.8	1.6	60.8	1.6	0.3	0.0
	2005	100.0	73.1	7.6	7.6	1.6	63.6	0.0	0.2	0.0
	2011	100.0	65.0	8.8	8.7	1.2	54.4	0.2	0.3	0.7
Manufactured goods	1995	100.0	72.2	8.6	7.9	2.1	60.0	1.1	0.4	0.1
(SITC 5 to 8 less 667 and 68)	2005	100.0	73.6	7.9	7.8	1.9	62.9	0.5	0.4	0.1
	2011	100.0	65.0	8.5	8.3	2.3	53.1	0.7	0.4	0.2
Share by major product group (percentage)										
All products	**1995**	**100.0**	**100.0**	**100.0**	**100.0**	**100.0**	**100.0**	**100.0**	**100.0**	**100.0**
	2005	**100.0**	**100.0**	**100.0**	**100.0**	**100.0**	**100.0**	**100.0**	**100.0**	**100.0**
	2011	**100.0**	**100.0**	**100.0**	**100.0**	**100.0**	**100.0**	**100.0**	**100.0**	**100.0**
All food items	1995	22.3	20.6	42.7	44.0	13.4	11.3	30.1	39.1	87.1
(SITC 0 + 1 + 22 + 4)	2005	16.1	13.3	34.0	34.6	9.9	7.2	30.9	33.2	86.5
	2011	18.9	14.7	30.6	32.7	11.4	8.3	27.4	33.1	71.2
Agricultural raw materials	1995	3.7	3.5	6.3	6.4	0.8	2.0	9.3	1.7	0.3
(SITC 2 - 22 - 27 - 28)	2005	2.0	1.9	3.9	3.9	0.8	1.3	5.6	2.9	1.9
	2011	1.9	1.7	3.5	3.8	0.5	1.0	4.0	2.7	3.0
Ores, metals, precious stones	1995	10.1	10.5	19.1	18.0	15.7	4.5	41.0	6.6	6.7
and non-monetary gold	2005	10.2	9.0	19.9	18.2	24.8	3.8	50.7	4.2	3.5
(SITC 27 + 28 + 68 + 667 + 971)	2011	16.1	14.5	27.6	22.1	38.0	5.8	54.4	21.2	1.7
Fuels (SITC 3)	1995	14.3	14.7	7.0	7.4	12.3	18.6	5.9	9.1	0.6
	2005	21.0	22.2	12.0	12.5	16.1	26.1	0.0	13.6	1.1
	2011	22.0	24.2	13.8	15.1	10.7	30.3	2.2	11.4	15.0
Manufactured goods	1995	49.0	50.1	23.6	23.0	57.5	63.2	13.6	43.2	5.2
(SITC 5 to 8 less 667 and 68)	2005	49.9	53.1	29.7	30.3	45.3	61.2	12.7	46.0	6.9
	2011	40.1	44.3	24.4	26.2	36.1	54.0	11.5	31.6	8.8

For sources and notes, see end of table 2.2.L.

Total	Africa / Afrique	America / Amérique	Asia / Asie Total	Eastern, Southern and South-Eastern Asia / Asie orientale, méridionale et du Sud-Est	China / Chine	Western Asia / Asie occidentale	Oceania (2) / Océanie (2)	Major petroleum exporters and gas exporters / Principaux exportateurs de pétrole et de gaz	Major manufactured goods exporters / Principaux exportateurs d'articles manufacturés	Year / Année	Destinations / Groupes de produits
Millions de dollars											
65 119	3 025	46 146	15 928	14 017	2 631	1 911	21	5 115	12 197	1995	Total tous produits
170 739	9 620	110 010	51 076	44 920	20 076	6 156	34	16 288	46 890	2005	
433 233	21 648	222 044	189 478	172 065	101 530	17 414	62	37 276	154 078	2011	
Parts par destinations (en pourcentage)											
28.3	1.3	20.0	6.9	6.1	1.1	0.8	0.0	2.2	5.3	1995	Total tous produits
29.2	1.6	18.8	8.7	7.7	3.4	1.1	0.0	2.8	8.0	2005	
39.3	2.0	20.1	17.2	15.6	9.2	1.6	0.0	3.4	14.0	2011	
31.7	3.3	17.1	11.3	9.4	2.8	1.9	0.0	4.3	6.2	1995	Produits alimentaires
37.3	5.3	14.3	17.6	14.0	6.3	3.6	0.0	6.2	11.2	2005	(CTCI 0 + 1 + 22 + 4)
49.9	7.3	17.0	25.6	20.9	10.8	4.7	0.0	9.7	16.7	2011	
33.5	1.0	15.0	17.5	15.8	3.2	1.7	0.0	2.6	13.5	1995	Matières premières
33.4	0.7	12.4	20.2	18.8	10.6	1.4	0.0	1.6	18.6	2005	d'origine agricole
47.6	1.0	11.6	34.9	32.8	20.1	2.1	0.0	2.1	30.6	2011	(CTCI 2 - 22 - 27 - 28)
25.6	1.2	10.7	13.7	12.8	2.0	1.0	0.0	1.6	12.2	1995	Minerais, métaux, pierres
38.7	1.1	10.9	26.7	25.3	14.3	1.4	0.0	1.6	24.8	2005	précieuses et or (non monétaire)
46.8	0.6	7.0	39.1	36.9	26.8	2.2	0.0	1.6	35.0	2011	(CTCI 27 + 28 + 68 + 667 + 971)
26.4	0.4	24.8	1.3	1.3	0.0	0.0	0.0	0.1	1.6	1995	Combustibles (CTCI 3)
26.5	0.6	22.7	3.2	3.1	0.9	0.2	0.0	0.3	3.0	2005	
34.0	0.2	18.4	15.4	15.1	8.1	0.3		0.5	11.0	2011	
27.6	0.8	22.4	4.4	3.9	0.4	0.5	0.0	2.0	4.0	1995	Articles manufacturés
26.1	1.1	20.8	4.2	3.7	1.1	0.5	0.0	3.1	5.4	2005	(CTCI 5 à 8 moins 667 et 68)
34.7	1.0	28.7	4.9	4.4	1.7	0.5	0.0	2.8	5.4	2011	
Parts par principaux groupes de produits (en pourcentage)											
100.0	100.0	100.0	100.0	100.0	100.0	100.0	100.0	100.0	100.0	1995	Total tous produits
100.0	100.0	100.0	100.0	100.0	100.0	100.0	100.0	100.0	100.0	2005	
100.0	100.0	100.0	100.0	100.0	100.0	100.0	100.0	100.0	100.0	2011	
25.0	55.9	19.0	36.5	34.5	55.2	50.9	38.7	43.6	26.1	1995	Produits alimentaires
20.4	52.0	12.2	32.2	29.1	29.4	54.9	61.8	35.6	22.5	2005	(CTCI 0 + 1 + 22 + 4)
24.0	70.2	16.0	28.1	25.3	22.2	56.1	37.2	54.1	22.6	2011	
4.4	2.8	2.8	9.4	9.7	10.6	7.6	0.4	4.4	9.5	1995	Matières premières
2.3	0.9	1.3	4.6	4.9	6.2	2.6	0.6	1.2	4.6	2005	d'origine agricole
2.4	1.0	1.1	3.9	4.1	4.3	2.6	1.3	1.2	4.3	2011	(CTCI 2 - 22 - 27 - 28)
9.2	9.0	5.4	20.1	21.3	17.9	11.7	0.1	7.3	23.3	1995	Minerais, métaux, pierres
13.5	6.8	5.9	31.1	33.5	42.3	13.7	0.2	6.0	31.5	2005	précieuses et or (non monétaire)
19.2	5.2	5.6	36.6	38.0	46.8	22.9	0.7	7.9	40.4	2011	(CTCI 27 + 28 + 68 + 667 + 971)
13.3	3.8	17.7	2.7	3.0	0.2	0.4	4.2	0.7	4.3	1995	Combustibles (CTCI 3)
19.0	7.2	25.3	7.7	8.4	5.6	3.0	1.5	2.3	7.9	2005	
19.0	2.4	20.1	19.7	21.2	19.3	4.5	..	3.4	17.3	2011	
47.9	28.4	54.9	31.3	31.5	16.1	29.4	56.5	44.1	36.7	1995	Articles manufacturés
44.6	33.0	55.0	24.2	24.1	16.5	25.5	35.5	54.8	33.4	2005	(CTCI 5 à 8 moins 667 et 68)
35.4	20.9	57.2	11.6	11.3	7.4	13.9	59.2	33.4	15.4	2011	

Developing economies - Économies en développement

Pour les sources et les notes, se reporter à la fin du tableau 2.2.L.

Product group	Year Année	World (1) Monde (1)	Developed economies - Économies développées							Transition economies Économies en transition
			Total	Europe		Canada	USA États-Unis	Japan Japon	Other developed countries Autres économies développées	
				Total	EU UE					
Millions of dollars										
All products	1995	242 996	173 176	48 336	45 289	5 291	104 307	13 636	1 606	1 182
	2005	523 425	309 960	79 576	74 905	10 363	189 841	25 994	4 187	3 792
	2011	1 073 503	543 956	150 783	142 111	19 454	324 037	41 472	8 209	12 375
Share by origin (percentage)										
All products	1995	100.0	71.3	19.9	18.6	2.2	42.9	5.6	0.7	0.5
	2005	100.0	59.2	15.2	14.3	2.0	36.3	5.0	0.8	0.7
	2011	100.0	50.7	14.0	13.2	1.8	30.2	3.9	0.8	1.2
All food items	1995	100.0	58.2	15.7	14.5	5.0	35.5	0.1	1.9	0.1
(SITC 0 + 1 + 22 + 4)	2005	100.0	58.2	9.3	8.7	4.9	41.7	0.0	2.2	0.1
	2011	100.0	51.5	8.0	7.4	4.8	37.0	0.0	1.6	0.1
Agricultural raw materials	1995	100.0	60.9	7.6	7.3	3.5	47.3	0.5	2.1	1.7
(SITC 2 - 22 - 27 - 28)	2005	100.0	63.5	8.4	8.2	2.8	50.7	0.6	1.0	0.5
	2011	100.0	56.7	7.5	7.4	2.1	45.6	0.8	0.8	1.6
Ores, metals, precious stones	1995	100.0	53.3	11.1	9.9	5.6	34.1	0.8	1.6	0.3
and non-monetary gold	2005	100.0	43.7	8.0	7.8	3.2	31.3	0.4	0.8	0.8
(SITC 27 + 28 + 68 + 667 + 971)	2011	100.0	39.9	7.4	6.9	3.9	26.8	0.4	1.4	1.7
Fuels (SITC 3)	1995	100.0	30.8	7.0	6.8	1.4	20.3	0.3	1.8	2.4
	2005	100.0	32.3	4.9	4.0	0.7	24.4	0.3	2.1	1.1
	2011	100.0	44.9	4.8	4.6	0.8	37.2	0.5	1.7	1.9
Manufactured goods	1995	100.0	76.6	22.5	21.0	1.7	45.5	6.6	0.4	0.4
(SITC 5 to 8 less 667 and 68)	2005	100.0	63.8	17.6	16.6	1.9	37.6	6.3	0.5	0.7
	2011	100.0	52.2	17.0	16.0	1.6	28.0	5.1	0.5	1.0
Share by major product group (percentage)										
All products	1995	100.0	100.0	100.0	100.0	100.0	100.0	100.0	100.0	100.0
	2005	100.0	100.0	100.0	100.0	100.0	100.0	100.0	100.0	100.0
	2011	100.0	100.0	100.0	100.0	100.0	100.0	100.0	100.0	100.0
All food items	1995	9.5	7.8	7.5	7.4	21.9	7.9	0.1	27.4	1.5
(SITC 0 + 1 + 22 + 4)	2005	7.1	7.0	4.3	4.3	17.6	8.1	0.1	19.4	0.5
	2011	7.7	7.8	4.4	4.3	20.6	9.4	0.1	15.9	0.9
Agricultural raw materials	1995	2.3	2.0	0.9	0.9	3.6	2.5	0.2	7.3	7.8
(SITC 2 - 22 - 27 - 28)	2005	1.3	1.4	0.7	0.8	1.9	1.9	0.1	1.7	0.9
	2011	1.2	1.4	0.7	0.7	1.4	1.9	0.3	1.3	1.7
Ores, metals, precious stones	1995	2.4	1.8	1.3	1.3	6.2	1.9	0.3	6.0	1.3
and non-monetary gold	2005	2.5	1.9	1.3	1.4	4.1	2.2	0.2	2.5	2.9
(SITC 27 + 28 + 68 + 667 + 971)	2011	2.6	2.0	1.4	1.3	5.6	2.3	0.3	4.7	3.8
Fuels (SITC 3)	1995	6.8	2.9	2.4	2.5	4.4	3.2	0.4	18.6	33.3
	2005	11.2	6.1	3.6	3.1	4.0	7.5	0.6	29.1	17.6
	2011	14.7	13.1	5.0	5.1	6.7	18.1	1.8	32.3	24.0
Manufactured goods	1995	76.1	81.7	85.9	85.9	59.6	80.6	89.2	40.6	56.0
(SITC 5 to 8 less 667 and 68)	2005	76.7	82.6	88.8	89.2	72.2	79.4	97.7	45.2	75.5
	2011	72.6	74.8	88.0	87.9	64.4	67.2	96.3	45.4	62.1

For sources and notes, see end of table 2.2.L.

Total	Africa Afrique	America Amérique	Asia Asie Total	Eastern, Southern and South-Eastern Asia Asie orientale, méridionale et du Sud-Est	China Chine	Western Asia Asie occidentale	Oceania (2) Océanie (2)	Major petroleum exporters and gas exporters Principaux exportateurs de pétrole et de gaz	Major manufactured goods exporters Principaux exportateurs d'articles manufacturés	Year Année	Origines Groupes de produits
Millions de dollars											
67 269	2 484	45 492	19 277	17 213	2 843	2 065	16	8 450	20 128	1995	**Total tous produits**
206 579	11 209	110 447	84 891	81 666	37 367	3 225	31	20 352	84 370	2005	
507 741	22 048	221 774	263 824	253 313	152 015	10 511	95	36 002	256 873	2011	
Parts par origines (en pourcentage)											
27.7	1.0	18.7	7.9	7.1	1.2	0.8	0.0	3.5	8.3	1995	**Total tous produits**
39.5	2.1	21.1	16.2	15.6	7.1	0.6	0.0	3.9	16.1	2005	
47.3	2.1	20.7	24.6	23.6	14.2	1.0	0.0	3.4	23.9	2011	
41.2	0.3	38.4	2.5	2.2	0.4	0.4	0.0	1.3	2.2	1995	Produits alimentaires
41.6	0.2	37.6	3.7	3.4	1.1	0.2	0.0	0.7	3.5	2005	(CTCI 0 + 1 + 22 + 4)
48.0	0.8	42.0	5.1	4.9	1.9	0.2	0.1	0.1	4.8	2011	
36.9	2.4	25.5	9.1	9.0	0.4	0.1	0.0	0.7	8.3	1995	Matières premières
36.0	0.6	23.9	11.3	11.1	1.4	0.2	0.1	0.5	8.8	2005	d'origine agricole
41.5	1.2	20.5	19.7	19.6	3.3	0.1	0.1	0.2	12.8	2011	(CTCI 2 - 22 - 27 - 28)
47.7	4.5	41.3	1.8	1.6	0.5	0.2	0.0	4.8	3.0	1995	Minerais, métaux, pierres
55.3	2.0	49.1	4.2	4.0	1.7	0.2	0.0	4.1	3.7	2005	précieuses et or (non monétaire)
58.3	2.5	44.5	11.3	10.1	8.0	1.3	0.0	2.9	12.2	2011	(CTCI 27 + 28 + 68 + 667 + 971)
66.7	8.8	44.2	13.6	3.0	0.9	10.6	..	35.1	4.4	1995	Combustibles (CTCI 3)
65.3	16.1	41.5	7.7	3.5	1.0	4.2	..	27.7	5.0	2005	
50.1	10.8	30.1	9.2	5.1	0.9	4.1	..	19.1	3.4	2011	
22.4	0.3	13.7	8.4	8.3	1.4	0.1	0.0	1.1	9.8	1995	Articles manufacturés
35.0	0.3	15.8	18.9	18.8	8.9	0.1	0.0	0.8	19.3	2005	(CTCI 5 à 8 moins 667 et 68)
46.4	0.4	15.9	30.1	29.6	18.6	0.4	0.0	0.6	30.5	2011	
Parts par principaux groupes de produits (en pourcentage)											
100.0	100.0	100.0	100.0	100.0	100.0	100.0	100.0	100.0	100.0	1995	**Total tous produits**
100.0	100.0	100.0	100.0	100.0	100.0	100.0	100.0	100.0	100.0	2005	
100.0	100.0	100.0	100.0	100.0	100.0	100.0	100.0	100.0	100.0	2011	
14.2	2.6	19.5	3.0	2.9	3.1	4.3	5.7	3.6	2.5	1995	Produits alimentaires
7.5	0.8	12.6	1.6	1.6	1.1	2.6	45.5	1.2	1.5	2005	(CTCI 0 + 1 + 22 + 4)
7.8	3.0	15.6	1.6	1.6	1.1	1.4	49.8	0.3	1.6	2011	
3.1	5.3	3.1	2.6	2.9	0.7	0.2	0.6	0.4	2.3	1995	Matières premières
1.2	0.4	1.5	0.9	1.0	0.3	0.5	12.0	0.2	0.7	2005	d'origine agricole
1.1	0.8	1.2	1.0	1.0	0.3	0.2	14.9	0.1	0.7	2011	(CTCI 2 - 22 - 27 - 28)
4.1	10.7	5.3	0.5	0.5	0.9	0.6	0.0	3.3	0.9	1995	Minerais, métaux, pierres
3.6	2.4	5.9	0.7	0.6	0.6	0.9	4.1	2.6	0.6	2005	précieuses et or (non monétaire)
3.2	3.1	5.6	1.2	1.1	1.5	3.3	0.0	2.2	1.3	2011	(CTCI 27 + 28 + 68 + 667 + 971)
16.4	58.9	16.1	11.7	2.9	5.3	84.9	..	68.7	3.6	1995	Combustibles (CTCI 3)
18.6	84.6	22.1	5.3	2.5	1.6	76.9	..	79.9	3.5	2005	
15.6	77.7	21.4	5.5	3.2	1.0	61.6	..	84.0	2.1	2011	
61.6	22.6	55.5	81.0	89.5	89.5	10.0	93.5	23.4	89.8	1995	Articles manufacturés
68.0	11.5	57.3	89.5	92.3	95.1	18.4	34.8	16.0	91.8	2005	(CTCI 5 à 8 moins 667 et 68)
71.1	15.1	55.8	88.8	91.1	95.4	32.9	35.0	13.2	92.6	2011	

Pour les sources et les notes, se reporter à la fin du tableau 2.2.L.

2.2.E Export structure by partner and product group
Developing economies: Asia

Destination / Product group	Year / Année	World (1) / Monde (1)	Developed economies - Économies développées							Transition economies / Économies en transition
			Total	Europe		Canada	USA / États-Unis	Japan / Japon	Other developed countries / Autres économies développées	
				Total	EU / UE					
Millions of dollars										
All products	1995	1 085 043	561 787	184 479	178 148	11 030	196 334	150 452	19 493	11 170
	2005	2 895 596	1 366 887	504 042	491 323	28 906	458 872	312 440	62 627	41 251
	2011	6 094 661	2 330 671	914 602	883 371	54 717	703 280	520 048	138 024	120 471
Share by destination (percentage)										
All products	1995	100.0	51.8	17.0	16.4	1.0	18.1	13.9	1.8	1.0
	2005	100.0	47.2	17.4	17.0	1.0	15.8	10.8	2.2	1.4
	2011	100.0	38.2	15.0	14.5	0.9	11.5	8.5	2.3	2.0
All food items	1995	100.0	46.7	15.0	14.3	0.8	7.4	22.1	1.4	3.4
(SITC 0 + 1 + 22 + 4)	2005	100.0	44.0	16.3	16.0	1.1	9.8	14.8	2.0	3.4
	2011	100.0	33.2	13.2	13.0	0.9	8.1	9.0	2.0	3.5
Agricultural raw materials	1995	100.0	44.0	15.9	15.7	0.8	9.6	16.3	1.2	0.4
(SITC 2 - 22 - 27 - 28)	2005	100.0	39.3	15.6	15.5	1.3	9.9	11.3	1.2	0.8
	2011	100.0	34.2	13.8	13.8	1.1	9.8	8.6	1.0	1.0
Ores, metals, precious stones	1995	100.0	39.8	11.8	10.8	0.2	7.5	18.4	1.8	1.4
and non-monetary gold	2005	100.0	32.9	14.2	12.2	0.5	6.7	8.1	3.3	0.6
(SITC 27 + 28 + 68 + 667 + 971)	2011	100.0	25.3	12.4	9.3	0.5	4.5	5.6	2.3	0.5
Fuels (SITC 3)	1995	100.0	54.7	13.5	13.5	0.3	7.7	31.3	1.9	0.1
	2005	100.0	47.4	11.8	11.7	0.5	10.0	22.5	2.6	0.1
	2011	100.0	36.0	9.4	9.3	0.5	6.9	16.7	2.4	0.1
Manufactured goods	1995	100.0	52.4	18.0	17.4	1.2	21.5	9.9	1.8	1.0
(SITC 5 to 8 less 667 and 68)	2005	100.0	48.2	19.1	18.7	1.1	18.3	7.7	2.0	1.7
	2011	100.0	40.5	17.1	16.6	1.1	13.9	6.2	2.3	2.6
Share by major product group (percentage)										
All products	1995	100.0	100.0	100.0	100.0	100.0	100.0	100.0	100.0	100.0
	2005	100.0	100.0	100.0	100.0	100.0	100.0	100.0	100.0	100.0
	2011	100.0	100.0	100.0	100.0	100.0	100.0	100.0	100.0	100.0
All food items	1995	6.7	6.1	5.9	5.9	5.3	2.7	10.7	5.3	22.1
(SITC 0 + 1 + 22 + 4)	2005	3.8	3.6	3.6	3.6	4.2	2.4	5.2	3.5	9.2
	2011	4.6	4.0	4.0	4.1	4.8	3.2	4.8	4.0	8.2
Agricultural raw materials	1995	2.2	1.9	2.1	2.1	1.8	1.2	2.6	1.5	0.8
(SITC 2 - 22 - 27 - 28)	2005	1.0	0.9	0.9	0.9	1.3	0.6	1.1	0.6	0.5
	2011	1.3	1.2	1.2	1.3	1.6	1.1	1.4	0.6	0.7
Ores, metals, precious stones	1995	3.2	2.5	2.2	2.1	0.8	1.3	4.2	3.3	4.2
and non-monetary gold	2005	3.3	2.3	2.7	2.4	1.8	1.4	2.5	5.1	1.3
(SITC 27 + 28 + 68 + 667 + 971)	2011	4.6	3.0	3.8	3.0	2.4	1.8	3.0	4.7	1.1
Fuels (SITC 3)	1995	13.0	13.7	10.4	10.7	4.5	5.5	29.3	13.5	1.9
	2005	18.9	18.9	12.8	13.0	10.1	11.9	39.3	22.5	1.2
	2011	21.0	19.8	13.2	13.5	12.2	12.6	41.1	22.7	1.2
Manufactured goods	1995	73.6	74.4	78.0	77.9	86.7	87.3	52.3	75.5	70.2
(SITC 5 to 8 less 667 and 68)	2005	72.2	73.8	79.3	79.4	82.3	83.2	51.4	67.1	87.3
	2011	67.3	71.3	76.8	77.3	78.7	80.9	49.1	67.3	88.6

For sources and notes, see end of table 2.2.L.

2.2.E Structure des exportations par partenaires et groupes de produits
Économies en développement : Asie

			Developing economies - Économies en développement							Destinations	
				Asia / Asie				Major petroleum exporters and gas exporters	Major manufactured goods exporters	Year	
Total	Africa / Afrique	America / Amérique	Total	Eastern, Southern and South-Eastern Asia / Asie orientale, méridionale et du Sud-Est	China / Chine	Western Asia / Asie occidentale	Oceania (2) / Océanie (2)	Principaux exportateurs de pétrole et de gaz	Principaux exportateurs d'articles manufacturés	Année	Groupes de produits
Millions de dollars											
507 183	21 350	24 993	460 082	421 947	79 067	38 135	759	30 475	355 576	1995	Total tous produits
1 479 982	71 117	63 300	1 340 531	1 218 052	327 272	122 479	5 033	114 441	1 004 398	2005	
3 611 362	202 665	235 918	3 153 894	2 837 070	762 121	316 824	18 885	323 614	2 159 499	2011	
Parts par destinations (en pourcentage)											
46.7	2.0	2.3	42.4	38.9	7.3	3.5	0.1	2.8	32.8	1995	Total tous produits
51.1	2.5	2.2	46.3	42.1	11.3	4.2	0.2	4.0	34.7	2005	
59.3	3.3	3.9	51.7	46.6	12.5	5.2	0.3	5.3	35.4	2011	
49.2	3.2	0.6	45.3	37.5	7.0	7.8	0.1	7.1	25.6	1995	Produits alimentaires
52.2	5.4	1.1	45.4	34.4	4.9	11.0	0.2	10.8	20.6	2005	(CTCI 0 + 1 + 22 + 4)
63.1	7.3	1.6	54.1	42.3	7.0	11.8	0.2	13.0	22.6	2011	
55.3	1.6	2.0	51.7	49.3	12.9	2.4	0.0	1.7	41.1	1995	Matières premières
59.5	1.7	2.3	55.5	52.4	23.6	3.2	0.0	2.0	40.7	2005	d'origine agricole
64.6	1.5	3.1	60.1	56.5	28.6	3.6	0.0	2.0	43.1	2011	(CTCI 2 - 22 - 27 - 28)
58.3	0.9	0.2	57.1	53.5	8.9	3.7	0.0	3.3	44.5	1995	Minerais, métaux, pierres
66.4	1.0	0.3	65.1	56.5	15.3	8.5	0.0	8.0	42.0	2005	précieuses et or (non monétaire)
73.6	1.8	1.1	70.8	61.4	21.5	9.3	0.0	8.7	44.9	2011	(CTCI 27 + 28 + 68 + 667 + 971)
44.2	2.1	1.4	40.6	36.6	3.5	4.0	0.1	0.3	28.8	1995	Combustibles (CTCI 3)
52.1	2.4	1.0	48.4	45.2	7.2	3.2	0.3	1.3	36.3	2005	
63.3	2.8	1.5	58.8	56.4	11.4	2.4	0.3	1.5	40.8	2011	
46.3	1.9	2.7	41.7	38.6	7.8	3.1	0.1	2.9	33.5	1995	Articles manufacturés
49.9	2.3	2.5	44.8	41.0	12.4	3.9	0.1	4.0	34.8	2005	(CTCI 5 à 8 moins 667 et 68)
56.7	3.4	4.8	48.2	43.0	12.4	5.3	0.3	5.9	34.1	2011	
Parts par principaux groupes de produits (en pourcentage)											
100.0	100.0	100.0	100.0	100.0	100.0	100.0	100.0	100.0	100.0	1995	Total tous produits
100.0	100.0	100.0	100.0	100.0	100.0	100.0	100.0	100.0	100.0	2005	
100.0	100.0	100.0	100.0	100.0	100.0	100.0	100.0	100.0	100.0	2011	
7.1	10.8	1.9	7.2	6.5	6.4	14.8	9.8	17.0	5.2	1995	Produits alimentaires
3.9	8.5	2.0	3.7	3.1	1.7	9.9	3.9	10.5	2.3	2005	(CTCI 0 + 1 + 22 + 4)
4.9	10.0	1.8	4.8	4.1	2.6	10.3	2.8	11.2	2.9	2011	
2.6	1.8	1.9	2.7	2.8	3.9	1.5	0.4	1.4	2.8	1995	Matières premières
1.2	0.7	1.1	1.2	1.3	2.1	0.8	0.1	0.5	1.2	2005	d'origine agricole
1.5	0.6	1.1	1.6	1.6	3.1	0.9	0.0	0.5	1.6	2011	(CTCI 2 - 22 - 27 - 28)
4.0	1.5	0.3	4.3	4.4	3.9	3.3	0.4	3.8	4.3	1995	Minerais, métaux, pierres
4.3	1.4	0.5	4.7	4.5	4.5	6.7	0.2	6.8	4.0	2005	précieuses et or (non monétaire)
5.7	2.5	1.2	6.3	6.1	7.9	8.2	0.1	7.5	5.8	2011	(CTCI 27 + 28 + 68 + 667 + 971)
12.3	13.9	8.1	12.4	12.2	6.3	14.8	15.5	1.3	11.4	1995	Combustibles (CTCI 3)
19.2	18.8	8.5	19.7	20.3	12.0	14.1	32.9	6.4	19.7	2005	
22.5	17.5	7.9	23.9	25.5	19.2	9.6	19.0	5.8	24.2	2011	
72.9	70.6	85.9	72.3	73.0	78.7	65.0	69.6	76.0	75.1	1995	Articles manufacturés
70.4	68.5	84.1	69.9	70.3	79.5	66.0	56.9	73.6	72.4	2005	(CTCI 5 à 8 moins 667 et 68)
64.4	69.1	83.4	62.7	62.1	66.8	67.9	67.4	74.6	64.8	2011	

Pour les sources et les notes, se reporter à la fin du tableau 2.2.L.

Origin / Product group	Year Année	World (1) Monde (1)	Developed economies - Économies développées							Transition economies Économies en transition
			Total	Europe		Canada	USA États-Unis	Japan Japon	Other developed countries Autres économies développées	
				Total	EU UE					
Millions of dollars										
All products	1995	1 127 236	634 531	217 540	199 477	12 804	153 053	222 234	28 901	19 682
	2005	2 608 508	1 077 122	424 676	388 800	19 452	220 919	339 477	72 598	66 435
	2011	5 659 211	2 033 265	839 382	725 640	48 092	410 767	530 522	204 502	161 221
Share by origin (percentage)										
All products	1995	100.0	56.3	19.3	17.7	1.1	13.6	19.7	2.6	1.7
	2005	100.0	41.3	16.3	14.9	0.7	8.5	13.0	2.8	2.5
	2011	100.0	35.9	14.8	12.8	0.8	7.3	9.4	3.6	2.8
All food items	1995	100.0	51.7	16.8	16.3	3.3	21.1	2.2	8.2	1.1
(SITC 0 + 1 + 22 + 4)	2005	100.0	39.4	13.7	12.8	2.3	12.8	1.8	8.9	2.5
	2011	100.0	36.8	11.7	10.9	2.6	14.0	1.0	7.5	2.7
Agricultural raw materials	1995	100.0	51.6	9.5	9.2	5.0	22.8	5.2	9.1	5.1
(SITC 2 - 22 - 27 - 28)	2005	100.0	49.0	13.2	12.8	5.3	18.2	4.6	7.8	8.3
	2011	100.0	46.4	11.7	11.5	6.2	16.9	4.0	7.7	6.3
Ores, metals, precious stones	1995	100.0	55.8	22.9	16.8	2.5	10.3	7.8	12.3	4.4
and non-monetary gold	2005	100.0	45.7	19.4	13.5	1.5	5.1	5.7	13.9	5.3
(SITC 27 + 28 + 68 + 667 + 971)	2011	100.0	44.3	16.6	9.4	1.4	5.6	4.4	16.2	4.0
Fuels (SITC 3)	1995	100.0	12.3	2.4	2.3	0.6	2.9	2.1	4.3	2.0
	2005	100.0	8.4	2.0	1.6	0.3	1.0	0.8	4.3	5.2
	2011	100.0	9.8	2.6	2.4	0.4	1.5	1.2	4.1	6.6
Manufactured goods	1995	100.0	60.6	21.1	19.6	0.7	13.5	24.4	0.9	1.4
(SITC 5 to 8 less 667 and 68)	2005	100.0	46.3	18.6	17.4	0.5	9.5	17.0	0.8	1.4
	2011	100.0	41.9	18.5	17.1	0.5	8.2	14.0	0.7	1.0
Share by major product group (percentage)										
All products	1995	100.0	100.0	100.0	100.0	100.0	100.0	100.0	100.0	100.0
	2005	100.0	100.0	100.0	100.0	100.0	100.0	100.0	100.0	100.0
	2011	100.0	100.0	100.0	100.0	100.0	100.0	100.0	100.0	100.0
All food items	1995	7.0	6.4	6.1	6.4	20.3	10.8	0.8	22.3	4.4
(SITC 0 + 1 + 22 + 4)	2005	4.9	4.7	4.1	4.2	15.3	7.4	0.7	15.7	4.9
	2011	6.0	6.2	4.7	5.1	18.3	11.6	0.7	12.6	5.7
Agricultural raw materials	1995	3.2	2.9	1.6	1.7	13.9	5.3	0.8	11.3	9.2
(SITC 2 - 22 - 27 - 28)	2005	2.1	2.4	1.7	1.8	14.7	4.4	0.7	5.7	6.7
	2011	2.3	3.0	1.8	2.1	16.7	5.4	1.0	4.9	5.1
Ores, metals, precious stones	1995	5.7	5.7	6.8	5.4	12.8	4.4	2.3	27.6	14.6
and non-monetary gold	2005	7.4	8.2	8.8	6.7	15.4	4.5	3.3	37.3	15.6
(SITC 27 + 28 + 68 + 667 + 971)	2011	11.1	13.7	12.5	8.1	18.4	8.7	5.3	49.9	15.8
Fuels (SITC 3)	1995	6.6	1.4	0.8	0.9	3.5	1.4	0.7	11.1	7.5
	2005	12.5	2.5	1.5	1.4	4.4	1.5	0.8	19.5	25.7
	2011	18.3	5.0	3.2	3.5	9.6	3.7	2.4	20.5	42.6
Manufactured goods	1995	75.8	81.7	83.0	84.0	49.0	75.1	93.9	26.4	62.2
(SITC 5 to 8 less 667 and 68)	2005	72.0	80.8	82.2	84.3	49.8	80.7	94.1	19.6	40.9
	2011	60.1	70.1	75.1	80.3	35.5	67.8	90.0	11.0	22.1

For sources and notes, see end of table 2.2.L.

			Developing economies - Économies en développement							Origines	
			Asia Asie					Major petroleum exporters and gas exporters	Major manufactured goods exporters	Year	
Total	Africa Afrique	America Amérique	Total	Eastern, Southern and South-Eastern Asia Asie orientale, méridionale et du Sud-Est	China Chine	Western Asia Asie occidentale	Oceania (2) Océanie (2)	Principaux exportateurs de pétrole et de gaz	Principaux exportateurs d'articles manufacturés	Année	Groupes de produits
Millions de dollars											
460 968	14 971	19 783	425 385	373 403	97 990	51 982	829	50 387	330 468	1995	Total tous produits
1 459 210	53 434	60 839	1 343 231	1 133 337	359 916	209 894	1 705	220 051	953 462	2005	
3 439 319	188 787	218 169	3 028 637	2 417 133	809 093	611 503	3 726	708 592	1 952 560	2011	
Parts par origines (en pourcentage)											
40.9	1.3	1.8	37.7	33.1	8.7	4.6	0.1	4.5	29.3	1995	Total tous produits
55.9	2.0	2.3	51.5	43.4	13.8	8.0	0.1	8.4	36.6	2005	
60.8	3.3	3.9	53.5	42.7	14.3	10.8	0.1	12.5	34.5	2011	
46.7	2.3	8.1	36.0	31.0	6.1	5.0	0.3	2.0	22.0	1995	Produits alimentaires
58.0	3.1	15.4	39.2	31.7	6.8	7.5	0.3	3.5	18.0	2005	(CTCI 0 + 1 + 22 + 4)
60.5	3.0	16.1	41.1	33.4	5.4	7.7	0.2	4.2	17.6	2011	
43.0	4.5	5.0	32.7	31.8	4.1	0.9	0.8	0.8	24.4	1995	Matières premières
42.6	5.5	5.2	30.9	29.7	3.0	1.2	1.0	0.9	19.3	2005	d'origine agricole
47.3	4.4	6.4	35.6	34.8	3.2	0.8	0.9	0.8	20.5	2011	(CTCI 2 - 22 - 27 - 28)
39.3	5.9	7.2	25.9	21.7	3.7	4.2	0.3	2.7	15.4	1995	Minerais, métaux, pierres
48.9	5.1	9.7	33.9	27.6	4.9	6.3	0.1	6.0	14.3	2005	précieuses et or (non monétaire)
51.5	7.0	12.8	31.6	24.3	3.6	7.3	0.2	7.2	12.2	2011	(CTCI 27 + 28 + 68 + 667 + 971)
85.0	5.7	0.7	78.5	34.4	3.3	44.1	0.1	50.7	21.7	1995	Combustibles (CTCI 3)
86.3	7.7	0.9	77.6	33.8	3.4	43.8	0.0	51.4	19.4	2005	
83.6	9.3	3.7	70.6	30.1	1.9	40.5	0.0	52.1	16.0	2011	
37.0	0.4	0.7	35.9	34.4	10.1	1.4	0.0	1.1	32.2	1995	Articles manufacturés
52.0	0.5	0.9	50.6	48.3	17.5	2.3	0.0	1.7	43.9	2005	(CTCI 5 à 8 moins 667 et 68)
56.9	0.5	1.0	55.3	51.8	21.8	3.5	0.0	2.9	47.2	2011	
Parts par principaux groupes de produits (en pourcentage)											
100.0	100.0	100.0	100.0	100.0	100.0	100.0	100.0	100.0	100.0	1995	Total tous produits
100.0	100.0	100.0	100.0	100.0	100.0	100.0	100.0	100.0	100.0	2005	
100.0	100.0	100.0	100.0	100.0	100.0	100.0	100.0	100.0	100.0	2011	
8.0	12.0	32.2	6.7	6.5	4.9	7.6	28.2	3.1	5.2	1995	Produits alimentaires
5.1	7.4	32.5	3.7	3.6	2.4	4.6	21.6	2.1	2.4	2005	(CTCI 0 + 1 + 22 + 4)
6.0	5.5	25.2	4.6	4.7	2.3	4.3	20.6	2.0	3.1	2011	
3.3	10.7	9.1	2.8	3.1	1.5	0.6	34.0	0.6	2.6	1995	Matières premières
1.6	5.6	4.5	1.2	1.4	0.4	0.3	32.5	0.2	1.1	2005	d'origine agricole
1.8	3.1	3.8	1.5	1.9	0.5	0.2	30.6	0.1	1.4	2011	(CTCI 2 - 22 - 27 - 28)
5.5	25.7	23.7	3.9	3.8	2.5	5.2	20.8	3.5	3.0	1995	Minerais, métaux, pierres
6.5	18.6	31.1	4.9	4.7	2.6	5.8	12.9	5.3	2.9	2005	précieuses et or (non monétaire)
9.4	23.3	36.9	6.6	6.3	2.8	7.5	27.5	6.4	3.9	2011	(CTCI 27 + 28 + 68 + 667 + 971)
13.6	28.2	2.6	13.6	6.8	2.5	62.8	8.4	74.3	4.8	1995	Combustibles (CTCI 3)
19.4	47.3	4.9	18.9	9.8	3.1	68.3	7.5	76.5	6.7	2005	
25.1	50.7	17.6	24.1	12.9	2.5	68.4	5.5	76.1	8.5	2011	
68.6	23.2	32.0	72.1	78.8	88.0	23.6	8.5	18.3	83.2	1995	Articles manufacturés
66.9	18.2	26.8	70.7	80.1	91.2	20.3	25.4	14.5	86.5	2005	(CTCI 5 à 8 moins 667 et 68)
56.3	8.8	16.0	62.2	73.0	91.6	19.5	15.7	13.7	82.2	2011	

Pour les sources et les notes, se reporter à la fin du tableau 2.2.L.

Product group	Year / Année	World (1) / Monde (1)	Developed economies - Économies développées							Transition economies / Économies en transition
			Total	Europe Total	EU / UE	Canada	USA / États-Unis	Japan / Japon	Other developed countries / Autres économies développées	
Millions of dollars										
All products	1995	949 867	489 248	155 886	150 094	10 540	183 710	121 511	17 602	8 583
	2005	2 380 897	1 110 915	400 581	390 145	25 559	400 964	226 466	57 345	34 066
	2011	4 966 497	1 908 332	750 447	723 497	46 664	612 278	373 094	125 849	101 912
Share by destination (percentage)										
All products	1995	100.0	51.5	16.4	15.8	1.1	19.3	12.8	1.9	0.9
	2005	100.0	46.7	16.8	16.4	1.1	16.8	9.5	2.4	1.4
	2011	100.0	38.4	15.1	14.6	0.9	12.3	7.5	2.5	2.1
All food items	1995	100.0	47.5	13.1	12.5	0.9	7.7	24.4	1.5	2.7
(SITC 0 + 1 + 22 + 4)	2005	100.0	45.5	13.9	13.7	1.2	11.0	17.2	2.1	3.0
	2011	100.0	35.3	12.9	12.7	1.0	9.1	10.2	2.0	3.2
Agricultural raw materials	1995	100.0	43.7	14.8	14.6	0.9	9.9	16.9	1.2	0.4
(SITC 2 - 22 - 27 - 28)	2005	100.0	39.4	14.9	14.8	1.4	10.2	11.7	1.2	0.7
	2011	100.0	34.4	13.6	13.5	1.1	10.0	8.8	1.0	0.9
Ores, metals, precious stones	1995	100.0	41.7	11.2	10.2	0.3	8.5	19.8	2.1	1.4
and non-monetary gold	2005	100.0	34.3	12.5	10.9	0.7	7.6	9.6	4.0	0.5
(SITC 27 + 28 + 68 + 667 + 971)	2011	100.0	26.8	11.2	8.1	0.5	5.3	7.0	2.9	0.4
Fuels (SITC 3)	1995	100.0	48.0	12.6	12.5	0.2	2.6	30.5	2.2	0.3
	2005	100.0	38.8	10.1	10.1	0.1	3.3	19.4	5.9	0.2
	2011	100.0	28.5	8.1	8.0	0.1	1.7	13.7	4.9	0.2
Manufactured goods	1995	100.0	52.6	17.2	16.5	1.2	22.1	10.2	1.9	0.8
(SITC 5 to 8 less 667 and 68)	2005	100.0	48.2	17.8	17.4	1.2	19.0	8.1	2.0	1.5
	2011	100.0	41.0	16.5	16.0	1.1	14.5	6.6	2.3	2.4
Share by major product group (percentage)										
All products	1995	100.0	100.0	100.0	100.0	100.0	100.0	100.0	100.0	100.0
	2005	100.0	100.0	100.0	100.0	100.0	100.0	100.0	100.0	100.0
	2011	100.0	100.0	100.0	100.0	100.0	100.0	100.0	100.0	100.0
All food items	1995	6.9	6.4	5.5	5.4	5.3	2.8	13.1	5.5	20.9
(SITC 0 + 1 + 22 + 4)	2005	4.0	3.8	3.3	3.3	4.5	2.6	7.1	3.4	8.3
	2011	4.9	4.5	4.2	4.2	5.3	3.6	6.6	3.9	7.5
Agricultural raw materials	1995	2.5	2.1	2.2	2.3	1.9	1.3	3.2	1.6	1.0
(SITC 2 - 22 - 27 - 28)	2005	1.2	1.0	1.1	1.1	1.5	0.7	1.5	0.6	0.6
	2011	1.6	1.4	1.4	1.5	1.9	1.3	1.9	0.6	0.7
Ores, metals, precious stones	1995	3.1	2.5	2.1	2.0	0.8	1.4	4.8	3.4	4.9
and non-monetary gold	2005	3.2	2.4	2.4	2.2	2.0	1.5	3.3	5.3	1.0
(SITC 27 + 28 + 68 + 667 + 971)	2011	4.3	3.0	3.2	2.4	2.1	1.9	4.0	4.9	0.8
Fuels (SITC 3)	1995	5.7	5.3	4.3	4.5	1.1	0.7	13.5	6.6	1.7
	2005	8.3	6.9	5.0	5.1	0.5	1.6	16.9	20.5	1.0
	2011	10.1	7.5	5.4	5.5	0.8	1.4	18.4	19.6	0.9
Manufactured goods	1995	80.5	82.2	84.3	84.3	89.9	91.9	64.3	81.8	70.5
(SITC 5 to 8 less 667 and 68)	2005	82.6	85.3	87.6	87.7	91.2	93.3	70.7	69.3	88.9
	2011	77.7	82.8	84.8	85.4	89.7	91.4	68.1	70.2	89.9

For sources and notes, see end of table 2.2.L.

2.2.F Structure des exportations par partenaires et groupes de produits
Économies en développement : Asie orientale, méridionale et du Sud-Est

Total	Africa / Afrique	America / Amérique	Asia / Asie — Total	Eastern, Southern and South-Eastern Asia / Asie orientale, méridionale et du Sud-Est	China / Chine	Western Asia / Asie occidentale	Oceania (2) / Océanie (2)	Major petroleum exporters and gas exporters / Principaux exportateurs de pétrole et de gaz	Major manufactured goods exporters / Principaux exportateurs d'articles manufacturés	Year / Année	Destinations / Groupes de produits
Millions de dollars											
448 178	17 296	23 190	406 935	383 750	77 150	23 185	758	20 888	329 999	1995	**Total tous produits**
1 231 929	50 735	59 599	1 116 687	1 040 501	302 249	76 186	4 908	73 538	869 157	2005	
2 927 387	153 832	225 108	2 529 727	2 310 145	660 699	219 582	18 720	222 256	1 817 009	2011	
Parts par destinations (en pourcentage)											
47.2	1.8	2.4	42.8	40.4	8.1	2.4	0.1	2.2	34.7	1995	**Total tous produits**
51.7	2.1	2.5	46.9	43.7	12.7	3.2	0.2	3.1	36.5	2005	
58.9	3.1	4.5	50.9	46.5	13.3	4.4	0.4	4.5	36.6	2011	
49.1	2.9	0.6	45.4	40.9	7.7	4.6	0.1	4.1	28.2	1995	Produits alimentaires
51.2	5.2	1.3	44.5	38.6	5.7	5.9	0.2	6.2	23.9	2005	(CTCI 0 + 1 + 22 + 4)
61.5	7.1	1.7	52.4	46.1	8.0	6.3	0.2	7.5	25.7	2011	
55.5	1.2	2.0	52.3	50.4	13.2	1.9	0.0	1.5	42.3	1995	Matières premières
59.6	1.4	2.4	55.8	53.5	24.5	2.3	0.0	1.5	42.1	2005	d'origine agricole
64.6	1.4	3.1	60.1	57.0	29.2	3.1	0.0	1.5	44.0	2011	(CTCI 2 - 22 - 27 - 28)
56.5	0.4	0.2	55.8	54.8	10.2	1.0	0.0	1.0	48.1	1995	Minerais, métaux, pierres
65.1	0.6	0.3	64.2	57.9	18.4	6.2	0.0	6.2	49.0	2005	précieuses et or (non monétaire)
72.0	1.3	1.2	69.5	62.4	26.3	7.1	0.0	7.2	53.8	2011	(CTCI 27 + 28 + 68 + 667 + 971)
49.3	2.8	0.8	45.5	44.1	7.0	1.4	0.2	0.3	37.6	1995	Combustibles (CTCI 3)
60.0	2.2	1.3	55.7	53.0	9.4	2.7	0.8	1.4	38.6	2005	
69.8	2.6	2.3	64.2	61.2	12.4	3.0	0.7	2.3	43.7	2011	
46.4	1.7	2.8	41.8	39.4	8.1	2.4	0.1	2.3	34.5	1995	Articles manufacturés
50.2	2.0	2.7	45.4	42.4	13.0	3.0	0.1	3.0	36.4	2005	(CTCI 5 à 8 moins 667 et 68)
56.6	3.1	5.0	48.2	44.0	12.9	4.2	0.3	4.5	35.5	2011	
Parts par principaux groupes de produits (en pourcentage)											
100.0	100.0	100.0	100.0	100.0	100.0	100.0	100.0	100.0	100.0	1995	**Total tous produits**
100.0	100.0	100.0	100.0	100.0	100.0	100.0	100.0	100.0	100.0	2005	
100.0	100.0	100.0	100.0	100.0	100.0	100.0	100.0	100.0	100.0	2011	
7.2	10.8	1.8	7.3	7.0	6.6	12.9	9.8	12.8	5.6	1995	Produits alimentaires
3.9	9.7	2.0	3.7	3.5	1.8	7.3	4.0	7.9	2.6	2005	(CTCI 0 + 1 + 22 + 4)
5.1	11.2	1.8	5.0	4.8	2.9	7.0	2.8	8.1	3.4	2011	
2.9	1.7	2.1	3.0	3.1	4.0	1.9	0.4	1.6	3.0	1995	Matières premières
1.4	0.8	1.1	1.4	1.5	2.3	0.9	0.1	0.6	1.4	2005	d'origine agricole
1.8	0.7	1.1	1.9	2.0	3.5	1.1	0.0	0.6	1.9	2011	(CTCI 2 - 22 - 27 - 28)
3.7	0.8	0.3	4.0	4.2	3.9	1.3	0.4	1.3	4.3	1995	Minerais, métaux, pierres
4.1	0.9	0.4	4.4	4.3	4.7	6.3	0.2	6.5	4.3	2005	précieuses et or (non monétaire)
5.3	1.8	1.2	5.9	5.8	8.6	7.0	0.1	7.0	6.4	2011	(CTCI 27 + 28 + 68 + 667 + 971)
5.9	8.8	1.8	6.0	6.2	4.8	3.2	15.5	0.9	6.1	1995	Combustibles (CTCI 3)
9.6	8.4	4.2	9.8	10.1	6.2	7.1	33.7	3.7	8.8	2005	
12.0	8.4	5.2	12.7	13.3	9.4	6.9	19.1	5.2	12.1	2011	
79.1	76.3	91.9	78.5	78.4	79.9	79.9	69.6	82.6	79.9	1995	Articles manufacturés
80.1	77.8	88.1	79.9	80.2	84.9	76.3	55.9	79.9	82.5	2005	(CTCI 5 à 8 moins 667 et 68)
74.6	77.6	85.9	73.4	73.4	75.1	73.9	67.2	78.9	75.5	2011	

Pour les sources et les notes, se reporter à la fin du tableau 2.2.L.

2.2.F Import structure by partner and product group
Developing Asia: Eastern, Southern and South-Eastern Asia

Product group	Year Année	World (1) Monde (1)	Developed economies - Économies développées							Transition economies Économies en transition
			Total	Europe		Canada	USA États-Unis	Japan Japon	Other developed countries Autres économies développées	
				Total	EU UE					
Millions of dollars										
All products	1995	1 001 530	557 868	166 726	152 320	11 825	137 868	213 991	27 458	15 182
	2005	2 244 990	882 193	288 195	261 004	17 596	191 108	320 753	64 542	43 493
	2011	4 874 487	1 692 833	610 757	511 868	43 292	346 199	503 234	189 352	117 291
Share by origin (percentage)										
All products	1995	100.0	55.7	16.6	15.2	1.2	13.8	21.4	2.7	1.5
	2005	100.0	39.3	12.8	11.6	0.8	8.5	14.3	2.9	1.9
	2011	100.0	34.7	12.5	10.5	0.9	7.1	10.3	3.9	2.4
All food items	1995	100.0	53.1	13.6	13.0	4.1	23.2	2.8	9.5	0.7
(SITC 0 + 1 + 22 + 4)	2005	100.0	39.5	10.3	9.5	3.0	14.1	2.4	9.7	2.2
	2011	100.0	38.2	9.3	8.5	3.0	16.4	1.4	8.1	1.9
Agricultural raw materials	1995	100.0	51.3	7.3	7.0	5.2	23.9	5.7	9.3	4.0
(SITC 2 - 22 - 27 - 28)	2005	100.0	48.0	10.9	10.5	5.7	18.2	5.0	8.3	8.1
	2011	100.0	45.8	10.0	9.8	6.6	16.7	4.3	8.2	6.2
Ores, metals, precious stones	1995	100.0	54.9	20.1	15.0	2.5	10.5	8.5	13.3	4.4
and non-monetary gold	2005	100.0	46.2	16.8	12.4	1.7	5.3	6.6	15.8	4.1
(SITC 27 + 28 + 68 + 667 + 971)	2011	100.0	45.7	15.4	8.3	1.5	5.6	5.1	18.1	3.4
Fuels (SITC 3)	1995	100.0	12.2	1.7	1.6	0.7	2.9	2.3	4.7	0.9
	2005	100.0	7.5	1.0	0.8	0.3	1.0	0.9	4.4	3.5
	2011	100.0	8.5	1.5	1.4	0.5	1.3	1.3	4.0	6.3
Manufactured goods	1995	100.0	59.7	18.3	16.9	0.7	13.5	26.2	1.0	1.3
(SITC 5 to 8 less 667 and 68)	2005	100.0	43.8	14.6	13.5	0.5	9.5	18.5	0.7	1.2
	2011	100.0	40.4	15.7	14.3	0.5	8.0	15.6	0.6	0.8
Share by major product group (percentage)										
All products	1995	100.0	100.0	100.0	100.0	100.0	100.0	100.0	100.0	100.0
	2005	100.0	100.0	100.0	100.0	100.0	100.0	100.0	100.0	100.0
	2011	100.0	100.0	100.0	100.0	100.0	100.0	100.0	100.0	100.0
All food items	1995	6.1	5.9	5.0	5.3	21.2	10.3	0.8	21.2	2.9
(SITC 0 + 1 + 22 + 4)	2005	4.2	4.2	3.3	3.4	15.9	6.9	0.7	14.0	4.7
	2011	5.2	5.7	3.8	4.2	17.6	11.9	0.7	10.9	4.2
Agricultural raw materials	1995	3.3	3.0	1.4	1.5	14.4	5.7	0.9	11.2	8.6
(SITC 2 - 22 - 27 - 28)	2005	2.2	2.7	1.8	2.0	15.7	4.6	0.8	6.3	9.1
	2011	2.5	3.2	2.0	2.3	18.3	5.8	1.0	5.2	6.3
Ores, metals, precious stones	1995	5.9	5.8	7.1	5.8	12.6	4.5	2.3	28.5	17.0
and non-monetary gold	2005	7.4	8.7	9.7	7.9	16.1	4.6	3.4	40.8	15.8
(SITC 27 + 28 + 68 + 667 + 971)	2011	11.3	14.8	13.9	8.9	18.5	9.0	5.5	52.6	15.7
Fuels (SITC 3)	1995	6.6	1.5	0.7	0.7	3.7	1.4	0.7	11.3	4.0
	2005	13.1	2.5	1.0	0.9	4.3	1.5	0.8	20.1	24.1
	2011	20.1	4.9	2.4	2.7	10.2	3.6	2.5	20.7	53.0
Manufactured goods	1995	76.4	81.8	83.8	84.8	47.7	75.0	93.7	26.6	64.8
(SITC 5 to 8 less 667 and 68)	2005	72.4	80.7	82.2	84.1	47.7	81.1	93.8	17.2	45.6
	2011	59.3	69.1	74.4	80.9	33.9	66.7	89.6	9.4	20.6

For sources and notes, see end of table 2.2.L.

2.2.F Structure des importations par partenaires et groupes de produits
Économies en développement : Asie orientale, méridionale et du Sud-Est

Total	Africa / Afrique	America / Amérique	Total	Eastern, Southern and South-Eastern Asia / Asie orientale, méridionale et du Sud-Est	China / Chine	Western Asia / Asie occidentale	Oceania (2) / Océanie (2)	Major petroleum exporters and gas exporters / Principaux exportateurs de pétrole et de gaz	Major manufactured goods exporters / Principaux exportateurs d'articles manufacturés	Year / Année	Origines / Groupes de produits
			Asia / Asie								
Millions de dollars											
421 584	12 016	17 493	391 251	353 157	94 928	38 094	824	39 761	316 667	1995	Total tous produits
1 315 079	41 873	53 440	1 218 084	1 055 828	335 732	162 256	1 681	183 554	900 948	2005	
3 052 194	167 690	198 662	2 682 123	2 168 917	723 794	513 206	3 719	634 657	1 798 607	2011	
Parts par origines (en pourcentage)											
42.1	1.2	1.7	39.1	35.3	9.5	3.8	0.1	4.0	31.6	1995	Total tous produits
58.6	1.9	2.4	54.3	47.0	15.0	7.2	0.1	8.2	40.1	2005	
62.6	3.4	4.1	55.0	44.5	14.8	10.5	0.1	13.0	36.9	2011	
45.9	1.7	8.5	35.3	34.8	7.5	0.6	0.4	0.5	26.2	1995	Produits alimentaires
58.3	2.2	17.1	38.5	37.0	8.8	1.6	0.4	1.6	22.5	2005	(CTCI 0 + 1 + 22 + 4)
59.9	2.3	17.7	39.6	37.6	6.6	2.0	0.3	1.8	21.4	2011	
44.4	4.4	5.2	34.0	33.4	4.5	0.6	0.9	0.6	25.8	1995	Matières premières
43.8	5.6	5.2	31.9	31.2	3.0	0.7	1.1	0.7	20.3	2005	d'origine agricole
48.0	4.4	6.4	36.2	35.6	2.9	0.6	0.9	0.6	20.9	2011	(CTCI 2 - 22 - 27 - 28)
40.4	5.9	7.5	26.7	23.3	4.1	3.3	0.3	2.1	16.8	1995	Minerais, métaux, pierres
49.6	4.7	10.7	34.0	28.3	5.4	5.7	0.1	5.7	15.5	2005	précieuses et or (non monétaire)
50.8	6.8	14.0	29.7	23.0	3.8	6.7	0.2	6.9	13.1	2011	(CTCI 27 + 28 + 68 + 667 + 971)
86.3	4.8	0.7	80.6	37.2	3.7	43.5	0.1	49.0	24.1	1995	Combustibles (CTCI 3)
88.9	7.4	0.9	80.5	36.2	3.7	44.3	0.0	51.8	21.3	2005	
85.2	9.5	3.9	71.8	30.6	2.0	41.3	0.0	53.7	16.7	2011	
38.4	0.4	0.7	37.3	36.4	10.9	0.9	0.0	0.7	34.3	1995	Articles manufacturés
54.7	0.4	0.9	53.4	52.2	18.8	1.2	0.0	1.2	47.9	2005	(CTCI 5 à 8 moins 667 et 68)
58.6	0.4	1.1	57.1	54.9	22.8	2.3	0.0	2.2	50.7	2011	
Parts par principaux groupes de produits (en pourcentage)											
100.0	100.0	100.0	100.0	100.0	100.0	100.0	100.0	100.0	100.0	1995	Total tous produits
100.0	100.0	100.0	100.0	100.0	100.0	100.0	100.0	100.0	100.0	2005	
100.0	100.0	100.0	100.0	100.0	100.0	100.0	100.0	100.0	100.0	2011	
6.7	8.6	29.8	5.5	6.0	4.8	0.9	27.9	0.7	5.1	1995	Produits alimentaires
4.1	4.9	29.9	3.0	3.3	2.4	0.9	21.9	0.8	2.3	2005	(CTCI 0 + 1 + 22 + 4)
5.0	3.5	22.5	3.7	4.4	2.3	1.0	20.7	0.7	3.0	2011	
3.5	12.0	9.7	2.9	3.1	1.5	0.5	34.3	0.5	2.7	1995	Matières premières
1.6	6.5	4.7	1.3	1.4	0.4	0.2	32.9	0.2	1.1	2005	d'origine agricole
1.9	3.1	3.9	1.6	2.0	0.5	0.1	30.6	0.1	1.4	2011	(CTCI 2 - 22 - 27 - 28)
5.6	29.1	25.2	4.0	3.9	2.5	5.1	21.0	3.2	3.1	1995	Minerais, métaux, pierres
6.3	18.8	33.5	4.7	4.5	2.7	5.9	13.1	5.2	2.9	2005	précieuses et or (non monétaire)
9.1	22.3	38.8	6.1	5.8	2.9	7.2	27.5	5.9	4.0	2011	(CTCI 27 + 28 + 68 + 667 + 971)
13.6	26.5	2.8	13.6	7.0	2.6	75.6	8.4	81.6	5.0	1995	Combustibles (CTCI 3)
19.9	52.2	5.2	19.5	10.1	3.3	80.6	7.6	83.3	7.0	2005	
27.4	55.4	19.2	26.3	13.8	2.7	78.9	5.5	83.0	9.1	2011	
69.7	23.7	32.0	72.9	78.9	87.9	17.6	8.4	13.8	83.0	1995	Articles manufacturés
67.6	16.4	26.5	71.3	80.3	90.9	12.2	24.4	10.3	86.3	2005	(CTCI 5 à 8 moins 667 et 68)
55.5	6.1	15.5	61.6	73.2	91.2	12.7	15.7	10.2	81.5	2011	

Developing economies - Économies en développement

Pour les sources et les notes, se reporter à la fin du tableau 2.2.L.

Destination / Product group	Year / Année	World (1) / Monde (1)	Developed economies - Économies développées							Transition economies / Économies en transition
			Total	Europe		Canada	USA / États-Unis	Japan / Japon	Other developed countries / Autres économies développées	
				Total	EU / UE					
Millions of dollars										
All products	1995	135 176	72 540	28 593	28 054	491	12 624	28 941	1 891	2 587
	2005	514 699	255 972	103 461	101 178	3 347	57 908	85 974	5 282	7 186
	2011	1 128 164	422 339	164 155	159 875	8 052	91 002	146 954	12 175	18 559
Share by destination (percentage)										
All products	1995	100.0	53.7	21.2	20.8	0.4	9.3	21.4	1.4	1.9
	2005	100.0	49.7	20.1	19.7	0.7	11.3	16.7	1.0	1.4
	2011	100.0	37.4	14.6	14.2	0.7	8.1	13.0	1.1	1.6
All food items	1995	100.0	39.4	32.3	31.1	0.4	4.7	1.0	0.9	9.3
(SITC 0 + 1 + 22 + 4)	2005	100.0	35.6	29.7	28.7	0.4	3.0	1.0	1.5	5.8
	2011	100.0	19.5	15.6	15.2	0.5	1.6	0.5	1.4	6.0
Agricultural raw materials	1995	100.0	50.8	46.1	45.3	0.1	1.7	1.2	1.6	0.5
(SITC 2 - 22 - 27 - 28)	2005	100.0	36.3	32.9	32.5	0.1	1.3	1.0	1.0	1.7
	2011	100.0	26.7	23.1	22.9	0.1	1.7	0.8	1.0	5.9
Ores, metals, precious stones	1995	100.0	29.0	15.6	14.2	0.1	2.1	10.7	0.6	1.0
and non-monetary gold	2005	100.0	27.1	20.6	17.3	0.0	3.2	2.4	0.8	1.0
(SITC 27 + 28 + 68 + 667 + 971)	2011	100.0	20.1	16.4	13.4	0.5	1.7	1.0	0.5	0.7
Fuels (SITC 3)	1995	100.0	58.8	14.1	14.1	0.4	10.9	31.8	1.7	0.1
	2005	100.0	52.2	12.7	12.7	0.8	13.8	24.2	0.7	0.0
	2011	100.0	40.8	10.2	10.2	0.8	10.2	18.6	0.9	0.1
Manufactured goods	1995	100.0	47.4	37.5	36.5	0.3	7.3	1.5	0.9	5.3
(SITC 5 to 8 less 667 and 68)	2005	100.0	48.6	39.6	38.6	0.4	6.3	0.5	1.8	4.6
	2011	100.0	33.8	27.5	26.7	0.5	3.6	0.4	1.8	6.2
Share by major product group (percentage)										
All products	1995	100.0	100.0	100.0	100.0	100.0	100.0	100.0	100.0	100.0
	2005	100.0	100.0	100.0	100.0	100.0	100.0	100.0	100.0	100.0
	2011	100.0	100.0	100.0	100.0	100.0	100.0	100.0	100.0	100.0
All food items	1995	5.4	3.9	8.2	8.0	5.7	2.7	0.3	3.5	26.0
(SITC 0 + 1 + 22 + 4)	2005	3.2	2.3	4.7	4.7	1.8	0.9	0.2	4.7	13.4
	2011	3.2	1.7	3.4	3.4	2.0	0.6	0.1	4.2	11.7
Agricultural raw materials	1995	0.7	0.6	1.4	1.4	0.2	0.1	0.0	0.8	0.2
(SITC 2 - 22 - 27 - 28)	2005	0.2	0.2	0.4	0.4	0.0	0.0	0.0	0.2	0.3
	2011	0.2	0.1	0.3	0.3	0.0	0.0	0.0	0.2	0.7
Ores, metals, precious stones	1995	3.9	2.1	2.8	2.6	0.6	0.9	1.9	1.6	2.1
and non-monetary gold	2005	3.8	2.1	3.9	3.4	0.3	1.1	0.5	3.0	2.7
(SITC 27 + 28 + 68 + 667 + 971)	2011	5.7	3.1	6.5	5.4	4.1	1.2	0.5	2.7	2.5
Fuels (SITC 3)	1995	64.7	70.9	43.1	43.9	75.5	75.3	96.0	77.4	2.6
	2005	67.8	71.2	42.9	43.6	83.3	83.0	98.4	44.9	2.4
	2011	69.0	75.2	48.6	49.7	78.7	87.7	98.7	54.7	2.5
Manufactured goods	1995	24.8	21.9	44.0	43.6	18.0	19.3	1.7	16.4	69.1
(SITC 5 to 8 less 667 and 68)	2005	24.1	23.5	47.4	47.2	14.3	13.4	0.7	43.3	80.0
	2011	21.5	19.5	40.6	40.6	15.0	9.6	0.7	36.8	81.5

For sources and notes, see end of table 2.2.L.

Total	Africa / Afrique	America / Amérique	Asia / Asie Total	Eastern, Southern and South-Eastern Asia / Asie orientale, méridionale et du Sud-Est	China / Chine	Western Asia / Asie occidentale	Oceania (2) / Océanie (2)	Major petroleum exporters and gas exporters / Principaux exportateurs de pétrole et de gaz	Major manufactured goods exporters / Principaux exportateurs d'articles manufacturés	Year / Année	Destinations / Groupes de produits
			**Developing economies - Économies en développement**								
Millions de dollars											
59 005	4 054	1 803	53 147	38 197	1 917	14 950	0	9 588	25 578	1995	Total tous produits
248 053	20 383	3 701	223 844	177 551	25 024	46 293	126	40 903	135 241	2005	
683 976	48 834	10 810	624 167	526 925	101 422	97 243	165	101 358	342 490	2011	
Parts par destinations (en pourcentage)											
43.7	3.0	1.3	39.3	28.3	1.4	11.1	0.0	7.1	18.9	1995	Total tous produits
48.2	4.0	0.7	43.5	34.5	4.9	9.0	0.0	7.9	26.3	2005	
60.6	4.3	1.0	55.3	46.7	9.0	8.6	0.0	9.0	30.4	2011	
50.7	6.0	0.6	44.1	7.3	0.1	36.7	0.0	34.6	2.2	1995	Produits alimentaires
57.6	6.5	0.5	50.5	10.9	0.2	39.6	0.0	37.2	1.5	2005	(CTCI 0 + 1 + 22 + 4)
73.8	8.2	0.4	65.2	16.7	0.3	48.5	0.0	50.5	1.8	2011	
47.9	10.1	0.2	37.6	22.7	3.0	14.9	0.0	9.3	7.9	1995	Matières premières
57.5	9.3	0.4	47.8	25.6	2.8	22.2	0.0	13.7	5.8	2005	d'origine agricole
64.7	5.3	1.1	58.4	38.6	6.3	19.7	0.0	20.3	8.9	2011	(CTCI 2 - 22 - 27 - 28)
68.3	3.5	0.2	64.7	45.9	1.6	18.8	0.0	16.6	24.1	1995	Minerais, métaux, pierres
71.5	2.8	0.2	68.5	51.1	3.1	17.4	0.0	15.0	14.7	2005	précieuses et or (non monétaire)
78.9	3.5	0.5	74.9	58.3	5.2	16.6	0.0	13.8	15.1	2011	(CTCI 27 + 28 + 68 + 667 + 971)
41.1	1.7	1.8	37.6	31.9	1.4	5.6	..	0.3	23.4	1995	Combustibles (CTCI 3)
47.7	2.6	0.8	44.3	40.9	5.9	3.4	0.0	1.3	34.9	2005	
59.2	2.9	0.9	55.4	53.4	10.8	2.0	0.0	0.9	39.0	2011	
45.7	5.6	0.4	39.6	21.0	1.7	18.7	0.0	17.6	10.7	1995	Articles manufacturés
44.4	7.5	0.6	36.2	17.9	3.0	18.3	0.1	20.5	8.0	2005	(CTCI 5 à 8 moins 667 et 68)
58.8	8.5	1.4	48.9	27.1	5.3	21.8	0.1	27.3	11.4	2011	
Parts par principaux groupes de produits (en pourcentage)											
100.0	100.0	100.0	100.0	100.0	100.0	100.0	100.0	100.0	100.0	1995	Total tous produits
100.0	100.0	100.0	100.0	100.0	100.0	100.0	100.0	100.0	100.0	2005	
100.0	100.0	100.0	100.0	100.0	100.0	100.0	100.0	100.0	100.0	2011	
6.2	10.7	2.5	6.0	1.4	0.3	17.8	5.4	26.1	0.6	1995	Produits alimentaires
3.8	5.3	2.4	3.7	1.0	0.1	14.2	1.3	15.0	0.2	2005	(CTCI 0 + 1 + 22 + 4)
3.9	6.0	1.5	3.8	1.1	0.1	18.0	1.8	18.0	0.2	2011	
0.7	2.2	0.1	0.6	0.5	1.4	0.9	11.0	0.9	0.3	1995	Matières premières
0.3	0.5	0.1	0.3	0.2	0.1	0.6	0.0	0.4	0.1	2005	d'origine agricole
0.2	0.2	0.2	0.2	0.2	0.1	0.4	0.0	0.4	0.1	2011	(CTCI 2 - 22 - 27 - 28)
6.0	4.6	0.4	6.3	6.3	4.4	6.5	16.7	9.0	4.9	1995	Minerais, métaux, pierres
5.7	2.7	0.8	6.0	5.7	2.4	7.4	0.1	7.2	2.1	2005	précieuses et or (non monétaire)
7.5	4.7	2.9	7.8	7.2	3.3	11.0	0.3	8.8	2.8	2011	(CTCI 27 + 28 + 68 + 667 + 971)
60.9	36.1	88.8	61.8	73.1	64.5	32.8	..	2.4	80.2	1995	Combustibles (CTCI 3)
67.1	44.8	76.1	69.0	80.3	82.0	25.7	0.1	11.2	90.1	2005	
67.4	46.4	64.0	69.1	78.9	83.2	15.9	8.6	7.2	88.7	2011	
26.0	46.4	8.2	25.0	18.4	29.4	41.9	66.9	61.5	14.0	1995	Articles manufacturés
22.2	45.5	19.6	20.0	12.5	14.8	48.9	97.3	62.2	7.3	2005	(CTCI 5 à 8 moins 667 et 68)
20.9	42.1	30.8	19.0	12.5	12.8	54.5	85.7	65.3	8.1	2011	

Pour les sources et les notes, se reporter à la fin du tableau 2.2.L.

Product group	Year / Année	World (1) / Monde (1)	Developed economies - Économies développées							Transition economies / Économies en transition
			Total	Europe		Canada	USA / États-Unis	Japan / Japon	Other developed countries / Autres économies développées	
				Total	EU / UE					
Millions of dollars										
All products	1995	125 707	76 664	50 814	47 157	980	15 185	8 243	1 443	4 500
	2005	363 517	194 930	136 481	127 797	1 857	29 811	18 725	8 056	22 943
	2011	784 724	340 431	228 625	213 772	4 800	64 567	27 288	15 150	43 930
Share by origin (percentage)										
All products	1995	100.0	61.0	40.4	37.5	0.8	12.1	6.6	1.1	3.6
	2005	100.0	53.6	37.5	35.2	0.5	8.2	5.2	2.2	6.3
	2011	100.0	43.4	29.1	27.2	0.6	8.2	3.5	1.9	5.6
All food items	1995	100.0	46.5	28.5	27.8	0.6	13.6	0.2	3.7	2.4
(SITC 0 + 1 + 22 + 4)	2005	100.0	39.4	22.7	21.8	0.5	9.3	0.1	6.7	3.4
	2011	100.0	32.9	18.5	17.5	1.3	7.1	0.1	5.8	4.9
Agricultural raw materials	1995	100.0	54.8	33.7	33.0	2.7	11.0	0.9	6.5	16.7
(SITC 2 - 22 - 27 - 28)	2005	100.0	58.7	36.0	35.6	2.0	17.7	0.6	2.4	10.5
	2011	100.0	52.9	29.8	29.5	1.3	19.3	0.8	1.8	7.6
Ores, metals, precious stones	1995	100.0	65.1	51.1	34.6	2.5	8.6	0.3	2.6	5.0
and non-monetary gold	2005	100.0	42.6	34.9	19.9	0.6	4.2	0.4	2.6	12.8
(SITC 27 + 28 + 68 + 667 + 971)	2011	100.0	34.6	24.6	16.6	1.0	5.7	0.2	3.0	8.8
Fuels (SITC 3)	1995	100.0	13.3	8.7	8.7	0.1	3.1	0.0	1.3	11.1
	2005	100.0	16.2	10.9	9.7	0.3	1.4	0.1	3.6	20.6
	2011	100.0	33.8	22.9	21.9	0.4	5.3	0.2	5.0	12.3
Manufactured goods	1995	100.0	68.9	45.7	42.8	0.7	13.0	9.1	0.4	2.7
(SITC 5 to 8 less 667 and 68)	2005	100.0	62.4	44.2	42.6	0.5	9.2	7.3	1.2	2.9
	2011	100.0	50.3	34.3	33.0	0.5	9.3	5.2	0.9	2.2
Share by major product group (percentage)										
All products	1995	100.0	100.0	100.0	100.0	100.0	100.0	100.0	100.0	100.0
	2005	100.0	100.0	100.0	100.0	100.0	100.0	100.0	100.0	100.0
	2011	100.0	100.0	100.0	100.0	100.0	100.0	100.0	100.0	100.0
All food items	1995	13.7	10.4	9.7	10.1	10.0	15.4	0.3	43.9	9.3
(SITC 0 + 1 + 22 + 4)	2005	9.6	7.0	5.8	5.9	10.1	10.8	0.2	29.2	5.2
	2011	11.3	8.5	7.1	7.2	24.6	9.7	0.3	34.0	9.9
Agricultural raw materials	1995	2.4	2.2	2.0	2.1	8.6	2.2	0.3	13.8	11.4
(SITC 2 - 22 - 27 - 28)	2005	1.4	1.5	1.3	1.4	5.3	2.9	0.2	1.5	2.3
	2011	1.4	1.7	1.4	1.5	2.9	3.2	0.3	1.3	1.9
Ores, metals, precious stones	1995	4.7	5.0	5.9	4.3	15.0	3.3	0.2	10.5	6.5
and non-monetary gold	2005	7.5	5.9	6.9	4.2	8.8	3.8	0.5	8.6	15.2
(SITC 27 + 28 + 68 + 667 + 971)	2011	10.3	8.2	8.7	6.3	17.0	7.1	0.7	16.2	16.1
Fuels (SITC 3)	1995	6.1	1.3	1.3	1.4	1.1	1.6	0.0	7.2	19.1
	2005	8.8	2.7	2.5	2.4	5.0	1.5	0.1	14.3	28.7
	2011	6.8	5.3	5.3	5.4	4.3	4.4	0.3	17.5	14.9
Manufactured goods	1995	71.1	80.3	80.4	81.1	65.0	76.7	98.7	22.3	53.7
(SITC 5 to 8 less 667 and 68)	2005	69.8	81.3	82.2	84.7	70.0	78.7	98.4	39.0	31.8
	2011	65.1	75.5	76.8	78.8	50.5	73.7	98.3	30.6	26.1

For sources and notes, see end of table 2.2.L.

			Developing economies - Économies en développement							Origines	
				Asia Asie				Major petroleum exporters and gas exporters	Major manufactured goods exporters	Year	
Total	Africa Afrique	America Amérique	Total	Eastern, Southern and South-Eastern Asia Asie orientale, méridionale et du Sud-Est	China Chine	Western Asia Asie occidentale	Oceania (2) Océanie (2)	Principaux exportateurs de pétrole et de gaz	Principaux exportateurs d'articles manufacturés	Année	Groupes de produits
Millions de dollars											
39 384	2 956	2 290	34 133	20 245	3 062	13 888	5	10 626	13 802	1995	**Total tous produits**
144 131	11 561	7 399	125 147	77 508	24 184	47 639	24	36 497	52 514	2005	
387 125	21 097	19 507	346 514	248 216	85 299	98 298	7	73 935	153 954	2011	
Parts par origines (en pourcentage)											
31.3	2.4	1.8	27.2	16.1	2.4	11.0	0.0	8.5	11.0	1995	**Total tous produits**
39.6	3.2	2.0	34.4	21.3	6.7	13.1	0.0	10.0	14.4	2005	
49.3	2.7	2.5	44.2	31.6	10.9	12.5	0.0	9.4	19.6	2011	
49.5	4.4	6.7	38.4	17.5	1.0	20.9	0.0	7.5	7.2	1995	Produits alimentaires
57.1	5.4	10.8	40.9	17.6	1.5	23.3	0.0	8.7	5.9	2005	(CTCI 0 + 1 + 22 + 4)
62.1	5.0	11.8	45.4	21.4	1.8	24.0	0.0	11.1	6.9	2011	
27.4	5.0	3.4	19.0	14.7	0.5	4.3	0.0	3.4	9.9	1995	Matières premières
30.5	4.8	4.6	21.1	15.6	2.4	5.6	..	2.9	9.9	2005	d'origine agricole
39.4	4.5	6.0	28.8	24.9	5.4	3.8	0.0	3.0	15.2	2011	(CTCI 2 - 22 - 27 - 28)
28.8	6.0	4.8	17.9	5.2	0.4	12.8	0.0	8.3	1.5	1995	Minerais, métaux, pierres
44.3	7.5	3.8	33.0	23.2	1.2	9.7	0.0	7.4	6.9	2005	précieuses et or (non monétaire)
56.6	8.1	4.1	44.4	33.3	2.0	11.2	0.0	9.2	5.8	2011	(CTCI 27 + 28 + 68 + 667 + 971)
74.2	13.6	0.1	60.4	10.6	0.3	49.8	..	65.2	1.0	1995	Combustibles (CTCI 3)
62.9	10.7	0.7	51.5	12.3	0.9	39.2	..	48.0	1.5	2005	
53.8	5.3	0.6	47.9	22.3	1.0	25.6	..	23.9	3.7	2011	
25.2	0.7	0.8	23.7	17.4	3.2	6.2	0.0	4.1	13.5	1995	Articles manufacturés
34.2	1.1	0.8	32.2	23.2	9.0	9.0	0.0	5.1	18.6	2005	(CTCI 5 à 8 moins 667 et 68)
47.3	1.2	0.8	45.2	34.6	15.8	10.6	0.0	6.4	27.3	2011	
Parts par principaux groupes de produits (en pourcentage)											
100.0	100.0	100.0	100.0	100.0	100.0	100.0	100.0	100.0	100.0	1995	**Total tous produits**
100.0	100.0	100.0	100.0	100.0	100.0	100.0	100.0	100.0	100.0	2005	
100.0	100.0	100.0	100.0	100.0	100.0	100.0	100.0	100.0	100.0	2011	
21.6	25.8	50.1	19.3	14.9	5.6	25.9	72.5	12.2	9.0	1995	Produits alimentaires
13.8	16.4	50.7	11.4	7.9	2.1	17.1	2.6	8.3	3.9	2005	(CTCI 0 + 1 + 22 + 4)
14.2	21.0	53.2	11.6	7.6	1.8	21.6	6.6	13.3	4.0	2011	
2.1	5.2	4.6	1.7	2.2	0.5	1.0	0.0	1.0	2.2	1995	Matières premières
1.1	2.0	3.1	0.8	1.0	0.5	0.6	..	0.4	0.9	2005	d'origine agricole
1.1	2.3	3.3	0.9	1.1	0.7	0.4	46.2	0.4	1.1	2011	(CTCI 2 - 22 - 27 - 28)
4.3	12.0	12.4	3.1	1.5	0.8	5.4	1.1	4.6	0.6	1995	Minerais, métaux, pierres
8.3	17.7	13.9	7.2	8.1	1.4	5.5	0.3	5.5	3.6	2005	précieuses et or (non monétaire)
11.8	30.8	16.9	10.3	10.8	1.9	9.2	1.2	10.0	3.0	2011	(CTCI 27 + 28 + 68 + 667 + 971)
14.5	35.5	0.4	13.6	4.0	0.8	27.7	..	47.3	0.5	1995	Combustibles (CTCI 3)
14.0	29.5	3.2	13.2	5.1	1.1	26.3	..	42.1	0.9	2005	
7.4	13.4	1.6	7.3	4.8	0.6	13.8	..	17.1	1.3	2011	
57.2	21.4	32.5	62.0	77.0	92.1	40.1	26.4	34.9	87.3	1995	Articles manufacturés
60.2	25.0	28.3	65.4	76.1	94.5	48.0	96.9	35.3	90.1	2005	(CTCI 5 à 8 moins 667 et 68)
62.4	30.2	21.7	66.7	71.3	94.9	55.0	45.9	44.3	90.6	2011	

Pour les sources et les notes, se reporter à la fin du tableau 2.2.L.

Product group	Year / Année	World (1) / Monde (1)	Developed economies - Économies développées							Transition economies / Économies en transition
			Total	Europe Total	Europe EU / UE	Canada	USA / États-Unis	Japan / Japon	Other developed countries / Autres économies développées	
Millions of dollars										
All products	1995	5 481	4 309	1 012	1 009	26	212	1 888	1 171	2
	2005	6 902	4 626	1 308	1 288	26	309	1 003	1 980	24
	2011	11 113	7 622	1 851	1 800	11	409	1 295	4 056	17
Share by destination (percentage)										
All products	1995	100.0	78.6	18.5	18.4	0.5	3.9	34.4	21.4	0.0
	2005	100.0	67.0	19.0	18.7	0.4	4.5	14.5	28.7	0.3
	2011	100.0	68.6	16.7	16.2	0.1	3.7	11.7	36.5	0.2
All food items	1995	100.0	81.7	53.1	53.1	2.2	5.2	12.7	8.4	0.1
(SITC 0 + 1 + 22 + 4)	2005	100.0	78.7	40.2	40.2	0.5	14.0	10.4	13.5	0.3
	2011	100.0	72.1	44.2	44.2	0.2	10.8	7.0	9.9	0.4
Agricultural raw materials	1995	100.0	61.6	1.5	1.5	0.0	0.3	58.2	1.6	..
(SITC 2 - 22 - 27 - 28)	2005	100.0	18.4	0.5	0.4	0.1	1.4	12.0	4.5	0.0
	2011	100.0	13.9	0.0	0.0	0.1	-0.3	8.8	5.3	0.0
Ores, metals, precious stones	1995	100.0	87.3	15.5	15.4	0.0	2.2	40.3	29.3	0.0
and non-monetary gold	2005	100.0	82.3	15.2	15.0	0.0	0.8	24.4	41.9	0.9
(SITC 27 + 28 + 68 + 667 + 971)	2011	100.0	80.5	10.5	10.5	0.0	0.7	16.7	52.6	0.0
Fuels (SITC 3)	1995	100.0	89.3	0.0	0.0	..	3.4	1.9	84.0	..
	2005	100.0	78.8	0.0	0.0	0.0	2.6	5.3	70.9	0.0
	2011	100.0	74.2	0.0	0.0	0.0	2.2	2.3	69.6	0.0
Manufactured goods	1995	100.0	85.7	25.5	25.3	0.4	10.1	34.7	14.9	0.1
(SITC 5 to 8 less 667 and 68)	2005	100.0	50.7	24.8	23.9	1.0	3.2	11.3	10.5	0.1
	2011	100.0	54.7	22.4	19.5	0.3	6.1	13.0	12.9	0.4
Share by major product group (percentage)										
All products	1995	100.0	100.0	100.0	100.0	100.0	100.0	100.0	100.0	100.0
	2005	100.0	100.0	100.0	100.0	100.0	100.0	100.0	100.0	100.0
	2011	100.0	100.0	100.0	100.0	100.0	100.0	100.0	100.0	100.0
All food items	1995	18.4	19.1	53.0	53.2	83.5	25.0	6.8	7.3	43.8
(SITC 0 + 1 + 22 + 4)	2005	19.5	22.9	41.4	42.0	27.0	61.1	14.0	9.2	15.3
	2011	20.0	21.0	53.1	54.5	46.8	58.8	11.9	5.4	58.4
Agricultural raw materials	1995	11.8	9.3	1.0	1.0	0.1	0.8	20.0	0.9	..
(SITC 2 - 22 - 27 - 28)	2005	8.4	2.3	0.2	0.2	1.1	2.6	6.9	1.3	0.1
	2011	8.4	1.7	0.0	0.0	5.8	-0.6	6.4	1.2	0.0
Ores, metals, precious stones	1995	25.1	27.9	21.0	21.0	0.4	14.6	29.3	34.4	0.2
and non-monetary gold	2005	28.1	34.5	22.5	22.7	2.7	5.0	47.2	41.1	75.7
(SITC 27 + 28 + 68 + 667 + 971)	2011	42.8	50.3	27.1	27.7	4.7	7.9	61.4	61.7	0.4
Fuels (SITC 3)	1995	11.5	13.1	0.0	0.0	..	10.1	0.6	45.4	..
	2005	14.5	17.1	0.0	0.0	0.0	8.3	5.3	35.9	0.1
	2011	13.5	14.7	0.0	0.0	0.0	8.3	2.7	25.8	0.1
Manufactured goods	1995	17.3	18.8	23.8	23.7	15.6	45.2	17.4	12.0	55.7
(SITC 5 to 8 less 667 and 68)	2005	27.3	20.6	35.7	34.9	68.9	19.2	21.1	10.0	8.7
	2011	14.7	11.7	19.8	17.7	38.2	24.4	16.4	5.2	41.2

For sources and notes, see end of table 2.2.L.

Structure des exportations par partenaires et groupes de produits
Économies en développement : Océanie

Total	Africa / Afrique	America / Amérique	Asia / Asie Total	Eastern, Southern and South-Eastern Asia / Asie orientale, méridionale et du Sud-Est	China / Chine	Western Asia / Asie occidentale	Oceania (2) / Océanie (2)	Major petroleum exporters and gas exporters / Principaux exportateurs de pétrole et de gaz	Major manufactured goods exporters / Principaux exportateurs d'articles manufacturés	Year / Année	Destinations / Groupes de produits
Millions de dollars											
810	6	9	776	771	84	5	18	1	658	1995	Total tous produits
2 243	87	173	1 742	1 732	433	10	241	3	1 452	2005	
3 460	153	46	2 901	2 896	978	5	361	5	2 238	2011	
Parts par destinations (en pourcentage)											
14.8	0.1	0.2	14.2	14.1	1.5	0.1	0.3	0.0	12.0	1995	Total tous produits
32.5	1.3	2.5	25.2	25.1	6.3	0.1	3.5	0.1	21.0	2005	
31.1	1.4	0.4	26.1	26.1	8.8	0.0	3.2	0.0	20.1	2011	
17.9	0.1	0.1	17.5	17.3	1.0	0.2	0.3	0.0	15.0	1995	Produits alimentaires
20.5	0.5	0.3	13.4	13.4	0.3	0.0	6.3	0.0	10.8	2005	(CTCI 0 + 1 + 22 + 4)
26.9	0.3	0.7	19.3	19.2	0.5	0.0	6.6	0.1	17.1	2011	
38.4	0.0	0.0	38.2	38.2	4.4	0.0	0.1	..	34.1	1995	Matières premières
81.6	0.4	0.8	79.8	79.8	45.3	0.0	0.7	0.0	57.1	2005	d'origine agricole
86.1	0.2	1.4	84.0	83.8	65.3	0.2	0.6	0.2	73.7	2011	(CTCI 2 - 22 - 27 - 28)
12.7	0.0	0.0	12.7	12.7	..	0.0	0.0	..	8.5	1995	Minerais, métaux, pierres
16.7	0.5	0.0	16.0	16.0	2.6	0.0	0.2	0.0	8.7	2005	précieuses et or (non monétaire)
19.5	0.4	0.0	19.1	19.1	2.5	0.0	0.1	0.0	12.2	2011	(CTCI 27 + 28 + 68 + 667 + 971)
10.7	..	..	10.3	10.3	7.2	..	0.4	..	10.3	1995	Combustibles (CTCI 3)
21.0	0.1	0.0	16.2	16.2	3.4	..	4.7	..	10.7	2005	
25.7	0.1	0.6	21.0	21.0	10.5	0.0	4.0	0.0	13.9	2011	
14.1	0.6	0.9	11.6	11.4	0.0	0.2	1.1	0.0	10.8	1995	Articles manufacturés
49.2	3.6	8.7	32.9	32.4	4.4	0.5	4.1	0.2	36.8	2005	(CTCI 5 à 8 moins 667 et 68)
44.9	7.4	0.6	28.3	28.2	4.8	0.1	8.6	0.1	23.0	2011	
Parts par principaux groupes de produits (en pourcentage)											
100.0	100.0	100.0	100.0	100.0	100.0	100.0	100.0	100.0	100.0	1995	Total tous produits
100.0	100.0	100.0	100.0	100.0	100.0	100.0	100.0	100.0	100.0	2005	
100.0	100.0	100.0	100.0	100.0	100.0	100.0	100.0	100.0	100.0	2011	
22.4	9.9	8.6	22.8	22.6	11.7	54.5	14.5	49.4	23.1	1995	Produits alimentaires
12.3	7.7	2.4	10.3	10.4	0.9	1.5	35.5	8.3	10.0	2005	(CTCI 0 + 1 + 22 + 4)
17.3	5.1	31.5	14.8	14.7	1.1	20.1	40.8	21.6	16.9	2011	
30.8	0.1	0.6	32.0	32.2	33.6	0.0	5.1	..	33.6	1995	Matières premières
21.1	2.6	2.7	26.6	26.7	60.7	0.0	1.6	0.0	22.8	2005	d'origine agricole
23.3	1.0	27.8	27.1	27.1	62.5	36.4	1.6	31.3	30.8	2011	(CTCI 2 - 22 - 27 - 28)
21.6	0.1	0.1	22.5	22.6	..	0.5	1.5	..	17.8	1995	Minerais, métaux, pierres
14.5	11.5	0.3	17.8	17.9	11.6	0.1	1.3	0.3	11.7	2005	précieuses et or (non monétaire)
26.9	12.0	0.0	31.3	31.3	12.3	2.9	1.2	2.5	26.1	2011	(CTCI 27 + 28 + 68 + 667 + 971)
8.3	..	..	8.4	8.5	54.5	..	13.3	..	9.9	1995	Combustibles (CTCI 3)
9.4	1.4	0.0	9.3	9.4	7.9	..	19.4	..	7.4	2005	
11.2	1.1	19.8	10.9	10.9	16.2	6.7	16.7	5.8	9.3	2011	
16.5	89.7	90.7	14.1	13.9	0.1	45.0	55.9	50.6	15.5	1995	Articles manufacturés
41.3	76.8	94.2	35.5	35.2	18.9	98.2	32.0	90.7	47.8	2005	(CTCI 5 à 8 moins 667 et 68)
21.2	79.7	20.5	15.9	15.9	8.0	33.9	39.1	18.8	16.8	2011	

Pour les sources et les notes, se reporter à la fin du tableau 2.2.L.

2.2.H Import structure by partner and product group
Developing economies: Oceania

Origin / Product group	Year / Année	World (1) / Monde (1)	Developed economies - Économies développées							Transition economies / Économies en transition
			Total	Europe		Canada	USA / États-Unis	Japan / Japon	Other developed countries / Autres économies développées	
				Total	EU / UE					
Millions of dollars										
All products	1995	6 585	4 437	1 322	1 310	13	356	804	1 942	1
	2005	9 602	5 728	1 973	1 945	30	484	510	2 731	3
	2011	15 397	8 292	2 495	2 434	86	810	599	4 301	9
Share by origin (percentage)										
All products	1995	100.0	67.4	20.1	19.9	0.2	5.4	12.2	29.5	0.0
	2005	100.0	59.7	20.5	20.3	0.3	5.0	5.3	28.4	0.0
	2011	100.0	53.9	16.2	15.8	0.6	5.3	3.9	27.9	0.1
All food items	1995	100.0	85.6	23.1	23.0	0.2	10.3	5.1	47.0	0.0
(SITC 0 + 1 + 22 + 4)	2005	100.0	71.2	16.9	16.7	0.3	8.7	2.6	42.8	0.0
	2011	100.0	66.6	15.0	14.8	0.4	9.2	1.2	40.9	0.0
Agricultural raw materials	1995	100.0	90.0	6.4	6.4	0.0	27.6	3.2	52.7	0.3
(SITC 2 - 22 - 27 - 28)	2005	100.0	83.5	5.7	5.7	7.3	12.9	0.7	56.8	0.0
	2011	100.0	79.1	5.7	5.7	5.0	8.4	1.5	58.4	0.0
Ores, metals, precious stones	1995	100.0	81.2	27.3	27.3	0.0	3.6	1.8	48.5	0.0
and non-monetary gold	2005	100.0	74.3	31.2	31.0	1.0	2.3	1.9	37.9	0.0
(SITC 27 + 28 + 68 + 667 + 971)	2011	100.0	62.1	13.4	13.3	0.0	19.1	1.9	27.8	0.0
Fuels (SITC 3)	1995	100.0	61.3	0.5	0.5	0.0	1.5	0.0	59.3	0.0
	2005	100.0	20.3	0.3	0.3	0.0	0.3	0.0	19.7	0.0
	2011	100.0	23.0	0.4	0.3	0.0	0.4	0.9	21.3	0.1
Manufactured goods	1995	100.0	77.8	27.1	26.8	0.3	5.2	18.5	26.7	0.0
(SITC 5 to 8 less 667 and 68)	2005	100.0	69.2	29.4	29.0	0.3	5.3	8.1	26.1	0.0
	2011	100.0	63.8	23.6	23.0	0.6	5.7	6.8	27.1	0.0
Share by major product group (percentage)										
All products	1995	100.0	100.0	100.0	100.0	100.0	100.0	100.0	100.0	100.0
	2005	100.0	100.0	100.0	100.0	100.0	100.0	100.0	100.0	100.0
	2011	100.0	100.0	100.0	100.0	100.0	100.0	100.0	100.0	100.0
All food items	1995	13.9	17.6	15.9	16.0	11.4	26.4	5.8	22.1	8.6
(SITC 0 + 1 + 22 + 4)	2005	17.4	20.7	14.2	14.3	18.6	29.9	8.4	26.1	7.9
	2011	18.9	23.4	17.5	17.7	12.4	32.9	5.8	27.7	11.6
Agricultural raw materials	1995	0.8	1.1	0.3	0.3	0.1	4.3	0.2	1.5	18.0
(SITC 2 - 22 - 27 - 28)	2005	0.9	1.3	0.3	0.3	21.2	2.4	0.1	1.8	0.6
	2011	0.7	1.0	0.2	0.3	6.2	1.1	0.3	1.5	0.0
Ores, metals, precious stones	1995	0.6	0.7	0.8	0.8	0.0	0.4	0.1	0.9	1.4
and non-monetary gold	2005	0.8	1.0	1.2	1.2	2.5	0.4	0.3	1.1	0.0
(SITC 27 + 28 + 68 + 667 + 971)	2011	1.0	1.1	0.8	0.8	0.1	3.5	0.5	1.0	0.1
Fuels (SITC 3)	1995	8.9	8.1	0.2	0.2	0.2	2.4	0.0	17.8	8.4
	2005	20.8	7.1	0.3	0.3	0.1	1.1	0.1	14.4	28.8
	2011	24.9	10.6	0.7	0.5	0.1	1.8	5.6	19.0	50.2
Manufactured goods	1995	60.8	70.1	82.1	82.0	86.6	58.4	92.0	55.0	63.5
(SITC 5 to 8 less 667 and 68)	2005	58.3	67.6	83.5	83.4	56.4	61.6	88.9	53.4	62.4
	2011	49.7	58.8	72.2	72.3	53.3	54.0	87.0	48.2	38.0

For sources and notes, see end of table 2.2.L.

| | | | Developing economies - Économies en développement | | | | | | | Origines |
Total	Africa / Afrique	America / Amérique	Asia / Asie Total	Eastern, Southern and South-Eastern Asia / Asie orientale, méridionale et du Sud-Est	China / Chine	Western Asia / Asie occidentale	Oceania (2) / Océanie (2)	Major petroleum exporters and gas exporters / Principaux exportateurs de pétrole et de gaz	Major manufactured goods exporters / Principaux exportateurs d'articles manufacturés	Year / Année	Groupes de produits
Millions de dollars											
1 182	6	33	1 125	1 123	70	1	19	1	1 048	1995	Total tous produits
3 845	33	49	3 499	3 483	344	17	263	3	3 215	2005	
7 089	55	64	6 608	6 578	1 335	30	362	5	5 982	2011	
Parts par origines (en pourcentage)											
18.0	0.1	0.5	17.1	17.1	1.1	0.0	0.3	0.0	15.9	1995	Total tous produits
40.0	0.3	0.5	36.4	36.3	3.6	0.2	2.7	0.0	33.5	2005	
46.0	0.4	0.4	42.9	42.7	8.7	0.2	2.3	0.0	38.9	2011	
13.3	0.4	1.4	11.3	11.2	0.7	0.0	0.3	0.0	9.3	1995	Produits alimentaires
27.4	1.0	1.7	17.1	17.0	2.6	0.1	7.6	0.1	14.8	2005	(CTCI 0 + 1 + 22 + 4)
33.4	0.8	1.2	25.7	25.6	10.7	0.1	5.7	0.0	22.7	2011	
9.5	0.1	0.2	7.3	7.1	0.0	0.2	1.9	0.2	6.5	1995	Matières premières
16.5	1.4	0.4	8.8	8.8	1.1	0.0	5.9	0.0	6.4	2005	d'origine agricole
20.9	1.9	1.3	12.1	12.1	1.9	0.0	5.6	0.0	7.1	2011	(CTCI 2 - 22 - 27 - 28)
12.9	1.2	0.1	10.8	10.6	0.1	0.2	0.8	0.0	9.6	1995	Minerais, métaux, pierres
25.7	0.6	0.4	20.3	20.1	2.3	0.2	4.4	0.2	11.5	2005	précieuses et or (non monétaire)
37.8	0.6	0.1	33.9	33.8	6.0	0.0	3.2	0.5	23.8	2011	(CTCI 27 + 28 + 68 + 667 + 971)
38.3	0.2	0.1	37.5	37.5	0.0	..	0.4	..	36.9	1995	Combustibles (CTCI 3)
79.7	0.0	0.0	77.6	77.6	0.1	0.0	2.1	0.0	76.9	2005	
76.9	0.1	0.0	75.3	75.3	0.5	0.1	1.4	0.0	74.6	2011	
19.9	0.0	0.5	19.1	19.1	1.6	0.0	0.3	0.0	17.8	1995	Articles manufacturés
30.7	0.3	0.4	28.8	28.5	5.2	0.3	1.3	0.0	24.9	2005	(CTCI 5 à 8 moins 667 et 68)
36.1	0.3	0.3	33.8	33.6	11.7	0.3	1.7	0.0	29.1	2011	
Parts par principaux groupes de produits (en pourcentage)											
100.0	100.0	100.0	100.0	100.0	100.0	100.0	100.0	100.0	100.0	1995	Total tous produits
100.0	100.0	100.0	100.0	100.0	100.0	100.0	100.0	100.0	100.0	2005	
100.0	100.0	100.0	100.0	100.0	100.0	100.0	100.0	100.0	100.0	2011	
10.3	57.6	39.3	9.1	9.1	9.7	11.1	13.3	16.1	8.1	1995	Produits alimentaires
11.9	50.4	56.6	8.2	8.1	12.5	12.8	48.2	31.5	7.7	2005	(CTCI 0 + 1 + 22 + 4)
13.7	40.0	52.4	11.3	11.3	23.3	9.2	46.2	10.8	11.0	2011	
0.4	0.7	0.4	0.4	0.3	0.0	7.3	5.6	15.5	0.3	1995	Matières premières
0.4	3.6	0.8	0.2	0.2	0.3	0.0	2.0	0.2	0.2	2005	d'origine agricole
0.3	3.7	2.2	0.2	0.2	0.2	0.0	1.7	1.0	0.1	2011	(CTCI 2 - 22 - 27 - 28)
0.4	7.3	0.1	0.4	0.4	0.0	4.9	1.6	1.3	0.3	1995	Minerais, métaux, pierres
0.5	1.5	0.6	0.5	0.4	0.5	0.8	1.3	4.5	0.3	2005	précieuses et or (non monétaire)
0.8	1.6	0.3	0.8	0.8	0.7	0.1	1.3	15.3	0.6	2011	(CTCI 27 + 28 + 68 + 667 + 971)
18.9	20.7	2.3	19.5	19.5	0.1	..	13.4	..	20.6	1995	Combustibles (CTCI 3)
41.4	0.7	0.1	44.3	44.5	0.6	0.8	15.7	4.1	47.8	2005	
41.6	10.4	0.0	43.7	43.9	1.3	6.8	14.8	32.3	47.8	2011	
67.2	13.7	57.9	68.0	68.0	90.2	76.7	55.6	67.1	68.0	1995	Articles manufacturés
44.7	43.2	41.5	46.0	45.8	84.7	84.5	27.6	59.7	43.3	2005	(CTCI 5 à 8 moins 667 et 68)
38.9	42.1	33.8	39.1	39.0	66.8	66.7	35.0	24.5	37.1	2011	

Pour les sources et les notes, se reporter à la fin du tableau 2.2.L.

2.2.I Export structure by partner and product group
Developing economies: Major petroleum and gas exporters

Destination / Product group	Year / Année	World (1) / Monde (1)	Developed economies - Économies développées							Transition economies / Économies en transition
			Total	Europe		Canada	USA / États-Unis	Japan / Japon	Other developed countries / Autres économies développées	
				Total	EU / UE					
Millions of dollars										
All products	1995	173 403	106 428	41 615	40 672	1 508	29 831	31 866	1 609	1 335
	2005	682 140	379 816	139 287	136 591	8 612	128 897	99 851	3 169	2 026
	2011	1 428 780	592 273	211 376	207 462	17 598	191 924	160 642	10 732	5 466
Share by destination (percentage)										
All products	1995	100.0	61.4	24.0	23.5	0.9	17.2	18.4	0.9	0.8
	2005	100.0	55.7	20.4	20.0	1.3	18.9	14.6	0.5	0.3
	2011	100.0	41.5	14.8	14.5	1.2	13.4	11.2	0.8	0.4
All food items	1995	100.0	27.5	22.1	21.8	0.5	3.0	1.7	0.2	8.7
(SITC 0 + 1 + 22 + 4)	2005	100.0	23.0	17.4	17.3	0.6	3.5	1.2	0.4	3.7
	2011	100.0	13.7	11.3	11.2	0.3	0.9	0.9	0.2	3.3
Agricultural raw materials	1995	100.0	53.8	49.6	48.1	0.2	3.4	0.5	0.0	0.7
(SITC 2 - 22 - 27 - 28)	2005	100.0	25.2	23.9	23.6	0.1	0.9	0.1	0.2	1.2
	2011	100.0	28.6	23.1	22.9	0.6	2.0	1.1	1.8	2.2
Ores, metals, precious stones	1995	100.0	46.4	20.7	19.9	0.4	10.4	14.7	0.0	1.1
and non-monetary gold	2005	100.0	29.4	20.8	18.0	0.8	4.9	2.8	0.1	0.5
(SITC 27 + 28 + 68 + 667 + 971)	2011	100.0	16.6	12.7	11.2	0.2	2.4	1.2	0.1	0.2
Fuels (SITC 3)	1995	100.0	66.9	24.5	24.1	1.0	18.8	21.5	1.0	0.3
	2005	100.0	60.1	20.4	20.1	1.4	21.0	16.9	0.4	0.0
	2011	100.0	46.6	15.5	15.3	1.4	15.6	13.4	0.7	0.2
Manufactured goods	1995	100.0	33.1	19.9	18.7	0.4	10.0	2.3	0.5	2.4
(SITC 5 to 8 less 667 and 68)	2005	100.0	30.7	21.8	20.9	0.5	6.8	0.8	0.9	2.2
	2011	100.0	16.0	10.9	10.4	0.5	2.9	0.6	1.0	1.7
Share by major product group (percentage)										
All products	1995	100.0	100.0	100.0	100.0	100.0	100.0	100.0	100.0	100.0
	2005	100.0	100.0	100.0	100.0	100.0	100.0	100.0	100.0	100.0
	2011	100.0	100.0	100.0	100.0	100.0	100.0	100.0	100.0	100.0
All food items	1995	2.3	1.0	2.1	2.1	1.2	0.4	0.2	0.6	25.9
(SITC 0 + 1 + 22 + 4)	2005	1.2	0.5	1.0	1.0	0.5	0.2	0.1	1.1	14.5
	2011	1.5	0.5	1.2	1.2	0.4	0.1	0.1	0.4	13.1
Agricultural raw materials	1995	0.5	0.4	1.0	1.0	0.1	0.1	0.0	0.0	0.5
(SITC 2 - 22 - 27 - 28)	2005	0.1	0.1	0.2	0.2	0.0	0.0	0.0	0.0	0.5
	2011	0.2	0.1	0.3	0.3	0.1	0.0	0.0	0.4	1.0
Ores, metals, precious stones	1995	2.5	1.9	2.1	2.1	1.2	1.5	2.0	0.1	3.7
and non-monetary gold	2005	2.7	1.4	2.7	2.4	1.7	0.7	0.5	0.4	4.3
(SITC 27 + 28 + 68 + 667 + 971)	2011	3.9	1.6	3.4	3.0	0.6	0.7	0.4	0.4	1.6
Fuels (SITC 3)	1995	82.3	89.7	84.2	84.6	92.1	90.2	96.2	92.4	28.5
	2005	85.4	92.2	85.2	85.7	94.0	95.0	98.7	74.1	6.1
	2011	83.2	93.6	87.3	87.9	94.5	96.6	98.8	82.7	34.9
Manufactured goods	1995	12.1	6.5	10.0	9.6	5.3	7.0	1.5	6.6	38.3
(SITC 5 to 8 less 667 and 68)	2005	10.0	5.5	10.7	10.4	3.7	3.6	0.5	18.6	72.5
	2011	10.6	4.1	7.8	7.5	4.4	2.3	0.6	14.6	47.7

For sources and notes, see end of table 2.2.L.

Structure des exportations par partenaires et groupes de produits
Économies en développement : principaux exportateurs de pétrole et de gaz

Total	Africa Afrique	America Amérique	Asia Asie Total	Eastern, Southern and South-Eastern Asia (Asie orientale, méridionale et du Sud-Est)	China Chine	Western Asia (Asie occidentale)	Oceania (2) Océanie (2)	Major petroleum exporters and gas exporters (Principaux exportateurs de pétrole et de gaz)	Major manufactured goods exporters (Principaux exportateurs d'articles manufacturés)	Year Année	Destinations / Groupes de produits
Millions de dollars											
65 620	5 485	8 856	51 280	38 579	1 889	12 701	0	6 433	26 060	1995	**Total tous produits**
298 575	24 244	25 353	248 974	209 534	38 592	39 440	4	26 621	160 708	2005	
830 860	53 109	38 428	739 273	657 941	166 113	81 331	50	67 932	438 075	2011	
Parts par destinations (en pourcentage)											
37.8	3.2	5.1	29.6	22.2	1.1	7.3	0.0	3.7	15.0	1995	**Total tous produits**
43.8	3.6	3.7	36.5	30.7	5.7	5.8	0.0	3.9	23.6	2005	
58.2	3.7	2.7	51.7	46.0	11.6	5.7	0.0	4.8	30.7	2011	
63.7	3.8	10.8	49.0	10.2	0.2	38.8	0.0	35.6	3.5	1995	Produits alimentaires
73.1	6.6	3.0	63.6	23.2	0.4	40.3	0.0	38.6	5.4	2005	(CTCI 0 + 1 + 22 + 4)
83.0	7.6	1.1	74.3	26.8	0.6	47.5	0.0	50.0	4.1	2011	
45.1	3.6	3.7	37.8	22.2	2.8	15.6	0.0	8.5	5.8	1995	Matières premières
72.0	12.1	3.2	56.7	37.2	2.9	19.6	0.0	16.5	6.9	2005	d'origine agricole
69.1	4.3	6.8	58.1	44.7	3.7	13.4	0.0	13.7	15.0	2011	(CTCI 2 - 22 - 27 - 28)
52.4	3.3	6.5	42.7	29.8	1.8	12.9	0.0	10.0	15.2	1995	Minerais, métaux, pierres
70.1	2.4	3.1	64.6	52.8	5.7	11.9	0.0	9.6	16.8	2005	précieuses et or (non monétaire)
83.2	2.3	1.3	79.7	67.0	9.0	12.8	0.0	10.0	19.2	2011	(CTCI 27 + 28 + 68 + 667 + 971)
32.8	2.7	4.4	25.8	21.6	0.8	4.2	..	0.3	15.4	1995	Combustibles (CTCI 3)
39.6	2.9	3.7	33.1	30.2	5.8	2.9	0.0	0.6	25.2	2005	
53.2	3.2	2.3	47.8	46.2	12.2	1.6	0.0	0.5	33.4	2011	
64.5	6.4	9.1	49.0	27.6	2.8	21.3	0.0	19.8	15.1	1995	Articles manufacturés
67.0	9.1	4.4	53.4	31.4	5.8	22.1	0.0	24.7	15.0	2005	(CTCI 5 à 8 moins 667 et 68)
82.1	8.3	6.9	66.9	42.8	10.3	24.1	0.0	30.2	19.6	2011	
Parts par principaux groupes de produits (en pourcentage)											
100.0	100.0	100.0	100.0	100.0	100.0	100.0	100.0	100.0	100.0	1995	**Total tous produits**
100.0	100.0	100.0	100.0	100.0	100.0	100.0	100.0	100.0	100.0	2005	
100.0	100.0	100.0	100.0	100.0	100.0	100.0	100.0	100.0	100.0	2011	
3.9	2.7	4.9	3.8	1.1	0.4	12.2	17.3	22.0	0.5	1995	Produits alimentaires
2.0	2.2	0.9	2.0	0.9	0.1	8.2	23.3	11.6	0.3	2005	(CTCI 0 + 1 + 22 + 4)
2.1	3.1	0.6	2.2	0.9	0.1	12.5	1.3	15.8	0.2	2011	
0.6	0.6	0.4	0.6	0.5	1.3	1.1	15.2	1.2	0.2	1995	Matières premières
0.2	0.4	0.1	0.2	0.2	0.1	0.4	0.0	0.5	0.0	2005	d'origine agricole
0.2	0.2	0.4	0.2	0.2	0.1	0.4	0.0	0.5	0.1	2011	(CTCI 2 - 22 - 27 - 28)
3.4	2.5	3.1	3.6	3.3	4.1	4.4	1.3	6.7	2.5	1995	Minerais, métaux, pierres
4.3	1.8	2.2	4.7	4.6	2.7	5.5	2.0	6.6	1.9	2005	précieuses et or (non monétaire)
5.6	2.4	1.8	6.0	5.7	3.0	8.8	1.7	8.2	2.5	2011	(CTCI 27 + 28 + 68 + 667 + 971)
71.3	69.5	70.2	71.8	79.8	63.6	47.2	..	5.6	84.6	1995	Combustibles (CTCI 3)
77.4	69.3	84.8	77.4	84.0	86.9	42.2	1.9	12.3	91.3	2005	
76.1	70.8	69.9	76.8	83.4	87.5	23.7	82.4	8.5	90.5	2011	
20.6	24.6	21.4	20.0	15.0	30.6	35.1	66.2	64.5	12.1	1995	Articles manufacturés
15.3	25.6	11.9	14.6	10.2	10.2	38.1	72.8	63.2	6.4	2005	(CTCI 5 à 8 moins 667 et 68)
14.9	23.5	27.2	13.6	9.8	9.4	44.6	13.6	66.9	6.7	2011	

Pour les sources et les notes, se reporter à la fin du tableau 2.2.L.

Origin / Product group	Year Année	World (1) Monde (1)	Developed economies - Économies développées								Transition economies Économies en transition
			Total	Europe		Canada	USA États-Unis	Japan Japon	Other developed countries Autres économies développées		
				Total	EU UE						
Millions of dollars											
All products	1995	117 575	74 973	46 069	42 764	2 245	16 767	8 366	1 527		1 687
	2005	315 283	170 665	110 538	105 160	2 328	35 253	17 770	4 776		7 699
	2011	714 995	296 924	187 903	176 961	4 639	68 149	26 377	9 857		12 233
Share by origin (percentage)											
All products	1995	100.0	63.8	39.2	36.4	1.9	14.3	7.1	1.3		1.4
	2005	100.0	54.1	35.1	33.4	0.7	11.2	5.6	1.5		2.4
	2011	100.0	41.5	26.3	24.8	0.6	9.5	3.7	1.4		1.7
All food items	1995	100.0	51.2	28.6	27.8	5.4	11.5	0.1	5.5		1.0
(SITC 0 + 1 + 22 + 4)	2005	100.0	41.3	24.9	23.4	1.3	10.3	0.1	4.8		2.6
	2011	100.0	33.7	20.4	19.2	1.5	7.2	0.1	4.5		1.8
Agricultural raw materials	1995	100.0	58.1	31.7	31.4	4.5	17.5	3.0	1.5		3.7
(SITC 2 - 22 - 27 - 28)	2005	100.0	55.5	40.2	38.9	3.1	8.8	1.8	1.6		6.8
	2011	100.0	48.4	32.9	32.2	1.7	8.7	2.8	2.3		5.3
Ores, metals, precious stones	1995	100.0	55.5	42.9	21.5	2.4	8.3	0.5	1.3		2.1
and non-monetary gold	2005	100.0	34.1	25.4	19.1	0.9	4.8	0.6	2.3		4.7
(SITC 27 + 28 + 68 + 667 + 971)	2011	100.0	25.8	18.0	12.3	0.8	2.9	0.3	3.8		2.2
Fuels (SITC 3)	1995	100.0	58.2	41.2	41.1	0.7	12.7	0.2	3.4		6.7
	2005	100.0	24.7	20.4	20.1	0.0	3.3	0.2	0.7		7.6
	2011	100.0	34.7	30.5	29.9	0.0	4.0	0.2	0.1		3.8
Manufactured goods	1995	100.0	67.1	41.3	38.8	1.0	15.2	9.4	0.2		1.4
(SITC 5 to 8 less 667 and 68)	2005	100.0	58.7	37.6	36.1	0.7	12.4	7.3	0.8		1.9
	2011	100.0	45.2	28.1	26.9	0.5	11.0	5.1	0.6		1.4
Share by major product group (percentage)											
All products	1995	100.0	100.0	100.0	100.0	100.0	100.0	100.0	100.0		100.0
	2005	100.0	100.0	100.0	100.0	100.0	100.0	100.0	100.0		100.0
	2011	100.0	100.0	100.0	100.0	100.0	100.0	100.0	100.0		100.0
All food items	1995	17.7	14.2	12.9	13.5	50.2	14.2	0.3	74.4		12.0
(SITC 0 + 1 + 22 + 4)	2005	12.7	9.7	9.0	8.9	21.6	11.7	0.3	39.9		13.4
	2011	14.5	11.7	11.2	11.2	34.2	10.9	0.4	47.4		15.5
Agricultural raw materials	1995	1.6	1.5	1.3	1.4	3.8	2.0	0.7	1.8		4.2
(SITC 2 - 22 - 27 - 28)	2005	0.8	0.9	1.0	1.0	3.5	0.7	0.3	0.9		2.3
	2011	0.9	1.0	1.1	1.1	2.2	0.8	0.7	1.4		2.7
Ores, metals, precious stones	1995	3.8	3.3	4.1	2.2	4.8	2.2	0.3	3.8		5.5
and non-monetary gold	2005	5.4	3.4	3.9	3.1	6.8	2.3	0.6	8.3		10.4
(SITC 27 + 28 + 68 + 667 + 971)	2011	7.7	4.8	5.3	3.8	9.0	2.4	0.7	21.2		10.0
Fuels (SITC 3)	1995	1.4	1.3	1.5	1.6	0.5	1.3	0.0	3.7		6.7
	2005	3.4	1.6	2.0	2.1	0.2	1.0	0.2	1.6		10.7
	2011	4.7	3.9	5.4	5.7	0.2	2.0	0.2	0.5		10.4
Manufactured goods	1995	74.7	78.6	78.7	79.7	40.5	79.5	98.4	14.2		71.5
(SITC 5 to 8 less 667 and 68)	2005	75.5	81.9	81.0	81.8	67.4	83.5	97.5	38.0		59.4
	2011	71.4	77.7	76.4	77.5	53.7	82.4	98.0	29.5		57.8

For sources and notes, see end of table 2.2.L.

2.2.I Structure des importations par partenaires et groupes de produits
Économies en développement : principaux exportateurs de pétrole et de gaz

Total	Africa / Afrique	America / Amérique	Asia / Asie Total	Eastern, Southern and South-Eastern Asia / Asie orientale, méridionale et du Sud-Est	China / Chine	Western Asia / Asie occidentale	Oceania (2) / Océanie (2)	Major petroleum exporters and gas exporters / Principaux exportateurs de pétrole et de gaz	Major manufactured goods exporters / Principaux exportateurs d'articles manufacturés	Year / Année	Origines / Groupes de produits
Millions de dollars											
37 124	2 531	5 824	28 767	19 254	2 942	9 513	2	5 224	13 954	1995	Total tous produits
134 427	7 202	16 632	110 562	70 085	21 857	40 477	31	22 516	50 982	2005	
402 356	18 609	40 338	343 115	241 400	94 631	101 716	293	62 182	165 920	2011	
Parts par origines (en pourcentage)											
31.6	2.2	5.0	24.5	16.4	2.5	8.1	0.0	4.4	11.9	1995	Total tous produits
42.6	2.3	5.3	35.1	22.2	6.9	12.8	0.0	7.1	16.2	2005	
56.3	2.6	5.6	48.0	33.8	13.2	14.2	0.0	8.7	23.2	2011	
46.4	3.9	13.3	29.2	13.8	1.0	15.5	0.0	5.2	5.3	1995	Produits alimentaires
55.4	4.6	15.3	35.4	16.4	1.8	19.0	0.0	7.2	6.5	2005	(CTCI 0 + 1 + 22 + 4)
64.4	4.3	19.0	41.1	20.0	2.1	21.1	0.0	10.1	8.0	2011	
37.1	4.5	10.9	21.7	17.0	0.5	4.7	..	2.8	13.0	1995	Matières premières
37.2	3.9	6.9	26.4	19.1	2.2	7.3	0.0	4.8	13.0	2005	d'origine agricole
45.9	3.9	8.7	33.1	25.0	3.6	8.2	0.1	5.9	17.7	2011	(CTCI 2 - 22 - 27 - 28)
40.2	7.4	10.3	22.5	7.7	0.6	14.8	..	8.4	2.7	1995	Minerais, métaux, pierres
60.9	6.2	5.3	49.5	37.0	1.9	12.5	0.0	9.3	11.3	2005	précieuses et or (non monétaire)
72.0	7.3	3.7	61.0	48.1	3.6	13.0	0.0	9.7	9.2	2011	(CTCI 27 + 28 + 68 + 667 + 971)
31.0	7.1	2.5	21.4	7.3	0.7	14.2	..	18.3	2.4	1995	Combustibles (CTCI 3)
66.9	3.0	2.2	61.6	16.4	1.5	45.2	0.0	25.4	4.8	2005	
61.5	4.8	4.6	52.0	28.6	2.2	23.5	0.0	16.9	5 4	2011	
27.8	1.4	2.7	23.7	17.7	3.1	6.0	0.0	3.9	14.1	1995	Articles manufacturés
38.5	1.6	3.8	33.1	22.9	8.6	10.2	0.0	5.9	19.0	2005	(CTCI 5 à 8 moins 667 et 68)
53.4	1.6	3.2	48.5	35.9	17.5	12.6	0.1	7.9	29.3	2011	
Parts par principaux groupes de produits (en pourcentage)											
100.0	100.0	100.0	100.0	100.0	100.0	100.0	100.0	100.0	100.0	1995	Total tous produits
100.0	100.0	100.0	100.0	100.0	100.0	100.0	100.0	100.0	100.0	2005	
100.0	100.0	100.0	100.0	100.0	100.0	100.0	100.0	100.0	100.0	2011	
26.0	31.6	47.3	21.1	14.9	7.2	33.8	85.0	20.8	7.9	1995	Produits alimentaires
16.5	25.8	36.9	12.8	9.4	3.3	18.8	52.8	12.9	5.1	2005	(CTCI 0 + 1 + 22 + 4)
16.6	23.9	48.8	12.4	8.6	2.3	21.4	0.8	16.8	5.0	2011	
1.9	3.4	3.6	1.5	1.7	0.3	1.0	..	1.0	1.8	1995	Matières premières
0.7	1.4	1.1	0.6	0.7	0.3	0.5	0.5	0.6	0.7	2005	d'origine agricole
0.7	1.3	1.3	0.6	0.6	0.2	0.5	1.4	0.6	0.7	2011	(CTCI 2 - 22 - 27 - 28)
4.8	12.9	7.8	3.5	1.8	1.0	6.9	..	7.1	0.9	1995	Minerais, métaux, pierres
7.7	14.5	5.4	7.6	8.9	1.4	5.2	1.3	7.0	3.8	2005	précieuses et or (non monétaire)
9.9	21.6	5.0	9.8	11.0	2.1	7.0	0.1	8.6	3.0	2011	(CTCI 27 + 28 + 68 + 667 + 971)
1.4	4.7	0.7	1.2	0.6	0.4	2.5	..	5.9	0.3	1995	Combustibles (CTCI 3)
5.4	4.5	1.5	6.0	2.5	0.7	12.1	4.3	12.2	1.0	2005	
5.1	8.7	3.8	5.1	4.0	0.8	7.7	0.5	9.1	1.1	2011	
65.7	47.3	40.5	72.4	80.7	91.1	55.8	15.0	65.0	89.0	1995	Articles manufacturés
68.3	53.2	54.7	71.3	77.7	93.8	60.2	41.0	62.1	88.8	2005	(CTCI 5 à 8 moins 667 et 68)
67.7	44.5	40.9	72.1	75.8	94.6	63.3	97.3	64.9	90.2	2011	

Pour les sources et les notes, se reporter à la fin du tableau 2.2.L.

Product group	Year / Année	World (1) / Monde (1)	Developed economies - Économies développées							Transition economies / Économies en transition
			Total	Europe		Canada	USA / États-Unis	Japan / Japon	Other developed countries / Autres économies développées	
				Total	EU / UE					
Millions of dollars										
All products	1995	887 071	476 681	125 187	119 731	11 153	226 636	98 264	15 441	5 997
	2005	2 223 477	1 121 061	333 132	323 899	26 690	532 288	180 170	48 781	30 947
	2011	4 431 058	1 869 845	617 595	593 545	50 635	798 445	294 393	108 778	92 897
Share by destination (percentage)										
All products	1995	100.0	53.7	14.1	13.5	1.3	25.5	11.1	1.7	0.7
	2005	100.0	50.4	15.0	14.6	1.2	23.9	8.1	2.2	1.4
	2011	100.0	42.2	13.9	13.4	1.1	18.0	6.6	2.5	2.1
All food items	1995	100.0	51.9	8.9	8.3	0.9	15.9	24.6	1.6	1.5
(SITC 0 + 1 + 22 + 4)	2005	100.0	55.8	10.2	10.0	1.4	22.8	19.3	2.1	2.4
	2011	100.0	44.2	9.4	9.2	1.5	18.5	12.4	2.5	2.5
Agricultural raw materials	1995	100.0	44.7	13.2	12.8	0.7	10.4	19.2	1.2	0.2
(SITC 2 - 22 - 27 - 28)	2005	100.0	41.2	14.6	14.6	1.3	11.4	12.7	1.2	0.7
	2011	100.0	33.4	14.2	14.1	1.0	7.8	9.5	1.0	0.9
Ores, metals, precious stones	1995	100.0	38.7	9.1	7.8	0.4	13.0	14.3	1.9	0.4
and non-monetary gold	2005	100.0	37.8	13.1	10.9	0.8	11.2	8.6	4.1	0.6
(SITC 27 + 28 + 68 + 667 + 971)	2011	100.0	33.9	12.5	8.1	0.9	11.5	6.3	2.7	0.4
Fuels (SITC 3)	1995	100.0	46.9	3.8	3.7	0.2	22.0	19.0	1.9	0.3
	2005	100.0	45.0	4.5	4.5	0.6	23.7	10.3	5.9	0.2
	2011	100.0	36.8	4.6	4.5	0.4	17.4	8.8	5.7	0.2
Manufactured goods	1995	100.0	54.9	15.0	14.4	1.4	27.2	9.5	1.7	0.7
(SITC 5 to 8 less 667 and 68)	2005	100.0	51.1	15.9	15.5	1.2	24.6	7.5	1.9	1.5
	2011	100.0	43.1	14.9	14.5	1.2	18.6	6.2	2.2	2.3
Share by major product group (percentage)										
All products	1995	100.0	100.0	100.0	100.0	100.0	100.0	100.0	100.0	100.0
	2005	100.0	100.0	100.0	100.0	100.0	100.0	100.0	100.0	100.0
	2011	100.0	100.0	100.0	100.0	100.0	100.0	100.0	100.0	100.0
All food items	1995	6.0	5.7	3.7	3.7	4.2	3.7	13.2	5.4	13.6
(SITC 0 + 1 + 22 + 4)	2005	3.2	3.5	2.1	2.2	3.7	3.0	7.5	3.0	5.4
	2011	3.7	3.9	2.5	2.6	4.9	3.8	6.9	3.7	4.4
Agricultural raw materials	1995	2.1	1.7	1.9	2.0	1.1	0.8	3.6	1.5	0.5
(SITC 2 - 22 - 27 - 28)	2005	0.9	0.8	0.9	0.9	1.0	0.4	1.5	0.5	0.4
	2011	1.1	0.9	1.1	1.2	0.9	0.5	1.6	0.4	0.5
Ores, metals, precious stones	1995	2.4	1.7	1.5	1.4	0.7	1.2	3.1	2.7	1.3
and non-monetary gold	2005	2.2	1.7	1.9	1.7	1.4	1.0	2.4	4.1	0.9
(SITC 27 + 28 + 68 + 667 + 971)	2011	3.5	2.8	3.2	2.1	2.6	2.3	3.3	3.9	0.7
Fuels (SITC 3)	1995	3.6	3.2	1.0	1.0	0.7	3.1	6.2	3.8	1.4
	2005	5.7	5.1	1.7	1.7	2.9	5.6	7.3	15.3	0.9
	2011	6.6	5.8	2.2	2.2	2.0	6.4	8.8	15.3	0.7
Manufactured goods	1995	85.3	87.1	90.7	91.0	93.1	90.9	73.5	85.7	82.4
(SITC 5 to 8 less 667 and 68)	2005	87.3	88.5	92.5	92.8	90.8	89.6	80.7	76.1	92.3
	2011	84.1	86.0	90.0	91.0	88.9	86.7	78.7	75.9	93.6

For sources and notes, see end of table 2.2.L.

2.2.J Structure des exportations par partenaires et groupes de produits
Économies en développement : principaux exportateurs d'articles manufacturés

Total	Africa / Afrique	America / Amérique	Asia / Asie – Total	Eastern, Southern and South-Eastern Asia / Asie orientale, méridionale et du Sud-Est	China / Chine	Western Asia / Asie occidentale	Oceania (2) / Océanie (2)	Major petroleum exporters and gas exporters / Principaux exportateurs de pétrole et de gaz	Major manufactured goods exporters / Principaux exportateurs d'articles manufacturés	Year / Année	Destinations / Groupes de produits
Millions de dollars											
401 818	13 085	25 996	362 025	345 502	73 786	16 523	711	15 495	299 052	1995	**Total tous produits**
1 068 060	37 466	64 923	961 000	910 382	272 531	50 618	4 671	53 479	765 989	2005	
2 458 408	115 383	229 687	2 095 415	1 958 445	570 229	136 971	17 923	155 802	1 551 283	2011	
Parts par destinations (en pourcentage)											
45.3	1.5	2.9	40.8	38.9	8.3	1.9	0.1	1.7	33.7	1995	**Total tous produits**
48.0	1.7	2.9	43.2	40.9	12.3	2.3	0.2	2.4	34.5	2005	
55.5	2.6	5.2	47.3	44.2	12.9	3.1	0.4	3.5	35.0	2011	
46.2	2.1	0.9	43.0	40.6	8.6	2.4	0.1	1.9	29.0	1995	Produits alimentaires
41.6	3.8	1.9	35.7	33.0	5.2	2.7	0.2	3.2	22.8	2005	(CTCI 0 + 1 + 22 + 4)
53.2	6.2	2.5	44.2	41.1	7.6	3.1	0.3	4.6	24.8	2011	
54.8	1.2	2.4	51.2	49.5	14.7	1.7	0.0	1.4	41.6	1995	Matières premières
58.0	1.4	2.5	54.1	52.0	24.2	2.2	0.0	1.4	41.6	2005	d'origine agricole
65.6	1.4	3.4	60.7	57.4	26.8	3.3	0.0	1.8	43.4	2011	(CTCI 2 - 22 - 27 - 28)
60.3	0.5	0.7	59.1	58.7	12.5	0.4	0.0	0.5	51.7	1995	Minerais, métaux, pierres
61.6	0.7	0.9	59.9	55.4	16.5	4.5	0.0	4.7	46.0	2005	précieuses et or (non monétaire)
65.7	1.0	2.1	62.5	60.1	26.1	2.4	0.0	2.6	50.6	2011	(CTCI 27 + 28 + 68 + 667 + 971)
50.1	0.2	1.9	47.6	47.4	8.2	0.1	0.4	0.1	39.4	1995	Combustibles (CTCI 3)
53.2	0.2	3.0	48.7	48.2	5.6	0.5	1.3	0.5	30.7	2005	
61.5	1.1	2.7	56.5	55.8	8.6	0.7	1.2	0.7	35.2	2011	
44.3	1.5	3.1	39.6	37.6	8.0	1.9	0.1	1.9	33.1	1995	Articles manufacturés
47.4	1.7	2.9	42.7	40.3	12.8	2.3	0.1	2.4	34.8	2005	(CTCI 5 à 8 moins 667 et 68)
54.5	2.7	5.4	46.1	42.8	12.8	3.3	0.3	3.8	34.9	2011	
Parts par principaux groupes de produits (en pourcentage)											
100.0	100.0	100.0	100.0	100.0	100.0	100.0	100.0	100.0	100.0	1995	**Total tous produits**
100.0	100.0	100.0	100.0	100.0	100.0	100.0	100.0	100.0	100.0	2005	
100.0	100.0	100.0	100.0	100.0	100.0	100.0	100.0	100.0	100.0	2011	
6.1	8.6	1.9	6.3	6.2	6.2	7.7	9.4	6.6	5.1	1995	Produits alimentaires
2.7	7.2	2.0	2.6	2.6	1.3	3.8	3.1	4.2	2.1	2005	(CTCI 0 + 1 + 22 + 4)
3.6	8.8	1.8	3.5	3.5	2.2	3.7	2.4	4.8	2.6	2011	
2.5	1.7	1.7	2.6	2.6	3.6	1.9	0.3	1.6	2.5	1995	Matières premières
1.1	0.8	0.8	1.2	1.2	1.8	0.9	0.1	0.6	1.1	2005	d'origine agricole
1.3	0.6	0.7	1.4	1.4	2.3	1.2	0.0	0.6	1.4	2011	(CTCI 2 - 22 - 27 - 28)
3.2	0.8	0.6	3.5	3.6	3.6	0.5	0.4	0.7	3.7	1995	Minerais, métaux, pierres
2.8	0.9	0.7	3.1	3.0	3.0	4.4	0.2	4.3	3.0	2005	précieuses et or (non monétaire)
4.2	1.4	1.4	4.7	4.8	7.2	2.7	0.1	2.7	5.1	2011	(CTCI 27 + 28 + 68 + 667 + 971)
4.0	0.5	2.4	4.2	4.4	3.6	0.3	16.0	0.2	4.2	1995	Combustibles (CTCI 3)
6.3	0.8	5.8	6.4	6.7	2.6	1.3	35.4	1.2	5.1	2005	
7.3	2.8	3.4	7.9	8.4	4.4	1.5	19.9	1.3	6.7	2011	
83.4	86.3	91.7	82.7	82.4	82.2	89.1	69.4	90.4	83.8	1995	Articles manufacturés
86.1	87.3	87.0	86.1	86.0	91.0	88.8	54.9	88.7	88.3	2005	(CTCI 5 à 8 moins 667 et 68)
82.7	86.0	88.1	82.1	81.5	83.8	90.4	66.4	90.4	83.8	2011	

Pour les sources et les notes, se reporter à la fin du tableau 2.2.L.

2.2.J Import structure by partner and product group
Developing economies: Major manufactured goods exporters

Origin / Product group	Year / Année	World (1) / Monde (1)	Developed economies - Économies développées							Transition economies / Économies en transition
			Total	Europe Total	EU / UE	Canada	USA / États-Unis	Japan / Japon	Other developed countries / Autres économies développées	
Millions of dollars										
All products	1995	911 557	539 863	136 610	124 433	11 106	176 513	193 664	21 970	11 550
	2005	2 057 264	890 856	234 359	214 957	20 700	282 012	302 726	51 058	32 487
	2011	4 192 640	1 661 411	520 056	444 113	45 888	471 591	464 598	159 279	95 694
Share by origin (percentage)										
All products	1995	100.0	59.2	15.0	13.7	1.2	19.4	21.2	2.4	1.3
	2005	100.0	43.3	11.4	10.4	1.0	13.7	14.7	2.5	1.6
	2011	100.0	39.6	12.4	10.6	1.1	11.2	11.1	3.8	2.3
All food items	1995	100.0	61.3	14.3	13.7	4.1	31.3	3.3	8.4	0.8
(SITC 0 + 1 + 22 + 4)	2005	100.0	51.9	9.9	9.3	3.7	26.4	2.7	9.1	1.9
	2011	100.0	49.4	9.9	9.1	3.6	26.9	1.6	7.4	1.4
Agricultural raw materials	1995	100.0	53.2	6.3	6.1	5.3	27.5	5.1	8.9	3.9
(SITC 2 - 22 - 27 - 28)	2005	100.0	52.4	9.8	9.6	6.0	23.2	5.1	8.2	8.1
	2011	100.0	49.9	9.9	9.8	7.4	19.6	4.3	8.6	6.2
Ores, metals, precious stones	1995	100.0	55.2	15.0	10.5	2.7	13.8	9.6	14.2	4.5
and non-monetary gold	2005	100.0	43.9	8.8	6.8	2.1	8.6	8.2	16.2	4.7
(SITC 27 + 28 + 68 + 667 + 971)	2011	100.0	46.3	11.0	6.2	1.8	7.1	5.9	20.4	3.7
Fuels (SITC 3)	1995	100.0	14.7	1.3	1.3	0.9	5.7	2.7	4.1	0.7
	2005	100.0	11.3	1.4	1.1	0.4	4.3	1.0	4.2	3.6
	2011	100.0	13.4	2.1	2.0	0.6	5.1	1.6	4.1	7.3
Manufactured goods	1995	100.0	62.6	16.4	15.1	0.8	19.2	25.4	0.8	1.0
(SITC 5 to 8 less 667 and 68)	2005	100.0	47.6	13.2	12.3	0.8	14.7	18.3	0.6	0.8
	2011	100.0	44.7	15.5	14.1	0.7	12.2	15.8	0.5	0.6
Share by major product group (percentage)										
All products	1995	100.0	100.0	100.0	100.0	100.0	100.0	100.0	100.0	100.0
	2005	100.0	100.0	100.0	100.0	100.0	100.0	100.0	100.0	100.0
	2011	100.0	100.0	100.0	100.0	100.0	100.0	100.0	100.0	100.0
All food items	1995	5.4	5.6	5.2	5.4	18.1	8.8	0.8	18.9	3.6
(SITC 0 + 1 + 22 + 4)	2005	3.8	4.5	3.3	3.4	14.0	7.3	0.7	14.0	4.7
	2011	4.7	5.9	3.8	4.1	15.4	11.2	0.7	9.2	2.9
Agricultural raw materials	1995	3.1	2.8	1.3	1.4	13.7	4.5	0.8	11.6	9.5
(SITC 2 - 22 - 27 - 28)	2005	2.0	2.4	1.7	1.9	12.1	3.4	0.7	6.7	10.4
	2011	2.4	3.0	1.9	2.2	16.4	4.2	0.9	5.5	6.5
Ores, metals, precious stones	1995	5.5	5.1	5.5	4.2	12.0	3.9	2.5	32.1	19.2
and non-monetary gold	2005	6.2	6.3	4.8	4.1	12.9	3.9	3.5	40.8	18.6
(SITC 27 + 28 + 68 + 667 + 971)	2011	10.5	12.2	9.3	6.1	17.3	6.6	5.6	56.3	17.2
Fuels (SITC 3)	1995	5.8	1.4	0.5	0.5	4.1	1.7	0.7	9.9	3.4
	2005	11.9	3.1	1.5	1.3	4.3	3.7	0.8	20.2	27.6
	2011	17.9	6.1	3.0	3.3	9.8	8.1	2.5	19.2	57.3
Manufactured goods	1995	78.7	83.2	86.0	87.1	50.6	77.9	94.3	27.0	60.9
(SITC 5 to 8 less 667 and 68)	2005	75.5	82.9	87.6	88.7	56.5	80.9	93.9	17.7	38.4
	2011	62.9	71.0	78.4	83.6	39.3	68.2	89.9	8.8	15.5

For sources and notes, see end of table 2.2.L.

2.2.J Structure des importations par partenaires et groupes de produits
Économies en développement : principaux exportateurs d'articles manufacturés

Total	Africa Afrique	America Amérique	Asia Asie Total	Eastern, Southern and South-Eastern Asia — Asie orientale, méridionale et du Sud-Est	China Chine	Western Asia Asie occidentale	Oceania (2) Océanie (2)	Major petroleum exporters and gas exporters — Principaux exportateurs de pétrole et de gaz	Major manufactured goods exporters — Principaux exportateurs d'articles manufacturés	Year Année	Groupes de produits
											Origines
Millions de dollars											
355 471	9 110	15 310	330 359	303 475	88 607	26 884	692	28 091	274 096	1995	**Total tous produits**
1 129 980	33 398	57 624	1 037 692	915 868	311 248	121 824	1 265	142 765	787 008	2005	
2 423 465	124 061	186 048	2 110 326	1 778 792	618 713	331 534	3 030	416 772	1 485 674	2011	
Parts par origines (en pourcentage)											
39.0	1.0	1.7	36.2	33.3	9.7	2.9	0.1	3.1	30.1	1995	**Total tous produits**
54.9	1.6	2.8	50.4	44.5	15.1	5.9	0.1	6.9	38.3	2005	
57.8	3.0	4.4	50.3	42.4	14.8	7.9	0.1	9.9	35.4	2011	
37.9	1.3	6.9	29.4	29.1	7.9	0.3	0.4	0.3	22.7	1995	Produits alimentaires
46.2	1.3	16.8	27.6	27.3	8.5	0.3	0.4	0.5	18.8	2005	(CTCI 0 + 1 + 22 + 4)
49.2	1.8	19.1	27.9	27.6	5.9	0.3	0.4	0.3	16.7	2011	
42.8	4.2	5.2	32.5	32.3	4.6	0.2	0.9	0.2	24.6	1995	Matières premières
39.5	4.6	6.3	27.6	27.3	2.5	0.2	1.1	0.2	17.9	2005	d'origine agricole
44.0	3.6	7.2	32.1	31.9	2.0	0.2	1.0	0.2	18.5	2011	(CTCI 2 - 22 - 27 - 28)
40.0	6.2	8.4	25.2	23.1	4.4	2.1	0.2	1.4	16.4	1995	Minerais, métaux, pierres
51.3	4.5	13.8	33.0	31.1	6.3	1.9	0.0	2.3	15.9	2005	précieuses et or (non monétaire)
49.8	6.9	16.9	25.9	23.5	4.0	2.4	0.1	2.9	12.0	2011	(CTCI 27 + 28 + 68 + 667 + 971)
83.9	4.1	1.2	78.6	37.5	3.7	41.0	0.1	45.0	23.3	1995	Combustibles (CTCI 3)
85.0	8.1	1.3	75.5	30.9	2.8	44.6	0.0	52.7	15.6	2005	
79.3	8.6	3.9	66.8	28.6	1.5	38.2	0.0	49.1	13.9	2011	
36.0	0.3	0.8	34.9	34.4	11.0	0.5	0.0	0.5	32.6	1995	Articles manufacturés
51.4	0.3	1.3	49.8	49.2	18.5	0.6	0.0	0.6	45.3	2005	(CTCI 5 à 8 moins 667 et 68)
54.5	0.2	1.4	52.9	51.6	21.8	1.2	0.0	1.3	48.0	2011	
Parts par principaux groupes de produits (en pourcentage)											
100.0	100.0	100.0	100.0	100.0	100.0	100.0	100.0	100.0	100.0	1995	**Total tous produits**
100.0	100.0	100.0	100.0	100.0	100.0	100.0	100.0	100.0	100.0	2005	
100.0	100.0	100.0	100.0	100.0	100.0	100.0	100.0	100.0	100.0	2011	
5.3	7.0	22.1	4.4	4.7	4.4	0.6	28.2	0.5	4.1	1995	Produits alimentaires
3.2	3.1	22.8	2.1	2.3	2.1	0.2	25.2	0.3	1.9	2005	(CTCI 0 + 1 + 22 + 4)
4.0	2.9	20.3	2.6	3.1	1.9	0.2	23.7	0.2	2.2	2011	
3.4	13.2	9.8	2.8	3.0	1.5	0.3	36.4	0.2	2.6	1995	Matières premières
1.5	5.7	4.5	1.1	1.2	0.3	0.1	34.8	0.0	0.9	2005	d'origine agricole
1.8	2.9	3.9	1.5	1.8	0.3	0.1	34.2	0.0	1.3	2011	(CTCI 2 - 22 - 27 - 28)
5.6	33.9	27.3	3.8	3.8	2.5	3.8	16.4	2.5	3.0	1995	Minerais, métaux, pierres
5.8	17.2	30.7	4.1	4.4	2.6	2.0	3.7	2.1	2.6	2005	précieuses et or (non monétaire)
9.0	24.4	40.0	5.4	5.8	2.9	3.2	18.2	3.0	3.5	2011	(CTCI 27 + 28 + 68 + 667 + 971)
12.5	23.8	4.0	12.6	6.6	2.2	81.0	10.0	85.0	4.5	1995	Combustibles (CTCI 3)
18.5	59.8	5.5	17.9	8.3	2.2	89.8	7.2	90.6	4.9	2005	
24.6	51.8	15.7	23.8	12.1	1.8	86.7	6.7	88.6	7.0	2011	
72.6	22.1	36.3	75.8	81.3	89.0	14.3	8.9	11.8	85.2	1995	Articles manufacturés
70.7	12.7	35.5	74.5	83.4	92.4	7.9	29.0	7.0	89.3	2005	(CTCI 5 à 8 moins 667 et 68)
59.4	5.1	19.6	66.1	76.6	92.8	9.9	17.1	8.2	85.3	2011	

Developing economies - Économies en développement

Pour les sources et les notes, se reporter à la fin du tableau 2.2.L.

Product group	Year / Année	World (1) / Monde (1)	Developed economies - Économies développées							Transition economies / Économies en transition
			Total	Europe		Canada	USA / États-Unis	Japan / Japon	Other developed countries / Autres économies développées	
				Total	EU / UE					
Millions of dollars										
All products	1995	117 538	55 170	47 928	43 728	126	4 174	2 568	375	31 869
	2005	360 203	222 141	204 785	186 512	983	9 211	4 185	2 976	69 941
	2011	778 196	421 762	374 896	356 222	4 232	22 165	15 482	4 987	113 834
Share by destination (percentage)										
All products	1995	100.0	46.9	40.8	37.2	0.1	3.6	2.2	0.3	27.1
	2005	100.0	61.7	56.9	51.8	0.3	2.6	1.2	0.8	19.4
	2011	100.0	54.2	48.2	45.8	0.5	2.8	2.0	0.6	14.6
All food items	1995	100.0	32.0	26.7	25.9	0.1	1.8	2.3	1.0	59.2
(SITC 0 + 1 + 22 + 4)	2005	100.0	25.1	21.8	21.1	0.1	0.8	1.3	1.2	53.5
	2011	100.0	23.4	20.7	20.4	0.1	0.4	0.8	1.4	42.3
Agricultural raw materials	1995	100.0	63.7	54.5	52.7	0.0	1.0	8.0	0.1	7.1
(SITC 2 - 22 - 27 - 28)	2005	100.0	48.3	41.5	41.2	0.1	0.6	5.8	0.3	11.4
	2011	100.0	34.7	31.0	30.4	0.1	0.9	2.6	0.2	11.6
Ores, metals, precious stones	1995	100.0	80.5	58.3	50.6	0.0	10.6	11.5	0.1	10.8
and non-monetary gold	2005	100.0	68.9	57.0	46.1	0.2	5.0	5.3	1.4	11.5
(SITC 27 + 28 + 68 + 667 + 971)	2011	100.0	55.3	48.1	41.4	0.3	3.7	2.4	0.9	11.2
Fuels (SITC 3)	1995	100.0	62.3	60.3	54.2	0.0	0.8	0.6	0.5	22.7
	2005	100.0	66.5	63.6	57.6	0.3	1.2	0.7	0.7	8.1
	2011	100.0	73.9	66.4	63.8	0.8	3.1	2.9	0.7	7.4
Manufactured goods	1995	100.0	39.0	31.5	29.5	0.3	6.2	0.8	0.2	30.8
(SITC 5 to 8 less 667 and 68)	2005	100.0	38.0	32.4	31.5	0.4	4.3	0.4	0.5	31.0
	2011	100.0	38.0	33.1	32.1	0.4	3.2	0.8	0.4	32.6
Share by major product group (percentage)										
All products	1995	100.0	100.0	100.0	100.0	100.0	100.0	100.0	100.0	100.0
	2005	100.0	100.0	100.0	100.0	100.0	100.0	100.0	100.0	100.0
	2011	100.0	100.0	100.0	100.0	100.0	100.0	100.0	100.0	100.0
All food items	1995	5.6	3.8	3.7	3.9	4.7	2.8	6.0	17.4	12.2
(SITC 0 + 1 + 22 + 4)	2005	4.0	1.6	1.5	1.6	1.2	1.2	4.4	6.0	11.1
	2011	5.1	2.2	2.2	2.3	0.7	0.8	2.1	11.3	14.8
Agricultural raw materials	1995	5.5	7.5	7.4	7.8	0.6	1.5	20.4	2.5	1.5
(SITC 2 - 22 - 27 - 28)	2005	2.8	2.2	2.1	2.2	1.2	0.7	14.1	0.9	1.7
	2011	2.3	1.4	1.5	1.5	0.3	0.7	3.0	0.6	1.8
Ores, metals, precious stones	1995	10.0	17.2	14.3	13.6	2.3	29.9	52.5	2.7	4.0
and non-monetary gold	2005	7.8	8.7	7.8	6.9	5.1	15.2	35.1	13.3	4.6
(SITC 27 + 28 + 68 + 667 + 971)	2011	6.9	7.0	6.9	6.3	4.0	8.9	8.2	9.4	5.3
Fuels (SITC 3)	1995	32.8	43.5	48.4	47.8	13.3	7.7	9.4	51.7	27.4
	2005	52.9	57.0	59.2	58.9	55.7	24.1	31.4	45.2	22.1
	2011	52.6	71.8	72.6	73.4	79.2	56.8	76.9	57.1	26.8
Manufactured goods	1995	33.3	27.6	25.7	26.4	78.7	58.0	11.7	25.6	37.8
(SITC 5 to 8 less 667 and 68)	2005	26.5	16.3	15.1	16.1	36.4	44.8	9.7	14.9	42.3
	2011	22.4	15.7	15.4	15.7	15.7	25.4	9.3	13.5	49.8

For sources and notes, see end of table 2.2.L.

2.2.K Structure des exportations par partenaires et groupes de produits
Économies en transition

Total	Africa Afrique	America Amérique	Asia Asie Total	Eastern, Southern and South-Eastern Asia / Asie orientale, méridionale et du Sud-Est	China Chine	Western Asia / Asie occidentale	Oceania (2) Océanie (2)	Major petroleum exporters and gas exporters / Principaux exportateurs de pétrole et de gaz	Major manufactured goods exporters / Principaux exportateurs d'articles manufacturés	Year Année	Destinations Groupes de produits
Millions de dollars											
17 407	1 001	2 956	13 449	10 416	4 794	3 033	1	1 158	8 210	1995	**Total tous produits**
67 422	5 610	6 706	55 089	35 862	17 499	19 227	17	8 281	24 572	2005	
175 292	13 414	11 815	150 047	112 593	59 951	37 453	17	18 311	86 221	2011	
Parts par destinations (en pourcentage)											
14.8	0.9	2.5	11.4	8.9	4.1	2.6	0.0	1.0	7.0	1995	**Total tous produits**
18.7	1.6	1.9	15.3	10.0	4.9	5.3	0.0	2.3	6.8	2005	
22.5	1.7	1.5	19.3	14.5	7.7	4.8	0.0	2.4	11.1	2011	
6.6	1.2	0.2	5.2	1.5	0.6	3.7	0.0	0.9	1.1	1995	Produits alimentaires
20.7	7.3	0.2	13.2	6.0	1.1	7.2	0.0	5.9	2.4	2005	(CTCI 0 + 1 + 22 + 4)
33.7	10.0	0.4	23.3	11.9	2.8	11.3	0.0	6.4	5.5	2011	
23.5	1.0	1.4	21.1	15.3	6.6	5.8	0.0	0.6	14.0	1995	Matières premières
40.3	2.4	0.1	37.7	33.1	25.1	4.6	..	2.1	27.6	2005	d'origine agricole
53.6	2.7	0.5	50.4	44.4	37.1	6.0	0.0	3.0	39.4	2011	(CTCI 2 - 22 - 27 - 28)
7.1	0.1	0.1	6.8	5.4	1.1	1.5	0.0	0.4	4.8	1995	Minerais, métaux, pierres
19.6	0.6	0.3	18.8	11.8	7.1	7.0	0.0	1.5	10.4	2005	précieuses et or (non monétaire)
33.4	1.0	0.7	31.7	20.8	16.4	11.0	0.0	0.9	18.8	2011	(CTCI 27 + 28 + 68 + 667 + 971)
9.7	0.1	5.5	4.1	2.2	0.1	1.9	0.0	0.6	1.3	1995	Combustibles (CTCI 3)
9.5	0.2	2.2	7.1	4.3	2.6	2.8	0.0	0.7	3.3	2005	
18.6	0.6	0.7	17.4	14.5	8.4	2.9	0.0	0.6	12.4	2011	
27.8	2.1	1.8	23.9	20.1	10.6	3.8	0.0	2.0	15.7	1995	Articles manufacturés
30.9	3.6	2.6	24.8	18.0	6.1	6.8	0.0	5.0	10.4	2005	(CTCI 5 à 8 moins 667 et 68)
29.3	2.5	4.1	22.7	15.6	5.0	7.1	0.0	5.0	8.7	2011	
Parts par principaux groupes de produits (en pourcentage)											
100.0	100.0	100.0	100.0	100.0	100.0	100.0	100.0	100.0	100.0	1995	**Total tous produits**
100.0	100.0	100.0	100.0	100.0	100.0	100.0	100.0	100.0	100.0	2005	
100.0	100.0	100.0	100.0	100.0	100.0	100.0	100.0	100.0	100.0	2011	
2.5	7.8	0.5	2.6	1.0	0.8	8.1	13.8	5.2	0.9	1995	Produits alimentaires
4.4	18.9	0.4	3.5	2.4	0.9	5.4	0.2	10.3	1.4	2005	(CTCI 0 + 1 + 22 + 4)
7.7	29.8	1.3	6.2	4.2	1.8	12.1	4.3	14.0	2.5	2011	
8.8	6.5	3.2	10.2	9.6	8.9	12.4	16.3	3.6	11.1	1995	Matières premières
6.1	4.4	0.2	7.0	9.4	14.6	2.4	..	2.6	11.4	2005	d'origine agricole
5.4	3.6	0.7	5.9	7.0	10.9	2.8	0.0	2.9	8.1	2011	(CTCI 2 - 22 - 27 - 28)
4.8	1.5	0.4	6.0	6.1	2.8	5.7	0.5	4.2	6.9	1995	Minerais, métaux, pierres
8.1	2.8	1.2	9.5	9.2	11.3	10.2	0.0	5.2	11.8	2005	précieuses et or (non monétaire)
10.3	3.8	3.4	11.4	9.9	14.7	15.7	0.0	2.6	11.7	2011	(CTCI 27 + 28 + 68 + 667 + 971)
21.4	2.4	71.7	11.8	8.1	0.8	24.6	9.9	18.5	6.2	1995	Combustibles (CTCI 3)
26.8	8.3	61.3	24.5	22.9	28.6	27.5	0.3	16.0	25.6	2005	
43.6	18.3	23.3	47.4	52.6	57.2	31.8	1.0	14.5	58.9	2011	
62.5	81.6	24.3	69.4	75.3	86.7	49.2	59.5	68.4	74.9	1995	Articles manufacturés
43.7	60.4	36.8	42.9	47.7	33.4	33.9	99.4	57.5	40.3	2005	(CTCI 5 à 8 moins 667 et 68)
29.1	32.4	61.1	26.3	24.1	14.4	32.8	91.0	47.1	17.5	2011	

Pour les sources et les notes, se reporter à la fin du tableau 2.2.L.

Product group	Year Année	World (1) Monde (1)	Developed economies - Économies développées							Transition economies Économies en transition
			Total	Europe		Canada	USA États-Unis	Japan Japon	Other developed countries Autres économies développées	
				Total	EU UE					

Millions of dollars

Product group	Year	World	Total	Europe Total	EU	Canada	USA	Japan	Other dev.	Transition
All products	1995	116 184	52 228	45 074	43 713	309	4 608	1 557	679	36 018
	2005	269 784	143 116	125 184	121 386	967	8 238	7 386	1 341	74 774
	2011	638 256	311 631	269 482	259 591	2 664	19 064	16 593	3 827	160 556

Share by origin (percentage)

Product group	Year	World	Total	Europe Total	EU	Canada	USA	Japan	Other dev.	Transition
All products	1995	100.0	45.0	38.8	37.6	0.3	4.0	1.3	0.6	31.0
	2005	100.0	53.0	46.4	45.0	0.4	3.1	2.7	0.5	27.7
	2011	100.0	48.8	42.2	40.7	0.4	3.0	2.6	0.6	25.2
All food items	1995	100.0	55.1	45.2	44.0	0.3	8.1	0.0	1.5	23.6
(SITC 0 + 1 + 22 + 4)	2005	100.0	42.2	36.4	33.3	0.5	4.4	0.1	0.8	25.7
	2011	100.0	42.5	36.6	33.6	1.1	3.0	0.1	1.7	23.9
Agricultural raw materials	1995	100.0	36.4	33.0	32.3	0.2	2.4	0.3	0.5	54.4
(SITC 2 - 22 - 27 - 28)	2005	100.0	44.7	40.5	40.3	0.3	3.4	0.3	0.2	42.0
	2011	100.0	45.1	39.2	38.9	0.2	3.4	1.0	1.3	30.4
Ores, metals, precious stones	1995	100.0	28.1	21.5	20.5	0.4	2.8	0.0	3.4	49.8
and non-monetary gold	2005	100.0	31.1	25.2	23.6	0.3	1.6	0.2	3.9	49.8
(SITC 27 + 28 + 68 + 667 + 971)	2011	100.0	32.0	28.2	25.7	0.1	0.5	0.1	3.1	48.1
Fuels (SITC 3)	1995	100.0	14.5	13.5	12.7	0.0	0.7	0.2	0.0	81.1
	2005	100.0	9.7	9.3	8.8	0.0	0.2	0.1	0.0	87.9
	2011	100.0	14.7	12.8	12.2	0.0	1.7	0.1	0.1	81.4
Manufactured goods	1995	100.0	63.5	55.6	53.9	0.4	4.5	2.6	0.4	22.3
(SITC 5 to 8 less 667 and 68)	2005	100.0	62.6	54.8	53.5	0.4	3.3	3.8	0.3	17.7
	2011	100.0	56.3	48.8	47.4	0.4	3.1	3.6	0.3	15.1

Share by major commodity group (percentage)

Product group	Year	World	Total	Europe Total	EU	Canada	USA	Japan	Other dev.	Transition
All products	1995	100.0	100.0	100.0	100.0	100.0	100.0	100.0	100.0	100.0
	2005	100.0	100.0	100.0	100.0	100.0	100.0	100.0	100.0	100.0
	2011	100.0	100.0	100.0	100.0	100.0	100.0	100.0	100.0	100.0
All food items	1995	17.5	21.5	20.4	20.5	18.0	35.8	0.6	45.4	13.3
(SITC 0 + 1 + 22 + 4)	2005	12.3	9.8	9.7	9.1	15.7	17.8	0.4	20.9	11.4
	2011	11.8	10.2	10.2	9.7	31.2	12.0	0.3	33.3	11.1
Agricultural raw materials	1995	1.3	1.0	1.1	1.1	0.8	0.8	0.3	1.1	2.2
(SITC 2 - 22 - 27 - 28)	2005	1.2	1.0	1.0	1.0	1.1	1.3	0.1	0.4	1.8
	2011	1.2	1.1	1.1	1.1	0.6	1.3	0.5	2.5	1.4
Ores, metals, precious stones	1995	2.9	1.8	1.6	1.6	4.0	2.0	0.0	16.6	4.6
and non-monetary gold	2005	3.1	1.8	1.7	1.7	2.5	1.6	0.2	24.6	5.7
(SITC 27 + 28 + 68 + 667 + 971)	2011	2.5	1.6	1.7	1.6	0.6	0.4	0.1	12.9	4.8
Fuels (SITC 3)	1995	11.2	3.6	3.9	3.8	1.0	2.1	1.8	0.5	29.2
	2005	10.8	2.0	2.2	2.1	0.2	0.8	0.4	0.2	34.1
	2011	12.0	3.6	3.6	3.6	1.2	7.0	0.5	1.6	39.0
Manufactured goods	1995	49.2	69.4	70.4	70.5	75.3	55.3	95.2	34.2	35.4
(SITC 5 to 8 less 667 and 68)	2005	71.1	83.9	84.0	84.6	76.6	76.5	98.3	42.1	45.5
	2011	71.0	81.8	82.1	82.7	66.1	74.4	98.0	38.1	42.5

For sources and notes, see end of table 2.2.L.

2.2.K Structure des importations par partenaires et groupes de produits
Économies en transition

| | Developing economies - Économies en développement | | | | | | Oceania (2) / Océanie (2) | Major petroleum exporters and gas exporters / Principaux exportateurs de pétrole et de gaz | Major manufactured goods exporters / Principaux exportateurs d'articles manufacturés | Year / Année | Origines |
Total	Africa / Afrique	America / Amérique	Asia / Asie — Total	Eastern, Southern and South-Eastern Asia / Asie orientale, méridionale et du Sud-Est	China / Chine	Western Asia / Asie occidentale					Groupes de produits
Millions de dollars											
12 552	814	1 933	9 798	7 452	1 819	2 346	6	1 096	5 130	1995	**Total tous produits**
50 718	1 825	6 880	41 988	35 081	20 701	6 907	24	1 803	31 397	2005	
163 532	5 076	15 328	143 112	123 698	82 801	19 414	16	5 056	111 349	2011	
Parts par origines (en pourcentage)											
10.8	0.7	1.7	8.4	6.4	1.6	2.0	0.0	0.9	4.4	1995	**Total tous produits**
18.8	0.7	2.6	15.6	13.0	7.7	2.6	0.0	0.7	11.6	2005	
25.6	0.8	2.4	22.4	19.4	13.0	3.0	0.0	0.8	17.4	2011	
20.3	1.3	7.8	11.2	8.2	2.7	3.0	0.0	1.4	3.8	1995	Produits alimentaires
32.0	2.6	17.4	12.0	9.2	3.0	2.7	0.0	0.8	5.4	2005	(CTCI 0 + 1 + 22 + 4)
33.6	3.1	15.5	15.0	11.6	4.0	3.3	0.0	1.0	6.3	2011	
7.7	0.3	1.3	6.1	5.7	0.9	0.4	..	0.1	2.1	1995	Matières premières
13.2	1.1	3.9	8.1	7.4	1.2	0.7	0.0	0.3	5.2	2005	d'origine agricole
24.5	2.8	7.0	14.7	13.0	4.1	1.7	0.0	0.6	8.4	2011	(CTCI 2 - 22 - 27 - 28)
21.2	3.8	5.4	12.0	10.5	1.9	1.6	0.0	1.7	2.6	1995	Minerais, métaux, pierres
19.0	7.1	3.4	8.2	5.9	3.1	2.3	0.2	1.2	3.6	2005	précieuses et or (non monétaire)
19.8	5.7	2.3	11.9	8.4	5.7	3.5	0.0	0.7	6.6	2011	(CTCI 27 + 28 + 68 + 667 + 971)
4.0	2.1	0.2	1.8	1.4	0.3	0.4	..	2.5	0.8	1995	Combustibles (CTCI 3)
2.4	0.3	0.2	2.0	1.3	0.8	0.7	..	0.4	1.0	2005	
3.8	0.1	1.6	2.1	1.6	0.8	0.6	0.0	1.9	1.2	2011	
12.2	0.2	0.2	11.7	8.9	2.0	2.8	0.0	0.6	7.2	1995	Articles manufacturés
19.4	0.1	0.3	18.9	16.1	10.0	2.9	0.0	0.7	15.0	2005	(CTCI 5 à 8 moins 667 et 68)
28.6	0.3	0.3	28.0	24.5	17.2	3.4	0.0	0.6	22.9	2011	
Parts par principaux groupes de produits (en pourcentage)											
100.0	100.0	100.0	100.0	100.0	100.0	100.0	100.0	100.0	100.0	1995	**Total tous produits**
100.0	100.0	100.0	100.0	100.0	100.0	100.0	100.0	100.0	100.0	2005	
100.0	100.0	100.0	100.0	100.0	100.0	100.0	100.0	100.0	100.0	2011	
32.9	32.4	82.1	23.3	22.5	30.8	25.9	17.5	26.0	15.0	1995	Produits alimentaires
20.9	47.3	84.0	9.5	8.7	4.7	13.2	14.8	15.4	5.7	2005	(CTCI 0 + 1 + 22 + 4)
15.4	45.9	75.7	7.9	7.1	3.6	12.9	80.2	14.2	4.2	2011	
0.9	0.5	1.0	0.9	1.1	0.7	0.2	..	0.1	0.6	1995	Matières premières
0.8	1.9	1.8	0.6	0.7	0.2	0.3	0.4	0.5	0.5	2005	d'origine agricole
1.1	4.1	3.4	0.8	0.8	0.4	0.6	0.0	1.0	0.6	2011	(CTCI 2 - 22 - 27 - 28)
5.6	15.6	9.3	4.1	4.7	3.5	2.2	0.0	5.2	1.7	1995	Minerais, métaux, pierres
3.2	33.1	4.3	1.7	1.4	1.3	2.8	78.3	5.5	1.0	2005	précieuses et or (non monétaire)
1.9	17.7	2.4	1.3	1.1	1.1	2.9	0.2	2.0	0.9	2011	(CTCI 27 + 28 + 68 + 667 + 971)
4.2	32.9	1.0	2.4	2.4	1.8	2.3	..	30.0	2.0	1995	Combustibles (CTCI 3)
1.4	4.6	0.6	1.4	1.0	1.1	2.9	..	6.6	0.9	2005	
1.8	1.6	8.0	1.1	1.0	0.8	2.3	0.9	28.9	0.8	2011	
55.5	17.2	6.0	68.4	68.1	63.2	69.1	81.7	33.4	80.1	1995	Articles manufacturés
73.3	12.4	8.7	86.6	88.0	92.7	79.5	5.8	69.5	91.8	2005	(CTCI 5 à 8 moins 667 et 68)
79.4	30.1	10.3	88.5	89.8	93.9	80.2	18.4	51.5	93.2	2011	

Pour les sources et les notes, se reporter à la fin du tableau 2.2.L.

2

Product group / Destination	Year / Année	World (1) / Monde (1)	Developed economies - Économies développées							Transition economies / Économies en transition
			Europe		Canada	USA / États-Unis	Japan / Japon	Other developed countries / Autres économies développées		
			Total	Total	EU / UE					

Millions of dollars										
All products	1995	3 571 460	2 622 250	1 835 015	1 724 666	148 777	432 214	135 845	70 400	53 047
	2005	6 299 815	4 708 333	3 391 741	3 215 545	258 069	801 762	147 622	109 139	142 042
	2011	9 518 978	6 485 326	4 885 246	4 583 765	338 998	891 439	205 282	164 361	292 526

Share by destination (percentage)										
All products	1995	100.0	73.4	51.4	48.3	4.2	12.1	3.8	2.0	1.5
	2005	100.0	74.7	53.8	51.0	4.1	12.7	2.3	1.7	2.3
	2011	100.0	68.1	51.3	48.2	3.6	9.4	2.2	1.7	3.1
All food items	1995	100.0	73.6	56.9	55.0	2.6	5.2	7.7	1.1	3.9
(SITC 0 + 1 + 22 + 4)	2005	100.0	78.8	61.3	59.4	3.4	7.7	5.1	1.3	3.0
	2011	100.0	73.0	58.5	56.6	3.3	5.7	4.0	1.5	3.5
Agricultural raw materials	1995	100.0	75.4	47.8	45.5	2.9	12.1	11.4	1.1	0.5
(SITC 2 - 22 - 27 - 28)	2005	100.0	70.0	47.6	45.6	3.1	13.5	4.9	0.9	1.3
	2011	100.0	57.7	45.8	44.2	2.1	5.6	3.3	0.8	2.0
Ores, metals, precious stones	1995	100.0	73.6	48.4	43.5	3.4	11.6	6.8	3.5	0.5
and non-monetary gold	2005	100.0	67.8	45.2	41.1	2.7	12.3	3.9	3.6	0.9
(SITC 27 + 28 + 68 + 667 + 971)	2011	100.0	60.3	44.7	37.9	2.2	7.8	3.5	2.1	0.6
Fuels (SITC 3)	1995	100.0	80.8	55.0	51.5	2.7	18.0	4.4	0.7	1.4
	2005	100.0	84.5	55.3	52.8	3.3	23.1	2.3	0.6	0.6
	2011	100.0	74.3	52.3	49.3	2.7	15.8	2.6	0.8	1.4
Manufactured goods	1995	100.0	72.6	50.2	47.1	4.6	12.7	3.0	2.1	1.3
(SITC 5 to 8 less 667 and 68)	2005	100.0	73.7	53.4	50.6	4.4	12.2	1.9	1.8	2.5
	2011	100.0	68.1	51.6	48.6	3.8	9.3	1.6	1.8	3.6

Share by major product group (percentage)										
All products	1995	100.0	100.0	100.0	100.0	100.0	100.0	100.0	100.0	100.0
	2005	100.0	100.0	100.0	100.0	100.0	100.0	100.0	100.0	100.0
	2011	100.0	100.0	100.0	100.0	100.0	100.0	100.0	100.0	100.0
All food items	1995	8.7	8.7	9.6	9.9	5.4	3.7	17.5	4.9	22.7
(SITC 0 + 1 + 22 + 4)	2005	7.0	7.4	7.9	8.1	5.7	4.2	15.1	5.3	9.3
	2011	8.5	9.1	9.7	10.0	7.9	5.2	15.7	7.3	9.7
Agricultural raw materials	1995	2.6	2.6	2.4	2.4	1.8	2.6	7.7	1.4	0.9
(SITC 2 - 22 - 27 - 28)	2005	1.7	1.6	1.5	1.5	1.3	1.8	3.5	0.9	1.0
	2011	1.7	1.5	1.6	1.6	1.0	1.1	2.7	0.8	1.1
Ores, metals, precious stones	1995	4.1	4.1	3.8	3.7	3.3	3.9	7.3	7.2	1.5
and non-monetary gold	2005	4.2	3.8	3.5	3.4	2.8	4.1	7.1	8.9	1.7
(SITC 27 + 28 + 68 + 667 + 971)	2011	6.5	5.8	5.7	5.1	4.1	5.4	10.7	7.9	1.4
Fuels (SITC 3)	1995	3.4	3.7	3.6	3.6	2.2	5.0	3.9	1.1	3.2
	2005	6.7	7.6	6.9	6.9	5.3	12.1	6.7	2.1	1.9
	2011	9.2	10.0	9.4	9.4	7.1	15.6	11.2	4.1	4.1
Manufactured goods	1995	76.8	75.9	75.0	74.8	84.2	80.8	61.0	80.3	66.6
(SITC 5 to 8 less 667 and 68)	2005	76.7	75.6	76.1	76.0	81.6	73.8	62.9	78.5	83.9
	2011	70.1	70.1	70.4	70.7	75.5	69.5	51.2	74.7	81.5

Source:
UNCTAD secretariat calculations, based on UNCTAD, *UNCTADstat* Merchandise Trade Matrix

Notes:

(1) Includes special category exports', ship stores and bunkers and other exports of minor importance whose destination could not be determined.

(2) It is recognized that the structure of trade and partner distribution for certain countries and years might vary. In this regard, reader should know the coverage and limitations of the main principal data used in this table. For further information, please visit
http://comtrade.un.org/db/help/uReadMeFirst.aspx.

2.2.L Structure des exportations par partenaires et groupes de produits
Économies développées

Developing economies - Économies en développement										Year	Destinations
			Asia Asie				Oceania (2)	Major petroleum exporters and gas exporters	Major manufactured goods exporters	Année	
Total	Africa Afrique	America Amérique	Total	Eastern, Southern and South-Eastern Asia Asie orientale, méridionale et du Sud-Est	China Chine	Western Asia Asie occidentale	Océanie (2)	Principaux exportateurs de pétrole et de gaz	Principaux exportateurs d'articles manufacturés		Groupes de produits
Millions de dollars											
833 170	80 236	169 164	579 848	500 024	59 497	79 824	3 923	75 777	473 786	1995	Total tous produits
1 416 460	135 313	304 905	969 916	784 344	209 521	185 572	6 326	167 256	803 557	2005	
2 673 411	244 363	578 690	1 839 339	1 505 610	562 171	333 728	11 019	279 365	1 495 987	2011	
Parts par destinations (en pourcentage)											
23.3	2.2	4.7	16.2	14.0	1.7	2.2	0.1	2.1	13.3	1995	Total tous produits
22.5	2.1	4.8	15.4	12.5	3.3	2.9	0.1	2.7	12.8	2005	
28.1	2.6	6.1	19.3	15.8	5.9	3.5	0.1	2.9	15.7	2011	
19.1	3.5	4.1	11.3	8.6	1.2	2.7	0.2	3.2	8.1	1995	Produits alimentaires
17.2	2.9	4.4	9.6	7.2	1.6	2.4	0.2	2.9	8.0	2005	(CTCI 0 + 1 + 22 + 4)
23.2	3.9	5.0	14.2	11.0	3.5	3.2	0.2	3.7	11.0	2011	
23.1	2.0	3.4	17.7	16.1	3.6	1.6	0.0	1.1	14.5	1995	Matières premières
27.8	2.0	4.1	21.6	19.2	9.5	2.4	0.1	1.2	18.3	2005	d'origine agricole
40.3	2.6	4.5	33.1	30.1	18.3	3.0	0.0	1.6	27.5	2011	(CTCI 2 - 22 - 27 - 28)
22.9	1.0	1.7	20.1	18.3	1.3	1.8	0.0	0.9	15.2	1995	Minerais, métaux, pierres
28.9	1.1	2.1	25.7	23.5	7.5	2.2	0.0	1.3	18.7	2005	précieuses et or (non monétaire)
37.7	1.2	1.9	34.6	31.8	14.3	2.8	0.0	1.2	27.3	2011	(CTCI 27 + 28 + 68 + 667 + 971)
12.6	1.4	3.7	7.3	6.4	0.4	0.9	0.2	0.8	6.2	1995	Combustibles (CTCI 3)
10.8	1.7	3.5	5.5	4.2	0.6	1.3	0.1	1.0	4.9	2005	
20.8	2.9	8.1	9.8	7.7	1.6	2.0	0.1	1.6	9.4	2011	
24.5	2.2	5.1	17.1	14.8	1.7	2.3	0.1	2.1	14.2	1995	Articles manufacturés
23.4	2.2	5.2	16.0	12.8	3.3	3.2	0.1	2.9	13.3	2005	(CTCI 5 à 8 moins 667 et 68)
28.2	2.5	6.3	19.2	15.5	5.7	3.7	0.1	3.1	15.7	2011	
Parts par principaux groupes de produits (en pourcentage)											
100.0	100.0	100.0	100.0	100.0	100.0	100.0	100.0	100.0	100.0	1995	Total tous produits
100.0	100.0	100.0	100.0	100.0	100.0	100.0	100.0	100.0	100.0	2005	
100.0	100.0	100.0	100.0	100.0	100.0	100.0	100.0	100.0	100.0	2011	
7.1	13.7	7.5	6.0	5.3	6.5	10.4	15.2	13.0	5.3	1995	Produits alimentaires
5.3	9.4	6.4	4.4	4.0	3.3	5.8	14.0	7.5	4.4	2005	(CTCI 0 + 1 + 22 + 4)
7.0	12.8	6.9	6.3	5.9	5.0	7.8	13.8	10.8	5.9	2011	
2.5	2.3	1.8	2.8	3.0	5.6	1.9	1.1	1.4	2.8	1995	Matières premières
2.1	1.6	1.4	2.3	2.6	4.7	1.4	1.6	0.8	2.4	2005	d'origine agricole
2.5	1.8	1.3	3.0	3.3	5.4	1.5	0.7	0.9	3.1	2011	(CTCI 2 - 22 - 27 - 28)
4.0	1.9	1.5	5.1	5.3	3.1	3.3	0.6	1.8	4.7	1995	Minerais, métaux, pierres
5.4	2.1	1.8	7.0	7.9	9.5	3.2	0.6	2.1	6.2	2005	précieuses et or (non monétaire)
8.8	3.1	2.1	11.7	13.1	15.8	5.2	0.9	2.6	11.4	2011	(CTCI 27 + 28 + 68 + 667 + 971)
1.8	2.1	2.6	1.5	1.5	0.7	1.4	7.1	1.2	1.6	1995	Combustibles (CTCI 3)
3.2	5.2	4.9	2.4	2.3	1.1	2.9	7.5	2.6	2.6	2005	
6.8	10.3	12.2	4.7	4.5	2.5	5.4	5.4	4.9	5.5	2011	
80.7	76.6	82.6	80.7	81.2	79.1	77.6	73.1	77.5	82.3	1995	Articles manufacturés
79.7	77.6	81.6	79.4	78.6	76.7	83.0	70.5	83.0	80.2	2005	(CTCI 5 à 8 moins 667 et 68)
70.4	68.4	72.9	69.8	68.7	67.4	74.8	73.9	75.2	69.8	2011	

Source :
Calculs du secrétariat de la CNUCED, basés sur la matrice du commerce de marchandises de *UNCTADstat* de la CNUCED

Notes :

(1) Y compris les exportations de catégorie spéciale, approvisionnements des navires et combustibles de soute et autres exportations de moindre importance dont la destination n'a pas pu être déterminée.

(2) Il est reconnu que la structure du commerce et la distribution au niveau partenaire pour certains pays et sur certaines années peuvent varier. À cet égard, le lecteur devrait connaître la couverture ainsi que les limites des données principales utilisées dans ce tableau. Pour de plus amples renseignements, veuillez visiter http://comtrade.un.org/db/help/uReadMeFirst.aspx.

2.2.L Import structure by partner and product group
Developed economies

Product group	Year / Année	World (1) / Monde (1)	Developed economies - Économies développées							Transition economies / Économies en transition
			Total	Europe		Canada	USA / États-Unis	Japan / Japon	Other developed countries / Autres économies développées	
				Total	EU / UE					
Millions of dollars										
All products	1995	3 573 361	2 604 167	1 775 218	1 660 281	177 666	362 908	234 357	54 019	66 282
	2005	7 048 788	4 567 491	3 346 776	3 138 552	329 759	504 255	286 151	100 549	224 549
	2011	10 329 468	6 156 206	4 680 845	4 366 570	378 240	649 275	287 980	159 867	449 810
Share by origin (percentage)										
All products	1995	100.0	72.9	49.7	46.5	5.0	10.2	6.6	1.5	1.9
	2005	100.0	64.8	47.5	44.5	4.7	7.2	4.1	1.4	3.2
	2011	100.0	59.6	45.3	42.3	3.7	6.3	2.8	1.5	4.4
All food items	1995	100.0	69.2	51.2	49.1	3.7	10.8	0.2	3.3	1.1
(SITC 0 + 1 + 22 + 4)	2005	100.0	70.6	55.3	53.3	4.1	7.1	0.2	3.9	1.1
	2011	100.0	68.6	55.4	52.9	3.8	6.4	0.1	2.9	1.4
Agricultural raw materials	1995	100.0	71.7	37.4	36.0	16.0	13.3	0.5	4.5	4.9
(SITC 2 - 22 - 27 - 28)	2005	100.0	69.1	44.1	43.1	13.7	7.7	0.6	3.0	4.7
	2011	100.0	62.1	45.5	44.4	6.8	6.6	0.8	2.4	4.2
Ores, metals, precious stones	1995	100.0	62.8	39.7	34.0	8.0	7.3	0.6	7.2	8.2
and non-monetary gold	2005	100.0	58.6	37.6	33.2	6.9	5.6	0.5	7.9	8.3
(SITC 27 + 28 + 68 + 667 + 971)	2011	100.0	57.9	38.2	32.7	6.7	5.4	0.8	6.9	5.9
Fuels (SITC 3)	1995	100.0	36.4	25.4	17.6	6.0	2.4	0.1	2.6	8.0
	2005	100.0	36.2	25.9	19.2	6.9	1.5	0.1	1.8	13.7
	2011	100.0	34.8	24.0	18.8	6.0	2.4	0.2	2.3	17.5
Manufactured goods	1995	100.0	77.3	52.2	49.5	4.3	11.1	8.9	0.7	0.6
(SITC 5 to 8 less 667 and 68)	2005	100.0	69.9	51.5	49.3	3.8	8.4	5.6	0.7	0.8
	2011	100.0	65.2	50.4	48.0	2.6	7.4	4.1	0.7	1.0
Share by major product group (percentage)										
All products	1995	100.0	100.0	100.0	100.0	100.0	100.0	100.0	100.0	100.0
	2005	100.0	100.0	100.0	100.0	100.0	100.0	100.0	100.0	100.0
	2011	100.0	100.0	100.0	100.0	100.0	100.0	100.0	100.0	100.0
All food items	1995	9.2	8.7	9.5	9.7	6.8	9.8	0.3	19.9	5.5
(SITC 0 + 1 + 22 + 4)	2005	6.9	7.6	8.1	8.3	6.1	6.9	0.3	19.1	2.5
	2011	7.9	9.1	9.6	9.9	8.1	8.0	0.4	14.6	2.5
Agricultural raw materials	1995	2.9	2.8	2.2	2.2	9.2	3.8	0.2	8.5	7.6
(SITC 2 - 22 - 27 - 28)	2005	1.5	1.7	1.4	1.5	4.5	1.7	0.2	3.3	2.3
	2011	1.4	1.5	1.4	1.5	2.7	1.5	0.4	2.2	1.4
Ores, metals, precious stones	1995	5.0	4.3	4.0	3.7	8.1	3.6	0.5	23.8	22.3
and non-monetary gold	2005	4.3	3.9	3.4	3.2	6.3	3.3	0.6	23.9	11.1
(SITC 27 + 28 + 68 + 667 + 971)	2011	5.5	5.3	4.6	4.2	10.0	4.7	1.5	24.2	7.4
Fuels (SITC 3)	1995	7.4	3.7	3.8	2.8	8.9	1.7	0.1	12.5	31.9
	2005	14.0	7.8	7.6	6.0	20.8	2.9	0.5	17.7	60.1
	2011	18.0	10.5	9.5	8.0	29.4	6.9	1.3	26.4	72.4
Manufactured goods	1995	71.7	76.1	75.4	76.4	62.5	78.6	97.2	32.6	25.0
(SITC 5 to 8 less 667 and 68)	2005	70.2	75.7	76.0	77.7	57.2	82.2	96.4	33.5	17.4
	2011	64.9	71.0	72.2	73.8	46.2	76.0	94.8	30.8	15.0

Source:
UNCTAD secretariat calculations, based on UNCTAD, *UNCTADstat* Merchandise Trade Matrix

Notes:

(1) Includes special category exports', ship stores and bunkers and other exports of minor importance whose destination could not be determined.

(2) It is recognized that the structure of trade and partner distribution for certain countries and years might vary. In this regard, reader should know the coverage and limitations of the main principal data used in this table. For further information, please visit
http://comtrade.un.org/db/help/uReadMeFirst.aspx.

Total	Africa Afrique	America Amérique	Asia Asie Total	Eastern, Southern and South-Eastern Asia / Asie orientale, méridionale et du Sud-Est	China Chine	Western Asia / Asie occidentale	Oceania (2) Océanie (2)	Major petroleum exporters and gas exporters / Principaux exportateurs de pétrole et de gaz	Major manufactured goods exporters / Principaux exportateurs d'articles manufacturés	Year Année	Origines / Groupes de produits
Developing economies - Économies en développement											
Millions de dollars											
846 423	83 232	174 868	584 477	511 608	127 476	72 870	3 845	108 316	484 538	1995	Total tous produits
2 207 446	219 929	437 999	1 544 544	1 306 306	638 803	238 238	4 974	351 024	1 291 751	2005	
3 632 612	346 650	698 668	2 578 229	2 151 191	1 182 116	427 038	9 064	595 280	2 092 447	2011	
Parts par origines (en pourcentage)											
23.7	2.3	4.9	16.4	14.3	3.6	2.0	0.1	3.0	13.6	1995	Total tous produits
31.3	3.1	6.2	21.9	18.5	9.1	3.4	0.1	5.0	18.3	2005	
35.2	3.4	6.8	25.0	20.8	11.4	4.1	0.1	5.8	20.3	2011	
28.1	3.9	12.3	11.6	10.7	2.2	0.9	0.3	0.4	8.7	1995	Produits alimentaires
28.1	3.7	13.2	11.0	9.8	3.2	1.2	0.2	0.4	8.6	2005	(CTCI 0 + 1 + 22 + 4)
29.8	3.4	14.2	12.0	11.1	3.1	0.9	0.2	0.3	9.5	2011	
22.5	3.6	6.0	12.4	11.9	1.9	0.5	0.4	0.5	8.9	1995	Matières premières
26.0	4.0	8.5	13.3	12.8	3.4	0.5	0.1	0.3	9.1	2005	d'origine agricole
33.6	3.8	8.8	21.0	20.4	4.1	0.5	0.1	0.3	12.1	2011	(CTCI 2 - 22 - 27 - 28)
25.5	6.3	10.1	8.5	7.6	1.3	0.8	0.7	1.2	4.9	1995	Minerais, métaux, pierres
32.6	8.4	12.5	11.2	9.7	2.6	1.5	0.5	1.5	6.4	2005	précieuses et or (non monétaire)
35.5	6.9	15.8	12.0	9.9	2.6	2.1	0.8	1.6	8.3	2011	(CTCI 27 + 28 + 68 + 667 + 971)
52.2	13.5	8.9	29.6	10.5	1.2	19.2	0.2	36.0	5.9	1995	Combustibles (CTCI 3)
47.5	13.5	10.0	23.9	7.4	0.6	16.5	0.1	32.8	5.8	2005	
45.1	11.8	8.7	24.5	7.6	0.2	16.9	0.1	30.0	5.8	2011	
20.7	0.6	3.2	16.8	16.2	4.4	0.6	0.0	0.3	16.1	1995	Articles manufacturés
29.1	0.8	4.4	24.0	22.7	12.1	1.3	0.0	0.4	23.0	2005	(CTCI 5 à 8 moins 667 et 68)
33.6	0.8	4.6	28.2	26.9	16.7	1.3	0.0	0.3	26.9	2011	
Parts par principaux groupes de produits (en pourcentage)											
100.0	100.0	100.0	100.0	100.0	100.0	100.0	100.0	100.0	100.0	1995	Total tous produits
100.0	100.0	100.0	100.0	100.0	100.0	100.0	100.0	100.0	100.0	2005	
100.0	100.0	100.0	100.0	100.0	100.0	100.0	100.0	100.0	100.0	2011	
10.9	15.6	23.2	6.5	6.8	5.6	4.1	25.6	1.1	5.9	1995	Produits alimentaires
6.2	8.2	14.8	3.5	3.7	2.4	2.4	21.7	0.6	3.3	2005	(CTCI 0 + 1 + 22 + 4)
6.7	8.1	16.5	3.8	4.2	2.2	1.7	20.9	0.4	3.7	2011	
2.7	4.5	3.5	2.2	2.4	1.5	0.7	11.4	0.4	1.9	1995	Matières premières
1.3	2.0	2.1	0.9	1.1	0.6	0.2	2.5	0.1	0.8	2005	d'origine agricole
1.4	1.7	1.9	1.2	1.4	0.5	0.2	1.2	0.1	0.9	2011	(CTCI 2 - 22 - 27 - 28)
5.4	13.5	10.4	2.6	2.7	1.9	2.0	32.4	2.0	1.8	1995	Minerais, métaux, pierres
4.5	11.6	8.6	2.2	2.2	1.2	1.8	32.7	1.3	1.5	2005	précieuses et or (non monétaire)
5.5	11.3	12.8	2.6	2.6	1.2	2.7	48.3	1.5	2.2	2011	(CTCI 27 + 28 + 68 + 667 + 971)
16.3	42.8	13.4	13.4	5.4	2.5	69.5	15.0	87.8	3.2	1995	Combustibles (CTCI 3)
21.2	60.5	22.6	15.3	5.6	0.9	68.4	18.6	92.3	4.4	2005	
23.1	63.4	23.2	17.7	6.6	0.3	73.6	15.1	93.8	5.2	2011	
62.7	19.4	46.9	73.8	81.2	87.7	22.4	14.8	6.4	85.3	1995	Articles manufacturés
65.2	17.0	49.4	76.7	85.9	94.0	26.2	21.9	5.2	88.2	2005	(CTCI 5 à 8 moins 667 et 68)
62.0	15.1	43.8	73.4	83.8	95.0	21.0	13.5	3.8	86.4	2011	

Source :
Calculs du secrétariat de la CNUCED, basés sur la matrice du commerce de marchandises de *UNCTADstat* de la CNUCED

Notes :

(1) Y compris les exportations de catégorie spéciale, approvisionnements des navires et combustibles de soute et autres exportations de moindre importance dont la destination n'a pas pu être déterminée.

(2) Il est reconnu que la structure du commerce et la distribution au niveau partenaire pour certains pays et sur certaines années peuvent varier. À cet égard, le lecteur devrait connaître la couverture ainsi que les limites des données principales utilisées dans ce tableau. Pour de plus amples renseignements, veuillez visiter http://comtrade.un.org/db/help/uReadMeFirst.aspx.

3

INTERNATIONAL **MERCHANDISE** TRADE BY PRODUCT

COMMERCE INTERNATIONAL DES **MARCHANDISES** PAR PRODUITS

Country or territory / Pays ou territoires	Year / Année	Total value (millions of dollars) / Valeur totale (millions de dollars)	By main SITC Revision 3 product group (percentage) / Par principaux groupes de produits de la CTCI Révision 3 (en pourcentage)					Of which: / dont :		
			All food items / Produits alimentaires	Agricultural raw materials / Matières premières agricoles	Fuels / Combustibles	Ores, metals, precious stones and non monetary gold / Minerais, métaux, pierres précieuses et or (non monétaire)	Manu-factured goods / Articles manu-facturés	Chemical products / Produits chimiques	Machinery and transport equipment / Machines et matériel de transport	Other manu-factured goods / Articles manu-facturés divers
			0 + 1 + 22 + 4	2 - (22 + 27 + 28)	3	27 + 28 + 68 + 667 + 971	5 + 6 +7 + 8- (667 + 68)	5	7	6 + 8 - (667 + 68)
Afghanistan	1995	(e)166	53.3	26.0	0.1	2.6	16.7	3.1	2.5	11.0
	2005	(e)384	36.6	18.6	9.9	7.2	14.0	2.2	6.0	5.8
	2011	(e)350	31.3	8.5	4.5	9.4	44.1	8.4	17.2	18.6
Albania - Albanie	1995	(e)202	11.2	12.4	2.7	12.3	60.0	1.7	3.4	54.9
	2005	(e)658	5.4	4.7	6.0	8.9	74.0	0.7	5.1	68.2
	2011	(e)1 948	3.8	2.7	17.8	15.0	60.4	1.8	7.2	51.5
Algeria - Algérie	1995	9 357	1.2	0.1	95.2	0.5	3.0	1.2	0.4	1.4
	2005	46 002	0.2	0.0	98.4	0.5	1.0	0.7	0.1	0.2
	2011	73 436	0.5	0.0	98.3	0.3	0.9	0.7	0.0	0.2
American Samoa - Samoa américaines	1995	272	..	..	..	..	..	..	..	..
	2005	(e)374	24.5	23.1	0.4	8.2	39.3	4.0	26.2	9.1
	2011	(e)310	23.9	1.4	0.0	6.6	68.0	31.2	13.6	23.2
Andorra - Andorre	1995	48	6.5	1.6	0.2	2.3	89.3	3.6	33.8	52.0
	2005	143	28.9	0.5	0.0	2.2	67.4	3.6	39.7	24.1
	2011	(e)77	1.3	0.0	0.0	0.6	59.2	1.6	29.1	28.4
Angola	1995	(e)3 723	1.0	0.0	93.9	4.5	0.5	0.0	0.2	0.3
	2005	(e)24 109	0.2	0.0	96.3	3.2	0.2	0.0	0.2	0.0
	2011	(e)65 689	0.0	0.0	98.9	0.9	0.1	0.0	0.1	0.0
Anguilla	1995	(e)1	13.8	2.2	3.2	1.8	78.1	16.1	29.2	32.8
	2005	(e)15	25.6	0.1	5.7	0.1	59.6	25.5	15.5	18.6
	2011	(e)16	15.6	0.3	0.4	1.1	76.4	6.1	42.3	28.0
Antigua and Barbuda - Antigua-et-Barbuda	1995	(e)53	18.8	4.2	47.4	4.4	23.2	6.3	11.0	5.8
	2005	(e)83	4.1	0.1	10.3	0.1	84.3	1.5	80.3	2.5
	2011	(e)43	9.1	0.6	3.3	0.7	86.0	7.7	51.7	26.6
Argentina - Argentine	1995	20 963	49.8	4.3	10.3	1.6	33.9	6.4	10.9	16.6
	2005	40 106	46.5	1.4	16.4	3.6	30.6	8.5	10.7	11.4
	2011	83 950	52.7	1.2	5.9	6.6	31.5	8.9	15.9	6.7
Armenia - Arménie	1995	(e)271	12.8	4.9	5.5	22.6	53.0	3.3	27.0	22.7
	2005	(e)937	12.2	0.8	2.5	40.1	43.5	0.4	3.2	39.9
	2011	(e)1 320	17.4	0.9	5.8	48.6	26.5	2.0	5.7	18.7
Aruba	1995	(e)1 347	2.9	0.1	93.6	0.4	2.0	0.9	0.5	0.5
	2005	(e)4 416	2.5	0.0	92.7	0.8	1.5	0.1	1.0	0.4
	2011	(e)5 179	7.6	0.0	89.7	0.3	1.0	0.1	0.3	0.5
Australia - Australie	1995	53 001	19.6	8.1	16.7	26.4	26.5	4.1	12.8	9.6
	2005	105 751	16.1	3.9	25.6	27.4	20.2	4.6	9.5	6.0
	2011	245 631	10.8	3.0	28.0	42.8	11.4	3.0	4.8	3.6
Austria - Autriche	1995	57 583	3.8	2.9	1.0	3.1	81.6	7.2	36.0	38.3
	2005	117 722	6.2	1.8	4.6	2.9	80.6	8.7	41.1	30.8
	2011	(e)168 435	8.3	2.0	2.9	4.0	82.8	11.1	38.4	33.3
Azerbaijan - Azerbaïdjan	1995	(e)547	10.1	13.0	46.0	3.9	26.9	5.3	12.6	9.0
	2005	(e)7 649	6.2	1.3	76.9	3.7	11.8	2.3	7.1	2.4
	2011	(e)34 495	1.8	0.2	94.7	0.3	2.9	0.9	0.5	1.6
Bahamas	1995	(e)176	20.2	0.8	10.6	6.7	60.2	17.0	36.2	7.0
	2005	(e)549	11.2	0.1	23.4	3.1	58.5	9.3	44.4	4.9
	2011	(e)835	4.3	0.4	65.7	3.3	23.6	9.6	7.4	6.6
Bahrain - Bahreïn	1995	(e)4 113	3.0	0.4	18.4	45.1	32.5	10.7	4.8	17.0
	2005	(e)10 239	1.4	-0.1	43.1	32.5	21.6	5.9	4.2	11.5
	2011	(e)19 648	3.6	0.5	33.9	38.3	22.8	4.8	6.3	11.7
Bangladesh	1995	(e)3 407	9.2	2.6	0.3	0.0	86.9	3.1	1.1	82.7
	2005	(e)9 332	5.8	1.4	0.4	0.2	92.0	1.9	1.3	88.8
	2011	(e)25 925	5.3	1.9	0.5	0.5	91.6	1.6	1.3	88.7

For sources and notes, see end of table.

Pour les sources et les notes, se reporter à la fin du tableau.

3.1 Country trade structure by product group
Exports

3.1 Structure du commerce des pays par groupes de produits
Exportations

Country or territory / Pays ou territoires	Year / Année	Total value (millions of dollars) / Valeur totale (millions de dollars)	All food items / Produits alimentaires	Agricultural raw materials / Matières premières agricoles	Fuels / Combustibles	Ores, metals, precious stones and non monetary gold / Minerais, métaux, pierres précieuses et or (non monétaire)	Manufactured goods / Articles manufacturés	Of which: / dont : Chemical products / Produits chimiques	Machinery and transport equipment / Machines et matériel de transport	Other manufactured goods / Articles manufacturés divers
			0 + 1 + 22 + 4	2 - (22 + 27 + 28)	3	27 + 28 + 68 + 667 + 971	5 + 6 +7 + 8- (667 + 68)	5	7	6 + 8 - (667 + 68)
Barbados - Barbade	1995	238	27.3	1.0	14.3	2.2	54.0	12.8	18.9	22.3
	2005	361	20.9	0.2	40.3	0.5	36.8	12.6	10.2	14.1
	2011	508	16.2	0.2	37.1	1.7	43.9	17.5	10.7	15.7
Belarus - Bélarus	1995	(a,e)4 804	1.9	5.0	4.6	3.8	33.0	10.8	9.0	13.2
	2005	15 977	8.3	2.5	34.8	0.5	51.9	11.1	18.7	22.2
	2011	40 294	9.4	1.6	35.5	0.6	49.9	17.6	15.8	16.4
Belgium - Belgique	1995	(e)177 831	7.6	0.8	1.8	8.7	53.4	12.7	22.3	18.4
	2005	334 106	8.1	1.2	6.9	7.6	73.9	27.6	25.2	21.1
	2011	477 925	8.8	1.4	10.8	8.4	68.5	28.3	20.6	19.6
Belize	1995	162	78.6	1.5	2.8	0.3	15.5	1.6	3.9	10.0
	2005	208	73.2	1.0	4.5	0.3	20.2	2.3	9.5	8.4
	2011	(e)348	57.3	0.9	31.4	1.7	8.6	1.5	4.8	2.3
Benin - Bénin	1995	420	17.6	71.6	4.7	1.7	5.5	0.6	0.4	4.4
	2005	(e)578	20.7	47.2	17.4	5.8	8.6	0.8	2.2	5.6
	2011	(e)1 849	28.6	25.7	17.8	15.8	12.1	2.2	3.2	6.7
Bermuda - Bermudes	1995	(e)56	7.3	12.9	2.1	0.2	68.3	18.5	45.6	4.2
	2005	(e)49	1.9	0.1	0.7	0.4	90.4	2.6	82.0	5.9
	2011	(e)13	5.0	0.1	10.4	1.6	61.0	18.3	38.4	4.3
Bhutan - Bhoutan	1995	(e)103	20.0	8.5	0.3	1.7	69.2	22.5	7.0	39.8
	2005	(e)258	9.2	0.3	28.9	10.1	51.3	8.1	3.5	39.7
	2011	(e)620	15.7	0.5	30.0	12.2	41.3	7.9	0.8	32.6
Bolivia (Plurinational State of) - Bolivie (État plurinational de)	1995	1 181	19.6	13.3	10.8	40.3	15.7	1.3	2.2	12.2
	2005	2 797	18.3	2.0	52.9	15.1	11.4	1.3	1.6	8.5
	2011	9 113	13.5	0.9	47.3	33.7	4.6	1.8	0.2	2.6
Bonaire, Sint Eustatius and Saba - Bonaire, Saint-Eustache et Saba	2011	(e)6	0.0	0.0	0.0	4.8	95.2	0.0	90.8	4.4
Bosnia and Herzegovina - Bosnie-Herzégovine	1995	(e)152	16.6	20.4	3.8	6.6	51.8	2.6	14.5	34.6
	2005	(e)2 388	5.1	8.4	8.9	23.0	53.7	3.2	16.6	33.9
	2011	(e)5 850	7.0	7.0	11.6	15.7	58.2	5.2	14.3	38.7
Botswana	1995	(e)2 142	7.2	1.0	0.1	54.7	36.9	6.0	18.1	12.8
	2005	4 431	2.2	0.1	0.1	91.0	6.5	0.6	2.6	3.3
	2011	5 882	1.7	0.1	0.4	89.8	7.9	1.0	3.3	3.6
Brazil - Brésil	1995	46 505	28.5	5.2	0.9	11.3	52.8	6.6	19.0	27.2
	2005	118 529	25.7	3.9	6.0	10.5	52.1	6.2	25.8	20.2
	2011	256 039	30.2	3.5	10.5	20.9	32.9	5.9	15.2	11.9
British Virgin Islands - Îles Vierges britanniques	1995	(e)11	6.2	0.6	4.3	6.4	75.0	22.6	39.3	13.1
Brunei Darussalam - Brunéi Darussalam	1995	(e)2 379	0.1	0.0	91.1	0.0	8.2	0.1	4.5	3.6
	2005	(e)6 268	0.1	0.1	92.4	0.5	7.0	0.0	1.2	5.8
	2011	(e)12 474	0.1	0.1	96.3	0.2	1.8	0.0	0.8	1.0
Bulgaria - Bulgarie	1995	(e)5 353	18.1	3.0	6.5	9.7	60.1	18.3	12.4	29.4
	2005	11 739	10.3	1.8	10.7	14.3	60.5	8.3	14.2	38.0
	2011	28 165	15.2	1.3	13.5	19.2	48.4	7.5	16.4	24.5
Burkina Faso	1995	(e)276	18.6	60.0	0.7	11.7	8.8	0.4	2.6	5.8
	2005	(e)468	13.7	76.4	0.1	2.0	7.4	0.8	2.2	4.4
	2011	(e)1 800	15.3	45.6	0.0	31.9	7.1	1.5	2.2	3.4
Burundi	1995	(e)106	57.5	3.8	0.0	36.5	2.1	0.2	0.4	1.5
	2005	(e)56	65.8	2.1	0.0	27.2	4.7	0.2	3.0	1.5
	2011	(e)122	71.6	4.2	1.1	13.2	9.9	1.7	4.5	3.6
Cambodia - Cambodge	1995	(e)855	4.0	74.4	0.0	0.3	20.8	0.3	0.7	19.7
	2005	(e)3 019	2.4	3.8	0.0	1.2	92.4	0.1	0.5	91.8
	2011	(e)7 554	4.3	6.2	0.0	2.9	86.5	0.3	3.0	83.2

For sources and notes, see end of table.

Pour les sources et les notes, se reporter à la fin du tableau.

133

3.1 Country trade structure
by product group
Exports

3.1 Structure du commerce des pays
par groupes de produits
Exportations

Country or territory / Pays ou territoires	Year / Année	Total value (millions of dollars) / Valeur totale (millions de dollars)	By main SITC Revision 3 product group (percentage) / Par principaux groupes de produits de la CTCI Révision 3 (en pourcentage)					Of which: / dont :		
			All food items / Produits alimentaires	Agricultural raw materials / Matières premières agricoles	Fuels / Combus-tibles	Ores, metals, precious stones and non monetary gold / Minerais, métaux, pierres précieuses et or (non monétaire)	Manu-factured goods / Articles manu-facturés	Chemical products / Produits chimiques	Machinery and transport equipment / Machines et matériel de transport	Other manu-factured goods / Articles manu-facturés divers
			0 + 1 + 22 + 4	2 - (22 + 27 + 28)	3	27 + 28 + 68 + 667 + 971	5 + 6 +7 + 8-(667 + 68)	5	7	6 + 8 - (667 + 68)
Cameroon - Cameroun	1995	(e)1 539	26.2	31.1	29.0	7.0	6.6	0.6	0.9	5.1
	2005	(e)2 861	18.9	18.0	49.4	4.8	6.0	0.9	1.2	3.9
	2011	(e)4 600	21.5	19.2	45.4	3.5	10.3	1.2	3.3	5.7
Canada	1995	191 118	7.6	9.2	9.1	7.8	62.0	5.9	38.5	17.6
	2005	360 552	6.7	4.7	20.2	7.0	56.9	7.2	32.8	16.8
	2011	450 397	9.7	3.7	25.7	13.1	44.9	8.8	24.4	11.8
Cape Verde - Cap-Vert	1995	9	14.0	0.5	9.1	6.0	68.6	1.8	15.7	51.0
	2005	(e)18	23.1	0.1	32.4	0.3	43.2	0.4	23.4	19.4
	2011	69	73.8	0.4	0.0	3.6	21.8	0.4	5.0	16.4
Cayman Islands - Îles Caïmanes	1995	(e)4	25.8	2.6	0.0	1.4	66.0	21.0	37.5	7.4
	2005	(e)60	0.5	0.1	8.7	0.1	84.5	0.4	82.6	1.4
	2011	(e)22	0.2	0.0	0.0	1.3	94.5	0.1	87.3	7.1
Central African Republic - République centrafricaine	1995	(e)171	14.3	17.7	0.1	57.0	8.2	0.5	5.3	2.5
	2005	(e)129	1.7	45.8	1.4	44.8	6.1	1.1	2.2	2.9
	2011	(e)156	9.6	46.5	0.0	34.7	8.6	0.7	4.6	3.3
Chad - Tchad	1995	(e)243	1.4	90.3	0.0	0.0	6.0	0.1	5.1	0.8
	2005	(e)3 144	0.1	6.4	90.9	0.1	2.2	0.1	1.8	0.3
	2011	(e)4 114	0.1	3.0	96.0	0.1	0.8	0.0	0.3	0.4
Chile - Chili	1995	15 901	23.7	13.6	0.2	49.5	11.7	3.5	1.8	6.5
	2005	41 973	19.3	6.3	2.7	57.1	14.6	5.0	2.7	6.9
	2011	81 411	17.6	5.8	1.0	62.6	13.0	4.3	2.9	5.8
China - Chine	1995	148 779	8.3	1.8	3.6	2.4	83.6	6.1	21.1	56.4
	2005	761 953	3.2	0.5	2.3	2.0	91.7	4.7	46.2	40.8
	2011	1 898 388	2.9	0.6	1.7	1.6	93.2	6.0	47.5	39.6
China, Hong Kong SAR - Chine (RAS de Hong Kong)	1995	173 871	3.0	1.3	1.0	2.6	91.6	6.2	32.4	53.1
	2005	292 119	0.9	0.6	0.3	4.1	94.0	4.8	52.3	36.9
	2011	455 573	1.6	0.5	0.2	11.6	86.1	4.4	56.3	25.4
China, Macao SAR - Chine (RAS de Macao)	1995	2 025	2.1	1.7	0.0	0.1	95.9	1.2	4.2	90.6
	2005	2 474	1.2	0.3	0.1	2.0	96.2	2.3	8.0	85.9
	2011	870	4.8	1.2	0.5	7.4	84.2	9.6	20.2	54.4
China, Taiwan Province of - Province chinoise de Taiwan	1995	(e)111 343	3.4	1.6	0.7	1.5	92.7	6.8	48.1	37.8
	2005	(e)189 393	1.2	1.2	4.7	1.8	90.7	10.5	49.8	30.4
	2011	(e)306 998	1.1	1.1	5.7	3.5	88.2	13.2	48.2	26.8
Colombia - Colombie	1995	10 201	30.8	5.4	27.2	6.8	29.8	7.9	2.6	19.3
	2005	21 190	17.2	4.5	39.2	4.6	34.4	8.4	6.0	20.0
	2011	56 954	10.0	2.3	64.1	6.3	17.2	5.8	3.0	8.4
Comoros - Comores	1995	11	60.4	0.4	0.0	0.0	38.6	35.0	1.8	1.8
	2005	(e)12	71.2	1.0	0.0	1.2	26.4	11.0	12.1	3.3
	2011	(e)25	33.7	0.4	0.0	1.0	64.9	12.3	50.8	1.8
Congo	1995	(e)1 090	1.7	11.8	79.7	1.8	4.7	0.3	0.4	4.0
	2005	(e)5 198	0.9	5.4	87.2	5.6	0.9	0.3	0.2	0.4
	2011	(e)10 800	0.4	3.1	84.1	4.3	8.1	0.7	6.2	1.1
Cook Islands - Îles Cook	1995	(e)5	32.7	5.0	0.5	33.8	24.7	5.4	4.6	14.7
	2005	(e)5	76.8	1.3	0.0	11.8	8.6	0.6	2.4	5.6
	2011	(e)3	61.0	0.2	0.0	4.2	33.5	1.7	28.8	3.0
Costa Rica	1995	(e)3 476	56.2	4.6	0.4	1.2	35.3	5.0	4.7	25.6
	2005	7 151	26.4	2.3	0.2	1.1	69.2	5.0	43.7	20.4
	2011	10 222	25.6	1.8	0.1	1.1	70.7	3.5	55.0	12.2
Côte d'Ivoire	1995	3 737	58.7	16.0	9.8	0.8	14.2	4.2	1.4	8.6
	2005	7 248	38.2	8.2	27.7	0.5	24.9	3.6	9.8	11.4
	2011	11 049	48.0	12.8	24.3	5.4	9.5	3.0	2.4	4.0

For sources and notes, see end of table.

Pour les sources et les notes, se reporter à la fin du tableau.

Country or territory / Pays ou territoires	Year / Année	Total value (millions of dollars) / Valeur totale (millions de dollars)	All food items / Produits alimentaires	Agricultural raw materials / Matières premières agricoles	Fuels / Combustibles	Ores, metals, precious stones and non monetary gold / Minerais, métaux, pierres précieuses et or (non monétaire)	Manufactured goods / Articles manufacturés	Chemical products / Produits chimiques	Machinery and transport equipment / Machines et matériel de transport	Other manufactured goods / Articles manufacturés divers
			0 + 1 + 22 + 4	2 - (22 + 27 + 28)	3	27 + 28 + 68 + 667 + 971	5 + 6 +7 + 8- (667 + 68)	5	7	6 + 8 - (667 + 68)
Croatia - Croatie	1995	4 633	10.8	4.6	8.4	2.3	73.8	17.6	16.8	39.5
	2005	8 773	10.5	3.4	13.9	3.8	68.5	9.9	28.9	29.6
	2011	12 289	11.3	3.9	12.3	5.6	66.8	11.3	30.4	25.1
Cuba	1995	(e)1 625	76.2	0.3	0.3	15.8	7.1	3.8	1.3	2.0
	2005	(e)2 319	28.2	0.6	2.2	32.8	14.4	4.3	3.6	6.5
	2011	(e)6 300	32.6	0.7	7.5	31.1	17.8	6.4	5.4	6.0
Cyprus - Chypre	1995	1 231	45.4	0.7	1.9	2.0	49.2	5.0	20.0	24.2
	2005	1 546	14.8	1.1	12.5	4.5	65.5	13.7	36.0	15.9
	2011	1 958	15.1	0.8	28.2	6.8	47.9	17.6	19.4	11.0
Czech Republic - République tchèque	1995	21 686	6.1	3.9	4.7	3.0	80.8	9.4	28.0	43.4
	2005	78 209	4.1	1.5	3.2	1.7	87.0	6.2	50.3	30.4
	2011	162 112	4.1	1.4	4.2	2.4	86.3	6.1	53.9	26.3
Dem. Rep. of the Congo - Rép. dém. du Congo	1995	(e)1 649	6.7	6.3	10.3	75.4	2.8	0.3	1.0	1.5
	2005	(e)2 403	2.8	6.5	16.3	70.1	3.3	0.7	1.0	1.6
	2011	(e)6 003	0.8	3.4	21.5	71.1	1.2	0.6	0.4	0.2
Denmark - Danemark	1995	48 789	24.0	2.9	2.6	1.2	59.8	9.7	25.1	25.0
	2005	82 415	17.6	2.5	9.4	1.3	65.3	13.2	28.1	24.1
	2011	112 784	17.7	3.0	9.1	1.8	60.6	11.3	25.2	24.1
Djibouti	1995	(e)14	18.7	5.0	10.2	11.4	53.3	7.9	19.1	26.4
	2005	(e)40	21.8	3.5	2.5	13.0	58.0	10.5	34.6	12.9
	2011	(e)95	37.9	5.9	5.1	12.6	33.4	2.6	14.3	16.5
Dominica - Dominique	1995	45	50.3	0.3	0.0	1.3	48.1	42.7	2.7	2.7
	2005	42	33.8	0.1	0.0	6.5	59.6	53.7	4.2	1.7
	2011	(e)29	31.9	0.1	0.0	7.4	60.7	45.0	7.0	8.7
Dominican Republic - République dominicaine	1995	(e)3 780	15.8	0.4	0.0	2.2	79.4	0.9	6.1	72.4
	2005	(e)6 183	14.4	0.4	0.0	2.7	80.7	2.8	14.3	63.6
	2011	(e)8 536	24.5	0.9	1.8	6.9	63.8	5.7	9.5	48.6
Ecuador - Équateur	1995	4 361	51.8	3.0	35.1	2.5	7.6	1.2	2.0	4.4
	2005	9 869	28.2	4.4	59.5	0.6	7.3	1.2	2.2	3.9
	2011	22 345	29.8	3.7	57.8	1.2	7.5	1.4	2.6	3.6
Egypt - Égypte	1995	3 444	9.9	6.1	37.3	6.4	40.3	5.8	0.6	33.8
	2005	10 646	8.8	2.3	51.3	2.9	23.6	5.0	1.2	17.4
	2011	30 782	14.1	2.7	30.0	11.2	41.9	14.5	4.8	22.7
El Salvador	1995	(e)1 651	44.2	1.1	0.2	1.9	52.3	9.0	3.9	39.4
	2005	3 436	18.8	0.4	1.5	1.5	76.7	6.9	5.4	64.4
	2011	(e)5 309	26.7	0.7	2.4	3.6	66.6	7.3	5.9	53.4
Equatorial Guinea - Guinée équatoriale	1995	86	7.5	52.1	33.1	0.0	6.9	0.0	0.5	6.3
	2005	7 064	0.0	1.4	94.0	0.0	4.2	3.7	0.1	0.4
	2011	(e)13 500	0.0	1.3	96.5	0.3	1.5	1.4	0.1	0.1
Eritrea - Érythrée	1995	(e)86	59.1	8.5	0.0	0.0	30.9	1.4	15.3	14.2
	2005	(e)11	28.4	16.3	0.0	2.4	49.7	3.7	9.6	36.4
	2011	(e)404	0.7	0.3	0.0	96.6	2.2	0.2	0.2	1.8
Estonia - Estonie	1995	1 840	13.9	9.9	10.8	5.2	59.9	8.1	17.8	34.1
	2005	8 247	7.1	6.3	14.0	2.7	65.7	5.0	32.2	28.5
	2011	18 158	8.7	5.0	13.3	3.6	65.0	6.1	33.9	24.9
Ethiopia - Éthiopie	1995	422	72.5	13.4	2.9	0.1	11.2	0.3	0.0	10.8
	2005	926	73.5	15.3	0.0	5.8	5.1	0.0	0.0	5.0
	2011	2 615	76.0	8.2	0.0	6.2	9.6	0.3	1.1	8.2
Faeroe Islands - Îles Féroé	1995	(e)362	91.1	2.2	0.0	0.0	6.7	0.1	4.8	1.8
	2005	602	91.6	1.5	0.0	0.0	6.9	0.1	5.4	1.4
	2011	(e)998	87.0	2.5	3.2	0.3	6.5	0.2	5.4	1.0

For sources and notes, see end of table.

Pour les sources et les notes, se reporter à la fin du tableau.

Country or territory Pays ou territoires	Year Année	Total value (millions of dollars) Valeur totale (millions de dollars)	By main SITC Revision 3 product group (percentage) Par principaux groupes de produits de la CTCI Révision 3 (en pourcentage)						Of which: / dont :		
			All food items Produits alimentaires	Agricultural raw materials Matières premières agricoles	Fuels Combus-tibles	Ores, metals, precious stones and non monetary gold Minerais, métaux, pierres précieuses et or (non monétaire)	Manu-factured goods Articles manu-facturés	Chemical products Produits chimiques	Machinery and transport equipment Machines et matériel de transport	Other manu-factured goods Articles manu-facturés divers
			0 + 1 + 22 + 4	2 - (22 + 27 + 28)	3	27 + 28 + 68 + 667 + 971	5 + 6 +7 + 8- (667 + 68)	5	7	6 + 8 - (667 + 68)
Falkland Islands (Malvinas) - Îles Falkland (Malvinas)	1995	(e)30	68.0	16.3	0.0	0.0	16.1	1.0	12.6	2.4
	2005	(e)173	95.0	2.4	0.0	0.5	0.8	0.1	0.5	0.3
	2011	(e)190	68.0	22.3	0.3	0.1	3.7	0.3	1.0	2.4
Fiji - Fidji	1995	(e)544	50.8	6.6	0.4	8.1	33.7	0.3	1.0	32.5
	2005	(e)702	55.1	4.9	6.8	6.7	23.7	1.8	2.0	19.9
	2011	(e)902	54.1	6.1	7.9	9.8	21.3	3.5	2.7	15.2
Finland - Finlande	1995	40 409	2.4	8.4	1.9	3.1	83.3	6.0	35.4	42.0
	2005	65 238	1.9	5.2	4.4	3.6	84.3	7.6	44.1	32.6
	2011	78 794	2.8	6.0	9.5	5.9	73.6	11.1	29.4	33.1
France	1995	277 845	14.3	1.5	2.4	2.7	76.6	12.9	39.4	24.3
	2005	434 354	10.7	0.9	4.1	2.3	80.1	15.9	41.6	22.5
	2011	581 542	12.7	1.0	4.6	3.1	76.0	17.1	37.6	21.3
French Polynesia - Polynésie française	1995	(e)196	2.7	1.0	0.0	61.8	28.6	0.8	20.8	7.1
	2005	210	12.9	2.2	0.0	61.4	23.5	1.3	13.6	8.6
	2011	150	18.8	2.3	0.0	52.6	26.3	2.1	17.8	6.3
Gabon	1995	(e)2 718	0.2	13.1	82.7	2.0	1.9	0.4	0.4	1.1
	2005	5 069	0.9	10.6	78.9	5.6	3.8	0.0	0.9	2.9
	2011	(e)12 175	0.5	9.9	78.2	6.7	4.7	0.2	2.4	2.0
Gambia - Gambie	1995	(e)16	28.4	0.8	0.5	61.5	8.5	2.1	1.7	4.8
	2005	(e)8	66.1	2.1	0.9	3.4	26.7	1.3	18.3	7.0
	2011	95	45.2	17.7	0.3	20.9	15.6	0.7	1.9	13.0
Georgia - Géorgie	1995	(e)158	29.3	3.3	18.8	8.0	40.6	11.1	5.7	23.8
	2005	865	34.9	2.1	3.2	21.1	38.5	6.8	16.9	14.8
	2011	(e)2 192	24.0	1.4	3.7	18.1	52.8	7.9	19.0	25.9
Germany - Allemagne	1995	523 697	5.1	1.1	1.0	2.8	83.4	13.2	46.1	24.2
	2005	977 132	4.5	0.8	2.2	2.7	86.0	13.9	50.2	21.8
	2011	1 482 202	5.4	0.9	2.2	4.0	82.7	14.4	47.0	21.4
Ghana	1995	(e)1 754	41.9	13.2	4.3	34.8	7.1	0.6	0.8	5.7
	2005	(e)3 060	54.9	8.3	8.1	13.9	13.1	0.7	2.3	10.1
	2011	(e)12 700	41.5	4.3	35.2	12.0	6.8	1.2	1.1	4.5
Gibraltar	1995	117	15.0	0.4	0.8	17.0	64.7	3.9	22.2	38.5
	2005	200	0.3	0.4	12.3	5.4	78.0	1.1	62.4	14.6
	2011	246	0.0	0.1	34.6	1.0	61.5	0.1	58.5	3.0
Greece - Grèce	1995	10 955	29.5	4.4	6.5	7.9	49.2	4.9	8.0	36.3
	2005	17 434	22.0	2.4	9.4	8.3	55.3	14.6	12.7	28.0
	2011	31 711	18.3	1.7	30.2	9.0	38.0	10.3	9.4	18.3
Greenland - Groenland	1995	364	94.6	0.3	0.0	0.0	3.5	0.0	2.5	0.9
	2005	402	89.9	0.5	0.0	5.0	1.7	0.0	0.5	1.2
	2011	(e)473	88.1	0.5	0.0	7.6	3.8	0.0	2.6	1.1
Grenada - Grenade	1995	22	70.2	0.2	1.5	0.4	26.7	2.3	8.0	16.4
	2005	28	64.1	0.2	0.1	0.2	33.9	3.7	16.9	13.3
	2011	(e)28	35.6	0.2	0.1	10.7	53.3	11.9	21.8	19.7
Guam	1995	84	..	..	..	..	..	..	..	..
	2005	(a,e)52	12.9	2.0	8.1	9.4	19.8	3.5	9.2	7.1
	2011	(a,e)43	6.0	0.4	0.1	31.7	22.6	0.2	7.5	14.8
Guatemala	1995	1 936	57.3	3.7	1.7	0.4	36.1	8.8	1.8	25.5
	2005	5 381	36.3	3.4	5.6	0.9	53.3	9.3	2.0	42.0
	2011	10 161	45.9	5.2	4.6	6.8	37.1	9.6	2.3	25.3
Guinea - Guinée	1995	(e)702	11.8	2.8	1.0	78.0	6.4	5.4	0.9	0.1
	2005	(e)796	8.4	1.9	6.3	81.6	1.6	0.1	0.5	1.0
	2011	(e)1 527	5.9	2.7	35.0	47.0	9.2	1.1	5.5	2.6

For sources and notes, see end of table.

Pour les sources et les notes, se reporter à la fin du tableau.

Country or territory / Pays ou territoires	Year / Année	Total value (millions of dollars) / Valeur totale (millions de dollars)	All food items / Produits alimentaires	Agricultural raw materials / Matières premières agricoles	Fuels / Combustibles	Ores, metals, precious stones and non monetary gold / Minerais, métaux, pierres précieuses et or (non monétaire)	Manufactured goods / Articles manufacturés	Of which: / dont : Chemical products / Produits chimiques	Machinery and transport equipment / Machines et matériel de transport	Other manufactured goods / Articles manufacturés divers
			0 + 1 + 22 + 4	2 - (22 + 27 + 28)	3	27 + 28 + 68 + 667 + 971	5 + 6 +7 + 8- (667 + 68)	5	7	6 + 8 - (667 + 68)
Guinea-Bissau - Guinée-Bissau	1995	(e)24	84.6	5.5	7.5	0.0	2.5	0.5	0.7	1.4
	2005	(e)89	96.3	1.3	0.3	0.8	1.2	0.0	0.2	0.9
	2011	(e)245	90.9	1.2	6.2	0.5	1.2	0.1	0.4	0.8
Guyana	1995	(e)455	44.9	2.2	0.0	42.1	10.8	0.7	1.1	9.0
	2005	539	45.3	6.6	0.0	38.1	9.0	1.6	1.9	5.6
	2011	1 049	31.4	5.7	0.0	55.0	7.9	1.1	4.6	2.3
Haiti - Haïti	1995	(e)110	25.4	0.8	0.3	0.3	69.4	7.2	2.8	59.4
	2005	(e)473	6.5	0.6	0.0	0.6	83.5	1.1	2.5	79.9
	2011	(e)772	9.0	0.7	0.0	1.1	89.3	1.4	3.4	84.5
Honduras	1995	(e)1 769	52.5	2.3	0.1	0.9	43.7	3.0	1.5	39.2
	2005	(e)5 048	32.4	2.2	0.3	4.0	59.8	2.5	6.7	50.6
	2011	(e)7 204	38.8	1.6	2.2	7.6	49.8	2.7	7.6	39.4
Hungary - Hongrie	1995	12 452	19.3	2.3	3.0	5.0	69.9	11.6	28.8	29.5
	2005	62 272	6.6	0.7	2.8	1.9	85.0	7.8	60.1	17.1
	2011	111 125	8.0	0.8	3.5	2.1	81.6	9.3	55.0	17.3
Iceland - Islande	1995	1 803	75.5	0.5	0.0	12.0	11.6	0.7	5.1	5.8
	2005	3 091	58.5	0.8	1.4	19.0	19.3	3.5	9.3	6.5
	2011	5 349	42.6	0.7	1.9	40.3	14.0	3.0	4.6	6.4
India - Inde	1995	31 699	18.7	1.3	1.7	18.6	58.2	8.1	7.5	42.5
	2005	100 353	9.0	1.3	10.5	19.8	58.4	11.4	10.5	36.4
	2011	301 483	9.0	2.5	18.8	14.9	50.3	10.4	13.9	26.1
Indonesia (...2002) - Indonésie (...2002)	1995	45 443	11.4	6.7	25.3	6.1	50.5	3.4	8.4	38.7
Indonesia - Indonésie	2005	85 660	11.7	5.1	27.7	8.7	46.9	5.2	15.9	25.8
	2011	203 497	16.2	7.5	33.9	8.9	33.6	5.7	10.7	17.2
Iran (Islamic Rep. of) - Iran (Rép. islamique d')	1995	(e)18 360	5.8	1.8	77.3	1.6	13.1	2.3	0.7	10.0
	2005	(e)60 012	2.7	0.4	85.3	2.2	8.1	2.8	1.3	4.0
	2011	(e)130 544	2.2	0.3	78.3	3.6	9.5	6.1	1.0	2.4
Iraq	1995	(e)1 963	0.1	0.2	95.3	0.0	4.1	0.4	3.4	0.3
	2005	(e)23 697	0.4	0.2	97.1	0.2	0.8	0.7	0.0	0.0
	2011	(e)84 673	0.2	0.1	98.8	0.3	0.6	0.5	0.1	0.0
Ireland - Irlande	1995	43 789	19.4	1.1	0.4	1.2	71.0	18.4	34.5	18.0
	2005	110 003	8.4	0.4	0.7	0.9	85.7	45.6	26.5	13.6
	2011	129 346	9.8	0.5	1.5	1.4	85.9	60.1	12.1	13.8
Israel - Israël	1995	19 047	5.8	1.9	0.4	31.9	58.0	14.4	24.8	18.8
	2005	42 771	3.2	0.9	1.6	37.1	49.7	15.7	19.4	14.6
	2011	67 796	3.4	0.8	2.8	31.2	60.9	27.8	19.7	13.5
Italy - Italie	1995	230 441	6.6	0.7	1.2	1.5	89.2	8.0	37.7	43.6
	2005	372 957	6.5	0.6	3.4	1.7	85.0	10.6	36.8	37.6
	2011	523 179	7.6	0.7	4.7	3.9	80.8	11.3	35.1	34.4
Jamaica - Jamaïque	1995	1 424	21.7	0.3	0.5	49.4	28.1	2.7	3.1	22.4
	2005	1 514	17.2	0.1	7.4	68.5	6.8	3.7	1.1	2.0
	2011	(e)1 603	18.3	0.2	16.2	44.2	20.2	8.7	8.3	3.1
Japan - Japon	1995	442 937	0.5	0.6	0.6	1.2	95.1	6.8	70.3	18.0
	2005	594 941	0.5	0.5	0.7	2.1	91.8	8.8	64.1	18.9
	2011	823 292	0.6	0.8	2.0	3.9	88.0	10.3	58.3	19.4
Jordan - Jordanie	1995	1 769	25.0	1.5	0.2	18.5	54.1	32.6	9.5	12.0
	2005	4 279	13.8	0.3	0.6	10.9	73.5	24.1	11.8	37.7
	2011	7 963	14.4	0.4	0.6	15.5	68.7	33.2	9.8	25.7
Kazakhstan	1995	5 227	9.9	2.8	25.0	24.1	38.1	10.3	6.0	21.9
	2005	27 846	2.4	0.7	70.1	14.7	12.0	1.9	1.2	8.9
	2011	(e)84 864	3.6	0.3	70.4	12.2	13.5	4.4	1.1	7.9

For sources and notes, see end of table.

Pour les sources et les notes, se reporter à la fin du tableau.

Country or territory / Pays ou territoires	Year / Année	Total value (millions of dollars) / Valeur totale (millions de dollars)	By main SITC Revision 3 product group (percentage) / Par principaux groupes de produits de la CTCI Révision 3 (en pourcentage)					Of which: / dont :		
			All food items / Produits alimentaires	Agricultural raw materials / Matières premières agricoles	Fuels / Combustibles	Ores, metals, precious stones and non monetary gold / Minerais, métaux, pierres précieuses et or (non monétaire)	Manu-factured goods / Articles manu-facturés	Chemical products / Produits chimiques	Machinery and transport equipment / Machines et matériel de transport	Other manu-factured goods / Articles manu-facturés divers
			0 + 1 + 22 + 4	2 - (22 + 27 + 28)	3	27 + 28 + 68 + 667 + 971	5 + 6 +7 + 8- (667 + 68)	5	7	6 + 8 - (667 + 68)
Kenya	1995	1 826	54.7	8.3	5.0	2.7	28.9	6.6	3.2	19.1
	2005	3 420	37.9	12.5	15.5	2.8	31.0	7.0	3.1	20.9
	2011	(e)5 775	43.1	13.6	4.5	4.3	34.5	8.7	5.1	20.7
Kiribati	1995	(e)7	84.3	1.9	0.0	0.6	5.9	0.1	0.4	5.4
	2005	(e)4	77.1	0.2	0.0	0.6	19.2	1.9	2.3	15.0
	2011	(e)20	85.4	0.1	0.0	0.3	6.6	0.0	5.2	1.3
Korea, Dem. People's Rep. of - Corée, Rép. populaire dém. de	1995	(e)959	15.5	2.7	2.0	9.5	69.3	5.4	27.6	36.2
	2005	(e)1 338	11.1	2.3	10.0	13.5	61.3	7.7	28.7	24.8
	2011	(e)3 700	3.9	0.7	36.4	16.9	42.1	4.1	13.1	24.8
Korea, Republic of - Corée, République de	1995	125 056	2.3	1.3	2.0	3.0	91.5	7.2	52.5	31.8
	2005	284 418	1.1	0.8	5.5	1.8	90.8	9.8	61.0	20.1
	2011	555 209	1.1	1.2	9.6	2.9	85.3	10.9	54.1	20.3
Kuwait - Koweït	1995	12 944	0.5	0.1	89.8	1.1	8.2	3.2	2.6	2.5
	2005	(e)44 909	0.3	0.1	90.7	0.8	8.2	6.4	0.5	1.2
	2011	(e)99 579	0.2	0.2	91.6	0.9	7.1	5.1	1.2	0.8
Kyrgyzstan - Kirghizistan	1995	(e)412	21.4	15.0	13.1	13.6	36.2	7.0	9.7	19.5
	2005	(e)672	12.4	9.3	10.2	34.0	32.5	1.1	8.9	22.6
	2011	(e)1 979	15.6	4.0	15.6	20.3	41.5	3.6	12.0	26.0
Lao People's Dem. Rep. - Rép. dém. populaire lao	1995	311	11.1	42.3	0.3	5.3	40.7	1.6	0.3	38.8
	2005	553	6.6	28.1	11.0	16.8	35.5	0.3	1.5	33.7
	2011	(e)2 400	7.3	14.1	19.4	46.4	12.7	2.0	1.2	9.4
Latvia - Lettonie	1995	1 305	14.4	23.0	1.7	1.0	58.1	6.9	16.3	34.9
	2005	5 303	11.3	17.1	8.9	3.5	55.4	6.0	12.4	37.0
	2011	12 015	14.7	10.9	7.9	4.5	54.6	8.4	17.5	28.7
Lebanon - Liban	1995	(e)656	19.5	1.5	0.1	10.6	68.3	12.5	14.4	41.4
	2005	(e)2 337	16.8	2.3	0.6	16.2	63.0	10.7	14.5	37.7
	2011	(e)5 664	16.2	1.2	0.2	28.6	53.5	12.4	17.0	24.2
Lesotho	1995	(e)160	11.3	4.5	0.0	0.1	84.0	1.1	14.6	68.4
	2005	(e)651	2.6	0.5	0.0	6.8	90.0	0.1	1.4	88.5
	2011	(e)1 010	4.3	2.5	0.0	25.5	67.7	0.2	4.0	63.5
Liberia - Libéria	1995	(e)820	0.1	1.9	2.1	81.5	14.4	0.4	13.6	0.3
	2005	(e)131	0.4	11.0	0.8	2.7	85.0	0.1	84.5	0.3
	2011	(e)358	3.6	51.7	9.7	6.2	23.1	0.2	22.0	0.9
Libya - Libye	1995	(e)9 364	0.2	0.2	92.0	0.0	7.4	4.1	0.1	3.2
	2005	(e)31 358	0.1	0.0	95.4	0.6	3.9	2.7	0.1	1.2
	2011	(e)16 463	0.2	-0.1	94.0	2.3	3.5	1.8	0.2	1.4
Lithuania - Lituanie	1995	2 706	18.1	7.8	11.4	5.0	57.7	14.3	15.7	27.7
	2005	12 070	12.4	3.3	26.6	1.5	55.5	8.4	21.5	25.5
	2011	28 154	15.8	2.4	25.5	1.8	52.7	13.5	17.4	21.8
Luxembourg	1995	(e)7 244	4.8	0.9	0.8	5.5	57.9	6.2	15.9	35.8
	2005	(e)18 790	6.0	0.6	0.9	5.5	84.4	8.6	29.1	46.7
	2011	(e)21 749	7.2	2.6	1.2	7.3	79.7	8.3	23.0	48.5
Madagascar	1995	(e)507	63.7	4.8	2.6	5.5	22.3	1.7	0.6	20.0
	2005	836	32.2	4.9	2.7	4.8	51.5	1.4	2.7	47.4
	2011	(e)1 593	32.4	4.7	3.6	10.5	48.8	13.1	5.1	30.6
Malawi	1995	433	86.2	2.3	0.1	0.1	11.1	0.3	1.7	9.1
	2005	495	79.8	4.0	0.1	0.3	15.3	0.6	2.4	12.3
	2011	1 425	75.4	5.1	0.1	5.6	13.7	6.1	2.3	5.3
Malaysia - Malaisie	1995	73 778	9.5	6.2	7.0	1.5	74.5	3.0	55.1	16.4
	2005	141 624	6.9	2.5	13.4	1.3	74.5	5.8	54.0	14.7
	2011	226 993	14.0	3.2	17.7	2.7	62.0	6.7	38.8	16.5
Maldives	1995	(e)85	68.7	0.6	0.0	0.2	30.0	0.3	0.5	29.2
	2005	154	77.8	0.1	6.6	0.9	14.4	1.9	3.8	8.7
	2011	(e)346	84.3	0.1	5.7	2.1	6.4	0.2	5.0	1.2

For sources and notes, see end of table.

Pour les sources et les notes, se reporter à la fin du tableau.

Country or territory / Pays ou territoires	Year / Année	Total value (millions of dollars) / Valeur totale (millions de dollars)	By main SITC Revision 3 product group (percentage) / Par principaux groupes de produits de la CTCI Révision 3 (en pourcentage)					Of which: / dont :		
			All food items / Produits alimentaires	Agricultural raw materials / Matières premières agricoles	Fuels / Combustibles	Ores, metals, precious stones and non monetary gold / Minerais, métaux, pierres précieuses et or (non monétaire)	Manufactured goods / Articles manufacturés	Chemical products / Produits chimiques	Machinery and transport equipment / Machines et matériel de transport	Other manufactured goods / Articles manufacturés divers
			0 + 1 + 22 + 4	2 - (22 + 27 + 28)	3	27 + 28 + 68 + 667 + 971	5 + 6 +7 + 8- (667 + 68)	5	7	6 + 8 - (667 + 68)
Mali	1995	(e)443	18.2	58.1	1.0	17.1	5.3	0.3	1.1	3.9
	2005	1 075	5.5	48.3	0.6	37.3	7.9	0.7	4.2	3.1
	2011	(e)2 389	5.7	22.0	5.0	59.1	8.1	2.4	3.6	2.2
Malta - Malte	1995	1 913	2.1	0.1	1.5	0.6	95.6	2.2	66.3	27.1
	2005	2 431	6.2	0.1	1.1	0.3	91.5	4.9	61.1	25.5
	2011	(e)4 105	8.0	0.2	5.1	0.8	85.9	9.4	58.0	18.5
Marshall Islands - Îles Marshall	1995	23	58.6	0.5	0.0	0.4	17.3	0.0	15.6	1.6
	2005	25	10.9	0.0	0.0	0.0	88.1	0.0	88.0	0.1
	2011	(e)35	31.0	0.0	0.7	0.1	67.7	0.0	67.2	0.5
Mauritania - Mauritanie	1995	(e)509	59.4	0.5	0.3	38.3	1.3	0.0	0.7	0.5
	2005	(e)556	44.5	0.2	0.0	49.6	1.4	0.1	0.8	0.6
	2011	(e)2 768	23.2	-0.3	5.3	58.3	0.7	0.1	0.4	0.2
Mauritius - Maurice	1995	1 538	28.9	0.7	0.0	2.0	68.4	0.8	2.3	65.3
	2005	2 144	26.9	0.3	0.1	2.8	63.0	1.4	15.1	46.6
	2011	(e)2 647	28.6	0.8	0.1	3.6	52.1	2.9	1.9	47.4
Mayotte	2005	6	19.4	0.1	0.2	0.1	80.2	15.1	50.4	14.8
	2011	(e)7	13.4	0.0	0.7	0.3	78.8	15.1	54.5	9.3
Mexico - Mexique	1995	79 541	7.7	1.3	10.3	3.1	77.5	5.0	52.3	20.2
	2005	214 207	5.4	0.5	14.9	2.0	77.0	3.7	53.2	20.1
	2011	349 569	6.2	0.4	15.9	6.2	70.7	4.1	52.6	14.0
Micronesia (Federated States of) - Micronésie (États fédérés de)	1995	21	86.3	0.3	0.0	0.0	8.8	0.0	0.0	8.8
	2005	19	94.3	0.9	0.0	1.5	2.9	0.0	0.3	2.6
	2011	(e)25	93.6	0.3	0.1	2.5	2.4	0.0	0.7	1.7
Mongolia - Mongolie	1995	(e)473	2.2	27.7	0.0	59.9	10.2	0.6	1.7	7.8
	2005	1 064	1.4	8.2	3.9	70.2	16.3	0.1	0.8	15.4
	2011	(e)4 774	1.9	8.4	10.7	75.4	3.6	0.2	0.6	2.8
Montenegro - Monténégro	2011	628	11.5	5.4	13.9	49.2	19.9	2.7	5.3	11.9
Montserrat	1995	(e)3	74.1	0.0	0.0	0.2	22.6	1.3	17.8	3.5
	2005	(e)1	0.2	1.1	13.7	6.4	69.4	7.1	44.3	18.0
	2011	(e)1	6.1	0.7	0.0	12.4	73.8	4.0	22.2	47.5
Morocco - Maroc	1995	(e)6 881	27.1	2.9	1.8	9.6	58.4	16.5	7.0	34.9
	2005	11 185	20.8	1.7	5.9	8.1	62.7	11.2	17.9	33.6
	2011	(e)21 518	19.9	1.2	4.6	11.3	63.0	20.9	16.8	25.3
Mozambique	1995	174	64.1	14.2	2.2	5.7	13.2	1.1	3.9	8.1
	2005	1 745	11.5	3.4	14.6	67.3	3.2	0.3	1.7	1.2
	2011	3 604	20.1	4.7	24.4	44.2	5.5	0.4	3.4	1.8
Myanmar	1995	(e)860	41.9	38.5	0.2	7.4	11.9	1.0	0.9	10.0
	2005	(e)3 950	20.7	19.0	33.3	4.2	22.8	0.2	0.7	21.9
	2011	(e)9 238	19.3	15.3	38.2	17.5	9.7	0.2	0.5	9.0
Namibia - Namibie	1995	(e)1 416	38.4	1.4	2.2	32.8	25.2	2.0	7.0	16.2
	2005	(e)2 070	30.2	0.6	1.2	42.6	25.0	10.8	4.4	9.8
	2011	(e)4 362	26.2	0.7	1.0	42.4	29.6	9.9	7.8	11.9
Nauru	1995	28	1.0	0.5	0.0	70.0	28.0	0.7	25.3	2.0
	2005	4	7.5	1.0	0.6	25.2	62.8	7.4	38.8	16.7
	2011	69	1.9	0.1	0.0	93.0	5.1	0.3	3.4	1.4
Nepal - Népal	1995	(e)359	7.8	1.1	0.0	0.1	83.7	1.2	0.1	82.4
	2005	(e)888	23.1	1.1	0.0	7.4	68.3	7.8	0.5	60.0
	2011	(e)918	27.4	2.3	0.0	6.6	63.7	5.4	1.5	56.9
Netherlands - Pays-Bas	1995	(e)203 187	20.5	4.1	8.1	3.2	61.4	17.4	24.3	19.7
	2005	(e)406 208	13.1	3.0	12.0	2.7	60.0	15.7	28.3	16.1
	2011	(e)666 207	17.2	3.3	17.5	3.6	58.3	17.5	24.7	16.1
Netherlands Antilles - Antilles néerlandaises	1995	(e)1 522	12.1	0.1	65.9	3.0	14.2	2.0	6.5	5.6
	2005	(e)608	1.9	0.1	76.2	1.0	15.2	3.6	6.2	5.3

For sources and notes, see end of table.

Pour les sources et les notes, se reporter à la fin du tableau.

139

Country or territory / Pays ou territoires	Year / Année	Total value (millions of dollars) / Valeur totale (millions de dollars)	By main SITC Revision 3 product group (percentage) / Par principaux groupes de produits de la CTCI Révision 3 (en pourcentage)					Of which: / dont :		
			All food items / Produits alimentaires	Agricultural raw materials / Matières premières agricoles	Fuels / Combustibles	Ores, metals, precious stones and non monetary gold / Minerais, métaux, pierres précieuses et or (non monétaire)	Manufactured goods / Articles manufacturés	Chemical products / Produits chimiques	Machinery and transport equipment / Machines et matériel de transport	Other manufactured goods / Articles manufacturés divers
			0 + 1 + 22 + 4	2 - (22 + 27 + 28)	3	27 + 28 + 68 + 667 + 971	5 + 6 +7 + 8- (667 + 68)	5	7	6 + 8 - (667 + 68)
New Caledonia - Nouvelle-Calédonie	1995	(e)471	2.7	0.3	0.0	42.1	54.5	0.1	0.7	53.7
	2005	(e)1 114	2.7	0.1	0.9	29.3	66.3	0.2	1.6	64.4
	2011	(e)1 658	1.3	1.6	0.2	37.6	58.1	2.9	1.6	53.5
New Zealand - Nouvelle-Zélande	1995	13 745	42.4	18.0	1.6	6.3	30.5	7.6	8.6	14.3
	2005	21 729	49.6	10.3	2.5	5.0	31.2	5.8	11.5	13.9
	2011	37 633	53.5	10.5	5.2	5.1	22.0	4.4	7.9	9.8
Nicaragua	1995	509	68.8	2.8	0.6	2.7	24.8	1.6	5.7	17.6
	2005	866	51.4	1.6	0.9	4.0	41.5	2.6	8.9	30.0
	2011	2 281	50.0	1.1	0.4	12.0	36.2	0.8	8.4	27.0
Niger	1995	273	15.9	4.6	4.6	20.9	53.8	40.7	5.9	7.3
	2005	(e)489	19.6	6.0	13.2	19.3	39.9	28.3	6.9	4.7
	2011	(e)1 250	20.6	1.8	22.8	24.6	30.2	26.1	2.3	1.7
Nigeria - Nigéria	1995	(e)12 342	2.8	2.4	92.4	0.3	2.1	0.4	0.2	1.5
	2005	(e)55 995	0.8	0.2	97.4	0.2	1.5	0.1	0.9	0.4
	2011	(e)108 296	1.7	0.9	94.0	0.6	2.9	0.6	1.0	1.3
Niue - Nioué	1995	0	62.1	0.4	2.5	0.2	38.5	5.0	12.7	20.8
	2005	0	6.2	1.4	0.1	25.9	66.4	5.9	28.9	31.7
	2011	(e)0	6.8	1.0	0.0	40.0	50.0	1.8	38.8	9.3
Northern Mariana Islands - Îles Mariannes du Nord	1995	(a,e)941	2.9	0.1	0.0	3.3	42.1	0.5	22.7	18.9
	2005	(e)651	0.8	2.1	0.0	4.5	88.7	1.2	13.1	74.5
	2011	(e)3	0.5	0.6	0.0	15.2	81.5	15.0	19.6	46.9
Norway - Norvège	1995	41 740	8.3	1.5	47.3	8.8	26.8	3.1	13.3	10.4
	2005	103 759	5.2	0.5	67.7	6.0	17.1	2.7	8.2	6.2
	2011	159 361	6.4	0.5	67.8	6.2	15.7	2.9	7.8	5.0
Occupied Palestinian territory - Territoire palestinien occupé	1995	394	..	..	..	..	..	..	..	..
	2005	(e)335	19.3	2.6	3.6	3.8	70.6	8.5	5.4	56.7
	2011	(e)759	20.9	1.6	0.7	13.2	63.4	14.6	5.6	43.2
Oman	1995	5 917	4.1	0.0	81.2	2.0	12.3	0.6	7.7	4.1
	2005	18 692	2.8	0.0	84.9	1.0	7.0	2.0	2.0	3.0
	2011	(e)47 090	4.0	0.0	76.6	3.6	15.7	7.8	4.4	3.6
Pakistan	1995	8 158	11.8	3.8	1.0	0.2	83.0	0.7	0.5	81.8
	2005	16 050	12.0	1.5	4.2	0.4	81.8	3.0	1.8	76.9
	2011	25 344	19.3	2.6	5.2	1.5	71.4	4.2	1.8	65.5
Palau - Palaos	1995	13	75.2	1.8	0.0	0.1	22.5	0.1	3.9	18.6
	2005	14	92.5	1.2	0.0	0.9	3.8	0.0	2.1	1.7
	2011	7	94.2	0.3	0.0	3.3	1.0	0.1	0.8	0.1
Panama	1995	577	32.6	0.4	2.8	1.8	61.7	5.1	40.3	16.3
	2005	(e)7 375	25.8	0.4	6.5	2.5	63.0	5.6	35.8	21.6
	2011	14 555	8.1	0.6	11.1	3.3	75.8	27.1	21.3	27.4
Papua New Guinea - Papouasie-Nouvelle-Guinée	1995	(e)2 654	20.4	18.9	23.7	36.1	0.8	0.1	0.6	0.1
	2005	(e)3 490	19.6	10.2	26.9	39.2	2.6	0.2	1.3	1.1
	2011	(e)7 368	18.8	8.0	19.4	52.0	1.7	0.1	0.8	0.8
Paraguay	1995	919	43.9	36.4	0.2	0.3	19.3	2.6	0.8	15.9
	2005	1 655	76.0	9.0	0.0	1.3	13.8	2.6	0.9	10.2
	2011	5 517	85.2	2.3	0.2	1.5	10.7	2.5	0.7	7.5
Peru - Pérou	1995	5 440	28.8	2.5	4.9	50.2	13.6	2.2	0.6	10.8
	2005	17 114	17.0	1.5	9.3	57.9	14.3	2.4	0.8	11.0
	2011	45 636	16.3	0.9	11.0	61.0	10.7	3.0	0.8	6.9
Philippines	1995	(a)17447	12.8	1.2	1.5	5.4	40.8	2.0	22.2	16.7
	2005	41 255	6.1	0.5	1.9	2.4	89.0	1.3	74.4	13.3
	2011	48 042	10.2	1.0	2.9	6.7	57.9	3.9	41.4	12.6

For sources and notes, see end of table.

Pour les sources et les notes, se reporter à la fin du tableau.

Country or territory Pays ou territoires	Year Année	Total value (millions of dollars) Valeur totale (millions de dollars)	By main SITC Revision 3 product group (percentage) Par principaux groupes de produits de la CTCI Révision 3 (en pourcentage)					Of which: / dont :		
			All food items Produits alimentaires	Agricultural raw materials Matières premières agricoles	Fuels Combustibles	Ores, metals, precious stones and non monetary gold Minerais, métaux, pierres précieuses et or (non monétaire)	Manufactured goods Articles manufacturés	Chemical products Produits chimiques	Machinery and transport equipment Machines et matériel de transport	Other manufactured goods Articles manufacturés divers
			0 + 1 + 22 + 4	2 - (22 + 27 + 28)	3	27 + 28 + 68 + 667 + 971	5 + 6 +7 + 8- (667 + 68)	5	7	6 + 8 - (667 + 68)
Poland - Pologne	1995	22 862	10.4	2.8	8.2	7.3	71.1	7.7	21.1	42.4
	2005	89 378	9.4	1.2	5.1	4.0	78.1	6.7	38.6	32.9
	2011	183 292	10.7	1.2	5.0	5.1	77.9	9.0	39.3	29.6
Portugal	1995	23 370	7.4	4.8	3.2	2.1	81.1	4.9	25.4	50.8
	2005	38 086	8.4	2.7	3.9	2.7	78.9	7.0	33.0	38.9
	2011	58 932	11.2	2.9	6.9	4.6	73.5	9.1	26.7	37.7
Qatar	1995	(e)3 557	0.3	0.1	81.4	0.8	17.1	9.2	1.3	6.6
	2005	(e)25 762	0.1	0.0	84.7	0.3	10.1	8.3	0.7	1.2
	2011	(e)114 298	0.0	0.0	92.2	1.2	6.4	5.3	0.4	0.7
Republic of Moldova - République de Moldova	1995	746	67.0	1.5	0.6	3.0	27.8	1.6	7.7	18.5
	2005	1 091	46.5	2.6	0.1	2.1	48.5	1.7	5.2	41.6
	2011	2 217	40.6	0.9	1.9	5.0	51.5	3.6	11.6	36.4
Romania - Roumanie	1995	7 910	6.6	3.3	7.9	3.5	78.3	10.7	13.1	54.4
	2005	27 730	3.0	2.3	10.7	4.2	79.2	5.7	25.4	48.1
	2011	62 692	8.6	2.1	5.5	4.1	77.8	6.2	40.9	30.7
Russian Federation - Fédération de Russie	1995	(e)78 217	1.8	3.3	43.1	9.9	26.1	5.9	7.0	13.1
	2005	241 452	1.6	2.8	61.8	7.2	18.2	4.2	4.1	9.9
	2011	478 009	2.4	2.1	59.1	6.0	13.5	4.6	2.5	6.5
Rwanda	1995	(e)52	72.7	9.7	0.1	8.3	7.8	1.2	2.5	4.1
	2005	(e)125	45.3	1.1	1.5	39.1	9.8	2.0	4.9	2.9
	2011	(e)417	46.1	2.6	3.5	36.3	11.3	0.5	2.7	8.1
Saint Helena - Sainte-Hélène	1995	(e)5	70.9	0.0	0.0	7.4	25.4	5.1	12.7	7.6
	2005	(e)20	40.0	0.7	0.0	0.1	56.9	6.4	28.8	21.7
	2011	(e)37	63.0	0.3	0.0	1.8	34.1	4.2	22.8	7.1
Saint Kitts and Nevis - Saint-Kitts-et-Nevis	1995	(e)19	40.0	0.2	0.1	0.1	56.7	0.4	50.1	6.2
	2005	(e)34	10.3	1.9	0.0	0.4	81.7	0.1	76.8	4.8
	2011	(e)55	6.0	0.0	0.0	1.8	81.7	0.4	77.5	3.9
Saint Lucia - Sainte-Lucie	1995	109	58.3	0.5	0.0	0.1	37.1	1.0	10.3	25.8
	2005	64	24.0	0.1	52.8	0.7	19.8	1.0	10.2	8.6
	2011	(e)161	31.5	0.1	29.9	2.5	35.9	3.2	13.6	19.2
Saint Pierre and Miquelon - Saint-Pierre-et-Miquelon	1995	6	82.5	1.9	0.0	0.1	14.2	0.9	4.8	8.5
	2005	(e)10	51.5	5.7	2.8	0.4	39.5	0.6	1.4	37.4
	2011	(e)5	59.8	0.1	0.0	0.0	38.4	0.0	1.9	36.4
Saint Vincent and the Grenadines - Saint-Vincent-et-les Grenadines	1995	(e)43	67.0	0.2	0.0	0.2	32.2	0.7	21.4	10.1
	2005	40	20.4	0.2	0.0	0.1	79.2	4.7	70.8	3.6
	2011	(e)42	21.4	0.0	0.3	0.8	77.4	0.4	70.8	6.2
Samoa	1995	(e)9	12.7	1.1	0.0	2.1	83.5	0.1	72.7	10.7
	2005	87	22.1	0.7	0.5	0.1	75.3	0.3	73.8	1.2
	2011	54	31.6	0.3	0.0	0.7	65.3	0.3	62.4	2.6
Sao Tome and Principe - Sao Tomé-et-Principe	1995	(e)5	58.6	2.2	0.0	0.1	38.1	5.0	18.4	14.8
	2005	(e)7	67.1	0.8	0.0	0.4	29.7	0.4	19.2	10.1
	2011	(e)13	70.0	0.6	0.0	0.9	28.5	1.5	11.8	15.2
Saudi Arabia - Arabie saoudite	1995	(e)49 030	1.1	0.2	83.8	1.0	13.7	9.0	1.8	3.0
	2005	(e)180 737	0.6	0.1	88.3	0.5	10.4	7.7	1.1	1.6
	2011	(e)360 093	1.4	0.0	84.1	0.8	13.5	10.4	0.9	2.2
Senegal - Sénégal	1995	(e)993	39.8	6.7	13.1	11.1	29.0	22.2	1.8	4.9
	2005	(e)1 471	32.6	2.5	18.9	4.4	41.5	23.1	8.2	10.1
	2011	(e)2 542	33.8	1.9	20.9	8.4	34.7	16.8	3.6	14.4
Serbia - Serbie	2011	11 775	22.3	2.1	4.2	10.4	60.0	8.5	16.7	34.9
Serbia and Montenegro - Serbie-et-Monténégro	1995	(e)1 531	28.2	4.0	2.1	14.8	49.0	9.0	12.1	27.9
	2005	(e)5 058	17.5	2.6	3.2	8.2	56.8	9.8	8.8	38.3

For sources and notes, see end of table.

Pour les sources et les notes, se reporter à la fin du tableau.

Country or territory / Pays ou territoires	Year / Année	Total value (millions of dollars) / Valeur totale (millions de dollars)	By main SITC Revision 3 product group (percentage) / Par principaux groupes de produits de la CTCI Révision 3 (en pourcentage)					Of which: / dont :		
			All food items / Produits alimentaires	Agricultural raw materials / Matières premières agricoles	Fuels / Combustibles	Ores, metals, precious stones and non monetary gold / Minerais, métaux, pierres précieuses et or (non monétaire)	Manufactured goods / Articles manufacturés	Chemical products / Produits chimiques	Machinery and transport equipment / Machines et matériel de transport	Other manufactured goods / Articles manufacturés divers
			0 + 1 + 22 + 4	2 - (22 + 27 + 28)	3	27 + 28 + 68 + 667 + 971	5 + 6 +7 + 8- (667 + 68)	5	7	6 + 8 - (667 + 68)
Seychelles	1995	53	68.4	0.2	19.2	0.2	10.6	1.3	5.5	3.7
	2005	340	68.9	0.0	10.2	0.3	20.3	2.7	10.9	6.7
	2011	(e)478	86.8	0.1	3.0	0.6	9.4	0.4	2.7	6.3
Sierra Leone	1995	(e)42	52.8	1.0	0.6	30.1	14.6	1.2	3.9	9.6
	2005	(e)159	10.7	0.8	0.7	58.2	29.1	4.0	13.1	12.0
	2011	(e)350	19.2	1.4	0.0	52.2	27.0	3.6	13.1	10.3
Singapore - Singapour	1995	118 263	3.9	1.1	6.8	2.3	83.6	6.0	65.6	12.0
	2005	229 652	1.7	0.3	12.2	2.1	79.9	11.4	58.7	9.8
	2011	409 504	2.1	0.3	19.8	1.8	68.1	12.6	45.8	9.8
Sint Maarten (Dutch part) - Saint-Martin (partie néerlandaise)	2011	127	2.1	0.1	0.7	14.1	5.4	0.4	3.6	1.4
Slovakia - Slovaquie	1995	8 374	5.7	3.6	4.1	3.7	82.2	12.3	20.3	49.6
	2005	31 852	4.2	1.6	7.0	2.6	82.4	5.4	44.4	32.6
	2011	78 487	4.3	1.0	7.4	3.2	82.9	4.9	52.5	25.5
Slovenia - Slovénie	1995	8 316	3.9	1.8	1.2	3.4	89.5	10.5	31.4	47.6
	2005	17 896	2.8	1.2	2.1	4.8	89.0	12.9	39.2	36.8
	2011	(e)34 709	3.4	1.4	5.1	4.1	67.9	13.0	30.3	24.6
Solomon Islands - Îles Salomon	1995	(e)168	36.7	61.9	0.0	0.1	1.2	0.0	0.5	0.8
	2005	(e)103	23.7	74.1	0.1	0.4	1.7	0.1	0.8	0.7
	2011	(e)389	23.8	65.6	0.1	9.5	0.9	0.1	0.3	0.4
Somalia - Somalie	1995	(e)170	90.1	6.8	0.0	0.2	2.6	0.5	0.8	1.3
	2005	(e)251	68.6	11.1	0.7	5.3	2.9	0.7	1.1	1.1
	2011	(e)518	56.1	33.1	0.1	0.5	10.1	2.6	0.2	7.3
South Africa - Afrique du Sud	1995	(e)29 784	14.7	3.0	8.9	21.0	52.5	9.0	20.1	23.3
	2005	(e)56 261	8.5	2.6	9.9	33.8	43.8	7.2	17.3	19.3
	2011	92 976	7.2	2.0	8.6	40.5	34.7	6.1	15.7	12.9
Spain - Espagne	1995	89 616	15.4	1.6	1.7	2.6	77.9	8.5	42.4	27.1
	2005	192 798	14.1	1.2	4.3	2.5	76.3	12.0	40.2	24.2
	2011	(e)296 496	16.8	1.3	4.3	4.1	73.5	14.1	33.9	25.6
Sri Lanka	1995	(e)3 798	18.7	4.3	0.4	6.9	69.0	0.9	3.6	64.5
	2005	6 160	22.2	2.1	0.0	8.6	65.2	1.3	4.5	59.4
	2011	10 011	25.7	4.0	0.4	5.2	64.6	1.4	5.3	57.9
Sudan (...2011) - Soudan (...2011)	1995	(e)556	47.7	41.6	0.2	3.1	7.2	0.2	0.9	6.2
	2005	4 506	5.4	4.1	85.5	3.0	1.8	0.2	1.3	0.3
	2011	(e)10 660	4.3	1.5	85.0	8.1	1.1	0.1	0.7	0.3
Suriname	1995	483	18.6	0.7	1.9	73.9	3.8	0.4	1.1	2.2
	2005	997	13.4	0.4	4.0	62.6	5.2	1.4	2.8	1.1
	2011	(e)2 345	12.9	1.1	8.4	72.9	4.8	2.1	1.7	1.0
Swaziland	1995	(e)844	39.8	12.1	1.1	1.5	45.6	14.9	8.7	22.0
	2005	(e)1 774	26.3	7.6	2.3	3.3	60.4	27.1	11.6	21.6
	2011	(e)2 049	34.9	3.6	0.2	7.2	46.9	15.0	13.3	18.6
Sweden - Suède	1995	77 436	2.2	6.5	1.9	3.2	78.6	6.6	42.1	29.9
	2005	130 264	3.5	4.0	5.0	3.3	78.4	10.6	41.8	26.1
	2011	187 179	4.4	3.6	7.3	5.7	73.9	10.1	38.7	25.1
Switzerland - Suisse	1995	81 641	3.0	0.7	0.1	5.3	90.9	26.0	31.4	33.5
	2005	130 930	2.6	0.4	2.1	4.3	90.6	34.7	25.5	30.4
	2011	234 426	3.7	0.3	3.1	5.7	85.5	35.6	20.8	29.0
Syrian Arab Republic - République arabe syrienne	1995	(e)3 563	12.8	9.0	63.4	1.0	13.7	0.6	1.1	12.0
	2005	(e)9 174	22.5	2.6	46.8	2.3	25.1	8.9	3.2	13.0
	2011	(e)7 843	29.5	1.3	37.6	3.4	28.1	5.7	3.9	18.5
Tajikistan - Tadjikistan	1995	(e)749	11.4	44.9	1.3	26.2	16.2	2.5	2.4	11.3
	2005	(e)874	2.8	7.7	7.9	67.6	10.9	0.7	2.2	8.0
	2011	(e)1 234	3.7	18.0	1.8	39.0	11.9	0.8	1.5	9.6

For sources and notes, see end of table.

Pour les sources et les notes, se reporter à la fin du tableau.

Country or territory / Pays ou territoires	Year / Année	Total value (millions of dollars) / Valeur totale (millions de dollars)	By main SITC Revision 3 product group (percentage) / Par principaux groupes de produits de la CTCI Révision 3 (en pourcentage)					Of which: / dont :		
			All food items / Produits alimentaires	Agricultural raw materials / Matières premières agricoles	Fuels / Combustibles	Ores, metals, precious stones and non monetary gold / Minerais, métaux, pierres précieuses et or (non monétaire)	Manufactured goods / Articles manufacturés	Chemical products / Produits chimiques	Machinery and transport equipment / Machines et matériel de transport	Other manufactured goods / Articles manufacturés divers
			0 + 1 + 22 + 4	2 - (22 + 27 + 28)	3	27 + 28 + 68 + 667 + 971	5 + 6 +7 + 8- (667 + 68)	5	7	6 + 8 - (667 + 68)
TFYR of Macedonia - LERY de Macédoine	1995	1 204	18.3	5.2	0.4	17.9	58.2	5.5	12.9	39.7
	2005	2 041	16.4	0.8	8.0	3.0	71.6	4.4	5.4	61.8
	2011	4 455	14.1	0.6	8.4	6.0	70.9	16.7	7.9	46.2
Thailand - Thaïlande	1995	56 439	19.3	5.4	0.7	2.9	70.9	4.4	33.7	32.9
	2005	110 110	11.6	4.5	4.3	2.4	75.7	8.1	44.7	22.9
	2011	228 824	13.8	7.1	5.6	4.9	68.6	10.0	37.5	21.2
Timor-Leste	2005	(e)8	7.6	0.6	83.8	0.5	7.2	0.2	3.5	3.5
	2011	(e)12	14.6	0.9	57.3	0.6	11.5	0.6	10.1	0.8
Togo	1995	383	16.8	30.1	6.5	35.1	11.4	0.9	3.7	6.8
	2005	(e)659	27.7	11.7	11.2	12.0	37.2	3.9	4.7	28.5
	2011	(e)1 100	31.4	15.7	0.7	17.6	34.5	7.4	3.2	23.9
Tokelau - Tokélaou	1995	(e)1	11.9	0.1	0.0	0.9	84.6	0.1	57.3	27.2
	2005	(e)0	1.6	30.9	0.3	3.0	46.3	2.9	9.8	33.6
	2011	(e)0	3.5	0.4	0.2	0.6	92.4	4.2	11.3	76.9
Tonga	1995	(e)15	84.1	0.5	0.0	0.5	2.9	0.2	1.1	1.6
	2005	(e)10	54.1	14.2	0.0	2.0	7.5	1.1	2.9	3.5
	2011	(e)11	55.1	12.2	1.1	3.4	23.2	5.9	10.5	6.8
Trinidad and Tobago - Trinité-et-Tobago	1995	2 467	10.3	0.2	43.0	1.5	44.6	26.5	2.4	15.7
	2005	9 611	2.7	0.0	66.7	0.7	28.8	21.7	1.2	5.9
	2011	(e)13 272	2.3	0.0	61.6	2.4	33.6	24.2	1.3	8.1
Tunisia - Tunisie	1995	5 475	9.8	0.6	8.5	1.8	79.3	11.9	9.4	57.9
	2005	10 494	10.4	0.6	12.9	1.2	74.9	9.4	19.2	46.3
	2011	(e)17 847	9.6	0.6	14.2	1.7	73.9	10.7	25.3	37.9
Turkey - Turquie	1995	21 599	19.6	1.5	1.3	3.3	74.3	4.1	11.1	59.1
	2005	73 476	10.5	0.5	3.6	2.7	81.4	3.8	29.3	48.3
	2011	134 915	10.5	0.5	4.8	5.3	77.3	5.3	27.8	44.3
Turkmenistan - Turkménistan	1995	(e)1 939	1.1	20.3	70.3	1.3	6.8	0.5	0.4	5.9
	2005	(e)4 944	0.2	2.5	89.1	0.3	7.6	1.3	0.9	5.4
	2011	(e)13 000	0.2	16.8	68.3	1.0	13.5	4.1	0.9	8.5
Turks and Caicos Islands - Îles Turques et Caïques	1995	(e)5	72.9	0.2	17.6	0.1	7.2	3.7	0.8	2.8
	2005	(e)15	51.7	24.4	0.1	0.1	21.1	0.1	12.4	8.6
	2011	(e)16	13.7	0.7	4.7	5.2	63.1	38.2	18.6	6.4
Tuvalu	1995	(e)0	1.0	1.2	0.0	1.3	96.4	14.5	31.0	50.9
	2005	(e)0	1.8	0.2	0.5	0.6	95.2	2.6	42.5	50.1
	2011	(e)0	76.7	0.0	1.6	3.0	12.8	1.0	3.6	8.2
Uganda - Ouganda	1995	(e)461	88.7	4.3	0.0	4.5	2.4	0.5	0.8	1.1
	2005	(e)1 016	60.4	12.7	1.9	9.4	14.8	2.2	4.8	7.7
	2011	(e)2 409	56.7	7.1	1.1	6.0	29.1	3.8	9.5	15.8
Ukraine	1995	(e)13 317	19.0	1.0	4.3	8.2	66.4	12.8	14.1	39.4
	2005	34 228	12.4	1.5	9.8	7.2	68.4	9.1	13.1	46.3
	2011	68 393	18.7	1.1	8.3	8.8	62.6	7.9	16.9	37.8
United Arab Emirates - Émirats arabes unis	1995	(e)27 753	3.3	0.3	72.4	5.1	18.0	2.9	6.3	8.8
	2005	(e)115 453	2.9	0.2	61.8	10.1	24.3	3.1	13.1	8.2
	2011	(e)236 017	3.7	0.2	57.2	16.7	21.9	3.4	9.2	9.4
United Kingdom - Royaume-Uni	1995	234 372	7.6	0.7	6.2	4.8	80.0	12.4	43.8	23.8
	2005	384 365	5.2	0.6	9.5	5.3	74.6	14.9	39.6	20.1
	2011	472 096	6.4	0.8	13.6	6.7	66.3	16.8	31.3	18.2
United Republic of Tanzania - République-Unie de Tanzanie	1995	(e)685	65.2	23.1	0.3	3.9	7.1	0.7	1.3	5.0
	2005	1 672	38.8	10.3	4.0	36.4	10.3	1.5	2.3	6.5
	2011	4 735	32.8	5.8	1.3	42.8	17.0	3.1	4.5	9.5
United States - États-Unis	1995	582 965	10.1	3.7	1.8	3.8	77.5	10.6	48.3	18.7
	2005	904 339	6.8	2.3	2.9	4.3	80.4	13.3	48.0	19.1
	2011	1 479 730	8.9	2.5	8.7	7.3	64.3	14.0	33.9	16.5

For sources and notes, see end of table.

Pour les sources et les notes, se reporter à la fin du tableau.

Country or territory / Pays ou territoires	Year / Année	Total value (millions of dollars) / Valeur totale (millions de dollars)	By main SITC Revision 3 product group (percentage) / Par principaux groupes de produits de la CTCI Révision 3 (en pourcentage)					Of which: / dont :		
			All food items / Produits alimentaires	Agricultural raw materials / Matières premières agricoles	Fuels / Combustibles	Ores, metals, precious stones and non monetary gold / Minerais, métaux, pierres précieuses et or (non monétaire)	Manufactured goods / Articles manufacturés	Chemical products / Produits chimiques	Machinery and transport equipment / Machines et matériel de transport	Other manufactured goods / Articles manufacturés divers
			0 + 1 + 22 + 4	2 - (22 + 27 + 28)	3	27 + 28 + 68 + 667 + 971	5 + 6 +7 + 8- (667 + 68)	5	7	6 + 8 - (667 + 68)
Uruguay	1995	2 106	44.2	14.9	1.0	0.9	38.7	5.6	6.0	27.1
	2005	3 405	54.5	9.2	4.8	1.9	29.6	5.8	2.9	20.9
	2011	(e)7 951	55.4	15.3	1.5	1.4	26.4	7.3	3.5	15.6
Uzbekistan - Ouzbékistan	1995	3 430	1.3	62.3	15.0	14.1	7.2	3.0	0.8	3.4
	2005	4 749	12.2	25.4	15.8	16.3	28.7	8.6	11.3	8.7
	2011	13 254	9.1	15.4	14.7	20.1	40.7	13.2	14.9	12.6
Vanuatu	1995	(e)28	82.7	4.8	0.0	0.0	12.3	0.0	6.1	6.1
	2005	(e)38	64.5	11.3	0.5	0.0	23.0	0.3	22.2	0.4
	2011	(e)67	72.6	0.7	0.9	0.6	24.9	0.4	23.8	0.6
Venezuela (Bolivarian Rep. of) - Venezuela (Rép. bolivarienne du)	1995	19 093	3.1	0.2	72.4	8.1	16.0	5.0	3.1	7.9
	2005	55 413	0.9	0.1	83.5	4.2	11.1	3.1	1.5	6.6
	2011	(e)92 602	0.3	0.1	84.3	2.9	12.3	4.4	1.1	6.8
Viet Nam	1995	(e)5 449	30.2	3.1	18.0	0.8	43.7	1.1	7.0	35.6
	2005	32 447	20.2	3.1	25.8	0.7	49.8	1.6	9.6	38.5
	2011	(e)96 906	19.9	5.3	15.5	1.7	57.5	2.5	12.6	42.4
Wallis and Futuna Islands - Îles Wallis-et-Futuna	1995	(e)1	16.4	0.0	0.0	0.0	83.6	7.9	49.0	26.7
	2005	(e)0	5.2	11.3	0.0	0.8	81.6	8.4	32.6	40.6
	2011	(e)0	0.7	0.0	0.0	0.0	84.5	8.1	22.5	53.9
Western Sahara - Sahara occidental	1995	(e)8	58.9	23.6	2.3	0.0	15.0	6.4	5.1	3.6
Yemen - Yémen	1995	(e)1 917	3.2	0.5	93.5	0.6	2.0	0.4	0.8	0.7
	2005	(e)5 608	5.7	0.3	90.3	1.9	1.6	0.4	0.8	0.4
	2011	(e)9 622	6.1	0.3	89.1	2.0	2.5	0.8	0.6	1.1
Zambia - Zambie	1995	1 055	3.6	0.8	2.3	87.4	5.8	0.3	1.5	4.0
	2005	1 810	12.3	6.3	0.6	68.8	10.9	0.7	1.6	8.6
	2011	(e)9 018	8.3	1.9	0.9	78.7	10.2	2.2	2.5	5.5
Zimbabwe	1995	(e)2 121	41.9	9.0	2.3	14.9	31.5	2.0	2.5	27.0
	2005	(e)1 850	25.2	10.1	0.9	36.9	26.6	1.9	2.3	22.3
	2011	(e)3 500	30.0	14.4	9.7	23.0	24.3	1.6	3.0	19.7

Source:
UNCTAD secretariat calculations, based on UNCTAD, *UNCTADstat* Merchandise Trade Matrix

Notes:
(a)   More than 30% of total trade under SITC Rev.3, code 931: "Special transactions & commodities not classified"

Source :
Calculs du secrétariat de la CNUCED, basés sur la matrice du commerce de marchandises de *UNCTADstat* de la CNUCED

Notes :
(a)   Plus de 30% du commerce sous la position 931 de la CTCI rév. 3 : "Transactions et articles spéciaux non classés"

Country or territory / Pays ou territoires	Year / Année	Total value (millions of dollars) / Valeur totale (millions de dollars)	All food items / Produits alimentaires	Agricultural raw materials / Matières premières agricoles	Fuels / Combustibles	Ores, metals, precious stones and non monetary gold / Minerais, métaux, pierres précieuses et or (non monétaire)	Manufactured goods / Articles manufacturés	Chemical products / Produits chimiques	Machinery and transport equipment / Machines et matériel de transport	Other manufactured goods / Articles manufacturés divers
			0 + 1 + 22 + 4	2 - (22 + 27 + 28)	3	27 + 28 + 68 + 667 + 971	5 + 6 +7 + 8- (667 + 68)	5	7	6 + 8 - (667 + 68)
Afghanistan	1995	(e)387	23.7	0.8	7.0	0.5	67.4	9.7	19.9	37.8
	2005	(e)2 470	22.1	1.3	17.3	0.4	56.7	6.3	22.3	28.1
	2011	(e)6 300	17.3	1.0	27.1	0.2	47.7	2.7	23.7	21.4
Albania - Albanie	1995	(e)714	55.8	1.5	4.2	1.7	99.6	9.6	37.1	52.9
	2005	2 614	17.7	1.1	8.0	2.4	70.4	8.6	22.7	39.0
	2011	5 396	16.6	1.0	17.1	3.8	61.3	9.8	19.2	32.2
Algeria - Algérie	1995	10 782	29.5	3.2	1.1	1.6	64.7	11.3	30.5	22.9
	2005	20 357	19.3	1.7	1.0	1.5	76.5	12.0	43.0	21.5
	2011	47 220	22.8	1.5	2.3	1.7	71.7	11.4	37.3	23.0
American Samoa - Samoa américaines	1995	416	..	..	..	..	..	..	..	..
	2005	(e)506	52.0	2.6	7.0	1.3	32.8	2.1	14.4	16.2
	2011	(e)690	21.1	1.0	45.8	1.0	29.5	7.9	11.4	10.1
Andorra - Andorre	1995	(e)1 025	28.4	0.8	4.3	1.2	65.2	9.5	20.4	35.2
	2005	(e)1 822	..	..	..	..	..	..	..	..
	2011	(e)1 615	23.1	0.3	12.4	1.0	63.1	9.3	22.9	31.0
Angola	1995	(e)1 468	26.2	0.9	0.6	0.4	70.5	6.1	42.4	22.0
	2005	(e)8 353	16.2	0.7	0.7	0.4	80.7	5.0	53.3	22.4
	2011	(e)21 736	21.9	0.9	5.7	0.7	67.9	7.0	32.0	28.8
Anguilla	1995	(e)53	24.8	0.2	67.1	0.1	7.1	0.8	2.8	3.5
	2005	(e)130	20.0	2.0	19.9	1.8	54.1	4.4	28.7	21.0
	2011	(e)153	12.3	1.9	1.5	2.0	79.8	5.9	35.5	38.4
Antigua and Barbuda - Antigua-et-Barbuda	1995	(e)346	15.5	1.8	4.7	0.4	69.9	7.4	46.4	16.1
	2005	(e)525	7.6	0.9	13.3	0.4	63.0	2.5	50.9	9.5
	2011	(a,e)471	6.5	0.5	9.7	0.2	49.7	2.4	41.6	5.7
Argentina - Argentine	1995	20 122	5.5	2.0	4.2	2.7	85.5	17.8	44.5	23.1
	2005	28 689	2.8	1.5	5.0	3.5	86.4	19.8	46.6	19.9
	2011	76 949	2.4	1.0	11.7	3.4	80.6	16.9	45.5	18.3
Armenia - Arménie	1995	(e)674	32.7	0.2	31.8	1.2	31.4	8.8	10.7	12.0
	2005	(e)1 692	16.9	0.8	12.9	20.1	48.3	7.8	20.9	19.6
	2011	(e)4 109	21.2	1.2	15.0	7.7	54.0	9.7	22.5	21.8
Aruba	1995	(e)1 772	27.9	2.0	14.0	2.9	50.0	6.9	19.6	23.5
	2005	(e)4 288	6.2	0.4	49.0	2.2	29.0	2.8	10.6	15.6
	2011	(e)5 891	15.6	0.5	40.0	1.2	40.6	6.0	15.0	19.5
Australia - Australie	1995	57 423	5.0	1.7	5.0	2.5	85.7	11.0	47.0	27.7
	2005	118 922	4.6	0.9	11.1	3.2	79.9	11.4	44.3	24.2
	2011	234 319	5.1	0.6	16.9	5.1	69.2	10.5	37.0	21.6
Austria - Autriche	1995	66 406	5.7	3.2	4.4	4.3	81.6	10.7	36.8	34.1
	2005	119 950	6.1	2.2	12.2	3.8	74.9	10.7	36.8	27.4
	2011	(e)181 217	8.3	2.6	10.9	7.1	71.1	12.4	30.6	28.1
Azerbaijan - Azerbaïdjan	1995	(e)668	37.2	0.9	6.5	1.0	53.9	10.2	14.1	29.6
	2005	4 211	10.5	1.0	11.9	2.2	74.2	5.5	43.5	25.2
	2011	9 733	14.1	2.0	0.9	1.2	81.7	8.8	48.6	24.3
Bahamas	1995	(e)1 243	18.8	1.9	12.6	0.5	64.5	8.1	25.8	30.6
	2005	2 567	15.6	2.3	19.8	0.6	57.8	8.5	22.1	27.2
	2011	3 410	15.9	1.3	27.3	0.5	51.2	11.3	17.1	22.8
Bahrain - Bahreïn	1995	(e)3 679	10.9	0.5	36.7	4.8	45.1	5.5	17.0	22.6
	2005	(e)9 339	6.7	0.4	32.2	4.9	53.6	4.4	29.3	19.9
	2011	(e)12 106	17.1	0.7	2.0	10.2	67.0	9.8	29.0	28.2
Bangladesh	1995	(e)6 694	16.6	3.4	5.7	2.1	70.9	9.3	18.3	43.3
	2005	12 631	13.1	5.3	12.8	2.7	65.5	11.4	24.5	29.5
	2011	(e)34 295	20.4	6.5	8.9	3.2	60.9	14.0	18.2	28.8

For sources and notes, see end of table.

Pour les sources et les notes, se reporter à la fin du tableau.

Country or territory / Pays ou territoires	Year / Année	Total value (millions of dollars) / Valeur totale (millions de dollars)	By main SITC Revision 3 product group (percentage) / Par principaux groupes de produits de la CTCI Révision 3 (en pourcentage)					Of which: / dont :		
			All food items / Produits alimentaires	Agricultural raw materials / Matières premières agricoles	Fuels / Combustibles	Ores, metals, precious stones and non-monetary gold / Minerais, métaux, pierres précieuses et or (non monétaire)	Manu-factured goods / Articles manufacturés	Chemical products / Produits chimiques	Machinery and transport equipment / Machines et matériel de transport	Other manu-factured goods / Articles manu-facturés divers
			0 + 1 + 22 + 4	2 - (22 + 27 + 28)	3	27 + 28 + 68 + 667 + 971	5 + 6 +7 + 8-(667 + 68)	5	7	6 + 8 - (667 + 68)
Barbados - Barbade	1995	766	18.5	2.3	8.4	1.3	67.4	11.3	26.8	29.3
	2005	1 672	14.4	1.9	21.7	1.2	59.0	8.2	26.4	24.4
	2011	1 775	13.7	1.0	45.0	0.9	37.3	6.5	15.5	15.3
Belarus - Bélarus	1995	(a,e)5 563	11.8	0.5	1.1	1.1	32.7	6.1	13.6	13.1
	2005	16 699	9.4	1.7	33.0	3.2	46.3	9.5	18.2	18.6
	2011	45 747	6.8	1.5	41.0	3.3	41.8	8.9	17.4	15.5
Belgium - Belgique	1995	(e)164 590	7.0	1.6	5.2	9.9	48.4	10.6	20.1	17.7
	2005	320 130	7.6	1.2	12.4	8.4	69.7	25.0	25.7	19.0
	2011	465 216	8.5	1.3	16.4	9.4	63.2	22.5	22.7	18.0
Belize	1995	259	16.3	0.7	14.5	0.5	65.6	9.2	28.0	28.4
	2005	(e)593	12.3	0.9	25.6	1.9	56.9	10.8	24.1	22.0
	2011	(e)831	16.7	0.9	22.4	0.8	59.2	10.6	22.4	26.1
Benin - Bénin	1995	(e)719	27.3	2.7	9.4	1.0	59.4	13.7	18.0	27.7
	2005	(e)1 018	21.4	2.3	12.3	0.7	63.0	7.4	17.8	37.7
	2011	(e)2 700	23.2	2.0	15.3	0.5	59.0	4.9	14.9	39.1
Bermuda - Bermudes	1995	(e)550	18.1	0.9	13.9	0.3	60.6	6.3	35.1	19.2
	2005	(e)988	9.1	0.4	5.5	0.3	80.8	3.2	64.0	13.5
	2011	(e)893	4.6	0.2	5.4	0.2	81.5	1.6	73.9	6.1
Bhutan - Bhoutan	1995	(e)113	16.1	1.0	1.7	1.7	60.7	5.3	40.3	15.1
	2005	(e)387	13.6	0.6	11.4	5.0	68.4	6.7	33.7	27.9
	2011	(e)949	11.9	1.5	14.2	7.3	64.9	4.3	36.9	23.7
Bolivia (Plurinational State of) - Bolivie (État plurinational de)	1995	1 396	14.3	1.5	3.7	2.7	77.3	13.7	35.9	27.7
	2005	2 343	9.5	1.3	8.7	1.0	79.1	17.5	31.9	29.7
	2011	7 673	8.9	0.7	9.6	0.8	79.2	13.9	37.7	27.6
Bonaire, Sint Eustatius and Saba - Bonaire, Saint-Eustache et Saba	2011	(e)55	1.7	0.0	0.0	0.0	98.2	7.8	62.4	28.0
Bosnia and Herzegovina - Bosnie-Herzégovine	1995	(e)1 082	37.8	0.9	10.7	1.0	46.4	9.0	12.6	24.8
	2005	(e)7 054	17.7	1.3	12.5	2.1	64.0	11.0	22.7	30.3
	2011	(e)11 051	18.7	1.9	16.9	2.7	59.6	13.1	18.7	27.8
Botswana	1995	(e)1 902	17.8	1.1	3.7	4.6	72.8	7.9	33.2	31.7
	2005	3 162	13.8	0.8	13.7	4.4	64.6	9.2	29.6	25.8
	2011	7 272	11.7	1.1	18.0	7.2	60.8	7.3	30.5	23.0
Brazil - Brésil	1995	53 734	10.7	2.7	12.1	3.4	71.1	15.2	39.2	16.7
	2005	73 600	4.4	1.5	18.3	3.9	71.9	19.9	37.9	14.2
	2011	226 243	4.5	1.5	18.5	3.4	72.0	18.5	38.3	15.2
British Virgin Islands - Îles Vierges britanniques	1995	(e)122	2.4	0.2	77.7	0.5	18.8	3.9	13.2	1.7
Brunei Darussalam - Brunéi Darussalam	1995	(e)2 078	13.6	0.6	0.2	3.3	81.8	6.4	39.0	36.5
	2005	(e)1 497	20.1	0.3	1.2	1.6	76.7	9.3	29.4	38.0
	2011	(e)2 950	19.6	0.3	2.1	1.5	76.2	10.7	26.9	38.7
Bulgaria - Bulgarie	1995	(e)5 651	7.6	2.6	33.7	4.4	47.9	11.1	16.0	20.8
	2005	18 162	5.0	1.4	11.1	6.8	66.9	9.8	29.8	27.2
	2011	32 494	9.7	1.2	19.7	12.0	55.2	11.4	22.3	21.5
Burkina Faso	1995	484	17.7	1.7	11.0	1.1	68.0	17.1	24.2	26.7
	2005	1 161	18.6	0.7	12.9	0.6	66.1	18.3	23.4	24.3
	2011	(e)2 600	17.1	1.1	18.2	1.3	62.2	15.4	20.8	26.1
Burundi	1995	(e)234	19.0	4.2	6.2	1.1	68.4	14.1	30.8	23.5
	2005	258	9.9	1.6	9.8	2.4	75.2	14.4	29.8	31.1
	2011	(e)752	16.6	1.7	6.2	1.7	73.9	16.9	23.2	33.7
Cambodia - Cambodge	1995	(e)1 187	23.8	1.6	9.0	7.8	56.3	5.9	34.2	16.2
	2005	(e)3 918	10.1	1.4	10.9	0.9	75.6	6.9	16.3	52.4
	2011	(e)9 300	12.6	0.9	16.9	5.1	65.7	5.9	18.4	41.4

For sources and notes, see end of table.

Pour les sources et les notes, se reporter à la fin du tableau.

Country or territory / Pays ou territoires	Year / Année	Total value (millions of dollars) / Valeur totale (millions de dollars)	By main SITC Revision 3 product group (percentage) / Par principaux groupes de produits de la CTCI Révision 3 (en pourcentage)						
			All food items / Produits alimentaires	Agricultural raw materials / Matières premières agricoles	Fuels / Combus-tibles	Ores, metals, precious stones and non monetary gold / Minerais, métaux, pierres précieuses et or (non monétaire)	Manu-factured goods / Articles manu-facturés	Of which: / dont :		
								Chemical products / Produits chimiques	Machinery and transport equipment / Machines et matériel de transport	Other manu-factured goods / Articles manu-facturés divers
			0 + 1 + 22 + 4	2 - (22 + 27 + 28)	3	27 + 28 + 68 + 667 + 971	5 + 6 +7 + 8- (667 + 68)	5	7	6 + 8 - (667 + 68)
Cameroon - Cameroun	1995	1 079	17.4	2.5	2.4	5.6	72.0	16.5	30.5	24.9
	2005	2 735	18.0	1.8	26.3	3.5	50.0	11.0	20.1	19.0
	2011	(e)6 500	19.6	1.7	23.7	2.1	52.8	10.4	23.9	18.5
Canada	1995	164 371	5.7	1.7	3.6	3.7	82.7	8.1	51.6	23.1
	2005	314 444	5.6	1.2	9.2	3.6	78.9	10.1	45.5	23.2
	2011	450 537	7.1	1.0	11.8	6.2	72.3	10.2	40.1	22.1
Cape Verde - Cap-Vert	1995	(e)252	32.0	2.1	14.5	0.4	49.9	5.8	19.6	24.6
	2005	(e)438	28.4	-0.3	10.6	5.7	53.7	6.8	20.8	26.1
	2011	(e)961	24.6	0.9	20.5	0.7	52.6	5.5	25.0	22.1
Cayman Islands - Îles Caïmanes	1995	(e)391	11.4	0.8	2.6	0.5	77.7	22.0	26.5	29.2
	2005	(e)1 191	10.5	0.5	4.9	0.4	73.8	1.4	61.3	11.1
	2011	(e)914	3.2	0.3	16.5	0.6	69.9	1.2	61.5	7.2
Central African Republic - République centrafricaine	1995	(e)174	14.2	1.3	0.9	2.0	81.0	12.0	50.3	18.6
	2005	185	19.6	3.7	16.0	1.5	58.2	10.1	28.6	19.5
	2011	(e)380	25.5	1.7	18.3	2.2	52.3	10.3	20.7	21.4
Chad - Tchad	1995	(e)488	17.5	0.5	14.0	0.5	66.8	9.3	31.2	26.3
	2005	(e)949	12.5	1.2	6.9	1.0	78.0	11.1	42.7	24.1
	2011	(e)2 100	16.0	0.8	9.3	1.0	70.2	10.8	38.5	20.9
Chile - Chili	1995	14 903	6.7	1.7	9.0	2.2	79.2	12.2	42.3	24.7
	2005	32 926	5.8	1.0	21.6	3.2	68.4	10.6	37.2	20.6
	2011	74 907	7.4	0.6	24.0	2.4	65.5	9.9	35.3	20.2
China - Chine	1995	132 083	7.0	5.2	3.9	4.6	78.1	12.9	39.8	25.4
	2005	659 953	3.3	3.6	9.7	8.8	74.4	11.8	44.0	18.6
	2011	1 743 395	4.3	4.0	15.8	14.2	58.8	10.4	36.2	12.3
China, Hong Kong SAR - Chine (RAS de Hong Kong)	1995	196 072	5.4	1.6	1.9	5.6	85.1	7.4	36.5	41.3
	2005	300 160	2.9	0.8	2.7	4.9	88.7	6.2	52.1	30.3
	2011	510 855	4.2	0.6	3.7	10.9	80.6	4.8	53.2	22.6
China, Macao SAR - Chine (RAS de Macao)	1995	2 025	18.8	2.6	3.9	1.0	73.2	5.9	20.2	47.2
	2005	(e)3 913	11.1	0.6	8.0	0.8	79.1	4.9	23.3	50.9
	2011	7 927	17.1	0.4	9.3	0.6	71.5	6.3	24.5	40.7
China, Taiwan Province of - Province chinoise de Taiwan	1995	(e)103 506	5.4	4.2	6.9	7.4	74.2	13.3	40.2	20.7
	2005	(e)181 592	3.6	1.6	15.5	6.3	72.1	12.6	41.0	18.4
	2011	(e)281 316	3.9	1.5	22.4	8.7	62.5	14.2	33.4	14.9
Colombia - Colombie	1995	13 883	9.4	2.5	2.8	2.5	78.0	18.1	37.3	22.6
	2005	21 204	8.7	1.6	2.6	2.6	83.7	20.8	40.4	22.5
	2011	54 675	9.3	1.2	7.0	1.8	79.8	16.8	40.7	22.3
Comoros - Comores	1995	62	25.1	1.5	5.0	0.5	67.4	7.4	32.5	27.5
	2005	(e)99	33.6	1.2	9.3	0.4	53.6	3.8	23.2	26.6
	2011	(e)277	35.0	0.9	5.2	0.4	58.5	3.6	29.3	25.5
Congo	1995	(e)670	11.9	0.4	15.6	0.6	70.6	8.8	26.6	35.1
	2005	(e)1 343	21.3	2.2	2.7	1.3	71.4	12.7	29.7	29.0
	2011	(e)5 501	15.6	1.5	3.4	0.7	78.1	7.7	49.5	20.9
Cook Islands - Îles Cook	1995	(e)49	22.7	1.7	11.5	1.2	62.5	5.8	31.0	25.6
	2005	(e)81	28.0	2.6	6.1	0.7	57.4	7.4	20.9	29.1
	2011	(e)81	29.4	2.1	11.3	0.7	54.8	5.9	22.9	26.0
Costa Rica	1995	(e)4 090	9.2	1.3	7.0	2.0	79.1	17.1	26.8	35.2
	2005	9 173	7.0	1.1	9.5	1.9	78.7	14.5	39.1	25.1
	2011	(e)16 218	8.7	1.2	13.1	2.0	74.1	13.1	37.2	23.7
Côte d'Ivoire	1995	(e)2 946	17.5	0.8	16.1	1.3	47.5	10.9	20.5	16.1
	2005	5 865	14.6	0.5	28.0	1.0	54.8	9.4	24.2	21.2
	2011	6 720	25.1	0.9	28.6	1.2	44.0	14.2	15.8	14.1

For sources and notes, see end of table.

Pour les sources et les notes, se reporter à la fin du tableau.

3

3.1   Country trade structure
      by product group
      Imports

3.1   Structure du commerce des pays
      par groupes de produits
      Importations

Country or territory Pays ou territoires	Year Année	Total value (millions of dollars) Valeur totale (millions de dollars)	By main SITC Revision 3 product group (percentage) Par principaux groupes de produits de la CTCI Révision 3 (en pourcentage)							
			All food items Produits alimentaires	Agricultural raw materials Matières premières agricoles	Fuels Combus-tibles	Ores, metals, precious stones and non monetary gold Minerais, métaux, pierres précieuses et or (non monétaire)	Manu-factured goods Articles manu-facturés	Of which: / dont :		
								Chemical products Produits chimiques	Machinery and transport equipment Machines et matériel de transport	Other manu-factured goods Articles manu-facturés divers
			0 + 1 + 22 + 4	2 - (22 + 27 + 28)	3	27 + 28 + 68 + 667 + 971	5 + 6 +7 + 8-(667 + 68)	5	7	6 + 8 - (667 + 68)
Croatia - Croatie	1995	7 509	11.8	1.8	11.6	2.5	66.6	10.8	26.7	29.0
	2005	18 560	8.3	1.3	15.1	2.3	72.9	11.1	32.9	28.9
	2011	20 397	10.6	1.1	21.7	2.7	63.8	13.8	22.7	27.4
Cuba	1995	(e)2 805	20.9	1.7	21.4	1.6	53.5	12.3	20.4	20.9
	2005	(e)8 084	19.2	0.7	26.3	1.5	51.1	7.5	24.7	18.9
	2011	(e)14 300	16.0	1.0	24.8	1.4	55.1	9.6	18.1	27.5
Cyprus - Chypre	1995	3 694	20.4	1.3	7.7	2.3	68.3	8.8	27.6	31.9
	2005	6 382	12.4	1.1	16.1	1.3	67.5	8.9	30.9	27.7
	2011	8 719	15.9	0.7	25.3	0.9	56.1	10.2	20.7	25.1
Czech Republic - République tchèque	1995	25 303	6.6	2.5	8.6	4.3	76.4	11.6	35.1	29.7
	2005	76 527	5.2	1.5	6.8	3.4	78.3	10.6	40.1	27.5
	2011	150 542	5.9	1.5	9.7	3.9	77.8	11.2	40.6	25.9
Dem. Rep. of the Congo - Rép. dém. du Congo	1995	(e)1 046	21.8	3.2	10.2	1.2	62.3	9.5	20.9	31.9
	2005	(e)2 690	22.9	2.8	13.6	0.9	59.0	11.0	26.3	21.6
	2011	(e)5 306	17.1	1.8	4.5	1.7	74.2	12.5	36.4	25.3
Denmark - Danemark	1995	43 142	12.0	3.0	3.3	2.1	72.7	11.2	32.0	29.5
	2005	74 265	11.3	2.2	6.7	1.8	76.4	10.9	36.3	29.2
	2011	97 831	13.5	2.5	9.3	1.7	70.1	11.1	30.0	29.1
Djibouti	1995	(e)177	28.8	11.3	2.1	0.3	56.7	5.3	15.3	36.2
	2005	(e)277	12.7	3.7	30.7	0.6	51.1	6.8	15.9	28.5
	2011	(e)416	27.6	1.0	14.4	1.2	55.0	8.2	18.9	28.0
Dominica - Dominique	1995	117	26.2	2.0	5.6	0.4	65.7	14.3	24.0	27.5
	2005	165	19.4	1.3	13.3	0.5	65.5	11.4	25.4	28.8
	2011	(e)221	22.6	2.3	16.9	0.6	57.6	8.5	22.4	26.6
Dominican Republic - République dominicaine	1995	(e)5 170	12.4	1.6	11.6	0.7	71.6	7.7	20.5	43.3
	2005	(e)9 869	11.6	1.3	13.2	1.5	70.6	9.5	24.4	36.7
	2011	(e)18 156	14.2	0.9	26.2	1.2	55.7	9.7	19.0	27.0
Ecuador - Équateur	1995	4 195	7.6	2.8	5.9	1.9	81.8	17.6	40.1	24.1
	2005	9 609	8.0	1.3	12.0	1.2	77.4	16.8	36.8	23.9
	2011	24 286	8.6	1.2	22.2	1.3	66.3	15.3	30.5	20.4
Egypt - Égypte	1995	11 739	28.4	7.1	1.2	2.7	60.6	13.2	25.3	22.1
	2005	19 812	20.1	4.1	13.5	3.4	46.2	11.3	18.6	16.3
	2011	59 269	22.9	3.1	15.7	5.7	52.6	12.6	20.1	19.9
El Salvador	1995	(e)3 329	14.3	2.4	7.8	1.4	73.0	15.1	27.4	30.5
	2005	6 809	14.3	1.4	13.3	1.4	66.6	13.9	18.0	34.7
	2011	(e)10 118	16.7	2.2	19.6	1.1	60.5	13.3	15.6	31.7
Equatorial Guinea - Guinée équatoriale	1995	121	25.7	2.6	3.2	0.6	69.0	9.7	27.9	31.4
	2005	1 310	10.3	0.8	9.5	0.4	77.1	2.8	56.3	17.9
	2011	(e)6 000	9.2	0.5	9.7	0.8	77.3	4.1	38.5	34.6
Eritrea - Érythrée	1995	(e)434	12.0	1.5	5.2	0.4	79.2	4.3	46.1	28.8
	2005	(e)487	33.2	0.7	2.3	1.2	59.4	6.5	33.2	19.6
	2011	(e)849	25.5	0.6	2.7	0.9	69.4	9.5	37.4	22.6
Estonia - Estonie	1995	2 546	14.2	2.6	11.5	2.4	68.5	8.9	29.1	30.5
	2005	11 018	8.0	3.4	12.7	1.5	69.2	8.9	35.3	24.9
	2011	18 780	9.7	2.0	18.6	1.9	62.7	10.0	30.5	22.1
Ethiopia - Éthiopie	1995	1 141	13.8	1.9	11.1	0.8	72.4	14.1	35.5	22.7
	2005	4 095	10.6	0.9	15.1	1.2	72.1	12.3	34.7	25.1
	2011	8 896	14.8	0.6	17.7	1.5	65.3	11.5	31.2	22.7
Faeroe Islands - Îles Féroé	1995	(e)314	22.3	3.5	11.7	1.2	57.9	7.3	27.5	23.0
	2005	747	13.2	2.3	16.2	1.1	65.6	6.4	36.8	22.3
	2011	(e)978	20.4	2.4	24.7	1.2	51.2	8.0	17.9	25.2

For sources and notes, see end of table.

Pour les sources et les notes, se reporter à la fin du tableau.

3.1 Country trade structure
by product group
Imports

3.1 Structure du commerce des pays
par groupes de produits
Importations

Country or territory / Pays ou territoires	Year / Année	Total value (millions of dollars) / Valeur totale (millions de dollars)	By main SITC Revision 3 product group (percentage) / Par principaux groupes de produits de la CTCI Révision 3 (en pourcentage)					Of which: / dont :		
			All food items / Produits alimentaires	Agricultural raw materials / Matières premières agricoles	Fuels / Combustibles	Ores, metals, precious stones and non monetary gold / Minerais, métaux, pierres précieuses et or (non monétaire)	Manufactured goods / Articles manufacturés	Chemical products / Produits chimiques	Machinery and transport equipment / Machines et matériel de transport	Other manufactured goods / Articles manufacturés divers
			0 + 1 + 22 + 4	2 - (22 + 27 + 28)	3	27 + 28 + 68 + 667 + 971	5 + 6 +7 + 8- (667 + 68)	5	7	6 + 8 - (667 + 68)
Falkland Islands (Malvinas) - Îles Falkland (Malvinas)	1995	(e)44	18.1	1.4	4.4	0.1	74.1	2.0	57.9	14.1
	2005	(a,e)59	1.5	0.1	1.6	0.1	12.1	0.2	5.4	6.5
	2011	(e)193	7.9	0.3	21.0	2.0	65.8	7.4	29.0	29.4
Fiji - Fidji	1995	(e)892	14.1	0.6	13.3	0.9	68.8	6.9	23.6	38.3
	2005	1 607	14.7	0.4	28.8	0.9	54.9	7.7	21.7	25.5
	2011	(e)2 300	17.5	0.3	33.0	1.1	48.1	8.1	17.5	22.5
Finland - Finlande	1995	29 520	6.0	3.6	8.8	5.7	74.3	12.2	38.7	23.3
	2005	58 473	5.2	2.9	13.7	6.5	70.0	11.3	39.2	19.5
	2011	83 862	6.8	2.4	21.7	7.8	57.9	11.0	27.8	19.2
France	1995	275 510	10.7	2.5	6.9	3.9	76.0	12.5	35.4	28.1
	2005	475 857	7.8	1.5	13.4	2.8	74.6	13.3	35.7	25.5
	2011	700 852	8.3	1.3	16.4	3.1	70.8	13.8	32.8	24.1
French Polynesia - Polynésie française	1995	(e)1 019	21.6	1.5	5.5	0.9	70.5	8.5	34.7	27.4
	2005	1 702	19.0	1.3	9.6	0.9	69.2	8.4	35.8	25.0
	2011	1 628	24.9	1.1	16.0	0.7	57.3	10.3	24.1	22.9
Gabon	1995	(e)884	19.1	0.7	3.4	1.1	75.6	10.7	39.3	25.7
	2005	1 472	16.9	0.5	4.1	1.3	76.2	9.1	41.9	25.2
	2011	(e)3 800	17.5	0.8	3.8	1.5	75.5	9.6	40.5	25.4
Gambia - Gambie	1995	(e)182	30.4	1.2	8.8	0.3	57.6	5.5	16.4	35.7
	2005	260	30.7	1.1	13.0	3.4	51.2	5.6	15.3	30.3
	2011	344	36.1	0.8	7.2	1.1	54.2	4.9	12.2	37.2
Georgia - Géorgie	1995	(e)489	31.6	0.2	32.8	0.3	29.4	12.1	8.9	8.4
	2005	(e)2 490	19.7	-0.3	20.1	3.2	55.1	8.9	25.7	20.4
	2011	(e)6 946	18.0	0.6	18.0	2.3	60.1	9.7	25.2	25.2
Germany - Allemagne	1995	464 145	9.8	2.6	6.2	4.4	69.9	9.1	31.8	28.9
	2005	779 819	7.0	1.5	11.5	4.1	71.6	11.7	37.4	22.4
	2011	1 260 298	7.3	1.6	13.2	5.8	67.2	12.5	33.0	21.7
Ghana	1995	(e)1 896	7.9	1.0	5.8	2.6	74.9	9.3	43.7	21.9
	2005	4 878	15.6	1.7	16.4	1.9	63.1	10.2	28.0	24.9
	2011	(e)15 300	15.9	1.2	3.0	1.9	77.4	13.3	34.7	29.5
Gibraltar	1995	411	12.0	0.6	51.9	1.3	33.2	2.8	15.8	14.6
	2005	551	3.7	0.1	67.1	1.2	24.7	1.3	18.2	5.3
	2011	867	1.2	0.0	81.2	0.0	9.0	2.6	5.8	0.7
Greece - Grèce	1995	25 927	16.0	2.5	7.2	3.2	70.6	13.2	27.4	30.0
	2005	54 894	11.2	1.2	17.9	3.1	66.4	14.4	28.9	23.1
	2011	60 832	13.9	1.1	27.5	3.9	53.5	15.7	18.5	19.4
Greenland - Groenland	1995	421	13.7	1.3	6.4	0.4	66.2	5.3	28.3	32.6
	2005	593	18.2	1.3	21.3	0.5	57.3	4.8	27.5	25.0
	2011	(e)965	22.5	1.2	22.1	0.4	53.8	5.6	22.7	25.5
Grenada - Grenade	1995	129	27.5	2.5	7.8	0.4	61.8	8.8	21.3	31.7
	2005	334	16.4	6.2	7.2	0.6	69.6	8.2	23.5	38.0
	2011	(e)329	23.4	2.0	17.1	0.9	56.5	8.2	19.5	28.8
Guam	1995	442	..	..	..	..	..	..	..	..
	2005	(e)533	9.4	0.1	58.0	0.0	31.5	2.0	11.6	17.9
	2011	(e)708	8.2	0.1	56.2	0.1	34.8	1.6	9.1	24.0
Guatemala	1995	3 292	11.9	1.5	12.4	1.2	73.0	17.2	31.5	24.3
	2005	10 500	10.9	1.2	15.5	1.3	71.1	15.8	23.1	32.3
	2011	16 611	13.2	1.4	19.9	1.4	64.0	16.9	21.4	25.7
Guinea - Guinée	1995	819	29.6	1.1	14.4	0.6	53.1	7.5	21.2	24.4
	2005	(e)820	20.3	0.8	12.2	0.5	55.4	9.0	21.0	25.4
	2011	(e)2 106	19.1	1.1	21.2	0.5	58.2	9.4	26.1	22.7

For sources and notes, see end of table.

Pour les sources et les notes, se reporter à la fin du tableau.

3.1 Country trade structure
by product group
Imports

3.1 Structure du commerce des pays
par groupes de produits
Importations

Country or territory Pays ou territoires	Year Année	Total value (millions of dollars) Valeur totale (millions de dollars)	By main SITC Revision 3 product group (percentage) Par principaux groupes de produits de la CTCI Révision 3 (en pourcentage)					Of which: / dont :		
			All food items Produits alimentaires	Agricultural raw materials Matières premières agricoles	Fuels Combustibles	Ores, metals, precious stones and non monetary gold Minerais, métaux, pierres précieuses et or (non monétaire)	Manufactured goods Articles manufacturés	Chemical products Produits chimiques	Machinery and transport equipment Machines et matériel de transport	Other manufactured goods Articles manufacturés divers
			0 + 1 + 22 + 4	2 - (22 + 27 + 28)	3	27 + 28 + 68 + 667 + 971	5 + 6 +7 + 8- (667 + 68)	5	7	6 + 8 - (667 + 68)
Guinea-Bissau - Guinée-Bissau	1995	(e)133	18.8	0.4	5.4	0.3	74.0	5.7	23.1	45.1
	2005	(e)112	30.6	0.5	36.0	0.1	30.8	5.3	13.2	12.3
	2011	(e)297	36.5	0.6	17.5	3.4	41.4	5.6	16.0	19.7
Guyana	1995	(e)528	14.1	0.4	5.6	0.5	68.7	11.1	34.8	22.8
	2005	778	14.9	0.3	25.3	1.2	54.1	9.2	25.4	19.4
	2011	1 684	12.7	0.3	29.6	0.7	54.7	8.0	27.0	19.7
Haiti - Haïti	1995	(e)654	38.5	1.8	3.8	0.6	48.1	5.6	21.7	20.8
	2005	(e)1 466	40.1	1.6	5.7	0.5	52.1	5.9	15.4	30.8
	2011	(e)3 045	46.0	1.6	6.0	0.4	46.0	5.6	12.2	28.2
Honduras	1995	1 728	11.5	1.1	6.0	1.2	77.9	14.2	26.1	37.6
	2005	(e)6 545	12.5	0.8	13.9	0.7	68.8	12.6	18.8	37.3
	2011	(e)10 338	15.2	1.4	16.0	0.8	66.7	14.2	16.5	36.0
Hungary - Hongrie	1995	15 186	5.7	3.0	11.9	4.3	75.2	14.5	30.1	30.6
	2005	65 920	4.1	1.1	10.1	1.9	77.5	9.1	48.9	19.5
	2011	101 520	4.9	1.3	12.2	3.1	69.3	10.6	42.3	16.4
Iceland - Islande	1995	1 751	11.8	1.6	7.2	4.6	74.6	9.3	32.4	32.9
	2005	4 979	7.8	1.3	9.4	4.1	77.3	7.8	41.9	27.6
	2011	4 846	10.5	1.1	14.4	15.4	58.4	9.3	29.6	19.6
India - Inde	1995	36 592	4.6	4.1	14.2	16.7	56.0	15.8	26.4	13.8
	2005	140 862	4.4	2.4	12.5	25.0	53.8	12.0	27.2	14.5
	2011	462 403	3.5	1.6	34.8	21.0	37.2	9.6	18.3	9.3
Indonesia (...2002) - Indonésie (...2002)	1995	(e)40 645	8.5	5.3	6.4	3.6	75.2	14.0	42.0	19.3
Indonesia - Indonésie	2005	(e)75 725	6.6	3.0	23.6	3.1	62.3	12.5	33.2	16.6
	2011	177 436	9.1	3.0	23.2	3.4	60.0	11.9	31.7	16.4
Iran (Islamic Rep. of) - Iran (Rép. islamique d')	1995	(e)13 882	20.9	2.4	1.8	5.1	69.8	13.3	35.6	20.9
	2005	38 675	8.1	1.8	7.9	2.4	73.1	9.6	39.5	24.0
	2011	(e)68 319	13.2	1.9	6.0	3.5	75.4	9.9	33.0	32.5
Iraq	1995	(e)2 891	63.9	0.2	0.1	0.1	34.8	30.6	1.4	2.8
	2005	(e)23 532	23.0	0.3	9.2	0.6	62.8	9.8	32.8	20.2
	2011	(e)50 581	28.5	0.4	4.2	0.7	63.4	6.7	31.1	25.6
Ireland - Irlande	1995	32 321	8.5	1.2	3.3	2.2	75.7	12.8	42.3	20.7
	2005	70 284	7.9	1.0	6.9	1.4	76.8	12.9	43.9	20.1
	2011	67 076	12.6	0.7	14.1	1.8	66.6	21.7	25.8	19.1
Israel - Israël	1995	28 344	6.9	1.6	1.6	20.2	67.8	9.2	35.9	22.7
	2005	45 032	5.8	1.0	4.9	26.0	60.1	10.7	30.9	18.5
	2011	73 526	8.6	1.2	4.6	19.4	64.6	11.7	32.9	20.0
Italy - Italie	1995	200 320	11.5	5.6	7.3	6.3	66.7	13.1	29.8	23.8
	2005	384 836	8.6	2.6	11.9	5.2	65.7	12.9	30.0	22.7
	2011	557 511	9.2	2.3	19.8	6.6	60.7	13.8	24.8	22.1
Jamaica - Jamaïque	1995	2 773	14.3	1.6	12.7	0.9	67.6	9.9	27.5	30.3
	2005	4 885	14.7	1.4	28.3	0.8	53.3	11.8	19.1	22.4
	2011	(e)6 489	15.6	0.9	37.6	0.4	45.6	12.5	13.7	19.3
Japan - Japon	1995	336 094	16.1	6.2	16.0	8.5	52.0	7.1	22.6	22.3
	2005	515 866	10.4	2.4	25.8	6.6	53.3	7.3	25.7	20.3
	2011	854 626	9.2	2.0	32.1	8.3	46.9	8.8	20.8	17.2
Jordan - Jordanie	1995	3 696	20.6	2.1	12.9	3.4	60.5	12.3	24.5	23.7
	2005	10 455	13.6	1.2	23.1	2.5	57.7	8.8	25.1	23.7
	2011	18 301	16.1	1.3	28.9	2.8	49.4	11.0	18.5	19.9
Kazakhstan	1995	3 805	10.0	2.1	23.5	4.2	59.5	9.9	26.4	23.2
	2005	17 333	6.3	0.9	11.0	1.5	79.6	8.5	36.8	34.3
	2011	(e)38 039	7.7	0.6	9.0	1.2	81.6	9.6	33.1	38.9

For sources and notes, see end of table.

Pour les sources et les notes, se reporter à la fin du tableau.

3.1 Country trade structure
by product group
Imports

3.1 Structure du commerce des pays
par groupes de produits
Importations

Country or territory / Pays ou territoires	Year / Année	Total value (millions of dollars) / Valeur totale (millions de dollars)	All food items / Produits alimentaires	Agricultural raw materials / Matières premières agricoles	Fuels / Combustibles	Ores, metals, precious stones and non monetary gold / Minerais, métaux, pierres précieuses et or (non monétaire)	Manufactured goods / Articles manufacturés	Of which: Chemical products / Produits chimiques	Of which: Machinery and transport equipment / Machines et matériel de transport	Of which: Other manufactured goods / Articles manufacturés divers
			0 + 1 + 22 + 4	2 - (22 + 27 + 28)	3	27 + 28 + 68 + 667 + 971	5 + 6 +7 + 8- (667 + 68)	5	7	6 + 8 - (667 + 68)
Kenya	1995	2 818	11.1	2.5	11.7	1.8	72.4	14.7	34.3	23.3
	2005	5 846	8.6	1.9	20.2	1.8	66.1	13.8	30.5	21.8
	2011	(e)14 818	13.1	1.5	24.0	1.5	59.9	12.8	25.8	21.2
Kiribati	1995	(e)34	32.9	1.8	10.2	0.4	51.1	8.9	16.4	25.8
	2005	(e)74	30.8	1.2	14.7	0.8	43.5	4.3	21.8	17.4
	2011	(e)110	23.8	-0.6	11.9	4.6	50.2	3.2	35.8	11.1
Korea, Dem. People's Rep. of - Corée, Rép. populaire dém. de	1995	(e)1 380	14.0	5.4	18.6	3.6	53.9	8.7	18.4	26.7
	2005	(e)2 718	18.4	2.4	28.4	4.3	44.4	6.9	16.6	20.9
	2011	(e)4 800	12.6	2.5	21.6	4.3	58.8	9.6	22.9	26.3
Korea, Republic of - Corée, République de	1995	135 113	5.4	5.5	14.1	8.4	66.6	9.7	36.6	20.3
	2005	261 236	4.4	2.0	25.8	7.1	60.6	9.4	31.6	19.7
	2011	524 405	4.8	1.8	33.1	9.2	51.0	9.1	25.4	16.5
Kuwait - Koweït	1995	7 790	15.5	1.1	0.5	2.0	80.8	7.3	41.2	32.3
	2005	(e)15 807	22.9	0.7	1.5	2.8	72.1	7.2	34.3	30.6
	2011	(e)25 228	18.6	0.7	0.7	3.7	76.3	8.6	34.3	33.3
Kyrgyzstan - Kirghizistan	1995	522	18.3	2.7	35.9	2.6	40.5	6.3	18.4	15.9
	2005	1 108	15.0	1.7	28.9	2.2	52.0	14.2	18.0	19.8
	2011	4 261	16.6	1.3	22.8	1.0	57.7	10.6	22.8	24.3
Lao People's Dem. Rep. - Rép. dém. populaire lao	1995	589	17.6	0.2	7.7	3.8	69.1	6.7	35.1	27.3
	2005	882	14.1	0.6	18.4	2.2	62.2	7.5	29.9	24.8
	2011	(e)2 650	12.6	0.3	20.4	1.8	64.4	6.3	38.4	19.6
Latvia - Lettonie	1995	1 818	10.5	1.7	21.2	1.1	65.6	12.7	25.4	27.5
	2005	8 770	10.8	2.7	15.1	1.5	66.5	10.2	28.7	27.6
	2011	15 167	12.7	1.3	16.6	2.3	57.1	11.2	22.7	23.2
Lebanon - Liban	1995	(e)7 278	20.1	1.9	7.5	6.0	64.2	8.5	25.0	30.7
	2005	(e)9 327	16.2	1.2	20.8	6.0	55.2	11.5	20.0	23.7
	2011	(e)20 163	15.3	1.2	20.8	10.1	52.6	10.3	18.0	24.4
Lesotho	1995	(e)1 107	24.6	1.3	7.7	2.0	64.4	8.8	13.6	42.0
	2005	(e)1 386	5.7	1.1	0.7	1.3	88.1	4.8	14.5	68.8
	2011	(e)2 525	24.5	2.8	10.4	0.8	61.6	7.8	18.5	35.3
Liberia - Libéria	1995	(e)510	1.5	0.1	0.7	0.1	93.1	0.5	92.0	0.6
	2005	(e)324	2.8	0.2	2.6	0.1	80.1	0.6	77.2	2.3
	2011	(e)1 044	1.7	0.4	4.9	0.1	92.7	0.6	89.3	2.9
Libya - Libye	1995	(e)5 033	21.6	0.9	4.4	2.0	69.6	8.9	31.1	29.7
	2005	(e)6 042	15.6	0.1	9.8	3.4	65.9	5.5	35.4	25.0
	2011	(e)4 988	28.0	1.2	6.9	1.5	61.3	7.4	24.4	29.5
Lithuania - Lituanie	1995	3 649	13.1	3.9	19.4	3.9	57.8	12.5	21.7	23.6
	2005	15 704	8.0	2.3	24.2	1.5	62.5	11.0	29.7	21.8
	2011	31 469	11.6	1.7	33.7	2.0	47.9	12.6	19.4	15.9
Luxembourg	1995	(e)8 983	8.7	0.9	2.0	5.8	54.2	7.1	28.9	18.3
	2005	(e)21 884	8.9	0.9	9.7	6.1	71.3	8.8	38.1	24.4
	2011	(e)28 684	9.3	2.5	13.1	10.0	61.2	9.3	29.0	22.9
Madagascar	1995	(e)628	14.0	2.0	11.7	0.6	70.4	11.5	26.9	32.0
	2005	1 686	14.6	0.5	16.0	0.4	66.8	7.6	24.7	34.5
	2011	(e)2 902	13.7	0.8	17.7	0.6	67.4	6.8	22.6	38.0
Malawi	1995	(e)500	17.7	0.8	8.4	0.6	71.3	16.6	30.4	24.3
	2005	(e)1 165	19.2	1.0	8.6	0.9	69.4	21.7	22.0	25.7
	2011	(e)2 428	15.6	1.0	8.3	2.4	72.1	22.8	23.3	26.1
Malaysia - Malaisie	1995	77 046	4.8	1.2	2.3	5.9	83.4	7.1	60.0	16.3
	2005	114 290	5.1	1.2	8.1	4.8	79.0	7.8	57.5	13.7
	2011	187 573	8.8	2.5	11.8	7.3	69.2	9.4	44.6	15.1
Maldives	1995	268	24.0	2.1	11.4	1.9	60.7	5.9	26.5	28.4
	2005	745	15.6	3.6	15.5	2.3	63.0	5.3	30.8	26.9
	2011	1 412	21.0	1.6	24.9	2.0	50.5	5.5	23.6	21.4

For sources and notes, see end of table.

Pour les sources et les notes, se reporter à la fin du tableau.

Country or territory / Pays ou territoires	Year / Année	Total value (millions of dollars) / Valeur totale (millions de dollars)	By main SITC Revision 3 product group (percentage) / Par principaux groupes de produits de la CTCI Révision 3 (en pourcentage)					Of which: / dont :		
			All food items / Produits alimentaires	Agricultural raw materials / Matières premières agricoles	Fuels / Combustibles	Ores, metals, precious stones and non monetary gold / Minerais, métaux, pierres précieuses et or (non monétaire)	Manufactured goods / Articles manufacturés	Chemical products / Produits chimiques	Machinery and transport equipment / Machines et matériel de transport	Other manufactured goods / Articles manufacturés divers
			0 + 1 + 22 + 4	2 - (22 + 27 + 28)	3	27 + 28 + 68 + 667 + 971	5 + 6 +7 + 8- (667 + 68)	5	7	6 + 8 - (667 + 68)
Mali	1995	(e)774	19.9	0.8	15.6	1.1	62.5	14.9	21.6	26.0
	2005	1 544	16.7	0.5	16.5	0.7	64.7	16.8	23.1	24.8
	2011	(e)3 250	14.3	0.7	20.8	1.3	62.9	14.8	21.9	26.2
Malta - Malte	1995	2 942	8.1	0.7	10.8	1.6	77.5	7.1	49.7	20.8
	2005	3 865	8.9	0.6	14.1	1.1	71.3	7.5	46.3	17.5
	2011	(e)6 284	12.4	0.6	26.7	2.1	58.3	7.9	33.6	16.7
Marshall Islands - Îles Marshall	1995	75	2.1	0.2	0.6	0.5	94.6	0.4	92.5	1.7
	2005	94	0.9	0.1	0.4	0.0	89.0	0.3	88.2	0.6
	2011	(e)140	0.1	0.0	2.2	0.0	84.0	0.1	83.4	0.6
Mauritania - Mauritanie	1995	(e)455	26.0	0.9	12.6	0.4	59.0	7.4	27.3	24.3
	2005	(e)1 342	25.2	0.6	6.2	0.4	66.2	6.7	34.8	24.7
	2011	(e)2 453	25.4	0.4	15.1	0.5	57.0	6.3	25.4	25.3
Mauritius - Maurice	1995	2 000	16.6	3.1	6.9	3.1	70.3	7.7	19.2	43.4
	2005	3 160	16.7	1.9	16.4	3.0	62.0	7.9	28.1	26.0
	2011	5 159	21.2	3.0	21.6	2.9	51.3	8.2	18.0	25.0
Mayotte	2005	309	22.4	1.5	13.4	0.4	62.3	8.5	27.2	26.7
	2011	(e)502	22.6	0.8	1.8	0.6	74.3	10.5	37.9	25.9
Mexico - Mexique	1995	72 453	6.3	2.3	2.1	2.3	80.1	9.8	43.2	27.1
	2005	221 819	6.0	1.4	5.5	2.6	83.4	11.0	48.1	24.2
	2011	350 842	7.0	1.3	10.0	3.1	76.5	11.3	45.3	19.9
Micronesia (Federated States of) - Micronésie (États fédérés de)	1995	89	37.2	2.1	1.0	0.9	52.5	2.7	28.2	21.7
	2005	130	33.8	3.1	1.2	0.5	51.5	3.7	18.8	29.0
	2011	(e)170	36.4	1.3	7.0	1.2	45.2	3.2	17.6	24.4
Mongolia - Mongolie	1995	(e)415	14.3	0.7	19.3	0.7	65.1	5.0	39.7	20.3
	2005	1,183	13.0	0.4	26.6	0.5	59.5	5.0	31.2	23.2
	2011	(e)6 526	12.8	0.5	19.2	0.5	67.0	6.3	28.2	32.6
Montenegro - Monténégro	2011	2 544	23.8	0.7	18.1	4.6	52.8	9.3	17.4	26.1
Montserrat	1995	(e)30	16.1	0.7	4.2	0.1	74.6	3.4	58.6	12.6
	2005	(e)30	16.8	2.2	18.9	2.5	56.7	5.5	27.7	23.5
	2011	(e)29	16.2	2.6	15.7	2.1	56.3	7.8	25.3	23.2
Morocco - Maroc	1995	(e)10 023	16.6	5.4	11.7	3.4	48.0	10.2	19.8	18.1
	2005	20 803	10.6	2.8	21.4	3.4	61.8	9.3	26.6	26.0
	2011	(e)44 286	13.2	2.1	23.4	4.0	57.3	9.6	24.7	23.0
Mozambique	1995	(e)727	25.7	1.4	5.8	0.7	65.2	9.7	31.6	24.0
	2005	(e)2 408	15.8	0.9	14.1	0.4	50.9	7.9	23.0	19.9
	2011	(e)6 306	14.5	1.0	19.8	2.8	56.8	9.5	27.6	19.7
Myanmar	1995	(e)1 348	21.7	0.7	4.0	1.8	71.0	9.5	32.8	28.7
	2005	(e)1 943	10.8	0.6	19.3	1.0	68.3	11.6	27.6	29.1
	2011	(e)9 019	12.0	0.7	23.3	1.1	63.0	10.5	23.3	29.2
Namibia - Namibie	1995	(e)1 496	16.6	1.1	3.9	3.7	74.6	9.8	37.0	27.8
	2005	2 516	16.8	0.7	2.0	2.8	76.3	10.6	35.4	30.2
	2011	(e)6 971	7.7	0.7	3.9	32.7	55.0	9.4	25.8	19.8
Nauru	1995	28	24.2	2.3	11.4	0.6	55.7	5.7	28.1	21.9
	2005	26	10.0	1.0	46.8	0.6	21.8	1.2	12.6	8.1
	2011	32	10.3	0.3	35.3	0.0	34.5	3.0	18.7	12.8
Nepal - Népal	1995	(e)1 292	9.8	2.3	9.5	22.3	37.1	8.6	15.0	13.4
	2005	(e)2 243	15.3	3.8	24.7	4.2	51.8	10.1	12.6	29.2
	2011	(e)5 773	13.4	2.1	21.3	11.9	51.3	9.3	17.1	24.9
Netherlands - Pays-Bas	1995	(e)185 240	14.0	2.3	7.2	4.1	70.9	12.1	33.2	25.5
	2005	(e)363 675	8.8	1.5	17.4	3.8	62.5	11.0	32.4	19.1
	2011	(e)598 232	11.3	1.7	23.6	4.3	59.1	11.7	27.6	19.8
Netherlands Antilles - Antilles néerlandaises	1995	(e)1 841	13.6	0.7	32.2	0.6	50.2	3.8	23.0	23.4
	2005	(e)1 950	3.9	0.2	76.4	1.8	16.7	2.6	5.8	8.4

For sources and notes, see end of table.

Pour les sources et les notes, se reporter à la fin du tableau.

3.1 Country trade structure
by product group
Imports

3.1 Structure du commerce des pays
par groupes de produits
Importations

Country or territory Pays ou territoires	Year Année	Total value (millions of dollars) Valeur totale (millions de dollars)	By main SITC Revision 3 product group (percentage) Par principaux groupes de produits de la CTCI Révision 3 (en pourcentage)					Of which: / dont :		
			All food items Produits alimentaires	Agricultural raw materials Matières premières agricoles	Fuels Combustibles	Ores, metals, precious stones and non monetary gold Minerais, métaux, pierres précieuses et or (non monétaire)	Manu-factured goods Articles manu-facturés	Chemical products Produits chimiques	Machinery and transport equipment Machines et matériel de transport	Other manu-factured goods Articles manu-facturés divers
			0 + 1 + 22 + 4	2 - (22 + 27 + 28)	3	27 + 28 + 68 + 667 + 971	5 + 6 +7 + 8- (667 + 68)	5	7	6 + 8 - (667 + 68)
New Caledonia - Nouvelle-Calédonie	1995	(e)967	15.4	1.0	11.2	0.8	69.9	9.0	33.7	27.2
	2005	1 774	13.2	0.8	15.8	1.0	68.9	9.2	35.0	24.7
	2011	3 697	11.6	0.6	18.1	1.4	51.0	7.2	25.2	18.6
New Zealand - Nouvelle-Zélande	1995	13 958	7.4	1.2	5.3	3.7	82.4	13.1	42.2	27.1
	2005	26 232	7.7	0.8	12.1	2.5	76.7	11.3	40.7	24.7
	2011	36 111	10.8	0.6	17.3	2.7	67.9	11.5	32.8	23.5
Nicaragua	1995	1 009	17.9	0.9	17.9	0.6	62.6	17.5	23.1	22.0
	2005	2 536	13.2	0.5	18.2	0.4	64.9	17.5	23.0	24.4
	2011	5 047	17.3	0.7	22.1	0.4	59.4	16.7	21.1	21.6
Niger	1995	345	28.2	2.5	8.1	2.6	57.8	10.2	23.5	24.2
	2005	(e)943	26.1	4.2	9.5	1.4	57.9	7.8	25.0	25.1
	2011	(e)2 400	19.3	2.6	13.5	2.3	61.9	12.5	27.8	21.5
Nigeria - Nigéria	1995	(e)8 222	11.6	0.9	5.2	1.0	79.5	17.6	34.9	27.1
	2005	(e)21 314	18.5	0.7	4.1	1.9	74.8	12.6	39.3	22.9
	2011	(e)64 103	12.9	0.8	13.2	1.7	71.3	10.8	38.8	21.8
Niue - Nioué	1995	4	4.0	0.3	0.1	0.1	91.4	3.4	22.8	65.2
	2005	8	13.1	2.1	12.7	5.6	66.3	4.6	29.5	32.2
	2011	(e)7	20.8	3.9	24.0	0.2	50.6	6.6	21.5	22.5
Northern Mariana Islands - Îles Mariannes du Nord	1995	(e)628	9.5	0.2	14.7	0.1	73.3	2.4	24.4	46.5
	2005	(e)591	3.4	0.2	27.1	0.0	68.7	0.7	4.0	64.0
	2011	(e)90	17.5	0.1	15.3	0.5	65.7	0.5	16.2	49.0
Norway - Norvège	1995	32 706	6.8	2.7	2.9	6.8	79.9	9.6	37.7	32.7
	2005	55 488	6.8	1.9	4.2	7.8	78.9	9.4	39.5	30.1
	2011	90 849	8.3	1.4	6.4	8.3	74.4	9.2	38.4	26.9
Occupied Palestinian territory - Territoire palestinien occupé	1995	1 658	..	..	..	..	..	..	..	..
	2005	(e)2 667	23.3	1.2	31.0	2.7	41.6	8.1	13.7	19.8
	2011	(e)4 492	24.1	0.5	34.1	1.7	39.5	7.1	11.0	21.5
Oman	1995	4 249	18.4	0.7	1.3	4.7	71.9	6.3	42.3	23.3
	2005	8 970	11.4	0.6	3.1	4.2	77.4	7.6	48.9	20.9
	2011	(e)23 857	13.8	0.6	6.8	4.9	74.0	8.1	43.7	22.2
Pakistan	1995	11 704	17.5	5.5	16.1	4.0	56.7	17.0	28.9	10.8
	2005	25 097	10.4	4.2	21.1	5.1	59.0	16.3	29.4	13.3
	2011	43 578	11.9	4.9	34.1	3.1	45.9	16.2	17.5	12.2
Palau - Palaos	1995	49	26.3	3.2	4.2	0.3	59.7	3.8	26.9	29.1
	2005	108	25.8	2.1	2.1	2.4	58.9	5.2	25.9	27.8
	2011	124	47.2	1.2	5.1	0.1	40.7	3.1	21.6	16.0
Panama	1995	2 511	3.2	0.2	4.4	0.7	89.6	5.5	62.0	22.1
	2005	(e)9 600	4.3	0.2	13.9	0.5	74.1	6.6	48.8	18.7
	2011	21 802	3.0	0.1	12.0	0.3	75.3	14.8	41.0	19.5
Papua New Guinea - Papouasie-Nouvelle-Guinée	1995	(e)1 452	14.3	0.8	10.8	0.6	69.8	6.4	39.4	24.0
	2005	(e)1 611	16.7	0.7	26.0	0.8	55.8	7.4	27.4	21.1
	2011	(e)4 241	22.2	0.7	25.5	0.7	50.8	8.4	22.4	20.0
Paraguay	1995	3 136	18.5	0.2	6.5	0.7	74.0	9.0	42.3	22.7
	2005	3 274	8.7	0.8	16.4	1.0	73.1	16.8	32.9	23.4
	2011	12 316	7.4	0.6	13.4	0.6	78.0	14.3	41.1	22.6
Peru - Pérou	1995	7 584	13.5	1.9	8.8	0.8	75.0	13.2	39.2	22.6
	2005	12 502	11.4	1.8	19.8	1.0	66.0	16.1	28.3	21.6
	2011	37 747	10.2	1.7	15.7	1.1	71.2	14.5	34.7	22.1
Philippines	1995	28 487	8.3	2.2	9.2	3.2	57.8	9.2	32.5	16.2
	2005	49 487	6.9	0.9	13.2	2.6	76.4	7.3	57.8	11.3
	2011	63 693	10.3	0.7	20.1	3.6	49.9	10.6	28.3	11.0

For sources and notes, see end of table.

Pour les sources et les notes, se reporter à la fin du tableau.

Country or territory / Pays ou territoires	Year / Année	Total value (millions of dollars) / Valeur totale (millions de dollars)	By main SITC Revision 3 product group (percentage) / Par principaux groupes de produits de la CTCI Révision 3 (en pourcentage)					Of which: / dont :		
			All food items / Produits alimentaires	Agricultural raw materials / Matières premières agricoles	Fuels / Combustibles	Ores, metals, precious stones and non monetary gold / Minerais, métaux, pierres précieuses et or (non monétaire)	Manufactured goods / Articles manufacturés	Chemical products / Produits chimiques	Machinery and transport equipment / Machines et matériel de transport	Other manufactured goods / Articles manufacturés divers
			0 + 1 + 22 + 4	2 - (22 + 27 + 28)	3	27 + 28 + 68 + 667 + 971	5 + 6 +7 + 8- (667 + 68)	5	7	6 + 8 - (667 + 68)
Poland - Pologne	1995	29 019	9.6	3.2	9.1	3.3	74.4	14.9	29.9	29.5
	2005	101 539	6.1	1.8	11.4	2.9	75.5	14.0	35.1	26.4
	2011	203 028	7.8	1.9	13.1	3.6	71.0	14.1	31.6	25.3
Portugal	1995	33 565	13.4	3.4	7.2	2.6	72.5	10.0	34.4	28.1
	2005	61 167	11.1	1.5	13.4	3.5	68.7	10.5	33.3	24.9
	2011	80 324	14.5	1.9	17.4	3.0	62.5	13.1	25.5	23.9
Qatar	1995	3 398	9.4	0.6	0.4	2.5	87.0	5.0	48.3	33.7
	2005	10 061	6.6	0.7	0.2	2.2	89.2	6.6	49.1	33.6
	2011	(e)25 672	8.7	0.4	1.0	7.8	68.7	6.7	38.0	23.9
Republic of Moldova - République de Moldova	1995	841	10.6	2.3	43.4	1.6	41.6	8.5	14.6	18.5
	2005	2 292	12.4	3.4	17.4	7.7	56.6	11.4	18.0	27.1
	2011	5 191	14.1	1.5	15.0	1.8	63.2	12.5	23.7	26.9
Romania - Roumanie	1995	10 278	8.5	2.3	21.4	3.6	63.3	10.6	24.8	28.0
	2005	40 463	6.0	1.0	13.9	2.7	76.0	10.2	33.2	32.6
	2011	76 365	7.4	1.6	11.3	2.8	74.3	12.9	33.8	27.6
Russian Federation - Fédération de Russie	1995	(e)68 955	19.9	0.9	2.3	2.8	48.8	6.7	21.9	20.2
	2005	(e)137 977	15.4	1.0	1.4	2.7	78.0	11.4	40.0	26.5
	2011	(e)354 549	13.6	1.1	2.4	1.8	79.8	11.9	43.0	24.9
Rwanda	1995	(e)241	27.3	2.7	10.0	2.0	56.5	7.5	30.1	18.9
	2005	(e)471	14.8	2.1	12.5	2.2	67.1	15.3	28.3	23.5
	2011	(e)1 730	18.3	2.1	5.7	1.9	65.8	14.5	23.4	27.9
Saint Helena - Sainte-Hélène	1995	(e)23	21.5	1.5	16.8	2.4	61.9	7.0	32.8	22.1
	2005	(e)56	12.0	1.9	15.5	13.4	56.5	3.3	37.7	15.4
	2011	56	16.0	0.9	30.5	1.2	47.0	3.9	26.6	16.4
Saint Kitts and Nevis - Saint-Kitts-et-Nevis	1995	132	21.1	2.5	4.3	0.9	71.2	8.3	27.8	35.1
	2005	210	18.5	1.5	8.8	0.8	70.4	6.9	31.2	32.3
	2011	(e)271	19.8	2.1	7.5	1.0	69.7	7.0	24.2	38.4
Saint Lucia - Sainte-Lucie	1995	306	20.4	1.8	23.6	0.7	51.4	7.7	17.4	26.3
	2005	486	15.1	1.3	41.0	1.0	39.7	4.8	15.3	19.5
	2011	(e)698	5.7	0.5	78.5	0.2	15.1	2.1	5.2	7.8
Saint Pierre and Miquelon - Saint-Pierre-et-Miquelon	1995	47	14.5	1.4	7.8	0.8	69.8	8.4	31.5	29.9
	2005	(e)50	22.5	1.6	2.6	0.3	68.6	8.4	32.3	27.9
	2011	(e)66	22.5	1.5	2.6	0.7	68.1	8.6	33.3	26.2
Saint Vincent and the Grenadines - Saint-Vincent-et-les Grenadines	1995	134	22.5	2.6	6.0	0.5	68.3	12.9	17.7	37.7
	2005	240	21.5	2.4	13.9	0.6	61.7	9.2	22.1	30.4
	2011	(e)348	23.4	2.1	20.1	0.7	53.7	7.3	18.7	27.8
Samoa	1995	(e)95	15.7	0.9	7.4	0.3	74.4	5.1	47.2	22.1
	2005	(e)239	20.7	2.2	14.1	0.7	47.2	5.2	16.5	25.5
	2011	(e)346	25.1	2.2	17.4	1.0	52.8	6.3	23.9	22.5
Sao Tome and Principe - Sao Tomé-et-Principe	1995	(e)29	25.3	0.4	1.9	0.5	71.5	6.6	39.0	25.9
	2005	50	38.5	0.9	20.2	0.2	40.1	4.5	21.3	14.4
	2011	(e)132	37.9	1.1	1.8	1.2	57.7	7.1	26.5	24.1
Saudi Arabia - Arabie saoudite	1995	28 085	16.1	1.2	0.2	7.0	75.0	9.6	35.6	29.7
	2005	59 510	14.6	0.7	0.2	5.4	79.0	9.7	45.2	24.0
	2011	(e)129 017	16.5	0.9	0.3	5.5	76.9	10.4	39.2	27.3
Senegal - Sénégal	1995	(e)1 412	28.2	1.9	8.7	1.4	46.5	12.1	15.7	18.8
	2005	3 498	26.6	1.8	22.4	2.0	46.6	9.1	21.0	16.5
	2011	5 909	21.2	1.3	31.7	1.5	43.7	8.4	19.2	16.1
Serbia - Serbie	2011	20 139	6.6	1.9	19.7	5.9	60.3	14.7	22.9	22.7
Serbia and Montenegro - Serbie-et-Monténégro	1995	(e)2 666	14.2	4.1	13.9	7.1	59.8	14.3	19.4	26.1
	2005	(e)10 461	7.1	1.5	19.4	6.2	65.5	14.0	25.7	25.8

For sources and notes, see end of table.

Pour les sources et les notes, se reporter à la fin du tableau.

Country or territory / Pays ou territoires	Year / Année	Total value (millions of dollars) / Valeur totale (millions de dollars)	By main SITC Revision 3 product group (percentage) / Par principaux groupes de produits de la CTCI Révision 3 (en pourcentage)					Of which: / dont :		
			All food items / Produits alimentaires	Agricultural raw materials / Matières premières agricoles	Fuels / Combustibles	Ores, metals, precious stones and non monetary gold / Minerais, métaux, pierres précieuses et or (non monétaire)	Manu-factured goods / Articles manu-facturés	Chemical products / Produits chimiques	Machinery and transport equipment / Machines et matériel de transport	Other manu-factured goods / Articles manu-facturés divers
			0 + 1 + 22 + 4	2 - (22 + 27 + 28)	3	27 + 28 + 68 + 667 + 971	5 + 6 +7 + 8- (667 + 68)	5	7	6 + 8 - (667 + 68)
Seychelles	1995	255	21.2	1.4	17.4	0.7	59.1	6.5	27.0	25.5
	2005	675	21.5	1.0	23.5	0.4	48.2	4.3	24.6	19.3
	2011	(e)850	21.4	2.1	25.8	0.8	50.0	4.1	24.4	21.4
Sierra Leone	1995	(e)134	31.1	3.0	10.0	0.9	53.4	7.5	26.9	19.0
	2005	(e)345	21.0	7.0	38.6	1.6	31.8	4.9	13.1	13.8
	2011	(e)1 717	23.5	7.4	40.0	1.5	27.6	4.6	10.9	12.1
Singapore - Singapour	1995	124 503	4.6	0.9	8.1	2.9	82.6	6.5	57.9	18.3
	2005	200 050	2.8	0.4	17.7	3.1	75.1	6.2	55.8	13.1
	2011	365 770	3.4	0.4	32.6	2.6	59.9	6.9	41.0	12.0
Sint Maarten (Dutch part) - Saint-Martin (partie néerlandaise)	2011	734	9.7	0.8	1.6	9.6	73.3	4.3	14.5	54.5
Slovakia - Slovaquie	1995	(e)9 225	7.9	2.5	11.2	5.3	61.6	12.8	26.7	22.0
	2005	34 226	6.1	1.3	13.2	3.4	75.3	9.8	37.8	27.7
	2011	76 690	6.4	1.5	14.7	3.7	73.5	8.8	39.9	24.8
Slovenia - Slovénie	1995	9 492	7.8	4.6	6.6	4.4	73.8	12.1	33.8	28.0
	2005	19 626	6.1	2.6	10.6	5.8	74.8	12.8	32.6	29.3
	2011	(e)35 480	7.0	2.3	13.7	5.8	57.9	11.6	24.6	21.7
Solomon Islands - Îles Salomon	1995	(e)154	12.4	0.6	15.4	0.6	67.6	4.1	34.2	29.2
	2005	(e)185	16.3	0.5	23.8	0.8	48.9	5.3	24.4	19.3
	2011	(e)462	20.2	0.5	26.0	0.8	47.3	6.5	22.6	18.3
Somalia - Somalie	1995	(c)268	65.5	2.7	1.3	0.1	31.2	8.3	7.3	15.6
	2005	(e)626	48.4	13.0	0.8	0.1	36.0	6.9	6.6	22.5
	2011	(e)1 175	74.4	0.3	2.5	0.1	22.0	4.2	5.8	12.0
South Africa - Afrique du Sud	1995	(e)30 979	15.3	3.1	6.3	3.7	71.5	11.8	41.8	17.9
	2005	(e)64 192	3.8	0.9	12.2	3.7	57.6	8.6	33.8	15.3
	2011	(e)122 418	5.0	0.8	17.3	2.4	50.9	8.4	28.7	13.9
Spain - Espagne	1995	113 399	13.6	3.0	8.3	4.3	70.8	12.1	35.6	23.1
	2005	289 611	9.2	1.4	14.0	3.5	71.4	11.6	37.9	22.0
	2011	(e)360 534	11.5	1.4	20.5	4.3	62.3	13.2	27.3	21.7
Sri Lanka	1995	(e)5 185	14.8	1.6	2.2	5.2	73.1	9.2	24.9	38.9
	2005	8 307	12.4	1.2	13.4	7.1	65.8	10.0	20.2	35.6
	2011	19 696	12.9	1.6	20.2	6.9	58.4	9.9	23.7	24.8
Sudan (...2011) - Soudan (...2011)	1995	1 185	20.0	1.9	10.4	0.5	66.9	10.7	24.1	32.1
	2005	7 367	11.9	0.6	4.6	0.9	79.4	8.5	43.5	27.4
	2011	(e)9 231	14.4	0.8	3.8	1.3	79.7	7.3	51.3	21.0
Suriname	1995	583	14.0	0.1	11.8	1.2	73.0	16.0	35.7	21.3
	2005	(a)1 050	9.5	0.0	17.2	0.3	41.0	3.9	23.1	13.9
	2011	(e)1 667	15.7	0.1	18.5	1.5	64.2	13.7	27.7	22.9
Swaziland	1995	(e)1 054	21.3	3.3	7.0	2.1	66.2	12.9	24.6	28.7
	2005	(e)1 904	16.8	1.1	11.7	0.9	68.6	20.9	18.8	28.9
	2011	(e)2 000	13.8	2.1	1.2	4.5	76.7	28.5	12.2	36.0
Sweden - Suède	1995	61 647	6.7	2.2	5.8	3.8	80.0	10.7	41.8	27.5
	2005	111 351	7.4	1.6	11.7	3.3	73.3	10.3	38.6	24.3
	2011	176 000	8.6	1.4	14.3	3.7	68.5	10.5	35.8	22.2
Switzerland - Suisse	1995	80 152	6.4	2.0	2.9	5.6	83.1	14.6	33.4	35.0
	2005	126 574	5.4	1.1	7.2	5.8	80.5	21.7	28.5	30.3
	2011	207 263	5.7	0.9	8.4	6.6	78.1	21.4	26.6	30.2
Syrian Arab Republic - République arabe syrienne	1995	(e)4 709	16.7	3.3	1.1	1.3	75.6	10.2	31.6	33.9
	2005	(e)10 862	14.3	2.6	10.8	2.3	67.9	17.2	26.2	24.5
	2011	(e)16 600	18.9	2.1	15.3	3.4	60.3	17.1	20.3	22.8
Tajikistan - Tadjikistan	1995	(e)810	25.4	0.9	14.5	12.1	46.4	7.3	26.5	12.6
	2005	(e)1 330	12.5	1.8	24.2	12.9	43.7	13.6	14.4	15.6
	2011	(e)3 186	14.3	1.4	15.1	7.8	58.0	8.8	12.7	36.5

For sources and notes, see end of table.

Pour les sources et les notes, se reporter à la fin du tableau.

Country or territory / Pays ou territoires	Year / Année	Total value (millions of dollars) / Valeur totale (millions de dollars)	All food items / Produits alimentaires	Agricultural raw materials / Matières premières agricoles	Fuels / Combustibles	Ores, metals, precious stones and non monetary gold / Minerais, métaux, pierres précieuses et or (non monétaire)	Manufactured goods / Articles manufacturés	Of which / dont : Chemical products / Produits chimiques	Of which / dont : Machinery and transport equipment / Machines et matériel de transport	Of which / dont : Other manufactured goods / Articles manufacturés divers
			0 + 1 + 22 + 4	2 - (22 + 27 + 28)	3	27 + 28 + 68 + 667 + 971	5 + 6 +7 + 8- (667 + 68)	5	7	6 + 8 - (667 + 68)
TFYR of Macedonia - LERY de Macédoine	1995	1 719	17.4	3.3	11.6	3.0	54.2	11.9	19.5	22.8
	2005	3 228	12.7	1.3	19.2	3.2	63.6	10.3	17.4	35.8
	2011	7 007	11.8	1.0	20.5	10.9	55.7	11.8	16.9	27.1
Thailand - Thaïlande	1995	70 781	3.8	4.1	6.7	5.4	78.7	10.5	47.5	20.7
	2005	118 164	4.0	2.0	17.7	6.8	68.2	10.2	38.0	20.0
	2011	228 483	4.7	1.9	19.0	12.7	61.6	10.4	32.7	18.5
Timor-Leste	2005	(e)102	20.6	2.3	25.7	1.6	42.8	5.2	18.0	19.7
	2011	(e)308	25.9	3.8	13.1	0.9	51.6	4.3	27.2	20.0
Togo	1995	556	19.8	2.6	16.5	0.9	59.7	8.0	16.1	35.7
	2005	(e)1 054	16.7	4.1	22.4	1.0	55.4	8.5	15.1	31.8
	2011	(e)1 700	13.4	1.3	36.3	0.7	48.0	6.3	13.6	28.1
Tokelau - Tokélaou	1995	(e)1	4.7	3.4	0.0	47.5	43.4	3.0	15.3	25.1
	2005	(e)0	1.1	25.7	0.4	0.6	69.0	18.1	32.2	18.7
	2011	(e)0	2.5	0.1	0.1	0.1	95.9	5.4	77.6	12.9
Tonga	1995	(e)77	33.3	3.8	4.3	0.7	53.8	6.6	25.4	21.8
	2005	(e)120	22.5	1.7	18.6	0.4	34.0	3.2	12.6	18.2
	2011	(e)184	34.6	1.6	19.3	0.8	39.2	4.9	14.0	20.3
Trinidad and Tobago - Trinité-et-Tobago	1995	1 724	15.1	0.3	0.5	4.6	59.4	6.5	32.7	20.2
	2005	5 694	9.0	0.6	34.8	4.3	51.2	7.3	26.4	17.4
	2011	(e)8 699	13.4	0.8	25.8	6.0	53.9	9.0	25.3	19.6
Tunisia - Tunisie	1995	7 903	12.5	4.2	7.2	3.3	72.8	9.1	25.9	37.8
	2005	13 174	8.5	2.6	13.7	3.2	72.0	10.5	28.8	32.7
	2011	(e)23 956	9.5	2.2	13.8	4.4	70.1	10.3	29.8	30.1
Turkey - Turquie	1995	35 707	7.0	5.6	12.9	5.9	68.6	15.0	32.2	21.5
	2005	116 774	2.8	2.7	13.5	9.2	66.4	13.8	32.4	20.2
	2011	240 839	4.4	2.9	8.2	10.8	59.0	12.8	27.8	18.4
Turkmenistan - Turkménistan	1995	(e)1 365	29.5	0.5	1.9	1.5	65.1	9.6	27.7	27.7
	2005	(e)2 947	7.2	0.6	0.8	0.7	89.2	7.9	55.3	26.0
	2011	(e)7 400	7.9	0.9	1.1	0.9	82.8	8.6	44.1	30.0
Turks and Caicos Islands - Îles Turques et Caïques	1995	(e)51	11.7	1.7	0.9	0.3	59.7	20.8	16.9	22.0
	2005	304	14.0	2.8	10.3	1.4	68.5	5.0	30.6	32.9
	2011	(e)302	16.3	2.0	11.9	1.3	59.4	5.1	21.0	33.3
Tuvalu	1995	(e)6	31.7	3.1	1.4	0.0	60.1	2.2	38.3	19.6
	2005	(e)13	18.4	1.2	10.4	0.2	56.7	1.7	45.2	9.8
	2011	(e)25	16.5	1.5	6.1	0.7	66.4	2.1	48.3	16.0
Uganda - Ouganda	1995	1 038	15.3	2.5	4.2	2.2	75.4	11.7	30.7	33.0
	2005	2 054	13.2	1.2	17.2	1.2	66.4	14.6	25.4	26.4
	2011	(e)4 561	11.7	1.3	17.6	1.4	67.9	14.4	28.0	25.5
Ukraine	1995	(e)16 052	7.9	2.4	47.8	3.1	37.9	6.7	17.0	14.2
	2005	36 122	7.2	1.3	29.5	4.3	57.0	11.8	26.4	18.7
	2011	82 608	7.4	1.0	34.6	3.7	52.8	12.8	23.0	16.9
United Arab Emirates - Émirats arabes unis	1995	(e)20 984	10.0	0.9	1.6	2.6	83.6	6.3	36.9	40.3
	2005	80 814	6.3	0.5	3.7	12.7	74.1	5.4	41.5	27.2
	2011	(e)207 835	7.8	0.5	5.8	18.6	67.3	5.6	31.5	30.1
United Kingdom - Royaume-Uni	1995	261 456	10.1	2.4	3.5	5.2	78.1	10.3	41.3	26.6
	2005	515 782	8.5	1.3	8.3	4.1	70.4	10.4	35.8	24.3
	2011	634 412	9.6	1.2	14.3	5.5	65.7	11.9	30.3	23.4
United Republic of Tanzania - République-Unie de Tanzanie	1995	1 653	14.4	1.7	5.0	3.0	75.0	13.7	34.7	26.6
	2005	3 247	10.7	1.3	13.8	2.3	70.3	15.2	29.8	25.4
	2011	11 184	10.2	0.9	23.8	0.9	63.6	12.6	29.9	21.0
United States - États-Unis	1995	770 821	4.8	2.1	8.2	3.8	78.1	5.5	46.4	26.2
	2005	1 732 321	4.2	1.3	17.2	3.4	70.6	7.6	38.3	24.7
	2011	2 262 586	5.0	1.0	20.5	4.3	66.4	8.9	35.8	21.7

For sources and notes, see end of table.

Pour les sources et les notes, se reporter à la fin du tableau.

Country or territory / Pays ou territoires	Year / Année	Total value (millions of dollars) / Valeur totale (millions de dollars)	By main SITC Revision 3 product group (percentage) / Par principaux groupes de produits de la CTCI Révision 3 (en pourcentage)					Of which: / dont :		
			All food items / Produits alimentaires	Agricultural raw materials / Matières premières agricoles	Fuels / Combustibles	Ores, metals, precious stones and non monetary gold / Minerais, métaux, pierres précieuses et or (non monétaire)	Manu-factured goods / Articles manu-facturés	Chemical products / Produits chimiques	Machinery and transport equipment / Machines et matériel de transport	Other manu-factured goods / Articles manu-facturés divers
			0 + 1 + 22 + 4	2 - (22 + 27 + 28)	3	27 + 28 + 68 + 667 + 971	5 + 6 +7 + 8- (667 + 68)	5	7	6 + 8 - (667 + 68)
Uruguay	1995	2 866	10.4	4.0	10.1	1.2	74.3	15.3	34.5	24.5
	2005	3 879	8.1	3.1	24.3	1.6	62.9	19.4	23.2	20.3
	2011	(e)10 623	9.9	2.7	26.1	1.1	60.2	16.9	25.0	18.3
Uzbekistan - Ouzbékistan	1995	2 750	19.6	0.4	2.3	2.8	73.3	8.9	41.7	22.7
	2005	3 666	7.7	3.2	2.8	2.9	80.9	11.1	43.5	26.3
	2011	9 953	7.3	4.2	2.6	1.8	82.8	12.2	44.7	25.9
Vanuatu	1995	(e)95	8.6	0.3	2.3	0.3	80.6	2.9	59.8	17.9
	2005	(e)149	18.9	0.7	17.9	1.0	61.6	6.8	33.8	21.0
	2011	(e)304	21.1	1.0	19.0	0.7	58.2	7.1	27.8	23.3
Venezuela (Bolivarian Rep. of) - Venezuela (Rép. bolivarienne du)	1995	10 791	13.8	4.3	1.3	3.5	75.5	15.2	38.7	21.6
	2005	21 848	10.5	1.1	1.2	1.6	85.0	13.7	48.5	22.7
	2011	(e)46 441	15.4	1.2	3.4	1.2	77.4	18.8	38.0	20.6
Viet Nam	1995	(e)8 155	4.9	2.4	10.3	2.4	75.9	16.7	28.3	30.9
	2005	36 761	6.3	3.7	14.6	5.4	69.7	14.4	25.1	30.2
	2011	(e)105 356	8.2	3.6	13.2	6.7	68.3	14.3	26.0	28.0
Wallis and Futuna Islands - Îles Wallis-et-Futuna	1995	(e)14	32.7	1.2	4.5	0.2	60.8	8.3	38.3	14.2
	2005	(e)51	27.1	0.8	11.2	1.2	55.7	11.1	22.0	22.5
	2011	(e)57	33.1	1.1	5.0	1.1	55.8	13.3	15.6	27.0
Western Sahara - Sahara occidental	1995	(e)14	19.5	21.0	9.3	1.5	48.6	8.1	5.8	34.8
Yemen - Yémen	1995	(e)1 582	32.2	1.8	9.9	1 0	54.4	7.3	21.0	26.1
	2005	(e)5 400	25.0	0.7	20.1	1.1	49.6	8.4	19.9	21.2
	2011	(e)10 034	33.4	0.7	26.9	0.8	38.0	7.4	12.9	17.7
Zambia - Zambie	1995	708	10.8	1.9	8.6	2.7	75.4	12.7	39.8	22.9
	2005	2 558	7.4	1.1	10.3	2.9	76.6	19.0	31.7	26.0
	2011	(e)7 191	5.8	0.6	10.2	19.4	64.0	16.3	30.2	17.5
Zimbabwe	1995	(e)2 659	8.1	2.4	6.7	4.7	77.0	17.5	38.8	20.7
	2005	(e)2 350	13.8	1.6	12.6	25.2	46.1	10.8	20.2	15.1
	2011	(e)4 400	22.9	1.3	11.1	7.2	57.5	12.6	26.3	18.6

3

Source:
UNCTAD secretariat calculations, based on UNCTAD, *UNCTADstat* Merchandise Trade Matrix

Notes:
(a)   More than 30% of total trade under SITC Rev.3, code 931: "Special transactions & commodities not classified".

Source :
Calculs du secrétariat de la CNUCED, basés sur la matrice du commerce de marchandises de *UNCTADstat* de la CNUCED

Notes :
(a)   Plus de 30% du commerce sous la position 931 de la CTCI rév. 3 : "Transactions et articles spéciaux non classés".

Products ranked by average 2010-2011 values SITC Revision 3 (3-digit level) / Produits classés d'après la moyenne des valeurs de 2010-2011 CTCI révision 3 (positions à 3 chiffres)	2005			2011			Growth rates (%) Taux d'accroissement (%) 2005-2011	
	Value (millions of dollars) Valeur (millions de dollars)	% of the country grouping exports En % des exportations du groupe de pays	% of world product exports En % des exportations mondiales des produits	Value (millions of dollars) Valeur (millions de dollars)	% of the country grouping exports En % des exportations du groupe de pays	% of world product exports En % des exportations mondiales des produits	Value Valeur	Difference from world Différence par rapport au monde
All commodity groups	10 465 300	100.00	100.00	18 087 096	100.00	100.00	7.35	_
333 Crude petroleum & bituminous oil	807 298	7.71	100.00	1 635 481	9.04	100.00	8.74	_
334 Heavy petroleum & bituminous oil	378 511	3.62	100.00	937 123	5.18	100.00	12.70	_
781 Passenger cars and race cars	488 412	4.67	100.00	639 948	3.54	100.00	1.91	_
776 Valves tubes; diodes, transistors	367 911	3.52	100.00	557 230	3.08	100.00	5.98	_
764 Telecommunicate equipment part nes	360 090	3.44	100.00	504 829	2.79	100.00	3.65	_
752 Computer equipment nes	276 218	2.64	100.00	343 596	1.90	100.00	2.37	_
542 Medicines including veterinary	207 901	1.99	100.00	340 956	1.89	100.00	8.22	_
784 Motor vehicle parts and accessories	234 910	2.24	100.00	356 900	1.97	100.00	4.76	_
343 Natural gas, liquefied or not	151 700	1.45	100.00	270 192	1.49	100.00	10.12	_
772 Electrical circuit equipment	142 267	1.36	100.00	231 682	1.28	100.00	6.52	_
778 Electrical machinery apparatus nes	148 517	1.42	100.00	224 557	1.24	100.00	5.33	_
759 Office equipment part & accessories	200 934	1.92	100.00	195 867	1.08	100.00	-1.67	_
971 Gold non-monetary excluding ores	38 961	0.37	100.00	222 100	1.23	100.00	31.08	_
793 Ships boats floating structures	71 286	0.68	100.00	184 085	1.02	100.00	17.26	_
728 Special industrial machine part nes	98 447	0.94	100.00	186 212	1.03	100.00	8.92	_
874 Measure analyze control device nes	111 840	1.07	100.00	178 913	0.99	100.00	6.15	_
713 Internal combustion engine part nes	113 461	1.08	100.00	164 986	0.91	100.00	3.61	_
667 Pearls, precious semiprecious stone	94 614	0.90	100.00	161 318	0.89	100.00	8.16	_
541 Pharmaceuticals excluding medicines	67 016	0.64	100.00	153 810	0.85	100.00	15.31	_
792 Aircraft, spacecraft & equipment	127 994	1.22	100.00	150 984	0.83	100.00	-0.86	_
682 Copper	64 242	0.61	100.00	149 197	0.82	100.00	9.26	_
821 Furniture part; bedding furnishing	97 487	0.93	100.00	147 585	0.82	100.00	5.40	_
845 Articles of apparel nes	95 923	0.92	100.00	141 834	0.78	100.00	4.75	_
699 Base metal manufactures nes	90 717	0.87	100.00	143 381	0.79	100.00	5.17	_
281 Iron ore and concentrates	29 234	0.28	100.00	144 346	0.80	100.00	30.00	_
893 Articles of plastic nes	86 035	0.82	100.00	133 718	0.74	100.00	5.96	_
641 Paper and paperboard	96 987	0.93	100.00	125 809	0.70	100.00	2.82	_
598 Miscellaneous chemical products nes	64 427	0.62	100.00	128 740	0.71	100.00	10.42	_
321 Coal excluding non-agglomomerated	47 144	0.45	100.00	133 534	0.74	100.00	19.41	_
782 Goods and service vehicles	90 503	0.86	100.00	129 199	0.71	100.00	2.24	_
684 Aluminium	79 417	0.76	100.00	126 237	0.70	100.00	3.61	_
743 Gas pump, compressor, fan, filter	69 946	0.67	100.00	124 521	0.69	100.00	8.18	_
723 Civil engineering plant & equipment	69 391	0.66	100.00	123 534	0.68	100.00	5.96	_
575 Other plastics, in primary forms	66 885	0.64	100.00	114 815	0.63	100.00	7.04	_
515 Organo-inorganic compound acid salt	80 063	0.77	100.00	112 004	0.62	100.00	4.62	_
851 Footwear	66 734	0.64	100.00	113 256	0.63	100.00	7.76	_
741 Heating cooling equipment parts nes	68 861	0.66	100.00	110 918	0.61	100.00	6.09	_
773 Electrical distribute equipment nes	61 397	0.59	100.00	111 840	0.62	100.00	7.28	_
871 Optical instruments apparatus nes	44 771	0.43	100.00	103 004	0.57	100.00	13.58	_
761 Television video receive project	57 572	0.55	100.00	96 687	0.53	100.00	7.49	_
582 Plastic sheet film foil & strips	57 954	0.55	100.00	99 491	0.55	100.00	7.63	_
897 Jewellery nes (667)	41 008	0.39	100.00	108 496	0.60	100.00	15.21	_
894 Baby carriage toy game sport good	64 758	0.62	100.00	96 933	0.54	100.00	5.78	_
775 Household equipment nes	64 008	0.61	100.00	93 245	0.52	100.00	5.08	_
771 Electric power machine part excluding 716	45 853	0.44	100.00	92 447	0.51	100.00	11.09	_
673 Flat iron non-alloy steel products	66 941	0.64	100.00	94 318	0.52	100.00	3.14	_
716 Rotating electric plant parts nes	51 571	0.49	100.00	92 924	0.51	100.00	8.64	_
511 Hydrocarbons nes; derivatives	50 777	0.49	100.00	96 566	0.53	100.00	7.86	_
679 Iron steel pipe tube fittings etc	54 469	0.52	100.00	96 152	0.53	100.00	6.12	_
676 Iron steel bar rod section piling	53 042	0.51	100.00	97 861	0.54	100.00	5.37	_
872 Medical instruments appliances nes	52 906	0.51	100.00	87 168	0.48	100.00	8.54	_
714 Non-electric engines excluding 712, 713, and 718	69 129	0.66	100.00	86 826	0.48	100.00	1.88	_
625 Rubber for wheels, incl inner tube	43 960	0.42	100.00	92 616	0.51	100.00	10.79	_
057 Fruit nut (exc oil), fresh or dried	48 824	0.47	100.00	86 471	0.48	100.00	9.47	_
842 Female clothing, woven	65 539	0.63	100.00	83 706	0.46	100.00	2.52	_
899 Manufactured articles nes	44 403	0.42	100.00	78 795	0.44	100.00	9.75	_
744 Mechanical handling equipment nes	52 399	0.50	100.00	80 738	0.45	100.00	4.28	_
571 Primary form ethylene polymers	42 047	0.40	100.00	79 114	0.44	100.00	8.92	_
747 Pipe, boiler, tank & vat appliances	40 995	0.39	100.00	78 173	0.43	100.00	8.91	_
553 Perfume toilet cosmetics, excluding soap	43 872	0.42	100.00	76 492	0.42	100.00	8.62	_

For sources and notes, see end of table.

Pour les sources et les notes, se reporter à la fin du tableau.

Products ranked by average 2010-2011 values SITC Revision 3 (3-digit level) Produits classés d'après la moyenne des valeurs de 2010-2011 CTCI révision 3 (positions à 3 chiffres)	2005			2011			Growth rates (%) Taux d'accroissement (%) 2005-2011	
	Value (millions of dollars) Valeur (millions de dollars)	% of the country grouping exports En % des exportations du groupe de pays	% of world product exports En % des exportations mondiales des produits	Value (millions of dollars) Valeur (millions de dollars)	% of the country grouping exports En % des exportations du groupe de pays	% of world product exports En % des exportations mondiales des produits	Value Valeur	Difference from world Différence par rapport au monde
112 Alcoholic beverages	46 499	0.44	100.00	74 375	0.41	100.00	6.62	_
012 Meat nes, fresh chilled frozen	40 026	0.38	100.00	75 292	0.42	100.00	10.52	_
675 Flat rolled products of alloy steel	44 455	0.42	100.00	74 721	0.41	100.00	4.15	_
841 Male clothing, woven	53 327	0.51	100.00	71 949	0.40	100.00	3.30	_
562 Manufactured fertilizer excluding crude	24 753	0.24	100.00	74 580	0.41	100.00	19.38	_
081 Animal feed excluding unmilled cereal	30 761	0.29	100.00	68 751	0.38	100.00	14.45	_
763 Sound TV recorder or reproducer	62 282	0.60	100.00	61 129	0.34	100.00	-0.47	_
681 Silver, platinum, platinum metals	22 354	0.21	100.00	73 573	0.41	100.00	14.52	_
054 Vegetable & vegetable products nes	33 862	0.32	100.00	64 561	0.36	100.00	10.43	_
898 Music instrument device recording	51 332	0.49	100.00	61 296	0.34	100.00	1.94	_
222 Oil seed etc for soft oil	21 450	0.20	100.00	65 050	0.36	100.00	21.24	_
533 Pigment, paint, varnish & related	39 328	0.38	100.00	64 607	0.36	100.00	6.59	_
522 Inorganic chemical elem oxide salt	29 179	0.28	100.00	67 040	0.37	100.00	11.90	_
098 Edible products & preparations nes	33 112	0.32	100.00	60 967	0.34	100.00	10.10	_
674 Flat plated iron non-alloy steel	34 991	0.33	100.00	62 447	0.35	100.00	6.97	_
642 Cut paper and paperboard articles	36 709	0.35	100.00	60 885	0.34	100.00	7.71	_
742 Liquid pump; liquid elevator parts	33 765	0.32	100.00	61 397	0.34	100.00	8.66	_
034 Fish, fresh live chilled frozen	34 728	0.33	100.00	60 939	0.34	100.00	8.80	_
651 Textile yarn	40 855	0.39	100.00	61 319	0.34	100.00	4.54	_
512 Alcohols, phenols; derivatives	32 295	0.31	100.00	63 144	0.35	100.00	8.73	_
574 Polyacetals and polyesters, etc	36 517	0.35	100.00	57 466	0.32	100.00	5.68	_
884 Optical goods fibres nes	30 637	0.29	100.00	55 119	0.30	100.00	9.17	_
745 Non-electrical machinery tool nes	39 779	0.38	100.00	56 152	0.31	100.00	3.66	_
751 Office machines	15 274	0.15	100.00	53 193	0.29	100.00	22.41	_
282 Ferrous iron & steel, waste & scrap	25 059	0.24	100.00	57 070	0.32	100.00	10.65	_
892 Printed matter	39 257	0.38	100.00	53 376	0.30	100.00	4.18	_
342 Liquefied propane and butane	28 838	0.28	100.00	55 298	0.31	100.00	8.85	_
514 Nitrogen function compounds	34 150	0.33	100.00	53 662	0.30	100.00	6.65	_
283 Copper ores and concentrates	19 544	0.19	100.00	53 178	0.29	100.00	13.28	_
748 Mechanical transmission equipment	29 562	0.28	100.00	54 996	0.30	100.00	8.72	_
691 Iron steel aluminium structures nes	27 211	0.26	100.00	54 800	0.30	100.00	9.93	_
844 Female clothing, knitted crocheted	25 920	0.25	100.00	54 011	0.30	100.00	10.65	_
658 Made-up textile articles nes	31 698	0.30	100.00	52 753	0.29	100.00	7.72	_
513 Carboxylic acid and compounds	33 262	0.32	100.00	53 466	0.30	100.00	5.46	_
251 Pulp and waste paper	26 417	0.25	100.00	49 637	0.27	100.00	9.23	_
831 Case bag: storage travel shopping	23 743	0.23	100.00	52 571	0.29	100.00	12.24	_
657 Special yarn and textile fabric etc	30 339	0.29	100.00	48 438	0.27	100.00	6.72	_
422 Fixed veg fat and oil, excluding "soft"	13 671	0.13	100.00	51 889	0.29	100.00	23.35	_
695 Tools for use in hand or in machine	30 653	0.29	100.00	48 515	0.27	100.00	5.51	_
288 Non ferrous base metal waste nes	17 466	0.17	100.00	48 670	0.27	100.00	11.70	_
785 Motorcycles, mopeds and cycles	32 478	0.31	100.00	47 645	0.26	100.00	4.58	_
335 Residual petroleum products nes	18 606	0.18	100.00	48 610	0.27	100.00	14.29	_
885 Watches and clocks	25 284	0.24	100.00	47 828	0.26	100.00	9.10	_
048 Cereal & preparation flour starch	25 364	0.24	100.00	45 760	0.25	100.00	9.54	_
061 Sugar, mollasses and honey	17 905	0.17	100.00	46 819	0.26	100.00	15.27	_
671 Pig & sponge iron, ferro alloys etc	27 039	0.26	100.00	44 365	0.25	100.00	6.04	_
672 Ingots, Iron steel primary products	29 077	0.28	100.00	45 368	0.25	100.00	4.20	_
041 Wheat meslin, incl spelt, unmilled	17 914	0.17	100.00	48 344	0.27	100.00	15.11	_
653 Man-made woven fabrics	32 053	0.31	100.00	44 456	0.25	100.00	3.63	_
774 Electrodiagnostic equipment	26 200	0.25	100.00	41 660	0.23	100.00	7.08	_
783 Road motor vehicles nes	30 496	0.29	100.00	46 355	0.26	100.00	2.37	_
022 Milk products, excluding butter & cheese	22 858	0.22	100.00	43 425	0.24	100.00	9.40	_
516 Other organic chemicals	25 607	0.24	100.00	42 836	0.24	100.00	7.09	_
292 Crude vegetable materials nes	24 471	0.23	100.00	43 529	0.24	100.00	8.43	_
554 Soaps cleansers polishes	22 727	0.22	100.00	40 633	0.22	100.00	9.19	_
011 Beef, fresh chilled frozen	21 805	0.21	100.00	41 413	0.23	100.00	9.76	_
664 Glass	25 532	0.24	100.00	39 658	0.22	100.00	5.94	_
071 Coffee and coffee substitutes	15 741	0.15	100.00	43 991	0.24	100.00	15.86	_
351 Electric current	25 244	0.24	100.00	39 938	0.22	100.00	5.60	_
248 Wood simply worked, railway sleeper	35 458	0.34	100.00	37 844	0.21	100.00	-1.58	_

For sources and notes, see end of table.

Pour les sources et les notes, se reporter à la fin du tableau.

Products ranked by average 2010-2011 values SITC Revision 3 (3-digit level) / Produits classés d'après la moyenne des valeurs de 2010-2011 CTCI révision 3 (positions à 3 chiffres)	2005			2011			Growth rates (%) Taux d'accroissement (%) 2005-2011	
	Value (millions of dollars) Valeur (millions de dollars)	% of the country grouping exports En % des exportations du groupe de pays	% of world product exports En % des exportations mondiales des produits	Value (millions of dollars) Valeur (millions de dollars)	% of the country grouping exports En % des exportations du groupe de pays	% of world product exports En % des exportations mondiales des produits	Value Valeur	Difference from world Différence par rapport au monde
421 Fixed veg fat and oil, "soft"	16 878	0.16	100.00	40 214	0.22	100.00	12.65	–
694 Nails screws nuts bolts rivets	21 459	0.21	100.00	38 000	0.21	100.00	7.23	–
721 Agricultural machine nes excluding tractor	20 724	0.20	100.00	37 225	0.21	100.00	8.17	–
731 Machine tools for material removal	27 275	0.26	100.00	38 687	0.21	100.00	0.97	–
746 Ball or roller bearings	19 761	0.19	100.00	35 888	0.20	100.00	8.22	–
634 Veneer, plywood & other wood nes	29 912	0.29	100.00	34 466	0.19	100.00	-0.11	–
663 Mineral manufactures nes	21 493	0.21	100.00	35 467	0.20	100.00	6.03	–
231 Natural rubber, latex, gum, etc	9 829	0.09	100.00	39 939	0.22	100.00	18.90	–
652 Woven cotton fabrics	29 014	0.28	100.00	35 157	0.19	100.00	1.09	–
786 Trailer caravan transport container	23 276	0.22	100.00	36 738	0.20	100.00	2.10	–
287 Base metal ores & concentrates nes	19 009	0.18	100.00	33 067	0.18	100.00	5.80	–
813 Lighting fixtures and fittings nes	19 139	0.18	100.00	33 857	0.19	100.00	8.18	–
036 Crustacean mollusc aquat invertebra	20 148	0.19	100.00	32 861	0.18	100.00	6.78	–
724 Textile leather machinery parts nes	25 502	0.24	100.00	31 172	0.17	100.00	0.45	–
044 Maize unmilled, excluding sweet corn	11 408	0.11	100.00	34 330	0.19	100.00	17.01	–
655 Knitted or crocheted fabrics nes	19 907	0.19	100.00	31 347	0.17	100.00	5.94	–
024 Cheese and curd	17 422	0.17	100.00	31 041	0.17	100.00	9.09	–
122 Manufactured tabacco	19 240	0.18	100.00	31 295	0.17	100.00	7.72	–
749 Non-electric machinery part nes	21 793	0.21	100.00	30 243	0.17	100.00	3.53	–
629 Articles of rubber nes	18 289	0.17	100.00	29 800	0.16	100.00	6.46	–
056 Vegetables roots tubers nes	16 189	0.15	100.00	30 154	0.17	100.00	9.69	–
661 Lime cement construction material	19 215	0.18	100.00	28 560	0.16	100.00	5.14	–
843 Male clothing, knitted crocheted	15 042	0.14	100.00	30 041	0.17	100.00	9.52	–
848 Headgear, non-textile clothing	21 131	0.20	100.00	29 513	0.16	100.00	4.84	–
697 Base metal household equipment nes	18 625	0.18	100.00	29 019	0.16	100.00	5.85	–
791 Railway vehicles and equipment	16 355	0.16	100.00	29 131	0.16	100.00	8.65	–
846 Clothing accessory excluding 831, 848, and 851	17 680	0.17	100.00	28 814	0.16	100.00	7.59	–
665 Glassware	17 451	0.17	100.00	29 273	0.16	100.00	6.40	–
591 Household and garden chemicals	16 298	0.16	100.00	28 355	0.16	100.00	9.59	–
232 Synthetic & reclaimed rubber; waste	11 987	0.11	100.00	29 496	0.16	100.00	12.68	–
572 Primary form styrene polymers	19 332	0.18	100.00	25 966	0.14	100.00	2.82	–
635 Wood manufactures nes	21 070	0.20	100.00	26 031	0.14	100.00	0.98	–
662 Clay and refractory materials	17 066	0.16	100.00	25 898	0.14	100.00	5.13	–
621 Rubber material e.g. paste tube rod	13 044	0.12	100.00	26 457	0.15	100.00	9.53	–
037 Fish shellfish, prepared preserved	14 887	0.14	100.00	26 161	0.14	100.00	7.60	–
611 Leather	20 678	0.20	100.00	24 824	0.14	100.00	0.16	–
592 Starches, glutenes, glues, etc	14 185	0.14	100.00	25 172	0.14	100.00	8.87	–
551 Essential oils, perfumes & flavours	15 608	0.15	100.00	24 527	0.14	100.00	7.02	–
263 Cotton	11 028	0.11	100.00	26 558	0.15	100.00	12.37	–
718 Power generating machinery part nes	11 428	0.11	100.00	24 171	0.13	100.00	12.12	–
042 Rice	10 170	0.10	100.00	23 319	0.13	100.00	16.09	–
073 Chocolate & cocoa preparations nes	12 743	0.12	100.00	23 658	0.13	100.00	9.86	–
072 Cocoa	9 343	0.09	100.00	22 353	0.12	100.00	17.39	–
683 Nickel	13 722	0.13	100.00	22 695	0.13	100.00	1.64	–
597 Additive e.g. lubricate, antifreeze	11 415	0.11	100.00	23 064	0.13	100.00	10.75	–
737 Metalwork machinery nes excluding tools	16 061	0.15	100.00	22 393	0.12	100.00	3.51	–
523 Inorganic acid metal salt peroxy	12 364	0.12	100.00	22 378	0.12	100.00	8.32	–
001 Live animal excluding fish & crustacean	13 780	0.13	100.00	21 458	0.12	100.00	7.03	–
722 Tractors	14 277	0.14	100.00	22 721	0.13	100.00	5.13	–
581 Plastic tube pipe hose & fittings	11 880	0.11	100.00	21 754	0.12	100.00	8.34	–
896 Work of art & collections; antiques	14 902	0.14	100.00	20 543	0.11	100.00	2.61	–
525 Radio active & associated materials	7 759	0.07	100.00	22 234	0.12	100.00	15.30	–
573 Vinyl chloride etc polymers	12 496	0.12	100.00	20 465	0.11	100.00	6.39	–
289 Prec metal ore concentrate excluding gold	4 134	0.04	100.00	20 241	0.11	100.00	27.35	–
692 Metal storage transport container	11 424	0.11	100.00	20 085	0.11	100.00	7.79	–
111 Non alcoholic beverage nes	11 149	0.11	100.00	20 637	0.11	100.00	8.62	–
017 Meat offal preserved nes	10 815	0.10	100.00	20 144	0.11	100.00	9.86	–
882 Photo cinematographic supply excluding 883	19 725	0.19	100.00	18 113	0.10	100.00	-2.42	–
058 Fruit preserve preparation excluding juice	10 156	0.10	100.00	19 101	0.11	100.00	9.22	–
278 Other crude minerals	10 859	0.10	100.00	17 271	0.10	100.00	6.47	–

For sources and notes, see end of table.

Pour les sources et les notes, se reporter à la fin du tableau.

Products ranked by average 2010-2011 values SITC Revision 3 (3-digit level) / Produits classés d'après la moyenne des valeurs de 2010-2011 CTCI révision 3 (positions à 3 chiffres)	2005			2011			Growth rates (%) Taux d'accroissement (%) 2005-2011	
	Value (millions of dollars) Valeur (millions de dollars)	% of the country grouping exports En % des exportations du groupe de pays	% of world product exports En % des exportations mondiales des produits	Value (millions of dollars) Valeur (millions de dollars)	% of the country grouping exports En % des exportations du groupe de pays	% of world product exports En % des exportations mondiales des produits	Value Valeur	Difference from world Différence par rapport au monde
762 Radio broadcast receivers	18 640	0.18	100.00	16 377	0.09	100.00	-4.12	_
059 Fruit & vegetable juice unferment	9 211	0.09	100.00	17 596	0.10	100.00	8.22	_
726 Printing bookbinding machines parts	18 717	0.18	100.00	16 055	0.09	100.00	-5.17	_
659 Floor coverings etc	11 718	0.11	100.00	16 839	0.09	100.00	4.17	_
735 Machine part accessory for 731 and 733	11 846	0.11	100.00	17 198	0.10	100.00	2.85	_
895 Office and stationery supplies nes	10 603	0.10	100.00	15 801	0.09	100.00	5.33	_
285 Aluminium ore concentrate alumina	10 613	0.10	100.00	15 474	0.09	100.00	3.04	_
812 Sanitary plumb heat fixtures nes	11 420	0.11	100.00	15 424	0.09	100.00	2.79	_
344 Petroleum and hydrocarbon gas nes	10 307	0.10	100.00	12 872	0.07	100.00	1.13	_
693 Wire products and fencing grills	9 126	0.09	100.00	15 806	0.09	100.00	6.68	_
247 Wood in rough or roughly squared	11 057	0.11	100.00	15 876	0.09	100.00	2.95	_
727 Food processing machine excluding domestic	9 360	0.09	100.00	15 041	0.08	100.00	5.71	_
524 Other inorganic chemicals	6 715	0.06	100.00	14 397	0.08	100.00	10.05	_
686 Zinc	6 917	0.07	100.00	13 948	0.08	100.00	2.81	_
531 Synthetic organic colour agents	10 417	0.10	100.00	12 771	0.07	100.00	2.20	_
431 Processed animal & veg fats & oils	5 736	0.05	100.00	14 732	0.08	100.00	14.36	_
678 Wire of iron or steel	7 224	0.07	100.00	13 717	0.08	100.00	8.16	_
891 Arms and ammunition	7 560	0.07	100.00	11 664	0.06	100.00	7.95	_
121 Unmanufactured tabacco and refuse	7 132	0.07	100.00	12 096	0.07	100.00	9.58	_
733 Metal work tool no material removal	9 065	0.09	100.00	13 316	0.07	100.00	2.79	_
873 Meters and counters nes	6 725	0.06	100.00	11 944	0.07	100.00	8.70	_
725 Paper & pulp mill, cut manufacture	9 403	0.09	100.00	11 789	0.07	100.00	1.64	_
654 Other woven textile fabrics nes	11 115	0.11	100.00	11 592	0.06	100.00	-1.54	_
284 Nickel ores, concentrates, etc	5 429	0.05	100.00	11 619	0.06	100.00	7.93	_
696 Cutlery	7 212	0.07	100.00	11 370	0.06	100.00	6.08	_
062 Sugar confectionery	6 634	0.06	100.00	10 791	0.06	100.00	7.47	_
689 Misc non-ferrous base metals	7 481	0.07	100.00	10 917	0.06	100.00	2.10	_
273 Stone, sand and gravel	6 310	0.06	100.00	10 226	0.06	100.00	6.57	_
656 Tulle lace embroidery trim etc	8 191	0.08	100.00	10 000	0.06	100.00	1.09	_
325 Coke, semi coke, retort carbon	6 180	0.06	100.00	10 005	0.06	100.00	6.07	_
711 Steam generating boilers & parts	3 930	0.04	100.00	9 963	0.06	100.00	18.03	_
712 Steam vapour turbines & parts nes	4 239	0.04	100.00	9 084	0.05	100.00	15.76	_
666 Pottery	6 351	0.06	100.00	9 238	0.05	100.00	4.88	_
266 Synthetic fibres for spinning	5 976	0.06	100.00	9 049	0.05	100.00	4.96	_
291 Crude animal materials nes	5 152	0.05	100.00	8 972	0.05	100.00	8.74	_
811 Prefabricated buildings	5 592	0.05	100.00	8 625	0.05	100.00	4.66	_
023 Butter fats oils derived from milk	4 357	0.04	100.00	8 653	0.05	100.00	11.26	_
074 Tea and maté	4 163	0.04	100.00	8 313	0.05	100.00	11.90	_
211 Raw hides & skins, excluding furskins	5 815	0.06	100.00	8 308	0.05	100.00	2.94	_
075 Spices	2 996	0.03	100.00	9 093	0.05	100.00	17.65	_
268 Wool & animal hair, incl wool tops	4 951	0.05	100.00	8 455	0.05	100.00	5.38	_
881 Photographic device nes	17 237	0.16	100.00	6 708	0.04	100.00	-16.49	_
579 Plastic waste, parings and scrap	3 699	0.04	100.00	7 396	0.04	100.00	10.32	_
687 Tin	3 215	0.03	100.00	8 050	0.04	100.00	13.32	_
685 Lead	2 877	0.03	100.00	6 875	0.04	100.00	11.59	_
043 Barley grain unmilled	3 631	0.03	100.00	7 404	0.04	100.00	9.85	_
091 Margarine and shortening	2 775	0.03	100.00	6 844	0.04	100.00	14.69	_
246 Wood chips, particles and waste	3 044	0.03	100.00	6 036	0.03	100.00	11.18	_
035 Fish, dried salted smoked	3 804	0.04	100.00	6 014	0.03	100.00	6.46	_
411 Animals oils and fats	2 525	0.02	100.00	6 364	0.04	100.00	14.98	_
025 Eggs, yolks and albumin	2 399	0.02	100.00	5 789	0.03	100.00	16.46	_
046 Wheat meal & flour, meslin flour	2 542	0.02	100.00	6 439	0.04	100.00	15.21	_
583 Plastic rod stick & profile shapes	3 667	0.04	100.00	5 672	0.03	100.00	5.18	_
016 Meat offal preserved	2 673	0.03	100.00	5 118	0.03	100.00	10.03	_
267 Man made fibre for spinning; waste	3 196	0.03	100.00	5 058	0.03	100.00	5.94	_
212 Raw furskins and furskin pieces	2 350	0.02	100.00	4 783	0.03	100.00	9.43	_
677 Iron steel rail railway materials	2 308	0.02	100.00	4 718	0.03	100.00	11.92	_
274 Sulphur and unroasted iron pyrites	1 632	0.02	100.00	5 498	0.03	100.00	17.63	_
272 Crude fertilizer, excluding manufactured	1 844	0.02	100.00	4 808	0.03	100.00	17.41	_
269 Worn clothing, textile article; rag	2 137	0.02	100.00	4 594	0.03	100.00	12.15	_

For sources and notes, see end of table.   Pour les sources et les notes, se reporter à la fin du tableau.

Products ranked by average 2010-2011 values SITC Revision 3 (3-digit level) / Produits classés d'après la moyenne des valeurs de 2010-2011 CTCI révision 3 (positions à 3 chiffres)	2005			2011			Growth rates (%) Taux d'accroissement (%) 2005-2011	
	Value (millions of dollars) Valeur (millions de dollars)	% of the country grouping exports En % des exportations du groupe de pays	% of world product exports En % des exportations mondiales des produits	Value (millions of dollars) Valeur (millions de dollars)	% of the country grouping exports En % des exportations du groupe de pays	% of world product exports En % des exportations mondiales des produits	Value Valeur	Difference from world Différence par rapport au monde
322 Briquettes, lignite and peat	991	0.01	100.00	3 995	0.02	100.00	30.02	–
593 Explosives and pyrotechnic products	1 931	0.02	100.00	3 530	0.02	100.00	9.48	–
612 Leather manufactures nes	3 092	0.03	100.00	3 461	0.02	100.00	-0.39	–
045 Grain, excluding wheat rice barley maize	1 603	0.02	100.00	3 573	0.02	100.00	11.29	–
223 Oil seed for non soft oil	1 465	0.01	100.00	2 964	0.02	100.00	11.64	–
532 Dyeing and tanning extracts	1 433	0.01	100.00	2 198	0.01	100.00	6.70	–
613 Furskin tanned dressed etc	1 722	0.02	100.00	1 965	0.01	100.00	-0.38	–
633 Cork manufactures	1 524	0.01	100.00	1 614	0.01	100.00	-0.95	–
277 Natural abrasives nes	1 164	0.01	100.00	1 629	0.01	100.00	5.08	–
047 Other cereal meals and flours	665	0.01	100.00	1 422	0.01	100.00	12.38	–
245 Fuel wood excluding waste; wood charcoal	552	0.01	100.00	1 333	0.01	100.00	14.75	–
265 Veg textile fibre, excluding cotton jute	698	0.01	100.00	1 008	0.01	100.00	3.92	–
286 Uranium & thorium ore concentrates	513	0.00	100.00	766	0.00	100.00	4.73	–
883 Cinematographic film, developed	672	0.01	100.00	497	0.00	100.00	-4.59	–
261 Silk	360	0.00	100.00	556	0.00	100.00	7.36	–
961 Coins, nongold and non currency	196	0.00	100.00	398	0.00	100.00	16.83	–
264 Jute & bast fibre nes, raw & retted	120	0.00	100.00	348	0.00	100.00	19.60	–
244 Natural cork, raw and wastes	238	0.00	100.00	218	0.00	100.00	-5.49	–
345 Coal, water, producer gas etc	17	0.00	100.00	26	0.00	100.00	13.44	–

Source:
UNCTAD secretariat calculations, based on UNCTAD, *UNCTADstat* Merchandise Trade Matrix

Source :
Calculs du secrétariat de la CNUCED, basés sur la matrice du commerce de marchandises de *UNCTADstat* de la CNUCED

Products ranked by average 2010-2011 values SITC Revision 3 (3-digit level) / Produits classés d'après la moyenne des valeurs de 2010-2011 CTCI révision 3 (positions à 3 chiffres)	2005			2011			Growth rates (%) Taux d'accroissement (%) 2005-2011	
	Value (millions of dollars) / Valeur (millions de dollars)	% of the country grouping exports / En % des exportations du groupe de pays	% of world product exports / En % des exportations mondiales des produits	Value (millions of dollars) / Valeur (millions de dollars)	% of the country grouping exports / En % des exportations du groupe de pays	% of world product exports / En % des exportations mondiales des produits	Value / Valeur	Difference from world / Différence par rapport au monde
All commodity groups	**3 805 282**	**100.00**	**36.36**	**7 789 922**	**100.00**	**43.07**	**10.42**	**3.07**
333 Crude petroleum & bituminous oil	588 493	15.47	72.90	1 175 967	15.10	71.90	8.35	-0.39
776 Valves tubes; diodes, transistors	214 599	5.64	58.33	396 030	5.08	71.07	9.35	3.37
334 Heavy petroleum & bituminous oil	174 463	4.58	46.09	410 697	5.27	43.83	12.07	-0.63
764 Telecommunicate equipment part nes	181 728	4.78	50.47	333 145	4.28	65.99	9.06	5.41
752 Computer equipment nes	154 004	4.05	55.75	239 344	3.07	69.66	6.53	4.17
343 Natural gas, liquefied or not	49 320	1.30	32.51	153 278	1.97	56.73	17.10	6.98
759 Office equipment part & accessories	113 686	2.99	56.58	114 945	1.48	58.69	-0.79	0.87
793 Ships boats floating structures	31 337	0.82	43.96	123 757	1.59	67.23	26.78	9.52
781 Passenger cars and race cars	62 578	1.64	12.81	111 070	1.43	17.36	7.31	5.40
778 Electrical machinery apparatus nes	60 740	1.60	40.90	108 396	1.39	48.27	8.40	3.07
971 Gold non-monetary excluding ores	19 796	0.52	50.81	111 898	1.44	50.38	32.06	0.98
772 Electrical circuit equipment	54 621	1.44	38.39	99 063	1.27	42.76	8.56	2.04
845 Articles of apparel nes	64 302	1.69	67.04	99 499	1.28	70.15	5.22	0.47
784 Motor vehicle parts and accessories	42 517	1.12	18.10	91 341	1.17	25.59	11.22	6.46
871 Optical instruments apparatus nes	33 929	0.89	75.78	81 708	1.05	79.33	14.34	0.77
667 Pearls, precious semiprecious stone	37 742	0.99	39.89	81 561	1.05	50.56	14.50	6.34
682 Copper	30 456	0.80	47.41	76 737	0.99	51.43	11.04	1.78
851 Footwear	37 582	0.99	56.32	68 834	0.88	60.78	9.40	1.64
821 Furniture part; bedding furnishing	34 369	0.90	35.25	67 828	0.87	45.96	10.69	5.29
281 Iron ore and concentrates	15 116	0.40	51.71	65 162	0.84	45.14	26.93	-3.07
761 Television video receive project	33 403	0.88	58.02	55 632	0.71	57.54	7.31	-0.18
897 Jewellery nes (667)	19 752	0.52	48.17	66 156	0.85	60.98	20.69	5.48
894 Baby carriage toy game sport good	38 308	1.01	59.16	56 749	0.73	58.55	5.53	-0.25
842 Female clothing, woven	42 570	1.12	64.95	54 870	0.70	65.55	2.77	0.25
775 Household equipment nes	27 717	0.73	43.30	52 167	0.67	55.95	9.84	4.76
773 Electrical distribute equipment nes	24 547	0.65	39.98	51 564	0.66	46.11	10.15	2.86
771 Electric power machine part excluding 716	23 414	0.62	51.06	48 088	0.62	52.02	11.33	0.24
893 Articles of plastic nes	27 954	0.73	32.49	49 205	0.63	36.80	8.35	2.39
699 Base metal manufactures nes	25 888	0.68	28.54	49 597	0.64	34.59	8.79	3.62
841 Male clothing, woven	34 683	0.91	65.04	49 056	0.63	68.18	4.09	0.79
321 Coal excluding non-agglomomerated	16 626	0.44	35.27	47 794	0.61	35.79	18.77	-0.65
422 Fixed veg fat and oil, excluding "soft"	11 741	0.31	85.88	46 080	0.59	88.81	24.26	0.91
057 Fruit nut (exc oil), fresh or dried	22 091	0.58	45.25	42 434	0.54	49.07	11.40	1.93
741 Heating cooling equipment parts nes	19 603	0.52	28.47	41 293	0.53	37.23	11.24	5.15
844 Female clothing, knitted crocheted	18 858	0.50	72.75	41 768	0.54	77.33	11.35	0.70
283 Copper ores and concentrates	15 668	0.41	80.17	39 115	0.50	73.55	12.13	-1.15
782 Goods and service vehicles	20 151	0.53	22.27	40 990	0.53	31.73	9.24	7.00
728 Special industrial machine part nes	15 735	0.41	15.98	41 337	0.53	22.20	15.15	6.23
658 Made-up textile articles nes	22 222	0.58	70.11	39 428	0.51	74.74	9.16	1.44
684 Aluminium	21 248	0.56	26.75	40 194	0.52	31.84	6.63	3.02
763 Sound TV recorder or reproducer	37 075	0.97	59.53	35 746	0.46	58.48	-0.41	0.06
651 Textile yarn	22 620	0.59	55.37	38 499	0.49	62.79	7.32	2.78
511 Hydrocarbons nes; derivatives	16 152	0.42	31.81	40 378	0.52	41.81	13.10	5.25
874 Measure analyze control device nes	16 606	0.44	14.85	37 537	0.48	20.98	12.70	6.55
342 Liquefied propane and butane	19 416	0.51	67.33	37 658	0.48	68.10	8.94	0.10
575 Other plastics, in primary forms	14 144	0.37	21.15	36 885	0.47	32.13	15.82	8.79
571 Primary form ethylene polymers	16 366	0.43	38.92	36 578	0.47	46.23	13.26	4.35
679 Iron steel pipe tube fittings etc	14 871	0.39	27.30	36 293	0.47	37.75	12.00	5.87
625 Rubber for wheels, incl inner tube	13 563	0.36	30.85	37 363	0.48	40.34	15.75	4.96
743 Gas pump, compressor, fan, filter	16 032	0.42	22.92	35 017	0.45	28.12	11.86	3.67
723 Civil engineering plant & equipment	13 579	0.36	19.57	36 666	0.47	29.68	14.26	8.30
713 Internal combustion engine part nes	16 280	0.43	14.35	35 556	0.46	21.55	11.36	7.75
751 Office machines	7 256	0.19	47.50	31 669	0.41	59.54	27.94	5.53
831 Case bag: storage travel shopping	14 311	0.38	60.28	34 273	0.44	65.19	14.11	1.87
231 Natural rubber, latex, gum, etc	9 577	0.25	97.43	37 901	0.49	94.90	18.27	-0.63
716 Rotating electric plant parts nes	16 346	0.43	31.70	32 408	0.42	34.88	10.28	1.64
061 Sugar, mollasses and honey	9 826	0.26	54.88	33 460	0.43	71.47	20.51	5.24
653 Man-made woven fabrics	19 574	0.51	61.07	32 585	0.42	73.30	7.00	3.37
512 Alcohols, phenols; derivatives	15 154	0.40	46.92	32 710	0.42	51.80	10.58	1.85
673 Flat iron non-alloy steel products	19 463	0.51	29.07	29 215	0.38	30.98	4.29	1.15

For sources and notes, see end of table.

Pour les sources et les notes, se reporter à la fin du tableau.

Products ranked by average 2010-2011 values SITC Revision 3 (3-digit level) / Produits classés d'après la moyenne des valeurs de 2010-2011 CTCI révision 3 (positions à 3 chiffres)	2005			2011			Growth rates (%) Taux d'accroissement (%) 2005-2011	
	Value (millions of dollars) / Valeur (millions de dollars)	% of the country grouping exports / En % des exportations du groupe de pays	% of world product exports / En % des exportations mondiales des produits	Value (millions of dollars) / Valeur (millions de dollars)	% of the country grouping exports / En % des exportations du groupe de pays	% of world product exports / En % des exportations mondiales des produits	Value / Valeur	Difference from world / Différence par rapport au monde
898 Music instrument device recording	15 935	0.42	31.04	29 357	0.38	47.89	9.41	7.47
598 Miscellaneous chemical products nes	10 026	0.26	15.56	30 540	0.39	23.72	18.22	7.81
081 Animal feed excluding unmilled cereal	12 151	0.32	39.50	29 725	0.38	43.24	16.52	2.08
676 Iron steel bar rod section piling	14 887	0.39	28.07	31 964	0.41	32.66	7.29	1.92
582 Plastic sheet film foil & strips	12 177	0.32	21.01	28 996	0.37	29.14	13.81	6.17
522 Inorganic chemical elem oxide salt	11 153	0.29	38.22	31 034	0.40	46.29	15.66	3.76
681 Silver, platinum, platinum metals	10 214	0.27	45.69	31 531	0.40	42.86	14.33	-0.19
222 Oil seed etc for soft oil	10 339	0.27	48.20	29 380	0.38	45.17	19.32	-1.91
899 Manufactured articles nes	13 503	0.35	30.41	27 320	0.35	34.67	11.49	1.74
542 Medicines including veterinary	9 805	0.26	4.72	27 850	0.36	8.17	16.57	8.35
513 Carboxylic acid and compounds	12 598	0.33	37.87	27 648	0.35	51.71	11.66	6.19
034 Fish, fresh live chilled frozen	13 959	0.37	40.19	26 688	0.34	43.80	10.19	1.39
884 Optical goods fibres nes	9 663	0.25	31.54	24 471	0.31	44.40	15.88	6.71
054 Vegetable & vegetable products nes	11 467	0.30	33.87	24 451	0.31	37.87	13.16	2.72
574 Polyacetals and polyesters, etc	13 493	0.35	36.95	25 051	0.32	43.59	8.95	3.27
652 Woven cotton fabrics	17 709	0.47	61.04	25 553	0.33	72.68	4.34	3.25
071 Coffee and coffee substitutes	10 132	0.27	64.37	27 841	0.36	63.29	15.20	-0.67
674 Flat plated iron non-alloy steel	10 189	0.27	29.12	26 256	0.34	42.05	12.87	5.90
785 Motorcycles, mopeds and cycles	12 538	0.33	38.61	24 851	0.32	52.16	10.40	5.83
843 Male clothing, knitted crocheted	11 945	0.31	79.41	25 036	0.32	83.34	10.20	0.69
562 Manufactured fertilizer excluding crude	6 941	0.18	28.04	24 839	0.32	33.30	23.34	3.96
671 Pig & sponge iron, ferro alloys etc	14 480	0.38	53.55	23 194	0.30	52.28	5.68	-0.36
655 Knitted or crocheted fabrics nes	12 789	0.34	64.24	23 622	0.30	75.36	8.93	2.99
792 Aircraft, spacecraft & equipment	10 509	0.28	8.21	22 725	0.29	15.05	11.41	12.28
641 Paper and paperboard	12 022	0.32	12.40	22 985	0.30	18.27	9.42	6.61
515 Organo-inorganic compound acid salt	9 692	0.25	12.10	23 431	0.30	20.92	13.74	9.12
691 Iron steel aluminium structures nes	7 421	0.20	27.27	21 969	0.28	40.09	17.56	7.63
747 Pipe, boiler, tank & vat appliances	8 600	0.23	20.98	21 295	0.27	27.24	13.47	4.55
036 Crustacean mollusc aquat invertebra	12 503	0.33	62.05	21 748	0.28	66.18	7.85	1.07
657 Special yarn and textile fabric etc	9 709	0.26	32.00	20 728	0.27	42.79	12.81	6.09
675 Flat rolled products of alloy steel	10 377	0.27	23.34	22 835	0.29	30.56	7.35	3.20
848 Headgear, non-textile clothing	15 001	0.39	70.99	20 427	0.26	69.21	4.92	0.08
287 Base metal ores & concentrates nes	10 590	0.28	55.71	19 316	0.25	58.42	7.77	1.97
541 Pharmaceuticals excluding medicines	6 715	0.18	10.02	19 479	0.25	12.66	19.62	4.31
042 Rice	7 791	0.20	76.60	18 993	0.24	81.45	17.28	1.18
872 Medical instruments appliances nes	9 640	0.25	18.22	18 503	0.24	21.23	11.15	2.61
642 Cut paper and paperboard articles	8 297	0.22	22.60	18 729	0.24	30.76	13.42	5.71
846 Clothing accessory excluding 831, 848, and 851	9 679	0.25	54.74	18 290	0.23	63.48	10.43	2.84
744 Mechanical handling equipment nes	7 281	0.19	13.90	18 467	0.24	22.87	14.53	10.25
813 Lighting fixtures and fittings nes	8 709	0.23	45.50	18 376	0.24	54.27	11.60	3.43
553 Perfume toilet cosmetics, excluding soap	6 935	0.18	15.81	17 635	0.23	23.06	15.84	7.21
335 Residual petroleum products nes	6 660	0.18	35.79	17 872	0.23	36.77	16.09	1.79
697 Base metal household equipment nes	9 447	0.25	50.72	17 197	0.22	59.26	8.86	3.01
514 Nitrogen function compounds	8 181	0.21	23.95	17 485	0.22	32.58	11.60	4.95
037 Fish shellfish, prepared preserved	9 280	0.24	62.34	17 828	0.23	68.15	8.88	1.28
661 Lime cement construction material	9 644	0.25	50.19	16 300	0.21	57.07	7.66	2.52
892 Printed matter	7 302	0.19	18.60	16 796	0.22	31.47	14.08	9.90
098 Edible products & preparations nes	6 706	0.18	20.25	16 025	0.21	26.28	15.44	5.34
885 Watches and clocks	9 931	0.26	39.28	16 096	0.21	33.65	7.13	-1.97
572 Primary form styrene polymers	10 421	0.27	53.90	15 142	0.19	58.31	5.06	2.24
695 Tools for use in hand or in machine	8 307	0.22	27.10	16 118	0.21	33.22	9.16	3.65
012 Meat nes, fresh chilled frozen	7 364	0.19	18.40	15 602	0.20	20.72	14.34	3.83
072 Cocoa	5 928	0.16	63.45	14 717	0.19	65.84	18.43	1.04
786 Trailer caravan transport container	8 723	0.23	37.47	16 934	0.22	46.09	5.42	3.32
634 Veneer, plywood & other wood nes	9 623	0.25	32.17	14 638	0.19	42.47	4.05	4.16
516 Other organic chemicals	8 370	0.22	32.69	14 819	0.19	34.60	9.30	2.22
611 Leather	11 235	0.30	54.33	13 321	0.17	53.66	0.05	-0.11
694 Nails screws nuts bolts rivets	7 218	0.19	33.64	14 224	0.18	37.43	9.02	1.78
112 Alcoholic beverages	6 794	0.18	14.61	13 090	0.17	17.60	10.77	4.15
664 Glass	6 484	0.17	25.40	13 537	0.17	34.13	11.00	5.06

For sources and notes, see end of table.

Pour les sources et les notes, se reporter à la fin du tableau.

Products ranked by average 2010-2011 values SITC Revision 3 (3-digit level) Produits classés d'après la moyenne des valeurs de 2010-2011 CTCI révision 3 (positions à 3 chiffres)	2005			2011			Growth rates (%) Taux d'accroissement (%) 2005-2011	
	Value (millions of dollars) Valeur (millions de dollars)	% of the country grouping exports En % des exportations du groupe de pays	% of world product exports En % des exportations mondiales des produits	Value (millions of dollars) Valeur (millions de dollars)	% of the country grouping exports En % des exportations du groupe de pays	% of world product exports En % des exportations mondiales des produits	Value Valeur	Difference from world Différence par rapport au monde
714 Non-electric engines excluding 712, 713, and 718	5 475	0.14	7.92	12 558	0.16	14.46	14.37	12.49
292 Crude vegetable materials nes	5 931	0.16	24.24	13 349	0.17	30.67	12.96	4.53
251 Pulp and waste paper	5 452	0.14	20.64	12 211	0.16	24.60	13.17	3.94
421 Fixed veg fat and oil, "soft"	6 599	0.17	39.10	13 339	0.17	33.17	8.95	-3.70
533 Pigment, paint, varnish & related	6 461	0.17	16.43	12 680	0.16	19.63	10.03	3.44
724 Textile leather machinery parts nes	7 139	0.19	27.99	12 285	0.16	39.41	7.38	6.93
745 Non-electrical machinery tool nes	5 951	0.16	14.96	12 339	0.16	21.97	11.03	7.37
742 Liquid pump; liquid elevator parts	4 480	0.12	13.27	12 308	0.16	20.05	16.24	7.58
672 Ingots, Iron steel primary products	9 552	0.25	32.85	12 616	0.16	27.81	0.69	-3.51
783 Road motor vehicles nes	4 865	0.13	15.95	13 047	0.17	28.15	15.36	12.99
665 Glassware	4 900	0.13	28.08	12 390	0.16	42.32	14.90	8.50
011 Beef, fresh chilled frozen	5 747	0.15	26.35	11 807	0.15	28.51	11.41	1.65
748 Mechanical transmission equipment	4 232	0.11	14.32	11 933	0.15	21.70	16.70	7.98
554 Soaps cleansers polishes	4 350	0.11	19.14	11 097	0.14	27.31	16.22	7.04
762 Radio broadcast receivers	12 293	0.32	65.95	10 304	0.13	62.92	-5.00	-0.88
749 Non-electric machinery part nes	5 572	0.15	25.57	10 671	0.14	35.28	10.04	6.51
662 Clay and refractory materials	4 518	0.12	26.47	10 344	0.13	39.94	13.66	8.53
056 Vegetables roots tubers nes	4 740	0.12	29.28	10 165	0.13	33.71	12.10	2.41
263 Cotton	3 938	0.10	35.71	10 816	0.14	40.73	15.59	3.22
288 Non ferrous base metal waste nes	3 702	0.10	21.20	9 766	0.13	20.07	10.76	-0.94
044 Maize unmilled, excluding sweet corn	3 211	0.08	28.14	10 679	0.14	31.11	20.36	3.35
344 Petroleum and hydrocarbon gas nes	3 339	0.09	32.39	6 245	0.08	48.52	11.22	10.09
746 Ball or roller bearings	4 239	0.11	21.45	9 577	0.12	26.68	12.60	4.38
523 Inorganic acid metal salt peroxy	4 310	0.11	34.86	9 592	0.12	42.86	12.27	3.95
048 Cereal & preparation flour starch	3 664	0.10	14.45	9 431	0.12	20.61	16.83	7.29
635 Wood manufactures nes	6 913	0.18	32.81	9 138	0.12	35.10	2.12	1.13
058 Fruit preserve preparation excluding juice	4 502	0.12	44.32	9 119	0.12	47.74	10.72	1.50
621 Rubber material e.g. paste tube rod	2 156	0.06	16.53	8 903	0.11	33.65	23.79	14.26
121 Unmanufactured tabacco and refuse	4 317	0.11	60.53	8 143	0.10	67.32	11.52	1.93
232 Synthetic & reclaimed rubber; waste	3 100	0.08	25.86	9 327	0.12	31.62	17.06	4.38
248 Wood simply worked, railway sleeper	7 253	0.19	20.45	7 968	0.10	21.05	-1.13	0.45
122 Manufactured tabacco	4 154	0.11	21.59	8 063	0.10	25.76	11.26	3.54
731 Machine tools for material removal	4 715	0.12	17.29	8 529	0.11	22.05	5.26	4.29
591 Household and garden chemicals	3 914	0.10	24.02	7 797	0.10	27.50	13.68	4.09
663 Mineral manufactures nes	3 598	0.09	16.74	8 323	0.11	23.47	12.01	5.98
629 Articles of rubber nes	3 795	0.10	20.75	8 006	0.10	26.87	10.86	4.40
431 Processed animal & veg fats & oils	3 002	0.08	52.34	8 595	0.11	58.34	15.84	1.48
659 Floor coverings etc	4 269	0.11	36.43	7 486	0.10	44.46	9.02	4.85
592 Starches, glutenes, glues, etc	2 850	0.07	20.09	7 568	0.10	30.06	16.74	7.87
059 Fruit & vegetable juice unferment	3 411	0.09	37.04	7 691	0.10	43.71	11.10	2.89
278 Other crude minerals	3 648	0.10	33.59	7 217	0.09	41.79	10.77	4.30
284 Nickel ores, concentrates, etc	2 713	0.07	49.97	6 534	0.08	56.24	12.37	4.44
017 Meat offal preserved nes	3 519	0.09	32.53	6 831	0.09	33.91	10.61	0.74
282 Ferrous iron & steel, waste & scrap	2 761	0.07	11.02	6 852	0.09	12.01	12.13	1.48
693 Wire products and fencing grills	3 264	0.09	35.77	6 965	0.09	44.06	10.40	3.71
656 Tulle lace embroidery trim etc	4 610	0.12	56.28	6 403	0.08	64.03	3.21	2.12
692 Metal storage transport container	2 649	0.07	23.19	6 542	0.08	32.57	13.54	5.76
285 Aluminium ore concentrate alumina	3 545	0.09	33.40	6 141	0.08	39.68	6.78	3.74
075 Spices	2 188	0.06	73.04	7 132	0.09	78.43	19.08	1.42
074 Tea and maté	3 087	0.08	74.15	6 247	0.08	75.15	12.45	0.55
289 Prec metal ore concentrate excluding gold	1 381	0.04	33.41	7 101	0.09	35.08	26.14	-1.21
687 Tin	2 742	0.07	85.29	6 764	0.09	84.02	13.47	0.15
531 Synthetic organic colour agents	3 508	0.09	33.68	5 866	0.08	45.93	7.80	5.60
696 Cutlery	3 524	0.09	48.87	6 216	0.08	54.07	7.80	1.71
666 Pottery	3 373	0.09	53.12	6 270	0.08	67.87	9.33	4.45
895 Office and stationery supplies nes	3 851	0.10	36.32	5 791	0.07	36.65	5.82	0.49
737 Metalwork machinery nes excluding tools	3 088	0.08	19.23	5 520	0.07	24.65	8.91	5.40
022 Milk products, excluding butter & cheese	2 691	0.07	11.77	5 948	0.08	13.70	12.47	3.07
573 Vinyl chloride etc polymers	3 145	0.08	25.17	5 902	0.08	28.84	8.44	2.05
774 Electrodiagnostic equipment	2 260	0.06	8.63	5 668	0.07	13.61	14.85	7.78

For sources and notes, see end of table.

Pour les sources et les notes, se reporter à la fin du tableau.

3

Products ranked by average 2010-2011 values SITC Revision 3 (3-digit level) / Produits classés d'après la moyenne des valeurs de 2010-2011 CTCI révision 3 (positions à 3 chiffres)	2005			2011			Growth rates (%) Taux d'accroissement (%) 2005-2011	
	Value (millions of dollars) / Valeur (millions de dollars)	% of the country grouping exports / En % des exportations du groupe de pays	% of world product exports / En % des exportations mondiales des produits	Value (millions of dollars) / Valeur (millions de dollars)	% of the country grouping exports / En % des exportations du groupe de pays	% of world product exports / En % des exportations mondiales des produits	Value / Valeur	Difference from world / Différence par rapport au monde
711 Steam generating boilers & parts	908	0.02	23.10	5 762	0.07	57.83	37.42	19.39
266 Synthetic fibres for spinning	3 378	0.09	56.53	5 735	0.07	63.37	7.24	2.28
678 Wire of iron or steel	2 259	0.06	31.27	5 684	0.07	41.44	13.64	5.49
791 Railway vehicles and equipment	1 572	0.04	9.61	5 919	0.08	20.32	18.96	10.31
654 Other woven textile fabrics nes	4 159	0.11	37.42	5 040	0.06	43.48	1.52	3.06
581 Plastic tube pipe hose & fittings	2 003	0.05	16.86	5 096	0.07	23.42	15.60	7.26
721 Agricultural machine nes excluding tractor	1 756	0.05	8.47	4 958	0.06	13.32	18.83	10.66
551 Essential oils, perfumes & flavours	2 081	0.05	13.33	5 082	0.07	20.72	14.73	7.71
247 Wood in rough or roughly squared	2 976	0.08	26.91	5 025	0.06	31.65	6.05	3.10
686 Zinc	2 246	0.06	32.47	4 778	0.06	34.26	3.09	0.27
689 Misc non-ferrous base metals	2 679	0.07	35.82	4 811	0.06	44.07	5.81	3.72
001 Live animal excluding fish & crustacean	2 919	0.08	21.18	4 428	0.06	20.63	8.29	1.26
111 Non alcoholic beverage nes	2 323	0.06	20.83	4 817	0.06	23.34	11.62	3.00
273 Stone, sand and gravel	2 240	0.06	35.50	4 450	0.06	43.52	10.53	3.96
351 Electric current	2 487	0.07	9.85	4 559	0.06	11.41	11.26	5.66
873 Meters and counters nes	1 672	0.04	24.86	4 291	0.06	35.92	17.23	8.53
062 Sugar confectionery	2 232	0.06	33.65	4 222	0.05	39.13	9.89	2.43
881 Photographic device nes	4 526	0.12	26.25	3 423	0.04	51.04	-3.77	12.72
041 Wheat meslin, incl spelt, unmilled	1 909	0.05	10.65	5 101	0.07	10.55	9.39	-5.72
524 Other inorganic chemicals	2 298	0.06	34.22	3 735	0.05	25.94	6.39	-3.67
812 Sanitary plumb heat fixtures nes	2 337	0.06	20.46	3 551	0.05	23.02	4.56	1.77
291 Crude animal materials nes	1 973	0.05	38.30	3 799	0.05	42.34	10.53	1.79
718 Power generating machinery part nes	916	0.02	8.01	3 697	0.05	15.30	25.16	13.04
597 Additive e.g. lubricate, antifreeze	1 492	0.04	13.07	3 352	0.04	14.54	14.39	3.64
882 Photo cinematographic supply excluding 883	3 593	0.09	18.22	3 121	0.04	17.23	-2.79	-0.37
272 Crude fertilizer, excluding manufactured	1 349	0.04	73.15	3 631	0.05	75.52	17.19	-0.22
683 Nickel	1 378	0.04	10.04	2 884	0.04	12.71	8.41	6.77
268 Wool & animal hair, incl wool tops	1 484	0.04	29.97	3 605	0.05	42.64	11.74	6.35
735 Machine part accessory for 731 733	1 751	0.05	14.78	3 375	0.04	19.63	7.81	4.95
325 Coke, semi coke, retort carbon	2 641	0.07	42.73	3 041	0.04	30.40	-2.94	-9.01
073 Chocolate & cocoa preparations nes	1 355	0.04	10.64	3 077	0.04	13.01	14.55	4.69
722 Tractors	1 595	0.04	11.17	3 224	0.04	14.19	10.53	5.40
733 Metal work tool no material removal	1 877	0.05	20.71	3 056	0.04	22.95	5.54	2.75
525 Radio active & associated materials	730	0.02	9.41	3 762	0.05	16.92	25.74	10.44
579 Plastic waste, parings and scrap	1 573	0.04	42.52	2 625	0.03	35.50	7.23	-3.10
046 Wheat meal & flour, meslin flour	1 058	0.03	41.64	2 983	0.04	46.32	17.50	2.29
811 Prefabricated buildings	854	0.02	15.27	2 671	0.03	30.97	16.47	11.81
712 Steam vapour turbines & parts nes	453	0.01	10.70	2 493	0.03	27.44	35.55	19.80
274 Sulphur and unroasted iron pyrites	763	0.02	46.74	2 953	0.04	53.72	20.59	2.96
726 Printing bookbinding machines parts	1 630	0.04	8.71	2 272	0.03	14.15	3.18	8.35
727 Food processing machine excluding domestic	893	0.02	9.55	2 400	0.03	15.95	15.27	9.56
024 Cheese and curd	667	0.02	3.83	2 026	0.03	6.53	23.13	14.04
091 Margarine and shortening	822	0.02	29.62	2 429	0.03	35.49	16.89	2.20
246 Wood chips, particles and waste	1 102	0.03	36.19	2 032	0.03	33.66	10.64	-0.54
267 Man made fibre for spinning; waste	618	0.02	19.34	2 085	0.03	41.22	19.76	13.82
685 Lead	1 009	0.03	35.07	2 070	0.03	30.12	6.25	-5.34
896 Work of art & collections; antiques	1 214	0.03	8.15	1 878	0.02	9.14	2.36	-0.25
725 Paper & pulp mill, cut manufacture	968	0.03	10.29	1 791	0.02	15.19	8.46	6.83
035 Fish, dried salted smoked	992	0.03	26.08	1 658	0.02	27.58	8.37	1.91
612 Leather manufactures nes	1 507	0.04	48.74	1 606	0.02	46.41	-2.03	-1.64
891 Arms and ammunition	986	0.03	13.04	1 397	0.02	11.98	6.72	-1.23
322 Briquettes, lignite and peat	22	0.00	2.25	1 938	0.02	48.50	92.03	62.00
593 Explosives and pyrotechnic products	679	0.02	35.19	1 277	0.02	36.17	9.46	-0.01
025 Eggs, yolks and albumin	390	0.01	16.24	1 234	0.02	21.32	24.59	8.13
269 Worn clothing, textile article; rag	565	0.01	26.46	1 354	0.02	29.46	13.17	1.02
613 Furskin tanned dressed etc	926	0.02	53.77	1 077	0.01	54.81	1.43	1.81
277 Natural abrasives nes	710	0.02	61.00	991	0.01	60.81	6.36	1.28
583 Plastic rod stick & profile shapes	315	0.01	8.59	1 067	0.01	18.81	17.46	12.28
411 Animals oils and fats	373	0.01	14.79	1 012	0.01	15.91	16.71	1.74
211 Raw hides & skins, excluding furskins	1 005	0.03	17.28	961	0.01	11.56	-3.24	-6.19

For sources and notes, see end of table.

Pour les sources et les notes, se reporter à la fin du tableau.

3

Products ranked by average 2010-2011 values SITC Revision 3 (3-digit level) Produits classés d'après la moyenne des valeurs de 2010-2011 CTCI révision 3 (positions à 3 chiffres)	2005			2011			Growth rates (%) Taux d'accroissement (%) 2005-2011	
	Value (millions of dollars) Valeur (millions de dollars)	% of the country grouping exports En % des exportations du groupe de pays	% of world product exports En % des exportations mondiales des produits	Value (millions of dollars) Valeur (millions de dollars)	% of the country grouping exports En % des exportations du groupe de pays	% of world product exports En % des exportations mondiales des produits	Value Valeur	Difference from world Différence par rapport au monde
212 Raw furskins and furskin pieces	518	0.01	22.05	784	0.01	16.39	6.28	-3.15
045 Grain, excluding wheat rice barley maize	178	0.00	11.11	897	0.01	25.10	29.14	17.86
532 Dyeing and tanning extracts	552	0.01	38.55	761	0.01	34.63	4.49	-2.21
016 Meat offal preserved	49	0.00	1.85	801	0.01	15.65	60.62	50.58
223 Oil seed for non soft oil	420	0.01	28.68	820	0.01	27.68	10.90	-0.74
286 Uranium & thorium ore concentrates	68	0.00	13.34	766	0.01	99.99	42.57	37.84
677 Iron steel rail railway materials	140	0.00	6.06	761	0.01	16.13	31.01	19.09
047 Other cereal meals and flours	294	0.01	44.18	579	0.01	40.69	12.72	0.34
023 Butter fats oils derived from milk	178	0.00	4.08	536	0.01	6.20	20.85	9.59
245 Fuel wood excluding waste; wood charcoal	205	0.01	37.18	507	0.01	38.06	16.03	1.28
043 Barley grain unmilled	91	0.00	2.51	619	0.01	8.36	27.57	17.72
261 Silk	299	0.01	82.95	425	0.01	76.50	5.64	-1.72
265 Veg textile fibre, excluding cotton jute	184	0.00	26.41	464	0.01	46.08	15.07	11.15
264 Jute & bast fibre nes, raw & retted	112	0.00	93.44	341	0.00	98.00	20.43	0.83
961 Coins, nongold and non currency	7	0.00	3.76	34	0.00	8.62	47.82	30.99
883 Cinematographic film, developed	64	0.00	9.52	95	0.00	19.13	9.88	14.47
633 Cork manufactures	109	0.00	7.16	86	0.00	5.30	-7.63	-6.68
345 Coal, water, producer gas etc	14	0.00	83.41	23	0.00	88.46	12.40	-1.04
244 Natural cork, raw and wastes	18	0.00	7.43	17	0.00	7.65	-5.12	0.37

Source:
UNCTAD secretariat calculations, based on UNCTAD, *UNCTADstat* Merchandise Trade Matrix

Source :
Calculs du secrétariat de la CNUCED, basés sur la matrice du commerce de marchandises de *UNCTADstat* de la CNUCED

3.2.C Export structure by product / Structure des exportations par produits
Developed economies / Économies développées

Products ranked by average 2010-2011 values SITC Revision 3 (3-digit level) / Produits classés d'après la moyenne des valeurs de 2010-2011 CTCI révision 3 (positions à 3 chiffres)	2005			2011			Growth rates (%) Taux d'accroissement (%) 2005-2011	
	Value (millions of dollars) / Valeur (millions de dollars)	% of the country grouping exports / En % des exportations du groupe de pays	% of world product exports / En % des exportations mondiales des produits	Value (millions of dollars) / Valeur (millions de dollars)	% of the country grouping exports / En % des exportations du groupe de pays	% of world product exports / En % des exportations mondiales des produits	Value / Valeur	Difference from world / Différence par rapport au monde
All commodity groups	6 299 815	100.00	60.20	9 518 978	100.00	52.63	5.03	-2.31
781 Passenger cars and race cars	424 688	6.74	86.95	526 042	5.53	82.20	0.95	-0.96
334 Heavy petroleum & bituminous oil	159 106	2.53	42.03	411 472	4.32	43.91	13.25	0.55
542 Medicines including veterinary	197 508	3.14	95.00	311 547	3.27	91.37	7.65	-0.57
784 Motor vehicle parts and accessories	191 376	3.04	81.47	264 330	2.78	74.06	3.04	-1.72
333 Crude petroleum & bituminous oil	116 504	1.85	14.43	201 737	2.12	12.34	6.54	-2.20
764 Telecommunicale equipment part nes	177 693	2.82	49.35	170 371	1.79	33.75	-3.48	-7.14
776 Valves tubes; diodes, transistors	153 078	2.43	41.61	160 796	1.69	28.86	-0.10	-6.08
728 Special industrial machine part nes	82 234	1.31	83.53	144 075	1.51	77.37	7.52	-1.40
874 Measure analyze control device nes	94 465	1.50	84.46	140 070	1.47	78.29	4.73	-1.42
541 Pharmaceuticals excluding medicines	60 102	0.95	89.68	134 114	1.41	87.19	14.80	-0.51
772 Electrical circuit equipment	86 992	1.38	61.15	131 390	1.38	56.71	5.09	-1.43
792 Aircraft, spacecraft & equipment	116 431	1.85	90.97	127 283	1.34	84.30	-2.33	-1.46
713 Internal combustion engine part nes	96 583	1.53	85.12	128 814	1.35	78.08	2.05	-1.56
778 Electrical machinery apparatus nes	86 963	1.38	58.55	114 774	1.21	51.11	2.84	-2.49
752 Computer equipment nes	122 036	1.94	44.18	103 956	1.09	30.26	-4.51	-6.88
641 Paper and paperboard	83 086	1.32	85.67	99 878	1.05	79.39	1.57	-1.25
343 Natural gas, liquefied or not	67 028	1.06	44.18	101 532	1.07	37.58	5.12	-4.99
971 Gold non-monetary excluding ores	18 449	0.29	47.35	108 581	1.14	48.89	30.29	-0.79
598 Miscellaneous chemical products nes	54 048	0.86	83.89	97 160	1.02	75.47	8.57	-1.84
515 Organo-inorganic compound acid salt	69 757	1.11	87.13	87 409	0.92	78.04	2.96	-1.66
699 Base metal manufactures nes	63 626	1.01	70.14	91 639	0.96	63.91	3.50	-1.67
743 Gas pump, compressor, fan, filter	53 394	0.85	76.34	88 523	0.93	71.09	6.92	-1.26
759 Office equipment part & accessories	87 193	1.38	43.39	80 767	0.85	41.24	-2.91	-1.25
893 Articles of plastic nes	57 585	0.91	66.93	83 326	0.88	62.31	4.64	-1.33
782 Goods and service vehicles	68 878	1.09	76.11	85 716	0.90	66.34	-0.34	-2.58
723 Civil engineering plant & equipment	55 163	0.88	79.50	86 017	0.90	69.63	3.42	-2.54
821 Furniture part; bedding furnishing	62 011	0.98	63.61	77 712	0.82	52.66	1.78	-3.62
575 Other plastics, in primary forms	52 398	0.83	78.34	76 989	0.81	67.05	3.99	-3.05
684 Aluminium	51 274	0.81	64.56	75 940	0.80	60.16	2.42	-1.19
667 Pearls, precious semiprecious stone	54 922	0.87	58.05	75 987	0.80	47.10	2.98	-5.18
714 Non-electric engines excluding 712, 713, and 718	62 632	0.99	90.60	72 110	0.76	83.05	0.17	-1.71
582 Plastic sheet film foil & strips	45 538	0.72	78.58	69 896	0.73	70.25	5.63	-2.00
321 Coal excluding non-agglomomerated	26 056	0.41	55.27	72 687	0.76	54.43	19.86	0.44
872 Medical instruments appliances nes	43 141	0.68	81.54	68 445	0.72	78.52	7.91	-0.63
741 Heating cooling equipment parts nes	48 793	0.77	70.86	68 876	0.72	62.10	3.65	-2.43
281 Iron ore and concentrates	11 604	0.18	39.69	70 790	0.74	49.04	34.90	4.90
793 Ships boats floating structures	37 772	0.60	52.99	57 807	0.61	31.40	6.85	-10.41
682 Copper	28 945	0.46	45.06	61 259	0.64	41.06	7.34	-1.92
716 Rotating electric plant parts nes	34 808	0.55	67.50	59 596	0.63	64.13	7.78	-0.86
744 Mechanical handling equipment nes	44 671	0.71	85.25	61 610	0.65	76.31	2.06	-2.21
112 Alcoholic beverages	38 532	0.61	82.87	59 910	0.63	80.55	5.92	-0.70
553 Perfume toilet cosmetics, excluding soap	36 675	0.58	83.60	58 194	0.61	76.08	6.89	-1.73
773 Electrical distribute equipment nes	36 098	0.57	58.79	57 718	0.61	51.61	4.77	-2.51
012 Meat nes, fresh chilled frozen	32 542	0.52	81.30	59 106	0.62	78.50	9.49	-1.03
747 Pipe, boiler, tank & vat appliances	32 084	0.51	78.26	56 374	0.59	72.11	7.49	-1.42
676 Iron steel bar rod section piling	33 307	0.53	62.79	58 399	0.61	59.68	4.78	-0.59
899 Manufactured articles nes	30 803	0.49	69.37	51 327	0.54	65.14	8.89	-0.86
679 Iron steel pipe tube fittings etc	36 700	0.58	67.38	55 903	0.59	58.14	3.47	-2.65
511 Hydrocarbons nes; derivatives	33 413	0.53	65.80	54 044	0.57	55.97	4.99	-2.86
673 Flat iron non-alloy steel products	37 584	0.60	56.15	53 486	0.56	56.71	3.04	-0.10
625 Rubber for wheels, incl inner tube	29 458	0.47	67.01	53 269	0.56	57.52	8.15	-2.64
675 Flat rolled products of alloy steel	32 761	0.52	73.70	50 583	0.53	67.70	3.34	-0.81
533 Pigment, paint, varnish & related	32 445	0.52	82.50	49 577	0.52	76.74	5.40	-1.19
742 Liquid pump; liquid elevator parts	28 934	0.46	85.69	48 455	0.51	78.92	7.22	-1.43
282 Ferrous iron & steel, waste & scrap	19 237	0.31	76.77	47 291	0.50	82.86	12.06	1.41
761 Television video receive project	24 051	0.38	41.78	40 308	0.42	41.69	7.43	-0.06
098 Edible products & preparations nes	25 896	0.41	78.21	44 031	0.46	72.22	8.53	-1.57
771 Electric power machine part excluding 716	21 958	0.35	47.89	43 100	0.45	46.62	10.74	-0.35
745 Non-electrical machinery tool nes	33 695	0.53	84.71	43 610	0.46	77.66	2.05	-1.61
057 Fruit nut (exc oil), fresh or dried	25 869	0.41	52.98	42 306	0.44	48.92	7.64	-1.83

For sources and notes, see end of table.

Pour les sources et les notes, se reporter à la fin du tableau.

Products ranked by average 2010-2011 values SITC Revision 3 (3-digit level) — Produits classés d'après la moyenne des valeurs de 2010-2011 CTCI révision 3 (positions à 3 chiffres)	2005			2011			Growth rates (%) Taux d'accroissement (%) 2005-2011	
	Value (millions of dollars) — Valeur (millions de dollars)	% of the country grouping exports — En % des exportations du groupe de pays	% of world product exports — En % des exportations mondiales des produits	Value (millions of dollars) — Valeur (millions de dollars)	% of the country grouping exports — En % des exportations du groupe de pays	% of world product exports — En % des exportations mondiales des produits	Value — Valeur	Difference from world — Différence par rapport au monde
851 Footwear	28 276	0.45	42.37	42 756	0.45	37.75	5.35	-2.41
642 Cut paper and paperboard articles	28 120	0.45	76.60	41 457	0.44	68.09	5.62	-2.09
748 Mechanical transmission equipment	25 089	0.40	84.87	42 645	0.45	77.54	7.08	-1.63
845 Articles of apparel nes	30 890	0.49	32.20	41 129	0.43	29.00	3.63	-1.12
775 Household equipment nes	35 677	0.57	55.74	39 940	0.42	42.83	0.34	-4.73
571 Primary form ethylene polymers	24 886	0.40	59.19	41 373	0.43	52.30	6.03	-2.88
897 Jewellery nes (667)	21 048	0.33	51.33	42 168	0.44	38.87	9.36	-5.85
894 Baby carriage toy game sport good	26 288	0.42	40.59	39 850	0.42	41.11	6.10	0.32
054 Vegetable & vegetable products nes	21 915	0.35	64.72	38 899	0.41	60.25	8.73	-1.70
081 Animal feed excluding unmilled cereal	18 289	0.29	59.45	37 682	0.40	54.81	12.72	-1.72
681 Silver, platinum, platinum metals	11 909	0.19	53.27	41 318	0.43	56.16	15.79	1.26
774 Electrodiagnostic equipment	23 898	0.38	91.21	35 893	0.38	86.16	6.14	-0.94
892 Printed matter	31 420	0.50	80.04	35 908	0.38	67.27	1.12	-3.06
288 Non ferrous base metal waste nes	13 545	0.22	77.55	38 150	0.40	78.39	11.91	0.21
251 Pulp and waste paper	20 174	0.32	76.37	35 977	0.38	72.48	8.10	-1.13
514 Nitrogen function compounds	25 793	0.41	75.53	35 756	0.38	66.63	4.71	-1.94
022 Milk products, excluding butter & cheese	19 533	0.31	85.45	36 261	0.38	83.50	8.93	-0.47
048 Cereal & preparation flour starch	21 327	0.34	84.08	35 379	0.37	77.32	7.92	-1.61
674 Flat plated iron non-alloy steel	23 781	0.38	67.96	34 829	0.37	55.77	3.93	-3.04
222 Oil seed etc for soft oil	10 853	0.17	50.60	33 851	0.36	52.04	22.30	1.06
041 Wheat meslin, incl spelt, unmilled	13 961	0.22	77.93	36 895	0.39	76.32	15.47	0.36
898 Music instrument device recording	35 288	0.56	68.75	31 758	0.33	51.81	-2.71	-4.65
574 Polyacetals and polyesters, etc	22 912	0.36	62.75	32 009	0.34	55.70	3.42	-2.26
034 Fish, fresh live chilled frozen	20 256	0.32	58.33	31 929	0.34	52.39	6.80	-1.99
695 Tools for use in hand or in machine	22 109	0.35	72.13	32 035	0.34	66.03	4.01	-1.51
351 Electric current	21 555	0.34	85.39	32 898	0.35	82.37	4.58	-1.02
884 Optical goods fibres nes	20 929	0.33	68.31	30 520	0.32	55.37	5.14	-4.03
691 Iron steel aluminium structures nes	19 178	0.30	70.48	31 936	0.34	58.28	6.15	-3.78
562 Manufactured fertilizer excluding crude	11 557	0.18	46.69	33 115	0.35	44.40	18.79	-0.59
522 Inorganic chemical elem oxide salt	16 005	0.25	54.85	31 742	0.33	47.35	9.40	-2.50
783 Road motor vehicles nes	25 174	0.40	82.55	32 567	0.34	70.26	-0.99	-3.36
721 Agricultural machine nes excluding tractor	18 616	0.30	89.83	31 599	0.33	84.89	6.87	-1.31
885 Watches and clocks	15 334	0.24	60.65	31 699	0.33	66.28	10.26	1.16
554 Soaps cleansers polishes	18 011	0.29	79.25	28 983	0.30	71.33	7.15	-2.03
292 Crude vegetable materials nes	18 453	0.29	75.41	29 900	0.31	68.69	6.68	-1.75
011 Beef, fresh chilled frozen	15 779	0.25	72.36	29 005	0.30	70.04	8.98	-0.78
512 Alcohols, phenols; derivatives	16 338	0.26	50.59	29 386	0.31	46.54	7.29	-1.44
842 Female clothing, woven	21 933	0.35	33.47	27 733	0.29	33.13	2.11	-0.40
763 Sound TV recorder or reproducer	25 190	0.40	40.44	25 330	0.27	41.44	-0.56	-0.09
024 Cheese and curd	16 240	0.26	93.21	27 904	0.29	89.89	8.08	-1.00
657 Special yarn and textile fabric etc	20 373	0.32	67.15	27 199	0.29	56.15	3.20	-3.52
516 Other organic chemicals	16 874	0.27	65.90	27 725	0.29	64.73	6.23	-0.86
731 Machine tools for material removal	22 432	0.36	82.24	30 030	0.32	77.62	-0.06	-1.03
335 Residual petroleum products nes	11 446	0.18	61.52	28 901	0.30	59.45	13.13	-1.16
664 Glass	18 811	0.30	73.68	25 787	0.27	65.02	3.95	-1.99
663 Mineral manufactures nes	17 591	0.28	81.85	26 501	0.28	74.72	4.48	-1.54
248 Wood simply worked, railway sleeper	25 452	0.40	71.78	25 455	0.27	67.26	-2.71	-1.13
746 Ball or roller bearings	15 220	0.24	77.02	25 814	0.27	71.93	6.93	-1.29
513 Carboxylic acid and compounds	20 215	0.32	60.78	25 320	0.27	47.36	0.83	-4.63
694 Nails screws nuts bolts rivets	14 061	0.22	65.53	23 433	0.25	61.66	6.23	-1.00
785 Motorcycles, mopeds and cycles	19 893	0.32	61.25	22 753	0.24	47.76	0.00	-4.58
751 Office machines	8 001	0.13	52.39	21 480	0.23	40.38	16.21	-6.20
629 Articles of rubber nes	14 365	0.23	78.54	21 585	0.23	72.43	5.13	-1.33
122 Manufactured tabacco	14 558	0.23	75.66	22 358	0.23	71.44	6.53	-1.19
841 Male clothing, woven	17 822	0.28	33.42	21 867	0.23	30.39	1.70	-1.60
421 Fixed veg fat and oil, "soft"	9 382	0.15	55.59	22 284	0.23	55.41	13.00	0.35
871 Optical instruments apparatus nes	10 717	0.17	23.94	21 034	0.22	20.42	10.76	-2.81
651 Textile yarn	17 580	0.28	43.03	20 993	0.22	34.24	-0.23	-4.77
591 Household and garden chemicals	12 341	0.20	75.72	20 445	0.21	72.10	8.18	-1.41
551 Essential oils, perfumes & flavours	13 507	0.21	86.54	19 400	0.20	79.10	5.55	-1.47

For sources and notes, see end of table.

Pour les sources et les notes, se reporter à la fin du tableau.

Products ranked by average 2010-2011 values SITC Revision 3 (3-digit level) Produits classés d'après la moyenne des valeurs de 2010-2011 CTCI révision 3 (positions à 3 chiffres)	2005			2011			Growth rates (%) Taux d'accroissement (%) 2005-2011	
	Value (millions of dollars) Valeur (millions de dollars)	% of the country grouping exports En % des exportations du groupe de pays	% of world product exports En % des exportations mondiales des produits	Value (millions of dollars) Valeur (millions de dollars)	% of the country grouping exports En % des exportations du groupe de pays	% of world product exports En % des exportations mondiales des produits	Value Valeur	Difference from world Différence par rapport au monde
791 Railway vehicles and equipment	13 279	0.21	81.19	18 637	0.20	63.98	5.69	-2.96
056 Vegetables roots tubers nes	11 268	0.18	69.60	19 667	0.21	65.22	8.57	-1.12
073 Chocolate & cocoa preparations nes	10 817	0.17	84.88	19 403	0.20	82.02	9.07	-0.79
749 Non-electric machinery part nes	16 126	0.26	74.00	19 404	0.20	64.16	0.77	-2.76
044 Maize unmilled, excluding sweet corn	7 785	0.12	68.24	20 948	0.22	61.02	14.19	-2.83
597 Additive e.g. lubricate, antifreeze	9 847	0.16	86.26	19 247	0.20	83.45	10.05	-0.70
724 Textile leather machinery parts nes	18 316	0.29	71.82	18 817	0.20	60.36	-2.93	-3.38
896 Work of art & collections; antiques	13 668	0.22	91.72	18 626	0.20	90.67	2.62	0.01
718 Power generating machinery part nes	9 560	0.15	83.66	19 007	0.20	78.64	10.66	-1.46
634 Veneer, plywood & other wood nes	19 303	0.31	64.53	18 163	0.19	52.70	-3.10	-2.99
786 Trailer caravan transport container	14 354	0.23	61.67	19 460	0.20	52.97	-0.37	-2.47
722 Tractors	12 127	0.19	84.95	18 365	0.19	80.83	4.28	-0.85
592 Starches, glutenes, glues, etc	11 112	0.18	78.34	17 382	0.18	69.05	6.47	-2.40
831 Case bag: storage travel shopping	9 395	0.15	39.57	18 219	0.19	34.66	9.16	-3.08
001 Live animal excluding fish & crustacean	10 840	0.17	78.66	16 778	0.18	78.19	6.48	-0.55
621 Rubber material e.g. paste tube rod	10 796	0.17	82.77	17 397	0.18	65.76	5.15	-4.38
737 Metalwork machinery nes excluding tools	12 761	0.20	79.45	16 616	0.17	74.20	1.98	-1.52
635 Wood manufactures nes	13 817	0.22	65.58	16 158	0.17	62.07	0.12	-0.86
581 Plastic tube pipe hose & fittings	9 710	0.15	81.73	16 378	0.17	75.29	6.60	-1.74
672 Ingots, Iron steel primary products	11 049	0.18	38.00	16 777	0.18	36.98	3.66	-0.54
232 Synthetic & reclaimed rubber; waste	7 876	0.13	65.70	17 184	0.18	58.26	10.33	-2.34
665 Glassware	12 323	0.20	70.61	16 399	0.17	56.02	1.85	-4.55
882 Photo cinematographic supply excluding 883	16 115	0.26	81.70	14 982	0.16	82.71	-2.33	0.09
342 Liquefied propane and butane	8 608	0.14	29.85	15 526	0.16	28.08	8.27	-0.58
813 Lighting fixtures and fittings nes	10 344	0.16	54.05	15 353	0.16	45.35	4.92	-3.25
111 Non alcoholic beverage nes	8 613	0.14	77.25	15 356	0.16	74.41	7.72	-0.91
662 Clay and refractory materials	12 192	0.19	71.44	15 021	0.16	58.00	1.01	-4.12
071 Coffee and coffee substitutes	5 572	0.09	35.40	16 012	0.17	36.40	16.98	1.11
573 Vinyl chloride etc polymers	9 193	0.15	73.57	14 324	0.15	69.99	5.67	-0.72
683 Nickel	8 747	0.14	63.75	15 160	0.16	66.80	1.59	-0.05
726 Printing bookbinding machines parts	17 066	0.27	91.18	13 741	0.14	85.59	-6.22	-1.05
289 Prec metal ore concentrate excluding gold	2 641	0.04	63.88	12 773	0.13	63.11	28.03	0.68
692 Metal storage transport container	8 615	0.14	75.41	13 209	0.14	65.77	5.52	-2.27
525 Radio active & associated materials	6 480	0.10	83.52	13 860	0.15	62.34	9.70	-5.60
735 Machine part accessory for 731 733	9 986	0.16	84.30	13 704	0.14	79.68	1.86	-1.00
017 Meat offal preserved nes	7 074	0.11	65.41	12 952	0.14	64.30	9.50	-0.36
658 Made-up textile articles nes	9 215	0.15	29.07	12 890	0.14	24.43	3.89	-3.83
287 Base metal ores & concentrates nes	7 964	0.13	41.89	12 223	0.13	36.97	2.15	-3.65
727 Food processing machine excluding domestic	8 413	0.13	89.88	12 552	0.13	83.45	4.36	-1.35
061 Sugar, mollasses and honey	7 336	0.12	40.97	12 198	0.13	26.05	6.56	-8.71
523 Inorganic acid metal salt peroxy	7 669	0.12	62.03	11 946	0.13	53.38	5.56	-2.76
812 Sanitary plumb heat fixtures nes	8 954	0.14	78.41	11 630	0.12	75.40	2.20	-0.59
653 Man-made woven fabrics	12 406	0.20	38.70	11 751	0.12	26.43	-3.02	-6.65
844 Female clothing, knitted crocheted	6 840	0.11	26.39	11 781	0.12	21.81	8.42	-2.23
283 Copper ores and concentrates	3 677	0.06	18.81	12 758	0.13	23.99	16.21	2.93
661 Lime cement construction material	8 913	0.14	46.38	11 465	0.12	40.14	2.39	-2.75
697 Base metal household equipment nes	8 897	0.14	47.77	11 288	0.12	38.90	2.07	-3.79
891 Arms and ammunition	6 479	0.10	85.70	10 093	0.11	86.53	8.13	0.18
572 Primary form styrene polymers	8 791	0.14	45.48	10 725	0.11	41.30	0.06	-2.76
036 Crustacean mollusc aquat invertebra	7 581	0.12	37.63	10 771	0.11	32.78	4.37	-2.41
611 Leather	8 785	0.14	42.48	10 661	0.11	42.95	0.46	0.30
263 Cotton	5 460	0.09	49.51	11 948	0.13	44.99	9.69	-2.69
671 Pig & sponge iron, ferro alloys etc	7 161	0.11	26.48	10 273	0.11	23.16	3.77	-2.27
895 Office and stationery supplies nes	6 740	0.11	63.57	9 990	0.10	63.22	5.05	-0.28
846 Clothing accessory excluding 831, 848, and 851	7 831	0.12	44.29	9 942	0.10	34.50	2.97	-4.62
725 Paper & pulp mill, cut manufacture	8 389	0.13	89.21	9 971	0.10	84.58	0.77	-0.87
733 Metal work tool no material removal	7 105	0.11	78.39	10 180	0.11	76.45	2.06	-0.73
059 Fruit & vegetable juice unferment	5 610	0.09	60.91	9 640	0.10	54.79	6.48	-1.74
278 Other crude minerals	6 690	0.11	61.60	8 967	0.09	51.92	3.33	-3.14
524 Other inorganic chemicals	4 047	0.06	60.27	9 381	0.10	65.16	11.08	1.03

For sources and notes, see end of table.

Pour les sources et les notes, se reporter à la fin du tableau.

Products ranked by average 2010-2011 values SITC Revision 3 (3-digit level) Produits classés d'après la moyenne des valeurs de 2010-2011 CTCI révision 3 (positions à 3 chiffres)	2005			2011			Growth rates (%) Taux d'accroissement (%) 2005-2011	
	Value (millions of dollars) Valeur (millions de dollars)	% of the country grouping exports En % des exportations du groupe de pays	% of world product exports En % des exportations mondiales des produits	Value (millions of dollars) Valeur (millions de dollars)	% of the country grouping exports En % des exportations du groupe de pays	% of world product exports En % des exportations mondiales des produits	Value Valeur	Difference from world Différence par rapport au monde
058 Fruit preserve preparation excluding juice	5 364	0.09	52.82	9 338	0.10	48.89	7.81	-1.41
652 Woven cotton fabrics	11 013	0.17	37.96	9 153	0.10	26.03	-5.64	-6.74
848 Headgear, non-textile clothing	6 034	0.10	28.55	8 989	0.09	30.46	4.82	-0.02
659 Floor coverings etc	7 354	0.12	62.76	9 196	0.10	54.61	0.86	-3.30
693 Wire products and fencing grills	5 597	0.09	61.33	8 460	0.09	53.52	4.42	-2.27
285 Aluminium ore concentrate alumina	6 110	0.10	57.56	8 218	0.09	53.11	1.52	-1.52
686 Zinc	4 234	0.07	61.21	8 029	0.08	57.56	2.34	-0.48
247 Wood in rough or roughly squared	4 965	0.08	44.90	8 396	0.09	52.89	6.64	3.69
037 Fish shellfish, prepared preserved	5 407	0.09	36.32	8 044	0.08	30.75	5.21	-2.40
072 Cocoa	3 400	0.05	36.39	7 593	0.08	33.97	15.42	-1.98
023 Butter fats oils derived from milk	4 029	0.06	92.48	7 787	0.08	89.99	10.54	-0.72
873 Meters and counters nes	5 002	0.08	74.38	7 584	0.08	63.50	5.20	-3.50
655 Knitted or crocheted fabrics nes	7 059	0.11	35.46	7 549	0.08	24.08	-1.17	-7.11
678 Wire of iron or steel	4 605	0.07	63.74	7 611	0.08	55.49	5.66	-2.50
531 Synthetic organic colour agents	6 898	0.11	66.22	6 891	0.07	53.95	-1.40	-3.60
211 Raw hides & skins, excluding furskins	4 594	0.07	79.00	7 082	0.07	85.24	4.06	1.11
712 Steam vapour turbines & parts nes	3 638	0.06	85.83	6 444	0.07	70.94	11.89	-3.87
654 Other woven textile fabrics nes	6 745	0.11	60.68	6 387	0.07	55.10	-3.47	-1.92
762 Radio broadcast receivers	6 339	0.10	34.01	6 062	0.06	37.01	-2.51	1.61
062 Sugar confectionery	4 246	0.07	64.00	6 201	0.07	57.46	5.65	-1.82
811 Prefabricated buildings	4 656	0.07	83.26	5 815	0.06	67.42	1.17	-3.50
431 Processed animal & veg fats & oils	2 663	0.04	46.42	6 014	0.06	40.82	12.48	-1.88
325 Coke, semi coke, retort carbon	2 746	0.04	44.43	5 445	0.06	54.42	10.72	4.66
273 Stone, sand and gravel	3 873	0.06	61.37	5 266	0.06	51.50	3.30	-3.27
344 Petroleum and hydrocarbon gas nes	6 754	0.11	65.53	5 802	0.06	45.07	-9.38	-10.51
696 Cutlery	3 637	0.06	50.43	5 102	0.05	44.87	4.36	-1.72
689 Misc non-ferrous base metals	4 244	0.07	56.73	5 299	0.06	48.55	-0.62	-2.71
043 Barley grain unmilled	2 867	0.05	78.96	5 625	0.06	75.98	8.82	-1.03
422 Fixed veg fat and oil, excluding "soft"	1 910	0.03	13.97	5 746	0.06	11.07	16.91	-6.44
291 Crude animal materials nes	3 128	0.05	60.72	5 094	0.05	56.77	7.61	-1.13
411 Animals oils and fats	2 145	0.03	84.95	5 331	0.06	83.77	14.63	-0.34
284 Nickel ores, concentrates, etc	2 714	0.04	49.99	5 054	0.05	43.50	2.90	-5.03
579 Plastic waste, parings and scrap	2 116	0.03	57.20	4 725	0.05	63.89	12.26	1.94
843 Male clothing, knitted crocheted	3 030	0.05	20.14	4 805	0.05	15.99	6.19	-3.32
583 Plastic rod stick & profile shapes	3 327	0.05	90.73	4 517	0.05	79.63	3.22	-1.95
042 Rice	2 362	0.04	23.23	4 211	0.04	18.06	11.34	-4.76
268 Wool & animal hair, incl wool tops	3 416	0.05	69.00	4 710	0.05	55.70	1.90	-3.48
025 Eggs, yolks and albumin	1 974	0.03	82.27	4 397	0.05	75.95	14.32	-2.14
685 Lead	1 751	0.03	60.87	4 332	0.05	63.01	13.63	2.05
035 Fish, dried salted smoked	2 775	0.04	72.94	4 278	0.05	71.15	5.73	-0.74
016 Meat offal preserved	2 616	0.04	97.88	4 297	0.05	83.97	6.98	-3.05
711 Steam generating boilers & parts	2 884	0.05	73.38	4 036	0.04	40.51	6.40	-11.62
091 Margarine and shortening	1 855	0.03	66.84	4 125	0.04	60.27	13.26	-1.43
121 Unmanufactured tabacco and refuse	2 643	0.04	37.05	3 671	0.04	30.35	5.91	-3.67
212 Raw furskins and furskin pieces	1 741	0.03	74.10	3 884	0.04	81.20	10.66	1.23
246 Wood chips, particles and waste	1 877	0.03	61.65	3 620	0.04	59.97	10.13	-1.05
677 Iron steel rail railway materials	1 976	0.03	85.63	3 661	0.04	77.60	10.03	-1.89
656 Tulle lace embroidery trim etc	3 565	0.06	43.52	3 531	0.04	35.31	-2.35	-3.45
881 Photographic device nes	12 702	0.20	73.69	3 277	0.03	48.86	-23.82	-7.33
269 Worn clothing, textile article; rag	1 556	0.02	72.83	3 185	0.03	69.33	11.68	-0.48
267 Man made fibre for spinning; waste	2 538	0.04	79.42	2 956	0.03	58.44	0.84	-5.10
666 Pottery	2 933	0.05	46.18	2 926	0.03	31.67	-1.47	-6.36
266 Synthetic fibres for spinning	2 433	0.04	40.72	3 057	0.03	33.79	1.30	-3.66
045 Grain, excluding wheat rice barley maize	1 404	0.02	87.57	2 614	0.03	73.15	7.90	-3.39
593 Explosives and pyrotechnic products	1 200	0.02	62.16	2 154	0.02	61.03	9.58	0.10
046 Wheat meal & flour, meslin flour	1 277	0.02	50.25	2 190	0.02	34.02	8.05	-7.16
074 Tea and maté	1 012	0.02	24.31	1 983	0.02	23.85	10.81	-1.09
223 Oil seed for non soft oil	1 021	0.02	69.67	1 952	0.02	65.87	10.70	-0.94
231 Natural rubber, latex, gum, etc	246	0.00	2.51	2 033	0.02	5.09	36.38	17.48
612 Leather manufactures nes	1 518	0.02	49.08	1 707	0.02	49.33	0.52	0.91

For sources and notes, see end of table.

Pour les sources et les notes, se reporter à la fin du tableau.

Products ranked by average 2010-2011 values SITC Revision 3 (3-digit level) Produits classés d'après la moyenne des valeurs de 2010-2011 CTCI révision 3 (positions à 3 chiffres)	2005			2011			Growth rates (%) Taux d'accroissement (%) 2005-2011	
	Value (millions of dollars) Valeur (millions de dollars)	% of the country grouping exports En % des exportations du groupe de pays	% of world product exports En % des exportations mondiales des produits	Value (millions of dollars) Valeur (millions de dollars)	% of the country grouping exports En % des exportations du groupe de pays	% of world product exports En % des exportations mondiales des produits	Value Valeur	Difference from world Différence par rapport au monde
075 Spices	789	0.01	26.34	1 909	0.02	20.99	13.11	-4.55
322 Briquettes, lignite and peat	912	0.01	92.03	1 592	0.02	39.84	9.11	-20.91
633 Cork manufactures	1 413	0.02	92.75	1 527	0.02	94.59	-0.50	0.45
274 Sulphur and unroasted iron pyrites	756	0.01	46.33	1 725	0.02	31.38	11.08	-6.55
532 Dyeing and tanning extracts	878	0.01	61.26	1 433	0.02	65.18	8.02	1.33
687 Tin	457	0.01	14.23	1 266	0.01	15.72	12.82	-0.50
272 Crude fertilizer, excluding manufactured	312	0.00	16.89	866	0.01	18.01	20.61	3.19
613 Furskin tanned dressed etc	775	0.01	45.03	846	0.01	43.07	-2.71	-2.33
047 Other cereal meals and flours	353	0.01	52.99	786	0.01	55.30	12.10	-0.28
245 Fuel wood excluding waste; wood charcoal	286	0.00	51.80	619	0.01	46.44	12.29	-2.46
277 Natural abrasives nes	433	0.01	37.25	554	0.01	34.01	0.82	-4.27
265 Veg textile fibre, excluding cotton jute	496	0.01	71.09	519	0.01	51.48	-1.81	-5.72
883 Cinematographic film, developed	605	0.01	90.12	400	0.00	80.46	-6.51	-1.92
961 Coins, nongold and non currency	189	0.00	96.06	363	0.00	91.30	10.78	-6.05
244 Natural cork, raw and wastes	221	0.00	92.55	201	0.00	92.35	-5.51	-0.02
261 Silk	45	0.00	12.51	57	0.00	10.23	-3.73	-11.09
286 Uranium & thorium ore concentrates	437	0.01	85.32	0	0.00	0.01	-69.74	-74.47
264 Jute & bast fibre nes, raw & retted	8	0.00	6.55	7	0.00	1.95	-2.36	-21.96
345 Coal, water, producer gas etc	3	0.00	16.59	3	0.00	11.14	1.88	-11.56

Source:
UNCTAD secretariat calculations, based on UNCTAD, *UNCTADstat* Merchandise Trade Matrix

Source :
Calculs du secrétariat de la CNUCED, basés sur la matrice du commerce de marchandises de *UNCTADstat* de la CNUCED

3.2.D Export structure by product
Individual countries and territories

3.2.D Structure des exportations par produits
Pays et territoires individuels

Leading products exported based on average 2010-2011 values SITC Revision 3 (3-digit level) / Principaux produits exportés d'après la moyenne des valeurs de 2010-2011 CTCI révision 3 (positions à 3 chiffres)	2010-2011			
	Value (f.o.b., thousands of dollars) / Valeur (f.a.b., milliers de dollars)	As percentage / En pourcentage		
		of country total / du total du pays	of ** (1) / des ** (1)	of world / du monde
Afghanistan (=Developing) (2)**				
All commodity groups	369 242	100.0	0.01	0.00
057 Fruit nut (exc oil), fresh or dried	76 361	20.7	0.19	0.10
292 Crude vegetable materials nes	23 016	6.2	0.20	0.06
263 Cotton	20 444	5.5	0.22	0.09
659 Floor coverings etc	19 680	5.3	0.28	0.13
282 Ferrous iron & steel, waste & scrap	17 817	4.8	0.29	0.03
661 Lime cement construction material	15 444	4.2	0.10	0.06
075 Spices	11 413	3.1	0.19	0.15
054 Vegetable & vegetable products nes	9 554	2.6	0.04	0.02
713 Internal combustion engine part nes	7 925	2.1	0.02	0.01
222 Oil seed etc for soft oil	6 433	1.7	0.03	0.01
Remainder	161 156	43.6		
Albania - Albanie (=Transition) (2)**				
All commodity groups	1 749 072	100.0	0.25	0.01
851 Footwear	274 846	15.7	17.95	0.26
333 Crude petroleum & bituminous oil	243 322	13.9	0.11	0.02
841 Male clothing, woven	107 852	6.2	10.95	0.16
287 Base metal ores & concentrates nes	106 983	6.1	7.97	0.34
672 Ingots, Iron steel primary products	83 021	4.7	0.56	0.20
845 Articles of apparel nes	80 436	4.6	7.33	0.06
699 Base metal manufactures nes	50 625	2.9	2.64	0.04
288 Non ferrous base metal waste nes	41 894	2.4	6.15	0.10
351 Electric current	39 690	2.3	1.74	0.11
842 Female clothing, woven	38 158	2.2	3.40	0.05
Remainder	682 244	39.0		
Algeria - Algérie (=Developing)**				
All commodity groups	65 243 640	100.0	0.92	0.39
333 Crude petroleum & bituminous oil	29 903 476	45.8	2.92	2.10
343 Natural gas, liquefied or not	18 583 143	28.5	14.58	7.36
334 Heavy petroleum & bituminous oil	9 676 336	14.8	2.73	1.20
342 Liquefied propane and butane	5 287 183	8.1	15.50	10.56
335 Residual petroleum products nes	696 973	1.1	4.31	1.63
522 Inorganic chemical elem oxide salt	325 640	0.5	1.24	0.56
061 Sugar, mollasses and honey	250 732	0.4	0.84	0.60
272 Crude fertilizer, excl. manufactured	86 110	0.1	2.83	2.07
686 Zinc	48 821	0.1	1.11	0.38
512 Alcohols, phenols; derivatives	34 676	0.1	0.12	0.06
Remainder	350 549	0.5		
American Samoa - Samoa américaines (=Developing) (2)**				
All commodity groups	305 000	100.0	0.00	0.00
542 Medicines including veterinary	39 795	13.0	0.16	0.01
034 Fish, fresh live chilled frozen	39 366	12.9	0.16	0.07
081 Animal feed excluding unmilled cereal	36 647	12.0	0.13	0.06
571 Primary form ethylene polymers	29 189	9.6	0.09	0.04
897 Jewellery nes (667)	23 488	7.7	0.04	0.03
743 Gas pump, compressor, fan, filter	18 843	6.2	0.06	0.02
282 Ferrous iron & steel, waste & scrap	11 023	3.6	0.18	0.02
288 Non ferrous base metal waste nes	8 461	2.8	0.09	0.02
263 Cotton	7 999	2.6	0.09	0.04
411 Animals oils and fats	7 758	2.5	0.88	0.14
Remainder	82 432	27.0		
Andorra - Andorre (=Developed) (2)**				
All commodity groups	65 662	100.0	0.00	0.00
781 Passenger cars and race cars	21 917	33.4	0.00	0.00
778 Electrical machinery apparatus nes	6 172	9.4	0.01	0.00
896 Work of art & collections; antiques	4 878	7.4	0.03	0.03
898 Music instrument device recording	2 453	3.7	0.01	0.00
844 Female clothing, knitted crocheted	1 510	2.3	0.01	0.00
061 Sugar, mollasses and honey	1 389	2.1	0.01	0.00
763 Sound TV recorder or reproducer	1 329	2.0	0.01	0.00
764 Telecommunicate equipment part nes	1 036	1.6	0.00	0.00
553 Perfume toilet cosmetics, excl. soap	754	1.1	0.00	0.00
845 Articles of apparel nes	634	1.0	0.00	0.00
Remainder	23 589	35.9		

For sources and notes, see end of table.

Leading products exported based on average 2010-2011 values SITC Revision 3 (3-digit level) / Principaux produits exportés d'après la moyenne des valeurs de 2010-2011 CTCI révision 3 (positions à 3 chiffres)	2010-2011			
	Value (f.o.b., thousands of dollars) / Valeur (f.a.b., milliers de dollars)	As percentage / En pourcentage		
		of country total / du total du pays	of ** (1) / des ** (1)	of world / du monde
Angola (=Developing) (2)**				
All commodity groups	58 141 950	100.0	0.82	0.35
333 Crude petroleum & bituminous oil	56 438 269	97.1	5.52	3.96
334 Heavy petroleum & bituminous oil	556 007	1.0	0.16	0.07
667 Pearls, precious semiprecious stone	470 467	0.8	0.63	0.32
342 Liquefied propane and butane	304 647	0.5	0.89	0.61
793 Ships boats floating structures	118 950	0.2	0.10	0.07
282 Ferrous iron & steel, waste & scrap	40 793	0.1	0.66	0.08
781 Passenger cars and race cars	26 532	0.0	0.03	0.00
273 Stone, sand and gravel	26 106	0.0	0.63	0.27
344 Petroleum and hydrocarbon gas nes	20 086	0.0	0.22	0.14
288 Non ferrous base metal waste nes	14 401	0.0	0.16	0.03
Remainder	125 692	0.2		
Anguilla (=Developing) (2)**				
All commodity groups	14 510	100.0	0.00	0.00
112 Alcoholic beverages	1 799	12.4	0.01	0.00
782 Goods and service vehicles	1 760	12.1	0.00	0.00
741 Heating cooling equipment parts nes	944	6.5	0.00	0.00
723 Civil engineering plant & equipment	551	3.8	0.00	0.00
896 Work of art & collections; antiques	509	3.5	0.03	0.00
781 Passenger cars and race cars	489	3.4	0.00	0.00
743 Gas pump, compressor, fan, filter	472	3.3	0.00	0.00
744 Mechanical handling equipment nes	419	2.9	0.00	0.00
691 Iron steel aluminium structures nes	413	2.8	0.00	0.00
674 Flat plated iron non-alloy steel	390	2.7	0.00	0.00
Remainder	6 764	46.6		
Antigua and Barbuda - Antigua-et-Barbuda (=Developing) (2)**				
All commodity groups	44 388	100.0	0.00	0.00
781 Passenger cars and race cars	4 395	9.9	0.00	0.00
782 Goods and service vehicles	3 799	8.6	0.01	0.00
783 Road motor vehicles nes	2 219	5.0	0.02	0.01
634 Veneer, plywood & other wood nes	2 134	4.8	0.02	0.01
793 Ships boats floating structures	1 810	4.1	0.00	0.00
699 Base metal manufactures nes	1 726	3.9	0.00	0.00
746 Ball or roller bearings	1 667	3.8	0.02	0.01
784 Motor vehicle parts and accessories	1 517	3.4	0.00	0.00
091 Margarine and shortening	1 445	3.3	0.07	0.02
334 Heavy petroleum & bituminous oil	1 372	3.1	0.00	0.00
Remainder	22 306	50.3		
Argentina - Argentine (=Developing)**				
All commodity groups	76 068 726	100.0	1.07	0.46
081 Animal feed excluding unmilled cereal	9 781 425	12.9	35.61	15.31
421 Fixed veg fat and oil, "soft"	5 715 022	7.5	49.85	16.47
222 Oil seed etc for soft oil	5 609 509	7.4	21.90	9.46
781 Passenger cars and race cars	4 317 842	5.7	4.18	0.72
044 Maize unmilled, excluding sweet corn	3 832 311	5.0	42.16	13.24
782 Goods and service vehicles	3 001 038	3.9	8.00	2.56
333 Crude petroleum & bituminous oil	2 382 879	3.1	0.23	0.17
971 Gold non-monetary excluding ores	2 169 276	2.9	2.25	1.15
598 Miscellaneous chemical products nes	1 898 875	2.5	6.86	1.60
041 Wheat meslin, incl spelt, unmilled	1 705 241	2.2	46.60	4.20
Remainder	35 655 308	46.9		
Armenia - Arménie (=Transition) (2)**				
All commodity groups	1 165 918	100.0	0.17	0.01
283 Copper ores and concentrates	171 341	14.7	15.82	0.34
671 Pig & sponge iron, ferro alloys etc	141 989	12.2	1.50	0.35
112 Alcoholic beverages	111 938	9.6	8.43	0.16
667 Pearls, precious semiprecious stone	102 578	8.8	3.16	0.07
682 Copper	99 784	8.6	1.00	0.07
684 Aluminium	85 507	7.3	0.90	0.07
971 Gold non-monetary excluding ores	50 767	4.4	3.21	0.03
351 Electric current	43 996	3.8	1.93	0.12
288 Non ferrous base metal waste nes	18 450	1.6	2.71	0.04
689 Misc non-ferrous base metals	17 762	1.5	2.42	0.18
Remainder	321 806	27.6		

Pour les sources et les notes, se reporter à la fin du tableau.

Header (applies to all tables):

Leading products exported based on average 2010-2011 values SITC Revision 3 (3-digit level) / Principaux produits exportés d'après la moyenne des valeurs de 2010-2011 CTCI révision 3 (positions à 3 chiffres)

Product	Value (f.o.b., thousands of dollars) / Valeur	As percentage — of country total / du total du pays	of ** (1) / des ** (1)	of world / du monde
Aruba (**=Developing) (2)				
All commodity groups	2 721 871	100.0	0.04	0.02
334 Heavy petroleum & bituminous oil	2 266 898	83.3	0.64	0.28
112 Alcoholic beverages	72 608	2.7	0.59	0.10
335 Residual petroleum products nes	60 429	2.2	0.37	0.14
044 Maize unmilled, excluding sweet corn	58 711	2.2	0.65	0.20
333 Crude petroleum & bituminous oil	51 320	1.9	0.01	0.00
122 Manufactured tabacco	34 265	1.3	0.46	0.12
081 Animal feed excluding unmilled cereal	33 068	1.2	0.12	0.05
041 Wheat meslin, incl spelt, unmilled	24 167	0.9	0.66	0.06
274 Sulphur and unroasted iron pyrites	6 431	0.2	0.28	0.15
897 Jewellery nes (667)	5 934	0.2	0.01	0.01
Remainder	108 039	4.0		
Australia - Australie (**=Developed)				
All commodity groups	226 168 082	100.0	2.55	1.36
281 Iron ore and concentrates	52 742 651	23.3	86.34	42.18
321 Coal excluding non-agglomomerated	41 116 519	18.2	62.75	34.82
971 Gold non-monetary excluding ores	13 301 683	5.9	14.74	7.06
333 Crude petroleum & bituminous oil	10 062 425	4.4	5.69	0.71
343 Natural gas, liquefied or not	9 425 624	4.2	10.26	3.73
285 Aluminium ore concentrate alumina	4 945 951	2.2	63.93	33.71
283 Copper ores and concentrates	4 776 094	2.1	43.97	9.58
041 Wheat meslin, incl spelt, unmilled	4 734 084	2.1	14.94	11.66
684 Aluminium	4 235 245	1.9	6.02	3.65
287 Base metal ores & concentrates nes	4 167 249	1.8	36.31	13.40
Remainder	76 660 557	33.9		
Austria - Autriche (**=Developed) (2)				
All commodity groups	156 658 372	100.0	1.77	0.94
713 Internal combustion engine part nes	6 096 813	3.9	5.14	4.04
542 Medicines including veterinary	5 173 470	3.3	1.69	1.56
781 Passenger cars and race cars	4 703 513	3.0	0.95	0.79
784 Motor vehicle parts and accessories	4 532 534	2.9	1.85	1.37
641 Paper and paperboard	3 929 095	2.5	4.13	3.31
699 Base metal manufactures nes	3 841 201	2.5	4.53	2.91
728 Special industrial machine part nes	3 517 867	2.2	2.60	2.03
541 Pharmaceuticals excluding medicines	3 153 728	2.0	2.47	2.16
772 Electrical circuit equipment	2 786 085	1.8	2.26	1.28
782 Goods and service vehicles	2 337 160	1.5	3.01	2.00
Remainder	116 586 906	74.4		
Azerbaijan - Azerbaïdjan (**=Transition) (2)				
All commodity groups	30 485 450	100.0	4.37	0.18
333 Crude petroleum & bituminous oil	27 016 394	88.6	12.08	1.90
334 Heavy petroleum & bituminous oil	1 162 347	3.8	1.16	0.14
343 Natural gas, liquefied or not	376 878	1.2	1.14	0.15
061 Sugar, mollasses and honey	180 090	0.6	16.52	0.43
057 Fruit nut (exc oil), fresh or dried	130 796	0.4	8.04	0.16
793 Ships boats floating structures	111 962	0.4	3.67	0.06
571 Primary form ethylene polymers	79 113	0.3	6.97	0.11
344 Petroleum and hydrocarbon gas nes	75 012	0.2	10.49	0.52
672 Ingots, Iron steel primary products	69 197	0.2	0.47	0.17
897 Jewellery nes (667)	67 730	0.2	42.49	0.07
Remainder	1 215 932	4.0		
Bahamas (**=Developing) (2)				
All commodity groups	768 676	100.0	0.01	0.00
334 Heavy petroleum & bituminous oil	420 939	54.8	0.12	0.05
793 Ships boats floating structures	82 288	10.7	0.07	0.05
335 Residual petroleum products nes	46 971	6.1	0.29	0.11
572 Primary form styrene polymers	42 452	5.5	0.29	0.17
036 Crustacean mollusc aquat invertebra	27 768	3.6	0.14	0.09
896 Work of art & collections; antiques	27 656	3.6	1.74	0.14
515 Organo-inorganic compound acid salt	18 178	2.4	0.09	0.02
553 Perfume toilet cosmetics, excl. soap	16 583	2.2	0.10	0.05
278 Other crude minerals	8 053	1.0	0.12	0.05
273 Stone, sand and gravel	6 868	0.9	0.17	0.07
Remainder	70 920	9.2		
Bahrain - Bahreïn (**=Developing) (2)				
All commodity groups	16 647 524	100.0	0.23	0.10
334 Heavy petroleum & bituminous oil	5 104 404	30.7	1.44	0.63
684 Aluminium	3 380 979	20.3	9.31	2.91
281 Iron ore and concentrates	2 050 914	12.3	3.60	1.64
693 Wire products and fencing grills	354 027	2.1	5.78	2.45
562 Manufactured fertilizer excl. crude	341 308	2.1	1.54	0.53
781 Passenger cars and race cars	337 213	2.0	0.33	0.06
335 Residual petroleum products nes	278 655	1.7	1.72	0.65
897 Jewellery nes (667)	264 876	1.6	0.48	0.28
344 Petroleum and hydrocarbon gas nes	250 256	1.5	2.80	1.72
671 Pig & sponge iron, ferro alloys etc	226 070	1.4	1.03	0.55
Remainder	4 058 824	24.4		
Bangladesh (**=Developing) (2)				
All commodity groups	23 117 054	100.0	0.33	0.14
845 Articles of apparel nes	7 165 294	31.0	7.68	5.39
841 Male clothing, woven	5 048 564	21.8	11.25	7.65
842 Female clothing, woven	2 354 656	10.2	4.57	3.01
843 Male clothing, knitted crocheted	1 337 049	5.8	5.89	4.92
844 Female clothing, knitted crocheted	1 308 400	5.7	3.42	2.64
658 Made-up textile articles nes	929 078	4.0	2.54	1.91
036 Crustacean mollusc aquat invertebra	729 213	3.2	3.79	2.48
651 Textile yarn	581 121	2.5	1.63	1.04
611 Leather	354 044	1.5	2.75	1.51
562 Manufactured fertilizer excl. crude	293 173	1.3	1.32	0.45
Remainder	3 016 463	13.0		
Barbados - Barbade (**=Developing) (2)				
All commodity groups	468 713	100.0	0.01	0.00
334 Heavy petroleum & bituminous oil	86 877	18.5	0.02	0.01
542 Medicines including veterinary	41 754	8.9	0.17	0.01
333 Crude petroleum & bituminous oil	38 885	8.3	0.00	0.00
112 Alcoholic beverages	29 609	6.3	0.24	0.04
793 Ships boats floating structures	17 455	3.7	0.02	0.01
747 Pipe, boiler, tank & vat appliances	10 526	2.2	0.05	0.01
091 Margarine and shortening	10 315	2.2	0.53	0.17
892 Printed matter	9 869	2.1	0.06	0.02
661 Lime cement construction material	9 650	2.1	0.06	0.04
899 Manufactured articles nes	8 900	1.9	0.04	0.01
Remainder	204 873	43.7		
Belarus - Bélarus (**=Transition)				
All commodity groups	32 759 938	100.0	4.69	0.20
334 Heavy petroleum & bituminous oil	9 644 571	29.4	9.67	1.20
562 Manufactured fertilizer excl. crude	3 114 741	9.5	22.16	4.79
782 Goods and service vehicles	1 167 356	3.6	56.67	1.00
533 Pigment, paint, varnish & related	911 842	2.8	58.16	1.55
722 Tractors	839 875	2.6	89.98	4.22
022 Milk products, excl. butter & cheese	732 968	2.2	63.16	1.87
333 Crude petroleum & bituminous oil	659 814	2.0	0.29	0.05
625 Rubber for wheels, incl inner tube	554 581	1.7	31.55	0.68
676 Iron steel bar rod section piling	544 151	1.7	8.16	0.64
024 Cheese and curd	540 928	1.7	50.02	1.89
Remainder	14 049 110	42.9		
Belgium - Belgique (**=Developed)				
All commodity groups	444 505 028	100.0	5.02	2.67
542 Medicines including veterinary	36 642 367	8.2	12.00	11.04
334 Heavy petroleum & bituminous oil	29 746 090	6.7	8.50	3.70
781 Passenger cars and race cars	25 980 541	5.8	5.27	4.34
667 Pearls, precious semiprecious stone	18 394 982	4.1	26.83	12.51
541 Pharmaceuticals excluding medicines	14 056 038	3.2	11.01	9.63
515 Organo-inorganic compound acid salt	12 183 214	2.7	14.35	11.49
575 Other plastics, in primary forms	10 395 780	2.3	14.50	9.78
784 Motor vehicle parts and accessories	7 330 412	1.6	2.99	2.22
343 Natural gas, liquefied or not	7 258 977	1.6	7.90	2.88
571 Primary form ethylene polymers	6 524 116	1.5	17.05	9.03
Remainder	275 992 510	62.1		

For sources and notes, see end of table.

Pour les sources et les notes, se reporter à la fin du tableau.

Leading products exported based on average 2010-2011 values SITC Revision 3 (3-digit level) / Principaux produits exportés d'après la moyenne des valeurs de 2010-2011 CTCI révision 3 (positions à 3 chiffres)	2010-2011 Value (f.o.b., thousands of dollars) / Valeur (f.a.b., milliers de dollars)	As percentage / En pourcentage: of country total / du total du pays	of ** (1) / des ** (1)	of world / du monde
Belize (=Developing) (2)**				
All commodity groups	315 232	100.0	0.00	0.00
333 Crude petroleum & bituminous oil	95 476	30.3	0.01	0.01
057 Fruit nut (exc oil), fresh or dried	59 936	19.0	0.15	0.07
061 Sugar, mollasses and honey	40 871	13.0	0.14	0.10
059 Fruit & vegetable juice unferment	33 504	10.6	0.49	0.21
036 Crustacean mollusc aquat invertebra	22 799	7.2	0.12	0.08
034 Fish, fresh live chilled frozen	10 926	3.5	0.05	0.02
793 Ships boats floating structures	8 662	2.7	0.01	0.00
054 Vegetable & vegetable products nes	4 296	1.4	0.02	0.01
081 Animal feed excluding unmilled cereal	2 891	0.9	0.01	0.00
282 Ferrous iron & steel, waste & scrap	1 988	0.6	0.03	0.00
Remainder	33 884	10.7		
Benin - Bénin (=Developing) (2)**				
All commodity groups	1 618 657	100.0	0.02	0.01
263 Cotton	313 872	19.4	3.42	1.40
334 Heavy petroleum & bituminous oil	272 011	16.8	0.08	0.03
057 Fruit nut (exc oil), fresh or dried	160 851	9.9	0.41	0.20
971 Gold non-monetary excluding ores	145 740	9.0	0.15	0.08
288 Non ferrous base metal waste nes	129 699	8.0	1.42	0.29
012 Meat nes, fresh chilled frozen	94 504	5.8	0.65	0.14
042 Rice	61 583	3.8	0.35	0.28
282 Ferrous iron & steel, waste & scrap	40 597	2.5	0.66	0.08
676 Iron steel bar rod section piling	38 893	2.4	0.14	0.05
247 Wood in rough or roughly squared	34 150	2.1	0.77	0.24
Remainder	326 758	20.2		
Bermuda - Bermudes (=Developed) (2)**				
All commodity groups	14 000	100.0	0.00	0.00
793 Ships boats floating structures	7 482	53.4	0.01	0.00
342 Liquefied propane and butane	1 347	9.6	0.01	0.00
542 Medicines including veterinary	1 279	9.1	0.00	0.00
831 Case bag; storage travel shopping	327	2.3	0.00	0.00
896 Work of art & collections; antiques	265	1.9	0.00	0.00
041 Wheat meslin, incl spelt, unmilled	185	1.3	0.00	0.00
044 Maize unmilled, excluding sweet corn	157	1.1	0.00	0.00
112 Alcoholic beverages	119	0.9	0.00	0.00
792 Aircraft, spacecraft & equipment	95	0.7	0.00	0.00
716 Rotating electric plant parts nes	78	0.6	0.00	0.00
Remainder	2 667	19.0		
Bhutan - Bhoutan (=Developing) (2)**				
All commodity groups	630 655	100.0	0.01	0.00
671 Pig & sponge iron, ferro alloys etc	165 789	26.3	0.76	0.41
351 Electric current	79 486	12.6	2.00	0.22
682 Copper	53 168	8.4	0.07	0.04
075 Spices	51 137	8.1	0.87	0.68
524 Other inorganic chemicals	40 233	6.4	1.21	0.31
676 Iron steel bar rod section piling	30 333	4.8	0.11	0.04
689 Misc non-ferrous base metals	26 640	4.2	0.61	0.27
672 Ingots, Iron steel primary products	25 756	4.1	0.23	0.06
057 Fruit nut (exc oil), fresh or dried	21 812	3.5	0.06	0.03
661 Lime cement construction material	19 885	3.2	0.13	0.07
Remainder	116 416	18.5		
Bolivia (Plurinational State of) - Bolivie (État plurinational de) (=Developing)**				
All commodity groups	7 992 428	100.0	0.11	0.05
343 Natural gas, liquefied or not	3 474 137	43.5	2.73	1.38
287 Base metal ores & concentrates nes	1 096 038	13.7	6.00	3.52
289 Prec metal ore concentrate excl. gold	679 003	8.5	11.58	3.62
081 Animal feed excluding unmilled cereal	390 068	4.9	1.42	0.61
687 Tin	377 560	4.7	6.58	5.51
421 Fixed veg fat and oil, "soft"	295 224	3.7	2.57	0.85
333 Crude petroleum & bituminous oil	243 709	3.0	0.02	0.02
681 Silver, platinum, platinum metals	155 569	1.9	0.60	0.25
971 Gold non-monetary excluding ores	150 746	1.9	0.16	0.08
057 Fruit nut (exc oil), fresh or dried	144 165	1.8	0.36	0.18
Remainder	986 209	12.3		

Leading products exported based on average 2010-2011 values SITC Revision 3 (3-digit level) / Principaux produits exportés d'après la moyenne des valeurs de 2010-2011 CTCI révision 3 (positions à 3 chiffres)	2010-2011 Value (f.o.b., thousands of dollars) / Valeur (f.a.b., milliers de dollars)	As percentage / En pourcentage: of country total / du total du pays	of ** (1) / des ** (1)	of world / du monde
Bosnia and Herzegovina - Bosnie-Herzégovine (=Transition) (2)**				
All commodity groups	5 326 593	100.0	0.76	0.03
684 Aluminium	427 327	8.0	4.49	0.37
851 Footwear	390 454	7.3	25.50	0.37
821 Furniture part; bedding furnishing	301 199	5.7	16.18	0.22
676 Iron steel bar rod section piling	183 183	3.4	2.75	0.22
325 Coke, semi coke, retort carbon	182 571	3.4	13.60	1.96
334 Heavy petroleum & bituminous oil	170 671	3.2	0.17	0.02
248 Wood simply worked, railway sleeper	161 434	3.0	3.87	0.45
351 Electric current	151 688	2.8	6.64	0.42
285 Aluminium ore concentrate alumina	138 973	2.6	14.65	0.95
743 Gas pump, compressor, fan, filter	138 088	2.6	15.60	0.12
Remainder	3 081 004	57.8		
Botswana (=Developing)**				
All commodity groups	5 287 578	100.0	0.07	0.03
667 Pearls, precious semiprecious stone	3 724 896	70.4	4.95	2.53
284 Nickel ores, concentrates, etc	605 997	11.5	9.68	5.65
011 Beef, fresh chilled frozen	100 585	1.9	0.92	0.27
283 Copper ores and concentrates	70 391	1.3	0.19	0.14
842 Female clothing, woven	49 615	0.9	0.10	0.06
971 Gold non-monetary excluding ores	47 821	0.9	0.05	0.03
662 Clay and refractory materials	45 088	0.9	0.47	0.19
841 Male clothing, woven	40 123	0.8	0.09	0.06
523 Inorganic acid metal salt peroxy	40 006	0.8	0.46	0.20
277 Natural abrasives nes	35 175	0.7	3.78	2.35
Remainder	527 881	10.0		
Brazil - Brésil (=Developing)**				
All commodity groups	226 697 569	100.0	3.20	1.36
281 Iron ore and concentrates	35 364 566	15.6	62.04	28.28
333 Crude petroleum & bituminous oil	18 948 367	8.4	1.85	1.33
061 Sugar, mollasses and honey	13 929 570	6.1	46.48	33.08
222 Oil seed etc for soft oil	13 759 613	6.1	53.73	23.20
012 Meat nes, fresh chilled frozen	8 169 412	3.6	56.19	12.11
071 Coffee and coffee substitutes	7 247 984	3.2	31.26	19.67
081 Animal feed excluding unmilled cereal	5 513 208	2.4	20.07	8.63
251 Pulp and waste paper	4 881 634	2.2	41.85	10.39
784 Motor vehicle parts and accessories	4 718 390	2.1	5.64	1.43
781 Passenger cars and race cars	4 395 914	1.9	4.26	0.73
Remainder	109 768 911	48.4		
Brunei Darussalam - Brunéi Darussalam (=Developing) (2)**				
All commodity groups	10 707 368	100.0	0.15	0.06
333 Crude petroleum & bituminous oil	5 993 335	56.0	0.59	0.42
343 Natural gas, liquefied or not	4 325 640	40.4	3.39	1.71
334 Heavy petroleum & bituminous oil	48 751	0.5	0.01	0.01
845 Articles of apparel nes	43 213	0.4	0.05	0.03
792 Aircraft, spacecraft & equipment	19 115	0.2	0.09	0.01
844 Female clothing, knitted crocheted	14 936	0.1	0.04	0.03
728 Special industrial machine part nes	14 921	0.1	0.04	0.01
731 Machine tools for material removal	11 878	0.1	0.16	0.04
282 Ferrous iron & steel, waste & scrap	11 454	0.1	0.18	0.02
843 Male clothing, knitted crocheted	10 170	0.1	0.04	0.04
Remainder	213 955	2.0		
Bulgaria - Bulgarie (=Developed)**				
All commodity groups	24 386 612	100.0	0.28	0.15
334 Heavy petroleum & bituminous oil	2 681 306	11.0	0.77	0.33
682 Copper	2 603 417	10.7	4.58	1.86
222 Oil seed etc for soft oil	789 822	3.2	2.46	1.33
542 Medicines including veterinary	562 027	2.3	0.18	0.17
842 Female clothing, woven	531 042	2.2	2.07	0.68
041 Wheat meslin, incl spelt, unmilled	491 344	2.0	1.55	1.21
351 Electric current	450 577	1.8	1.52	1.25
841 Male clothing, woven	446 428	1.8	2.22	0.68
845 Articles of apparel nes	413 640	1.7	1.07	0.31
676 Iron steel bar rod section piling	400 405	1.6	0.79	0.47
Remainder	15 016 604	61.6		

For sources and notes, see end of table.

Pour les sources et les notes, se reporter à la fin du tableau.

Leading products exported based on average 2010-2011 values SITC Revision 3 (3-digit level) / Principaux produits exportés d'après la moyenne des valeurs de 2010-2011 CTCI révision 3 (positions à 3 chiffres)	Value (f.o.b., thousands of dollars) / Valeur (f.a.b., milliers de dollars)	of country total / du total du pays	of ** (1) / des ** (1)	of world / du monde
Burkina Faso (**=Developing) (2)				
All commodity groups	1 544 067	100.0	0.02	0.01
263 Cotton	633 948	41.1	6.91	2.82
971 Gold non-monetary excluding ores	537 233	34.8	0.56	0.29
222 Oil seed etc for soft oil	106 069	6.9	0.41	0.18
223 Oil seed for non soft oil	39 062	2.5	5.45	1.51
001 Live animal excl. fish & crustacean	26 320	1.7	0.61	0.13
057 Fruit nut (exc oil), fresh or dried	20 098	1.3	0.05	0.03
054 Vegetable & vegetable products nes	15 433	1.0	0.07	0.03
598 Miscellaneous chemical products nes	10 335	0.7	0.04	0.01
676 Iron steel bar rod section piling	10 270	0.7	0.04	0.01
287 Base metal ores & concentrates nes	8 819	0.6	0.05	0.03
Remainder	136 480	8.8		
Burundi (**=Developing) (2)				
All commodity groups	111 180	100.0	0.00	0.00
071 Coffee and coffee substitutes	61 448	55.3	0.26	0.17
074 Tea and maté	13 535	12.2	0.23	0.17
971 Gold non-monetary excluding ores	9 760	8.8	0.01	0.01
287 Base metal ores & concentrates nes	4 052	3.6	0.02	0.01
211 Raw hides & skins, excluding furskins	2 193	2.0	0.25	0.03
263 Cotton	1 819	1.6	0.02	0.01
554 Soaps cleansers polishes	1 429	1.3	0.01	0.00
061 Sugar, mollasses and honey	1 357	1.2	0.00	0.00
334 Heavy petroleum & bituminous oil	1 345	1.2	0.00	0.00
112 Alcoholic beverages	1 033	0.9	0.01	0.00
Remainder	13 209	11.9		
Cambodia - Cambodge (**=Developing) (2)				
All commodity groups	6 571 988	100.0	0.09	0.04
845 Articles of apparel nes	1 947 187	29.6	2.09	1.47
844 Female clothing, knitted crocheted	1 172 961	17.8	3.07	2.36
843 Male clothing, knitted crocheted	526 861	8.0	2.32	1.94
851 Footwear	491 872	7.5	0.77	0.47
842 Female clothing, woven	469 969	7.2	0.91	0.60
841 Male clothing, woven	403 946	6.1	0.90	0.61
892 Printed matter	334 493	5.1	2.18	0.66
231 Natural rubber, latex, gum, etc	233 290	3.5	0.77	0.72
785 Motorcycles, mopeds and cycles	82 928	1.3	0.36	0.19
793 Ships boats floating structures	70 728	1.1	0.06	0.04
Remainder	837 752	12.7		
Cameroon - Cameroun (**=Developing) (2)				
All commodity groups	4 239 216	100.0	0.06	0.03
333 Crude petroleum & bituminous oil	1 546 612	36.5	0.15	0.11
072 Cocoa	598 422	14.1	4.14	2.76
248 Wood simply worked, railway sleeper	328 425	7.7	4.33	0.91
334 Heavy petroleum & bituminous oil	327 007	7.7	0.09	0.04
247 Wood in rough or roughly squared	191 147	4.5	4.33	1.34
057 Fruit nut (exc oil), fresh or dried	184 826	4.4	0.47	0.23
231 Natural rubber, latex, gum, etc	138 219	3.3	0.45	0.43
263 Cotton	118 245	2.8	1.29	0.53
684 Aluminium	94 000	2.2	0.26	0.08
071 Coffee and coffee substitutes	79 625	1.9	0.34	0.22
Remainder	632 689	14.9		
Canada (**=Developed)				
All commodity groups	418 488 402	100.0	4.72	2.51
333 Crude petroleum & bituminous oil	59 967 994	14.3	33.94	4.21
781 Passenger cars and race cars	38 335 547	9.2	7.78	6.41
334 Heavy petroleum & bituminous oil	16 084 296	3.8	4.60	2.00
971 Gold non-monetary excluding ores	15 813 118	3.8	17.52	8.39
343 Natural gas, liquefied or not	14 332 287	3.4	15.59	5.68
792 Aircraft, spacecraft & equipment	9 717 651	2.3	8.05	6.81
784 Motor vehicle parts and accessories	9 417 696	2.3	3.85	2.86
684 Aluminium	7 941 527	1.9	11.29	6.84
641 Paper and paperboard	7 525 236	1.8	7.91	6.33
251 Pulp and waste paper	7 341 462	1.8	21.59	15.62
Remainder	232 011 588	55.4		
Cape Verde - Cap-Vert (**=Developing) (2)				
All commodity groups	57 725	100.0	0.00	0.00
037 Fish shellfish, prepared preserved	21 726	37.6	0.14	0.09
034 Fish, fresh live chilled frozen	17 121	29.7	0.07	0.03
851 Footwear	3 998	6.9	0.01	0.00
841 Male clothing, woven	2 817	4.9	0.01	0.00
845 Articles of apparel nes	1 293	2.2	0.00	0.00
843 Male clothing, knitted crocheted	1 104	1.9	0.00	0.00
282 Ferrous iron & steel, waste & scrap	1 079	1.9	0.02	0.00
793 Ships boats floating structures	842	1.5	0.00	0.00
112 Alcoholic beverages	762	1.3	0.01	0.00
036 Crustacean mollusc aquat invertebra	555	1.0	0.00	0.00
Remainder	6 429	11.1		
Cayman Islands - Îles Caïmanes (**=Developing) (2)				
All commodity groups	17 500	100.0	0.00	0.00
793 Ships boats floating structures	14 727	84.2	0.01	0.01
792 Aircraft, spacecraft & equipment	783	4.5	0.00	0.00
897 Jewellery nes (667)	555	3.2	0.00	0.00
896 Work of art & collections; antiques	196	1.1	0.01	0.00
781 Passenger cars and race cars	137	0.8	0.00	0.00
282 Ferrous iron & steel, waste & scrap	80	0.5	0.00	0.00
714 Non-electric engines excl. 712 713 718	78	0.4	0.00	0.00
334 Heavy petroleum & bituminous oil	58	0.3	0.00	0.00
971 Gold non-monetary excluding ores	45	0.3	0.00	0.00
321 Coal excluding non-agglomerated	33	0.2	0.00	0.00
Remainder	809	4.6		
Central African Republic - République centrafricaine (**=Developing) (2)				
All commodity groups	147 532	100.0	0.00	0.00
247 Wood in rough or roughly squared	33 577	22.8	0.76	0.23
667 Pearls, precious semiprecious stone	33 161	22.5	0.04	0.02
248 Wood simply worked, railway sleeper	21 094	14.3	0.28	0.06
277 Natural abrasives nes	16 499	11.2	1.77	1.10
263 Cotton	12 446	8.4	0.14	0.06
071 Coffee and coffee substitutes	4 686	3.2	0.02	0.01
061 Sugar, mollasses and honey	3 761	2.5	0.01	0.01
781 Passenger cars and race cars	1 832	1.2	0.00	0.00
098 Edible products & preparations nes	890	0.6	0.01	0.00
971 Gold non-monetary excluding ores	863	0.6	0.00	0.00
Remainder	18 724	12.7		
Chad - Tchad (**=Developing) (2)				
All commodity groups	3 823 890	100.0	0.05	0.02
333 Crude petroleum & bituminous oil	3 437 044	89.9	0.34	0.24
334 Heavy petroleum & bituminous oil	213 740	5.6	0.06	0.03
263 Cotton	80 442	2.1	0.88	0.36
292 Crude vegetable materials nes	26 221	0.7	0.22	0.07
792 Aircraft, spacecraft & equipment	6 558	0.2	0.03	0.00
657 Special yarn and textile fabric etc	6 546	0.2	0.03	0.01
523 Inorganic acid metal salt peroxy	5 694	0.1	0.07	0.03
662 Clay and refractory materials	5 338	0.1	0.06	0.02
267 Man made fibre for spinning; waste	5 165	0.1	0.28	0.11
691 Iron steel aluminium structures nes	4 022	0.1	0.02	0.01
Remainder	33 120	0.9		
Chile - Chili (**=Developing)				
All commodity groups	76 152 777	100.0	1.07	0.46
682 Copper	28 356 916	37.2	38.79	20.26
283 Copper ores and concentrates	14 059 610	18.5	37.10	28.21
057 Fruit nut (exc oil), fresh or dried	4 288 161	5.6	10.85	5.34
034 Fish, fresh live chilled frozen	2 751 082	3.6	11.37	4.88
251 Pulp and waste paper	2 634 423	3.5	22.58	5.61
112 Alcoholic beverages	1 655 154	2.2	13.39	2.39
287 Base metal ores & concentrates nes	1 399 203	1.8	7.66	4.50
281 Iron ore and concentrates	1 398 088	1.8	2.45	1.12
971 Gold non-monetary excluding ores	1 237 920	1.6	1.28	0.66
288 Non ferrous base metal waste nes	1 055 960	1.4	11.54	2.40
Remainder	17 316 260	22.7		

For sources and notes, see end of table.

Pour les sources et les notes, se reporter à la fin du tableau.

176

Leading products exported based on average 2010-2011 values SITC Revision 3 (3-digit level) / Principaux produits exportés d'après la moyenne des valeurs de 2010-2011 CTCI révision 3 (positions à 3 chiffres)	2010-2011 Value (f.o.b., thousands of dollars) / Valeur (f.a.b., milliers de dollars)	As percentage / En pourcentage — of country total / du total du pays	of ** (1) / des ** (1)	of world / du monde
China - Chine (**=Developing)				
All commodity groups	1 738 076 093	100.0	24.51	10.44
752 Computer equipment nes	154 462 221	8.9	65.94	46.18
764 Telecommunicate equipment part nes	147 804 162	8.5	47.45	31.06
776 Valves tubes; diodes, transistors	66 244 252	3.8	17.01	11.99
845 Articles of apparel nes	42 871 199	2.5	45.96	32.26
778 Electrical machinery apparatus nes	42 416 602	2.4	41.38	20.02
793 Ships boats floating structures	41 960 746	2.4	36.59	23.67
821 Furniture part; bedding furnishing	41 845 599	2.4	65.58	30.27
759 Office equipment part & accessories	38 719 998	2.2	32.35	19.44
851 Footwear	38 678 092	2.2	60.59	37.05
894 Baby carriage toy game sport good	33 962 491	2.0	63.23	36.95
Remainder	1 089 110 731	62.7		
China, Hong Kong SAR - Chine (RAS de Hong Kong) (**=Developing)				
All commodity groups	428 132 698	100.0	6.04	2.57
776 Valves tubes; diodes, transistors	66 365 804	15.5	17.04	12.01
764 Telecommunicate equipment part nes	60 484 088	14.1	19.42	12.71
759 Office equipment part & accessories	29 052 786	6.8	24.28	14.59
772 Electrical circuit equipment	19 140 751	4.5	20.47	8.77
971 Gold non-monetary excluding ores	18 452 512	4.3	19.10	9.79
752 Computer equipment nes	15 363 203	3.6	6.56	4.59
667 Pearls, precious semiprecious stone	14 258 369	3.3	18.96	9.70
894 Baby carriage toy game sport good	11 559 830	2.7	21.52	12.58
778 Electrical machinery apparatus nes	11 149 346	2.6	10.88	5.26
845 Articles of apparel nes	10 470 010	2.4	11.23	7.88
Remainder	171 836 001	40.1		
China, Macao SAR - Chine (RAS de Macao) (**=Developing)				
All commodity groups	869 852	100.0	0.01	0.01
897 Jewellery nes (667)	100 707	11.6	0.18	0.11
885 Watches and clocks	59 701	6.9	0.40	0.14
845 Articles of apparel nes	50 443	5.8	0.05	0.04
579 Plastic waste, parings and scrap	41 712	4.8	1.68	0.60
842 Female clothing, woven	37 866	4.4	0.07	0.05
682 Copper	35 781	4.1	0.05	0.03
841 Male clothing, woven	31 345	3.6	0.07	0.05
764 Telecommunicate equipment part nes	30 724	3.5	0.01	0.01
844 Female clothing, knitted crocheted	22 904	2.6	0.06	0.05
759 Office equipment part & accessories	16 554	1.9	0.01	0.01
Remainder	442 116	50.8		
China, Taiwan Province of - Province chinoise de Taiwan (**=Developing) (2)				
All commodity groups	290 351 926	100.0	4.09	1.74
776 Valves tubes; diodes, transistors	63 210 439	21.8	16.23	11.44
871 Optical instruments apparatus nes	17 611 845	6.1	21.72	17.56
334 Heavy petroleum & bituminous oil	15 390 040	5.3	4.34	1.91
764 Telecommunicate equipment part nes	14 862 502	5.1	4.77	3.12
778 Electrical machinery apparatus nes	8 688 224	3.0	8.48	4.10
772 Electrical circuit equipment	8 671 738	3.0	9.28	3.97
759 Office equipment part & accessories	7 042 360	2.4	5.88	3.54
898 Music instrument device recording	5 954 490	2.1	21.26	10.01
728 Special industrial machine part nes	4 588 594	1.6	12.36	2.64
513 Carboxylic acid and compounds	4 439 322	1.5	18.00	9.20
Remainder	139 892 372	48.2		
Colombia - Colombie (**=Developing)				
All commodity groups	48 386 522	100.0	0.68	0.29
333 Crude petroleum & bituminous oil	18 207 053	37.6	1.78	1.28
321 Coal excluding non-agglomomerated	6 688 597	13.8	16.34	5.66
334 Heavy petroleum & bituminous oil	3 718 359	7.7	1.05	0.46
071 Coffee and coffee substitutes	2 551 695	5.3	11.00	6.92
971 Gold non-monetary excluding ores	2 455 208	5.1	2.54	1.30
292 Crude vegetable materials nes	1 269 674	2.6	10.82	3.28
671 Pig & sponge iron, ferro alloys etc	897 603	1.9	4.09	2.20
057 Fruit nut (exc oil), fresh or dried	833 164	1.7	2.11	1.04
061 Sugar, mollasses and honey	529 111	1.1	1.77	1.26
325 Coke, semi coke, retort carbon	517 416	1.1	17.46	5.55
Remainder	10 718 641	22.2		
Comoros - Comores (**=Developing) (2)				
All commodity groups	22 889	100.0	0.00	0.00
793 Ships boats floating structures	9 990	43.6	0.01	0.01
075 Spices	7 013	30.6	0.12	0.09
551 Essential oils, perfumes & flavours	3 012	13.2	0.07	0.01
751 Office machines	1 709	7.5	0.01	0.00
673 Flat iron non-alloy steel products	173	0.8	0.00	0.00
971 Gold non-monetary excluding ores	156	0.7	0.00	0.00
034 Fish, fresh live chilled frozen	146	0.6	0.00	0.00
282 Ferrous iron & steel, waste & scrap	69	0.3	0.00	0.00
513 Carboxylic acid and compounds	63	0.3	0.00	0.00
247 Wood in rough or roughly squared	59	0.3	0.00	0.00
Remainder	500	2.2		
Congo (**=Developing) (2)				
All commodity groups	10 054 668	100.0	0.14	0.06
333 Crude petroleum & bituminous oil	8 006 391	79.6	0.78	0.56
793 Ships boats floating structures	587 989	5.8	0.51	0.33
334 Heavy petroleum & bituminous oil	277 142	2.8	0.08	0.03
682 Copper	241 791	2.4	0.33	0.17
247 Wood in rough or roughly squared	221 950	2.2	5.03	1.55
287 Base metal ores & concentrates nes	98 647	1.0	0.54	0.32
342 Liquefied propane and butane	76 620	0.8	0.22	0.15
679 Iron steel pipe tube fittings etc	74 510	0.7	0.23	0.09
283 Copper ores and concentrates	70 515	0.7	0.19	0.14
248 Wood simply worked, railway sleeper	43 803	0.4	0.58	0.12
Remainder	355 311	3.5		
Cook Islands - Îles Cook (**=Developing) (2)				
All commodity groups	4 000	100.0	0.00	0.00
034 Fish, fresh live chilled frozen	2 395	59.9	0.01	0.00
793 Ships boats floating structures	418	10.5	0.00	0.00
059 Fruit & vegetable juice unferment	271	6.8	0.00	0.00
667 Pearls, precious semiprecious stone	240	6.0	0.00	0.00
778 Electrical machinery apparatus nes	71	1.8	0.00	0.00
533 Pigment, paint, varnish & related	60	1.5	0.00	0.00
896 Work of art & collections; antiques	47	1.2	0.00	0.00
036 Crustacean mollusc aquat invertebra	29	0.7	0.00	0.00
511 Hydrocarbons nes; derivatives	25	0.6	0.00	0.00
747 Pipe, boiler, tank & vat appliances	21	0.5	0.00	0.00
Remainder	423	10.6		
Costa Rica (**=Developing) (2)				
All commodity groups	9 633 541	100.0	0.14	0.06
776 Valves tubes; diodes, transistors	3 804 244	39.5	0.98	0.69
057 Fruit nut (exc oil), fresh or dried	1 410 265	14.6	3.57	1.76
759 Office equipment part & accessories	1 058 155	11.0	0.88	0.53
872 Medical instruments appliances nes	418 512	4.3	2.40	0.50
071 Coffee and coffee substitutes	180 227	1.9	0.78	0.49
098 Edible products & preparations nes	162 044	1.7	1.10	0.28
899 Manufactured articles nes	139 674	1.4	0.55	0.18
772 Electrical circuit equipment	139 479	1.4	0.15	0.06
292 Crude vegetable materials nes	122 464	1.3	1.04	0.32
542 Medicines including veterinary	114 176	1.2	0.46	0.03
Remainder	2 084 301	21.6		
Côte d'Ivoire (**=Developing)				
All commodity groups	10 666 286	100.0	0.15	0.06
072 Cocoa	3 876 622	36.3	26.81	17.85
334 Heavy petroleum & bituminous oil	1 247 936	11.7	0.35	0.16
333 Crude petroleum & bituminous oil	1 198 675	11.2	0.12	0.08
231 Natural rubber, latex, gum, etc	908 412	8.5	2.98	2.82
057 Fruit nut (exc oil), fresh or dried	468 779	4.4	1.19	0.58
971 Gold non-monetary excluding ores	378 295	3.5	0.39	0.20
793 Ships boats floating structures	363 236	3.4	0.32	0.20
422 Fixed veg fat and oil, excl. "soft"	233 948	2.2	0.59	0.52
071 Coffee and coffee substitutes	172 993	1.6	0.75	0.47
553 Perfume toilet cosmetics, excl. soap	142 667	1.3	0.88	0.20
Remainder	1 674 723	15.7		

For sources and notes, see end of table.   Pour les sources et les notes, se reporter à la fin du tableau.

177

Leading products exported based on average 2010-2011 values SITC Revision 3 (3-digit level) / Principaux produits exportés d'après la moyenne des valeurs de 2010-2011 CTCI révision 3 (positions à 3 chiffres)	Value (f.o.b., thousands of dollars) Valeur (f.a.b., milliers de dollars)	of country total du total du pays	of ** (1) des ** (1)	of world du monde
Croatia - Croatie (=Transition)**				
All commodity groups	12 049 754	100.0	1.73	0.07
793 Ships boats floating structures	1 456 657	12.1	47.80	0.82
334 Heavy petroleum & bituminous oil	1 160 809	9.6	1.16	0.14
542 Medicines including veterinary	420 661	3.5	29.04	0.13
771 Electric power machine part excl. 716	369 276	3.1	31.63	0.41
821 Furniture part; bedding furnishing	313 666	2.6	16.85	0.23
562 Manufactured fertilizer excl. crude	298 947	2.5	2.13	0.46
248 Wood simply worked, railway sleeper	259 671	2.2	6.23	0.72
684 Aluminium	223 244	1.9	2.35	0.19
851 Footwear	196 686	1.6	12.85	0.19
845 Articles of apparel nes	184 781	1.5	16.83	0.14
Remainder	7 165 356	59.5		
Cuba (=Developing) (2)**				
All commodity groups	5 632 833	100.0	0.08	0.03
284 Nickel ores, concentrates, etc	1 589 237	28.2	25.38	14.82
061 Sugar, mollasses and honey	925 465	16.4	3.09	2.20
122 Manufactured tabacco	422 828	7.5	5.64	1.48
334 Heavy petroleum & bituminous oil	264 556	4.7	0.07	0.03
542 Medicines including veterinary	206 174	3.7	0.82	0.06
672 Ingots, Iron steel primary products	160 734	2.9	1.45	0.39
288 Non ferrous base metal waste nes	151 445	2.7	1.65	0.34
036 Crustacean mollusc aquat invertebra	130 714	2.3	0.68	0.44
541 Pharmaceuticals excluding medicines	105 976	1.9	0.59	0.07
287 Base metal ores & concentrates nes	105 351	1.9	0.58	0.34
Remainder	1 570 353	27.9		
Cyprus - Chypre (=Developed)**				
All commodity groups	1 732 003	100.0	0.02	0.01
334 Heavy petroleum & bituminous oil	398 389	23.0	0.11	0.05
542 Medicines including veterinary	142 681	8.2	0.05	0.04
776 Valves tubes; diodes, transistors	100 898	5.8	0.06	0.02
793 Ships boats floating structures	74 455	4.3	0.13	0.04
515 Organo-inorganic compound acid salt	54 119	3.1	0.06	0.05
054 Vegetable & vegetable products nes	43 580	2.5	0.12	0.07
024 Cheese and curd	39 403	2.3	0.15	0.14
282 Ferrous iron & steel, waste & scrap	31 686	1.8	0.07	0.06
764 Telecommunicate equipment part nes	29 478	1.7	0.02	0.01
541 Pharmaceuticals excluding medicines	29 015	1.7	0.02	0.02
Remainder	788 299	45.5		
Czech Republic - République tchèque (=Developed)**				
All commodity groups	147 126 320	100.0	1.66	0.88
781 Passenger cars and race cars	14 202 587	9.7	2.88	2.37
784 Motor vehicle parts and accessories	10 132 623	6.9	4.14	3.07
752 Computer equipment nes	8 902 050	6.1	8.90	2.66
772 Electrical circuit equipment	4 044 582	2.7	3.27	1.85
699 Base metal manufactures nes	3 775 630	2.6	4.46	2.86
764 Telecommunicate equipment part nes	3 764 324	2.6	2.31	0.79
778 Electrical machinery apparatus nes	3 548 620	2.4	3.28	1.67
761 Television video receive project	3 124 084	2.1	7.54	3.16
741 Heating cooling equipment parts nes	2 794 230	1.9	4.35	2.71
773 Electrical distribute equipment nes	2 499 545	1.7	4.70	2.43
Remainder	90 338 045	61.4		
Dem. Rep. of the Congo - Rép. dém. du Congo (=Developing) (2)**				
All commodity groups	5 701 740	100.0	0.08	0.03
682 Copper	2 030 079	35.6	2.78	1.45
287 Base metal ores & concentrates nes	967 587	17.0	5.29	3.11
333 Crude petroleum & bituminous oil	856 739	15.0	0.08	0.06
689 Misc non-ferrous base metals	579 411	10.2	13.36	5.88
283 Copper ores and concentrates	382 565	6.7	1.01	0.77
667 Pearls, precious semiprecious stone	232 753	4.1	0.31	0.16
247 Wood in rough or roughly squared	105 249	1.8	2.38	0.74
522 Inorganic chemical elem oxide salt	98 037	1.7	0.37	0.17
334 Heavy petroleum & bituminous oil	93 651	1.6	0.03	0.01
248 Wood simply worked, railway sleeper	44 091	0.8	0.58	0.12
Remainder	311 578	5.5		

Leading products exported based on average 2010-2011 values SITC Revision 3 (3-digit level) / Principaux produits exportés d'après la moyenne des valeurs de 2010-2011 CTCI révision 3 (positions à 3 chiffres)	Value (f.o.b., thousands of dollars) Valeur (f.a.b., milliers de dollars)	of country total du total du pays	of ** (1) des ** (1)	of world du monde
Denmark - Danemark (=Developed)**				
All commodity groups	104 641 645	100.0	1.18	0.63
333 Crude petroleum & bituminous oil	5 060 433	4.8	2.86	0.36
012 Meat nes, fresh chilled frozen	3 906 470	3.7	7.44	5.79
334 Heavy petroleum & bituminous oil	3 309 080	3.2	0.95	0.41
542 Medicines including veterinary	2 952 075	2.8	0.97	0.89
716 Rotating electric plant parts nes	2 668 171	2.5	4.78	3.07
541 Pharmaceuticals excluding medicines	2 600 768	2.5	2.04	1.78
821 Furniture part; bedding furnishing	2 133 819	2.0	2.94	1.54
874 Measure analyze control device nes	1 821 931	1.7	1.40	1.10
098 Edible products & preparations nes	1 634 862	1.6	3.96	2.87
741 Heating cooling equipment parts nes	1 514 390	1.4	2.36	1.47
Remainder	77 039 646	73.6		
Djibouti (=Developing) (2)**				
All commodity groups	90 067	100.0	0.00	0.00
001 Live animal excl. fish & crustacean	26 280	29.2	0.61	0.13
971 Gold non-monetary excluding ores	10 597	11.8	0.01	0.01
071 Coffee and coffee substitutes	4 421	4.9	0.02	0.01
811 Prefabricated buildings	3 352	3.7	0.14	0.04
781 Passenger cars and race cars	2 837	3.2	0.00	0.00
247 Wood in rough or roughly squared	2 262	2.5	0.05	0.02
334 Heavy petroleum & bituminous oil	2 100	2.3	0.00	0.00
782 Goods and service vehicles	1 551	1.7	0.00	0.00
278 Other crude minerals	1 195	1.3	0.02	0.01
723 Civil engineering plant & equipment	1 105	1.2	0.00	0.00
Remainder	34 367	38.2		
Dominica - Dominique (=Developing) (2)**				
All commodity groups	31 540	100.0	0.00	0.00
554 Soaps cleansers polishes	11 948	37.9	0.12	0.03
057 Fruit nut (exc oil), fresh or dried	5 280	16.7	0.01	0.01
892 Printed matter	3 102	9.8	0.02	0.01
533 Pigment, paint, varnish & related	2 004	6.4	0.02	0.00
054 Vegetable & vegetable products nes	1 985	6.3	0.01	0.00
273 Stone, sand and gravel	1 933	6.1	0.05	0.02
764 Telecommunicate equipment part nes	657	2.1	0.00	0.00
551 Essential oils, perfumes & flavours	495	1.6	0.01	0.00
111 Non alcoholic beverage nes	357	1.1	0.01	0.00
716 Rotating electric plant parts nes	350	1.1	0.00	0.00
Remainder	3 430	10.9		
Dominican Republic - République dominicaine (=Developing) (2)**				
All commodity groups	7 644 697	100.0	0.11	0.05
872 Medical instruments appliances nes	784 447	10.3	4.50	0.95
845 Articles of apparel nes	408 743	5.3	0.44	0.31
122 Manufactured tabacco	401 510	5.3	5.35	1.40
057 Fruit nut (exc oil), fresh or dried	389 180	5.1	0.98	0.48
772 Electrical circuit equipment	383 655	5.0	0.41	0.18
652 Woven cotton fabrics	331 281	4.3	1.43	1.04
893 Articles of plastic nes	287 183	3.8	0.63	0.23
851 Footwear	283 559	3.7	0.44	0.27
897 Jewellery· nes (667)	253 453	3.3	0.46	0.27
971 Gold non-monetary excluding ores	189 617	2.5	0.20	0.10
Remainder	3 932 069	51.4		
Ecuador - Équateur (=Developing)**				
All commodity groups	19 917 563	100.0	0.28	0.12
333 Crude petroleum & bituminous oil	10 377 297	52.1	1.01	0.73
057 Fruit nut (exc oil), fresh or dried	2 212 981	11.1	5.60	2.76
036 Crustacean mollusc aquat invertebra	1 015 930	5.1	5.29	3.45
334 Heavy petroleum & bituminous oil	855 522	4.3	0.24	0.11
037 Fish shellfish, prepared preserved	741 890	3.7	4.66	3.15
292 Crude vegetable materials nes	652 114	3.3	5.56	1.69
072 Cocoa	491 762	2.5	3.40	2.26
034 Fish, fresh live chilled frozen	266 784	1.3	1.10	0.47
422 Fixed veg fat and oil, excl. "soft"	234 333	1.2	0.59	0.52
071 Coffee and coffee substitutes	209 769	1.1	0.90	0.57
Remainder	2 859 181	14.4		

For sources and notes, see end of table.

Pour les sources et les notes, se reporter à la fin du tableau.

Egypt - Égypte (**=Developing)

Leading products exported based on average 2010-2011 values SITC Revision 3 (3-digit level) / Principaux produits exportés d'après la moyenne des valeurs de 2010-2011 CTCI révision 3 (positions à 3 chiffres)	Value (f.o.b., thousands of dollars) / Valeur (f.a.b., milliers de dollars)	of country total du total du pays	of ** (1) des ** (1)	of world du monde
All commodity groups	28 556 930	100.0	0.40	0.17
334 Heavy petroleum & bituminous oil	3 243 928	11.4	0.91	0.40
333 Crude petroleum & bituminous oil	2 403 748	8.4	0.23	0.17
343 Natural gas, liquefied or not	1 874 344	6.6	1.47	0.74
971 Gold non-monetary excluding ores	1 372 089	4.8	1.42	0.73
562 Manufactured fertilizer excl. crude	1 265 903	4.4	5.70	1.95
057 Fruit nut (exc oil), fresh or dried	969 574	3.4	2.45	1.21
054 Vegetable & vegetable products nes	893 773	3.1	3.83	1.48
773 Electrical distribute equipment nes	759 796	2.7	1.60	0.74
682 Copper	633 389	2.2	0.87	0.45
845 Articles of apparel nes	602 913	2.1	0.65	0.45
Remainder	14 537 473	50.9		

El Salvador (**=Developing) (2)

	Value	of country total	of ** (1)	of world
All commodity groups	4 904 024	100.0	0.07	0.03
845 Articles of apparel nes	1 035 839	21.1	1.11	0.78
071 Coffee and coffee substitutes	357 338	7.3	1.54	0.97
843 Male clothing, knitted crocheted	258 109	5.3	1.14	0.95
061 Sugar, mollasses and honey	230 249	4.7	0.77	0.55
778 Electrical machinery apparatus nes	206 244	4.2	0.20	0.10
642 Cut paper and paperboard articles	177 410	3.6	1.04	0.31
844 Female clothing, knitted crocheted	175 775	3.6	0.46	0.35
893 Articles of plastic nes	162 543	3.3	0.36	0.13
846 Clothing accessory excl. 831 848 851	148 914	3.0	0.89	0.56
048 Cereal & preparation flour starch	133 406	2.7	1.55	0.32
Remainder	2 018 198	41.2		

Equatorial Guinea - Guinée équatoriale (**=Developing) (2)

	Value	of country total	of ** (1)	of world
All commodity groups	11 732 000	100.0	0.17	0.07
333 Crude petroleum & bituminous oil	8 412 015	71.7	0.82	0.59
343 Natural gas, liquefied or not	2 428 169	20.7	1.91	0.96
342 Liquefied propane and butane	294 244	2.5	0.86	0.59
512 Alcohols, phenols; derivatives	153 300	1.3	0.53	0.28
247 Wood in rough or roughly squared	134 033	1.1	3.03	0.94
334 Heavy petroleum & bituminous oil	68 460	0.6	0.02	0.01
793 Ships boats floating structures	55 557	0.5	0.05	0.03
971 Gold non-monetary excluding ores	47 857	0.4	0.05	0.03
511 Hydrocarbons nes; derivatives	19 005	0.2	0.05	0.02
634 Veneer, plywood & other wood nes	9 488	0.1	0.07	0.03
Remainder	109 871	0.9		

Eritrea - Érythrée (**=Developing) (2)

	Value	of country total	of ** (1)	of world
All commodity groups	207 779	100.0	0.00	0.00
971 Gold non-monetary excluding ores	192 092	92.5	0.20	0.10
611 Leather	1 755	0.8	0.01	0.01
681 Silver, platinum, platinum metals	1 327	0.6	0.01	0.00
651 Textile yarn	1 164	0.6	0.00	0.00
841 Male clothing, woven	987	0.5	0.00	0.00
282 Ferrous iron & steel, waste & scrap	928	0.4	0.01	0.00
001 Live animal excl. fish & crustacean	812	0.4	0.02	0.00
075 Spices	679	0.3	0.01	0.01
054 Vegetable & vegetable products nes	506	0.2	0.00	0.00
667 Pearls, precious semiprecious stone	498	0.2	0.00	0.00
Remainder	7 030	3.4		

Estonia - Estonie (**=Developed)

	Value	of country total	of ** (1)	of world
All commodity groups	15 484 833	100.0	0.17	0.09
764 Telecommunicate equipment part nes	1 885 693	12.2	1.16	0.40
334 Heavy petroleum & bituminous oil	1 533 073	9.9	0.44	0.19
821 Furniture part; bedding furnishing	548 370	3.5	0.76	0.40
773 Electrical distribute equipment nes	359 066	2.3	0.68	0.35
772 Electrical circuit equipment	335 204	2.2	0.27	0.15
635 Wood manufactures nes	330 921	2.1	2.19	1.36
248 Wood simply worked, railway sleeper	327 948	2.1	1.36	0.91
781 Passenger cars and race cars	324 279	2.1	0.07	0.05
351 Electric current	299 008	1.9	1.01	0.83
282 Ferrous iron & steel, waste & scrap	295 253	1.9	0.69	0.57
Remainder	9 246 020	59.7		

Ethiopia - Éthiopie (**=Developing)

	Value	of country total	of ** (1)	of world
All commodity groups	2 472 342	100.0	0.03	0.01
071 Coffee and coffee substitutes	773 007	31.3	3.33	2.10
054 Vegetable & vegetable products nes	407 293	16.5	1.75	0.68
222 Oil seed etc for soft oil	329 585	13.3	1.29	0.56
292 Crude vegetable materials nes	192 550	7.8	1.64	0.50
001 Live animal excl. fish & crustacean	161 391	6.5	3.76	0.80
971 Gold non-monetary excluding ores	153 477	6.2	0.16	0.08
611 Leather	94 956	3.8	0.74	0.41
012 Meat nes, fresh chilled frozen	58 296	2.4	0.40	0.09
075 Spices	33 221	1.3	0.56	0.44
223 Oil seed for non soft oil	25 425	1.0	3.55	0.98
Remainder	243 141	9.8		

Faeroe Islands - Îles Féroé (**=Developed) (2)

	Value	of country total	of ** (1)	of world
All commodity groups	911 560	100.0	0.01	0.01
034 Fish, fresh live chilled frozen	627 654	68.9	2.10	1.11
035 Fish, dried salted smoked	87 693	9.6	2.21	1.57
081 Animal feed excluding unmilled cereal	41 338	4.5	0.12	0.06
036 Crustacean mollusc aquat invertebra	32 731	3.6	0.33	0.11
793 Ships boats floating structures	29 079	3.2	0.05	0.02
334 Heavy petroleum & bituminous oil	24 883	2.7	0.01	0.00
291 Crude animal materials nes	20 874	2.3	0.45	0.26
037 Fish shellfish, prepared preserved	4 699	0.5	0.06	0.02
792 Aircraft, spacecraft & equipment	4 662	0.5	0.00	0.00
251 Pulp and waste paper	4 322	0.5	0.01	0.01
Remainder	33 626	3.7		

Falkland Islands (Malvinas) - Îles Falkland (Malvinas) (**=Developing) (2)

	Value	of country total	of ** (1)	of world
All commodity groups	184 605	100.0	0.00	0.00
036 Crustacean mollusc aquat invertebra	95 282	51.6	0.50	0.32
034 Fish, fresh live chilled frozen	46 007	24.9	0.19	0.08
268 Wool & animal hair, incl wool tops	24 550	13.3	0.81	0.34
012 Meat nes, fresh chilled frozen	7 264	3.9	0.05	0.01
874 Measure analyze control device nes	760	0.4	0.00	0.00
897 Jewellery nes (667)	398	0.2	0.00	0.00
342 Liquefied propane and butane	288	0.2	0.00	0.00
713 Internal combustion engine part nes	257	0.1	0.00	0.00
721 Agricultural machine nes excl. tractor	218	0.1	0.00	0.00
699 Base metal manufactures nes	206	0.1	0.00	0.00
Remainder	9 376	5.1		

Fiji - Fidji (**=Developing) (2)

	Value	of country total	of ** (1)	of world
All commodity groups	874 062	100.0	0.01	0.01
334 Heavy petroleum & bituminous oil	106 147	12.1	0.03	0.01
034 Fish, fresh live chilled frozen	100 441	11.5	0.42	0.18
111 Non alcoholic beverage nes	79 193	9.1	1.90	0.43
061 Sugar, mollasses and honey	77 920	8.9	0.26	0.19
971 Gold non-monetary excluding ores	65 470	7.5	0.07	0.03
048 Cereal & preparation flour starch	43 221	4.9	0.50	0.10
037 Fish shellfish, prepared preserved	42 297	4.8	0.27	0.18
841 Male clothing, woven	24 651	2.8	0.05	0.04
046 Wheat meal & flour, meslin flour	22 339	2.6	0.91	0.42
246 Wood chips, particles and waste	21 025	2.4	1.11	0.37
Remainder	291 356	33.3		

Finland - Finlande (**=Developed)

	Value	of country total	of ** (1)	of world
All commodity groups	74 455 360	100.0	0.84	0.45
641 Paper and paperboard	9 819 599	13.2	10.32	8.26
334 Heavy petroleum & bituminous oil	6 085 715	8.2	1.74	0.76
675 Flat rolled products of alloy steel	3 281 986	4.4	6.97	4.88
764 Telecommunicate equipment part nes	3 241 127	4.4	1.99	0.68
251 Pulp and waste paper	1 792 644	2.4	5.27	3.81
728 Special industrial machine part nes	1 660 538	2.2	1.23	0.96
248 Wood simply worked, railway sleeper	1 648 586	2.2	6.83	4.59
716 Rotating electric plant parts nes	1 638 705	2.2	2.93	1.89
679 Iron steel pipe tube fittings etc	1 414 401	1.9	2.83	1.64
723 Civil engineering plant & equipment	1 412 582	1.9	1.85	1.29
Remainder	42 459 476	57.0		

For sources and notes, see end of table.

Pour les sources et les notes, se reporter à la fin du tableau.

3

Leading products exported based on average 2010-2011 values SITC Revision 3 (3-digit level) / Principaux produits exportés d'après la moyenne des valeurs de 2010-2011 CTCI révision 3 (positions à 3 chiffres)	Value (f.o.b., thousands of dollars) Valeur (f.a.b., milliers de dollars)	2010-2011 As percentage En pourcentage — of country total du total du pays	of ** (1) des ** (1)	of world du monde
France (**=Developed)				
All commodity groups	546 596 457	100.0	6.17	3.28
792 Aircraft, spacecraft & equipment	48 090 825	8.8	39.82	33.71
542 Medicines including veterinary	27 197 374	5.0	8.91	8.20
781 Passenger cars and race cars	22 126 063	4.0	4.49	3.70
784 Motor vehicle parts and accessories	18 755 110	3.4	7.66	5.69
334 Heavy petroleum & bituminous oil	14 611 270	2.7	4.18	1.82
112 Alcoholic beverages	13 817 380	2.5	24.85	19.94
553 Perfume toilet cosmetics, excl. soap	13 259 252	2.4	24.15	18.49
776 Valves tubes; diodes, transistors	10 134 036	1.9	6.22	1.83
714 Non-electric engines excl. 712 713 718	10 077 061	1.8	14.82	12.30
772 Electrical circuit equipment	9 430 742	1.7	7.63	4.32
Remainder	359 097 344	65.7		
French Polynesia - Polynésie française (**=Developing)				
All commodity groups	151 504	100.0	0.00	0.00
667 Pearls, precious semiprecious stone	79 661	52.6	0.11	0.05
793 Ships boats floating structures	9 723	6.4	0.01	0.01
792 Aircraft, spacecraft & equipment	7 391	4.9	0.03	0.01
034 Fish, fresh live chilled frozen	6 960	4.6	0.03	0.01
058 Fruit preserve preparation excl. juice	6 779	4.5	0.08	0.04
422 Fixed veg fat and oil, excl. "soft"	6 088	4.0	0.02	0.01
897 Jewellery nes (667)	4 920	3.2	0.01	0.00
714 Non-electric engines excl. 712 713 718	4 523	3.0	0.04	0.01
291 Crude animal materials nes	2 985	2.0	0.09	0.04
553 Perfume toilet cosmetics, excl. soap	2 648	1.7	0.02	0.00
Remainder	19 825	13.1		
Gabon (**=Developing) (2)				
All commodity groups	10 165 547	100.0	0.14	0.06
333 Crude petroleum & bituminous oil	7 615 734	74.9	0.74	0.53
247 Wood in rough or roughly squared	791 151	7.8	17.91	5.53
287 Base metal ores & concentrates nes	711 301	7.0	3.89	2.29
334 Heavy petroleum & bituminous oil	222 453	2.2	0.06	0.03
634 Veneer, plywood & other wood nes	180 784	1.8	1.33	0.56
793 Ships boats floating structures	145 433	1.4	0.13	0.08
248 Wood simply worked, railway sleeper	137 713	1.4	1.81	0.38
231 Natural rubber, latex, gum, etc	102 767	1.0	0.34	0.32
792 Aircraft, spacecraft & equipment	26 786	0.3	0.13	0.02
122 Manufactured tabacco	21 902	0.2	0.29	0.08
Remainder	209 523	2.1		
Gambia - Gambie (**=Developing)				
All commodity groups	64 858	100.0	0.00	0.00
057 Fruit nut (exc oil), fresh or dried	13 343	20.6	0.03	0.02
247 Wood in rough or roughly squared	8 743	13.5	0.20	0.06
287 Base metal ores & concentrates nes	7 498	11.6	0.04	0.02
421 Fixed veg fat and oil, "soft"	5 363	8.3	0.05	0.02
653 Man-made woven fabrics	4 454	6.9	0.02	0.01
034 Fish, fresh live chilled frozen	4 223	6.5	0.02	0.01
282 Ferrous iron & steel, waste & scrap	3 624	5.6	0.06	0.01
222 Oil seed etc for soft oil	2 985	4.6	0.01	0.01
288 Non ferrous base metal waste nes	1 349	2.1	0.01	0.00
035 Fish, dried salted smoked	1 032	1.6	0.07	0.02
Remainder	12 244	18.9		
Georgia - Géorgie (**=Transition) (2)				
All commodity groups	1 887 509	100.0	0.27	0.01
671 Pig & sponge iron, ferro alloys etc	292 952	15.5	3.09	0.72
781 Passenger cars and race cars	240 533	12.7	10.60	0.04
112 Alcoholic beverages	128 007	6.8	9.64	0.18
282 Ferrous iron & steel, waste & scrap	102 209	5.4	4.04	0.20
057 Fruit nut (exc oil), fresh or dried	94 578	5.0	5.81	0.12
283 Copper ores and concentrates	91 880	4.9	8.48	0.18
971 Gold non-monetary excluding ores	86 422	4.6	5.46	0.05
562 Manufactured fertilizer excl. crude	71 099	3.8	0.51	0.11
288 Non ferrous base metal waste nes	65 262	3.5	9.59	0.15
111 Non alcoholic beverage nes	64 306	3.4	14.43	0.35
Remainder	650 261	34.5		
Germany - Allemagne (**=Developed)				
All commodity groups	1 376 649 302	100.0	15.54	8.27
781 Passenger cars and race cars	141 480 315	10.3	28.70	23.64
784 Motor vehicle parts and accessories	49 678 308	3.6	20.29	15.07
542 Medicines including veterinary	45 359 767	3.3	14.85	13.67
792 Aircraft, spacecraft & equipment	33 721 894	2.4	27.92	23.64
772 Electrical circuit equipment	30 022 161	2.2	24.30	13.76
874 Measure analyze control device nes	28 816 833	2.1	22.12	17.32
728 Special industrial machine part nes	25 728 056	1.9	18.98	14.82
713 Internal combustion engine part nes	24 534 515	1.8	20.69	16.26
541 Pharmaceuticals excluding medicines	22 381 114	1.6	17.54	15.34
776 Valves tubes; diodes, transistors	21 148 831	1.5	12.99	3.83
Remainder	953 777 509	69.3		
Ghana (**=Developing) (2)				
All commodity groups	10 330 040	100.0	0.15	0.06
072 Cocoa	3 984 797	38.6	27.56	18.35
333 Crude petroleum & bituminous oil	1 823 965	17.7	0.18	0.13
971 Gold non-monetary excluding ores	887 364	8.6	0.92	0.47
287 Base metal ores & concentrates nes	410 144	4.0	2.24	1.32
057 Fruit nut (exc oil), fresh or dried	382 419	3.7	0.97	0.48
342 Liquefied propane and butane	277 445	2.7	0.81	0.55
334 Heavy petroleum & bituminous oil	183 797	1.8	0.05	0.02
037 Fish shellfish, prepared preserved	182 751	1.8	1.15	0.78
248 Wood simply worked, railway sleeper	158 477	1.5	2.09	0.44
634 Veneer, plywood & other wood nes	155 610	1.5	1.15	0.48
Remainder	1 883 268	18.2		
Gibraltar (**=Developed)				
All commodity groups	252 385	100.0	0.00	0.00
334 Heavy petroleum & bituminous oil	141 848	56.2	0.04	0.02
793 Ships boats floating structures	65 026	25.8	0.11	0.04
781 Passenger cars and race cars	13 549	5.4	0.00	0.00
714 Non-electric engines excl. 712 713 718	5 672	2.2	0.01	0.01
792 Aircraft, spacecraft & equipment	3 736	1.5	0.00	0.00
778 Electrical machinery apparatus nes	2 700	1.1	0.00	0.00
683 Nickel	1 980	0.8	0.01	0.01
885 Watches and clocks	1 378	0.5	0.01	0.00
671 Pig & sponge iron, ferro alloys etc	1 101	0.4	0.01	0.00
335 Residual petroleum products nes	780	0.3	0.00	0.00
Remainder	14 615	5.8		
Greece - Grèce (**=Developed)				
All commodity groups	26 730 530	100.0	0.30	0.16
334 Heavy petroleum & bituminous oil	5 608 927	21.0	1.60	0.70
684 Aluminium	1 256 204	4.7	1.79	1.08
542 Medicines including veterinary	1 246 733	4.7	0.41	0.38
057 Fruit nut (exc oil), fresh or dried	862 396	3.2	2.20	1.07
034 Fish, fresh live chilled frozen	665 099	2.5	2.22	1.18
676 Iron steel bar rod section piling	582 935	2.2	1.16	0.69
682 Copper	579 026	2.2	1.02	0.41
056 Vegetables roots tubers nes	550 570	2.1	3.05	1.99
058 Fruit preserve preparation excl. juice	465 620	1.7	5.50	2.71
263 Cotton	434 437	1.6	4.41	1.93
Remainder	14 478 583	54.2		
Greenland - Groenland (**=Developed) (2)				
All commodity groups	431 704	100.0	0.00	0.00
036 Crustacean mollusc aquat invertebra	148 368	34.4	1.50	0.50
034 Fish, fresh live chilled frozen	119 573	27.7	0.40	0.21
037 Fish shellfish, prepared preserved	104 533	24.2	1.42	0.44
289 Prec metal ore concentrate excl. gold	25 219	5.8	0.20	0.13
035 Fish, dried salted smoked	5 910	1.4	0.15	0.11
689 Misc non-ferrous base metals	4 988	1.2	0.10	0.05
793 Ships boats floating structures	4 313	1.0	0.01	0.00
772 Electrical circuit equipment	4 170	1.0	0.00	0.00
273 Stone, sand and gravel	2 291	0.5	0.05	0.02
291 Crude animal materials nes	1 641	0.4	0.04	0.02
Remainder	10 697	2.5		

For sources and notes, see end of table.

Pour les sources et les notes, se reporter à la fin du tableau.

Leading products exported based on average 2010-2011 values SITC Revision 3 (3-digit level) / Principaux produits exportés d'après la moyenne des valeurs de 2010-2011 CTCI révision 3 (positions à 3 chiffres)	2010-2011 Value (f.o.b., thousands of dollars) / Valeur (f.a.b., milliers de dollars)	As percentage / En pourcentage: of country total / du total du pays	of ** (1) / des ** (1)	of world / du monde
Grenada - Grenade (=Developing) (2)**				
All commodity groups	25 871	100.0	0.00	0.00
046 Wheat meal & flour, meslin flour	3 266	12.6	0.13	0.06
793 Ships boats floating structures	2 479	9.6	0.00	0.00
684 Aluminium	2 376	9.2	0.01	0.00
581 Plastic tube pipe hose & fittings	2 184	8.4	0.05	0.01
075 Spices	1 914	7.4	0.03	0.03
034 Fish, fresh live chilled frozen	1 625	6.3	0.01	0.00
892 Printed matter	1 495	5.8	0.01	0.00
642 Cut paper and paperboard articles	1 057	4.1	0.01	0.00
081 Animal feed excluding unmilled cereal	1 007	3.9	0.00	0.00
748 Mechanical transmission equipment	777	3.0	0.01	0.00
Remainder	7 690	29.7		
Guam (=Developing) (2)**				
All commodity groups	44 500	100.0	0.00	0.00
282 Ferrous iron & steel, waste & scrap	8 814	19.8	0.14	0.02
288 Non ferrous base metal waste nes	2 620	5.9	0.03	0.01
034 Fish, fresh live chilled frozen	1 998	4.5	0.01	0.00
831 Case bag: storage travel shopping	1 875	4.2	0.01	0.00
713 Internal combustion engine part nes	1 587	3.6	0.00	0.00
885 Watches and clocks	1 431	3.2	0.01	0.00
897 Jewellery nes (667)	908	2.0	0.00	0.00
781 Passenger cars and race cars	550	1.2	0.00	0.00
776 Valves tubes; diodes, transistors	520	1.2	0.00	0.00
612 Leather manufactures nes	446	1.0	0.03	0.01
Remainder	23 752	53.4		
Guatemala (=Developing)**				
All commodity groups	9 310 597	100.0	0.13	0.06
071 Coffee and coffee substitutes	966 751	10.4	4.17	2.62
061 Sugar, mollasses and honey	850 151	9.1	2.84	2.02
057 Fruit nut (exc oil), fresh or dried	790 648	8.5	2.00	0.98
845 Articles of apparel nes	465 942	5.0	0.50	0.35
289 Prec metal ore concentrate excl. gold	338 507	3.6	5.77	1.81
844 Female clothing, knitted crocheted	325 082	3.5	0.85	0.66
075 Spices	310 486	3.3	5.26	4.13
231 Natural rubber, latex, gum, etc	310 001	3.3	1.02	0.96
333 Crude petroleum & bituminous oil	268 129	2.9	0.03	0.02
842 Female clothing, woven	218 312	2.3	0.42	0.28
Remainder	4 466 586	48.0		
Guinea - Guinée (=Developing) (2)**				
All commodity groups	1 547 722	100.0	0.02	0.01
285 Aluminium ore concentrate alumina	598 512	38.7	10.00	4.08
343 Natural gas, liquefied or not	391 845	25.3	0.31	0.16
333 Crude petroleum & bituminous oil	197 368	12.8	0.02	0.01
971 Gold non-monetary excluding ores	60 079	3.9	0.06	0.03
283 Copper ores and concentrates	31 477	2.0	0.08	0.06
071 Coffee and coffee substitutes	26 121	1.7	0.11	0.07
231 Natural rubber, latex, gum, etc	21 814	1.4	0.07	0.07
072 Cocoa	20 042	1.3	0.14	0.09
034 Fish, fresh live chilled frozen	17 098	1.1	0.07	0.03
667 Pearls, precious semiprecious stone	16 439	1.1	0.02	0.01
Remainder	166 928	10.8		
Guinea-Bissau - Guinée-Bissau (=Developing) (2)**				
All commodity groups	182 468	100.0	0.00	0.00
057 Fruit nut (exc oil), fresh or dried	164 380	90.1	0.42	0.20
333 Crude petroleum & bituminous oil	10 895	6.0	0.00	0.00
247 Wood in rough or roughly squared	1 017	0.6	0.02	0.01
282 Ferrous iron & steel, waste & scrap	953	0.5	0.02	0.00
672 Ingots, Iron steel primary products	844	0.5	0.01	0.00
263 Cotton	659	0.4	0.01	0.00
036 Crustacean mollusc aquat invertebra	293	0.2	0.00	0.00
725 Paper & pulp mill, cut manufacture	282	0.2	0.02	0.00
034 Fish, fresh live chilled frozen	274	0.2	0.00	0.00
231 Natural rubber, latex, gum, etc	254	0.1	0.00	0.00
Remainder	2 616	1.4		

Leading products exported based on average 2010-2011 values SITC Revision 3 (3-digit level) / Principaux produits exportés d'après la moyenne des valeurs de 2010-2011 CTCI révision 3 (positions à 3 chiffres)	2010-2011 Value (f.o.b., thousands of dollars) / Valeur (f.a.b., milliers de dollars)	As percentage / En pourcentage: of country total / du total du pays	of ** (1) / des ** (1)	of world / du monde
Guyana (=Developing)**				
All commodity groups	992 702	100.0	0.01	0.01
971 Gold non-monetary excluding ores	402 585	40.6	0.42	0.21
061 Sugar, mollasses and honey	119 922	12.1	0.40	0.28
285 Aluminium ore concentrate alumina	114 406	11.5	1.91	0.78
042 Rice	110 250	11.1	0.62	0.50
248 Wood simply worked, railway sleeper	46 600	4.7	0.61	0.13
112 Alcoholic beverages	29 964	3.0	0.24	0.04
036 Crustacean mollusc aquat invertebra	29 754	3.0	0.15	0.10
034 Fish, fresh live chilled frozen	20 443	2.1	0.08	0.04
786 Trailer caravan transport container	19 160	1.9	0.14	0.06
247 Wood in rough or roughly squared	11 828	1.2	0.27	0.08
Remainder	87 790	8.8		
Haiti - Haïti (=Developing) (2)**				
All commodity groups	677 639	100.0	0.01	0.00
845 Articles of apparel nes	352 124	52.0	0.38	0.26
844 Female clothing, knitted crocheted	67 297	9.9	0.18	0.14
843 Male clothing, knitted crocheted	50 454	7.4	0.22	0.19
841 Male clothing, woven	40 245	5.9	0.09	0.06
057 Fruit nut (exc oil), fresh or dried	22 236	3.3	0.06	0.03
773 Electrical distribute equipment nes	16 417	2.4	0.03	0.02
658 Made-up textile articles nes	14 114	2.1	0.04	0.03
846 Clothing accessory excl. 831 848 851	12 985	1.9	0.08	0.05
072 Cocoa	11 789	1.7	0.08	0.05
071 Coffee and coffee substitutes	10 515	1.6	0.05	0.03
Remainder	79 463	11.7		
Honduras (=Developing) (2)**				
All commodity groups	6 473 110	100.0	0.09	0.04
845 Articles of apparel nes	1 204 185	18.6	1.29	0.91
071 Coffee and coffee substitutes	827 345	12.8	3.57	2.25
057 Fruit nut (exc oil), fresh or dried	480 882	7.4	1.22	0.60
773 Electrical distribute equipment nes	380 944	5.9	0.80	0.37
843 Male clothing, knitted crocheted	285 128	4.4	1.26	1.05
422 Fixed veg fat and oil, excl. "soft"	241 698	3.7	0.61	0.54
971 Gold non-monetary excluding ores	232 685	3.6	0.24	0.12
841 Male clothing, woven	210 647	3.3	0.47	0.32
844 Female clothing, knitted crocheted	205 257	3.2	0.54	0.41
036 Crustacean mollusc aquat invertebra	205 139	3.2	1.07	0.70
Remainder	2 199 199	34.0		
Hungary - Hongrie (=Developed)**				
All commodity groups	102 908 790	100.0	1.16	0.62
764 Telecommunicate equipment part nes	13 268 085	12.9	8.13	2.79
713 Internal combustion engine part nes	6 335 473	6.2	5.34	4.20
761 Television video receive project	5 260 003	5.1	12.70	5.32
781 Passenger cars and race cars	4 514 239	4.4	0.92	0.75
784 Motor vehicle parts and accessories	3 947 885	3.8	1.61	1.20
542 Medicines including veterinary	3 232 335	3.1	1.06	0.97
752 Computer equipment nes	3 119 972	3.0	3.12	0.93
772 Electrical circuit equipment	2 928 952	2.8	2.37	1.34
874 Measure analyze control device nes	2 275 621	2.2	1.75	1.37
778 Electrical machinery apparatus nes	2 263 899	2.2	2.09	1.07
Remainder	55 762 326	54.2		
Iceland - Islande (=Developed)**				
All commodity groups	4 974 360	100.0	0.06	0.03
684 Aluminium	2 009 938	40.4	2.86	1.73
034 Fish, fresh live chilled frozen	1 288 599	25.9	4.30	2.29
035 Fish, dried salted smoked	360 380	7.2	9.07	6.46
671 Pig & sponge iron, ferro alloys etc	186 872	3.8	1.98	0.46
081 Animal feed excluding unmilled cereal	134 544	2.7	0.38	0.21
542 Medicines including veterinary	125 028	2.5	0.04	0.04
411 Animals oils and fats	88 703	1.8	1.91	1.60
036 Crustacean mollusc aquat invertebra	79 698	1.6	0.80	0.27
037 Fish shellfish, prepared preserved	77 316	1.6	1.05	0.33
334 Heavy petroleum & bituminous oil	75 341	1.5	0.02	0.01
Remainder	547 940	11.0		

For sources and notes, see end of table.

Pour les sources et les notes, se reporter à la fin du tableau.

Leading products exported based on average 2010-2011 values SITC Revision 3 (3-digit level) / Principaux produits exportés d'après la moyenne des valeurs de 2010-2011 CTCI révision 3 (positions à 3 chiffres)	2010-2011			
	Value (f.o.b., thousands of dollars) / Valeur (f.a.b., milliers de dollars)	As percentage / En pourcentage		
		of country total / du total du pays	of ** (1) / des ** (1)	of world / du monde
India - Inde (=Developing)**				
All commodity groups	260 945 873	100.0	3.68	1.57
334 Heavy petroleum & bituminous oil	45 626 194	17.5	12.86	5.67
667 Pearls, precious semiprecious stone	27 590 698	10.6	36.68	18.76
897 Jewellery nes (667)	12 757 206	4.9	23.28	13.73
542 Medicines including veterinary	6 720 641	2.6	26.85	2.03
793 Ships boats floating structures	5 635 805	2.2	4.91	3.18
281 Iron ore and concentrates	5 153 095	2.0	9.04	4.12
651 Textile yarn	4 740 173	1.8	13.32	8.48
781 Passenger cars and race cars	4 067 726	1.6	3.94	0.68
842 Female clothing, woven	3 925 380	1.5	7.62	5.01
682 Copper	3 915 843	1.5	5.36	2.80
Remainder	140 813 113	54.0		
Indonesia - Indonésie (=Developing)**				
All commodity groups	180 637 861	100.0	2.55	1.08
321 Coal excluding non-agglomomerated	21 835 705	12.1	53.34	18.49
422 Fixed veg fat and oil, excl. "soft"	18 047 631	10.0	45.20	40.39
343 Natural gas, liquefied or not	18 022 645	10.0	14.14	7.14
333 Crude petroleum & bituminous oil	12 115 773	6.7	1.18	0.85
231 Natural rubber, latex, gum, etc	9 547 651	5.3	31.32	29.67
283 Copper ores and concentrates	5 791 263	3.2	15.28	11.62
641 Paper and paperboard	3 721 789	2.1	17.80	3.13
682 Copper	3 345 769	1.9	4.58	2.39
851 Footwear	2 901 896	1.6	4.55	2.78
334 Heavy petroleum & bituminous oil	2 546 338	1.4	0.72	0.32
Remainder	82 761 403	45.8		
Iran (Islamic Rep. of) - Iran (Rép. islamique d') (=Developing) (2)**				
All commodity groups	116 246 890	100.0	1.64	0.70
333 Crude petroleum & bituminous oil	84 142 176	72.4	8.22	5.91
334 Heavy petroleum & bituminous oil	4 630 285	4.0	1.30	0.58
342 Liquefied propane and butane	2 391 909	2.1	7.01	4.78
511 Hydrocarbons nes; derivatives	1 859 589	1.6	5.28	2.16
571 Primary form ethylene polymers	1 812 966	1.6	5.52	2.51
281 Iron ore and concentrates	1 778 192	1.5	3.12	1.42
512 Alcohols, phenols; derivatives	1 666 002	1.4	5.75	2.99
057 Fruit nut (exc oil), fresh or dried	1 519 762	1.3	3.85	1.89
682 Copper	703 303	0.6	0.96	0.50
344 Petroleum and hydrocarbon gas nes	669 877	0.6	7.50	4.61
Remainder	15 072 832	13.0		
Iraq (=Developing) (2)**				
All commodity groups	69 329 022	100.0	0.98	0.42
333 Crude petroleum & bituminous oil	67 767 286	97.7	6.62	4.76
334 Heavy petroleum & bituminous oil	510 613	0.7	0.14	0.06
971 Gold non-monetary excluding ores	172 904	0.2	0.18	0.09
598 Miscellaneous chemical products nes	126 417	0.2	0.46	0.11
525 Radio active & associated materials	104 829	0.2	3.83	0.55
057 Fruit nut (exc oil), fresh or dried	89 262	0.1	0.23	0.11
274 Sulphur and unroasted iron pyrites	72 127	0.1	3.20	1.71
511 Hydrocarbons nes; derivatives	55 843	0.1	0.16	0.06
522 Inorganic chemical elem oxide salt	40 647	0.1	0.15	0.07
728 Special industrial machine part nes	40 354	0.1	0.11	0.02
Remainder	348 740	0.5		
Ireland - Irlande (=Developed)**				
All commodity groups	123 841 995	100.0	1.40	0.74
542 Medicines including veterinary	25 084 975	20.3	8.21	7.56
515 Organo-inorganic compound acid salt	23 652 341	19.1	27.86	22.31
541 Pharmaceuticals excluding medicines	9 513 697	7.7	7.46	6.52
551 Essential oils, perfumes & flavours	6 716 525	5.4	36.28	29.18
899 Manufactured articles nes	4 774 190	3.9	9.53	6.31
872 Medical instruments appliances nes	3 601 760	2.9	5.52	4.34
752 Computer equipment nes	3 424 250	2.8	3.42	1.02
598 Miscellaneous chemical products nes	3 184 454	2.6	3.53	2.68
776 Valves tubes; diodes, transistors	2 535 806	2.0	1.56	0.46
759 Office equipment part & accessories	2 401 819	1.9	3.03	1.21
Remainder	38 952 178	31.5		

Leading products exported based on average 2010-2011 values SITC Revision 3 (3-digit level) / Principaux produits exportés d'après la moyenne des valeurs de 2010-2011 CTCI révision 3 (positions à 3 chiffres)	2010-2011			
	Value (f.o.b., thousands of dollars) / Valeur (f.a.b., milliers de dollars)	As percentage / En pourcentage		
		of country total / du total du pays	of ** (1) / des ** (1)	of world / du monde
Israel - Israël (=Developed)**				
All commodity groups	63 104 678	100.0	0.71	0.38
667 Pearls, precious semiprecious stone	17 793 833	28.2	25.95	12.10
542 Medicines including veterinary	7 427 990	11.8	2.43	2.24
764 Telecommunicate equipment part nes	2 624 879	4.2	1.61	0.55
562 Manufactured fertilizer excl. crude	2 014 336	3.2	7.01	3.10
776 Valves tubes; diodes, transistors	1 976 959	3.1	1.21	0.36
874 Measure analyze control device nes	1 747 169	2.8	1.34	1.05
334 Heavy petroleum & bituminous oil	1 702 202	2.7	0.49	0.21
598 Miscellaneous chemical products nes	1 629 188	2.6	1.81	1.37
778 Electrical machinery apparatus nes	1 012 049	1.6	0.94	0.48
772 Electrical circuit equipment	891 138	1.4	0.72	0.41
Remainder	24 284 935	38.5		
Italy - Italie (=Developed)**				
All commodity groups	485 009 449	100.0	5.47	2.91
334 Heavy petroleum & bituminous oil	20 163 607	4.2	5.76	2.51
542 Medicines including veterinary	15 580 265	3.2	5.10	4.70
784 Motor vehicle parts and accessories	14 458 441	3.0	5.91	4.39
728 Special industrial machine part nes	12 626 265	2.6	9.31	7.28
821 Furniture part; bedding furnishing	11 012 909	2.3	15.17	7.97
851 Footwear	10 633 455	2.2	27.24	10.19
699 Base metal manufactures nes	9 710 368	2.0	11.46	7.35
741 Heating cooling equipment parts nes	8 932 731	1.8	13.90	8.66
781 Passenger cars and race cars	8 827 214	1.8	1.79	1.48
745 Non-electrical machinery tool nes	8 105 339	1.7	20.07	15.63
Remainder	364 958 857	75.2		
Jamaica - Jamaïque (=Developing) (2)**				
All commodity groups	1 465 306	100.0	0.02	0.01
285 Aluminium ore concentrate alumina	592 518	40.4	9.90	4.04
334 Heavy petroleum & bituminous oil	270 690	18.5	0.08	0.03
112 Alcoholic beverages	82 980	5.7	0.67	0.12
512 Alcohols, phenols; derivatives	71 381	4.9	0.25	0.13
061 Sugar, mollasses and honey	52 201	3.6	0.17	0.12
282 Ferrous iron & steel, waste & scrap	25 812	1.8	0.42	0.05
071 Coffee and coffee substitutes	25 686	1.8	0.11	0.07
098 Edible products & preparations nes	24 207	1.7	0.16	0.04
752 Computer equipment nes	24 090	1.6	0.01	0.01
054 Vegetable & vegetable products nes	23 880	1.6	0.10	0.04
Remainder	271 859	18.6		
Japan - Japon (=Developed)**				
All commodity groups	796 565 920	100.0	8.99	4.78
781 Passenger cars and race cars	88 862 098	11.2	18.03	14.85
776 Valves tubes; diodes, transistors	46 075 345	5.8	28.30	8.34
784 Motor vehicle parts and accessories	37 319 648	4.7	15.24	11.32
728 Special industrial machine part nes	34 130 008	4.3	25.18	19.67
793 Ships boats floating structures	26 047 962	3.3	43.77	14.70
778 Electrical machinery apparatus nes	22 476 275	2.8	20.79	10.61
772 Electrical circuit equipment	20 569 697	2.6	16.65	9.43
713 Internal combustion engine part nes	19 837 092	2.5	16.73	13.15
874 Measure analyze control device nes	17 678 490	2.2	13.57	10.63
759 Office equipment part & accessories	14 832 431	1.9	18.69	7.45
Remainder	468 736 874	58.8		
Jordan - Jordanie (=Developing)**				
All commodity groups	7 493 312	100.0	0.11	0.05
562 Manufactured fertilizer excl. crude	1 103 094	14.7	4.97	1.70
542 Medicines including veterinary	632 254	8.4	2.53	0.19
845 Articles of apparel nes	612 074	8.2	0.66	0.46
272 Crude fertilizer, excl. manufactured	594 262	7.9	19.56	14.30
054 Vegetable & vegetable products nes	385 057	5.1	1.65	0.64
971 Gold non-monetary excluding ores	222 666	3.0	0.23	0.12
522 Inorganic chemical elem oxide salt	197 086	2.6	0.75	0.34
773 Electrical distribute equipment nes	175 203	2.3	0.37	0.17
523 Inorganic acid metal salt peroxy	155 587	2.1	1.81	0.76
842 Female clothing, woven	128 718	1.7	0.25	0.16
Remainder	3 287 309	43.9		

For sources and notes, see end of table.

Pour les sources et les notes, se reporter à la fin du tableau.

3.2.D Export structure by product
Individual countries and territories

3.2.D Structure des exportations par produits
Pays et territoires individuels

Leading products exported based on average 2010-2011 values SITC Revision 3 (3-digit level) / Principaux produits exportés d'après la moyenne des valeurs de 2010-2011 CTCI révision 3 (positions à 3 chiffres)	Value (f.o.b., thousands of dollars) Valeur (f.a.b., milliers de dollars)	of country total du total du pays	of ** (1) des ** (1)	of world du monde
Kazakhstan (**=Transition) (2)				
All commodity groups	71 053 887	100.0	10.18	0.43
333 Crude petroleum & bituminous oil	45 066 716	63.4	20.14	3.17
682 Copper	2 759 885	3.9	27.66	1.97
671 Pig & sponge iron, ferro alloys etc	2 612 571	3.7	27.56	6.39
525 Radio active & associated materials	2 535 737	3.6	62.57	13.33
334 Heavy petroleum & bituminous oil	2 081 504	2.9	2.09	0.26
343 Natural gas, liquefied or not	1 922 674	2.7	5.81	0.76
281 Iron ore and concentrates	1 257 327	1.8	18.07	1.01
041 Wheat meslin, incl spelt, unmilled	1 131 054	1.6	21.57	2.79
673 Flat iron non-alloy steel products	1 001 671	1.4	9.40	1.13
971 Gold non-monetary excluding ores	824 414	1.2	52.09	0.44
Remainder	9 860 333	13.9		
Kenya (**=Developing) (2)				
All commodity groups	5 471 978	100.0	0.08	0.03
074 Tea and maté	1 005 130	18.4	17.12	12.83
292 Crude vegetable materials nes	669 976	12.2	5.71	1.73
054 Vegetable & vegetable products nes	280 299	5.1	1.20	0.46
071 Coffee and coffee substitutes	278 563	5.1	1.20	0.76
334 Heavy petroleum & bituminous oil	232 305	4.2	0.07	0.03
523 Inorganic acid metal salt peroxy	110 569	2.0	1.28	0.54
122 Manufactured tabacco	97 011	1.8	1.29	0.34
554 Soaps cleansers polishes	96 932	1.8	0.94	0.26
661 Lime cement construction material	92 078	1.7	0.59	0.34
893 Articles of plastic nes	88 251	1.6	0.19	0.07
Remainder	2 520 864	46.1		
Kiribati (**=Developing) (2)				
All commodity groups	17 500	100.0	0.00	0.00
034 Fish, fresh live chilled frozen	12 346	70.5	0.05	0.02
422 Fixed veg fat and oil, excl. "soft"	1 115	6.4	0.00	0.00
793 Ships boats floating structures	693	4.0	0.00	0.00
728 Special industrial machine part nes	286	1.6	0.00	0.00
036 Crustacean mollusc aquat invertebra	238	1.4	0.00	0.00
786 Trailer caravan transport container	145	0.8	0.00	0.00
081 Animal feed excluding unmilled cereal	113	0.6	0.00	0.00
541 Pharmaceuticals excluding medicines	98	0.6	0.00	0.00
573 Vinyl chloride etc polymers	92	0.5	0.00	0.00
872 Medical instruments appliances nes	91	0.5	0.00	0.00
Remainder	2 283	13.0		
Korea, Dem. People's Rep. of - Corée, Rép. populaire dém. de (**=Developing) (2)				
All commodity groups	3 127 500	100.0	0.04	0.02
321 Coal excluding non-agglomomerated	882 883	28.2	2.16	0.75
281 Iron ore and concentrates	295 906	9.5	0.52	0.24
841 Male clothing, woven	175 552	5.6	0.39	0.27
842 Female clothing, woven	131 715	4.2	0.26	0.17
671 Pig & sponge iron, ferro alloys etc	122 193	3.9	0.56	0.30
036 Crustacean mollusc aquat invertebra	76 617	2.4	0.40	0.26
781 Passenger cars and race cars	76 564	2.4	0.07	0.01
845 Articles of apparel nes	68 913	2.2	0.07	0.05
334 Heavy petroleum & bituminous oil	68 665	2.2	0.02	0.01
686 Zinc	65 158	2.1	1.48	0.50
Remainder	1 163 333	37.2		
Korea, Republic of - Corée, République de (**=Developing)				
All commodity groups	510 794 759	100.0	7.20	3.07
793 Ships boats floating structures	50 434 211	9.9	43.97	28.45
776 Valves tubes; diodes, transistors	44 272 768	8.7	11.37	8.01
334 Heavy petroleum & bituminous oil	40 267 217	7.9	11.35	5.01
781 Passenger cars and race cars	36 345 793	7.1	35.20	6.07
764 Telecommunicate equipment part nes	35 341 943	6.9	11.35	7.43
871 Optical instruments apparatus nes	28 912 566	5.7	35.66	28.83
784 Motor vehicle parts and accessories	19 775 623	3.9	23.62	6.00
778 Electrical machinery apparatus nes	11 910 112	2.3	11.62	5.62
673 Flat iron non-alloy steel products	9 563 520	1.9	33.25	10.83
511 Hydrocarbons nes; derivatives	9 420 823	1.8	26.76	10.93
Remainder	224 550 133	44.0		

Leading products exported based on average 2010-2011 values SITC Revision 3 (3-digit level) / Principaux produits exportés d'après la moyenne des valeurs de 2010-2011 CTCI révision 3 (positions à 3 chiffres)	Value (f.o.b., thousands of dollars) Valeur (f.a.b., milliers de dollars)	of country total du total du pays	of ** (1) des ** (1)	of world du monde
Kuwait - Koweït (**=Developing) (2)				
All commodity groups	82 070 653	100.0	1.16	0.49
333 Crude petroleum & bituminous oil	59 965 082	73.1	5.86	4.21
334 Heavy petroleum & bituminous oil	12 125 199	14.8	3.42	1.51
342 Liquefied propane and butane	2 553 573	3.1	7.49	5.10
571 Primary form ethylene polymers	2 186 099	2.7	6.65	3.03
512 Alcohols, phenols; derivatives	848 288	1.0	2.93	1.52
562 Manufactured fertilizer excl. crude	576 068	0.7	2.59	0.89
274 Sulphur and unroasted iron pyrites	340 226	0.4	15.07	8.06
781 Passenger cars and race cars	329 411	0.4	0.32	0.06
575 Other plastics, in primary forms	238 146	0.3	0.71	0.22
282 Ferrous iron & steel, waste & scrap	169 119	0.2	2.73	0.33
Remainder	2 739 441	3.3		
Kyrgyzstan - Kirghizistan (**=Transition) (2)				
All commodity groups	1 869 366	100.0	0.27	0.01
971 Gold non-monetary excluding ores	190 446	10.2	12.03	0.10
334 Heavy petroleum & bituminous oil	153 248	8.2	0.15	0.02
842 Female clothing, woven	132 903	7.1	11.84	0.17
054 Vegetable & vegetable products nes	111 372	6.0	9.89	0.18
351 Electric current	101 039	5.4	4.42	0.28
057 Fruit nut (exc oil), fresh or dried	75 458	4.0	4.64	0.09
525 Radio active & associated materials	68 344	3.7	1.69	0.36
778 Electrical machinery apparatus nes	55 655	3.0	4.38	0.03
782 Goods and service vehicles	54 323	2.9	2.64	0.05
282 Ferrous iron & steel, waste & scrap	50 209	2.7	1.98	0.10
Remainder	876 368	46.9		
Lao People's Dem. Rep. - Rép. dém. populaire lao (**=Developing) (2)				
All commodity groups	2 073 185	100.0	0.03	0.01
682 Copper	493 269	23.8	0.67	0.35
283 Copper ores and concentrates	438 612	21.2	1.16	0.88
351 Electric current	343 979	16.6	8.67	0.96
248 Wood simply worked, railway sleeper	145 276	7.0	1.91	0.40
247 Wood in rough or roughly squared	133 560	6.4	3.02	0.93
841 Male clothing, woven	88 105	4.2	0.20	0.13
071 Coffee and coffee substitutes	60 887	2.9	0.26	0.17
845 Articles of apparel nes	39 223	1.9	0.04	0.03
044 Maize unmilled, excluding sweet corn	28 438	1.4	0.31	0.10
231 Natural rubber, latex, gum, etc	26 986	1.3	0.09	0.08
Remainder	274 849	13.3		
Latvia - Lettonie (**=Developed)				
All commodity groups	10 432 942	100.0	0.12	0.06
248 Wood simply worked, railway sleeper	588 250	5.6	2.44	1.64
676 Iron steel bar rod section piling	434 398	4.2	0.86	0.51
334 Heavy petroleum & bituminous oil	395 319	3.8	0.11	0.05
634 Veneer, plywood & other wood nes	354 129	3.4	2.03	1.09
542 Medicines including veterinary	349 952	3.4	0.11	0.11
112 Alcoholic beverages	345 840	3.3	0.62	0.50
781 Passenger cars and race cars	322 863	3.1	0.07	0.05
247 Wood in rough or roughly squared	289 179	2.8	3.83	2.02
635 Wood manufactures nes	235 573	2.3	1.56	0.97
761 Television video receive project	227 281	2.2	0.55	0.23
Remainder	6 890 157	66.0		
Lebanon - Liban (**=Developing)				
All commodity groups	5 342 540	100.0	0.08	0.03
971 Gold non-monetary excluding ores	612 791	11.5	0.63	0.33
667 Pearls, precious semiprecious stone	342 974	6.4	0.46	0.23
282 Ferrous iron & steel, waste & scrap	289 465	5.4	4.67	0.56
716 Rotating electric plant parts nes	258 359	4.8	0.85	0.30
897 Jewellery nes (667)	218 733	4.1	0.40	0.24
288 Non ferrous base metal waste nes	160 761	3.0	1.76	0.37
892 Printed matter	142 584	2.7	0.93	0.28
562 Manufactured fertilizer excl. crude	140 881	2.6	0.63	0.22
642 Cut paper and paperboard articles	135 431	2.5	0.79	0.24
891 Arms and ammunition	126 567	2.4	8.98	1.07
Remainder	2 913 994	54.5		

For sources and notes, see end of table.

Pour les sources et les notes, se reporter à la fin du tableau.

Leading products exported based on average 2010-2011 values SITC Revision 3 (3-digit level) Principaux produits exportés d'après la moyenne des valeurs de 2010-2011 CTCI révision 3 (positions à 3 chiffres)	2010-2011			
	Value (f.o.b., thousands of dollars) Valeur (f.a.b., milliers de dollars)	of country total du total du pays	of ** (1) des ** (1)	of world du monde

Lesotho (**=Developing) (2)				
All commodity groups	930 835	100.0	0.01	0.01
667 Pearls, precious semiprecious stone	228 797	24.6	0.30	0.16
845 Articles of apparel nes	168 033	18.1	0.18	0.13
841 Male clothing, woven	140 216	15.1	0.31	0.21
842 Female clothing, woven	79 284	8.5	0.15	0.10
843 Male clothing, knitted crocheted	75 845	8.1	0.33	0.28
844 Female clothing, knitted crocheted	70 009	7.5	0.18	0.14
652 Woven cotton fabrics	30 746	3.3	0.13	0.10
761 Television video receive project	22 844	2.5	0.04	0.02
851 Footwear	16 372	1.8	0.03	0.02
268 Wool & animal hair, incl wool tops	15 734	1.7	0.52	0.22
Remainder	82 956	8.9		

Liberia - Libéria (**=Developing) (2)				
All commodity groups	299 640	100.0	0.00	0.00
231 Natural rubber, latex, gum, etc	115 939	38.7	0.38	0.36
793 Ships boats floating structures	71 689	23.9	0.06	0.04
334 Heavy petroleum & bituminous oil	27 042	9.0	0.01	0.00
333 Crude petroleum & bituminous oil	17 334	5.8	0.00	0.00
971 Gold non-monetary excluding ores	8 986	3.0	0.01	0.00
072 Cocoa	7 724	2.6	0.05	0.04
247 Wood in rough or roughly squared	5 986	2.0	0.14	0.04
667 Pearls, precious semiprecious stone	4 694	1.6	0.01	0.00
281 Iron ore and concentrates	4 526	1.5	0.01	0.00
282 Ferrous iron & steel, waste & scrap	4 210	1.4	0.07	0.01
Remainder	31 512	10.5		

Libya - Libye (**=Developing) (2)				
All commodity groups	32 699 000	100.0	0.46	0.20
333 Crude petroleum & bituminous oil	26 221 644	80.2	2.56	1.84
334 Heavy petroleum & bituminous oil	2 196 018	6.7	0.62	0.27
343 Natural gas, liquefied or not	2 076 913	6.4	1.63	0.82
342 Liquefied propane and butane	383 180	1.2	1.12	0.77
971 Gold non-monetary excluding ores	362 120	1.1	0.37	0.19
344 Petroleum and hydrocarbon gas nes	200 998	0.6	2.25	1.38
562 Manufactured fertilizer excl. crude	190 185	0.6	0.86	0.29
511 Hydrocarbons nes; derivatives	178 757	0.5	0.51	0.21
671 Pig & sponge iron, ferro alloys etc	131 594	0.4	0.60	0.32
673 Flat iron non-alloy steel products	110 371	0.3	0.38	0.12
Remainder	647 221	2.0		

Lithuania - Lituanie (**=Developed)				
All commodity groups	24 483 860	100.0	0.28	0.15
334 Heavy petroleum & bituminous oil	5 607 004	22.9	1.60	0.70
821 Furniture part; bedding furnishing	1 091 783	4.5	1.50	0.79
562 Manufactured fertilizer excl. crude	1 070 963	4.4	3.73	1.65
781 Passenger cars and race cars	862 560	3.5	0.17	0.14
574 Polyacetals and polyesters, etc	701 069	2.9	2.34	1.31
893 Articles of plastic nes	396 514	1.6	0.51	0.32
057 Fruit nut (exc oil), fresh or dried	396 094	1.6	1.01	0.49
054 Vegetable & vegetable products nes	325 353	1.3	0.91	0.54
635 Wood manufactures nes	308 437	1.3	2.04	1.27
542 Medicines including veterinary	302 646	1.2	0.10	0.09
Remainder	13 421 438	54.8		

Luxembourg (**=Developed) (2)				
All commodity groups	20 739 080	100.0	0.23	0.12
676 Iron steel bar rod section piling	2 827 834	13.6	5.60	3.35
625 Rubber for wheels, incl inner tube	928 254	4.5	1.95	1.14
764 Telecommunicate equipment part nes	880 421	4.2	0.54	0.19
674 Flat plated iron non-alloy steel	876 870	4.2	2.70	1.54
893 Articles of plastic nes	759 469	3.7	0.98	0.61
684 Aluminium	695 299	3.4	0.99	0.60
582 Plastic sheet film foil & strips	593 216	2.9	0.90	0.64
657 Special yarn and textile fabric etc	589 280	2.8	2.30	1.30
641 Paper and paperboard	526 923	2.5	0.55	0.44
781 Passenger cars and race cars	461 033	2.2	0.09	0.08
Remainder	11 600 482	55.9		

Madagascar (**=Developing) (2)				
All commodity groups	1 337 660	100.0	0.02	0.01
845 Articles of apparel nes	176 475	13.2	0.19	0.13
075 Spices	155 316	11.6	2.63	2.07
551 Essential oils, perfumes & flavours	113 429	8.5	2.54	0.49
036 Crustacean mollusc aquat invertebra	99 947	7.5	0.52	0.34
287 Base metal ores & concentrates nes	77 625	5.8	0.42	0.25
841 Male clothing, woven	74 114	5.5	0.17	0.11
842 Female clothing, woven	63 509	4.7	0.12	0.08
334 Heavy petroleum & bituminous oil	47 249	3.5	0.01	0.01
037 Fish shellfish, prepared preserved	43 212	3.2	0.27	0.18
971 Gold non-monetary excluding ores	27 382	2.0	0.03	0.01
Remainder	459 402	34.3		

Malawi (**=Developing) (2)				
All commodity groups	1 245 746	100.0	0.02	0.01
121 Unmanufactured tabacco and refuse	612 124	49.1	7.82	5.25
061 Sugar, mollasses and honey	112 980	9.1	0.38	0.27
074 Tea and maté	85 615	6.9	1.46	1.09
286 Uranium & thorium ore concentrates	63 195	5.1	9.02	8.91
525 Radio active & associated materials	53 540	4.3	1.96	0.28
263 Cotton	41 275	3.3	0.45	0.18
044 Maize unmilled, excluding sweet corn	33 306	2.7	0.37	0.12
054 Vegetable & vegetable products nes	33 029	2.7	0.14	0.05
222 Oil seed etc for soft oil	17 472	1.4	0.07	0.03
057 Fruit nut (exc oil), fresh or dried	15 272	1.2	0.04	0.02
Remainder	177 939	14.3		

Malaysia - Malaisie (**=Developing)				
All commodity groups	212 891 686	100.0	3.00	1.28
776 Valves tubes; diodes, transistors	32 773 065	15.4	8.42	5.93
422 Fixed veg fat and oil, excl. "soft"	16 195 083	7.6	40.56	36.24
343 Natural gas, liquefied or not	14 087 142	6.6	11.06	5.58
752 Computer equipment nes	10 689 069	5.0	4.56	3.20
333 Crude petroleum & bituminous oil	10 203 202	4.8	1.00	0.72
334 Heavy petroleum & bituminous oil	9 369 294	4.4	2.64	1.16
759 Office equipment part & accessories	9 110 896	4.3	7.61	4.57
764 Telecommunicate equipment part nes	5 330 794	2.5	1.71	1.12
772 Electrical circuit equipment	5 041 238	2.4	5.39	2.31
761 Television video receive project	4 724 216	2.2	8.34	4.78
Remainder	95 367 687	44.8		

Maldives (**=Developing) (2)				
All commodity groups	271 950	100.0	0.00	0.00
034 Fish, fresh live chilled frozen	166 774	61.3	0.69	0.30
342 Liquefied propane and butane	27 839	10.2	0.08	0.06
035 Fish, dried salted smoked	23 058	8.5	1.50	0.41
037 Fish shellfish, prepared preserved	14 838	5.5	0.09	0.06
344 Petroleum and hydrocarbon gas nes	5 347	2.0	0.06	0.04
764 Telecommunicate equipment part nes	5 211	1.9	0.00	0.00
036 Crustacean mollusc aquat invertebra	4 124	1.5	0.02	0.01
282 Ferrous iron & steel, waste & scrap	2 898	1.1	0.05	0.01
288 Non ferrous base metal waste nes	1 952	0.7	0.02	0.00
723 Civil engineering plant & equipment	1 734	0.6	0.01	0.00
Remainder	18 175	6.7		

Mali (**=Developing) (2)				
All commodity groups	2 192 648	100.0	0.03	0.01
971 Gold non-monetary excluding ores	1 326 891	60.5	1.37	0.70
263 Cotton	412 251	18.8	4.49	1.83
334 Heavy petroleum & bituminous oil	137 171	6.3	0.04	0.02
001 Live animal excl. fish & crustacean	46 184	2.1	1.08	0.23
562 Manufactured fertilizer excl. crude	31 376	1.4	0.14	0.05
222 Oil seed etc for soft oil	24 655	1.1	0.10	0.04
057 Fruit nut (exc oil), fresh or dried	17 981	0.8	0.05	0.02
723 Civil engineering plant & equipment	14 814	0.7	0.05	0.01
611 Leather	13 451	0.6	0.10	0.06
782 Goods and service vehicles	8 799	0.4	0.02	0.01
Remainder	159 074	7.3		

For sources and notes, see end of table.

Pour les sources et les notes, se reporter à la fin du tableau.

184

3.2.D Export structure by product
Individual countries and territories

3.2.D Structure des exportations par produits
Pays et territoires individuels

Leading products exported based on average 2010-2011 values SITC Revision 3 (3-digit level) / Principaux produits exportés d'après la moyenne des valeurs de 2010-2011 CTCI révision 3 (positions à 3 chiffres)	2010-2011 Value (f.o.b., thousands of dollars) / Valeur (f.a.b., milliers de dollars)	As percentage / En pourcentage: of country total / du total du pays	of ** (1) / des ** (1)	of world / du monde
Malta - Malte (=Developed) (2)**				
All commodity groups	3 731 113	100.0	0.04	0.02
776 Valves tubes; diodes, transistors	1 689 406	45.3	1.04	0.31
542 Medicines including veterinary	222 690	6.0	0.07	0.07
772 Electrical circuit equipment	220 047	5.9	0.18	0.10
334 Heavy petroleum & bituminous oil	197 002	5.3	0.06	0.02
892 Printed matter	133 182	3.6	0.39	0.26
034 Fish, fresh live chilled frozen	133 095	3.6	0.44	0.24
098 Edible products & preparations nes	132 064	3.5	0.32	0.23
894 Baby carriage toy game sport good	120 765	3.2	0.32	0.13
655 Knitted or crocheted fabrics nes	90 409	2.4	1.31	0.31
893 Articles of plastic nes	59 813	1.6	0.08	0.05
Remainder	732 639	19.6		
Marshall Islands - Îles Marshall (=Developing) (2)**				
All commodity groups	33 650	100.0	0.00	0.00
793 Ships boats floating structures	23 892	71.0	0.02	0.01
034 Fish, fresh live chilled frozen	7 901	23.5	0.03	0.01
334 Heavy petroleum & bituminous oil	556	1.7	0.00	0.00
037 Fish shellfish, prepared preserved	370	1.1	0.00	0.00
422 Fixed veg fat and oil, excl. "soft"	110	0.3	0.00	0.00
035 Fish, dried salted smoked	91	0.3	0.01	0.00
894 Baby carriage toy game sport good	69	0.2	0.00	0.00
288 Non ferrous base metal waste nes	41	0.1	0.00	0.00
344 Petroleum and hydrocarbon gas nes	37	0.1	0.00	0.00
081 Animal feed excluding unmilled cereal	36	0.1	0.00	0.00
Remainder	547	1.6		
Mauritania - Mauritanie (=Developing) (2)**				
All commodity groups	2 426 602	100.0	0.03	0.01
281 Iron ore and concentrates	1 158 613	47.7	2.03	0.93
034 Fish, fresh live chilled frozen	326 006	13.4	1.35	0.58
283 Copper ores and concentrates	265 814	11.0	0.70	0.53
036 Crustacean mollusc aquat invertebra	187 947	7.7	0.98	0.64
333 Crude petroleum & bituminous oil	130 006	5.4	0.01	0.01
971 Gold non-monetary excluding ores	70 547	2.9	0.07	0.04
081 Animal feed excluding unmilled cereal	33 342	1.4	0.12	0.05
287 Base metal ores & concentrates nes	7 076	0.3	0.04	0.02
037 Fish shellfish, prepared preserved	4 560	0.2	0.03	0.02
282 Ferrous iron & steel, waste & scrap	4 514	0.2	0.07	0.01
Remainder	238 177	9.8		
Mauritius - Maurice (=Developing) (2)**				
All commodity groups	2 454 010	100.0	0.03	0.01
845 Articles of apparel nes	368 300	15.0	0.39	0.28
061 Sugar, mollasses and honey	285 540	11.6	0.95	0.68
037 Fish shellfish, prepared preserved	263 929	10.8	1.66	1.12
841 Male clothing, woven	220 269	9.0	0.49	0.33
844 Female clothing, knitted crocheted	77 124	3.1	0.20	0.16
034 Fish, fresh live chilled frozen	63 404	2.6	0.26	0.11
897 Jewellery nes (667)	62 030	2.5	0.11	0.07
667 Pearls, precious semiprecious stone	60 821	2.5	0.08	0.04
842 Female clothing, woven	51 608	2.1	0.10	0.07
843 Male clothing, knitted crocheted	41 364	1.7	0.18	0.15
Remainder	959 622	39.1		
Mayotte (=Developing)**				
All commodity groups	6 780	100.0	0.00	0.00
723 Civil engineering plant & equipment	633	9.3	0.00	0.00
781 Passenger cars and race cars	567	8.4	0.00	0.00
775 Household equipment nes	555	8.2	0.00	0.00
034 Fish, fresh live chilled frozen	529	7.8	0.00	0.00
741 Heating cooling equipment parts nes	502	7.4	0.00	0.00
542 Medicines including veterinary	368	5.4	0.00	0.00
551 Essential oils, perfumes & flavours	338	5.0	0.01	0.00
744 Mechanical handling equipment nes	209	3.1	0.00	0.00
699 Base metal manufactures nes	198	2.9	0.00	0.00
778 Electrical machinery apparatus nes	186	2.7	0.00	0.00
Remainder	2 697	39.8		

Leading products exported based on average 2010-2011 values SITC Revision 3 (3-digit level) / Principaux produits exportés d'après la moyenne des valeurs de 2010-2011 CTCI révision 3 (positions à 3 chiffres)	2010-2011 Value (f.o.b., thousands of dollars) / Valeur (f.a.b., milliers de dollars)	As percentage / En pourcentage: of country total / du total du pays	of ** (1) / des ** (1)	of world / du monde
Mexico - Mexique (=Developing)**				
All commodity groups	323 937 062	100.0	4.57	1.95
333 Crude petroleum & bituminous oil	42 635 346	13.2	4.17	2.99
781 Passenger cars and race cars	24 967 638	7.7	24.18	4.17
764 Telecommunicate equipment part nes	19 624 802	6.1	6.30	4.12
761 Television video receive project	19 400 980	6.0	34.23	19.64
784 Motor vehicle parts and accessories	15 408 251	4.8	18.41	4.67
752 Computer equipment nes	15 259 429	4.7	6.51	4.56
782 Goods and service vehicles	11 508 428	3.6	30.69	9.83
773 Electrical distribute equipment nes	7 457 170	2.3	15.71	7.25
778 Electrical machinery apparatus nes	6 951 591	2.1	6.78	3.28
971 Gold non-monetary excluding ores	6 865 273	2.1	7.11	3.64
Remainder	153 858 153	47.5		
Micronesia (Federated States of) - Micronésie (États fédérés de) (=Developing) (2)**				
All commodity groups	25 000	100.0	0.00	0.00
034 Fish, fresh live chilled frozen	23 020	92.1	0.10	0.04
036 Crustacean mollusc aquat invertebra	478	1.9	0.00	0.00
689 Misc non-ferrous base metals	175	0.7	0.00	0.00
896 Work of art & collections; antiques	150	0.6	0.01	0.00
288 Non ferrous base metal waste nes	101	0.4	0.00	0.00
851 Footwear	92	0.4	0.00	0.00
035 Fish, dried salted smoked	82	0.3	0.01	0.00
282 Ferrous iron & steel, waste & scrap	76	0.3	0.00	0.00
657 Special yarn and textile fabric etc	76	0.3	0.00	0.00
899 Manufactured articles nes	75	0.3	0.00	0.00
Remainder	675	2.7		
Mongolia - Mongolie (=Developing) (2)**				
All commodity groups	3 834 825	100.0	0.05	0.02
283 Copper ores and concentrates	1 940 201	50.6	5.12	3.89
287 Base metal ores & concentrates nes	422 112	11.0	2.31	1.36
971 Gold non-monetary excluding ores	418 214	10.9	0.43	0.22
321 Coal excluding non-agglomomerated	296 391	7.7	0.72	0.25
268 Wool & animal hair, incl wool tops	278 815	7.3	9.23	3.86
333 Crude petroleum & bituminous oil	95 667	2.5	0.01	0.01
278 Other crude minerals	49 695	1.3	0.74	0.30
611 Leather	42 320	1.1	0.33	0.18
281 Iron ore and concentrates	38 902	1.0	0.07	0.03
682 Copper	32 369	0.8	0.04	0.02
Remainder	220 140	5.7		
Montenegro - Monténégro (=Transition)**				
All commodity groups	532 054	100.0	0.08	0.00
684 Aluminium	213 050	40.0	2.24	0.18
351 Electric current	45 367	8.5	1.99	0.13
112 Alcoholic beverages	28 857	5.4	2.17	0.04
676 Iron steel bar rod section piling	18 159	3.4	0.27	0.02
248 Wood simply worked, railway sleeper	17 394	3.3	0.42	0.05
282 Ferrous iron & steel, waste & scrap	17 374	3.3	0.69	0.03
288 Non ferrous base metal waste nes	15 481	2.9	2.27	0.04
334 Heavy petroleum & bituminous oil	14 854	2.8	0.01	0.00
672 Ingots, Iron steel primary products	12 997	2.4	0.09	0.03
542 Medicines including veterinary	9 702	1.8	0.67	0.00
Remainder	138 819	26.1		
Montserrat (=Developing) (2)**				
All commodity groups	1 178	100.0	0.00	0.00
692 Metal storage transport container	202	17.2	0.00	0.00
273 Stone, sand and gravel	182	15.4	0.00	0.00
821 Furniture part; bedding furnishing	135	11.4	0.00	0.00
714 Non-electric engines excl. 712 713 718	68	5.8	0.00	0.00
743 Gas pump, compressor, fan, filter	67	5.7	0.00	0.00
782 Goods and service vehicles	56	4.7	0.00	0.00
282 Ferrous iron & steel, waste & scrap	51	4.3	0.00	0.00
872 Medical instruments appliances nes	51	4.3	0.00	0.00
045 Grain, excl. wheat rice barley maize	28	2.3	0.00	0.00
764 Telecommunicate equipment part nes	27	2.3	0.00	0.00
Remainder	311	26.4		

For sources and notes, see end of table.

Pour les sources et les notes, se reporter à la fin du tableau.

Morocco - Maroc (**=Developing) (2)

Leading products exported based on average 2010-2011 values SITC Revision 3 (3-digit level) / Principaux produits exportés d'après la moyenne des valeurs de 2010-2011 CTCI révision 3 (positions à 3 chiffres)	Value (f.o.b., thousands of dollars) / Valeur (f.a.b., milliers de dollars)	As percentage / En pourcentage		
		of country total / du total du pays	of ** (1) / des ** (1)	of world / du monde
All commodity groups	19 641 640	100.0	0.28	0.12
522 Inorganic chemical elem oxide salt	2 082 343	10.6	7.93	3.61
773 Electrical distribute equipment nes	1 674 632	8.5	3.53	1.63
842 Female clothing, woven	1 523 773	7.8	2.96	1.95
562 Manufactured fertilizer excl. crude	1 436 057	7.3	6.47	2.21
272 Crude fertilizer, excl. manufactured	1 153 520	5.9	37.96	27.77
845 Articles of apparel nes	849 311	4.3	0.91	0.64
054 Vegetable & vegetable products nes	844 563	4.3	3.62	1.40
776 Valves tubes; diodes, transistors	774 327	3.9	0.20	0.14
037 Fish shellfish, prepared preserved	690 759	3.5	4.34	2.94
841 Male clothing, woven	648 410	3.3	1.44	0.98
Remainder	7 963 946	40.5		

Mozambique (**=Developing) (2)

	Value	of country total	of ** (1)	of world
All commodity groups	2 923 593	100.0	0.04	0.02
684 Aluminium	1 266 174	43.3	3.49	1.09
351 Electric current	247 056	8.5	6.23	0.69
334 Heavy petroleum & bituminous oil	172 617	5.9	0.05	0.02
343 Natural gas, liquefied or not	164 816	5.6	0.13	0.07
121 Unmanufactured tabacco and refuse	121 856	4.2	1.56	1.04
061 Sugar, mollasses and honey	119 503	4.1	0.40	0.28
287 Base metal ores & concentrates nes	112 356	3.8	0.61	0.36
057 Fruit nut (exc oil), fresh or dried	98 013	3.4	0.25	0.12
036 Crustacean mollusc aquat invertebra	55 685	1.9	0.29	0.19
247 Wood in rough or roughly squared	49 455	1.7	1.12	0.35
Remainder	516 062	17.7		

Myanmar (**=Developing) (2)

	Value	of country total	of ** (1)	of world
All commodity groups	8 949 560	100.0	0.13	0.05
343 Natural gas, liquefied or not	3 148 087	35.2	2.47	1.25
667 Pearls, precious semiprecious stone	1 613 155	18.0	2.14	1.10
054 Vegetable & vegetable products nes	898 824	10.0	3.86	1.49
247 Wood in rough or roughly squared	753 797	8.4	17.07	5.27
231 Natural rubber, latex, gum, etc	192 328	2.1	0.63	0.60
841 Male clothing, woven	188 241	2.1	0.42	0.29
034 Fish, fresh live chilled frozen	183 267	2.0	0.76	0.33
036 Crustacean mollusc aquat invertebra	174 429	1.9	0.91	0.59
845 Articles of apparel nes	156 439	1.7	0.17	0.12
042 Rice	125 773	1.4	0.71	0.57
Remainder	1 515 219	16.9		

Namibia - Namibie (**=Developing) (2)

	Value	of country total	of ** (1)	of world
All commodity groups	4 186 538	100.0	0.06	0.03
034 Fish, fresh live chilled frozen	581 468	13.9	2.40	1.03
667 Pearls, precious semiprecious stone	566 023	13.5	0.75	0.38
686 Zinc	410 740	9.8	9.33	3.16
286 Uranium & thorium ore concentrates	384 111	9.2	54.85	54.13
525 Radio active & associated materials	373 856	8.9	13.68	1.97
892 Printed matter	265 494	6.3	1.73	0.53
682 Copper	171 265	4.1	0.23	0.12
793 Ships boats floating structures	88 133	2.1	0.08	0.05
121 Unmanufactured tabacco and refuse	78 876	1.9	1.01	0.68
112 Alcoholic beverages	75 329	1.8	0.61	0.11
Remainder	1 191 242	28.5		

Nauru (**=Developing)

	Value	of country total	of ** (1)	of world
All commodity groups	61 984	100.0	0.00	0.00
272 Crude fertilizer, excl. manufactured	53 028	85.6	1.75	1.28
874 Measure analyze control device nes	3 097	5.0	0.01	0.00
335 Residual petroleum products nes	1 179	1.9	0.01	0.00
022 Milk products, excl. butter & cheese	405	0.7	0.01	0.00
034 Fish, fresh live chilled frozen	396	0.6	0.00	0.00
772 Electrical circuit equipment	387	0.6	0.00	0.00
744 Mechanical handling equipment nes	285	0.5	0.00	0.00
776 Valves tubes; diodes, transistors	257	0.4	0.00	0.00
282 Ferrous iron & steel, waste & scrap	221	0.4	0.00	0.00
288 Non ferrous base metal waste nes	221	0.4	0.00	0.00
Remainder	2 507	4.0		

Nepal - Népal (**=Developing) (2)

	Value	of country total	of ** (1)	of world
All commodity groups	876 063	100.0	0.01	0.01
651 Textile yarn	77 316	8.8	0.22	0.14
674 Flat plated iron non-alloy steel	68 944	7.9	0.30	0.12
659 Floor coverings etc	67 659	7.7	0.96	0.44
054 Vegetable & vegetable products nes	46 549	5.3	0.20	0.08
653 Man-made woven fabrics	45 606	5.2	0.16	0.11
431 Processed animal & veg fats & oils	37 599	4.3	0.52	0.30
658 Made-up textile articles nes	34 938	4.0	0.10	0.07
075 Spices	29 135	3.3	0.49	0.39
842 Female clothing, woven	23 396	2.7	0.05	0.03
292 Crude vegetable materials nes	22 372	2.6	0.19	0.06
Remainder	422 549	48.2		

Netherlands - Pays-Bas (**=Developed) (2)

	Value	of country total	of ** (1)	of world
All commodity groups	619 952 851	100.0	7.00	3.72
334 Heavy petroleum & bituminous oil	67 639 169	10.9	19.33	8.41
752 Computer equipment nes	18 799 827	3.0	18.80	5.62
333 Crude petroleum & bituminous oil	16 524 496	2.7	9.35	1.16
764 Telecommunicate equipment part nes	16 352 807	2.6	10.02	3.44
759 Office equipment part & accessories	15 150 647	2.4	19.09	7.61
542 Medicines including veterinary	14 236 703	2.3	4.66	4.29
292 Crude vegetable materials nes	14 113 248	2.3	52.93	36.50
511 Hydrocarbons nes; derivatives	11 417 307	1.8	23.20	13.25
728 Special industrial machine part nes	9 754 290	1.6	7.20	5.62
776 Valves tubes; diodes, transistors	9 751 603	1.6	5.99	1.76
Remainder	426 212 754	68.7		

New Caledonia - Nouvelle-Calédonie (**=Developing) (2)

	Value	of country total	of ** (1)	of world
All commodity groups	1 570 482	100.0	0.02	0.01
671 Pig & sponge iron, ferro alloys etc	825 350	52.6	3.76	2.02
284 Nickel ores, concentrates, etc	522 372	33.3	8.34	4.87
281 Iron ore and concentrates	66 980	4.3	0.12	0.05
522 Inorganic chemical elem oxide salt	33 493	2.1	0.13	0.06
036 Crustacean mollusc aquat invertebra	11 767	0.7	0.06	0.04
334 Heavy petroleum & bituminous oil	9 513	0.6	0.00	0.00
034 Fish, fresh live chilled frozen	8 017	0.5	0.03	0.01
282 Ferrous iron & steel, waste & scrap	4 497	0.3	0.07	0.01
892 Printed matter	3 949	0.3	0.03	0.01
792 Aircraft, spacecraft & equipment	3 009	0.2	0.01	0.00
Remainder	81 535	5.2		

New Zealand - Nouvelle-Zélande (**=Developed)

	Value	of country total	of ** (1)	of world
All commodity groups	34 282 514	100.0	0.39	0.21
022 Milk products, excl. butter & cheese	5 590 252	16.3	17.04	14.23
012 Meat nes, fresh chilled frozen	2 487 159	7.3	4.74	3.69
023 Butter fats oils derived from milk	1 756 559	5.1	24.82	22.28
333 Crude petroleum & bituminous oil	1 545 653	4.5	0.87	0.11
011 Beef, fresh chilled frozen	1 498 608	4.4	5.81	4.01
057 Fruit nut (exc oil), fresh or dried	1 136 810	3.3	2.90	1.42
247 Wood in rough or roughly squared	1 135 446	3.3	15.05	7.94
024 Cheese and curd	1 050 574	3.1	4.10	3.67
098 Edible products & preparations nes	963 861	2.8	2.34	1.69
112 Alcoholic beverages	918 513	2.7	1.65	1.33
Remainder	16 199 077	47.3		

Nicaragua (**=Developing)

	Value	of country total	of ** (1)	of world
All commodity groups	2 064 250	100.0	0.03	0.01
845 Articles of apparel nes	294 568	14.3	0.32	0.22
071 Coffee and coffee substitutes	290 370	14.1	1.25	0.79
971 Gold non-monetary excluding ores	200 186	9.7	0.21	0.11
011 Beef, fresh chilled frozen	186 282	9.0	1.70	0.50
773 Electrical distribute equipment nes	147 980	7.2	0.31	0.14
061 Sugar, mollasses and honey	113 891	5.5	0.38	0.27
841 Male clothing, woven	105 288	5.1	0.23	0.16
036 Crustacean mollusc aquat invertebra	94 032	4.6	0.49	0.32
222 Oil seed etc for soft oil	53 031	2.6	0.21	0.09
024 Cheese and curd	47 757	2.3	2.44	0.17
Remainder	530 866	25.7		

For sources and notes, see end of table.

Pour les sources et les notes, se reporter à la fin du tableau.

Leading products exported based on average 2010-2011 values SITC Revision 3 (3-digit level) / Principaux produits exportés d'après la moyenne des valeurs de 2010-2011 CTCI révision 3 (positions à 3 chiffres)	2010-2011			
	Value (f.o.b., thousands of dollars) / Valeur (f.a.b., milliers de dollars)	As percentage / En pourcentage		
		of country total / du total du pays	of ** (1) / des ** (1)	of world / du monde
Niger (=Developing) (2)**				
All commodity groups	1 144 810	100.0	0.02	0.01
286 Uranium & thorium ore concentrates	248 240	21.7	35.45	34.98
525 Radio active & associated materials	248 113	21.7	9.08	1.30
001 Live animal excl. fish & crustacean	235 594	20.6	5.49	1.16
334 Heavy petroleum & bituminous oil	160 082	14.0	0.05	0.02
054 Vegetable & vegetable products nes	70 533	6.2	0.30	0.12
971 Gold non-monetary excluding ores	47 489	4.1	0.05	0.03
269 Worn clothing, textile article; rag	15 639	1.4	1.37	0.38
652 Woven cotton fabrics	8 043	0.7	0.03	0.03
782 Goods and service vehicles	7 221	0.6	0.02	0.01
723 Civil engineering plant & equipment	7 153	0.6	0.02	0.01
Remainder	96 703	8.4		
Nigeria - Nigéria (=Developing) (2)**				
All commodity groups	93 070 290	100.0	1.31	0.56
333 Crude petroleum & bituminous oil	74 583 068	80.1	7.29	5.24
343 Natural gas, liquefied or not	5 233 617	5.6	4.11	2.07
334 Heavy petroleum & bituminous oil	4 997 953	5.4	1.41	0.62
342 Liquefied propane and butane	1 191 870	1.3	3.49	2.38
611 Leather	1 051 834	1.1	8.18	4.49
072 Cocoa	938 690	1.0	6.49	4.32
793 Ships boats floating structures	550 425	0.6	0.48	0.31
231 Natural rubber, latex, gum, etc	402 593	0.4	1.32	1.25
222 Oil seed etc for soft oil	376 000	0.4	1.47	0.63
344 Petroleum and hydrocarbon gas nes	368 181	0.4	4.12	2.53
Remainder	3 376 059	3.6		
Niue - Nioué (=Developing) (2)**				
All commodity groups	20	100.0	0.00	0.00
272 Crude fertilizer, excl. manufactured	4	19.7	0.00	0.00
771 Electric power machine part excl. 716	3	16.3	0.00	0.00
761 Television video receive project	3	13.6	0.00	0.00
728 Special industrial machine part nes	2	11.8	0.00	0.00
513 Carboxylic acid and compounds	2	9.2	0.00	0.00
333 Crude petroleum & bituminous oil	2	8.6	0.00	0.00
059 Fruit & vegetable juice unferment	0	2.3	0.00	0.00
745 Non-electrical machinery tool nes	0	1.6	0.00	0.00
582 Plastic sheet film foil & strips	0	1.0	0.00	0.00
655 Knitted or crocheted fabrics nes	0	1.0	0.00	0.00
Remainder	3	14.9		
Northern Mariana Islands - Îles Mariannes du Nord (=Developing) (2)**				
All commodity groups	4 000	100.0	0.00	0.00
287 Base metal ores & concentrates nes	699	17.5	0.00	0.00
288 Non ferrous base metal waste nes	459	11.5	0.01	0.00
282 Ferrous iron & steel, waste & scrap	416	10.4	0.01	0.00
831 Case bag: storage travel shopping	315	7.9	0.00	0.00
533 Pigment, paint, varnish & related	285	7.1	0.00	0.00
034 Fish, fresh live chilled frozen	202	5.1	0.00	0.00
885 Watches and clocks	137	3.4	0.00	0.00
851 Footwear	111	2.8	0.00	0.00
845 Articles of apparel nes	108	2.7	0.00	0.00
778 Electrical machinery apparatus nes	98	2.4	0.00	0.00
Remainder	1 170	29.2		
Norway - Norvège (=Developed)**				
All commodity groups	145 377 996	100.0	1.64	0.87
333 Crude petroleum & bituminous oil	52 885 387	36.4	29.93	3.71
343 Natural gas, liquefied or not	31 544 226	21.7	34.32	12.50
034 Fish, fresh live chilled frozen	7 752 370	5.3	25.89	13.76
334 Heavy petroleum & bituminous oil	7 144 113	4.9	2.04	0.89
684 Aluminium	4 661 570	3.2	6.63	4.01
342 Liquefied propane and butane	3 198 610	2.2	22.29	6.39
683 Nickel	2 071 834	1.4	15.57	9.70
598 Miscellaneous chemical products nes	1 834 395	1.3	2.03	1.55
874 Measure analyze control device nes	1 458 377	1.0	1.12	0.88
793 Ships boats floating structures	1 404 568	1.0	2.36	0.79
Remainder	31 422 546	21.6		

Leading products exported based on average 2010-2011 values SITC Revision 3 (3-digit level) / Principaux produits exportés d'après la moyenne des valeurs de 2010-2011 CTCI révision 3 (positions à 3 chiffres)	2010-2011			
	Value (f.o.b., thousands of dollars) / Valeur (f.a.b., milliers de dollars)	As percentage / En pourcentage		
		of country total / du total du pays	of ** (1) / des ** (1)	of world / du monde
Occupied Palestinian territory - Territoire palestinien occupé (=Developing) (2)**				
All commodity groups	667 256	100.0	0.01	0.00
661 Lime cement construction material	112 224	16.8	0.71	0.41
542 Medicines including veterinary	50 086	7.5	0.20	0.02
282 Ferrous iron & steel, waste & scrap	40 827	6.1	0.66	0.08
821 Furniture part; bedding furnishing	37 876	5.7	0.06	0.03
893 Articles of plastic nes	29 163	4.4	0.06	0.02
851 Footwear	24 041	3.6	0.04	0.02
288 Non ferrous base metal waste nes	23 037	3.5	0.25	0.05
122 Manufactured tabacco	20 165	3.0	0.27	0.07
635 Wood manufactures nes	14 972	2.2	0.18	0.06
421 Fixed veg fat and oil, "soft"	14 381	2.2	0.13	0.04
Remainder	300 484	45.0		
Oman (=Developing) (2)**				
All commodity groups	41 844 728	100.0	0.59	0.25
333 Crude petroleum & bituminous oil	24 922 173	59.6	2.44	1.75
343 Natural gas, liquefied or not	4 289 994	10.3	3.37	1.70
334 Heavy petroleum & bituminous oil	2 102 330	5.0	0.59	0.26
562 Manufactured fertilizer excl. crude	866 207	2.1	3.90	1.33
684 Aluminium	848 087	2.0	2.34	0.73
773 Electrical distribute equipment nes	698 260	1.7	1.47	0.68
511 Hydrocarbons nes; derivatives	605 918	1.4	1.72	0.70
022 Milk products, excl. butter & cheese	408 035	1.0	7.66	1.04
512 Alcohols, phenols; derivatives	379 321	0.9	1.31	0.68
582 Plastic sheet film foil & strips	366 990	0.9	1.39	0.39
Remainder	6 357 413	15.2		
Pakistan (=Developing)**				
All commodity groups	23 378 436	100.0	0.33	0.14
658 Made-up textile articles nes	3 402 644	14.6	9.30	6.99
652 Woven cotton fabrics	2 364 873	10.1	10.20	7.41
042 Rice	2 169 594	9.3	12.22	9.85
651 Textile yarn	1 876 629	8.0	5.27	3.36
334 Heavy petroleum & bituminous oil	1 252 786	5.4	0.35	0.16
841 Male clothing, woven	983 741	4.2	2.19	1.49
843 Male clothing, knitted crocheted	977 231	4.2	4.31	3.60
653 Man-made woven fabrics	564 808	2.4	1.94	1.41
842 Female clothing, woven	538 315	2.3	1.05	0.69
845 Articles of apparel nes	537 632	2.3	0.58	0.40
Remainder	8 710 184	37.3		
Palau - Palaos (=Developing)**				
All commodity groups	7 000	100.0	0.00	0.00
034 Fish, fresh live chilled frozen	6 375	91.1	0.03	0.01
282 Ferrous iron & steel, waste & scrap	144	2.1	0.00	0.00
112 Alcoholic beverages	75	1.1	0.00	0.00
288 Non ferrous base metal waste nes	64	0.9	0.00	0.00
793 Ships boats floating structures	45	0.6	0.00	0.00
641 Paper and paperboard	37	0.5	0.00	0.00
652 Woven cotton fabrics	28	0.4	0.00	0.00
778 Electrical machinery apparatus nes	21	0.3	0.00	0.00
776 Valves tubes; diodes, transistors	14	0.2	0.00	0.00
048 Cereal & preparation flour starch	13	0.2	0.00	0.00
Remainder	185	2.6		
Panama (=Developing)**				
All commodity groups	12 770 709	100.0	0.18	0.08
541 Pharmaceuticals excluding medicines	1 591 240	12.5	8.80	1.09
793 Ships boats floating structures	1 150 270	9.0	1.00	0.65
542 Medicines including veterinary	1 001 166	7.8	4.00	0.30
851 Footwear	707 334	5.5	1.11	0.68
334 Heavy petroleum & bituminous oil	505 289	4.0	0.14	0.06
333 Crude petroleum & bituminous oil	454 701	3.6	0.04	0.03
842 Female clothing, woven	371 774	2.9	0.72	0.47
057 Fruit nut (exc oil), fresh or dried	353 106	2.8	0.89	0.44
845 Articles of apparel nes	329 255	2.6	0.35	0.25
553 Perfume toilet cosmetics, excl. soap	327 105	2.6	2.02	0.46
Remainder	5 979 469	46.8		

For sources and notes, see end of table.

Pour les sources et les notes, se reporter à la fin du tableau.

Papua New Guinea - Papouasie-Nouvelle-Guinée (**=Developing) (2)

Leading products exported based on average 2010-2011 values SITC Revision 3 (3-digit level) / Principaux produits exportés d'après la moyenne des valeurs de 2010-2011 CTCI révision 3 (positions à 3 chiffres)	Value (f.o.b., thousands of dollars) / Valeur (f.a.b., milliers de dollars)	of country total / du total du pays	of ** (1) / des ** (1)	of world / du monde
All commodity groups	6 744 379	100.0	0.10	0.04
971 Gold non-monetary excluding ores	1 765 436	26.2	1.83	0.94
283 Copper ores and concentrates	1 471 764	21.8	3.88	2.95
333 Crude petroleum & bituminous oil	1 109 951	16.5	0.11	0.08
422 Fixed veg fat and oil, excl. "soft"	492 417	7.3	1.23	1.10
247 Wood in rough or roughly squared	446 909	6.6	10.12	3.13
289 Prec metal ore concentrate excl. gold	283 038	4.2	4.83	1.51
071 Coffee and coffee substitutes	216 830	3.2	0.94	0.59
072 Cocoa	136 939	2.0	0.95	0.63
681 Silver, platinum, platinum metals	124 546	1.8	0.48	0.20
334 Heavy petroleum & bituminous oil	113 398	1.7	0.03	0.01
Remainder	583 150	8.6		

Paraguay (**=Developing)

	Value	of country total	of ** (1)	of world
All commodity groups	5 025 566	100.0	0.07	0.03
222 Oil seed etc for soft oil	2 021 840	40.2	7.89	3.41
011 Beef, fresh chilled frozen	801 549	15.9	7.29	2.15
081 Animal feed excluding unmilled cereal	372 782	7.4	1.36	0.58
044 Maize unmilled, excluding sweet corn	295 655	5.9	3.25	1.02
421 Fixed veg fat and oil, "soft"	292 339	5.8	2.55	0.84
041 Wheat meslin, incl spelt, unmilled	207 836	4.1	5.68	0.51
611 Leather	95 720	1.9	0.74	0.41
042 Rice	74 722	1.5	0.42	0.34
061 Sugar, mollasses and honey	64 534	1.3	0.22	0.15
893 Articles of plastic nes	54 790	1.1	0.12	0.04
Remainder	743 800	14.8		

Peru - Pérou (**=Developing)

	Value	of country total	of ** (1)	of world
All commodity groups	40 420 577	100.0	0.57	0.24
971 Gold non-monetary excluding ores	8 828 149	21.8	9.14	4.68
283 Copper ores and concentrates	6 978 630	17.3	18.42	14.00
287 Base metal ores & concentrates nes	3 431 789	8.5	18.78	11.04
682 Copper	3 197 839	7.9	4.37	2.28
334 Heavy petroleum & bituminous oil	2 617 307	6.5	0.74	0.33
081 Animal feed excluding unmilled cereal	1 807 623	4.5	6.58	2.83
071 Coffee and coffee substitutes	1 237 544	3.1	5.34	3.36
343 Natural gas, liquefied or not	783 528	1.9	0.61	0.31
281 Iron ore and concentrates	773 208	1.9	1.36	0.62
845 Articles of apparel nes	676 601	1.7	0.73	0.51
Remainder	10 088 360	25.0		

Philippines (**=Developing)

	Value	of country total	of ** (1)	of world
All commodity groups	49 769 822	100.0	0.70	0.30
776 Valves tubes; diodes, transistors	12 285 046	24.7	3.16	2.22
752 Computer equipment nes	5 595 887	11.2	2.39	1.67
784 Motor vehicle parts and accessories	1 870 023	3.8	2.23	0.57
759 Office equipment part & accessories	1 771 485	3.6	1.48	0.89
635 Wood manufactures nes	1 356 276	2.7	15.98	5.59
422 Fixed veg fat and oil, excl. "soft"	1 350 479	2.7	3.38	3.02
771 Electric power machine part excl. 716	1 243 619	2.5	2.65	1.40
773 Electrical distribute equipment nes	1 158 085	2.3	2.44	1.13
682 Copper	1 136 162	2.3	1.55	0.81
778 Electrical machinery apparatus nes	922 119	1.9	0.90	0.44
Remainder	21 080 640	42.4		

Poland - Pologne (**=Developed)

	Value	of country total	of ** (1)	of world
All commodity groups	170 178 458	100.0	1.92	1.02
781 Passenger cars and race cars	9 133 692	5.4	1.85	1.53
784 Motor vehicle parts and accessories	8 688 966	5.1	3.55	2.64
821 Furniture part; bedding furnishing	8 385 103	4.9	11.55	6.06
761 Television video receive project	6 589 299	3.9	15.91	6.67
713 Internal combustion engine part nes	4 566 969	2.7	3.85	3.03
793 Ships boats floating structures	4 116 340	2.4	6.92	2.32
682 Copper	4 073 634	2.4	7.16	2.91
775 Household equipment nes	3 803 595	2.2	9.89	4.26
893 Articles of plastic nes	3 263 179	1.9	4.19	2.62
699 Base metal manufactures nes	3 044 126	1.8	3.59	2.30
Remainder	114 513 556	67.3		

Portugal (**=Developed)

	Value	of country total	of ** (1)	of world
All commodity groups	53 837 873	100.0	0.61	0.32
334 Heavy petroleum & bituminous oil	3 054 371	5.7	0.87	0.38
781 Passenger cars and race cars	2 632 021	4.9	0.53	0.44
784 Motor vehicle parts and accessories	2 394 327	4.4	0.98	0.73
851 Footwear	1 981 082	3.7	5.08	1.90
641 Paper and paperboard	1 605 587	3.0	1.69	1.35
845 Articles of apparel nes	1 431 867	2.7	3.72	1.08
821 Furniture part; bedding furnishing	1 347 347	2.5	1.86	0.97
112 Alcoholic beverages	1 159 609	2.2	2.09	1.67
762 Radio broadcast receivers	999 188	1.9	17.21	6.26
633 Cork manufactures	943 772	1.8	65.28	61.94
Remainder	36 288 701	67.4		

Qatar (**=Developing) (2)

	Value	of country total	of ** (1)	of world
All commodity groups	95 207 737	100.0	1.34	0.57
343 Natural gas, liquefied or not	37 046 806	38.9	29.08	14.68
333 Crude petroleum & bituminous oil	33 592 742	35.3	3.28	2.36
342 Liquefied propane and butane	6 313 567	6.6	18.51	12.61
334 Heavy petroleum & bituminous oil	6 199 627	6.5	1.77	0.77
344 Petroleum and hydrocarbon gas nes	3 700 480	3.9	41.43	25.44
571 Primary form ethylene polymers	1 773 144	1.9	5.40	2.45
562 Manufactured fertilizer excl. crude	1 194 559	1.3	5.38	1.84
511 Hydrocarbons nes; derivatives	804 116	0.8	2.28	0.93
684 Aluminium	528 663	0.6	1.46	0.46
516 Other organic chemicals	499 248	0.5	3.72	1.28
Remainder	3 554 786	3.7		

Republic of Moldova - République de Moldova (**=Transition)

	Value	of country total	of ** (1)	of world
All commodity groups	1 879 151	100.0	0.27	0.01
057 Fruit nut (exc oil), fresh or dried	161 479	8.6	9.92	0.20
112 Alcoholic beverages	158 016	8.4	11.90	0.23
222 Oil seed etc for soft oil	150 680	8.0	9.74	0.25
773 Electrical distribute equipment nes	95 191	5.1	4.30	0.09
842 Female clothing, woven	78 800	4.2	7.02	0.10
676 Iron steel bar rod section piling	76 089	4.0	1.14	0.09
851 Footwear	70 853	3.8	4.63	0.07
421 Fixed veg fat and oil, "soft"	67 097	3.6	1.67	0.19
841 Male clothing, woven	57 070	3.0	5.79	0.09
845 Articles of apparel nes	54 955	2.9	5.01	0.04
Remainder	908 920	48.4		

Romania - Roumanie (**=Developed)

	Value	of country total	of ** (1)	of world
All commodity groups	56 052 694	100.0	0.63	0.34
784 Motor vehicle parts and accessories	3 079 477	5.5	1.26	0.93
773 Electrical distribute equipment nes	3 023 978	5.4	5.69	2.94
764 Telecommunicate equipment part nes	3 011 191	5.4	1.84	0.63
781 Passenger cars and race cars	2 999 066	5.4	0.61	0.50
334 Heavy petroleum & bituminous oil	2 467 003	4.4	0.71	0.31
821 Furniture part; bedding furnishing	1 680 423	3.0	2.31	1.22
851 Footwear	1 647 108	2.9	4.22	1.58
772 Electrical circuit equipment	1 432 958	2.6	1.16	0.66
793 Ships boats floating structures	1 215 450	2.2	2.04	0.69
625 Rubber for wheels, incl inner tube	1 197 244	2.1	2.52	1.46
Remainder	34 298 797	61.2		

Russian Federation - Fédération de Russie (**=Transition) (2)

	Value	of country total	of ** (1)	of world
All commodity groups	439 054 598	100.0	62.92	2.64
333 Crude petroleum & bituminous oil	150 411 073	34.3	67.23	10.56
334 Heavy petroleum & bituminous oil	80 513 776	18.3	80.69	10.01
343 Natural gas, liquefied or not	25 187 323	5.7	76.12	9.98
321 Coal excluding non-agglomerated	10 276 408	2.3	88.29	8.70
562 Manufactured fertilizer excl. crude	8 727 619	2.0	62.10	13.43
672 Ingots, Iron steel primary products	7 594 532	1.7	51.51	18.62
684 Aluminium	7 236 592	1.6	76.02	6.23
683 Nickel	5 008 843	1.1	99.69	23.45
682 Copper	4 919 429	1.1	49.31	3.51
673 Flat iron non-alloy steel products	4 478 158	1.0	42.02	5.07
Remainder	134 700 845	30.7		

For sources and notes, see end of table.

Pour les sources et les notes, se reporter à la fin du tableau.

Leading products exported based on average 2010-2011 values SITC Revision 3 (3-digit level) / Principaux produits exportés d'après la moyenne des valeurs de 2010-2011 CTCI révision 3 (positions à 3 chiffres)	Value (f.o.b., thousands of dollars) Valeur (f.a.b., milliers de dollars)	of country total du total du pays	of ** (1) des ** (1)	of world du monde
Rwanda (**=Developing) (2)				
All commodity groups	357 311	100.0	0.01	0.00
287 Base metal ores & concentrates nes	110 280	30.9	0.60	0.35
074 Tea and maté	92 467	25.9	1.58	1.18
071 Coffee and coffee substitutes	55 243	15.5	0.24	0.15
211 Raw hides & skins, excluding furskins	9 073	2.5	1.03	0.12
851 Footwear	8 977	2.5	0.01	0.01
334 Heavy petroleum & bituminous oil	8 535	2.4	0.00	0.00
001 Live animal excl. fish & crustacean	7 325	2.1	0.17	0.04
081 Animal feed excluding unmilled cereal	5 155	1.4	0.02	0.01
675 Flat rolled products of alloy steel	5 068	1.4	0.03	0.01
112 Alcoholic beverages	3 421	1.0	0.03	0.00
Remainder	51 766	14.5		
Saint Helena - Sainte-Hélène (**=Developing) (2)				
All commodity groups	33 895	100.0	0.00	0.00
034 Fish, fresh live chilled frozen	10 473	30.9	0.04	0.02
036 Crustacean mollusc aquat invertebra	8 768	25.9	0.05	0.03
743 Gas pump, compressor, fan, filter	2 033	6.0	0.01	0.00
764 Telecommunicate equipment part nes	2 033	6.0	0.00	0.00
792 Aircraft, spacecraft & equipment	1 825	5.4	0.01	0.00
776 Valves tubes; diodes, transistors	1 278	3.8	0.00	0.00
744 Mechanical handling equipment nes	832	2.5	0.00	0.00
582 Plastic sheet film foil & strips	610	1.8	0.00	0.00
899 Manufactured articles nes	602	1.8	0.00	0.00
752 Computer equipment nes	318	0.9	0.00	0.00
Remainder	5 123	15.1		
Saint Kitts and Nevis - Saint-Kitts-et-Nevis (**=Developing) (2)				
All commodity groups	49 790	100.0	0.00	0.00
772 Electrical circuit equipment	12 142	24.4	0.01	0.01
764 Telecommunicate equipment part nes	9 660	19.4	0.00	0.00
842 Female clothing, woven	4 430	8.9	0.01	0.01
716 Rotating electric plant parts nes	4 088	8.2	0.01	0.00
793 Ships boats floating structures	2 992	6.0	0.00	0.00
771 Electric power machine part excl. 716	1 973	4.0	0.00	0.00
112 Alcoholic beverages	1 148	2.3	0.01	0.00
778 Electrical machinery apparatus nes	971	2.0	0.00	0.00
792 Aircraft, spacecraft & equipment	723	1.5	0.00	0.00
111 Non alcoholic beverage nes	658	1.3	0.02	0.00
Remainder	11 003	22.1		
Saint Lucia - Sainte-Lucie (**=Developing) (2)				
All commodity groups	187 979	100.0	0.00	0.00
334 Heavy petroleum & bituminous oil	52 241	27.8	0.01	0.01
057 Fruit nut (exc oil), fresh or dried	37 511	20.0	0.09	0.05
112 Alcoholic beverages	15 189	8.1	0.12	0.02
764 Telecommunicate equipment part nes	6 132	3.3	0.00	0.00
642 Cut paper and paperboard articles	5 673	3.0	0.03	0.01
874 Measure analyze control device nes	3 877	2.1	0.01	0.00
885 Watches and clocks	3 740	2.0	0.03	0.01
897 Jewellery nes (667)	3 538	1.9	0.01	0.00
321 Coal excluding non-agglomerated	2 804	1.5	0.01	0.00
111 Non alcoholic beverage nes	2 744	1.5	0.07	0.01
Remainder	54 528	29.0		
Saint Pierre and Miquelon - Saint-Pierre-et-Miquelon (**=Developed) (2)				
All commodity groups	4 880	100.0	0.00	0.00
034 Fish, fresh live chilled frozen	1 801	36.9	0.01	0.00
035 Fish, dried salted smoked	952	19.5	0.02	0.02
036 Crustacean mollusc aquat invertebra	938	19.2	0.01	0.00
842 Female clothing, woven	304	6.2	0.00	0.00
845 Articles of apparel nes	282	5.8	0.00	0.00
844 Female clothing, knitted crocheted	129	2.6	0.00	0.00
684 Aluminium	67	1.4	0.00	0.00
851 Footwear	42	0.9	0.00	0.00
874 Measure analyze control device nes	37	0.8	0.00	0.00
291 Crude animal materials nes	32	0.7	0.00	0.00
Remainder	296	6.1		

Leading products exported based on average 2010-2011 values SITC Revision 3 (3-digit level) / Principaux produits exportés d'après la moyenne des valeurs de 2010-2011 CTCI révision 3 (positions à 3 chiffres)	Value (f.o.b., thousands of dollars) Valeur (f.a.b., milliers de dollars)	of country total du total du pays	of ** (1) des ** (1)	of world du monde
St Vincent and the Grenadines - St-Vincent-et-les Grenadines (**=Developing) (2)				
All commodity groups	41 752	100.0	0.00	0.00
793 Ships boats floating structures	24 651	59.0	0.02	0.01
046 Wheat meal & flour, meslin flour	3 225	7.7	0.13	0.06
057 Fruit nut (exc oil), fresh or dried	2 128	5.1	0.01	0.00
054 Vegetable & vegetable products nes	1 325	3.2	0.01	0.00
845 Articles of apparel nes	1 163	2.8	0.00	0.00
042 Rice	1 063	2.5	0.01	0.00
111 Non alcoholic beverage nes	982	2.4	0.02	0.01
081 Animal feed excluding unmilled cereal	627	1.5	0.00	0.00
674 Flat plated iron non-alloy steel	624	1.5	0.00	0.00
896 Work of art & collections; antiques	481	1.2	0.03	0.00
Remainder	5 484	13.1		
Samoa (**=Developing) (2)				
All commodity groups	56 952	100.0	0.00	0.00
773 Electrical distribute equipment nes	38 591	67.8	0.08	0.04
034 Fish, fresh live chilled frozen	7 065	12.4	0.03	0.01
422 Fixed veg fat and oil, excl. "soft"	2 983	5.2	0.01	0.01
112 Alcoholic beverages	1 404	2.5	0.01	0.00
059 Fruit & vegetable juice unferment	1 165	2.0	0.02	0.01
057 Fruit nut (exc oil), fresh or dried	548	1.0	0.00	0.00
111 Non alcoholic beverage nes	528	0.9	0.01	0.00
054 Vegetable & vegetable products nes	467	0.8	0.00	0.00
898 Music instrument device recording	397	0.7	0.00	0.00
786 Trailer caravan transport container	321	0.6	0.00	0.00
Remainder	3 483	6.1		
Sao Tome and Principe - Sao Tomé-et-Principe (**=Developing) (2)				
All commodity groups	12 000	100.0	0.00	0.00
072 Cocoa	5 999	50.0	0.04	0.03
885 Watches and clocks	1 081	9.0	0.01	0.00
897 Jewellery nes (667)	800	6.7	0.00	0.00
776 Valves tubes; diodes, transistors	384	3.2	0.00	0.00
874 Measure analyze control device nes	263	2.2	0.00	0.00
792 Aircraft, spacecraft & equipment	235	2.0	0.00	0.00
764 Telecommunicate equipment part nes	233	1.9	0.00	0.00
073 Chocolate & cocoa preparations nes	193	1.6	0.01	0.00
058 Fruit preserve preparation excl. juice	167	1.4	0.00	0.00
679 Iron steel pipe tube fittings etc	158	1.3	0.00	0.00
Remainder	2 487	20.7		
Saudi Arabia - Arabie saoudite (**=Developing) (2)				
All commodity groups	305 617 780	100.0	4.31	1.84
333 Crude petroleum & bituminous oil	228 380 411	74.7	22.32	16.04
334 Heavy petroleum & bituminous oil	18 052 506	5.9	5.09	2.24
571 Primary form ethylene polymers	8 909 563	2.9	27.11	12.33
512 Alcohols, phenols; derivatives	7 397 642	2.4	25.53	13.29
342 Liquefied propane and butane	5 733 371	1.9	16.81	11.45
575 Other plastics, in primary forms	5 073 722	1.7	15.03	4.77
511 Hydrocarbons nes; derivatives	3 437 669	1.1	9.76	3.99
516 Other organic chemicals	2 125 624	0.7	15.85	5.43
562 Manufactured fertilizer excl. crude	1 531 047	0.5	6.89	2.36
022 Milk products, excl. butter & cheese	962 836	0.3	18.07	2.45
Remainder	24 013 388	7.9		
Senegal - Sénégal (**=Developing) (2)				
All commodity groups	2 351 416	100.0	0.03	0.01
334 Heavy petroleum & bituminous oil	536 557	22.8	0.15	0.07
522 Inorganic chemical elem oxide salt	239 570	10.2	0.91	0.42
034 Fish, fresh live chilled frozen	201 623	8.6	0.83	0.36
661 Lime cement construction material	188 188	8.0	1.20	0.69
971 Gold non-monetary excluding ores	110 891	4.7	0.11	0.06
036 Crustacean mollusc aquat invertebra	108 718	4.6	0.57	0.37
421 Fixed veg fat and oil, "soft"	103 907	4.4	0.91	0.30
122 Manufactured tabacco	53 286	2.3	0.71	0.19
676 Iron steel bar rod section piling	51 267	2.2	0.19	0.06
098 Edible products & preparations nes	50 632	2.2	0.34	0.09
Remainder	706 777	30.1		

For sources and notes, see end of table.   Pour les sources et les notes, se reporter à la fin du tableau.

Leading products exported based on average 2010-2011 values SITC Revision 3 (3-digit level) / Principaux produits exportés d'après la moyenne des valeurs de 2010-2011 CTCI révision 3 (positions à 3 chiffres)	2010-2011 Value (f.o.b., thousands of dollars) / Valeur (f.a.b., milliers de dollars)	As percentage / En pourcentage: of country total / du total du pays	of ** (1) / des ** (1)	of world / du monde
Serbia - Serbie (=Transition)**				
All commodity groups	10 784 976	100.0	1.55	0.06
673 Flat iron non-alloy steel products	675 305	6.3	6.34	0.76
682 Copper	514 216	4.8	5.15	0.37
044 Maize unmilled, excluding sweet corn	395 214	3.7	20.05	1.37
058 Fruit preserve preparation excl. juice	294 708	2.7	51.96	1.72
625 Rubber for wheels, incl inner tube	286 669	2.7	16.31	0.35
773 Electrical distribute equipment nes	268 975	2.5	12.16	0.26
851 Footwear	239 832	2.2	15.66	0.23
684 Aluminium	239 271	2.2	2.51	0.21
893 Articles of plastic nes	212 698	2.0	19.28	0.17
351 Electric current	209 011	1.9	9.15	0.58
Remainder	7 449 077	69.1		
Seychelles (=Developing) (2)**				
All commodity groups	439 100	100.0	0.01	0.00
037 Fish shellfish, prepared preserved	197 342	44.9	1.24	0.84
034 Fish, fresh live chilled frozen	98 315	22.4	0.41	0.17
035 Fish, dried salted smoked	53 957	12.3	3.52	0.97
872 Medical instruments appliances nes	14 961	3.4	0.09	0.02
334 Heavy petroleum & bituminous oil	12 754	2.9	0.00	0.00
036 Crustacean mollusc aquat invertebra	5 809	1.3	0.03	0.02
899 Manufactured articles nes	5 314	1.2	0.02	0.01
411 Animals oils and fats	5 263	1.2	0.60	0.10
282 Ferrous iron & steel, waste & scrap	4 139	0.9	0.07	0.01
081 Animal feed excluding unmilled cereal	3 557	0.8	0.01	0.01
Remainder	37 690	8.6		
Sierra Leone (=Developing) (2)**				
All commodity groups	346 173	100.0	0.00	0.00
667 Pearls, precious semiprecious stone	86 157	24.9	0.11	0.06
285 Aluminium ore concentrate alumina	47 363	13.7	0.79	0.32
072 Cocoa	36 017	10.4	0.25	0.17
287 Base metal ores & concentrates nes	26 632	7.7	0.15	0.09
793 Ships boats floating structures	20 390	5.9	0.02	0.01
571 Primary form ethylene polymers	8 453	2.4	0.03	0.01
282 Ferrous iron & steel, waste & scrap	6 713	1.9	0.11	0.01
821 Furniture part; bedding furnishing	6 558	1.9	0.01	0.00
625 Rubber for wheels, incl inner tube	5 888	1.7	0.02	0.01
061 Sugar, mollasses and honey	4 586	1.3	0.02	0.01
Remainder	97 416	28.1		
Singapore - Singapour (=Developing)**				
All commodity groups	380 685 399	100.0	5.37	2.29
776 Valves tubes; diodes, transistors	84 928 374	22.3	21.81	15.37
334 Heavy petroleum & bituminous oil	67 205 229	17.7	18.94	8.35
759 Office equipment part & accessories	17 927 049	4.7	14.98	9.00
764 Telecommunicate equipment part nes	9 868 065	2.6	3.17	2.07
752 Computer equipment nes	8 985 782	2.4	3.84	2.69
778 Electrical machinery apparatus nes	6 481 999	1.7	6.32	3.06
728 Special industrial machine part nes	6 354 194	1.7	17.12	3.66
772 Electrical circuit equipment	6 194 534	1.6	6.63	2.84
874 Measure analyze control device nes	5 659 755	1.5	16.26	3.40
515 Organo-inorganic compound acid salt	5 305 999	1.4	26.36	5.00
Remainder	161 774 419	42.5		
Slovakia - Slovaquie (=Developed)**				
All commodity groups	71 242 928	100.0	0.80	0.43
781 Passenger cars and race cars	10 205 539	14.3	2.07	1.71
761 Television video receive project	7 636 429	10.7	18.43	7.73
784 Motor vehicle parts and accessories	4 725 921	6.6	1.93	1.43
334 Heavy petroleum & bituminous oil	3 343 970	4.7	0.96	0.42
764 Telecommunicate equipment part nes	1 951 695	2.7	1.20	0.41
673 Flat iron non-alloy steel products	1 679 391	2.4	3.43	1.90
773 Electrical distribute equipment nes	1 450 218	2.0	2.73	1.41
699 Base metal manufactures nes	1 266 035	1.8	1.49	0.96
625 Rubber for wheels, incl inner tube	1 215 500	1.7	2.55	1.49
674 Flat plated iron non-alloy steel	1 199 965	1.7	3.70	2.11
Remainder	36 568 265	51.3		

Leading products exported based on average 2010-2011 values SITC Revision 3 (3-digit level) / Principaux produits exportés d'après la moyenne des valeurs de 2010-2011 CTCI révision 3 (positions à 3 chiffres)	2010-2011 Value (f.o.b., thousands of dollars) / Valeur (f.a.b., milliers de dollars)	As percentage / En pourcentage: of country total / du total du pays	of ** (1) / des ** (1)	of world / du monde
Slovenia - Slovénie (=Developed) (2)**				
All commodity groups	31 940 487	100.0	0.36	0.19
781 Passenger cars and race cars	2 506 221	7.8	0.51	0.42
542 Medicines including veterinary	2 132 671	6.7	0.70	0.64
775 Household equipment nes	1 186 066	3.7	3.08	1.33
778 Electrical machinery apparatus nes	958 641	3.0	0.89	0.45
821 Furniture part; bedding furnishing	751 908	2.4	1.04	0.54
351 Electric current	711 148	2.2	2.40	1.98
684 Aluminium	707 793	2.2	1.01	0.61
334 Heavy petroleum & bituminous oil	680 740	2.1	0.19	0.08
784 Motor vehicle parts and accessories	666 086	2.1	0.27	0.20
699 Base metal manufactures nes	547 380	1.7	0.65	0.41
Remainder	21 091 834	66.0		
Solomon Islands - Îles Salomon (=Developing) (2)**				
All commodity groups	301 044	100.0	0.00	0.00
247 Wood in rough or roughly squared	200 243	66.5	4.53	1.40
422 Fixed veg fat and oil, excl. "soft"	20 104	6.7	0.05	0.04
971 Gold non-monetary excluding ores	17 599	5.8	0.02	0.01
034 Fish, fresh live chilled frozen	14 683	4.9	0.06	0.03
037 Fish shellfish, prepared preserved	13 704	4.6	0.09	0.06
072 Cocoa	8 854	2.9	0.06	0.04
223 Oil seed for non soft oil	8 221	2.7	1.15	0.32
248 Wood simply worked, railway sleeper	4 661	1.5	0.06	0.01
035 Fish, dried salted smoked	2 883	1.0	0.19	0.05
001 Live animal excl. fish & crustacean	1 060	0.4	0.02	0.01
Remainder	9 032	3.0		
Somalia - Somalie (=Developing) (2)**				
All commodity groups	483 750	100.0	0.01	0.00
001 Live animal excl. fish & crustacean	235 075	48.6	5.47	1.16
245 Fuel wood excl. waste; wood charcoal	72 121	14.9	15.52	6.00
971 Gold non-monetary excluding ores	47 036	9.7	0.05	0.02
211 Raw hides & skins, excluding furskins	38 544	8.0	4.37	0.51
222 Oil seed etc for soft oil	19 501	4.0	0.08	0.03
611 Leather	19 034	3.9	0.15	0.08
057 Fruit nut (exc oil), fresh or dried	12 317	2.5	0.03	0.02
012 Meat nes, fresh chilled frozen	12 159	2.5	0.08	0.02
292 Crude vegetable materials nes	8 989	1.9	0.08	0.02
574 Polyacetals and polyesters, etc	5 639	1.2	0.02	0.01
Remainder	13 336	2.8		
South Africa - Afrique du Sud (=Developing) (2)**				
All commodity groups	89 337 806	100.0	1.26	0.54
681 Silver, platinum, platinum metals	10 656 399	11.9	41.05	17.44
281 Iron ore and concentrates	6 564 456	7.3	11.52	5.25
971 Gold non-monetary excluding ores	5 802 250	6.5	6.01	3.08
321 Coal excluding non-agglomomerated	5 528 829	6.2	13.51	4.68
671 Pig & sponge iron, ferro alloys etc	4 940 125	5.5	22.53	12.09
781 Passenger cars and race cars	4 109 301	4.6	3.98	0.69
287 Base metal ores & concentrates nes	3 642 306	4.1	19.93	11.71
667 Pearls, precious semiprecious stone	3 592 581	4.0	4.78	2.44
057 Fruit nut (exc oil), fresh or dried	2 626 625	2.9	6.65	3.27
743 Gas pump, compressor, fan, filter	2 398 269	2.7	7.46	2.08
Remainder	39 476 665	44.2		
Spain - Espagne (=Developed) (2)**				
All commodity groups	271 380 839	100.0	3.06	1.63
781 Passenger cars and race cars	28 664 454	10.6	5.82	4.79
784 Motor vehicle parts and accessories	11 533 154	4.2	4.71	3.50
542 Medicines including veterinary	10 430 602	3.8	3.42	3.14
334 Heavy petroleum & bituminous oil	9 746 225	3.6	2.79	1.21
057 Fruit nut (exc oil), fresh or dried	8 110 413	3.0	20.71	10.10
054 Vegetable & vegetable products nes	6 235 213	2.3	17.37	10.34
676 Iron steel bar rod section piling	5 906 196	2.2	11.71	7.00
782 Goods and service vehicles	5 876 721	2.2	7.58	5.02
792 Aircraft, spacecraft & equipment	3 821 827	1.4	3.16	2.68
012 Meat nes, fresh chilled frozen	3 746 499	1.4	7.14	5.55
Remainder	177 309 534	65.3		

For sources and notes, see end of table.

Pour les sources et les notes, se reporter à la fin du tableau.

3.2.D Export structure by product
Individual countries and territories

3.2.D Structure des exportations par produits
Pays et territoires individuels

Leading products exported based on average 2010-2011 values SITC Revision 3 (3-digit level) / Principaux produits exportés d'après la moyenne des valeurs de 2010-2011 CTCI révision 3 (positions à 3 chiffres)	2010-2011 Value (f.o.b., thousands of dollars) / Valeur (f.a.b., milliers de dollars)	As percentage / En pourcentage: of country total / du total du pays	of ** (1) / des ** (1)	of world / du monde
Sri Lanka (=Developing)**				
All commodity groups	9 157 667	100.0	0.13	0.05
074 Tea and maté	1 433 911	15.7	24.42	18.30
845 Articles of apparel nes	1 089 413	11.9	1.17	0.82
842 Female clothing, woven	768 621	8.4	1.49	0.98
844 Female clothing, knitted crocheted	763 189	8.3	1.99	1.54
841 Male clothing, woven	563 410	6.2	1.26	0.85
625 Rubber for wheels, incl inner tube	459 493	5.0	1.42	0.56
667 Pearls, precious semiprecious stone	450 986	4.9	0.60	0.31
843 Male clothing, knitted crocheted	234 013	2.6	1.03	0.86
846 Clothing accessory excl. 831 848 851	229 586	2.5	1.37	0.86
848 Headgear, non-textile clothing	203 211	2.2	1.08	0.75
Remainder	2 961 834	32.3		
Sudan (...2011) - Soudan (...2011) (=Developing) (2)**				
All commodity groups	11 599 873	100.0	0.16	0.07
333 Crude petroleum & bituminous oil	8 701 343	75.0	0.85	0.61
334 Heavy petroleum & bituminous oil	1 141 066	9.8	0.32	0.14
971 Gold non-monetary excluding ores	850 927	7.3	0.88	0.45
222 Oil seed etc for soft oil	169 319	1.5	0.66	0.29
001 Live animal excl. fish & crustacean	165 062	1.4	3.84	0.81
292 Crude vegetable materials nes	85 388	0.7	0.73	0.22
263 Cotton	80 917	0.7	0.88	0.36
061 Sugar, mollasses and honey	47 750	0.4	0.16	0.11
282 Ferrous iron & steel, waste & scrap	25 962	0.2	0.42	0.05
054 Vegetable & vegetable products nes	25 146	0.2	0.11	0.04
Remainder	306 994	2.6		
Suriname (=Developing) (2)**				
All commodity groups	2 185 123	100.0	0.03	0.01
971 Gold non-monetary excluding ores	804 678	36.8	0.83	0.43
285 Aluminium ore concentrate alumina	553 991	25.4	9.26	3.78
334 Heavy petroleum & bituminous oil	196 982	9.0	0.06	0.02
034 Fish, fresh live chilled frozen	73 090	3.3	0.30	0.13
057 Fruit nut (exc oil), fresh or dried	48 669	2.2	0.12	0.06
036 Crustacean mollusc aquat invertebra	36 559	1.7	0.19	0.12
042 Rice	29 638	1.4	0.17	0.13
522 Inorganic chemical elem oxide salt	15 083	0.7	0.06	0.03
247 Wood in rough or roughly squared	10 390	0.5	0.24	0.07
283 Copper ores and concentrates	10 185	0.5	0.03	0.02
Remainder	405 858	18.6		
Swaziland (=Developing) (2)**				
All commodity groups	1 927 175	100.0	0.03	0.01
061 Sugar, mollasses and honey	404 437	21.0	1.35	0.96
551 Essential oils, perfumes & flavours	266 774	13.8	5.98	1.16
971 Gold non-monetary excluding ores	75 011	3.9	0.08	0.04
845 Articles of apparel nes	73 129	3.8	0.08	0.06
098 Edible products & preparations nes	72 276	3.8	0.49	0.13
251 Pulp and waste paper	68 481	3.6	0.59	0.15
598 Miscellaneous chemical products nes	61 415	3.2	0.22	0.05
671 Pig & sponge iron, ferro alloys etc	56 193	2.9	0.26	0.14
057 Fruit nut (exc oil), fresh or dried	51 002	2.6	0.13	0.06
842 Female clothing, woven	43 771	2.3	0.08	0.06
Remainder	754 686	39.2		
Sweden - Suède (=Developed)**				
All commodity groups	172 794 812	100.0	1.95	1.04
764 Telecommunicate equipment part nes	10 748 116	6.2	6.59	2.26
334 Heavy petroleum & bituminous oil	10 353 011	6.0	2.96	1.29
641 Paper and paperboard	10 129 258	5.9	10.64	8.53
542 Medicines including veterinary	7 404 478	4.3	2.42	2.23
784 Motor vehicle parts and accessories	6 539 439	3.8	2.67	1.98
781 Passenger cars and race cars	6 078 019	3.5	1.23	1.02
675 Flat rolled products of alloy steel	3 609 071	2.1	7.66	5.37
248 Wood simply worked, railway sleeper	3 440 364	2.0	14.24	9.58
713 Internal combustion engine part nes	3 082 446	1.8	2.60	2.04
281 Iron ore and concentrates	3 050 465	1.8	4.99	2.44
Remainder	108 360 144	62.7		

Leading products exported based on average 2010-2011 values SITC Revision 3 (3-digit level) / Principaux produits exportés d'après la moyenne des valeurs de 2010-2011 CTCI révision 3 (positions à 3 chiffres)	2010-2011 Value (f.o.b., thousands of dollars) / Valeur (f.a.b., milliers de dollars)	As percentage / En pourcentage: of country total / du total du pays	of ** (1) / des ** (1)	of world / du monde
Switzerland - Suisse (=Developed)**				
All commodity groups	215 017 813	100.0	2.43	1.29
542 Medicines including veterinary	29 840 710	13.9	9.77	8.99
541 Pharmaceuticals excluding medicines	24 056 977	11.2	18.85	16.49
885 Watches and clocks	18 641 975	8.7	67.69	44.02
515 Organo-inorganic compound acid salt	7 780 573	3.6	9.16	7.34
897 Jewellery nes (667)	7 510 342	3.5	19.77	8.08
899 Manufactured articles nes	6 277 199	2.9	12.53	8.29
351 Electric current	5 563 211	2.6	18.74	15.48
728 Special industrial machine part nes	5 264 720	2.4	3.88	3.03
681 Silver, platinum, platinum metals	4 909 313	2.3	14.20	8.04
874 Measure analyze control device nes	4 896 818	2.3	3.76	2.94
Remainder	100 275 977	46.6		
Syrian Arab Republic - République arabe syrienne (=Developing) (2)**				
All commodity groups	9 597 945	100.0	0.14	0.06
333 Crude petroleum & bituminous oil	2 849 411	29.7	0.28	0.20
334 Heavy petroleum & bituminous oil	973 286	10.1	0.27	0.12
054 Vegetable & vegetable products nes	465 493	4.8	2.00	0.77
057 Fruit nut (exc oil), fresh or dried	388 685	4.0	0.98	0.48
111 Non alcoholic beverage nes	315 725	3.3	7.58	1.71
554 Soaps cleansers polishes	273 720	2.9	2.66	0.72
001 Live animal excl. fish & crustacean	246 865	2.6	5.75	1.22
893 Articles of plastic nes	182 244	1.9	0.40	0.15
651 Textile yarn	173 659	1.8	0.49	0.31
272 Crude fertilizer, excl. manufactured	172 209	1.8	5.67	4.15
Remainder	3 556 646	37.1		
Tajikistan - Tadjikistan (=Transition) (2)**				
All commodity groups	1 208 715	100.0	0.17	0.01
684 Aluminium	463 384	38.3	4.87	0.40
263 Cotton	234 454	19.4	6.80	1.04
287 Base metal ores & concentrates nes	77 088	6.4	5.74	0.25
652 Woven cotton fabrics	47 120	3.9	11.79	0.15
057 Fruit nut (exc oil), fresh or dried	24 730	2.0	1.52	0.03
351 Electric current	17 222	1.4	0.75	0.05
845 Articles of apparel nes	15 597	1.3	1.42	0.01
288 Non ferrous base metal waste nes	13 470	1.1	1.98	0.03
651 Textile yarn	13 308	1.1	0.86	0.02
792 Aircraft, spacecraft & equipment	12 320	1.0	1.80	0.01
Remainder	290 022	24.0		
Thailand - Thaïlande (=Developing)**				
All commodity groups	212 067 746	100.0	2.99	1.27
752 Computer equipment nes	12 155 009	5.7	5.19	3.63
231 Natural rubber, latex, gum, etc	10 536 188	5.0	34.56	32.74
776 Valves tubes; diodes, transistors	9 303 721	4.4	2.39	1.68
334 Heavy petroleum & bituminous oil	8 945 508	4.2	2.52	1.11
781 Passenger cars and race cars	6 646 149	3.1	6.44	1.11
971 Gold non-monetary excluding ores	6 219 575	2.9	6.44	3.30
042 Rice	5 924 278	2.8	33.37	26.90
782 Goods and service vehicles	5 618 437	2.6	14.98	4.80
037 Fish shellfish, prepared preserved	4 580 667	2.2	28.78	19.47
784 Motor vehicle parts and accessories	4 394 046	2.1	5.25	1.33
Remainder	137 744 169	65.0		
TFYR of Macedonia - LERY de Macédoine (=Transition) (2)**				
All commodity groups	3 877 168	100.0	0.56	0.02
671 Pig & sponge iron, ferro alloys etc	487 397	12.6	5.14	1.19
842 Female clothing, woven	330 667	8.5	29.47	0.42
673 Flat iron non-alloy steel products	281 503	7.3	2.64	0.32
598 Miscellaneous chemical products nes	279 156	7.2	37.41	0.24
841 Male clothing, woven	246 976	6.4	25.07	0.37
334 Heavy petroleum & bituminous oil	178 992	4.6	0.18	0.02
679 Iron steel pipe tube fittings etc	108 707	2.8	3.21	0.13
121 Unmanufactured tabacco and refuse	108 337	2.8	38.65	0.93
674 Flat plated iron non-alloy steel	98 362	2.5	7.94	0.17
287 Base metal ores & concentrates nes	79 625	2.1	5.93	0.26
Remainder	1 677 444	43.3		

For sources and notes, see end of table.

Pour les sources et les notes, se reporter à la fin du tableau.

3

Left side:

Leading products exported based on average 2010-2011 values SITC Revision 3 (3-digit level) / Principaux produits exportés d'après la moyenne des valeurs de 2010-2011 CTCI révision 3 (positions à 3 chiffres)	2010-2011 Value (f.o.b., thousands of dollars) Valeur (f.a.b., milliers de dollars)	As percentage En pourcentage of country total du total du pays	of ** (1) des ** (1)	of world du monde
Timor-Leste (**=Developing) (2)				
All commodity groups	14 500	100.0	0.00	0.00
333 Crude petroleum & bituminous oil	4 279	29.5	0.00	0.00
342 Liquefied propane and butane	4 097	28.3	0.01	0.01
071 Coffee and coffee substitutes	2 332	16.1	0.01	0.01
782 Goods and service vehicles	675	4.7	0.00	0.00
723 Civil engineering plant & equipment	432	3.0	0.00	0.00
772 Electrical circuit equipment	296	2.0	0.00	0.00
764 Telecommunicate equipment part nes	137	0.9	0.00	0.00
891 Arms and ammunition	105	0.7	0.01	0.00
792 Aircraft, spacecraft & equipment	95	0.7	0.00	0.00
892 Printed matter	71	0.5	0.00	0.00
Remainder	1 982	13.7		
Togo (**=Developing) (2)				
All commodity groups	996 619	100.0	0.01	0.01
072 Cocoa	171 814	17.2	1.19	0.79
661 Lime cement construction material	126 603	12.7	0.80	0.46
263 Cotton	113 062	11.3	1.23	0.50
272 Crude fertilizer, excl. manufactured	81 956	8.2	2.70	1.97
971 Gold non-monetary excluding ores	62 948	6.3	0.07	0.03
071 Coffee and coffee substitutes	35 934	3.6	0.15	0.10
351 Electric current	32 386	3.2	0.82	0.09
553 Perfume toilet cosmetics, excl. soap	29 828	3.0	0.18	0.04
893 Articles of plastic nes	26 749	2.7	0.06	0.02
562 Manufactured fertilizer excl. crude	25 755	2.6	0.12	0.04
Remainder	289 585	29.1		
Tokelau - Tokélaou (**=Developing) (2)				
All commodity groups	101	100.0	0.00	0.00
676 Iron steel bar rod section piling	32	31.6	0.00	0.00
042 Rice	5	5.4	0.00	0.00
741 Heating cooling equipment parts nes	4	3.9	0.00	0.00
714 Non-electric engines excl. 712 713 718	3	3.3	0.00	0.00
695 Tools for use in hand or in machine	2	2.2	0.00	0.00
057 Fruit nut (exc oil), fresh or dried	2	1.9	0.00	0.00
694 Nails screws nuts bolts rivets	2	1.9	0.00	0.00
896 Work of art & collections; antiques	2	1.8	0.00	0.00
542 Medicines including veterinary	2	1.7	0.00	0.00
845 Articles of apparel nes	2	1.5	0.00	0.00
Remainder	45	44.7		
Tonga (**=Developing) (2)				
All commodity groups	9 630	100.0	0.00	0.00
054 Vegetable & vegetable products nes	1 853	19.2	0.01	0.00
036 Crustacean mollusc aquat invertebra	1 514	15.7	0.01	0.01
034 Fish, fresh live chilled frozen	1 203	12.5	0.00	0.00
292 Crude vegetable materials nes	617	6.4	0.01	0.00
793 Ships boats floating structures	457	4.8	0.00	0.00
533 Pigment, paint, varnish & related	378	3.9	0.00	0.00
057 Fruit nut (exc oil), fresh or dried	375	3.9	0.00	0.00
035 Fish, dried salted smoked	327	3.4	0.02	0.01
072 Cocoa	277	2.9	0.00	0.00
532 Dyeing and tanning extracts	218	2.3	0.03	0.01
Remainder	2 411	25.0		
Trinidad and Tobago - Trinité-et-Tobago (**=Developing) (2)				
All commodity groups	12 126 605	100.0	0.17	0.07
343 Natural gas, liquefied or not	3 010 532	24.8	2.36	1.19
334 Heavy petroleum & bituminous oil	2 596 869	21.4	0.73	0.32
522 Inorganic chemical elem oxide salt	1 719 162	14.2	6.54	2.98
333 Crude petroleum & bituminous oil	1 254 239	10.3	0.12	0.09
512 Alcohols, phenols; derivatives	874 664	7.2	3.02	1.57
671 Pig & sponge iron, ferro alloys etc	610 944	5.0	2.79	1.50
342 Liquefied propane and butane	312 348	2.6	0.92	0.62
562 Manufactured fertilizer excl. crude	252 646	2.1	1.14	0.39
281 Iron ore and concentrates	242 773	2.0	0.43	0.19
676 Iron steel bar rod section piling	193 763	1.6	0.71	0.23
Remainder	1 058 666	8.7		

Right side:

Leading products exported based on average 2010-2011 values SITC Revision 3 (3-digit level) / Principaux produits exportés d'après la moyenne des valeurs de 2010-2011 CTCI révision 3 (positions à 3 chiffres)	2010-2011 Value (f.o.b., thousands of dollars) Valeur (f.a.b., milliers de dollars)	As percentage En pourcentage of country total du total du pays	of ** (1) des ** (1)	of world du monde
Tunisia - Tunisie (**=Developing) (2)				
All commodity groups	17 136 769	100.0	0.24	0.10
333 Crude petroleum & bituminous oil	2 154 221	12.6	0.21	0.15
845 Articles of apparel nes	1 708 838	10.0	1.83	1.29
773 Electrical distribute equipment nes	1 340 073	7.8	2.82	1.30
562 Manufactured fertilizer excl. crude	854 167	5.0	3.85	1.31
841 Male clothing, woven	826 417	4.8	1.84	1.25
772 Electrical circuit equipment	810 725	4.7	0.87	0.37
851 Footwear	565 276	3.3	0.89	0.54
842 Female clothing, woven	534 430	3.1	1.04	0.68
421 Fixed veg fat and oil, "soft"	518 499	3.0	4.52	1.49
764 Telecommunicate equipment part nes	402 822	2.4	0.13	0.08
Remainder	7 421 299	43.3		
Turkey - Turquie (**=Developing)				
All commodity groups	124 447 352	100.0	1.75	0.75
781 Passenger cars and race cars	6 347 921	5.1	6.15	1.06
676 Iron steel bar rod section piling	6 141 666	4.9	22.52	7.28
334 Heavy petroleum & bituminous oil	4 900 727	3.9	1.38	0.61
845 Articles of apparel nes	4 671 537	3.8	5.01	3.51
782 Goods and service vehicles	3 749 882	3.0	10.00	3.20
057 Fruit nut (exc oil), fresh or dried	3 649 619	2.9	9.23	4.54
775 Household equipment nes	3 178 193	2.6	6.39	3.56
784 Motor vehicle parts and accessories	3 070 330	2.5	3.67	0.93
842 Female clothing, woven	2 685 722	2.2	5.21	3.43
773 Electrical distribute equipment nes	2 098 587	1.7	4.42	2.04
Remainder	83 953 167	67.5		
Turkmenistan - Turkménistan (**=Transition) (2)				
All commodity groups	9 750 000	100.0	1.40	0.06
343 Natural gas, liquefied or not	4 427 337	45.4	13.38	1.75
334 Heavy petroleum & bituminous oil	1 389 713	14.3	1.39	0.17
263 Cotton	1 179 882	12.1	34.21	5.25
322 Briquettes, lignite and peat	317 617	3.3	28.17	8.33
651 Textile yarn	314 807	3.2	20.37	0.56
333 Crude petroleum & bituminous oil	282 252	2.9	0.13	0.02
575 Other plastics, in primary forms	181 345	1.9	22.58	0.17
652 Woven cotton fabrics	141 516	1.5	35.41	0.44
522 Inorganic chemical elem oxide salt	136 498	1.4	4.03	0.24
657 Special yarn and textile fabric etc	126 029	1.3	26.74	0.28
Remainder	1 253 005	12.9		
Turks and Caicos Islands - Îles Turques et Caïques (**=Developing) (2)				
All commodity groups	16 000	100.0	0.00	0.00
541 Pharmaceuticals excluding medicines	2 431	15.2	0.01	0.00
036 Crustacean mollusc aquat invertebra	1 181	7.4	0.01	0.00
781 Passenger cars and race cars	910	5.7	0.00	0.00
723 Civil engineering plant & equipment	639	4.0	0.00	0.00
037 Fish shellfish, prepared preserved	539	3.4	0.00	0.00
334 Heavy petroleum & bituminous oil	386	2.4	0.00	0.00
288 Non ferrous base metal waste nes	385	2.4	0.00	0.00
716 Rotating electric plant parts nes	346	2.2	0.00	0.00
523 Inorganic acid metal salt peroxy	274	1.7	0.00	0.00
772 Electrical circuit equipment	269	1.7	0.00	0.00
Remainder	8 641	54.0		
Tuvalu (**=Developing) (2)				
All commodity groups	299	100.0	0.00	0.00
034 Fish, fresh live chilled frozen	148	49.6	0.00	0.00
793 Ships boats floating structures	39	12.9	0.00	0.00
421 Fixed veg fat and oil, "soft"	8	2.8	0.00	0.00
122 Manufactured tabacco	7	2.2	0.00	0.00
831 Case bag: storage travel shopping	6	1.9	0.00	0.00
653 Man-made woven fabrics	5	1.6	0.00	0.00
282 Ferrous iron & steel, waste & scrap	5	1.5	0.00	0.00
692 Metal storage transport container	4	1.5	0.00	0.00
894 Baby carriage toy game sport good	4	1.5	0.00	0.00
334 Heavy petroleum & bituminous oil	4	1.4	0.00	0.00
Remainder	69	23.1		

For sources and notes, see end of table.

Pour les sources et les notes, se reporter à la fin du tableau.

3.2.D Export structure by product
Individual countries and territories

3.2.D Structure des exportations par produits
Pays et territoires individuels

Leading products exported based on average 2010-2011 values SITC Revision 3 (3-digit level) / Principaux produits exportés d'après la moyenne des valeurs de 2010-2011 CTCI révision 3 (positions à 3 chiffres)	2010-2011			
	Value (f.o.b., thousands of dollars) / Valeur (f.a.b., milliers de dollars)	As percentage / En pourcentage		
		of country total / du total du pays	of ** (1) / des ** (1)	of world / du monde
Uganda - Ouganda (=Developing) (2)**				
All commodity groups	2 757 900	100.0	0.04	0.02
071 Coffee and coffee substitutes	551 637	20.0	2.38	1.50
034 Fish, fresh live chilled frozen	204 552	7.4	0.85	0.36
121 Unmanufactured tabacco and refuse	162 301	5.9	2.07	1.39
661 Lime cement construction material	120 387	4.4	0.77	0.44
764 Telecommunicate equipment part nes	110 924	4.0	0.04	0.02
292 Crude vegetable materials nes	102 781	3.7	0.88	0.27
971 Gold non-monetary excluding ores	101 295	3.7	0.10	0.05
074 Tea and maté	88 116	3.2	1.50	1.12
061 Sugar, mollasses and honey	77 803	2.8	0.26	0.18
072 Cocoa	58 165	2.1	0.40	0.27
Remainder	1 179 939	42.8		
Ukraine (=Transition)**				
All commodity groups	59 911 660	100.0	8.59	0.36
672 Ingots, Iron steel primary products	6 018 535	10.0	40.82	14.76
673 Flat iron non-alloy steel products	4 200 532	7.0	39.42	4.76
676 Iron steel bar rod section piling	3 727 547	6.2	55.92	4.42
281 Iron ore and concentrates	3 121 230	5.2	44.85	2.50
791 Railway vehicles and equipment	3 095 553	5.2	80.93	11.50
421 Fixed veg fat and oil, "soft"	2 818 345	4.7	70.20	8.12
334 Heavy petroleum & bituminous oil	2 767 336	4.6	2.77	0.34
671 Pig & sponge iron, ferro alloys etc	1 835 503	3.1	19.36	4.49
679 Iron steel pipe tube fittings etc	1 721 481	2.9	50.75	2.00
044 Maize unmilled, excluding sweet corn	1 384 314	2.3	70.24	4.78
Remainder	29 221 283	48.8		
United Arab Emirates - Émirats arabes unis (=Developing) (2)**				
All commodity groups	217 189 560	100.0	3.06	1.30
333 Crude petroleum & bituminous oil	93 120 925	42.9	9.10	6.54
334 Heavy petroleum & bituminous oil	18 774 515	8.6	5.29	2.33
667 Pearls, precious semiprecious stone	15 506 679	7.1	20.61	10.55
971 Gold non-monetary excluding ores	14 266 319	6.6	14.77	7.57
342 Liquefied propane and butane	5 260 546	2.4	15.42	10.50
343 Natural gas, liquefied or not	4 374 515	2.0	3.43	1.73
684 Aluminium	3 177 515	1.5	8.75	2.74
781 Passenger cars and race cars	2 773 735	1.3	2.69	0.46
897 Jewellery nes (667)	2 563 421	1.2	4.68	2.76
764 Telecommunicate equipment part nes	2 386 749	1.1	0.77	0.50
Remainder	54 984 641	25.3		
United Kingdom - Royaume-Uni (=Developed)**				
All commodity groups	438 982 263	100.0	4.95	2.64
781 Passenger cars and race cars	29 288 089	6.7	5.94	4.89
542 Medicines including veterinary	27 278 842	6.2	8.93	8.22
333 Crude petroleum & bituminous oil	25 882 671	5.9	14.65	1.82
334 Heavy petroleum & bituminous oil	24 533 964	5.6	7.01	3.05
714 Non-electric engines excl. 712 713 718	17 267 134	3.9	25.39	21.07
112 Alcoholic beverages	9 167 673	2.1	16.49	13.23
874 Measure analyze control device nes	8 981 238	2.0	6.89	5.40
764 Telecommunicate equipment part nes	8 827 937	2.0	5.41	1.86
667 Pearls, precious semiprecious stone	8 552 204	1.9	12.47	5.82
713 Internal combustion engine part nes	7 868 090	1.8	6.64	5.21
Remainder	271 334 422	61.8		
United Republic of Tanzania - République-Unie de Tanzanie (=Developing)**				
All commodity groups	4 392 753	100.0	0.06	0.03
971 Gold non-monetary excluding ores	689 642	15.7	0.71	0.37
289 Prec metal ore concentrate excl. gold	552 671	12.6	9.43	2.95
287 Base metal ores & concentrates nes	315 061	7.2	1.72	1.01
121 Unmanufactured tabacco and refuse	238 115	5.4	3.04	2.04
057 Fruit nut (exc oil), fresh or dried	189 652	4.3	0.48	0.24
071 Coffee and coffee substitutes	188 123	4.3	0.81	0.51
034 Fish, fresh live chilled frozen	171 760	3.9	0.71	0.30
054 Vegetable & vegetable products nes	130 773	3.0	0.56	0.22
682 Copper	123 566	2.8	0.17	0.09
263 Cotton	119 188	2.7	1.30	0.53
Remainder	1 674 203	38.1		

Leading products exported based on average 2010-2011 values SITC Revision 3 (3-digit level) / Principaux produits exportés d'après la moyenne des valeurs de 2010-2011 CTCI révision 3 (positions à 3 chiffres)	2010-2011			
	Value (f.o.b., thousands of dollars) / Valeur (f.a.b., milliers de dollars)	As percentage / En pourcentage		
		of country total / du total du pays	of ** (1) / des ** (1)	of world / du monde
United States - États-Unis (=Developed)**				
All commodity groups	1 378 419 665	100.0	15.56	8.28
334 Heavy petroleum & bituminous oil	72 357 649	5.2	20.68	8.99
776 Valves tubes; diodes, transistors	45 959 186	3.3	28.23	8.32
781 Passenger cars and race cars	43 836 831	3.2	8.89	7.33
764 Telecommunicate equipment part nes	35 827 372	2.6	21.95	7.53
784 Motor vehicle parts and accessories	35 645 137	2.6	14.56	10.81
874 Measure analyze control device nes	30 500 752	2.2	23.41	18.33
752 Computer equipment nes	26 946 833	2.0	26.94	8.06
971 Gold non-monetary excluding ores	25 475 773	1.8	28.23	13.52
542 Medicines including veterinary	25 133 329	1.8	8.23	7.57
728 Special industrial machine part nes	21 392 832	1.6	15.78	12.33
Remainder	1 015 343 973	73.7		
Uruguay (=Developing) (2)**				
All commodity groups	7 309 504	100.0	0.10	0.04
011 Beef, fresh chilled frozen	1 400 897	19.2	12.75	3.75
268 Wool & animal hair, incl wool tops	720 685	9.9	23.85	9.99
042 Rice	426 726	5.8	2.40	1.94
022 Milk products, excl. butter & cheese	319 608	4.4	6.00	0.81
611 Leather	292 583	4.0	2.28	1.25
048 Cereal & preparation flour starch	243 058	3.3	2.83	0.58
034 Fish, fresh live chilled frozen	233 634	3.2	0.97	0.41
222 Oil seed etc for soft oil	225 869	3.1	0.88	0.38
024 Cheese and curd	195 309	2.7	9.99	0.68
012 Meat nes, fresh chilled frozen	189 897	2.6	1.31	0.28
Remainder	3 061 238	41.9		
Uzbekistan - Ouzbékistan (=Transition)**				
All commodity groups	12 420 500	100.0	1.78	0.07
263 Cotton	1 825 197	14.7	52.92	8.12
682 Copper	1 379 388	11.1	13.83	0.99
781 Passenger cars and race cars	1 260 599	10.1	55.55	0.21
525 Radio active & associated materials	1 060 229	8.5	26.16	5.58
343 Natural gas, liquefied or not	1 022 418	8.2	3.09	0.41
651 Textile yarn	774 129	6.2	50.10	1.38
322 Briquettes, lignite and peat	678 113	5.5	60.14	17.79
057 Fruit nut (exc oil), fresh or dried	677 645	5.5	41.64	0.84
562 Manufactured fertilizer excl. crude	362 061	2.9	2.58	0.56
971 Gold non-monetary excluding ores	351 338	2.8	22.20	0.19
Remainder	3 029 382	24.4		
Vanuatu (=Developing) (2)**				
All commodity groups	57 976	100.0	0.00	0.00
034 Fish, fresh live chilled frozen	34 069	58.8	0.14	0.06
793 Ships boats floating structures	15 582	26.9	0.01	0.01
223 Oil seed for non soft oil	2 299	4.0	0.32	0.09
422 Fixed veg fat and oil, excl. "soft"	1 347	2.3	0.00	0.00
011 Beef, fresh chilled frozen	600	1.0	0.01	0.00
292 Crude vegetable materials nes	570	1.0	0.00	0.00
072 Cocoa	431	0.7	0.00	0.00
344 Petroleum and hydrocarbon gas nes	410	0.7	0.00	0.00
054 Vegetable & vegetable products nes	346	0.6	0.00	0.00
248 Wood simply worked, railway sleeper	188	0.3	0.00	0.00
Remainder	2 134	3.7		
Venezuela (Bolivarian Rep.of)-Venezuela (Rép.bolivarienne du) (=Developing) (2)**				
All commodity groups	79 782 336	100.0	1.12	0.48
333 Crude petroleum & bituminous oil	53 287 601	66.8	5.21	3.74
334 Heavy petroleum & bituminous oil	13 917 416	17.4	3.92	1.73
684 Aluminium	1 218 743	1.5	3.36	1.05
676 Iron steel bar rod section piling	1 193 750	1.5	4.38	1.41
281 Iron ore and concentrates	1 077 296	1.4	1.89	0.86
674 Flat plated iron non-alloy steel	1 037 777	1.3	4.48	1.83
671 Pig & sponge iron, ferro alloys etc	1 018 197	1.3	4.64	2.49
542 Medicines including veterinary	725 852	0.9	2.90	0.22
591 Household and garden chemicals	604 771	0.8	8.19	2.31
335 Residual petroleum products nes	523 689	0.7	3.24	1.22
Remainder	5 177 244	6.5		

For sources and notes, see end of table.

Pour les sources et les notes, se reporter à la fin du tableau.

Leading products exported based on average 2010-2011 values SITC Revision 3 (3-digit level) / Principaux produits exportés d'après la moyenne des valeurs de 2010-2011 CTCI révision 3 (positions à 3 chiffres)	Value (f.o.b., thousands of dollars) Valeur (f.a.b., milliers de dollars)	As percentage / En pourcentage		
		of country total du total du pays	of ** (1) des ** (1)	of world du monde
Viet Nam (**=Developing) (2)				
All commodity groups	84 571 159	100.0	1.19	0.51
333 Crude petroleum & bituminous oil	7 554 046	8.9	0.74	0.53
851 Footwear	6 129 987	7.2	9.60	5.87
845 Articles of apparel nes	3 474 019	4.1	3.72	2.61
821 Furniture part; bedding furnishing	3 444 297	4.1	5.40	2.49
231 Natural rubber, latex, gum, etc	3 122 618	3.7	10.24	9.70
042 Rice	2 983 019	3.5	16.80	13.55
071 Coffee and coffee substitutes	2 759 848	3.3	11.90	7.49
841 Male clothing, woven	2 688 474	3.2	5.99	4.07
842 Female clothing, woven	2 653 368	3.1	5.15	3.39
036 Crustacean mollusc aquat invertebra	2 547 140	3.0	13.25	8.65
Remainder	47 214 342	55.8		
Wallis and Futuna Islands - Îles Wallis-et-Futuna (**=Developing) (2)				
All commodity groups	36	100.0	0.00	0.00
676 Iron steel bar rod section piling	14	38.1	0.00	0.00
772 Electrical circuit equipment	5	14.7	0.00	0.00
571 Primary form ethylene polymers	2	6.3	0.00	0.00
675 Flat rolled products of alloy steel	2	6.3	0.00	0.00
598 Miscellaneous chemical products nes	2	5.2	0.00	0.00
741 Heating cooling equipment parts nes	1	4.0	0.00	0.00
592 Starches, glutenes, glues, etc	1	2.1	0.00	0.00
871 Optical instruments apparatus nes	0	1.2	0.00	0.00
759 Office equipment part & accessories	0	1.1	0.00	0.00
664 Glass	0	1.1	0.00	0.00
Remainder	7	19.9		
Yemen - Yémen (**=Developing) (2)				
All commodity groups	9 059 250	100.0	0.13	0.05
333 Crude petroleum & bituminous oil	5 456 189	60.2	0.53	0.38
343 Natural gas, liquefied or not	1 684 769	18.6	1.32	0.67
334 Heavy petroleum & bituminous oil	620 573	6.9	0.17	0.08
971 Gold non-monetary excluding ores	170 041	1.9	0.18	0.09
034 Fish, fresh live chilled frozen	160 829	1.8	0.66	0.29
057 Fruit nut (exc oil), fresh or dried	94 714	1.0	0.24	0.12
335 Residual petroleum products nes	75 758	0.8	0.47	0.18
036 Crustacean mollusc aquat invertebra	44 988	0.5	0.23	0.15
122 Manufactured tabacco	35 193	0.4	0.47	0.12
098 Edible products & preparations nes	33 532	0.4	0.23	0.06
Remainder	682 664	7.5		

Leading products exported based on average 2010-2011 values SITC Revision 3 (3-digit level) / Principaux produits exportés d'après la moyenne des valeurs de 2010-2011 CTCI révision 3 (positions à 3 chiffres)	Value (f.o.b., thousands of dollars) Valeur (f.a.b., milliers de dollars)	As percentage / En pourcentage		
		of country total du total du pays	of ** (1) des ** (1)	of world du monde
Zambia - Zambie (**=Developing) (2)				
All commodity groups	8 108 999	100.0	0.11	0.05
682 Copper	5 557 790	68.5	7.60	3.97
283 Copper ores and concentrates	385 870	4.8	1.02	0.77
699 Base metal manufactures nes	252 848	3.1	0.56	0.19
121 Unmanufactured tabacco and refuse	235 629	2.9	3.01	2.02
061 Sugar, mollasses and honey	152 341	1.9	0.51	0.36
689 Misc non-ferrous base metals	121 474	1.5	2.80	1.23
661 Lime cement construction material	90 559	1.1	0.58	0.33
263 Cotton	88 932	1.1	0.97	0.40
287 Basc metal ores & concentrates nes	87 010	1.1	0.48	0.28
288 Non ferrous base metal waste nes	79 810	1.0	0.87	0.18
Remainder	1 056 739	13.0		
Zimbabwe (**=Developing) (2)				
All commodity groups	3 000 000	100.0	0.04	0.02
121 Unmanufactured tabacco and refuse	462 336	15.4	5.91	3.96
671 Pig & sponge iron, ferro alloys etc	295 445	9.8	1.35	0.72
325 Coke, semi coke, retort carbon	256 794	8.6	8.66	2.76
263 Cotton	238 225	7.9	2.60	1.06
284 Nickel ores, concentrates, etc	189 600	6.3	3.03	1.77
971 Gold non-monetary excluding ores	139 615	4.7	0.14	0.07
061 Sugar, mollasses and honey	139 257	4.6	0.46	0.33
683 Nickel	93 183	3.1	3.07	0.44
122 Manufactured tabacco	83 305	2.8	1.11	0.29
661 Lime cement construction material	72 651	2.4	0.46	0.27
Remainder	1 029 588	34.3		

Source:
UNCTAD secretariat calculations, based on UNCTAD, *UNCTADstat* Merchandise Trade Matrix

Notes:
(1) The symbol ** indicates the grouping to which the country belongs and the percentage share shown applies. The percentage is the share of exports of each commodity shown by the country in the relevant grouping total exports for that commodity (i.e. "developing", which refers to developing economies; "transition", which refers to transition economies and "developed", which refers to developed economies).
(2) Data are estimated at least for one of the reference years.

Source :
Calculs du secrétariat de la CNUCED, basés sur la matrice du commerce de marchandises de *UNCTADstat* de la CNUCED

Notes :
(1) Le symbole ** indique le groupement auquel le pays appartient et par rapport auquel est calculé le pourcentage. Ce pourcentage est la part que représentent les exportations du produit par le pays par rapport aux exportations du même produit par le groupement auquel le pays appartient («developing» se réfère aux économies en développement, «transition» aux économies en transition et «developed» aux économies développées).
(2) Données estimées pour au moins une des années de référence

3.2.E Export structure by product
Major exporters for leading products
among developing economies

3.2.E Structure des exportations par produits
Principaux exportateurs de produits majeurs
parmi les économies en développement

Leading exporting developing economies (1) based on average 2010-11 exports (2) SITC Revision 3 (3-digit level) / Principales économies en dévelopement exportatrices (1) d'après la moyenne des exportations de 2010-11 (2) CTCI révision 3 (positions à 3 chiffres)	Value (f.o.b., thousands of dollars) Valeur (f.a.b., milliers de dollars)	2010-2011		
		As percentage / En pourcentage		
		of country total du total du pays	of developing economies des économies en déve-loppement	of world du monde
057 - Fruit nut (exc oil), fresh or dried				
World	80 309 010	0.48	_	100.00
Developed economies	39 159 659	0.44	_	48.76
Transition economies	1 627 480	0.23	_	2.03
Developing economies	39 521 871	0.56	100.00	49.21
Chile	4 288 161	5.63	10.85	5.34
Turkey	3 649 619	2.93	9.23	4.54
South Africa	2 626 625	2.94	6.65	3.27
China	2 624 848	0.15	6.64	3.27
Mexico	2 397 817	0.74	6.07	2.99
Ecuador	2 212 981	11.11	5.60	2.76
Viet Nam	1 524 051	1.80	3.86	1.90
Iran (Islamic Rep. of)	1 519 762	1.31	3.85	1.89
Costa Rica	1 410 265	14.64	3.57	1.76
China, Hong Kong SAR	1 381 802	0.32	3.50	1.72
061 - Sugar, mollasses and honey				
World	42 111 312	0.25	_	100.00
Developed economies	11 055 408	0.12	_	26.25
Transition economies	1 090 137	0.16	_	2.59
Developing economies	29 965 767	0.42	100.00	71.16
Brazil	13 929 570	6.14	46.48	33.08
Thailand	2 987 948	1.41	9.97	7.10
India	1 570 093	0.60	5.24	3.73
United Arab Emirates	1 249 998	0.58	4.17	2.97
Mexico	1 136 136	0.35	3.79	2.70
Cuba	925 465	16.43	3.09	2.20
Guatemala	850 151	9.13	2.84	2.02
China	805 282	0.05	2.69	1.91
Colombia	529 111	1.09	1.77	1.26
Saudi Arabia	451 483	0.15	1.51	1.07
081 - Animal feed excluding unmilled cereal				
World	63 909 432	0.38	_	100.00
Developed economies	35 252 620	0.40	_	55.16
Transition economies	1 186 989	0.17	_	1.86
Developing economies	27 469 823	0.39	100.00	42.98
Argentina	9 781 425	12.86	35.61	15.31
Brazil	5 513 208	2.43	20.07	8.63
India	2 410 535	0.92	8.78	3.77
China	2 032 263	0.12	7.40	3.18
Peru	1 807 623	4.47	6.58	2.83
Thailand	1 068 061	0.50	3.89	1.67
Chile	554 952	0.73	2.02	0.87
Indonesia	423 893	0.23	1.54	0.66
Bolivia (Plurinational State of)	390 068	4.88	1.42	0.61
Malaysia	389 575	0.18	1.42	0.61
222 - Oil seed etc for soft oil				
World	59 320 386	0.36	_	100.00
Developed economies	32 164 229	0.36	_	54.22
Transition economies	1 546 246	0.22	_	2.61
Developing economies	25 609 911	0.36	100.00	43.17
Brazil	13 759 613	6.07	53.73	23.20
Argentina	5 609 509	7.37	21.90	9.46
Paraguay	2 021 840	40.23	7.89	3.41
India	1 216 585	0.47	4.75	2.05
China	678 605	0.04	2.65	1.14
Nigeria	376 000	0.40	1.47	0.63
Ethiopia	329 585	13.33	1.29	0.56
Uruguay	225 869	3.09	0.88	0.38
Sudan (...2011)	169 319	1.46	0.66	0.29
United Arab Emirates	139 343	0.06	0.54	0.23

Leading exporting developing economies (1) based on average 2010-11 exports (2) SITC Revision 3 (3-digit level) / Principales économies en dévelopement exportatrices (1) d'après la moyenne des exportations de 2010-11 (2) CTCI révision 3 (positions à 3 chiffres)	Value (f.o.b., thousands of dollars) Valeur (f.a.b., milliers de dollars)	2010-2011		
		As percentage / En pourcentage		
		of country total du total du pays	of developing economies des économies en déve-loppement	of world du monde
231 - Natural rubber, latex, gum, etc				
World	32 182 429	0.19	_	100.00
Developed economiës	1 696 285	0.02	_	5.27
Transition economies	3 684	0.00	_	0.01
Developing economies	30 482 459	0.43	100.00	94.72
Thailand	10 536 188	4.97	34.56	32.74
Indonesia	9 547 651	5.29	31.32	29.67
Malaysia	3 601 629	1.69	11.82	11.19
Viet Nam	3 122 618	3.69	10.24	9.70
Côte d'Ivoire	908 412	8.52	2.98	2.82
Singapore	453 543	0.12	1.49	1.41
Nigeria	402 593	0.43	1.32	1.25
Guatemala	310 001	3.33	1.02	0.96
Cambodia	233 290	3.55	0.77	0.72
Myanmar	192 328	2.15	0.63	0.60
281 - Iron ore and concentrates				
World	125 049 442	0.75	_	100.00
Developed economies	61 085 184	0.69	_	48.85
Transition economies	6 959 098	1.00	_	5.57
Developing economies	57 005 159	0.80	100.00	45.59
Brazil	35 364 566	15.60	62.04	28.28
South Africa	6 564 456	7.35	11.52	5.25
India	5 153 095	1.97	9.04	4.12
Bahrain	2 050 914	12.32	3.60	1.64
Iran (Islamic Rep. of)	1 778 192	1.53	3.12	1.42
Chile	1 398 088	1.84	2.45	1.12
Mauritania	1 158 613	47.75	2.03	0.93
Venezuela (Bolivarian Rep. of)	1 077 296	1.35	1.89	0.86
Peru	773 208	1.91	1.36	0.62
Korea, Dem. People's Rep. of	295 906	9.46	0.52	0.24
283 - Copper ores and concentrates				
World	49 839 596	0.30	_	100.00
Developed economies	10 862 197	0.12	_	21.79
Transition economies	1 083 256	0.16	_	2.17
Developing economies	37 894 143	0.53	100.00	76.03
Chile	14 059 610	18.46	37.10	28.21
Peru	6 978 630	17.27	18.42	14.00
Indonesia	5 791 263	3.21	15.28	11.62
Mongolia	1 940 201	50.59	5.12	3.89
Papua New Guinea	1 471 764	21.82	3.88	2.95
Argentina	1 442 059	1.90	3.81	2.89
Brazil	1 407 325	0.62	3.71	2.82
Mexico	985 896	0.30	2.60	1.98
South Africa	442 933	0.50	1.17	0.89
Lao People's Dem. Rep.	438 612	21.16	1.16	0.88
321 - Coal excluding non-agglomomerated				
World	118 099 088	0.71	_	100.00
Developed economies	65 524 063	0.74	_	55.48
Transition economies	11 639 224	1.67	_	9.86
Developing economies	40 935 802	0.58	100.00	34.66
Indonesia	21 835 705	12.09	53.34	18.49
Colombia	6 688 597	13.82	16.34	5.66
South Africa	5 528 829	6.19	13.51	4.68
China	2 454 276	0.14	6.00	2.08
Viet Nam	2 216 130	2.62	5.41	1.88
Korea, Dem. People's Rep. of	882 883	28.23	2.16	0.75
Venezuela (Bolivarian Rep. of)	336 708	0.42	0.82	0.29
Mongolia	296 391	7.73	0.72	0.25
Philippines	180 578	0.36	0.44	0.15
India	178 855	0.07	0.44	0.15

For sources and notes, see end of table.

Pour les sources et les notes, se reporter à la fin du tableau.

3.2.E Export structure by product
Major exporters for leading products
among developing economies

3.2.E Structure des exportations par produits
Principaux exportateurs de produits majeurs
parmi les économies en développement

Leading exporting developing economies (1) based on average 2010-11 exports (2) SITC Revision 3 (3-digit level) / Principales économies en dévelopement exportatrices (1) d'après la moyenne des exportations de 2010-11 (2) CTCI révision 3 (positions à 3 chiffres)	2010-2011				Leading exporting developing economies (1) based on average 2010-11 exports (2) SITC Revision 3 (3-digit level) / Principales économies en dévelopement exportatrices (1) d'après la moyenne des exportations de 2010-11 (2) CTCI révision 3 (positions à 3 chiffres)	2010-2011			
	Value (f.o.b., thousands of dollars) Valeur (f.a.b., milliers de dollars)	As percentage / En pourcentage				Value (f.o.b., thousands of dollars) Valeur (f.a.b., milliers de dollars)	As percentage / En pourcentage		
		of country total du total du pays	of developing economies des économies en déve-loppement	of world du monde			of country total du total du pays	of developing economies des économies en déve-loppement	of world du monde
333 - Crude petroleum & bituminous oil					**422 - Fixed veg fat and oil, excl. "soft"**				
World	1 423 731 084	8.55	_	100.00	World	44 688 581	0.27	_	100.00
Developed economies	176 694 051	1.99	_	12.41	Developed economies	4 670 050	0.05	_	10.45
Transition economies	223 722 042	32.06	_	15.71	Transition economies	90 832	0.01	_	0.20
Developing economies	1 023 314 990	14.43	100.00	71.88	Developing economies	39 927 699	0.56	100.00	89.35
Saudi Arabia	228 380 411	74.73	22.32	16.04	Indonesia	18 047 631	9.99	45.20	40.39
United Arab Emirates	93 120 925	42.88	9.10	6.54	Malaysia	16 195 083	7.61	40.56	36.24
Iran (Islamic Rep. of)	84 142 176	72.38	8.22	5.91	Philippines	1 350 479	2.71	3.38	3.02
Nigeria	74 583 068	80.14	7.29	5.24	India	753 561	0.29	1.89	1.69
Iraq	67 767 286	97.75	6.62	4.76	Papua New Guinea	492 417	7.30	1.23	1.10
Kuwait	59 965 082	73.07	5.86	4.21	Thailand	398 793	0.19	1.00	0.89
Angola	56 438 269	97.07	5.52	3.96	United Arab Emirates	264 518	0.12	0.66	0.59
Venezuela (Bolivarian Rep. of)	53 287 601	66.79	5.21	3.74	Honduras	241 698	3.73	0.61	0.54
Mexico	42 635 346	13.16	4.17	2.99	Ecuador	234 333	1.18	0.59	0.52
Qatar	33 592 742	35.28	3.28	2.36	Côte d'Ivoire	233 948	2.19	0.59	0.52
334 - Heavy petroleum & bituminous oil					**511 - Hydrocarbons nes; derivatives**				
World	804 456 362	4.83	_	100.00	World	86 179 182	0.52	_	100.00
Developed economies	349 860 091	3.95	_	43.49	Developed economies	49 216 466	0.56	_	57.11
Transition economies	99 778 285	14.30	_	12.40	Transition economies	1 756 575	0.25	_	2.04
Developing economies	354 817 986	5.00	100.00	44.11	Developing economies	35 206 141	0.50	100.00	40.85
Singapore	67 205 229	17.65	18.94	8.35	Korea, Republic of	9 420 823	1.84	26.76	10.93
India	45 626 194	17.48	12.86	5.67	Saudi Arabia	3 437 669	1.12	9.76	3.99
Korea, Republic of	40 267 217	7.88	11.35	5.01	China	3 385 662	0.19	9.62	3.93
China	18 897 006	1.09	5.33	2.35	China, Taiwan Province of	2 908 412	1.00	8.26	3.37
United Arab Emirates	18 774 515	8.64	5.29	2.33	Singapore	2 713 639	0.71	7.71	3.15
Saudi Arabia	18 052 506	5.91	5.09	2.24	India	2 398 905	0.92	6.81	2.78
China, Taiwan Province of	15 390 040	5.30	4.34	1.91	Thailand	1 962 366	0.93	5.57	2.28
Venezuela (Bolivarian Rep. of)	13 917 416	17.44	3.92	1.73	Iran (Islamic Rep. of)	1 859 589	1.60	5.28	2.16
Kuwait	12 125 199	14.77	3.42	1.51	Indonesia	1 342 929	0.74	3.81	1.56
Algeria	9 676 336	14.83	2.73	1.20	Brazil	1 112 217	0.49	3.16	1.29
342 - Liquefied propane and butane					**512 - Alcohols, phenols; derivatives**				
World	50 086 098	0.30	_	100.00	World	55 674 228	0.33	_	100.00
Developed economies	14 348 847	0.16	_	28.65	Developed economies	25 718 415	0.29	_	46.19
Transition economies	1 627 342	0.23	_	3.25	Transition economies	978 904	0.14	_	1.76
Developing economies	34 109 909	0.48	100.00	68.10	Developing economies	28 976 909	0.41	100.00	52.05
Qatar	6 313 567	6.63	18.51	12.61	Saudi Arabia	7 397 642	2.42	25.53	13.29
Saudi Arabia	5 733 371	1.88	16.81	11.45	China, Taiwan Province of	2 914 538	1.00	10.06	5.23
Algeria	5 287 183	8.10	15.50	10.56	Singapore	2 551 104	0.67	8.80	4.58
United Arab Emirates	5 260 546	2.42	15.42	10.50	Malaysia	1 743 615	0.82	6.02	3.13
Kuwait	2 553 573	3.11	7.49	5.10	Iran (Islamic Rep. of)	1 666 002	1.43	5.75	2.99
Iran (Islamic Rep. of)	2 391 909	2.06	7.01	4.78	Brazil	1 514 819	0.67	5.23	2.72
Nigeria	1 191 870	1.28	3.49	2.38	Korea, Republic of	1 484 872	0.29	5.12	2.67
China	832 562	0.05	2.44	1.66	China	1 456 697	0.08	5.03	2.62
Argentina	644 579	0.85	1.89	1.29	Indonesia	1 002 203	0.55	3.46	1.80
Malaysia	640 429	0.30	1.88	1.28	Trinidad and Tobago	874 664	7.21	3.02	1.57
343 - Natural gas, liquefied or not					**522 - Inorganic chemical elem oxide salt**				
World	252 411 633	1.52	_	100.00	World	57 708 842	0.35	_	100.00
Developed economies	91 908 092	1.04	_	36.41	Developed economies	28 049 651	0.32	_	48.61
Transition economies	33 087 419	4.74	_	13.11	Transition economies	3 389 989	0.49	_	5.87
Developing economies	127 416 123	1.80	100.00	50.48	Developing economies	26 269 201	0.37	100.00	45.52
Qatar	37 046 806	38.91	29.08	14.68	China	7 225 061	0.42	27.50	12.52
Algeria	18 583 143	28.48	14.58	7.36	Korea, Republic of	2 891 816	0.57	11.01	5.01
Indonesia	18 022 645	9.98	14.14	7.14	Morocco	2 082 343	10.60	7.93	3.61
Malaysia	14 087 142	6.62	11.06	5.58	Trinidad and Tobago	1 719 162	14.18	6.54	2.98
Nigeria	5 233 617	5.62	4.11	2.07	China, Taiwan Province of	1 099 676	0.38	4.19	1.91
United Arab Emirates	4 374 515	2.01	3.43	1.73	Brazil	874 687	0.39	3.33	1.52
Brunei Darussalam	4 325 640	40.40	3.39	1.71	Saudi Arabia	852 461	0.28	3.25	1.48
Oman	4 289 994	10.25	3.37	1.70	Chile	789 799	1.04	3.01	1.37
Bolivia (Plurinational State of)	3 474 137	43.47	2.73	1.38	South Africa	666 308	0.75	2.54	1.15
Myanmar	3 148 087	35.18	2.47	1.25	India	591 561	0.23	2.25	1.03

For sources and notes, see end of table.

Pour les sources et les notes, se reporter à la fin du tableau.

3.2.E **Export structure by product**
Major exporters for leading products
among developing economies

3.2.E **Structure des exportations par produits**
Principaux exportateurs de produits majeurs
parmi les économies en développement

Leading exporting developing economies (1) based on average 2010-11 exports (2) SITC Revision 3 (3-digit level) / Principales économies en dévelopement exportatrices (1) d'après la moyenne des exportations de 2010-11 (2) CTCI révision 3 (positions à 3 chiffres)	Value (f.o.b., thousands of dollars) Valeur (f.a.b., milliers de dollars)	2010-2011 As percentage / En pourcentage		
		of country total du total du pays	of developing economies des économies en déve-loppement	of world du monde
542 - Medicines including veterinary				
World	331 846 801	1.99	_	100.00
Developed economies	305 366 092	3.45	_	92.02
Transition economies	1 448 727	0.21	_	0.44
Developing economies	25 031 982	0.35	100.00	7.54
India	6 720 641	2.58	26.85	2.03
Singapore	4 530 949	1.19	18.10	1.37
China	1 944 313	0.11	7.77	0.59
China, Hong Kong SAR	1 555 507	0.36	6.21	0.47
Mexico	1 325 559	0.41	5.30	0.40
Panama	1 001 166	7.84	4.00	0.30
Brazil	985 838	0.43	3.94	0.30
Venezuela (Bolivarian Rep. of)	725 852	0.91	2.90	0.22
Jordan	632 254	8.44	2.53	0.19
Argentina	624 246	0.82	2.49	0.19
571 - Primary form ethylene polymers				
World	72 262 102	0.43	_	100.00
Developed economies	38 263 841	0.43	_	52.95
Transition economies	1 134 851	0.16	_	1.57
Developing economies	32 863 410	0.46	100.00	45.48
Saudi Arabia	8 909 563	2.92	27.11	12.33
Korea, Republic of	3 494 167	0.68	10.63	4.84
Singapore	3 493 139	0.92	10.63	4.83
Thailand	2 513 736	1.19	7.65	3.48
Kuwait	2 186 099	2.66	6.65	3.03
Iran (Islamic Rep. of)	1 812 966	1.56	5.52	2.51
Qatar	1 773 144	1.86	5.40	2.45
United Arab Emirates	1 467 602	0.68	4.47	2.03
China, Taiwan Province of	1 307 685	0.45	3.98	1.81
Brazil	1 281 545	0.57	3.90	1.77
575 - Other plastics, in primary forms				
World	106 258 635	0.64	_	100.00
Developed economies	71 701 650	0.81	_	67.48
Transition economies	803 240	0.12	_	0.76
Developing economies	33 753 744	0.48	100.00	31.77
Korea, Republic of	6 013 105	1.18	17.81	5.66
Saudi Arabia	5 073 722	1.66	15.03	4.77
Singapore	4 357 955	1.14	12.91	4.10
China, Taiwan Province of	3 763 280	1.30	11.15	3.54
China	3 563 365	0.21	10.56	3.35
China, Hong Kong SAR	2 368 553	0.55	7.02	2.23
Thailand	1 749 567	0.83	5.18	1.65
India	1 311 253	0.50	3.88	1.23
Brazil	946 525	0.42	2.80	0.89
Malaysia	730 591	0.34	2.16	0.69
582 - Plastic sheet film foil & strips				
World	93 015 227	0.56	_	100.00
Developed economies	66 083 213	0.75	_	71.05
Transition economies	565 294	0.08	_	0.61
Developing economies	26 366 721	0.37	100.00	28.35
China	6 128 125	0.35	23.24	6.59
Korea, Republic of	4 220 813	0.83	16.01	4.54
China, Taiwan Province of	3 586 973	1.24	13.60	3.86
China, Hong Kong SAR	2 022 696	0.47	7.67	2.17
Malaysia	1 113 807	0.52	4.22	1.20
Thailand	1 040 050	0.49	3.94	1.12
Turkey	979 105	0.79	3.71	1.05
India	921 918	0.35	3.50	0.99
Singapore	889 475	0.23	3.37	0.96
Mexico	882 496	0.27	3.35	0.95

For sources and notes, see end of table.

Leading exporting developing economies (1) based on average 2010-11 exports (2) SITC Revision 3 (3-digit level) / Principales économies en dévelopement exportatrices (1) d'après la moyenne des exportations de 2010-11 (2) CTCI révision 3 (positions à 3 chiffres)	Value (f.o.b., thousands of dollars) Valeur (f.a.b., milliers de dollars)	2010-2011 As percentage / En pourcentage		
		of country total du total du pays	of developing economies des économies en déve-loppement	of world du monde
598 - Miscellaneous chemical products nes				
World	118 687 003	0.71	_	100.00
Developed economies	90 243 830	1.02	_	76.04
Transition economies	746 265	0.11	_	0.63
Developing economies	27 696 908	0.39	100.00	23.34
China	8 333 914	0.48	30.09	7.02
China, Taiwan Province of	3 122 029	1.08	11.27	2.63
Korea, Republic of	2 970 585	0.58	10.73	2.50
Singapore	2 187 974	0.57	7.90	1.84
Argentina	1 898 875	2.50	6.86	1.60
China, Hong Kong SAR	1 409 397	0.33	5.09	1.19
Malaysia	1 337 799	0.63	4.83	1.13
Indonesia	1 318 267	0.73	4.76	1.11
India	747 847	0.29	2.70	0.63
Mexico	570 584	0.18	2.06	0.48
625 - Rubber for wheels, incl inner tube				
World	81 778 017	0.49	_	100.00
Developed economies	47 590 570	0.54	_	58.19
Transition economies	1 757 883	0.25	_	2.15
Developing economies	32 429 564	0.46	100.00	39.66
China	13 259 518	0.76	40.89	16.21
Korea, Republic of	3 997 491	0.78	12.33	4.89
Thailand	3 236 551	1.53	9.98	3.96
Indonesia	1 684 788	0.93	5.20	2.06
Brazil	1 526 771	0.67	4.71	1.87
India	1 339 908	0.51	4.13	1.64
Turkey	1 189 970	0.96	3.67	1.46
China, Taiwan Province of	1 084 762	0.37	3.34	1.33
United Arab Emirates	972 670	0.45	3.00	1.19
Mexico	708 196	0.22	2.18	0.87
651 - Textile yarn				
World	55 926 107	0.34	_	100.00
Developed economies	18 792 098	0.21	_	33.60
Transition economies	1 545 128	0.22	_	2.76
Developing economies	35 588 882	0.50	100.00	63.64
China	10 794 172	0.62	30.33	19.30
India	4 740 173	1.82	13.32	8.48
China, Hong Kong SAR	3 157 673	0.74	8.87	5.65
China, Taiwan Province of	2 433 872	0.84	6.84	4.35
Indonesia	2 298 924	1.27	6.46	4.11
Pakistan	1 876 629	8.03	5.27	3.36
Viet Nam	1 721 089	2.04	4.84	3.08
Korea, Republic of	1 695 850	0.33	4.77	3.03
Turkey	1 489 776	1.20	4.19	2.66
Thailand	1 141 113	0.54	3.21	2.04
653 - Man-made woven fabrics				
World	40 150 709	0.24	_	100.00
Developed economies	10 941 046	0.12	_	27.25
Transition economies	101 969	0.01	_	0.25
Developing economies	29 107 694	0.41	100.00	72.50
China	14 602 858	0.84	50.17	36.37
Korea, Republic of	2 448 749	0.48	8.41	6.10
China, Taiwan Province of	2 280 250	0.79	7.83	5.68
India	2 125 540	0.81	7.30	5.29
Turkey	1 447 826	1.16	4.97	3.61
United Arab Emirates	1 170 977	0.54	4.02	2.92
Indonesia	1 170 369	0.65	4.02	2.91
China, Hong Kong SAR	978 832	0.23	3.36	2.44
Thailand	709 357	0.33	2.44	1.77
Pakistan	564 808	2.42	1.94	1.41

Pour les sources et les notes, se reporter à la fin du tableau.

3

3.2.E Export structure by product
Major exporters for leading products among developing economies

3.2.E Structure des exportations par produits
Principaux exportateurs de produits majeurs parmi les économies en développement

Leading exporting developing economies (1) based on average 2010-11 exports (2) SITC Revision 3 (3-digit level) Principales économies en dévelopement exportatrices (1) d'après la moyenne des exportations de 2010-11 (2) CTCI révision 3 (positions à 3 chiffres)	2010-2011			
	Value (f.o.b., thousands of dollars) Valeur (f.a.b., milliers de dollars)	As percentage / En pourcentage		
		of country total du total du pays	of developing economies des économies en déve-loppement	of world du monde
658 - Made-up textile articles nes				
World	48 683 935	0.29	_	100.00
Developed economies	11 723 044	0.13	_	24.08
Transition economies	392 180	0.06	_	0.81
Developing economies	36 568 710	0.52	100.00	75.11
China	21 002 173	1.21	57.43	43.14
Pakistan	3 402 644	14.55	9.30	6.99
India	3 303 882	1.27	9.03	6.79
Turkey	1 977 941	1.59	5.41	4.06
Viet Nam	948 048	1.12	2.59	1.95
Bangladesh	929 078	4.02	2.54	1.91
Mexico	737 934	0.23	2.02	1.52
Korea, Republic of	337 579	0.07	0.92	0.69
Thailand	334 737	0.16	0.92	0.69
China, Hong Kong SAR	331 540	0.08	0.91	0.68
667 - Pearls, precious semiprecious stone				
World	147 033 195	0.88	_	100.00
Developed economies	68 563 832	0.77	_	46.63
Transition economies	3 247 417	0.47	_	2.21
Developing economies	75 221 946	1.06	100.00	51.16
India	27 590 698	10.57	36.68	18.76
United Arab Emirates	15 506 679	7.14	20.61	10.55
China, Hong Kong SAR	14 258 369	3.33	18.96	9.70
Botswana	3 724 896	70.45	4.95	2.53
South Africa	3 592 581	4.02	4.78	2.44
China	2 919 934	0.17	3.88	1.99
Thailand	1 930 074	0.91	2.57	1.31
Myanmar	1 613 155	18.02	2.14	1.10
Singapore	580 979	0.15	0.77	0.40
Namibia	566 023	13.52	0.75	0.38
673 - Flat iron non-alloy steel products				
World	88 321 984	0.53	_	100.00
Developed economies	48 898 161	0.55	_	55.36
Transition economies	10 657 040	1.53	_	12.07
Developing economies	28 766 783	0.41	100.00	32.57
Korea, Republic of	9 563 520	1.87	33.25	10.83
China	5 995 435	0.34	20.84	6.79
China, Taiwan Province of	3 149 070	1.08	10.95	3.57
India	1 387 828	0.53	4.82	1.57
Turkey	1 087 340	0.87	3.78	1.23
Brazil	1 082 666	0.48	3.76	1.23
United Arab Emirates	874 788	0.40	3.04	0.99
South Africa	779 897	0.87	2.71	0.88
Viet Nam	655 342	0.77	2.28	0.74
Singapore	613 421	0.16	2.13	0.69
676 - Iron steel bar rod section piling				
World	84 396 417	0.51	_	100.00
Developed economies	50 453 705	0.57	_	59.78
Transition economies	6 666 135	0.96	_	7.90
Developing economies	27 276 577	0.38	100.00	32.32
China	6 610 377	0.38	24.23	7.83
Turkey	6 141 666	4.94	22.52	7.28
Korea, Republic of	2 790 607	0.55	10.23	3.31
China, Taiwan Province of	1 495 312	0.51	5.48	1.77
Venezuela (Bolivarian Rep. of)	1 193 750	1.50	4.38	1.41
United Arab Emirates	1 150 755	0.53	4.22	1.36
India	1 074 845	0.41	3.94	1.27
Brazil	912 808	0.40	3.35	1.08
Mexico	801 631	0.25	2.94	0.95
Thailand	531 249	0.25	1.95	0.63

Leading exporting developing economies (1) based on average 2010-11 exports (2) SITC Revision 3 (3-digit level) Principales économies en dévelopement exportatrices (1) d'après la moyenne des exportations de 2010-11 (2) CTCI révision 3 (positions à 3 chiffres)	2010-2011			
	Value (f.o.b., thousands of dollars) Valeur (f.a.b., milliers de dollars)	As percentage / En pourcentage		
		of country total du total du pays	of developing economies des économies en déve-loppement	of world du monde
679 - Iron steel pipe tube fittings etc				
World	86 044 273	0.52	_	100.00
Developed economies	50 062 216	0.57	_	58.18
Transition economies	3 391 785	0.49	_	3.94
Developing economies	32 590 272	0.46	100.00	37.88
China	12 633 467	0.73	38.76	14.68
Korea, Republic of	3 923 375	0.77	12.04	4.56
India	3 031 722	1.16	9.30	3.52
Turkey	1 677 672	1.35	5.15	1.95
Mexico	1 532 583	0.47	4.70	1.78
Singapore	1 383 935	0.36	4.25	1.61
China, Taiwan Province of	1 201 754	0.41	3.69	1.40
Argentina	1 072 808	1.41	3.29	1.25
Malaysia	936 622	0.44	2.87	1.09
United Arab Emirates	782 993	0.36	2.40	0.91
681 - Silver, platinum, platinum metals				
World	61 087 056	0.37	_	100.00
Developed economies	34 583 626	0.39	_	56.61
Transition economies	544 987	0.08	_	0.89
Developing economies	25 958 443	0.37	100.00	42.49
South Africa	10 656 399	11.93	41.05	17.44
China, Hong Kong SAR	3 952 040	0.92	15.22	6.47
Mexico	3 533 237	1.09	13.61	5.78
Korea, Republic of	1 712 987	0.34	6.60	2.80
China, Taiwan Province of	1 394 846	0.48	5.37	2.28
China	1 253 015	0.07	4.83	2.05
United Arab Emirates	1 153 351	0.53	4.44	1.89
Chile	517 901	0.68	2.00	0.85
Argentina	324 680	0.43	1.25	0.53
Singapore	285 394	0.07	1.10	0.47
682 - Copper				
World	139 971 829	0.84	_	100.00
Developed economies	56 884 606	0.64	_	40.64
Transition economies	9 977 442	1.43	_	7.13
Developing economies	73 109 781	1.03	100.00	52.23
Chile	28 356 916	37.24	38.79	20.26
Zambia	5 557 790	68.54	7.60	3.97
China	5 098 938	0.29	6.97	3.64
Korea, Republic of	4 265 960	0.84	5.84	3.05
India	3 915 843	1.50	5.36	2.80
Indonesia	3 345 769	1.85	4.58	2.39
China, Taiwan Province of	3 203 706	1.10	4.38	2.29
Peru	3 197 839	7.91	4.37	2.28
China, Hong Kong SAR	2 156 757	0.50	2.95	1.54
Dem. Rep. of the Congo	2 030 079	35.60	2.78	1.45
684 - Aluminium				
World	116 140 614	0.70	_	100.00
Developed economies	70 324 437	0.79	_	60.55
Transition economies	9 519 676	1.36	_	8.20
Developing economies	36 296 502	0.51	100.00	31.25
China	10 614 420	0.61	29.24	9.14
Bahrain	3 380 979	20.31	9.31	2.91
United Arab Emirates	3 177 515	1.46	8.75	2.74
South Africa	1 961 973	2.20	5.41	1.69
Korea, Republic of	1 900 019	0.37	5.23	1.64
Brazil	1 614 522	0.71	4.45	1.39
Turkey	1 462 931	1.18	4.03	1.26
Mozambique	1 266 174	43.31	3.49	1.09
Venezuela (Bolivarian Rep. of)	1 218 743	1.53	3.36	1.05
Malaysia	1 106 080	0.52	3.05	0.95

For sources and notes, see end of table.

Pour les sources et les notes, se reporter à la fin du tableau.

3.2.E Export structure by product
Major exporters for leading products among developing economies

3.2.E Structure des exportations par produits
Principaux exportateurs de produits majeurs parmi les économies en développement

Leading exporting developing economies (1) based on average 2010-11 exports (2) SITC Revision 3 (3-digit level) / Principales économies en dévelopement exportatrices (1) d'après la moyenne des exportations de 2010-11 (2) CTCI révision 3 (positions à 3 chiffres)	2010-2011		
	Value (f.o.b., thousands of dollars) Valeur (f.a.b., milliers de dollars)	As percentage / En pourcentage	
		of country total / du total du pays	of developing economies / des économies en développement	of world / du monde

699 - Base metal manufactures nes

	Value	of country total	of developing economies	of world
World	132 171 572	0.79	_	100.00
Developed economies	84 743 022	0.96	_	64.12
Transition economies	1 915 287	0.27	_	1.45
Developing economies	45 513 262	0.64	100.00	34.43
China	19 708 302	1.13	43.30	14.91
China, Taiwan Province of	3 890 229	1.34	8.55	2.94
Mexico	3 353 625	1.04	7.37	2.54
Korea, Republic of	2 975 601	0.58	6.54	2.25
India	2 263 814	0.87	4.97	1.71
Thailand	2 038 909	0.96	4.48	1.54
China, Hong Kong SAR	1 905 025	0.44	4.19	1.44
Turkey	1 630 359	1.31	3.58	1.23
Brazil	1 461 976	0.64	3.21	1.11
Malaysia	1 161 213	0.55	2.55	0.88

713 - Internal combustion engine part nes

	Value	of country total	of developing economies	of world
World	150 891 186	0.91	_	100.00
Developed economies	118 565 479	1.34	_	78.58
Transition economies	555 946	0.08	_	0.37
Developing economies	31 769 761	0.45	100.00	21.05
Mexico	6 831 959	2.11	21.50	4.53
China	6 107 061	0.35	19.22	4.05
Korea, Republic of	4 945 523	0.97	15.57	3.28
Brazil	2 897 138	1.28	9.12	1.92
Thailand	2 726 769	1.29	8.58	1.81
Singapore	2 183 041	0.57	6.87	1.45
Turkey	1 566 488	1.26	4.93	1.04
India	1 207 193	0.46	3.80	0.80
South Africa	554 276	0.62	1.74	0.37
China, Hong Kong SAR	468 070	0.11	1.47	0.31

716 - Rotating electric plant parts nes

	Value	of country total	of developing economies	of world
World	86 919 904	0.52	_	100.00
Developed economies	55 844 374	0.63	_	64.25
Transition economies	832 959	0.12	_	0.96
Developing economies	30 242 570	0.43	100.00	34.79
China	14 226 561	0.82	47.04	16.37
Mexico	2 994 625	0.92	9.90	3.45
China, Hong Kong SAR	2 600 966	0.61	8.60	2.99
Korea, Republic of	1 631 965	0.32	5.40	1.88
Singapore	1 395 206	0.37	4.61	1.61
Brazil	1 225 409	0.54	4.05	1.41
Thailand	1 224 047	0.58	4.05	1.41
China, Taiwan Province of	899 860	0.31	2.98	1.04
India	821 078	0.31	2.71	0.94
Viet Nam	762 403	0.90	2.52	0.88

723 - Civil engineering plant & equipment

	Value	of country total	of developing economies	of world
World	109 231 532	0.66	_	100.00
Developed economies	76 465 713	0.86	_	70.00
Transition economies	817 547	0.12	_	0.75
Developing economies	31 948 273	0.45	100.00	29.25
China	9 449 651	0.54	29.58	8.65
Korea, Republic of	6 739 117	1.32	21.09	6.17
Singapore	4 841 446	1.27	15.15	4.43
Brazil	1 961 719	0.87	6.14	1.80
Mexico	1 298 125	0.40	4.06	1.19
United Arab Emirates	1 271 875	0.59	3.98	1.16
Thailand	918 340	0.43	2.87	0.84
India	675 324	0.26	2.11	0.62
Turkey	624 754	0.50	1.96	0.57
China, Hong Kong SAR	622 357	0.15	1.95	0.57

728 - Special industrial machine part nes

	Value	of country total	of developing economies	of world
World	173 550 116	1.04	_	100.00
Developed economies	135 548 883	1.53	_	78.10
Transition economies	890 211	0.13	_	0.51
Developing economies	37 111 022	0.52	100.00	21.38
China	9 218 623	0.53	24.84	5.31
Korea, Republic of	7 720 550	1.51	20.80	4.45
Singapore	6 354 194	1.67	17.12	3.66
China, Taiwan Province of	4 588 594	1.58	12.36	2.64
China, Hong Kong SAR	2 569 209	0.60	6.92	1.48
Malaysia	1 302 475	0.61	3.51	0.75
Mexico	872 241	0.27	2.35	0.50
India	779 699	0.30	2.10	0.45
Turkey	674 872	0.54	1.82	0.39
Brazil	635 920	0.28	1.71	0.37

741 - Heating cooling equipment parts nes

	Value	of country total	of developing economies	of world
World	103 158 158	0.62	_	100.00
Developed economies	64 245 716	0.73	_	62.28
Transition economies	633 194	0.09	_	0.61
Developing economies	38 279 247	0.54	100.00	37.11
China	17 513 744	1.01	45.75	16.98
Thailand	4 268 592	2.01	11.15	4.14
Korea, Republic of	3 721 041	0.73	9.72	3.61
Mexico	3 453 260	1.07	9.02	3.35
Malaysia	1 565 009	0.74	4.09	1.52
Singapore	1 032 852	0.27	2.70	1.00
Turkey	966 447	0.78	2.52	0.94
India	884 240	0.34	2.31	0.86
China, Taiwan Province of	842 399	0.29	2.20	0.82
China, Hong Kong SAR	827 684	0.19	2.16	0.80

743 - Gas pump, compressor, fan, filter

	Value	of country total	of developing economies	of world
World	115 253 676	0.69	_	100.00
Developed economies	82 241 185	0.93	_	71.36
Transition economies	885 152	0.13	_	0.77
Developing economies	32 127 339	0.45	100.00	27.88
China	12 062 640	0.69	37.55	10.47
Mexico	3 196 348	0.99	9.95	2.77
Korea, Republic of	2 823 190	0.55	8.79	2.45
South Africa	2 398 269	2.68	7.46	2.08
Thailand	2 195 121	1.04	6.83	1.90
Singapore	1 616 063	0.42	5.03	1.40
Brazil	1 295 041	0.57	4.03	1.12
China, Taiwan Province of	1 157 912	0.40	3.60	1.00
China, Hong Kong SAR	1 136 442	0.27	3.54	0.99
India	869 178	0.33	2.71	0.75

751 - Office machines

	Value	of country total	of developing economies	of world
World	51 522 315	0.31	_	100.00
Developed economies	20 326 346	0.23	_	39.45
Transition economies	44 396	0.01	_	0.09
Developing economies	31 151 573	0.44	100.00	60.46
China	19 043 574	1.10	61.13	36.96
China, Hong Kong SAR	2 253 317	0.53	7.23	4.37
Singapore	1 787 933	0.47	5.74	3.47
Viet Nam	1 687 284	2.00	5.42	3.27
Thailand	1 300 296	0.61	4.17	2.52
Korea, Republic of	1 155 325	0.23	3.71	2.24
Indonesia	1 107 308	0.61	3.55	2.15
Malaysia	999 171	0.47	3.21	1.94
Mexico	901 443	0.28	2.89	1.75
China, Taiwan Province of	342 694	0.12	1.10	0.67

For sources and notes, see end of table.

Pour les sources et les notes, se reporter à la fin du tableau.

199

3.2.E **Export structure by product**
Major exporters for leading products
among developing economies

3.2.E **Structure des exportations par produits**
Principaux exportateurs de produits majeurs
parmi les économies en développement

Left column

Leading exporting developing economies (1) based on average 2010-11 exports (2) SITC Revision 3 (3-digit level) / Principales économies en dévelopement exportatrices (1) d'après la moyenne des exportations de 2010-11 (2) CTCI révision 3 (positions à 3 chiffres)	Value (f.o.b., thousands of dollars) Valeur (f.a.b., milliers de dollars)	2010-2011 As percentage En pourcentage		
		of country total du total du pays	of developing economies des économies en déve- loppement	of world du monde
752 - Computer equipment nes				
World	334 503 627	2.01	_	100.00
Developed economies	100 008 519	1.13	_	29.90
Transition economies	261 937	0.04	_	0.08
Developing economies	234 233 171	3.30	100.00	70.02
China	154 462 221	8.89	65.94	46.18
China, Hong Kong SAR	15 363 203	3.59	6.56	4.59
Mexico	15 259 429	4.71	6.51	4.56
Thailand	12 155 009	5.73	5.19	3.63
Malaysia	10 689 069	5.02	4.56	3.20
Singapore	8 985 782	2.36	3.84	2.69
Philippines	5 595 887	11.24	2.39	1.67
Korea, Republic of	5 008 753	0.98	2.14	1.50
China, Taiwan Province of	3 725 728	1.28	1.59	1.11
United Arab Emirates	888 944	0.41	0.38	0.27
759 - Office equipment part & accessories				
World	199 191 649	1.20	_	100.00
Developed economies	79 369 287	0.90	_	39.85
Transition economies	142 008	0.02	_	0.07
Developing economies	119 680 355	1.69	100.00	60.08
China	38 719 998	2.23	32.35	19.44
China, Hong Kong SAR	29 052 786	6.79	24.28	14.59
Singapore	17 927 049	4.71	14.98	9.00
Malaysia	9 110 896	4.28	7.61	4.57
Korea, Republic of	7 333 966	1.44	6.13	3.68
China, Taiwan Province of	7 042 360	2.43	5.88	3.54
Thailand	4 024 900	1.90	3.36	2.02
Philippines	1 771 485	3.56	1.48	0.89
Mexico	1 159 182	0.36	0.97	0.58
Costa Rica	1 058 155	10.98	0.88	0.53
761 - Television video receive project				
World	98 790 483	0.59	_	100.00
Developed economies	41 425 257	0.47	_	41.93
Transition economies	694 448	0.10	_	0.70
Developing economies	56 670 779	0.80	100.00	57.36
China	22 173 788	1.28	39.13	22.45
Mexico	19 400 980	5.99	34.23	19.64
Malaysia	4 724 216	2.22	8.34	4.78
Korea, Republic of	1 962 583	0.38	3.46	1.99
Turkey	1 807 602	1.45	3.19	1.83
Thailand	1 431 152	0.67	2.53	1.45
Indonesia	1 177 331	0.65	2.08	1.19
China, Taiwan Province of	1 089 880	0.38	1.92	1.10
China, Hong Kong SAR	867 825	0.20	1.53	0.88
Singapore	591 485	0.16	1.04	0.60
763 - Sound TV recorder or reproducer				
World	61 860 907	0.37	_	100.00
Developed economies	25 617 807	0.29	_	41.41
Transition economies	46 681	0.01	_	0.08
Developing economies	36 196 419	0.51	100.00	58.51
China	20 567 265	1.18	56.82	33.25
China, Hong Kong SAR	5 759 680	1.35	15.91	9.31
Thailand	1 874 976	0.88	5.18	3.03
Indonesia	1 686 276	0.93	4.66	2.73
Malaysia	1 504 142	0.71	4.16	2.43
China, Taiwan Province of	1 304 621	0.45	3.60	2.11
Singapore	1 110 139	0.29	3.07	1.79
Korea, Republic of	1 064 169	0.21	2.94	1.72
Viet Nam	396 040	0.47	1.09	0.64
Mexico	323 614	0.10	0.89	0.52

Right column

Leading exporting developing economies (1) based on average 2010-11 exports (2) SITC Revision 3 (3-digit level) / Principales économies en dévelopement exportatrices (1) d'après la moyenne des exportations de 2010-11 (2) CTCI révision 3 (positions à 3 chiffres)	Value (f.o.b., thousands of dollars) Valeur (f.a.b., milliers de dollars)	2010-2011 As percentage En pourcentage		
		of country total du total du pays	of developing economies des économies en déve- loppement	of world du monde
764 - Telecommunicate equipment part nes				
World	475 843 273	2.86	_	100.00
Developed economies	163 210 016	1.84	_	34.30
Transition economies	1 140 114	0.16	_	0.24
Developing economies	311 493 143	4.39	100.00	65.46
China	147 804 162	8.50	47.45	31.06
China, Hong Kong SAR	60 484 088	14.13	19.42	12.71
Korea, Republic of	35 341 992	6.92	11.35	7.43
Mexico	19 624 802	6.06	6.30	4.12
China, Taiwan Province of	14 862 502	5.12	4.77	3.12
Singapore	9 868 065	2.59	3.17	2.07
Malaysia	5 330 794	2.50	1.71	1.12
Thailand	4 202 568	1.98	1.35	0.88
India	3 468 891	1.33	1.11	0.73
Viet Nam	2 499 363	2.96	0.80	0.53
771 - Electric power machine part excl. 716				
World	89 086 543	0.54	_	100.00
Developed economies	41 019 563	0.46	_	46.04
Transition economies	1 167 582	0.17	_	1.31
Developing economies	46 899 398	0.66	100.00	52.64
China	21 250 628	1.22	45.31	23.85
China, Hong Kong SAR	9 834 792	2.30	20.97	11.04
Korea, Republic of	2 823 085	0.55	6.02	3.17
Mexico	2 299 901	0.71	4.90	2.58
China, Taiwan Province of	1 685 983	0.58	3.59	1.89
Singapore	1 516 803	0.40	3.23	1.70
Thailand	1 359 088	0.64	2.90	1.53
Philippines	1 243 619	2.50	2.65	1.40
India	978 433	0.37	2.09	1.10
Turkey	717 307	0.58	1.53	0.81
772 - Electrical circuit equipment				
World	218 181 616	1.31	_	100.00
Developed economies	123 543 230	1.39	_	56.62
Transition economies	1 154 243	0.17	_	0.53
Developing economies	93 484 143	1.32	100.00	42.85
China	29 314 315	1.69	31.36	13.44
China, Hong Kong SAR	19 140 751	4.47	20.47	8.77
China, Taiwan Province of	8 671 738	2.99	9.28	3.97
Korea, Republic of	7 114 310	1.39	7.61	3.26
Mexico	6 578 760	2.03	7.04	3.02
Singapore	6 194 534	1.63	6.63	2.84
Malaysia	5 041 238	2.37	5.39	2.31
Thailand	3 138 530	1.48	3.36	1.44
India	1 659 562	0.64	1.78	0.76
Turkey	1 027 296	0.83	1.10	0.47
773 - Electrical distribute equipment nes				
World	102 830 680	0.62	_	100.00
Developed economies	53 164 541	0.60	_	51.70
Transition economies	2 212 317	0.32	_	2.15
Developing economies	47 453 822	0.67	100.00	46.15
China	15 003 006	0.86	31.62	14.59
Mexico	7 457 170	2.30	15.71	7.25
Korea, Republic of	3 457 015	0.68	7.29	3.36
China, Hong Kong SAR	3 006 846	0.70	6.34	2.92
Turkey	2 098 587	1.69	4.42	2.04
Morocco	1 674 632	8.53	3.53	1.63
Viet Nam	1 482 448	1.75	3.12	1.44
Tunisia	1 340 073	7.82	2.82	1.30
Philippines	1 158 085	2.33	2.44	1.13
Thailand	1 114 692	0.53	2.35	1.08

For sources and notes, see end of table.

Pour les sources et les notes, se reporter à la fin du tableau.

3.2.E Export structure by product
Major exporters for leading products
among developing economies

3.2.E Structure des exportations par produits
Principaux exportateurs de produits majeurs
parmi les économies en développement

Left table

Leading exporting developing economies (1) based on average 2010-11 exports (2) SITC Revision 3 (3-digit level) / Principales économies en dévelopement exportatrices (1) d'après la moyenne des exportations de 2010-11 (2) CTCI révision 3 (positions à 3 chiffres)	2010-2011			
	Value (f.o.b., thousands of dollars) Valeur (f.a.b., milliers de dollars)	As percentage / En pourcentage		
		of country total / du total du pays	of developing economies / des économies en déve-loppement	of world / du monde
775 - Household equipment nes				
World	89 316 614	0.54	_	100.00
Developed economies	38 472 454	0.43	_	43.07
Transition economies	1 102 503	0.16	_	1.23
Developing economies	49 741 657	0.70	100.00	55.69
China	27 917 021	1.61	56.12	31.26
Mexico	4 521 370	1.40	9.09	5.06
Korea, Republic of	3 528 018	0.69	7.09	3.95
Turkey	3 178 193	2.55	6.39	3.56
Thailand	3 035 204	1.43	6.10	3.40
China, Hong Kong SAR	2 404 533	0.56	4.83	2.69
Malaysia	1 172 413	0.55	2.36	1.31
Singapore	1 147 612	0.30	2.31	1.28
United Arab Emirates	546 173	0.25	1.10	0.61
Indonesia	522 382	0.29	1.05	0.58
776 - Valves tubes; diodes, transistors				
World	552 611 280	3.32	_	100.00
Developed economies	162 802 343	1.84	_	29.46
Transition economies	427 877	0.06	_	0.08
Developing economies	389 381 061	5.49	100.00	70.46
Singapore	84 928 374	22.31	21.81	15.37
China, Hong Kong SAR	66 365 804	15.50	17.04	12.01
China	66 244 252	3.81	17.01	11.99
China, Taiwan Province of	63 210 439	21.77	16.23	11.44
Korea, Republic of	44 272 768	8.67	11.37	8.01
Malaysia	32 773 065	15.39	8.42	5.93
Philippines	12 285 046	24.68	3.16	2.22
Thailand	9 303 721	4.39	2.39	1.68
Costa Rica	3 804 244	39.49	0.98	0.69
Mexico	2 384 242	0.74	0.61	0.43
778 - Electrical machinery apparatus nes				
World	211 908 822	1.27	_	100.00
Developed economies	108 133 892	1.22	_	51.03
Transition economies	1 271 791	0.18	_	0.60
Developing economies	102 503 139	1.45	100.00	48.37
China	42 416 602	2.44	41.38	20.02
Korea, Republic of	11 910 112	2.33	11.62	5.62
China, Hong Kong SAR	11 149 346	2.60	10.88	5.26
China, Taiwan Province of	8 688 224	2.99	8.48	4.10
Mexico	6 951 591	2.15	6.78	3.28
Singapore	6 481 999	1.70	6.32	3.06
Thailand	3 624 018	1.71	3.54	1.71
Malaysia	2 701 208	1.27	2.64	1.27
Indonesia	1 752 625	0.97	1.71	0.83
India	1 106 365	0.42	1.08	0.52
781 - Passenger cars and race cars				
World	598 446 919	3.59	_	100.00
Developed economies	492 920 912	5.56	_	82.37
Transition economies	2 269 457	0.33	_	0.38
Developing economies	103 256 549	1.46	100.00	17.25
Korea, Republic of	36 345 793	7.12	35.20	6.07
Mexico	24 967 638	7.71	24.18	4.17
Thailand	6 646 149	3.13	6.44	1.11
Turkey	6 347 921	5.10	6.15	1.06
Brazil	4 395 914	1.94	4.26	0.73
Argentina	4 317 842	5.68	4.18	0.72
South Africa	4 109 301	4.60	3.98	0.69
India	4 067 726	1.56	3.94	0.68
China	2 972 228	0.17	2.88	0.50
United Arab Emirates	2 773 735	1.28	2.69	0.46

For sources and notes, see end of table.

Right table

Leading exporting developing economies (1) based on average 2010-11 exports (2) SITC Revision 3 (3-digit level) / Principales économies en dévelopement exportatrices (1) d'après la moyenne des exportations de 2010-11 (2) CTCI révision 3 (positions à 3 chiffres)	2010-2011			
	Value (f.o.b., thousands of dollars) Valeur (f.a.b., milliers de dollars)	As percentage / En pourcentage		
		of country total / du total du pays	of developing economies / des économies en déve-loppement	of world / du monde
782 - Goods and service vehicles				
World	117 088 130	0.70	_	100.00
Developed economies	77 533 193	0.88	_	66.22
Transition economies	2 059 759	0.30	_	1.76
Developing economies	37 495 179	0.53	100.00	32.02
Mexico	11 508 428	3.55	30.69	9.83
Thailand	5 618 437	2.65	14.98	4.80
China	4 179 218	0.24	11.15	3.57
Turkey	3 749 882	3.01	10.00	3.20
Argentina	3 001 038	3.95	8.00	2.56
Korea, Republic of	2 461 495	0.48	6.56	2.10
Brazil	1 955 180	0.86	5.21	1.67
South Africa	1 462 062	1.64	3.90	1.25
India	814 554	0.31	2.17	0.70
United Arab Emirates	701 443	0.32	1.87	0.60
784 - Motor vehicle parts and accessories				
World	329 685 670	1.98	_	100.00
Developed economies	244 804 364	2.76	_	74.25
Transition economies	1 168 969	0.17	_	0.35
Developing economies	83 712 336	1.18	100.00	25.39
Korea, Republic of	19 775 623	3.87	23.62	6.00
China	18 692 711	1.08	22.33	5.67
Mexico	15 408 251	4.76	18.41	4.67
Brazil	4 718 390	2.08	5.64	1.43
Thailand	4 394 046	2.07	5.25	1.33
China, Taiwan Province of	3 187 935	1.10	3.81	0.97
Turkey	3 070 330	2.47	3.67	0.93
Singapore	2 597 428	0.68	3.10	0.79
India	2 552 181	0.98	3.05	0.77
Philippines	1 870 023	3.76	2.23	0.57
793 - Ships boats floating structures				
World	177 245 232	1.06	_	100.00
Developed economies	59 509 459	0.67	_	33.57
Transition economies	3 047 193	0.44	_	1.72
Developing economies	114 688 580	1.62	100.00	64.71
Korea, Republic of	50 434 211	9.87	43.97	28.45
China	41 960 746	2.41	36.59	23.67
India	5 635 805	2.16	4.91	3.18
Singapore	3 997 494	1.05	3.49	2.26
Turkey	1 194 064	0.96	1.04	0.67
Indonesia	1 167 215	0.65	1.02	0.66
Panama	1 150 270	9.01	1.00	0.65
China, Taiwan Province of	994 721	0.34	0.87	0.56
Thailand	992 396	0.47	0.87	0.56
Brazil	664 228	0.29	0.58	0.37
821 - Furniture part; bedding furnishing				
World	138 258 919	0.83	_	100.00
Developed economies	72 589 955	0.82	_	52.50
Transition economies	1 861 080	0.27	_	1.35
Developing economies	63 807 884	0.90	100.00	46.15
China	41 845 599	2.41	65.58	30.27
Mexico	4 590 741	1.42	7.19	3.32
Viet Nam	3 444 297	4.07	5.40	2.49
Malaysia	2 565 206	1.20	4.02	1.86
Indonesia	1 851 362	1.02	2.90	1.34
Turkey	1 512 635	1.22	2.37	1.09
China, Taiwan Province of	1 292 133	0.45	2.03	0.93
Thailand	1 166 693	0.55	1.83	0.84
Korea, Republic of	809 164	0.16	1.27	0.59
Brazil	772 392	0.34	1.21	0.56

Pour les sources et les notes, se reporter à la fin du tableau.

3.2.E Export structure by product
Major exporters for leading products
among developing economies

3.2.E Structure des exportations par produits
Principaux exportateurs de produits majeurs
parmi les économies en développement

831 - Case bag: storage travel shopping

Leading exporting developing economies (1) based on average 2010-11 exports (2) SITC Revision 3 (3-digit level) / Principales économies en dévelopement exportatrices (1) d'après la moyenne des exportations de 2010-11 (2) CTCI révision 3 (positions à 3 chiffres)	Value (f.o.b., thousands of dollars) Valeur (f.a.b., milliers de dollars)	2010-2011 As percentage / En pourcentage		
		of country total / du total du pays	of developing economies / des économies en développement	of world / du monde
World	46 662 837	0.28	_	100.00
Developed economies	16 092 524	0.18	_	34.49
Transition economies	71 363	0.01	_	0.15
Developing economies	30 498 950	0.43	100.00	65.36
China	21 115 194	1.21	69.23	45.25
China, Hong Kong SAR	5 739 964	1.34	18.82	12.30
Viet Nam	860 667	1.02	2.82	1.84
India	851 154	0.33	2.79	1.82
Singapore	396 420	0.10	1.30	0.85
Thailand	264 060	0.12	0.87	0.57
Turkey	163 600	0.13	0.54	0.35
Indonesia	158 160	0.09	0.52	0.34
Panama	129 944	1.02	0.43	0.28
United Arab Emirates	109 143	0.05	0.36	0.23

841 - Male clothing, woven

	Value	of country total	of developing economies	of world
World	65 985 804	0.40	_	100.00
Developed economies	20 107 480	0.23	_	30.47
Transition economies	985 210	0.14	_	1.49
Developing economies	44 893 113	0.63	100.00	68.03
China	19 301 592	1.11	42.99	29.25
Bangladesh	5 048 564	21.84	11.25	7.65
China, Hong Kong SAR	2 936 416	0.69	6.54	4.45
Viet Nam	2 688 474	3.18	5.99	4.07
Turkey	1 966 662	1.58	4.38	2.98
Mexico	1 832 520	0.57	4.08	2.78
India	1 782 664	0.68	3.97	2.70
Indonesia	1 595 121	0.88	3.55	2.42
Pakistan	983 741	4.21	2.19	1.49
Tunisia	826 417	4.82	1.84	1.25

842 - Female clothing, woven

	Value	of country total	of developing economies	of world
World	78 311 447	0.47	_	100.00
Developed economies	25 676 713	0.29	_	32.79
Transition economies	1 122 231	0.16	_	1.43
Developing economies	51 512 503	0.73	100.00	65.78
China	25 068 217	1.44	48.66	32.01
China, Hong Kong SAR	5 159 400	1.21	10.02	6.59
India	3 925 380	1.50	7.62	5.01
Turkey	2 685 722	2.16	5.21	3.43
Viet Nam	2 653 368	3.14	5.15	3.39
Bangladesh	2 354 656	10.19	4.57	3.01
Indonesia	1 671 665	0.93	3.25	2.13
Morocco	1 523 773	7.76	2.96	1.95
Sri Lanka	768 621	8.39	1.49	0.98
Pakistan	538 315	2.30	1.05	0.69

844 - Female clothing, knitted crocheted

	Value	of country total	of developing economies	of world
World	49 626 912	0.30	_	100.00
Developed economies	10 935 106	0.12	_	22.03
Transition economies	432 696	0.06	_	0.87
Developing economies	38 259 110	0.54	100.00	77.09
China	22 313 467	1.28	58.32	44.96
China, Hong Kong SAR	2 690 360	0.63	7.03	5.42
Turkey	2 009 636	1.61	5.25	4.05
Viet Nam	1 508 307	1.78	3.94	3.04
Bangladesh	1 308 400	5.66	3.42	2.64
Cambodia	1 172 961	17.85	3.07	2.36
India	1 166 274	0.45	3.05	2.35
Indonesia	908 200	0.50	2.37	1.83
Sri Lanka	763 189	8.33	1.99	1.54
Thailand	457 386	0.22	1.20	0.92

845 - Articles of apparel nes

Leading exporting developing economies (1) based on average 2010-11 exports (2) SITC Revision 3 (3-digit level) / Principales économies en dévelopement exportatrices (1) d'après la moyenne des exportations de 2010-11 (2) CTCI révision 3 (positions à 3 chiffres)	Value (f.o.b., thousands of dollars) Valeur (f.a.b., milliers de dollars)	2010-2011 As percentage / En pourcentage		
		of country total / du total du pays	of developing economies / des économies en développement	of world / du monde
World	132 910 645	0.80	_	100.00
Developed economies	38 541 244	0.43	_	29.00
Transition economies	1 097 896	0.16	_	0.83
Developing economies	93 271 506	1.32	100.00	70.18
China	42 871 199	2.47	45.96	32.26
China, Hong Kong SAR	10 470 010	2.45	11.23	7.88
Bangladesh	7 165 294	31.00	7.68	5.39
Turkey	4 671 537	3.75	5.01	3.51
Viet Nam	3 474 019	4.11	3.72	2.61
India	3 261 630	1.25	3.50	2.45
Indonesia	2 238 422	1.24	2.40	1.68
Cambodia	1 947 187	29.63	2.09	1.47
Tunisia	1 708 838	9.97	1.83	1.29
Mexico	1 471 601	0.45	1.58	1.11

851 - Footwear

	Value	of country total	of developing economies	of world
World	104 395 567	0.63	_	100.00
Developed economies	39 032 373	0.44	_	37.39
Transition economies	1 531 091	0.22	_	1.47
Developing economies	63 832 103	0.90	100.00	61.14
China	38 678 092	2.23	60.59	37.05
Viet Nam	6 129 987	7.25	9.60	5.87
China, Hong Kong SAR	5 614 088	1.31	8.80	5.38
Indonesia	2 901 896	1.61	4.55	2.78
India	1 866 716	0.72	2.92	1.79
Brazil	1 565 142	0.69	2.45	1.50
Thailand	873 794	0.41	1.37	0.84
Panama	707 334	5.54	1.11	0.68
Tunisia	565 276	3.30	0.89	0.54
Cambodia	491 872	7.48	0.77	0.47

871 - Optical instruments apparatus nes

	Value	of country total	of developing economies	of world
World	100 269 981	0.60	_	100.00
Developed economies	18 928 681	0.21	_	18.88
Transition economies	269 809	0.04	_	0.27
Developing economies	81 071 491	1.14	100.00	80.85
China	30 220 966	1.74	37.28	30.14
Korea, Republic of	28 912 566	5.66	35.66	28.83
China, Taiwan Province of	17 611 845	6.07	21.72	17.56
China, Hong Kong SAR	3 166 330	0.74	3.91	3.16
Singapore	456 323	0.12	0.56	0.46
Thailand	253 868	0.12	0.31	0.25
Malaysia	123 404	0.06	0.15	0.12
Mexico	104 134	0.03	0.13	0.10
United Arab Emirates	57 785	0.03	0.07	0.06
India	27 860	0.01	0.03	0.03

874 - Measure analyze control device nes

	Value	of country total	of developing economies	of world
World	166 360 210	1.00	_	100.00
Developed economies	130 283 025	1.47	_	78.31
Transition economies	1 279 379	0.18	_	0.77
Developing economies	34 797 806	0.49	100.00	20.92
China	9 336 086	0.54	26.83	5.61
Singapore	5 659 755	1.49	16.26	3.40
China, Hong Kong SAR	4 491 560	1.05	12.91	2.70
Malaysia	3 995 565	1.88	11.48	2.40
Mexico	3 248 351	1.00	9.33	1.95
Korea, Republic of	2 516 928	0.49	7.23	1.51
China, Taiwan Province of	1 917 639	0.66	5.51	1.15
Thailand	835 485	0.39	2.40	0.50
India	582 255	0.22	1.67	0.35
Brazil	346 946	0.15	1.00	0.21

For sources and notes, see end of table.

Pour les sources et les notes, se reporter à la fin du tableau.

3.2.E Export structure by product
Major exporters for leading products
among developing economies

3.2.E Structure des exportations par produits
Principaux exportateurs de produits majeurs
parmi les économies en développement

Leading exporting developing economies (1) based on average 2010-11 exports (2) SITC Revision 3 (3-digit level) — Principales économies en développement exportatrices (1) d'après la moyenne des exportations de 2010-11 (2) CTCI révision 3 (positions à 3 chiffres)	2010-2011				Leading exporting developing economies (1) based on average 2010-11 exports (2) SITC Revision 3 (3-digit level) — Principales économies en développement exportatrices (1) d'après la moyenne des exportations de 2010-11 (2) CTCI révision 3 (positions à 3 chiffres)	2010-2011			
	Value (f.o.b., thousands of dollars) Valeur (f.a.b., milliers de dollars)	As percentage / En pourcentage				Value (f.o.b., thousands of dollars) Valeur (f.a.b., milliers de dollars)	As percentage / En pourcentage		
		of country total / du total du pays	of developing economies / des économies en déve-loppement	of world / du monde			of country total / du total du pays	of developing economies / des économies en déve-loppement	of world / du monde
893 - Articles of plastic nes					**898 - Music instrument device recording**				
World	124 501 571	0.75	_	100.00	World	59 465 006	0.36	_	100.00
Developed economies	77 832 069	0.88	_	62.51	Developed economies	31 300 949	0.35	_	52.64
Transition economies	1 103 055	0.16	_	0.89	Transition economies	155 472	0.02	_	0.26
Developing economies	45 566 447	0.64	100.00	36.60	Developing economies	28 008 586	0.39	100.00	47.10
China	21 078 641	1.21	46.26	16.93	China	7 243 000	0.42	25.86	12.18
China, Taiwan Province of	2 931 003	1.01	6.43	2.35	China, Taiwan Province of	5 954 490	2.05	21.26	10.01
China, Hong Kong SAR	2 844 067	0.66	6.24	2.28	Singapore	5 053 399	1.33	18.04	8.50
Mexico	2 427 320	0.75	5.33	1.95	China, Hong Kong SAR	3 548 602	0.83	12.67	5.97
Korea, Republic of	2 227 105	0.44	4.89	1.79	Korea, Republic of	1 901 422	0.37	6.79	3.20
Thailand	1 975 881	0.93	4.34	1.59	Malaysia	1 707 998	0.80	6.10	2.87
Malaysia	1 850 156	0.87	4.06	1.49	Mexico	682 427	0.21	2.44	1.15
Turkey	1 411 257	1.13	3.10	1.13	Indonesia	507 307	0.28	1.81	0.85
Singapore	1 197 982	0.31	2.63	0.96	India	464 461	0.18	1.66	0.78
Viet Nam	976 443	1.15	2.14	0.78	Thailand	329 936	0.16	1.18	0.55
894 - Baby carriage toy game sport good					**899 - Manufactured articles nes**				
World	91 903 093	0.55	_	100.00	World	75 688 593	0.45	_	100.00
Developed economies	37 874 326	0.43	_	41.21	Developed economies	50 111 844	0.57	_	66.21
Transition economies	317 048	0.05	_	0.34	Transition economies	255 858	0.04	_	0.34
Developing economies	53 711 719	0.76	100.00	58.44	Developing economies	25 320 891	0.36	100.00	33.45
China	33 962 491	1.95	63.23	36.95	China	16 130 899	0.93	63.71	21.31
China, Hong Kong SAR	11 559 830	2.70	21.52	12.58	China, Hong Kong SAR	2 249 236	0.53	8.88	2.97
China, Taiwan Province of	1 991 671	0.69	3.71	2.17	Mexico	956 452	0.30	3.78	1.26
Mexico	1 262 532	0.39	2.35	1.37	Singapore	942 008	0.25	3.72	1.24
Singapore	795 934	0.21	1.48	0.87	Korea, Republic of	642 103	0.13	2.54	0.85
Thailand	795 579	0.30	1.48	0.87	China, Taiwan Province of	623 382	0.21	2.46	0.82
Indonesia	468 632	0.26	0.87	0.51	Indonesia	544 305	0.30	2.15	0.72
Korea, Republic of	443 291	0.09	0.83	0.48	Viet Nam	540 078	0.64	2.13	0.71
Viet Nam	387 763	0.46	0.72	0.42	India	489 239	0.19	1.93	0.65
Pakistan	330 430	1.41	0.62	0.36	Thailand	335 459	0.16	1.32	0.44
897 - Jewellery nes (667)					**971 - Gold non-monetary excluding ores**				
World	92 942 460	0.56	_	100.00	World	188 453 479	1.13	_	100.00
Developed economies	37 987 642	0.43	_	40.87	Developed economies	90 257 750	1.02	_	47.89
Transition economies	159 387	0.02	_	0.17	Transition economies	1 582 816	0.23	_	0.84
Developing economies	54 795 430	0.77	100.00	58.96	Developing economies	96 612 914	1.36	100.00	51.27
China	15 643 490	0.90	28.55	16.83	China, Hong Kong SAR	18 452 512	4.31	19.10	9.79
India	12 757 206	4.89	23.28	13.73	United Arab Emirates	14 266 319	6.57	14.77	7.57
China, Hong Kong SAR	6 436 110	1.50	11.75	6.92	Peru	8 828 149	21.84	9.14	4.68
Thailand	3 762 531	1.77	6.87	4.05	Mexico	6 865 273	2.12	7.11	3.64
Singapore	2 601 124	0.68	4.75	2.80	Thailand	6 219 575	2.93	6.44	3.30
United Arab Emirates	2 563 421	1.18	4.68	2.76	South Africa	5 802 250	6.49	6.01	3.08
Viet Nam	2 187 460	2.59	3.99	2.35	Korea, Republic of	3 063 122	0.60	3.17	1.63
Malaysia	2 177 939	1.02	3.97	2.34	Singapore	2 859 199	0.75	2.96	1.52
Turkey	1 759 942	1.41	3.21	1.89	Colombia	2 455 208	5.07	2.54	1.30
Mexico	642 931	0.20	1.17	0.69	China, Taiwan Province of	2 351 938	0.81	2.43	1.25

Source:
UNCTAD secretariat calculations, based on UNCTAD, *UNCTADstat* Merchandise Trade Matrix

Notes:
(1) In addition, are presented for each product group the world total exports and the exports from developed, transition and developing economies.
(2) Commodity groups are selected on the basis of ranking by value.

Source :
Calculs du secrétariat de la CNUCED, basés sur la matrice du commerce de marchandises de *UNCTADstat* de la CNUCED

Notes :
(1) Les exportations mondiales totales et les exportations des économies développées, en transition et en développement sont également présentées pour chaque groupe de produits.
(2) Les groupes de produits sont sélectionnés d'après le classement par valeur.

SITC group Revision 3 (3-digit level) ranked according to the concentration index in 2011 Groupes de la CTCI Révision 3 (positions à 3 chiffres) classés d'après l'indice de concentration en 2011	Concentration index (1) Indice de concentration (1)			Structural change index (2) Indice de changement structurel (2) 1995=0	
	2005	2010	2011	2005	2011
264 Jute, other textile bast fibres n.e.s., raw, processed, not spun; waste of	0.826	0.775	0.748	0.144	0.162
261 Silk	0.738	0.625	0.693	0.292	0.307
633 Cork manufactures	0.601	0.612	0.597	0.076	0.100
286 Uranium or thorium ores and concentrates	0.816	0.551	0.576	0.213	0.286
345 Coal gas, water gas, producer gas, similar gas (exclude other gas hydrocarbons)	0.685	0.353	0.567	0.835	0.422
244 Cork, natural, raw and waste (including natural cork in blocks or sheets)	0.581	0.565	0.561	0.116	0.073
666 Pottery	0.356	0.494	0.526	0.276	0.435
422 Fixed vegetable fats and oils, crude, refined or fractionated, other than "soft"	0.459	0.521	0.506	0.181	0.197
281 Iron ore and concentrates	0.351	0.459	0.474	0.168	0.220
885 Watches & clocks	0.432	0.443	0.466	0.168	0.229
831 Cases bags(storage hand executive equipment instrument gun travel shopping back)	0.364	0.450	0.460	0.222	0.331
752 Automatic data-processing transcibing machines; magnetic optical readers, n.e.s.	0.284	0.441	0.450	0.436	0.607
883 Cinematographic film, exposed developed, whether or not incorporating soundtrack	0.494	0.462	0.444	0.541	0.545
844 Women's textiles, knitted (articles as code 841, plus dresses skirts)	0.235	0.412	0.432	0.320	0.522
231 Natural rubber, balata, gutta-percha, guayule, chicle, natural gums	0.445	0.416	0.420	0.159	0.199
843 Men's textile, knitted (coat suit trouser short shirt underwear nightwear)	0.244	0.414	0.416	0.335	0.496
871 Optical instruments and apparatus, n.e.s.	0.379	0.429	0.416	0.551	0.604
322 Briquettes, lignites and peat	0.292	0.363	0.410	0.262	0.370
896 Works of art, collectors' pieces and antiques	0.440	0.441	0.408	0.162	0.178
658 Made-up articles, wholly or chiefly of textile materials, n.e.s.	0.314	0.417	0.404	0.259	0.330
044 Maize (not including sweet corn), unmilled	0.443	0.425	0.403	0.283	0.362
813 Lighting fixtures and fittings, n.e.s.	0.277	0.390	0.398	0.261	0.374
786 Trailers semi-trailers vehicles not mechanically-propelled; transport containers	0.339	0.374	0.398	0.244	0.313
846 Clothing accessories of textiles, knitted or crocheted or not (exluding babies)	0.260	0.370	0.386	0.262	0.421
891 Arms and ammunition	0.396	0.393	0.386	0.254	0.309
697 Household equipment of base metal, n.e.s.	0.271	0.364	0.385	0.292	0.417
792 Aircraft, associated equipment; spacecraft, satellites, launch vehicles; parts	0.424	0.385	0.382	0.158	0.477
652 Cotton fabrics, woven (not including narrow or special fabrics)	0.260	0.379	0.376	0.181	0.346
894 Baby carriages, toys, games and sporting goods	0.344	0.364	0.373	0.241	0.352
751 Office machines	0.319	0.360	0.367	0.374	0.419
793 Ships, boats (including hovercraft) and floating structures	0.269	0.354	0.366	0.308	0.455
212 Furskins, raw, other than hides and skins of group 211	0.339	0.367	0.363	0.218	0.243
321 Coal, whether or not pulverized, excluding agglomerated	0.350	0.392	0.361	0.206	0.205
292 Crude vegetable materials, n.e.s.	0.358	0.325	0.358	0.091	0.139
653 Fabrics, woven, of man-made textiles (excluding narrow or special fabrics)	0.252	0.332	0.357	0.292	0.429
222 Oil-seed, oleaginous fruit for soft fixed vegetable oils (exclude flours, meals)	0.380	0.394	0.357	0.303	0.340
851 Footwear	0.297	0.361	0.357	0.275	0.386
711 Steam vapour superheated water boiler, auxiliary plant for use with; parts of	0.186	0.316	0.355	0.266	0.551
848 Apparel articles accessories other than textile fabrics; headgear (all material)	0.374	0.346	0.350	0.217	0.251
655 Knitted, crocheted fabric (include tubular knit, pile, openwork fabric), n.e.s.	0.259	0.342	0.347	0.249	0.395
284 Nickel ores, concentrates; mattes, oxide sinters, intermediate product of	0.295	0.323	0.346	0.196	0.175
961 Coin (other than gold coin), not being legal tender	0.314	0.360	0.344	0.351	0.518
763 Sound or television image recorder reproducer; prepared unrecorded media	0.369	0.350	0.340	0.407	0.441
583 Plastic monofilament, cross-section > 1 mm, rods, sticks, profile shapes	0.358	0.363	0.338	0.172	0.257
263 Cotton	0.348	0.340	0.329	0.231	0.323
696 Cutlery	0.301	0.319	0.329	0.324	0.477
285 Aluminium ores and concentrates (including alumina)	0.308	0.333	0.328	0.164	0.221
042 Rice	0.306	0.313	0.327	0.184	0.186
764 Telecommunications equipment and parts, n.e.s.; accessories within division 76	0.212	0.309	0.326	0.295	0.480
045 Cereals, unmilled (excluding wheat, rice, barley, maize)	0.366	0.327	0.325	0.176	0.316
025 Eggs, birds', yolks, fresh, dried, preserved, sweetened or not; albumin	0.283	0.281	0.325	0.202	0.239
431 Animal, vegetable fats, oils, processed; waxes; inedible preparations of, n.e.s.	0.280	0.332	0.325	0.208	0.244
268 Wool and other animal hair (including wool tops)	0.344	0.334	0.324	0.175	0.307
731 Machine tools working by removing metal or other material	0.320	0.308	0.322	0.093	0.162
687 Tin	0.302	0.313	0.322	0.277	0.249
775 Household-type electrical and non-electrical equipment, n.e.s.	0.236	0.299	0.312	0.274	0.450
882 Photographic and cinematographic supplies	0.281	0.311	0.312	0.142	0.210
774 Electrodiagnostic apparatus, medical surgical dental veterinary radiological	0.326	0.313	0.307	0.114	0.161
845 Articles of apparel, textile fabrics, knitted or crocheted or not, n.e.s.	0.243	0.305	0.306	0.252	0.384
662 Clay construction materials and refractory construction materials	0.298	0.299	0.305	0.223	0.346
842 Women's textiles not knitted (articles as code 841, plus dresses skirts)	0.242	0.309	0.301	0.232	0.319
061 Sugar, molasses and honey	0.208	0.313	0.300	0.316	0.424
551 Essential oils, perfume and flavour materials	0.369	0.312	0.296	0.328	0.307
265 Vegetable textile fibre (exclu cotton, jute), raw, processed, not spun; waste of	0.370	0.331	0.295	0.191	0.283

For sources and notes, see end of table 3.3 Imports.

Pour les sources et les notes, se reporter à la fin du tableau 3.3 Importations.

SITC group Revision 3 (3-digit level) ranked according to the concentration index in 2011 Groupes de la CTCI Révision 3 (positions à 3 chiffres) classés d'après l'indice de concentration en 2011	Concentration index (1) Indice de concentration (1)			Structural change index (2) Indice de changement structurel (2) 1995=0	
	2005	2010	2011	2005	2011
821 Furniture and parts; bedding, mattresses, mattress supports, cushions	0.202	0.294	0.295	0.249	0.394
785 Motor cycles, mopeds, cycles, motorized and non-motorized; invalid carriages	0.291	0.290	0.294	0.254	0.400
654 Other textile fabrics, woven n.e.s.	0.271	0.287	0.293	0.187	0.270
726 Printing and bookbinding machinery, and parts thereof	0.352	0.304	0.290	0.127	0.170
656 Tulles, lace, embroidery, ribbons, trimmings and other smallwares	0.210	0.284	0.286	0.215	0.348
272 Fertilizers, crude (excluding those of division 56)	0.298	0.274	0.283	0.201	0.268
761 Television receiver, video monitor projector, w wo radio video-record reproduce	0.222	0.285	0.283	0.363	0.563
072 Cocoa	0.288	0.283	0.281	0.112	0.149
283 Copper ores and concentrates; copper mattes; cement copper	0.388	0.310	0.281	0.258	0.262
593 Explosives and pyrotechnic products	0.306	0.282	0.280	0.255	0.264
841 Men's textile, not knitted (coat suit trouser short shirt underwear nightwear)	0.217	0.278	0.279	0.225	0.316
667 Pearls and precious or semiprecious stones, unworked or worked	0.262	0.266	0.277	0.212	0.349
041 Wheat (including spelt) and meslin, unmilled	0.287	0.264	0.276	0.202	0.234
762 Radio-broadcast receivers, with without sound-recording reproducing or clock	0.249	0.265	0.274	0.322	0.448
325 Coke, semi-coke of coal, lignite, peat, agglomerated or not; retort carbon	0.374	0.264	0.273	0.291	0.436
023 Butter and other fats and oils derived from milk	0.227	0.254	0.272	0.189	0.242
613 Furskin, tanned, dressed, unassembled, assembled (without other materials)	0.310	0.291	0.271	0.410	0.427
712 Steam turbines and other vapour turbines, and parts thereof, n.e.s.	0.309	0.267	0.271	0.265	0.321
597 Prepared additives: mineral oil; transmission; anti-freeze, de-ice; lubricating	0.286	0.274	0.270	0.120	0.175
781 Vehicles to transport less than 10 persons, including station-wagons race cars	0.273	0.272	0.269	0.122	0.202
211 Hides and skins (except furskins), raw	0.267	0.290	0.267	0.197	0.181
745 Non-electrical machinery, tools and mechanical apparatus, parts thereof, n.e.s.	0.280	0.265	0.267	0.107	0.180
759 Parts, accessories for machines of groups 751, 752	0.231	0.254	0.266	0.318	0.390
037 Fish, crustaceans, molluscs, aquatic invertebrates (prepared preserved) n.e.s.	0.236	0.255	0.266	0.246	0.305
748 Transmission shaft camshaft crankshaft; bearing housing; gearbox speed changer	0.282	0.267	0.266	0.143	0.202
267 Other man-made fibres suitable for spinning; waste of man-made fibres	0.371	0.269	0.263	0.176	0.361
515 Organo-inorganic and heterocyclic compounds, nucleic acids-salts, sulphonamides	0.279	0.267	0.260	0.282	0.303
714 Engines, motors, non-electric (exclude group 712, 713 and 718); parts of, n.e.s.	0.353	0.253	0.260	0.126	0.266
016 Meat, edible meat offal (salted dried); flours, meals	0.304	0.260	0.260	0.197	0.331
525 Radio-actives and associated materials	0.316	0.281	0.260	0.258	0.404
724 Textile and leather machinery, and parts thereof, n.e.s.	0.252	0.245	0.260	0.174	0.282
899 Miscellaneous manufactured articles, n.e.s.	0.222	0.244	0.259	0.233	0.283
122 Tobacco, manufactured (whether or not containing tobacco substitutes)	0.271	0.242	0.258	0.398	0.483
771 Electric power machinery parts (excluding rotating electric plant, group 716)	0.225	0.254	0.257	0.212	0.290
897 Jewellery, articles of goldsmiths' silversmiths' B2 semiprecious, n.e.s.	0.206	0.200	0.255	0.232	0.361
728 Other machinery or specialized industrial equipment; parts thereof, n.e.s.	0.262	0.259	0.254	0.089	0.175
776 Thermionic cold cathode photo-cathode valves tubes; diodes, transistors	0.235	0.252	0.254	0.248	0.357
872 Instruments and appliances, n.e.s., (medical, surgical, dental or veterinary)	0.244	0.255	0.252	0.171	0.179
733 Machine tool to work metal sintered metal carbide cermet, not removing material	0.249	0.233	0.250	0.156	0.198
722 Tractors (excluding headings 714.14 & 744.15)	0.261	0.245	0.249	0.159	0.215
541 Medicinal and pharmaceutical products, excluding medicines of group 542	0.246	0.257	0.249	0.145	0.226
874 Measuring, checking, analysing and controlling instruments and apparatus, n.e.s.	0.273	0.249	0.248	0.123	0.196
895 Office and stationery supplies, n.e.s.	0.205	0.240	0.247	0.214	0.316
289 Ores and concentrates of precious metals; waste of (excluding gold)	0.257	0.398	0.247	0.292	0.359
251 Pulp and waste paper	0.262	0.247	0.245	0.141	0.203
884 Optical goods, n.e.s.	0.279	0.245	0.245	0.169	0.247
683 Nickel	0.280	0.270	0.245	0.131	0.169
725 Paper mill pulp mill paper-cutting other paper manufacture machines; parts of	0.252	0.247	0.243	0.140	0.206
531 Synthetic organic colouring matter and colour lakes, preparations based thereon	0.231	0.234	0.241	0.217	0.335
266 Synthetic fibres suitable for spinning	0.219	0.223	0.240	0.198	0.338
727 Food-processing machines (excluding domestic); parts thereof	0.250	0.237	0.239	0.108	0.145
024 Cheese and curd	0.239	0.227	0.239	0.170	0.208
112 Alcoholic beverages	0.248	0.232	0.239	0.142	0.158
694 Nails, screws, nuts, bolts, rivets, of iron, steel, copper or aluminium	0.224	0.233	0.238	0.134	0.199
659 Floor coverings, etc.	0.234	0.227	0.236	0.168	0.328
721 Agricultural machinery (excluding tractors), and parts thereof	0.245	0.228	0.235	0.118	0.182
056 Vegetables, roots and tubers (prepared preserved) n.e.s.	0.203	0.222	0.235	0.169	0.199
074 Tea and maté	0.240	0.237	0.234	0.203	0.214
747 Appliances for pipes boiler shells tanks vats; pressure and temperature valves	0.224	0.232	0.234	0.163	0.233
778 Electrical machinery and apparatus, n.e.s.	0.200	0.224	0.234	0.208	0.280
742 Liquid pump, with without a fitted measuring device; liquid elevator; parts for	0.256	0.231	0.234	0.153	0.220
746 Ball or roller bearings	0.224	0.235	0.233	0.146	0.212
737 Metalworking machinery (other than machine tools), and parts thereof, n.e.s.	0.222	0.236	0.233	0.146	0.218
657 Special yarns, special textile fabrics and related products	0.180	0.218	0.232	0.172	0.297

For sources and notes, see end of table 3.3 Imports.

Pour les sources et les notes, se reporter à la fin du tableau 3.3 Importations.

3

SITC group Revision 3 (3-digit level) ranked according to the concentration index in 2011 / Groupes de la CTCI Révision 3 (positions à 3 chiffres) classés d'après l'indice de concentration en 2011	Concentration index (1) Indice de concentration (1)			Structural change index (2) Indice de changement structurel (2) 1995=0	
	2005	2010	2011	2005	2011
043 Barley, unmilled	0.263	0.240	0.232	0.313	0.372
121 Tobacco, unmanufactured; tobacco refuse	0.241	0.236	0.229	0.263	0.347
572 Polymers of styrene, in primary forms	0.216	0.239	0.229	0.179	0.273
223 Oil-seed, oleaginous fruit to extract other vegetable oil; flour, meal of n.e.s.	0.279	0.239	0.228	0.418	0.477
783 Road motor vehicles, n.e.s.	0.246	0.215	0.226	0.235	0.365
291 Crude animal materials, nes	0.222	0.219	0.225	0.157	0.185
723 Civil engineering and contractors' plant and equipment; parts thereof	0.243	0.229	0.225	0.123	0.228
735 Parts, n.e.s. and accessories for machines of groups 731, 733; tool holder	0.243	0.227	0.225	0.135	0.196
282 Ferrous waste and scrap; remelting scrap ingots of iron or steel	0.200	0.217	0.222	0.229	0.177
523 Metallic salts and peroxysalts, of inorganic acids	0.212	0.214	0.221	0.209	0.285
695 Tools for use in the hand or in machine	0.211	0.215	0.221	0.138	0.206
579 Waste, parings and scrap, of plastics	0.255	0.245	0.221	0.252	0.333
744 Mechanical handling equipment, and parts thereof, n.e.s.	0.212	0.219	0.219	0.141	0.215
573 Polymers of vinyl chloride or of other halogenated olefins, in primary forms	0.186	0.227	0.219	0.168	0.271
081 Feeding stuff for animals (excluding unmilled cereals)	0.213	0.220	0.219	0.150	0.205
232 Synthetic rubber; reclaimed rubber; waste, parings, scrap of unhardened rubber	0.222	0.224	0.219	0.190	0.283
672 Ingots, other primary forms of iron or steel; semi-finished products of	0.209	0.230	0.219	0.213	0.301
689 Miscellaneous non-ferrous base metals employed in metallurgy, and cermets	0.258	0.229	0.219	0.308	0.264
791 Railway vehicles (including hovertrains) and associated equipment	0.232	0.228	0.218	0.257	0.339
516 Other organic chemicals	0.198	0.209	0.218	0.187	0.248
677 Rails or railway track construction material, of iron or steel	0.197	0.208	0.218	0.245	0.272
713 Internal combustion piston engines, and parts thereof, n.e.s.	0.238	0.221	0.217	0.194	0.239
716 Rotating electric plant, and parts thereof, n.e.s.	0.189	0.212	0.217	0.189	0.274
691 Structures and parts of structures, n.e.s., of iron, steel or aluminium	0.179	0.214	0.215	0.248	0.312
553 Perfumery, cosmetic or toilet preparations (excluding soaps)	0.254	0.219	0.215	0.151	0.226
743 Pump (non liquid), air gas compressor, fan ventilation filter; centrifuge; parts	0.219	0.215	0.215	0.155	0.231
741 Heating and cooling equipment, and parts thereof, n.e.s.	0.193	0.208	0.214	0.217	0.311
411 Animals oils and fats	0.206	0.230	0.212	0.236	0.228
675 Flat-rolled products of alloy steel	0.189	0.199	0.212	0.231	0.288
772 Electrical apparatus to switch protect circuits or make circuit connections	0.201	0.211	0.212	0.185	0.258
054 Vegetables and veg products (fresh chilled frozen preserved dried edible) n.e.s.	0.210	0.196	0.211	0.149	0.172
012 Other meat and edible meat offal (fresh chilled frozen)	0.206	0.207	0.211	0.277	0.314
612 Manufactures of leather or of composition leather, n.e.s.; saddlery and harness	0.219	0.217	0.211	0.362	0.385
749 Non-electric parts and accessories of machinery, n.e.s.	0.204	0.206	0.210	0.141	0.248
663 Mineral manufactures, n.e.s.	0.200	0.208	0.210	0.136	0.224
524 Other inorganic chemicals; organic and inorganic compounds of precious metals	0.251	0.220	0.210	0.215	0.239
071 Coffee and coffee substitutes	0.207	0.206	0.210	0.228	0.296
665 Glassware	0.180	0.218	0.210	0.209	0.342
898 Musical instrument, parts accessory; tape, sound recording (excluding 763 & 883)	0.207	0.211	0.209	0.246	0.371
542 Medicines (including veterinary medicines)	0.229	0.216	0.209	0.186	0.206
343 Natural gas, whether or not liquefied	0.257	0.212	0.209	0.276	0.486
598 Miscellaneous chemical products, n.e.s.	0.232	0.213	0.208	0.118	0.193
421 Fixed vegetable fats and oils, "soft", crude, refined or fractioned	0.224	0.207	0.208	0.213	0.257
782 Motor vehicles for the transport of goods and special-purpose motor vehicles	0.219	0.211	0.208	0.197	0.323
812 Sanitary, plumbing and heating fixtures and fittings, n.e.s.	0.212	0.208	0.207	0.204	0.289
718 Power-generating machinery, and parts thereof, n.e.s.	0.223	0.215	0.207	0.195	0.247
674 Flat-rolled products of iron or non-alloy steel, clad, plated or coated	0.180	0.194	0.207	0.223	0.362
581 Tubes, pipes and hoses, and fittings therefor, of plastics	0.206	0.205	0.207	0.198	0.253
784 Parts and accessories of the motor vehicles of groups 722, 781, 782 and 783	0.215	0.207	0.206	0.209	0.317
611 Leather	0.223	0.206	0.206	0.192	0.200
288 Non-ferrous base metal waste and scrap, n.e.s.	0.185	0.195	0.205	0.201	0.220
893 Articles, n.e.s., of plastics	0.188	0.197	0.205	0.176	0.233
513 Carboxylic acid, anhydrides, halides, peroxides, peroxyacids; halogenate derivatives	0.187	0.198	0.204	0.290	0.410
681 Silver, platinum, other metals of the platinum group	0.296	0.241	0.204	0.179	0.281
514 Nitrogen-function compounds	0.189	0.203	0.203	0.254	0.307
073 Chocolate and other food preparations containing cocoa, n.e.s.	0.199	0.197	0.203	0.200	0.224
022 Milk, cream and milk products (excluding butter, cheese)	0.209	0.200	0.203	0.203	0.294
664 Glass	0.182	0.208	0.202	0.164	0.242
699 Manufactures of base metal, n.e.s.	0.196	0.197	0.200	0.155	0.237
651 Textile yarn	0.169	0.202	0.200	0.160	0.322
274 Sulphur and unroasted iron pyrites	0.251	0.190	0.199	0.269	0.380
873 Meters and counters, n.e.s.	0.219	0.201	0.199	0.268	0.389
342 Liquefied propane and butane	0.219	0.193	0.199	0.189	0.347
591 Insecticide, rodenticide, fungicide, herbicide, plant-growth reg, disinfectant	0.210	0.192	0.199	0.203	0.247

For sources and notes, see end of table 3.3 Imports.

Pour les sources et les notes, se reporter à la fin du tableau 3.3 Importations.

SITC group Revision 3 (3-digit level) ranked according to the concentration index in 2011 Groupes de la CTCI Révision 3 (positions à 3 chiffres) classés d'après l'indice de concentration en 2011	Concentration index (1) Indice de concentration (1)			Structural change index (2) Indice de changement structurel (2) 1995=0	
	2005	2010	2011	2005	2011
881 Photographic apparatus and equipment, n.e.s.	0.338	0.201	0.199	0.228	0.373
011 Meat of bovine animals (fresh chilled frozen)	0.215	0.191	0.198	0.298	0.287
661 Lime, cement, fabricated construction material (excluding glass, clay material)	0.175	0.190	0.198	0.292	0.371
091 Margarine and shortening	0.171	0.178	0.198	0.257	0.281
533 Pigments, paints, varnishes and related materials	0.209	0.204	0.198	0.104	0.171
075 Spices	0.162	0.199	0.198	0.211	0.263
682 Copper	0.191	0.200	0.196	0.183	0.248
001 Live animals other than animals of division 03	0.198	0.186	0.196	0.158	0.232
511 Hydrocarbons, n.e.s., halogenated, sulphonated, nitrated, nitrosated derivatives	0.204	0.195	0.195	0.165	0.262
269 Worn clothing and other worn textile articles; rags	0.202	0.202	0.195	0.286	0.345
335 Residual petroleum products, n.e.s., related mater.	0.161	0.190	0.195	0.216	0.217
592 Starches, inulin and wheat gluten; albuminoidal substances; glues	0.196	0.192	0.193	0.133	0.202
634 Veneers, plywood, particle board, and other wood, worked, n.e.s.	0.185	0.183	0.193	0.238	0.330
035 Fish (dried, salted, in brine, smoked); flours, meals, pellets for human consump	0.203	0.200	0.192	0.243	0.350
582 Plates, sheets, film, foil and strip, of plastics	0.201	0.199	0.192	0.124	0.230
059 Fruit and vegetable juice (unfermented, no added spirit, sweetened or not)	0.185	0.187	0.192	0.213	0.226
679 Tubes, pipes and hollow profiles, and tube or pipe fittings, of iron or steel	0.175	0.183	0.192	0.162	0.255
971 Gold, non-monetary (excluding gold ores and concentrates)	0.199	0.166	0.192	0.374	0.413
693 Wire products (excluding insulated electrical wiring) and fencing grills	0.167	0.185	0.192	0.205	0.296
017 Meat, edible meat offal (prepared preserved) n.e.s.	0.188	0.193	0.191	0.267	0.304
625 Rubber tyres, interchangeable tyre treads, tyre flaps, inner tubes for wheels	0.172	0.187	0.191	0.187	0.314
575 Other plastics, in primary forms	0.230	0.193	0.190	0.143	0.249
811 Prefabricated buildings	0.143	0.188	0.190	0.257	0.375
287 Ores and concentrates of base metals, n.e.s.	0.210	0.195	0.190	0.269	0.223
277 Natural abrasives, n.e.s. (including industrial diamonds)	0.168	0.164	0.189	0.411	0.504
629 Articles of rubber, n.e.s.	0.192	0.188	0.189	0.159	0.239
248 Wood, simply worked, and railway sleepers of wood	0.251	0.189	0.187	0.211	0.307
892 Printed matter	0.214	0.189	0.186	0.130	0.251
046 Meal and flour of wheat and flour of meslin	0.182	0.179	0.186	0.414	0.511
621 Materials of rubber (e.g., pastes, plates, sheets, rods, thread, tubes, of rubber)	0.217	0.192	0.185	0.131	0.312
333 Petroleum oils and oils obtained from bituminous minerals, crude	0.180	0.172	0.185	0.142	0.203
562 Fertilizers (excluding group 272)	0.184	0.178	0.183	0.214	0.302
635 Wood manufactures, n.e.s.	0.185	0.188	0.183	0.234	0.299
641 Paper and paperboard	0.201	0.188	0.183	0.120	0.197
512 Alcohol, phenol, phenol-alcohol;halogenate, sulphonate, nitrate, nitrosate deriv	0.164	0.169	0.181	0.231	0.317
247 Wood in the rough or roughly squared	0.264	0.192	0.181	0.318	0.314
111 Non-alcoholic beverages, n.e.s.	0.198	0.177	0.180	0.270	0.319
673 Flat-rolled products of iron or non-alloy steel, not clad, plated or coated	0.157	0.184	0.180	0.171	0.195
642 Paper and paperboard, cut to size or shape, and articles of paper or paperboard	0.182	0.176	0.180	0.178	0.262
574 Polyacetal, polyether, epoxide resin; polycarbonate, alkyd resin, polyester	0.188	0.178	0.178	0.182	0.259
678 Wire of iron or steel	0.146	0.174	0.177	0.187	0.300
571 Polymers of ethylene, in primary forms	0.179	0.179	0.174	0.223	0.310
671 Pig-iron, spiegeleisen, sponge iron, iron steel granules, powders, ferro-alloys	0.187	0.169	0.173	0.267	0.283
773 Equipment for distributing electricity, n.e.s.	0.169	0.171	0.170	0.224	0.343
532 Dyeing and tanning extracts, and synthetic tanning materials	0.171	0.169	0.170	0.201	0.244
278 Other crude minerals	0.163	0.167	0.169	0.170	0.240
048 Cereal preparations and preparations of flour or starch of fruits or vegetables	0.190	0.172	0.168	0.155	0.193
522 Inorganic chemical elements, oxides and halogen salts	0.173	0.178	0.168	0.153	0.234
034 Fish, fresh (live dead chilled frozen)	0.151	0.169	0.168	0.180	0.274
351 Electric current	0.198	0.167	0.167	0.372	0.394
058 Fruit, preserved, and fruit preparations (excluding fruit juices)	0.157	0.165	0.167	0.189	0.238
554 Soaps, cleansing and polishing preparations	0.182	0.167	0.167	0.129	0.182
685 Lead	0.212	0.163	0.165	0.210	0.281
047 Other cereal meals and flours	0.190	0.183	0.164	0.233	0.354
057 Fruits and nuts (excluding oil nuts), fresh or dried	0.165	0.159	0.161	0.168	0.204
334 Petroleum oil, oil from bituminous (excl crude); preparations, n.e.s., > 70% oil	0.129	0.153	0.159	0.186	0.247
686 Zinc	0.156	0.155	0.159	0.232	0.272
692 Metal containers for storage or transport	0.158	0.156	0.158	0.181	0.266
246 Wood in chips or particles and wood waste	0.227	0.172	0.157	0.347	0.443
098 Edible products and preparations, n.e.s.	0.170	0.155	0.156	0.213	0.242
036 Crustaceans, mollusks and aquatic invertebrates	0.133	0.147	0.152	0.231	0.246
676 Iron and steel bars, rods, angles, shapes and sections (including sheet piling)	0.143	0.144	0.146	0.183	0.276
684 Aluminium	0.142	0.139	0.143	0.144	0.221
344 Petroleum gases and other gaseous hydrocarbons, n.e.s.	0.374	0.388	0.138	0.454	0.566
273 Stone, sand and gravel	0.135	0.137	0.138	0.216	0.298
062 Sugar confectionery	0.139	0.131	0.136	0.214	0.259
245 Fuel wood (excluding wood waste) and wood charcoal	0.100	0.118	0.115	0.301	0.374

For sources and notes, see end of table 3.3 Imports.

Pour les sources et les notes, se reporter à la fin du tableau 3.3 Importations.

SITC group Revision 3 (3-digit level) ranked according to the concentration index in 2011 Groupes de la CTCI Révision 3 (positions à 3 chiffres) classés d'après l'indice de concentration en 2011	Concentration index (1) Indice de concentration (1)			Structural change index (2) Indice de changement structurel (2) 1995=0	
	2005	2010	2011	2005	2011
286 Uranium or thorium ores and concentrates	0.883	0.994	0.954	0.275	0.289
961 Coin (other than gold coin), not being legal tender	0.173	0.444	0.701	0.445	0.421
579 Waste, parings and scrap, of plastics	0.498	0.604	0.605	0.361	0.567
281 Iron ore and concentrates	0.432	0.587	0.603	0.376	0.524
871 Optical instruments and apparatus, n.e.s.	0.596	0.617	0.593	0.641	0.684
244 Cork, natural, raw and waste (including natural cork in blocks or sheets)	0.511	0.431	0.513	0.268	0.298
322 Briquettes, lignites and peat	0.211	0.377	0.496	0.261	0.644
265 Vegetable textile fibre (exclu cotton, jute), raw, processed, not spun; waste of	0.357	0.467	0.493	0.460	0.549
883 Cinematographic film, exposed developed, whether or not incorporating soundtrack	0.511	0.453	0.423	0.364	0.376
247 Wood in the rough or roughly squared	0.261	0.390	0.422	0.396	0.581
222 Oil-seed, oleaginous fruit for soft fixed vegetable oils (exclude flours, meals)	0.306	0.426	0.420	0.384	0.517
613 Furskin, tanned, dressed, unassembled, assembled (without other materials)	0.374	0.487	0.419	0.401	0.456
284 Nickel ores, concentrates; mattes, oxide sinters, intermediate product of	0.295	0.349	0.414	0.239	0.428
896 Works of art, collectors' pieces and antiques	0.439	0.426	0.410	0.120	0.202
261 Silk	0.429	0.401	0.382	0.406	0.442
268 Wool and other animal hair (including wool tops)	0.296	0.385	0.382	0.277	0.376
263 Cotton	0.291	0.345	0.370	0.355	0.453
264 Jute, other textile bast fibres n.e.s., raw, processed, not spun; waste of	0.345	0.338	0.366	0.331	0.422
345 Coal gas, water gas, producer gas, similar gas (exclude other gas hydrocarbons)	0.438	0.367	0.360	0.796	0.572
211 Hides and skins (except furskins), raw	0.276	0.333	0.352	0.318	0.404
287 Ores and concentrates of base metals, n.e.s.	0.217	0.363	0.352	0.240	0.409
212 Furskins, raw, other than hides and skins of group 211	0.373	0.378	0.347	0.288	0.278
288 Non-ferrous base metal waste and scrap, n.e.s.	0.255	0.346	0.347	0.267	0.386
246 Wood in chips or particles and wood waste	0.526	0.373	0.347	0.241	0.493
283 Copper ores and concentrates; copper mattes; cement copper	0.329	0.349	0.335	0.360	0.470
274 Sulphur and unroasted iron pyrites	0.343	0.362	0.324	0.425	0.421
251 Pulp and waste paper	0.228	0.282	0.321	0.238	0.366
776 Thermionic cold cathode photo-cathode valves tubes; diodes, transistors	0.250	0.301	0.313	0.314	0.384
016 Meat, edible meat offal (salted dried); flours, meals	0.379	0.325	0.303	0.200	0.307
667 Pearls and precious or semiprecious stones, unworked or worked	0.293	0.312	0.299	0.201	0.322
289 Ores and concentrates of precious metals; waste of (excluding gold)	0.366	0.307	0.279	0.270	0.343
525 Radio-actives and associated materials	0.317	0.294	0.278	0.234	0.223
043 Barley, unmilled	0.260	0.324	0.275	0.246	0.230
761 Television receiver, video monitor projector, w wo radio video-record reproduce	0.338	0.286	0.272	0.317	0.268
231 Natural rubber, balata, gutta-percha, guayule, chicle, natural gums	0.243	0.257	0.271	0.193	0.301
891 Arms and ammunition	0.243	0.329	0.270	0.312	0.324
731 Machine tools working by removing metal or other material	0.199	0.270	0.267	0.204	0.307
971 Gold, non-monetary (excluding gold ores and concentrates)	0.243	0.253	0.256	0.528	0.502
036 Crustaceans, mollusks and aquatic invertebrates	0.299	0.264	0.256	0.234	0.264
512 Alcohol, phenol, phenol-alcohol;halogenate, sulphonate, nitrate, nitrosate deriv	0.208	0.251	0.253	0.262	0.324
894 Baby carriages, toys, games and sporting goods	0.316	0.280	0.253	0.097	0.150
683 Nickel	0.202	0.243	0.251	0.184	0.305
321 Coal, whether or not pulverized, excluding agglomerated	0.233	0.251	0.248	0.164	0.276
843 Men's textile, knitted (coat suit trouser short shirt underwear nightwear)	0.315	0.258	0.243	0.178	0.203
515 Organo-inorganic and heterocyclic compounds, nucleic acids-salts, sulphonamides	0.266	0.241	0.241	0.205	0.232
572 Polymers of styrene, in primary forms	0.248	0.262	0.240	0.200	0.261
762 Radio-broadcast receivers, with without sound-recording reproducing or clock	0.276	0.252	0.240	0.169	0.225
897 Jewellery, articles of goldsmiths' silversmiths' B2 semiprecious, n.e.s.	0.268	0.243	0.240	0.159	0.350
681 Silver, platinum, other metals of the platinum group	0.266	0.253	0.239	0.229	0.273
752 Automatic data-processing transcibing machines; magnetic optical readers, n.e.s.	0.231	0.236	0.239	0.145	0.219
633 Cork manufactures	0.251	0.243	0.239	0.157	0.232
682 Copper	0.184	0.251	0.238	0.217	0.319
821 Furniture and parts; bedding, mattresses, mattress supports, cushions	0.303	0.251	0.235	0.210	0.183
845 Articles of apparel, textile fabrics, knitted or crocheted or not, n.e.s.	0.269	0.241	0.233	0.164	0.179
333 Petroleum oils and oils obtained from bituminous minerals, crude	0.242	0.234	0.233	0.118	0.204
848 Apparel articles accessories other than textile fabrics; headgear (all material)	0.274	0.239	0.233	0.168	0.192
885 Watches & clocks	0.232	0.224	0.232	0.120	0.125
658 Made-up articles, wholly or chiefly of textile materials, n.e.s.	0.298	0.262	0.231	0.194	0.190
511 Hydrocarbons, n.e.s., halogenated, sulphonated, nitrated, nitrosated derivatives	0.190	0.220	0.231	0.203	0.256
844 Women's textiles, knitted (articles as code 841, plus dresses skirts)	0.285	0.237	0.228	0.153	0.213
045 Cereals, unmilled (excluding wheat, rice, barley, maize)	0.270	0.228	0.224	0.257	0.301
689 Miscellaneous non-ferrous base metals employed in metallurgy, and cermets	0.250	0.228	0.223	0.135	0.232
611 Leather	0.227	0.223	0.222	0.207	0.227
841 Men's textile, not knitted (coat suit trouser short shirt underwear nightwear)	0.277	0.229	0.219	0.140	0.178

For sources and notes, see end of table.

Pour les sources et les notes, se reporter à la fin du tableau.

SITC group Revision 3 (3-digit level) ranked according to the concentration index in 2011 Groupes de la CTCI Révision 3 (positions à 3 chiffres) classés d'après l'indice de concentration en 2011	Concentration index (1) Indice de concentration (1)			Structural change index (2) Indice de changement structurel (2) 1995=0	
	2005	2010	2011	2005	2011
884 Optical goods, n.e.s.	0.215	0.222	0.218	0.289	0.330
792 Aircraft, associated equipment; spacecraft, satellites, launch vehicles; parts	0.215	0.224	0.215	0.306	0.355
072 Cocoa	0.225	0.211	0.215	0.140	0.161
343 Natural gas, whether or not liquefied	0.259	0.210	0.215	0.333	0.339
759 Parts, accessories for machines of groups 751, 752	0.204	0.216	0.212	0.238	0.338
071 Coffee and coffee substitutes	0.212	0.204	0.212	0.118	0.119
842 Women's textiles not knitted (articles as code 841, plus dresses skirts)	0.282	0.224	0.212	0.172	0.234
774 Electrodiagnostic apparatus, medical surgical dental veterinary radiological	0.243	0.209	0.211	0.174	0.166
112 Alcoholic beverages	0.256	0.222	0.211	0.172	0.190
831 Cases bags(storage hand executive equipment instrument gun travel shopping back)	0.266	0.221	0.210	0.172	0.240
017 Meat, edible meat offal (prepared preserved) n.e.s.	0.229	0.211	0.210	0.201	0.256
342 Liquefied propane and butane	0.265	0.212	0.208	0.267	0.293
851 Footwear	0.252	0.216	0.207	0.143	0.206
037 Fish, crustaceans, molluscs, aquatic invertebrates (prepared preserved) n.e.s.	0.247	0.214	0.207	0.168	0.216
285 Aluminium ores and concentrates (including alumina)	0.234	0.209	0.206	0.248	0.286
714 Engines, motors, non-electric (exclude group 712, 713 and 718); parts of, n.e.s.	0.225	0.203	0.206	0.148	0.234
751 Office machines	0.249	0.210	0.204	0.117	0.192
697 Household equipment of base metal, n.e.s.	0.267	0.215	0.204	0.179	0.169
272 Fertilizers, crude (excluding those of division 56)	0.175	0.168	0.202	0.242	0.340
344 Petroleum gases and other gaseous hydrocarbons, n.e.s.	0.232	0.208	0.200	0.497	0.529
781 Vehicles to transport less than 10 persons, including station-wagons race cars	0.259	0.209	0.200	0.166	0.252
718 Power-generating machinery, and parts thereof, n.e.s.	0.187	0.185	0.199	0.234	0.307
687 Tin	0.207	0.193	0.198	0.337	0.343
728 Other machinery or specialized industrial equipment; parts thereof, n.e.s.	0.158	0.199	0.198	0.152	0.181
273 Stone, sand and gravel	0.151	0.205	0.198	0.254	0.398
025 Eggs, birds', yolks, fresh, dried, preserved, sweetened or not; albumin	0.216	0.218	0.198	0.179	0.305
763 Sound or television image recorder reproducer; prepared unrecorded media	0.262	0.206	0.198	0.133	0.247
899 Miscellaneous manufactured articles, n.e.s.	0.201	0.197	0.198	0.166	0.178
282 Ferrous waste and scrap; remelting scrap ingots of iron or steel	0.178	0.189	0.197	0.258	0.300
267 Other man-made fibres suitable for spinning; waste of man-made fibres	0.164	0.189	0.197	0.234	0.342
621 Materials of rubber (e.g., pastes, plates, sheets, rods, thread, tubes, of rubber)	0.155	0.200	0.195	0.176	0.322
813 Lighting fixtures and fittings, n.e.s.	0.273	0.199	0.194	0.186	0.160
724 Textile and leather machinery, and parts thereof, n.e.s.	0.174	0.188	0.194	0.193	0.204
035 Fish (dried, salted, in brine, smoked); flours, meals, pellets for human consump	0.196	0.184	0.193	0.151	0.249
422 Fixed vegetable fats and oils, crude, refined or fractionated, other than "soft"	0.174	0.191	0.192	0.209	0.292
671 Pig-iron, spiegeleisen, sponge iron, iron steel granules, powders, ferro-alloys	0.192	0.195	0.192	0.167	0.233
513 Carboxylic acid, anhydrides, halides, peroxides, peroxyacids; halogenate derivatives	0.216	0.189	0.191	0.249	0.287
541 Medicinal and pharmaceutical products, excluding medicines of group 542	0.195	0.183	0.191	0.159	0.177
612 Manufactures of leather or of composition leather, n.e.s.; saddlery and harness	0.217	0.188	0.190	0.280	0.288
058 Fruit, preserved, and fruit preparations (excluding fruit juices)	0.217	0.192	0.190	0.155	0.219
325 Coke, semi-coke of coal, lignite, peat, agglomerated or not; retort carbon	0.193	0.165	0.189	0.284	0.370
872 Instruments and appliances, n.e.s., (medical, surgical, dental or veterinary)	0.208	0.186	0.188	0.181	0.167
764 Telecommunications equipment and parts, n.e.s.; accessories within division 76	0.183	0.189	0.188	0.159	0.192
635 Wood manufactures, n.e.s.	0.272	0.194	0.187	0.219	0.192
277 Natural abrasives, n.e.s. (including industrial diamonds)	0.179	0.191	0.186	0.274	0.393
122 Tobacco, manufactured (whether or not containing tobacco substitutes)	0.185	0.166	0.186	0.288	0.314
733 Machine tool to work metal sintered metal carbide cermet, not removing material	0.188	0.176	0.185	0.228	0.302
059 Fruit and vegetable juice (unfermented, no added spirit, sweetened or not)	0.189	0.178	0.185	0.150	0.169
771 Electric power machinery parts (excluding rotating electric plant, group 716)	0.193	0.187	0.184	0.163	0.229
772 Electrical apparatus to switch protect circuits or make circuit connections	0.171	0.184	0.183	0.216	0.287
846 Clothing accessories of textiles, knitted or crocheted or not (exluding babies)	0.194	0.183	0.183	0.205	0.225
666 Pottery	0.251	0.198	0.182	0.157	0.243
873 Meters and counters, n.e.s.	0.200	0.178	0.181	0.163	0.198
874 Measuring, checking, analysing and controlling instruments and apparatus, n.e.s.	0.171	0.175	0.181	0.123	0.194
784 Parts and accessories of the motor vehicles of groups 722, 781, 782 and 783	0.212	0.178	0.178	0.150	0.265
713 Internal combustion piston engines, and parts thereof, n.e.s.	0.209	0.174	0.178	0.184	0.277
292 Crude vegetable materials, n.e.s.	0.193	0.173	0.177	0.126	0.179
248 Wood, simply worked, and railway sleepers of wood	0.284	0.170	0.176	0.218	0.322
335 Residual petroleum products, n.e.s., related mater.	0.165	0.176	0.175	0.253	0.327
712 Steam turbines and other vapour turbines, and parts thereof, n.e.s.	0.161	0.147	0.174	0.394	0.423
775 Household-type electrical and non-electrical equipment, n.e.s.	0.187	0.175	0.174	0.183	0.206
024 Cheese and curd	0.191	0.171	0.174	0.188	0.235
232 Synthetic rubber; reclaimed rubber; waste, parings, scrap of unhardened rubber	0.165	0.190	0.173	0.167	0.291
034 Fish, fresh (live dead chilled frozen)	0.210	0.175	0.173	0.204	0.261

For sources and notes, see end of table.

Pour les sources et les notes, se reporter à la fin du tableau.

SITC group Revision 3 (3-digit level) ranked according to the concentration index in 2011 / Groupes de la CTCI Révision 3 (positions à 3 chiffres) classés d'après l'indice de concentration en 2011	Concentration index (1) / Indice de concentration (1)			Structural change index (2) / Indice de changement structurel (2) 1995=0	
	2005	2010	2011	2005	2011
524 Other inorganic chemicals; organic and inorganic compounds of precious metals	0.169	0.168	0.172	0.147	0.223
686 Zinc	0.179	0.174	0.172	0.241	0.253
778 Electrical machinery and apparatus, n.e.s.	0.170	0.173	0.171	0.166	0.218
514 Nitrogen-function compounds	0.158	0.168	0.170	0.175	0.194
735 Parts, n.e.s. and accessories for machines of groups 731, 733; tool holder	0.167	0.167	0.169	0.164	0.232
748 Transmission shaft camshaft crankshaft; bearing housing; gearbox speed changer	0.178	0.165	0.168	0.164	0.239
725 Paper mill pulp mill paper-cutting other paper manufacture machines; parts of	0.139	0.161	0.167	0.199	0.236
542 Medicines (including veterinary medicines)	0.202	0.179	0.167	0.233	0.206
562 Fertilizers (excluding group 272)	0.148	0.159	0.167	0.211	0.304
746 Ball or roller bearings	0.159	0.164	0.165	0.147	0.227
659 Floor coverings, etc.	0.220	0.173	0.164	0.241	0.237
291 Crude animal materials, nes	0.185	0.164	0.164	0.208	0.225
696 Cutlery	0.192	0.166	0.163	0.182	0.237
812 Sanitary, plumbing and heating fixtures and fittings, n.e.s.	0.181	0.169	0.163	0.237	0.225
882 Photographic and cinematographic supplies	0.147	0.157	0.162	0.211	0.305
593 Explosives and pyrotechnic products	0.220	0.187	0.161	0.262	0.286
625 Rubber tyres, interchangeable tyre treads, tyre flaps, inner tubes for wheels	0.186	0.163	0.161	0.155	0.197
881 Photographic apparatus and equipment, n.e.s.	0.225	0.154	0.161	0.245	0.263
895 Office and stationery supplies, n.e.s.	0.177	0.160	0.161	0.149	0.209
571 Polymers of ethylene, in primary forms	0.159	0.166	0.160	0.204	0.258
747 Appliances for pipes boiler shells tanks vats; pressure and temperature valves	0.173	0.156	0.159	0.163	0.199
551 Essential oils, perfume and flavour materials	0.184	0.159	0.158	0.221	0.231
057 Fruits and nuts (excluding oil nuts), fresh or dried	0.176	0.158	0.158	0.163	0.229
044 Maize (not including sweet corn), unmilled	0.192	0.162	0.158	0.195	0.271
001 Live animals other than animals of division 03	0.201	0.166	0.158	0.223	0.285
711 Steam vapour superheated water boiler, auxiliary plant for use with; parts of	0.124	0.161	0.158	0.305	0.392
898 Musical instrument, parts accessory; tape, sound recording (excluding 763 & 883)	0.172	0.151	0.157	0.159	0.279
516 Other organic chemicals	0.162	0.155	0.155	0.150	0.237
694 Nails, screws, nuts, bolts, rivets, of iron, steel, copper or aluminium	0.194	0.155	0.155	0.151	0.235
791 Railway vehicles (including hovertrains) and associated equipment	0.139	0.145	0.155	0.311	0.358
522 Inorganic chemical elements, oxides and halogen salts	0.175	0.159	0.155	0.140	0.194
629 Articles of rubber, n.e.s.	0.173	0.151	0.154	0.137	0.197
056 Vegetables, roots and tubers (prepared preserved) n.e.s.	0.183	0.158	0.154	0.155	0.190
011 Meat of bovine animals (fresh chilled frozen)	0.203	0.155	0.154	0.245	0.277
266 Synthetic fibres suitable for spinning	0.186	0.150	0.154	0.167	0.273
054 Vegetables and veg products (fresh chilled frozen preserved dried edible) n.e.s.	0.187	0.155	0.154	0.175	0.259
223 Oil-seed, oleaginous fruit to extract other vegetable oil; flour, meal of n.e.s.	0.192	0.169	0.153	0.383	0.406
742 Liquid pump, with without a fitted measuring device; liquid elevator; parts for	0.151	0.143	0.153	0.164	0.228
575 Other plastics, in primary forms	0.147	0.158	0.153	0.167	0.246
351 Electric current	0.181	0.144	0.153	0.335	0.356
786 Trailers semi-trailers vehicles not mechanically-propelled; transport containers	0.163	0.150	0.152	0.192	0.223
245 Fuel wood (excluding wood waste) and wood charcoal	0.173	0.152	0.152	0.223	0.319
023 Butter and other fats and oils derived from milk	0.185	0.155	0.151	0.234	0.270
893 Articles, n.e.s., of plastics	0.174	0.155	0.151	0.142	0.157
685 Lead	0.159	0.156	0.150	0.249	0.276
574 Polyacetal, polyether, epoxide resin; polycarbonate, alkyd resin, polyester	0.144	0.165	0.150	0.234	0.292
773 Equipment for distributing electricity, n.e.s.	0.185	0.155	0.149	0.148	0.218
684 Aluminium	0.177	0.151	0.149	0.155	0.193
598 Miscellaneous chemical products, n.e.s.	0.146	0.145	0.147	0.144	0.184
737 Metalworking machinery (other than machine tools), and parts thereof, n.e.s.	0.180	0.153	0.147	0.194	0.264
695 Tools for use in the hand or in machine	0.162	0.148	0.147	0.140	0.189
722 Tractors (excluding headings 714.14 & 744.15)	0.212	0.153	0.146	0.182	0.269
075 Spices	0.165	0.149	0.145	0.142	0.223
663 Mineral manufactures, n.e.s.	0.163	0.139	0.143	0.159	0.168
592 Starches, inulin and wheat gluten; albuminoidal substances; glues	0.142	0.141	0.142	0.142	0.217
062 Sugar confectionery	0.183	0.150	0.141	0.199	0.213
012 Other meat and edible meat offal (fresh chilled frozen)	0.181	0.144	0.140	0.237	0.319
743 Pump (non liquid), air gas compressor, fan ventilation filter; centrifuge; parts	0.159	0.138	0.140	0.143	0.193
582 Plates, sheets, film, foil and strip, of plastics	0.135	0.142	0.140	0.167	0.250
664 Glass	0.147	0.137	0.140	0.170	0.233
073 Chocolate and other food preparations containing cocoa, n.e.s.	0.154	0.138	0.140	0.198	0.208
745 Non-electrical machinery, tools and mechanical apparatus, parts thereof, n.e.s.	0.153	0.140	0.139	0.141	0.173
675 Flat-rolled products of alloy steel	0.190	0.140	0.139	0.240	0.229
111 Non-alcoholic beverages, n.e.s.	0.165	0.142	0.139	0.271	0.278

For sources and notes, see end of table.

Pour les sources et les notes, se reporter à la fin du tableau.

SITC group Revision 3 (3-digit level) ranked according to the concentration index in 2011 Groupes de la CTCI Révision 3 (positions à 3 chiffres) classés d'après l'indice de concentration en 2011	Concentration index (1) Indice de concentration (1)			Structural change index (2) Indice de changement structurel (2) 1995=0	
	2005	2010	2011	2005	2011
699 Manufactures of base metal, n.e.s.	0.169	0.136	0.138	0.124	0.175
532 Dyeing and tanning extracts, and synthetic tanning materials	0.137	0.138	0.138	0.204	0.263
278 Other crude minerals	0.142	0.136	0.138	0.142	0.203
672 Ingots, other primary forms of iron or steel; semi-finished products of	0.165	0.149	0.137	0.256	0.347
411 Animals oils and fats	0.130	0.139	0.137	0.281	0.318
793 Ships, boats (including hovercraft) and floating structures	0.126	0.166	0.137	0.420	0.400
785 Motor cycles, mopeds, cycles, motorized and non-motorized; invalid carriages	0.203	0.142	0.137	0.232	0.217
721 Agricultural machinery (excluding tractors), and parts thereof	0.150	0.136	0.137	0.155	0.207
121 Tobacco, unmanufactured; tobacco refuse	0.148	0.127	0.135	0.265	0.354
716 Rotating electric plant, and parts thereof, n.e.s.	0.165	0.133	0.134	0.186	0.225
782 Motor vehicles for the transport of goods and special-purpose motor vehicles	0.195	0.142	0.134	0.183	0.279
749 Non-electric parts and accessories of machinery, n.e.s.	0.145	0.137	0.133	0.164	0.219
726 Printing and bookbinding machinery, and parts thereof	0.148	0.129	0.133	0.166	0.279
074 Tea and maté	0.133	0.129	0.133	0.213	0.228
634 Veneers, plywood, particle board, and other wood, worked, n.e.s.	0.242	0.136	0.132	0.288	0.283
334 Petroleum oil, oil from bituminous (excl crude); preparations, n.e.s., > 70% oil	0.169	0.134	0.131	0.229	0.241
654 Other textile fabrics, woven n.e.s.	0.140	0.138	0.130	0.242	0.275
573 Polymers of vinyl chloride or of other halogenated olefins, in primary forms	0.150	0.137	0.130	0.266	0.329
651 Textile yarn	0.150	0.147	0.129	0.200	0.306
655 Knitted, crocheted fabric (include tubular knit, pile, openwork fabric), n.e.s.	0.163	0.143	0.128	0.304	0.420
783 Road motor vehicles, n.e.s.	0.136	0.118	0.127	0.286	0.326
048 Cereal preparations and preparations of flour or starch of fruits or vegetables	0.152	0.134	0.127	0.214	0.233
892 Printed matter	0.155	0.134	0.126	0.134	0.169
641 Paper and paperboard	0.164	0.128	0.125	0.128	0.198
597 Prepared additives: mineral oil; transmission; anti-freeze, de-ice; lubricating	0.113	0.124	0.125	0.166	0.211
642 Paper and paperboard, cut to size or shape, and articles of paper or paperboard	0.148	0.130	0.123	0.133	0.171
531 Synthetic organic colouring matter and colour lakes, preparations based thereon	0.127	0.125	0.123	0.152	0.234
679 Tubes, pipes and hollow profiles, and tube or pipe fittings, of iron or steel	0.130	0.120	0.123	0.190	0.231
744 Mechanical handling equipment, and parts thereof, n.e.s.	0.157	0.115	0.122	0.173	0.193
741 Heating and cooling equipment, and parts thereof, n.e.s.	0.127	0.116	0.122	0.188	0.234
431 Animal, vegetable fats, oils, processed; waxes; inedible preparations of, n.e.s.	0.124	0.113	0.121	0.258	0.313
583 Plastic monofilament, cross-section > 1 mm, rods, sticks, profile shapes	0.146	0.122	0.121	0.304	0.306
678 Wire of iron or steel	0.150	0.125	0.121	0.158	0.242
665 Glassware	0.153	0.131	0.121	0.182	0.276
421 Fixed vegetable fats and oils, "soft", crude, refined or fractionated	0.146	0.131	0.120	0.241	0.260
657 Special yarns, special textile fabrics and related products	0.133	0.123	0.119	0.157	0.210
673 Flat-rolled products of iron or non-alloy steel, not clad, plated or coated	0.137	0.123	0.117	0.247	0.271
553 Perfumery, cosmetic or toilet preparations (excluding soaps)	0.133	0.116	0.116	0.140	0.177
723 Civil engineering and contractors' plant and equipment; parts thereof	0.147	0.113	0.114	0.192	0.263
693 Wire products (excluding insulated electrical wiring) and fencing grills	0.148	0.112	0.114	0.176	0.211
652 Cotton fabrics, woven (not including narrow or special fabrics)	0.129	0.116	0.112	0.244	0.369
674 Flat-rolled products of iron or non-alloy steel, clad, plated or coated	0.142	0.113	0.111	0.210	0.276
656 Tulles, lace, embroidery, ribbons, trimmings and other smallwares	0.124	0.114	0.110	0.236	0.331
677 Rails or railway track construction material, of iron or steel	0.140	0.126	0.110	0.300	0.350
046 Meal and flour of wheat and flour of meslin	0.148	0.106	0.110	0.419	0.433
081 Feeding stuff for animals (excluding unmilled cereals)	0.122	0.110	0.108	0.146	0.224
653 Fabrics, woven, of man-made textiles (excluding narrow or special fabrics)	0.116	0.110	0.107	0.253	0.349
091 Margarine and shortening	0.116	0.103	0.106	0.349	0.404
047 Other cereal meals and flours	0.117	0.107	0.106	0.394	0.416
811 Prefabricated buildings	0.124	0.101	0.106	0.447	0.395
581 Tubes, pipes and hoses, and fittings therefor, of plastics	0.122	0.103	0.105	0.174	0.211
042 Rice	0.088	0.104	0.103	0.289	0.300
022 Milk, cream and milk products (excluding butter, cheese)	0.121	0.104	0.103	0.263	0.317
591 Insecticide, rodenticide, fungicide, herbicide, plant-growth reg, disinfectant	0.114	0.100	0.103	0.162	0.224
533 Pigments, paints, varnishes and related materials	0.110	0.102	0.102	0.138	0.167
691 Structures and parts of structures, n.e.s., of iron, steel or aluminium	0.124	0.102	0.100	0.263	0.292
041 Wheat (including spelt) and meslin, unmilled	0.102	0.093	0.099	0.277	0.305
676 Iron and steel bars, rods, angles, shapes and sections (including sheet piling)	0.122	0.098	0.099	0.206	0.281
692 Metal containers for storage or transport	0.114	0.096	0.097	0.170	0.211
661 Lime, cement, fabricated construction material (excluding glass, clay material)	0.226	0.101	0.096	0.338	0.323
554 Soaps, cleansing and polishing preparations	0.114	0.095	0.095	0.133	0.169
098 Edible products and preparations, n.e.s.	0.109	0.096	0.093	0.166	0.196
727 Food-processing machines (excluding domestic); parts thereof	0.105	0.089	0.093	0.198	0.209
523 Metallic salts and peroxysalts, of inorganic acids	0.106	0.098	0.093	0.122	0.178
061 Sugar, molasses and honey	0.108	0.088	0.092	0.241	0.244
662 Clay construction materials and refractory construction materials	0.144	0.090	0.089	0.252	0.300
269 Worn clothing and other worn textile articles; rags	0.075	0.069	0.069	0.358	0.410

For sources and notes, see next page.

Pour les sources et les notes, se reporter à la page suivante.

Source:
UNCTAD secretariat calculations, based on UNCTAD, *UNCTADstat* Merchandise Trade Matrix

Source :
Calculs du secrétariat de la CNUCED, basés sur la matrice du commerce de marchandises de *UNCTADstat* de la CNUCED

Notes:

(1) Concentration index:

The Herfindahl-Hirschmann index is a measure of the degree of market concentration. It has been normalized to obtain values ranking from 0 to 1 (maximum concentration), according to the following formula:

$$H_i = \frac{\sqrt{\sum_{j=1}^{n}(\frac{x_{ij}}{X_i})^2} - \sqrt{\frac{1}{n}}}{1 - \sqrt{\frac{1}{n}}}$$

where

H_i = Value of concentration index for product i

x_{ij} = Value of exports or imports for country j and product i

$$X_i = \sum_{j=1}^{n} x_{ij}$$

and

n = maximum number of individual economies

An index value that is close to 1 indicates a very concentrated market. On the contrary, values closer to 0 reflect a more equal distribution of market shares among exporters or importers.

(2)

Structural change index:

This index, ranging from 0 to 1 reveals the structural change in trade for a particular product as compared to the reference year (1995 = 0).

An index value close to 1 indicates a significant change in the composition of exporters (importers). On the contrary, values closer to 0 would demonstrate a higher degree of "traditionality" in the markets over the period concerned.

The value is calculated as follows:

$$I_i = \frac{\sum_{j} \left| S^1_{ij} - S^0_{ij} \right|}{2}$$

where

I_i = Value of structure index for product *i*

S^0_{ij} = Share of trade of product *i* for country *j* in 1995

S^1_{ij} = Share of trade of product *i* for the country *j* in the concerned year

Notes :

(1) Indice de concentration :

L'indice Herfindahl-Hirschmann mesure le degré de concentration des marchés. Il a été normalisé afin d'obtenir des valeurs comprises entre 0 et 1 (concentration maximale), d'après la formule suivante :

$$H_i = \frac{\sqrt{\sum_{j=1}^{n}(\frac{x_{ij}}{X_i})^2} - \sqrt{\frac{1}{n}}}{1 - \sqrt{\frac{1}{n}}}$$

où

H_i = Valeur de l'indice de concentration pour le produit i

x_{ij} = Valeur des exportations ou des importations du pays j pour le produit i

$$X_i = \sum_{j=1}^{n} x_{ij}$$

et

n = nombre maximum d'économies individuelles

Un indice proche de 1 indique une concentration très forte du marché pour ce produit en particulier. En revanche, une valeur proche de 0 démontre une répartition plus homogène du commerce entre les exportateurs ou les importateurs.

(2)

Indice de changement structurel :

Cet indice, dont la valeur est comprise entre 0 et 1, représente les changements de structure du commerce par rapport à une année de référence (1995 = 0).

Une valeur proche de 1 indique un important changement structurel du commerce de ce produit, c'est à dire une grande variation des parts de marché au sein des exportateurs ou importateurs, par rapport à l'année de référence. Plus la valeur de l'indice est proche de 0, plus la structure du commerce de ce produit est stable.

Il est calculé comme suit :

$$I_i = \frac{\sum_{j} \left| S^1_{ij} - S^0_{ij} \right|}{2}$$

où

I_i = Valeur de l'indice de changement structurel, pour le produit *i*

S^0_{ij} = Part du commerce du produit *i* pour le pays *j* par rapport au commerce total de ce produit pour l'année 1995

S^1_{ij} = Part du commerce du produit *i* pour le pays *j*, par rapport au commerce total de ce produit pour l'année concernée

4

INTERNATIONAL MERCHANDISE TRADE INDICATORS

INDICATEURS DU COMMERCE INTERNATIONAL DES MARCHANDISES

Region, country or territory	Exports - Exportations					
	2005			2011		
	Number of products exported	Diversification index	Concentration index	Number of products exported	Diversification index	Concentration index
	Nombre de produits exportés (1)	Indice de diversification (2)	Indice de concentration (3)	Nombre de produits exportés (1)	Indice de diversification (2)	Indice de concentration (3)
WORLD	260	0.000	0.077	260	0.000	0.083
DEVELOPING ECONOMIES	260	0.246	0.141	260	0.202	0.134
TRANSITION ECONOMIES	259	0.578	0.293	259	0.553	0.342
DEVELOPED ECONOMIES	260	0.160	0.066	260	0.177	0.060
Developing economies: Africa	260	0.603	0.441	260	0.548	0.411
Eastern Africa	259	0.676	0.115	260	0.684	0.151
Burundi	17	0.789	0.608	50	0.740	0.537
Comoros	9	0.679	0.543	7	0.747	0.514
Djibouti	217	0.650	0.152	214	0.602	0.240
Eritrea	178	0.658	0.168	30	0.815	0.947
Ethiopia	119	0.643	0.379	115	0.796	0.361
Kenya	227	0.709	0.209	237	0.650	0.191
Madagascar	231	0.732	0.228	162	0.760	0.211
Malawi	215	0.825	0.565	115	0.809	0.449
Mauritius	231	0.703	0.280	236	0.709	0.246
Mayotte	16	0.525	0.167	15	0.557	0.197
Mozambique	101	0.812	0.633	229	0.739	0.368
Rwanda	186	0.756	0.444	77	0.849	0.422
Seychelles	197	0.830	0.460	67	0.838	0.523
Somalia	153	0.777	0.567	32	0.734	0.497
Uganda	239	0.749	0.259	213	0.730	0.211
United Republic of Tanzania	174	0.760	0.235	254	0.762	0.198
Zambia	245	0.876	0.519	211	0.850	0.646
Zimbabwe	247	0.754	0.204	201	0.731	0.198
Middle Africa	252	0.831	0.817	236	0.815	0.826
Angola	71	0.833	0.944	72	0.816	0.971
Cameroon	234	0.760	0.421	191	0.709	0.380
Central African Republic	32	0.798	0.440	50	0.758	0.339
Chad	162	0.774	0.720	53	0.793	0.927
Congo	91	0.824	0.786	126	0.806	0.785
Dem. Rep. of the Congo	193	0.778	0.415	214	0.784	0.430
Equatorial Guinea	32	0.787	0.922	131	0.749	0.705
Gabon	85	0.856	0.770	150	0.821	0.750
Sao Tome and Principe	136	0.675	0.614	15	0.611	0.586
Northern Africa	257	0.696	0.480	258	0.613	0.365
Algeria	108	0.809	0.588	98	0.724	0.538
Egypt	242	0.674	0.318	238	0.551	0.145
Libya	116	0.816	0.833	116	0.785	0.793
Morocco	250	0.670	0.157	243	0.700	0.169
Sudan (...2011)	75	0.804	0.607	136	0.786	0.772
Tunisia	200	0.598	0.180	225	0.546	0.160
Southern Africa	260	0.580	0.146	260	0.591	0.150
Botswana	142	0.916	0.776	158	0.891	0.783
Lesotho	43	0.852	0.414	63	0.834	0.326
Namibia	188	0.808	0.320	223	0.764	0.223
South Africa	260	0.584	0.140	260	0.599	0.161
Swaziland	180	0.763	0.230	190	0.750	0.243
Western Africa	244	0.766	0.703	251	0.714	0.621
Benin	90	0.778	0.435	147	0.767	0.276
Burkina Faso	96	0.812	0.743	143	0.808	0.525
Cape Verde	198	0.699	0.376	32	0.717	0.469
Côte d'Ivoire	230	0.731	0.319	161	0.705	0.382
Gambia	177	0.692	0.340	50	0.751	0.271
Ghana	248	0.813	0.396	218	0.749	0.400
Guinea	51	0.845	0.643	151	0.755	0.456
Guinea-Bissau	11	0.722	0.926	21	0.753	0.894
Liberia	8	0.852	0.838	171	0.732	0.475
Mali	215	0.812	0.576	186	0.804	0.602
Mauritania	156	0.858	0.540	187	0.820	0.482
Niger	228	0.776	0.314	98	0.843	0.388
Nigeria	196	0.855	0.917	232	0.790	0.815

For sources and notes, see end of table.

Imports - Importations						Régions, pays ou territoires
2005			2011			
Number of products imported	Diversification index	Concentration index	Number of products imported	Diversification index	Concentration index	
Nombre de produits importés	Indice de diversification	Indice de concentration	Nombre de produits importés	Indice de diversification	Indice de concentration	
(1)	(2)	(3)	(1)	(2)	(3)	
260	0.000	0.074	260	0.000	0.082	**MONDE**
260	0.191	0.091	260	0.147	0.092	ÉCONOMIES EN DÉVELOPPEMENT
259	0.251	0.055	260	0.265	0.056	ÉCONOMIES EN TRANSITION
260	0.091	0.080	260	0.100	0.086	ÉCONOMIES DÉVELOPPÉES
260	0.281	0.077	260	0.297	0.077	**Économies en développement : Afrique**
260	0.388	0.097	260	0.406	0.114	*Afrique orientale*
241	0.492	0.103	198	0.505	0.084	Burundi
231	0.551	0.121	154	0.539	0.111	Comores
246	0.558	0.268	250	0.517	0.136	Djibouti
247	0.520	0.099	235	0.540	0.116	Érythrée
212	0.481	0.139	222	0.503	0.150	Éthiopie
258	0.413	0.132	249	0.395	0.145	Kenya
249	0.525	0.139	228	0.516	0.149	Madagascar
255	0.543	0.124	257	0.528	0.103	Malawi
218	0.450	0.140	224	0.383	0.153	Maurice
161	0.431	0.115	180	0.497	0.092	Mayotte
257	0.515	0.166	257	0.479	0.102	Mozambique
246	0.419	0.110	257	0.473	0.080	Rwanda
247	0.604	0.253	196	0.569	0.245	Seychelles
213	0.697	0.165	178	0.640	0.256	Somalie
254	0.481	0.145	236	0.464	0.146	Ouganda
259	0.438	0.113	260	0.498	0.203	République-Unie de Tanzanie
256	0.441	0.085	242	0.457	0.123	Zambie
259	0.546	0.133	258	0.477	0.082	Zimbabwe
259	0.450	0.095	259	0.422	0.062	*Afrique centrale*
254	0.565	0.180	255	0.460	0.065	Angola
243	0.494	0.211	222	0.475	0.179	Cameroun
217	0.498	0.143	177	0.525	0.156	République centrafricaine
234	0.525	0.100	217	0.471	0.109	Tchad
247	0.473	0.061	258	0.531	0.172	Congo
253	0.484	0.115	251	0.455	0.061	Rép. dém. du Congo
223	0.621	0.212	231	0.478	0.111	Guinée équatoriale
250	0.444	0.070	228	0.474	0.072	Gabon
60	0.581	0.203	132	0.498	0.090	Sao Tomé-et-Principe
260	0.317	0.061	259	0.353	0.063	*Afrique septentrionale*
236	0.455	0.086	236	0.484	0.083	Algérie
255	0.458	0.124	246	0.395	0.085	Égypte
254	0.462	0.096	255	0.462	0.066	Libye
249	0.356	0.109	252	0.332	0.092	Maroc
258	0.454	0.080	245	0.512	0.170	Soudan (...2011)
242	0.396	0.087	246	0.388	0.081	Tunisie
260	0.280	0.181	260	0.289	0.195	*Afrique australe*
259	0.428	0.100	259	0.468	0.127	Botswana
185	0.782	0.310	231	0.534	0.082	Lesotho
258	0.394	0.070	238	0.585	0.254	Namibie
257	0.302	0.209	259	0.316	0.228	Afrique du Sud
260	0.478	0.103	211	0.595	0.138	Swaziland
260	0.402	0.076	258	0.404	0.099	*Afrique occidentale*
239	0.551	0.141	210	0.599	0.202	Bénin
246	0.524	0.120	221	0.512	0.152	Burkina Faso
245	0.470	0.093	249	0.532	0.165	Cap-Vert
248	0.527	0.254	215	0.506	0.241	Côte d'Ivoire
245	0.585	0.134	248	0.607	0.140	Gambie
259	0.413	0.125	258	0.464	0.070	Ghana
245	0.557	0.137	217	0.521	0.183	Guinée
227	0.622	0.327	243	0.578	0.159	Guinée-Bissau
235	0.855	0.747	111	0.871	0.856	Libéria
243	0.544	0.138	224	0.521	0.175	Mali
240	0.490	0.091	251	0.566	0.139	Mauritanie
251	0.514	0.096	246	0.519	0.112	Niger
247	0.480	0.077	255	0.429	0.110	Nigéria

Pour les sources et les notes, se reporter à la fin du tableau.

Region, country or territory	Exports - Exportations					
	2005			2011		
	Number of products exported	Diversification index	Concentration index	Number of products exported	Diversification index	Concentration index
	Nombre de produits exportés	Indice de diversification	Indice de concentration	Nombre de produits exportés	Indice de diversification	Indice de concentration
	(1)	(2)	(3)	(1)	(2)	(3)
Saint Helena	118	0.555	0.270	115	0.586	0.436
Senegal	182	0.679	0.208	206	0.728	0.227
Sierra Leone	211	0.677	0.498	127	0.676	0.274
Togo	143	0.718	0.211	123	0.733	0.235
Developing economies: America	**260**	**0.326**	**0.122**	**259**	**0.347**	**0.139**
Caribbean	*257*	*0.644*	*0.268*	*259*	*0.604*	*0.228*
Anguilla	148	0.538	0.235	140	0.490	0.132
Antigua and Barbuda	203	0.773	0.769	76	0.526	0.121
Aruba	216	0.834	0.910	218	0.851	0.855
Bahamas	194	0.794	0.464	200	0.787	0.582
Barbados	227	0.638	0.348	218	0.660	0.321
Bonaire, Sint Eustatius and Saba	–	–		8	0.475	0.345
Cayman Islands	145	0.780	0.811	124	0.733	0.779
Cuba	210	0.784	0.366	241	0.737	0.306
Dominica	20	0.728	0.356	20	0.710	0.379
Dominican Republic	244	0.723	0.175	249	0.676	0.127
Grenada	166	0.701	0.322	27	0.680	0.190
Haiti	59	0.771	0.552	64	0.749	0.494
Jamaica	111	0.785	0.657	145	0.704	0.416
Montserrat	97	0.480	0.250	110	0.618	0.300
Netherlands Antilles	232	0.798	0.718	–	–	–
Saint Kitts and Nevis	164	0.689	0.374	183	0.670	0.328
Saint Lucia	185	0.665	0.520	92	0.617	0.316
Saint Vincent and the Grenadines	18	0.828	0.674	24	0.823	0.631
Sint Maarten (Dutch part)	–	–	–	(a)159	(a)0.737	(a)0.767
Trinidad and Tobago	248	0.769	0.370	199	0.736	0.355
Turks and Caicos Islands	120	0.674	0.341	172	0.602	0.286
Central America	*259*	*0.355*	*0.125*	*259*	*0.364*	*0.133*
Belize	200	0.785	0.302	87	0.736	0.360
Costa Rica	245	0.661	0.268	246	0.748	0.471
El Salvador	246	0.730	0.260	213	0.688	0.201
Guatemala	255	0.682	0.157	224	0.679	0.149
Honduras	241	0.792	0.288	220	0.777	0.215
Mexico	252	0.386	0.144	257	0.410	0.154
Nicaragua	229	0.774	0.187	239	0.815	0.228
Panama	246	0.610	0.222	250	0.570	0.161
South America	*259*	*0.486*	*0.153*	*259*	*0.493*	*0.175*
Argentina	254	0.556	0.136	253	0.617	0.152
Bolivia (Plurinational State of)	153	0.766	0.393	138	0.833	0.439
Brazil	258	0.476	0.087	257	0.519	0.170
Chile	229	0.743	0.322	232	0.720	0.378
Colombia	231	0.581	0.210	232	0.648	0.405
Ecuador	170	0.745	0.535	204	0.714	0.515
Falkland Islands (Malvinas)	78	0.697	0.807	71	0.615	0.426
Guyana	224	0.812	0.287	84	0.865	0.440
Paraguay	115	0.780	0.364	139	0.773	0.428
Peru	215	0.787	0.243	234	0.748	0.268
Suriname	207	0.780	0.441	131	0.780	0.484
Uruguay	181	0.669	0.209	209	0.674	0.200
Venezuela (Bolivarian Rep. of)	233	0.775	0.649	200	0.743	0.660
Developing economies: Asia	**260**	**0.281**	**0.129**	**260**	**0.239**	**0.121**
Eastern Asia	*258*	*0.396*	*0.107*	*259*	*0.394*	*0.103*
China	256	0.460	0.110	255	0.458	0.099
China, Hong Kong SAR	242	0.512	0.150	239	0.543	0.193
China, Macao SAR	155	0.753	0.332	207	0.545	0.149
China, Taiwan Province of	254	0.455	0.156	254	0.464	0.198
Korea, Dem. People's Rep. of	231	0.467	0.102	187	0.645	0.339
Korea, Republic of	242	0.441	0.161	247	0.454	0.152
Mongolia	84	0.861	0.395	131	0.842	0.522
Southern Asia	*259*	*0.539*	*0.232*	*260*	*0.461*	*0.203*
Afghanistan	229	0.710	0.260	234	0.618	0.176
Bangladesh	166	0.828	0.381	221	0.876	0.364
Bhutan	55	0.761	0.278	82	0.807	0.322

For sources and notes, see end of table.

Imports - Importations						Régions, pays ou territoires
2005			2011			
Number of products imported / Nombre de produits importés (1)	Diversification index / Indice de diversification (2)	Concentration index / Indice de concentration (3)	Number of products imported / Nombre de produits importés (1)	Diversification index / Indice de diversification (2)	Concentration index / Indice de concentration (3)	
205	0.612	0.287	195	0.569	0.275	Sainte-Hélène
251	0.418	0.131	253	0.440	0.190	Sénégal
183	0.616	0.352	217	0.630	0.366	Sierra Leone
241	0.610	0.201	185	0.578	0.238	Togo
260	**0.196**	**0.063**	**260**	**0.208**	**0.077**	**Économies en développement : Amérique**
259	*0.354*	*0.148*	*259*	*0.345*	*0.140*	*Caraïbes*
246	0.533	0.136	246	0.510	0.085	Anguilla
247	0.667	0.415	(a)246	(a)0.747	(a)0.478	Antigua-et-Barbuda
242	0.606	0.424	253	0.453	0.261	Aruba
256	0.488	0.162	256	0.521	0.233	Bahamas
255	0.437	0.151	254	0.541	0.401	Barbade
–	–	–	17	0.496	0.424	Bonaire, Saint-Eustache et Saba
234	0.656	0.449	236	0.650	0.506	Îles Caïmanes
250	0.432	0.145	255	0.426	0.146	Cuba
145	0.414	0.100	157	0.497	0.130	Dominique
256	0.381	0.077	258	0.380	0.132	République dominicaine
156	0.459	0.080	170	0.506	0.131	Grenade
207	0.587	0.134	225	0.600	0.148	Haïti
249	0.428	0.203	217	0.449	0.228	Jamaïque
219	0.472	0.136	218	0.397	0.124	Montserrat
256	0.700	0.674				Antilles néerlandaises
144	0.412	0.084	159	0.481	0.084	Saint-Kitts-et-Nevis
242	0.503	0.264	157	0.654	0.683	Sainte-Lucie
155	0.427	0.102	172	0.517	0.157	Saint-Vincent-et-les Grenadines
			212	0.554	0.359	Saint-Martin (partie néerlandaise)
226	0.447	0.275	237	0.413	0.205	Trinité-et-Tobago
208	0.464	0.094	152	0.505	0.119	Îles Turques et Caïques
260	*0.256*	*0.072*	*259*	*0.271*	*0.091*	*Amérique centrale*
247	0.493	0.183	203	0.462	0.157	Belize
258	0.347	0.146	258	0.330	0.118	Costa Rica
255	0.404	0.080	242	0.405	0.108	El Salvador
235	0.430	0.112	241	0.426	0.138	Guatemala
254	0.485	0.117	239	0.492	0.129	Honduras
258	0.243	0.079	259	0.305	0.097	Mexique
249	0.387	0.105	219	0.404	0.124	Nicaragua
256	0.546	0.343	257	0.574	0.281	Panama
260	*0.210*	*0.068*	*260*	*0.228*	*0.077*	*Amérique du Sud*
256	0.325	0.071	255	0.325	0.096	Argentine
257	0.426	0.081	257	0.412	0.088	Bolivie (État plurinational de)
250	0.293	0.100	254	0.258	0.091	Brésil
250	0.294	0.107	249	0.277	0.114	Chili
255	0.341	0.072	257	0.348	0.083	Colombie
232	0.388	0.080	256	0.392	0.110	Équateur
(a)184	(a)0.747	(a)0.835	195	0.522	0.224	Îles Falkland (Malvinas)
247	0.524	0.209	252	0.527	0.210	Guyana
207	0.432	0.132	221	0.465	0.127	Paraguay
242	0.341	0.114	246	0.306	0.091	Pérou
(a)209	(a)0.502	(a)0.320	203	0.435	0.154	Suriname
233	0.356	0.156	244	0.324	0.129	Uruguay
258	0.343	0.072	259	0.390	0.054	Venezuela (Rép. bolivarienne du)
260	**0.232**	**0.108**	**260**	**0.186**	**0.106**	**Économies en développement : Asie**
259	*0.309*	*0.129*	*260*	*0.284*	*0.131*	*Asie orientale*
259	0.386	0.140	258	0.349	0.141	Chine
249	0.442	0.153	253	0.486	0.184	Chine (RAS de Hong Kong)
250	0.470	0.117	245	0.481	0.124	Chine (RAS de Macao)
257	0.376	0.156	256	0.343	0.149	Province chinoise de Taiwan
252	0.450	0.156	226	0.371	0.124	Corée, Rép. populaire dém. de
256	0.353	0.155	257	0.323	0.173	Corée, République de
188	0.502	0.226	227	0.482	0.166	Mongolie
259	*0.352*	*0.081*	*260*	*0.358*	*0.184*	*Asie méridionale*
252	0.495	0.143	256	0.601	0.184	Afghanistan
254	0.533	0.112	251	0.556	0.104	Bangladesh
251	0.467	0.090	205	0.512	0.101	Bhoutan

Pour les sources et les notes, se reporter à la fin du tableau.

Region, country or territory	Exports - Exportations					
	2005			2011		
	Number of products exported / Nombre de produits exportés (1)	Diversification index / Indice de diversification (2)	Concentration index / Indice de concentration (3)	Number of products exported / Nombre de produits exportés (1)	Diversification index / Indice de diversification (2)	Concentration index / Indice de concentration (3)
India	259	0.542	0.133	258	0.493	0.183
Iran (Islamic Rep. of)	258	0.777	0.795	260	0.738	0.719
Maldives	35	0.760	0.545	154	0.727	0.671
Nepal	100	0.520	0.136	136	0.648	0.142
Pakistan	207	0.770	0.226	226	0.698	0.184
Sri Lanka	247	0.747	0.211	175	0.767	0.202
South-Eastern Asia	*260*	*0.346*	*0.152*	*260*	*0.329*	*0.119*
Brunei Darussalam	108	0.831	0.641	125	0.836	0.676
Cambodia	98	0.829	0.354	165	0.803	0.348
Indonesia	247	0.493	0.130	241	0.560	0.172
Lao People's Dem. Rep.	189	0.767	0.266	103	0.785	0.341
Malaysia	258	0.467	0.186	260	0.470	0.168
Myanmar	149	0.827	0.337	168	0.817	0.381
Philippines	227	0.621	0.356	245	0.597	0.245
Singapore	257	0.489	0.246	259	0.506	0.256
Thailand	259	0.389	0.086	248	0.396	0.080
Timor-Leste	173	0.789	0.825	187	0.746	0.419
Viet Nam	249	0.637	0.226	248	0.545	0.126
Western Asia	*260*	*0.590*	*0.518*	*260*	*0.570*	*0.518*
Bahrain	245	0.755	0.425	244	0.709	0.342
Iraq	184	0.824	0.952	129	0.873	0.979
Jordan	243	0.594	0.135	245	0.648	0.174
Kuwait	224	0.814	0.633	234	0.788	0.738
Lebanon	251	0.635	0.106	226	0.640	0.123
Occupied Palestinian territory	127	0.591	0.167	138	0.631	0.166
Oman	238	0.768	0.717	237	0.671	0.593
Qatar	238	0.790	0.571	215	0.787	0.537
Saudi Arabia	248	0.808	0.745	254	0.758	0.749
Syrian Arab Republic	252	0.664	0.345	232	0.613	0.254
Turkey	258	0.529	0.091	258	0.480	0.074
United Arab Emirates	259	0.593	0.458	260	0.559	0.421
Yemen	135	0.814	0.817	177	0.744	0.587
Developing economies: Oceania	**254**	**0.698**	**0.182**	**258**	**0.727**	**0.239**
American Samoa	180	0.633	0.245	80	0.696	0.282
Cook Islands	86	0.654	0.543	101	0.666	0.572
Fiji	244	0.757	0.229	256	0.726	0.188
French Polynesia	38	0.785	0.594	42	0.727	0.487
Guam	(a)134	(a)0.649	(a)0.461	(a)118	(a)0.640	(a)0.423
Kiribati	91	0.663	0.303	99	0.734	0.794
Marshall Islands	113	0.763	0.866	94	0.729	0.696
Micronesia (Federated States of)	95	0.745	0.928	83	0.690	0.894
Nauru	107	0.560	0.231	14	0.722	0.910
New Caledonia	218	0.874	0.654	233	0.903	0.591
Niue	..	0.515	0.266	98	0.565	0.405
Northern Mariana Islands	85	0.584	0.328	70	0.560	0.181
Palau	50	0.644	0.898	39	0.579	0.913
Papua New Guinea	120	0.817	0.327	138	0.812	0.345
Samoa	139	0.707	0.717	143	0.731	0.579
Solomon Islands	16	0.824	0.705	33	0.842	0.615
Tokelau	129	0.585	0.307	137	0.551	0.532
Tonga	111	0.674	0.404	152	0.657	0.232
Tuvalu	84	0.588	0.254	1	0.652	0.682
Vanuatu	140	0.781	0.563	16	0.826	0.632
Wallis and Futuna Islands	71	0.546	0.291	49	0.499	0.455
Transition economies	**259**	**0.578**	**0.293**	**259**	**0.553**	**0.342**
Albania	233	0.718	0.265	188	0.658	0.201
Armenia	220	0.779	0.350	240	0.758	0.206
Azerbaijan	172	0.763	0.579	151	0.785	0.889
Belarus	236	0.570	0.276	238	0.572	0.292
Bosnia and Herzegovina	248	0.663	0.135	253	0.624	0.107
Croatia	232	0.458	0.110	235	0.460	0.126
Georgia	122	0.747	0.198	190	0.689	0.185
Kazakhstan	195	0.756	0.605	231	0.733	0.608
Kyrgyzstan	231	0.717	0.238	245	0.636	0.142

For sources and notes, see end of table.

Imports - Importations						Régions, pays ou territoires
2005			2011			
Number of products imported	Diversification index	Concentration index	Number of products imported	Diversification index	Concentration index	
Nombre de produits importés	Indice de diversification	Indice de concentration	Nombre de produits importés	Indice de diversification	Indice de concentration	
(1)	(2)	(3)	(1)	(2)	(3)	
259	0.412	0.115	259	0.440	0.252	Inde
259	0.427	0.084	253	0.397	0.057	Iran (Rép. islamique d')
170	0.500	0.123	180	0.479	0.184	Maldives
220	0.561	0.195	236	0.505	0.155	Népal
243	0.439	0.128	247	0.449	0.206	Pakistan
234	0.445	0.094	240	0.422	0.118	Sri Lanka
260	*0.288*	*0.162*	*260*	*0.246*	*0.136*	*Asie du Sud-Est*
210	0.468	0.078	229	0.478	0.070	Brunéi Darussalam
244	0.551	0.159	237	0.577	0.174	Cambodge
259	0.348	0.136	260	0.349	0.137	Indonésie
238	0.466	0.142	246	0.454	0.159	Rép. dém. populaire lao
259	0.374	0.221	260	0.321	0.144	Malaisie
220	0.471	0.119	242	0.519	0.166	Myanmar
250	0.470	0.319	256	0.339	0.177	Philippines
257	0.380	0.217	257	0.373	0.245	Singapour
257	0.322	0.135	258	0.310	0.134	Thaïlande
254	0.510	0.227	258	0.533	0.123	Timor-Leste
256	0.455	0.114	256	0.400	0.092	Viet Nam
259	*0.242*	*0.062*	*260*	*0.295*	*0.065*	*Asie occidentale*
256	0.419	0.270	259	0.475	0.074	Bahreïn
256	0.504	0.077	259	0.491	0.064	Iraq
247	0.347	0.143	252	0.326	0.144	Jordanie
198	0.415	0.058	253	0.419	0.086	Koweït
256	0.426	0.162	256	0.447	0.173	Liban
205	0.517	0.184	205	0.590	0.178	Territoire palestinien occupé
257	0.416	0.138	252	0.445	0.120	Oman
258	0.446	0.105	255	0.467	0.121	Qatar
249	0.338	0.092	244	0.314	0.065	Arabie saoudite
251	0.446	0.093	249	0.469	0.108	République arabe syrienne
257	0.286	0.083	257	0.314	0.131	Turquie
259	0.365	0.110	257	0.376	0.104	Émirats arabes unis
253	0.515	0.169	235	0.570	0.240	Yémen
258	**0.428**	**0.162**	**260**	**0.442**	**0.194**	**Économies en développement : Océanie**
199	0.565	0.250	196	0.667	0.440	Samoa américaines
238	0.483	0.068	246	0.501	0.095	Îles Cook
247	0.478	0.244	216	0.505	0.286	Fidji
201	0.426	0.103	196	0.372	0.127	Polynésie française
212	0.665	0.558	211	0.649	0.534	Guam
224	0.552	0.155	234	0.621	0.191	Kiribati
199	0.844	0.842	198	0.833	0.818	Îles Marshall
185	0.507	0.100	188	0.507	0.109	Micronésie (États fédérés de)
144	0.592	0.466	137	0.508	0.354	Nauru
208	0.417	0.129	245	0.404	0.195	Nouvelle-Calédonie
23	0.483	0.110	184	0.493	0.198	Nioué
185	0.712	0.390	159	0.566	0.248	Îles Mariannes du Nord
195	0.504	0.102	196	0.505	0.192	Palaos
216	0.500	0.195	232	0.508	0.200	Papouasie-Nouvelle-Guinée
232	0.573	0.164	243	0.524	0.144	Samoa
235	0.530	0.215	252	0.558	0.231	Îles Salomon
202	0.591	0.267	113	0.574	0.486	Tokélaou
233	0.613	0.229	254	0.559	0.168	Tonga
197	0.630	0.386	229	0.532	0.282	Tuvalu
150	0.512	0.169	179	0.534	0.142	Vanuatu
226	0.470	0.107	240	0.484	0.067	Îles Wallis-et-Futuna
259	**0.251**	**0.055**	**260**	**0.265**	**0.056**	**Économies en transition**
254	0.452	0.062	236	0.453	0.095	Albanie
254	0.455	0.141	256	0.402	0.094	Arménie
216	0.484	0.126	225	0.511	0.098	Azerbaïdjan
247	0.414	0.225	247	0.371	0.210	Bélarus
257	0.400	0.077	248	0.369	0.071	Bosnie-Herzégovine
249	0.245	0.075	249	0.258	0.092	Croatie
255	0.447	0.130	257	0.422	0.120	Géorgie
256	0.372	0.065	251	0.391	0.063	Kazakhstan
206	0.531	0.201	248	0.437	0.170	Kirghizistan

Pour les sources et les notes, se reporter à la fin du tableau.

4

Region, country or territory	Exports - Exportations					
	2005			2011		
	Number of products exported	Diversification index	Concentration index	Number of products exported	Diversification index	Concentration index
	Nombre de produits exportés	Indice de diversification	Indice de concentration	Nombre de produits exportés	Indice de diversification	Indice de concentration
	(1)	(2)	(3)	(1)	(2)	(3)
Montenegro	–	–	–	116	0.756	0.389
Republic of Moldova	163	0.719	0.252	187	0.640	0.133
Russian Federation	254	0.661	0.352	254	0.644	0.407
Serbia and Montenegro	235	0.580	0.105			
Serbia	–	–	–	254	0.553	0.071
Tajikistan	53	0.846	0.656	73	0.817	0.503
TFYR of Macedonia	185	0.646	0.174	198	0.623	0.168
Turkmenistan	99	0.767	0.662	131	0.791	0.551
Ukraine	253	0.609	0.144	253	0.571	0.132
Uzbekistan	217	0.729	0.279	157	0.703	0.240
Developed economies: America	**260**	**0.227**	**0.072**	**260**	**0.224**	**0.079**
Bermuda	187	0.777	0.526	197	0.750	0.424
Canada	260	0.367	0.126	259	0.358	0.151
Greenland	141	0.819	0.482	29	0.828	0.469
Saint Pierre and Miquelon	8	0.628	0.434	52	0.574	0.282
United States	258	0.269	0.074	260	0.258	0.084
Developed economies: Asia	**258**	**0.400**	**0.127**	**258**	**0.418**	**0.107**
Israel	251	0.566	0.334	253	0.586	0.284
Japan	255	0.419	0.135	254	0.398	0.115
Developed economies: Europe	**260**	**0.179**	**0.065**	**260**	**0.212**	**0.060**
Andorra	166	0.630	0.258	30	0.587	0.281
Austria	256	0.328	0.072	249	0.350	0.054
Belgium	259	0.356	0.106	258	0.365	0.095
Bulgaria	258	0.533	0.111	255	0.445	0.130
Cyprus	245	0.442	0.153	244	0.521	0.235
Czech Republic	259	0.394	0.095	259	0.426	0.106
Denmark	258	0.399	0.084	254	0.409	0.081
Estonia	252	0.488	0.157	255	0.488	0.150
Faeroe Islands	14	0.533	0.575	48	0.752	0.691
Finland	257	0.520	0.194	256	0.492	0.134
France	259	0.298	0.082	260	0.334	0.083
Germany	258	0.294	0.096	258	0.334	0.092
Gibraltar	150	0.689	0.552	109	0.630	0.490
Greece	251	0.488	0.100	255	0.504	0.255
Hungary	257	0.405	0.149	255	0.392	0.128
Iceland	200	0.777	0.385	219	0.776	0.452
Ireland	256	0.657	0.224	250	0.690	0.260
Italy	260	0.369	0.055	259	0.369	0.053
Latvia	247	0.527	0.124	252	0.451	0.092
Lithuania	252	0.531	0.213	253	0.479	0.209
Luxembourg	256	0.524	0.125	257	0.554	0.131
Malta	217	0.634	0.393	174	0.659	0.412
Netherlands	260	0.343	0.101	257	0.330	0.094
Norway	254	0.647	0.453	253	0.618	0.403
Poland	257	0.438	0.081	253	0.419	0.072
Portugal	257	0.374	0.081	258	0.434	0.076
Romania	247	0.505	0.124	248	0.424	0.091
Slovakia	256	0.455	0.131	256	0.444	0.156
Slovenia	236	0.498	0.119	252	0.493	0.172
Spain	259	0.350	0.110	255	0.373	0.093
Sweden	258	0.383	0.117	258	0.368	0.096
Switzerland	244	0.540	0.136	258	0.594	0.168
United Kingdom	258	0.258	0.098	258	0.304	0.105
Developed economies: Oceania	**259**	**0.576**	**0.139**	**258**	**0.641**	**0.240**
Australia	259	0.590	0.167	258	0.664	0.280
New Zealand	254	0.638	0.130	253	0.645	0.172

For sources and notes, see next page.

Imports - Importations						Régions, pays ou territoires
2005			2011			
Number of products imported	Diversification index	Concentration index	Number of products imported	Diversification index	Concentration index	
Nombre de produits importés	Indice de diversification	Indice de concentration	Nombre de produits importés	Indice de diversification	Indice de concentration	
(1)	(2)	(3)	(1)	(2)	(3)	
–	–	–	217	0.487	0.095	Monténégro
252	0.460	0.103	252	0.444	0.104	République de Moldova
258	0.336	0.062	259	0.342	0.062	Fédération de Russie
248	0.315	0.084				Serbie-et-Monténégro
–	–	–	256	0.303	0.078	Serbie
247	0.575	0.154	248	0.522	0.103	Tadjikistan
234	0.391	0.103	238	0.377	0.090	LERY de Macédoine
253	0.494	0.123	254	0.453	0.086	Turkménistan
256	0.336	0.135	255	0.373	0.160	Ukraine
250	0.409	0.091	250	0.467	0.086	Ouzbékistan
260	**0.167**	**0.105**	**260**	**0.190**	**0.124**	**Économies développées : Amérique**
258	0.595	0.330	260	0.757	0.607	Bermudes
260	0.213	0.082	260	0.219	0.075	Canada
244	0.465	0.176	189	0.538	0.186	Groenland
195	0.391	0.072	208	0.420	0.079	Saint-Pierre-et-Miquelon
260	0.189	0.112	260	0.212	0.138	États-Unis
259	**0.264**	**0.121**	**258**	**0.269**	**0.137**	**Économies développées : Asie**
257	0.327	0.206	257	0.313	0.152	Israël
258	0.283	0.131	258	0.295	0.150	Japon
260	**0.103**	**0.069**	**260**	**0.117**	**0.070**	**Économies développées : Europe**
..	..	..	182	0.588	0.142	Andorre
259	0.227	0.062	253	0.243	0.057	Autriche
260	0.282	0.103	260	0.262	0.091	Belgique
258	0.306	0.092	258	0.278	0.099	Bulgarie
254	0.370	0.152	250	0.435	0.207	Chypre
259	0.247	0.064	260	0.279	0.065	République tchèque
259	0.253	0.058	260	0.280	0.057	Danemark
259	0.327	0.109	256	0.347	0.143	Estonie
254	0.480	0.191	196	0.545	0.214	Îles Féroé
258	0.196	0.085	258	0.195	0.099	Finlande
259	0.160	0.073	259	0.188	0.079	France
258	0.144	0.072	259	0.169	0.067	Allemagne
249	0.725	0.584	213	0.829	0.798	Gibraltar
254	0.283	0.116	253	0.321	0.150	Grèce
256	0.275	0.101	258	0.321	0.115	Hongrie
229	0.400	0.102	233	0.450	0.162	Islande
260	0.300	0.113	259	0.353	0.093	Irlande
258	0.211	0.096	259	0.213	0.094	Italie
255	0.344	0.098	256	0.373	0.114	Lettonie
256	0.332	0.179	256	0.369	0.212	Lituanie
260	0.370	0.114	259	0.382	0.108	Luxembourg
255	0.431	0.203	238	0.464	0.224	Malte
260	0.220	0.105	257	0.226	0.116	Pays-Bas
257	0.299	0.059	257	0.344	0.066	Norvège
259	0.238	0.061	258	0.206	0.073	Pologne
259	0.171	0.076	259	0.234	0.085	Portugal
251	0.288	0.074	252	0.261	0.063	Roumanie
255	0.279	0.075	253	0.297	0.093	Slovaquie
249	0.309	0.066	254	0.335	0.131	Slovénie
260	0.179	0.091	257	0.186	0.099	Espagne
259	0.174	0.076	258	0.193	0.082	Suède
252	0.287	0.076	255	0.342	0.083	Suisse
259	0.214	0.088	258	0.208	0.079	Royaume-Uni
259	**0.230**	**0.092**	**258**	**0.226**	**0.104**	**Économies développées : Océanie**
259	0.231	0.092	258	0.234	0.106	Australie
249	0.268	0.095	257	0.277	0.106	Nouvelle-Zélande

Pour les sources et les notes, se reporter à la page suivante.

4

4.1.1 Export and import concentration and diversification indices of countries and geographical regions

Source:
UNCTAD secretariat calculations, based on UNCTAD, *UNCTADstat* Merchandise Trade Matrix

Notes:

(a) More than 30% of total trade under SITC Rev.3, code 931: "Special transactions & commodities not classified"

(1) Number of products exported (or imported) at the three-digit SITC, Rev. 3 level; this figure includes only those products that are greater than $100,000 or more than 0.3 per cent of the country's total exports (or imports).
Data for the country groupings are calculated as weighted averages of individual countries data, including those that are estimated and not shown separately.

(2) The diversification index signals whether the structure of exports or imports by product of a given country or group of countries differ from the structure of product of the world. This index that ranges from 0 to 1 reveals the extent of the differences between the structure of trade of the country or country group and the world average. The index value closer to 1 indicates a bigger difference from the world average.

Diversification index is computed by measuring absolute deviation of the country share from world structure, as follows:

$$S_j = \frac{\sum_i \left| h_{ij} - h_i \right|}{2}$$

where
h_{ij} = share of product i in total exports or imports of country or country group *j*
h_i = share of product i in total world exports or imports.

This index is a modified Finger-Kreinin measure of similarity in trade. For more information, please consult the article of Finger, J. M. and M. E. Kreinin (1979), "A measure of 'export similarity' and its possible uses" in the *Economic Journal*, 89: 905-12.

(3) Concentration index, also named Herfindahl-Hirschmann index, is a measure of the degree of market concentration. It has been normalized to obtain values ranking from 0 to 1 (maximum concentration), according to the following formula:

$$H_j = \frac{\sqrt{\sum_{i=1}^{n} \left(\frac{x_{ij}}{X_j} \right)^2} - \sqrt{1/n}}{1 - \sqrt{1/n}}$$

where
H_j = country or country group index
X_{ij} = value of exports for country j and product i

$$X_j = \sum_{i=1}^{n} x_{ij}$$

and
n = number of products (SITC Revision 3 at 3-digit group level)

Source :
Calculs du secrétariat de la CNUCED, basés sur la matrice du commerce de marchandises de *UNCTADstat* de la CNUCED

Notes :

(a)   Plus de 30% du commerce sous la position 931 de la CTCI rév. 3 : "Transactions et articles spéciaux non classés"

(1)   Nombre de produits au niveau de groupes de la CTCI (rév. 3, position à 3 chiffres) exportés (ou importés) par chaque pays ; cependant, seuls les produits ayant une valeur supérieure à 100.000 dollars ou comptant pour plus de 0,3 % des exportations (ou des importations) totales du pays sont inclus.
Les indices de concentration et de diversification calculés au niveau des groupes de pays et du monde sont les moyennes arithmétiques des indices respectifs des pays, pondérées par la valeur de leurs exportations.

(2)   L'indice de Diversification indique si la structure par produits des exportations d'un pays ou groupe de pays diverge peu ou beaucoup de la structure par produits des exportations totales dans le monde. Cet indice dont la valeur est comprise entre de 0 à 1, révèle l'ampleur des différences entre la structure des échanges d'un pays ou du groupe de pays et la moyenne mondiale. Plus l'indice est proche de 1, plus la divergence est forte.

L'indice de diversification mesure la déviation absolue de la structure du pays par rapport à la structure mondiale comme ci-dessous :

$$S_j = \frac{\sum_i \left| h_{ij} - h_i \right|}{2}$$

où

h_{ij} = part du produit i dans le total des exportations (ou importations) du pays j
h_i = part du produit i dans le total des exportations (ou importations) mondiales.

Cet indice est une variante de l'indicateur de Finger-Kreinin sur la similarité de la structure du commerce. Pour plus d'information, veuillez consulter l'article de Finger, J. M. et M. E. Kreinin (1979), "A measure of 'export similarity' and its possible uses", dans l'*Economic Journal*, 89: 905-12.

(3)   L'indice de concentration, aussi appelé indice de Herfindahl-Hirschmann, mesure le degré de concentration des marchés. Il a été normalisé afin d'obtenir des valeurs comprises entre 0 et 1 (concentration maximale), d'après la formule suivante :

$$H_j = \frac{\sqrt{\sum_{i=1}^{n} \left(\frac{x_{ij}}{X_j} \right)^2} - \sqrt{1/n}}{1 - \sqrt{1/n}}$$

où

H_j = Indice du pays ou groupe de pays
X_{ij} = valeur des exportations du pays j pour le produit i

$$X_j = \sum_{i=1}^{n} x_{ij}$$

et

n = nombre de produits (de la CTCI Révision 3, position à 3 chiffres)

223

4.1.2 Export and import concentration and diversification indices of economic groupings

Region, country or territory	Exports - Exportations					
	2005			2011		
	Number of products exported Nombre de produits exportés (1)	Diversification index Indice de diversification (2)	Concentration index Indice de concentration (3)	Number of products exported Nombre de produits exportés (1)	Diversification index Indice de diversification (2)	Concentration index Indice de concentration (3)
DEVELOPING ECONOMIES	**260**	**0.246**	**0.141**	**260**	**0.202**	**0.134**
Developing economies excluding China	260	0.259	0.174	260	0.240	0.179
Developing economies excluding LDCs	260	0.243	0.136	260	0.198	0.128
High-income developing economies	260	0.283	0.174	260	0.264	0.179
Middle-income developing economies	260	0.280	0.087	260	0.273	0.078
Low-income developing economies	260	0.512	0.271	260	0.460	0.244
Heavily indebted poor countries (IMF)	260	0.639	0.208	260	0.603	0.226
Landlocked developing countries	260	0.622	0.304	259	0.625	0.384
Small island developing States	258	0.664	0.208	260	0.619	0.196
Least developed countries	*260*	*0.686*	*0.457*	*260*	*0.671*	*0.434*
Africa and Haiti	260	0.728	0.579	260	0.699	0.578
Asia	257	0.719	0.265	250	0.701	0.232
Islands	222	0.852	0.375	233	0.868	0.425
Major petroleum and gas exporters	*260*	*0.736*	*0.689*	*260*	*0.686*	*0.657*
Africa	219	0.838	0.790	239	0.805	0.758
America	233	0.775	0.649	200	0.743	0.660
Asia	260	0.713	0.662	260	0.671	0.633
Major exporters of manufactured goods	*260*	*0.336*	*0.109*	*260*	*0.319*	*0.098*
America	252	0.386	0.144	257	0.410	0.154
Asia	260	0.361	0.116	260	0.343	0.103
Emerging economies	*260*	*0.268*	*0.108*	*260*	*0.256*	*0.100*
America	260	0.317	0.085	259	0.374	0.102
Asia	260	0.367	0.151	260	0.350	0.143
Newly industrialized Asian economies	*260*	*0.346*	*0.137*	*260*	*0.322*	*0.127*
First tier	259	0.390	0.151	260	0.389	0.159
Second tier	260	0.373	0.127	260	0.376	0.097
Developing economies: Africa	**260**	**0.603**	**0.441**	**260**	**0.548**	**0.411**
Northern Africa excluding Sudan	257	0.696	0.477	257	0.608	0.343
Sub-Saharan Africa	260	0.610	0.432	260	0.593	0.449
Sub-Saharan Africa excluding South Africa	260	0.706	0.608	260	0.684	0.589
Developing economies: America	**260**	**0.326**	**0.122**	**259**	**0.347**	**0.139**
Central America and Greater Caribbean Islands excluding Puerto Rico	259	0.349	0.120	259	0.356	0.126
Central America and Greater Caribbean Islands excluding Mexico and Puerto Rico	258	0.574	0.118	259	0.548	0.104
South America and Central America	260	0.326	0.125	259	0.357	0.142
South America excluding Brazil	258	0.595	0.239	259	0.543	0.235
Developing economies: Asia	**260**	**0.281**	**0.129**	**260**	**0.239**	**0.121**
Eastern and South-Eastern Asia excluding China	260	0.336	0.132	260	0.308	0.120
Southern Asia excluding India	259	0.696	0.497	260	0.657	0.470

For sources and notes, see end of table 4.1.1.

| Imports - Importations | | | | | | Régions, pays ou territoires |
| 2005 | | | 2011 | | | |
Number of products imported / Nombre de produits importés (1)	Diversification index / Indice de diversification (2)	Concentration index / Indice de concentration (3)	Number of products imported / Nombre de produits importés (1)	Diversification index / Indice de diversification (2)	Concentration index / Indice de concentration (3)	
260	0.191	0.091	260	0.147	0.092	**ÉCONOMIES EN DÉVELOPPEMENT**
260	0.167	0.084	260	0.145	0.087	Économies en développement sans la Chine
260	0.192	0.093	260	0.147	0.094	Économies en développement sans les PMA
260	0.180	0.101	260	0.169	0.095	Économies en développement à revenu élevé
260	0.248	0.102	260	0.209	0.101	Économies en développement à revenu intermédiaire
260	0.316	0.072	260	0.280	0.117	Économies en développement à revenu faible
260	0.373	0.081	260	0.391	0.087	Pays pauvres très endettés (FMI)
260	0.344	0.066	260	0.340	0.066	Pays en développement sans littoral
259	0.353	0.141	260	0.360	0.161	Petits États insulaires en développement
260	*0.426*	*0.085*	260	*0.418*	*0.093*	*Pays les moins avancés*
260	0.419	0.077	260	0.415	0.090	Afrique et Haïti
259	0.471	0.115	260	0.487	0.109	Asie
257	0.516	0.152	258	0.491	0.124	Îles
260	*0.311*	*0.061*	260	*0.325*	*0.053*	*Principaux exportateurs de pétrole et de gaz*
260	0.411	0.067	260	0.387	0.071	Afrique
258	0.343	0.072	259	0.390	0.054	Amérique
259	0.319	0.066	260	0.351	0.059	Asie
260	*0.264*	*0.128*	260	*0.231*	*0.124*	*Principaux exportateurs d'articles manufacturés*
258	0.243	0.079	259	0.305	0.097	Amérique
260	0.290	0.140	260	0.253	0.132	Asie
260	*0.219*	*0.122*	260	*0.176*	*0.115*	*Économies émergentes*
260	0.219	0.068	260	0.225	0.082	Amérique
260	0.289	0.158	260	0.252	0.148	Asie
260	*0.261*	*0.145*	260	*0.222*	*0.132*	*Économies nouvellement industrialisées d'Asie*
260	0.278	0.143	260	0.268	0.145	Première génération
260	0.295	0.153	260	0.225	0.105	Deuxième génération
260	0.281	0.077	260	0.297	0.077	**Économies en développement : Afrique**
260	0.315	0.063	259	0.355	0.064	Afrique septentrionale sans le Soudan
260	0.294	0.090	260	0.311	0.096	Afrique subsaharienne
260	0.375	0.067	260	0.377	0.085	Afrique subsaharienne sans l'Afrique du Sud
260	0.196	0.063	260	0.208	0.077	**Économies en développement : Amérique**
260	0.245	0.069	259	0.261	0.088	Amérique centrale et Grandes Antilles sans Porto Rico
260	0.334	0.092	259	0.333	0.108	Amérique centrale et Grandes Antilles sans le Mexique et Porto Rico
260	0.207	0.062	260	0.214	0.076	Amérique du Sud et Amérique centrale
259	0.232	0.063	260	0.250	0.073	Amérique du Sud sans le Brésil
260	0.232	0.108	260	0.186	0.106	**Économies en développement : Asie**
260	0.254	0.139	260	0.214	0.126	Asie orientale et Asie du Sud-Est sans la Chine
259	0.370	0.078	259	0.382	0.086	Asie méridionale sans l'Inde

Pour les sources et les notes, se reporter à la fin du tableau 4.1.1.

Region, country or territory	Exports (1) - Exportations (1)							
	2004	2005	2006	2007	2008	2009	2010	2011
WORLD	**123**	**131**	**142**	**151**	**155**	**134**	**153**	**162**
DEVELOPING ECONOMIES	142	156	172	188	194	175	202	216
TRANSITION ECONOMIES	142	141	151	165	165	141	157	166
DEVELOPED ECONOMIES	114	120	130	135	139	118	133	140
Developing economies: Africa	**117**	**127**	**125**	**134**	**129**	**117**	**127**	**120**
Eastern Africa	*131*	*134*	*138*	*151*	*156*	*154*	*166*	*166*
Burundi	88	81	76	75	54	64	85	79
Comoros	206	135	104	113	63	107	98	98
Djibouti	106	103	130	124	125	171	177	170
Eritrea	60	58	59	55	43	43	42	(c)1 189
Ethiopia	120	141	150	164	174	184	233	212
Kenya	145	156	153	175	183	166	179	173
Madagascar	124	103	118	147	166	113	103	128
Malawi	135	135	161	193	174	206	175	182
Mauritius	120	131	144	130	130	119	143	145
Mayotte	162	210	233	237	218	195	200	182
Mozambique	354	357	397	387	373	382	426	467
Rwanda	142	120	130	144	142	112	153	196
Seychelles	153	164	178	170	178	164	150	154
Somalia	83	107	107	119	123	125	125	129
Uganda	155	181	192	300	350	398	372	235
United Republic of Tanzania	172	178	164	174	203	201	230	214
Zambia	134	127	163	187	202	213	261	275
Zimbabwe	78	74	66	65	57	59	57	69
Middle Africa	*141*	*159*	*163*	*185*	*196*	*192*	*194*	*194*
Angola	128	163	176	222	241	239	232	230
Cameroon	101	94	101	93	87	81	77	75
Central African Republic	75	71	83	86	69	60	61	61
Chad	894	922	823	806	685	705	698	618
Congo	105	104	110	93	102	107	130	119
Dem. Rep. of the Congo	211	206	195	206	226	248	299	279
Equatorial Guinea	313	344	336	381	394	370	334	354
Gabon	110	107	98	102	111	94	115	137
Sao Tome and Principe	136	172	191	149	187	136	177	207
Northern Africa	*119*	*121*	*123*	*131*	*130*	*115*	*122*	*94*
Algeria	111	110	106	109	100	89	98	99
Egypt	129	136	147	163	203	209	214	203
Libya	121	130	138	138	144	133	134	37
Morocco	109	122	132	143	121	91	107	104
Sudan (...2011)	160	148	146	208	202	207	226	147
Tunisia	154	156	167	199	208	170	182	171
Southern Africa	*107*	*129*	*127*	*133*	*120*	*99*	*116*	*114*
Botswana	121	147	133	135	141	107	131	147
Lesotho	323	298	319	347	390	313	360	382
Namibia	126	132	129	127	137	143	168	161
South Africa	103	126	125	132	119	97	113	111
Swaziland	180	154	139	142	111	99	103	103
Western Africa	*111*	*128*	*117*	*118*	*108*	*107*	*121*	*137*
Benin	126	122	139	180	183	193	175	182
Burkina Faso	205	217	252	234	220	306	325	336
Cape Verde	141	137	148	133	195	212	254	335
Côte d'Ivoire	119	116	115	104	97	108	91	83
Gambia	59	45	59	59	51	276	132	115
Ghana	106	109	132	134	121	133	161	228
Guinea	96	94	86	94	95	103	120	120
Guinea-Bissau	127	136	96	138	132	127	119	216
Liberia	31	41	42	45	44	29	33	33
Mali	142	163	193	173	192	159	137	132
Mauritania	119	124	230	224	208	179	273	307
Niger	118	110	100	96	127	157	157	150
Nigeria	110	139	120	124	111	111	133	154
Saint Helena	262	244	248	290	384	360	341	363
Senegal	142	132	119	116	123	133	125	116
Sierra Leone	1 012	1 115	1 502	1 495	1 124	1 307	1 735	2 425
Togo	199	256	229	220	169	208	181	187

For sources and notes, see end of table.

Imports (1) - Importations (1)								Régions, pays ou territoires
2004	2005	2006	2007	2008	2009	2010	2011	
125	**134**	**145**	**155**	**159**	**138**	**157**	**165**	**MONDE**
140	154	170	189	201	182	217	231	ÉCONOMIES EN DÉVELOPPEMENT
189	212	256	325	375	268	310	365	ÉCONOMIES EN TRANSITION
117	124	133	138	138	118	131	136	ÉCONOMIES DÉVELOPPÉES
135	**156**	**170**	**193**	**213**	**205**	**220**	**229**	**Économies en développement : Afrique**
136	*150*	*166*	*182*	*205*	*205*	*219*	*226*	*Afrique orientale*
104	148	226	154	174	184	223	285	Burundi
176	187	209	232	241	242	241	224	Comores
107	95	106	135	139	121	91	88	Djibouti
89	88	80	71	69	71	77	84	Érythrée
200	258	308	318	405	423	428	379	Éthiopie
123	147	160	183	192	199	217	225	Kenya
148	137	134	173	239	213	160	151	Madagascar
156	182	181	186	247	245	252	235	Malawi
138	146	160	160	158	152	167	165	Maurice
180	181	204	258	281	247	235	213	Mayotte
154	165	184	180	194	203	228	273	Mozambique
117	180	216	246	347	415	431	455	Rwanda
120	143	147	157	166	143	118	120	Seychelles
161	155	178	182	190	159	151	166	Somalie
98	105	121	154	176	183	190	160	Ouganda
152	166	200	231	264	265	311	369	République-Unie de Tanzanie
210	230	261	315	349	297	368	425	Zambie
96	89	77	76	76	84	97	100	Zimbabwe
176	*213*	*235*	*301*	*371*	*413*	*365*	*402*	*Afrique centrale*
179	252	254	368	515	586	415	483	Angola
140	140	146	178	185	173	182	197	Cameroun
118	122	134	152	157	153	159	167	République centrafricaine
263	247	334	393	410	431	434	380	Tchad
185	237	340	393	429	414	546	624	Congo
260	312	316	338	379	362	405	428	Rép. dém. du Congo
194	216	318	404	501	838	831	775	Guinée équatoriale
128	133	151	173	189	191	182	250	Gabon
122	129	171	174	213	219	223	225	Sao Tomé-et-Principe
128	*145*	*150*	*171*	*215*	*210*	*218*	*212*	*Afrique septentrionale*
176	188	187	215	280	294	300	300	Algérie
78	111	108	126	196	199	218	209	Égypte
150	131	123	123	146	172	171	146	Libye
127	140	155	183	207	180	179	190	Maroc
234	366	419	429	422	460	455	373	Soudan (...2011)
132	126	133	156	176	150	162	149	Tunisie
136	*157*	*182*	*191*	*180*	*163*	*189*	*210*	*Afrique australe*
139	127	113	138	159	157	176	200	Botswana
163	156	161	179	186	196	199	192	Lesotho
141	147	158	182	203	252	232	236	Namibie
135	161	189	198	183	161	191	215	Afrique du Sud
155	143	137	120	94	106	110	92	Swaziland
138	*169*	*185*	*223*	*228*	*205*	*238*	*255*	*Afrique occidentale*
128	135	157	240	221	223	206	213	Bénin
187	168	190	194	215	206	212	231	Burkina Faso
164	154	179	225	220	211	205	229	Cap-Vert
167	181	164	174	163	167	172	126	Côte d'Ivoire
109	110	104	117	98	99	84	87	Gambie
123	145	170	188	206	177	226	286	Ghana
110	105	115	135	128	111	136	159	Guinée
139	148	161	192	180	217	199	244	Guinée-Bissau
49	57	75	76	95	58	66	73	Libéria
153	155	172	188	246	199	211	209	Mali
183	269	204	225	261	211	261	282	Mauritanie
163	191	184	204	239	396	369	339	Niger
144	202	237	305	304	263	329	363	Nigéria
91	113	147	185	83	76	88	68	Sainte-Hélène
154	168	164	196	209	176	163	168	Sénégal
156	155	157	163	153	185	240	293	Sierra Leone
56	57	54	58	60	64	58	57	Togo

Pour les sources et les notes, se reporter à la fin du tableau.

4.2.1 Volume indices of exports and imports
of countries and geographical regions
2000 = 100

Region, country or territory	Exports (1) - Exportations (1)							
	2004	2005	2006	2007	2008	2009	2010	2011
Developing economies: America	**118**	**127**	**134**	**137**	**136**	**121**	**134**	**139**
Caribbean	*92*	*92*	*98*	*90*	*85*	*63*	*66*	*75*
Anguilla	138	319	213	155	180	375	208	184
Antigua and Barbuda	77	112	92	66	51	45	39	42
Aruba	83	72	65	43	45	27	4	16
Bahamas	78	81	96	102	99	91	77	72
Barbados	85	90	100	113	88	73	78	73
Cuba	98	91	91	102	102	84	109	120
Curaçao	–	–	–	–	–	–	–	(a)14
Dominica	65	62	60	50	46	41	38	34
Dominican Republic	100	100	103	103	92	80	94	110
Grenada	68	61	51	59	45	46	35	40
Haiti	117	135	139	143	127	138	140	199
Jamaica	93	100	111	107	118	95	80	81
Montserrat	359	114	101	196	276	233	80	117
Netherlands Antilles	21	18	18	16	20	20	17	–
Saint Kitts and Nevis	132	103	119	103	137	138	146	189
Saint Lucia	159	100	129	139	185	210	285	244
Saint Vincent and the Grenadines	70	79	69	78	67	58	45	43
Trinidad and Tobago	121	136	159	140	134	92	101	90
Turks and Caicos Islands	148	177	211	186	265	229	168	150
Central America	*108*	*117*	*130*	*133*	*134*	*117*	*139*	*147*
Belize	96	84	94	88	87	72	80	83
Costa Rica	114	127	148	168	168	162	178	189
El Salvador	113	112	118	121	135	117	132	143
Guatemala	187	185	197	214	218	210	227	249
Honduras	163	166	167	174	173	145	152	157
Mexico	106	112	124	126	127	109	132	138
Nicaragua	130	136	156	175	199	195	237	261
Panama (2)	109	827	883	932	988	1 101	1 096	1 356
South America	*133*	*143*	*146*	*150*	*151*	*138*	*146*	*150*
Argentina	118	136	144	155	157	150	174	181
Bolivia (Plurinational State of)	154	174	179	183	269	204	216	234
Brazil	164	179	185	195	190	170	186	185
Chile	136	141	145	155	154	141	149	147
Colombia	116	131	139	147	156	167	168	192
Ecuador	162	173	186	184	202	193	202	213
Falkland Islands (Malvinas)	188	224	189	219	216	176	198	168
Guyana	108	88	77	89	82	78	77	87
Paraguay	166	178	195	270	363	293	399	433
Peru	151	173	174	178	191	186	190	198
Suriname	179	200	183	200	223	196	229	215
Uruguay	124	140	152	158	171	173	192	197
Venezuela (Bolivarian Rep. of)	93	96	92	84	85	77	70	74
Developing economies: Asia	**151**	**167**	**189**	**209**	**219**	**199**	**233**	**254**
Eastern Asia	*174*	*205*	*242*	*280*	*300*	*268*	*333*	*367*
China	236	300	376	458	507	436	564	638
China, Hong Kong SAR	135	149	162	172	174	151	177	180
China, Macao SAR	109	95	96	93	70	34	30	28
China, Taiwan Province of	136	147	166	180	175	165	199	204
Korea, Dem. People's Rep. of	177	167	169	185	185	187	235	284
Korea, Republic of	161	178	202	224	244	250	288	321
Mongolia	117	119	118	131	138	124	144	193
Southern Asia	*137*	*146*	*167*	*176*	*188*	*177*	*190*	*205*
Afghanistan	168	194	185	203	186	144	122	95
Bangladesh	130	144	183	190	222	213	265	301
Bhutan	125	152	219	350	199	229	265	206
India	155	180	210	224	262	244	262	294
Iran (Islamic Rep. of)	118	109	125	131	123	127	131	132
Maldives	159	127	155	173	211	109	113	174
Nepal	87	93	82	79	77	71	66	61
Pakistan	144	172	177	180	182	161	177	179
Sri Lanka	106	113	117	128	122	103	116	125
South-Eastern Asia	*133*	*141*	*155*	*166*	*169*	*151*	*180*	*188*
Brunei Darussalam	103	88	86	81	78	79	86	93
Cambodia	195	202	253	273	296	257	302	374
Indonesia	92	95	99	102	95	95	109	114
Lao People's Dem. Rep.	102	141	169	170	184	197	274	318

For sources and notes, see end of table.

			Imports (1) - Importations (1)					Régions, pays ou territoires
2004	2005	2006	2007	2008	2009	2010	2011	
108	**119**	**136**	**152**	**164**	**135**	**167**	**179**	**Économies en développement : Amérique**
92	*101*	*112*	*113*	*119*	*96*	*97*	*103*	*Caraïbes*
97	111	180	187	187	119	106	87	Anguilla
106	122	128	135	111	77	65	58	Antigua-et-Barbuda
93	85	82	56	70	35	23	29	Aruba
85	98	108	104	95	90	87	89	Bahamas
109	111	105	102	96	83	77	75	Barbade
108	142	176	167	195	139	150	156	Cuba
–	–	–	–	–	–	–	(a)32	Curaçao
86	90	86	93	105	111	98	87	Dominique
78	93	109	116	123	110	126	126	République dominicaine
95	119	102	116	103	88	91	79	Grenade
115	118	132	122	116	126	181	149	Haïti
98	101	111	130	134	94	87	88	Jamaïque
115	108	103	94	105	103	..	..	Montserrat
48	40	39	41	40	42	38	–	Antilles néerlandaises
83	90	102	104	114	106	94	85	Saint-Kitts-et-Nevis
112	102	114	112	87	100	98	78	Sainte-Lucie
124	122	130	144	145	147	154	121	Saint-Vincent-et-les Grenadines
126	124	128	139	143	120	101	117	Trinité-et-Tobago
134	172	269	293	269	185	140	124	Îles Turques et Caïques
110	*117*	*132*	*139*	*144*	*116*	*141*	*151*	*Amérique centrale*
86	86	92	86	90	84	84	93	Belize
126	143	163	180	201	165	192	214	Costa Rica
125	128	140	150	156	125	135	147	El Salvador
170	173	184	194	184	164	180	188	Guatemala
153	157	161	183	187	150	160	169	Honduras
107	114	126	132	136	109	134	143	Mexique
112	119	129	147	157	142	161	174	Nicaragua
101	111	274	321	346	326	375	446	Panama (2)
109	*126*	*147*	*178*	*204*	*170*	*218*	*236*	*Amérique du Sud*
88	108	126	153	178	139	190	202	Argentine
92	110	122	135	187	172	195	253	Bolivie (État plurinational de)
104	109	126	154	182	150	207	217	Brésil
134	162	181	213	245	195	262	300	Chili
138	165	193	231	251	226	261	300	Colombie
208	239	258	270	332	305	382	399	Équateur
133	91	90	123	67	72	132	222	Îles Falkland (Malvinas)
97	102	108	117	124	124	138	145	Guyana
114	132	184	216	303	259	357	400	Paraguay
125	141	161	194	235	185	231	247	Pérou
124	155	140	134	147	175	163	158	Suriname
87	96	107	119	149	142	163	175	Uruguay
93	127	172	227	220	196	193	209	Venezuela (Rép. bolivarienne du)
150	**164**	**180**	**200**	**212**	**193**	**231**	**247**	**Économies en développement : Asie**
160	*171*	*189*	*208*	*209*	*198*	*247*	*266*	*Asie orientale*
231	251	284	324	332	326	426	472	Chine
133	143	157	169	171	153	179	185	Chine (RAS de Hong Kong)
145	155	175	195	179	164	187	244	Chine (RAS de Macao)
122	119	125	126	117	103	127	124	Province chinoise de Taiwan
117	119	119	109	102	100	106	123	Corée, Rép. populaire dém. de
130	139	153	166	167	163	192	205	Corée, République de
143	145	169	222	321	215	306	520	Mongolie
146	*196*	*227*	*249*	*302*	*285*	*324*	*343*	*Asie méridionale*
170	174	171	170	155	186	276	279	Afghanistan
118	125	136	141	145	145	163	175	Bangladesh
213	184	182	204	177	193	291	281	Bhoutan
143	224	280	321	416	413	469	505	Inde
197	206	199	202	221	204	243	231	Iran (Rép. islamique d')
148	157	183	201	220	172	178	206	Maldives
104	106	104	118	112	151	160	149	Népal
136	170	181	179	182	124	131	134	Pakistan
111	113	121	122	127	103	124	153	Sri Lanka
131	*141*	*150*	*161*	*174*	*145*	*177*	*188*	*Asie du Sud-Est*
117	118	127	147	158	159	151	150	Brunéi Darussalam
154	173	200	214	224	218	223	254	Cambodge
112	135	132	141	164	135	180	203	Indonésie
118	130	147	138	160	178	243	271	Rép. dém. populaire lao

Pour les sources et les notes, se reporter à la fin du tableau.

4.2.1 Volume indices of exports and imports of countries and geographical regions
2000 = 100

Region, country or territory	Exports (1) - Exportations (1)							
	2004	2005	2006	2007	2008	2009	2010	2011
Malaysia	127	134	147	154	158	132	157	161
Myanmar	128	167	171	228	195	218	279	257
Philippines	134	121	137	143	136	110	145	125
Singapore	156	174	192	208	218	196	236	247
Thailand	133	142	160	178	185	159	187	206
Viet Nam	168	181	206	238	256	249	292	329
Western Asia	*124*	*125*	*130*	*132*	*138*	*136*	*140*	*158*
Bahrain	103	109	107	111	113	102	103	124
Iraq	68	62	66	78	92	100	92	111
Jordan	182	173	190	177	157	145	178	181
Kuwait	111	124	132	134	140	131	130	155
Lebanon	265	270	298	343	372	361	405	398
Occupied Palestinian territory	70	72	76	96	94	92	96	112
Oman	91	88	83	87	88	117	113	106
Qatar	126	122	132	154	141	187	245	262
Saudi Arabia	114	113	110	96	102	98	97	132
Syrian Arab Republic	129	130	139	133	136	118	115	81
Turkey	181	199	223	248	265	244	260	275
United Arab Emirates	148	149	159	180	189	188	196	191
Yemen	76	76	75	65	58	70	77	84
Developing economies: Oceania	**97**	**93**	**75**	**78**	**68**	**64**	**64**	**69**
American Samoa	105	90	62	60	70	60	35	35
Cook Islands	76	51	32	..	..	..	..	..
Fiji	124	110	92	98	105	70	84	71
French Polynesia	75	82	70	59	66	51	51	45
Guam	60	52	48	80	80	38	32	27
Kiribati	73	121	160	225	286	389	265	301
Marshall Islands	224	304	196	181	155	188	176	216
Micronesia (Federated States of)	86	81	68	93	98	91	85	73
Nauru	46	12	10	31	45	21	45	30
New Caledonia	111	115	111	137	77	62	62	73
Niue	56	61	342	849	5	6	6	5
Northern Mariana Islands	79	62	45	26	11	0	0	0
Palau	49	104	92	83	71	74	70	60
Papua New Guinea	98	101	81	83	84	96	96	106
Samoa	600	568	394	565	395	274	321	260
Solomon Islands	111	115	124	145	171	159	193	300
Tokelau	..	..	..	..	..	..	..	..
Tonga	152	92	86	81	71	64	62	57
Vanuatu	140	135	155	173	156	158	122	142
Wallis and Futuna Islands	97	77	71	65	51	58	55	41
Transition economies	**142**	**141**	**151**	**165**	**165**	**141**	**157**	**166**
Albania	215	222	255	326	357	308	399	448
Armenia	211	261	229	259	192	141	171	193
Azerbaijan	160	253	361	538	571	600	595	594
Belarus	158	153	175	194	206	166	176	234
Bosnia and Herzegovina	154	180	226	264	285	244	274	291
Croatia	170	170	185	206	203	160	169	159
Georgia	160	199	194	220	216	172	218	263
Kazakhstan	174	177	193	216	242	202	217	261
Kyrgyzstan	111	96	114	156	191	178	168	160
Republic of Moldova	217	261	254	285	289	312	355	448
Russian Federation	133	133	140	148	144	127	144	147
Serbia and Montenegro	206	229	289	359	—	—	—	—
Tajikistan	97	86	104	106	92	88	78	67
TFYR of Macedonia	112	125	138	176	178	124	145	170
Turkmenistan	134	115	127	138	138	105	95	127
Ukraine	172	159	167	188	204	133	163	183
Uzbekistan	125	123	121	162	158	197	179	165
Developed economies: America	**99**	**106**	**114**	**120**	**123**	**104**	**118**	**126**
Bermuda	142	96	47	43	30	50	24	20
Canada	94	100	101	100	97	80	87	92
Greenland	168	168	157	170	172	134	129	132
Saint Pierre and Miquelon	48	69	243	94	57	33	27	21
United States	101	109	120	128	135	115	133	142
Developed economies: Asia	**122**	**128**	**142**	**156**	**159**	**120**	**152**	**152**
Israel	116	119	125	136	132	111	131	131
Japan	123	129	144	157	161	121	154	153

For sources and notes, see end of table.

2004	2005	2006	2007	2008	2009	2010	2011	Régions, pays ou territoires
			Imports (1) - Importations (1)					
129	133	147	156	155	124	156	160	Malaisie
79	62	77	89	100	114	115	180	Myanmar
155	139	130	133	121	101	121	115	Philippines
124	134	149	158	175	151	177	184	Singapour
140	164	168	175	197	153	194	217	Thaïlande
177	184	207	265	295	280	313	334	Viet Nam
154	*171*	*185*	*221*	*248*	*220*	*231*	*241*	*Asie occidentale*
141	153	147	148	176	123	137	131	Bahreïn
134	147	131	106	174	200	221	236	Iraq
136	154	154	160	165	161	135	133	Jordanie
160	191	199	231	249	207	221	225	Koweït
134	119	111	130	154	167	171	164	Liban
80	77	72	77	69	85	87	88	Territoire palestinien occupé
153	145	169	230	305	249	263	277	Oman
166	267	418	559	624	565	489	520	Qatar
141	169	187	224	255	219	236	223	Arabie saoudite
191	223	219	259	275	256	271	215	République arabe syrienne
139	156	171	190	188	163	198	222	Turquie
206	212	233	326	395	345	327	348	Émirats arabes unis
148	175	180	227	235	238	232	162	Yémen
129	*122*	*128*	*138*	*134*	*122*	*134*	*136*	*Économies en développement : Océanie*
114	88	93	102	83	76	64	65	Samoa américaines
137	139	164	161	..	..	..	..	Îles Cook
150	143	148	135	144	106	121	128	Fidji
125	134	125	130	137	118	111	92	Polynésie française
99	81	67	87	68	85	81	64	Guam
133	152	118	119	102	103	101	135	Kiribati
173	208	184	180	140	105	134	121	Îles Marshall
114	106	109	105	101	117	111	97	Micronésie (États fédérés de)
59	65	76	124	160	265	51	62	Nauru
161	159	181	224	230	199	242	237	Nouvelle-Calédonie
371	353	148	256	255	187	182	218	Nioué
100	77	60	34	15	8	9	9	Îles Mariannes du Nord
76	74	76	65	69	57	60	56	Palaos
126	111	137	161	153	155	178	209	Papouasie-Nouvelle-Guinée
205	209	226	201	189	170	210	202	Samoa
114	150	163	198	178	166	235	230	Îles Salomon
92	57	9	8	6	7	6	6	Tokélaou
133	134	120	134	136	130	130	127	Tonga
137	145	200	193	215	218	196	176	Vanuatu
141	125	133	121	109	116	107	94	Îles Wallis-et-Futuna
189	*212*	*256*	*325*	*375*	*268*	*310*	*365*	*Économies en transition*
184	196	216	275	305	287	263	280	Albanie
139	163	186	259	304	248	270	263	Arménie
259	283	327	329	377	331	348	468	Azerbaïdjan
158	135	162	192	213	187	212	233	Bélarus
134	146	140	172	189	149	146	153	Bosnie-Herzégovine
188	193	209	236	241	183	163	145	Croatie
226	268	365	481	489	396	429	509	Géorgie
241	290	368	474	487	377	308	433	Kazakhstan
145	156	231	306	392	308	301	344	Kirghizistan
232	318	392	488	525	486	566	672	République de Moldova
198	245	310	400	488	330	414	497	Fédération de Russie
276	243	286	390	–	–	–	–	Serbie-et-Monténégro
147	141	161	213	234	207	194	201	Tadjikistan
118	117	126	161	179	140	138	149	LERY de Macédoine
167	144	120	158	225	272	222	261	Turkménistan
177	188	212	268	311	191	243	286	Ukraine
111	114	130	175	232	236	210	230	Ouzbékistan
117	*124*	*130*	*132*	*128*	*108*	*123*	*128*	*Économies développées : Amérique*
133	131	136	131	107	94	80	71	Bermudes
108	119	120	125	128	109	120	128	Canada
137	134	139	146	156	136	138	126	Groenland
58	40	50	45	40	53	44	42	Saint-Pierre-et-Miquelon
118	125	132	133	129	107	123	128	États-Unis
114	*116*	*121*	*122*	*122*	*106*	*118*	*120*	*Économies développées : Asie*
102	104	105	113	114	97	113	122	Israël
115	118	123	124	123	108	118	121	Japon.

Pour les sources et les notes, se reporter à la fin du tableau.

4.2.1 Volume indices of exports and imports
of countries and geographical regions
2000 = 100

Region, country or territory	Exports (1) - Exportations (1)							
	2004	2005	2006	2007	2008	2009	2010	2011
Developed economies: Europe	**120**	**125**	**136**	**141**	**144**	**124**	**138**	**147**
Andorra	268	290	266	227	160	102	86	116
Austria	160	162	169	190	196	155	167	177
Belgium	121	125	131	135	132	116	125	129
Bulgaria	156	172	194	199	206	185	222	259
Cyprus	89	128	111	108	110	93	96	108
Czech Republic	161	173	201	230	242	207	248	283
Denmark	111	116	121	125	129	116	121	129
Estonia	80	101	121	117	119	94	120	155
Faeroe Islands	125	112	101	125	121	109	107	114
Finland	114	119	134	139	144	108	122	125
France	109	112	118	120	120	104	115	121
Germany	128	136	152	163	165	138	160	170
Gibraltar	166	164	177	202	164	196	165	145
Greece	85	92	105	106	103	90	92	117
Hungary	149	168	199	230	244	213	249	269
Iceland	139	139	138	170	170	172	163	170
Ireland	111	116	114	119	120	115	119	125
Italy	104	104	110	115	110	89	97	101
Latvia	148	181	195	213	225	200	240	279
Lithuania	229	254	286	317	363	286	333	389
Luxembourg	171	191	222	203	208	190	167	159
Malta	99	95	114	124	134	112	141	153
Netherlands	122	131	142	135	158	142	161	165
Norway	107	107	105	107	108	104	100	96
Poland	171	188	219	239	257	235	228	245
Portugal	138	142	158	176	175	143	149	160
Romania	205	222	246	287	311	266	313	361
Slovakia	212	229	288	385	434	363	409	468
Slovenia	169	193	222	269	282	228	246	269
Spain	119	120	126	133	135	124	142	164
Sweden	117	121	130	131	135	109	126	134
Switzerland	139	145	157	172	188	168	186	206
United Kingdom	100	107	120	107	107	94	109	114
Developed economies: Oceania	**105**	**107**	**110**	**113**	**119**	**111**	**126**	**127**
Australia	105	108	111	113	120	114	129	130
New Zealand	105	103	111	116	122	101	125	118

Sources:
UNCTAD secretariat calculations, based on:
- ECLAC, *CEPALSTAT* external trade deflator
- IMF, *International Financial Statistics*
- U.S. Bureau of Labor Statistics, external trade price indices
- Unit value indices of Japan Customs and price indices of Bank of Japan
- UNCTAD, *UNCTADstat Commodity Price Statistics*
- UNCTAD, *UNCTADstat Merchandise Trade Matrix*
- UNCTAD secretariat estimates

Notes:
(a) Data refer to Netherlands Antilles.
(c) From 2011 onwards, exports include commercial mining.
(1) Volume indices or quantum: The ratio of the export or import value index to the corresponding unit value index.
(2) From 2005 onwards, including customs free zones.

Imports (1) - Importations (1)								Régions, pays ou territoires
2004	2005	2006	2007	2008	2009	2010	2011	
119	**126**	**137**	**144**	**145**	**124**	**137**	**142**	**Économies développées : Europe**
161	..	..	..	..	..	..	..	Andorre
150	148	149	167	168	140	148	159	Autriche
118	126	132	138	138	122	129	133	Belgique
173	201	232	256	276	203	221	245	Bulgarie
129	136	141	163	180	146	149	130	Chypre
150	154	177	203	212	181	215	235	République tchèque
113	121	132	133	139	118	125	133	Danemark
123	145	181	187	169	119	139	175	Estonie
107	118	117	141	123	104	95	103	Îles Féroé
114	122	133	140	144	110	124	134	Finlande
114	123	126	132	133	118	127	134	France
120	127	142	148	150	135	153	160	Allemagne
91	71	76	87	65	86	73	55	Gibraltar
102	96	107	118	121	97	88	74	Grèce
141	151	173	193	202	167	192	203	Hongrie
118	141	176	174	136	94	94	102	Islande
101	112	115	121	110	91	88	86	Irlande
108	108	113	116	109	94	105	104	Italie
159	182	219	252	227	155	182	221	Lettonie
210	234	271	321	330	226	265	304	Lituanie
159	162	188	185	189	163	151	153	Luxembourg
88	84	94	97	91	82	85	88	Malte
112	126	138	144	158	138	157	162	Pays-Bas
111	122	135	148	155	133	144	150	Norvège
141	148	173	199	218	178	167	175	Pologne
124	127	138	150	152	125	124	116	Portugal
223	253	301	389	411	285	312	343	Roumanie
199	212	259	332	361	290	328	353	Slovaquie
156	165	183	224	234	182	195	204	Slovénie
127	135	148	158	153	126	141	146	Espagne
105	111	118	127	128	107	125	131	Suède
108	117	127	135	134	123	133	142	Suisse
117	123	138	130	127	111	126	127	Royaume-Uni
136	**148**	**159**	**174**	**193**	**167**	**184**	**197**	**Économies développées : Océanie**
138	150	163	181	200	178	195	209	Australie
127	139	142	145	165	121	141	151	Nouvelle-Zélande

Sources :
Calculs du secrétariat de la CNUCED, basés sur :
- CEPALC, *CEPALSTAT* déflateur du commerce extérieur
- FMI, *Statistiques financières internationales*
- Bureau des statistiques du travail des États-Unis (BLS), indices de prix du commerce extérieur
- Indices des valeurs unitaires des douanes japonaises et indices des prix de la Banque du Japon
- CNUCED, *UNCTADstat Statistiques de prix des produits de base*
- CNUCED, *UNCTADstat Matrice du commerce de marchandises*
- Estimations du secrétariat de la CNUCED

Notes :
(a) Les données se réfèrent aux Antilles néerlandaises.
(c) À partir de 2011, les exportations comprennent l'exploitation minière commerciale.
(1) Indices du volume ou quantum : représentent le rapport de l'indice de la valeur des exportations ou des importations à l'indice de la valeur unitaire correspondant.
(2) À partir de 2005, y compris les zones franches douanières.

4

4.2.1 Unit value indices of exports and imports of countries and geographical regions
2000 = 100

Region, country or territory	Exports (1) - Exportations (1)							
	2004	2005	2006	2007	2008	2009	2010	2011
WORLD	116	125	132	144	162	145	155	174
DEVELOPING ECONOMIES	106	119	128	137	158	139	155	176
TRANSITION ECONOMIES	129	167	196	216	290	219	254	320
DEVELOPED ECONOMIES	120	125	130	143	155	142	146	161
Developing economies: Africa	133	168	199	218	290	226	267	335
Eastern Africa	110	122	148	160	179	167	195	231
Burundi	106	137	154	167	201	195	237	308
Comoros	66	66	74	90	106	109	123	150
Djibouti	114	122	136	148	174	143	152	177
Eritrea	100	103	110	127	140	134	152	(c)186
Ethiopia	117	135	143	161	189	181	206	254
Kenya	107	121	129	134	156	155	166	192
Madagascar	91	94	99	106	117	113	122	144
Malawi	94	99	109	118	133	152	161	180
Mauritius	91	90	89	95	102	90	87	101
Mayotte	110	111	115	120	129	127	123	135
Mozambique	117	134	165	171	195	155	187	212
Rwanda	130	197	215	231	357	325	365	402
Seychelles	98	107	110	109	125	124	137	160
Somalia	116	122	138	150	175	175	186	207
Uganda	106	122	135	145	169	164	182	223
United Republic of Tanzania	117	129	160	174	204	202	240	301
Zambia	132	160	259	277	282	227	310	367
Zimbabwe	125	131	157	192	200	200	227	262
Middle Africa	132	183	218	240	327	218	275	354
Angola	134	187	224	248	336	217	276	362
Cameroon	134	166	193	211	269	227	274	333
Central African Republic	111	113	117	128	135	128	141	160
Chad	134	186	223	246	333	217	277	364
Congo	132	184	221	244	328	228	287	366
Dem. Rep. of the Congo	110	141	168	183	236	172	219	261
Equatorial Guinea	134	187	223	245	346	225	272	348
Gabon	131	181	214	237	330	224	279	350
Sao Tome and Principe	148	147	150	167	211	222	231	233
Northern Africa	129	174	206	224	310	228	265	331
Algeria	131	190	235	251	359	229	265	337
Egypt	127	168	200	213	277	236	264	322
Libya	133	187	224	247	338	219	273	354
Morocco	127	128	135	149	233	215	229	283
Sudan (...2011)	131	180	214	236	320	221	279	365
Tunisia	107	115	120	130	159	145	154	178
Western Sahara	93	..	..	..	..	..	..	..
Southern Africa	141	136	161	176	217	205	226	274
Botswana	105	109	124	139	127	117	130	144
Lesotho	99	99	99	101	104	105	107	120
Namibia	110	119	155	173	176	164	181	206
South Africa	147	139	165	181	227	214	237	290
Swaziland	119	126	142	145	170	183	192	217
Western Africa	137	184	218	241	325	244	298	378
Benin	115	120	135	149	178	161	202	259
Burkina Faso	114	105	114	129	153	143	193	261
Cape Verde	101	120	131	136	154	156	165	194
Côte d'Ivoire	149	171	190	214	273	250	296	341
Gambia	114	119	129	141	178	159	177	194
Ghana	138	154	168	194	261	264	295	333
Guinea	119	135	179	191	211	154	184	220
Guinea-Bissau	96	105	124	125	156	153	162	182
Liberia	101	98	112	125	160	162	219	269
Mali	126	124	147	165	201	204	262	342
Mauritania	104	143	167	177	246	214	215	254
Niger	131	157	180	244	253	225	234	294
Nigeria	135	189	228	251	345	228	283	368
Saint Helena	90	92	95	94	100	95	101	113
Senegal	115	130	142	155	195	165	187	238
Sierra Leone	105	109	118	125	147	137	151	163
Togo	83	71	75	87	138	119	135	161

For sources and notes, see end of table.

4.2.1 Indices de la valeur unitaire des exportations et importations
des pays et des régions géographiques
2000 = 100

Imports (1) - Importations (1)								Régions, pays ou territoires
2004	2005	2006	2007	2008	2009	2010	2011	
114	121	128	138	155	138	147	166	**MONDE**
108	115	122	130	149	134	145	164	ÉCONOMIES EN DÉVELOPPEMENT
113	122	129	137	154	144	150	167	ÉCONOMIES EN TRANSITION
117	123	130	141	158	139	146	165	ÉCONOMIES DÉVELOPPÉES
120	127	135	148	170	154	165	189	**Économies en développement : Afrique**
114	126	135	147	172	153	165	194	*Afrique orientale*
114	122	129	140	157	148	155	179	Burundi
112	122	128	138	169	162	173	197	Comores
118	141	154	170	200	180	193	227	Djibouti
114	120	131	153	185	175	189	227	Érythrée
114	126	134	145	170	149	159	186	Éthiopie
120	135	147	158	185	165	180	212	Kenya
112	124	132	142	162	149	159	193	Madagascar
112	120	126	139	167	155	162	183	Malawi
91	98	103	110	134	111	119	141	Maurice
113	123	129	139	156	147	154	170	Mayotte
114	126	134	146	178	160	170	198	Mozambique
114	123	128	141	159	148	156	178	Rwanda
121	137	150	160	185	165	182	213	Seychelles
110	118	130	142	173	171	184	207	Somalie
114	127	137	147	168	151	161	187	Ouganda
118	130	139	152	176	156	169	199	République-Unie de Tanzanie
115	125	133	143	163	144	163	191	Zambie
124	142	161	180	208	185	205	238	Zimbabwe
111	117	124	134	150	139	148	166	*Afrique centrale*
107	109	114	122	134	127	132	148	Angola
115	132	146	159	197	173	190	222	Cameroun
110	121	129	140	164	151	164	194	République centrafricaine
114	121	127	140	156	146	152	174	Tchad
113	118	124	134	149	146	155	171	Congo
113	124	131	144	163	151	159	178	Rép. dém. du Congo
112	120	126	136	149	123	136	154	Guinée équatoriale
111	116	120	131	144	137	144	160	Gabon
114	129	139	153	180	158	169	194	Sao Tomé-et-Principe
116	124	131	146	167	153	163	188	*Afrique septentrionale*
114	118	125	140	154	146	149	169	Algérie
117	128	138	153	179	162	174	202	Égypte
114	124	133	148	169	158	166	191	Libye
121	129	134	152	177	158	172	201	Maroc
112	119	124	132	143	136	142	159	Soudan (…2011)
113	122	132	143	163	149	160	188	Tunisie
95	..	..	..	..	..	..	..	Sahara occidental
132	130	139	149	171	153	165	187	*Afrique australe*
112	122	131	141	158	144	154	175	Botswana
110	112	115	120	135	124	137	162	Lesotho
109	113	118	124	138	127	149	176	Namibie
135	132	142	151	175	156	167	189	Afrique du Sud
119	126	134	147	175	161	173	206	Swaziland
116	128	137	150	175	159	169	192	*Afrique occidentale*
114	123	128	138	169	151	171	207	Bénin
111	122	129	141	168	149	158	184	Burkina Faso
114	123	132	145	163	146	157	183	Cap-Vert
114	131	143	155	195	168	184	215	Côte d'Ivoire
112	126	133	146	176	164	181	212	Gambie
112	124	133	144	167	153	162	180	Ghana
116	127	135	147	174	156	168	200	Guinée
116	140	151	167	212	182	193	225	Guinée-Bissau
90	85	93	104	133	146	162	166	Libéria
111	124	131	144	169	151	164	193	Mali
111	117	126	141	166	148	163	193	Mauritanie
116	125	131	142	166	151	157	179	Niger
112	121	129	141	160	148	154	174	Nigéria
113	128	141	148	168	157	181	213	Sainte-Hélène
118	134	144	160	201	172	189	226	Sénégal
123	149	166	184	233	189	215	264	Sierra Leone
281	330	355	383	450	416	461	531	Togo

Pour les sources et les notes, se reporter à la fin du tableau.

4

Region, country or territory	Exports (1) - Exportations (1)							
	2004	2005	2006	2007	2008	2009	2010	2011
Developing economies: America	111	126	142	156	182	157	181	216
Caribbean	*119*	*147*	*171*	*189*	*241*	*195*	*218*	*266*
Anguilla	108	117	142	147	158	152	151	162
Antigua and Barbuda	92	91	100	111	139	140	143	155
Aruba	131	191	225	247	325	209	239	323
Bahamas	107	117	127	137	168	136	159	202
Barbados	120	146	162	172	203	190	203	232
British Virgin Islands	102	..	..	..	..	..	..	..
Cayman Islands	95	93	102	113	136	148	163	165
Cuba	142	152	196	233	232	220	271	313
Curaçao	–	–	–	–	–	–	–	(a)307
Dominica	118	124	133	140	162	165	169	186
Dominican Republic	103	107	111	121	128	119	125	135
Grenada	96	94	104	119	140	132	145	172
Haiti	105	110	112	115	119	131	130	133
Jamaica	115	115	130	161	160	107	128	153
Montserrat	106	113	116	124	132	121	122	135
Netherlands Antilles	122	170	196	214	276	197	236	–
Saint Kitts and Nevis	97	100	102	106	108	106	106	109
Saint Lucia	116	148	168	177	205	178	193	227
Saint Vincent and the Grenadines	103	100	109	121	155	167	181	191
Trinidad and Tobago	126	171	208	223	325	232	254	343
Turks and Caicos Islands	93	94	95	99	106	102	107	121
Central America	*106*	*113*	*119*	*127*	*135*	*125*	*133*	*149*
Belize	102	114	130	132	152	142	161	194
Costa Rica	95	95	95	96	98	92	90	93
El Salvador	99	104	107	113	117	112	116	126
Guatemala	99	107	112	119	131	127	137	155
Honduras	83	91	95	99	107	100	113	137
Mexico	108	115	121	129	138	127	136	152
Nicaragua	90	98	102	106	115	111	121	137
Panama (2)	101	104	106	110	116	113	117	125
South America	*114*	*133*	*159*	*177*	*217*	*179*	*217*	*269*
Argentina	111	113	122	137	171	142	149	177
Bolivia (Plurinational State of)	113	130	176	199	213	196	237	288
Brazil	107	120	135	150	189	164	197	250
Chile	125	152	210	227	225	191	248	285
Colombia	108	124	135	155	188	150	182	225
Ecuador	97	119	139	153	189	146	175	213
Falkland Islands (Malvinas)	81	83	86	88	96	87	97	121
Guyana	109	125	152	151	193	196	227	271
Paraguay	108	107	109	120	141	125	131	146
Peru	121	143	195	223	235	205	267	326
Suriname	114	126	162	172	197	180	223	275
Uruguay	103	106	113	124	163	136	153	177
Venezuela (Bolivarian Rep. of)	128	174	214	244	334	223	281	373
Developing economies: Asia	103	113	119	127	143	128	140	156
Eastern Asia	*95*	*97*	*98*	*101*	*106*	*100*	*105*	*113*
China	101	102	104	107	113	111	112	119
China, Hong Kong SAR	95	96	97	99	103	104	109	118
China, Macao SAR	102	103	105	108	112	110	116	123
China, Taiwan Province of	86	91	91	93	98	84	93	102
Korea, Dem. People's Rep. of	102	113	122	129	157	151	153	184
Korea, Republic of	92	93	93	96	101	84	94	101
Mongolia	139	166	245	269	343	286	375	463
Southern Asia	*118*	*139*	*153*	*170*	*203*	*174*	*213*	*258*
Afghanistan	132	144	160	178	211	205	231	268
Bangladesh	100	101	101	103	108	111	114	127
Bhutan	143	165	184	187	253	210	235	292
India	116	130	137	158	175	159	200	239
Iran (Islamic Rep. of)	132	182	217	239	325	219	271	350
Maldives	105	117	134	122	144	143	161	183
Nepal	110	116	128	138	151	144	156	191
Pakistan	103	103	106	110	123	120	134	157
Sri Lanka	100	104	109	112	123	126	132	148
South-Eastern Asia	*99*	*107*	*115*	*120*	*137*	*125*	*136*	*153*
Brunei Darussalam	126	182	227	243	353	234	265	336
Cambodia	103	104	105	108	115	117	123	134

For sources and notes, see end of table.

		Imports (1) - Importations (1)						Régions, pays ou territoires
2004	2005	2006	2007	2008	2009	2010	2011	
107	**114**	**120**	**128**	**144**	**131**	**138**	**156**	**Économies en développement : Amérique**
113	*127*	*136*	*147*	*175*	*153*	*168*	*198*	*Caraïbes*
111	124	132	140	154	150	158	174	Anguilla
106	111	120	132	164	171	189	206	Antigua-et-Barbuda
126	158	179	196	231	211	230	273	Aruba
113	126	134	144	164	145	158	186	Bahamas
112	125	134	145	169	153	175	209	Barbade
118	..	..	..	..	..	..	..	Îles Vierges britanniques
105	104	112	126	167	178	197	212	Îles Caïmanes
107	117	119	135	163	143	158	189	Cuba
–	–	–	–	–	–	–	(a)307	Curaçao
114	124	130	142	158	142	153	178	Dominique
107	112	117	123	137	118	128	146	République dominicaine
110	118	122	132	148	134	145	168	Grenade
110	119	126	133	192	163	167	206	Haïti
116	134	145	157	191	163	181	222	Jamaïque
116	128	136	145	168	133	..	..	Montserrat
126	169	197	215	267	216	249	–	Antilles néerlandaises
112	120	125	134	145	138	115	163	Saint-Kitts-et-Nevis
110	133	146	160	212	152	187	239	Sainte-Lucie
112	122	129	140	159	141	153	178	Saint-Vincent-et-les Grenadines
116	139	153	167	202	175	193	225	Trinité-et-Tobago
111	119	124	133	148	136	145	164	Îles Turques et Caïques
106	*111*	*116*	*123*	*132*	*124*	*130*	*142*	*Amérique centrale*
115	131	140	151	177	151	160	185	Belize
103	107	110	113	119	109	111	119	Costa Rica
102	108	112	119	127	118	127	139	El Salvador
108	117	125	136	153	136	149	171	Guatemala
96	104	114	122	140	122	134	153	Honduras
106	111	116	123	131	124	129	141	Mexique
109	120	129	135	153	135	145	165	Nicaragua
106	111	117	122	135	126	132	145	Panama (2)
106	*115*	*122*	*130*	*152*	*135*	*142*	*163*	*Amérique du Sud*
102	105	108	116	128	112	118	131	Argentine
109	117	126	140	148	141	151	164	Bolivie (État plurinational de)
109	121	130	140	171	152	158	185	Brésil
100	109	115	120	137	115	122	134	Chili
105	111	117	125	136	126	135	158	Colombie
106	116	126	135	153	133	145	164	Équateur
102	108	115	122	136	117	124	144	Îles Falkland (Malvinas)
116	133	142	156	181	160	175	209	Guyana
104	110	114	120	132	119	125	136	Paraguay
109	119	128	142	172	159	175	205	Pérou
113	129	138	148	169	151	162	194	Suriname
103	117	128	139	174	141	153	175	Uruguay
108	113	116	121	134	123	130	144	Venezuela (Rép. bolivarienne du)
107	**114**	**121**	**129**	**147**	**132**	**144**	**163**	**Économies en développement : Asie**
104	*111*	*118*	*124*	*142*	*126*	*137*	*154*	*Asie orientale*
108	117	124	131	152	137	146	164	Chine
96	98	100	103	107	107	114	123	Chine (RAS de Hong Kong)
107	112	116	122	133	125	131	141	Chine (RAS de Macao)
99	109	116	124	147	121	142	162	Province chinoise de Taiwan
116	135	150	166	208	184	198	231	Corée, Rép. populaire dém. de
107	117	126	134	162	123	138	160	Corée, République de
116	133	143	155	183	161	174	204	Mongolie
127	*126*	*129*	*143*	*161*	*139*	*162*	*194*	*Asie méridionale*
109	121	128	141	166	153	159	183	Afghanistan
115	125	133	149	186	170	192	232	Bangladesh
110	120	132	147	174	157	167	193	Bhoutan
135	124	124	138	150	121	145	176	Inde
118	128	134	147	171	163	170	193	Iran (Rép. islamique d')
112	122	130	140	162	145	158	183	Maldives
118	137	152	169	204	184	203	245	Népal
122	138	151	167	214	236	266	299	Pakistan
114	124	135	147	175	156	173	205	Sri Lanka
103	*112*	*121*	*127*	*143*	*132*	*142*	*161*	*Asie du Sud-Est*
110	114	118	130	145	139	147	168	Brunéi Darussalam
109	117	123	131	150	138	158	189	Cambodge

Pour les sources et les notes, se reporter à la fin du tableau.

Region, country or territory	Exports (1) - Exportations (1)							
	2004	2005	2006	2007	2008	2009	2010	2011
Indonesia	120	139	160	178	224	193	222	271
Lao People's Dem. Rep.	108	119	158	164	180	155	193	228
Malaysia	101	107	111	117	135	121	129	144
Myanmar	113	139	163	169	217	187	191	221
Philippines	74	83	87	88	91	88	89	97
Singapore	93	96	103	104	113	100	108	120
Thailand	105	113	118	125	138	138	151	160
Viet Nam	109	124	134	141	169	158	170	199
Western Asia	*131*	*175*	*204*	*234*	*302*	*219*	*266*	*316*
Bahrain	119	151	184	198	248	187	214	255
Iraq	133	188	226	250	340	218	278	366
Jordan	114	131	143	170	261	237	207	231
Kuwait	132	185	218	240	321	212	264	343
Lebanon	116	121	132	146	167	162	174	199
Occupied Palestinian territory	112	117	121	134	148	140	149	170
Oman	129	188	231	244	378	212	287	385
Qatar	128	182	223	236	341	226	258	328
Saudi Arabia	143	206	248	313	397	252	335	358
Syrian Arab Republic	125	153	169	188	244	199	231	287
Turkey	126	133	138	155	180	151	158	176
United Arab Emirates	124	158	183	199	254	205	241	300
Yemen	131	182	217	239	321	219	269	343
Developing economies: Oceania	**124**	**141**	**202**	**227**	**274**	**217**	**271**	**341**
American Samoa	122	121	203	216	236	227	251	265
Cook Islands	104	113	121	..	..	..	..	..
Fiji	104	119	140	142	163	167	187	225
French Polynesia	102	105	109	115	121	119	124	137
Guam	120	134	149	155	177	180	195	215
Kiribati	95	99	110	121	146	143	157	185
Marshall Islands	97	91	100	111	143	152	168	177
Micronesia (Federated States of)	95	105	120	107	129	126	135	159
Nauru	113	117	124	170	805	346	354	521
New Caledonia	153	157	201	254	280	274	337	389
Niue	108	113	116	115	124	120	122	152
Northern Mariana Islands	102	103	107	114	130	130	147	158
Palau	105	117	134	118	144	139	150	175
Papua New Guinea	126	157	248	272	329	222	290	378
Samoa	100	108	116	121	128	118	130	147
Solomon Islands	127	131	142	164	178	150	170	195
Tokelau	112	109	113	120	135	133	135	188
Tonga	113	122	127	123	143	139	152	169
Vanuatu	102	107	121	111	140	139	154	177
Wallis and Futuna Islands	121	123	127	138	177	156	165	222
Transition economies	**129**	**167**	**196**	**216**	**290**	**219**	**254**	**320**
Albania	108	113	120	126	145	136	148	166
Armenia	115	124	149	160	187	168	201	232
Azerbaijan	129	173	207	227	307	202	255	333
Belarus	119	142	154	171	215	175	196	235
Bosnia and Herzegovina	116	125	137	147	165	152	164	188
Croatia	107	116	126	135	157	147	158	176
Georgia	126	135	158	175	216	205	225	257
Kazakhstan	134	181	227	254	337	243	300	384
Kyrgyzstan	127	138	153	166	191	183	206	243
Republic of Moldova	96	89	88	100	117	87	92	105
Russian Federation	131	175	207	229	312	227	265	338
Serbia and Montenegro	116	129	146	157	–	–	–	–
Tajikistan	121	133	171	177	194	147	197	240
TFYR of Macedonia	113	124	131	142	167	164	172	194
Turkmenistan	115	171	224	228	346	252	274	346
Ukraine	131	148	158	180	225	205	216	256
Uzbekistan	122	137	165	176	231	194	229	286
Developed economies: America	**107**	**113**	**118**	**125**	**134**	**125**	**133**	**145**
Bermuda	101	100	112	122	158	113	125	130
Canada	117	130	140	150	169	142	160	177
Greenland	83	88	93	92	104	99	109	134
Saint Pierre and Miquelon	100	104	111	105	132	120	137	151
United States	104	107	111	116	123	117	123	133

For sources and notes, see end of table.

			Imports (1) - Importations (1)					Régions, pays ou territoires
2004	2005	2006	2007	2008	2009	2010	2011	
114	130	142	153	181	161	174	202	Indonésie
113	126	135	145	164	148	158	183	Rép. dém. populaire lao
100	105	109	115	130	122	129	143	Malaisie
115	129	138	153	180	160	174	211	Myanmar
80	96	112	117	135	122	130	149	Philippines
104	111	119	123	135	121	130	148	Singapour
109	116	124	130	147	142	154	170	Thaïlande
115	128	139	151	175	160	171	199	Viet Nam
117	*125*	*134*	*146*	*166*	*152*	*162*	*185*	*Asie occidentale*
113	132	146	159	175	169	177	199	Bahreïn
113	121	127	140	154	145	151	173	Iraq
130	148	162	184	221	197	243	303	Jordanie
111	115	121	129	140	137	142	157	Koweït
116	130	140	152	175	159	173	203	Liban
124	145	160	172	216	178	192	215	Territoire palestinien occupé
115	121	128	138	149	142	149	167	Oman
112	116	121	129	138	136	139	154	Qatar
111	116	123	133	150	145	150	166	Arabie saoudite
115	128	138	148	172	158	170	200	République arabe syrienne
129	138	150	164	197	159	172	199	Turquie
109	114	123	131	145	141	149	168	Émirats arabes unis
116	132	145	162	191	166	180	218	Yémen
112	**126**	**134**	**145**	**172**	**155**	**167**	**195**	**Économies en développement : Océanie**
104	114	123	126	162	157	169	206	Samoa américaines
109	115	120	130	..	..	..	..	Îles Cook
113	131	142	155	183	158	175	209	Fidji
111	118	124	133	147	135	146	165	Polynésie française
121	156	177	189	226	178	204	253	Guam
113	127	136	149	183	167	182	205	Kiribati
89	82	90	101	131	148	164	166	Îles Marshall
110	115	118	127	144	138	144	163	Micronésie (États fédérés de)
112	146	159	164	200	138	155	185	Nauru
110	121	127	136	153	140	148	169	Nouvelle-Calédonie
111	123	128	138	158	140	143	168	Nioué
109	126	135	144	172	147	162	183	Îles Mariannes du Nord
112	116	120	129	149	144	149	168	Palaos
116	135	145	159	202	179	193	228	Papouasie-Nouvelle-Guinée
114	127	135	146	169	151	164	190	Samoa
116	134	145	157	201	176	188	222	Îles Salomon
106	104	106	116	145	143	147	158	Tokélaou
114	130	139	153	176	160	176	208	Tonga
108	118	125	136	167	154	167	193	Vanuatu
102	111	117	128	143	134	145	165	Îles Wallis-et-Futuna
113	**122**	**129**	**137**	**154**	**144**	**150**	**167**	**Économies en transition**
115	123	130	140	158	145	154	177	Albanie
110	123	134	144	165	151	159	181	Arménie
116	127	138	148	162	158	162	177	Azerbaïdjan
121	143	160	173	214	176	190	227	Bélarus
115	125	134	145	165	151	162	185	Bosnie-Herzégovine
112	122	131	139	161	147	156	178	Croatie
115	131	142	153	175	156	168	192	Géorgie
114	123	130	139	157	149	155	174	Kazakhstan
117	137	150	163	186	177	192	222	Kirghizistan
98	93	89	97	120	87	88	99	République de Moldova
109	114	118	125	133	130	134	145	Fédération de Russie
116	130	141	150	–	–	–	–	Serbie-et-Monténégro
120	140	158	171	207	184	203	234	Tadjikistan
118	131	142	154	183	172	188	224	LERY de Macédoine
111	115	120	128	141	139	141	156	Turkménistan
117	137	152	162	197	171	179	207	Ukraine
113	120	125	134	148	142	148	160	Ouzbékistan
103	**111**	**116**	**121**	**134**	**120**	**128**	**141**	**Économies développées : Amérique**
103	104	112	124	151	157	173	179	Bermudes
106	114	122	127	133	124	133	145	Canada
109	123	130	140	158	146	160	185	Groenland
112	116	118	126	132	132	138	148	Saint-Pierre-et-Miquelon
102	110	115	120	134	119	127	141	États-Unis

Pour les sources et les notes, se reporter à la fin du tableau.

Region, country or territory	Exports (1) - Exportations (1)							
	2004	2005	2006	2007	2008	2009	2010	2011
Developed economies: Asia	**97**	**97**	**95**	**97**	**104**	**103**	**107**	**115**
Israel	106	114	119	126	147	138	141	156
Japan	96	96	94	95	101	100	104	112
Developed economies: Europe	**128**	**132**	**138**	**155**	**168**	**152**	**153**	**169**
Andorra	100	108	125	124	133	137	139	147
Austria	109	115	120	127	137	130	135	148
Belgium	135	142	149	170	189	168	173	196
Bulgaria	133	142	162	193	224	182	193	226
Cyprus	111	120	126	135	155	142	154	178
Czech Republic	147	156	163	184	208	187	185	197
Denmark	136	143	149	162	176	158	157	172
Estonia	194	199	209	245	273	250	253	281
Faeroe Islands	104	113	135	125	148	146	161	184
Finland	117	120	126	140	145	126	124	136
France	127	126	129	142	156	143	139	151
Germany	129	130	132	147	158	147	143	157
Gibraltar	93	96	108	118	136	106	128	145
Greece	154	160	169	190	217	193	200	228
Hungary	133	134	135	148	158	138	137	149
Iceland	110	117	132	149	166	125	149	166
Ireland	122	123	124	132	135	130	127	131
Italy	142	149	158	181	204	190	192	216
Latvia	145	153	169	209	240	206	213	252
Lithuania	114	131	139	152	183	161	175	203
Luxembourg	114	118	123	135	147	134	141	164
Malta	103	103	101	102	106	104	104	109
Netherlands	126	133	141	175	173	151	154	172
Norway	127	161	193	212	266	194	219	276
Poland	138	150	160	185	209	183	221	242
Portugal	107	111	116	122	134	127	135	151
Romania	111	121	127	136	153	147	153	167
Slovakia	110	117	122	128	137	129	133	142
Slovenia	111	114	120	128	138	131	136	148
Spain	133	140	148	165	180	159	156	163
Sweden	121	124	131	148	156	138	145	161
Switzerland	110	113	117	124	132	128	130	141
United Kingdom	122	126	131	144	151	131	130	146
Developed economies: Oceania	**131**	**153**	**170**	**192**	**235**	**207**	**248**	**314**
Australia	129	153	174	195	244	212	259	328
New Zealand	141	153	148	174	182	177	181	230

Sources:
UNCTAD secretariat calculations, based on:
- ECLAC, *CEPALSTAT* external trade deflator
- IMF, *International Financial Statistics* on CD-ROM
- U.S. Bureau of Labor Statistics, external trade prices indices
- Unit value indices of Japan Customs and price indices of Bank of Japan
- UNCTAD, *UNCTADstat Commodity Price Statistics*
- UNCTAD, *UNCTADstat Merchandise Trade Matrix*
- UNCTAD secretariat estimates

Notes:
(a)   Data refer to Netherlands Antilles
(c)   From 2011 onwards, exports include commercial mining.
(1)   To improve data coverage, especially for the latest periods, the following procedure was used in the calculation of unit value indices:
   - A set of average prices indices at SITC (Revision 3, 3-digit) group level was constructed using UNCTAD, Commodity Price Statistics, international and national sources and UNCTAD secretariat estimates.
   - At the country level, unit value indices were calculated using previous year's trade values at the SITC 3-digit level, available in table 3.2 as weights.
   In some instances these indices may differ from the estimates published in official sources, since the main aim is to provide tentative estimates for most countries on a comparable basis.

(2)   From 2005 onwards, including customs free zones.

4.2.1 Indices de la valeur unitaire des exportations et importations des pays et des régions géographiques
2000 = 100

Imports (1) - Importations (1)								Régions, pays ou territoires
2004	2005	2006	2007	2008	2009	2010	2011	
105	**116**	**125**	**133**	**163**	**135**	**154**	**185**	**Économies développées : Asie**
112	120	127	138	158	134	144	165	Israël
104	115	125	132	164	135	154	186	Japon
126	**131**	**138**	**153**	**169**	**149**	**154**	**173**	**Économies développées : Europe**
106	..	..	..	..	..	..	..	Andorre
110	119	127	135	151	141	148	167	Autriche
136	143	150	168	189	164	172	196	Belgique
128	139	154	180	205	178	177	204	Bulgarie
110	121	128	137	153	139	149	172	Chypre
137	146	156	172	197	170	174	190	République tchèque
132	138	142	161	172	154	149	162	Danemark
134	140	147	165	187	168	175	198	Estonie
110	119	126	135	151	141	153	178	Îles Féroé
131	140	151	169	185	160	161	183	Finlande
122	121	128	142	159	140	142	158	France
120	123	129	143	158	138	139	158	Allemagne
122	161	186	204	263	180	219	290	Gibraltar
155	169	178	199	228	213	216	243	Grèce
134	138	141	155	168	145	143	158	Hongrie
116	124	131	148	175	148	161	184	Islande
120	121	125	136	149	134	134	152	Irlande
138	149	165	184	216	184	194	226	Italie
140	150	166	191	222	198	202	229	Lettonie
113	128	137	146	180	155	169	198	Lituanie
112	120	125	134	150	138	148	166	Luxembourg
121	129	135	145	170	160	178	204	Malte
131	133	138	156	168	147	151	170	Pays-Bas
126	132	139	158	170	151	156	176	Norvège
130	141	150	170	195	171	217	242	Pologne
111	121	129	137	156	144	153	174	Portugal
112	122	130	138	156	145	153	170	Roumanie
111	122	130	136	152	142	147	163	Slovaquie
113	122	130	139	156	143	152	171	Slovénie
131	137	143	158	175	149	149	165	Espagne
131	138	148	166	180	154	163	184	Suède
130	132	135	145	166	153	161	177	Suisse
116	120	126	138	144	125	129	144	Royaume-Uni
114	**120**	**122**	**132**	**142**	**133**	**147**	**166**	**Économies développées : Océanie**
111	117	120	128	140	130	145	163	Australie
130	136	132	153	145	146	152	173	Nouvelle-Zélande

Sources :
Calculs du secrétariat de la CNUCED, basés sur :
- CEPALC, *CEPALSTAT* déflateur du commerce extérieur
- FMI, *Statistiques financières internationales* sur CD-ROM
- Bureau des statistiques du travail des États-Unis (BLS), indices de prix du commerce extérieur
- Indices des valeurs unitaires des douanes japonaises et indices des prix de la Banque du Japon
- CNUCED, *UNCTADstat Statistiques de prix des produits de base*
- CNUCED, *UNCTADstat Matrice du commerce de marchandises*
- Estimations du secrétariat de la CNUCED

Notes :
(a) Les données se réfèrent aux Antilles néerlandaises.
(c) À partir de 2011, les exportations comprennent l'exploitation minière commerciale.
(1) Afin d'améliorer la couverture des données et spécialement pour les années récentes, la méthode suivante a été utilisée pour le calcul des valeurs unitaires :
  - Un ensemble d'indices de prix moyens au niveau des groupes de la CTCI (révision 3, position à 3 chiffres) a été construit en utilisant les données de CNUCED, Statistiques des produits de base, des sources internationales et nationales ainsi que des estimations du secrétariat de la CNUCED.
  - Au niveau des pays individuels, les indices de la valeur unitaire ont été calculés en utilisant comme pondération les valeurs des exportations et des importations de l'année précédente, disponibles dans la table 3.2.
  Dans certains cas ces indices peuvent différer des estimations publiées dans les sources officielles, le but principal étant de fournir des estimations approximatives et comparables pour la plupart des pays.
(2) À partir de 2005, y compris les zones franches douanières.

Region, country or territory	Terms of trade (1) - Termes de l'échange (1)							
	2004	2005	2006	2007	2008	2009	2010	2011
WORLD	**102**	**103**	**103**	**104**	**104**	**105**	**105**	**105**
DEVELOPING ECONOMIES	98	103	105	105	106	104	107	107
TRANSITION ECONOMIES	114	137	151	158	188	151	169	192
DEVELOPED ECONOMIES	103	101	100	101	98	102	100	98
Developing economies: Africa	**111**	**132**	**147**	**147**	**171**	**146**	**162**	**177**
Eastern Africa	*97*	*97*	*109*	*109*	*104*	*109*	*118*	*119*
Burundi	93	112	120	119	128	132	153	173
Comoros	59	54	58	65	63	67	71	76
Djibouti	96	87	89	87	87	80	79	78
Eritrea	88	86	84	83	76	76	80	(c)82
Ethiopia	102	108	107	111	111	121	129	136
Kenya	89	90	88	85	84	94	92	91
Madagascar	81	76	75	75	72	76	77	75
Malawi	84	83	87	85	80	98	99	98
Mauritius	101	92	87	86	76	81	73	71
Mayotte	97	90	89	86	83	86	80	80
Mozambique	103	107	123	118	110	97	110	107
Rwanda	115	160	167	164	224	220	235	226
Seychelles	81	78	73	68	68	75	75	75
Somalia	105	103	106	105	101	102	101	100
Uganda	93	96	98	98	101	109	113	120
United Republic of Tanzania	99	99	115	114	116	130	142	151
Zambia	114	128	195	193	173	158	190	193
Zimbabwe	101	92	98	107	96	108	111	110
Middle Africa	*119*	*156*	*176*	*179*	*218*	*156*	*186*	*213*
Angola	125	172	198	203	251	170	209	245
Cameroon	116	126	132	133	137	131	144	150
Central African Republic	101	93	91	91	82	84	86	82
Chad	118	154	175	176	214	148	182	209
Congo	117	155	179	182	221	156	185	215
Dem. Rep. of the Congo	97	114	128	127	145	114	137	147
Equatorial Guinea	120	156	177	180	233	182	200	226
Gabon	118	156	178	181	229	163	194	219
Sao Tome and Principe	129	114	107	110	117	140	137	120
Northern Africa	*111*	*140*	*157*	*153*	*186*	*148*	*162*	*176*
Algeria	115	161	188	179	233	157	177	199
Egypt	109	131	145	139	155	146	152	159
Libya	116	150	168	167	200	139	164	185
Morocco	105	99	100	98	131	136	133	141
Sudan (…2011)	116	152	173	179	224	163	197	229
Tunisia	94	94	91	91	97	97	96	95
Western Sahara	98	..	..	..	..	..	..	..
Southern Africa	*107*	*104*	*115*	*118*	*126*	*133*	*137*	*146*
Botswana	94	90	94	99	81	81	85	82
Lesotho	90	89	86	84	77	85	78	74
Namibia	100	105	132	139	127	129	121	117
South Africa	108	105	116	119	130	138	142	154
Swaziland	100	100	106	99	97	113	111	105
Western Africa	*118*	*144*	*159*	*161*	*186*	*154*	*177*	*196*
Benin	100	98	105	107	106	107	118	125
Burkina Faso	102	86	88	92	91	96	122	141
Cape Verde	88	97	100	93	95	107	105	106
Côte d'Ivoire	131	131	133	138	140	149	161	159
Gambia	101	95	97	97	101	97	98	92
Ghana	124	124	126	135	156	173	182	185
Guinea	103	106	132	130	122	98	109	110
Guinea-Bissau	83	75	82	75	74	84	84	81
Liberia	113	114	120	120	120	111	135	162
Mali	114	100	112	115	119	135	160	177
Mauritania	94	122	133	125	148	145	132	131
Niger	112	126	137	172	152	149	149	164
Nigeria	120	157	177	178	216	155	184	211
Saint Helena	80	72	67	64	59	61	56	53
Senegal	97	96	99	97	97	96	99	105
Sierra Leone	86	73	71	68	63	72	70	62
Togo	30	21	21	23	31	29	29	30

For sources and notes, see end of table.

Purchasing power of exports (2) - Pouvoir d'achat des exportations (2)								Régions, pays ou territoires
2004	2005	2006	2007	2008	2009	2010	2011	
125	**135**	**147**	**158**	**161**	**141**	**161**	**170**	**MONDE**
140	160	181	197	206	181	216	231	ÉCONOMIES EN DÉVELOPPEMENT
163	193	229	260	311	214	265	319	ÉCONOMIES EN TRANSITION
117	121	129	137	136	120	133	137	ÉCONOMIES DÉVELOPPÉES
129	**167**	**184**	**197**	**221**	**171**	**206**	**213**	**Économies en développement : Afrique**
127	*130*	*150*	*164*	*163*	*168*	*196*	*198*	*Afrique orientale*
82	91	91	89	69	84	130	136	Burundi
122	72	60	74	40	72	70	75	Comores
101	89	115	108	109	136	140	132	Djibouti
53	50	50	46	32	33	34	(c)973	Érythrée
122	152	161	182	194	223	301	289	Éthiopie
129	141	135	148	155	156	165	156	Kenya
100	78	89	110	120	85	79	96	Madagascar
113	111	140	164	138	202	173	179	Malawi
121	121	125	112	99	96	105	103	Maurice
157	189	208	204	181	168	160	145	Mayotte
363	381	489	455	409	370	469	499	Mozambique
163	191	217	237	318	246	360	442	Rwanda
125	128	131	116	120	124	113	116	Seychelles
87	111	114	126	124	128	127	130	Somalie
144	174	188	295	352	432	420	281	Ouganda
171	176	188	199	235	261	326	324	République-Unie de Tanzanie
153	162	318	361	350	336	496	530	Zambie
79	68	65	69	55	64	64	77	Zimbabwe
169	*247*	*287*	*332*	*427*	*299*	*361*	*413*	*Afrique centrale*
160	281	347	451	604	407	486	562	Angola
117	118	134	123	119	106	111	113	Cameroun
76	66	76	79	57	51	53	50	République centrafricaine
1 053	1 419	1 440	1 418	1 466	1 044	1 268	1 290	Tchad
122	161	198	168	225	167	241	254	Congo
205	236	250	261	328	282	412	410	Rép. dém. du Congo
375	536	594	686	916	673	669	800	Guinée équatoriale
129	167	174	185	253	154	224	300	Gabon
176	196	205	164	219	191	242	249	Sao Tomé-et-Principe
132	*169*	*193*	*201*	*241*	*171*	*198*	*166*	*Afrique septentrionale*
128	176	198	195	233	141	173	197	Algérie
140	178	213	226	314	305	325	323	Égypte
140	196	233	232	288	184	219	68	Libye
114	121	132	141	160	123	142	147	Maroc
186	224	253	373	452	337	444	337	Soudan (...2011)
146	147	151	181	203	165	175	163	Tunisie
..	..	..	..	..	..	..	..	Sahara occidental
115	*134*	*146*	*157*	*152*	*132*	*158*	*167*	*Afrique australe*
114	131	125	133	114	87	111	121	Botswana
292	264	275	290	300	264	282	282	Lesotho
127	138	170	178	175	185	204	187	Namibie
112	133	146	158	154	134	161	171	Afrique du Sud
180	154	147	140	108	113	114	109	Swaziland
130	*184*	*186*	*191*	*201*	*165*	*214*	*270*	*Afrique occidentale*
127	120	147	193	193	207	207	227	Bénin
210	186	222	214	200	294	396	475	Burkina Faso
124	134	147	125	185	226	266	355	Cap-Vert
156	152	153	144	136	161	147	132	Côte d'Ivoire
59	42	57	57	52	269	129	105	Gambie
131	135	167	180	189	229	294	422	Ghana
98	100	114	123	116	101	131	132	Guinée
105	103	79	103	97	107	100	174	Guinée-Bissau
35	47	50	54	53	32	45	54	Libéria
162	163	217	198	228	215	220	234	Mali
112	151	307	280	307	258	362	404	Mauritanie
133	138	137	165	194	233	234	247	Niger
132	217	212	220	240	171	244	326	Nigéria
210	175	167	185	228	218	190	193	Sainte-Hélène
138	127	117	112	119	127	124	122	Sénégal
869	816	1 069	1 021	711	947	1 220	1 496	Sierra Leone
59	55	49	50	52	60	53	57	Togo

Pour les sources et les notes, se reporter à la fin du tableau.

4

4.2.1 Terms of trade indices and purchasing power indices of exports of countries and geographical regions
2000 = 100

Region, country or territory	Terms of trade (1) - Termes de l'échange (1)							
	2004	2005	2006	2007	2008	2009	2010	2011
Developing economies: America	**104**	**110**	**118**	**121**	**126**	**120**	**131**	**139**
Caribbean	*105*	*115*	*126*	*128*	*137*	*128*	*129*	*134*
Anguilla	97	94	108	105	103	102	95	93
Antigua and Barbuda	87	82	83	84	84	82	75	75
Aruba	104	121	126	126	141	99	104	119
Bahamas	95	93	95	95	102	93	100	109
Barbados	107	117	120	119	120	124	116	111
British Virgin Islands	86	..	..	..	..	..	..	..
Cayman Islands	91	90	91	89	81	83	83	78
Cuba	133	130	164	173	143	154	172	166
Curaçao	–	–	–	–	–	–	–	(a)100
Dominica	104	101	102	99	103	116	110	104
Dominican Republic	97	96	95	98	94	101	98	92
Grenada	88	80	85	90	95	99	100	102
Haiti	96	92	89	86	62	80	78	65
Jamaica	99	86	90	102	83	66	71	69
Montserrat	91	88	86	85	78	91	..	..
Netherlands Antilles	96	101	100	99	103	92	95	–
Saint Kitts and Nevis	87	84	82	79	74	77	73	67
Saint Lucia	105	112	115	110	97	117	103	95
Saint Vincent and the Grenadines	92	81	85	86	97	119	118	107
Trinidad and Tobago	108	123	136	134	161	133	131	153
Turks and Caicos Islands	84	79	76	74	71	75	74	73
Central America	*101*	*102*	*102*	*103*	*103*	*101*	*103*	*105*
Belize	88	87	93	87	86	94	101	104
Costa Rica	92	88	86	85	82	84	81	78
El Salvador	97	97	95	95	92	95	91	90
Guatemala	92	91	90	88	86	93	92	91
Honduras	87	87	83	82	77	82	84	90
Mexico	102	104	104	105	106	103	105	108
Nicaragua	82	81	79	79	75	82	83	83
Panama (3)	95	94	91	90	86	90	88	86
South America	*107*	*116*	*131*	*136*	*143*	*133*	*152*	*165*
Argentina	109	107	113	118	133	127	127	135
Bolivia (Plurinational State of)	104	112	140	142	144	139	158	175
Brazil	98	99	104	107	110	108	125	136
Chile	125	140	183	189	165	167	204	213
Colombia	102	111	115	124	138	119	134	142
Ecuador	91	102	110	113	124	110	121	130
Falkland Islands (Malvinas)	79	77	74	72	70	74	78	84
Guyana	95	94	107	97	106	122	130	130
Paraguay	104	97	96	100	107	105	105	107
Peru	111	119	152	158	137	129	152	159
Suriname	101	97	118	116	117	119	138	142
Uruguay	100	91	89	89	94	97	100	101
Venezuela (Bolivarian Rep. of)	118	154	184	202	249	182	216	259
Developing economies: Asia	**96**	**99**	**98**	**98**	**97**	**97**	**98**	**96**
Eastern Asia	*92*	*87*	*83*	*81*	*75*	*79*	*77*	*73*
China	93	87	84	81	75	81	77	73
China, Hong Kong SAR	99	98	97	97	96	98	96	96
China, Macao SAR	96	92	91	88	84	88	89	87
China, Taiwan Province of	87	83	78	74	67	69	66	63
Korea, Dem. People's Rep. of	88	84	81	78	76	82	78	80
Korea, Republic of	85	79	74	72	62	68	68	63
Mongolia	120	125	171	173	187	178	216	227
Southern Asia	*93*	*111*	*118*	*119*	*126*	*125*	*132*	*133*
Afghanistan	122	119	125	127	127	134	145	146
Bangladesh	87	81	76	69	58	65	59	55
Bhutan	129	137	140	127	145	134	140	152
India	86	105	111	114	117	132	138	136
Iran (Islamic Rep. of)	112	142	162	163	190	135	160	181
Maldives	94	96	103	87	89	99	102	100
Nepal	93	85	84	82	74	78	77	78
Pakistan	85	75	70	66	58	51	50	52
Sri Lanka	88	83	81	76	70	81	76	72
South-Eastern Asia	*96*	*96*	*95*	*95*	*95*	*95*	*96*	*95*
Brunei Darussalam	115	160	192	187	243	168	180	201
Cambodia	94	88	85	82	76	85	78	71

For sources and notes, see end of table.

Purchasing power of exports (2) - Pouvoir d'achat des exportations (2)								Régions, pays ou territoires
2004	2005	2006	2007	2008	2009	2010	2011	
123	**139**	**158**	**166**	**172**	**145**	**175**	**193**	**Économies en développement : Amérique**
98	*106*	*124*	*115*	*117*	*80*	*85*	*100*	*Caraïbes*
134	299	230	162	185	381	199	172	Anguilla
67	92	76	55	43	37	30	32	Antigua-et-Barbuda
86	87	81	55	64	27	5	19	Aruba
74	76	91	97	101	85	77	78	Bahamas
91	106	121	133	106	91	90	82	Barbade
..	..	..	..	..	..	..	..	Îles Vierges britanniques
..	..	..	..	..	..	..	..	Îles Caïmanes
130	118	149	176	145	129	187	199	Cuba
							(a)14	Curaçao
–	63	–	–	–	–	–	35	Dominique
68	96	61	50	47	48	42	102	République dominicaine
97		98	101	86	81	92		
60	49	43	53	43	46	35	41	Grenade
112	125	124	123	79	111	109	129	Haïti
92	86	100	109	98	62	57	56	Jamaïque
327	101	86	166	216	211	..	..	Montserrat
21	18	18	16	20	19	16	–	Antilles néerlandaises
115	86	97	81	101	106	106	126	Saint-Kitts-et-Nevis
167	112	148	153	178	247	295	232	Sainte-Lucie
65	64	58	67	65	69	54	47	Saint-Vincent-et-les Grenadines
131	168	216	188	216	122	133	138	Trinité-et-Tobago
125	140	160	138	189	172	125	110	Îles Turques et Caïques
109	*120*	*133*	*137*	*138*	*117*	*143*	*154*	*Amérique centrale*
85	73	87	77	75	68	80	87	Belize
105	112	127	142	137	137	144	148	Costa Rica
110	109	113	115	124	111	121	129	El Salvador
173	169	177	188	186	195	210	226	Guatemala
142	145	139	142	133	119	128	141	Honduras
107	116	130	133	134	111	139	149	Mexique
107	111	124	137	150	161	198	216	Nicaragua
104	773	802	839	849	991	967	1 172	Panama (3)
142	*165*	*190*	*205*	*216*	*184*	*222*	*248*	*Amérique du Sud*
129	145	164	182	209	190	220	244	Argentine
160	195	250	259	387	284	340	410	Bolivie (État plurinational de)
161	177	193	208	210	183	232	252	Brésil
169	197	266	294	253	236	304	314	Chili
118	145	160	183	216	199	225	274	Colombie
148	177	205	208	250	212	244	277	Équateur
149	172	141	157	152	131	156	142	Îles Falkland (Malvinas)
102	83	82	87	87	95	100	113	Guyana
173	174	186	270	390	307	419	466	Paraguay
168	207	264	280	261	241	289	315	Pérou
180	195	215	231	261	234	315	305	Suriname
124	127	135	140	161	168	192	199	Uruguay
109	148	169	171	212	140	151	192	Venezuela (Rép. bolivarienne du)
145	**165**	**186**	**205**	**213**	**192**	**227**	**243**	**Économies en développement : Asie**
160	*178*	*202*	*228*	*224*	*213*	*256*	*268*	*Asie orientale*
220	262	314	373	378	352	435	465	Chine
134	146	157	167	168	148	170	173	Chine (RAS de Hong Kong)
104	87	87	82	59	30	26	24	Chine (RAS de Macao)
119	123	130	134	117	114	131	129	Province chinoise de Taiwan
156	140	138	144	140	153	183	226	Corée, Rép. populaire dém. de
137	141	149	161	151	170	196	202	Corée, République de
140	149	201	227	259	221	311	437	Mongolie
127	*162*	*197*	*210*	*237*	*221*	*250*	*273*	*Asie méridionale*
204	232	232	257	237	193	178	139	Afghanistan
113	117	139	131	130	139	157	165	Bangladesh
161	209	306	445	289	307	372	312	Bhoutan
134	190	232	256	307	322	363	399	Inde
133	155	202	214	235	171	210	239	Iran (Rép. islamique d')
149	121	159	149	188	107	115	174	Maldives
81	78	69	64	57	56	51	48	Népal
122	129	124	118	105	82	89	94	Pakistan
93	94	94	97	86	84	88	90	Sri Lanka
128	*135*	*148*	*158*	*161*	*143*	*172*	*179*	*Asie du Sud-Est*
118	141	165	152	189	133	155	186	Brunéi Darussalam
184	179	216	224	226	218	235	264	Cambodge

Pour les sources et les notes, se reporter à la fin du tableau.

Region, country or territory	Terms of trade (1) - Termes de l'échange (1)							
	2004	2005	2006	2007	2008	2009	2010	2011
Indonesia	105	107	113	116	124	120	127	134
Lao People's Dem. Rep.	95	94	117	114	109	104	122	125
Malaysia	101	102	102	102	104	99	100	101
Myanmar	98	108	118	110	121	117	109	105
Philippines	93	86	77	75	67	72	69	65
Singapore	89	87	86	84	83	83	83	81
Thailand	96	97	96	96	94	97	98	94
Viet Nam	95	97	96	93	97	99	99	100
Western Asia	*112*	*140*	*152*	*161*	*183*	*143*	*164*	*171*
Bahrain	105	114	126	125	142	111	121	129
Iraq	118	155	177	179	220	150	184	212
Jordan	87	88	88	92	118	120	85	76
Kuwait	120	161	181	186	230	154	186	219
Lebanon	100	93	95	96	96	102	100	98
Occupied Palestinian territory	91	81	75	78	69	79	78	79
Oman	112	156	180	177	253	149	193	231
Qatar	115	156	184	183	248	166	186	213
Saudi Arabia	129	177	201	235	266	174	223	216
Syrian Arab Republic	108	120	123	127	142	126	136	144
Turkey	98	97	92	95	91	95	92	89
United Arab Emirates	113	139	149	152	176	145	162	178
Yemen	113	137	150	148	168	132	149	157
Developing economies: Oceania	**111**	**112**	**150**	**156**	**159**	**140**	**162**	**175**
American Samoa	117	106	165	172	145	145	148	129
Cook Islands	95	99	101	..	..	..	..	..
Fiji	93	91	99	92	89	106	107	108
French Polynesia	92	88	88	86	83	88	85	83
Guam	99	86	84	82	78	101	96	85
Kiribati	84	78	81	81	80	86	86	90
Marshall Islands	109	111	111	109	109	103	103	107
Micronesia (Federated States of)	86	92	102	84	89	92	94	97
Nauru	100	80	78	103	402	251	229	281
New Caledonia	139	130	159	187	183	196	228	230
Niue	98	92	91	83	78	86	85	91
Northern Mariana Islands	94	82	79	79	75	88	90	86
Palau	94	101	112	91	97	97	101	104
Papua New Guinea	108	116	170	171	163	124	150	166
Samoa	88	85	86	83	76	78	80	78
Solomon Islands	109	98	98	104	89	86	91	88
Tokelau	106	105	106	103	93	93	91	119
Tonga	99	94	91	81	81	87	87	81
Vanuatu	95	91	97	81	83	90	92	92
Wallis and Futuna Islands	119	111	109	108	124	116	114	134
Transition economies	**114**	**137**	**151**	**158**	**188**	**151**	**169**	**192**
Albania	94	92	92	90	92	93	96	94
Armenia	105	100	112	111	113	111	127	129
Azerbaijan	112	136	150	153	189	128	157	188
Belarus	98	99	97	99	101	99	103	104
Bosnia and Herzegovina	102	100	103	101	100	100	101	101
Croatia	96	95	97	97	97	100	101	99
Georgia	109	103	112	114	124	131	134	134
Kazakhstan	118	147	175	182	215	163	194	220
Kyrgyzstan	109	101	103	101	102	104	107	109
Republic of Moldova	97	96	99	102	98	100	105	106
Russian Federation	120	153	175	184	234	175	198	234
Serbia and Montenegro	100	100	103	105	–	–	–	–
Tajikistan	100	95	108	103	94	80	97	102
TFYR of Macedonia	96	94	93	92	91	95	91	87
Turkmenistan	104	149	188	178	246	181	194	221
Ukraine	111	107	104	111	114	120	121	124
Uzbekistan	108	114	133	131	156	137	155	178
Developed economies: America	**104**	**102**	**102**	**103**	**100**	**104**	**104**	**102**
Bermuda	98	96	100	98	105	72	72	72
Canada	110	114	114	118	127	115	120	122
Greenland	76	72	71	66	66	68	68	72
Saint Pierre and Miquelon	89	90	94	84	99	91	100	102
United States	101	97	96	97	92	99	97	95

For sources and notes, see end of table.

Purchasing power of exports (2) - Pouvoir d'achat des exportations (2)								Régions, pays ou territoires
2004	2005	2006	2007	2008	2009	2010	2011	
96	101	112	118	118	113	139	152	Indonésie
97	133	198	193	201	205	334	398	Rép. dém. populaire lao
128	137	150	156	164	132	157	162	Malaisie
125	180	202	250	235	255	305	269	Myanmar
124	104	106	108	91	79	100	81	Philippines
139	151	165	176	181	162	196	201	Singapour
128	138	153	171	174	155	184	193	Thaïlande
159	176	198	222	248	248	290	328	Viet Nam
139	*175*	*197*	*212*	*252*	*195*	*229*	*269*	*Asie occidentale*
108	125	135	138	160	114	125	160	Bahreïn
81	96	118	139	202	150	169	235	Iraq
159	153	168	164	185	175	152	139	Jordanie
133	200	239	249	322	203	243	340	Koweït
266	251	282	330	357	368	407	391	Liban
63	58	57	74	64	72	75	88	Territoire palestinien occupé
103	137	149	155	223	174	217	246	Oman
145	191	244	282	349	312	456	558	Qatar
146	200	221	226	270	172	216	284	Arabie saoudite
140	155	171	168	193	148	156	116	République arabe syrienne
177	192	206	235	241	232	238	244	Turquie
167	206	238	273	332	273	317	340	Émirats arabes unis
86	104	112	96	97	93	115	132	Yémen
107	**104**	**112**	**121**	**108**	**90**	**104**	**121**	**Économies en développement : Océanie**
123	95	103	103	101	86	51	45	Samoa américaines
72	50	32	44	..	..	..	..	Îles Cook
115	100	91	90	94	74	90	76	Fidji
68	73	62	51	54	45	43	37	Polynésie française
59	45	41	65	63	39	31	23	Guam
61	95	129	183	228	332	229	271	Kiribati
245	337	217	198	169	193	181	232	Îles Marshall
74	75	69	78	87	84	80	71	Micronésie (États fédérés de)
46	9	8	32	179	53	104	85	Nauru
155	149	176	256	141	121	142	168	Nouvelle-Calédonie
55	56	311	708	4	5	5	4	Nioué
74	51	35	21	8	0	0	0	Îles Mariannes du Nord
46	105	103	76	69	71	70	62	Palaos
106	117	138	142	137	119	144	176	Papouasie-Nouvelle-Guinée
526	484	340	468	300	214	255	201	Samoa
122	112	122	151	151	136	175	264	Îles Salomon
..	..	..	..	..	..	..	..	Tokélaou
150	87	78	65	58	56	53	46	Tonga
133	123	150	140	130	142	112	131	Vanuatu
115	86	77	70	63	67	62	55	Îles Wallis-et-Futuna
163	**193**	**229**	**260**	**311**	**214**	**265**	**319**	**Économies en transition**
201	205	235	295	329	287	385	422	Albanie
221	262	256	288	218	157	216	248	Arménie
179	346	542	821	1 079	766	938	1 115	Azerbaïdjan
156	152	169	192	208	165	181	243	Bélarus
156	180	232	267	284	245	278	295	Bosnie-Herzégovine
162	162	179	201	197	161	170	157	Croatie
174	205	216	251	267	226	292	353	Géorgie
206	261	338	394	522	328	420	573	Kazakhstan
121	97	117	158	195	185	180	174	Kirghizistan
212	250	252	292	282	313	372	474	République de Moldova
159	203	245	271	337	223	285	344	Fédération de Russie
206	228	298	375	–	–	–	–	Serbie-et-Monténégro
97	81	113	109	87	70	76	68	Tadjikistan
107	118	128	162	162	119	132	148	LERY de Macédoine
139	172	239	246	338	189	184	281	Turkménistan
191	171	173	209	233	160	197	227	Ukraine
134	141	160	212	246	269	278	293	Ouzbékistan
103	**108**	**116**	**123**	**124**	**108**	**123**	**129**	**Économies développées : Amérique**
139	92	47	43	31	36	17	14	Bermudes
104	114	115	118	122	92	105	113	Canada
128	121	112	112	113	90	88	95	Groenland
43	62	228	79	57	30	26	21	Saint-Pierre-et-Miquelon
102	105	115	124	124	114	129	135	États-Unis

Pour les sources et les notes, se reporter à la fin du tableau.

4

4.2.1 Terms of trade indices and purchasing power indices of exports of countries and geographical regions
2000 = 100

Región, country or territory	Terms of trade (1) - Termes de l'échange (1)							
	2004	2005	2006	2007	2008	2009	2010	2011
Developed economies: Asia	**92**	**84**	**76**	**73**	**64**	**76**	**69**	**62**
Israel	95	95	94	91	93	103	98	95
Japan	92	83	75	72	62	74	68	60
Developed economies: Europe	**102**	**101**	**100**	**102**	**99**	**102**	**100**	**98**
Andorra	95	..	..	..	..	..	..	..
Austria	99	96	94	94	90	92	91	89
Belgium	99	99	99	101	100	103	101	100
Bulgaria	103	102	105	108	109	103	109	111
Cyprus	101	99	98	98	101	102	103	103
Czech Republic	107	106	105	107	106	110	106	104
Denmark	103	104	105	100	102	103	106	106
Estonia	144	143	143	148	146	149	144	142
Faeroe Islands	95	95	107	92	98	104	105	103
Finland	90	86	83	83	79	79	77	75
France	104	104	101	100	98	102	98	96
Germany	107	105	102	103	100	106	103	99
Gibraltar	77	60	58	58	52	59	58	50
Greece	99	95	95	96	95	91	93	94
Hungary	99	97	96	95	94	96	95	94
Iceland	95	94	101	101	95	84	92	90
Ireland	102	102	99	97	91	97	94	86
Italy	103	100	96	98	95	103	99	96
Latvia	104	102	102	109	108	104	105	110
Lithuania	101	102	102	105	102	104	104	102
Luxembourg	101	98	98	100	98	97	96	98
Malta	85	80	75	70	62	65	59	54
Netherlands	96	100	102	112	103	103	102	102
Norway	100	122	139	134	157	129	140	157
Poland	107	107	107	109	107	107	102	100
Portugal	96	92	90	89	86	88	88	87
Romania	99	99	98	98	98	101	100	98
Slovakia	99	97	94	94	90	91	90	87
Slovenia	98	94	92	92	89	91	89	86
Spain	102	102	104	105	103	107	105	99
Sweden	92	90	88	89	87	90	89	87
Switzerland	85	85	87	86	80	83	81	80
United Kingdom	105	105	104	104	105	105	101	101
Developed economies: Oceania	**115**	**128**	**140**	**146**	**166**	**156**	**169**	**189**
Australia	116	131	146	152	175	163	179	201
New Zealand	108	113	112	114	126	121	119	133

Sources:
UNCTAD secretariat calculations, based on:
- ECLAC, *CEPALSTAT* external trade deflator
- IMF, *International Financial Statistics*
- U.S. Bureau of Labor Statistics, external trade price indices
- Unit value indices of Japan Customs and price indices of Bank of Japan
- UNCTAD, *UNCTADstat Commodity Price Statistics*
- UNCTAD, *UNCTADstat Merchandise Trade Matrix*
- UNCTAD secretariat estimates

Notes:
(a)   Data refer to Netherlands Antilles.
(c)   From 2011 onwards, exports include commercial mining.
(1)   The "net barter" terms of trade, defined as the ratio of the export unit value index to the import unit value index.
(2)   The purchasing power index of exports is the value index of exports deflated by the import unit value index.
(3)   From 2005 onwards, including customs free zones.

Purchasing power of exports (2) - Pouvoir d'achat des exportations (2)								Régions, pays ou territoires
2004	2005	2006	2007	2008	2009	2010	2011	
113	**108**	**109**	**113**	**101**	**91**	**106**	**94**	**Économies développées : Asie**
110	114	117	125	123	114	129	125	Israël
114	108	108	113	100	90	104	92	Japon
122	**127**	**136**	**143**	**143**	**127**	**138**	**144**	**Économies développées : Europe**
253	..	..	..	..	..	..	..	Andorre
158	155	159	179	177	143	152	158	Autriche
120	125	130	136	132	120	126	129	Belgique
161	176	204	214	226	190	242	287	Bulgarie
90	128	109	107	111	95	99	111	Chypre
173	184	210	246	256	228	264	294	République tchèque
114	121	127	125	132	119	128	136	Danemark
115	144	172	174	173	140	173	220	Estonie
118	106	108	116	118	114	113	117	Îles Féroé
102	102	111	116	113	85	94	94	Finlande
113	117	119	121	118	105	113	116	France
137	143	156	167	165	147	164	170	Allemagne
127	98	102	117	85	115	96	72	Gibraltar
84	87	99	101	98	82	85	110	Grèce
148	163	190	220	229	204	237	253	Hongrie
132	131	139	170	162	145	151	154	Islande
113	118	112	115	109	111	113	108	Irlande
107	104	105	113	104	92	96	96	Italie
154	184	199	233	244	208	253	307	Lettonie
232	261	291	331	369	299	346	398	Lituanie
173	187	218	204	204	185	160	156	Luxembourg
85	76	85	87	84	73	83	82	Malte
117	132	144	151	163	145	163	167	Pays-Bas
108	130	146	144	169	133	140	150	Norvège
182	201	233	260	275	252	232	244	Pologne
132	130	143	157	151	126	131	139	Portugal
202	219	240	282	305	268	313	355	Roumanie
209	221	272	361	392	330	368	408	Slovaquie
166	181	204	248	250	208	219	232	Slovénie
121	122	130	139	139	133	148	163	Espagne
108	109	114	117	117	97	112	117	Suède
118	124	136	147	150	140	151	165	Suisse
105	113	125	112	112	99	111	115	Royaume-Uni
120	**137**	**154**	**165**	**198**	**173**	**213**	**240**	**Économies développées : Océanie**
122	142	161	173	209	186	230	260	Australie
114	116	125	133	154	122	148	157	Nouvelle-Zélande

Sources :
Calculs du secrétariat de la CNUCED, basés sur :
- CEPALC, *CEPALSTAT* déflateur du commerce extérieur
- FMI, *Statistiques financières internationales*
- Bureau des statistiques du travail des États-Unis (BLS), indices de prix du commerce extérieur
- Indices des valeurs unitaires des douanes japonaises et indices des prix de la Banque du Japon
- CNUCED, *UNCTADstat Statistiques de prix des produits de base*
- CNUCED, *UNCTADstat Matrice du commerce de marchandises*
- Estimations du secrétariat de la CNUCED

Notes :
(a) Les données se réfèrent aux Antilles néerlandaises.
(c) À partir de 2011, les exportations comprennent l'exploitation minière commerciale.
(1) Le terme de l'échange, appelé aussi "troc net", est le rapport de l'indice de la valeur unitaire des exportations à l'indice de la valeur unitaire des importations exprimé en pourcentage.
(2) Le pouvoir d'achat des exportations est l'indice de la valeur des exportations corrigé par l'indice de la valeur unitaire des importations.
(3) À partir de 2005, y compris les zones franches douanières.

4.2.2   Volume indices of exports and imports
of economic groupings
2000 = 100

Economic grouping	Exports (1) - Exportations (1)							
	2004	2005	2006	2007	2008	2009	2010	2011
DEVELOPING ECONOMIES	**142**	**156**	**172**	**188**	**194**	**175**	**202**	**216**
Developing economies excluding China	129	137	146	154	156	143	160	169
Developing economies excluding LDCs	142	156	173	188	194	175	202	217
High-income developing economies	131	139	150	157	160	147	165	175
Middle-income developing economies	175	204	237	273	287	249	303	329
Low-income developing economies	118	128	135	146	151	146	159	173
Heavily indebted poor countries (IMF)	136	134	138	145	148	146	154	150
Landlocked developing countries	146	152	164	191	203	182	190	207
Small island developing States	110	116	123	114	110	88	92	90
Least developed countries	*139*	*150*	*160*	*184*	*189*	*184*	*195*	*194*
Africa and Haiti	155	169	176	209	217	212	215	206
Asia	117	127	144	152	153	154	185	200
Islands	178	174	164	199	194	179	193	257
Major petroleum and gas exporters	*114*	*116*	*118*	*119*	*121*	*120*	*123*	*133*
Africa	114	129	125	133	129	123	132	121
America	93	96	92	84	85	77	70	74
Asia	117	116	120	121	125	127	130	146
Major exporters of manufactured goods	*156*	*179*	*208*	*234*	*248*	*220*	*270*	*293*
America	106	112	124	126	127	109	132	138
Asia	165	190	222	252	269	239	294	320
Emerging economies	*137*	*149*	*164*	*175*	*179*	*164*	*192*	*202*
America	121	130	138	144	142	126	144	147
Asia	145	158	177	193	200	186	220	235
Newly industrialized Asian economies	*138*	*149*	*165*	*178*	*182*	*167*	*197*	*207*
First tier	146	161	179	194	201	187	220	233
Second tier	120	124	136	144	144	126	149	155
Developing economies: Africa	**117**	**127**	**125**	**134**	**129**	**117**	**127**	**120**
Northern Africa excluding Sudan	118	120	123	129	128	112	119	93
Sub-Saharan Africa	117	131	127	137	131	121	133	136
Sub-Saharan Africa excluding South Africa	125	138	133	144	142	136	147	154
Developing economies: America	**118**	**127**	**134**	**137**	**136**	**121**	**134**	**139**
Central America and Greater Caribbean Islands excluding Puerto Rico	108	116	129	132	132	115	137	145
Central America and Greater Caribbean Islands excluding Mexico and Puerto Rico	121	148	158	167	169	158	171	191
South America and Central America	119	129	136	139	139	125	138	143
South America excluding Brazil	117	126	127	130	132	124	128	133
Developing economies: Asia	**151**	**167**	**189**	**209**	**219**	**199**	**233**	**254**
Eastern and South-Eastern Asia excluding China	138	149	165	178	182	167	197	208
Southern Asia excluding India	121	119	133	140	135	129	138	141

For sources and notes, see end of table 4.2.1 (Volume indices of exports and imports).

4.2.2   Indices du volume des exportations et importations
des groupements économiques
2000 = 100

			Imports (1) - Importations (1)					Groupements économiques
2004	2005	2006	2007	2008	2009	2010	2011	
140	**154**	**170**	**189**	**201**	**182**	**217**	**231**	**ÉCONOMIES EN DÉVELOPPEMENT**
128	141	155	171	184	162	188	198	Économies en développement sans la Chine
140	154	170	189	201	180	216	231	Économies en développement sans les PMA
126	135	148	163	170	147	171	179	Économies en développement à revenu élevé
170	186	206	231	245	227	285	309	Économies en développement à revenu intermédiaire
136	172	191	214	254	240	272	292	Économies en développement à revenu faible
145	163	178	197	216	207	225	233	Pays pauvres très endettés (FMI)
156	169	192	229	261	241	245	279	Pays en développement sans littoral
116	118	127	135	135	115	112	118	Petits États insulaires en développement
142	*161*	*175*	*197*	*220*	*229*	*233*	*239*	*Pays les moins avancés*
157	184	201	232	270	282	273	279	Afrique et Haïti
123	130	140	153	157	164	182	190	Asie
151	166	187	192	191	183	205	200	Îles
161	*182*	*199*	*246*	*287*	*262*	*268*	*276*	*Principaux exportateurs de pétrole et de gaz*
161	192	203	251	294	297	304	319	Afrique
93	127	172	227	220	196	193	209	Amérique
171	188	203	248	296	265	271	277	Asie
144	*155*	*170*	*185*	*189*	*171*	*213*	*228*	*Principaux exportateurs d'articles manufacturés*
107	114	126	132	136	109	134	143	Amérique
151	162	179	195	199	183	227	244	Asie
120	*128*	*140*	*150*	*157*	*134*	*165*	*173*	*Économies émergentes*
106	116	130	144	158	126	164	175	Amérique
127	135	145	154	158	138	167	174	Asie
129	*137*	*146*	*155*	*159*	*139*	*167*	*175*	*Économies nouvellement industrialisées d'Asie*
128	134	146	156	157	142	167	173	Première génération
132	144	147	155	164	131	167	180	Deuxième génération
135	**156**	**170**	**193**	**213**	**205**	**220**	**229**	**Économies en développement : Afrique**
125	137	141	163	208	202	210	206	Afrique septentrionale sans le Soudan
141	166	187	210	216	207	225	242	Afrique subsaharienne
147	172	188	220	239	238	249	262	Afrique subsaharienne sans l'Afrique du Sud
108	**119**	**136**	**152**	**164**	**135**	**167**	**179**	**Économies en développement : Amérique**
108	117	132	138	144	116	140	149	Amérique centrale et Grandes Antilles sans Porto Rico
115	127	153	165	175	146	163	174	Amérique centrale et Grandes Antilles sans le Mexique et Porto Rico
109	121	138	155	169	139	174	187	Amérique du Sud et Amérique centrale
113	137	161	194	219	184	225	247	Amérique du Sud sans le Brésil
150	**164**	**180**	**200**	**212**	**193**	**231**	**247**	**Économies en développement : Asie**
129	137	147	157	162	142	170	178	Asie orientale et Asie du Sud-Est sans la Chine
150	164	167	169	177	153	176	179	Asie méridionale sans l'Inde

Pour les sources et les notes, se reporter à la fin du tableau 4.2.1 (Indices du volume des exportations et importations).

4.2.2 Unit value indices of exports and imports
of economic groupings
2000 = 100

Economic grouping	Exports (1) - Exportations (1)							
	2004	2005	2006	2007	2008	2009	2010	2011
DEVELOPING ECONOMIES	**106**	**119**	**128**	**137**	**158**	**139**	**155**	**176**
Developing economies excluding China	108	123	135	146	173	146	167	194
Developing economies excluding LDCs	106	118	127	136	156	138	153	174
High-income developing economies	104	118	127	136	157	132	149	169
Middle-income developing economies	106	113	120	127	143	134	143	160
Low-income developing economies	120	145	164	182	224	189	226	277
Heavily indebted poor countries (IMF)	122	146	172	189	233	202	243	294
Landlocked developing countries	125	155	192	211	270	213	257	322
Small island developing States	117	145	179	195	258	195	222	286
Least developed countries	*121*	*152*	*178*	*193*	*247*	*194*	*232*	*288*
Africa and Haiti	125	164	197	216	284	209	260	331
Asia	110	125	136	142	166	153	164	191
Islands	107	112	122	133	149	135	151	174
Major petroleum and gas exporters	*133*	*185*	*222*	*252*	*337*	*230*	*286*	*352*
Africa	134	190	230	251	347	225	277	358
America	128	174	214	244	334	223	281	373
Asia	133	185	220	253	334	231	288	348
Major exporters of manufactured goods	*97*	*100*	*103*	*106*	*113*	*106*	*112*	*121*
America	108	115	121	129	138	127	136	152
Asia	96	98	100	103	110	104	109	118
Emerging economies	*99*	*104*	*111*	*116*	*128*	*113*	*125*	*140*
America	110	121	136	148	169	149	171	202
Asia	94	97	100	103	112	99	108	118
Newly industrialized Asian economies	*95*	*99*	*103*	*106*	*115*	*104*	*114*	*125*
First tier	92	94	96	99	104	94	102	111
Second tier	102	112	119	127	147	136	148	167
Developing economies: Africa	**133**	**168**	**199**	**218**	**290**	**226**	**267**	**335**
Northern Africa excluding Sudan	129	174	205	223	309	228	263	329
Sub-Saharan Africa	135	164	195	214	279	223	267	334
Sub-Saharan Africa excluding South Africa	129	169	202	222	292	220	269	339
Developing economies: America	**111**	**126**	**142**	**156**	**182**	**157**	**181**	**216**
Central America and Greater Caribbean Islands excluding Puerto Rico	107	114	119	128	136	126	135	150
Central America and Greater Caribbean Islands excluding Mexico and Puerto Rico	101	105	110	118	124	117	125	138
South America and Central America	111	125	141	154	180	155	179	214
South America excluding Brazil	118	142	175	196	236	188	228	279
Developing economies: Asia	**103**	**113**	**119**	**127**	**143**	**128**	**140**	**156**
Eastern and South-Eastern Asia excluding China	95	100	104	107	117	106	116	128
Southern Asia excluding India	121	150	170	184	236	186	219	272

For sources and notes, see end of table 4.2.1 (Unit value indices).

Indices de la valeur unitaire des exportations et importations des groupements économiques
2000 = 100

	Imports (1) - Importations (1)								Groupements économiques
2004	2005	2006	2007	2008	2009	2010	2011		
108	**115**	**122**	**130**	**149**	**134**	**145**	**164**		**ÉCONOMIES EN DÉVELOPPEMENT**
108	115	122	130	148	133	145	165		Économies en développement sans la Chine
108	115	122	130	148	133	144	164		Économies en développement sans les PMA
105	112	118	125	140	126	136	153		Économies en développement à revenu élevé
109	118	126	134	155	141	151	171		Économies en développement à revenu intermédiaire
121	127	133	146	167	147	165	195		Économies en développement à revenu faible
113	125	133	145	169	153	165	190		Pays pauvres très endettés (FMI)
113	123	131	142	161	149	158	180		Pays en développement sans littoral
112	127	137	149	179	156	171	202		Petits États insulaires en développement
115	*125*	*133*	*145*	*170*	*154*	*167*	*196*		*Pays les moins avancés*
115	124	132	143	165	150	161	186		Afrique et Haïti
114	126	135	149	180	163	181	217		Asie
113	126	134	146	178	162	174	202		Îles
112	*118*	*125*	*134*	*149*	*143*	*149*	*168*		*Principaux exportateurs de pétrole et de gaz*
112	119	126	139	154	145	150	170		Afrique
108	113	116	121	134	123	130	144		Amérique
112	118	125	135	150	145	151	170		Asie
104	*112*	*118*	*124*	*140*	*127*	*137*	*153*		*Principaux exportateurs d'articles manufacturés*
106	111	116	123	131	124	129	141		Amérique
104	111	118	124	141	127	137	154		Asie
105	*113*	*120*	*127*	*146*	*127*	*139*	*157*		*Économies émergentes*
106	113	119	127	142	130	136	153		Amérique
104	113	120	127	147	125	139	158		Asie
101	*109*	*116*	*122*	*138*	*123*	*135*	*152*		*Économies nouvellement industrialisées d'Asie*
101	108	115	120	136	119	131	148		Première génération
102	111	120	126	145	135	145	163		Deuxième génération
120	**127**	**135**	**148**	**170**	**154**	**165**	**189**		**Économies en développement : Afrique**
116	124	132	147	169	155	164	190		Afrique septentrionale sans le Soudan
122	128	137	148	170	154	165	189		Afrique subsaharienne
114	124	132	144	166	151	161	185		Afrique subsaharienne sans l'Afrique du Sud
107	**114**	**120**	**128**	**144**	**131**	**138**	**156**		**Économies en développement : Amérique**
106	112	117	124	134	125	131	145		Amérique centrale et Grandes Antilles sans Porto Rico
106	114	120	128	145	129	138	157		Amérique centrale et Grandes Antilles sans le Mexique et Porto Rico
106	113	119	127	142	129	136	153		Amérique du Sud et Amérique centrale
105	112	117	125	141	125	134	151		Amérique du Sud sans le Brésil
107	**114**	**121**	**129**	**147**	**132**	**144**	**163**		**Économies en développement : Asie**
102	110	117	123	139	124	136	154		Asie orientale et Asie du Sud-Est sans la Chine
117	129	139	152	185	181	197	228		Asie méridionale sans l'Inde

Pour les sources et les notes, se reporter à la fin du tableau 4.2.1 (Indices de la valeur unitaire).

4.2.2   Terms of trade indices and purchasing power indices
of exports of economic groupings
2000 = 100

Economic grouping	Terms of trade (1) - Termes de l'échange (1)							
	2004	2005	2006	2007	2008	2009	2010	2011
DEVELOPING ECONOMIES	**98**	**103**	**105**	**105**	**106**	**104**	**107**	**107**
Developing economies excluding China	100	107	111	112	117	110	116	118
Developing economies excluding LDCs	98	102	104	105	106	103	106	106
High-income developing economies	100	105	108	109	112	105	110	110
Middle-income developing economies	97	96	96	95	92	95	95	94
Low-income developing economies	99	114	123	124	134	128	137	142
Heavily indebted poor countries (IMF)	108	117	129	131	138	132	148	155
Landlocked developing countries	110	126	146	149	168	143	163	179
Small island developing States	105	114	131	131	145	125	130	142
Least developed countries	*105*	*122*	*134*	*133*	*145*	*126*	*139*	*147*
Africa and Haiti	109	131	150	151	172	139	162	178
Asia	96	100	101	95	92	94	91	88
Islands	95	89	91	91	84	84	87	86
Major petroleum and gas exporters	*119*	*157*	*178*	*188*	*226*	*161*	*191*	*210*
Africa	119	160	182	181	225	156	184	211
America	118	154	184	202	249	182	216	259
Asia	119	157	176	188	223	159	190	205
Major exporters of manufactured goods	*93*	*90*	*87*	*86*	*80*	*84*	*82*	*79*
America	102	104	104	105	106	103	105	108
Asia	92	88	85	84	78	82	80	76
Emerging economies	*94*	*92*	*92*	*91*	*88*	*88*	*90*	*89*
America	104	107	115	117	118	115	125	132
Asia	90	87	83	82	76	79	78	75
Newly industrialized Asian economies	*93*	*91*	*88*	*87*	*83*	*85*	*84*	*82*
First tier	91	87	84	82	77	79	78	75
Second tier	101	100	100	101	101	101	102	103
Developing economies: Africa	**111**	**132**	**147**	**147**	**171**	**146**	**162**	**177**
Northern Africa excluding Sudan	111	139	156	151	183	147	160	173
Sub-Saharan Africa	111	128	142	145	164	145	162	177
Sub-Saharan Africa excluding South Africa	113	137	152	155	176	146	167	183
Developing economies: America	**104**	**110**	**118**	**121**	**126**	**120**	**131**	**139**
Central America and Greater Caribbean Islands excluding Puerto Rico	101	102	102	103	101	100	102	104
Central America and Greater Caribbean Islands excluding Mexico and Puerto Rico	95	92	92	92	85	91	90	88
South America and Central America	104	110	119	122	127	120	132	140
South America excluding Brazil	113	127	149	157	168	151	171	186
Developing economies: Asia	**96**	**99**	**98**	**98**	**97**	**97**	**98**	**96**
Eastern and South-Eastern Asia excluding China	94	91	89	88	84	85	85	83
Southern Asia excluding India	103	116	123	121	127	103	111	120

For sources and notes, see end of table 4.2.1 (Terms of trade and purchasing power indices).

Purchasing power of exports (2) - Pouvoir d'achat des exportations (2)								Groupements économiques
2004	2005	2006	2007	2008	2009	2010	2011	
140	**160**	**181**	**197**	**206**	**181**	**216**	**231**	**ÉCONOMIES EN DÉVELOPPEMENT**
129	146	162	173	182	158	185	199	Économies en développement sans la Chine
140	160	180	196	205	181	215	231	Économies en développement sans les PMA
131	146	161	171	179	154	181	193	Économies en développement à revenu élevé
169	195	227	258	265	237	289	308	Économies en développement à revenu intermédiaire
117	147	167	181	203	187	218	245	Économies en développement à revenu faible
146	157	179	189	204	192	227	233	Pays pauvres très endettés (FMI)
160	191	240	285	341	259	309	372	Pays en développement sans littoral
115	132	160	150	160	109	120	127	Petits États insulaires en développement
146	*183*	*214*	*244*	*275*	*231*	*270*	*284*	*Pays les moins avancés*
168	222	263	316	375	295	347	367	Afrique et Haïti
113	127	146	145	141	144	168	176	Asie
169	155	150	181	162	149	168	221	Îles
135	*183*	*209*	*224*	*274*	*193*	*236*	*279*	*Principaux exportateurs de pétrole et de gaz*
136	207	228	241	291	191	244	254	Afrique
109	148	169	171	212	140	151	192	Amérique
139	181	210	227	278	202	247	299	Asie
146	*161*	*181*	*200*	*200*	*184*	*221*	*231*	*Principaux exportateurs d'articles manufacturés*
107	116	130	133	134	111	139	149	Amérique
152	168	189	211	210	196	235	245	Asie
128	*137*	*151*	*160*	*157*	*145*	*174*	*180*	*Économies émergentes*
126	139	159	168	169	145	181	194	Amérique
130	137	148	157	153	146	172	175	Asie
129	*135*	*146*	*155*	*152*	*141*	*166*	*170*	*Économies nouvellement industrialisées d'Asie*
132	140	150	160	154	147	171	175	Première génération
120	125	136	145	146	127	153	158	Deuxième génération
129	**167**	**184**	**197**	**221**	**171**	**206**	**213**	**Économies en développement : Afrique**
131	167	191	195	234	165	190	160	Afrique septentrionale sans le Soudan
129	168	181	198	215	175	215	242	Afrique subsaharienne
142	189	203	223	250	199	246	282	Afrique subsaharienne sans l'Afrique du Sud
123	**139**	**158**	**166**	**172**	**145**	**175**	**193**	**Économies en développement : Amérique**
108	118	131	135	134	115	140	150	Amérique centrale et Grandes Antilles sans Porto Rico
115	137	145	154	144	144	155	168	Amérique centrale et Grandes Antilles sans le Mexique et Porto Rico
124	142	161	170	177	150	182	200	Amérique du Sud et Amérique centrale
132	160	190	204	222	186	218	247	Amérique du Sud sans le Brésil
145	**165**	**186**	**205**	**213**	**192**	**227**	**243**	**Économies en développement : Asie**
129	136	147	156	153	143	168	173	Asie orientale et Asie du Sud-Est sans la Chine
124	138	164	168	171	132	154	169	Asie méridionale sans l'Inde

Pour les sources et les notes, se reporter à la fin du tableau 4.2.1 (Indices des termes de l'échange et du pouvoir d'achat).

4

Market / Marchés	Year / Année	MFN rate - Simple average (2) / Droit NPF - Moyenne simple (2)						MFN rate - Weighted average (3) / Droit NPF - Moyenne pondérée (3)					
		Total of non-agricultural and non-fuel products / Total des produits non-agricoles et non-pétroliers	Ores and metals / Minérais et métaux	Manufactured products / Produits manufacturés	Chemical products / Produits chimiques	Machinery and transport equipment / Machines et matériel de transport	Other manufactured products / Produits manufacturés divers	Total of non-agricultural and non-fuel products / Total des produits non-agricoles et non-pétroliers	Ores and metals / Minérais et métaux	Manufactured products / Produits manufacturés	Chemical products / Produits chimiques	Machinery and transport equipment / Machines et matériel de transport	Other manufactured products / Produits manufacturés divers
SITC Rev.3 (1) / CTCI Rév.3 (1)		5+6+7+8 +27+28-667	27+28+68	(5+6+7+8) -(667+68)	5	7	(6+8) -(667+68)	5+6+7+8 +27+28-667	27+28+68	(5+6+7+8) -(667+68)	5	7	(6+8) -(667+68)
Afghanistan	2006	6.1	5.5	6.1	5.0	5.1	6.9	5.6	7.4	5.6	4.0	5.5	6.1
	2007	6.1	5.7	6.1	5.1	5.0	6.9	6.2	6.1	6.2	4.5	6.7	6.2
	2008	6.1	5.4	6.1	5.0	4.8	7.0	6.3	4.8	6.3	4.9	6.9	5.4
Albania - Albanie	2005	6.5	3.0	6.6	2.8	2.6	9.4	7.4	0.9	7.6	3.2	4.2	10.7
	2007	5.7	2.8	5.8	2.3	2.5	8.2	6.0	1.4	6.2	2.5	3.6	8.5
	2008	5.4	3.0	5.5	2.2	1.6	8.2	5.1	1.1	5.3	2.6	1.5	8.4
	2009	5.4	1.0	5.6	2.4	1.6	8.2	4.8	0.6	5.0	2.7	1.4	8.0
	2011	5.3	1.1	5.4	2.2	1.6	8.1	4.6	1.2	4.9	2.7	1.5	7.6
Algeria - Algérie	2005	18.2	11.9	18.6	14.2	12.1	23.2	11.9	9.3	12.0	8.8	10.5	16.7
	2006	18.2	11.9	18.5	14.2	12.1	23.2	12.1	9.5	12.2	8.4	11.1	15.5
	2007	17.9	11.9	18.2	14.2	11.4	22.9	12.1	9.4	12.1	8.2	11.3	15.2
	2008	17.9	12.0	18.2	14.2	11.3	23.0	11.7	9.7	11.7	8.3	11.1	14.2
	2009	17.9	12.2	18.2	14.2	11.3	22.9	12.0	9.8	12.0	8.3	11.2	14.8
Angola	2005	6.7	7.9	6.7	5.2	3.1	8.8	5.0	6.5	5.0	7.9	2.8	9.9
	2006	6.7	7.9	6.7	5.2	3.1	8.8	5.0	6.5	5.0	7.9	2.8	9.9
	2008	6.5	7.3	6.5	5.1	2.8	8.6	6.2	8.1	6.2	8.8	3.3	10.9
	2009	6.5	7.3	6.5	5.1	2.8	8.6	5.9	8.0	5.9	8.7	3.2	10.9
Antigua and Barbuda - Antigua-et-Barbuda	2000	12.1	5.4	12.4	8.5	9.7	14.4	15.3	10.0	15.4	16.7	13.6	17.0
	2006	10.3	5.0	10.5	6.7	8.9	12.0	13.4	6.4	13.5	9.3	14.4	13.5
	2007	10.3	5.0	10.5	6.7	8.9	12.0	13.4	6.4	13.5	9.3	14.4	13.5
	2008	10.2	5.2	10.3	6.5	8.7	12.0	14.1	6.0	14.2	11.7	13.3	15.5
	2009	10.3	5.2	10.4	7.2	8.7	12.0	14.4	5.9	14.5	14.2	13.3	15.5
Argentina - Argentine	2000	15.8	9.7	16.2	11.6	14.8	18.6	15.1	8.2	15.3	12.6	15.1	18.0
	2005	11.8	6.5	12.1	8.1	8.6	15.2	12.5	4.0	12.8	8.7	14.3	13.6
	2006	11.8	6.5	12.1	8.1	8.6	15.2	12.6	4.3	13.0	8.6	14.4	13.8
	2007	11.7	6.5	12.0	8.1	8.5	15.1	12.8	4.7	13.1	8.3	14.7	13.8
	2008	10.3	6.5	10.5	8.1	7.8	13.4	11.1	4.6	11.4	8.1	12.2	12.9
	2009	10.5	6.5	10.8	8.1	8.4	13.7	13.1	3.7	13.5	7.8	16.1	13.4
	2010	13.4	6.5	13.8	8.1	8.5	18.4	13.5	4.4	13.8	8.7	15.2	15.8
	2011	10.5	6.5	10.8	8.1	8.4	13.7	13.9	4.0	14.4	8.2	17.0	13.7
Armenia - Arménie	2006	2.6	0.7	2.7	0.0	2.0	3.9	2.8	0.1	2.9	0.0	3.4	3.8
	2008	2.5	0.7	2.6	0.1	1.8	3.8	2.9	0.1	3.0	0.2	3.2	3.9
Australia - Australie	2000	5.2	1.2	5.5	2.0	3.9	7.5	4.7	2.4	4.7	1.8	4.2	7.1
	2005	4.1	1.1	4.2	1.6	3.0	5.8	3.8	2.6	3.8	1.6	3.4	5.6
	2006	4.0	1.1	4.2	1.5	3.0	5.8	3.8	2.5	3.8	1.6	3.4	5.6
	2007	4.1	1.2	4.3	1.6	3.2	5.8	4.2	2.2	4.2	1.6	4.0	5.7
	2008	4.1	1.2	4.3	1.6	3.2	5.8	4.2	2.2	4.2	1.6	4.0	5.7
	2009	4.1	1.2	4.3	1.6	3.2	5.8	4.1	2.0	4.1	1.5	4.0	5.6
	2010	3.2	1.2	3.3	1.6	2.9	4.2	3.4	2.0	3.4	1.5	3.4	4.3
	2011	3.2	1.2	3.3	1.6	2.9	4.2	3.3	1.2	3.4	1.4	3.4	4.4
Azerbaijan - Azerbaïdjan	2005	9.2	4.9	9.4	5.2	6.2	12.1	5.8	2.1	6.0	5.7	2.9	10.8
	2007	8.6	5.0	8.7	5.2	5.0	12.0	5.5	2.4	5.6	4.8	3.4	10.0
	2008	8.6	5.0	8.7	5.2	5.0	12.0	5.5	2.4	5.6	4.8	3.4	10.0
	2009	8.5	4.4	8.7	5.1	4.8	12.1	5.3	4.0	5.4	5.3	3.2	10.0
	2011	8.5	4.8	8.7	5.0	4.7	12.0	5.2	4.1	5.2	5.3	2.8	10.0
Bahamas	2006	31.1	33.0	31.0	32.8	34.3	28.9	29.7	27.3	29.7	27.1	34.5	26.5
	2010	37.8	41.7	37.6	40.2	38.0	36.6	32.5	29.3	32.6	31.5	32.0	33.5
	2011	37.7	40.7	37.6	40.2	37.9	36.5	31.5	30.9	31.5	26.7	33.0	32.7
Bahrain - Bahreïn	2005	4.9	5.0	4.9	4.8	4.9	5.0	4.9	5.0	4.9	4.3	5.0	5.0
	2006	4.9	4.9	4.9	4.7	4.9	5.0	4.9	5.0	4.9	4.3	5.0	5.0
	2007	4.8	5.0	4.8	4.6	4.6	4.9	4.8	5.0	4.7	4.1	4.8	5.0
	2008	4.8	4.8	4.8	4.6	4.5	4.9	4.6	5.0	4.6	3.5	4.5	4.9
	2009	4.8	4.8	4.8	4.6	4.5	4.9	4.5	5.0	4.5	3.6	4.2	4.9
	2011	4.8	5.2	4.8	4.7	4.5	5.0	4.8	5.2	4.7	3.8	4.6	5.1

For sources and notes, see end of table.

Pour les sources et les notes, se reporter à la fin du tableau.

Market / Marchés	Year / Année	MFN rate - Simple average (2) / Droit NPF - Moyenne simple (2)						MFN rate - Weighted average (3) / Droit NPF - Moyenne pondérée (3)					
		Total of non-agricultural and non-fuel products / Total des produits non-agricoles et non-pétroliers	Ores and metals / Minérais et métaux	Manufactured products / Produits manufacturés	Chemical products / Produits chimiques	Machinery and transport equipment / Machines et matériel de transport	Other manufactured products / Produits manufacturés divers	Total of non-agricultural and non-fuel products / Total des produits non-agricoles et non-pétroliers	Ores and metals / Minérais et métaux	Manufactured products / Produits manufacturés	Chemical products / Produits chimiques	Machinery and transport equipment / Machines et matériel de transport	Other manufactured products / Produits manufacturés divers
SITC Rev.3 (1) / CTCI Rév.3 (1)		5+6+7+8 +27+28-667	27+28+68	(5+6+7+8) -(667+68)	5	7	(6+8) -(667+68)	5+6+7+8 +27+28-667	27+28+68	(5+6+7+8) -(667+68)	5	7	(6+8) -(667+68)
Bangladesh	2000	21.9	14.9	22.2	17.0	13.6	28.1	18.5	11.7	18.7	11.7	10.8	25.9
	2005	15.2	10.5	15.5	11.5	10.7	19.1	25.5	9.5	26.0	8.7	14.7	43.0
	2006	15.2	10.5	15.5	11.5	10.7	19.1	25.5	9.5	26.0	8.7	14.7	43.0
	2007	14.4	9.7	14.7	10.2	9.8	18.5	12.9	8.7	13.0	6.8	9.4	19.1
	2008	14.3	10.4	14.5	11.1	8.6	18.3	13.9	8.6	14.0	8.0	8.9	20.1
Barbados - Barbade	2000	17.9	18.7	17.9	12.2	16.9	19.1	21.5	18.2	21.5	14.4	26.1	21.1
	2006	11.6	6.1	11.9	6.7	8.3	15.1	15.6	7.1	15.8	12.1	11.4	21.5
	2007	11.6	5.4	11.8	6.7	8.2	15.2	13.8	5.4	14.0	12.0	12.0	16.9
Belarus - Bélarus	2008	8.9	7.7	8.9	6.7	6.4	11.3	7.8	6.8	7.9	8.6	6.1	9.6
	2009	8.8	7.5	8.9	6.7	6.3	11.3	7.6	5.4	7.7	8.7	5.4	10.2
	2010	7.8	7.0	7.8	6.3	4.7	10.2	6.6	3.8	6.9	8.1	4.2	9.1
	2011	7.7	6.6	7.8	6.2	4.7	10.1	6.4	3.3	6.6	8.0	4.0	8.9
Belize	2006	10.1	4.9	10.3	6.6	8.1	12.3	11.9	8.1	11.9	9.3	10.7	13.9
	2007	10.1	4.9	10.2	6.7	8.1	12.3	11.5	8.8	11.5	9.5	10.6	13.1
	2008	10.1	4.9	10.2	6.7	8.1	12.3	11.5	8.8	11.5	9.5	10.6	13.1
	2009	10.0	4.8	10.1	7.0	7.7	12.3	9.3	4.3	9.4	8.0	6.8	13.6
	2010	10.3	4.8	10.4	7.1	7.7	12.7	10.0	4.3	10.1	8.1	6.9	14.6
	2011	9.8	4.9	10.0	6.6	7.5	12.2	12.9	11.0	12.9	9.4	9.9	15.1
Benin - Bénin	2005	13.2	8.9	13.3	7.9	9.5	16.9	12.7	6.9	12.8	4.6	11.6	15.6
	2006	13.2	8.9	13.3	7.9	9.5	16.8	12.8	6.9	12.9	4.6	11.8	15.6
	2007	13.0	9.1	13.1	8.0	9.1	16.7	12.7	7.0	12.9	4.4	11.9	15.6
	2008	13.0	8.6	13.1	8.0	8.7	16.5	17.6	10.7	17.6	6.8	16.3	19.1
	2009	13.0	8.4	13.1	8.0	8.7	16.5	17.6	10.2	17.6	6.9	16.3	19.0
	2010	12.7	8.4	12.8	7.6	8.6	16.3	17.1	9.1	17.2	6.5	15.4	19.2
	2011	12.8	8.5	12.9	7.6	8.6	16.3	17.2	9.1	17.2	7.8	16.1	19.1
Bermuda - Bermudes	2005	19.5	19.8	19.5	17.8	24.2	17.6	28.2	21.9	28.2	13.8	31.0	14.8
	2007	19.7	20.4	19.7	18.3	24.6	17.7	30.8	21.7	30.8	13.8	31.9	16.3
	2008	19.7	20.9	19.7	17.9	24.9	17.7	31.0	22.2	31.4	13.6	33.4	15.8
	2009	19.6	20.9	19.6	17.9	24.6	17.7	28.8	22.2	28.9	13.6	30.3	15.9
	2010	19.6	20.2	19.6	18.2	24.2	17.8	27.7	21.0	27.7	13.8	29.9	16.8
	2011	19.3	19.5	19.3	18.9	23.8	17.4	18.5	17.1	18.5	13.5	29.2	14.1
Bhutan - Bhoutan	2005	18.0	25.8	17.7	19.6	11.3	21.4	14.7	26.0	14.5	27.0	9.1	21.4
	2007	16.6	22.5	16.4	15.6	11.0	21.4	16.2	26.2	16.0	6.4	16.0	18.1
Bolivia (Plurinational State of) - Bolivie (État plurinational de)	2000	9.2	9.9	9.1	9.9	6.9	9.9	8.2	10.0	8.2	9.7	6.4	9.7
	2005	8.2	8.5	8.1	7.7	5.7	9.4	8.4	9.5	8.4	9.5	6.6	9.5
	2006	8.1	8.5	8.1	7.6	5.7	9.4	8.1	9.5	8.1	9.4	6.3	9.5
	2007	8.0	8.5	8.0	7.5	5.5	9.3	8.1	9.4	8.1	9.3	6.5	9.5
	2008	8.0	8.5	8.0	7.5	5.5	9.3	8.0	9.4	7.9	9.2	6.3	9.5
	2009	9.8	6.9	10.0	7.0	5.4	13.2	8.0	8.1	8.0	8.2	6.0	10.6
	2010	11.1	6.9	11.3	7.0	5.4	15.6	8.3	8.1	8.3	8.2	6.0	11.4
	2011	11.1	6.8	11.3	7.0	5.3	15.5	8.2	8.4	8.2	8.1	5.9	11.9
Bosnia and Herzegovina - Bosnie-Herzégovine	2006	6.8	2.3	7.0	3.1	6.4	8.6	7.3	3.7	7.6	5.9	7.4	8.3
	2007	6.8	2.3	7.0	3.1	6.4	8.6	7.3	3.7	7.6	6.0	7.5	8.2
	2008	6.5	2.3	6.7	3.1	5.9	8.4	7.2	3.5	7.5	5.9	7.6	8.0
	2009	6.5	2.3	6.7	3.1	5.9	8.3	7.3	4.6	7.5	6.0	7.4	8.2
	2010	6.5	2.2	6.7	3.0	5.9	8.4	7.3	4.3	7.4	5.9	7.4	8.2
	2011	6.5	2.3	6.7	3.1	5.9	8.3	7.1	4.5	7.2	5.7	7.3	7.9
Botswana	2005	11.5	2.5	11.7	5.2	4.0	16.8	12.0	0.1	13.6	1.0	10.7	22.7
	2006	11.4	2.5	11.6	5.2	4.0	16.8	14.8	0.1	13.4	1.0	10.3	22.7
	2007	10.7	2.0	10.9	6.3	4.1	15.6	13.1	0.7	13.2	1.2	5.2	26.4
	2008	10.8	2.3	11.0	6.0	3.8	15.9	14.3	0.4	14.4	1.4	5.0	26.5
	2009	10.6	2.0	10.9	6.0	3.8	15.6	13.9	0.4	13.9	1.5	7.1	23.1
	2010	10.5	1.1	10.7	4.9	3.6	15.6	8.0	0.2	8.0	0.9	2.5	17.2
	2011	10.0	1.1	10.2	4.1	3.7	14.8	4.6	0.2	4.7	1.3	4.8	4.8

For sources and notes, see end of table.

Pour les sources et les notes, se reporter à la fin du tableau.

4.3 Average applied import MFN tariff rates on non-agricultural and non-fuel products

4.3 Droits de douane moyens NPF appliqués à l'importation des produits non-agricoles et non-pétroliers

Market Marchés	Year Année	MFN rate - Simple average (2) / Droit NPF - Moyenne simple (2)						MFN rate - Weighted average (3) / Droit NPF - Moyenne pondérée (3)					
		Total of non-agricultural and non-fuel products Total des produits non-agricoles et non-pétroliers	of which: / dont :					Total of non-agricultural and non-fuel products Total des produits non-agricoles et non-pétroliers	of which: / dont :				
			Ores and metals Minérais et métaux	Manu-factured products Produits manu-facturés	Of which: / dont :				Ores and metals Minérais et métaux	Manu-factured products Produits manu-facturés	Of which: / dont :		
					Chemical products Produits chimiques	Machinery and transport equipment Machines et matériel de transport	Other manu-factured products Produits manu-facturés divers				Chemical products Produits chimiques	Machinery and transport equipment Machines et matériel de transport	Other manu-factured products Produits manu-facturés divers
SITC Rev.3 (1) / CTCI Rév.3 (1)		5+6+7+8 +27+28-667	27+28+68	(5+6+7+8) -(667+68)	5	7	(6+8) -(667+68)	5+6+7+8 +27+28-667	27+28+68	(5+6+7+8) -(667+68)	5	7	(6+8) -(667+68)
Brazil - Brésil	2000	16.4	9.3	16.8	11.6	17.6	18.6	14.7	8.2	15.0	11.1	16.1	16.5
	2005	13.1	6.1	13.5	8.3	13.9	15.5	10.5	4.7	10.8	7.4	11.5	13.5
	2006	13.0	6.0	13.5	8.2	13.6	15.5	10.5	4.7	10.9	7.4	11.6	13.2
	2007	13.0	6.0	13.4	8.2	13.7	15.4	11.0	4.8	11.5	6.8	13.6	13.2
	2008	14.2	6.0	14.7	8.2	13.7	17.7	11.1	4.2	11.5	6.1	13.9	13.8
	2009	14.8	6.1	15.3	8.1	13.8	18.7	12.2	5.0	12.5	6.9	14.5	14.7
	2010	14.9	6.1	15.4	8.1	13.7	19.0	12.3	5.0	12.6	6.9	14.5	15.1
	2011	14.9	6.1	15.4	8.1	13.8	18.9	13.0	5.2	13.4	6.8	15.9	15.8
Brunei Darussalam - Brunéi Darussalam	2005	3.7	0.1	3.8	0.5	9.7	2.1	6.5	0.0	6.6	0.9	11.4	2.5
	2006	3.7	0.1	3.8	0.5	9.7	2.1	6.5	0.0	6.6	0.9	11.4	2.5
	2007	3.8	0.1	3.9	0.5	10.0	2.1	6.3	0.0	6.3	1.1	10.0	2.7
	2008	3.5	0.0	3.6	0.5	9.1	2.0	4.2	0.0	4.3	1.1	5.8	2.7
	2010	3.5	0.1	3.6	0.5	9.4	1.9	4.9	0.0	5.0	1.2	7.2	2.9
Bulgaria - Bulgarie (4)	2005	9.3	3.3	9.6	7.5	5.9	11.9	8.2	1.5	8.9	7.2	6.8	12.0
	2006	9.4	3.4	9.7	7.4	6.3	12.0	8.1	1.4	9.0	6.9	7.2	11.9
Burkina Faso	2005	12.7	8.6	12.9	7.4	9.3	16.3	12.6	8.4	12.6	5.9	13.8	14.8
	2006	12.7	8.6	12.9	7.4	9.3	16.3	12.7	8.4	12.7	5.9	14.0	14.8
	2007	12.6	8.9	12.7	7.5	8.7	16.2	12.6	8.5	12.7	5.1	14.0	14.6
	2008	12.4	8.6	12.5	7.9	8.7	16.2	9.9	8.2	9.9	6.0	9.0	16.1
	2009	12.3	8.7	12.4	7.8	8.7	16.2	9.7	8.3	9.8	5.8	8.8	16.0
	2010	12.5	8.8	12.7	7.6	8.6	16.2	10.5	7.2	10.5	5.0	10.2	14.0
	2011	12.5	8.6	12.6	7.4	8.4	16.3	10.4	7.7	10.5	4.5	10.4	13.8
Burundi	2005	18.6	11.1	18.7	16.0	15.5	21.5	17.9	14.9	18.0	15.8	16.5	21.2
	2006	14.6	5.8	14.8	11.2	10.2	18.2	15.5	5.4	16.2	14.1	15.6	17.7
	2007	14.8	6.0	15.0	11.9	10.3	18.1	14.0	9.2	14.1	14.2	15.0	13.0
	2008	14.7	5.8	14.8	11.9	10.3	17.8	13.6	8.5	13.6	14.5	13.0	13.7
	2009	12.8	10.7	12.9	6.8	7.3	17.7	16.4	16.6	16.4	6.3	8.1	24.1
	2010	12.5	12.0	12.5	6.3	7.3	17.7	14.6	19.3	14.5	5.6	7.5	22.9
	2011	13.0	9.4	13.1	6.4	6.8	17.8	12.1	16.9	12.1	4.6	8.4	18.6
Cambodia - Cambodge	2005	14.5	9.3	14.6	9.8	17.4	14.8	10.9	9.9	10.9	6.0	16.4	10.2
	2007	14.3	9.3	14.5	9.8	17.3	14.5	10.9	9.9	10.9	6.0	16.4	10.2
	2008	14.5	8.9	14.6	10.1	17.2	14.8	11.2	11.3	11.2	5.9	16.7	9.1
Cameroon - Cameroun	2005	18.0	10.9	18.3	11.3	14.4	22.5	14.8	10.7	15.1	7.8	16.5	17.7
	2007	17.4	11.0	17.7	11.2	13.9	22.0	14.3	10.4	14.6	8.9	16.7	16.1
	2009	17.7	10.7	18.0	11.6	13.9	22.1	15.8	13.9	15.9	8.5	16.0	18.9
	2011	17.8	10.7	18.1	11.3	14.4	22.2	14.2	10.5	14.3	8.1	15.5	16.5
Canada	2000	4.7	0.7	5.0	2.9	2.1	7.0	3.1	0.6	3.2	3.3	2.5	4.7
	2005	4.2	0.7	4.4	2.6	2.2	6.0	3.1	0.6	3.2	2.6	2.8	4.2
	2006	3.9	0.7	4.1	2.5	2.2	5.6	3.1	0.6	3.2	2.7	2.8	4.2
	2007	3.9	0.7	4.1	2.6	2.2	5.5	3.3	0.6	3.4	2.6	3.0	4.4
	2008	3.9	0.7	4.1	2.6	2.3	5.5	3.3	0.6	3.4	2.6	3.0	4.4
	2009	3.8	0.7	4.0	2.6	1.7	5.5	3.1	0.7	3.2	2.3	2.6	4.7
	2010	2.8	0.0	2.9	0.8	1.3	4.5	2.7	0.0	2.8	1.3	2.4	4.2
Cape Verde - Cap-Vert	2005	12.6	1.4	12.9	5.1	9.1	16.6	13.4	1.5	13.5	11.4	12.9	14.6
	2007	11.5	1.2	11.8	4.9	7.9	15.7	9.5	0.1	10.8	11.8	8.4	12.9
	2008	12.0	1.4	12.4	4.9	7.9	16.4	11.6	1.7	11.8	9.6	12.4	11.9
	2009	12.1	1.7	12.4	4.8	7.7	16.5	11.4	2.1	11.6	8.9	10.5	13.4
	2010	11.6	1.7	11.9	4.8	6.7	16.2	10.8	2.1	11.0	8.6	9.8	12.8
	2011	11.5	1.2	11.8	4.9	6.7	16.0	9.6	2.1	9.7	9.1	8.1	11.6
Central African Republic - République centrafricaine	2005	18.8	13.3	18.9	13.3	15.7	22.1	15.4	22.2	15.2	7.5	15.7	18.9
	2007	17.8	12.7	18.0	12.1	15.0	21.5	13.4	13.3	13.4	7.0	14.2	17.8

For sources and notes, see end of table.

Pour les sources et les notes, se reporter à la fin du tableau.

Market / Marchés	Year / Année	MFN rate - Simple average (2) / Droit NPF - Moyenne simple (2)						MFN rate - Weighted average (3) / Droit NPF - Moyenne pondérée (3)					
		Total of non-agricultural and non-fuel products / Total des produits non-agricoles et non-pétroliers	Ores and metals / Minérais et métaux	Manu-factured products / Produits manu-facturés	of which: / dont : Chemical products / Produits chimiques	Machinery and transport equipment / Machines et matériel de transport	Other manu-factured products / Produits manu-facturés divers	Total of non-agricultural and non-fuel products / Total des produits non-agricoles et non-pétroliers	Ores and metals / Minérais et métaux	Manu-factured products / Produits manu-facturés	of which: / dont : Chemical products / Produits chimiques	Machinery and transport equipment / Machines et matériel de transport	Other manu-factured products / Produits manu-facturés divers
SITC Rev.3 (1) / CTCI Rév.3 (1)		5+6+7+8 +27+28-667	27+28+68	(5+6+7+8) -(667+68)	5	7	(6+8) -(667+68)	5+6+7+8 +27+28-667	27+28+68	(5+6+7+8) -(667+68)	5	7	(6+8) -(667+68)
Chad - Tchad	2005	17.9	13.6	18.0	13.0	14.9	21.7	11.4	14.5	11.3	9.1	10.6	16.0
	2007	17.5	12.7	17.6	12.9	14.4	21.3	12.6	8.9	12.7	8.1	12.2	17.7
	2009	17.4	11.3	17.5	12.5	14.3	21.3	13.8	6.8	13.9	9.2	13.2	17.8
	2011	17.7	11.0	17.8	12.5	14.1	21.5	14.3	8.8	14.3	9.5	13.0	18.3
Chile - Chili	2000	9.0	9.0	9.0	9.0	9.0	9.0	9.0	9.0	9.0	9.0	9.0	9.0
	2005	6.0	6.0	6.0	6.0	6.0	6.0	6.0	6.0	6.0	6.0	6.0	6.0
	2006	6.0	6.0	6.0	6.0	6.0	6.0	6.0	6.0	6.0	6.0	5.9	6.0
	2007	6.0	6.0	6.0	6.0	6.0	6.0	6.0	6.0	6.0	6.0	5.9	6.0
	2008	6.0	6.0	6.0	6.0	6.0	6.0	6.0	6.0	6.0	6.0	5.9	6.0
	2009	6.0	6.0	6.0	6.0	5.9	6.0	6.0	6.0	6.0	6.0	5.9	6.0
	2010	6.0	6.0	6.0	6.0	5.9	6.0	6.0	6.0	6.0	6.0	6.0	6.0
China - Chine	2000	15.9	5.3	16.5	11.2	16.2	18.7	13.0	5.2	13.7	13.0	12.6	16.1
	2005	9.2	3.7	9.6	6.9	9.2	10.8	5.0	1.8	5.4	7.3	4.0	7.3
	2006	9.1	3.6	9.5	6.8	9.0	10.7	4.3	1.3	4.7	6.3	3.4	7.0
	2007	9.2	3.7	9.6	6.9	8.9	10.9	5.6	1.5	6.4	6.4	5.5	7.9
	2008	8.9	3.4	9.3	6.6	8.4	10.8	5.1	0.7	6.1	5.9	5.1	7.7
	2009	8.9	3.3	9.3	6.6	8.4	10.7	5.1	0.5	6.3	6.0	5.6	7.6
	2010	9.0	3.3	9.3	6.5	8.6	10.7	5.3	0.4	6.6	5.8	6.2	7.9
	2011	9.0	3.3	9.3	6.5	8.6	10.7	5.2	0.3	6.9	5.6	7.0	7.8
China, Taiwan Province of - Province chinoise de Taiwan	2000	6.1	1.6	6.4	3.9	6.0	7.5	2.9	1.4	3.0	3.4	2.5	4.1
	2005	4.5	0.9	4.7	2.8	4.5	5.5	2.3	0.6	2.4	1.9	2.7	2.2
	2006	4.4	0.9	4.6	2.9	4.4	5.4	2.3	0.6	2.4	2.0	2.6	2.2
	2007	4.3	0.9	4.5	2.8	4.1	5.4	1.8	0.5	1.9	1.9	1.7	2.3
	2008	4.3	0.9	4.5	2.8	4.0	5.4	1.7	0.4	1.9	1.8	1.8	2.2
	2009	4.3	0.8	4.6	2.8	4.1	5.5	2.4	0.6	2.7	1.8	3.4	2.6
	2010	4.3	0.9	4.6	2.8	4.1	5.4	2.6	0.5	2.9	2.0	3.8	2.7
Colombia - Colombie	2000	11.9	6.7	12.2	8.1	10.0	14.8	10.5	6.6	10.6	8.0	10.7	13.0
	2005	11.9	6.5	12.2	8.1	9.8	14.9	10.7	6.4	10.9	8.2	10.9	13.2
	2006	11.9	6.5	12.2	8.1	9.9	14.9	11.1	6.2	11.3	8.4	11.7	13.2
	2007	11.9	6.5	12.2	8.1	9.8	14.8	11.8	6.1	12.1	8.5	13.0	13.1
	2008	11.8	6.6	12.1	8.1	9.7	14.8	12.1	6.1	12.4	8.5	14.0	13.1
	2009	11.8	6.5	12.2	8.0	9.8	14.8	10.6	6.8	10.7	7.7	10.7	13.3
	2010	11.9	6.5	12.2	8.0	9.9	14.8	10.5	6.8	10.6	7.5	10.7	13.3
	2011	7.3	4.8	7.4	5.6	6.4	8.6	8.8	4.9	8.9	5.5	11.0	8.0
Comoros - Comores	2008	11.5	14.5	11.5	11.3	13.3	10.5	11.2	13.0	11.2	7.9	12.4	10.4
	2010	11.4	13.7	11.3	11.5	13.2	10.3	12.2	11.7	12.2	5.5	13.1	11.6
	2011	11.2	14.5	11.1	10.6	13.0	10.3	8.8	13.5	8.7	9.1	12.9	6.3
Congo	2005	18.4	11.5	18.6	11.7	14.5	22.7	15.9	17.0	15.9	9.4	14.3	20.6
	2007	18.0	11.8	18.2	11.7	14.0	22.3	14.1	14.9	14.1	10.8	12.6	18.3
Cook Islands - Îles Cook	2010	0.5	0.0	0.5	0.0	2.1	0.0	1.7	0.0	1.7	0.0	4.0	0.0
Costa Rica	2000	4.8	1.6	5.0	1.4	2.2	7.5	3.8	1.6	3.9	3.1	1.9	6.9
	2005	5.1	1.3	5.3	1.4	2.3	8.0	3.6	1.3	3.7	3.0	1.9	6.8
	2007	4.9	1.3	5.1	1.5	2.1	7.8	4.0	0.9	4.1	2.8	3.1	6.0
	2009	4.6	1.3	4.7	1.4	1.8	7.3	3.5	0.9	3.5	2.3	2.0	5.7
Côte d'Ivoire	2005	12.3	8.2	12.4	6.8	8.9	16.1	10.4	7.0	10.4	5.1	8.2	15.3
	2006	12.3	8.3	12.4	6.8	8.9	16.1	10.5	7.0	10.6	5.4	9.9	14.7
	2007	12.1	8.2	12.2	6.9	8.4	16.0	10.6	7.1	10.7	5.3	10.3	14.6
	2008	12.0	8.1	12.2	6.9	8.3	15.9	9.7	6.8	9.8	5.1	10.9	12.6
	2009	12.0	8.1	12.2	6.9	8.3	15.9	9.7	6.8	9.8	5.1	10.9	12.6
	2010	12.0	8.1	12.2	6.9	8.3	16.0	9.4	7.2	9.5	5.0	10.0	12.6
	2011	11.9	7.9	12.1	6.8	8.3	15.8	9.2	6.5	9.3	4.6	10.2	12.9

For sources and notes, see end of table.   Pour les sources et les notes, se reporter à la fin du tableau.

259

Market / Marchés	Year / Année	MFN rate - Simple average (2) / Droit NPF - Moyenne simple (2)						MFN rate - Weighted average (3) / Droit NPF - Moyenne pondérée (3)					
		Total of non-agricultural and non-fuel products / Total des produits non-agricoles et non-pétroliers	of which: / dont :					Total of non-agricultural and non-fuel products / Total des produits non-agricoles et non-pétroliers	of which: / dont :				
			Ores and metals / Minérais et métaux	Manu-factured products / Produits manu-facturés	Of which: / dont :				Ores and metals / Minérais et métaux	Manu-factured products / Produits manu-facturés	Of which: / dont :		
					Chemical products / Produits chimiques	Machinery and transport equipment / Machines et matériel de transport	Other manu-factured products / Produits manu-facturés divers				Chemical products / Produits chimiques	Machinery and transport equipment / Machines et matériel de transport	Other manu-factured products / Produits manu-facturés divers
SITC Rev.3 (1) / CTCI Rév.3 (1)		5+6+7+8 +27+28-667	27+28+68	(5+6+7+8) -(667+68)	5	7	(6+8) -(667+68)	5+6+7+8 +27+28-667	27+28+68	(5+6+7+8) -(667+68)	5	7	(6+8) -(667+68)
Croatia - Croatie	2005	4.0	1.8	4.2	1.3	3.1	5.6	3.8	2.0	3.9	2.3	3.6	4.9
	2006	4.1	1.7	4.2	1.3	3.3	5.7	4.0	1.7	4.1	2.3	3.7	5.1
	2007	4.2	1.6	4.3	1.4	3.6	5.7	4.2	1.8	4.3	2.3	4.1	5.2
	2008	4.1	1.6	4.3	1.4	3.6	5.7	4.2	1.8	4.3	2.3	4.1	5.2
	2009	4.1	1.6	4.3	1.4	3.5	5.7	4.2	2.1	4.3	2.3	4.1	5.4
	2010	4.1	1.6	4.3	1.3	3.5	5.7	4.2	2.1	4.3	2.2	4.1	5.4
	2011	4.1	1.6	4.3	1.3	3.6	5.7	4.0	1.7	4.2	2.0	4.2	5.2
Cuba	2005	11.5	5.6	11.7	9.3	10.1	13.5	9.8	3.9	9.9	8.1	9.3	11.4
	2006	11.5	5.9	11.7	9.1	10.1	13.5	9.8	2.6	10.0	8.2	9.4	11.7
	2007	11.5	5.6	11.7	9.2	10.1	13.5	10.0	3.9	10.1	8.6	9.4	11.6
	2008	11.4	5.9	11.7	9.1	10.1	13.4	9.8	2.6	10.0	8.1	9.4	11.7
	2009	11.3	5.3	11.6	9.3	9.8	13.3	10.0	6.3	10.0	9.4	9.1	11.7
	2010	11.4	5.7	11.6	9.4	9.9	13.3	10.3	6.0	10.4	9.9	9.5	11.6
	2011	11.3	5.1	11.6	9.3	9.8	13.3	10.2	4.5	10.3	9.6	9.7	11.3
Dem. Rep. of the Congo - Rép. dém. du Congo	2006	12.4	9.8	12.5	9.2	8.6	15.5	11.4	8.4	11.5	14.6	8.0	14.7
	2007	12.4	9.7	12.5	8.9	8.6	15.6	11.3	9.6	11.3	14.0	7.7	15.2
	2008	12.0	8.9	12.2	8.8	8.3	15.3	10.8	6.0	11.1	13.1	7.6	15.2
	2009	12.0	8.9	12.2	8.8	8.3	15.3	10.8	6.0	11.1	13.0	7.6	15.1
Djibouti	2006	32.1	29.3	32.2	30.4	33.0	32.2	31.3	31.1	31.3	24.9	33.0	31.9
	2009	21.6	22.7	21.5	23.6	20.5	21.4	18.6	21.1	18.6	16.0	18.1	19.9
	2011	22.1	20.6	22.2	22.9	21.7	22.3	19.9	16.1	20.0	20.8	19.4	20.6
Dominica - Dominique	2000	14.1	12.8	14.1	10.6	16.1	14.6	15.0	14.4	15.0	10.3	21.8	12.5
	2006	10.5	4.4	10.6	9.3	8.0	12.1	11.9	4.7	11.9	10.0	9.9	14.6
	2007	10.2	4.4	10.4	9.3	7.7	11.8	11.7	4.6	11.7	10.7	10.7	13.0
	2011	10.0	4.4	10.2	9.6	7.0	11.7	12.6	6.6	12.6	15.5	10.4	13.6
Dominican Republic - République dominicaine	2000	18.2	10.2	18.5	10.4	13.4	24.1	17.5	13.6	17.6	9.8	17.8	21.3
	2005	8.1	4.7	8.3	4.9	5.5	10.7	9.1	5.1	9.2	6.2	8.1	10.7
	2006	8.3	5.0	8.4	4.7	5.5	11.1	8.8	5.2	8.8	5.2	8.9	9.9
	2007	6.5	2.7	6.6	2.5	3.2	9.8	7.7	3.1	7.8	3.7	8.3	8.7
	2008	8.1	5.2	8.2	4.9	5.1	10.9	8.7	5.5	8.7	5.3	9.0	9.8
	2010	6.3	2.1	6.5	2.4	3.2	9.4	7.5	6.1	7.5	3.8	7.2	9.2
Ecuador - Équateur	2005	11.5	6.0	11.7	7.2	8.3	15.0	10.3	6.6	10.4	7.1	10.5	12.5
	2006	11.5	6.0	11.8	7.2	8.4	15.0	10.3	6.9	10.4	7.2	10.5	12.4
	2007	11.5	6.0	11.8	7.2	8.4	15.0	10.2	6.6	10.2	7.3	10.1	12.5
	2008	10.8	4.4	11.1	4.7	6.2	15.9	8.5	6.1	8.5	5.0	8.5	10.9
	2009	10.1	1.1	10.6	3.1	4.8	16.1	7.3	2.7	7.3	4.6	6.8	10.2
	2010	10.1	1.1	10.6	3.1	4.8	16.1	7.2	2.7	7.3	4.6	6.8	10.2
	2011	8.6	0.9	9.0	3.1	5.1	13.1	7.0	2.3	7.1	4.3	7.4	8.8
Egypt - Égypte	2005	13.1	5.6	13.5	6.8	8.0	18.5	11.6	2.3	12.1	16.5	10.0	13.0
	2008	10.2	5.1	10.4	6.1	7.0	13.6	9.1	1.8	10.3	10.7	11.5	8.8
	2009	10.0	4.9	10.3	5.9	6.7	13.6	8.9	1.8	10.0	10.1	11.2	8.8
El Salvador	2000	6.7	1.2	7.0	1.6	2.4	11.2	5.4	1.6	5.5	4.6	3.5	8.4
	2005	5.3	1.3	5.5	1.7	2.3	8.3	6.0	1.3	6.1	6.0	4.6	7.5
	2006	6.8	1.4	7.0	1.7	2.1	11.2	7.8	1.3	7.9	10.2	5.0	8.5
	2007	5.2	1.3	5.3	1.7	2.1	8.1	6.8	1.2	6.9	8.4	4.8	7.4
	2008	5.2	1.3	5.3	1.7	2.1	8.1	6.7	1.2	6.8	8.4	4.8	7.2
	2009	5.1	1.4	5.3	1.6	2.0	8.0	6.6	1.8	6.7	5.9	4.0	8.4
	2010	5.1	1.4	5.3	1.7	2.0	8.0	6.6	1.8	6.7	5.9	4.0	8.4
Equatorial Guinea - Guinée équatoriale	2005	18.5	12.1	18.7	13.0	14.6	22.4	14.3	9.9	14.3	16.4	12.9	18.3
	2007	18.0	11.0	18.2	12.6	14.3	21.9	14.3	11.5	14.3	14.2	12.1	18.7
Eritrea - Érythrée	2006	8.7	2.2	9.0	3.4	6.5	11.4	7.3	2.1	7.4	3.2	8.3	7.7
Estonia - Estonie (5)	2000	0.1	0.0	0.1	0.3	0.0	0.0	0.0	0.0	0.0	0.1	0.0	0.0

For sources and notes, see end of table.   Pour les sources et les notes, se reporter à la fin du tableau.

Market / Marchés	Year / Année	MFN rate - Simple average (2) / Droit NPF - Moyenne simple (2) Total of non-agricultural and non-fuel products / Total des produits non-agricoles et non-pétroliers	Ores and metals / Minérais et métaux	Manu-factured products / Produits manu-facturés	Chemical products / Produits chimiques	Machinery and transport equipment / Machines et matériel de transport	Other manu-factured products / Produits manu-facturés divers	MFN rate - Weighted average (3) / Droit NPF - Moyenne pondérée (3) Total of non-agricultural and non-fuel products / Total des produits non-agricoles et non-pétroliers	Ores and metals / Minérais et métaux	Manu-factured products / Produits manu-facturés	Chemical products / Produits chimiques	Machinery and transport equipment / Machines et matériel de transport	Other manu-factured products / Produits manu-facturés divers
SITC Rev.3 (1) / CTCI Rév.3 (1)		5+6+7+8 +27+28-667	27+28+68	(5+6+7+8) -(667+68)	5	7	(6+8) -(667+68)	5+6+7+8 +27+28-667	27+28+68	(5+6+7+8) -(667+68)	5	7	(6+8) -(667+68)
Ethiopia - Éthiopie	2006	17.3	8.5	17.7	10.8	12.1	22.8	13.8	7.0	13.9	7.3	12.9	18.7
	2008	16.9	8.3	17.3	10.7	11.3	22.7	12.7	6.9	12.8	6.5	12.1	17.2
	2009	16.9	8.3	17.3	10.7	11.3	22.7	12.7	6.9	12.8	6.5	12.1	17.2
	2010	16.9	8.3	17.3	10.6	11.3	22.7	13.1	6.7	13.2	6.5	12.1	18.3
	2011	16.8	8.3	17.2	10.4	11.2	22.7	12.9	6.9	13.0	6.5	11.3	18.5
EU - UE	2000	4.2	1.6	4.4	4.2	2.3	5.4	3.3	1.8	3.4	2.9	2.3	5.4
	2005	3.9	1.6	4.1	4.6	2.3	4.7	3.3	1.7	3.4	3.2	2.4	5.0
	2006	3.9	1.6	4.1	4.6	2.2	4.7	3.2	1.6	3.4	3.1	2.5	4.8
	2007	3.7	1.6	3.9	3.7	2.2	4.6	3.3	1.7	3.5	2.2	2.8	4.7
	2008	3.7	1.6	3.9	3.7	2.2	4.6	3.2	1.3	3.4	2.2	2.7	4.7
	2009	3.7	1.6	3.8	3.7	2.2	4.6	3.2	1.3	3.4	2.1	2.7	4.7
	2010	3.9	1.6	4.0	4.6	2.2	4.6	3.2	1.3	3.4	2.9	2.2	5.0
	2011	3.9	1.6	4.0	4.6	2.2	4.6	3.3	1.3	3.5	3.0	2.3	5.1
Fiji - Fidji	2008	9.6	5.5	9.8	6.6	7.9	11.7	10.4	5.0	10.5	7.0	9.4	12.9
	2009	10.8	5.3	10.9	7.2	8.7	12.9	12.8	5.0	12.9	7.1	13.9	14.6
	2010	10.5	5.2	10.7	6.9	8.4	12.9	12.0	5.0	12.2	8.2	11.1	14.6
	2011	10.2	5.0	10.4	6.9	8.1	12.6	11.7	5.0	11.9	7.5	11.1	14.2
French Polynesia - Polynésie française	2008	11.7	10.0	11.7	10.9	10.1	12.6	11.3	11.1	11.3	13.5	10.6	11.4
	2009	11.7	9.9	11.8	11.1	10.3	12.6	11.7	10.9	11.7	13.8	11.2	11.3
	2011	11.7	9.8	11.8	11.1	10.4	12.6	11.8	10.8	11.8	13.8	11.3	11.3
Gabon	2005	18.3	11.5	18.5	11.6	14.8	22.5	15.5	16.4	15.5	9.7	15.2	18.2
	2007	17.8	11.0	18.1	11.6	14.2	22.1	14.9	14.8	14.9	11.4	14.4	16.9
	2008	17.9	11.1	18.2	11.8	14.0	22.1	14.2	14.4	14.2	9.8	13.5	17.3
	2009	17.9	11.1	18.1	11.8	14.0	22.0	14.3	14.2	14.3	9.8	13.6	17.4
Gambia - Gambie	2007	19.3	19.0	19.3	18.5	19.1	19.5	17.0	17.7	17.0	12.1	18.1	16.7
	2008	19.3	18.9	19.3	18.6	19.3	19.6	17.4	16.4	17.4	11.7	18.8	17.0
	2009	19.3	18.8	19.3	18.7	19.2	19.6	16.9	15.2	17.0	14.5	18.2	16.6
	2011	14.3	8.5	14.5	12.2	10.8	17.1	13.0	13.4	13.0	7.4	15.2	12.7
Georgia - Géorgie	2006	6.5	7.0	6.5	5.9	3.8	7.9	6.0	7.4	6.0	4.6	5.4	7.2
	2007	0.3	3.2	0.2	0.1	0.0	0.3	0.3	3.3	0.2	0.0	0.0	0.6
	2008	0.3	3.2	0.2	0.1	0.0	0.3	0.3	3.3	0.2	0.0	0.0	0.6
	2009	0.3	3.5	0.2	0.1	0.0	0.3	0.3	1.7	0.3	0.0	0.0	0.7
	2010	0.3	3.5	0.2	0.1	0.0	0.3	0.3	1.7	0.3	0.0	0.0	0.7
	2011	0.8	3.6	0.7	0.7	0.1	1.0	1.2	2.4	1.1	1.7	0.0	1.9
Ghana	2000	13.8	11.2	13.9	12.1	5.4	18.6	8.9	10.2	8.9	11.4	5.2	13.3
	2007	12.4	11.0	12.4	11.2	5.9	15.9	8.9	10.2	8.8	10.2	6.4	13.1
	2008	12.3	11.0	12.4	11.2	5.8	15.9	8.8	10.2	8.8	10.2	6.4	13.1
	2009	12.4	11.4	12.4	11.2	5.8	15.9	8.5	10.8	8.5	9.2	5.5	13.0
Grenada - Grenade	2006	10.5	6.4	10.6	7.9	8.5	12.2	11.6	6.5	11.6	13.3	10.3	12.3
	2007	10.2	5.7	10.3	7.7	8.4	11.9	11.1	7.0	11.1	12.8	10.3	11.2
	2008	10.2	5.8	10.4	7.6	8.5	12.0	10.5	8.1	10.5	13.0	11.0	9.7
	2010	10.7	6.3	10.8	9.1	9.1	12.0	11.3	6.9	11.4	12.1	10.8	11.7
	2011	10.6	6.3	10.7	8.9	9.1	11.9	12.0	6.0	12.1	12.2	12.3	11.9
Guatemala	2000	6.7	1.4	7.0	1.5	2.6	11.0	5.1	2.0	5.2	3.5	4.7	7.0
	2005	5.2	1.4	5.3	1.6	2.5	8.0	5.9	1.7	6.0	3.2	5.5	7.7
	2007	5.0	1.3	5.2	1.5	2.3	7.8	5.6	1.7	5.7	3.0	5.3	7.3
	2008	5.0	1.3	5.2	1.5	2.3	7.8	5.6	1.7	5.7	3.0	5.3	7.3
	2009	5.0	1.2	5.2	1.6	2.3	7.8	5.4	1.9	5.4	3.1	5.4	6.9
	2010	5.0	1.3	5.2	1.6	2.3	7.8	5.4	2.1	5.5	3.4	5.7	7.1
	2011	5.0	1.3	5.2	1.6	2.3	7.8	5.3	2.2	5.3	3.4	4.9	6.9
Guinea - Guinée	2005	12.7	9.8	12.8	7.8	9.2	16.2	11.2	8.8	11.2	4.3	11.8	15.0
	2008	12.6	9.6	12.6	7.5	9.2	16.0	11.2	8.0	11.2	4.1	11.8	15.1
	2009	12.6	10.2	12.7	7.3	8.9	16.0	10.2	9.9	10.2	5.2	8.9	14.7
	2010	12.6	10.2	12.7	7.3	8.9	16.0	10.2	9.9	10.2	5.2	8.9	14.7

For sources and notes, see end of table.

Pour les sources et les notes, se reporter à la fin du tableau.

Market / Marchés	Year / Année	MFN rate - Simple average (2) / Droit NPF - Moyenne simple (2)						MFN rate - Weighted average (3) / Droit NPF - Moyenne pondérée (3)					
		Total of non-agricultural and non-fuel products / Total des produits non-agricoles et non-pétroliers	Ores and metals / Minérais et métaux	Manufactured products / Produits manufacturés	Chemical products / Produits chimiques	Machinery and transport equipment / Machines et matériel de transport	Other manufactured products / Produits manufacturés divers	Total of non-agricultural and non-fuel products / Total des produits non-agricoles et non-pétroliers	Ores and metals / Minérais et métaux	Manufactured products / Produits manufacturés	Chemical products / Produits chimiques	Machinery and transport equipment / Machines et matériel de transport	Other manufactured products / Produits manufacturés divers
SITC Rev.3 (1) / CTCI Rév.3 (1)		5+6+7+8 +27+28-667	27+28+68	(5+6+7+8) -(667+68)	5	7	(6+8) -(667+68)	5+6+7+8 +27+28-667	27+28+68	(5+6+7+8) -(667+68)	5	7	(6+8) -(667+68)
Guinea-Bissau - Guinée-Bissau	2005	13.7	11.0	13.7	9.6	10.0	16.9	13.5	13.4	13.5	10.9	10.2	17.0
	2006	13.7	11.0	13.7	9.6	10.1	16.9	13.5	13.4	13.5	10.9	10.2	17.1
	2007	13.5	10.1	13.6	10.3	9.4	16.9	12.4	7.6	12.4	9.7	9.8	16.5
	2008	13.5	10.7	13.5	9.8	9.4	16.5	13.8	10.8	13.8	11.2	10.3	16.9
	2009	13.4	10.7	13.5	9.8	9.4	16.5	13.8	10.8	13.8	11.5	10.4	16.8
	2010	13.5	10.0	13.6	9.7	9.3	16.6	12.3	11.1	12.3	11.4	8.5	16.2
	2011	13.5	10.7	13.6	9.3	9.5	16.6	13.6	10.6	13.6	11.0	10.0	16.3
Guyana	2000	17.7	14.1	17.7	13.6	16.9	18.7	16.1	16.2	16.1	12.2	20.3	14.9
	2006	10.1	5.4	10.2	7.3	8.2	12.2	9.5	7.5	9.5	10.4	8.8	10.1
	2008	9.6	5.8	9.7	7.1	6.7	11.9	9.1	8.1	9.1	10.2	7.8	10.0
	2010	9.5	5.6	9.6	7.3	6.5	11.9	9.5	6.4	9.5	11.1	7.5	11.1
	2011	9.5	5.6	9.7	7.1	6.5	12.1	8.7	6.8	8.7	10.6	6.8	10.6
Haiti - Haïti	2007	2.4	0.8	2.4	2.2	0.9	3.3	1.9	0.5	2.0	3.5	1.6	2.0
	2008	2.3	0.8	2.4	2.0	0.9	3.3	5.5	0.0	5.6	3.5	2.4	7.6
	2009	2.4	0.8	2.4	2.1	0.9	3.3	5.8	0.0	5.9	3.6	2.7	7.8
	2011	5.4	3.1	5.4	5.0	3.7	6.4	7.8	1.7	7.9	6.1	5.9	9.1
Honduras	2000	7.2	2.1	7.4	2.5	3.6	10.8	6.0	3.8	6.0	2.5	8.0	8.7
	2005	5.3	1.4	5.4	1.6	2.5	8.1	5.3	2.6	5.3	2.7	5.0	7.5
	2007	5.1	1.5	5.2	1.6	2.2	7.9	5.6	2.6	5.7	2.6	5.8	7.7
	2008	5.1	1.5	5.2	1.6	2.2	7.9	5.6	2.6	5.7	2.6	5.8	7.7
	2009	5.1	1.5	5.2	1.6	2.1	7.9	5.4	2.6	5.5	2.6	5.3	7.7
Iceland - Islande	2006	2.9	0.0	3.0	1.0	1.4	4.4	2.2	0.0	2.4	3.0	0.5	5.4
	2007	2.7	0.0	2.8	0.9	1.2	4.2	2.3	0.0	2.5	3.0	0.5	5.4
	2008	2.7	0.0	2.8	0.9	1.2	4.2	2.3	0.0	2.5	3.0	0.5	5.4
	2009	2.8	0.0	2.9	1.0	1.3	4.2	2.2	0.0	2.6	2.7	0.5	5.4
	2010	2.7	0.0	2.9	0.9	1.2	4.2	2.1	0.0	2.7	2.7	0.6	5.3
	2011	2.7	0.0	2.9	0.9	1.2	4.2	2.0	0.0	2.5	2.6	0.5	5.4
India - Inde	2005	15.3	14.0	15.4	15.9	15.1	15.3	12.0	13.6	11.8	14.5	9.4	14.9
	2007	13.1	11.8	13.2	13.4	13.3	13.0	11.1	9.6	11.4	11.9	9.7	14.1
	2008	8.6	5.2	8.9	8.5	9.0	9.0	6.9	4.7	7.1	7.0	6.8	7.9
	2009	9.0	5.3	9.3	8.8	9.6	9.3	7.6	6.2	7.8	7.5	7.8	8.1
Indonesia (...2002) - Indonésie (...2002)	2000	8.7	4.8	8.9	6.1	5.4	11.6	6.5	2.9	6.7	5.6	6.1	8.9
Indonesia - Indonésie	2005	7.0	4.3	7.2	5.2	4.8	8.9	6.4	3.4	6.5	5.8	5.5	9.1
	2006	7.0	4.3	7.2	5.2	4.8	8.9	6.4	3.4	6.5	5.8	5.5	9.1
	2007	6.9	4.3	7.1	5.1	4.5	9.0	6.3	3.5	6.5	5.9	5.5	8.5
	2009	6.8	4.2	7.0	4.9	4.3	8.9	6.3	3.2	6.4	5.5	5.7	8.4
	2010	7.2	4.2	7.4	5.5	6.1	8.7	6.7	3.0	6.8	7.1	6.0	8.1
	2011	7.2	4.3	7.4	5.5	6.1	8.7	6.5	2.9	6.7	6.2	6.4	7.6
Iran (Islamic Rep. of) - Iran (Rép. islamique d')	2000	41.8	16.8	43.1	17.0	42.0	60.1	28.1	13.3	28.6	12.7	34.8	28.9
	2007	24.0	9.0	24.7	11.2	16.7	35.1	18.3	8.5	18.5	14.0	20.9	17.2
	2008	27.0	8.1	28.0	11.2	16.0	39.8	21.0	9.4	21.2	13.2	20.5	25.1
	2011	27.2	8.0	28.2	11.1	17.1	39.9	23.2	8.2	23.6	13.2	23.8	27.4
Israel - Israël	2005	4.6	0.7	4.8	1.8	3.6	6.5	3.7	0.5	3.8	3.0	2.6	6.4
	2006	4.6	0.7	4.8	1.8	3.6	6.5	3.7	0.7	3.8	3.1	2.6	6.3
	2007	4.5	0.7	4.7	1.7	3.8	6.3	3.9	0.7	4.1	2.9	3.1	6.2
	2008	4.5	0.7	4.7	1.7	3.8	6.2	3.9	0.7	4.0	2.8	3.1	6.0
	2009	4.5	0.7	4.7	1.8	3.8	6.2	4.3	0.8	4.4	3.4	3.3	6.7
Jamaica - Jamaïque	2000	6.1	1.4	6.3	2.5	4.2	8.6	9.9	1.1	10.0	6.9	10.4	10.9
	2006	6.1	1.4	6.3	2.6	4.1	8.7	8.5	2.5	8.6	6.4	8.6	9.6
	2007	6.1	1.6	6.3	2.8	3.9	8.6	9.3	2.4	9.4	9.4	9.9	9.0
	2010	6.1	1.7	6.2	2.8	3.9	8.6	9.9	3.5	9.9	9.1	9.9	10.5
	2011	6.1	1.5	6.3	2.8	3.9	8.7	10.4	3.2	10.4	9.9	10.8	10.6

For sources and notes, see end of table.

Pour les sources et les notes, se reporter à la fin du tableau.

Market / Marchés	Year / Année	MFN rate - Simple average (2) / Droit NPF - Moyenne simple (2)						MFN rate - Weighted average (3) / Droit NPF - Moyenne pondérée (3)					
		Total of non-agricultural and non-fuel products / Total des produits non-agricoles et non-pétroliers	Ores and metals / Minérais et métaux	Manufactured products / Produits manufacturés	Chemical products / Produits chimiques	Machinery and transport equipment / Machines et matériel de transport	Other manufactured products / Produits manufacturés divers	Total of non-agricultural and non-fuel products / Total des produits non-agricoles et non-pétroliers	Ores and metals / Minérais et métaux	Manufactured products / Produits manufacturés	Chemical products / Produits chimiques	Machinery and transport equipment / Machines et matériel de transport	Other manufactured products / Produits manufacturés divers
SITC Rev.3 (1) / CTCI Rév.3 (1)		5+6+7+8 +27+28-667	27+28+68	(5+6+7+8) -(667+68)	5	7	(6+8) -(667+68)	5+6+7+8 +27+28-667	27+28+68	(5+6+7+8) -(667+68)	5	7	(6+8) -(667+68)
Japan - Japon	2000	2.8	1.2	2.9	2.8	0.1	4.2	2.0	0.1	2.2	1.8	0.1	5.1
	2005	2.5	1.2	2.6	2.7	0.1	3.6	1.7	0.2	1.8	1.7	0.1	4.1
	2006	2.5	1.2	2.6	2.7	0.1	3.6	1.6	0.1	1.8	1.7	0.1	4.0
	2007	2.5	1.3	2.6	2.8	0.1	3.6	1.9	0.6	2.1	1.8	0.1	4.2
	2008	2.5	1.2	2.6	2.7	0.1	3.6	1.7	0.1	2.0	1.7	0.1	3.9
	2009	2.5	1.2	2.6	2.8	0.1	3.6	1.7	0.1	2.0	1.7	0.1	3.9
	2010	2.5	1.2	2.6	2.8	0.1	3.5	2.0	0.1	2.2	1.6	0.1	4.3
	2011	2.5	1.2	2.6	2.7	0.0	3.6	1.7	0.1	2.1	1.5	0.0	4.1
Jordan - Jordanie	2000	22.5	17.9	22.7	18.2	15.4	27.6	19.7	14.2	19.9	14.0	18.7	24.8
	2005	13.3	9.1	13.5	3.0	11.5	18.2	12.1	6.6	12.3	4.2	12.4	15.1
	2006	10.9	7.1	11.0	1.7	9.9	15.0	8.3	6.3	8.4	3.2	8.7	9.9
	2007	10.5	7.4	10.6	1.5	8.8	14.7	8.7	5.9	8.8	2.7	9.9	10.4
	2008	10.0	6.9	10.1	1.3	8.8	14.1	8.0	5.4	8.1	1.5	9.1	10.1
	2009	9.3	6.2	9.4	1.2	8.0	13.2	7.4	5.4	7.5	1.6	7.6	10.2
Kazakhstan	2008	4.6	4.2	4.6	4.6	0.8	6.7	4.0	4.8	4.0	3.8	0.7	7.9
	2010	7.3	5.9	7.4	5.4	4.3	10.1	7.1	3.8	7.2	5.5	3.9	11.7
	2011	7.4	6.5	7.4	5.4	4.4	10.1	7.2	5.2	7.3	5.5	4.0	11.9
Kenya	2000	17.6	11.8	17.9	11.6	13.6	23.8	12.9	7.7	13.0	7.2	12.3	19.7
	2005	11.9	7.2	12.1	3.4	6.4	18.1	6.9	3.4	7.0	3.4	4.7	13.4
	2006	11.8	6.7	12.0	3.3	6.3	18.0	6.9	3.0	7.1	2.6	5.4	13.6
	2007	11.7	7.0	11.9	3.4	6.3	17.8	7.1	3.8	7.3	2.8	5.5	13.0
	2008	11.4	7.0	11.6	3.6	5.8	17.6	7.2	4.8	7.2	2.5	5.8	12.7
	2009	11.4	7.0	11.6	3.6	5.8	17.5	7.2	4.8	7.2	2.5	5.8	12.7
	2010	11.5	6.8	11.7	3.6	5.7	17.6	7.2	5.0	7.3	2.8	5.8	13.0
	2011	11.4	7.2	11.6	3.6	5.7	17.5	7.1	4.9	7.2	3.0	5.5	12.7
Korea, Republic of - Corée, République de	2006	7.3	4.2	7.5	9.5	6.0	7.3	4.2	2.5	4.5	7.2	3.5	4.8
	2007	7.3	3.7	7.5	9.7	6.1	7.3	4.6	1.5	5.2	6.8	4.9	4.7
	2009	7.2	3.7	7.5	9.6	6.2	7.2	4.3	1.5	4.9	6.6	4.9	4.0
	2010	7.3	3.7	7.5	9.6	6.1	7.2	4.8	1.5	5.3	6.9	4.9	4.8
Kuwait - Koweït	2005	4.9	4.8	4.9	4.7	4.9	5.0	4.8	5.0	4.8	3.2	4.8	5.0
	2006	4.9	4.8	4.9	4.6	4.9	5.0	4.8	5.0	4.8	3.2	4.8	5.0
	2007	4.8	4.8	4.8	4.6	4.6	4.9	4.4	5.0	4.4	3.4	4.3	4.9
	2008	4.8	4.8	4.8	4.5	4.6	4.9	4.7	5.0	4.6	3.1	4.7	4.9
	2009	4.8	4.8	4.8	4.5	4.6	4.9	4.7	5.0	4.6	3.2	4.7	4.9
Kyrgyzstan - Kirghizistan	2006	4.0	2.1	4.1	2.1	3.2	5.1	1.9	3.0	1.9	0.8	1.4	3.1
	2007	3.9	2.5	4.0	1.9	3.2	5.0	2.1	2.3	2.1	0.8	2.1	2.7
	2008	4.2	1.5	4.3	1.8	3.0	5.5	9.4	0.2	9.5	0.6	4.5	10.0
	2009	4.2	1.5	4.3	1.8	3.0	5.5	9.4	0.2	9.4	0.5	5.0	10.0
	2010	4.1	2.1	4.2	2.2	2.9	5.4	4.1	2.3	4.1	0.4	4.6	5.5
	2011	4.1	2.0	4.2	2.2	2.9	5.4	4.3	2.5	4.4	0.3	5.4	5.4
Lao People's Dem. Rep. - Rép. dém. populaire lao	2000	8.3	5.3	8.4	8.3	7.5	9.0	12.6	5.0	12.7	9.7	16.6	8.4
	2005	8.4	5.1	8.5	8.0	7.7	9.1	12.3	5.0	12.4	11.7	15.4	8.6
	2006	8.4	5.1	8.5	8.0	7.7	9.1	12.3	5.0	12.4	11.7	15.4	8.6
	2007	8.4	5.5	8.5	8.1	7.8	9.0	13.3	5.0	13.4	12.5	16.8	8.3
	2008	8.3	5.4	8.4	7.9	7.6	8.9	12.7	6.5	12.7	12.5	16.2	8.0
Lebanon - Liban	2000	14.6	7.6	14.9	7.9	12.0	18.6	16.1	6.4	16.6	10.7	15.7	19.6
	2005	4.5	2.6	4.6	2.7	3.8	5.5	6.1	1.5	6.3	5.5	4.9	7.9
	2006	4.5	2.7	4.6	2.7	3.8	5.5	6.1	1.6	6.3	5.5	4.9	7.9
	2007	4.2	2.8	4.3	2.9	3.8	5.0	5.8	1.6	6.0	5.6	4.9	7.4

For sources and notes, see end of table.

Pour les sources et les notes, se reporter à la fin du tableau.

Market / Marchés	Year / Année	MFN rate - Simple average (2) / Droit NPF - Moyenne simple (2)						MFN rate - Weighted average (3) / Droit NPF - Moyenne pondérée (3)					
		Total of non-agricultural and non-fuel products / Total des produits non-agricoles et non-pétroliers	Ores and metals / Minérais et métaux	Manufactured products / Produits manufacturés	Chemical products / Produits chimiques	Machinery and transport equipment / Machines et matériel de transport	Other manufactured products / Produits manufacturés divers	Total of non-agricultural and non-fuel products / Total des produits non-agricoles et non-pétroliers	Ores and metals / Minérais et métaux	Manufactured products / Produits manufacturés	Chemical products / Produits chimiques	Machinery and transport equipment / Machines et matériel de transport	Other manufactured products / Produits manufacturés divers
SITC Rev.3 (1) / CTCI Rév.3 (1)		5+6+7+8 +27+28-667	27+28+68	(5+6+7+8) -(667+68)	5	7	(6+8) -(667+68)	5+6+7+8 +27+28-667	27+28+68	(5+6+7+8) -(667+68)	5	7	(6+8) -(667+68)
Lesotho	2005	10.4	3.5	10.6	4.8	4.1	14.7	17.3	2.4	17.4	2.4	8.0	20.2
	2006	10.4	3.5	10.5	4.8	4.0	14.7	17.3	2.4	17.4	2.4	7.9	20.2
	2007	9.6	2.5	9.7	5.8	4.2	13.9	14.3	0.4	14.3	3.8	4.6	19.9
	2008	10.0	0.4	10.1	5.3	4.0	14.3	17.3	0.0	17.4	1.0	5.8	20.0
	2009	9.9	0.4	10.1	5.5	4.0	14.2	13.7	0.0	13.8	0.9	4.1	20.0
	2010	9.6	2.2	9.7	4.1	4.1	13.7	12.0	4.3	12.0	0.8	5.8	19.0
	2011	11.1	5.0	11.2	3.7	4.2	15.8	9.4	0.9	9.4	0.8	4.0	13.3
Madagascar	2005	11.1	10.1	11.2	9.8	6.8	13.6	6.1	8.4	6.1	7.9	4.9	6.5
	2006	13.6	9.2	13.8	10.1	11.1	16.2	12.9	7.6	13.0	7.6	11.7	14.9
	2007	12.4	8.2	12.6	7.3	10.9	15.1	11.9	8.4	11.9	6.9	10.9	13.6
	2008	12.5	8.2	12.7	7.3	10.9	15.3	11.9	8.4	11.9	6.9	10.8	13.6
	2010	11.6	8.4	11.7	7.3	8.2	14.7	9.8	7.3	9.9	6.6	7.1	11.9
	2011	11.5	8.3	11.6	7.3	7.9	14.6	8.9	9.3	8.9	6.6	6.8	11.5
Malawi	2006	13.7	7.1	13.9	6.9	10.0	18.0	10.1	2.9	10.2	3.9	10.4	15.0
	2008	13.2	7.4	13.4	7.1	8.9	17.5	7.7	3.2	7.8	2.3	7.1	15.0
	2009	13.1	7.4	13.3	7.1	8.6	17.5	7.6	3.2	7.7	2.3	6.9	15.0
	2010	12.6	10.2	12.6	4.0	7.9	17.9	8.7	6.1	8.7	2.1	9.3	14.4
	2011	12.8	10.4	12.9	3.9	8.2	18.5	8.1	2.9	8.5	4.0	4.3	14.5
Malaysia - Malaisie	2005	8.4	2.6	8.8	3.0	5.5	12.5	4.8	4.0	4.9	5.1	2.8	13.3
	2006	8.2	2.5	8.6	2.9	5.1	12.3	4.5	3.7	4.5	4.9	2.2	13.5
	2007	8.2	2.5	8.6	2.9	5.2	12.4	4.7	3.9	4.7	4.8	2.2	14.0
	2008	8.0	2.7	8.3	2.8	4.7	12.1	5.5	3.9	5.6	4.1	3.2	13.4
	2009	8.0	2.7	8.3	2.8	4.7	12.1	5.5	3.9	5.6	4.1	3.2	13.4
Maldives	2000	22.1	23.9	22.0	15.6	24.4	22.4	21.4	19.2	21.5	19.5	23.8	20.0
	2005	21.7	23.6	21.6	14.8	24.3	22.3	21.9	20.1	22.0	20.3	23.7	20.3
	2006	21.9	23.5	21.8	15.1	24.4	22.4	22.2	20.0	22.3	20.7	24.1	20.7
	2008	22.2	23.6	22.1	15.0	26.0	22.4	22.6	19.9	22.8	20.9	25.3	20.7
	2009	22.2	23.6	22.1	15.0	26.0	22.4	22.6	19.9	22.8	20.9	25.3	20.7
Mali	2005	12.5	9.0	12.6	7.6	9.0	16.1	10.6	8.1	10.6	5.2	9.7	15.4
	2006	12.4	8.4	12.6	7.4	9.1	16.1	10.7	8.7	10.7	5.2	9.7	15.4
	2007	12.4	8.8	12.5	7.6	8.5	16.1	11.3	8.4	11.3	4.6	10.9	16.2
	2008	12.4	8.6	12.5	7.4	8.5	16.1	10.8	8.1	10.8	5.1	9.3	15.4
	2009	12.4	8.6	12.5	7.4	8.5	16.1	10.8	8.1	10.8	5.1	9.3	15.4
	2010	12.4	8.6	12.5	7.4	8.5	16.1	10.8	8.1	10.8	5.1	9.3	15.4
	2011	12.3	7.9	12.4	7.3	8.5	16.0	10.4	7.8	10.5	3.5	9.8	15.6
Malta - Malte (5)	2000	8.0	7.7	8.0	7.1	7.2	8.7	10.3	4.5	10.3	4.3	11.7	8.1
Mauritania - Mauritanie	2006	11.0	5.3	11.2	5.6	9.2	13.7	6.6	5.0	6.6	7.9	5.8	11.6
	2007	12.7	9.0	12.8	8.3	9.8	15.8	11.0	8.2	11.0	6.9	9.5	14.0
Mauritius - Maurice	2005	6.1	1.5	6.3	4.2	5.9	7.3	4.9	1.7	4.9	6.0	3.6	6.1
	2006	2.8	0.4	2.9	1.7	2.8	3.4	1.9	0.3	1.9	3.1	1.2	2.5
	2007	2.7	0.3	2.8	1.7	2.8	3.2	2.7	0.3	2.8	3.4	1.9	3.2
	2008	2.7	0.4	2.8	1.8	2.3	3.3	3.0	0.3	3.0	3.9	1.9	3.5
	2009	1.4	0.1	1.4	0.9	0.8	1.9	1.8	0.5	1.8	2.4	0.5	2.6
	2010	1.4	0.1	1.4	0.9	0.8	1.9	1.8	0.4	1.8	2.5	0.4	2.7
	2011	1.3	0.1	1.4	0.9	0.8	1.9	2.0	0.2	2.0	2.8	0.6	2.7
Mayotte	2007	8.9	4.6	9.0	8.6	10.2	8.6	9.5	3.5	9.5	6.0	12.1	6.8
	2008	8.9	4.6	9.0	8.7	10.2	8.6	9.4	3.5	9.5	6.0	12.1	6.8
	2009	8.9	4.6	9.0	8.6	10.1	8.6	9.4	3.5	9.5	6.0	12.1	6.8
	2010	8.9	4.2	9.0	8.8	10.1	8.7	8.1	4.3	8.2	4.6	9.8	7.1
	2011	8.9	4.2	9.0	8.8	10.1	8.7	8.1	4.3	8.2	4.6	9.8	7.1

For sources and notes, see end of table.

Pour les sources et les notes, se reporter à la fin du tableau.

Market / Marchés	Year / Année	MFN rate - Simple average (2) / Droit NPF - Moyenne simple (2)						MFN rate - Weighted average (3) / Droit NPF - Moyenne pondérée (3)					
		Total of non-agricultural and non-fuel products / Total des produits non-agricoles et non-pétroliers	Ores and metals / Minérais et métaux	Manu-factured products / Produits manu-facturés	Chemical products / Produits chimiques	Machinery and transport equipment / Machines et matériel de transport	Other manu-factured products / Produits manu-facturés divers	Total of non-agricultural and non-fuel products / Total des produits non-agricoles et non-pétroliers	Ores and metals / Minérais et métaux	Manu-factured products / Produits manu-facturés	Chemical products / Produits chimiques	Machinery and transport equipment / Machines et matériel de transport	Other manu-factured products / Produits manu-facturés divers
SITC Rev.3 (1) / CTCI Rév.3 (1)		5+6+7+8 +27+28-667	27+28+68	(5+6+7+8)-(667+68)	5	7	(6+8)-(667+68)	5+6+7+8 +27+28-667	27+28+68	(5+6+7+8)-(667+68)	5	7	(6+8)-(667+68)
Mexico - Mexique	2000	17.1	12.4	17.4	12.4	14.1	20.7	14.6	11.9	14.7	11.8	13.2	18.4
	2005	13.6	9.4	13.8	9.3	10.4	17.0	11.8	9.4	11.9	9.0	11.1	14.7
	2006	13.5	9.4	13.7	9.3	10.4	16.9	11.7	9.6	11.8	9.0	11.2	14.1
	2008	11.2	6.5	11.5	6.9	8.8	14.5	10.0	5.6	10.2	6.4	10.8	11.0
	2009	10.0	4.8	10.4	5.3	7.3	13.7	8.4	4.5	8.6	5.2	9.0	9.5
	2010	7.3	0.7	7.7	2.5	4.0	11.2	4.9	1.3	5.0	3.0	4.5	6.9
Mongolia - Mongolie	2005	4.2	5.0	4.2	5.0	2.1	5.0	3.8	5.0	3.7	5.0	2.6	5.0
	2006	4.2	5.0	4.2	5.0	2.1	5.0	3.9	5.0	3.9	5.0	2.8	5.0
	2007	4.9	5.0	4.9	5.0	4.8	5.0	4.9	5.0	4.9	5.0	4.8	5.0
	2008	4.9	5.0	4.9	5.0	4.8	5.0	4.9	5.0	4.9	5.0	4.8	5.0
	2009	4.9	5.0	4.9	5.0	4.8	5.0	4.9	5.0	4.9	5.0	4.8	5.0
	2011	4.9	5.0	4.9	5.0	4.8	5.0	4.9	5.0	4.9	5.0	4.8	5.0
Montenegro - Monténégro	2008	4.6	3.4	4.6	2.7	2.5	6.1	5.0	2.5	5.2	4.8	2.9	7.2
	2009	4.6	3.4	4.6	2.7	2.6	6.1	5.0	2.5	5.2	4.8	2.9	7.2
	2010	4.5	3.7	4.6	2.6	2.6	6.0	5.1	2.0	5.3	4.6	2.9	7.2
	2011	4.5	3.7	4.6	2.6	2.6	6.0	5.5	1.7	5.8	4.7	3.6	7.6
Morocco - Maroc	2000	28.2	24.1	28.4	26.7	13.2	35.7	25.9	12.8	26.4	26.1	15.5	36.2
	2005	23.7	13.6	24.2	17.6	11.1	32.2	21.2	7.5	21.8	19.4	14.3	30.2
	2006	21.5	13.4	21.9	17.3	11.0	28.2	18.9	8.4	19.5	19.2	14.9	24.6
	2007	20.2	13.3	20.6	15.5	9.0	27.4	17.9	7.9	18.5	17.0	13.4	24.9
	2008	18.0	12.7	18.3	14.5	8.3	24.0	16.3	7.7	16.8	15.5	12.4	22.4
	2009	15.0	10.4	15.3	11.3	8.1	19.9	12.9	3.1	13.9	10.7	11.9	17.6
Mozambique	2005	11.9	4.9	12.2	5.5	8.3	16.2	8.8	6.2	8.8	5.7	8.1	11.1
	2006	11.6	4.8	11.9	5.4	8.2	15.9	8.4	5.9	8.4	5.2	7.6	11.0
	2007	10.1	4.7	10.4	5.1	7.6	13.4	7.9	7.0	7.9	4.7	7.6	9.6
	2009	9.7	4.7	9.9	5.0	6.8	13.1	7.6	2.7	7.9	5.6	6.9	10.2
	2010	9.6	4.7	9.9	5.0	6.9	13.0	7.9	3.5	8.0	5.5	6.2	11.4
Myanmar	2005	4.9	3.1	5.0	2.2	3.0	6.9	4.1	2.8	4.1	2.6	3.0	5.6
	2006	4.9	3.1	5.0	2.2	3.0	6.9	4.1	2.8	4.1	2.6	3.0	5.6
	2007	4.9	2.9	4.9	2.1	3.0	6.8	4.1	2.6	4.1	2.6	3.2	5.4
	2008	5.0	3.1	5.1	2.2	2.8	7.1	3.9	2.9	3.9	2.7	3.2	5.2
Namibia - Namibie	2005	8.6	1.6	9.0	3.1	3.1	13.4	11.0	1.9	11.1	6.0	10.6	13.7
	2006	8.6	1.7	9.0	3.0	3.1	13.4	10.5	1.7	10.6	6.4	9.6	13.4
	2007	8.4	1.7	8.8	3.2	3.1	13.1	10.5	1.5	10.6	6.1	9.3	13.5
	2008	8.4	1.7	8.8	3.1	3.1	13.1	10.3	1.5	10.4	6.1	9.1	13.3
	2009	8.3	1.7	8.6	3.1	3.1	12.9	10.1	1.8	10.2	5.8	9.5	13.0
	2010	8.2	1.1	8.6	2.4	2.9	13.2	10.2	1.2	10.3	5.5	9.2	13.6
	2011	8.1	1.1	8.5	2.4	2.9	13.1	10.0	0.4	10.5	5.2	9.9	13.6
Nepal - Népal	2000	13.7	8.0	13.9	12.6	12.3	15.2	19.5	5.4	20.4	12.1	33.2	12.5
	2005	14.1	10.0	14.3	13.0	11.4	16.0	16.4	7.2	17.0	14.8	19.6	16.4
	2006	12.4	9.4	12.6	11.8	10.2	13.9	15.0	7.0	15.5	12.9	17.0	15.6
	2007	12.5	9.2	12.7	11.9	10.4	14.0	15.6	7.0	16.2	13.0	18.8	16.0
	2009	12.8	9.8	12.9	12.6	10.2	14.2	16.5	6.0	16.9	13.1	18.9	16.3
	2010	12.3	9.2	12.4	11.6	9.7	14.0	14.4	6.9	14.9	12.5	18.9	11.7
	2011	12.2	9.1	12.4	11.5	9.8	13.9	14.3	6.9	14.8	12.0	18.9	11.6
New Zealand - Nouvelle-Zélande	2000	3.0	0.8	3.1	0.7	3.2	4.1	3.6	1.3	3.7	1.4	3.8	4.6
	2005	3.6	1.0	3.8	0.9	3.9	4.8	4.3	2.2	4.4	1.8	4.6	5.3
	2006	3.5	1.0	3.6	0.9	3.9	4.5	4.1	2.0	4.2	1.9	4.2	5.1
	2007	3.5	1.1	3.6	1.0	4.0	4.5	4.5	2.0	4.6	2.0	5.0	5.3
	2008	2.6	0.8	2.7	0.8	2.9	3.3	3.3	1.5	3.4	1.6	3.7	3.8
	2009	2.4	0.8	2.5	0.7	2.9	3.0	2.8	1.5	2.9	1.6	2.8	3.5
	2010	2.4	0.8	2.5	0.7	2.9	3.0	2.8	1.6	2.9	1.6	2.8	3.5

For sources and notes, see end of table.   Pour les sources et les notes, se reporter à la fin du tableau.

Market / Marchés	Year / Année	MFN rate - Simple average (2) / Droit NPF - Moyenne simple (2)						MFN rate - Weighted average (3) / Droit NPF - Moyenne pondérée (3)					
		Total of non-agricultural and non-fuel products / Total des produits non-agricoles et non-pétroliers	Ores and metals / Minérais et métaux	Manufactured products / Produits manufacturés	Chemical products / Produits chimiques	Machinery and transport equipment / Machines et matériel de transport	Other manufactured products / Produits manufacturés divers	Total of non-agricultural and non-fuel products / Total des produits non-agricoles et non-pétroliers	Ores and metals / Minérais et métaux	Manufactured products / Produits manufacturés	Chemical products / Produits chimiques	Machinery and transport equipment / Machines et matériel de transport	Other manufactured products / Produits manufacturés divers
SITC Rev.3 (1) / CTCI Rév.3 (1)		5+6+7+8 +27+28-667	27+28+68	(5+6+7+8) -(667+68)	5	7	(6+8) -(667+68)	5+6+7+8 +27+28-667	27+28+68	(5+6+7+8) -(667+68)	5	7	(6+8) -(667+68)
Nicaragua	2000	3.5	1.3	3.6	1.3	1.7	5.2	3.9	2.3	3.9	3.0	3.5	4.9
	2005	5.4	1.6	5.5	1.8	2.4	8.1	5.4	4.7	5.4	3.6	4.2	7.9
	2007	5.1	1.7	5.2	1.8	2.1	7.9	5.6	3.8	5.6	3.7	4.2	7.9
	2009	5.1	1.7	5.2	1.8	2.1	7.8	5.3	3.8	5.3	3.8	4.3	7.1
	2010	5.1	1.5	5.2	1.8	2.1	7.8	5.0	4.7	5.0	3.6	3.9	7.1
Niger	2005	12.8	8.1	13.0	7.3	9.5	16.3	11.8	5.6	12.0	5.6	11.0	15.6
	2006	12.8	8.5	12.9	7.4	9.4	16.3	11.3	6.2	11.4	4.9	10.9	15.1
	2007	12.7	7.8	12.8	7.4	9.0	16.2	11.8	5.6	12.0	5.5	11.2	15.4
	2008	12.8	8.5	12.9	7.6	8.8	16.2	9.6	5.4	9.7	3.1	9.3	15.7
	2009	12.8	8.5	12.9	7.6	8.8	16.2	9.6	5.4	9.7	3.1	9.3	15.7
	2010	12.8	8.5	12.9	7.6	8.8	16.2	9.6	5.4	9.7	3.1	9.3	15.7
	2011	12.6	9.1	12.7	7.7	8.7	16.1	10.5	5.3	10.6	3.4	9.8	16.1
Nigeria - Nigéria	2000	24.6	17.0	24.9	18.3	16.7	31.9	18.2	15.4	18.2	17.0	17.6	20.5
	2005	11.6	7.5	11.8	7.3	6.0	16.3	9.8	10.1	9.8	10.2	6.6	14.8
	2006	10.6	7.3	10.8	7.2	5.6	15.6	8.3	9.1	8.2	6.9	5.4	14.3
	2008	10.8	7.4	11.0	7.2	5.6	16.0	8.7	10.1	8.7	7.7	5.3	15.4
	2009	10.7	6.6	10.9	7.2	5.2	15.0	10.0	11.9	10.0	8.6	8.1	14.7
	2010	10.7	6.8	10.9	7.1	7.4	14.8	10.8	9.6	10.8	8.1	10.0	14.2
Norway - Norvège	2000	2.5	0.3	2.6	1.6	0.3	4.0	1.6	0.3	1.7	3.3	0.2	3.9
	2006	0.7	0.0	0.8	0.4	0.0	1.2	0.4	0.0	0.5	0.5	0.0	1.1
	2007	0.7	0.0	0.8	0.4	0.0	1.2	0.4	0.0	0.5	0.5	0.0	1.1
	2008	0.7	0.0	0.8	0.4	0.0	1.2	0.4	0.0	0.5	0.4	0.0	1.1
	2009	0.6	0.0	0.7	0.4	0.0	1.0	0.5	0.0	0.5	0.5	0.0	1.2
	2010	0.7	0.0	0.7	0.7	0.0	1.0	0.5	0.0	0.5	0.7	0.0	1.2
	2011	0.7	0.0	0.7	0.7	0.0	1.0	0.5	0.0	0.5	0.6	0.0	1.2
Oman	2005	4.9	4.9	4.9	4.8	4.9	5.0	4.7	5.0	4.7	3.8	4.8	5.0
	2006	4.9	4.8	4.9	4.7	4.9	5.0	4.9	5.0	4.9	4.2	5.0	5.0
	2007	4.8	4.8	4.8	4.5	4.6	5.0	4.8	5.0	4.8	4.2	4.7	4.9
	2008	4.8	4.8	4.8	4.5	4.6	5.0	4.8	5.0	4.8	4.2	4.7	4.9
	2009	4.8	4.8	4.8	4.5	4.6	5.0	4.8	5.0	4.8	4.2	4.7	4.9
Pakistan	2005	14.5	8.9	14.8	9.9	13.7	17.4	14.4	9.4	14.7	8.5	18.0	14.9
	2006	14.6	8.9	14.9	9.8	13.9	17.5	14.3	8.7	14.6	8.7	17.0	15.3
	2007	14.3	8.4	14.6	9.5	12.9	17.5	13.1	8.1	13.4	8.2	15.5	15.3
	2008	13.8	7.3	14.1	9.2	12.4	16.9	12.0	5.5	12.5	6.8	16.1	14.0
	2009	14.0	7.2	14.4	9.6	12.9	17.1	11.8	5.2	12.3	6.9	15.3	14.6
Palau - Palaos	2005	3.2	2.9	3.2	3.9	3.1	3.0	3.2	3.0	3.2	2.6	3.5	3.0
	2006	3.2	2.9	3.2	3.9	3.1	3.0	3.2	3.0	3.2	2.6	3.5	3.0
	2010	3.2	2.8	3.2	4.8	3.0	3.0	3.1	2.9	3.1	4.1	3.0	3.0
	2011	3.4	2.5	3.4	6.2	3.0	3.0	3.1	3.0	3.1	6.0	2.9	3.0
Panama	2000	7.2	7.4	7.2	4.2	6.8	8.4	7.7	6.9	7.7	5.0	7.8	8.6
	2005	6.4	7.0	6.4	2.1	6.6	7.8	6.7	4.3	6.7	2.8	7.5	7.7
	2006	6.4	6.6	6.4	2.1	6.6	7.9	6.7	4.3	6.7	2.9	7.6	7.5
	2007	6.4	6.6	6.4	1.9	6.6	7.9	6.7	4.6	6.8	2.6	7.6	7.5
	2008	6.3	6.8	6.3	1.9	6.5	7.7	7.0	4.9	7.1	2.7	8.1	7.5
	2009	6.2	6.8	6.2	1.8	6.4	7.7	7.0	5.3	7.0	2.9	8.3	7.4
Papua New Guinea - Papoúasie-Nouvelle-Guinée	2005	4.5	0.0	4.6	1.5	0.2	7.9	1.7	0.0	1.8	2.7	0.1	3.7
	2006	3.6	0.0	3.7	1.1	0.2	6.3	1.3	0.0	1.3	1.9	0.1	2.9
	2007	3.3	0.1	3.4	1.1	0.2	5.9	1.1	1.3	1.1	1.3	0.0	2.6
	2008	3.4	0.1	3.5	1.4	0.3	5.7	2.2	1.2	2.2	2.1	0.1	5.9
	2010	3.2	0.1	3.4	0.9	0.2	5.7	2.8	0.6	2.8	1.9	0.1	8.1

For sources and notes, see end of table.

Pour les sources et les notes, se reporter à la fin du tableau.

Market / Marchés	Year / Année	MFN rate - Simple average (2) / Droit NPF - Moyenne simple (2)						MFN rate - Weighted average (3) / Droit NPF - Moyenne pondérée (3)					
		Total of non-agricultural and non-fuel products / Total des produits non-agricoles et non-pétroliers	Ores and metals / Minérais et métaux	Manufactured products / Produits manu-facturés	Chemical products / Produits chimiques	Machinery and transport equipment / Machines et matériel de transport	Other manu-factured products / Produits manu-facturés divers	Total of non-agricultural and non-fuel products / Total des produits non-agricoles et non-pétroliers	Ores and metals / Minérais et métaux	Manufactured products / Produits manu-facturés	Chemical products / Produits chimiques	Machinery and transport equipment / Machines et matériel de transport	Other manu-factured products / Produits manu-facturés divers
SITC Rev.3 (1) / CTCI Rév.3 (1)		5+6+7+8 +27+28-667	27+28+68	(5+6+7+8) -(667+68)	5	7	(6+8) -(667+68)	5+6+7+8 +27+28-667	27+28+68	(5+6+7+8) -(667+68)	5	7	(6+8) -(667+68)
Paraguay	2000	13.9	9.6	14.0	11.2	9.1	17.3	11.7	8.8	11.7	11.2	10.0	14.1
	2005	11.4	7.1	11.5	8.2	6.3	15.2	10.1	6.2	10.1	7.4	9.0	13.6
	2006	10.4	6.8	10.5	7.4	5.3	14.2	6.0	4.4	6.0	5.2	4.5	10.1
	2007	11.0	6.4	11.1	7.9	5.7	14.9	6.9	6.8	6.9	5.8	5.2	12.2
	2008	11.0	6.5	11.2	8.1	5.6	15.0	7.1	7.0	7.1	5.4	5.6	11.9
	2009	11.0	6.6	11.1	8.1	5.6	14.9	8.0	6.9	8.0	5.9	6.7	11.0
	2010	11.0	6.6	11.1	8.1	5.2	15.0	8.2	7.0	8.2	6.1	6.8	11.3
	2011	11.0	6.8	11.2	8.1	5.2	15.1	8.8	8.3	8.8	6.2	7.4	12.2
Peru - Pérou	2000	13.2	12.0	13.3	12.0	12.3	14.2	12.3	12.0	12.4	12.0	12.2	12.8
	2005	9.6	8.5	9.7	6.7	6.1	12.4	8.2	9.4	8.1	6.9	7.3	10.2
	2006	9.7	8.3	9.7	6.6	6.2	12.5	7.9	9.2	7.9	7.0	6.6	10.3
	2007	9.6	8.3	9.7	6.6	6.1	12.5	7.6	8.4	7.6	6.6	6.5	10.0
	2008	5.4	3.9	5.5	2.9	1.5	8.3	3.0	5.6	2.9	3.1	1.8	4.5
	2009	5.5	4.0	5.5	2.9	1.5	8.4	3.0	5.6	2.9	3.1	1.9	4.5
	2010	5.4	3.3	5.5	2.8	1.5	8.3	3.3	3.0	3.4	3.6	2.0	5.0
	2011	3.8	1.2	3.9	1.8	1.0	6.0	2.3	1.5	2.3	2.2	1.3	3.7
Philippines	2000	7.2	3.4	7.4	3.9	5.1	9.8	3.5	3.4	3.5	5.2	2.1	7.7
	2005	5.8	2.5	6.0	3.4	3.5	8.1	3.3	2.5	3.3	5.5	2.0	6.2
	2006	5.8	2.5	6.0	3.4	3.5	8.1	3.3	2.5	3.3	5.5	2.0	6.2
	2007	5.8	2.5	6.0	3.4	3.6	8.0	3.8	2.7	3.8	4.7	2.9	6.2
	2008	5.8	2.5	6.0	3.6	3.6	8.0	4.9	2.6	5.0	4.8	4.1	6.5
	2009	5.8	2.5	6.0	3.6	3.6	8.0	5.6	2.9	5.8	5.0	5.0	7.2
	2010	5.8	2.5	6.0	3.6	3.6	8.0	5.6	2.9	5.8	5.0	5.0	7.2
Poland - Pologne (5)	2000	10.5	6.0	10.8	9.0	9.2	12.1	10.0	5.6	10.1	7.8	10.7	10.7
Qatar	2005	4.9	4.9	4.9	4.8	4.9	5.0	4.9	5.0	4.9	4.2	5.0	5.0
	2006	4.9	4.9	4.9	4.7	4.9	5.0	4.9	5.0	4.9	4.2	5.0	5.0
	2007	4.8	4.9	4.8	4.6	4.6	4.9	4.7	5.0	4.7	4.1	4.6	4.9
	2008	4.8	4.9	4.8	4.5	4.5	4.9	4.4	5.0	4.4	3.8	4.1	4.9
	2009	4.8	4.9	4.8	4.5	4.5	4.9	4.4	5.0	4.3	3.9	4.0	4.9
Republic of Moldova - République de Moldova	2000	4.5	1.9	4.6	3.5	1.7	6.1	2.8	1.8	2.8	1.5	1.2	4.1
	2006	4.4	1.4	4.5	2.8	1.6	6.4	3.3	0.6	3.3	2.2	1.6	4.7
	2008	4.0	1.1	4.1	2.7	1.7	5.5	2.9	0.1	3.1	2.5	1.8	4.4
	2010	3.9	1.0	4.0	2.8	1.7	5.5	3.2	0.6	3.2	2.1	2.0	4.7
Romania - Roumanie (4)	2005	15.5	6.7	16.0	13.9	12.8	18.2	13.9	4.3	14.3	10.1	13.9	15.9
Russian Federation - Fédération de Russie	2005	9.5	7.6	9.6	6.6	8.4	11.6	8.4	5.6	8.5	8.9	7.6	10.5
	2007	8.6	7.7	8.7	6.6	6.0	11.1	6.8	3.6	6.9	8.8	5.4	9.5
	2008	8.5	7.3	8.6	6.6	5.7	11.0	6.5	3.8	6.6	8.8	5.2	9.2
	2009	8.5	7.2	8.6	6.5	5.7	11.0	6.7	3.8	6.8	8.8	5.5	9.2
	2010	7.8	6.5	7.8	6.2	4.8	10.1	5.8	3.5	5.9	8.5	3.5	9.2
	2011	7.7	6.5	7.8	6.2	4.8	10.1	5.8	4.4	5.8	8.4	3.8	9.0
Rwanda	2005	21.6	13.4	21.8	16.4	19.2	24.8	16.2	15.2	16.2	9.8	15.5	22.3
	2006	21.8	11.7	22.1	15.9	20.0	24.6	16.0	6.2	16.4	9.6	16.2	19.6
	2008	21.2	11.4	21.6	16.0	19.1	24.5	17.1	6.8	17.5	10.5	19.5	18.6
	2009	12.4	8.2	12.6	5.2	6.2	17.7	12.9	11.9	12.9	6.1	8.2	20.6
	2010	12.5	7.6	12.7	5.0	6.1	17.8	11.2	11.1	11.3	6.7	7.2	18.7
	2011	12.5	8.0	12.7	5.1	6.0	18.0	11.1	11.0	11.1	6.7	8.5	15.5
Saint Kitts and Nevis - Saint-Kitts-et-Nevis	2000	11.1	3.8	11.3	7.1	9.6	13.1	13.3	4.4	13.4	13.5	12.5	14.1
	2006	11.1	4.1	11.4	7.4	8.9	13.5	13.7	7.6	13.8	13.1	12.2	15.3
	2007	11.1	4.1	11.4	7.4	8.9	13.5	13.7	7.6	13.8	13.1	12.2	15.3
	2008	11.0	3.9	11.3	7.3	9.1	13.3	13.6	5.3	13.7	14.2	11.9	15.4
	2009	11.0	3.9	11.3	7.3	9.1	13.3	13.6	5.3	13.7	14.2	11.9	15.4
	2010	11.2	4.8	11.4	9.6	8.9	13.1	12.9	5.9	13.0	14.9	10.0	16.0
	2011	11.9	4.8	12.1	9.6	9.5	13.8	13.4	1.7	13.7	13.8	9.6	18.5

For sources and notes, see end of table.

Pour les sources et les notes, se reporter à la fin du tableau.

Market / Marchés	Year / Année	MFN rate - Simple average (2) / Droit NPF - Moyenne simple (2)						MFN rate - Weighted average (3) / Droit NPF - Moyenne pondérée (3)					
		Total of non-agricultural and non-fuel products / Total des produits non-agricoles et non-pétroliers	Ores and metals / Minérais et métaux	Manufactured products / Produits manu-facturés	Chemical products / Produits chimiques	Machinery and transport equipment / Machines et matériel de transport	Other manu-factured products / Produits manu-facturés divers	Total of non-agricultural and non-fuel products / Total des produits non-agricoles et non-pétroliers	Ores and metals / Minérais et métaux	Manufactured products / Produits manu-facturés	Chemical products / Produits chimiques	Machinery and transport equipment / Machines et matériel de transport	Other manu-factured products / Produits manu-facturés divers
SITC Rev.3 (1) / CTCI Rév.3 (1)		5+6+7+8 +27+28-667	27+28+68	(5+6+7+8) -(667+68)	5	7	(6+8) -(667+68)	5+6+7+8 +27+28-667	27+28+68	(5+6+7+8) -(667+68)	5	7	(6+8) -(667+68)
Saint Lucia - Sainte-Lucie	2000	17.6	13.3	17.6	12.8	18.8	18.1	17.7	13.1	17.7	14.3	24.3	15.6
	2005	9.6	2.7	9.8	7.3	6.3	11.9	13.5	2.8	13.6	13.2	12.8	14.3
	2006	9.6	2.7	9.8	7.3	6.3	11.9	13.5	2.8	13.6	13.2	12.8	14.3
	2007	9.5	2.2	9.7	7.2	6.4	11.8	14.0	3.7	14.1	13.8	14.2	14.1
Saint Vincent and the Grenadines - Saint-Vincent-et-les Grenadines	2000	17.2	12.3	17.2	13.2	17.4	17.8	16.5	14.5	16.6	12.8	22.3	15.5
	2006	1.7	2.3	1.7	5.7	0.8	1.2	3.6	3.5	3.6	8.9	3.5	2.2
	2007	10.1	5.0	10.3	7.6	8.3	11.8	10.8	5.8	10.8	11.8	9.9	11.2
Saudi Arabia - Arabie saoudite	2000	12.1	12.2	12.0	11.8	11.8	12.3	11.3	13.1	11.2	8.5	11.4	12.0
	2005	4.9	4.8	4.9	4.8	4.9	5.0	4.7	5.0	4.7	3.4	4.8	5.0
	2006	4.9	4.9	4.9	4.6	4.9	5.0	4.7	5.0	4.7	3.4	4.8	5.0
	2007	4.8	4.8	4.7	4.4	4.6	5.0	4.5	5.0	4.4	3.1	4.4	4.9
	2008	4.7	4.8	4.7	4.5	4.6	4.9	4.5	5.0	4.4	3.1	4.4	4.9
	2009	4.7	4.8	4.7	4.4	4.6	4.9	4.5	5.0	4.4	3.1	4.4	4.9
Senegal - Sénégal	2005	12.5	8.7	12.7	7.0	8.9	16.2	10.2	6.0	10.4	5.8	10.1	13.6
	2006	12.5	8.6	12.6	6.9	8.9	16.3	10.5	7.7	10.6	5.8	10.2	13.9
	2007	12.3	8.1	12.4	7.0	8.3	16.0	10.7	6.9	10.8	5.9	10.5	13.6
	2008	12.2	8.0	12.4	7.1	8.3	16.0	10.4	5.9	10.6	6.3	9.9	13.7
	2009	12.2	8.0	12.4	7.1	8.3	16.0	10.4	5.9	10.6	6.3	9.9	13.7
	2010	12.3	8.3	12.4	7.1	8.4	16.1	10.4	7.8	10.4	6.2	9.7	13.8
	2011	12.1	8.3	12.3	7.0	8.3	16.0	10.0	7.6	10.0	5.9	9.4	13.5
Serbia and Montenegro - Serbie-et-Monténégro	2005	6.6	3.6	6.8	3.1	5.2	8.8	6.4	2.3	6.8	4.2	7.2	7.9
Seychelles	2000	25.3	21.2	25.4	32.1	21.4	25.7	18.5	21.3	18.5	23.1	17.3	20.9
	2005	7.5	2.1	7.7	1.4	8.1	9.1	11.3	1.4	11.3	3.8	17.2	5.6
	2006	5.2	0.0	5.4	1.6	4.4	6.9	6.7	0.0	6.8	2.3	13.5	2.2
	2007	4.6	0.0	4.8	1.6	3.6	6.2	6.4	0.0	6.4	1.9	10.2	2.4
Sierra Leone	2010	12.0	5.7	12.1	8.2	9.1	15.0	9.2	5.6	9.2	7.1	8.5	12.0
	2011	12.0	5.5	12.1	8.2	9.0	15.1	9.1	5.1	9.1	7.9	7.3	14.1
Solomon Islands - Îles Salomon	2006	14.2	10.8	14.2	11.2	13.2	15.5	12.8	14.3	12.8	12.0	12.2	13.6
	2007	9.1	8.2	9.1	8.4	9.1	9.3	7.6	7.8	7.6	8.5	7.0	8.5
	2008	9.1	8.5	9.1	8.5	9.1	9.3	8.6	8.0	8.6	8.7	8.5	8.8
	2010	9.2	8.5	9.2	8.9	9.2	9.3	8.8	7.3	8.8	8.0	8.7	9.0
	2011	9.2	8.5	9.2	9.0	9.2	9.3	9.1	6.7	9.1	8.5	9.0	9.3
South Africa - Afrique du Sud	2005	8.2	1.3	8.6	2.6	3.0	13.4	7.2	0.6	7.4	3.1	7.0	10.9
	2006	8.1	1.3	8.5	2.6	3.0	13.3	7.1	0.6	7.4	3.2	6.8	11.1
	2007	8.0	1.3	8.4	2.6	3.0	13.0	7.4	0.6	7.8	3.3	7.6	10.8
	2008	8.0	1.3	8.4	2.6	3.0	13.0	7.2	0.6	7.6	3.3	7.4	10.3
	2009	7.9	1.3	8.4	2.6	3.0	13.0	6.4	0.7	6.8	3.0	6.1	10.5
	2010	7.8	0.9	8.3	2.0	2.8	13.1	7.1	0.4	7.3	2.4	6.4	11.8
	2011	7.8	0.9	8.3	2.0	2.8	13.1	7.4	0.4	7.7	2.4	7.3	11.7
Sri Lanka	2000	8.0	5.5	8.2	6.4	6.2	9.7	5.7	5.3	5.7	5.4	6.9	5.1
	2005	9.7	5.8	9.9	5.3	8.0	12.4	6.8	4.4	7.0	5.0	9.8	5.9
	2006	9.4	5.7	9.6	5.1	7.6	12.2	6.4	4.1	6.6	4.5	9.5	5.5
	2007	9.3	5.6	9.5	5.2	7.2	12.2	6.7	3.9	6.9	4.3	10.8	5.6
	2009	9.0	5.5	9.2	5.1	7.1	11.8	6.3	4.1	6.4	4.0	10.0	5.5
	2010	8.0	4.6	8.2	3.3	4.7	11.7	6.6	2.2	6.7	2.9	10.3	5.7
	2011	7.5	4.1	7.7	3.1	4.5	11.0	6.7	2.0	6.9	2.7	10.8	4.9
Sudan (...2011) - Soudan (...2011)	2006	18.8	13.9	19.0	8.6	11.1	26.3	15.0	10.3	15.0	10.1	11.5	23.6
	2008	18.8	16.0	18.9	7.4	10.9	27.1	14.0	12.6	14.0	10.3	11.0	24.4
	2009	19.1	15.2	19.2	7.8	10.9	27.5	10.6	12.7	10.6	10.9	5.8	30.7
	2010	18.0	14.5	18.1	8.4	10.6	25.7	19.1	13.1	19.2	10.7	15.0	26.9
	2011	18.0	14.5	18.1	8.4	10.6	25.7	19.1	13.1	19.2	10.7	15.0	26.9

For sources and notes, see end of table.

Pour les sources et les notes, se reporter à la fin du tableau.

Market / Marchés	Year / Année	MFN rate - Simple average (2) / Droit NPF - Moyenne simple (2)						MFN rate - Weighted average (3) / Droit NPF - Moyenne pondérée (3)					
		Total of non-agricultural and non-fuel products / Total des produits non-agricoles et non-pétroliers	Ores and metals / Minérais et métaux	Manu-factured products / Produits manu-facturés	Chemical products / Produits chimiques	Machinery and transport equipment / Machines et matériel de transport	Other manu-factured products / Produits manu-facturés divers	Total of non-agricultural and non-fuel products / Total des produits non-agricoles et non-pétroliers	Ores and metals / Minérais et métaux	Manu-factured products / Produits manu-facturés	Chemical products / Produits chimiques	Machinery and transport equipment / Machines et matériel de transport	Other manu-factured products / Produits manu-facturés divers
SITC Rev.3 (1) / CTCI Rév.3 (1)		5+6+7+8 +27+28-667	27+28+68	(5+6+7+8) -(667+68)	5	7	(6+8) -(667+68)	5+6+7+8 +27+28-667	27+28+68	(5+6+7+8) -(667+68)	5	7	(6+8) -(667+68)
Suriname	2000	10.6	11.5	10.6	9.5	7.1	12.1	11.7	14.1	11.6	9.7	10.9	12.9
	2007	9.9	6.2	10.0	7.8	7.9	11.8	11.7	9.7	11.7	9.6	11.0	12.8
	2010	9.5	5.9	9.7	7.7	7.5	11.3	10.3	9.9	10.3	8.3	10.7	11.2
Swaziland	2005	11.2	2.9	11.3	4.7	4.2	16.2	10.1	1.9	10.1	2.1	5.2	16.3
	2006	11.1	2.9	11.3	4.7	4.1	16.1	10.0	1.9	10.1	2.1	5.2	16.2
	2007	10.6	2.1	10.7	5.4	3.8	15.4	9.4	1.0	10.0	3.8	4.2	15.6
	2008	11.1	2.0	11.2	5.6	4.4	16.0	6.8	0.3	7.4	2.8	2.8	16.5
	2009	10.7	1.8	10.8	5.4	4.4	15.4	6.1	0.1	7.6	2.6	2.9	15.3
	2010	11.0	1.3	11.2	3.6	3.8	16.3	14.6	0.0	16.3	0.6	4.7	26.2
	2011	11.3	1.4	11.6	3.2	4.0	16.6	4.3	0.1	4.6	0.7	1.3	15.4
Syrian Arab Republic - République arabe syrienne	2009	13.5	2.3	13.9	4.8	7.2	20.1	12.7	1.3	13.1	6.3	16.1	12.2
	2010	10.0	1.7	10.3	4.5	7.5	15.0	6.8	1.4	7.3	3.4	16.6	4.8
Tajikistan - Tadjikistan	2006	7.3	7.0	7.3	6.1	5.0	8.7	7.0	5.1	7.4	5.7	5.0	9.8
	2010	7.2	7.9	7.2	6.2	5.0	8.6	8.9	4.2	9.0	6.0	5.0	10.5
TFYR of Macedonia - LERY de Macédoine	2005	8.4	3.4	8.6	3.6	6.3	11.3	7.0	1.9	7.3	5.7	5.9	8.4
	2006	7.9	3.1	8.2	3.4	6.5	10.5	6.4	1.7	6.7	5.3	6.0	7.5
	2007	7.4	2.6	7.6	3.2	6.5	9.7	5.6	0.7	6.2	4.4	6.4	6.5
	2008	7.4	2.6	7.6	3.1	6.5	9.7	5.6	0.7	6.1	4.2	6.4	6.5
	2009	7.1	2.5	7.3	2.8	5.6	9.6	6.3	2.5	6.4	3.8	6.0	7.5
	2010	6.6	2.5	6.8	2.8	5.6	8.7	5.9	2.5	6.0	3.6	5.5	7.2
	2011	6.6	2.6	6.7	2.7	5.7	8.6	5.4	3.9	5.7	3.7	5.6	6.6
Thailand - Thaïlande	2000	15.7	6.7	16.2	11.3	12.2	19.8	10.2	5.4	10.4	10.6	8.8	14.0
	2005	10.4	2.5	10.9	4.7	8.1	14.4	6.5	2.0	6.8	7.0	6.1	7.9
	2006	10.3	2.5	10.8	4.7	8.1	14.3	6.3	2.1	6.7	6.9	5.7	8.4
	2007	8.3	1.2	8.8	2.9	7.2	12.3	5.1	1.2	5.5	3.6	5.8	6.2
	2008	8.3	1.2	8.8	3.0	7.2	12.3	5.5	1.1	5.9	3.8	6.4	6.4
	2009	8.4	1.2	8.9	3.0	7.2	12.3	5.9	1.2	6.2	4.1	6.3	7.3
Togo	2005	13.5	9.1	13.6	8.4	9.9	16.8	10.8	5.6	11.0	4.3	10.7	13.1
	2006	13.5	9.1	13.6	8.4	9.9	16.8	10.8	5.6	11.0	4.3	10.8	13.1
	2007	13.3	8.9	13.4	8.5	9.3	16.7	10.8	5.6	11.0	4.1	10.8	13.0
	2008	13.0	9.2	13.1	7.9	8.7	16.6	16.2	8.9	16.2	8.5	13.6	18.6
	2009	13.0	8.7	13.1	7.8	8.7	16.6	16.1	7.9	16.1	8.3	13.6	18.6
	2010	12.7	8.9	12.8	7.4	8.7	16.4	15.1	7.2	15.1	6.7	11.9	18.4
	2011	12.9	9.9	12.9	8.3	8.9	16.4	11.8	6.1	12.0	5.7	11.6	14.0
Tonga	2009	10.8	14.0	10.7	12.2	4.8	13.2	9.0	10.8	9.0	9.7	3.2	13.2
	2010	10.9	13.5	10.8	12.0	4.8	13.3	9.0	12.4	9.0	10.8	4.0	12.5
	2011	10.9	14.4	10.8	12.0	4.4	13.5	7.9	11.5	7.9	8.7	2.4	12.0
Trinidad and Tobago - Trinité-et-Tobago	2006	6.9	1.8	7.1	2.6	5.5	9.7	6.6	0.6	7.2	6.6	6.9	7.8
	2007	5.9	1.4	6.1	2.5	3.9	8.5	5.0	0.4	5.8	6.4	5.5	6.0
	2008	5.9	1.4	6.1	2.5	3.9	8.5	5.0	0.4	5.8	6.4	5.5	6.0
Tunisia - Tunisie	2005	21.4	15.0	21.7	14.3	14.2	27.7	20.2	9.3	20.7	13.1	16.8	26.5
	2006	21.2	14.4	21.6	14.0	13.8	27.6	19.9	10.1	20.4	13.2	16.6	26.4
	2008	18.7	7.8	19.3	12.0	11.7	25.2	16.9	3.6	18.2	11.4	15.1	23.5
Turkey - Turquie	2005	4.2	1.9	4.3	4.7	2.2	5.1	4.0	1.5	4.2	4.1	3.9	4.8
	2006	4.3	2.5	4.4	4.9	2.3	5.1	3.7	1.6	3.9	4.6	3.1	4.6
	2007	4.3	2.7	4.3	4.9	2.3	5.0	3.7	1.5	4.0	4.6	3.1	4.6
	2008	4.2	1.9	4.3	4.7	2.3	5.0	3.9	1.3	4.2	4.3	3.6	4.9
	2009	4.2	1.9	4.4	4.7	2.3	5.1	3.9	1.2	4.3	4.0	3.3	5.8
	2010	4.2	1.8	4.4	4.8	2.3	5.1	3.9	1.1	4.3	4.2	3.6	5.3
	2011	4.2	1.8	4.3	4.8	2.3	4.9	3.9	1.1	4.3	4.4	3.7	5.0
Tuvalu	2010	7.5	0.0	7.6	4.5	5.9	9.1	0.4	0.0	0.4	1.2	0.3	2.6

For sources and notes, see end of table.

Pour les sources et les notes, se reporter à la fin du tableau.

Market / Marchés	Year / Année	MFN rate - Simple average (2) / Droit NPF - Moyenne simple (2)						MFN rate - Weighted average (3) / Droit NPF - Moyenne pondérée (3)					
		Total of non-agricultural and non-fuel products / Total des produits non-agricoles et non-pétroliers	Ores and metals / Minérais et métaux	Manufactured products / Produits manufacturés	Chemical products / Produits chimiques	Machinery and transport equipment / Machines et matériel de transport	Other manufactured products / Produits manufacturés divers	Total of non-agricultural and non-fuel products / Total des produits non-agricoles et non-pétroliers	Ores and metals / Minérais et métaux	Manufactured products / Produits manufacturés	Chemical products / Produits chimiques	Machinery and transport equipment / Machines et matériel de transport	Other manufactured products / Produits manufacturés divers
SITC Rev.3 (1) / CTCI Rév.3 (1)		5+6+7+8 +27+28-667	27+28+68	(5+6+7+8) -(667+68)	5	7	(6+8) -(667+68)	5+6+7+8 +27+28-667	27+28+68	(5+6+7+8) -(667+68)	5	7	(6+8) -(667+68)
Uganda - Ouganda	2000	8.6	7.9	8.6	7.3	4.1	11.2	7.0	7.2	7.0	4.9	6.3	8.6
	2005	12.3	7.7	12.5	4.1	6.6	18.1	11.5	12.5	11.5	6.1	8.1	17.7
	2006	12.3	7.3	12.5	4.0	6.5	18.2	10.5	12.4	10.5	4.2	6.8	18.0
	2007	12.2	8.0	12.3	3.9	6.6	18.1	10.2	11.7	10.2	3.9	6.8	17.8
	2008	11.7	6.9	11.9	4.0	5.8	17.7	10.6	12.7	10.5	3.8	7.6	17.0
	2009	11.7	6.9	11.9	4.0	5.8	17.7	10.6	12.7	10.5	3.8	7.6	17.0
	2010	11.7	6.9	11.9	4.0	5.8	17.7	10.6	12.7	10.6	3.8	7.6	17.1
	2011	11.6	6.8	11.8	3.9	5.7	17.6	10.2	12.5	10.2	4.5	7.2	16.4
Ukraine	2006	4.6	2.5	4.8	3.2	4.3	5.6	5.7	2.2	5.9	2.2	8.4	4.5
	2008	4.7	2.6	4.8	3.2	4.2	5.6	6.4	1.9	6.7	2.5	9.7	4.5
	2009	4.0	1.9	4.1	3.3	3.1	4.9	3.6	1.3	3.8	2.5	4.6	3.3
	2010	4.0	1.9	4.1	3.3	3.0	4.9	2.9	1.1	3.1	2.3	3.2	3.6
	2011	4.0	1.6	4.1	3.2	2.9	5.0	3.2	0.9	3.3	2.3	4.0	3.4
United Arab Emirates - Émirats arabes unis	2005	4.9	4.8	4.9	4.8	4.9	5.0	4.6	4.8	4.6	4.3	4.5	5.0
	2006	4.9	4.8	4.9	4.6	4.9	5.0	4.6	4.8	4.6	4.3	4.5	5.0
	2007	4.8	4.8	4.8	4.5	4.6	4.9	4.6	3.1	4.7	4.3	4.4	4.9
	2008	4.8	4.8	4.8	4.5	4.5	4.9	4.5	2.4	4.7	4.3	4.5	5.0
	2009	4.8	4.8	4.8	4.5	4.5	4.9	4.5	2.4	4.7	4.3	4.5	5.0
United Republic of Tanzania - République-Unie de Tanzanie	2000	16.5	11.9	16.7	8.7	13.4	21.2	13.0	10.4	13.0	8.9	11.0	18.4
	2005	11.8	7.5	12.0	3.7	6.4	17.9	8.6	8.5	8.6	4.3	7.8	13.0
	2006	11.8	7.2	12.0	3.6	6.3	17.9	8.3	4.0	8.3	2.9	7.4	13.3
	2007	11.9	7.8	12.0	3.7	6.4	17.9	7.9	4.1	8.0	2.3	8.0	12.1
	2008	11.9	7.1	12.0	4.4	5.9	17.6	11.6	10.5	11.6	4.6	8.1	18.1
	2009	11.8	7.1	12.0	4.3	5.9	17.6	11.5	10.4	11.5	4.4	8.1	18.1
	2010	11.5	7.2	11.7	3.9	5.6	17.6	8.7	7.4	8.7	3.1	7.3	14.3
	2011	11.5	6.9	11.7	4.1	5.6	17.5	7.7	5.8	7.8	3.8	6.2	13.1
United States - États-Unis	2000	3.9	1.3	4.0	3.4	1.7	5.3	3.0	1.1	3.0	3.1	1.8	5.2
	2005	3.5	1.3	3.6	3.1	1.6	4.7	2.8	1.4	2.8	2.3	1.9	4.4
	2006	3.5	1.3	3.6	3.1	1.6	4.7	2.7	1.4	2.7	2.2	1.9	4.3
	2007	3.5	1.3	3.7	3.0	1.7	4.8	2.9	1.3	3.0	2.0	2.1	4.5
	2008	3.5	1.4	3.7	3.0	1.7	4.8	2.7	1.3	2.8	2.0	1.9	4.3
	2009	3.5	1.4	3.7	3.1	1.7	4.8	2.8	1.3	2.9	1.9	1.7	4.7
	2010	3.5	1.4	3.7	3.1	1.7	4.8	2.8	1.3	2.9	1.9	1.7	4.7
	2011	3.3	1.2	3.4	2.7	1.4	4.6	2.3	1.3	2.4	1.5	1.1	4.6
Uruguay	2000	14.9	10.5	15.1	11.4	10.9	18.4	14.4	9.6	14.5	12.6	12.8	17.6
	2005	11.8	7.0	12.0	8.4	7.1	15.3	10.5	4.5	10.6	9.2	8.7	14.2
	2006	11.4	6.3	11.7	7.9	6.8	15.1	9.7	2.9	9.9	7.4	8.6	13.7
	2007	11.4	6.3	11.6	7.9	6.8	15.0	9.6	2.8	9.8	7.2	8.7	13.9
	2008	11.4	6.3	11.6	7.9	6.6	15.2	10.0	2.8	10.2	6.7	9.5	14.4
	2009	11.4	6.3	11.6	7.8	6.6	15.1	10.2	3.5	10.3	7.4	8.8	14.9
	2010	11.4	6.3	11.6	7.8	6.6	15.1	10.5	3.5	10.6	7.4	9.4	14.9
	2011	11.4	6.3	11.6	7.8	6.6	15.1	10.5	3.9	10.6	7.5	9.4	14.8
Uzbekistan - Ouzbékistan	2006	15.0	14.8	15.1	9.5	10.9	19.3	11.1	10.2	11.1	11.0	9.8	13.4
	2007	14.7	15.0	14.7	9.3	10.8	19.0	10.4	7.8	10.5	10.3	9.6	12.2
	2008	14.9	15.7	14.9	9.7	10.2	19.3	10.4	10.7	10.4	10.0	10.0	11.0
	2009	14.6	15.6	14.5	9.4	9.1	19.3	10.1	10.7	10.0	9.9	9.4	11.2
Vanuatu	2006	15.1	11.2	15.1	11.4	15.3	15.8	7.0	10.3	7.0	7.5	4.9	13.2
	2007	15.3	10.1	15.5	12.4	15.1	16.2	9.9	7.0	10.0	9.4	7.4	15.2
	2008	14.8	11.5	14.9	11.4	13.8	16.3	14.3	9.5	14.4	14.5	12.7	16.0
	2009	14.8	11.5	14.9	11.4	13.8	16.3	14.3	9.5	14.4	14.5	12.7	16.0

For sources and notes, see end of table.

Pour les sources et les notes, se reporter à la fin du tableau.

Market / Marchés	Year / Année	MFN rate - Simple average (2) / Droit NPF - Moyenne simple (2)						MFN rate - Weighted average (3) / Droit NPF - Moyenne pondérée (3)					
		Total of non-agricultural and non-fuel products / Total des produits non-agricoles et non-pétroliers	Ores and metals / Minérais et métaux	Manufactured products / Produits manufacturés	Chemical products / Produits chimiques	Machinery and transport equipment / Machines et matériel de transport	Other manufactured products / Produits manufacturés divers	Total of non-agricultural and non-fuel products / Total des produits non-agricoles et non-pétroliers	Ores and metals / Minérais et métaux	Manufactured products / Produits manufacturés	Chemical products / Produits chimiques	Machinery and transport equipment / Machines et matériel de transport	Other manufactured products / Produits manufacturés divers
SITC Rev.3 (1) / CTCI Rév.3 (1)		5+6+7+8 +27+28-667	27+28+68	(5+6+7+8) -(667+68)	5	7	(6+8) -(667+68)	5+6+7+8 +27+28-667	27+28+68	(5+6+7+8) -(667+68)	5	7	(6+8) -(667+68)
Venezuela (Bolivarian Rep. of) - Venezuela (Rép. bolivarienne du)	2000	12.1	6.8	12.4	8.4	10.3	14.9	13.3	8.5	13.4	9.5	14.0	14.4
	2005	12.1	7.0	12.4	8.4	10.4	14.9	13.5	8.7	13.5	10.1	14.4	13.7
	2006	12.9	7.0	13.2	8.4	10.5	16.3	14.1	8.9	14.2	9.8	14.3	16.6
	2007	12.9	7.0	13.2	8.4	10.5	16.3	14.1	8.9	14.2	9.8	14.3	16.6
	2008	13.1	7.0	13.4	8.3	10.6	16.6	15.5	9.0	15.7	10.1	16.4	16.8
	2009	13.0	7.0	13.4	8.4	10.5	16.5	13.5	8.3	13.7	10.0	12.2	17.6
	2010	13.0	7.0	13.4	8.3	10.5	16.6	12.1	7.8	12.2	9.6	10.4	16.5
	2011	13.0	7.1	13.3	8.4	10.5	16.5	10.6	8.3	10.7	8.7	9.6	14.6
Viet Nam	2005	15.8	1.9	16.6	4.3	10.1	24.2	13.9	1.1	14.3	4.4	13.2	19.8
	2006	15.3	2.0	16.1	4.2	9.8	23.7	11.8	0.9	12.5	3.9	9.5	19.1
	2007	15.3	2.0	16.1	4.1	10.1	23.6	13.0	1.1	13.5	3.9	12.5	19.0
	2008	9.4	1.9	9.9	3.7	7.3	13.5	6.8	0.9	7.2	3.0	7.4	8.9
	2010	8.7	1.9	9.1	3.3	6.7	12.5	6.8	1.0	7.1	2.8	7.9	8.7
Yemen - Yémen	2000	12.5	11.3	12.6	9.8	11.1	14.3	12.5	10.5	12.5	8.5	13.2	13.2
	2006	6.2	6.6	6.2	5.8	4.9	7.0	5.6	5.5	5.6	5.2	4.7	6.7
	2009	6.2	6.8	6.1	5.9	5.0	6.8	5.3	5.6	5.3	5.2	4.5	6.5
	2011	6.2	6.9	6.2	5.9	5.0	6.9	5.1	5.7	5.0	5.2	4.5	5.4
Zambia - Zambie	2005	13.6	9.5	13.7	7.3	10.6	17.5	9.9	3.6	10.1	3.9	11.2	12.8
	2008	12.8	9.6	12.9	6.9	9.7	16.9	7.9	0.8	9.2	3.7	9.3	13.7
	2009	12.8	9.4	12.9	7.1	9.5	16.6	8.1	3.8	9.0	4.0	8.9	14.2
	2011	12.3	9.1	12.5	5.6	9.3	16.6	7.2	3.2	8.7	3.2	8.4	15.2
Zimbabwe	2007	13.1	7.7	13.4	7.9	9.3	18.1	9.7	5.1	14.7	7.5	16.7	16.4

Source:
UNCTAD/WITS, TRAINS

Source :
CNUCED/WITS, TRAINS

Notes:
(1) Product categories are defined in terms of SITC Revision 3, and all corresponding Harmonized System (HS) 6-digit codes have been aggregated for each category.

(2) Simple average for each product group calculated from simple average at HS 6-digit level.

(3) Weighted average for each product group calculated from simple average at HS 6-digit level. Country's own imports at HS 6-digit level for corresponding years are used as weights. Where imports are not reported, mirror imports have been compiled using exports of partner countries.

(4) From 2008 onwards, member of the European Union.
(5) From 2004 onwards, member of the European Union.

Notes :
(1) Les catégories de produits sont définies sur la base de la CTCI, révision 3, et pour chaque catégorie, les codes à 6 chiffres du Système harmonisé (SH) correspondants ont été agrégés.

(2) Moyenne arithmétique, pour chaque catégorie de produits, calculée à partir des moyennes arithmétiques au niveau du code à 6 chiffres du SH.

(3) Moyenne arithmétique pondérée, pour chaque catégorie de produits, calculée à partir des moyennes simples au niveau du code à 6 chiffres du SH. Pour chaque année, les coefficients de pondération sont les importations de chaque marché au niveau du code à 6 chiffres du SH. Lorsque les importations n'étaient pas disponibles, elles ont été évaluées par les données miroir basées sur les exportations des pays partenaires.

(4) À partir de 2008, membre de l'Union européenne.
(5) À partir de 2004, membre de l'Union européenne.

5

INTERNATIONAL TRADE IN **SERVICES**

COMMERCE INTERNATIONAL DES **SERVICES**

1

2

3

4

5

6

7

8

5.1.1 Value of exports and imports of services of countries and geographical regions

Region, country or territory	Exports - Exportations Millions of dollars							
	1980	1990	2000	2005	2008	2009	2010	2011
WORLD	**395 659**	**830 236**	**1 521 680**	**2 563 438**	**3 914 741**	**3 486 623**	**3 834 989**	**4 243 259**
DEVELOPING ECONOMIES	73 389	150 390	350 998	629 352	1 036 588	940 483	1 137 766	1 265 634
TRANSITION ECONOMIES	9 812	16 685	24 260	57 496	113 276	94 616	103 089	120 970
DEVELOPED ECONOMIES	312 459	663 161	1 146 422	1 876 591	2 764 877	2 451 524	2 594 134	2 856 655
Developing economies: Africa	**13 438**	**21 711**	**33 120**	**59 654**	**90 363**	**81 581**	**90 541**	**91 731**
Eastern Africa	*1 836*	*3 144*	*5 160*	*8 733*	*14 556*	*13 347*	*15 889*	*17 843*
Burundi	-	17	4	35	83	50	79	-
Comoros	2	17	-	43	64	59	65	-
Djibouti	-	-	162	248	297	322	336	
Eritrea			61	-	-	-	-	-
Ethiopia (…1991)	125	305						
Ethiopia	–	–	506	1 012	1 959	1 895	2 244	(e)2 938
Kenya	577	1 138	993	1 880	3 251	2 883	3 675	(e)3 604
Madagascar	79	153	364	498	1 296	862	1 030	(e)1 045
Malawi	32	37	34	107	124	131	(e)141	-
Mauritius	140	484	1 070	1 618	2 544	2 239	2 695	(e)3 277
Mozambique	118	103	325	342	555	612	647	676
Rwanda	34	42	59	129	408	341	310	(e)431
Seychelles	91	172	287	369	608	600	592	(e)614
Somalia	66	-	-	-	-	-	-	-
Uganda	10	-	213	525	799	984	1 376	1 452
United Republic of Tanzania	165	131	627	1 269	1 999	1 855	2 092	(e)2 415
Zambia	151	107	115	273	300	241	311	375
Zimbabwe	169	264	291	267	150	167	175	-
Middle Africa	*1 132*	*1 180*	*1 431*	*2 019*	*3 469*	*3 545*	*3 497*	*3 935*
Angola	-	109	267	177	329	623	857	-
Cameroon	401	382	682	970	1 484	1 249	1 159	-
Central African Republic	54	69	31	44	68	65	(e)69	-
Chad	0	41	51	108	252	457	(e)390	-
Congo	111	99	137	220	372	378	(e)399	-
Dem. Rep. of the Congo	103	230	62	308	703	541	389	-
Equatorial Guinea	-	5	9	36	57	48	(e)50	-
Gabon	325	242	178	146	-	-	(e)172	-
Sao Tome and Principe	3	4	14	9	10	11	12	-
Northern Africa	*5 175*	*10 455*	*16 713*	*29 917*	*48 532*	*43 114*	*46 388*	*43 108*
Algeria	476	497	910	2 507	3 490	2 983	3 566	(e)3 857
Egypt	2 393	5 971	9 803	14 643	24 912	21 520	23 807	(e)19 140
Libya	164	117	172	534	208	385	410	-
Morocco	783	2 009	3 034	8 098	13 416	12 336	12 545	13 963
Sudan (…2011)	292	173	(b)27	114	493	392	254	-
Tunisia	1 067	1 688	2 767	4 021	6 014	5 499	5 805	(e)4 865
Southern Africa	*2 683*	*3 897*	*5 841*	*12 865*	*14 500*	*13 282*	*15 557*	*16 406*
Botswana	101	210	325	834	872	496	394	(e)334
Lesotho	32	41	24	36	43	44	48	-
Namibia	-	132	174	413	555	521	853	(e)909
South Africa	2 463	3 407	5 046	11 300	12 805	12 020	14 004	14 824
Swaziland	36	108	273	283	225	200	257	-
Western Africa	*2 611*	*3 035*	*3 975*	*6 119*	*9 306*	*8 293*	*9 211*	*10 439*
Benin	62	126	136	194	348	221	376	-
Burkina Faso	49	69	31	68	132	153	(e)301	-
Cape Verde	10	35	108	269	601	486	518	(e)593
Côte d'Ivoire	564	590	482	832	1 025	975	(e)1 045	-
Gambia	19	59	-	82	118	104	88	153
Ghana	107	86	504	1 106	1 801	1 770	1 477	(e)1 751
Guinea	-	157	68	83	103	72	62	77
Guinea-Bissau	-	7	5	5	44	33	(e)44	-
Liberia	13	-	-	213	510	274	158	-
Mali	58	85	99	274	454	354	384	-
Mauritania	56	27	47	80	138	159	119	210
Niger	41	44	38	88	131	100	(e)126	-
Nigeria	1 127	965	1 833	(b)1 793	2 263	2 218	3 081	3 386
Senegal	337	515	387	777	1 294	1 022	(e)1 051	-
Sierra Leone	49	61	42	78	61	58	60	-
Togo	74	149	62	177	283	294	(e)320	-

For sources and notes, see end of table.

1980	1990	2000	2005	2008	2009	2010	2011	Régions, pays ou territoires
447 772	877 742	1 515 961	2 467 444	3 759 273	3 366 539	3 685 107	4 081 900	**MONDE**
139 580	193 761	415 182	700 428	1 186 860	1 087 216	1 298 742	1 482 159	ÉCONOMIES EN DÉVELOPPEMENT
12 415	30 580	28 388	68 469	131 310	107 272	123 709	145 957	ÉCONOMIES EN TRANSITION
295 777	653 401	1 072 391	1 698 546	2 441 103	2 172 052	2 262 655	2 453 784	ÉCONOMIES DÉVELOPPÉES
29 408	30 315	41 266	77 117	152 430	135 571	151 273	168 310	**Économies en développement : Afrique**
3 419	*4 176*	*5 743*	*8 505*	*14 387*	*13 512*	*15 295*	*18 669*	*Afrique orientale*
-	129	43	134	259	177	168	-	Burundi
12	44	-	46	79	83	93	-	Comores
-	-	71	84	130	128	119	-	Djibouti
-	-	28	-	-	-	-	-	Érythrée
208	359	-	-	-	-	-	-	Éthiopie (...1991)
-	-	490	1 194	2 410	2 227	2 546	(e)3 409	Éthiopie
502	700	719	1 137	1 870	1 812	2 016	(e)2 586	Kenya
311	242	522	615	1 579	1 218	1 017	(e)1 101	Madagascar
179	268	167	143	99	110	(e)126	-	Malawi
174	421	763	1 198	1 920	1 607	1 984	(e)2 480	Maurice
124	206	446	649	965	1 069	1 198	1 472	Mozambique
133	129	200	304	521	519	557	(e)613	Rwanda
40	80	190	235	371	392	441	(e)429	Seychelles
133	-	-	-	-	-	-	-	Somalie
123	195	459	609	1 257	1 417	1 880	2 280	Ouganda
295	288	682	1 207	1 649	1 709	1 850	(e)2 160	République-Unie de Tanzanie
651	386	335	471	906	705	940	1 193	Zambie
394	495	443	304	195	182	187	-	Zimbabwe
3 559	*5 828*	*6 448*	*14 477*	*35 825*	*31 295*	*34 256*	*40 822*	*Afrique centrale*
-	1 807	2 699	6 791	22 139	19 169	18 754	-	Angola
717	1 045	1 017	1 455	2 668	1 780	1 746	-	Cameroun
142	169	114	105	165	156	(e)183	-	République centrafricaine
24	228	241	1 567	1 868	1 881	(e)2 176	-	Tchad
480	769	738	1 417	3 571	3 213	(e)4 854	-	Congo
834	758	215	1 167	2 097	1 783	2 663	-	Rép. dém. du Congo
-	36	552	921	1 663	2 015	(e)1 889	-	Guinée équatoriale
789	1 007	858	1 042	-	-	(e)1 956	-	Gabon
6	9	13	11	22	19	34	-	Sao Tomé-et-Principe
9 733	*9 013*	*14 526*	*25 521*	*45 725*	*42 458*	*45 854*	*46 242*	*Afrique septentrionale*
2 697	1 321	2 360	4 783	11 082	11 679	11 906	(e)11 534	Algérie
2 343	3 788	7 513	10 508	17 615	13 935	14 718	(e)13 962	Égypte
2 303	1 385	895	2 349	4 344	5 063	6 127	-	Libye
1 436	1 445	1 892	3 845	6 694	6 899	7 436	8 574	Maroc
353	228	(b)648	1 844	2 620	1 907	2 321	(e)2 114	Soudan (...2011)
600	846	1 218	2 191	3 370	2 974	3 345	(e)3 312	Tunisie
3 815	*4 728*	*7 250*	*14 130*	*19 369*	*17 316*	*21 224*	*22 826*	*Afrique australe*
216	376	547	864	783	952	877	(e)1 134	Botswana
50	81	249	369	371	385	516	-	Lesotho
-	354	320	369	589	609	705	(e)721	Namibie
3 295	3 738	5 823	12 125	16 976	14 808	18 456	19 664	Afrique du Sud
80	179	310	403	651	562	670	-	Swaziland
8 882	*6 570*	*7 299*	*14 485*	*37 124*	*30 990*	*34 644*	*39 751*	*Afrique occidentale*
109	131	192	279	510	496	515	-	Bénin
209	216	140	360	605	559	(e)832	-	Burkina Faso
7	28	100	209	359	318	296	(e)311	Cap-Vert
1 531	1 626	1 227	2 124	2 660	2 485	(e)2 824	-	Côte d'Ivoire
43	53	-	47	86	83	72	68	Gambie
270	301	584	1 273	2 298	2 943	3 003	(e)3 670	Ghana
-	367	285	278	444	331	396	572	Guinée
-	20	29	42	85	87	(e)103	-	Guinée-Bissau
73	-	-	855	1 411	1 145	1 079	-	Libéria
212	374	335	588	1 024	826	1 017	-	Mali
128	137	149	379	769	638	670	765	Mauritanie
279	227	132	279	601	735	(e)843	-	Niger
5 285	1 976	3 300	(b)6 624	24 373	18 697	21 332	24 564	Nigéria
340	676	405	806	1 415	1 151	(e)1 121	-	Sénégal
85	74	113	91	125	122	144	-	Sierra Leone
167	244	118	251	359	375	(e)398	-	Togo

Pour les sources et les notes, se reporter à la fin du tableau.

5

Region, country or territory	Exports - Exportations Millions of dollars							
	1980	1990	2000	2005	2008	2009	2010	2011
Developing economies: America	18 982	31 595	61 760	88 077	129 346	117 819	133 305	148 305
Caribbean	3 878	7 473	15 485	23 060	27 920	25 935	29 965	30 553
Anguilla	-	41	65	99	117	108	111	119
Antigua and Barbuda	45	312	415	463	560	511	479	493
Aruba	-	411	1 012	1 308	1 599	1 523	1 546	1 677
Bahamas	746	1 500	1 973	2 511	2 534	2 351	2 494	2 605
Barbados	345	654	1 020	1 454	1 822	1 503	1 638	(e)1 579
Cuba	-	525	2 642	7 075	9 252	8 384	10 433	-
Curaçao								1 227
Dominica	6	33	90	86	118	120	131	133
Dominican Republic	309	1 097	3 228	3 935	4 951	4 836	5 099	(e)5 283
Grenada	21	64	153	116	149	139	138	148
Haiti	90	52	172	141	339	375	238	(e)258
Jamaica	401	1 027	2 026	2 330	2 795	2 651	2 634	(e)2 659
Montserrat	-	18	16	15	14	12	11	10
Netherlands Antilles	878	1 161	1 571	1 875	2 055	2 035	(e)3 452	–
Saint Kitts and Nevis	8	54	99	163	161	132	160	173
Saint Lucia	41	151	324	436	364	353	390	380
Saint Vincent and the Grenadines	18	45	128	158	153	139	139	143
Sint Maarten (Dutch part)	–	–	–	–	–	–	–	902
Trinidad and Tobago	411	329	554	897	936	765	874	-
Central America	6 196	10 793	19 767	25 083	32 176	28 493	30 783	32 972
Belize	-	115	153	302	386	344	354	344
Costa Rica	194	609	1 936	2 622	4 083	3 593	4 330	5 006
El Salvador	139	329	698	(b)946	1 058	863	976	1 073
Guatemala	211	356	777	1 308	1 873	1 925	2 291	2 359
Honduras	82	137	507	700	885	953	1 022	1 083
Mexico	4 591	8 094	13 480	15 666	17 575	14 730	15 168	15 298
Nicaragua	44	60	221	309	526	560	573	660
Panama, excl. Canal Zone	902	–	–	–	–	–	–	–
Panama	–	1 092	1 994	3 231	5 788	5 525	6 070	7 150
South America	8 908	13 328	26 508	39 935	69 250	63 391	72 557	84 779
Argentina	1 876	2 446	4 936	6 634	12 156	10 967	13 117	14 193
Bolivia (Plurinational State of)	88	146	224	489	500	515	550	801
Brazil	1 737	3 762	9 498	16 048	30 451	27 728	31 821	38 434
Chile	1 263	1 848	4 083	7 134	10 824	8 634	10 797	(e)12 361
Colombia	1 342	1 600	2 049	2 668	4 137	4 202	4 446	4 907
Ecuador	367	538	849	1 012	1 442	1 337	1 473	(e)1 567
Guyana	20	-	169	148	212	170	248	(e)240
Paraguay	164	418	595	656	1 150	1 432	1 473	1 917
Peru	715	798	1 555	2 289	3 649	3 645	3 956	(e)4 724
Suriname	176	37	91	204	285	287	241	201
Uruguay	468	466	1 276	1 311	2 277	2 245	2 576	3 405
Venezuela (Bolivarian Rep. of)	693	1 183	1 182	1 342	2 170	2 227	1 857	2 031
Developing economies: Asia	40 657	96 306	255 162	478 642	813 259	738 130	910 624	1 021 847
Eastern Asia	15 210	42 918	125 772	222 657	385 121	340 546	434 190	485 989
China	-	5 855	30 431	74 404	147 112	129 549	171 203	(e)183 101
China, Hong Kong SAR	5 876	18 294	40 433	63 700	92 286	86 407	106 159	121 470
China, Macao SAR	379	1 473	3 280	8 567	17 760	18 821	28 703	(e)39 526
China, Taiwan Province of	1 944	7 008	20 010	25 827	36 829	31 774	40 357	46 270
Korea, Republic of	4 915	10 240	31 540	49 745	90 635	73 580	87 282	95 000
Mongolia	-	48	78	414	499	415	486	622
Southern Asia	5 044	7 656	22 491	64 846	125 007	109 181	145 155	158 988
Afghanistan	36	-	-	-	-	-	-	-
Bangladesh	211	392	815	1 249	1 996	1 976	2 418	2 645
Bhutan	-	28	20	42	55	57	69	82
India	2 971	4 625	16 685	(b)52 527	107 131	93 036	123 762	(e)137 149
Iran (Islamic Rep. of)	731	436	1 797	4 999	8 009	6 777	8 282	-
Maldives	52	101	348	323	721	660	769	(e)852
Nepal	155	204	506	380	724	705	672	863
Pakistan	652	1 429	1 380	3 678	4 263	3 983	6 593	5 041
Sri Lanka	231	440	939	1 540	2 002	1 892	2 474	3 084
South-Eastern Asia	9 689	29 505	68 922	119 081	197 837	185 577	221 406	254 721
Brunei Darussalam	-	-	198	616	867	915	(e)1 054	(e)1 255
Cambodia	-	-	428	1 118	1 645	1 625	1 744	(e)2 256
Indonesia (...2002)	-	2 488	5 214					
Indonesia	–	–	–	12 927	15 247	13 156	16 766	20 532

For sources and notes, see end of table.

Imports - Importations Millions de dollars								Régions, pays ou territoires
1980	1990	2000	2005	2008	2009	2010	2011	
29 929	**37 863**	**74 085**	**95 325**	**151 015**	**140 432**	**168 674**	**197 707**	**Économies en développement : Amérique**
2 850	*4 821*	*7 693*	*9 495*	*12 316*	*10 929*	*12 693*	*12 740*	*Caraïbes*
-	15	41	56	87	62	57	56	Anguilla
17	105	156	227	272	228	226	217	Antigua-et-Barbuda
-	135	644	712	785	686	672	857	Aruba
226	573	1 026	1 286	1 403	1 196	1 181	1 292	Bahamas
129	250	485	656	736	711	733	(e)730	Barbade
-	(b)1 313	778	1 015	2 079	1 670	1 918	-	Cuba
							794	Curaçao
6	30	53	50	70	66	67	68	Dominique
399	440	1 373	1 478	1 989	1 849	2 163	(e)2 192	République dominicaine
11	33	89	96	113	98	94	96	Grenade
162	72	282	544	757	772	1 275	(e)1 097	Haïti
370	697	1 423	1 722	2 367	1 881	1 824	(e)1 938	Jamaïque
-	12	23	26	23	18	17	16	Montserrat
529	518	668	734	871	930	(e)1 686	_	Antilles néerlandaises
6	35	76	95	120	96	99	97	Saint-Kitts-et-Nevis
22	81	133	177	215	190	203	207	Sainte-Lucie
11	32	56	79	102	94	91	92	Saint-Vincent-et-les Grenadines
							237	Saint-Martin (partie néerlandaise)
645	479	388	541	326	383	387	-	Trinité-et-Tobago
8 460	*12 652*	*22 231*	*28 200*	*34 593*	*31 618*	*35 269*	*40 677*	*Amérique centrale*
-	60	123	159	170	162	162	170	Belize
286	550	1 273	1 506	1 882	1 405	1 783	1 806	Costa Rica
273	315	933	(b)1 075	1 271	953	1 070	1 106	El Salvador
487	384	825	1 450	2 149	2 084	2 381	2 504	Guatemala
174	220	694	929	1 213	1 103	1 331	1 556	Honduras
6 514	10 323	16 891	20 823	24 526	23 047	25 175	29 361	Mexique
104	112	351	448	750	664	719	838	Nicaragua
588		_	_	_	_	_	_	Panama, sans la zone du canal
_	689	1 141	1 811	2 633	2 201	2 648	3 336	Panama
18 620	*20 390*	*44 162*	*57 630*	*104 106*	*97 885*	*120 711*	*144 291*	*Amérique du Sud*
3 788	3 120	9 219	7 626	13 440	12 252	14 125	16 423	Argentine
259	311	468	683	1 017	1 015	1 152	1 661	Bolivie (État plurinational de)
4 871	7 523	16 660	24 356	47 140	46 974	62 592	76 340	Brésil
1 583	2 076	4 802	7 756	11 787	10 078	11 816	(e)13 951	Chili
1 170	1 750	3 307	4 770	7 210	7 023	8 070	9 528	Colombie
704	804	1 269	2 142	3 013	2 618	3 010	(e)3 191	Équateur
107	-	193	201	323	272	344	(e)408	Guyana
165	434	420	343	592	538	755	903	Paraguay
880	1 164	2 290	3 123	5 704	4 789	5 993	(e)6 830	Pérou
364	171	216	352	398	285	259	563	Suriname
476	393	882	939	1 523	1 315	1 548	1 968	Uruguay
4 253	2 534	4 435	5 339	11 958	10 724	11 048	12 527	Venezuela (Rép. bolivarienne du)
79 744	**124 753**	**298 448**	**524 279**	**878 345**	**806 644**	**972 920**	**1 109 743**	**Économies en développement : Asie**
12 603	*42 690*	*121 944*	*212 809*	*343 637*	*318 396*	*386 382*	*446 975*	*Asie orientale*
-	4 352	36 031	83 796	158 924	158 947	193 321	(e)237 583	Chine
4 029	12 937	24 699	33 977	47 064	43 937	51 006	55 877	Chine (RAS de Hong Kong)
22	247	828	2 384	5 687	4 950	7 502	(e)10 329	Chine (RAS de Macao)
2 554	14 658	26 647	32 480	34 982	29 783	37 864	42 026	Province chinoise de Taiwan
3 738	10 341	33 577	59 696	96 369	80 221	95 908	99 378	Corée, République de
-	155	163	476	610	558	780	1 782	Mongolie
10 216	*13 807*	*28 231*	*70 792*	*124 007*	*112 649*	*156 212*	*169 036*	*Asie méridionale*
144	-	-	-	-	-	-	-	Afghanistan
481	700	1 620	2 207	3 664	3 396	4 396	5 218	Bangladesh
-	28	46	128	93	75	90	117	Bhoutan
2 981	6 090	19 188	(b)47 287	88 349	81 049	116 842	(e)124 566	Inde
5 223	3 962	3 127	10 840	17 885	17 847	23 394	-	Iran (Rép. islamique d')
43	38	110	213	351	286	306	(e)337	Maldives
88	167	200	435	852	842	871	782	Népal
877	2 073	2 252	7 508	9 717	6 551	7 105	7 969	Pakistan
351	639	1 621	2 089	3 010	2 522	3 113	4 012	Sri Lanka
14 097	*28 814*	*87 918*	*138 629*	*212 049*	*187 059*	*225 146*	*264 081*	*Asie du Sud-Est*
-	-	768	1 110	1 403	1 434	(e)1 612	(e)1 891	Brunéi Darussalam
-	-	328	642	1 036	1 018	1 088	(e)1 480	Cambodge
-	6 056	15 637					_	Indonésie (...2002)
_	_	_	22 049	28 245	22 896	26 089	32 354	Indonésie

Pour les sources et les notes, se reporter à la fin du tableau.

5

Region, country or territory	Exports - Exportations Millions of dollars							
	1980	1990	2000	2005	2008	2009	2010	2011
Lao People's Dem. Rep.	-	24	176	204	402	397	511	-
Malaysia	1 135	3 859	13 941	19 576	30 321	28 769	32 760	35 001
Myanmar	53	93	471	257	303	313	363	-
Philippines	1 447	3 244	3 377	4 525	9 717	11 014	14 095	15 450
Singapore	4 856	12 811	28 547	55 702	99 249	93 474	112 308	(e)129 182
Thailand	1 490	6 419	13 868	19 892	33 037	30 103	34 298	(e)41 144
Timor-Leste	–			–	44	46	47	
Viet Nam	-	182	2 702	4 265	7 006	5 766	7 460	(e)8 879
Western Asia	*10 714*	*16 228*	*37 978*	*72 058*	*105 294*	*102 826*	*109 872*	*122 148*
Bahrain	333	359	933	3 048	3 740	3 653	4 047	3 040
Iraq	-		-	355	1 967	2 623	(e)3 382	-
Jordan	1 003	1 447	1 640	2 334	4 478	4 554	5 600	5 138
Kuwait	1 225	1 279	1 823	4 775	11 959	11 309	9 323	10 131
Lebanon	-	-	-	10 858	17 574	16 889	15 976	-
Occupied Palestinian territory	-	-	473	282	496	579	831	(e)662
Oman	9	-	452	(b)939	1 826	1 620	1 899	2 148
Qatar	-	-	363	3 221	3 425	2 002	3 011	7 394
Saudi Arabia	5 191	3 027	4 779	(b)11 410	(b)9 370	9 749	10 683	11 489
Syrian Arab Republic	365	874	1 699	2 910	4 415	4 798	7 333	
Turkey	711	8 016	19 528	26 770	35 243	33 655	34 440	(e)38 342
United Arab Emirates	789	764	2 170	4 784	9 596	10 157	11 736	12 798
Yemen, Arab Republic	164	–	–	–	–	–	–	–
Yemen, Democratic	87	–	–	–	–	–	–	–
Yemen	–	106	211	372	1 205	1 237	1 612	1 248
Developing economies: Oceania	**312**	**778**	**956**	**2 979**	**3 620**	**2 953**	**3 296**	**3 752**
Fiji	201	417	432	851	978	706	861	-
French Polynesia	-	-	-	1 081	1 192	1 030	955	-
Kiribati	4	8	6	11	5	5	-	-
Micronesia (Federated States of)	–	-	18	19	26	-	-	-
New Caledonia	-	-	-	380	583	499	547	
Papua New Guinea	43	206	243	305	369	185	310	(e)484
Samoa	8	36	59	113	133	148	158	171
Solomon Islands	12	25	52	41	59	70	106	(e)128
Tonga	9	26	14	35	38	35	(e)42	(e)54
Tuvalu	-	-	1	2	2	-	-	-
Vanuatu	-	60	130	139	234	248	277	286
Transition economies	**9 812**	**16 685**	**24 260**	**57 496**	**113 276**	**94 616**	**103 089**	**120 970**
Albania	11	32	448	1 165	2 478	2 484	2 308	2 437
Armenia			137	411	645	590	762	827
Azerbaijan	–	–	260	683	1 548	1 779	2 114	2 732
Belarus	–	–	1 000	2 073	4 258	3 504	4 501	5 261
Bosnia and Herzegovina	–	–	450	989	1 672	1 431	1 286	1 287
Croatia	–	–	4 071	9 967	14 751	11 725	11 275	(e)12 389
Georgia	–	–	360	715	1 260	1 314	1 599	1 980
Kazakhstan	–	–	1 053	2 228	4 426	4 236	4 253	4 509
Kyrgyzstan	–	–	62	259	896	860	693	1 117
Montenegro	–	–	–	–	1 099	945	989	1 175
Republic of Moldova	–	–	165	399	844	673	701	869
Russian Federation	–	–	9 758	24 970	51 178	41 594	44 981	54 025
Serbia and Montenegro	–	–	624	2 239				
Serbia	–	–	–	-	4 543	4 156	4 233	5 105
SFR of Yugoslavia	4 541	6 374			–	–	–	–
Tajikistan	–	–	-	146	181	180	209	(e)400
TFYR of Macedonia	–	–	317	517	1 017	862	917	1 114
Ukraine	–	–	3 896	9 354	17 895	13 859	17 064	19 426
USSR	5 260	10 280			–	–	–	–
Uzbekistan	–	–	447	660	1 196	1 036	1 328	1 773
Developed economies: America	**54 995**	**167 042**	**329 371**	**432 503**	**607 814**	**569 873**	**621 338**	**677 253**
Bermuda	-	-	-	-	1 580	1 328	1 426	(e)1 450
Canada	7 445	19 210	40 230	55 829	68 359	60 089	69 166	76 154
United States	47 550	147 832	289 141	376 674	537 875	508 456	550 746	599 649
Developed economies: Asia	**22 962**	**45 953**	**86 066**	**121 278**	**172 660**	**149 653**	**165 515**	**172 296**
Israel	2 722	4 569	15 701	16 873	23 917	21 411	24 229	26 860
Japan	20 240	41 384	70 365	104 406	148 743	128 242	141 286	145 437
Developed economies: Europe	**229 631**	**437 469**	**706 686**	**1 283 071**	**1 929 688**	**1 682 828**	**1 750 521**	**1 945 272**
Austria	9 423	23 279	23 093	42 446	63 569	54 497	54 484	(e)61 752
Belgium (1)	12 925	28 417	49 789	56 166	88 221	84 017	87 058	(e)89 426

For sources and notes, see end of table.

Imports - Importations Millions de dollars								Régions, pays ou territoires
1980	1990	2000	2005	2008	2009	2010	2011	
-	26	43	39	108	136	263	-	Rép. dém. populaire lao
2 957	5 485	16 747	21 956	30 270	27 472	32 216	37 729	Malaisie
74	72	324	497	617	617	789	-	Myanmar
1 439	1 761	5 247	5 865	8 557	8 900	11 360	11 857	Philippines
2 912	8 642	30 112	55 259	87 442	79 351	96 463	(e)114 069	Singapour
1 644	6 309	15 460	26 762	45 926	36 484	44 847	(e)51 090	Thaïlande
-	-	-	-	490	564	496	-	Timor-Leste
-	126	3 252	4 450	7 956	8 187	9 921	(e)11 859	Viet Nam
42 827	*39 441*	*60 355*	*102 049*	*198 652*	*188 540*	*205 181*	*229 652*	*Asie occidentale*
474	474	757	1 416	2 030	1 741	1 905	1 778	Bahreïn
-	-	-	6 095	7 225	8 568	(e)9 861	-	Iraq
1 094	1 268	1 722	2 542	4 127	3 818	4 419	4 406	Jordanie
3 067	3 359	4 921	8 715	15 777	13 850	14 965	17 664	Koweït
-	-	-	7 895	13 464	14 051	13 428	-	Liban
-	-	548	504	836	931	1 143	(e)922	Territoire palestinien occupé
518	719	1 759	3 145	5 878	5 482	6 291	7 066	Oman
-	-	1 640	4 144	7 222	5 918	8 780	16 867	Qatar
30 231	22 384	25 228	(b)33 120	(b)75 234	74 991	76 772	78 025	Arabie saoudite
521	892	1 667	2 359	3 153	2 719	3 473		République arabe syrienne
569	3 071	8 153	11 505	17 932	16 906	19 695	(e)21 288	Turquie
2 279	3 075	8 574	19 367	43 427	37 433	42 100	49 594	Émirats arabes unis
375	–	–	–	–	–	–	–	Yémen, République arabe du
130	–	–	–	–	–	–	–	Yémen, Démocratique
–	683	809	1 241	2 348	2 133	2 349	2 273	Yémen
499	**830**	**1 383**	**3 707**	**5 070**	**4 568**	**5 876**	**6 398**	**Économies en développement : Océanie**
124	257	329	506	597	451	509	-	Fidji
-	-	-	737	719	713	637	-	Polynésie française
9	19	23	44	58	50	-	-	Kiribati
–	-	57	60	64	-	-	-	Micronésie (États fédérés de)
-	-	-	841	1 390	1 102	1 384	-	Nouvelle-Calédonie
302	403	772	1 278	1 843	1 840	2 757	(e)2 879	Papouasie-Nouvelle-Guinée
15	25	29	56	73	78	87	75	Samoa
28	79	73	58	116	105	187	(e)203	Îles Salomon
6	23	18	41	55	49	(e)47	(e)61	Tonga
-	-	11	12	19	-	-	-	Tuvalu
-	24	70	74	135	109	121	145	Vanuatu
12 415	**30 580**	**28 388**	**68 469**	**131 310**	**107 272**	**123 709**	**145 957**	**Économies en transition**
18	29	429	1 383	2 379	2 233	2 008	2 249	Albanie
–	–	193	531	973	858	1 004	1 126	Arménie
–	–	485	2 653	3 891	3 389	3 846	5 729	Azerbaïdjan
–	–	536	1 093	2 630	2 116	2 878	3 183	Bélarus
–	–	263	436	692	647	536	529	Bosnie-Herzégovine
–	–	1 822	3 401	4 577	3 853	3 505	(e)3 612	Croatie
–	–	295	631	1 239	974	1 085	1 253	Géorgie
–	–	1 850	7 496	11 119	10 040	11 332	10 921	Kazakhstan
–	–	148	290	993	867	924	1 138	Kirghizistan
–	–	–	–	593	460	446	440	Monténégro
–	–	202	420	837	713	771	895	République de Moldova
–	–	16 847	38 745	75 468	61 429	73 682	89 972	Fédération de Russie
–	–	293	1 818					Serbie-et-Monténégro
–	–	–	–	4 692	3 856	4 036	4 511	Serbie
5 211	15 012	–	–	–	–	–	–	RSF de Yougoslavie
–	–	-	252	456	291	393	(e)458	Tadjikistan
–	–	268	556	1 001	838	853	978	LERY de Macédoine
–	–	3 004	7 548	16 154	11 505	12 660	14 539	Ukraine
7 186	15 539	–	–	–	–	–	–	URSS
–	–	-	-	-	415	486	557	Ouzbékistan
51 636	**145 960**	**264 226**	**370 315**	**495 939**	**464 068**	**497 181**	**531 468**	**Économies développées : Amérique**
-	-	-	-	1 042	984	1 007	(e)967	Bermudes
10 666	28 303	44 118	65 749	88 791	79 268	91 255	101 188	Canada
40 970	117 657	220 108	304 566	406 106	383 816	404 919	429 313	États-Unis
34 670	**89 203**	**118 455**	**137 850**	**189 195**	**165 779**	**175 450**	**187 500**	**Économies développées : Asie**
2 310	4 921	12 047	13 826	19 769	17 089	18 055	19 841	Israël
32 360	84 281	106 408	124 024	169 426	148 690	157 395	167 659	Japon
201 060	**401 142**	**666 320**	**1 151 636**	**1 697 762**	**1 492 761**	**1 529 831**	**1 663 419**	**Économies développées : Europe**
6 204	14 197	16 462	30 791	42 697	36 883	37 112	(e)42 254	Autriche
12 827	26 581	41 868	51 190	83 167	75 968	78 561	(e)84 897	Belgique (1)

Pour les sources et les notes, se reporter à la fin du tableau.

Region, country or territory	Exports - Exportations Millions of dollars							
	1980	1990	2000	2005	2008	2009	2010	2011
Bulgaria	1 211	837	2 175	4 428	7 833	6 836	6 837	(e)7 540
Cyprus	482	2 004	4 068	6 511	9 577	8 028	8 012	(e)8 579
Czechoslovakia	–	2 673						
Czech Republic	–	–	6 839	11 856	21 783	19 295	20 910	(e)23 031
Denmark	4 785	12 830	23 721	43 436	72 572	55 131	60 444	(e)65 605
Estonia	–	–	1 486	3 248	5 175	4 411	4 534	(e)5 473
Faeroe Islands	-	-	54	133	252	170	191	-
Finland	2 733	4 649	7 728	16 995	31 922	27 884	27 807	(e)27 453
France	43 506	67 782	82 703	122 331	165 364	144 047	145 491	(e)167 812
Germany, Federal Republic of	32 817							
Germany	–	62 447	82 929	164 238	254 449	231 602	237 574	(e)258 129
Greece	3 947	6 560	19 239	34 273	49 898	37 484	37 717	(e)38 279
Hungary	-	2 884	5 901	12 867	20 112	18 399	19 410	(e)21 662
Iceland	280	560	1 044	(e)2 034	2 115	2 324	2 455	(e)2 833
Ireland	1 381	3 445	18 538	59 965	99 531	93 262	97 792	(e)109 942
Italy	19 192	49 666	56 556	89 410	115 391	94 185	98 833	(e)106 614
Latvia	–	–	1 150	2 169	4 513	3 831	3 693	(e)4 470
Lithuania	–	–	1 059	3 115	4 748	3 693	4 127	(e)5 231
Luxembourg	-	-	-	40 477	68 096	58 148	66 686	(e)72 999
Malta	481	752	1 098	2 011	4 325	3 970	4 108	(e)4 432
Netherlands	17 150	29 302	49 319	92 023	125 880	113 808	118 005	(e)136 184
Norway	8 615	12 765	17 718	29 318	44 848	38 446	39 734	(e)42 144
Poland	2 018	3 200	10 398	16 292	35 240	28 679	32 746	(e)36 957
Portugal	2 006	5 096	9 026	15 206	26 169	22 669	23 273	(e)26 623
Romania	1 063	610	1 747	5 089	(e)12 799	9 817	8 780	(e)10 232
Slovakia	–	–	2 241	4 408	8 464	6 282	5 824	(e)6 608
Slovenia	–	–	1 888	3 995	7 260	6 039	6 136	(e)6 701
Spain	11 593	27 937	52 453	94 820	143 042	122 548	123 851	(e)141 257
Sweden	7 489	13 726	21 624	43 043	70 264	59 481	66 246	(e)76 360
Switzerland	6 888	19 001	30 707	49 821	77 298	76 305	83 632	96 666
United Kingdom	36 452	56 422	120 397	207 672	285 376	244 735	250 044	(e)277 669
Developed economies: Oceania	**4 871**	**12 698**	**24 299**	**39 738**	**54 716**	**49 169**	**56 759**	**61 833**
Australia	3 862	10 204	19 894	31 047	45 240	41 005	47 726	51 760
New Zealand	1 009	2 494	4 405	8 691	9 476	8 164	9 033	10 074

Sources:
UNCTAD and WTO secretariats' calculations, based on:
- IMF, *Balance of Payments Statistics*
- Eurostat, online database
- UN/DESA/Statistics Division, *UN Service Trade*
- OECD, *OECD.Stat*
- Other international and national sources

Notes:
- The statistics presented correspond to the concepts and definitions from the IMF *Balance of Payments Manual* (*BPM5, 1993*).

  Total services cover the following main categories: transport, travel, communications, construction, insurance, financial services, computer and information services, royalties and license fees, other business services, personal, cultural and recreational services, and government services.

(1) Data from 1980 to 2001 inclusive refer to Belgium-Luxembourg Economic Union and from 2002 onwards to Belgium only.

Imports - Importations Millions de dollars								Régions, pays ou territoires
1980	1990	2000	2005	2008	2009	2010	2011	
549	600	1 670	3 411	5 918	5 028	4 168	(e)4 345	Bulgarie
268	674	1 585	2 708	4 302	3 357	3 267	(e)3 432	Chypre
–	2 472	–	–	–	–	–	–	Tchécoslovaquie
–	–	5 436	10 274	17 456	15 416	16 966	(e)19 268	République tchèque
3 596	10 218	21 063	37 047	62 361	50 662	51 884	(e)57 019	Danemark
–	–	886	2 204	3 355	2 523	2 795	(e)3 735	Estonie
-	-	97	230	382	343	366	-	Îles Féroé
2 555	7 627	8 440	17 720	30 660	27 083	27 624	(e)26 173	Finlande
32 148	51 947	65 509	107 026	141 255	129 926	132 242	(e)144 274	France
45 143								Allemagne, Rép. fédérale d'
–	85 125	137 943	211 342	290 289	256 249	263 615	(e)290 281	Allemagne
1 428	3 000	11 286	14 748	24 800	19 923	20 170	(e)19 114	Grèce
-	2 400	4 775	11 354	17 945	15 674	15 555	(e)17 209	Hongrie
263	556	1 164	(e)2 550	2 432	2 032	2 177	(e)2 550	Islande
1 593	5 178	31 272	71 533	110 766	104 448	107 187	(e)114 397	Irlande
16 249	46 795	55 601	90 076	127 996	105 903	110 785	(e)115 977	Italie
–	–	690	1 562	3 172	2 269	2 226	(e)2 611	Lettonie
–	–	679	2 060	4 153	2 974	2 836	(e)3 689	Lituanie
-	-	-	24 243	38 865	33 203	36 643	(e)41 059	Luxembourg
243	514	761	1 205	2 658	2 525	2 523	(e)2 591	Malte
18 148	29 708	51 339	84 482	112 016	108 348	106 244	(e)118 893	Pays-Bas
6 996	12 358	14 991	29 568	44 570	36 724	42 842	(e)45 207	Norvège
2 023	2 847	8 995	15 562	30 104	23 935	29 651	(e)30 920	Pologne
1 525	4 005	7 031	10 341	16 498	14 354	14 392	(e)15 868	Portugal
1 045	787	1 993	5 518	(e)11 822	10 223	9 500	(e)11 240	Roumanie
–	–	1 805	4 087	9 151	8 013	6 809	(e)7 118	Slovaquie
–	–	1 438	2 851	5 175	4 420	4 404	(e)4 713	Slovénie
5 732	16 055	33 171	67 164	105 264	87 119	87 036	(e)93 604	Espagne
7 018	17 058	23 977	35 349	53 608	45 867	48 345	(e)55 838	Suède
4 885	11 202	14 646	25 753	35 370	38 136	39 612	47 061	Suisse
27 933	48 737	99 747	162 950	202 408	164 687	166 731	(e)176 384	Royaume-Uni
8 411	**17 096**	**23 390**	**38 744**	**58 207**	**49 445**	**60 194**	**71 397**	**Économies développées : Océanie**
6 568	13 772	18 934	30 505	48 338	41 379	50 850	60 433	Australie
1 843	3 324	4 456	8 239	9 869	8 066	9 343	10 964	Nouvelle-Zélande

Sources :
Calculs des secrétariats de la CNUCED et de l'OMC, sur la base de :
- FMI, *Statistiques de la balance des paiements*
- Eurostat, base de données en ligne
- ONU/DAES/Division des statistiques, *ONU Service Trade*
- OCDE, *OECD.Stat*
- Autres sources internationales et nationales

Notes :
-   Les statistiques présentées correspondent aux concepts et définitions du *Manuel de la balance des paiements* du FMI (*MBP5, 1993*).

    Les services totaux comprennent les catégories suivantes : transports, voyages, communications, bâtiment et travaux publics (BTP), assurances, services financiers, informatique et information, redevances et droits de licence, autres services aux entreprises, services personnels, culturels et relatifs aux loisirs, et les services fournis ou reçus par les administrations publiques.

(1) Les données de 1980 à 2001 se réfèrent à l'Union belgo-luxembourgeoise et à partir de 2002 uniquement à la Belgique.

5

5.1.2 Value of exports and imports of services of economic groupings

Economic grouping	Exports - Exportations Millions of dollars							
	1980	1990	2000	2005	2008	2009	2010	2011
DEVELOPING ECONOMIES	**73 389**	**150 390**	**350 998**	**629 352**	**1 036 588**	**940 483**	**1 137 766**	**1 265 634**
Developing economies excluding China	71 329	144 535	320 568	554 948	889 476	810 934	966 563	1 082 533
Developing economies excluding LDCs	70 222	146 205	343 897	617 624	1 015 762	920 700	1 115 516	1 239 916
High-income developing economies	39 732	87 177	206 168	335 867	522 573	477 025	561 291	636 074
Middle-income developing economies	22 663	46 356	106 306	200 271	346 422	314 967	384 520	415 654
Low-income developing economies	10 994	16 857	38 525	93 213	167 593	148 491	191 955	213 906
Heavily indebted poor countries (IMF)	3 584	4 461	6 752	12 333	20 993	19 346	20 140	24 017
Landlocked developing countries	1 386	2 341	7 347	12 399	23 575	22 897	25 337	30 599
Small island developing States	2 650	5 758	9 610	12 762	16 030	14 187	15 568	16 920
Least developed countries	*3 167*	*4 185*	*7 102*	*11 727*	*20 826*	*19 783*	*22 250*	*25 718*
Africa and Haiti	2 368	3 146	4 163	7 639	13 839	12 789	14 071	16 789
Asia	734	890	2 628	3 729	6 435	6 405	7 505	8 198
Islands	64	149	311	359	552	589	675	731
Major petroleum and gas exporters	*11 375*	*8 734*	*15 893*	*36 834*	*54 612*	*52 673*	*58 086*	*67 587*
Africa	1 899	1 688	3 182	5 010	6 291	6 209	7 913	8 728
America	693	1 183	1 182	1 342	2 170	2 227	1 857	2 031
Asia	8 782	5 863	11 529	30 482	46 151	44 237	48 316	56 828
Major exporters of manufactured goods	*26 866*	*72 580*	*192 249*	*324 512*	*547 044*	*488 386*	*599 535*	*666 466*
America	4 591	8 094	13 480	15 666	17 575	14 730	15 168	15 298
Asia	22 275	64 486	178 769	308 845	529 469	473 656	584 368	651 168
Emerging economies	*24 521*	*57 285*	*141 458*	*218 513*	*364 725*	*323 404*	*381 865*	*431 606*
America	10 182	16 948	33 552	47 772	74 654	65 704	74 859	85 008
Asia	14 340	40 337	107 906	170 741	290 071	257 700	307 006	346 597
Newly industrialized Asian economies	*22 104*	*64 363*	*156 930*	*251 893*	*407 320*	*368 276*	*444 026*	*504 049*
First tier	17 591	48 353	120 530	194 974	318 999	285 235	346 106	391 922
Second tier	4 514	16 010	36 400	56 919	88 322	83 041	97 919	112 127
Developing economies: Africa	**13 438**	**21 711**	**33 120**	**59 654**	**90 363**	**81 581**	**90 541**	**91 731**
Northern Africa excluding Sudan	4 883	10 283	16 686	29 803	48 040	42 722	46 134	42 275
Sub-Saharan Africa	8 555	11 428	16 435	29 851	42 323	38 858	44 407	49 456
Sub-Saharan Africa excluding South Africa	6 092	8 021	11 389	18 551	29 518	26 838	30 404	34 632
Developing economies: America	**18 982**	**31 595**	**61 760**	**88 077**	**129 346**	**117 819**	**133 305**	**148 305**
Central America and Greater Caribbean Islands excluding Puerto Rico	7 364	13 494	27 834	38 563	49 513	44 739	49 186	52 930
Central America and Greater Caribbean Islands excluding Mexico and Puerto Rico	2 773	5 400	14 354	22 896	31 938	30 009	34 019	37 633
South America and Central America	15 104	24 121	46 275	65 017	101 426	91 884	103 340	117 752
South America excluding Brazil	7 171	9 566	17 009	23 887	38 800	35 662	40 736	46 346
Developing economies: Asia	**40 657**	**96 306**	**255 162**	**478 642**	**813 259**	**738 130**	**910 624**	**1 021 847**
Eastern and South-Eastern Asia excluding China	22 839	66 568	164 263	267 334	435 846	396 574	484 394	557 609
Southern Asia excluding India	2 073	3 031	5 806	12 318	17 876	16 145	21 393	21 839

Sources:
UNCTAD and WTO secretariats' calculations, based on:
- IMF, *Balance of Payments Statistics*
- Eurostat, online database
- UN/DESA/Statistics Division, *UN Service Trade*
- OECD, *OECD.Stat*
- Other international and national sources

Imports - Importations Millions de dollars								Groupements économiques
1980	1990	2000	2005	2008	2009	2010	2011	
139 580	**193 761**	**415 182**	**700 428**	**1 186 860**	**1 087 216**	**1 298 742**	**1 482 159**	**ÉCONOMIES EN DÉVELOPPEMENT**
137 350	189 409	379 151	616 633	1 027 936	928 269	1 105 421	1 244 576	Économies en développement sans la Chine
131 872	183 264	400 809	671 699	1 127 998	1 033 843	1 240 161	1 413 749	Économies en développement sans les PMA
75 188	109 360	229 888	349 752	562 622	510 124	587 742	661 007	Économies en développement à revenu élevé
36 016	50 191	120 609	220 304	388 183	367 453	449 010	525 316	Économies en développement à revenu intermédiaire
28 376	34 210	64 684	130 372	236 054	209 638	261 991	295 836	Économies en développement à revenu faible
9 357	11 091	12 645	23 949	40 442	36 879	43 381	49 606	Pays pauvres très endettés (FMI)
3 766	5 042	10 510	23 297	37 959	34 836	40 397	47 434	Pays en développement sans littoral
2 227	3 765	6 478	8 970	12 277	10 966	12 412	13 557	Petits États insulaires en développement
7 708	*10 497*	*14 372*	*28 729*	*58 861*	*53 373*	*58 581*	*68 410*	*Pays les moins avancés*
6 218	8 455	10 682	23 152	49 065	44 051	47 541	56 023	Afrique et Haïti
1 404	1 843	3 436	5 276	8 805	8 297	9 941	11 182	Asie
86	199	254	302	992	1 025	1 100	1 206	Îles
59 964	*46 038*	*60 814*	*111 312*	*246 544*	*229 422*	*251 332*	*285 123*	*Principaux exportateurs de pétrole et de gaz*
10 823	6 490	9 255	20 546	61 939	54 608	58 120	66 441	Afrique
4 253	2 534	4 435	5 339	11 958	10 724	11 048	12 527	Amérique
44 887	37 015	47 125	85 427	172 647	164 090	182 164	206 155	Asie
26 578	*73 047*	*200 164*	*334 749*	*525 502*	*479 242*	*576 801*	*667 113*	*Principaux exportateurs d'articles manufacturés*
6 514	10 323	16 891	20 823	24 526	23 047	25 175	29 361	Amérique
20 064	62 724	183 273	313 925	500 977	456 195	551 626	637 752	Asie
31 441	*69 641*	*172 406*	*259 837*	*397 586*	*350 450*	*427 001*	*487 195*	*Économies émergentes*
17 636	24 206	49 862	63 685	102 598	97 140	119 702	142 904	Amérique
13 805	45 435	122 543	196 153	294 989	253 311	307 299	344 291	Asie
24 133	*66 189*	*168 126*	*258 044*	*378 855*	*329 044*	*395 754*	*444 380*	*Économies nouvellement industrialisées d'Asie*
13 233	46 578	115 035	181 412	265 856	233 292	281 241	311 350	Première génération
10 900	19 611	53 092	76 631	112 998	95 752	114 513	133 030	Deuxième génération
29 408	**30 315**	**41 266**	**77 117**	**152 430**	**135 571**	**151 273**	**168 310**	**Économies en développement : Afrique**
9 380	8 785	13 879	23 677	43 105	40 551	43 533	44 127	Afrique septentrionale sans le Soudan
20 028	21 530	27 387	53 441	109 324	95 020	107 740	124 183	Afrique subsaharienne
16 733	17 792	21 564	41 315	92 349	80 212	89 284	104 519	Afrique subsaharienne sans l'Afrique du Sud
29 929	**37 863**	**74 085**	**95 325**	**151 015**	**140 432**	**168 674**	**197 707**	**Économies en développement : Amérique**
9 642	15 175	26 086	32 960	41 786	37 790	42 449	48 200	Amérique centrale et Grandes Antilles sans Porto Rico
3 128	4 852	9 195	12 137	17 260	14 743	17 274	18 839	Amérique centrale et Grandes Antilles sans le Mexique et Porto Rico
27 079	33 042	66 392	85 830	138 700	129 503	155 980	184 967	Amérique du Sud et Amérique centrale
13 749	12 867	27 501	33 274	56 966	50 911	58 119	67 951	Amérique du Sud sans le Brésil
79 744	**124 753**	**298 448**	**524 279**	**878 345**	**806 644**	**972 920**	**1 109 743**	**Économies en développement : Asie**
24 470	67 153	173 831	267 642	396 762	346 508	418 206	473 473	Asie orientale et Asie du Sud-Est sans la Chine
7 235	7 718	9 043	23 505	35 659	31 600	39 370	44 469	Asie méridionale sans l'Inde

Sources :
Calculs des secrétariats de la CNUCED et de l'OMC, sur la base de :
- FMI, *Statistiques de la balance des paiements*
- Eurostat, base de données en ligne
- ONU/DAES/Division des statistiques, *ONU Service Trade*
- OCDE, *OECD.Stat*
- Autres sources internationales et nationales

Trade group	Exports - Exportations Millions of dollars							
	1980	1990	2000	2005	2008	2009	2010	2011
AFRICA								
CEMAC	894	837	1 087	1 525	2 427	2 370	2 240	2 462
CEPGL	140	289	125	472	1 195	932	779	940
COMESA	4 475	9 509	14 545	23 003	38 542	33 919	38 267	35 884
EAC	789	1 363	1 897	3 838	6 540	6 112	7 532	7 987
ECCAS	1 169	1 238	1 494	2 183	3 961	3 936	3 887	4 451
ECOWAS	2 555	3 008	3 928	6 040	9 168	8 134	9 092	10 229
MRU	665	867	664	1 207	1 698	1 380	1 325	1 463
SADC	3 784	5 532	8 920	17 595	21 812	20 291	23 455	25 587
UMA	2 547	4 339	6 929	15 240	23 266	21 361	22 446	23 345
WAEMU	1 191	1 585	1 240	2 415	3 711	3 152	3 647	4 033
AMERICA								
ANCOM	2 511	3 082	4 677	6 458	9 727	9 700	10 426	11 999
CACM	670	1 491	4 140	5 883	8 426	7 894	9 192	10 180
CARICOM	2 366	4 476	7 381	9 423	10 829	9 851	10 168	10 372
FTAA	72 538	196 480	385 825	510 210	722 543	674 303	737 665	808 414
LAIA	13 671	21 824	42 369	62 324	95 581	86 047	97 668	111 394
MERCOSUR	4 245	7 092	16 305	24 649	46 033	42 373	48 987	57 948
NAFTA	59 586	175 136	342 851	448 170	623 809	583 275	635 080	691 100
OAS	72 905	197 005	388 467	517 284	731 795	682 686	748 097	820 172
OECS	145	717	1 288	1 536	1 637	1 513	1 559	1 600
ASIA								
APTA	10 397	21 575	80 585	179 670	349 278	300 431	387 651	421 562
ASEAN	9 689	29 505	68 922	119 081	197 793	185 531	221 359	254 671
ECO	2 130	9 882	25 742	40 251	59 255	55 989	61 906	67 730
GCC	7 732	5 564	10 521	28 176	39 916	38 490	40 699	47 000
SAARC	4 313	7 220	20 694	59 847	116 998	102 404	136 873	149 847
EUROPE								
EFTA	15 783	32 325	49 469	81 173	124 260	117 075	125 822	141 642
EU	213 848	405 143	657 163	1 201 765	1 805 176	1 565 583	1 624 509	(e)1 803 419
Euro area	157 635	311 336	462 152	848 522	1 266 331	1 112 880	1 147 185	1 268 264
OCEANIA								
MSG	291	708	857	1 336	1 639	1 210	1 555	1 859
INTERREGIONAL								
ACP	11 902	18 287	30 624	51 785	69 230	63 388	71 937	79 037
APEC	111 125	302 812	643 414	958 190	1 455 593	1 319 250	1 516 912	1 667 247
BSEC	6 943	16 055	57 711	108 257	186 165	154 239	161 535	181 794
CIS	–	–	17 991	41 904	86 454	71 699	80 482	95 484

Sources:
UNCTAD and WTO secretariats' calculations, based on:
- IMF, *Balance of Payments Statistics*
- Eurostat, online database
- UN/DESA/Statistics Division, *UN Service Trade*
- OECD, *OECD.Stat*
- Other international and national sources

Imports - Importations Millions de dollars								Groupements commerciaux
1980	1990	2000	2005	2008	2009	2010	2011	
								AFRIQUE
2 181	3 253	3 521	6 507	11 567	10 324	12 804	14 222	CEMAC
1 060	1 017	458	1 605	2 877	2 478	3 388	3 766	CEPGL
8 781	9 884	14 044	22 769	38 947	33 847	38 596	41 394	COMESA
1 145	1 441	2 103	3 391	5 556	5 633	6 470	7 828	CAE
3 785	6 086	6 691	14 915	36 605	31 991	34 980	41 624	CEEAC
8 755	6 433	7 150	14 106	36 355	30 352	33 974	38 986	CEDEAO
1 817	2 188	1 755	3 349	4 641	4 083	4 442	4 975	UFM
7 043	9 438	13 189	26 294	49 711	44 042	49 366	57 449	SADC
7 164	5 134	6 515	13 547	26 259	27 253	29 485	30 930	UMA
2 863	3 513	2 577	4 729	7 259	6 714	7 653	8 535	UEMOA
								AMÉRIQUE
3 013	4 029	7 335	10 718	16 944	15 446	18 224	21 209	ANCOM
1 325	1 580	4 077	5 407	7 266	6 209	7 284	7 809	MCAC
2 118	2 741	4 720	6 211	7 396	6 452	6 963	7 448	CARICOM
80 721	181 831	336 158	463 097	642 067	600 151	660 498	723 952	ZLEA
24 913	31 745	61 421	78 916	129 990	122 044	147 201	174 978	ALADI
9 300	11 470	27 181	33 265	62 695	61 080	79 020	95 633	MERCOSUR
58 150	156 283	281 117	391 139	519 422	486 131	521 349	559 862	ALENA
80 972	183 144	336 935	464 112	644 146	601 821	662 416	726 248	OEA
81	343	627	806	1 003	852	855	849	OECO
								ASIE
9 842	22 149	92 080	195 113	350 424	326 271	413 843	471 062	ACAP
14 097	28 814	87 918	138 629	211 559	186 495	224 649	263 533	ANASE
6 813	9 216	17 835	41 846	65 695	59 175	70 535	77 961	ECO
37 421	30 997	42 878	69 909	149 567	139 416	150 814	170 994	CCG
4 993	9 845	25 104	59 952	106 122	94 802	132 818	143 109	SAARC
								EUROPE
12 144	24 116	30 801	57 871	82 372	76 892	84 631	94 818	AELE
188 916	377 026	635 421	1 093 536	1 615 008	1 415 526	1 444 834	(e)1 568 202	UE
144 062	291 405	466 398	793 712	1 148 912	1 020 245	1 041 408	1 128 381	Zone euro
								OCÉANIE
470	763	1 244	1 916	2 691	2 505	3 574	3 809	MSG
								INTERRÉGIONAUX
23 289	26 842	35 618	64 248	124 216	108 291	123 119	140 767	ACP
128 174	332 252	643 804	952 208	1 388 996	1 260 013	1 433 794	1 608 263	CEAP
3 609	7 487	44 556	87 093	166 106	137 037	152 625	176 261	CEMN
–	–	25 018	60 244	116 136	94 413	111 241	132 384	CEI

Sources :
Calculs des secrétariats de la CNUCED et de l'OMC, sur la base de :
- FMI, *Statistiques de la balance des paiements*
- Eurostat, base de données en ligne
- ONU/DAES/Division des statistiques, *ONU Service Trade*
- OCDE, *OECD.Stat*
- Autres sources internationales et nationales

5

Country or territory Pays ou territoires	Exports (2) - Exportations (2)							
	Millions of dollars / Millions de dollars				As % of total services En % du total des services			
	2000	2005	2010	2011	2000	2005	2010	2011
SELECTED COUNTRY GROUPINGS **SÉLECTION DE GROUPEMENTS DE PAYS**								
World - Monde	343 143	569 047	790 847	860 128	22.6	22.2	20.6	20.3
Developing economies - Économies en développement	83 943	157 531	258 525	281 443	23.9	25.0	22.7	22.2
Transition economies - Économies en transition	9 535	19 350	35 176	40 282	39.3	33.7	34.1	33.3
Developed economies - Économies développées	249 664	392 167	497 146	538 403	21.8	20.9	19.2	18.8
Developing economies: Africa - Économies en développement : Afrique	7 863	14 910	22 852	23 896	23.7	25.0	25.2	26.1
Developing economies: America - Économies en développement : Amérique	11 088	17 824	26 119	29 601	18.0	20.2	19.6	20.0
Developing economies: Asia - Économies en développement : Asie	64 814	124 113	208 856	227 210	25.4	25.9	22.9	22.2
Developing economies: Oceania - Économies en développement : Océanie	178	684	698	736	18.6	23.0	21.2	19.6
Developed economies: America - Économies développées : Amérique	53 054	62 041	82 326	92 462	16.1	14.3	13.2	13.7
Developed economies: Asia - Économies développées : Asie	28 083	39 437	43 154	42 840	32.6	32.5	26.1	24.9
Developed economies: Europe - Économies développées : Europe	162 993	282 825	364 954	395 697	23.1	22.0	20.8	20.3
Developed economies: Oceania - Économies développées : Océanie	5 534	7 864	6 712	7 404	22.8	19.8	11.8	12.0
Least developed countries - Pays les moins avancés	1 179	2 095	4 023	4 884	16.6	17.9	18.1	19.0
Developing economies excluding LDCs - Économies en développement sans les PMA	82 765	155 436	254 502	276 559	24.1	25.2	22.8	22.3
Developing economies excluding China - Économies en développement sans la Chine	80 272	142 104	224 315	245 832	25.0	25.6	23.2	22.7
25 LEADING EXPORTERS: DEVELOPING AND TRANSITION ECONOMIES **25 PRINCIPAUX EXPORTATEURS : ÉCONOMIES EN DÉVELOPPEMENT ET EN TRANSITION**								
Korea, Republic of - Corée, République de	13 687	23 877	38 982	37 057	43.4	48.0	44.7	39.0
China - Chine	3 671	15 427	34 211	(e)35 611	12.1	20.7	20.0	(e)19.4
Singapore - Singapour	11 729	19 574	32 738	(e)37 093	41.1	35.1	29.2	(e)28.7
China, Hong Kong SAR - Chine (RAS de Hong Kong)	12 773	20 317	29 888	32 652	31.6	31.9	28.2	26.9
Russian Federation - Fédération de Russie	3 555	9 113	14 911	16 992	36.4	36.5	33.1	31.5
India - Inde	1 979	5 754	13 248	(e)17 486	11.9	(b)11.0	10.7	(e)12.7
China, Taiwan Province of - Province chinoise de Taiwan	4 121	5 924	9 765	9 696	20.6	22.9	24.2	21.0
Turkey - Turquie	2 955	4 919	9 022	(e)10 387	15.1	18.4	26.2	(e)27.1
Egypt - Égypte	2 645	4 746	7 916	(e)8 199	27.0	32.4	33.3	(e)42.8
Ukraine	2 920	4 481	7 805	9 004	75.0	47.9	45.7	46.4
Chile - Chili	2 188	4 301	6 466	(e)7 300	53.6	60.3	59.9	(e)59.1
Thailand - Thaïlande	3 250	4 626	5 916	(e)5 830	23.4	23.3	17.2	(e)14.2
Brazil - Brésil	1 409	3 139	4 931	5 819	14.8	19.6	15.5	15.1
Malaysia - Malaisie	2 802	4 056	4 692	4 851	20.1	20.7	14.3	13.9
Kuwait - Koweït	1 383	2 260	4 414	5 497	75.9	47.3	47.3	54.3
Iran (Islamic Rep. of) - Iran (Rép. islamique d')	561	2 327	3 651	-	31.2	46.5	44.1	-
Panama	1 153	1 791	3 341	3 935	57.8	55.4	55.0	55.0
Belarus - Bélarus	584	1 338	3 006	3 538	58.3	64.5	66.8	67.3
Indonesia - Indonésie	. _	2 842	2 665	3 425	_	22.0	15.9	16.7
United Arab Emirates - Émirats arabes unis	781	1 059	2 451	2 859	36.0	22.1	20.9	22.3
Viet Nam	-	1 167	2 306	(e)2 505	-	27.4	30.9	(e)28.2
Kazakhstan	461	1 021	2 276	2 221	43.8	45.8	53.5	49.3
Morocco - Maroc	485	1 300	2 152	2 724	16.0	16.1	17.2	19.5
Argentina - Argentine	1 145	1 264	2 034	2 252	23.2	19.1	15.5	15.9
Saudi Arabia - Arabie saoudite	-	1 820	2 031	1 975	-	(b)16.0	19.0	17.2
15 LEADING EXPORTERS: DEVELOPED ECONOMIES **15 PRINCIPAUX EXPORTATEURS : ÉCONOMIES DÉVELOPPÉES**								
United States - États-Unis	45 515	52 313	70 637	78 929	15.7	13.9	12.8	13.2
Germany - Allemagne	19 734	41 240	57 554	(e)60 307	23.8	25.1	24.2	(e)23.4
Japan - Japon	25 604	35 752	38 901	38 366	36.4	34.2	27.5	26.4
Denmark - Danemark	(e)14 114	27 006	36 639	(e)39 877	(e)59.5	62.2	60.6	(e)60.8
France	18 462	28 245	35 938	(e)38 697	22.3	23.1	24.7	(e)23.1
United Kingdom - Royaume-Uni	19 149	31 516	31 412	(e)35 276	15.9	15.2	12.6	(e)12.7
Netherlands - Pays-Bas	16 787	21 461	25 573	(e)30 035	34.0	23.3	21.7	(e)22.1
Belgium - Belgique	(a)10 665	13 866	25 389	(e)25 128	(a)21.4	24.7	29.2	(e)28.1
Spain - Espagne	8 432	16 146	20 804	(e)23 450	16.1	17.0	16.8	(e)16.6
Greece - Grèce	7 923	17 249	20 421	(e)19 597	41.2	50.3	54.1	(e)51.9
Norway - Norvège	9 606	15 391	15 679	(e)15 119	54.2	52.5	39.5	(e)35.9
Italy - Italie	9 291	14 546	14 555	(e)15 202	16.4	16.3	14.7	(e)14.3
Austria - Autriche	4 208	8 985	12 881	(e)14 477	18.2	21.2	23.6	(e)23.4
Canada	7 539	9 728	11 656	13 503	18.7	17.4	16.9	17.7
Sweden - Suède	4 965	8 717	10 269	(e)11 129	23.0	20.3	15.5	(e)14.6

For sources and notes, see end of table.

Pour les sources et les notes, se reporter à la fin du tableau.

5.2 Exports and imports of services
by service category
Transport

5.2 Exportations et importations des services
par catégories de services
Transports

Country or territory / Pays ou territoires	Imports (2) - Importations (2)							
	Millions of dollars / Millions de dollars				As % of total services En % du total des services			
	2000	2005	2010	2011	2000	2005	2010	2011
SELECTED COUNTRY GROUPINGS (1) **SÉLECTION DE GROUPEMENTS DE PAYS (1)**								
World - Monde	418 767	683 994	972 199	1 101 409	27.6	27.7	26.4	27.0
Developing economies - Économies en développement	138 408	254 523	449 643	526 120	33.3	36.3	34.6	35.5
Transition economies - Économies en transition	4 885	12 056	25 614	31 263	17.2	17.6	20.7	21.4
Developed economies - Économies développées	275 474	417 415	496 942	544 026	25.7	24.6	22.0	22.2
Developing economies: Africa - Économies en développement : Afrique	14 470	30 975	55 309	61 526	35.1	40.2	36.6	36.6
Developing economies: America - Économies en développement : Amérique	26 348	34 555	55 157	64 099	35.6	36.2	32.7	32.4
Developing economies: Asia - Économies en développement : Asie	97 135	187 828	337 481	398 601	32.5	35.8	34.7	35.9
Developing economies: Oceania - Économies en développement : Océanie	456	1 165	1 698	1 894	33.0	31.4	28.9	29.6
Developed economies: America - Économies développées : Amérique	69 698	93 250	98 813	108 907	26.4	25.2	19.9	20.5
Developed economies: Asia - Économies développées : Asie	37 543	45 087	52 234	55 986	31.7	32.7	29.8	29.9
Developed economies: Europe - Économies développées : Europe	160 514	265 518	329 774	360 558	24.1	23.1	21.6	21.7
Developed economies: Oceania - Économies développées : Océanie	7 719	13 560	16 121	18 575	33.0	35.0	26.8	26.0
Least developed countries - Pays les moins avancés	6 095	12 337	23 006	27 097	42.4	42.9	39.3	39.6
Developing economies excluding LDCs - Économies en développement sans les PMA	132 313	242 186	426 637	499 023	33.0	36.1	34.4	35.3
Developing economies excluding China - Économies en développement sans la Chine	128 012	226 075	386 387	445 675	33.8	36.7	35.0	35.8
25 LEADING IMPORTERS: DEVELOPING AND TRANSITION ECONOMIES **25 PRINCIPAUX IMPORTATEURS : ÉCONOMIES EN DÉVELOPPEMENT ET EN TRANSITION**								
China - Chine	10 396	28 448	63 257	(e)80 445	28.9	33.9	32.7	(e)33.9
India - Inde	8 703	20 678	46 422	(e)56 860	45.4	(b)43.7	39.7	(e)45.6
Korea, Republic of - Corée, République de	11 048	20 144	29 675	27 797	32.9	33.7	30.9	28.0
Singapore - Singapour	12 617	20 380	28 411	(e)33 361	41.9	36.9	29.5	(e)29.2
United Arab Emirates - Émirats arabes unis	4 557	11 012	25 780	30 976	53.2	56.9	61.2	62.5
Thailand - Thaïlande	6 760	14 442	22 414	(e)26 674	43.7	54.0	50.0	(e)52.2
China, Hong Kong SAR - Chine (RAS de Hong Kong)	6 242	10 462	14 623	15 717	25.3	30.8	28.7	28.1
Saudi Arabia - Arabie saoudite	2 244	4 792	12 724	15 355	8.9	(b)14.5	16.6	19.7
Russian Federation - Fédération de Russie	2 330	5 137	12 058	15 303	13.8	13.3	16.4	17.0
Malaysia - Malaisie	5 890	8 396	11 905	13 081	35.2	38.2	37.0	34.7
Brazil - Brésil	4 305	5 089	11 339	14 154	25.8	20.9	18.1	18.5
Mexico - Mexique	6 186	8 117	10 774	12 120	36.6	39.0	42.8	41.3
China, Taiwan Province of - Province chinoise de Taiwan	6 247	8 439	9 895	10 268	23.4	26.0	26.1	24.4
Indonesia - Indonésie	_	7 451	8 673	12 139		33.8	33.2	37.5
Nigeria - Nigéria	624	(b)2 801	8 493	8 053	18.9	(b)42.3	39.8	32.8
Turkey - Turquie	2 463	4 861	8 288	(e)8 766	30.2	42.3	42.1	(e)41.2
South Africa - Afrique du Sud	2 441	5 328	7 088	8 262	41.9	43.9	38.4	42.0
Chile - Chili	2 191	4 135	6 661	(e)7 978	45.6	53.3	56.4	(e)57.2
Viet Nam	-	2 190	6 596	(e)8 226	-	49.2	66.5	(e)69.4
Egypt - Égypte	2 212	3 731	6 575	(e)6 391	29.4	35.5	44.7	(e)45.8
Qatar	293	1 737	5 758	9 845	17.9	41.9	65.6	58.4
Iraq	-	2 811	-	-	-	46.1	-	-
Kuwait - Koweït	1 536	2 646	5 485	6 232	31.2	30.4	36.7	35.3
Iran (Islamic Rep. of) - Iran (Rép. islamique d')	1 148	2 324	5 005	-	36.7	21.4	21.4	-
Philippines	2 052	3 125	4 965	4 859	39.1	53.3	43.7	41.0
15 LEADING IMPORTERS: DEVELOPED ECONOMIES **15 PRINCIPAUX IMPORTATEURS : ÉCONOMIES DÉVELOPPÉES**								
United States - États-Unis	60 325	78 766	78 122	85 237	27.4	25.9	19.3	19.9
Germany - Allemagne	26 209	46 101	62 851	(e)67 162	19.0	21.8	23.8	(e)23.1
Japan - Japon	33 325	40 376	46 448	49 515	31.3	32.6	29.5	29.5
France	17 859	32 495	35 865	(e)40 852	27.3	30.4	27.1	(e)28.3
United Kingdom - Royaume-Uni	24 132	36 176	28 910	(e)33 003	24.2	22.2	17.3	(e)18.7
Denmark - Danemark	(e)11 109	17 864	26 297	(e)29 730	(e)52.7	48.2	50.7	(e)52.1
Italy - Italie	13 140	21 154	25 647	(e)26 742	23.6	23.5	23.2	(e)23.1
Spain - Espagne	10 117	18 500	20 955	(e)22 836	30.5	27.5	24.1	(e)24.4
Canada	9 373	14 484	20 422	23 424	21.2	22.0	22.4	23.1
Belgium - Belgique	(a)8 386	12 272	19 625	(e)19 620	(a)20.0	24.0	25.0	(e)23.1
Netherlands - Pays-Bas	12 888	14 954	18 831	(e)21 095	25.1	17.7	17.7	(e)17.7
Australia - Australie	6 292	10 759	13 372	15 530	33.2	35.3	26.3	25.7
Austria - Autriche	3 749	8 674	12 154	(e)14 481	22.8	28.2	32.8	(e)34.3
Norway - Norvège	5 138	9 547	11 684	(e)10 880	34.3	32.3	27.3	(e)24.1
Greece - Grèce	4 088	7 757	10 801	(e)10 055	36.2	52.6	53.6	(e)52.6

For sources and notes, see end of table.

Pour les sources et les notes, se reporter à la fin du tableau.

5

Country or territory	Exports (3) - Exportations (3)							
Pays ou territoires	Millions of dollars / Millions de dollars				As % of total services En % du total des services			
	2000	2005	2010	2011	2000	2005	2010	2011
SELECTED COUNTRY GROUPINGS **SÉLECTION DE GROUPEMENTS DE PAYS**								
World - Monde	479 424	694 567	950 465	1 067 408	31.5	27.1	24.8	25.2
Developing economies - Économies en développement	130 310	213 600	362 430	411 374	37.1	33.9	31.9	32.5
Transition economies - Économies en transition	8 438	20 489	29 499	35 818	34.8	35.6	28.6	29.6
Developed economies - Économies développées	340 677	460 478	558 536	620 216	29.7	24.5	21.5	21.7
Developing economies: Africa - Économies en développement : Afrique	14 472	28 782	42 200	40 491	43.7	48.2	46.6	44.1
Developing economies: America - Économies en développement : Amérique	31 642	42 932	55 806	58 752	51.2	48.7	41.9	39.6
Developing economies: Asia - Économies en développement : Asie	83 876	140 520	262 922	310 402	32.9	29.4	28.9	30.4
Developing economies: Oceania - Économies en développement : Océanie	319	1 366	1 501	1 729	33.4	45.9	45.6	46.1
Developed economies: America - Économies développées : Amérique	111 494	119 929	150 979	166 800	33.9	27.7	24.3	24.6
Developed economies: Asia - Économies développées : Asie	8 608	9 491	17 967	15 851	10.0	7.8	10.9	9.2
Developed economies: Europe - Économies développées : Europe	209 013	308 979	354 885	400 630	29.6	24.1	20.3	20.6
Developed economies: Oceania - Économies développées : Océanie	11 561	22 079	34 705	36 936	47.6	55.6	61.1	59.7
Least developed countries - Pays les moins avancés	2 546	4 849	9 822	11 305	35.9	41.3	44.1	44.0
Developing economies excluding LDCs - Économies en développement sans les PMA	127 764	208 751	352 608	400 069	37.2	33.8	31.6	32.3
Developing economies excluding China - Économies en développement sans la Chine	114 079	184 304	316 616	362 859	35.6	33.2	32.8	33.5
25 LEADING EXPORTERS: DEVELOPING AND TRANSITION ECONOMIES **25 PRINCIPAUX EXPORTATEURS : ÉCONOMIES EN DÉVELOPPEMENT ET EN TRANSITION**								
China - Chine	16 231	29 296	45 814	(e)48 515	53.3	39.4	26.8	(e)26.5
China, Macao SAR - Chine (RAS de Macao)	3 011	7 933	27 805	(e)38 530	91.8	92.6	96.9	(e)97.5
China, Hong Kong SAR - Chine (RAS de Hong Kong)	5 907	10 295	22 200	27 686	14.6	16.2	20.9	22.8
Turkey - Turquie	7 636	18 152	20 807	(e)22 712	39.1	67.8	60.4	(e)59.2
Thailand - Thaïlande	7 483	9 577	20 127	(e)26 740	54.0	48.1	58.7	(e)65.0
Malaysia - Malaisie	5 011	8 846	18 315	18 247	35.9	45.2	55.9	52.1
Singapore - Singapour	5 142	6 211	14 181	(e)19 094	18.0	11.1	12.6	(e)14.8
India - Inde	3 460	7 493	14 160	(e)17 520	20.7	(b)14.3	11.4	(e)12.8
Egypt - Égypte	4 345	6 851	12 528	(e)8 707	44.3	46.8	52.6	(e)45.5
Mexico - Mexique	8 294	11 803	11 992	11 869	61.5	75.3	79.1	77.6
Korea, Republic of - Corée, République de	6 834	5 806	10 359	12 304	21.7	11.7	11.9	13.0
South Africa - Afrique du Sud	2 677	7 516	9 085	9 515	53.0	66.5	64.9	64.2
Russian Federation - Fédération de Russie	3 429	5 870	8 830	11 398	35.1	23.5	19.6	21.1
China, Taiwan Province of - Province chinoise de Taiwan	3 738	4 977	8 721	11 044	18.7	19.3	21.6	23.9
United Arab Emirates - Émirats arabes unis	1 062	3 218	8 577	9 204	48.9	67.3	73.1	71.9
Croatia - Croatie	2 758	7 415	8 220	(e)9 141	67.7	74.4	72.9	(e)73.8
Lebanon - Liban	-	5 532	8 019	-	-	50.9	50.2	-
Indonesia - Indonésie	_	4 522	6 958	7 953	_	35.0	41.5	38.7
Saudi Arabia - Arabie saoudite	-	4 626	6 712	8 459	-	(b)40.5	62.8	73.6
Morocco - Maroc	2 039	4 610	6 702	7 321	67.2	56.9	53.4	52.4
Syrian Arab Republic - République arabe syrienne	1 082	1 944	6 190	-	63.7	66.8	84.4	-
Brazil - Brésil	1 810	3 861	5 919	6 775	19.1	24.1	18.6	17.6
Argentina - Argentine	2 904	2 729	4 942	5 352	58.8	41.1	37.7	37.7
Viet Nam	-	2 300	4 450	(e)5 620	-	53.9	59.7	(e)63.3
Dominican Republic - République dominicaine	2 860	3 518	4 209	(e)4 353	88.6	89.4	82.6	(e)82.4
15 LEADING EXPORTERS: DEVELOPED ECONOMIES **15 PRINCIPAUX EXPORTATEURS : ÉCONOMIES DÉVELOPPÉES**								
United States - États-Unis	100 716	106 161	134 846	149 640	34.8	28.2	24.5	25.0
Spain - Espagne	29 802	47 951	52 475	(e)59 810	56.8	50.6	42.4	(e)42.3
France	32 855	44 005	46 514	(e)53 773	39.7	36.0	32.0	(e)32.0
Italy - Italie	27 493	35 318	38 749	(e)42 925	48.6	39.5	39.2	(e)40.3
Germany - Allemagne	18 611	29 161	34 642	(e)38 789	22.4	17.8	14.6	(e)15.0
United Kingdom - Royaume-Uni	21 769	30 675	32 401	(e)35 706	18.1	14.8	13.0	(e)12.9
Australia - Australie	9 289	16 868	29 798	31 443	46.7	54.3	62.4	60.7
Austria - Autriche	9 899	16 047	18 578	(e)19 833	42.9	37.8	34.1	(e)32.1
Canada	10 778	13 768	15 711	16 716	26.8	24.7	22.7	21.9
Switzerland - Suisse	6 652	10 041	14 978	17 650	21.7	20.2	17.9	18.3
Japan - Japon	(e)4 494	(e)6 626	13 199	11 002	(e)6.4	(e)6.3	9.3	7.6
Netherlands - Pays-Bas	7 197	10 473	12 870	(e)14 499	14.6	11.4	10.9	(e)10.6
Greece - Grèce	9 219	13 725	12 729	(e)14 604	47.9	40.0	33.7	(e)38.2
Sweden - Suède	4 068	7 415	11 076	(e)13 822	18.8	17.2	16.7	(e)18.1
Belgium - Belgique	(a)7 447	9 867	10 254	(e)11 189	(a)15.0	17.6	11.8	(e)12.5

For sources and notes, see end of table.

Pour les sources et les notes, se reporter à la fin du tableau.

5.2   Exports and imports of services
       by service category
       Travel

5.2   Exportations et importations des services
       par catégories de services
       Voyages

Country or territory / Pays ou territoires	Imports (3) - Importations (3)							
	Millions of dollars / Millions de dollars				As % of total services / En % du total des services			
	2000	2005	2010	2011	2000	2005	2010	2011
SELECTED COUNTRY GROUPINGS (1) / **SÉLECTION DE GROUPEMENTS DE PAYS (1)**								
World - Monde	437 125	641 715	857 214	949 145	28.8	26.0	23.3	23.3
Developing economies - Économies en développement	103 787	163 499	295 492	339 966	25.0	23.3	22.8	22.9
Transition economies - Économies en transition	11 646	24 364	38 558	47 209	41.0	35.6	31.2	32.3
Developed economies - Économies développées	321 691	453 852	523 164	561 969	30.0	26.7	23.1	22.9
Developing economies: Africa - Économies en développement : Afrique	8 282	12 658	25 556	27 262	20.1	16.4	16.9	16.2
Developing economies: America - Économies en développement : Amérique	20 673	24 163	41 741	49 630	27.9	25.3	24.7	25.1
Developing economies: Asia - Économies en développement : Asie	74 661	126 035	227 527	262 260	25.0	24.0	23.4	23.6
Developing economies: Oceania - Économies en développement : Océanie	170	643	669	814	12.3	17.4	11.4	12.7
Developed economies: America - Économies développées : Amérique	80 298	92 807	112 555	120 203	30.4	25.1	22.6	22.6
Developed economies: Asia - Économies développées : Asie	26 004	30 228	31 280	30 816	22.0	21.9	17.8	16.4
Developed economies: Europe - Économies développées : Europe	207 553	316 894	354 120	380 578	31.1	27.5	23.1	22.9
Developed economies: Oceania - Économies développées : Océanie	7 837	13 923	25 209	30 373	33.5	35.9	41.9	42.5
Least developed countries - Pays les moins avancés	2 278	3 729	6 491	6 896	15.9	13.0	11.1	10.1
Developing economies excluding LDCs - Économies en développement sans les PMA	101 509	159 770	289 001	333 070	25.3	23.8	23.3	23.6
Developing economies excluding China - Économies en développement sans la Chine	90 673	141 740	240 612	267 492	23.9	23.0	21.8	21.5
25 LEADING IMPORTERS: DEVELOPING AND TRANSITION ECONOMIES / **25 PRINCIPAUX IMPORTATEURS : ÉCONOMIES EN DÉVELOPPEMENT ET EN TRANSITION**								
China - Chine	13 114	21 759	54 880	(e)72 474	36.4	26.0	28.4	(e)30.5
Russian Federation - Fédération de Russie	8 848	17 314	26 587	32 466	52.5	44.7	36.1	36.1
Saudi Arabia - Arabie saoudite	-	9 087	21 135	17 271	-	(b)27.4	27.5	22.1
Korea, Republic of - Corée, République de	7 132	15 406	18 780	19 463	21.2	25.8	19.6	19.6
China, Hong Kong SAR - Chine (RAS de Hong Kong)	12 502	13 305	17 504	19 138	50.6	39.2	34.3	34.3
Singapore - Singapour	4 938	10 072	16 770	(e)20 205	16.4	18.2	17.4	(e)17.7
Brazil - Brésil	3 894	4 720	16 422	21 234	23.4	19.4	26.2	27.8
Iran (Islamic Rep. of) - Iran (Rép. islamique d')	668	3 723	14 186	-	21.4	34.3	60.6	-
United Arab Emirates - Émirats arabes unis	3 017	6 186	11 818	13 206	35.2	31.9	28.1	26.6
India - Inde	2 690	6 187	10 628	(e)13 827	14.0	(b)13.1	9.1	(e)11.1
China, Taiwan Province of - Province chinoise de Taiwan	8 107	8 682	9 357	10 112	30.4	26.7	24.7	24.1
Malaysia - Malaisie	2 075	3 711	7 943	10 320	12.4	16.9	24.7	27.4
Mexico - Mexique	5 499	7 600	7 255	7 832	32.6	36.5	28.8	26.7
Kuwait - Koweït	2 495	4 532	6 427	8 131	50.7	52.0	42.9	46.0
Indonesia - Indonésie	_	3 584	6 395	7 279	_	16.3	24.5	22.5
South Africa - Afrique du Sud	2 085	3 374	5 595	5 283	35.8	27.8	30.3	26.9
Nigeria - Nigéria	591	(b)240	5 566	6 597	17.9	(b)3.6	26.1	26.9
Thailand - Thaïlande	2 772	3 800	5 514	(e)5 594	17.9	14.2	12.3	(e)10.9
Lebanon - Liban	-	2 908	4 911	-	-	36.8	36.6	-
Argentina - Argentine	4 425	2 790	4 878	5 516	48.0	36.6	34.5	33.6
Turkey - Turquie	1 713	2 872	4 826	(e)4 970	21.0	25.0	24.5	(e)23.3
Ukraine	470	2 805	3 742	4 461	15.6	37.2	29.6	30.7
Philippines	1 642	1 279	3 416	3 646	31.3	21.8	30.1	30.7
Egypt - Égypte	1 072	1 629	2 240	(e)2 203	14.3	15.5	15.2	(e)15.8
Libya - Libye	397	680	2 047	-	44.4	28.9	33.4	-
15 LEADING IMPORTERS: DEVELOPED ECONOMIES / **15 PRINCIPAUX IMPORTATEURS : ÉCONOMIES DÉVELOPPÉES**								
United States - États-Unis	67 860	74 790	82 696	86 734	30.8	24.6	20.4	20.2
Germany - Allemagne	52 824	74 325	78 054	(e)84 237	38.3	35.2	29.6	(e)29.0
United Kingdom - Royaume-Uni	38 262	59 602	50 002	(e)50 163	38.4	36.6	30.0	(e)28.4
France	22 533	31 814	38 493	(e)41 594	34.4	29.7	29.1	(e)28.8
Canada	12 438	18 017	29 558	33 166	28.2	27.4	32.4	32.8
Japan - Japon	(e)23 200	(e)27 333	27 866	27 278	(e)21.8	(e)22.0	17.7	16.3
Italy - Italie	15 685	22 335	27 039	(e)28 790	28.2	24.8	24.4	(e)24.8
Australia - Australie	6 387	11 253	22 171	26 914	33.7	36.9	43.6	44.5
Netherlands - Pays-Bas	12 191	16 162	19 611	(e)20 774	23.7	19.1	18.5	(e)17.5
Belgium - Belgique	(a)10 182	14 982	18 739	(e)22 136	(a)24.3	29.3	23.9	(e)26.1
Spain - Espagne	5 922	15 079	16 771	(e)17 268	17.9	22.5	19.3	(e)18.4
Norway - Norvège	4 601	10 178	13 974	(e)16 741	30.7	34.4	32.6	(e)37.0
Sweden - Suède	8 036	10 772	13 369	(e)15 908	33.5	30.5	27.7	(e)28.5
Switzerland - Suisse	5 419	8 782	11 159	12 657	37.0	34.1	28.2	26.9
Austria - Autriche	6 232	9 334	10 222	(e)10 470	37.9	30.3	27.5	(e)24.8

For sources and notes, see end of table.

Pour les sources et les notes, se reporter à la fin du tableau.

5

Country or territory / Pays ou territoires	Exports (4) - Exportations (4)							
	Millions of dollars / Millions de dollars				As % of total services / En % du total des services			
	2000	2005	2010	2011	2000	2005	2010	2011
SELECTED COUNTRY GROUPINGS / SÉLECTION DE GROUPEMENTS DE PAYS								
World - Monde	33 500	59 424	93 968	102 160	2.2	2.3	2.5	2.4
Developing economies - Économies en développement	9 119	15 715	23 844	23 962	2.6	2.5	2.1	1.9
Transition economies - Économies en transition	941	1 803	3 524	3 934	3.9	3.1	3.4	3.3
Developed economies - Économies développées	23 439	41 907	66 601	74 264	2.0	2.2	2.6	2.6
Developing economies: Africa - Économies en développement : Afrique	893	1 893	3 885	3 361	2.7	3.2	4.3	3.7
Developing economies: America - Économies en développement : Amérique	3 211	3 238	4 051	3 526	5.2	3.7	3.0	2.4
Developing economies: Asia - Économies en développement : Asie	4 972	10 511	15 857	17 055	1.9	2.2	1.7	1.7
Developing economies: Oceania - Économies en développement : Océanie	-	-	-	-	-	-	-	-
Developed economies: America - Économies développées : Amérique	5 507	7 015	14 352	16 494	1.7	1.6	2.3	2.4
Developed economies: Asia - Économies développées : Asie	998	556	1 025	1 036	1.2	0.5	0.6	0.6
Developed economies: Europe - Économies développées : Europe	15 853	33 437	50 026	55 372	2.2	2.6	2.9	2.8
Developed economies: Oceania - Économies développées : Océanie	1 082	898	1 199	1 362	4.5	2.3	2.1	2.2
Least developed countries - Pays les moins avancés	342	572	1 568	1 275	4.8	4.9	7.0	5.0
Developing economies excluding LDCs - Économies en développement sans les PMA	8 777	15 143	22 276	22 687	2.6	2.5	2.0	1.8
Developing economies excluding China - Économies en développement sans la Chine	7 774	15 230	22 623	22 273	2.4	2.7	2.3	2.1
25 LEADING EXPORTERS: DEVELOPING AND TRANSITION ECONOMIES / 25 PRINCIPAUX EXPORTATEURS : ÉCONOMIES EN DÉVELOPPEMENT ET EN TRANSITION								
Kuwait - Koweït	-	1 295	3 559	3 602	-	27.1	38.2	35.6
India - Inde	599	1 566	1 411	(e)1 601	3.6	(b)3.0	1.1	(e)1.2
Russian Federation - Fédération de Russie	385	658	1 351	1 473	3.9	2.6	3.0	2.7
Singapore - Singapour	433	560	1 347	(e)1 486	1.5	1.0	1.2	(e)1.2
China, Hong Kong SAR - Chine (RAS de Hong Kong)	362	942	1 241	-	0.9	1.5	1.2	-
China - Chine	1 345	485	1 220	(e)1 689	4.4	0.7	0.7	(e)0.9
Indonesia - Indonésie	_	998	1 126	1 421	_	7.7	6.7	6.9
Egypt - Égypte	306	362	844	-	3.1	2.5	3.5	-
Korea, Republic of - Corée, République de	387	443	834	792	1.2	0.9	1.0	0.8
Bahrain - Bahreïn	-	638	799	627	-	20.9	19.8	20.6
Morocco - Maroc	114	328	713	772	3.7	4.0	5.7	5.5
Turkey - Turquie	-	412	538	(e)522	-	1.5	1.6	(e)1.4
Cuba	-	-	-	-	-	. .	-	-
Ukraine	89	203	518	577	2.3	2.2	3.0	3.0
Thailand - Thaïlande	132	285	471	-	1.0	1.4	1.4	-
Brazil - Brésil	36	239	435	320	0.4	1.5	1.4	0.8
China, Taiwan Province of - Province chinoise de Taiwan	294	320	392	439	1.5	1.2	1.0	0.9
Lebanon - Liban	-	241	387	-	-	2.2	2.4	-
Kenya	22	178	360	-	2.2	9.4	9.8	-
Guatemala	0	174	316	343	0.0	13.3	13.8	14.6
Philippines	182	522	305	391	5.4	11.5	2.2	2.5
Tunisia - Tunisie	12	45	302	-	0.4	1.1	5.2	-
Argentina - Argentine	175	210	293	299	3.5	3.2	2.2	2.1
Saudi Arabia - Arabie saoudite	-	193	293	264	-	(b)1.7	2.7	2.3
Bangladesh	22	24	278	399	2.6	1.9	11.5	15.1
15 LEADING EXPORTERS: DEVELOPED ECONOMIES / 15 PRINCIPAUX EXPORTATEURS : ÉCONOMIES DÉVELOPPÉES								
United States - États-Unis	4 128	5 057	11 324	12 988	1.4	1.3	2.1	2.2
United Kingdom - Royaume-Uni	2 812	6 722	8 251	(e)9 917	2.3	3.2	3.3	(e)3.6
Italy - Italie	1 274	2 174	6 783	(e)6 839	2.3	2.4	6.9	(e)6.4
Germany - Allemagne	1 454	3 432	5 409	(e)5 697	1.8	2.1	2.3	(e)2.2
Netherlands - Pays-Bas	1 441	3 761	4 931	(e)5 978	2.9	4.1	4.2	(e)4.4
France	1 328	3 524	4 481	(e)4 863	1.6	2.9	3.1	(e)2.9
Belgium - Belgique	(a)1 894	2 201	4 043	(e)4 560	(a)3.8	3.9	4.6	(e)5.1
Canada	1 379	1 958	2 959	3 440	3.4	3.5	4.3	4.5
Luxembourg	. .	1 104	2 622	(e)2 566		2.7	3.9	(e)3.5
Spain - Espagne	668	. .	2 118	(e)2 295	1.3	. .	1.7	(e)1.6
Sweden - Suède	647	1 448	1 832	(e)2 179	3.0	3.4	2.8	(e)2.9
Switzerland - Suisse	879	1 183	1 431	1 533	2.9	2.4	1.7	1.6
Austria - Autriche	478	1 007	1 385	(e)1 414	2.1	2.4	2.5	(e)2.3
Australia - Australie	889	625	1 042	1 164	4.5	2.0	2.2	2.2
Norway - Norvège	291	378	737	-	1.6	1.3	1.9	-

For sources and notes, see end of table.   Pour les sources et les notes, se reporter à la fin du tableau.

Country or territory / Pays ou territoires	Imports (4) - Importations (4)							
	Millions of dollars / Millions de dollars				As % of total services / En % du total des services			
	2000	2005	2010	2011	2000	2005	2010	2011
SELECTED COUNTRY GROUPINGS (1) / **SÉLECTION DE GROUPEMENTS DE PAYS (1)**								
World - Monde	..	..	..	..	..	..	..	..
Developing economies - Économies en développement	..	..	..	..	..	..	..	..
Transition economies - Économies en transition	..	..	..	..	..	..	..	..
Developed economies - Économies développées	..	..	..	..	..	..	..	..
Developing economies: Africa - Économies en développement : Afrique	..	..	..	..	..	..	..	..
Developing economies: America - Économies en développement : Amérique	..	..	..	..	..	..	..	..
Developing economies: Asia - Économies en développement : Asie	..	..	..	..	..	..	..	..
Developing economies: Oceania - Économies en développement : Océanie	..	..	..	..	..	..	..	..
Developed economies: America - Économies développées : Amérique	..	..	..	..	..	..	..	..
Developed economies: Asia - Économies développées : Asie	..	..	..	..	..	..	..	..
Developed economies: Europe - Économies développées : Europe	..	..	..	..	..	..	..	..
Developed economies: Oceania - Économies développées : Océanie	..	..	..	..	..	..	..	..
Least developed countries - Pays les moins avancés	..	..	..	..	..	..	..	..
Developing economies excluding LDCs - Économies en développement sans les PMA	..	..	..	..	..	..	..	..
Developing economies excluding China - Économies en développement sans la Chine	..	..	..	..	..	..	..	..
25 LEADING IMPORTERS: DEVELOPING AND TRANSITION ECONOMIES / **25 PRINCIPAUX IMPORTATEURS : ÉCONOMIES EN DÉVELOPPEMENT ET EN TRANSITION**								
Saudi Arabia - Arabie saoudite	-	344	2 197	2 599	-	(b)1.0	2.9	3.3
Russian Federation - Fédération de Russie	288	746	2 100	2 530	1.7	1.9	2.8	2.8
Singapore - Singapour	621	889	1 758	(e)1 941	2.1	1.6	1.8	(e)1.7
China, Hong Kong SAR - Chine (RAS de Hong Kong)	698	1 141	1 673	-	2.8	3.4	3.3	-
Korea, Republic of - Corée, République de	623	773	1 460	1 464	1.9	1.3	1.5	1.5
India - Inde	105	418	1 194	(e)1 394	0.5	(b)0.9	1.0	(e)1.1
China - Chine	242	603	1 137	(e)1 042	0.7	0.7	0.6	(e)0.4
Indonesia - Indonésie	_	495	547	804	_	2.2	2.1	2.5
China, Taiwan Province of - Province chinoise de Taiwan	528	505	454	542	2.0	1.6	1.2	1.3
South Africa - Afrique du Sud	83	168	397	309	1.4	1.4	2.2	1.6
Venezuela (Bolivarian Rep. of) - Venezuela (Rép. bolivarienne du)	84	76	369	357	1.9	1.4	3.3	2.8
Argentina - Argentine	205	269	367	443	2.2	3.5	2.6	2.7
Qatar	-	427	365	253	-	10.3	4.2	1.5
Thailand - Thaïlande	39	248	363	-	0.3	0.9	0.8	-
Angola	-	23	362	-	-	0.3	1.9	-
Egypt - Égypte	102	406	338	-	1.4	3.9	2.3	-
Malaysia - Malaisie	231	680	-	-	1.4	3.1	-	-
Lebanon - Liban	-	138	309	-	-	1.8	2.3	-
Nigeria - Nigéria	-	159	285	229	-	(b)2.4	1.3	0.9
Brazil - Brésil	32	112	271	204	0.2	0.5	0.4	0.3
Turkey - Turquie	84	228	270	(e)344	1.0	2.0	1.4	(e)1.6
Iran (Islamic Rep. of) - Iran (Rép. islamique d')	-	152	234	-	-	1.4	1.0	-
Honduras	26	19	220	132	3.7	2.1	16.5	8.5
Colombia - Colombie	123	152	210	239	3.7	3.2	2.6	2.5
Congo	8	-	-	-	1.1	-	-	-
15 LEADING IMPORTERS: DEVELOPED ECONOMIES / **15 PRINCIPAUX IMPORTATEURS : ÉCONOMIES DÉVELOPPÉES**								
United States - États-Unis	5 926	5 153	8 367	8 174	2.7	1.7	2.1	1.9
Germany - Allemagne	3 148	5 010	7 402	(e)7 511	2.3	2.4	2.8	(e)2.6
United Kingdom - Royaume-Uni	2 823	5 820	6 793	(e)7 081	2.8	3.6	4.1	(e)4.0
Italy - Italie	1 935	3 075	6 558	(e)6 508	3.5	3.4	5.9	(e)5.6
Netherlands - Pays-Bas	1 416	3 191	4 086	(e)4 703	2.8	3.8	3.8	(e)4.0
France	1 148	2 179	3 849	(e)3 639	1.8	2.0	2.9	(e)2.5
Belgium - Belgique	(a)988	1 326	3 187	(e)3 532	(a)2.4	2.6	4.1	(e)4.2
Spain - Espagne	744	..	2 669	(e)2 821	2.2	..	3.1	(e)3.0
Canada	1 381	1 489	2 287	2 231	3.1	2.3	2.5	2.2
Sweden - Suède	792	1 586	2 231	(e)2 435	3.3	4.5	4.6	(e)4.4
Norway - Norvège	165	286	1 620	-	1.1	1.0	3.8	-
Ireland - Irlande	794	882	1 601	(e)1 635	2.5	1.2	1.5	(e)1.4
Austria - Autriche	431	823	1 086	(e)1 183	2.6	2.7	2.9	(e)2.8
Switzerland - Suisse	885	938	1 056	1 069	6.0	3.6	2.7	2.3
Japan - Japon	1 152	616	1 026	975	1.1	0.5	0.7	0.6

For sources and notes, see end of table.   Pour les sources et les notes, se reporter à la fin du tableau.

Country or territory / Pays ou territoires	Exports (5) - Exportations (5)							
	Millions of dollars / Millions de dollars				As % of total services / En % du total des services			
	2000	2005	2010	2011	2000	2005	2010	2011
SELECTED COUNTRY GROUPINGS / SÉLECTION DE GROUPEMENTS DE PAYS								
World - Monde	30 858	56 483	94 458	101 813	2.0	2.2	2.5	2.4
Developing economies - Économies en développement	5 489	14 349	35 914	40 126	1.6	2.3	3.2	3.2
Transition economies - Économies en transition	605	2 860	4 102	4 737	2.5	5.0	4.0	3.9
Developed economies - Économies développées	24 764	39 274	54 441	56 949	2.2	2.1	2.1	2.0
Developing economies: Africa - Économies en développement : Afrique	407	1 146	1 994	1 938	1.2	1.9	2.2	2.1
Developing economies: America - Économies en développement : Amérique	387	139	239	183	0.6	0.2	0.2	0.1
Developing economies: Asia - Économies en développement : Asie	4 670	13 030	33 535	37 940	1.8	2.7	3.7	3.7
Developing economies: Oceania - Économies en développement : Océanie	-	-	-	-	-	-	-	-
Developed economies: America - Économies développées : Amérique	2 033	1 527	2 905	2 955	0.6	0.4	0.5	0.4
Developed economies: Asia - Économies développées : Asie	6 031	7 572	11 475	11 972	7.0	6.2	6.9	6.9
Developed economies: Europe - Économies développées : Europe	16 665	30 043	39 838	41 741	2.4	2.3	2.3	2.1
Developed economies: Oceania - Économies développées : Océanie	35	131	222	281	0.1	0.3	0.4	0.5
Least developed countries - Pays les moins avancés	117	189	387	485	1.6	1.6	1.7	1.9
Developing economies excluding LDCs - Économies en développement sans les PMA	5 372	14 161	35 528	39 641	1.6	2.3	3.2	3.2
Developing economies excluding China - Économies en développement sans la Chine	4 886	11 757	21 420	25 332	1.5	2.1	2.2	2.3
25 LEADING EXPORTERS: DEVELOPING AND TRANSITION ECONOMIES / 25 PRINCIPAUX EXPORTATEURS : ÉCONOMIES EN DÉVELOPPEMENT ET EN TRANSITION								
China - Chine	602	2 593	14 495	(e)14 795	2.0	3.5	8.5	(e)8.1
Korea, Republic of - Corée, République de	933	4 707	11 977	15 185	3.0	9.5	13.7	16.0
Russian Federation - Fédération de Russie	170	2 209	2 625	3 119	1.7	8.8	5.8	5.8
Turkey - Turquie	1 033	882	1 120	(e)1 250	5.3	3.3	3.3	(e)3.3
Singapore - Singapour	134	542	1 049	(e)1 179	0.5	1.0	0.9	(e)0.9
Iran (Islamic Rep. of) - Iran (Rép. islamique d')	-	1 475	951	-	-	29.5	11.5	-
Malaysia - Malaisie	314	811	-	-	2.3	4.1	-	-
Egypt - Égypte	93	503	711	-	0.9	3.4	3.0	-
Lebanon - Liban	-	0	598	-	-	0.0	3.7	-
India - Inde	502	346	524	-	3.0	(b)0.7	0.4	-
Indonesia - Indonésie	_	484	520	549	_	3.7	3.1	2.7
Tunisia - Tunisie	50	151	479	-	1.8	3.8	8.2	-
Thailand - Thaïlande	230	255	472	(e)444	1.7	1.3	1.4	(e)1.1
China, Taiwan Province of - Province chinoise de Taiwan	119	121	355	348	0.6	0.5	0.9	0.8
Serbia - Serbie	_	_	239	307	_	_	5.6	6.0
Ukraine	38	115	234	255	1.0	1.2	1.4	1.3
Algeria - Algérie	-	167	180	-	-	6.7	5.0	-
Bosnia and Herzegovina - Bosnie-Herzégovine	73	150	169	86	16.1	15.1	13.1	6.6
Croatia - Croatie	199	43	156	(e)88	4.9	0.4	1.4	(e)0.7
Turkmenistan - Turkménistan	-	-	-	-	-	-	-	-
Azerbaijan - Azerbaïdjan	5	9	153	113	1.9	1.4	7.2	4.1
China, Hong Kong SAR - Chine (RAS de Hong Kong)	338	313	145	-	0.8	0.5	0.1	-
Belarus - Bélarus	42	60	126	195	4.2	2.9	2.8	3.7
Philippines	97	66	121	45	2.9	1.5	0.9	0.3
Papua New Guinea - Papouasie-Nouvelle-Guinée	-	15	95	(e)14	-	5.0	30.7	(e)3.0
15 LEADING EXPORTERS: DEVELOPED ECONOMIES / 15 PRINCIPAUX EXPORTATEURS : ÉCONOMIES DÉVELOPPÉES								
Germany - Allemagne	4 244	10 431	11 619	(e)11 901	5.1	6.4	4.9	(e)4.6
Japan - Japon	5 849	7 224	10 637	10 968	8.3	6.9	7.5	7.5
France	2 871	3 633	6 310	(e)6 123	3.5	3.0	4.3	(e)3.6
Spain - Espagne	588	..	4 163	(e)4 274	1.1	..	3.4	(e)3.0
Netherlands - Pays-Bas	2 581	2 757	2 784	(e)2 945	5.2	3.0	2.4	(e)2.2
United States - États-Unis	1 815	1 346	2 611	-	0.6	0.4	0.5	-
United Kingdom - Royaume-Uni	333	1 091	1 882	(e)2 524	0.3	0.5	0.8	(e)0.9
Belgium - Belgique	(a)924	1 908	1 543	(e)1 676	(a)1.9	3.4	1.8	(e)1.9
Switzerland - Suisse	-	-	-	-	-	-	-	-
Poland - Pologne	296	866	1 323	(e)1 486	2.8	5.3	4.0	(e)4.0
Austria - Autriche	586	989	1 164	(e)780	2.5	2.3	2.1	(e)1.3
Finland - Finlande	439	572	1 109	(e)1 207	5.7	3.4	4.0	(e)4.4
Czech Republic - République tchèque	167	238	975	(e)847	2.4	2.0	4.7	(e)3.7
Sweden - Suède	681	667	840	(e)902	3.1	1.6	1.3	(e)1.2
Israel - Israël	182	348	838	1 004	1.2	2.1	3.5	3.7

For sources and notes, see end of table.

Pour les sources et les notes, se reporter à la fin du tableau.

Country or territory / Pays ou territoires	Imports (5) - Importations (5)							
	Millions of dollars / Millions de dollars				As % of total services / En % du total des services			
	2000	2005	2010	2011	2000	2005	2010	2011
SELECTED COUNTRY GROUPINGS (1) **SÉLECTION DE GROUPEMENTS DE PAYS (1)**								
World - Monde	..	..	..	..	..	..	..	..
Developing economies - Économies en développement	..	..	..	..	..	..	..	..
Transition economies - Économies en transition	..	..	..	..	..	..	..	..
Developed economies - Économies développées	..	..	..	..	..	..	..	..
Developing economies: Africa - Économies en développement : Afrique	..	..	..	..	..	..	..	..
Developing economies: America - Économies en développement : Amérique	..	..	..	..	..	..	..	..
Developing economies: Asia - Économies en développement : Asie	..	..	..	..	..	..	..	..
Developing economies: Oceania - Économies en développement : Océanie	..	..	..	..	..	..	..	..
Developed economies: America - Économies développées : Amérique	..	..	..	..	..	..	..	..
Developed economies: Asia - Économies développées : Asie	..	..	..	..	..	..	..	..
Developed economies: Europe - Économies développées : Europe	..	..	..	..	..	..	..	..
Developed economies: Oceania - Économies développées : Océanie	..	..	..	..	..	..	..	..
Least developed countries - Pays les moins avancés	..	..	..	..	..	..	..	..
Developing economies excluding LDCs - Économies en développement sans les PMA	..	..	..	..	..	..	..	..
Developing economies excluding China - Économies en développement sans la Chine	..	..	..	..	..	..	..	..
25 LEADING IMPORTERS: DEVELOPING AND TRANSITION ECONOMIES **25 PRINCIPAUX IMPORTATEURS : ÉCONOMIES EN DÉVELOPPEMENT ET EN TRANSITION**								
China - Chine	994	1 619	5 072	(e)3 753	2.8	1.9	2.6	(e)1.6
Angola	-	1 323	4 643	-	-	19.5	24.8	-
Russian Federation - Fédération de Russie	406	4 034	4 382	5 655	2.4	10.4	5.9	6.3
Saudi Arabia - Arabie saoudite	-	1 416	3 789	2 578	-	(b)4.3	4.9	3.3
Algeria - Algérie	-	548	2 556	-	-	11.5	21.5	-
Korea, Republic of - Corée, République de	187	879	2 302	3 092	0.6	1.5	2.4	3.1
Kazakhstan	539	1 941	1 666	1 900	29.1	25.9	14.7	17.4
Kuwait - Koweït	26	42	1 546	1 250	0.5	0.5	10.3	7.1
India - Inde	127	602	991	-	0.7	(b)1.3	0.8	-
Iran (Islamic Rep. of) - Iran (Rép. islamique d')	-	2 956	794	-	-	27.3	3.4	-
Thailand - Thaïlande	105	314	713	(e)308	0.7	1.2	1.6	(e)0.6
Papua New Guinea - Papouasie-Nouvelle-Guinée	-	58	676	(e)1 016	-	4.6	24.5	(e)35.3
Indonesia - Indonésie	–	726	592	489	–	3.3	2.3	1.5
Malaysia - Malaisie	1 091	1 087	-	-	6.5	5.0	-	-
Lebanon - Liban	-	0	508	-	-	0.0	3.8	-
Singapore - Singapour	124	203	500	(e)561	0.4	0.4	0.5	(e)0.5
China, Macao SAR - Chine (RAS de Macao)	-	-	-	-	-	-	-	-
Tunisia - Tunisie	112	197	399	-	9.2	9.0	11.9	-
Egypt - Égypte	-	231	386	-	-	2.2	2.6	-
Ethiopia - Éthiopie	10	121	361	(e)367	2.1	10.1	14.2	(e)10.8
Azerbaijan - Azerbaïdjan	91	1 499	325	514	18.7	56.5	8.5	9.0
Haiti - Haïti	-	-	290	-	-	-	22.7	-
Turkey - Turquie	65	8	261	(e)409	0.8	0.1	1.3	(e)1.9
Turkmenistan - Turkménistan	-	-	-	-	-	-	-	-
China, Taiwan Province of - Province chinoise de Taiwan	439	376	241	233	1.6	1.2	0.6	0.6
15 LEADING IMPORTERS: DEVELOPED ECONOMIES **15 PRINCIPAUX IMPORTATEURS : ÉCONOMIES DÉVELOPPÉES**								
Japan - Japon	4 000	4 765	7 883	7 711	3.8	3.8	5.0	4.6
Germany - Allemagne	4 931	6 595	7 796	(e)8 146	3.6	3.1	3.0	(e)2.8
France	1 528	1 629	2 979	(e)2 565	2.3	1.5	2.3	(e)1.8
United States - États-Unis	1 326	1 171	2 351	-	0.6	0.4	0.6	-
Netherlands - Pays-Bas	977	1 418	2 012	(e)2 337	1.9	1.7	1.9	(e)2.0
United Kingdom - Royaume-Uni	82	1 036	1 899	(e)1 600	0.1	0.6	1.1	(e)0.9
Spain - Espagne	218	..	1 879	(e)1 582	0.7	..	2.2	(e)1.7
Belgium - Belgique	(a)609	848	1 246	(e)1 421	(a)1.5	1.7	1.6	(e)1.7
Sweden - Suède	322	482	1 164	(e)1 901	1.3	1.4	2.4	(e)3.4
Austria - Autriche	311	846	901	(e)790	1.9	2.7	2.4	(e)1.9
Poland - Pologne	316	514	710	(e)643	3.5	3.3	2.4	(e)2.1
Czech Republic - République tchèque	146	190	623	(e)537	2.7	1.9	3.7	(e)2.8
Luxembourg	..	426	558	(e)525	..	1.8	1.5	(e)1.3
Finland - Finlande	52	482	538	(e)400	0.6	2.7	1.9	(e)1.5
Romania - Roumanie	28	196	494	(e)340	1.4	3.5	5.2	(e)3.0

For sources and notes, see end of table.

Pour les sources et les notes, se reporter à la fin du tableau.

Country or territory Pays ou territoires	Exports (6) - Exportations (6)							
	Millions of dollars / Millions de dollars				As % of total services En % du total des services			
	2000	2005	2010	2011	2000	2005	2010	2011
SELECTED COUNTRY GROUPINGS **SÉLECTION DE GROUPEMENTS DE PAYS**								
World - Monde	48 545	107 434	216 149	249 502	3.2	4.2	5.6	5.9
Developing economies - Économies en développement	6 913	22 400	63 801	75 966	2.0	3.6	5.6	6.0
Transition economies - Économies en transition	155	750	2 757	3 687	0.6	1.3	2.7	3.0
Developed economies - Économies développées	41 477	84 284	149 591	169 849	3.6	4.5	5.8	5.9
Developing economies: Africa - Économies en développement : Afrique	316	397	1 104	1 348	1.0	0.7	1.2	1.5
Developing economies: America - Économies en développement : Amérique	461	981	3 737	4 642	0.7	1.1	2.8	3.1
Developing economies: Asia - Économies en développement : Asie	6 121	21 000	58 953	69 908	2.4	4.4	6.5	6.8
Developing economies: Oceania - Économies en développement : Océanie	-	-	-	-	-	-	-	-
Developed economies: America - Économies développées : Amérique	9 377	13 034	18 697	20 444	2.8	3.0	3.0	3.0
Developed economies: Asia - Économies développées : Asie	5 815	5 655	8 745	10 933	6.8	4.7	5.3	6.3
Developed economies: Europe - Économies développées : Europe	25 709	64 517	120 473	136 596	3.6	5.0	6.9	7.0
Developed economies: Oceania - Économies développées : Océanie	576	1 079	1 676	1 877	2.4	2.7	3.0	3.0
Least developed countries - Pays les moins avancés	88	83	200	358	1.2	0.7	0.9	1.4
Developing economies excluding LDCs - Économies en développement sans les PMA	6 825	22 317	63 601	75 609	2.0	3.6	5.7	6.1
Developing economies excluding China - Économies en développement sans la Chine	6 557	20 560	54 544	63 792	2.0	3.7	5.6	5.9
25 LEADING EXPORTERS: DEVELOPING AND TRANSITION ECONOMIES **25 PRINCIPAUX EXPORTATEURS : ÉCONOMIES EN DÉVELOPPEMENT ET EN TRANSITION**								
India - Inde	-	-	-	-	-	-	-	-
China - Chine	356	1 840	9 256	(e)12 174	1.2	2.5	5.4	(e)6.6
Philippines	76	89	1 928	2 062	2.3	2.0	13.7	13.3
Singapore - Singapour	247	514	1 790	(e)2 039	0.9	0.9	1.6	(e)1.6
Russian Federation - Fédération de Russie	59	422	1 359	1 753	0.6	1.7	3.0	3.2
Malaysia - Malaisie	82	435	-	-	0.6	2.2	-	-
Argentina - Argentine	147	238	1 241	1 594	3.0	3.6	9.5	11.2
Costa Rica	60	255	1 217	1 534	3.1	9.7	28.1	30.6
Thailand - Thaïlande	-	-	-	-	-	-	-	-
China, Hong Kong SAR - Chine (RAS de Hong Kong)	60	265	885	-	0.1	0.4	0.8	-
Cuba	-	-	-	-	-	-	-	-
Ukraine	6	44	429	698	0.2	0.5	2.5	3.6
Morocco - Maroc	-	-	297	378	-	-	2.4	2.7
South Africa - Afrique du Sud	-	109	290	319	-	1.0	2.1	2.2
Sri Lanka	-	82	265	355	-	5.4	10.7	11.5
Korea, Republic of - Corée, République de	11	57	234	424	0.0	0.1	0.3	0.4
Croatia - Croatie	33	86	234	(e)335	0.8	0.9	2.1	(e)2.7
Belarus - Bélarus	5	26	223	279	0.4	1.3	5.0	5.3
China, Taiwan Province of - Province chinoise de Taiwan	117	105	218	388	0.6	0.4	0.5	0.8
Brazil - Brésil	34	88	210	236	0.4	0.5	0.7	0.6
Pakistan	22	59	193	240	1.6	1.6	2.9	4.8
Uruguay	10	83	180	180	0.8	6.3	7.0	5.3
Serbia - Serbie	_	_	172	206	_	_	4.1	4.0
Egypt - Égypte	23	25	152	-	0.2	0.2	0.6	-
Indonesia - Indonésie	_	147	114	203	_	1.1	0.7	1.0
15 LEADING EXPORTERS: DEVELOPED ECONOMIES **15 PRINCIPAUX EXPORTATEURS : ÉCONOMIES DÉVELOPPÉES**								
Ireland - Irlande	7 490	19 593	37 330	(e)44 484	40.4	32.7	38.2	(e)40.5
Germany - Allemagne	3 798	8 415	16 305	(e)18 343	4.6	5.1	6.9	(e)7.1
United States - États-Unis	6 949	9 434	13 766	15 313	2.4	2.5	2.5	2.6
United Kingdom - Royaume-Uni	4 319	10 829	13 508	(e)14 074	3.6	5.2	5.4	(e)5.1
Israel - Israël	4 246	4 529	7 700	9 737	27.0	26.8	31.8	36.3
Sweden - Suède	1 200	2 700	7 208	(e)8 749	5.5	6.3	10.9	(e)11.5
Finland - Finlande	203	1 509	6 510	(e)6 360	2.6	8.9	23.4	(e)23.2
Spain - Espagne	2 043	..	6 408	(e)6 662	3.9	..	5.2	(e)4.7
Netherlands - Pays-Bas	1 166	3 727	6 302	(e)6 260	2.4	4.0	5.3	(e)4.6
Canada	2 428	3 600	4 893	5 095	6.0	6.4	7.1	6.7
Switzerland - Suisse	-	-	-	-	-	-	-	-
Belgium - Belgique	(a)1 786	2 583	4 001	(e)4 819	(a)3.6	4.6	4.6	(e)5.4
Norway - Norvège	660	898	3 023	-	3.7	3.1	7.6	-
Italy - Italie	448	596	2 020	(e)2 377	0.8	0.7	2.0	(e)2.2
Austria - Autriche	296	1 245	2 014	(e)2 600	1.3	2.9	3.7	(e)4.2

For sources and notes, see end of table.   Pour les sources et les notes, se reporter à la fin du tableau.

Country or territory / Pays ou territoires	Imports (6) - Importations (6)							
	Millions of dollars / Millions de dollars				As % of total services / En % du total des services			
	2000	2005	2010	2011	2000	2005	2010	2011
SELECTED COUNTRY GROUPINGS (1) **SÉLECTION DE GROUPEMENTS DE PAYS (1)**								
World - Monde	..	..	..	..	..	..	..	..
Developing economies - Économies en développement	..	..	..	..	..	..	..	..
Transition economies - Économies en transition	..	..	..	..	..	..	..	..
Developed economies - Économies développées	..	..	..	..	..	..	..	..
Developing economies: Africa - Économies en développement : Afrique	..	..	..	..	..	..	..	..
Developing economies: America - Économies en développement : Amérique	..	..	..	..	..	..	..	..
Developing economies: Asia - Économies en développement : Asie	..	..	..	..	..	..	..	..
Developing economies: Oceania - Économies en développement : Océanie	..	..	..	..	..	..	..	..
Developed economies: America - Économies développées : Amérique	..	..	..	..	..	..	..	..
Developed economies: Asia - Économies développées : Asie	..	..	..	..	..	..	..	..
Developed economies: Europe - Économies développées : Europe	..	..	..	..	..	..	..	..
Developed economies: Oceania - Économies développées : Océanie	..	..	..	..	..	..	..	..
Least developed countries - Pays les moins avancés	..	..	..	..	..	..	..	..
Developing economies excluding LDCs - Économies en développement sans les PMA	..	..	..	..	..	..	..	..
Developing economies excluding China - Économies en développement sans la Chine	..	..	..	..	..	..	..	..
25 LEADING IMPORTERS: DEVELOPING AND TRANSITION ECONOMIES **25 PRINCIPAUX IMPORTATEURS : ÉCONOMIES EN DÉVELOPPEMENT ET EN TRANSITION**								
Brazil - Brésil	1 145	1 713	3 505	4 036	6.9	7.0	5.6	5.3
China - Chine	265	1 623	2 965	(e)3 855	0.7	1.9	1.5	(e)1.6
India - Inde	577	1 266	2 531	(e)1 457	3.0	(b)2.7	2.2	(e)1.2
Russian Federation - Fédération de Russie	474	482	1 884	2 433	2.8	1.2	2.6	2.7
Singapore - Singapour	226	386	1 230	(e)1 402	0.8	0.7	1.3	(e)1.2
Saudi Arabia - Arabie saoudite	-	-	-	-	-	-	-	-
Thailand - Thaïlande	-	-	-	-	-	-	-	-
Indonesia - Indonésie	_	561	585	715	_	2.5	2.2	2.2
China, Hong Kong SAR - Chine (RAS de Hong Kong)	128	427	564	-	0.5	1.3	1.1	-
Korea, Republic of - Corée, République de	92	183	496	559	0.3	0.3	0.5	0.6
Argentina - Argentine	149	195	468	577	1.6	2.6	3.3	3.5
China, Taiwan Province of - Province chinoise de Taiwan	217	315	435	479	0.8	1.0	1.1	1.1
Malaysia - Malaisie	201	379	-	-	1.2	1.7	-	-
Iran (Islamic Rep. of) - Iran (Rép. islamique d')	-	216	399	-	-	2.0	1.7	-
Croatia - Croatie	57	148	292	(e)326	3.1	4.4	8.3	(e)9.0
Congo	-	-	-	-	-	-	-	-
Ukraine	51	128	247	296	1.7	1.7	2.0	2.0
United Arab Emirates - Émirats arabes unis	-	-	-	-	-	-	-	-
Peru - Pérou	-	-	206	(e)216	-	-	3.4	(e)3.2
Iraq	-	205	-	-	-	3.4	-	-
Serbia - Serbie	_	_	188	160	_	_	4.7	3.6
South Africa - Afrique du Sud	-	114	186	201	-	0.9	1.0	1.0
Pakistan	-	34	168	192	-	0.5	2.4	2.4
Egypt - Égypte	20	27	161	-	0.3	0.3	1.1	-
Colombia - Colombie	46	119	152	203	1.4	2.5	1.9	2.1
15 LEADING IMPORTERS: DEVELOPED ECONOMIES **15 PRINCIPAUX IMPORTATEURS : ÉCONOMIES DÉVELOPPÉES**								
United States - États-Unis	6 230	10 596	19 385	23 977	2.8	3.5	4.8	5.6
Germany - Allemagne	4 970	8 587	14 067	(e)16 150	3.6	4.1	5.3	(e)5.6
United Kingdom - Royaume-Uni	1 270	4 013	6 131	(e)5 646	1.3	2.5	3.7	(e)3.2
Netherlands - Pays-Bas	1 187	3 709	5 331	(e)5 151	2.3	4.4	5.0	(e)4.3
Italy - Italie	926	1 499	4 391	(e)4 641	1.7	1.7	4.0	(e)4.0
Japan - Japon	3 066	2 432	3 573	4 214	2.9	2.0	2.3	2.5
Canada	899	1 802	2 904	3 272	2.0	2.7	3.2	3.2
Belgium - Belgique	(a)1 322	1 867	2 858	(e)3 550	(a)3.2	3.6	3.6	(e)4.2
Spain - Espagne	1 227	..	2 809	(e)3 078	3.7	..	3.2	(e)3.3
Sweden - Suède	1 078	1 519	2 663	(e)3 445	4.5	4.3	5.5	(e)6.2
Finland - Finlande	307	1 155	2 150	(e)1 820	3.6	6.5	7.8	(e)7.0
Denmark - Danemark	-	1 142	2 014	(e)2 216	-	3.1	3.9	(e)3.9
France	744	1 781	1 918	(e)2 666	1.1	1.7	1.5	(e)1.8
Norway - Norvège	243	1 135	1 674	-	1.6	3.8	3.9	-
Poland - Pologne	217	419	1 664	(e)1 849	2.4	2.7	5.6	(e)6.0

For sources and notes, see end of table.

Pour les sources et les notes, se reporter à la fin du tableau.

Country or territory Pays ou territoires	Exports (7) - Exportations (7)							
	Millions of dollars / Millions de dollars				As % of total services En % du total des services			
	2000	2005	2010	2011	2000	2005	2010	2011
SELECTED COUNTRY GROUPINGS **SÉLECTION DE GROUPEMENTS DE PAYS**								
World - Monde	25 597	48 984	80 967	86 047	1.7	1.9	2.1	2.0
Developing economies - Économies en développement	6 245	9 806	15 509	17 478	1.8	1.6	1.4	1.4
Transition economies - Économies en transition	120	487	788	788	0.5	0.8	0.8	0.7
Developed economies - Économies développées	19 232	38 691	64 670	67 781	1.7	2.1	2.5	2.4
Developing economies: Africa - Économies en développement : Afrique	755	1 150	1 041	1 033	2.3	1.9	1.2	1.1
Developing economies: America - Économies en développement : Amérique	2 831	2 856	3 562	4 054	4.6	3.2	2.7	2.7
Developing economies: Asia - Économies en développement : Asie	2 652	5 781	10 897	12 368	1.0	1.2	1.2	1.2
Developing economies: Oceania - Économies en développement : Océanie	-	-	-	-	-	-	-	-
Developed economies: America - Économies développées : Amérique	5 570	10 778	19 040	19 992	1.7	2.5	3.1	3.0
Developed economies: Asia - Économies développées : Asie	191	889	1 299	1 663	0.2	0.7	0.8	1.0
Developed economies: Europe - Économies développées : Europe	13 020	26 466	43 999	45 653	1.8	2.1	2.5	2.3
Developed economies: Oceania - Économies développées : Océanie	450	557	332	473	1.9	1.4	0.6	0.8
Least developed countries - Pays les moins avancés	88	95	144	169	1.2	0.8	0.6	0.7
Developing economies excluding LDCs - Économies en développement sans les PMA	6 157	9 712	15 365	17 309	1.8	1.6	1.4	1.4
Developing economies excluding China - Économies en développement sans la Chine	6 137	9 257	13 783	14 132	1.9	1.7	1.4	1.3
25 LEADING EXPORTERS: DEVELOPING AND TRANSITION ECONOMIES **25 PRINCIPAUX EXPORTATEURS : ÉCONOMIES EN DÉVELOPPEMENT ET EN TRANSITION**								
Singapore - Singapour	559	1 296	2 837	(e)2 024	2.0	2.3	2.5	(e)1.6
Mexico - Mexique	1 799	1 550	1 831	2 262	13.3	9.9	12.1	14.8
India - Inde	257	941	1 782	(e)2 575	1.5	(b)1.8	1.4	(e)1.9
China - Chine	108	549	1 727	(e)3 346	0.4	0.7	1.0	(e)1.8
Bahrain - Bahreïn	-	655	906	352	-	21.5	22.4	11.6
Turkey - Turquie	32	323	719	(e)867	0.2	1.2	2.1	(e)2.3
China, Hong Kong SAR - Chine (RAS de Hong Kong)	443	414	538	578	1.1	0.6	0.5	0.5
Korea, Republic of - Corée, République de	68	169	515	419	0.2	0.3	0.6	0.4
Russian Federation - Fédération de Russie	35	323	462	440	0.4	1.3	1.0	0.8
China, Taiwan Province of - Province chinoise de Taiwan	607	365	430	513	3.0	1.4	1.1	1.1
Brazil - Brésil	312	134	416	505	3.3	0.8	1.3	1.3
Qatar	-	18	311	368	-	0.6	10.3	5.0
Saudi Arabia - Arabie saoudite	-	-	290	251	-	-	2.7	2.2
Chile - Chili	76	163	286	(e)346	1.9	2.3	2.6	(e)2.8
South Africa - Afrique du Sud	451	124	273	319	8.9	1.1	1.9	2.2
Cuba	-	-	-	-	-	-	-	-
Malaysia - Malaisie	156	278	-	-	1.1	1.4	-	-
Peru - Pérou	113	118	166	(e)228	7.2	5.2	4.2	(e)4.8
Morocco - Maroc	30	72	153	133	1.0	0.9	1.2	0.9
Trinidad and Tobago - Trinité-et-Tobago	46	135	139	-	8.3	15.1	15.9	-
Egypt - Égypte	30	58	97	-	0.3	0.4	0.4	-
Panama	39	31	90	106	1.9	1.0	1.5	1.5
Sri Lanka	41	73	80	91	4.3	4.7	3.2	2.9
Iran (Islamic Rep. of) - Iran (Rép. islamique d')	-	35	78	-	-	0.7	0.9	-
Philippines	12	17	77	78	0.4	0.4	0.5	0.5
15 LEADING EXPORTERS: DEVELOPED ECONOMIES **15 PRINCIPAUX EXPORTATEURS : ÉCONOMIES DÉVELOPPÉES**								
United States - États-Unis	3 631	7 566	14 605	15 351	1.3	2.0	2.7	2.6
Ireland - Irlande	1 122	8 592	10 300	(e)10 640	6.1	14.3	10.5	(e)9.7
United Kingdom - Royaume-Uni	4 062	2 822	8 135	(e)6 948	3.4	1.4	3.3	(e)2.5
Germany - Allemagne	554	2 222	6 098	(e)6 664	0.7	1.4	2.6	(e)2.6
Switzerland - Suisse	1 509	3 326	4 918	5 671	4.9	6.7	5.9	5.9
Canada	1 939	3 212	4 392	4 593	4.8	5.8	6.4	6.0
Luxembourg	..	1 957	3 549	(e)3 143	..	4.8	5.3	(e)4.3
Italy - Italie	821	1 512	2 895	(e)2 520	1.5	1.7	2.9	(e)2.4
Japan - Japon	174	873	1 274	1 638	0.2	0.8	0.9	1.1
France	1 326	1 130	1 234	(e)2 313	1.6	0.9	0.8	(e)1.4
Spain - Espagne	213	..	1 175	(e)1 503	0.4	..	0.9	(e)1.1
Austria - Autriche	670	805	1 148	(e)934	2.9	1.9	2.1	(e)1.5
Belgium - Belgique	(a)1 068	831	1 107	(e)1 162	(a)2.1	1.5	1.3	(e)1.3
Sweden - Suède	518	862	805	(e)915	2.4	2.0	1.2	(e)1.2
Netherlands - Pays-Bas	204	450	625	(e)716	0.4	0.5	0.5	(e)0.5

For sources and notes, see end of table.   Pour les sources et les notes, se reporter à la fin du tableau.

Country or territory / Pays ou territoires	Imports (7) - Importations (7)							
	Millions of dollars / Millions de dollars				As % of total services / En % du total des services			
	2000	2005	2010	2011	2000	2005	2010	2011
SELECTED COUNTRY GROUPINGS (1) / **SÉLECTION DE GROUPEMENTS DE PAYS (1)**								
World - Monde	..	..	..	..	..	..	..	..
Developing economies - Économies en développement	..	..	..	..	..	..	..	..
Transition economies - Économies en transition	..	..	..	..	..	..	..	..
Developed economies - Économies développées	..	..	..	..	..	..	..	..
Developing economies: Africa - Économies en développement : Afrique	..	..	..	..	..	..	..	..
Developing economies: America - Économies en développement : Amérique	..	..	..	..	..	..	..	..
Developing economies: Asia - Économies en développement : Asie	..	..	..	..	..	..	..	..
Developing economies: Oceania - Économies en développement : Océanie	..	..	..	..	..	..	..	..
Developed economies: America - Économies développées : Amérique	..	..	..	..	..	..	..	..
Developed economies: Asia - Économies développées : Asie	..	..	..	..	..	..	..	..
Developed economies: Europe - Économies développées : Europe	..	..	..	..	..	..	..	..
Developed economies: Oceania - Économies développées : Océanie	..	..	..	..	..	..	..	..
Least developed countries - Pays les moins avancés	..	..	..	..	..	..	..	..
Developing economies excluding LDCs - Économies en développement sans les PMA	..	..	..	..	..	..	..	..
Developing economies excluding China - Économies en développement sans la Chine	..	..	..	..	..	..	..	..
25 LEADING IMPORTERS: DEVELOPING AND TRANSITION ECONOMIES / **25 PRINCIPAUX IMPORTATEURS : ÉCONOMIES EN DÉVELOPPEMENT ET EN TRANSITION**								
China - Chine	2 471	7 200	15 755	(e)19 769	6.9	8.6	8.1	(e)8.3
India - Inde	813	2 330	5 004	(e)6 078	4.2	(b)4.9	4.3	(e)4.9
Singapore - Singapour	1 537	1 922	3 479	(e)3 250	5.1	3.5	3.6	(e)2.8
Mexico - Mexique	1 359	2 340	2 626	4 086	8.0	11.2	10.4	13.9
Thailand - Thaïlande	801	1 389	2 107	(e)2 634	5.2	5.2	4.7	(e)5.2
Saudi Arabia - Arabie saoudite	249	491	1 669	1 950	1.0	(b)1.5	2.2	2.5
Brazil - Brésil	317	702	1 529	1 717	1.9	2.9	2.4	2.2
Egypt - Égypte	450	781	1 459	-	6.0	7.4	9.9	-
Turkey - Turquie	342	891	1 188	(e)1 279	4.2	7.7	6.0	(e)6.0
Malaysia - Malaisie	289	518	-	-	1.7	2.4	-	-
Indonesia - Indonésie	_	338	1 153	1 290	_	1.5	4.4	4 0
Russian Federation - Fédération de Russie	412	698	1 037	1 293	2.4	1.8	1.4	1.4
China, Taiwan Province of - Province chinoise de Taiwan	587	967	999	1 155	2.2	3.0	2.6	2.7
Korea, Republic of - Corée, République de	146	733	882	805	0.4	1.2	0.9	0.8
China, Hong Kong SAR - Chine (RAS de Hong Kong)	528	606	826	971	2.1	1.8	1.6	1.7
Oman	114	285	715	759	6.5	9.0	11.4	10.7
Libya - Libye	5	160	651	-	0.6	6.8	10.6	-
Colombia - Colombie	202	290	576	716	6.1	6.1	7.1	7.5
Argentina - Argentine	200	230	541	691	2.2	3.0	3.8	4.2
South Africa - Afrique du Sud	380	478	527	635	6.5	3.9	2.9	3.2
Chile - Chili	192	463	510	(e)517	4.0	6.0	4.3	(e)3.7
Nigeria - Nigéria	88	(b)4	501	703	2.7	(b)0.1	2.4	2.9
Peru - Pérou	150	233	491	(e)578	6.5	7.5	8.2	(e)8.5
Viet Nam	-	249	481	(e)567	-	5.6	4.8	(e)4.8
Venezuela (Bolivarian Rep. of) - Venezuela (Rép. bolivarienne du)	181	222	478	526	4.1	4.2	4.3	4.2
15 LEADING IMPORTERS: DEVELOPED ECONOMIES / **15 PRINCIPAUX IMPORTATEURS : ÉCONOMIES DÉVELOPPÉES**								
United States - États-Unis	11 284	28 710	61 767	57 562	5.1	9.4	15.3	13.4
Ireland - Irlande	1 354	7 432	8 104	(e)8 242	4.3	10.4	7.6	(e)7.2
Japan - Japon	2 025	1 894	6 799	6 771	1.9	1.5	4.3	4.0
Canada	2 840	5 008	6 240	6 847	6.4	7.6	6.8	6.8
Italy - Italie	1 104	2 053	4 237	(e)3 722	2.0	2.3	3.8	(e)3.2
Germany - Allemagne	1 033	4 799	4 006	(e)4 607	0.7	2.3	1.5	(e)1.6
France	-331	2 255	2 948	(e)2 751	-0.5	2.1	2.2	(e)1.9
United Kingdom - Royaume-Uni	1 089	1 620	2 412	(e)2 582	1.1	1.0	1.4	(e)1.5
Luxembourg	..	1 233	2 106	(e)1 833	..	5.1	5.7	(e)4.5
Spain - Espagne	328	..	1 869	(e)1 956	1.0	..	2.1	(e)2.1
Greece - Grèce	210	..	1 451	(e)1 487	1.9	..	7.2	(e)7.8
Switzerland - Suisse	216	535	1 234	1 455	1.5	2.1	3.1	3.1
Belgium - Belgique	(a)868	509	1 163	(e)1 261	(a)2.1	1.0	1.5	(e)1.5
Netherlands - Pays-Bas	534	803	1 066	(e)1 204	1.0	1.0	1.0	(e)1.0
Austria - Autriche	85	930	1 020	(e)1 101	0.5	3.0	2.7	(e)2.6

For sources and notes, see end of table.

Pour les sources et les notes, se reporter à la fin du tableau.

5

Country or territory / Pays ou territoires	Exports (8) - Exportations (8)							
	Millions of dollars / Millions de dollars				As % of total services / En % du total des services			
	2000	2005	2010	2011	2000	2005	2010	2011
SELECTED COUNTRY GROUPINGS / SÉLECTION DE GROUPEMENTS DE PAYS								
World - Monde	99 814	178 689	275 926	310 282	6.6	7.0	7.2	7.3
Developing economies - Économies en développement	11 566	20 178	46 923	52 479	3.3	3.2	4.1	4.1
Transition economies - Économies en transition	250	743	1 836	1 748	1.0	1.3	1.8	1.4
Developed economies - Économies développées	87 998	157 768	227 167	256 056	7.7	8.4	8.8	9.0
Developing economies: Africa - Économies en développement : Afrique	720	1 412	1 986	2 313	2.2	2.4	2.2	2.5
Developing economies: America - Économies en développement : Amérique	998	1 258	3 597	4 542	1.6	1.4	2.7	3.1
Developing economies: Asia - Économies en développement : Asie	9 797	17 471	41 301	45 546	3.8	3.7	4.5	4.5
Developing economies: Oceania - Économies en développement : Océanie	-	-	-	-	-	-	-	-
Developed economies: America - Économies développées : Amérique	22 996	41 832	69 915	76 967	7.0	9.7	11.3	11.4
Developed economies: Asia - Économies développées : Asie	3 739	6 059	4 776	5 376	4.3	5.0	2.9	3.1
Developed economies: Europe - Économies développées : Europe	60 712	109 027	151 473	172 148	8.6	8.5	8.7	8.8
Developed economies: Oceania - Économies développées : Océanie	552	850	1 002	1 566	2.3	2.1	1.8	2.5
Least developed countries - Pays les moins avancés	181	189	305	541	2.5	1.6	1.4	2.1
Developing economies excluding LDCs - Économies en développement sans les PMA	11 385	19 989	46 617	51 938	3.3	3.2	4.2	4.2
Developing economies excluding China - Économies en développement sans la Chine	11 488	20 033	45 592	51 680	3.6	3.6	4.7	4.8
25 LEADING EXPORTERS: DEVELOPING AND TRANSITION ECONOMIES / 25 PRINCIPAUX EXPORTATEURS : ÉCONOMIES EN DÉVELOPPEMENT ET EN TRANSITION								
China, Hong Kong SAR - Chine (RAS de Hong Kong)	4 371	6 269	13 141	15 288	10.8	9.8	12.4	12.6
Singapore - Singapour	1 814	4 511	12 182	(e)14 099	6.4	8.1	10.8	(e)10.9
India - Inde	276	1 143	6 003	(e)6 414	1.7	(b)2.2	4.9	(e)4.7
Korea, Republic of - Corée, République de	705	1 651	2 736	3 367	2.2	3.3	3.1	3.5
Lebanon - Liban	-	58	(b)2 076	-	-	0.5	(b)13.0	-
Brazil - Brésil	376	507	2 073	2 662	4.0	3.2	6.5	6.9
China - Chine	78	145	1 331	(e)799	0.3	0.2	0.8	(e)0.4
Russian Federation - Fédération de Russie	100	390	1 053	1 103	1.0	1.6	2.3	2.0
Saudi Arabia - Arabie saoudite	-	-	951	96	-	-	8.9	0.8
China, Taiwan Province of - Province chinoise de Taiwan	805	1 517	847	922	4.0	5.9	2.1	2.0
South Africa - Afrique du Sud	-	534	827	901	-	4.7	5.9	6.1
Cuba	-	-	-	-	-	-	-	-
Turkey - Turquie	368	345	490	(e)530	1.9	1.3	1.4	(e)1.4
Ukraine	22	36	475	312	0.6	0.4	2.8	1.6
Panama	141	198	438	653	7.0	6.1	7.2	9.1
Indonesia - Indonésie	–	367	332	407	_	2.8	2.0	2.0
Algeria - Algérie	-	48	221	-	-	1.9	6.2	-
Viet Nam	-	220	192	(e)208	-	5.2	2.6	(e)2.3
Thailand - Thaïlande	-	72	188	(e)269	-	0.4	0.5	(e)0.7
Egypt - Égypte	52	137	180	-	0.5	0.9	0.8	-
Uruguay	62	66	121	138	4.9	5.0	4.7	4.1
Kenya	-	-	109	-	-	-	3.0	-
China, Macao SAR - Chine (RAS de Macao)	-	32	108	-	-	0.4	0.4	-
Malaysia - Malaisie	160	60	-	-	1.1	0.3	-	-
Netherlands Antilles - Antilles néerlandaises	14	6	-	_	0.9	0.3	-	-
15 LEADING EXPORTERS: DEVELOPED ECONOMIES / 15 PRINCIPAUX EXPORTATEURS : ÉCONOMIES DÉVELOPPÉES								
United States - États-Unis	22 117	39 878	66 387	72 989	7.6	10.6	12.1	12.2
United Kingdom - Royaume-Uni	22 122	42 551	50 841	(e)59 396	18.4	20.5	20.3	(e)21.4
Luxembourg	..	24 491	40 497	(e)43 878	..	60.5	60.7	(e)60.1
Switzerland - Suisse	10 637	14 071	15 791	17 034	34.6	28.2	18.9	17.6
Germany - Allemagne	3 536	6 610	11 779	(e)13 633	4.3	4.0	5.0	(e)5.3
Ireland - Irlande	2 069	6 031	7 917	(e)9 103	11.2	10.1	8.1	(e)8.3
Spain - Espagne	1 394	..	4 560	(e)5 374	2.7	..	3.7	(e)3.8
Japan - Japon	2 865	5 044	3 607	4 106	4.1	4.8	2.6	2.8
Belgium - Belgique	(a)13 122	3 393	3 316	(e)3 703	(a)26.4	6.0	3.8	(e)4.1
Canada	879	1 954	3 312	3 766	2.2	3.5	4.8	4.9
France	1 265	1 434	2 581	(e)4 595	1.5	1.2	1.8	(e)2.7
Italy - Italie	428	1 230	2 522	(e)2 593	0.8	1.4	2.6	(e)2.4
Netherlands - Pays-Bas	735	1 078	1 402	(e)1 648	1.5	1.2	1.2	(e)1.2
Norway - Norvège	386	734	1 374	-	2.2	2.5	3.5	-
Israel - Israël	-	-	-	-	-	-	-	-

For sources and notes, see end of table.

Pour les sources et les notes, se reporter à la fin du tableau.

Country or territory / Pays ou territoires	Imports (8) - Importations (8)							
	Millions of dollars / Millions de dollars				As % of total services / En % du total des services			
	2000	2005	2010	2011	2000	2005	2010	2011
SELECTED COUNTRY GROUPINGS (1) **SÉLECTION DE GROUPEMENTS DE PAYS (1)**								
World - Monde	..	..	..	..	..	..	..	..
Developing economies - Économies en développement	..	..	..	..	..	..	..	..
Transition economies - Économies en transition	..	..	..	..	..	..	..	..
Developed economies - Économies développées	..	..	..	..	..	..	..	..
Developing economies: Africa - Économies en développement : Afrique	..	..	..	..	..	..	..	..
Developing economies: America - Économies en développement : Amérique	..	..	..	..	..	..	..	..
Developing economies: Asia - Économies en développement : Asie	..	..	..	..	..	..	..	..
Developing economies: Oceania - Économies en développement : Océanie	..	..	..	..	..	..	..	..
Developed economies: America - Économies développées : Amérique	..	..	..	..	..	..	..	..
Developed economies: Asia - Économies développées : Asie	..	..	..	..	..	..	..	..
Developed economies: Europe - Économies développées : Europe	..	..	..	..	..	..	..	..
Developed economies: Oceania - Économies développées : Océanie	..	..	..	..	..	..	..	..
Least developed countries - Pays les moins avancés	..	..	..	..	..	..	..	..
Developing economies excluding LDCs - Économies en développement sans les PMA	..	..	..	..	..	..	..	..
Developing economies excluding China - Économies en développement sans la Chine	..	..	..	..	..	..	..	..
25 LEADING IMPORTERS: DEVELOPING AND TRANSITION ECONOMIES **25 PRINCIPAUX IMPORTATEURS : ÉCONOMIES EN DÉVELOPPEMENT ET EN TRANSITION**								
India - Inde	1 277	869	6 787	(e)8 210	6.7	(b)1.8	5.8	(e)6.6
China, Hong Kong SAR - Chine (RAS de Hong Kong)	824	1 406	3 532	3 985	3.3	4.1	6.9	7.1
Singapore - Singapour	603	916	2 369	(e)2 604	2.0	1.7	2.5	(e)2.3
Russian Federation - Fédération de Russie	36	892	1 720	1 744	0.2	2.3	2.3	1.9
Brazil - Brésil	670	737	1 679	1 779	4.0	3.0	2.7	2.3
China - Chine	97	159	1 387	(e)694	0.3	0.2	0.7	(e)0.3
Ukraine	74	256	1 086	954	2.5	3.4	8.6	6.6
Saudi Arabia - Arabie saoudite	-	3 532	1 034	1 619	-	(b)10.7	1.3	2.1
Lebanon - Liban	-	10	1 010	-	-	0.1	7.5	-
Korea, Republic of - Corée, République de	191	235	843	884	0.6	0.4	0.9	0.9
Angola	-	16	830	-	-	0.2	4.4	-
Turkey - Turquie	671	386	724	(e)1 219	8.2	3.4	3.7	(e)5.7
Malaysia - Malaisie	175	119	-	-	1.0	0.5	-	-
Mexico - Mexique	918	550	548	452	5.4	2.6	2.2	1.5
Chile - Chili	222	256	459	-	4.6	3.3	3.9	-
Indonesia - Indonésie	_	539	450	635	_	2.4	1.7	2.0
Iran (Islamic Rep. of) - Iran (Rép. islamique d')	-	157	386	-	-	1.4	1.6	-
Congo	-	-	-	-	-	-	-	-
United Arab Emirates - Émirats arabes unis	-	-	-	-	-	-	-	-
Papua New Guinea - Papouasie-Nouvelle-Guinée	-	53	260	(e)113	-	4.2	9.4	(e)3.9
Kazakhstan	13	48	255	187	0.7	0.6	2.3	1.7
Panama	36	157	237	589	3.2	8.7	9.0	17.7
Iraq	-	40	-	-	-	0.6	-	-
China, Taiwan Province of - Province chinoise de Taiwan	1 037	1 370	197	267	3.9	4.2	0.5	0.6
Viet Nam	-	230	195	(e)217	-	5.2	2.0	(e)1.8
15 LEADING IMPORTERS: DEVELOPED ECONOMIES **15 PRINCIPAUX IMPORTATEURS : ÉCONOMIES DÉVELOPPÉES**								
Luxembourg	..	12 707	18 908	(e)21 223	..	52.4	51.6	(e)51.7
United States - États-Unis	10 936	12 126	13 803	15 070	5.0	4.0	3.4	3.5
United Kingdom - Royaume-Uni	4 471	9 251	9 685	(e)12 618	4.5	5.7	5.8	(e)7.2
Germany - Allemagne	1 995	4 593	6 867	(e)9 154	1.4	2.2	2.6	(e)3.2
Ireland - Irlande	1 448	3 301	5 977	(e)6 485	4.6	4.6	5.6	(e)5.7
Spain - Espagne	1 082	..	4 597	(e)4 935	3.3	..	5.3	(e)5.3
Italy - Italie	545	1 203	4 539	(e)5 349	1.0	1.3	4.1	(e)4.6
Canada	1 546	2 732	3 658	3 506	3.5	4.2	4.0	3.5
Japan - Japon	1 883	2 687	3 150	3 347	1.8	2.2	2.0	2.0
France	1 452	2 378	2 061	(e)3 071	2.2	2.2	1.6	(e)2.1
Belgium - Belgique	(a)7 904	3 495	1 886	(e)2 226	(a)18.9	6.8	2.4	(e)2.6
Switzerland - Suisse	783	1 055	1 722	1 898	5.3	4.1	4.3	4.0
Netherlands - Pays-Bas	961	1 588	1 579	(e)1 828	1.9	1.9	1.5	(e)1.5
Norway - Norvège	585	1 238	1 260	-	3.9	4.2	2.9	-
Poland - Pologne	220	385	851	(e)736	2.4	2.5	2.9	(e)2.4

For sources and notes, see end of table.

Pour les sources et les notes, se reporter à la fin du tableau.

**5.2   Exports and imports of services
by service category**
Royalties and license fees

**5.2   Exportations et importations des services
par catégories de services**
Redevances et droits de licence

Country or territory Pays ou territoires	Exports (9) - Exportations (9)							
	Millions of dollars / Millions de dollars				As % of total services En % du total des services			
	2000	2005	2010	2011	2000	2005	2010	2011
SELECTED COUNTRY GROUPINGS **SÉLECTION DE GROUPEMENTS DE PAYS**								
World - Monde	84 448	150 669	237 888	267 894	5.5	5.9	6.2	6.3
Developing economies - Économies en développement	3 701	6 069	9 641	12 238	1.1	1.0	0.8	1.0
Transition economies - Économies en transition	220	479	943	1 214	0.9	0.8	0.9	1.0
Developed economies - Économies développées	80 527	144 121	227 304	254 441	7.0	7.7	8.8	8.9
Developing economies: Africa - Économies en développement : Afrique	541	562	708	781	1.6	0.9	0.8	0.9
Developing economies: America - Économies en développement : Amérique	514	644	1 203	1 522	0.8	0.7	0.9	1.0
Developing economies: Asia - Économies en développement : Asie	2 617	4 829	7 711	9 839	1.0	1.0	0.8	1.0
Developing economies: Oceania - Économies en développement : Océanie	-	-	-	-	-	-	-	-
Developed economies: America - Économies développées : Amérique	45 492	67 161	96 084	107 968	13.8	15.5	15.5	15.9
Developed economies: Asia - Économies développées : Asie	10 723	18 229	27 533	30 083	12.5	15.0	16.6	17.5
Developed economies: Europe - Économies développées : Europe	23 891	58 085	102 578	115 232	3.4	4.5	5.9	5.9
Developed economies: Oceania - Économies développées : Océanie	421	645	1 109	1 159	1.7	1.6	2.0	1.9
Least developed countries Pays les moins avancés	104	126	167	301	1.5	1.1	0.8	1.2
Developing economies excluding LDCs - Économies en développement sans les PMA	3 597	5 943	9 474	11 938	1.0	1.0	0.8	1.0
Developing economies excluding China - Économies en développement sans la Chine	3 621	5 911	8 810	11 408	1.1	1.1	0.9	1.1
25 LEADING EXPORTERS: DEVELOPING AND TRANSITION ECONOMIES **25 PRINCIPAUX EXPORTATEURS : ÉCONOMIES EN DÉVELOPPEMENT ET EN TRANSITION**								
Korea, Republic of - Corée, République de	688	1 908	3 145	4 321	2.2	3.8	3.6	4.5
Singapore - Singapour	85	907	1 867	(e)2 230	0.3	1.6	1.7	(e)1.7
China - Chine	80	157	830	(e)830	0.3	0.2	0.5	(e)0.5
Russian Federation - Fédération de Russie	91	260	625	868	0.9	1.0	1.4	1.6
China, Taiwan Province of - Province chinoise de Taiwan	371	234	460	838	1.9	0.9	1.1	1.8
China, Hong Kong SAR - Chine (RAS de Hong Kong)	107	245	400	-	0.3	0.4	0.4	-
Brazil - Brésil	125	102	397	591	1.3	0.6	1.2	1.5
Malaysia - Malaisie	18	27	-	-	0.1	0.1	-	-
Paraguay	203	219	254	297	34.0	33.3	17.2	15.5
Egypt - Égypte	59	136	-	-	0.6	0.9	-	-
Cuba	-	-	-	-	-	-	-	-
Thailand - Thaïlande	9	17	153	(e)177	0.1	0.1	0.4	(e)0.4
Ukraine	1	22	132	107	0.0	0.2	0.8	0.6
India - Inde	83	206	129	-	0.5	(b)0.4	0.1	-
Argentina - Argentine	37	51	119	170	0.7	0.8	0.9	1.2
Kuwait - Koweït	-	-	-	-	-	-	-	-
Chile - Chili	10	54	64	(e)75	0.2	0.8	0.6	(e)0.6
Jordan - Jordanie	-	-	-	-	-	-	-	-
Indonesia - Indonésie	_	263	60	78	_	2.0	0.4	0.4
South Africa - Afrique du Sud	49	45	59	66	1.0	0.4	0.4	0.4
Colombia - Colombie	5	10	56	59	0.3	0.4	1.3	1.2
Côte d'Ivoire	0	-	-	-	0.0	-	-	-
Kenya	7	18	54	-	0.7	0.9	1.5	-
Oman	-	-	-	-	-	-	-	-
United Republic of Tanzania - République-Unie de Tanzanie	0	-	-	-	0.0	-	-	-
15 LEADING EXPORTERS: DEVELOPED ECONOMIES **15 PRINCIPAUX EXPORTATEURS : ÉCONOMIES DÉVELOPPÉES**								
United States - États-Unis	43 233	64 396	92 054	103 797	15.0	17.1	16.7	17.3
Japan - Japon	10 227	17 655	26 684	29 016	14.5	16.9	18.9	20.0
Netherlands - Pays-Bas	2 171	10 240	24 593	(e)29 572	4.4	11.1	20.8	(e)21.7
Switzerland - Suisse	2 744	8 608	16 405	-	8.9	17.3	19.6	-
Germany - Allemagne	2 910	7 071	14 234	(e)13 834	3.5	4.3	6.0	(e)5.4
United Kingdom - Royaume-Uni	8 151	13 300	13 409	(e)13 503	6.8	6.4	5.4	(e)4.9
France	2 319	6 237	10 391	(e)12 396	2.8	5.1	7.1	(e)7.4
Sweden - Suède	1 282	3 501	5 972	(e)6 018	5.9	8.1	9.0	(e)7.9
Canada	2 259	2 765	3 813	3 946	5.6	5.0	5.5	5.2
Italy - Italie	563	1 116	3 608	(e)3 637	1.0	1.2	3.7	(e)3.4
Denmark - Danemark	-	1 567	2 362	(e)2 674	-	3.6	3.9	(e)4.1
Finland - Finlande	886	1 205	2 335	(e)3 046	11.5	7.1	8.4	(e)11.1
Ireland - Irlande	638	775	2 245	(e)2 583	3.4	1.3	2.3	(e)2.3
Belgium - Belgique	(a)779	1 360	2 140	(e)2 313	(a)1.6	2.4	2.5	(e)2.6
Hungary - Hongrie	112	840	1 055	(e)1 056	1.9	6.5	5.4	(e)4.9

For sources and notes, see end of table.   Pour les sources et les notes, se reporter à la fin du tableau.

Country or territory / Pays ou territoires	Imports (9) - Importations (9)							
	Millions of dollars / Millions de dollars				As % of total services / En % du total des services			
	2000	2005	2010	2011	2000	2005	2010	2011
SELECTED COUNTRY GROUPINGS (1) **SÉLECTION DE GROUPEMENTS DE PAYS (1)**								
World - Monde	..	..	..	..	..	..	..	..
Developing economies - Économies en développement	..	..	..	..	..	..	..	..
Transition economies - Économies en transition	..	..	..	..	..	..	..	..
Developed economies - Économies développées	..	..	..	..	..	..	..	..
Developing economies: Africa - Économies en développement : Afrique	..	..	..	..	..	..	..	..
Developing economies: America - Économies en développement : Amérique	..	..	..	..	..	..	..	..
Developing economies: Asia - Économies en développement : Asie	..	..	..	..	..	..	..	..
Developing economies: Oceania - Économies en développement : Océanie	..	..	..	..	..	..	..	..
Developed economies: America - Économies développées : Amérique	..	..	..	..	..	..	..	..
Developed economies: Asia - Économies développées : Asie	..	..	..	..	..	..	..	..
Developed economies: Europe - Économies développées : Europe	..	..	..	..	..	..	..	..
Developed economies: Oceania - Économies développées : Océanie	..	..	..	..	..	..	..	..
Least developed countries - Pays les moins avancés	..	..	..	..	..	..	..	..
Developing economies excluding LDCs - Économies en développement sans les PMA	..	..	..	..	..	..	..	..
Developing economies excluding China - Économies en développement sans la Chine	..	..	..	..	..	..	..	..
25 LEADING IMPORTERS: DEVELOPING AND TRANSITION ECONOMIES **25 PRINCIPAUX IMPORTATEURS : ÉCONOMIES EN DÉVELOPPEMENT ET EN TRANSITION**								
Singapore - Singapour	5 047	9 348	15 857	(e)19 391	16.8	16.9	16.4	(e)17.0
China - Chine	1 281	5 321	13 040	(e)14 632	3.6	6.4	6.7	(e)6.2
Korea, Republic of - Corée, République de	3 221	4 561	9 031	7 302	9.6	7.6	9.4	7.3
Russian Federation - Fédération de Russie	69	1 593	5 066	6 105	0.4	4.1	6.9	6.8
China, Taiwan Province of - Province chinoise de Taiwan	1 834	1 796	4 943	5 788	6.9	5.5	13.1	13.8
Thailand - Thaïlande	710	1 674	3 084	(e)3 119	4.6	6.3	6.9	(e)6.1
Brazil - Brésil	1 415	1 404	2 850	3 301	8.5	5.8	4.6	4.3
India - Inde	282	672	2 438	-	1.5	(b)1.4	2.1	-
Malaysia - Malaisie	546	1 370	-	-	3.3	6.2	-	-
China, Hong Kong SAR - Chine (RAS de Hong Kong)	461	1 289	1 978	-	1.9	3.8	3.9	-
South Africa - Afrique du Sud	246	1 071	1 941	2 118	4.2	8.8	10.5	10.8
Saudi Arabia - Arabie saoudite	-	-	-	-	-	-	-	-
Indonesia - Indonésie	_	961	1 616	1 786	_	4.4	6.2	5.5
Argentina - Argentine	580	651	1 541	1 735	6.3	8.5	10.9	10.6
Turkey - Turquie	173	439	816	(e)678	2.1	3.8	4.1	(e)3.2
Ukraine	663	421	744	746	22.1	5.6	5.9	5.1
Congo	-	-	-	-	-	-	-	-
United Arab Emirates - Émirats arabes unis	-	-	-	-	-	-	-	-
Chile - Chili	297	348	496	(e)532	6.2	4.5	4.2	(e)3.8
Iraq	-	29	-	-	-	0.5	-	-
Philippines	197	265	445	440	3.8	4.5	3.9	3.7
Colombia - Colombie	74	118	362	423	2.2	2.5	4.5	4.4
Oman	-	-	-	-	-	-	-	-
Venezuela (Bolivarian Rep. of) - Venezuela (Rép. bolivarienne du)	184	239	340	364	4.1	4.5	3.1	2.9
Papua New Guinea - Papouasie-Nouvelle-Guinée	-	-	-	-	-	-	-	-
15 LEADING IMPORTERS: DEVELOPED ECONOMIES **15 PRINCIPAUX IMPORTATEURS : ÉCONOMIES DÉVELOPPÉES**								
Ireland - Irlande	8 329	19 253	37 790	(e)40 791	26.6	26.9	35.3	(e)35.7
United States - États-Unis	16 468	24 612	31 784	34 813	7.5	8.1	7.8	8.1
Netherlands - Pays-Bas	2 505	8 582	20 038	(e)20 696	4.9	10.2	18.9	(e)17.4
Japan - Japon	11 007	14 654	18 773	19 160	10.3	11.8	11.9	11.4
Switzerland - Suisse	1 828	7 819	14 910	-	12.5	30.4	37.6	-
Germany - Allemagne	5 673	8 566	12 918	(e)12 863	4.1	4.1	4.9	(e)4.4
Canada	3 768	6 902	8 665	9 218	8.5	10.5	9.5	9.1
United Kingdom - Royaume-Uni	6 637	9 458	8 160	(e)10 225	6.7	5.8	4.9	(e)5.8
Italy - Italie	1 198	1 910	6 966	(e)7 596	2.2	2.1	6.3	(e)6.5
France	2 041	3 093	5 552	(e)5 765	3.1	2.9	4.2	(e)4.0
Australia - Australie	1 160	2 005	3 411	4 073	6.1	6.6	6.7	6.7
Spain - Espagne	1 681	..	2 642	(e)2 621	5.1	..	3.0	(e)2.8
Poland - Pologne	555	1 037	2 242	(e)2 481	6.2	6.7	7.6	(e)8.0
Belgium - Belgique	(a)918	1 048	1 895	(e)2 363	(a)2.2	2.0	2.4	(e)2.8
Denmark - Danemark	-	1 106	1 470	(e)1 578	-	3.0	2.8	(e)2.8

For sources and notes, see end of table.   Pour les sources et les notes, se reporter à la fin du tableau.

5

Country or territory / Pays ou territoires	Exports (10) - Exportations (10)							
	Millions of dollars / Millions de dollars				As % of total services / En % du total des services			
	2000	2005	2010	2011	2000	2005	2010	2011
SELECTED COUNTRY GROUPINGS / SÉLECTION DE GROUPEMENTS DE PAYS								
World - Monde	322 213	608 794	977 641	1 069 882	21.2	23.7	25.5	25.2
Developing economies - Économies en développement	81 299	149 906	294 820	321 583	23.2	23.8	25.9	25.4
Transition economies - Économies en transition	3 274	8 906	21 178	25 173	13.5	15.5	20.5	20.8
Developed economies - Économies développées	237 640	449 982	661 643	723 126	20.7	24.0	25.5	25.3
Developing economies: Africa - Économies en développement : Afrique	5 312	5 313	9 493	10 049	16.0	8.9	10.5	11.0
Developing economies: America - Économies en développement : Amérique	8 183	14 792	30 563	36 800	13.2	16.8	22.9	24.8
Developing economies: Asia - Économies en développement : Asie	67 565	129 399	254 332	274 161	26.5	27.0	27.9	26.8
Developing economies: Oceania - Économies en développement : Océanie	-	-	-	-	-	-	-	-
Developed economies: America - Économies développées : Amérique	55 971	82 546	129 927	134 255	17.0	19.1	20.9	19.8
Developed economies: Asia - Économies développées : Asie	20 533	30 735	46 601	49 199	23.9	25.3	28.2	28.6
Developed economies: Europe - Économies développées : Europe	158 774	332 449	477 264	531 053	22.5	25.9	27.3	27.3
Developed economies: Oceania - Économies développées : Océanie	2 363	4 253	7 850	8 619	9.7	10.7	13.8	13.9
Least developed countries - Pays les moins avancés	1 034	963	2 061	2 235	14.6	8.2	9.3	8.7
Developing economies excluding LDCs - Économies en développement sans les PMA	80 265	148 943	292 759	319 348	23.3	24.1	26.2	25.8
Developing economies excluding China - Économies en développement sans la Chine	73 636	126 624	233 579	257 055	23.0	22.8	24.2	23.7
25 LEADING EXPORTERS: DEVELOPING AND TRANSITION ECONOMIES / 25 PRINCIPAUX EXPORTATEURS : ÉCONOMIES EN DÉVELOPPEMENT ET EN TRANSITION								
China - Chine	7 663	23 283	61 242	(e)64 528	25.2	31.3	35.8	(e)35.2
India - Inde	-	-	-	-	-	-	-	-
Singapore - Singapour	8 264	21 226	43 851	(e)49 384	28.9	38.1	39.0	(e)38.2
China, Hong Kong SAR - Chine (RAS de Hong Kong)	15 954	24 312	37 516	-	39.5	38.2	35.3	-
China, Taiwan Province of - Province chinoise de Taiwan	9 692	11 950	18 818	21 669	48.4	46.3	46.6	46.8
Korea, Republic of - Corée, République de	7 200	9 422	16 834	18 911	22.8	18.9	19.3	19.9
Brazil - Brésil	4 568	6 722	15 777	19 626	48.1	41.9	49.6	51.1
Russian Federation - Fédération de Russie	-	5 309	12 775	15 692	-	21.3	28.4	29.0
Philippines	285	525	7 600	8 306	8.4	11.6	53.9	53.8
Malaysia - Malaisie	5 055	-	-	-	36.3	-	-	-
Thailand - Thaïlande	-	-	-	-	-	-	-	-
Cuba	-	-	-	-	-	-	-	-
Indonesia - Indonésie	_	2 876	4 309	5 725	_	22.2	25.7	27.9
Argentina - Argentine	324	-	3 856	3 950	6.6	-	29.4	27.8
Lebanon - Liban	-	4 362	(b)3 817	-	-	40.2	(b)23.9	-
Ukraine	323	846	2 940	3 392	8.3	9.0	17.2	17.5
Morocco - Maroc	-	-	1 994	2 065	-	-	15.9	14.8
Algeria - Algérie	-	-	1 901	-	-	-	53.3	-
Chile - Chili	-	-	-	-	-	-	-	-
Serbia - Serbie	_	_	1 163	1 295	_	_	27.5	25.4
Croatia - Croatie	266	934	1 137	(e)1 216	6.5	9.4	10.1	(e)9.8
South Africa - Afrique du Sud	-	837	1 115	1 231	-	7.4	8.0	8.3
Egypt - Égypte	2 119	1 549	-	-	21.6	10.6	-	-
Turkmenistan - Turkménistan	-	-	-	-	-	-	-	-
Mauritius - Maurice	208	265	758	-	19.4	16.4	28.1	-
15 LEADING EXPORTERS: DEVELOPED ECONOMIES / 15 PRINCIPAUX EXPORTATEURS : ÉCONOMIES DÉVELOPPÉES								
United States - États-Unis	45 569	67 363	111 397	-	15.8	17.9	20.2	-
United Kingdom - Royaume-Uni	33 878	60 478	80 599	(e)89 627	28.1	29.1	32.2	(e)32.3
Germany - Allemagne	24 203	48 094	74 401	(e)83 334	29.2	29.3	31.3	(e)32.3
Japan - Japon	17 709	27 279	42 473	45 273	25.2	26.1	30.1	31.1
Netherlands - Pays-Bas	15 527	35 274	35 779	(e)41 053	31.5	38.3	30.3	(e)30.1
France	19 299	29 431	33 326	(e)39 602	23.3	24.1	22.9	(e)23.6
Belgium - Belgique	(a)10 243	17 578	31 150	(e)30 764	(a)20.6	31.3	35.8	(e)34.4
Ireland - Irlande	-	16 256	29 580	(e)31 120	-	27.1	30.2	(e)28.3
Spain - Espagne	8 018	..	28 645	(e)33 756	15.3	..	23.1	(e)23.9
Sweden - Suède	7 212	15 625	26 220	(e)30 142	33.4	36.3	39.6	(e)39.5
Italy - Italie	13 789	28 942	26 071	(e)28 556	24.4	32.4	26.4	(e)26.8
Canada	10 402	15 183	18 236	20 682	25.9	27.2	26.4	27.2
Switzerland - Suisse	-	-	-	-	-	-	-	-
Austria - Autriche	5 384	11 431	14 737	(e)18 738	23.3	26.9	27.0	(e)30.3
Norway - Norvège	4 014	6 902	12 673	-	22.7	23.5	31.9	-

For sources and notes, see end of table.

Pour les sources et les notes, se reporter à la fin du tableau.

Country or territory / Pays ou territoires	Imports (10) - Importations (10)							
	Millions of dollars / Millions de dollars				As % of total services / En % du total des services			
	2000	2005	2010	2011	2000	2005	2010	2011
SELECTED COUNTRY GROUPINGS (1) / **SÉLECTION DE GROUPEMENTS DE PAYS (1)**								
World - Monde	..	..	..	..	..	..	..	..
Developing economies - Économies en développement	..	..	..	..	..	..	..	..
Transition economies - Économies en transition	..	..	..	..	..	..	..	..
Developed economies - Économies développées	..	..	..	..	..	..	..	..
Developing economies: Africa - Économies en développement : Afrique	..	..	..	..	..	..	..	..
Developing economies: America - Économies en développement : Amérique	..	..	..	..	..	..	..	..
Developing economies: Asia - Économies en développement : Asie	..	..	..	..	..	..	..	..
Developing economies: Oceania - Économies en développement : Océanie	..	..	..	..	..	..	..	..
Developed economies: America - Économies développées : Amérique	..	..	..	..	..	..	..	..
Developed economies: Asia - Économies développées : Asie	..	..	..	..	..	..	..	..
Developed economies: Europe - Économies développées : Europe	..	..	..	..	..	..	..	..
Developed economies: Oceania - Économies développées : Océanie	..	..	..	..	..	..	..	..
Least developed countries - Pays les moins avancés	..	..	..	..	..	..	..	..
Developing economies excluding LDCs - Économies en développement sans les PMA	..	..	..	..	..	..	..	..
Developing economies excluding China - Économies en développement sans la Chine	..	..	..	..	..	..	..	..
25 LEADING IMPORTERS: DEVELOPING AND TRANSITION ECONOMIES / **25 PRINCIPAUX IMPORTATEURS : ÉCONOMIES EN DÉVELOPPEMENT ET EN TRANSITION**								
India - Inde	-	(b)13 694	39 678	-	-	(b)29.0	34.0	-
China - Chine	6 959	16 287	34 310	(e)39 497	19.3	19.4	17.7	(e)16.6
Korea, Republic of - Corée, République de	10 328	15 538	30 422	35 827	30.8	26.0	31.7	36.1
Singapore - Singapour	4 190	10 677	25 418	(e)30 559	13.9	19.3	26.4	(e)26.8
Brazil - Brésil	3 434	7 480	20 874	25 256	20.6	30.7	33.3	33.1
Russian Federation - Fédération de Russie	-	6 459	15 796	19 278	-	16.7	21.4	21.4
China, Taiwan Province of - Province chinoise de Taiwan	6 348	8 669	10 381	12 240	23.8	26.7	27.4	29.1
China, Hong Kong SAR - Chine (RAS de Hong Kong)	2 726	4 877	10 020	-	11.0	14.4	19.6	-
Thailand - Thaïlande	-	-	-	-	-	-	-	-
Malaysia - Malaisie	6 035	-	-	-	36.0	-	-	-
Angola	-	3 265	6 470	-	-	48.1	34.5	-
Saudi Arabia - Arabie saoudite	-	-	-	-	-	-	-	-
Indonesia - Indonésie	_	7 017	5 456	6 471	_	31.8	20.9	20.0
Kazakhstan	447	3 120	5 412	4 181	24.2	41.6	47.8	38.3
Algeria - Algérie	-	1 448	4 849	-	-	30.3	40.7	-
China, Macao SAR - Chine (RAS de Macao)	-	-	-	-	-	-	-	-
Nigeria - Nigéria	-	(b)2 890	4 461	6 019	-	(b)43.6	20.9	24.5
Lebanon - Liban	-	-	4 347	-	-	-	32.4	-
Venezuela (Bolivarian Rep. of) - Venezuela (Rép. bolivarienne du)	-	-	-	-	-	-	-	-
South Africa - Afrique du Sud	-	1 104	2 133	2 255	-	9.1	11.6	11.5
Congo	-	-	-	-	-	-	-	-
United Arab Emirates - Émirats arabes unis	-	-	-	-	-	-	-	-
Colombia - Colombie	-	-	1 798	2 290	-	-	22.3	24.0
Argentina - Argentine	-	896	1 796	2 183	-	11.8	12.7	13.3
Turkey - Turquie	-	-	1 673	(e)1 743	-	-	8.5	(e)8.2
15 LEADING IMPORTERS: DEVELOPED ECONOMIES / **15 PRINCIPAUX IMPORTATEURS : ÉCONOMIES DÉVELOPPÉES**								
United States - États-Unis	24 446	36 493	69 418	-	11.1	12.0	17.1	-
Germany - Allemagne	32 158	47 464	65 690	(e)76 557	23.3	22.5	24.9	(e)26.4
United Kingdom - Royaume-Uni	16 946	29 944	43 994	(e)45 033	17.0	18.4	26.4	(e)25.5
Ireland - Irlande	13 814	31 479	42 751	(e)46 229	44.2	44.0	39.9	(e)40.4
Japan - Japon	24 296	26 497	39 164	45 859	22.8	21.4	24.9	27.4
France	15 461	25 621	34 038	(e)36 612	23.6	23.9	25.7	(e)25.4
Netherlands - Pays-Bas	16 687	32 238	32 256	(e)39 609	32.5	38.2	30.4	(e)33.3
Spain - Espagne	10 094	..	30 380	(e)34 002	30.4	..	34.9	(e)36.3
Italy - Italie	17 799	31 485	28 506	(e)29 985	32.0	35.0	25.7	(e)25.9
Belgium - Belgique	(a)9 440	13 611	24 991	(e)25 379	(a)22.5	26.6	31.8	(e)29.9
Sweden - Suède	8 029	12 259	17 664	(e)20 147	33.5	34.7	36.5	(e)36.1
Canada	9 626	12 459	13 392	15 060	21.8	18.9	14.7	14.9
Finland - Finlande	-	6 413	12 025	(e)10 911	-	36.2	43.5	(e)41.7
Norway - Norvège	3 100	5 007	10 887	-	20.7	16.9	25.4	-
Denmark - Danemark	-	6 364	8 813	(e)9 181	-	17.2	17.0	(e)16.1

For sources and notes, see end of table.   Pour les sources et les notes, se reporter à la fin du tableau.

5.2 **Exports and imports of services**
by service category
Personal, cultural and recreational services

5.2 **Exportations et importations des services**
par catégories de services
Services personnels, culturels et relatifs aux loisirs

Country or territory / Pays ou territoires	Exports (11) - Exportations (11)							
	Millions of dollars / Millions de dollars				As % of total services / En % du total des services			
	2000	2005	2010	2011	2000	2005	2010	2011
SELECTED COUNTRY GROUPINGS **SÉLECTION DE GROUPEMENTS DE PAYS**								
World - Monde	23 670	32 121	44 844	52 085	1.6	1.3	1.2	1.2
Developing economies - Économies en développement	3 936	3 824	4 653	5 452	1.1	0.6	0.4	0.4
Transition economies - Économies en transition	62	314	1 177	1 131	0.3	0.5	1.1	0.9
Developed economies - Économies développées	19 673	27 983	39 014	45 502	1.7	1.5	1.5	1.6
Developing economies: Africa - Économies en développement : Afrique	175	299	344	388	0.5	0.5	0.4	0.4
Developing economies: America - Économies en développement : Amérique	549	893	1 044	909	0.9	1.0	0.8	0.6
Developing economies: Asia - Économies en développement : Asie	3 207	2 623	3 247	4 144	1.3	0.5	0.4	0.4
Developing economies: Oceania - Économies en développement : Océanie	-	-	-	-	-	-	-	-
Developed economies: America - Économies développées : Amérique	10 167	12 370	16 715	18 433	3.1	2.9	2.7	2.7
Developed economies: Asia - Économies développées : Asie	327	279	339	372	0.4	0.2	0.2	0.2
Developed economies: Europe - Économies développées : Europe	7 985	14 724	20 913	25 565	1.1	1.1	1.2	1.3
Developed economies: Oceania - Économies développées : Océanie	1 194	610	1 047	1 131	4.9	1.5	1.8	1.8
Least developed countries - Pays les moins avancés	35	28	52	104	0.5	0.2	0.2	0.4
Developing economies excluding LDCs - Économies en développement sans les PMA	3 900	3 796	4 601	5 348	1.1	0.6	0.4	0.4
Developing economies excluding China - Économies en développement sans la Chine	3 924	3 690	4 530	5 305	1.2	0.7	0.5	0.5
25 LEADING EXPORTERS: DEVELOPING AND TRANSITION ECONOMIES **25 PRINCIPAUX EXPORTATEURS : ÉCONOMIES EN DÉVELOPPEMENT ET EN TRANSITION**								
Turkey - Turquie	2 591	1 079	912	(e)1 263	13.3	4.0	2.6	(e)3.3
Korea, Republic of - Corée, République de	137	268	637	794	0.4	0.5	0.7	0.8
Russian Federation - Fédération de Russie	-	187	474	493	-	0.8	1.1	0.9
Argentina - Argentine	18	203	361	310	0.4	3.1	2.8	2.2
India - Inde	-	111	335	-	-	(b)0.2	0.3	-
Singapore - Singapour	19	180	219	(e)262	0.1	0.3	0.2	(e)0.2
Lebanon - Liban	-	0	(b)202	-	-	0.0	(b)1.3	-
Serbia - Serbie	–	–	186	199	–	–	4.4	3.9
Iran (Islamic Rep. of) - Iran (Rép. islamique d')	-	55	145	-	-	1.1	1.8	-
China, Hong Kong SAR - Chine (RAS de Hong Kong)	51	270	135	-	0.1	0.4	0.1	-
Cuba	-	-	-	-	-	-	-	-
China - Chine	11	134	123	(e)147	0.0	0.2	0.1	(e)0.1
Thailand - Thaïlande	-	58	121	(e)92	-	0.3	0.4	(e)0.2
Ukraine	3	16	113	93	0.1	0.2	0.7	0.5
Brazil - Brésil	63	56	108	108	0.7	0.3	0.3	0.3
Indonesia - Indonésie	–	57	104	157	–	0.4	0.6	0.8
Egypt - Égypte	15	83	99	-	0.2	0.6	0.4	-
China, Taiwan Province of - Province chinoise de Taiwan	26	61	98	136	0.1	0.2	0.2	0.3
Croatia - Croatie	30	29	90	(e)57	0.7	0.3	0.8	(e)0.5
Chile - Chili	22	69	87	(e)81	0.5	1.0	0.8	(e)0.7
Colombia - Colombie	23	41	84	86	1.1	1.6	1.9	1.8
Mexico - Mexique	328	373	80	80	2.4	2.4	0.5	0.5
Kyrgyzstan - Kirghizistan	3	7	68	94	4.4	2.6	9.8	8.4
South Africa - Afrique du Sud	-	114	67	66	-	1.0	0.5	0.4
Ecuador - Équateur	39	39	66	(e)82	4.6	3.8	4.5	(e)5.2
15 LEADING EXPORTERS: DEVELOPED ECONOMIES **15 PRINCIPAUX EXPORTATEURS : ÉCONOMIES DÉVELOPPÉES**								
United States - États-Unis	8 716	10 300	14 515	15 906	3.0	2.7	2.6	2.7
United Kingdom - Royaume-Uni	1 973	4 078	6 199	(e)6 762	1.6	2.0	2.5	(e)2.4
Canada	1 451	2 070	2 198	2 488	3.6	3.7	3.2	3.3
France	1 590	2 136	2 016	(e)2 338	1.9	1.7	1.4	(e)1.4
Luxembourg	..	242	1 979	(e)2 786	..	0.6	3.0	(e)3.8
Spain - Espagne	535	..	1 775	(e)2 174	1.0	..	1.4	(e)1.5
Hungary - Hongrie	207	1 278	1 251	(e)1 306	3.5	9.9	6.4	(e)6.0
Germany - Allemagne	395	1 195	1 073	(e)878	0.5	0.7	0.5	(e)0.3
Australia - Australie	1 058	438	702	886	5.3	1.4	1.5	1.7
Netherlands - Pays-Bas	552	904	699	(e)819	1.1	1.0	0.6	(e)0.6
Denmark - Danemark	-	276	641	(e)553	-	0.6	1.1	(e)0.8
Belgium - Belgique	(a)628	519	612	(e)666	(a)1.3	0.9	0.7	(e)0.7
Norway - Norvège	139	351	398	-	0.8	1.2	1.0	-
Sweden - Suède	113	222	397	(e)562	0.5	0.5	0.6	(e)0.7
Portugal	136	205	359	(e)332	1.5	1.3	1.5	(e)1.2

For sources and notes, see end of table.

Pour les sources et les notes, se reporter à la fin du tableau.

5.2 **Exports and imports of services by service category**
Personal, cultural and recreational services

5.2 **Exportations et importations des services par catégories de services**
Services personnels, culturels et relatifs aux loisirs

Country or territory Pays ou territoires	Imports (11) - Importations (11)							
	Millions of dollars / Millions de dollars				As % of total services En % du total des services			
	2000	2005	2010	2011	2000	2005	2010	2011
SELECTED COUNTRY GROUPINGS (1) **SÉLECTION DE GROUPEMENTS DE PAYS (1)**								
World - Monde	..	..	..	..	..	..	..	..
Developing economies - Économies en développement	..	..	..	..	..	..	..	..
Transition economies - Économies en transition	..	..	..	..	..	..	..	..
Developed economies - Économies développées	..	..	..	..	..	..	..	..
Developing economies: Africa - Économies en développement : Afrique	..	..	..	..	..	..	..	..
Developing economies: America - Économies en développement : Amérique	..	..	..	..	..	..	..	..
Developing economies: Asia - Économies en développement : Asie	..	..	..	..	..	..	..	..
Developing economies: Oceania - Économies en développement : Océanie	..	..	..	..	..	..	..	..
Developed economies: America - Économies développées : Amérique	..	..	..	..	..	..	..	..
Developed economies: Asia - Économies développées : Asie	..	..	..	..	..	..	..	..
Developed economies: Europe - Économies développées : Europe	..	..	..	..	..	..	..	..
Developed economies: Oceania - Économies développées : Océanie	..	..	..	..	..	..	..	..
Least developed countries - Pays les moins avancés	..	..	..	..	..	..	..	..
Developing economies excluding LDCs - Économies en développement sans les PMA	..	..	..	..	..	..	..	..
Developing economies excluding China - Économies en développement sans la Chine	..	..	..	..	..	..	..	..
25 LEADING IMPORTERS: DEVELOPING AND TRANSITION ECONOMIES **25 PRINCIPAUX IMPORTATEURS : ÉCONOMIES EN DÉVELOPPEMENT ET EN TRANSITION**								
Brazil - Brésil	363	451	1 271	1 426	2.2	1.9	2.0	1.9
Korea, Republic of - Corée, République de	160	477	1 022	1 018	0.5	0.8	1.1	1.0
Russian Federation - Fédération de Russie	-	440	1 000	1 059	-	1.1	1.4	1.2
Venezuela (Bolivarian Rep. of) - Venezuela (Rép. bolivarienne du)	72	197	751	658	1.6	3.7	6.8	5.3
India - Inde	-	105	467	-	-	(b)0.2	0.4	-
Singapore - Singapour	82	279	462	(e)554	0.3	0.5	0.5	(e)0.5
China - Chine	37	154	371	(e)371	0.1	0.2	0.2	(e)0.2
Argentina - Argentine	171	165	363	434	1.9	2.2	2.6	2.6
Iran (Islamic Rep. of) - Iran (Rép. islamique d')	-	196	322	-	-	1.8	1.4	-
Mexico - Mexique	245	275	272	272	1.4	1.3	1.1	0.9
Saudi Arabia - Arabie saoudite	-	-	-	-	-	-	-	-
Turkey - Turquie	1 541	88	259	(e)293	18.9	0.8	1.3	(e)1.4
Haiti - Haïti	-	218	250	-	-	40.0	19.6	-
Ukraine	11	109	221	234	0.4	1.4	1.7	1.6
China, Taiwan Province of - Province chinoise de Taiwan	163	301	215	237	0.6	0.9	0.6	0.6
Ecuador - Équateur	52	106	168	(e)188	4.1	5.0	5.6	(e)5.9
Angola	-	45	156		-	0.7	0.8	
Malaysia - Malaisie	70	-	-	-	0.4	-	-	-
Indonesia - Indonésie	—	166	133	212	—	0.8	0.5	0.7
Lebanon - Liban	-	0	114	-	-	0.0	0.9	-
Colombia - Colombie	27	44	111	82	0.8	0.9	1.4	0.9
Croatia - Croatie	30	56	111	(e)109	1.7	1.7	3.2	(e)3.0
China, Macao SAR - Chine (RAS de Macao)	-	-	-	..				
Congo	5	-	-	-	0.6	-	-	-
Serbia - Serbie	—	—	90	90	—	—	2.2	2.0
15 LEADING IMPORTERS: DEVELOPED ECONOMIES **15 PRINCIPAUX IMPORTATEURS : ÉCONOMIES DÉVELOPPÉES**								
France	1 964	2 803	3 718	(e)3 959	3.0	2.6	2.8	(e)2.7
Germany - Allemagne	3 558	3 523	2 771	(e)2 705	2.6	1.7	1.1	(e)0.9
Canada	1 647	1 838	2 608	2 679	3.7	2.8	2.9	2.6
United Kingdom - Royaume-Uni	1 181	1 511	2 335	(e)2 476	1.2	0.9	1.4	(e)1.4
United States - États-Unis	223	1 128	2 214	-	0.1	0.4	0.5	-
Spain - Espagne	1 425	..	2 090	(e)2 110	4.3	..	2.4	(e)2.3
Luxembourg	..	331	1 567	(e)2 122	..	1.4	4.3	(e)5.2
Australia - Australie	509	774	1 260	1 629	2.7	2.5	2.5	2.7
Denmark - Danemark	-	1 162	1 032	(e)1 071	-	3.1	2.0	(e)1.9
Hungary - Hongrie	151	1 148	972	(e)1 011	3.2	10.1	6.2	(e)5.9
Japan - Japon	1 275	1 115	934	978	1.2	0.9	0.6	0.6
Austria - Autriche	209	725	934	(e)1 037	1.3	2.4	2.5	(e)2.5
Poland - Pologne	139	159	862	(e)962	1.5	1.0	2.9	(e)3.1
Belgium - Belgique	(a)826	469	763	(e)782	(a)2.0	0.9	1.0	(e)0.9
Netherlands - Pays-Bas	597	945	701	(e)778	1.2	1.1	0.7	(e)0.7

For sources and notes, see next page.

Pour les sources et les notes, se reporter à la page suivante.

Sources:
UNCTAD and WTO secretariats, based on:
- IMF, *Balance of Payments Statistics*
- Eurostat, *Statistics database*
- UN DESA Statistics Division, *UN Service Trade*
- OECD, *OECD.Stat*
- Other international and national sources

Notes:

- The statistics presented correspond to the concepts and definitions from the IMF *Balance of Payments Manual*, fifth edition (*BPM5*, 1993).
  UNCTAD and WTO may use different definitions for certain country groups ("developed" and "developing" economies, for example). Consequently, some aggregates will be different, although the individual-country underlying data are the same.
  Individual economies are ranked based on both reported and estimated 2010 figures. Non-publishable estimates are indicated by a - sign.

(a) Refers to Belgium-Luxembourg Economic Union.
(1) Owing to the lack of data, the country groups aggregates for imports are available only for Transport and Travel categories.

(2) Covers all transportation services that involve carriage of passengers, movement of goods (freight), rentals with crew, and related supporting services. Excludes freight insurance, which is included with insurance services. Excludes goods procured in ports by non-resident carriers and repairs on transport equipment, which are included in goods.

(3) Includes goods and services acquired from an economy by non-resident travellers during visits shorter than one year.
(4) Consists of postal, courier and telecommunications services between residents and non-residents.
(5) Covers the work performed on construction projects and installations by an enterprise outside the economy of residence of that enterprise.
(6) (1) Computer services consist of hardware and software-related services and data-processing.
(2) New agency services include the provision of news, photographs and feature articles to the media.
(3) Other information services cover database services: database conception, data storage and dissemination of data. Direct non-bulk subscriptions to periodicals regardless of means of information transmission also belong to this service category.
(7) Covers all types of insurance, reinsurance and related auxiliary services. Insurance services are estimated or valued by the service charges included in total premiums rather than by total value of the premiums.
(8) Includes financial intermediation and auxiliary services, except those directly related to life insurance and pension funds (covered under insurance services).

(9) Covers franchising fees, royalties paid for the use of registered trade marks, and other fees paid for authorised use of intangible, non-produced non-financial assets and proprietary rights. Distributive rights with limitations for audiovisual products are not included here.

(10) Includes merchanting and other trade-related services; operational leasing services; and miscellaneous business, professional and technical services (legal, advertising, consulting, accounting, R&D, etc.)
(11) (1) Audiovisual and related services cover the production of motion pictures, video and radio programmes, musical recordings, (and similar) including fees paid to personnel involved. Related limited distribution rights are also covered. Fees paid for sporting, theatrical and similar events belong to this category as well.
(2) Other personal cultural and recreational services encompass services associated with museums, libraries, archives, and other cultural and sporting activities. Education and health services are covered under this category (excluding, however, the expenses for health and education services paid by travellers, which belong to travel services).

Sources :
Secrétariats de la CNUCED et de l'OMC, basés sur :
- FMI, *Statistiques de la balance des paiements*
- Eurostat, *Base de données statistiques*
- ONU DAES Division de statistique, *ONU Service Trade*
- OCDE, *OECD.Stat*
- Autres sources internationales et nationales

Notes :

- Les statistiques présentées correspondent aux concepts et définitions du *Manuel de la balance des paiements* du FMI, cinquième édition (*MBP5*, 1993).
  La composition de certains groupements de pays peut être différente pour la CNUCED et l'OMC ("pays en développement" et "pays développés", par exemple). Par conséquent, certains agrégats seront différents bien que les données des pays individuels soient les mêmes.
  Les économies individuelles sont classées en fonction des données rapportées et estimées de l'année 2010. Les estimations qui ne sont pas publiables sont indiquées par le signe -.

(a) Se réfère à l'Union économique belgo-luxembourgeoise.
(1) En raison du manque de données, les aggrégats pour les groupements de pays ne sont pas disponibles pour les importations, hormis pour les catégories des transports et voyages.

(2) Recouvre tous les services de transport de passagers, l'acheminement des marchandises (fret), la location de moyens de transports avec leur équipage et les services annexes qui s'y rapportent. L'assurance du fret n'est pas comprise. Elle fait partie des services d'assurance. Les achats effectués dans les ports par les transporteurs non résidents, ainsi que les réparations du matériel de transport ne sont pas compris. Ils sont classés dans les biens.

(3) Comprend les biens et services acquis dans une économie par les voyageurs non-résidents au cours d'un séjour inférieur à un an.
(4) Englobe les services postaux (y compris les messageries) et les services de télécommunication, entre résidents et non-résidents.
(5) Recouvre les travaux de construction et d'installation par une entreprise en dehors de l'économie dans laquelle l'entreprise est résidente.
(6) (1) Les services informatiques englobent les services liés aux matériels et logiciels informatiques et les services de traitement de données.
(2) Les services d'agence de presse incluent la communication d'informations, de photographies et d'articles de fond aux médias.
(3) Les autres services d'information couvrent les services concernant les bases de données : leur conception, le stockage et la diffusion des données. Les abonnements directs individuels aux périodiques font partie de cette catégorie de services.
(7) Comprend diverses formes d'assurances, réassurances et services auxiliaires connexes. Ces services sont évalués ou estimés au montant des frais de service inclus dans le total des primes perçues, et non au montant total des primes proprement dites.
(8) Comprend les services d'intermédiation financière et les services auxiliaires, à l'exception de ceux directement liés à l'assurance-vie ou aux fonds de pension (déjà compris dans les services d'assurance).
(9) Recouvre les redevances de franchises et les redevances payées pour l'utilisation des marques déposées, ainsi que les autres redevances et droits de licence liés à l'utilisation légale d'actifs intangibles non produits non financiers et de droits de propriété. Les droits de distribution limitée des produits audiovisuels ne sont pas compris dans cette catégorie.
(10) Y compris le négoce international et les autres services liés au commerce, la location-exploitation et divers services aux entreprises, spécialisés et techniques (juridiques, comptabilité, conseil, publicité, R&D, etc.).
(11) (1) Les services audiovisuels et connexes sont attachés à la production de films cinématographiques, d'émissions de radio et de télévision, d'enregistrements musicaux (et similaires). Les cachets versés au personnel impliqué et les droits limités de distributions figurent également dans cette catégorie, ainsi que les paiements liés aux événements sportifs, théâtraux et spectacles divers.
(2) Les autres services personnels, culturels et relatifs aux loisirs englobent les services associés aux musées, bibliothèques, archives et autres activités culturelles et sportives. Les services d'éducation et de santé figurent aussi dans cette catégorie. Cependant, ne sont pas comprises les dépenses liées à l'éducation ou à la santé encourues par des voyageurs (et qui figurent sous la catégorie 'voyages').

5.3 World merchant fleet by flag of registration and type of ship of countries and geographical regions

5.3 Flotte marchande mondiale par pavillons d'immatriculation et par types de navires des pays et des régions géographiques

Region, country or territory / Régions pays ou territoires	Year / Année	Total fleet (thousands of DWT) / Flotte totale (milliers de TPL) (1)	As percentage of world total fleet / En pourcentage de la flotte mondiale					As percentage of the country or region total fleet / En pourcentage de la flotte totale du pays ou de la région				
			Oil tankers / Pétroliers	Bulk carriers / Vraquiers	General cargo / Navires de charge classique (2)	Container ships / Porte-conteneurs	Other types / Autres navires	Oil tankers / Pétroliers	Bulk carriers / Vraquiers	General cargo / Navires de charge classique (2)	Container ships / Porte-conteneurs	Other types / Autres navires
WORLD - MONDE	**1990**	**629 976.0**	**100.0**	**100.0**	**100.0**	**100.0**	**100.0**	**37.4**	**35.5**	**15.9**	**3.5**	**7.6**
	2000	**793 770.8**	**100.0**	**100.0**	**100.0**	**100.0**	**100.0**	**35.7**	**34.6**	**12.8**	**8.0**	**9.0**
	2010	**1276 137.2**	**100.0**	**100.0**	**100.0**	**100.0**	**100.0**	**35.3**	**35.8**	**8.5**	**13.3**	**7.2**
	2012	**1534 019.5**	**100.0**	**100.0**	**100.0**	**100.0**	**100.0**	**33.1**	**40.6**	**6.9**	**12.9**	**6.5**
DEVELOPING ECONOMIES - ÉCONOMIES EN DÉVELOPPEMENT (3)	1990	334 184.0	52.2	56.5	54.4	43.1	43.1	36.8	37.8	16.4	2.9	6.2
	2000	487 692.9	56.6	68.5	63.7	58.3	53.0	32.9	38.5	13.3	7.6	7.7
	2010	915 129.5	69.1	77.6	70.0	68.4	63.6	34.0	38.7	8.3	12.6	6.4
	2012	1135 291.4	70.4	79.6	71.0	71.7	65.2	31.5	43.7	6.7	12.5	5.7
TRANSITION ECONOMIES - ÉCONOMIES EN TRANSITION	1990	35 090.0	2.9	4.4	12.4	3.2	11.0	19.2	28.4	35.4	2.0	15.0
	2000	13 598.3	0.9	0.9	5.4	0.7	3.8	18.5	18.0	40.2	3.4	19.9
	2010	12 777.5	0.8	0.4	4.5	0.1	2.1	29.6	15.7	38.5	1.3	14.8
	2012	12 574.0	0.8	0.3	4.2	0.1	1.9	31.9	16.3	35.8	1.3	14.7
DEVELOPED ECONOMIES - ÉCONOMIES DÉVELOPPÉES (3)	1990	260 702.0	45.0	39.1	33.2	53.7	45.8	40.7	33.5	12.8	4.6	8.4
	2000	292 479.6	42.5	30.6	30.9	40.9	43.2	41.1	28.7	10.7	8.9	10.5
	2010	342 619.1	29.8	21.8	23.4	31.4	33.3	39.1	29.0	7.4	15.5	9.0
	2012	381 521.3	28.7	19.9	23.2	28.2	31.7	38.1	32.5	6.5	14.6	8.3
Developing economies: Africa - Économies en développement : Afrique	**1990**	**97 139.0**	**23.1**	**12.7**	**6.1**	**5.4**	**14.6**	**56.0**	**29.3**	**6.4**	**1.2**	**7.2**
	2000	**91 552.9**	**14.7**	**9.7**	**6.5**	**9.5**	**15.1**	**45.3**	**29.2**	**7.2**	**6.6**	**11.8**
	2010	**150 731.7**	**14.8**	**8.0**	**5.4**	**20.2**	**8.4**	**44.1**	**24.3**	**3.9**	**22.6**	**5.2**
	2012	**199 888.4**	**15.1**	**10.2**	**6.4**	**22.6**	**8.4**	**38.2**	**31.8**	**3.4**	**22.3**	**4.2**
Eastern Africa - Afrique orientale	*1990*	*482.0*	*0.0*	*0.0*	*0.2*	*0.1*	*0.1*	*22.2*	*13.7*	*50.4*	*6.0*	*7.5*
	2000	*437.0*	*0.0*	*0.0*	*0.2*	*0.2*	*0.1*	*6.8*	*1.2*	*49.6*	*30.0*	*12.5*
	2010	*1 930.1*	*0.1*	*0.1*	*0.8*	*0.0*	*0.3*	*29.8*	*13.7*	*43.3*	*0.9*	*12.3*
	2012	*2 278.6*	*0.1*	*0.1*	*1.1*	*0.0*	*0.2*	*23.8*	*14.6*	*51.3*	*0.2*	*10.2*
Comoros - Comores	1990	3.0	..	..	0.0	..	..	..	..	100.0	..	..
	2000	1.0	..	..	0.0	..	..	..	..	100.0	..	..
	2010	1 211.8	0.1	0.1	0.5	0.0	0.1	27.3	20.5	42.0	1.4	8.8
	2012	945.9	0.0	0.0	0.4	0.0	0.1	18.8	28.4	43.3	0.5	9.0
Djibouti	2000	4.9	..	..	0.0	..	..	..	..	90.8	..	9.2
	2010	0.7	..	..	..	..	0.0	..	..	..	..	100.0
	2012	0.9	..	..	..	..	0.0	..	..	..	..	100.0
Eritrea - Érythrée	2010	14.0	0.0	..	0.0	..	0.0	22.7	..	73.3	..	4.0
	2012	14.0	0.0	..	0.0	..	0.0	22.7	..	73.3	..	4.0
Ethiopia (...1991) - Éthiopie (...1991)	1990	94.0	0.0	..	0.1	..	..	2.1	..	96.8	..	..
Ethiopia - Éthiopie	2000	119.7	0.0	..	0.1	..	..	3.0	..	97.0	..	..
	2010	150.0	..	..	0.1	..	..	..	..	100.0	..	..
	2012	146.5	..	..	0.1	..	..	..	..	100.0	..	..
Kenya	1990	5.0	..	..	..	..	0.0	..	..	..	..	100.0
	2000	19.1	0.0	..	0.0	..	0.0	40.0	..	10.4	..	49.7
	2010	14.0	0.0	..	0.0	..	0.0	54.4	..	3.3	..	42.4
	2012	7.9	0.0	..	..	..	0.0	26.3	..	..	..	73.7
Madagascar	1990	88.0	0.0	..	0.1	..	0.0	8.0	..	80.7	..	11.4
	2000	45.1	0.0	..	0.0	..	0.0	37.5	..	47.5	..	15.0
	2010	30.6	0.0	..	0.0	..	0.0	22.9	..	53.6	..	23.5
	2012	12.7	0.0	..	0.0	..	0.0	1.4	..	63.7	..	34.8
Mauritius - Maurice	1990	216.0	0.0	0.0	0.0	0.1	0.0	42.6	30.6	11.1	13.4	2.3
	2000	189.7	..	0.0	0.0	0.2	0.0	..	2.8	21.4	69.0	6.8
	2010	63.8	..	..	0.0	..	0.1	..	..	18.3	..	81.7
	2012	142.4	0.0	..	0.0	..	0.1	54.3	..	8.2	..	37.5
Mozambique	1990	27.0	0.0	..	0.0	..	0.0	7.4	..	66.7	..	25.9
	2000	25.2	..	..	0.0	..	0.0	..	..	49.9	..	50.1
	2010	35.0	..	..	0.0	..	0.0	..	..	30.2	..	69.8
	2012	37.0	..	..	0.0	..	0.0	..	..	32.5	..	67.5
Seychelles	1990	2.0	..	..	0.0	..	..	..	..	100.0	..	..
	2000	22.7	..	..	0.0	..	0.0	..	..	50.9	..	49.1
	2010	288.0	0.0	..	0.1	..	0.0	69.6	..	19.4	..	10.9
	2012	287.1	0.0	..	0.1	..	0.0	69.9	..	19.5	..	10.6

For sources and notes, see end of table.

Pour les sources et les notes, se reporter à la fin du tableau.

5

5.3 World merchant fleet by flag of registration and type of ship of countries and geographical regions

5.3 Flotte marchande mondiale par pavillons d'immatriculation et par types de navires des pays et des régions géographiques

Region, country or territory / Régions pays ou territoires	Year / Année	Total fleet (thousands of DWT) / Flotte totale (milliers de TPL) (1)	As percentage of world total fleet / En pourcentage de la flotte mondiale					As percentage of the country or region total fleet / En pourcentage de la flotte totale du pays ou de la région				
			Oil tankers / Pétroliers	Bulk carriers / Vraquiers	General cargo / Navires de charge classique (2)	Container ships / Porte-conteneurs	Other types / Autres navires	Oil tankers / Pétroliers	Bulk carriers / Vraquiers	General cargo / Navires de charge classique (2)	Container ships / Porte-conteneurs	Other types / Autres navires
Somalia - Somalie	1990	14.0	..	..	0.0	..	0.0	..	..	71.4	..	28.6
	2000	6.8	0.0	..	0.0	..	0.0	22.6	..	59.5	..	17.9
	2010	5.5	0.0	..	0.0	..	0.0	27.9	..	25.9	..	46.3
	2012	5.3	..	..	0.0	..	0.0	..	..	65.4	..	34.6
Uganda - Ouganda	1990	1.0	..	..	..	..	0.0	..	..	..	..	100.0
	2000	2.7	..	..	0.0	..	..	..	..	100.0	..	..
United Republic of Tanzania - République-Unie de Tanzanie	1990	32.0	0.0	..	0.0	..	0.0	12.5	..	75.0	..	12.5
	2010	116.6	0.0	0.0	0.1	..	0.0	21.3	13.9	60.7	..	4.1
	2012	679.0	0.0	0.0	0.5	..	0.0	12.0	9.2	75.2	..	3.7
Middle Africa - Afrique centrale	*1990*	*285.0*	*0.0*	*..*	*0.2*	*..*	*0.1*	*0.7*	*..*	*82.8*	*..*	*16.5*
	2000	*143.3*	*0.0*	*..*	*0.1*	*0.0*	*0.1*	*4.9*	*..*	*65.6*	*1.0*	*28.5*
	2010	*132.2*	*0.0*	*0.0*	*0.0*	*..*	*0.1*	*11.7*	*5.2*	*32.7*	*..*	*50.3*
	2012	*165.3*	*0.0*	*..*	*0.0*	*..*	*0.1*	*27.1*	*..*	*24.7*	*..*	*48.2*
Angola	1990	122.0	0.0	..	0.1	..	0.0	1.6	..	86.9	..	11.5
	2000	69.7	0.0	..	0.0	..	0.0	6.5	..	69.1	..	24.4
	2010	52.2	0.0	..	0.0	..	0.0	15.7	..	29.3	..	55.0
	2012	57.8	0.0	..	0.0	..	0.0	17.6	..	23.2	..	59.2
Cameroon - Cameroun	1990	39.0	..	..	0.0	..	0.0	..	..	92.3	..	7.7
	2000	5.7	..	..	0.0	..	0.0	..	..	5.3	..	94.7
	2010	9.1	..	..	0.0	..	0.0	..	..	28.3	..	71.7
	2012	8.8	..	..	0.0	..	0.0	..	..	28.4	..	71.6
Congo	1990	11.0	..	..	..	..	0.0	..	..	..	..	100.0
	2000	0.7	..	..	..	..	0.0	..	..	..	..	100.0
	2010	0.7	..	..	..	..	0.0	..	..	..	..	100.0
	2012	0.8	..	..	..	..	0.0	..	..	..	..	100.0
Dem. Rep. of the Congo - Rép. dém. du Congo	1990	76.0	..	..	0.1	..	0.0	..	..	80.3	..	19.7
	2010	16.7	0.0	..	0.0	..	0.0	9.8	..	3.6	..	86.6
	2012	14.3	0.0	..	0.0	..	0.0	11.5	..	4.2	..	84.3
Equatorial Guinea - Guinée équatoriale	1990	7.0	..	..	0.0	..	..	..	..	100.0	..	..
	2000	19.4	..	..	0.0	..	0.0	..	..	53.1	..	46.9
	2010	16.9	0.0	..	0.0	..	0.0	23.2	..	13.1	..	63.7
	2012	63.5	0.0	..	0.0	..	0.0	51.3	..	17.1	..	31.6
Gabon	1990	29.0	..	..	0.0	..	0.0	..	..	89.7	..	10.3
	2000	11.6	0.0	..	0.0	..	0.0	6.4	..	61.0	..	32.6
	2010	8.9	0.0	..	0.0	..	0.0	8.4	..	50.6	..	41.0
	2012	9.6	0.0	..	0.0	..	0.0	5.0	..	56.0	..	39.0
Sao Tome and Principe - Sao Tomé-et-Principe	1990	1.0	..	..	..	..	0.0	..	..	..	..	100.0
	2000	36.3	0.0	..	0.0	0.0	0.0	4.8	..	77.6	4.1	13.5
	2010	27.8	0.0	0.0	0.0	..	0.0	3.6	24.8	64.9	..	6.7
	2012	10.5	..	..	0.0	..	0.0	..	..	76.7	..	23.3
Northern Africa - Afrique septentrionale	*1990*	*5 391.0*	*0.7*	*0.4*	*1.4*	*0.0*	*2.9*	*31.0*	*17.5*	*25.7*	*0.2*	*25.6*
	2000	*4 477.3*	*0.4*	*0.5*	*1.1*	*0.1*	*1.3*	*22.5*	*30.1*	*25.1*	*1.0*	*21.3*
	2010	*4 143.9*	*0.4*	*0.2*	*0.4*	*0.1*	*1.0*	*43.2*	*22.0*	*9.8*	*3.2*	*21.9*
	2012	*4 391.5*	*0.4*	*0.2*	*0.3*	*0.1*	*0.9*	*44.0*	*25.8*	*7.5*	*3.2*	*19.5*
Algeria - Algérie	1990	964.0	0.0	0.1	0.3	..	1.0	4.8	16.2	30.7	..	48.3
	2000	1 110.8	0.0	0.1	0.3	..	0.7	4.7	25.9	26.6	..	42.7
	2010	764.6	0.0	0.0	0.1	..	0.5	3.3	26.7	8.4	..	61.6
	2012	808.7	0.0	0.0	0.1	..	0.5	3.4	25.3	8.1	..	63.3
Egypt - Égypte	1990	1 796.0	0.2	0.3	0.7	..	0.2	25.9	31.5	37.4	..	5.3
	2000	2 092.6	0.1	0.4	0.5	0.0	0.2	17.4	49.5	26.0	0.8	6.3
	2010	1 517.9	0.1	0.1	0.2	0.0	0.2	24.7	44.7	16.0	4.2	10.4
	2012	1 630.0	0.1	0.1	0.2	0.0	0.2	19.6	55.2	11.7	3.9	9.7
Libya - Libye	1990	1 463.0	0.5	..	0.1	..	0.6	74.7	..	6.8	..	18.5
	2000	667.1	0.2	..	0.1	..	0.1	80.5	..	13.7	..	5.8
	2010	1 404.9	0.3	..	0.0	..	0.0	95.8	..	2.2	..	2.0
	2012	1 491.6	0.3	..	0.0	..	0.0	98.0	..	0.3	..	1.7

For sources and notes, see end of table.

Pour les sources et les notes, se reporter à la fin du tableau.

5.3 World merchant fleet by flag of registration and type of ship of countries and geographical regions

5.3 Flotte marchande mondiale par pavillons d'immatriculation et par types de navires des pays et des régions géographiques

Region, country or territory / Régions pays ou territoires	Year / Année	Total fleet (thousands of DWT) / Flotte totale (milliers de TPL) (1)	As percentage of world total fleet / En pourcentage de la flotte mondiale					As percentage of the country or region total fleet / En pourcentage de la flotte totale du pays ou de la région				
			Oil tankers / Pétroliers	Bulk carriers / Vraquiers	General cargo / Navires de charge classique (2)	Container ships / Porte-conteneurs	Other types / Autres navires	Oil tankers / Pétroliers	Bulk carriers / Vraquiers	General cargo / Navires de charge classique (2)	Container ships / Porte-conteneurs	Other types / Autres navires
Morocco - Maroc	1990	594.0	0.0	0.1	0.1	0.0	0.6	3.2	27.4	21.7	1.7	46.0
	2000	383.8	0.0	..	0.1	0.0	0.3	5.3	..	29.2	6.6	58.9
	2010	332.0	0.0	..	0.0	0.0	0.2	6.0	..	5.8	20.9	67.3
	2012	238.9	0.0	..	0.0	0.0	0.1	8.5	..	3.4	32.8	55.3
Sudan (...2011) - Soudan (...2011)	1990	127.0	0.0	..	0.1	..	0.0	0.8	..	98.4	..	0.8
	2000	53.2	0.0	..	0.1	..	0.0	2.3	..	96.2	..	1.5
	2010	27.6	..	..	0.0	..	0.0	..	..	95.0	..	5.0
Sudan - Soudan	2012	26.9	..	..	0.0	..	0.0	..	..	93.0	..	7.0
Tunisia - Tunisie	1990	447.0	0.0	0.0	0.1	..	0.6	10.5	13.2	14.8	..	61.5
	2000	169.9	0.0	0.0	0.0	..	0.1	19.1	15.5	17.9	..	47.5
	2010	96.9	0.0	0.0	0.0	..	0.0	24.8	27.2	21.8	..	26.2
	2012	195.4	0.0	0.0	0.0	..	0.0	54.6	13.5	18.1	..	13.9
Southern Africa - Afrique australe	*1990*	*352.0*	*0.0*	*..*	*..*	*1.1*	*0.2*	*9.1*	*..*	*..*	*68.2*	*22.7*
	2000	*369.0*	*0.0*	*..*	*0.0*	*0.4*	*0.1*	*1.4*	*..*	*0.0*	*71.1*	*27.4*
	2010	*196.2*	*0.0*	*..*	*0.0*	*0.0*	*0.2*	*4.6*	*..*	*0.9*	*15.1*	*79.4*
	2012	*170.7*	*0.0*	*..*	*0.0*	*..*	*0.2*	*10.4*	*..*	*1.2*	*..*	*88.4*
Namibia - Namibie	2010	70.4	..	..	0.0	..	0.1	..	..	2.2	..	97.8
	2012	70.2	..	..	0.0	..	0.1	..	..	2.2	..	97.8
South Africa - Afrique du Sud	1990	352.0	0.0	..	..	1.1	0.2	9.1	..	..	68.2	22.7
	2000	369.0	0.0	..	0.0	0.4	0.1	1.4	..	0.0	71.1	27.4
	2010	125.9	0.0	..	0.0	0.0	0.1	7.1	..	0.1	23.6	69.2
	2012	100.5	0.0	..	0.0	..	0.1	17.7	..	0.5	..	81.8
Western Africa - Afrique occidentale	*1990*	*90 629.0*	*22.3*	*12.3*	*4.3*	*4.2*	*11.3*	*58.0*	*30.2*	*4.7*	*1.0*	*6.0*
	2000	*86 126.4*	*14.3*	*9.2*	*5.1*	*8.8*	*13.5*	*47.0*	*29.4*	*6.0*	*6.5*	*11.2*
	2010	*144 329.3*	*14.2*	*7.7*	*4.2*	*20.1*	*7.0*	*44.4*	*24.5*	*3.1*	*23.5*	*4.4*
	2012	*192 882.3*	*14.6*	*10.0*	*5.0*	*22.5*	*7.1*	*38.3*	*32.2*	*2.7*	*23.1*	*3.7*
Benin - Bénin	1990	5.0	..	..	0.0	..	0.0	..	..	80.0	..	20.0
	2000	0.2	..	..	..	..	0.0	..	..	..	..	100.0
	2010	0.4	..	..	..	..	0.0	..	..	..	..	100.0
	2012	0.4	..	..	..	..	0.0	..	..	..	..	100.0
Cape Verde - Cap-Vert	1990	26.0	..	..	0.0	..	0.0	..	..	92.3	..	7.7
	2000	24.0	0.0	..	0.0	..	0.0	6.4	..	78.4	..	15.3
	2010	23.5	0.0	..	0.0	..	0.0	26.6	..	48.7	..	24.7
	2012	26.3	0.0	..	0.0	..	0.0	37.8	..	44.1	..	18.2
Côte d'Ivoire	1990	100.0	..	..	0.1	..	0.0	..	..	85.0	..	15.0
	2000	5.9	0.0	..	..	..	0.0	19.9	..	..	..	80.1
	2010	5.1	0.0	..	..	..	0.0	22.8	..	..	..	77.2
	2012	4.1	0.0	..	..	..	0.0	28.6	..	..	..	71.4
Gambia - Gambie	1990	2.0	..	..	..	..	0.0	..	..	..	..	100.0
	2000	1.9	..	..	..	..	0.0	..	..	..	..	100.0
	2010	11.7	0.0	..	0.0	..	0.0	42.7	..	38.4	..	18.9
	2012	1.9	..	..	..	..	0.0	..	..	..	..	100.0
Ghana	1990	114.0	0.0	..	0.1	..	0.1	0.9	..	69.3	..	29.8
	2000	92.1	0.0	0.0	0.0	..	0.1	9.3	0.3	19.2	..	71.1
	2010	84.7	0.0	0.0	0.0	..	0.1	5.4	0.3	20.9	..	73.4
	2012	86.8	0.0	..	0.0	..	0.1	2.5	..	22.8	..	74.6
Guinea - Guinée	1990	3.0	..	..	..	..	0.0	..	..	..	..	100.0
	2000	4.8	..	..	0.0	..	0.0	..	..	6.0	..	94.0
	2010	11.6	..	..	0.0	..	0.0	..	..	2.5	..	97.5
	2012	12.5	..	..	0.0	..	0.0	..	..	2.3	..	97.7
Guinea-Bissau - Guinée-Bissau	1990	2.0	..	..	..	..	0.0	..	..	..	..	100.0
	2000	2.2	..	..	0.0	..	0.0	..	..	24.7	..	75.3
	2010	2.2	..	..	0.0	..	0.0	..	..	10.2	..	89.8
	2012	2.2	..	..	0.0	..	0.0	..	..	10.2	..	89.8
Liberia - Libéria	1990	89 501.0	22.1	12.3	3.8	4.2	10.9	58.3	30.6	4.2	1.0	5.8
	2000	85 186.9	14.1	9.2	4.9	8.8	13.3	46.8	29.7	5.8	6.6	11.1
	2010	142 121.0	14.0	7.7	3.5	20.0	6.5	44.5	24.8	2.7	23.9	4.2
	2012	189 910.9	14.3	9.9	4.2	22.4	6.7	38.2	32.5	2.3	23.4	3.5

For sources and notes, see end of table.

Pour les sources et les notes, se reporter à la fin du tableau.

5

5.3 World merchant fleet by flag of registration and type of ship of countries and geographical regions

5.3 Flotte marchande mondiale par pavillons d'immatriculation et par types de navires des pays et des régions géographiques

Region, country or territory / Régions pays ou territoires	Year / Année	Total fleet (thousands of DWT) / Flotte totale (milliers de TPL) (1)	As percentage of world total fleet / En pourcentage de la flotte mondiale					As percentage of the country or region total fleet / En pourcentage de la flotte totale du pays ou de la région				
			Oil tankers / Pétroliers	Bulk carriers / Vraquiers	General cargo / Navires de charge classique (2)	Container ships / Porte-conteneurs	Other types / Autres navires	Oil tankers / Pétroliers	Bulk carriers / Vraquiers	General cargo / Navires de charge classique (2)	Container ships / Porte-conteneurs	Other types / Autres navires
Mauritania - Mauritanie	1990	22.0	..	..	0.0	..	0.0	..	..	18.2	..	81.8
	2000	22.2	..	..	0.0	..	0.0	..	..	3.2	..	96.8
	2010	24.7	..	..	0.0	..	0.0	..	..	3.5	..	96.5
	2012	21.6	0.0	..	0.0	..	0.0	11.1	..	4.0	..	84.8
Nigeria - Nigéria	1990	737.0	0.2	..	0.3	..	0.1	59.0	..	35.7	..	5.3
	2000	677.9	0.2	..	0.1	..	0.1	76.6	..	17.0	..	6.4
	2010	989.4	0.2	0.0	0.0	..	0.2	75.8	1.3	1.9	..	20.9
	2012	938.9	0.1	..	0.0	..	0.2	77.8	..	0.9	..	21.3
Saint Helena - Sainte-Hélène	1990	2.0	..	..	..	..	0.0	..	..	..	..	100.0
	2000	0.5	..	..	..	..	0.0	..	..	..	..	100.0
	2010	0.8	..	..	..	..	0.0	..	..	..	..	100.0
	2012	0.8	..	..	..	..	0.0	..	..	..	..	100.0
Senegal - Sénégal	1990	36.0	..	..	0.0	..	0.0	..	..	47.2	..	52.8
	2000	22.4	..	..	0.0	..	0.0	..	..	9.1	..	90.9
	2010	19.3	0.0	..	0.0	..	0.0	1.4	..	8.0	..	90.5
	2012	22.2	0.0	..	0.0	..	0.0	1.3	..	13.4	..	85.3
Sierra Leone	1990	14.0	0.0	..	0.0	..	0.0	7.1	..	21.4	..	71.4
	2000	11.2	0.0	..	0.0	..	0.0	55.0	..	8.5	..	36.5
	2010	792.2	0.0	0.0	0.5	0.0	0.0	12.9	9.6	70.3	1.4	5.7
	2012	1 268.4	0.1	0.0	0.6	0.0	0.1	21.8	20.9	46.3	2.4	8.7
Togo	1990	65.0	0.0	..	0.0	..	0.1	1.5	..	32.3	..	67.7
	2000	74.4	..	0.0	..	..	0.0	..	99.1	..	..	0.9
	2010	242.8	0.0	0.0	0.1	0.0	0.0	3.3	31.2	57.9	3.4	4.1
	2012	585.5	0.0	0.0	0.2	0.0	0.0	41.1	12.5	37.9	6.7	1.8
Developing economies: America - Économies en développement : Amérique	**1990**	**119 936.0**	**16.4**	**20.2**	**24.0**	**19.3**	**16.2**	**32.2**	**37.6**	**20.1**	**3.6**	**6.4**
	2000	**237 755.2**	**26.8**	**34.5**	**31.6**	**28.8**	**23.7**	**31.9**	**39.8**	**13.5**	**7.7**	**7.1**
	2010	**395 591.2**	**24.8**	**38.9**	**33.7**	**25.6**	**28.6**	**28.2**	**45.0**	**9.2**	**11.0**	**6.7**
	2012	**440 727.1**	**21.6**	**35.2**	**34.2**	**24.2**	**27.8**	**24.9**	**49.7**	**8.2**	**10.9**	**6.3**
Caribbean - Caraïbes	*1990*	*24 104.0*	*5.1*	*2.7*	*4.3*	*1.1*	*3.0*	*49.8*	*25.2*	*18.0*	*1.0*	*5.9*
	2000	*62 854.5*	*9.5*	*5.3*	*13.4*	*6.1*	*5.4*	*42.6*	*23.4*	*21.7*	*6.2*	*6.1*
	2010	*94 721.4*	*8.2*	*4.6*	*15.1*	*5.4*	*12.1*	*39.1*	*22.3*	*17.3*	*9.6*	*11.7*
	2012	*99 992.8*	*7.6*	*3.5*	*15.4*	*4.9*	*13.2*	*38.6*	*22.1*	*16.4*	*9.7*	*13.2*
Anguilla	1990	4.0	..	..	0.0	..	..	..	..	75.0	..	..
	2000	2.0	..	..	0.0	..	..	..	..	100.0	..	..
	2010	0.9	..	..	0.0	..	..	..	..	100.0	..	..
	2012	0.3	..	..	0.0	..	..	..	..	100.0	..	..
Antigua and Barbuda - Antigua-et-Barbuda	1990	696.0	0.0	0.0	0.5	0.3	0.1	12.2	0.7	70.3	11.2	5.6
	2000	4 677.6	0.0	0.1	1.8	3.9	0.1	0.2	6.7	39.2	53.0	0.9
	2010	13 033.6	0.0	0.3	4.0	4.3	0.1	0.2	9.8	33.1	56.0	0.9
	2012	14 402.4	0.0	0.2	5.0	3.7	0.2	0.1	10.4	36.9	51.4	1.2
Aruba	2010	0.1	..	..	..	..	0.0	..	..	..	..	100.0
	2012	0.1	..	..	..	..	0.0	..	..	..	..	100.0
Bahamas	1990	19 228.0	4.8	2.2	1.8	0.4	2.2	59.2	25.3	9.6	0.5	5.4
	2000	44 941.4	8.8	3.2	7.3	1.9	3.9	55.4	19.3	16.5	2.7	6.1
	2010	64 109.1	7.4	2.8	6.0	0.9	10.5	52.2	20.1	10.2	2.4	15.1
	2012	69 105.1	6.8	2.4	5.5	1.0	11.9	50.1	21.5	8.5	2.8	17.2
Barbados - Barbade	1990	8.0	..	..	0.0	..	..	..	..	100.0	..	..
	2000	1 162.0	0.2	0.1	0.2	0.0	0.1	55.0	22.7	13.3	1.5	7.4
	2010	1 181.1	0.1	0.1	0.3	..	0.1	23.9	43.4	27.7	..	5.0
	2012	2 040.1	0.1	0.1	0.3	0.1	0.1	23.2	44.8	16.8	10.3	4.9
British Virgin Islands - Îles Vierges britanniques	1990	5.0	..	..	0.0	..	..	..	..	100.0	..	..
	2000	2.1	..	..	0.0	..	0.0	..	..	68.8	..	31.2
	2010	11.0	..	..	0.0	..	0.0	..	..	5.1	..	94.9
	2012	1.4	0.0	..	0.0	..	0.0	42.8	..	39.5	..	17.7
Cayman Islands - Îles Caïmanes	1990	566.0	0.0	0.1	0.2	..	0.2	11.0	33.2	38.9	..	17.0
	2000	1 756.2	0.1	0.3	0.4	0.1	0.3	11.9	52.7	22.1	2.2	11.1
	2010	3 960.6	0.5	0.3	0.3	..	0.4	55.0	29.4	7.4	..	8.2
	2012	3 803.6	0.4	0.2	0.4	..	0.2	54.0	28.5	12.0	..	5.4

For sources and notes, see end of table.

Pour les sources et les notes, se reporter à la fin du tableau.

310

5.3 World merchant fleet by flag of registration and type of ship of countries and geographical regions

5.3 Flotte marchande mondiale par pavillons d'immatriculation et par types de navires des pays et des régions géographiques

Region, country or territory / Régions pays ou territoires	Year / Année	Total fleet (thousands of DWT) / Flotte totale (milliers de TPL) (1)	As percentage of world total fleet / En pourcentage de la flotte mondiale					As percentage of the country or region total fleet / En pourcentage de la flotte totale du pays ou de la région				
			Oil tankers / Pétroliers	Bulk carriers / Vraquiers	General cargo / Navires de charge classique (2)	Container ships / Porte-conteneurs	Other types / Autres navires	Oil tankers / Pétroliers	Bulk carriers / Vraquiers	General cargo / Navires de charge classique (2)	Container ships / Porte-conteneurs	Other types / Autres navires
Cuba	1990	1 198.0	0.0	0.0	0.8	..	0.3	9.8	8.3	68.1	..	13.8
	2000	156.3	0.0	0.0	0.1	..	0.1	3.0	2.0	53.3	..	41.6
	2010	49.4	0.0	0.0	0.0	..	0.0	2.1	7.0	28.8	..	62.1
	2012	30.5	0.0	0.0	0.0	..	0.0	3.4	2.1	16.7	..	77.9
Curaçao	2012	1 561.0	0.0	0.0	1.0	..	0.2	11.0	4.7	69.6	..	14.6
Dominica - Dominique	1990	5.0	..	..	0.0	..	..	..	..	100.0	..	..
	2000	2.7	..	..	0.0	..	0.0	..	..	79.9	..	20.1
	2010	1 610.4	0.1	0.2	0.1	..	0.0	28.5	62.1	7.1	..	2.3
	2012	1 843.0	0.1	0.2	0.1	..	0.0	38.0	54.4	5.5	..	2.1
Dominican Republic - République dominicaine	1990	68.0	0.0	0.0	0.0	..	..	2.9	27.9	69.1	..	..
	2000	8.4	..	..	0.0	..	0.0	..	..	85.6	..	14.4
	2010	5.6	..	..	0.0	..	0.0	..	..	89.0	..	11.0
	2012	0.8	..	..	..	..	0.0	..	..	..	..	100.0
Grenada - Grenade	1990	1.0	..	..	..	..	0.0	..	..	..	..	100.0
	2000	1.0	..	..	0.0	..	..	..	..	100.0	..	..
	2010	1.0	..	..	0.0	..	0.0	..	..	95.5	..	4.5
	2012	1.0	..	..	0.0	..	0.0	..	..	95.5	..	4.5
Haiti - Haïti	2000	1.0	..	..	0.0	..	0.0	..	..	82.3	..	17.7
	2010	1.5	..	..	0.0	..	0.0	..	..	88.9	..	11.1
	2012	0.7	..	..	0.0	..	0.0	..	..	77.1	..	22.9
Jamaica - Jamaïque	1990	21.0	0.0	0.0	0.0	0.0	0.0	14.3	19.0	38.1	23.8	4.8
	2000	3.3	0.0	..	..	..	0.0	92.9	..	..	..	7.1
	2010	353.3	..	0.1	0.1	0.0	0.0	..	74.4	15.6	9.9	0.2
	2012	217.1	..	0.0	0.1	0.0	0.0	..	58.7	25.0	16.1	0.2
Montserrat	1990	1.0	..	..	0.0	..	..	..	..	100.0	..	..
Netherlands Antilles - Antilles néerlandaises	2010	1 836.7	0.0	0.0	1.1	0.0	0.3	9.4	8.1	66.7	0.5	15.4
Saint Kitts and Nevis - Saint-Kitts-et-Nevis	1990	1.0	..	..	0.0	..	..	..	..	100.0	..	..
	2000	0.6	..	..	0.0	..	..	..	..	100.0	..	..
	2010	1 219.2	0.0	0.1	0.5	0.0	0.1	10.5	39.3	45.0	0.9	4.3
	2012	1 328.6	0.1	0.1	0.5	0.0	0.1	21.1	28.2	38.8	3.3	8.6
Saint Lucia - Sainte-Lucie	1990	2.0	..	..	0.0	..	..	..	..	100.0	..	..
Saint Vincent and the Grenadines - Saint-Vincent-et-les Grenadines	1990	2 282.0	0.2	0.4	0.9	0.3	0.2	15.6	39.7	38.9	2.7	3.2
	2000	10 131.0	0.4	1.6	3.7	0.3	1.0	10.0	44.4	36.8	1.8	7.0
	2010	7 329.2	0.1	0.7	2.8	0.1	0.5	4.3	46.1	40.7	2.1	6.7
	2012	5 636.2	0.1	0.4	2.4	0.1	0.4	5.7	38.7	46.1	1.9	7.5
Trinidad and Tobago - Trinité-et-Tobago	1990	16.0	..	..	0.0	..	0.0	..	..	37.5	..	62.5
	2000	8.9	0.0	..	0.0	..	0.0	16.6	..	28.9	..	54.5
	2010	18.3	0.0	..	..	..	0.0	22.6	..	..	..	77.4
	2012	20.8	0.0	..	..	..	0.0	19.8	..	..	..	80.2
Turks and Caicos Islands - Îles Turques et Caïques	1990	2.0	..	..	0.0	..	0.0	..	..	50.0	..	50.0
	2000	0.2	..	..	0.0	..	..	..	..	100.0	..	..
	2010	0.2	..	..	0.0	..	..	..	..	100.0	..	..
	2012	0.0	..	..	..	..	0.0	..	..	..	..	100.0
Central America - Amérique centrale	*1990*	*78 245.0*	*8.9*	*14.3*	*16.4*	*17.2*	*10.3*	*27.0*	*40.7*	*21.1*	*4.9*	*6.3*
	2000	*164 753.9*	*15.8*	*27.9*	*17.2*	*22.3*	*16.4*	*27.2*	*46.6*	*10.6*	*8.6*	*7.1*
	2010	*292 694.0*	*15.7*	*34.0*	*17.9*	*20.0*	*14.8*	*24.2*	*53.0*	*6.6*	*11.6*	*4.7*
	2012	*332 619.0*	*13.2*	*31.4*	*18.2*	*19.0*	*12.9*	*20.2*	*58.8*	*5.8*	*11.3*	*3.9*
Belize	2000	3 052.4	0.2	0.1	1.7	0.1	0.6	18.8	10.6	55.5	1.8	13.2
	2010	1 451.1	0.0	0.1	0.8	..	0.3	2.2	20.4	61.4	..	16.0
	2012	1 815.2	0.0	0.1	0.9	..	0.2	7.1	26.3	53.5	..	13.1
Costa Rica	1990	7.0	..	..	0.0	..	0.0	..	..	42.9	..	57.1
	2000	1.2	..	..	..	..	0.0	..	..	..	..	100.0
	2010	0.4	..	..	..	..	0.0	..	..	..	..	100.0
	2012	1.7	..	..	..	..	0.0	..	..	..	..	100.0
El Salvador	1990	3.0	..	..	..	..	0.0	..	..	..	..	100.0
	2010	1.7	..	..	..	..	0.0	..	..	..	..	100.0
	2012	1.7	..	..	..	..	0.0	..	..	..	..	100.0

For sources and notes, see end of table.

Pour les sources et les notes, se reporter à la fin du tableau.

5.3   World merchant fleet by flag of registration and type of ship of countries and geographical regions

5.3   Flotte marchande mondiale par pavillons d'immatriculation et par types de navires des pays et des régions géographiques

Region, country or territory / Régions pays ou territoires	Year / Année	Total fleet (thousands of DWT) / Flotte totale (milliers de TPL) (1)	As percentage of world total fleet / En pourcentage de la flotte mondiale					As percentage of the country or region total fleet / En pourcentage de la flotte totale du pays ou de la région				
			Oil tankers / Pétroliers	Bulk carriers / Vraquiers	General cargo / Navires de charge classique (2)	Container ships / Porte-conteneurs	Other types / Autres navires	Oil tankers / Pétroliers	Bulk carriers / Vraquiers	General cargo / Navires de charge classique (2)	Container ships / Porte-conteneurs	Other types / Autres navires
Guatemala	1990	7.0	..	..	0.0	..	0.0	..	..	85.7	..	14.3
	2000	3.8	..	..	..	..	0.0	..	..	..	..	100.0
	2010	2.8	0.0	..	..	..	0.0	33.4	..	..	..	66.6
	2012	2.8	0.0	..	..	..	0.0	33.4	..	..	..	66.6
Honduras	1990	982.0	0.1	0.1	0.6	0.0	0.1	14.1	17.6	62.8	0.9	4.6
	2000	1 520.7	0.1	0.1	0.9	0.0	0.3	15.8	14.6	57.0	0.5	12.1
	2010	702.2	0.0	0.0	0.3	0.0	0.1	26.7	10.1	44.3	0.3	18.5
	2012	514.3	0.0	0.0	0.2	..	0.1	31.1	8.7	45.7	..	14.5
Mexico - Mexique	1990	1 883.0	0.3	0.2	0.1	0.1	1.4	42.9	18.4	3.3	0.6	34.8
	2000	1 226.6	0.3	..	0.0	..	0.6	62.3	..	2.0	..	35.8
	2010	1 775.7	0.3	0.0	0.0	..	0.6	63.7	5.2	2.0	..	29.1
	2012	2 071.1	0.2	0.0	0.0	..	0.6	60.0	12.2	1.3	..	26.6
Nicaragua	1990	3.0	..	..	0.0	..	..	..	..	100.0	..	..
	2000	2.0	..	..	0.0	..	0.0	..	..	59.4	..	40.6
	2010	2.7	0.0	..	0.0	..	0.0	33.9	..	43.4	..	22.7
	2012	2.7	0.0	..	0.0	..	0.0	33.9	..	43.4	..	22.7
Panama	1990	75 360.0	8.5	14.0	15.7	17.1	8.8	26.7	41.6	21.0	5.1	5.6
	2000	158 947.3	15.3	27.7	14.6	22.2	15.0	27.2	47.9	9.3	8.9	6.7
	2010	288 757.6	15.4	33.9	16.7	20.0	13.9	24.0	53.6	6.3	11.7	4.4
	2012	328 209.5	12.9	31.3	17.0	19.0	12.0	20.0	59.4	5.5	11.5	3.6
South America - Amérique du Sud	*1990*	*17 587.0*	*2.4*	*3.2*	*3.3*	*1.0*	*2.9*	*31.6*	*40.5*	*18.9*	*1.3*	*7.8*
	2000	*10 146.7*	*1.5*	*1.2*	*1.0*	*0.4*	*1.9*	*42.5*	*32.0*	*10.2*	*2.3*	*13.0*
	2010	*8 175.8*	*0.8*	*0.4*	*0.7*	*0.2*	*1.7*	*46.5*	*19.9*	*9.1*	*5.0*	*19.5*
	2012	*8 115.3*	*0.8*	*0.2*	*0.6*	*0.3*	*1.7*	*49.2*	*15.7*	*7.9*	*6.8*	*20.3*
Argentina - Argentine	1990	2 764.0	0.4	0.4	0.8	0.3	0.5	32.6	29.1	27.6	2.6	8.2
	2000	599.3	0.1	0.0	0.1	..	0.3	30.1	8.7	21.9	..	39.3
	2010	980.9	0.1	0.0	0.1	0.0	0.3	54.7	11.7	7.2	1.9	24.6
	2012	818.5	0.1	0.0	0.0	0.0	0.2	66.1	2.9	6.2	2.2	22.5
Bolivia (Plurinational State of) - Bolivie (État plurinational de)	1990	16.0	..	..	0.0	..	..	..	..	100.0	..	..
	2000	244.5	0.0	0.0	0.1	0.0	0.0	11.4	35.7	44.1	3.4	5.5
	2010	166.0	0.0	0.0	0.1	..	0.0	14.5	28.7	48.1	..	8.7
	2012	124.1	0.0	0.0	0.1	..	0.0	2.3	23.1	73.4	..	1.2
Brazil - Brésil	1990	10 063.0	1.4	2.3	1.1	0.5	1.1	32.2	50.6	10.9	1.1	5.2
	2000	6 383.6	1.1	0.9	0.4	0.3	0.3	48.0	39.8	6.1	2.6	3.5
	2010	3 406.8	0.3	0.2	0.3	0.2	0.5	42.4	25.3	8.2	10.5	13.6
	2012	3 360.3	0.3	0.1	0.2	0.2	0.5	45.2	18.3	7.7	14.2	14.6
Chile - Chili	1990	870.0	..	0.2	0.2	..	0.3	..	63.4	22.8	..	13.8
	2000	1 012.0	0.1	0.1	0.1	0.1	0.5	16.4	34.5	12.0	5.0	32.1
	2010	1 095.8	0.1	0.1	0.1	0.0	0.2	36.1	34.8	6.9	1.9	20.3
	2012	1 065.8	0.1	0.1	0.0	0.0	0.2	34.0	39.3	4.4	2.8	19.6
Colombia - Colombie	1990	546.0	0.0	0.1	0.4	..	0.0	2.7	28.8	65.0	..	3.5
	2000	119.4	0.0	..	0.1	..	0.0	8.3	..	67.7	..	24.1
	2010	109.0	0.0	..	0.0	..	0.1	7.1	..	49.4	..	43.4
	2012	112.6	0.0	..	0.0	..	0.0	21.6	..	35.9	..	42.5
Ecuador - Équateur	1990	531.0	0.1	0.0	0.2	..	0.1	39.4	7.2	47.1	..	6.4
	2000	446.6	0.1	..	0.0	..	0.1	86.3	..	0.8	..	12.9
	2010	400.6	0.1	..	0.0	..	0.1	81.6	..	1.5	..	16.9
	2012	420.5	0.1	..	0.0	..	0.1	81.9	..	2.0	..	16.1
Falkland Islands (Malvinas) - Îles Falkland (Malvinas)	1990	4.0	..	..	..	..	0.0	..	..	..	..	100.0
	2000	31.1	..	..	0.0	..	0.0	..	..	2.0	..	98.0
	2010	34.6	..	..	..	..	0.0	..	..	..	..	100.0
	2012	33.7	..	..	..	..	0.0	..	..	..	..	100.0
Guyana	1990	11.0	..	..	0.0	..	0.0	..	..	45.5	..	54.5
	2000	12.5	..	..	0.0	..	0.0	..	..	53.8	..	46.2
	2010	41.7	0.0	..	0.0	..	0.0	16.4	..	67.1	..	16.5
	2012	45.5	0.0	..	0.0	..	0.0	20.6	..	63.0	..	16.4
Paraguay	1990	44.0	0.0	..	0.0	..	0.0	2.3	..	59.1	..	38.6
	2000	48.8	0.0	..	0.0	0.0	0.0	18.2	..	73.3	4.5	4.0
	2010	63.3	0.0	..	0.0	0.0	0.0	10.3	..	73.9	13.4	2.4
	2012	67.4	0.0	..	0.0	0.0	0.0	5.4	..	77.9	14.6	2.1

For sources and notes, see end of table.

Pour les sources et les notes, se reporter à la fin du tableau.

5.3 World merchant fleet by flag of registration and type of ship of countries and geographical regions

5.3 Flotte marchande mondiale par pavillons d'immatriculation et par types de navires des pays et des régions géographiques

Region, country or territory / Régions pays ou territoires	Year / Année	Total fleet (thousands of DWT) / Flotte totale (milliers de TPL) (1)	As percentage of world total fleet / En pourcentage de la flotte mondiale					As percentage of the country or region total fleet / En pourcentage de la flotte totale du pays ou de la région				
			Oil tankers / Pétroliers	Bulk carriers / Vraquiers	General cargo / Navires de charge classique (2)	Container ships / Porte-conteneurs	Other types / Autres navires	Oil tankers / Pétroliers	Bulk carriers / Vraquiers	General cargo / Navires de charge classique (2)	Container ships / Porte-conteneurs	Other types / Autres navires
Peru - Pérou	1990	841.0	0.1	0.1	0.2	..	0.1	40.1	25.7	28.2	..	6.1
	2000	267.0	0.0	0.0	0.1	..	0.1	29.7	9.6	30.4	..	30.4
	2010	317.9	0.0	..	0.0	..	0.1	55.7	..	9.3	..	35.0
	2012	546.3	0.1	..	0.0	0.0	0.1	79.2	..	2.5	2.7	15.5
Suriname	1990	15.0	0.0	..	0.0	0.0	0.0	13.3	..	66.7	13.3	6.7
	2000	7.2	0.0	..	0.0	..	0.0	42.1	..	43.8	..	14.2
	2010	5.7	0.0	..	0.0	..	0.0	59.7	..	31.3	..	9.0
	2012	5.7	0.0	..	0.0	..	0.0	59.7	..	31.3	..	9.0
Uruguay	1990	155.0	0.0	..	0.0	0.2	0.1	60.6	..	1.9	21.9	15.5
	2000	38.1	0.0	..	0.0	..	0.0	22.0	..	3.3	..	74.7
	2010	69.9	0.0	0.0	0.0	..	0.0	22.3	4.6	12.4	..	60.6
	2012	60.3	0.0	0.0	0.0	..	0.0	32.3	5.4	12.6	..	49.7
Venezuela (Bolivarian Rep. of) - Venezuela (Rép. bolivarienne du)	1990	1 727.0	0.3	0.1	0.4	0.0	0.7	43.9	15.3	21.1	0.2	19.5
	2000	936.7	0.1	0.1	0.1	0.0	0.4	40.1	20.7	8.1	0.1	31.0
	2010	1 483.6	0.2	0.0	0.1	..	0.4	58.0	14.8	4.2	..	22.9
	2012	1 454.7	0.1	0.0	0.0	..	0.5	50.3	12.9	2.9	..	33.9
Developing economies: Asia - Économies en développement : Asie	**1990**	**115 295.0**	**12.6**	**23.2**	**23.8**	**18.2**	**12.1**	**25.7**	**45.0**	**20.7**	**3.5**	**5.0**
	2000	**156 453.2**	**15.1**	**24.0**	**25.1**	**20.0**	**13.4**	**27.4**	**42.1**	**16.3**	**8.1**	**6.1**
	2010	**285 345.4**	**20.3**	**24.9**	**28.7**	**19.4**	**17.6**	**32.1**	**39.9**	**10.9**	**11.5**	**5.7**
	2012	**366 203.0**	**22.0**	**26.6**	**28.1**	**20.6**	**18.4**	**30.5**	**45.2**	**8.1**	**11.1**	**5.0**
Eastern Asia - Asie orientale	*1990*	*43 401.0*	*2.4*	*10.8*	*9.8*	*9.3*	*3.8*	*12.8*	*55.5*	*22.8*	*4.8*	*4.2*
	2000	*54 642.3*	*2.4*	*11.0*	*9.2*	*9.8*	*3.2*	*12.2*	*55.1*	*17.1*	*11.4*	*4.2*
	2010	*146 890.9*	*7.0*	*17.8*	*11.9*	*10.1*	*4.5*	*21.5*	*55.4*	*8.7*	*11.6*	*2.8*
	2012	*200 339.4*	*8.0*	*19.3*	*11.6*	*11.5*	*4.7*	*20.3*	*59.8*	*6.2*	*11.4*	*2.4*
China - Chine	1990	20 200.0	1.1	3.6	7.7	4.0	1.8	13.2	39.9	38.2	4.5	4.2
	2000	23 701.2	1.2	4.0	6.4	2.6	1.6	14.3	46.8	27.2	7.0	4.7
	2010	45 157.3	2.1	5.0	5.6	3.1	1.7	20.5	51.0	13.4	11.7	3.4
	2012	58 194.8	2.5	5.1	4.7	3.2	2.1	22.0	55.1	8.5	10.9	3.6
China, Hong Kong SAR - Chine (RAS de Hong Kong)	1990	10 337.0	0.6	3.5	0.4	2.1	0.6	13.1	75.2	4.2	4.5	2.8
	2000	13 190.9	0.3	3.6	0.9	2.3	0.1	7.1	73.9	7.2	11.2	0.6
	2010	74 513.5	4.1	9.0	3.5	6.0	1.2	24.9	55.0	5.0	13.6	1.5
	2012	116 805.7	5.0	11.4	4.2	7.4	1.2	21.9	60.8	3.8	12.5	1.0
China, Macao SAR - Chine (RAS de Macao)	2010	2.2	..	..	..	..	0.0	..	..	..	..	100.0
China, Taiwan Province of - Province chinoise de Taiwan	2000	8 248.1	0.6	1.6	0.2	3.4	0.1	18.9	51.8	2.4	26.3	0.7
	2010	3 944.1	0.3	0.4	0.1	0.4	0.1	29.0	46.4	4.1	18.0	2.4
	2012	4 328.4	0.1	0.4	0.1	0.4	0.1	16.8	58.9	3.6	18.1	2.7
Korea, Dem. People's Rep. of - Corée, Rép. populaire dém. de	1990	529.0	0.0	0.0	0.4	..	0.0	3.8	20.6	71.6	..	4.0
	2000	846.6	0.0	0.0	0.7	..	0.1	1.4	10.4	80.7	..	7.6
	2010	1 265.6	0.0	0.0	0.8	0.0	0.1	9.3	12.8	71.1	2.5	4.3
	2012	1 023.3	0.0	0.0	0.7	0.0	0.0	6.6	16.2	71.9	2.2	3.2
Korea, Republic of - Corée, République de	1990	12 335.0	0.6	3.6	1.4	3.2	1.3	12.2	65.8	11.0	5.8	5.2
	2000	8 655.5	0.3	1.8	1.1	1.5	1.3	8.9	56.8	12.3	11.0	11.1
	2010	20 818.6	0.5	3.2	1.6	0.5	1.4	11.7	69.7	8.4	4.1	6.2
	2012	19 157.3	0.3	2.2	1.7	0.5	1.3	7.5	71.0	9.6	5.2	6.7
Mongolia - Mongolie	2010	1 189.6	0.0	0.2	0.2	..	0.0	1.6	75.9	21.0	..	1.5
	2012	830.0	0.0	0.1	0.2	0.0	0.0	3.8	64.8	27.3	1.3	2.8
Southern Asia - Asie méridionale	*1990*	*20 524.0*	*3.9*	*3.2*	*3.5*	*..*	*1.4*	*45.3*	*34.6*	*16.9*	*..*	*3.3*
	2000	*18 704.6*	*3.0*	*2.3*	*2.4*	*0.3*	*1.7*	*45.2*	*34.5*	*13.1*	*1.0*	*6.3*
	2010	*18 185.6*	*2.1*	*1.1*	*1.3*	*0.4*	*1.6*	*52.6*	*28.4*	*7.6*	*3.5*	*8.0*
	2012	*20 384.9*	*2.0*	*1.1*	*1.3*	*0.2*	*1.5*	*49.3*	*34.8*	*6.8*	*1.9*	*7.2*
Bangladesh	1990	587.0	0.0	..	0.5	..	0.0	14.1	..	83.5	..	2.4
	2000	518.7	0.0	0.0	0.4	..	0.0	19.6	1.7	74.9	..	3.8
	2010	975.3	0.0	0.1	0.3	0.0	0.0	11.4	47.4	33.7	5.0	2.5
	2012	2 041.0	0.0	0.2	0.5	0.0	0.0	10.7	61.9	24.2	1.9	1.3
India - Inde	1990	10 207.0	1.2	2.3	1.6	..	1.0	28.5	50.9	15.9	..	4.7
	2000	11 209.3	1.7	1.7	0.6	0.2	1.4	43.1	41.3	5.9	1.2	8.6
	2010	14 969.6	2.0	0.9	0.3	0.2	1.3	60.2	27.5	2.4	2.2	7.8
	2012	16 141.3	1.8	0.8	0.3	0.1	1.2	56.1	32.4	2.2	1.8	7.5

For sources and notes, see end of table.

Pour les sources et les notes, se reporter à la fin du tableau.

5.3 World merchant fleet by flag of registration and type of ship of countries and geographical regions

5.3 Flotte marchande mondiale par pavillons d'immatriculation et par types de navires des pays et des régions géographiques

Region, country or territory / Régions pays ou territoires	Year / Année	Total fleet (thousands of DWT) / Flotte totale (milliers de TPL) (1)	As percentage of world total fleet / En pourcentage de la flotte mondiale					As percentage of the country or region total fleet / En pourcentage de la flotte totale du pays ou de la région				
			Oil tankers / Pétroliers	Bulk carriers / Vraquiers	General cargo / Navires de charge classique (2)	Container ships / Porte-conteneurs	Other types / Autres navires	Oil tankers / Pétroliers	Bulk carriers / Vraquiers	General cargo / Navires de charge classique (2)	Container ships / Porte-conteneurs	Other types / Autres navires
Iran (Islamic Rep. of) - Iran (Rép. islamique d')	1990	8 685.0	2.6	0.8	0.6	..	0.3	71.3	20.4	6.5	..	1.8
	2000	6 097.3	1.2	0.6	0.9	0.0	0.2	55.9	26.4	14.8	0.2	2.6
	2010	1 333.3	0.0	0.1	0.3	0.1	0.2	9.0	34.0	22.3	18.9	15.7
	2012	1 179.3	0.1	0.0	0.3	0.0	0.2	35.2	19.7	26.3	3.7	15.0
Maldives	1990	148.0	0.0	0.0	0.1	..	0.0	6.8	48.6	43.2	..	1.4
	2000	132.8	0.0	..	0.1	..	0.0	6.5	..	88.5	..	4.9
	2010	187.5	0.0	0.0	0.1	..	0.0	8.4	0.9	86.0	..	4.7
	2012	116.1	0.0	0.0	0.1	..	0.0	10.1	1.5	82.6	..	5.9
Pakistan	1990	526.0	0.0	..	0.4	..	0.0	17.1	..	80.8	..	2.1
	2000	458.7	0.0	0.0	0.3	0.1	0.0	19.8	11.4	56.8	9.1	2.9
	2010	481.1	0.1	0.0	0.1	..	0.0	58.5	13.7	22.3	..	5.5
	2012	662.6	0.1	0.0	0.0	..	0.0	49.7	40.8	5.5	..	4.0
Sri Lanka	1990	371.0	0.0	0.0	0.3	..	0.0	4.0	14.8	80.1	..	1.1
	2000	287.6	0.0	0.1	0.1	..	0.0	3.5	52.0	42.2	..	2.4
	2010	238.9	0.0	0.0	0.1	..	0.0	10.9	31.5	51.2	..	6.3
	2012	244.6	0.0	0.0	0.1	0.0	0.0	5.5	40.5	40.6	6.9	6.5
South-Eastern Asia - Asie du Sud-Est	*1990*	*35 050.0*	*2.8*	*7.9*	*6.9*	*6.5*	*4.9*	*19.0*	*50.2*	*19.9*	*4.1*	*6.7*
	2000	*62 945.1*	*7.7*	*7.9*	*9.4*	*8.0*	*6.9*	*34.5*	*34.5*	*15.2*	*8.1*	*7.8*
	2010	*101 728.6*	*9.4*	*5.1*	*12.8*	*7.7*	*10.0*	*41.5*	*23.0*	*13.6*	*12.8*	*9.1*
	2012	*125 886.6*	*10.4*	*5.4*	*12.8*	*7.8*	*10.7*	*41.8*	*26.5*	*10.8*	*12.3*	*8.5*
Brunei Darussalam - Brunéi Darussalam	1990	346.0	..	..	0.0	..	0.7	..	..	0.3	..	99.7
	2000	349.6	0.0	..	0.0	..	0.5	0.1	..	0.7	..	99.2
	2010	448.9	0.0	0.0	0.0	..	0.5	0.1	4.5	0.7	..	94.6
	2012	420.9	0.0	..	0.0	..	0.4	1.6	..	0.8	..	97.6
Cambodia - Cambodge	1990	4.0	..	..	0.0	..	0.0	..	..	25.0	..	75.0
	2010	2 517.0	0.0	0.1	1.8	0.0	0.1	2.6	14.6	78.2	0.6	4.0
	2012	1 739.7	0.0	0.0	1.3	0.0	0.1	1.4	13.3	81.5	0.8	3.1
Indonesia (...2002) - Indonésie (...2002)	1990	2 742.0	0.4	0.1	1.2	0.3	0.5	35.2	7.7	45.4	2.7	9.0
	2000	4 153.7	0.5	0.2	1.8	0.1	0.5	32.1	14.8	43.5	1.4	8.2
Indonesia - Indonésie	2010	10 470.7	0.9	0.5	2.7	0.5	0.8	36.9	19.9	28.0	7.9	7.3
	2012	13 512.0	1.0	0.4	3.1	0.6	1.5	36.4	20.4	24.1	8.1	11.1
Lao People's Dem. Rep. - Rép. dém. populaire lao	2010	1.6	..	..	0.0	..	..	..	..	100.0	..	..
	2012	21.6	..	0.0	0.0	..	..	..	92.8	7.2	..	..
Malaysia - Malaisie	1990	2 364.0	0.1	0.3	0.7	1.0	1.1	12.0	26.9	29.6	9.8	21.8
	2000	7 577.5	0.6	1.0	0.8	1.3	2.3	21.6	35.3	11.4	10.5	21.3
	2010	10 224.8	1.2	0.1	0.5	0.5	3.3	51.1	4.9	5.8	8.4	29.8
	2012	10 894.9	1.2	0.1	0.4	0.4	3.2	55.8	3.3	4.3	7.3	29.3
Myanmar	1990	907.0	0.0	0.3	0.2	..	0.1	0.4	72.5	23.5	..	3.5
	2000	792.3	0.0	0.2	0.2	0.0	0.0	0.6	63.7	30.8	3.2	1.7
	2010	210.1	0.0	0.0	0.2	..	0.0	2.2	11.3	79.9	..	6.6
	2012	198.2	0.0	..	0.2	..	0.0	3.4	..	89.7	..	7.0
Philippines	1990	15 468.0	0.3	5.5	2.1	0.3	0.3	5.0	79.9	13.7	0.4	1.1
	2000	11 112.0	0.1	3.0	2.0	0.2	0.5	2.1	74.7	18.5	1.4	3.2
	2010	7 032.8	0.2	0.8	1.6	0.2	0.4	11.1	54.6	24.1	5.0	5.2
	2012	6 694.1	0.2	0.6	1.6	0.2	0.4	11.9	51.4	25.6	5.7	5.3
Singapore - Singapour	1990	11 888.0	1.9	1.7	1.7	4.6	2.1	37.6	31.2	14.2	8.6	8.4
	2000	34 635.5	6.2	3.2	2.6	6.1	2.6	50.9	25.0	7.5	11.2	5.4
	2010	61 660.4	6.6	3.2	2.7	6.2	4.4	48.3	23.4	4.7	17.0	6.6
	2012	82 083.5	7.3	3.8	3.4	6.5	4.8	45.4	28.8	4.4	15.6	5.8
Thailand - Thaïlande	1990	805.0	0.1	0.0	0.6	0.2	0.1	16.0	2.1	70.2	6.2	5.5
	2000	3 068.4	0.2	0.3	1.3	0.3	0.2	22.4	25.6	42.7	5.2	4.1
	2010	3 746.8	0.2	0.2	1.2	0.2	0.2	27.7	23.6	34.7	8.4	5.7
	2012	4 249.1	0.4	0.2	0.7	0.1	0.3	47.3	22.7	16.4	7.0	6.6
Timor-Leste	2010	0.3	..	..	..	..	0.0	..	..	..	..	100.0
	2012	0.3	..	..	..	..	0.0	..	..	..	..	100.0

For sources and notes, see end of table.

Pour les sources et les notes, se reporter à la fin du tableau.

5.3 World merchant fleet by flag of registration and type of ship of countries and geographical regions

5.3 Flotte marchande mondiale par pavillons d'immatriculation et par types de navires des pays et des régions géographiques

Region, country or territory / Régions pays ou territoires	Year / Année	Total fleet (thousands of DWT) / Flotte totale (milliers de TPL) (1)	As percentage of world total fleet / En pourcentage de la flotte mondiale					As percentage of the country or region total fleet / En pourcentage de la flotte totale du pays ou de la région				
			Oil tankers / Pétroliers	Bulk carriers / Vraquiers	General cargo / Navires de charge classique (2)	Container ships / Porte-conteneurs	Other types / Autres navires	Oil tankers / Pétroliers	Bulk carriers / Vraquiers	General cargo / Navires de charge classique (2)	Container ships / Porte-conteneurs	Other types / Autres navires
Viet Nam	1990	526.0	0.0	0.0	0.4	..	0.0	6.5	4.6	85.9	..	3.0
	2000	1 256.1	0.1	0.1	0.7	0.0	0.3	13.5	12.0	54.3	1.3	18.9
	2010	5 415.2	0.3	0.3	2.1	0.1	0.3	27.3	22.6	42.2	3.0	4.8
	2012	6 072.4	0.3	0.3	2.1	0.1	0.1	25.1	32.4	37.3	2.7	2.4
Western Asia - Asie occidentale	*1990*	*16 320.0*	*3.5*	*1.4*	*3.5*	*2.4*	*1.9*	*50.2*	*19.0*	*21.8*	*3.3*	*5.7*
	2000	*20 161.2*	*2.1*	*2.8*	*4.1*	*1.9*	*1.7*	*30.1*	*37.5*	*20.5*	*5.9*	*6.0*
	2010	*18 540.3*	*1.8*	*0.8*	*2.7*	*1.3*	*1.6*	*44.0*	*20.8*	*15.9*	*11.6*	*7.8*
	2012	*19 592.1*	*1.6*	*0.8*	*2.3*	*1.1*	*1.4*	*42.5*	*27.0*	*12.5*	*10.7*	*7.3*
Bahrain - Bahreïn	1990	65.0	0.0	0.0	0.0	..	0.0	3.1	30.8	41.5	..	24.6
	2000	369.8	0.0	0.0	0.1	0.2	0.0	26.2	11.9	26.5	27.0	8.3
	2010	613.4	0.0	0.0	0.0	0.2	0.1	25.2	13.9	0.3	44.2	16.4
	2012	630.2	0.0	0.0	0.0	0.1	0.1	30.5	7.0	0.1	43.0	19.4
Iraq	1990	1 813.0	0.7	..	0.1	..	0.3	85.6	..	7.5	..	6.9
	2000	834.7	0.2	..	0.1	..	0.1	79.0	..	12.6	..	8.4
	2010	180.1	0.0	..	0.1	..	0.1	37.7	..	30.2	..	32.1
	2012	29.3	0.0	..	..	..	0.0	91.7	..	..	..	8.3
Jordan - Jordanie	1990	48.0	..	0.0	..	..	0.0	..	91.7	..	..	8.3
	2000	59.3	..	0.0	0.0	0.0	0.0	..	56.3	32.1	11.2	0.4
	2010	369.3	0.1	..	0.1	..	0.0	78.5	..	16.1	..	5.4
	2012	343.7	0.1	..	0.0	..	0.0	84.4	..	13.0	..	2.6
Kuwait - Koweït	1990	2 887.0	0.8	..	0.5	0.7	0.6	65.9	..	18.8	5.1	10.2
	2000	3 884.4	1.0	0.0	0.3	0.4	0.5	76.2	0.7	7.9	5.8	9.4
	2010	3 856.2	0.7	0.0	0.1	0.2	0.3	83.4	1.0	2.0	7.6	6.0
	2012	3 976.0	0.6	0.0	0.1	0.1	0.2	82.8	2.0	1.9	7.3	6.0
Lebanon - Liban	1990	593.0	0.0	0.1	0.4	0.0	0.0	3.9	26.3	68.1	0.5	1.2
	2000	483.2	0.0	0.1	0.2	0.0	0.0	0.3	52.5	44.7	1.5	1.0
	2010	158.6	0.0	0.0	0.1	..	0.0	0.9	33.9	63.2	..	2.0
	2012	143.1	0.0	0.0	0.1	..	0.0	0.6	25.2	72.1	..	2.2
Oman	1990	13.0	..	..	0.0	..	0.0	..	..	53.8	..	46.2
	2000	10.9	0.0	..	0.0	..	0.0	4.2	..	27.5	..	68.2
	2010	14.3	0.0	..	0.0	..	0.0	15.5	..	11.5	..	73.0
	2012	16.6	0.0	..	0.0	..	0.0	13.3	..	17.1	..	69.6
Qatar	1990	459.0	0.1	..	0.2	0.4	0.0	43.8	..	32.9	20.0	3.3
	2000	1 154.0	0.2	0.1	0.2	0.3	0.0	40.4	23.4	17.5	17.1	1.5
	2010	1 363.4	0.1	0.0	0.0	0.2	0.3	40.0	8.5	0.0	29.6	21.8
	2012	1 147.1	0.1	0.0	0.0	0.2	0.3	34.2	10.1	0.0	28.9	26.8
Saudi Arabia - Arabie saoudite	1990	3 535.0	1.0	0.1	0.7	0.3	0.5	63.4	8.8	18.6	2.1	7.0
	2000	1 443.0	0.1	..	0.6	0.3	0.3	28.4	..	39.6	15.0	17.1
	2010	2 319.3	0.3	..	0.3	0.1	0.3	65.1	..	12.7	9.5	12.6
	2012	2 332.9	0.3	..	0.3	0.1	0.2	70.5	..	11.5	7.9	10.0
Syrian Arab Republic - République arabe syrienne	1990	102.0	..	..	0.1	..	0.0	..	..	97.1	..	2.9
	2000	679.4	..	0.0	0.6	..	0.0	..	6.5	92.1	..	1.4
	2010	344.2	..	0.0	0.2	0.0	0.0	..	22.4	74.9	2.5	0.3
	2012	129.4	..	0.0	0.1	..	0.0	..	49.6	50.1	..	0.2
Turkey - Turquie	1990	5 477.0	0.6	1.1	1.3	..	0.2	27.0	46.3	24.6	..	2.2
	2000	10 174.2	0.4	2.5	1.7	0.3	0.4	10.4	67.3	17.2	2.1	3.0
	2010	7 878.0	0.4	0.7	1.9	0.3	0.3	21.5	42.6	25.5	7.3	3.1
	2012	9 535.2	0.4	0.8	1.7	0.4	0.3	19.3	51.1	19.0	7.5	3.1
United Arab Emirates - Émirats arabes unis	1990	1 316.0	0.3	0.0	0.2	1.0	0.2	59.4	2.9	14.6	16.6	6.5
	2000	1 042.5	0.1	0.0	0.2	0.4	0.2	39.3	3.5	22.6	21.8	12.8
	2010	1 412.3	0.1	0.0	0.1	0.2	0.2	46.0	8.5	5.8	26.8	12.9
	2012	1 273.0	0.1	0.0	0.1	0.2	0.2	48.8	5.6	5.9	24.1	15.6
Yemen - Yémen	1990	12.0	0.0	..	0.0	..	0.0	25.0	..	33.3	..	41.7
	2000	25.8	0.0	..	0.0	..	0.0	12.3	..	11.9	..	75.8
	2010	31.2	0.0	..	0.0	..	0.0	69.3	..	10.9	..	19.9
	2012	35.7	0.0	..	0.0	..	0.0	78.0	..	4.7	..	17.3

For sources and notes, see end of table.

Pour les sources et les notes, se reporter à la fin du tableau.

5.3 World merchant fleet by flag of registration and type of ship of countries and geographical regions

5.3 Flotte marchande mondiale par pavillons d'immatriculation et par types de navires des pays et des régions géographiques

Region, country or territory Régions pays ou territoires	Year Année	Total fleet (thousands of DWT) Flotte totale (milliers de TPL) (1)	As percentage of world total fleet En pourcentage de la flotte mondiale					As percentage of the country or region total fleet En pourcentage de la flotte totale du pays ou de la région				
			Oil tankers Pétroliers	Bulk carriers Vraquiers	General cargo Navires de charge classique (2)	Container ships Porte-conteneurs	Other types Autres navires	Oil tankers Pétroliers	Bulk carriers Vraquiers	General cargo Navires de charge classique (2)	Container ships Porte-conteneurs	Other types Autres navires
Developing economies: Oceania - Économies en développement : Océanie (3)	1990	1 814.0	0.1	0.4	0.4	0.2	0.3	15.5	48.5	24.9	2.8	8.4
	2000	1 931.6	0.0	0.3	0.5	0.1	0.7	1.2	44.4	25.4	1.8	27.2
	2010	83 461.2	9.2	5.7	2.2	3.2	8.9	49.6	31.2	2.9	6.4	9.9
	2012	128 472.9	11.7	7.6	2.4	4.3	10.6	46.2	37.0	2.0	6.6	8.3
Fiji - Fidji	1990	64.0	0.0	..	0.0	..	0.0	10.9	..	71.9	..	17.2
	2000	24.4	0.0	..	0.0	..	0.0	14.8	..	23.6	..	61.6
	2010	17.0	..	..	0.0	..	0.0	..	..	40.0	..	60.0
	2012	16.2	..	..	0.0	..	0.0	..	..	31.1	..	68.9
French Polynesia - Polynésie française	2010	1.1	..	..	0.0	..	..	..	..	100.0	..	..
Kiribati	1990	3.0	..	..	0.0	..	..	..	..	100.0	..	..
	2000	4.1	..	..	0.0	..	0.0	..	..	84.0	..	16.0
	2010	828.8	0.0	0.1	0.3	..	0.1	19.7	41.5	33.3	..	5.6
	2012	469.2	0.0	0.0	0.2	..	0.0	12.2	25.7	51.8	..	10.3
Marshall Islands - Îles Marshall (4)	2010	77 827.4	8.9	5.2	1.4	3.1	8.0	51.3	30.3	2.0	6.8	9.5
	2012	122 856.9	11.4	7.3	1.7	4.3	9.5	47.0	37.0	1.4	6.9	7.7
Micronesia (Federated States of) - Micronésie (États fédérés de)	2010	9.8	..	0.0	0.0	..	0.0	..	3.8	64.8	..	31.5
	2012	11.3	..	0.0	0.0	..	0.0	..	3.3	56.6	..	40.1
Nauru	1990	45.0	..	0.0	0.0	..	0.0	..	60.0	42.2	..	2.2
New Caledonia - Nouvelle-Calédonie	2010	2.7	..	..	0.0	..	..	..	..	100.0	..	..
Papua New Guinea - Papouasie-Nouvelle-Guinée	1990	42.0	0.0	0.0	0.0	..	0.0	4.8	11.9	57.1	..	26.2
	2000	70.9	0.0	..	0.1	..	0.0	3.9	..	77.8	..	18.4
	2010	111.1	0.0	0.0	0.1	..	0.0	2.5	5.7	80.8	..	11.0
	2012	140.7	0.0	0.0	0.1	..	0.0	4.2	17.0	66.2	..	12.6
Samoa	1990	35.0	..	..	0.0	..	0.0	..	..	97.1	..	2.9
	2010	9.8	..	..	0.0	..	0.0	..	..	93.9	..	6.1
	2012	10.1	..	..	0.0	..	0.0	..	..	91.9	..	8.1
Solomon Islands - Îles Salomon	1990	7.0	..	..	0.0	..	0.0	..	..	71.4	..	28.6
	2000	6.9	..	..	0.0	..	0.0	..	..	35.9	..	64.1
	2010	8.0	..	..	0.0	..	0.0	..	..	24.9	..	75.1
	2012	6.6	..	..	0.0	..	0.0	..	..	23.3	..	76.7
Tonga	1990	43.0	..	..	0.0	0.1	0.0	..	..	27.9	69.8	2.3
	2000	29.3	..	..	0.0	..	0.0	..	..	63.1	..	36.9
	2010	77.5	0.0	0.0	0.1	..	0.0	2.1	8.6	77.5	..	11.8
	2012	35.4	0.0	..	0.0	..	0.0	4.1	..	84.6	..	11.2
Tuvalu	1990	1.0	..	..	0.0	..	..	..	..	100.0	..	..
	2000	68.4	..	..	0.0	..	0.1	..	..	37.6	..	62.4
	2010	1 884.1	0.3	0.1	0.1	0.0	0.1	67.3	19.2	7.8	0.8	4.9
	2012	1 868.5	0.3	0.0	0.1	0.0	0.1	77.3	6.7	6.0	2.0	8.0
Vanuatu	1990	1 574.0	0.1	0.4	0.3	0.1	0.3	17.3	53.9	19.5	1.3	8.0
	2000	1 727.7	0.0	0.3	0.4	0.1	0.6	1.0	49.7	21.9	2.0	25.4
	2010	2 683.7	..	0.4	0.2	0.0	0.7	..	65.2	8.9	1.1	24.9
	2012	3 058.1	..	0.3	0.2	0.0	0.9	..	61.5	7.6	0.9	30.0
Transition economies - Économies en transition	1990	35 090.0	2.9	4.4	12.4	3.2	11.0	19.2	28.4	35.4	2.0	15.0
	2000	13 598.3	0.9	0.9	5.4	0.7	3.8	18.5	18.0	40.2	3.4	19.9
	2010	12 777.5	0.8	0.4	4.5	0.1	2.1	29.6	15.7	38.5	1.3	14.8
	2012	12 574.0	0.8	0.3	4.2	0.1	1.9	31.9	16.3	35.8	1.3	14.7
Albania - Albanie	1990	63.0	..	..	0.1	..	..	..	..	100.0	..	..
	2000	20.1	..	..	0.0	..	0.0	..	..	93.8	..	6.2
	2010	96.8	..	..	0.1	..	0.0	..	..	98.5	..	1.5
	2012	62.6	..	..	0.1	..	0.0	..	..	99.7	..	0.3
Azerbaijan - Azerbaïdjan	2000	507.5	0.1	..	0.1	..	0.2	45.8	..	20.2	..	33.9
	2010	662.6	0.1	..	0.1	..	0.2	53.3	..	18.4	..	28.3
	2012	670.4	0.1	..	0.1	..	0.2	53.2	..	19.9	..	26.9
Croatia - Croatie	2000	1 227.7	0.0	0.3	0.2	0.2	0.0	1.1	70.7	17.7	8.0	2.5
	2010	2 277.1	0.3	0.2	0.0	..	0.0	54.4	41.6	2.4	..	1.6
	2012	2 570.7	0.3	0.2	0.0	..	0.0	50.2	47.2	1.3	..	1.3

For sources and notes, see end of table.

Pour les sources et les notes, se reporter à la fin du tableau.

5.3 World merchant fleet by flag of registration and type of ship of countries and geographical regions

5.3 Flotte marchande mondiale par pavillons d'immatriculation et par types de navires des pays et des régions géographiques

Region, country or territory / Régions pays ou territoires	Year / Année	Total fleet (thousands of DWT) / Flotte totale (milliers de TPL) (1)	As percentage of world total fleet / En pourcentage de la flotte mondiale					As percentage of the country or region total fleet / En pourcentage de la flotte totale du pays ou de la région				
			Oil tankers / Pétroliers	Bulk carriers / Vraquiers	General cargo / Navires de charge classique (2)	Container ships / Porte-conteneurs	Other types / Autres navires	Oil tankers / Pétroliers	Bulk carriers / Vraquiers	General cargo / Navires de charge classique (2)	Container ships / Porte-conteneurs	Other types / Autres navires
Georgia - Géorgie	2000	183.8	0.0	0.0	0.0	..	0.0	65.3	0.1	24.8	..	9.8
	2010	935.2	0.0	0.0	0.6	0.0	0.0	4.0	22.1	68.2	1.3	4.5
	2012	331.2	0.0	0.0	0.2	0.0	0.0	10.2	21.2	59.2	3.5	5.9
Kazakhstan	2000	4.7	..	..	0.0	..	0.0	..	..	16.6	..	83.4
	2010	91.3	0.0	..	0.0	..	0.0	69.4	..	2.2	..	28.4
	2012	144.6	0.0	..	0.0	..	0.0	71.4	..	1.3	..	27.2
Montenegro - Monténégro	2010	6.1	..	..	0.0	..	0.0	..	..	87.7	..	12.3
	2012	37.5	..	0.0	0.0	..	0.0	..	93.5	4.7	..	1.8
Republic of Moldova - République de Moldova	2010	459.8	0.0	0.0	0.3	0.0	0.0	7.1	25.9	64.3	1.2	1.4
	2012	584.1	0.0	0.0	0.4	..	0.0	5.3	19.2	69.9	...	5.6
Russian Federation - Fédération de Russie	2000	9 950.4	0.7	0.5	4.1	0.5	2.9	20.6	13.2	42.0	3.2	21.0
	2010	7 283.0	0.4	0.1	2.9	0.1	1.5	27.2	8.6	43.5	2.1	18.6
	2012	7 413.2	0.4	0.1	3.1	0.1	1.3	28.6	7.6	44.0	2.0	17.8
SFR of Yugoslavia - RSF de Yougoslavie	1990	5 815.0	0.2	1.5	1.8	0.5	0.1	9.1	57.2	30.9	2.0	0.8
Turkmenistan - Turkménistan	2000	36.5	0.0	0.0	0.0	..	0.0	9.3	18.3	41.6	..	30.8
	2010	61.8	0.0	..	0.0	..	0.0	36.4	..	25.1	..	38.5
	2012	80.9	0.0	..	0.0	..	0.0	42.0	..	19.1	..	38.8
Ukraine	2000	1 667.5	0.0	0.1	0.9	0.1	0.5	5.4	15.9	52.8	2.7	23.1
	2010	903.9	0.0	0.0	0.5	..	0.2	5.8	12.3	58.2	..	23.6
	2012	678.8	0.0	0.0	0.4	..	0.2	6.6	8.3	57.2	..	27.9
USSR - URSS	1990	29 212.0	2.6	3.0	10.5	2.7	10.9	21.2	22.7	36.2	2.1	17.9
Developed economies: America - Économies développées : Amérique (3)	**1990**	**31 335.0**	**9.0**	**0.9**	**2.0**	**13.0**	**6.7**	**67.6**	**6.3**	**6.5**	**9.3**	**10.2**
	2000	**37 163.0**	**7.3**	**2.4**	**2.0**	**6.8**	**5.1**	**55.4**	**17.8**	**5.4**	**11.7**	**9.7**
	2010	**26 299.5**	**1.6**	**1.6**	**1.1**	**2.7**	**6.6**	**27.5**	**27.8**	**4.5**	**17.2**	**23.1**
	2012	**27 127.6**	**1.4**	**1.2**	**1.1**	**2.2**	**7.0**	**26.4**	**27.6**	**4.2**	**15.9**	**25.8**
Bermuda - Bermudes	1990	7 625.0	2.8	0.1	0.2	0.1	1.0	86.7	3.6	2.8	0.4	6.4
	2000	10 468.5	1.9	1.3	0.3	0.9	0.8	51.0	35.3	3.0	5.3	5.4
	2010	10 106.6	0.5	0.7	0.1	0.4	4.0	22.3	33.0	1.1	7.0	36.5
	2012	11 598.4	0.5	0.6	0.1	0.3	4.6	23.9	30.1	1.0	5.4	39.6
Canada	1990	756.0	0.1	0.2	0.0	0.0	0.1	34.5	53.2	6.3	0.9	5.0
	2000	1 018.4	0.1	0.1	0.1	0.0	0.5	40.1	16.0	11.6	0.2	32.2
	2010	3 401.1	0.2	0.4	0.1	0.0	0.6	29.6	50.8	2.9	0.5	16.2
	2012	3 532.4	0.2	0.3	0.1	0.0	0.5	26.1	54.2	3.8	0.5	15.4
United States - États-Unis (5)	1990	22 954.0	6.1	0.6	1.8	12.8	5.6	62.4	5.7	7.8	12.5	11.7
	2000	25 676.0	5.2	1.0	1.6	5.9	3.8	57.8	10.8	6.2	14.7	10.5
	2010	12 791.8	0.9	0.5	0.9	2.2	2.0	31.1	17.5	7.6	29.6	14.4
	2012	11 996.8	0.7	0.3	0.8	1.9	1.9	29.0	17.3	7.5	30.7	15.5
Developed economies: Asia - Économies développées : Asie	**1990**	**42 943.0**	**6.1**	**7.7**	**6.4**	**7.7**	**6.7**	**33.2**	**40.3**	**15.0**	**4.0**	**7.5**
	2000	**23 554.9**	**3.2**	**2.4**	**2.7**	**2.5**	**5.3**	**38.2**	**27.8**	**11.4**	**6.6**	**16.0**
	2010	**18 193.3**	**1.1**	**1.4**	**2.3**	**0.4**	**3.8**	**27.7**	**36.3**	**13.7**	**3.3**	**19.0**
	2012	**23 881.6**	**1.3**	**1.8**	**2.4**	**0.2**	**2.9**	**27.5**	**47.9**	**10.5**	**1.8**	**12.3**
Israel - Israël	1990	586.0	0.0	0.0	0.1	1.7	0.0	0.2	8.9	24.7	65.9	0.3
	2000	832.1	0.0	..	0.0	1.3	0.0	0.3	..	0.9	98.3	0.5
	2010	486.1	0.0	..	0.0	0.3	0.0	1.1	..	1.1	96.8	1.0
	2012	309.4	0.0	..	0.0	0.1	0.0	1.8	..	0.9	95.9	1.5
Japan - Japon	1990	42 357.0	6.1	7.7	6.3	6.0	6.7	33.7	40.7	14.8	3.2	7.6
	2000	22 722.9	3.2	2.4	2.6	1.2	5.3	39.6	28.8	11.8	3.3	16.5
	2010	17 707.2	1.1	1.4	2.3	0.1	3.8	28.4	37.3	14.1	0.7	19.5
	2012	23 572.3	1.3	1.8	2.4	0.1	2.9	27.8	48.5	10.7	0.5	12.4
Developed economies: Europe - Économies développées : Europe	**1990**	**182 418.0**	**29.4**	**29.6**	**24.5**	**32.4**	**31.5**	**38.0**	**36.3**	**13.5**	**4.0**	**8.2**
	2000	**228 742.9**	**31.9**	**25.3**	**26.2**	**31.6**	**31.4**	**39.4**	**30.4**	**11.6**	**8.8**	**9.8**
	2010	**295 627.9**	**27.0**	**18.6**	**19.7**	**28.4**	**21.7**	**41.0**	**28.7**	**7.2**	**16.3**	**6.8**
	2012	**328 243.2**	**25.9**	**16.8**	**19.5**	**25.8**	**20.5**	**40.1**	**31.8**	**6.3**	**15.6**	**6.2**
Austria - Autriche	1990	355.0	..	0.1	0.1	..	..	..	69.3	30.7	..	..
	2000	100.3	..	..	0.1	..	..	..	..	100.0	..	..
	2010	11.7	..	..	0.0	..	..	..	..	100.0	..	..

For sources and notes, see end of table.

Pour les sources et les notes, se reporter à la fin du tableau.

5.3 World merchant fleet by flag of registration and type of ship of countries and geographical regions

5.3 Flotte marchande mondiale par pavillons d'immatriculation et par types de navires des pays et des régions géographiques

Region, country or territory / Régions pays ou territoires	Year / Année	Total fleet (thousands of DWT) / Flotte totale (milliers de TPL) (1)	As percentage of world total fleet / En pourcentage de la flotte mondiale					As percentage of the country or region total fleet / En pourcentage de la flotte totale du pays ou de la région				
			Oil tankers / Pétroliers	Bulk carriers / Vraquiers	General cargo / Navires de charge classique (2)	Container ships / Porte-conteneurs	Other types / Autres navires	Oil tankers / Pétroliers	Bulk carriers / Vraquiers	General cargo / Navires de charge classique (2)	Container ships / Porte-conteneurs	Other types / Autres navires
Belgium - Belgique	1990	3 282.0	0.1	0.9	0.1	1.0	1.5	6.3	62.5	3.4	6.6	21.2
	2000	149.5	0.0	..	0.0	..	0.2	4.5	..	0.4	..	95.1
	2010	6 575.1	0.5	0.6	0.1	0.1	1.5	33.0	41.5	2.3	2.0	21.2
	2012	6 662.7	0.3	0.5	0.1	0.0	1.6	24.5	47.8	2.3	1.4	24.0
Bulgaria - Bulgarie	1990	1 956.0	0.2	0.4	0.4	0.1	0.2	23.6	49.5	22.3	0.9	3.7
	2000	1 501.6	0.1	0.3	0.3	0.1	0.1	18.0	54.1	20.8	4.5	2.7
	2010	696.8	0.0	0.1	0.1	0.0	0.0	3.7	66.6	16.8	9.2	3.8
	2012	440.1	0.0	0.0	0.1	..	0.0	2.2	67.5	27.9	..	2.4
Cyprus - Chypre	1990	32 699.0	4.7	7.1	4.9	1.9	0.9	33.9	48.5	14.9	1.3	1.3
	2000	36 669.4	2.4	7.2	5.7	4.6	1.7	18.8	54.1	15.9	7.9	3.4
	2010	31 305.2	2.3	3.0	1.6	2.9	0.9	32.4	43.7	5.6	15.6	2.7
	2012	32 986.5	1.9	2.6	1.5	2.4	0.9	28.7	49.4	4.9	14.3	2.8
Czechoslovakia - Tchécoslovaquie	1990	279.0	..	0.1	0.1	..	0.0	..	54.8	44.8	..	0.4
Denmark - Danemark	1990	6 926.0	1.2	0.3	0.8	5.5	2.8	42.0	8.7	12.0	17.7	19.6
	2000	7 420.8	0.4	0.3	0.8	5.0	2.0	16.1	11.8	10.8	42.5	18.8
	2010	13 813.8	1.2	0.1	0.3	4.0	1.1	38.1	3.7	2.4	48.5	7.2
	2012	14 186.9	1.0	0.1	0.2	3.7	0.8	37.3	3.0	1.9	52.3	5.6
Estonia - Estonie	2000	363.1	0.0	0.0	0.2	..	0.1	3.7	27.8	51.9	..	16.7
	2010	98.7	0.0	..	0.0	..	0.1	12.9	..	15.6	..	71.6
	2012	85.9	0.0	..	0.0	..	0.1	14.8	..	17.5	..	67.7
Finland - Finlande	1990	838.0	0.1	0.1	0.3	..	0.5	21.4	14.8	35.2	..	28.6
	2000	1 239.5	0.2	0.0	0.4	..	0.3	41.0	10.8	31.2	..	17.0
	2010	1 171.3	0.1	0.0	0.4	0.0	0.1	52.0	0.3	34.2	3.2	10.3
	2012	1 257.8	0.1	0.0	0.4	0.0	0.1	48.4	6.4	32.4	2.9	9.8
France	1990	6 653.0	1.6	0.5	0.6	2.6	1.1	57.3	16.3	9.4	8.8	8.2
	2000	7 292.5	1.6	0.4	0.4	0.8	1.4	60.8	14.0	4.9	7.1	13.2
	2010	8 822.3	1.3	0.1	0.1	1.1	1.0	64.0	3.9	1.0	20.3	10.7
	2012	8 890.1	1.1	0.1	0.1	1.1	0.9	60.4	3.9	1.0	24.2	10.6
Germany - Allemagne	1990	6 778.0	0.1	0.5	2.5	9.1	2.0	4.6	14.9	36.9	29.9	13.8
	2000	7 788.3	0.0	0.0	1.0	9.9	0.5	0.1	0.1	13.6	81.2	4.9
	2010	17 570.2	0.1	0.2	0.5	9.0	0.4	3.2	4.7	3.1	86.9	2.1
	2012	17 482.0	0.1	0.1	0.4	7.8	0.4	3.0	4.3	2.2	88.3	2.2
Gibraltar	1990	5 026.0	1.7	0.3	0.2	..	0.1	80.7	14.0	3.9	..	1.4
	2000	728.5	0.2	0.0	0.0	0.1	0.1	76.0	3.7	4.9	8.6	6.8
Greece - Grèce	1990	38 465.0	6.8	8.2	2.9	1.0	2.1	41.6	47.7	7.5	0.6	2.6
	2000	42 532.1	8.9	5.1	0.9	2.2	1.8	58.9	32.7	2.1	3.3	3.0
	2010	67 629.2	9.4	4.7	0.3	1.4	1.2	62.6	31.6	0.5	3.6	1.7
	2012	72 558.2	8.8	3.8	0.3	1.3	1.1	61.9	32.8	0.4	3.4	1.5
Hungary - Hongrie	1990	108.0	..	..	0.1	..	..	..	..	100.0	..	..
	2000	14.9	..	..	0.0	..	..	..	..	100.0	..	..
Iceland - Islande	1990	155.0	0.0	0.0	0.1	..	0.1	0.6	12.3	49.7	..	37.4
	2000	83.6	0.0	0.0	0.0	0.0	0.1	3.2	0.8	3.5	14.8	77.7
	2010	69.4	0.0	0.0	0.0	..	0.1	0.7	0.9	1.0	..	97.4
	2012	75.8	0.0	0.0	0.0	..	0.1	0.6	0.9	0.9	..	97.6
Ireland - Irlande	1990	178.0	0.0	..	0.1	0.1	0.1	6.2	..	55.1	14.0	24.7
	2000	154.4	0.0	0.0	0.1	0.0	0.0	0.2	7.9	65.5	4.4	22.0
	2010	196.2	0.0	..	0.1	0.0	0.0	9.4	..	73.9	3.8	12.9
	2012	262.8	0.0	..	0.2	0.0	0.0	7.0	..	80.7	2.8	9.4
Italy - Italie (6)	1990	11 524.0	1.8	1.9	1.2	1.5	2.9	37.7	36.5	10.7	2.9	12.2
	2000	9 768.8	1.0	1.3	0.9	1.0	2.7	28.7	35.8	9.5	6.7	19.4
	2010	17 276.0	1.8	1.1	1.4	0.6	1.6	47.3	29.0	8.8	6.3	8.7
	2012	21 763.4	1.8	1.4	1.6	0.5	1.6	40.9	39.7	7.8	4.4	7.3
Latvia - Lettonie	2000	101.5	0.0	..	0.0	..	0.1	15.1	..	47.0	..	37.9
	2010	180.3	0.0	..	0.0	..	0.1	58.9	..	12.5	..	28.6
	2012	78.5	0.0	..	0.0	..	0.0	15.6	..	24.0	..	60.4
Lithuania - Lituanie	2000	414.6	0.0	0.1	0.2	..	0.1	1.8	38.6	45.8	..	13.8
	2010	364.2	0.0	..	0.3	0.0	0.1	0.4	..	75.2	3.8	20.6
	2012	325.0	..	..	0.2	0.0	0.1	..	..	73.2	4.2	22.6

For sources and notes, see end of table.

Pour les sources et les notes, se reporter à la fin du tableau.

5.3 World merchant fleet by flag of registration and type of ship of countries and geographical regions

5.3 Flotte marchande mondiale par pavillons d'immatriculation et par types de navires des pays et des régions géographiques

Region, country or territory / Régions pays ou territoires	Year / Année	Total fleet (thousands of DWT) / Flotte totale (milliers de TPL) (1)	As percentage of world total fleet / En pourcentage de la flotte mondiale					As percentage of the country or region total fleet / En pourcentage de la flotte totale du pays ou de la région				
			Oil tankers / Pétroliers	Bulk carriers / Vraquiers	General cargo / Navires de charge classique (2)	Container ships / Porte-conteneurs	Other types / Autres navires	Oil tankers / Pétroliers	Bulk carriers / Vraquiers	General cargo / Navires de charge classique (2)	Container ships / Porte-conteneurs	Other types / Autres navires
Luxembourg	1990	6.0	0.0	..	..	..	0.0	50.0	..	..	..	50.0
	2000	1 959.6	0.4	0.1	0.1	0.0	1.0	51.0	8.8	2.9	1.2	36.1
	2010	1 099.8	0.1	0.0	0.1	0.1	0.4	23.2	17.5	10.2	17.1	32.0
	2012	1 231.0	0.1	0.0	0.1	0.0	0.6	22.6	6.9	12.8	8.0	49.8
Malta - Malte	1990	5 691.0	1.1	0.9	1.1	0.0	0.3	43.5	35.2	19.0	0.1	2.2
	2000	46 749.4	7.8	6.2	5.3	1.5	1.7	47.4	36.5	11.5	2.0	2.6
	2010	56 156.1	4.6	6.1	3.4	1.7	1.2	36.8	49.4	6.6	5.1	2.0
	2012	71 286.9	5.5	5.4	3.1	2.7	1.4	39.0	47.1	4.6	7.4	1.9
Netherlands - Pays-Bas	1990	4 557.0	0.2	0.2	1.8	2.3	2.4	12.6	12.0	38.7	11.2	25.6
	2000	6 607.3	0.1	0.0	2.8	2.8	2.3	4.0	1.6	42.4	27.0	25.0
	2010	7 252.5	0.1	0.0	3.3	1.1	1.2	9.0	0.7	49.7	25.6	15.0
	2012	8 279.0	0.1	0.1	4.0	0.6	1.2	8.1	9.7	52.0	15.2	15.0
Norway - Norvège	1990	26 568.0	5.5	3.5	1.7	0.3	8.3	48.9	29.6	6.3	0.2	14.9
	2000	35 388.0	6.2	2.6	3.8	0.2	9.8	49.2	19.9	10.8	0.3	19.7
	2010	20 811.2	2.1	0.9	3.1	0.0	4.4	45.0	19.4	15.9	0.0	19.6
	2012	19 773.8	1.7	0.7	2.7	..	4.1	43.7	21.3	14.4	..	20.6
Poland - Pologne	1990	4 490.0	0.1	1.2	1.4	0.2	0.5	4.9	57.6	31.6	1.0	4.9
	2000	1 855.4	0.0	0.6	0.1	..	0.2	0.4	88.8	3.8	..	6.9
	2010	130.9	0.0	..	0.0	..	0.1	5.7	..	22.7	..	71.6
	2012	73.2	0.0	..	0.0	..	0.0	9.2	..	26.9	..	63.9
Portugal	1990	1 102.0	0.3	0.1	0.1	0.0	0.2	54.8	26.3	9.5	0.9	8.4
	2000	1 630.0	0.3	0.1	0.4	0.1	0.3	44.9	17.6	23.7	2.5	11.3
	2010	1 288.3	0.2	0.0	0.2	0.0	0.2	52.5	11.4	20.1	2.7	13.3
	2012	1 236.1	0.1	0.0	0.3	0.0	0.2	51.8	7.1	23.6	5.1	12.3
Romania - Roumanie	1990	5 711.0	0.4	1.3	1.6	0.1	0.3	18.5	51.1	27.8	0.3	2.3
	2000	1 618.3	0.0	0.2	0.8	0.0	0.2	6.4	32.1	51.3	0.5	9.6
	2010	244.1	0.0	..	0.1	..	0.1	19.3	..	33.6	..	47.1
	2012	58.7	0.0	..	0.0	..	0.0	10.5	..	16.4	..	73.1
Slovakia - Slovaquie	2000	19.5	..	..	0.0	..	..	..	..	100.0	..	..
	2010	192.9	..	0.0	0.2	..	0.0	..	7.9	92.0	..	0.1
	2012	21.8	..	..	0.0	..	0.0	..	..	99.1	..	0.9
Slovenia - Slovénie	2000	0.8	..	..	0.0	..	0.0	..	..	29.9	..	70.1
	2010	0.4	..	..	..	..	0.0	..	..	..	..	100.0
	2012	1.2	..	..	..	..	0.0	..	..	..	..	100.0
Spain - Espagne	1990	6 461.0	1.3	0.8	0.8	0.5	1.6	47.4	27.3	12.0	1.7	11.6
	2000	2 053.0	0.4	0.0	0.3	0.2	0.7	51.1	3.4	14.3	6.6	24.6
	2010	2 554.7	0.2	0.0	0.2	0.1	1.2	40.5	1.4	8.1	6.5	43.5
	2012	2 646.9	0.2	0.0	0.2	0.0	1.3	38.7	1.8	8.4	1.8	49.4
Sweden - Suède	1990	1 995.0	0.1	0.1	0.9	0.3	0.9	14.6	13.7	46.8	3.6	21.3
	2000	1 846.0	0.1	0.0	1.0	..	0.9	8.7	2.4	55.9	..	33.0
	2010	2 206.3	0.1	0.0	1.2	..	0.3	28.0	1.6	57.1	..	13.3
	2012	1 619.4	0.1	0.0	1.0	..	0.3	15.8	1.6	65.4	..	17.2
Switzerland - Suisse	1990	363.0	..	0.1	0.0	..	0.1	..	83.7	9.4	..	6.9
	2000	779.0	..	0.3	0.0	..	0.1	..	91.7	3.6	..	4.7
	2010	1 023.1	0.0	0.1	0.1	0.1	0.0	8.6	61.3	10.3	19.2	0.5
	2012	1 189.4	0.0	0.1	0.1	0.1	0.0	7.3	73.3	8.9	9.9	0.6
United Kingdom - Royaume-Uni	1990	10 252.0	2.0	1.0	0.7	5.9	2.7	46.1	21.8	6.9	12.8	12.4
	2000	11 913.1	2.0	0.5	0.6	3.0	3.3	46.9	11.8	5.5	16.3	19.6
	2010	36 887.2	2.9	1.5	2.5	6.1	4.3	34.9	18.9	7.4	28.0	10.8
	2012	43 770.1	3.0	1.8	2.8	5.5	3.5	35.3	25.1	6.7	24.8	8.1
Developed economies: Oceania - Économies développées : Océanie	**1990**	**4 006.0**	**0.5**	**0.9**	**0.3**	**0.6**	**0.9**	**30.7**	**48.4**	**7.0**	**3.1**	**10.8**
	2000	**3 018.8**	**0.2**	**0.5**	**0.1**	**0.1**	**1.5**	**17.6**	**44.0**	**2.3**	**1.6**	**34.5**
	2010	**2 498.5**	**0.1**	**0.1**	**0.3**	**0.0**	**1.2**	**19.3**	**24.0**	**11.6**	**0.3**	**44.8**
	2012	**2 268.9**	**0.0**	**0.1**	**0.3**	**0.0**	**1.2**	**6.2**	**26.7**	**13.8**	**0.4**	**52.9**
Australia - Australie	1990	3 707.0	0.5	0.8	0.2	0.5	0.8	29.8	51.1	5.3	3.0	10.8
	2000	2 686.2	0.1	0.5	0.1	0.1	1.2	15.2	48.9	2.2	1.8	32.0
	2010	2 171.1	0.1	0.1	0.1	..	1.2	18.1	26.7	6.1	..	49.1
	2012	1 814.6	0.0	0.1	0.1	..	1.1	2.9	26.5	7.9	..	62.7

For sources and notes, see end of table.

Pour les sources et les notes, se reporter à la fin du tableau.

5.3 World merchant fleet by flag of registration and type of ship of countries and geographical regions

5.3 Flotte marchande mondiale par pavillons d'immatriculation et par types de navires des pays et des régions géographiques

Region, country or territory / Régions pays ou territoires	Year / Année	Total fleet (thousands of DWT) / Flotte totale (milliers de TPL) (1)	As percentage of world total fleet / En pourcentage de la flotte mondiale					As percentage of the country or region total fleet / En pourcentage de la flotte totale du pays ou de la région				
			Oil tankers / Pétroliers	Bulk carriers / Vraquiers	General cargo / Navires de charge classique (2)	Container ships / Porte-conteneurs	Other types / Autres navires	Oil tankers / Pétroliers	Bulk carriers / Vraquiers	General cargo / Navires de charge classique (2)	Container ships / Porte-conteneurs	Other types / Autres navires
New Zealand - Nouvelle-Zélande	1990	299.0	0.1	0.0	0.1	0.1	0.1	42.1	14.0	27.8	4.7	11.4
	2000	332.7	0.0	0.0	0.0	..	0.3	37.1	5.1	3.2	..	54.6
	2010	327.4	0.0	0.0	0.1	0.0	0.1	27.2	6.2	47.6	2.5	16.5
	2012	454.3	0.0	0.0	0.2	0.0	0.1	19.5	27.4	37.4	1.8	13.9
World n.e.s. - Monde n.d.a.	2010	5 611.0	0.3	0.2	2.1	0.1	1.0	22.5	17.5	40.4	3.5	16.2
	2012	4 632.8	0.2	0.1	1.5	0.1	1.2	19.6	15.5	35.6	2.7	26.7
Major 10 open and international registries - 10 principaux pays de libre immatriculation et de registre international (7)	**1990**	**233 082.0**	**44.2**	**37.0**	**28.9**	**24.4**	**24.4**	**44.7**	**35.5**	**12.4**	**2.3**	**5.0**
	2000	**405 458.6**	**52.3**	**57.2**	**44.0**	**44.6**	**38.4**	**36.5**	**38.7**	**11.0**	**7.0**	**6.7**
	2010	**707 456.7**	**55.5**	**61.3**	**40.0**	**53.6**	**47.7**	**35.3**	**39.6**	**6.1**	**12.8**	**6.2**
	2012	**868 534.5**	**55.9**	**61.3**	**41.0**	**55.9**	**49.5**	**32.6**	**43.9**	**5.0**	**12.8**	**5.7**
Developing economies excluding major open and international registries - Économies en développement sans les principaux pays de libre immatriculation et de registre international	1990	147 117.0	16.5	27.6	31.7	20.8	20.9	26.4	42.0	21.6	3.2	6.8
	2000	183 808.6	18.1	26.6	31.4	21.3	19.9	27.9	39.8	17.3	7.4	7.7
	2010	321 951.6	23.2	27.0	35.6	19.8	24.0	32.5	38.3	12.0	10.4	6.9
	2012	405 170.4	24.9	28.1	35.2	21.2	24.6	31.1	43.2	9.2	10.3	6.0
Developing economies: Africa excluding major open and international registries - Économies en développement : Afrique sans les principaux pays de libre immatriculation et de registre international	1990	7 638.0	1.0	0.5	2.4	1.2	3.6	29.5	13.2	31.0	3.7	22.7
	2000	6 365.9	0.6	0.5	1.6	0.7	1.9	24.9	22.4	25.0	6.9	20.8
	2010	8 610.8	0.7	0.3	1.9	0.1	1.9	37.9	15.6	23.7	2.3	20.4
	2012	9 977.5	0.7	0.3	2.2	0.1	1.8	38.1	18.0	24.0	2.2	17.7
Developing economies: America excluding major open and international registries - Économies en développement : Amérique sans les principaux pays de libre immatriculation et de registre international	1990	22 370.0	2.8	3.6	5.1	1.1	4.9	29.9	35.5	22.9	1.1	10.5
	2000	19 057.9	2.4	1.8	4.2	0.5	3.8	35.4	26.2	22.4	1.8	14.2
	2010	22 361.7	1.9	1.2	4.2	0.3	3.6	37.5	25.3	20.4	2.1	14.7
	2012	23 373.9	1.8	0.9	4.2	0.4	3.3	39.4	24.1	19.0	3.6	13.9
Developed economies excluding major open and international registries - Économies développées sans les principaux pays de libre immatriculation et de registre international (8)	1990	204 435.0	34.4	30.0	26.4	45.7	41.0	39.7	32.8	12.9	5.0	9.6
	2000	186 679.2	28.4	15.3	19.0	31.0	35.7	43.1	22.5	10.3	10.6	13.6
	2010	208 164.0	19.6	10.4	15.7	20.3	22.9	42.4	22.9	8.2	16.5	10.1
	2012	221 879.4	17.7	9.6	15.8	17.3	21.2	40.5	26.9	7.6	15.5	9.5

Source:
UNCTAD secretariat calculations, based on data supplied by IHS Fairplay,
www.ihsfairplay.com

Source :
Calculs du secrétariat de la CNUCED, basés sur les données fournies par IHS Fairplay,
www.ihsfairplay.com

Notes:

(1) DWT (deadweight ton) is the weight measure of a vessel's carrying capacity. It includes cargo, fuel and stores.

(2) Including passenger/cargo combined.

(3) Year 2002: break in series; from 2002 onwards, ships registered under the flag of the Marshall Islands (developing country) are shown separately; before they were included with the United States of America (developed country).

(4) From 2002 onwards, ships registered under the flag of the Marshall Islands are shown separately; before they were included with the United States of America.

(5) Year 2002: break in series; from 2002 onwards, ships registered under the flag of the Marshall Islands are shown separately; before they were included with the United States of America.

(6) Including San Marino.

(7) UNCTAD has grouped the 10 major open and international registries to include the 10 largest fleets with more than 90 per cent foreign-controlled tonnage. Accordingly, the following 10 economies appear in the group: Antigua and Barbuda, Bahamas, Bermuda, Cyprus, Isle of Man, Liberia, Malta, Marshall Islands, Panama, and Saint Vincent and Grenadines. From 1995 onwards, the data for this group cover also the fleet of the Isle of Man, included otherwise with figures of the United Kingdom and not shown separately.

(8) Before 1995, Isle of Man is included.

Notes :

(1) TPL (Tonne de port en lourd) : c'est une mesure de poids de la capacité de charge d'un navire. Il inclut la cargaison, le carburant et les magasins.

(2) Y compris les cargos mixtes.

(3) Année 2002 : rupture de série ; les navires immatriculés aux Îles Marshall (pays en développement) sont présentés séparément à partir de 2002 ; avant, ils étaient compris dans les chiffres des États-Unis (pays développé).

(4) Les navires immatriculés aux Îles Marshall sont présentés séparément à partir de 2002 ; avant, ils étaient compris dans les chiffres des États-Unis.

(5) Année 2002 : rupture de série ; les navires immatriculés aux Îles Marshall sont présentés séparément à partir de 2002 ; avant, ils étaient compris dans les chiffres des États-Unis.

(6) Y compris Saint-Marin.

(7) La CNUCED a regroupé les pays de libre immatriculation en incluant les 10 plus grandes flottes dont le tonnage, contrôlé par les non-résidents, dépasse 90% du tonnage total du pays. Par conséquent, les 10 pays suivants font partie du groupe : Antigua-et-Barbuda, Bahamas, Bermudes, Chypre, Îles Marshall, Île de Man, Libéria, Malte, Panama et Saint-Vincent-et-les Grenadines. À partir de 1995, les données de ce groupe comprennent aussi la flotte de l'Île de Man. Les données de l'Île de Man ne sont pas présentées séparément, mais inclues dans la flotte du Royaume-Uni.

(8) Y compris l'île de Man avant 1995.

6 | COMMODITIES

PRODUITS DE BASE

6.1 Annual and quaterly indices of free-market prices of selected primary commodities
2000 = 100

Primary commodity	Level (1) Niveau (1) 2000	1985	1990	1995	2004	2005	2006	2007	2008	2009	2010	2011
ALL COMMODITIES	_	96.2	124.0	137.6	125.8	140.4	182.8	206.5	256.0	212.7	251.4	295.1
All food	_	103.4	121.8	138.9	120.8	128.4	149.4	169.2	235.6	215.6	231.6	272.8
Food and tropical beverages	_	*98.8*	*123.5*	*135.5*	*116.7*	*127.0*	*149.6*	*162.5*	*228.2*	*215.9*	*227.9*	*265.6*
Food	_	*89.6*	*125.4*	*132.3*	*118.6*	*127.2*	*151.3*	*164.1*	*233.9*	*219.9*	*229.6*	*265.1*
1. Wheat*	119.6	91.4	88.9	139.4	114.9	109.2	128.5	209.1	246.0	183.1	210.8	256.5
2. Wheat	119.2	115.6	114.8	150.0	134.8	132.9	168.2	225.9	288.0	197.4	204.0	275.6
3. Maize	86.8	..	123.9	142.7	120.3	103.8	138.6	188.8	237.9	195.9	226.8	332.5
4. Maize*	90.0	..	121.9	139.0	124.9	109.9	136.8	189.0	253.2	191.4	216.8	325.5
5. Rice	203.8	106.7	140.9	157.8	120.6	141.2	149.0	163.1	343.6	289.2	255.8	270.9
6. Sugar (2)	8.2	49.6	153.4	162.4	87.6	120.9	180.6	123.3	156.5	221.9	260.2	317.9
7. Beef (2)	87.8	111.2	131.5	98.5	129.8	135.2	131.9	134.5	138.0	136.3	173.8	208.6
8. Bananas (2)	19.0	90.7	123.6	104.7	125.1	137.4	162.8	161.4	201.1	202.6	210.0	232.6
9. Pepper	4 341.6	93.0	41.3	87.3	59.1	57.1	74.5	109.3	119.9	105.4	139.0	219.3
10. Soybean meal	199.7	78.7	107.1	105.5	128.6	116.5	110.3	160.5	226.2	210.4	196.0	200.9
11. Fish meal	413.0	67.8	99.8	119.9	157.1	172.2	281.9	285.0	274.4	297.7	408.6	372.3
Tropical beverages	_	*179.1*	*107.6*	*163.3*	*100.2*	*125.7*	*134.1*	*148.0*	*178.0*	*181.5*	*213.2*	*270.3*
12. Coffee (2)	102.6	151.9	94.1	154.3	82.0	114.0	115.4	123.5	142.1	176.3	218.1	276.6
13. Coffee (2)	79.9	190.0	103.7	182.7	85.4	126.9	128.8	138.6	153.4	139.5	182.5	305.1
14. Coffee (2)	85.1	171.1	104.7	175.4	94.2	134.3	133.9	144.8	162.5	166.5	228.4	321.1
15. Coffee (2)	42.1	288.2	130.5	301.0	88.5	126.7	166.9	209.6	252.4	183.2	199.6	275.4
16. Coffee* (2)	63.6	209.8	113.3	217.0	92.3	131.8	144.8	166.3	192.3	172.0	218.9	305.9
17. Cocoa (2)	40.3	254.0	143.2	161.5	174.5	173.3	179.4	219.9	290.7	325.4	353.0	335.7
18. Tea (3)	248.1	..	..	71.1	79.9	87.2	97.4	85.4	108.6	126.5	125.3	139.5
Vegetable oilseeds and oils	_	*141.2*	*107.0*	*167.1*	*155.3*	*140.6*	*147.7*	*225.7*	*297.8*	*213.3*	*261.7*	*332.8*
19. Soybeans	211.8	106.3	116.5	122.4	144.7	129.7	126.8	181.3	246.8	205.9	212.3	255.2
20. Soybean oil	338.1	169.2	132.3	184.9	182.2	161.2	177.1	260.7	372.2	251.0	297.2	384.3
21. Sunflower oil	391.8	153.7	124.9	176.9	174.6	172.9	167.9	260.8	382.5	218.1	274.2	347.2
22. Groundnut oil	713.7	126.8	135.0	138.8	162.7	148.6	135.9	189.4	292.7	165.9	196.7	263.7
23. Copra	304.8	126.7	75.7	143.9	147.7	135.8	132.1	199.3	267.7	157.4	246.0	379.8
24. Coconut oil	450.3	131.1	74.8	148.7	146.7	137.0	134.8	204.1	271.8	161.1	249.5	384.2
25. Palm kernel oil	443.5	124.3	75.3	152.8	146.1	141.4	131.0	200.3	254.7	158.4	267.0	371.6
26. Palm oil	310.3	161.3	93.4	202.5	151.9	136.1	154.2	251.5	305.8	220.1	290.4	362.7
Agricultural raw materials	_	94.0	128.2	150.4	125.4	129.4	146.6	164.2	197.9	163.3	225.7	289.1
27. Linseed oil	398.4	157.5	177.9	165.0	218.5	276.5	168.6	251.3	389.3	246.6	292.0	358.0
28. Tobacco	2 988.1	87.4	113.7	88.5	91.7	93.4	99.4	110.9	120.1	141.8	144.4	149.8
29. Cotton (2)	83.8	117.6	112.1	133.8	97.1	88.0	102.5	..	116.1	105.0	126.9	291.3
30. Cotton (2)	65.5	108.9	127.9	159.4	95.8	89.9	92.8	98.8	111.1	100.4	156.8	244.3
31. Cotton (2)	57.3	111.8	138.4	176.0	107.3	97.6	101.6	111.2	124.7	113.8	180.1	276.6
32. Cotton* (2)	51.7	90.7	150.3	161.5	92.5	101.1	110.9	135.3	..	..	..	..
33. Cotton* (2)	59.2	101.0	139.5	164.4	103.6	91.5	97.0	106.8	120.5	105.8	175.0	258.1
34. Cotton (2)	108.5	147.9	236.0	..	109.5	93.2	126.3	114.8	113.8	106.4	156.9	201.4
35. Wool	7 335.4	..	..	..	97.2	92.4	97.6	132.6	132.0	106.1	139.5	223.2
36. Wool	2 809.8	..	..	..	196.9	188.8	192.4	272.2	252.4	217.6	291.7	430.5
37. Jute	278.8	204.2	146.5	131.2	106.3	135.4	136.3	119.6	167.7	201.0	309.9	228.9
38. Sisal	782.1	79.2	95.0	97.4	123.7	128.0	134.2	130.9	145.4	104.5	142.0	183.0
39. Sisal	628.7	83.6	113.7	113.0	139.0	143.3	150.7	152.4	171.3	122.6	160.6	210.4
40. Hides (2)	80.2	63.8	115.0	109.9	83.7	82.0	86.1	90.0	79.8	55.9	89.7	102.2
41. Non-coniferous woods*	85.2	..	..	103.6	111.1	117.4	131.8	145.5	154.0	154.4	160.7	158.1
42. Tropical logs (4)	244.6	71.1	140.4	139.4	136.3	136.7	130.2	155.7	216.8	172.1	175.2	199.4
43. Tropical sawnwood* (4)	531.8	51.9	98.6	144.2	103.4	103.4	103.4	103.4	103.4	103.4	..	..
44. Plywood* (5)	448.5	47.0	79.1	129.9	103.6	113.4	132.8	143.9	143.9	125.9	126.9	135.5
45. Rubber	726.5	..	119.6	226.9	185.9	210.9	289.5	319.4	372.7	270.6	492.4	660.0

For sources and notes, see end of table.

2009		2010				2011				2012		Produits de base
III	IV	I	II	III	IV	I	II	III	IV	I	II	
222.6	**237.0**	**244.9**	**230.9**	**245.7**	**284.1**	**312.4**	**300.3**	**297.9**	**269.7**	**276.3**	**271.1**	**TOTAL DES PRODUITS**
222.6	**229.0**	**229.0**	**207.4**	**228.3**	**261.5**	**284.1**	**271.8**	**275.9**	**259.3**	**261.1**	**264.3**	**Total des produits alimentaires**
223.6	*229.5*	*228.4*	*204.3*	*224.8*	*254.2*	*274.6*	*263.0*	*270.1*	*254.5*	*254.4*	*257.9*	***Produits alimentaires et boissons tropicales***
227.9	*232.9*	*231.9*	*204.7*	*225.3*	*256.7*	*274.3*	*260.8*	*269.7*	*255.4*	*257.0*	*263.6*	*Produits alimentaires*
186.4	186.7	184.7	185.8	223.2	249.3	285.3	289.5	250.2	200.9	215.7	213.2	1. Blé*
181.5	183.8	173.7	160.8	226.0	255.4	291.7	292.9	270.5	247.5	248.4	236.6	2. Blé
189.0	201.4	192.1	190.6	234.4	290.1	330.5	353.1	343.5	302.8	304.3	285.1	3. Maïs
176.7	198.9	188.2	181.1	222.2	275.5	320.0	347.4	334.1	300.4	310.7	304.4	4. Maïs*
293.3	284.3	282.5	234.8	242.1	263.9	257.3	248.5	284.5	293.2	272.5	295.2	5. Riz
260.6	278.9	287.5	193.4	238.3	321.7	347.7	291.5	336.8	295.5	292.6	261.0	6. Sucre (2)
141.2	141.6	162.5	177.6	171.2	183.8	211.5	210.9	202.9	209.2	220.0	213.7	7. Viande de boeuf (2)
197.0	194.3	191.8	211.7	219.9	216.7	234.9	240.1	228.1	227.4	249.5	233.7	8. Bananes (2)
111.2	119.9	118.5	128.2	144.9	164.5	184.4	205.2	229.3	258.3	235.6	233.3	9. Poivre
221.6	213.7	198.5	178.8	193.0	213.9	221.1	201.0	200.8	180.6	197.3	244.7	10. Farine de soja
309.0	371.6	401.9	439.1	402.7	390.5	421.3	399.0	345.3	323.4	314.7	358.7	11. Farine de poisson
185.7	*200.7*	*198.3*	*201.0*	*220.4*	*232.9*	*277.7*	*283.0*	*273.6*	*246.9*	*231.8*	*208.2*	*Boissons tropicales*
176.6	180.2	204.4	202.0	231.3	234.5	282.8	294.3	278.9	250.5	237.6	197.5	12. Café (2)
138.9	158.7	156.5	159.7	192.7	220.8	293.8	327.5	311.4	287.7	259.8	208.4	13. Café (2)
168.6	179.4	185.0	211.1	250.8	266.8	331.2	342.5	320.1	290.4	261.2	215.2	14. Café (2)
179.8	177.6	175.0	186.0	210.6	227.0	271.5	292.8	276.2	261.0	264.5	269.9	15. Café (2)
172.3	178.8	181.7	202.8	237.5	253.7	311.4	326.1	305.6	280.7	262.3	233.4	16. Café* (2)
333.9	385.0	371.4	361.7	344.6	334.1	376.6	346.2	341.9	278.0	263.7	257.1	17. Cacao (2)
139.7	145.1	128.7	114.1	120.8	137.5	140.9	132.6	144.6	140.0	136.9	137.4	18. Thé (3)
214.5	*224.5*	*233.6*	*233.2*	*257.6*	*322.4*	*363.6*	*344.8*	*323.9*	*298.8*	*316.4*	*317.8*	***Graines oléagineuses et huiles végétales***
213.1	207.2	196.7	192.9	213.4	246.4	266.7	262.8	261.2	230.2	244.4	269.9	19. Fèves de soja
253.3	272.4	271.3	259.0	291.0	367.3	398.9	387.8	391.6	359.0	370.7	365.6	20. Huile de soja
207.0	234.2	243.7	231.6	265.8	355.5	369.0	363.9	345.3	310.5	316.7	322.5	21. Huile de tournesol
158.8	161.4	190.4	189.4	182.4	224.7	241.4	256.4	297.1	311.8	..	355.6	22. Huile d'arachide
153.8	161.0	182.6	208.2	252.4	340.6	452.5	440.4	325.2	301.0	306.1	260.3	23. Coprah
158.0	163.1	185.3	212.0	257.3	343.4	460.4	443.3	327.3	305.8	310.9	263.6	24. Huile de coprah
157.8	173.5	208.0	233.1	261.9	365.1	480.5	422.6	301.7	281.8	308.0	280.1	25. Huile de palmiste
218.8	236.1	260.3	262.0	281.9	357.1	403.2	369.7	347.8	330.3	356.7	350.8	26. Huile de palme
164.4	**193.1**	**210.1**	**208.6**	**215.9**	**268.3**	**314.9**	**303.4**	**289.7**	**248.2**	**245.9**	**228.9**	**Matières premières d'origine agricole**
249.0	290.0	265.0	240.9	322.9	339.0	380.5	388.0	349.6	313.9	322.8	331.4	27. Huile de lin
143.1	147.6	145.7	141.7	145.0	144.9	146.6	149.5	152.0	151.1	147.3	144.9	28. Tabac
99.1	107.7	119.4	125.5	140.0	..	..	293.1	289.4	..	..	..	29. Coton (2)
103.8	118.4	118.2	138.5	142.6	228.1	310.4	293.5	187.2	166.9	161.1	142.0	30. Coton (2)
118.8	135.7	143.3	157.1	161.3	258.9	352.5	329.7	213.9	189.5	180.8	162.3	31. Coton (2)
..	..	..	..	..	..	..	..	..	..	..	..	32. Coton* (2)
108.7	120.8	136.9	152.6	157.1	253.4	349.9	309.1	198.7	174.8	169.6	151.1	33. Coton* (2)
97.1	112.8	125.2	136.3	141.6	219.5	257.2	..	..	164.3	140.9	136.8	34. Coton (2)
111.5	130.3	135.4	128.6	129.1	164.8	222.0	245.4	228.8	197.2	209.2	184.8	35. Laine
232.0	270.5	297.7	278.2	279.7	311.3	393.4	474.5	452.1	401.9	476.2	442.5	36. Laine
197.3	230.7	316.2	373.6	260.6	289.3	271.4	245.1	223.6	175.7	188.9	181.1	37. Jute
91.8	107.0	126.2	142.8	148.3	150.9	162.8	166.2	198.2	204.6	198.2	196.1	38. Sisal
106.0	124.6	143.2	157.5	168.9	172.9	186.6	190.9	230.6	233.3	229.3	228.0	39. Sisal
66.9	74.4	83.9	90.5	90.6	93.7	98.0	109.7	107.1	94.2	96.4	104.7	40. Peaux (2)
152.5	149.0	147.6	162.0	166.5	166.7	158.8	157.0	160.7	156.0	152.8	155.3	41. Bois non conifères*
169.7	182.7	176.4	166.5	174.4	183.5	182.3	201.1	210.8	197.5	189.7	185.2	42. Grumes tropicales (4)
..	..	..	..	..	..	..	..	..	..	..	..	43. Grumes tropicales sciées* (4)
125.2	124.5	124.2	126.3	127.6	129.4	131.2	134.5	138.5	137.7	136.6	136.1	44. Contre-plaqué* (5)
273.2	368.7	452.6	443.2	459.5	614.4	759.7	679.9	661.9	538.5	548.0	490.0	45. Caoutchouc

Pour les sources et les notes, se reporter à la fin du tableau.

6

6.1 Annual and quaterly indices of free-market prices of selected primary commodities
2000 = 100

Primary commodity	Level (1) Niveau (1) 2000	1985	1990	1995	2004	2005	2006	2007	2008	2009	2010	2011
Minerals, ores and metals	_	81.2	127.0	128.1	137.3	173.2	277.7	313.2	332.5	231.6	309.7	348.9
46. Phosphate rock	43.8	76.6	92.6	80.0	93.7	96.0	101.1	162.1	789.9	278.1	281.2	422.6
47. Manganese ore	186.0	74.5	213.1	109.7	106.7	175.8	139.7	191.9	758.5	293.8	415.0	324.4
48. Iron ore (6)	27.7	96.0	111.3	97.4	131.7	225.9	268.8	294.4	485.8	348.8	348.8	..
49. Iron ore* (6)	27.5	96.5	109.8	97.4	126.2	201.0	256.4	286.1	467.6	396.0	352.7	..
50. Aluminium	1 549.2	69.8	105.8	116.6	110.8	122.5	165.9	170.3	166.1	107.4	140.2	154.8
51. Copper	1 813.1	78.2	146.8	161.8	158.0	202.9	370.7	392.6	383.6	282.8	415.6	486.6
52. Copper* (2)	86.8	75.6	140.4	158.4	152.8	198.4	361.2	376.5	366.3	276.4	399.9	466.7
53. Nickel*	8 637.7	56.8	102.6	95.3	160.0	170.6	280.7	430.9	244.3	169.6	252.4	265.0
54. Nickel (2)	397.9	56.8	102.3	98.1	159.4	171.2	276.0	424.8	248.1	174.0	262.3	264.1
55. Lead	454.0	86.1	178.5	138.9	195.2	215.0	283.8	568.2	460.2	378.6	473.2	529.0
56. Lead* (2)	43.6	43.8	103.4	96.3	126.6	140.1	178.0	284.2	276.2	199.4	250.0	279.3
57. Zinc	1 128.1	67.0	134.6	91.4	92.9	122.5	290.3	287.4	166.2	146.7	191.5	194.4
58. Zinc* (2)	55.6	72.6	134.1	95.9	94.4	120.7	285.7	277.6	159.9	139.8	183.4	191.0
59. Tin	5 432.8	221.8	114.8	114.3	156.5	135.8	161.5	267.4	340.5	249.6	375.4	480.5
60. Tin*	5 382.0	221.5	113.1	113.1	157.8	136.7	162.9	269.9	341.6	248.9	377.8	486.7
61. Tungsten (7)	44.9	150.9	103.4	141.2	122.9	271.3	369.7	367.4	366.5	334.0	334.0	334.0
62. Gold* (8)	279.0	113.7	137.4	137.7	146.6	159.4	216.6	249.7	312.4	348.7	439.9	562.2
63. Silver* (9)	499.9	122.9	96.4	103.8	133.3	146.8	231.4	268.3	300.1	294.0	404.1	705.4
MEMO ITEM:												
64. Crude petroleum (10)	28.2	95.6	78.1	59.9	133.8	189.1	227.8	252.1	343.8	219.0	280.2	368.3
65. Unit value index of manufactured goods exports	100.0	70.9	110.9	122.3	116.5	119.4	123.5	132.8	139.3	131.5	(r)135.5	147.8

Sources:
- The prices used in the calculation of the indices shown in this table are extracted from *UNCTADstat* Commodity Price Statistics

Notes:
- The group indices include all commodities shown except for those with an asterisk (*).
- The average annual indices are calculated from monthly data and may not correspond to the average from quarterly data.

(1) Dollars per metric ton (unless otherwise specified).
(2) Cents per pound.
(3) Cents per kilogram.
(4) Dollars per cubic meter.
(5) Cents per sheet.
(6) Cents per Fe unit.
(7) Dollars per metric ton unit of WO3.
(8) Dollars per troy ounce.
(9) Cents per troy ounce.
(10) Dollars per barrel.

- For specifications, see next page.

6.1 Indices annuels et trimestriels des prix d'une sélection de produits de base sur le marché libre
2000 = 100

2009		2010				2011				2012		Produits de base
III	IV	I	II	III	IV	I	II	III	IV	I	II	
252.4	**277.8**	**298.9**	**295.9**	**300.6**	**343.6**	**375.6**	**363.5**	**352.3**	**304.4**	**326.8**	**308.2**	**Minéraux, minerais et métaux**
205.7	205.7	233.4	285.7	285.7	320.0	361.9	417.1	451.4	460.1	447.6	410.0	46. Phosphate brut
232.2	297.0	384.5	438.6	447.0	389.8	376.4	340.6	290.4	290.4	249.0	249.0	47. Minerai de manganèse
348.8	348.8	348.8	348.8	348.8	348.8	..	..	..	..	..	..	48. Minerai de fer (6)
352.7	352.7	352.7	352.7	352.7	352.7	..	..	..	..	..	..	49. Minerai de fer* (6)
116.9	129.2	139.6	135.3	134.9	151.2	161.3	168.0	154.9	134.8	140.5	127.6	50. Aluminium
323.1	366.7	399.1	387.5	399.5	476.3	532.3	504.7	496.2	413.0	458.2	433.8	51. Cuivre
312.9	354.8	383.6	372.5	385.5	457.9	510.5	484.1	474.5	397.7	441.3	413.8	52. Cuivre* (2)
204.8	202.9	231.0	260.1	245.3	273.3	311.4	281.2	255.4	211.9	227.6	198.5	53. Nickel*
211.3	207.8	240.7	280.0	255.2	273.3	307.2	280.5	258.5	210.0	227.2	197.4	54. Nickel (2)
424.4	504.6	489.4	429.5	447.5	526.2	573.2	563.6	542.4	436.7	461.1	434.3	55. Plomb
221.3	254.7	254.1	249.3	224.3	272.2	278.4	285.0	292.7	261.2	262.0	261.0	56. Plomb* (2)
156.1	196.2	202.9	179.6	178.4	205.1	212.3	199.8	197.3	168.1	179.4	170.9	57. Zinc
147.4	185.7	191.8	171.7	172.4	197.6	205.0	195.9	195.1	168.2	178.0	170.3	58. Zinc* (2)
268.4	278.9	316.5	328.6	378.1	478.5	550.4	532.2	456.2	383.1	422.0	378.5	59. Étain
267.8	279.6	319.5	332.0	379.2	480.3	556.6	540.8	460.1	389.1	426.7	384.0	60. Étain*
334.0	334.0	334.0	334.0	334.0	334.0	334.0	334.0	334.0	334.0	334.0	334.0	61. Tungstène (7)
344.1	394.8	397.4	432.4	439.6	490.1	496.1	539.1	609.3	604.1	606.0	577.3	62. Or* (8)
294.8	351.9	338.6	367.5	380.4	529.8	635.8	770.2	778.1	637.4	654.4	589.9	63. Argent* (9)
												POUR MÉMOIRE :
241.8	267.7	273.1	277.2	267.8	302.8	353.2	390.1	365.2	364.6	398.5	364.6	64. Pétrole brut (10)
134.0	137.0	134.0	(r)132.0	(r)135.0	(r)141.0	(r)144.0	(r)151.0	(p)150.0	(p)146.0	(p)145.0	..	65. Valeur unitaire des exportations d'articles manufacturés en dollars

Sources :
- Les prix utilisés pour le calcul des indices présentés dans ce tableau sont extraits des statistiques des prix des produits de base de *UNCTADstat*

Notes :

- Les indices agrégés recouvrent tous les produits présentés à l'exception de ceux munis d'un astérisque (*).
- Les indices moyens annuels sont calculés sur la base de données mensuelles et peuvent ne pas correspondre aux moyennes calculées sur la base de données trimestrielles.

(1) Dollars par tonne métrique (sauf mention spéciale).
(2) Cents par livre.
(3) Cents par kilogramme.
(4) Dollars par mètre cube.
(5) Cents par feuille.
(6) Cents par unité de Fe.
(7) Dollars par tonne métrique d'unité de WO3.
(8) Dollars par once troy.
(9) Cents par once troy.
(10) Dollars par baril.

- Pour les spécifications, se reporter à la page suivante.

6

Specifications

Food

1. Wheat: Argentina, Trigo Pan Upriver, f.o.b.
2. Wheat: United States, no. 2, Hard Red Winter (ordinary), f.o.b. Gulf ports.
3. Maize: Argentina, Rosario, f.o.b.
4. Maize: United States, no. 3 yellow, f.o.b. Gulf ports.
5. Rice: Thailand, white milled, 5 % broken, nominal price quotes, f.o.b. Bangkok.
6. Sugar: Caribbean ports, f.o.b. bulk basis (I.S.A.).
7. Beef: Australia and New-Zealand, frozen and boneless, 85 % visible lean, U.S. import price, f.o.b. port of entry.
8. Bananas: Central America and Ecuador, fresh, U.S. importer's price, f.o.b. U.S. ports.
9. Pepper: Muntok, white, fair average quality (faq) spot Prior to June 2003, Singapore.
10. Soybean meal: Hamburg, 44/45% protein, f.o.b. ex-mill.
11. Fish meal: Any origin, 64/65% protein, Bremen free carrier price. Prior to March 2006, cost and freight Hamburg.

Tropical beverages

12. Coffee: Colombian mild Arabicas, ex-dock New York (I.C.A.).
13. Coffee: Brazilian and other natural Arabicas, ex-dock New York (I.C.A.).
14. Coffee: Other mild Arabicas, ex-dock New York (I.C.A.).
15. Coffee: Robustas, ex-dock New York (I.C.A.).
16. Coffee: Composite indicator price 1976 (I.C.A.).
17. Cocoa: Average of daily prices, New York/London, 3 months futures (I.C.C.A.).
18. Tea: Best Pekoe Fannings 1, Mombasa auction prices.

Vegetable oils and oilseeds

19. Soybeans: United States, no. 2 yellow, c.i.f. Rotterdam.
20. Soybean oil: Any origin, crude oil, the Netherlands, f.o.b. ex-mill.
21. Sunflower oil: European Union, f.o.b. N.W. European ports.
22. Groundnut oil: Any origin, c.i.f. Rotterdam.
23. Copra: Philippines/Indonesia, bulk, c.i.f. N.W. European ports.
24. Coconut oil: Philippines, c.i.f. Rotterdam.
25. Palm kernel oil: Malaysia, c.i.f. Rotterdam.
26. Palm oil: generally Indonesia, 5% ffa, c.i.f. N.W. European ports.

Agricultural raw materials

27. Linseed oil: Any origin, ex-tank, c.i.f. Rotterdam.
28. Tobacco: Unmanufactured tobacco, US general import price.
29. Cotton: Sudan, Barakat, X4B, CFR Far Eastern quotations. Prior to August 2005, c.i.f. North Europe.
30. Cotton: United States, Memphis/Eastern Midd 1-3/32", c.i.f. North Europe.
31. Cotton: United States; Memphis/Orleans/Texas, Midd 1-3/32", CFR Far Eastern quotations. Prior to June 2005, Memphis/Orleans/Texas, Midd 1-3/32", c.i.f. North Europe.
32. Cotton: Pakistan, Sind/Punjab, Afzal 1-1/32", c.i.f. North Europe.
33. Cotton: Cotton Outlook Index A, Middling 1-3/32", CFR Far Eastern quotations. Prior to August 2004, c.i.f. North Europe.
34. Cotton: Egypt, Giza 88, good + 3/8, CFR Far Eastern quotations. Prior to August 2005, Giza 70, good + 3/8, f.o.b. Alexandria.
35. Wool: fine, 19 micron, Australia.
36. Wool: coarse, 23 micron, Australia.
37. Jute: Bangladesh, Bangladesh White D (BWD), f.o.b. Mongla.
38. Sisal: Tanzania/Kenya, no. 2 & 3 long, f.o.b. Prior to 2007, c.i.f. main European ports.
39. Sisal: Tanzania/Kenya no. 3 & UG, f.o.b. Prior to 2007, c.i.f. main European ports.
40. Hides: US, Chicago packer's heavy native steers over 53lbs., wholesale dealer's price, f.o.b. shipping point.
41. Non-coniferous woods: United Kingdom, import price index 2005=100, dollar equivalent.
42. Tropical logs: Sapele, loyal and marchand, UK import price, f.o.b. plus commission. Prior to June 2000, Cameroon f.o.b.
43. Tropical sawnwood: Malaysia, Dark Red Meranti, select and better, c.i.f. French ports.
44. Plywood: Southeast Asia, Lauan, 3-ply, Extra, 91 cm x 182 cm x 4 mm, wholesale price, spot Tokyo.
45. Rubber: TSR 20 New York.

Spécifications

Produits alimentaires

1. Blé : Argentine, Trigo Pan Upriver, f.a.b.
2. Blé : États-Unis, Hard Red Winter, n° 2 (ordinaire), f.a.b. ports du Golfe.
3. Maïs : Argentine, Rosario, f.a.b.
4. Maïs : États-Unis, jaune n° 3, f.a.b. ports du Golfe.
5. Riz : Thaïlande, blanchi, 5 % brisures, prix nominal, f.a.b. Bangkok.
6. Sucre : Ports des Caraïbes, f.a.b. en vrac (A.I.S.).
7. Viande de boeuf : Australie et Nouvelle-Zélande, désossée et congelée, maigres à 85 % visibles, prix à l'importation aux États-Unis, f.a.b. port d'entrée.
8. Bananes : Amérique centrale et Equateur, fraîches, f.a.b. ports des États-Unis.
9. Poivre : Muntok blanc, 'fair average quality' (faq) au comptant. Avant juin 2003, Singapour.
10. Farine de soja : Hambourg, 44/45 % protéines, f.a.b. départ moulin.
11. Farine de poisson : toutes origines, 64/65 % protéines, Brême, prix franco transporteur. Avant mars 2006, coût et fret Hambourg.

Boissons tropicales

12. Café : Arabicas doux colombiens, ex-dock New York (A.I.C.).
13. Café : Brésilien et autres Arabicas naturels, ex-dock New York (A.I.C.).
14. Café : autres Arabicas doux, ex-dock New York (A.I.C.).
15. Café : Robustas, ex-dock New York (A.I.C.).
16. Café : Prix indicatif composite de 1976 (A.I.C.).
17. Cacao : moyenne des cours quotidiens New York/Londres, 3 mois à terme (A.I.C.C.).
18. Thé : Best Pekoe Fannings 1, cours aux enchères à Mombasa.

Huiles végétales et graines oléagineuses

19. Fèves de soja : États-Unis, n° 2 jaune, c.a.f. Rotterdam.
20. Huile de soja : toutes origines, huile brute, f.a.b. Pays-Bas, départ raffinerie.
21. Huile de tournesol : Union européenne, f.a.b. ports de l'Europe du Nord-Ouest.
22. Huile d'arachide : toutes origines, c.a.f. Rotterdam.
23. Coprah : Philippines/Indonésie, en vrac, c.a.f. ports de l'Europe du Nord-Ouest.
24. Huile de coprah : Philippines, c.a.f. Rotterdam.
25. Huile de palmiste : Malaisie, c.a.f. Rotterdam.
26. Huile de palme : généralement Indonésie, 5 % ffa, c.a.f. ports de l'Europe du Nord-Ouest.

Matières premières d'origine agricole

27. Huile de lin : toutes origines, cours du disponible, c.a.f. Rotterdam.
28. Tabac : tabac non fabriqué, prix général à l'importation aux États-Unis.
29. Coton : Soudan, Barakat, classe X4B, cotations coût et fret Extrême Orient. Avant août 2005, c.a.f. Europe septentrionale.
30. Coton : États-Unis, Memphis, oriental Midd 1-3/32", c.a.f. Europe septentrionale.
31. Coton : États-Unis, Memphis/Orléans/Texas, Midd 1-3/32", cotations coût et fret Extrême Orient. Avant juin 2005, Memphis/Orléans/Texas, Midd 1-3/32", c.a.f. Europe septentrionale.
32. Coton : Pakistan, Sind/Punjab, Afzal 1-1/32", c.a.f. Europe septentrionale.
33. Coton : Indice A de "Cotton Outlook", Middling 1-3/32", cotations coût et fret Extrême Orient. Avant août 2005, c.a.f. Europe septentrionale.
34. Coton : Égypte, Giza 88, good + 3/8, cotations coût et fret Extrême Orient. Avant août 2005, Giza 70, good + 3/8, f.a.b. Alexandrie.
35. Laine : fine, 19 microns, Australie.
36. Laine : grossière, 23 microns, Australie.
37. Jute : Bengladesh, Bengladesh White D (BWD), f.a.b. Mongla.
38. Sisal : Tanzanie/Kenya, n° 2 et 3 long, f.a.b. Avant 2007 : c.a.f. principaux ports européens.
39. Sisal : Tanzanie/Kenya, n° 3 et UG, f.a.b. Avant 2007 : c.a.f. principaux ports européens.
40. Peaux : États-Unis, lourdes de bouvillons de plus de 24 kgs, abattus à Chicago, prix de gros, f.a.b. point d'expédition.
41. Bois non conifères : Royaume-Uni, indice des prix à l'importation 2005=100, équivalent dollar.
42. Grumes tropicales : Sapelli, loyal et marchand, prix d'importation au Royaume-Uni, f.a.b plus commission. Avant juin 2000, Cameroun, f.a.b.
43. Grumes tropicales sciées : Malaisie, Meranti rouge foncé, select and better, c.a.f. ports français.
44. Contre-plaqué : Asie du Sud-Est, Lauan, 3-feuilles, extra, 91 cm x 182 cm x 4 mm, prix de gros, cours du disponible à Tokyo.
45. Caoutchouc : TSR 20 New York.

Minerals, ores and metals

46. Phosphate rock: Morocco, 70% BPL, contract f.a.s. Casablanca.
47. Manganese ore: Metallurgical 48/50% Mn content, f.o.b. United Kingdom.
48. Iron ore: Brazilian to Europe, fines, Vale, Itabira, f.o.b.
49. Iron ore: Australian to Japan, fines, Hamersley, f.o.b.
50. Aluminium: London Metal Exchange, high grade, cash.
51. Copper: London Metal Exchange, grade A, cash.
52. Copper: United States producer, wire bars, f.o.b. refinery.
53. Nickel: London Metal Exchange, cash.
54. Nickel: New York dealer, 4x4 cathodes, free market.
55. Lead: London Metal Exchange, settlement and cash seller's price in warehouse, excluding duty, range main United Kingdom ports; purity 99.97% Pb.
56. Lead: North America, producer price, refined.
57. Zinc: London Metal Exchange, cash settlement.
58. Zinc: North America, special high grade, daily weighted average, delivered basis.
59. Tin: London Metal Exchange, high grade, cash.
60. Tin: Ex-smelter price, Kuala Lumpur market.
61. Tungsten ore: wolframite and sheelite, c.i.f. European ports, basis minimum 65% WO3. Prior to April 1992, Wolfram.
62. Gold: United Kingdom, 99.5% fine, London afternoon fixing, average of daily rates.
63. Silver: Handy & Harman, 99.9% grade refined, average of daily quotations, New York.

MEMO ITEM:

64. Crude petroleum: Average of United Kingdom Brent, Dubai, and West Texas crude prices, reflecting relatively equal consumption of light, medium and heavy crudes worldwide.
65. Unit value index of manufactured goods exports: Developed economies, sections 5-8 less 68 of the Standard International Trade Classification (SITC), Revision 2.

Minéraux, minerais et métaux

46. Phosphate brut : Maroc, 70 % BPL, f.a.s. Casablanca.
47. Minerai de manganèse : 48/50 % teneur en Mn, f.a.b. Royaume-Uni.
48. Minerai de fer : Brésilien vers l'Europe, minerai fin, Vale, Itabira, f.a.b.
49. Minerai de fer : Australien vers le Japon, minerai fin, Hamersley, f.a.b.
50. Aluminium : Bourse des métaux de Londres, haute qualité, cours au comptant.
51. Cuivre : Bourse des métaux de Londres, grade A, comptant.
52. Cuivre : Producteur États-Unis, barres à fil, f.a.b. sortie affinerie.
53. Nickel : Bourse des métaux de Londres, cours au comptant.
54. Nickel : Prix du négociant à New York, cathodes 4x4, marché libre.
55. Plomb : Bourse des métaux de Londres, prix vendeur, à terme et au comptant, à l'entrepôt, droits non acquittés, principaux ports du Royaume-Uni; pureté : 99,97 % Pb.
56. Plomb : Amérique du Nord, prix des producteurs, raffiné.
57. Zinc : Bourse des métaux de Londres, cours de vente au comptant.
58. Zinc : Amérique du Nord, haute qualité spéciale, moyenne pondérée des prix journaliers à la livraison.
59. Étain : Bourse des métaux de Londres, haute qualité, cours au comptant.
60. Étain : Prix départ fonderie, marché de Kuala Lumpur.
61. Minerai de tungstène : wolframite et scheelite, c.a.f. ports européens, minimum 65 % de WO3. Avant avril 1992, Wolfram.
62. Or : Royaume-Uni, 99,5 % fin, cotation de l'après-midi à Londres, moyenne des taux journaliers.
63. Argent : Handy & Harman, 99,9 % raffiné, moyenne des cotations journalières à New York.

POUR MÉMOIRE :

64. Pétrole brut : moyenne des prix du Brent du Royaume-Uni, de Dubaï et du Texas de l'Ouest, correspondant aux parts relatives de la consommation mondiale du brut léger, moyen et lourd.
65. Valeur unitaire des exportations des produits manufacturés : Économies développées, sections 5 à 8 moins 68 de la Classification type pour le commerce international (CTCI), révision 2.

6

Primary commodity	Price instability indices (1) / Indices d'instabilité des prix (1)			Price trends (2) (annual average rate of change in percentage) / Tendances des prix (2) (taux de variation annuel en pourcentage)						Produits de base
				In current dollars / En dollars courants			In constant dollars (3) / En dollars constants (3)			
	82-91	92-01	02-11	82-91	92-01	02-11	82-91	92-01	02-11	
ALL COMMODITIES (4)	**9.5**	**10.1**	**9.3**	**1.9**	**-2.4**	**12.5**	**-2.8**	**-2.4**	**8.7**	**TOTAL DES PRODUITS (4)**
All food	**9.1**	**11.7**	**7.0**	**0.4**	**-2.4**	**11.5**	**-4.3**	**-2.4**	**7.7**	**Total des produits alimentaires**
Food and tropical beverages	***9.2***	***11.1***	***6.7***	***0.9***	***-2.4***	***11.6***	***-3.8***	***-2.4***	***7.8***	***Produits alimentaires et boissons tropicales***
Food	*11.6*	*10.0*	*7.1*	*2.0*	*-2.5*	*11.5*	*-2.7*	*-2.5*	*7.8*	*Produits alimentaires*
Wheat	12.4	13.5	15.3	-1.5	-3.1	9.0	-6.2	-3.1	5.2	Blé
Maize	14.5	13.8	16.2	-2.0	-2.5	11.3	-6.7	-2.4	7.6	Maïs
Rice	12.5	16.2	15.1	1.9	-5.2	14.1	-2.8	-5.2	10.3	Riz
Sugar	29.0	19.1	17.2	6.7	-3.9	14.9	2.0	-3.9	11.1	Sucre
Beef	5.7	10.2	8.2	1.5	-2.9	5.7	-3.2	-2.9	1.9	Viande de bœuf
Bananas	16.0	17.1	13.0	3.7	0.9	9.2	-1.0	0.9	5.4	Bananes
Pepper	51.6	35.9	16.7	-0.2	9.3	14.5	-4.9	9.3	10.7	Poivre
Soybean meal	13.2	13.5	14.2	1.1	-1.8	9.3	-3.6	-1.8	5.6	Farine de soja
Fishmeal	15.7	18.8	12.2	2.9	1.3	12.1	-1.8	1.3	8.3	Farine de poisson
Tropical beverages	*14.0*	*26.9*	*6.8*	*-6.9*	*-0.9*	*12.0*	*-11.5*	*-0.9*	*8.2*	*Boissons tropicales*
Coffee	16.5	36.3	11.1	-5.9	-0.3	15.0	-10.6	-0.3	11.2	Café
Cocoa	14.6	18.6	14.4	-6.9	-1.3	8.2	-11.5	-1.2	4.4	Cacao
Tea	18.1	12.0	7.9	-2.6	2.2	7.3	-7.3	2.2	3.5	Thé
Vegetable oilseeds and oils	***17.9***	***18.3***	***15.5***	***-3.4***	***-2.9***	***11.0***	***-8.0***	***-2.8***	***7.2***	***Graines oléagineuses et huiles végétales***
Soybeans	11.5	11.2	13.4	-0.2	-2.6	9.8	-4.8	-2.6	6.1	Fèves de soja
Soybean oil	19.0	18.6	16.1	-2.4	-3.6	11.1	-7.1	-3.6	7.3	Huile de soja
Sunflower oil	18.1	16.9	17.9	-2.8	-1.5	9.2	-7.5	-1.5	5.5	Huile de tournesol
Groundnut oil	24.7	15.9	20.6	2.2	-0.4	7.4	-2.5	-0.3	3.6	Huile d'arachide
Copra	30.6	22.3	20.6	-5.4	-3.3	13.3	-10.1	-3.3	9.5	Coprah
Coconut oil	32.6	22.9	19.6	-5.7	-2.9	12.9	-10.4	-2.8	9.2	Huile de coprah
Palm kernel oil	30.0	23.5	20.1	-5.6	-3.1	12.7	-10.3	-3.1	9.0	Huile de palmiste
Palm oil	22.9	26.6	17.3	-5.9	-3.1	11.5	-10.5	-3.0	7.8	Huile de palme
Cotton oil	15.5	11.1	24.4	-1.1	-4.1	7.2	-5.8	-4.0	3.5	Huile de coton
Agricultural raw materials	**5.7**	**9.7**	**8.3**	**3.1**	**-3.2**	**10.7**	**-1.6**	**-3.2**	**7.0**	**Matières premières d'origine agricole**
Linseed oil	24.6	19.6	21.8	1.0	-0.5	9.2	-3.6	-0.5	5.5	Huile de lin
Tobacco	6.7	8.1	5.0	3.0	0.3	6.6	-1.6	0.3	2.8	Tabac
Cotton	14.9	18.4	19.5	0.3	-3.1	8.9	-4.3	-3.1	5.1	Coton
Wool	21.3	15.4	14.7	4.8	2.6	7.7	0.1	2.6	3.9	Laine
Jute	26.3	18.2	15.2	0.3	0.1	13.5	-4.4	0.2	9.5	Jute
Sisal	5.0	12.1	9.9	1.5	4.3	4.8	-3.1	4.3	0.9	Sisal
Hides	12.5	8.6	11.5	9.5	-0.2	-1.1	4.8	-0.2	-4.8	Peaux
Non-coniferous woods	8.7	5.5	4.1	6.3	1.6	5.3	1.6	1.6	1.6	Bois non conifères
Tropical logs	8.1	7.7	9.3	8.7	-3.9	7.5	3.9	-3.9	3.8	Grumes tropicales
Tropical sawnwood	14.4	15.6	5.6	5.9	-2.3	4.5	1.2	-2.3	0.8	Grumes tropicales sciées
Plywood	11.2	13.0	8.6	6.9	-3.0	4.5	2.2	-3.0	0.7	Contre-plaqué
Rubber	12.8	25.7	16.4	-0.1	-6.3	17.6	-4.7	-6.3	13.8	Caoutchouc
Minerals, ores and metals	**14.0**	**10.1**	**21.7**	**5.3**	**-1.8**	**15.3**	**0.6**	**-1.8**	**11.5**	**Minéraux, minerais et métaux**
Phosphate rock	7.5	6.9	42.6	2.0	2.3	20.5	-2.6	2.3	16.7	Phosphate brut
Manganese ore	23.8	11.5	35.6	11.8	-5.3	17.6	7.1	-5.3	13.8	Minerai de manganèse
Iron ore	9.9	4.5	18.7	0.2	-0.2	18.5	-4.5	-0.2	14.6	Minerai de fer
Aluminium	22.3	11.2	17.0	4.7	1.3	5.3	0.0	1.4	1.5	Aluminium
Copper	16.6	14.8	26.0	8.1	-4.4	18.4	3.4	-4.4	14.6	Cuivre
Nickel	29.1	18.6	34.1	10.5	-0.3	11.0	5.8	-0.2	7.2	Nickel
Lead	17.2	15.5	24.9	5.3	-0.9	18.8	0.6	-0.8	15.1	Plomb
Zinc	19.8	10.2	34.6	8.0	-0.8	11.5	3.3	-0.8	7.7	Zinc
Tin	13.8	7.9	18.8	-10.2	-1.9	19.5	-14.9	-1.8	15.7	Étain
Tungsten ore	13.4	18.7	31.6	-7.2	1.0	16.4	-11.9	1.1	12.6	Minerai de tungstène
Gold	9.8	7.4	6.1	0.2	-3.9	18.0	-4.4	-3.9	14.2	Or
Silver	15.0	9.4	14.8	-8.1	1.3	20.8	-12.8	1.3	17.0	Argent
Crude petroleum	18.9	16.3	19.5	-6.6	3.9	14.7	-11.3	3.9	10.9	Pétrole brut

For sources and notes, see next page.

Pour les sources et les notes, se reporter à la page suivante.

6.2 Instability indices and trends in free-market prices for selected primary commodities
2000 = 100

6.2 Indices d'instabilité et tendances des prix d'une sélection de produits de base sur le marché libre
2000 = 100

Source:
UNCTAD calculations based on *UNCTADstat* Commodity Price Statistics

Notes:

(1) The measure of price instability is

$$1/n\sum_{t=1}^{n}\left[\left(|Y(t)-y(t)|\right)/y(t)\right]*100$$

where

$Y(t)$ is the observed magnitude of the variable

$y(t)$ is the magnitude estimated by fitting an exponential trend to the observed value

n is the number of observations

Accordingly, instability is measured as the percentage deviation of the variables concerned from their exponential trend levels for a given period.

(2) The growth rate of each period has been calculated using the formula:

$$\log(p) = a + b(t)$$

where

p is the price index and t is time.

(3) Constant 2000 dollars (current dollars divided by the United Nations unit value index of manufactured goods exported by developed economies).

(4) Excluding petroleum

Source :
Calculs du secrétariat de la CNUCED basés sur les statistiques des prix des produits de base de *UNCTADstat*

Notes :

(1) L'indice d'instabilité des prix est calculé selon

$$1/n\sum_{t=1}^{n}\left[\left(|Y(t)-y(t)|\right)/y(t)\right]*100$$

où

$Y(t)$ est la valeur observée de la variable

$y(t)$ est la valeur estimée par ajustement à la tendance exponentielle des valeurs observées

n est le nombre d'observations

L'instabilité est le pourcentage de déviation des variables en question par rapport à la ligne de tendance exponentielle pour une période donnée.

(2) Le taux de croissance de chaque période a été calculé selon la formule :

$$\log(p) = a + b(t)$$

où

p est l'indice de prix et t le temps.

(3) Dollars constants 2000 (dollar courant divisé par l'index des Nations Unies de la valeur unitaire des exportations des produits manufacturés par les économies développées).

(4) Pétrole exclu

6

7 INTERNATIONAL FINANCE

FINANCE INTERNATIONALE

1

2

3

4

5

6

7

8

7.1.1 Balance of payments: Current account net of countries and geographical regions

Region, country or territory	Millions of dollars - Millions de dollars							
	1980	1990	2000	2005	2008	2009	2010	2011
DEVELOPING ECONOMIES	28 455	14 617	103 220	482 234	743 189	426 576	490 240	496 365
TRANSITION ECONOMIES	-2 301	-2 482	47 094	83 116	84 069	30 660	66 530	105 352
DEVELOPED ECONOMIES	-78 726	-104 763	-324 016	-524 571	-669 494	-238 274	-240 265	-251 544
Developing economies: Africa	**6 656**	**3 635**	**16 833**	**60 327**	**53 052**	**-33 314**	**2 657**	**-21 318**
Eastern Africa	*-3 801*	*-3 451*	*-3 066*	*-6 652*	*-15 709*	*-13 470*	*-12 769*	*-15 833*
Burundi	-83	-69	-50	-6	-259	-164	-301	(e)- 253
Comoros	-9	-10	0	-29	-58	-41	-37	-60
Djibouti	31	-11	-19	20	-225	-71	50	-157
Eritrea	_	_	-105	-	-	-	-	-
Ethiopia (...1991)	-226	-294						
Ethiopia	_	_	13	-1 568	-1 806	-2 191	-425	-69
Kenya	-876	-527	-199	-252	-1 983	-1 689	-2 512	-3 536
Madagascar	-556	-265	-260	-554	-2 142	-2 495	(e)-2 477	(e)- 743
Malawi	-260	-86	-73	-620	-808	-563	(e)- 440	(e)- 678
Mauritius	-117	-119	-37	-324	-976	-655	-800	(e)-1 164
Mozambique	-367	-415	-764	-761	-1 179	-1 220	-1 250	-1 615
Rwanda	-52	-85	-94	-52	-252	-383	-421	(e)- 692
Seychelles	-16	-13	-43	-174	-201	-91	-225	(e)- 210
Uganda	-83	-263	-359	-26	-1 314	-1 251	-1 859	-2 276
United Republic of Tanzania	-521	-559	-428	-1 105	-2 675	-1 934	-1 978	(e)-3 874
Zambia	-516	-594	-662	-600	-1 039	537	1 144	215
Zimbabwe	-149	-140	-	-	-	-	-	-
Middle Africa	*-465*	*-1 751*	*1 611*	*5 783*	*7 161*	*-13 542*	*2 604*	*6 144*
Angola	68	-236	796	5 138	7 194	-7 572	7 421	8 183
Cameroon	-445	-551	-218	-493	-450	-1 119	-856	-913
Central African Republic	-43	-89	-13	-88	-196	-160	-197	-150
Chad	12	-46	-213	50	-1 146	(e)-1 218	(e)-2 958	(e)-2 386
Congo	-167	-251	648	696	-1 316	(e)- 819	(e)606	(e)1 850
Dem. Rep. of the Congo	-254	-715	-173	-955	-2 025	-1 166	-904	-1 360
Equatorial Guinea	-21	-19	-196	-511	1 672	-2 094	(e)-1 596	(e)- 945
Gabon	384	168	1 001	1 983	3 520	685	1 196	1 943
Sao Tome and Principe	1	-12	-20	-36	-94	-79	-107	(e)-78
Northern Africa	*5 951*	*4 917*	*12 627*	*36 201*	*61 174*	*-2 771*	*18 570*	*8 327*
Algeria	249	1 420	9 142	21 180	34 440	401	12 146	21 080
Egypt	-436	2 327	-971	2 103	-1 415	-3 349	-4 504	-4 647
Libya	8 214	2 201	6 270	14 945	35 702	9 381	16 801	1 628
Morocco	-1 407	-196	-475	1 041	-4 528	-4 971	-3 925	-8 000
Sudan (...2011)	-316	-372	-518	-2 768	-1 314	-2 998	157	1 330
Tunisia	-353	-463	-821	-299	-1 711	-1 234	-2 104	(e)-3 064
Southern Africa	*2 947*	*1 676*	*429*	*-6 742*	*-19 078*	*-12 145*	*-10 851*	*-16 475*
Botswana	-151	-19	545	1 562	868	-521	46	-1 191
Lesotho	56	65	-71	-17	144	-2	-421	(e)- 545
Namibia	-	28	192	333	225	120	30	-776
South Africa	3 161	1 552	-191	-8 518	-20 083	-11 327	-10 117	-13 683
Swaziland	-130	51	-46	-103	-231	-414	-388	(e)- 281
Western Africa	*2 024*	*2 244*	*5 232*	*31 738*	*19 505*	*8 614*	*5 103*	*-3 480*
Benin	-36	-18	-81	-226	-536	-649	-530	(e)- 700
Burkina Faso	-49	-77	-319	-634	-963	-380	(e)- 206	(e)- 126
Cape Verde	4	-4	-58	-41	-205	-239	-184	(e)- 299
Côte d'Ivoire	-1 826	-1 214	-241	40	452	1 670	(e)555	(e)- 257
Gambia	-91	24	38	-43	11	63	52	67
Ghana	30	-223	-386	-1 105	-3 327	-1 688	-2 700	-3 715
Guinea	54	-203	-140	-160	-438	-403	-327	-1 161
Guinea-Bissau	-61	-45	32	-10	-29	-48	(e)-90	(e)-96
Mali	-124	-221	-255	-438	-1 063	-655	-1 190	(e)-1 301
Mauritania	-133	-10	-98	-877	-523	-323	-319	-272
Niger	-276	-236	-104	-312	-651	-1 320	(e)-1 256	(e)-1 697
Nigeria	5 178	4 988	7 427	36 529	29 108	13 821	13 260	8 686
Senegal	-386	-363	-332	-676	-1 884	-865	(e)-1 412	(e)-1 685
Sierra Leone	-165	-69	-112	-105	-225	-194	-320	(e)- 661
Togo	-95	-84	-140	-204	-219	-177	(e)- 230	(e)- 264
Developing economies: America	**-29 931**	**-4 028**	**-49 380**	**51 333**	**-34 669**	**-22 727**	**-56 145**	**-66 342**
Caribbean	*-769*	*-3 225*	*-2 873*	*520*	*-5 859*	*-3 908*	*-4 887*	*-4 220*
Anguilla	..	-9	-61	-52	-211	-84	-66	-54
Antigua and Barbuda	-19	-31	-42	-171	-349	-169	-162	-120

For sources and notes, see end of table.

As percentage of GDP - En pourcentage du PIB (1)								Régions, pays ou territoires
1980	1990	2000	2005	2008	2009	2010	2011	
1.17	0.38	1.48	4.47	4.24	2.47	2.40	2.09	ÉCONOMIES EN DÉVELOPPEMENT
-3.19	-3.04	11.84	7.57	3.59	1.72	3.14	4.08	ÉCONOMIES EN TRANSITION
-0.95	-0.60	-1.30	-1.55	-1.62	-0.61	-0.59	-0.58	ÉCONOMIES DÉVELOPPÉES
1.54	**0.74**	**2.82**	**6.01**	**3.39**	**-2.25**	**0.16**	**-1.13**	**Économies en développement : Afrique**
-7.48	*-5.38*	*-4.48*	*-6.88*	*-9.99*	*-8.46*	*-7.58*	*-8.49*	*Afrique orientale*
-6.27	-4.32	-5.04	-0.51	-19.77	-12.38	-20.32	(e)-14.73	Burundi
-7.21	-4.29	-0.20	-7.37	-10.99	-7.73	-6.90	-9.95	Comores
10.23	-2.30	-3.40	2.84	-22.94	-6.78	4.43	-12.47	Djibouti
–	–	-14.82	-	-	-	-	-	Érythrée
-3.84	-2.52							Éthiopie (...1991)
–	–	0.17	-12.76	-6.98	-7.69	-1.58	-0.23	Éthiopie
-9.56	-4.78	-1.58	-1.35	-6.50	-5.52	-7.73	-10.38	Kenya
-17.04	-8.60	-6.72	-11.00	-22.76	-29.18	(e)-28.34	(e)-7.42	Madagascar
-15.23	-3.57	-3.06	-22.52	-19.14	-11.49	(e)-8.27	(e)-12.00	Malawi
-10.10	-4.55	-0.79	-4.99	-10.12	-7.39	-8.22	(e)-10.27	Maurice
-7.60	-13.99	-17.72	-11.56	-11.92	-12.61	-13.11	-12.17	Mozambique
-3.72	-3.29	-5.33	-2.02	-5.35	-7.28	-7.45	(e)-11.05	Rwanda
-8.52	-2.83	-5.58	-18.75	-21.85	-11.51	-22.72	(e)-20.13	Seychelles
-2.67	-6.52	-5.66	-0.26	-8.02	-7.43	-10.93	-13.85	Ouganda
-7.13	-10.20	-4.11	-7.62	-12.53	-8.78	-8.54	(e)-16.20	République-Unie de Tanzanie
-13.29	-15.88	-20.45	-8.25	-7.09	4.20	7.06	1.12	Zambie
-2.09	-1.19	-	-	-	-	-	-	Zimbabwe
-1.40	*-4.04*	*4.48*	*6.84*	*4.15*	*-8.87*	*1.52*	*2.95*	*Afrique centrale*
1.26	-2.29	8.71	16.77	8.55	-10.03	9.00	8.10	Angola
-5.02	-4.65	-2.35	-2.97	-1.93	-4.78	-3.62	-3.42	Cameroun
-3.87	-6.19	-1.38	-6.52	-9.87	-8.09	-9.94	-6.93	République centrafricaine
1.34	-2.96	-15.39	0.86	-13.72	(e)-17.66	(e)-36.22	(e)-26.73	Tchad
-9.77	-8.98	20.13	11.43	-12.93	(e)-10.00	(e)5.62	(e)13.97	Congo
-2.58	-7.65	-3.28	-13.33	-16.97	-10.46	-6.83	-8.57	Rép. dém. du Congo
-38.17	-14.25	-16.68	-7.09	10.67	-21.01	(e)-13.52	(e)-5.86	Guinée équatoriale
7.32	2.87	18.24	20.96	20.92	4.45	6.37	8.05	Gabon
0.81	-10.01	-26.67	-29.41	-51.32	-39.78	-50.59	(e)-29.61	Sao Tomé-et-Principe
4.32	*2.67*	*4.85*	*9.78*	*9.93*	*-0.47*	*2.81*	*1.23*	*Afrique septentrionale*
0.59	2.29	16.69	20.52	20.09	0.29	7.66	11.32	Algérie
-2.17	6.47	-1.01	2.23	-0.86	-1.78	-2.09	-2.00	Égypte
21.51	7.08	16.30	32.88	43.87	15.96	23.35	4.93	Libye
-6.69	-0.68	-1.28	1.75	-5.10	-5.44	-4.29	-7.98	Maroc
-4.96	-2.94	-3.95	-7.87	-2.03	-4.55	0.20	1.67	Soudan (...2011)
-3.66	-3.41	-3.83	-0.93	-3.82	-2.83	-4.76	(e)-6.61	Tunisie
3.46	*1.40*	*0.30*	*-2.51*	*-6.31*	*-3.94*	*-2.74*	*-3.70*	*Afrique australe*
-14.42	-0.52	9.68	15.23	6.44	-4.54	0.31	-6.80	Botswana
16.04	11.94	-9.27	-1.25	8.97	-0.14	-19.79	(e)-22.81	Lesotho
-	1.03	4.90	4.59	2.51	1.31	0.26	-6.01	Namibie
3.93	1.39	-0.14	-3.45	-7.30	-4.01	-2.78	-3.36	Afrique du Sud
-18.16	4.82	-2.99	-3.95	-7.66	-13.11	-9.89	(e)-6.66	Swaziland
1.61	*2.73*	*5.98*	*17.24*	*6.12*	*3.11*	*1.64*	*-0.95*	*Afrique occidentale*
-2.60	-0.98	-3.42	-5.19	-8.08	-9.85	-8.09	(e)-9.59	Bénin
-2.52	-2.46	-12.11	-11.61	-11.47	-4.55	(e)-2.40	(e)-1.30	Burkina Faso
3.04	-1.24	-10.76	-4.18	-13.42	-15.45	-11.45	(e)-16.22	Cap-Vert
-17.95	-10.21	-2.26	0.24	1.94	7.25	(e)2.44	(e)-1.08	Côte d'Ivoire
-17.97	3.42	4.89	-6.89	1.10	6.94	5.23	6.55	Gambie
0.58	-2.24	-4.84	-6.42	-11.66	-6.50	-8.30	-9.73	Ghana
3.63	-6.95	-4.39	-5.46	-11.60	-9.08	-7.66	-23.34	Guinée
-11.90	-7.45	8.63	-1.83	-3.39	-5.52	(e)-10.96	(e)-10.13	Guinée-Bissau
-8.74	-8.81	-9.58	-7.98	-12.17	-7.31	-12.93	(e)-12.57	Mali
-8.91	-0.59	-7.55	-40.14	-14.12	-10.48	-8.16	-5.97	Mauritanie
-10.22	-8.94	-6.03	-9.25	-12.06	-24.82	(e)-22.64	(e)-27.49	Niger
5.56	14.24	16.01	32.54	13.99	8.16	6.75	3.66	Nigéria
-11.86	-5.85	-7.10	-7.76	-14.18	-6.78	(e)-11.00	(e)-11.68	Sénégal
-11.50	-7.34	-12.13	-7.04	-10.46	-9.15	-15.51	(e)-27.77	Sierra Leone
-8.40	-4.71	-10.79	-9.66	-6.92	-5.59	(e)-7.27	(e)-7.39	Togo
-4.07	**-0.36**	**-2.32**	**1.90**	**-0.79**	**-0.56**	**-1.12**	**-1.18**	**Économies en développement : Amérique**
-3.37	*-5.31*	*-3.13*	*0.41*	*-3.30*	*-2.30*	*-2.73*	*-2.21*	*Caraïbes*
..	-15.61	-56.43	-30.67	-72.73	-38.70	-31.13	-25.72	Anguilla
-17.09	-7.91	-6.37	-19.78	-28.96	-14.94	-14.51	-10.61	Antigua-et-Barbuda

Pour les sources et les notes, se reporter à la fin du tableau.

Region, country or territory	Millions of dollars - Millions de dollars							
	1980	1990	2000	2005	2008	2009	2010	2011
Aruba	..	-158	207	114	19	194	-426	-235
Bahamas	-75	-37	-633	-701	-1 222	-809	-814	-1 091
Barbados	-17	-8	-213	-466	-476	-260	-218	-506
Dominica	-14	-44	-60	-76	-124	-102	-82	-85
Dominican Republic	-720	-280	-1 027	-473	-4 519	-2 331	-4 435	-4 499
Grenada	0	-46	-88	-193	-274	-188	-221	-217
Haiti	-101	-22	-114	7	-292	-227	-166	(e)-28
Jamaica	-136	-312	-367	-1 071	-2 793	-1 128	-934	-2 069
Montserrat	..	-23	-8	-16	-20	-13	-20	-10
Netherlands Antilles	1	-44	-48	-106	-846	-340	-968	_
Saint Kitts and Nevis	-3	-47	-66	-65	-175	-172	-129	-60
Saint Lucia	-33	-57	-95	-129	-340	-140	-183	-284
Saint Vincent and the Grenadines	-9	-24	-24	-102	-230	-197	-213	-208
Trinidad and Tobago	357	459	544	3 881	8 499	1 633	4 172	4 911
Central America	*-12 276*	*-8 372*	*-23 207*	*-10 965*	*-27 897*	*-7 454*	*-10 148*	*-20 621*
Belize	-4	15	-162	-151	-145	-83	-46	-31
Costa Rica	-664	-424	-707	-981	-2 787	-576	-1 274	-2 200
El Salvador	34	-152	-431	-622	-1 532	-312	-658	-1 223
Guatemala	-163	-213	-1 050	-1 241	-1 681	8	-626	-1 457
Honduras	-317	-51	-508	-304	-1 782	-515	-955	-1 503
Mexico	-10 422	-7 451	-18 743	-5 861	-15 741	-5 021	-2 844	-9 030
Nicaragua	-411	-305	-936	-784	-1 507	-775	-883	-1 302
Panama, excl. Canal Zone	-329							
Panama	_	209	-673	-1 022	-2 722	-179	-2 862	-3 874
South America	*-16 886*	*7 569*	*-23 300*	*61 778*	*-912*	*-11 365*	*-41 110*	*-41 501*
Argentina	-4 774	4 552	-8 981	5 274	6 756	8 338	2 932	21
Bolivia (Plurinational State of)	-6	-199	-446	622	1 993	814	874	(e)878
Brazil	-12 831	-3 823	-24 225	13 985	-28 192	-24 302	-47 323	-52 612
Chile	-1 971	-485	-898	1 449	-3 307	2 570	3 802	-3 220
Colombia	-206	542	795	-1 886	-6 699	-4 960	-8 760	-9 980
Ecuador	-642	-360	926	347	1 467	-90	-1 785	-259
Guyana	-129	-161	-82	-96	-192	-165	-160	(e)- 373
Paraguay	-277	390	-163	16	-319	68	-654	-270
Peru	-101	-1 419	-1 546	1 148	-5 318	211	-2 315	-2 267
Suriname	32	67	32	-144	353	210	653	251
Uruguay	-709	186	-566	42	-1 729	-92	-446	-875
Venezuela (Bolivarian Rep. of)	4 728	8 279	11 853	41 021	34 275	6 035	12 072	27 205
Developing economies: Asia	**52 066**	**15 208**	**135 497**	**370 642**	**726 669**	**484 318**	**546 621**	**584 849**
Eastern Asia	*-7 380*	*25 654*	*51 143*	*190 531*	*471 871*	*354 454*	*386 144*	*277 110*
China	286	11 997	20 518	134 082	412 364	261 120	305 374	201 700
China, Hong Kong SAR	-1 432	4 764	6 993	20 181	29 494	17 963	12 390	10 080
China, Taiwan Province of	-818	10 923	8 899	17 578	27 505	42 923	39 873	41 585
Korea, Republic of	-5 071	-1 390	14 803	18 607	3 198	32 791	29 394	26 505
Mongolia	-346	-640	-70	84	-690	-342	-886	-2 760
Southern Asia	*-6 440*	*-9 374*	*6 224*	*350*	*-26 601*	*-17 866*	*-27 293*	*-2 430*
Afghanistan	54	..	..	-168	89	-349	266	-17
Bangladesh	-702	-398	-306	-176	926	3 556	2 109	244
Bhutan	14	-28	-39	-38	-28	-20	-142	-355
India	-1 785	-7 036	-4 601	-10 284	-30 972	-25 922	-51 781	(p)-46 912
Iran (Islamic Rep. of)	-2 438	327	12 481	15 392	22 837	9 477	25 276	51 427
Maldives	-22	10	-51	-273	-647	-419	-463	-257
Nepal	-39	-289	-131	153	733	18	-128	289
Pakistan	-866	-1 661	-85	-3 606	-15 655	-3 993	-1 354	-2 234
Sri Lanka	-655	-298	-1 044	-650	-3 885	-215	-1 075	-4 615
South-Eastern Asia	*-6 768*	*-8 961*	*37 558*	*44 856*	*71 461*	*107 663*	*107 739*	*111 670*
Brunei Darussalam	..	2 531	2 998	4 033	6 939	3 977	5 623	8 421
Cambodia	..	-35	-136	-307	-1 051	-931	-879	(e)-1 137
Indonesia (...2002)	..	-2 988	7 992					
Indonesia	_			278	125	10 629	5 144	2 070
Lao People's Dem. Rep.	-43	-55	-8	-174	78	-61	29	-1 530
Malaysia	-266	-870	8 488	19 980	38 914	31 801	27 291	32 025
Myanmar	-350	-431	-210	582	1 532	1 076	1 511	(e)105
Philippines	-1 904	-2 695	-2 228	1 980	3 627	9 358	8 922	7 078
Singapore	-1 563	3 122	10 244	26 429	27 887	35 207	49 558	(e)50 158
Thailand	-2 076	-7 281	9 313	-7 647	2 211	21 891	13 099	11 870
Timor-Leste	_	_	_	262	2 022	1 325	1 717	2 375
Viet Nam	-565	-259	1 106	-560	-10 823	-6 608	-4 276	236

For sources and notes, see end of table.

As percentage of GDP - En pourcentage du PIB (1)								Régions, pays ou territoires
1980	1990	2000	2005	2008	2009	2010	2011	
..	-19.10	11.06	4.87	0.69	7.74	-17.36	-8.37	Aruba
-4.76	-0.99	-10.00	-9.09	-14.83	-10.36	-10.57	-13.51	Bahamas
-1.73	-0.40	-7.31	-12.64	-11.93	-6.67	-5.51	-12.10	Barbade
-20.22	-21.75	-18.44	-21.04	-26.89	-21.33	-17.26	-17.13	Dominique
-8.80	-2.98	-4.34	-1.41	-9.93	-5.00	-8.60	-7.89	République dominicaine
0.36	-20.91	-16.95	-27.71	-33.07	-24.75	-28.48	-26.96	Grenade
-7.29	-0.84	-3.40	0.18	-4.98	-3.82	-2.70	(e)-0.41	Haïti
-4.47	-6.47	-4.10	-9.60	-20.13	-9.15	-6.96	-14.06	Jamaïque
..	-34.13	-22.20	-36.71	-39.31	-24.10	-35.61	-17.39	Montserrat
0.06	-2.22	-1.69	-3.23	-21.44	-8.57	-23.74		Antilles néerlandaises
-5.56	-29.50	-20.11	-14.75	-30.72	-31.48	-23.49	-10.32	Saint-Kitts-et-Nevis
-24.58	-13.71	-13.54	-15.29	-31.37	-13.15	-15.71	-23.15	Sainte-Lucie
-13.26	-10.02	-6.02	-18.53	-32.94	-29.35	-31.57	-29.00	Saint-Vincent-et-les Grenadines
5.72	9.06	6.67	24.29	31.27	8.32	20.46	22.27	Trinité-et-Tobago
-4.88	*-2.62*	*-3.28*	*-1.16*	*-2.27*	*-0.74*	*-0.86*	*-1.56*	**Amérique centrale**
-1.90	3.79	-19.43	-13.56	-10.66	-6.14	-3.26	-2.12	Belize
-10.81	-5.84	-4.43	-4.91	-9.34	-1.97	-3.55	-5.41	Costa Rica
2.89	-3.16	-3.28	-3.64	-7.15	-1.51	-3.10	-5.37	El Salvador
-2.32	-3.12	-6.10	-4.56	-4.29	0.02	-1.51	-3.08	Guatemala
-10.35	-1.41	-7.07	-3.12	-12.83	-3.64	-6.20	-8.65	Honduras
-4.58	-2.59	-2.94	-0.69	-1.44	-0.57	-0.28	-0.78	Mexique
-18.90	-11.10	-23.76	-16.08	-23.66	-12.47	-13.48	-17.95	Nicaragua
-8.11								Panama, sans la zone du canal
	3.44	-5.79	-6.61	-11.83	-0.74	-10.69	-12.58	Panama
-3.66	*1.02*	*-1.75*	*3.79*	*-0.03*	*-0.40*	*-1.13*	*-1.01*	**Amérique du Sud**
-6.32	3.22	-3.16	2.88	2.06	2.70	0.79	0.00	Argentine
-0.18	-4.09	-5.32	6.52	11.95	4.69	4.45	(e)3.59	Bolivie (État plurinational de)
-6.71	-0.95	-3.76	1.59	-1.71	-1.53	-2.27	-2.18	Brésil
-6.69	-1.45	-1.19	1.23	-1.94	1.60	1.87	-1.38	Chili
-0.44	0.95	0.80	-1.29	-2.74	-2.11	-3.04	-3.00	Colombie
-5.19	-3.20	5.68	0.94	2.71	-0.17	-3.03	-0.38	Équateur
-13.63	-25.45	-7.23	-7.32	-9.97	-8.16	-7.06	(e)-14.92	Guyana
-7.05	8.38	-2.29	0.21	-1.89	0.48	-3.65	-1.21	Paraguay
-0.60	-4.85	-2.90	1.45	-4.12	0.16	-1.47	-1.26	Pérou
3.54	10.87	3.42	-8.05	11.52	6.44	17.74	6.44	Suriname
-6.66	2.01	-2.48	0.24	-5.55	-0.29	-1.11	-1.83	Uruguay
6.84	17.60	10.12	28.19	11.02	1.85	3.09	8.67	Venezuela (Rép. bolivarienne du)
4.13	**0.68**	**3.19**	**5.24**	**6.29**	**4.15**	**3.99**	**3.61**	**Économies en développement : Asie**
-1.67	*2.79*	*2.30*	*5.19*	*7.76*	*5.47*	*5.21*	*3.11*	**Asie orientale**
0.09	2.97	1.72	5.87	9.10	5.17	5.32	2.86	Chine
-4.97	6.20	4.13	11.35	13.70	8.58	5.52	4.14	Chine (RAS de Hong Kong)
-1.94	6.62	2.73	4.82	6.87	11.37	9.27	8.91	Province chinoise de Taiwan
-7.88	-0.51	2.78	2.20	0.34	3.93	2.90	2.38	Corée, République de
-51.80	-42.45	-6.15	3.34	-12.27	-7.46	-14.31	-32.30	Mongolie
-1.94	*-1.85*	*0.87*	*0.03*	*-1.37*	*-0.88*	*-1.11*	*-0.09*	**Asie méridionale**
1.47	..	..	-2.45	0.83	-2.80	1.69	-0.09	Afghanistan
-4.20	-1.41	-0.67	-0.31	1.16	3.99	2.12	0.22	Bangladesh
11.06	-10.01	-8.93	-4.63	-2.23	-1.59	-9.57	-21.95	Bhoutan
-0.97	-2.15	-0.98	-1.23	-2.41	-1.92	-3.01	(p)-2.41	Inde
-2.65	0.36	12.00	7.49	6.23	2.69	6.54	10.93	Iran (Rép. islamique d')
-41.40	4.98	-8.24	-36.41	-51.36	-31.75	-31.27	-17.56	Maldives
-1.86	-7.65	-2.28	1.85	6.27	0.14	-0.80	1.59	Népal
-3.01	-3.47	-0.12	-3.30	-10.76	-2.56	-0.78	-1.07	Pakistan
-15.33	-3.64	-6.24	-2.66	-9.54	-0.51	-2.17	-7.81	Sri Lanka
-5.92	*-2.47*	*6.19*	*4.92*	*4.71*	*7.15*	*5.78*	*5.16*	**Asie du Sud-Est**
..	71.91	49.96	42.31	48.21	37.06	43.17	51.50	Brunéi Darussalam
..	-2.04	-3.71	-4.87	-10.15	-8.95	-7.80	(e)-8.85	Cambodge
..	-2.37	4.83						Indonésie (…2002)
			0.10	0.02	1.97	0.73	0.24	Indonésie
-13.35	-6.34	-0.51	-6.34	1.47	-1.09	0.45	-19.56	Rép. dém. populaire lao
-1.05	-1.90	9.05	14.48	17.48	16.48	11.48	11.49	Malaisie
-5.93	-8.34	-2.89	4.88	5.93	3.28	3.60	(e)0.19	Myanmar
-5.30	-5.49	-2.75	1.92	2.08	5.56	4.47	3.15	Philippines
-12.97	8.04	10.86	21.07	14.73	19.20	22.25	(e)19.71	Singapour
-6.42	-8.53	7.59	-4.34	0.81	8.30	4.11	3.43	Thaïlande
			74.91	359.62	188.17	216.30	238.28	Timor-Leste
-23.60	-4.00	3.55	-1.06	-11.88	-6.80	-4.12	0.20	Viet Nam

Pour les sources et les notes, se reporter à la fin du tableau.

7

7.1.1 Balance of payments: Current account net of countries and geographical regions

Region, country or territory	Millions of dollars - Millions de dollars							
	1980	1990	2000	2005	2008	2009	2010	2011
Western Asia	*72 653*	*7 888*	*40 571*	*134 904*	*209 939*	*40 067*	*80 031*	*198 499*
Bahrain	184	70	830	1 474	2 257	560	770	(e)1 090
Jordan	374	-227	27	-2 272	-2 054	-1 244	-1 882	-2 885
Kuwait	15 302	3 886	14 672	30 071	60 239	25 774	36 822	70 776
Lebanon	-	-	-	-2 748	-4 103	-6 741	-7 462	(e)-10 975
Occupied Palestinian territory	..	..	-990	-1 152	764	-737	-691	-1 894
Oman	942	1 106	3 129	5 178	5 019	-596	5 871	10 263
Qatar	8 364	-657	4 128	13 301	33 039	9 987	21 027	24 449
Saudi Arabia	41 503	-4 147	14 317	90 061	132 314	20 955	66 751	158 492
Syrian Arab Republic	251	1 762	1 061	299	472	-1 030	-367	(e)-5 858
Turkey	-3 408	-2 625	-9 920	-22 309	-41 524	-13 370	-46 643	-77 238
United Arab Emirates	10 089	7 942	16 696	22 378	24 766	9 073	7 216	33 308
Yemen, Arab Republic	-685	–	–	–	–	–	–	–
Yemen, Democratic	-124	–	–	–	–	–	–	–
Yemen	–	739	1 337	624	-1 251	-2 565	-1 381	-1 029
Developing economies: Oceania	*-336*	*-198*	*271*	*-68*	*-1 863*	*-1 701*	*-2 894*	*-825*
Fiji	-17	-94	-26	-300	-645	-236	-411	(e)- 429
French Polynesia	..	..	..	9	-91	154	2	..
Kiribati	2	-9	-2	-36	-22	-32	-22	-37
New Caledonia	..	..	..	-112	-1 419	-824	-1 463	..
Papua New Guinea	-289	-76	351	539	708	-585	-633	(e)-49
Samoa	-13	9	-4	-25	-53	-9	-59	-76
Solomon Islands	-12	-28	-41	-90	-124	-129	-204	-98
Tonga	-7	6	-12	-21	-66	-54	-15	-17
Tuvalu	..	..	..	3	-9	4	-5	-3
Vanuatu	..	-6	5	-34	-142	10	-84	-116
Transition economies	*-2 301*	*-2 482*	*47 094*	*83 116*	*84 069*	*30 660*	*66 530*	*105 352*
Albania	16	-118	-156	-571	-2 018	-1 851	-1 353	-1 588
Armenia	–	–	-278	-52	-1 383	-1 369	-1 373	-1 120
Azerbaijan	–	–	-168	167	16 453	10 175	15 040	17 145
Belarus	–	–	-338	436	-4 988	-6 178	-8 278	-5 775
Bosnia and Herzegovina	–	–	-396	-1 844	-2 605	-1 088	-946	-1 588
Croatia	–	–	-533	-2 460	-6 083	-3 057	-863	-449
Georgia	–	–	-177	-710	-2 824	-1 144	-1 197	-1 682
Kazakhstan	–	–	366	-1 056	6 326	-4 114	2 409	14 110
Kyrgyzstan	–	–	-76	-37	-701	-102	-385	-253
Montenegro	–	–	–	–	-2 286	-1 224	-1 012	-882
Republic of Moldova	–	–	-98	-226	-979	-465	-460	-802
Russian Federation	–	–	46 839	84 602	103 530	48 605	71 080	98 834
Serbia and Montenegro	–	–	35	-308	–	–	–	–
Serbia	–	–	–	–	-10 395	-2 867	-2 820	-4 113
SFR of Yugoslavia	-2 317	-2 364	–	–	–	–	–	–
Tajikistan	–	–	-62	-19	48	-180	-383	(e)- 293
TFYR of Macedonia	–	–	-103	-159	-1 236	-610	-200	-274
Turkmenistan	–	–	412	875	3 560	-2 981	-2 349	466
Ukraine	–	–	1 481	2 531	-12 763	-1 732	-3 018	-9 006
Uzbekistan	–	–	345	1 948	2 413	(e)843	(e)2 637	(e)2 621
Developed economies: America	*-3 961*	*-98 716*	*-396 721*	*-724 067*	*-669 525*	*-415 999*	*-519 380*	*-514 286*
Bermuda	..	..	..	..	1 239	579	829	(e)726
Canada	-6 088	-19 764	19 622	21 714	6 376	-40 024	-49 307	-49 086
United States	2 127	-78 952	-416 343	-745 780	-677 141	-376 554	-470 902	-465 926
Developed economies: Asia	*-11 621*	*44 242*	*117 604*	*169 884*	*161 193*	*153 992*	*210 252*	*119 258*
Israel	-871	163	-2 056	4 101	1 830	6 975	6 336	194
Japan	-10 750	44 078	119 660	165 783	159 363	147 017	203 916	119 064
Developed economies: Europe	*-57 724*	*-32 888*	*-27 730*	*79 420*	*-101 809*	*70 873*	*105 848*	*183 075*
Austria	-3 865	1 166	-1 339	6 245	20 127	10 291	11 671	7 988
Belgium (2)	-4 931	3 627	9 352	7 703	-7 110	-7 309	6 132	-3 709
Bulgaria	954	-1 710	-703	-3 347	-11 875	-4 256	-591	579
Cyprus	-258	-154	-488	-971	-3 878	-2 480	-2 309	-2 546
Czechoslovakia	-	-1 227	–	–	–	–	–	–
Czech Republic	–	–	-2 690	-1 210	-4 774	-4 849	-7 602	-6 349
Denmark	-2 389	1 372	2 262	11 104	10 001	10 402	17 134	22 077
Estonia	..	..	-299	-1 386	-2 217	682	549	477
Faeroe Islands	..	..	99	31	-31	-16	135	..
Finland	-1 403	-6 962	10 526	6 469	6 930	4 549	3 495	-1 860
France	-4 208	-9 944	19 674	-10 260	-49 877	-39 867	-44 499	-54 126
Germany, Federal Republic of	-15 656	–	–	–	–	–	–	–

For sources and notes, see end of table.

	As percentage of GDP - En pourcentage du PIB (1)							Régions, pays ou territoires
1980	1990	2000	2005	2008	2009	2010	2011	
19.58	*1.82*	*5.78*	*10.93*	*10.46*	*2.39*	*4.07*	*8.56*	*Asie occidentale*
5.60	1.62	10.34	10.95	10.19	2.90	3.36	(e)4.08	Bahreïn
9.32	-5.65	0.32	-18.05	-9.05	-4.96	-6.84	-9.48	Jordanie
53.33	21.04	38.90	37.22	40.87	24.34	29.62	40.08	Koweït
-	-	-	-12.57	-13.71	-19.52	-19.01	(e)-26.59	Liban
..	..	-23.61	-24.86	12.23	-10.89	-9.40	-25.77	Territoire palestinien occupé
15.06	9.57	16.09	16.75	8.29	-1.27	10.15	14.28	Oman
106.72	-8.93	23.24	29.87	28.66	10.21	16.51	14.06	Qatar
25.22	-3.56	7.60	28.54	27.78	5.62	15.36	28.50	Arabie saoudite
1.91	15.81	5.40	1.05	0.90	-1.90	-0.61	(e)-10.14	République arabe syrienne
-3.69	-1.30	-3.72	-4.62	-5.69	-2.18	-6.35	-9.91	Turquie
23.14	15.67	16.00	12.39	7.87	3.36	2.42	9.25	Émirats arabes unis
-28.02	–	–	–	–	–	–	–	Yémen, République arabe du
-20.52	–	–	–	–	–	–	–	Yémen, Démocratique
–	15.78	13.31	3.49	-4.36	-9.27	-4.00	-2.74	Yémen
-7.62	*-3.72*	*4.29*	*-0.32*	*-6.22*	*-5.94*	*-9.37*	*-4.25*	*Économies en développement : Océanie*
-1.44	-6.96	-1.48	-9.97	-18.09	-8.35	-13.48	(e)-11.70	Fidji
..	..	..	0.16	-1.30	2.25	0.03	..	Polynésie française
7.00	-22.25	-3.68	-34.33	-16.33	-25.80	-14.94	-21.72	Kiribati
..	..	..	-1.80	-15.55	-9.41	-16.51	..	Nouvelle-Calédonie
-10.23	-2.30	10.02	11.08	8.85	-7.26	-6.46	(e)-0.38	Papouasie-Nouvelle-Guinée
-11.52	7.68	-1.81	-5.78	-9.74	-1.76	-9.58	-11.16	Samoa
-8.48	-13.34	-12.11	-21.00	-20.45	-21.53	-31.83	-12.27	Îles Salomon
-8.64	3.58	-6.13	-8.22	-19.39	-16.96	-4.11	-3.98	Tonga
..	..	..	14.65	-31.39	14.80	-15.52	-9.59	Tuvalu
..	-3.57	1.83	-8.66	-23.86	1.74	-11.79	-14.40	Vanuatu
-3.19	*-3.04*	*11.84*	*7.57*	*3.59*	*1.72*	*3.14*	*4.08*	*Économies en transition*
0.72	-5.32	-4.29	-7.00	-15.56	-15.38	-11.48	-12.39	Albanie
–	–	-14.56	-1.06	-11.86	-15.84	-14.65	-10.80	Arménie
–	–	-3.18	1.26	33.68	22.97	29.04	27.01	Azerbaïdjan
–	–	-3.25	1.44	-8.21	-12.54	-15.13	-10.50	Bélarus
–	–	-7.13	-16.91	-14.07	-6.38	-5.62	-8.70	Bosnie-Herzégovine
–	–	-2.48	-5.49	-8.70	-4.82	-1.42	-0.70	Croatie
–	–	-5.78	-11.07	-22.07	-10.63	-10.26	-11.68	Géorgie
–	–	2.00	-1.85	4.74	-3.57	1.64	7.91	Kazakhstan
–	–	-5.55	-1.52	-13.64	-2.18	-8.34	-4.44	Kirghizistan
–	–	–	–	-50.58	-29.56	-24.62	-19.40	Monténégro
–	–	-7.62	-7.56	-16.17	-8.55	-7.92	-11.46	République de Moldova
–	–	18.05	11.07	6.23	3.98	4.80	5.37	Fédération de Russie
–	–	0.31	-0.99	–	–	–	–	Serbie-et-Monténégro
–	–	–	–	-19.47	-6.29	-6.51	-8.07	Serbie
-3.31	-2.97	–	–	–	–	–	–	RSF de Yougoslavie
–	–	-7.20	-0.82	0.92	-3.61	-6.82	(e)-4.50	Tadjikistan
–	–	-2.87	-2.66	-12.57	-6.54	-2.19	-2.69	LERY de Macédoine
–	–	8.36	7.03	18.64	-14.95	-10.15	1.56	Turkménistan
–	–	4.74	2.94	-7.09	-1.48	-2.19	-5.46	Ukraine
–	–	2.51	13.53	8.40	(e)2.56	(e)6.73	(e)5.78	Ouzbékistan
-0.13	*-1.55*	*-3.71*	*-5.25*	*-4.23*	*-2.72*	*-3.22*	*-3.05*	*Économies développées : Amérique*
..	..	..	..	20.42	10.13	13.78	(e)12.07	Bermudes
-2.26	-3.39	2.71	1.92	0.42	-2.99	-3.13	-2.83	Canada
0.08	-1.36	-4.18	-5.90	-4.73	-2.70	-3.24	-3.08	États-Unis
-1.06	*1.42*	*2.45*	*3.63*	*3.17*	*2.95*	*3.70*	*1.96*	*Économies développées : Asie*
-3.67	0.28	-1.65	3.06	0.91	3.58	2.91	0.08	Israël
-1.00	1.44	2.56	3.64	3.27	2.92	3.74	2.04	Japon
-1.46	*-0.43*	*-0.31*	*0.55*	*-0.53*	*0.41*	*0.61*	*0.98*	*Économies développées : Europe*
-4.74	0.71	-0.70	2.05	4.86	2.70	3.08	1.91	Autriche
-3.93	1.79	4.02	2.04	-1.40	-1.55	1.31	-0.72	Belgique (2)
8.85	-8.25	-5.45	-11.58	-22.91	-8.76	-1.24	1.08	Bulgarie
-11.58	-2.67	-5.32	-5.74	-15.43	-10.59	-10.06	-10.21	Chypre
-	-2.34	–	–	–	–	–	–	Tchécoslovaquie
–	–	-4.57	-0.93	-2.12	-2.47	-3.85	-2.95	République tchèque
-3.43	1.01	1.41	4.31	2.93	3.37	5.53	6.67	Danemark
–	–	-5.26	-9.97	-9.29	3.55	2.90	2.15	Estonie
..	..	..	..	..	..	..	..	Îles Féroé
-2.65	-5.01	8.65	3.31	2.55	1.89	1.46	-0.70	Finlande
-0.61	-0.80	1.48	-0.48	-1.76	-1.52	-1.73	-1.95	France
-1.70	–	–	–	–	–	–	–	Allemagne, Rép. fédérale d'

Pour les sources et les notes, se reporter à la fin du tableau.

7.1.1 Balance of payments: Current account net of countries and geographical regions

Region, country or territory	Millions of dollars - Millions de dollars							
	1980	1990	2000	2005	2008	2009	2010	2011
Germany	–	46 456	-32 484	140 216	226 272	198 096	200 708	204 252
Greece	-2 209	-3 537	-9 820	-18 233	-51 313	-35 913	-30 897	-29 227
Hungary	-1 102	379	-4 004	-8 238	-11 119	-107	1 515	2 054
Iceland	-76	-134	-847	-2 648	-4 472	-1 433	-1 024	-952
Ireland	-2 132	-361	-356	-7 150	-15 297	-6 293	954	144
Italy	-10 588	-16 479	-5 781	-29 744	-66 252	-41 004	-72 015	-71 874
Latvia	–	–	-371	-1 992	-4 492	2 284	731	-362
Lithuania	–	–	-675	-1 831	-6 310	1 725	534	-619
Luxembourg	..	..	2 562	4 406	3 040	3 307	4 122	4 185
Malta	39	-56	-480	-524	-454	-662	-536	-282
Netherlands	-855	8 089	7 264	46 618	38 036	32 931	55 393	76 312
Norway	1 079	3 992	25 079	49 003	79 235	44 543	51 444	(e)70 000
Poland	-3 417	3 067	-10 343	-7 242	-34 957	-17 155	-21 873	-22 128
Portugal	-1 064	-181	-12 189	-19 821	-31 852	-25 596	-22 813	-15 437
Romania	-2 420	-3 254	-1 355	-8 504	-23 719	-6 955	-7 284	-8 541
Slovakia	–	–	-694	-4 005	-6 185	-3 161	-3 009	12
Slovenia	–	–	-548	-681	-3 763	-625	-388	-528
Spain	-5 580	-18 009	-23 185	-83 388	-154 529	-69 775	-63 129	-52 281
Sweden	-4 331	-6 339	10 074	25 057	44 499	30 115	30 513	38 286
Switzerland	-201	6 124	32 830	53 149	5 686	36 453	74 015	74 064
United Kingdom	6 862	-38 811	-38 800	-59 406	-41 159	-37 051	-75 229	-46 535
Developed economies: Oceania	**-5 420**	**-17 401**	**-17 170**	**-49 809**	**-59 353**	**-47 139**	**-36 985**	**-39 590**
Australia	-4 447	-15 948	-14 763	-41 032	-47 786	-43 891	-31 991	-32 881
New Zealand	-973	-1 453	-2 407	-8 777	-11 567	-3 248	-4 994	-6 709

Sources:
UNCTAD secretariat calculations, based on:
- IMF, *Balance of Payments Statistics*
- IMF, *World Economic Outlook*
- Economist Intelligence Unit, *Country Data*
- OECD, *OECD.Stat*
- national sources

Notes:
- Balance-of-payments current account data cover all transactions between residents and non-residents of a reporting economy, involving economic values and mainly concerning goods, services, income and current transfers. In general, the current account balance describes the difference between current receipts and expenditures for internationally traded goods, services and income payments. At the same time, from a national perspective, the current account balance would equal the gap between national savings and domestic investment.

(1)   Source of GDP data: UNCTAD, based on UN DESA Statistics Division (UNSD)
(2)   Data from 1980 to 1994 inclusive refer to Belgium-Luxembourg.

As percentage of GDP - En pourcentage du PIB (1)								Régions, pays ou territoires
1980	1990	2000	2005	2008	2009	2010	2011	
_	2.71	-1.72	5.07	6.24	6.01	6.12	5.72	Allemagne
-4.04	-3.75	-7.73	-7.59	-15.04	-11.16	-10.26	-9.78	Grèce
-4.41	1.04	-8.63	-7.47	-7.21	-0.08	1.18	1.47	Hongrie
-2.29	-2.10	-9.74	-16.26	-26.54	-11.83	-8.14	-6.75	Islande
-9.95	-0.75	-0.37	-3.52	-5.80	-2.82	0.46	0.07	Irlande
-2.30	-1.45	-0.53	-1.67	-2.88	-1.94	-3.51	-3.28	Italie
_	_	-4.77	-12.50	-13.43	8.83	3.04	-1.28	Lettonie
_	_	-5.87	-7.02	-13.27	4.66	1.46	-1.45	Lituanie
..	..	12.64	11.70	5.26	6.37	7.73	7.13	Luxembourg
3.10	-2.19	-12.14	-8.75	-5.31	-8.18	-6.57	-3.16	Malte
-0.47	2.74	1.89	7.30	4.37	4.15	7.11	9.09	Pays-Bas
1.69	3.39	14.90	16.23	17.80	12.02	12.45	(e)14.67	Norvège
-5.91	4.75	-6.04	-2.38	-6.60	-3.98	-4.66	-4.31	Pologne
-3.28	-0.23	-10.42	-10.37	-12.64	-10.93	-9.97	-6.47	Portugal
-6.64	-8.02	-3.63	-8.57	-11.61	-4.23	-4.51	-4.58	Roumanie
_	_	-3.40	-8.36	-6.55	-3.62	-3.45	0.01	Slovaquie
_	_	-2.74	-1.91	-6.89	-1.27	-0.83	-1.07	Slovénie
-2.47	-3.46	-3.99	-7.38	-9.69	-4.77	-4.49	-3.47	Espagne
-3.28	-2.59	4.07	6.76	9.15	7.46	6.65	7.17	Suède
-0.18	2.56	13.01	14.13	1.12	7.33	13.88	11.50	Suisse
1.27	-3.83	-2.63	-2.60	-1.56	-1.71	-3.34	-1.93	Royaume-Uni
-2.74	**-4.68**	**-3.70**	**-5.67**	**-5.02**	**-4.21**	**-2.62**	**-2.35**	**Économies développées : Océanie**
-2.54	-4.87	-3.59	-5.37	-4.54	-4.38	-2.52	-2.16	Australie
-4.21	-3.27	-4.51	-7.76	-8.87	-2.77	-3.53	-4.13	Nouvelle-Zélande

Sources :
Calculs du secrétariat de la CNUCED, sur la base de :
- FMI, *Statistiques de la balance des paiements*
- FMI, *World Economic Outlook*
- Economist Intelligence Unit, *Country Data*
- OCDE, *OECD.Stat*
- sources nationales

Notes:
- Les données du compte des transactions courantes de la balance des paiements recouvrent toutes les transactions, entre entités résidentes et non résidentes, portant sur des valeurs économiques, concernant notamment les biens, les services, les revenus et les transferts courants. En général, la balance du compte courant indique la différence entre les recettes et les paiements pour les biens, les services et les revenus faisant partie des transactions internationales. De même, d'une perspective nationale, la balance du compte courant représente l'écart entre les épargnes nationales et l'investissement intérieur.

(1)   Source des données du PIB : CNUCED, sur la base des données de ONU DAES Division de statistiques (UNSD)
(2)   Les données de 1980 à 1994 se réfèrent à Belgique-Luxembourg.

Economic grouping	Millions of dollars - Millions de dollars							
	1980	1990	2000	2005	2008	2009	2010	2011
DEVELOPING ECONOMIES	**28 455**	**14 617**	**103 220**	**482 234**	**743 189**	**426 576**	**490 240**	**496 365**
Developing economies excluding China	28 169	2 620	82 702	348 152	330 825	165 456	184 866	294 665
Developing economies excluding LDCs	34 954	20 549	107 592	489 814	755 016	455 071	500 390	511 925
High-income developing economies	58 265	31 567	79 136	301 601	403 955	227 924	277 426	393 864
Middle-income developing economies	-20 864	-242	18 188	167 968	388 336	242 937	269 257	168 602
Low-income developing economies	-8 946	-16 708	5 896	12 665	-49 101	-44 285	-56 443	-66 101
Heavily indebted poor countries (IMF)	-7 954	-8 157	-7 590	-14 416	-30 052	-23 698	-21 970	-26 317
Landlocked developing countries	-2 716	-2 924	-2 205	-1 525	17 040	-8 474	4 466	15 786
Small island developing States	-444	-493	-983	328	2 002	-2 762	-317	-246
Least developed countries	*-6 500*	*-5 932*	*-4 371*	*-7 580*	*-11 827*	*-28 495*	*-10 150*	*-15 560*
Africa and Haiti	-4 593	-5 378	-4 814	-8 091	-14 375	-30 269	-12 732	-14 036
Asia	-1 876	-497	506	497	1 029	725	1 384	-3 430
Islands	-31	-57	-63	15	1 519	1 049	1 199	1 906
Major petroleum and gas exporters	*92 199*	*25 111*	*100 911*	*295 192*	*418 933*	*96 735*	*224 664*	*415 497*
Africa	13 708	8 374	23 635	77 792	106 444	16 031	49 628	39 577
America	4 728	8 279	11 853	41 021	34 275	6 035	12 072	27 205
Asia	73 763	8 458	65 423	176 380	278 214	74 669	162 964	348 715
Major exporters of manufactured goods	*-21 362*	*13 814*	*60 515*	*223 349*	*525 832*	*438 674*	*474 134*	*364 893*
America	-10 422	-7 451	-18 743	-5 861	-15 741	-5 021	-2 844	-9 030
Asia	-10 940	21 265	79 258	229 210	541 573	443 694	476 978	373 923
Emerging economies	*-39 893*	*-4 122*	*-2 644*	*90 941*	*53 913*	*146 407*	*113 466*	*95 035*
America	-30 099	-8 626	-54 391	15 994	-45 802	-18 205	-45 748	-67 108
Asia	-9 794	4 503	51 747	74 947	99 715	164 612	159 214	162 143
Newly industrialized Asian economies	*-13 130*	*3 585*	*64 504*	*97 385*	*132 961*	*202 561*	*185 670*	*181 371*
First tier	-8 883	17 419	40 938	82 795	88 084	128 883	131 215	128 329
Second tier	-4 246	-13 834	23 565	14 591	44 877	73 678	54 455	53 042
Developing economies: Africa	**6 656**	**3 635**	**16 833**	**60 327**	**53 052**	**-33 314**	**2 657**	**-21 318**
Northern Africa excluding Sudan	6 267	5 289	13 145	38 969	62 487	227	18 413	6 997
Sub-Saharan Africa	390	-1 655	3 688	21 358	-9 436	-33 541	-15 756	-28 315
Sub-Saharan Africa excluding South Africa	-2 772	-3 206	3 878	29 876	10 648	-22 214	-5 639	-14 632
Developing economies: America	**-29 931**	**-4 028**	**-49 380**	**51 333**	**-34 669**	**-22 727**	**-56 145**	**-66 342**
Central America and Greater Caribbean Islands excluding Puerto Rico	-13 233	-11 530	-25 494	-12 363	-38 007	-10 714	-15 704	-26 883
Central America and Greater Caribbean Islands excluding Mexico and Puerto Rico	-2 811	-4 079	-6 751	-6 502	-22 266	-5 694	-12 860	-17 852
South America and Central America	-29 162	-802	-46 508	50 813	-28 809	-18 819	-51 258	-62 122
South America excluding Brazil	-4 055	11 392	924	47 793	27 280	12 937	6 213	11 111
Developing economies: Asia	**52 066**	**15 208**	**135 497**	**370 642**	**726 669**	**484 318**	**546 621**	**584 849**
Eastern and South-Eastern Asia excluding China	-14 434	4 697	68 183	101 306	130 968	200 997	188 509	187 081
Southern Asia excluding India	-4 654	-2 338	10 825	10 634	4 371	8 055	24 488	44 482

Sources:
For sources and notes, see end of table 7.1.1.

As percentage of GDP - En pourcentage du PIB (1)								Groupements économiques
1980	1990	2000	2005	2008	2009	2010	2011	
1.17	**0.38**	**1.48**	**4.47**	**4.24**	**2.47**	**2.40**	**2.09**	**ÉCONOMIES EN DÉVELOPPEMENT**
1.32	0.08	1.43	4.09	2.55	1.36	1.26	1.77	Économies en développement sans la Chine
1.50	0.56	1.58	4.67	4.45	2.72	2.52	2.22	Économies en développement sans les PMA
5.88	1.99	2.55	7.08	6.74	4.36	4.48	5.72	Économies en développement à revenu élevé
-2.13	-0.02	0.63	3.54	4.50	2.69	2.54	1.33	Économies en développement à revenu intermédiaire
-1.93	-2.22	0.58	0.71	-1.70	-1.49	-1.55	-1.58	Économies en développement à revenu faible
-7.29	-5.87	-5.36	-5.87	-7.51	-5.95	-5.02	-5.41	Pays pauvres très endettés (FMI)
-5.55	-4.16	-1.79	-0.66	3.71	-1.94	0.87	2.60	Pays en développement sans littoral
-2.40	-1.87	-2.31	0.53	2.31	-3.67	-0.39	-0.27	Petits États insulaires en développement
-6.02	*-4.04*	*-2.50*	*-2.46*	*-2.20*	*-5.24*	*-1.66*	*-2.25*	*Pays les moins avancés*
-6.07	-5.30	-4.83	-4.17	-3.97	-8.69	-3.34	-3.27	Afrique et Haïti
-5.89	-1.11	0.68	0.44	0.59	0.38	0.61	-1.32	Asie
-6.23	-6.35	-5.35	0.66	47.67	31.77	32.50	43.75	Îles
15.60	*5.22*	*13.68*	*22.79*	*17.93*	*4.80*	*9.65*	*15.50*	*Principaux exportateurs de pétrole et de gaz*
7.65	6.05	15.89	26.68	19.53	3.63	9.74	7.10	Afrique
6.84	17.60	10.12	28.19	11.02	1.85	3.09	8.67	Amérique
21.51	2.86	13.87	20.56	18.79	5.99	11.41	19.28	Asie
-2.89	*1.00*	*1.91*	*4.51*	*6.69*	*5.49*	*5.14*	*3.34*	*Principaux exportateurs d'articles manufacturés*
-4.58	-2.59	-2.94	-0.69	-1.44	-0.57	-0.28	-0.78	Amérique
-2.14	1.96	3.13	5.58	8.01	6.24	5.83	3.83	Asie
-5.56	*-0.27*	*-0.09*	*2.42*	*1.00*	*2.97*	*1.87*	*1.38*	*Économies émergentes*
-5.57	-0.96	-3.21	0.76	-1.36	-0.59	-1.19	-1.52	Amérique
-5.55	0.74	4.42	4.54	4.95	8.89	7.16	6.59	Asie
-5.44	*0.42*	*4.07*	*4.39*	*4.56*	*7.32*	*5.53*	*4.80*	*Économies nouvellement industrialisées d'Asie*
-6.02	3.16	3.65	5.47	5.07	8.03	6.94	6.17	Première génération
-4.53	-4.52	5.09	2.07	3.80	6.33	3.72	3.13	Deuxième génération
1.54	**0.74**	**2.82**	**6.01**	**3.39**	**-2.25**	**0.16**	**-1.13**	**Économies en développement : Afrique**
4.77	3.09	5.31	11.63	11.33	0.04	3.17	1.17	Afrique septentrionale sans le Soudan
0.13	-0.51	1.05	3.19	-0.93	-3.48	-1.40	-2.20	Afrique subsaharienne
-1.25	-1.52	1.79	7.08	1.44	-3.27	-0.74	-1.67	Afrique subsaharienne sans l'Afrique du Sud
-4.07	**-0.36**	**-2.32**	**1.90**	**-0.79**	**-0.56**	**-1.12**	**-1.18**	**Économies en développement : Amérique**
-5.01	-3.16	-3.30	-1.20	-2.81	-0.94	-1.19	-1.83	Amérique centrale et Grandes Antilles sans Porto Rico
-7.72	-5.28	-4.95	-3.48	-8.53	-2.19	-4.53	-5.65	Amérique centrale et Grandes Antilles sans le Mexique et Porto Rico
-4.09	-0.08	-2.28	1.98	-0.69	-0.48	-1.06	-1.15	Amérique du Sud et Amérique centrale
-1.50	3.36	0.13	6.40	2.09	1.01	0.40	0.66	Amérique du Sud sans le Brésil
4.13	**0.68**	**3.19**	**5.24**	**6.29**	**4.15**	**3.99**	**3.61**	**Économies en développement : Asie**
-5.76	0.54	4.17	4.40	4.27	6.86	5.33	4.68	Asie orientale et Asie du Sud-Est sans la Chine
-3.15	-1.30	4.43	2.57	0.67	1.21	3.29	5.02	Asie méridionale sans l'Inde

Sources :
Pour les sources et les notes, se reporter à la fin du tableau 7.1.1.

Trade group	Millions of dollars - Millions de dollars							
	1980	1990	2000	2005	2008	2009	2010	2011
AFRICA								
CEMAC	-279	-788	1 009	1 636	2 085	-4 725	-3 805	-602
CEPGL	-389	-869	-317	-1 013	-2 536	-1 713	-1 626	-2 306
COMESA	4 165	1 015	2 688	8 435	18 862	-8 864	1 621	-13 675
EAC	-1 616	-1 503	-1 131	-1 441	-6 483	-5 419	-7 072	-10 631
ECCAS	-600	-1 905	1 467	5 725	6 649	-14 089	1 882	5 198
ECOWAS	2 158	2 254	5 329	32 615	20 028	8 937	5 422	-3 208
MRU	-1 937	-1 487	-494	-226	-212	1 073	-92	-2 079
SADC	815	-1 202	-941	-6 755	-21 387	-25 921	-8 837	-17 598
UMA	6 570	2 953	14 018	35 990	63 379	3 254	22 598	11 373
WAEMU	-2 853	-2 259	-1 439	-2 460	-4 894	-2 423	-4 359	-6 125
AMERICA								
ANCOM	-955	-1 436	-271	231	-8 558	-4 026	-11 986	-11 628
CACM	-1 522	-1 145	-3 631	-3 931	-9 289	-2 171	-4 396	-7 686
CARICOM	-151	-269	-1 378	507	2 220	-1 810	1 478	81
FTAA	-33 893	-99 966	-445 413	-672 813	-701 870	-439 487	-574 852	-581 389
LAIA	-27 211	-2 332	-42 771	56 297	-19 321	-16 006	-44 470	-50 075
MERCOSUR	-18 591	1 305	-33 934	19 317	-23 484	-15 988	-45 491	-53 736
NAFTA	-14 383	-106 167	-415 463	-729 927	-686 506	-421 599	-523 054	-524 043
OAS	-33 893	-102 510	-446 191	-672 673	-704 376	-439 062	-574 874	-581 055
OECS	-78	-280	-444	-805	-1 724	-1 065	-1 076	-1 038
ASIA								
APTA	-7 970	2 820	29 362	141 405	381 708	271 269	284 049	175 392
ASEAN	-6 768	-8 961	37 558	44 594	69 439	106 338	106 022	109 296
ECO	-6 658	-3 959	3 294	-8 813	-6 154	-4 595	-5 486	5 735
GCC	76 385	8 201	53 773	162 462	257 634	65 752	138 458	298 378
SAARC	-4 002	-9 701	-6 257	-15 042	-49 438	-27 343	-52 569	-53 858
EUROPE								
EFTA	801	9 982	57 062	99 504	80 448	79 563	124 435	143 112
EU	-58 525	-42 869	-84 891	-20 115	-182 227	-8 674	-18 723	39 962
Euro area	-52 710	3 654	-38 286	35 494	-98 322	17 172	43 429	61 500
OCEANIA								
MSG	-318	-204	289	115	-203	-940	-1 333	-691
INTERREGIONAL								
ACP	-817	-4 924	784	21 845	-12 553	-36 951	-18 431	-30 840
APEC	-46 323	-63 615	-179 100	-291 275	50 559	190 130	208 203	40 458
BSEC	-7 067	-11 244	25 645	33 349	-38 810	-11 143	-9 515	-16 759
CIS	–	–	48 423	89 169	111 515	42 501	74 920	115 928

Sources:
For sources and notes, see end of table 7.1.1.

As percentage of GDP - En pourcentage du PIB (1)								Groupements commerciaux
1980	1990	2000	2005	2008	2009	2010	2011	
								AFRIQUE
-1.56	-3.34	4.70	3.51	2.73	-7.18	-5.06	-0.66	CEMAC
-3.10	-6.43	-3.95	-9.33	-14.12	-9.66	-7.99	-9.66	CEPGL
3.66	0.70	1.29	3.24	4.17	-1.95	0.31	-2.66	COMESA
-7.24	-6.08	-3.52	-3.07	-8.73	-7.13	-8.86	-12.90	CAE
-1.67	-4.01	3.79	6.49	3.72	-8.85	1.06	2.40	CEEAC
1.73	2.80	6.18	17.93	6.36	3.27	1.76	-0.89	CEDEAO
-14.79	-9.43	-3.34	-1.09	-0.73	3.62	-0.32	-6.65	UFM
0.64	-0.71	-0.49	-1.92	-4.60	-5.64	-1.57	-2.73	SADC
5.83	2.15	9.16	14.83	16.24	0.97	6.10	3.07	UMA
-12.68	-7.38	-5.45	-5.30	-7.02	-3.51	-6.27	-8.02	UEMOA
								AMÉRIQUE
-1.20	-1.40	-0.15	0.08	-1.93	-0.93	-2.29	-1.92	ANCOM
-7.77	-4.53	-6.33	-4.98	-8.39	-2.01	-3.65	-5.68	MCAC
-0.96	-1.25	-3.87	1.01	3.15	-2.97	2.32	0.12	CARICOM
-0.89	-1.34	-3.48	-4.09	-3.49	-2.28	-2.73	-2.60	ZLEA
-3.96	-0.22	-2.14	2.24	-0.47	-0.42	-0.94	-0.94	ALADI
-6.61	0.23	-3.54	1.77	-1.16	-0.82	-1.81	-1.83	MERCOSUR
-0.44	-1.59	-3.67	-4.99	-4.06	-2.61	-3.05	-2.91	ALENA
-0.89	-1.37	-3.48	-4.08	-3.49	-2.27	-2.72	-2.59	OEA
-15.34	-16.03	-14.42	-20.25	-33.22	-21.64	-21.41	-19.86	OECO
								ASIE
-1.38	0.27	1.30	3.49	5.55	3.68	3.29	1.70	ACAP
-5.92	-2.47	6.19	4.89	4.58	7.07	5.69	5.06	ANASE
-3.07	-1.16	0.68	-0.97	-0.41	-0.34	-0.35	0.32	ECO
30.05	3.92	14.31	24.40	22.67	7.20	13.00	21.85	CCG
-1.66	-2.34	-1.03	-1.44	-3.14	-1.64	-2.53	-2.28	SAARC
								EUROPE
0.45	2.74	13.29	14.33	8.29	9.04	12.98	12.61	AELE
-1.55	-0.59	-1.00	-0.15	-1.00	-0.05	-0.12	0.23	UE
-1.85	0.06	-0.61	0.35	-0.73	0.14	0.36	0.47	Zone euro
								OCÉANIE
-7.61	-4.06	4.96	1.33	-1.59	-7.78	-9.38	-3.82	MSG
								INTERRÉGIONAUX
-0.25	-1.27	0.18	2.71	-1.04	-3.22	-1.39	-2.05	ACP
-0.90	-0.56	-0.91	-1.14	0.16	0.60	0.59	0.10	CEAP
-3.59	-3.12	3.42	1.92	-1.17	-0.43	-0.32	-0.48	CEMN
–	–	13.88	9.00	5.16	2.62	3.82	4.81	CEI

Sources :
Pour les sources et les notes, se reporter à la fin du tableau 7.1.1.

Region, country or territory	Inward flows - Flux entrants Millions of dollars							
	1980	1990	2000	2005	2008	2009	2010	2011
WORLD	54 078	207 455	1 400 541	980 727	1 790 706	1 197 824	1 309 001	1 524 422
DEVELOPING ECONOMIES	7 479	34 853	255 506	327 248	650 017	519 225	616 661	684 399
TRANSITION ECONOMIES	24	75	7 038	30 854	121 041	72 386	73 755	92 163
DEVELOPED ECONOMIES	46 576	172 526	1 137 996	622 625	1 019 648	606 212	618 586	747 860
Developing economies: Africa	400	2 845	9 671	30 505	57 842	52 645	43 122	42 652
Eastern Africa	197	389	1 468	2 501	5 943	5 652	6 667	8 585
Burundi	5	1	12	1	4	0	1	2
Comoros	..	0	0	1	5	14	4	7
Djibouti	0	0	3	22	229	100	27	78
Eritrea			28	-1	0	0	56	19
Ethiopia (...1991)	1	12						
Ethiopia	–	–	135	265	109	221	288	206
Kenya	79	57	111	21	96	116	178	335
Madagascar	-1	22	83	86	1 169	1 066	860	907
Malawi	9	23	40	52	71	55	58	56
Mauritius	1	41	277	42	383	248	430	273
Mayotte	0	0	0	5	0	0	0	0
Mozambique	4	9	139	108	592	893	989	2 093
Rwanda	16	8	8	14	103	119	42	106
Seychelles	10	0	24	86	130	118	160	144
Somalia	0	6	0	24	87	108	112	102
Uganda	4	-6	181	380	729	842	544	792
United Republic of Tanzania	5	0	282	936	1 247	953	1 023	1 095
Zambia	62	203	122	357	939	695	1 729	1 982
Zimbabwe	2	12	23	103	52	105	166	387
Middle Africa	353	-345	1 503	1 365	5 752	8 310	6 231	2 840
Angola	37	-335	879	-1 304	1 679	2 205	-3 227	-5 586
Cameroon	130	-113	159	234	-24	668	354	360
Central African Republic	5	1	1	32	117	121	92	109
Chad	0	9	115	-99	234	1 105	1 940	1 855
Congo	40	23	162	1 475	2 526	1 862	2 209	2 931
Dem. Rep. of the Congo	110	-14	72	0	1 727	664	2 939	1 687
Equatorial Guinea	..	11	154	769	-794	1 636	1 369	737
Gabon	32	73	-43	242	209	33	531	728
Sao Tome and Principe	..	0	4	16	79	16	25	18
Northern Africa	152	1 155	3 250	12 236	23 114	18 224	15 709	7 686
Algeria	349	40	280	1 081	2 594	2 746	2 264	2 571
Egypt	548	734	1 235	5 376	9 495	6 712	6 386	-483
Libya	-1 089	159	141	1 038	3 180	3 310	1 909	0
Morocco	89	165	422	1 654	2 487	1 952	1 574	2 519
Sudan (...2011)	9	-31	392	2 305	2 601	1 816	2 064	1 936
Tunisia	246	89	779	783	2 759	1 688	1 513	1 143
Southern Africa	132	92	1 268	7 285	10 416	6 999	2 690	7 441
Botswana	112	96	57	279	528	968	559	587
Lesotho	4	16	32	57	56	48	55	52
Namibia	..	30	186	348	720	552	712	900
South Africa	-10	-78	887	6 647	9 006	5 365	1 228	5 807
Swaziland	26	28	106	-46	106	66	136	95
Western Africa	-434	1 553	2 182	7 118	12 617	13 461	11 825	16 100
Benin	4	62	60	53	170	134	177	118
Burkina Faso	0	0	23	34	238	101	35	7
Cape Verde	0	0	43	82	209	119	111	93
Côte d'Ivoire	95	48	235	312	446	377	339	344
Gambia	0	14	44	45	70	40	37	36
Ghana	16	15	166	145	1 220	1 685	2 527	3 222
Guinea	1	18	10	105	382	141	101	1 211
Guinea-Bissau	..	2	1	8	6	18	33	19
Liberia	72	225	21	83	284	218	450	508
Mali	2	6	82	224	180	748	406	178
Mauritania	27	7	40	814	343	-3	131	45
Niger	49	41	8	30	340	791	940	1 014
Nigeria	-739	1 003	1 310	4 978	8 249	8 650	6 099	8 915
Saint Helena	0	0	-4	0	0	0	0	0
Senegal	14	57	63	45	398	320	266	286
Sierra Leone	-19	32	39	83	58	74	87	49
Togo	43	23	41	77	24	49	86	54

For sources and notes, see end of table.

7.2.1 Investissement étranger direct : flux entrants et sortants des pays et des régions géographiques

Outward flows - Flux sortants Millions de dollars								Régions, pays ou territoires
1980	1990	2000	2005	2008	2009	2010	2011	
51 590	241 498	1 226 633	888 561	1 969 336	1 175 108	1 451 365	1 694 396	**MONDE**
3 192	11 914	135 116	132 507	328 121	268 476	400 144	383 754	ÉCONOMIES EN DÉVELOPPEMENT
0	0	3 195	14 310	60 462	48 840	61 644	73 135	ÉCONOMIES EN TRANSITION
48 397	229 584	1 088 321	741 744	1 580 753	857 792	989 576	1 237 508	ÉCONOMIES DÉVELOPPÉES
1 097	659	1 534	1 820	7 896	3 169	7 027	3 512	**Économies en développement : Afrique**
5	21	28	92	98	356	1 272	1 266	*Afrique orientale*
..	0	0	0	1	0	0	0	Burundi
0	1	0	0	0	0	0	0	Comores
0	0	0	0	0	0	0	0	Djibouti
–	–	0	0	0	0	0	0	Érythrée
0	0							Éthiopie (…1991)
–	–	0	0	0	0	0	0	Éthiopie
1	0	0	10	44	46	2	9	Kenya
0	1	0	0	0	0	0	0	Madagascar
0	0	-1	0	-19	0	0	0	Malawi
..	1	13	48	52	37	129	89	Maurice
0	0	0	0	0	0	0	0	Mayotte
0	0	0	0	0	-3	1	-3	Mozambique
0	0	0	0	0	0	0	0	Rwanda
4	1	8	33	13	5	6	8	Seychelles
0	0	0	0	0	0	0	0	Somalie
0	0	0	0	0	0	-3	0	Ouganda
0	0	0	0	0	0	0	0	République-Unie de Tanzanie
0	0	0	0	0	270	1 095	1 150	Zambie
0	17	8	1	8	0	43	14	Zimbabwe
0	52	33	70	2 673	-12	1 393	1 404	*Afrique centrale*
0	1	0	0	2 570	7	1 340	1 300	Angola
-8	15	10	-23	-47	-141	-36	-75	Cameroun
..	4	0	0	0	0	0	0	République centrafricaine
0	0	0	0	0	0	0	0	Tchad
..	3	4	0	0	0	0	0	Congo
0	0	-2	13	54	35	7	91	Rép. dém. du Congo
..	0	-4	0	0	0	0	0	Guinée équatoriale
8	29	25	65	96	87	81	88	Gabon
0	0	0	15	0	0	0	0	Sao Tomé-et-Principe
87	135	223	289	8 752	2 588	4 847	1 753	*Afrique septentrionale*
34	5	14	-20	318	215	220	534	Algérie
7	12	51	92	1 920	571	1 176	626	Égypte
47	105	98	128	5 888	1 165	2 722	233	Libye
..	13	59	77	485	470	589	247	Maroc
0	0	0	0	98	89	66	84	Soudan (…2011)
..	0	1	12	42	77	74	28	Tunisie
766	39	285	951	-3 228	1 204	-64	-630	*Afrique australe*
2	7	2	56	-91	48	3	4	Botswana
0	0	0	0	0	0	0	0	Lesotho
..	1	3	-13	5	-3	5	-3	Namibie
755	27	271	930	-3 134	1 151	-76	-635	Afrique du Sud
9	3	10	-22	-8	7	4	4	Swaziland
238	412	965	418	-398	-967	-421	-281	*Afrique occidentale*
..	0	4	0	-4	31	-18	3	Bénin
0	-1	0	0	8	8	-4	4	Burkina Faso
0	0	0	0	0	0	0	0	Cap-Vert
0	0	8	0	0	-9	25	8	Côte d'Ivoire
0	0	0	0	0	0	0	0	Gambie
0	0	0	0	9	7	8	8	Ghana
0	0	..	0	126	0	0	5	Guinée
..	..	0	1	0	-3	6	1	Guinée-Bissau
236	6	780	437	382	364	369	372	Libéria
0	0	4	-1	1	-1	7	2	Mali
0	0	0	2	4	4	4	4	Mauritanie
-4	0	-1	-4	24	59	60	48	Niger
5	415	169	15	-1 058	-1 542	-923	-824	Nigéria
0	0	0	0	0	0	0	0	Sainte-Hélène
2	-10	1	-8	126	77	2	66	Sénégal
0	0	0	-8	0	0	5	0	Sierra Leone
0	0	0	-15	-16	37	37	20	Togo

Pour les sources et les notes, se reporter à la fin du tableau.

Region, country or territory	Inward flows - Flux entrants Millions of dollars							
	1980	1990	2000	2005	2008	2009	2010	2011
Developing economies: America	**6 416**	**8 926**	**97 824**	**78 057**	**209 517**	**149 402**	**187 401**	**216 988**
Caribbean	*390*	*828*	*20 475*	*5 799*	*81 823*	*72 322*	*70 194*	*67 622*
Anguilla	0	11	43	117	99	37	25	11
Antigua and Barbuda	20	59	43	221	174	81	97	59
Aruba	0	131	-128	-208	14	-33	160	544
Bahamas	4	-17	609	1 054	1 512	873	1 142	1 533
Barbados	3	11	55	240	464	247	290	334
British Virgin Islands	-1	18	9 877	-9 090	51 722	46 503	49 058	53 717
Cayman Islands	20	49	7 627	10 221	19 634	20 426	15 875	7 408
Cuba	0	1	-10	16	24	24	86	110
Curaçao	–	–	–	–	–	–	–	69
Dominica	..	8	18	19	57	41	24	25
Dominican Republic	93	133	953	1 123	2 870	2 165	1 896	2 371
Grenada	..	13	37	70	142	103	60	40
Haiti	13	8	13	26	30	38	150	181
Jamaica	28	175	469	682	1 437	541	228	242
Montserrat	..	10	2	5	13	3	3	3
Netherlands Antilles	35	8	-1	42	232	95	122	–
Saint Kitts and Nevis	1	49	96	93	178	131	120	142
Saint Lucia	31	46	54	78	161	146	110	76
Saint Vincent and the Grenadines	1	8	38	40	159	97	103	135
Sint Maarten (Dutch part)	–	–	–	–	–	–	–	-48
Trinidad and Tobago	143	109	680	940	2 801	709	549	574
Turks and Caicos Islands	0	0	0	108	99	95	97	97
Central America	*2 505*	*3 056*	*20 293*	*28 217*	*34 874*	*20 757*	*26 849*	*27 895*
Belize	..	19	23	127	170	109	97	94
Costa Rica	53	162	409	861	2 078	1 347	1 466	2 104
El Salvador	6	2	173	511	903	366	117	386
Guatemala	111	59	230	508	754	600	806	985
Honduras	6	44	382	600	1 006	523	797	1 014
Mexico	2 099	2 633	18 110	24 407	27 140	16 119	20 709	19 554
Nicaragua	13	1	267	241	626	434	508	968
Panama, excl. Canal Zone	219							
Panama	–	136	700	962	2 196	1 259	2 350	2 790
South America	*3 521*	*5 042*	*57 056*	*44 041*	*92 820*	*56 323*	*90 357*	*121 472*
Argentina	678	1 836	10 418	5 265	9 726	4 017	7 055	7 243
Bolivia (Plurinational State of)	47	67	736	-288	513	423	643	859
Brazil	1 910	989	32 779	15 066	45 058	25 949	48 506	66 660
Chile	213	661	4 860	7 097	15 518	12 887	15 373	17 299
Colombia	157	500	2 436	10 252	10 620	7 137	6 899	13 234
Ecuador	70	126	-23	493	1 006	321	158	568
Falkland Islands (Malvinas)	0	..	45	0	0	0	0	0
Guyana	1	8	67	77	178	164	154	165
Paraguay	30	71	100	35	209	94	228	303
Peru	27	41	810	2 579	6 924	6 431	8 455	8 233
Suriname	18	-77	-148	28	-231	-93	-612	-585
Uruguay	290	42	273	847	2 106	1 529	2 289	2 191
Venezuela (Bolivarian Rep. of)	80	778	4 701	2 589	1 195	-2 536	1 209	5 302
Developing economies: Asia	**543**	**22 628**	**147 787**	**218 420**	**380 360**	**315 238**	**384 063**	**423 157**
Eastern Asia	*950*	*8 791*	*116 641*	*116 189*	*185 253*	*159 183*	*201 364*	*218 974*
China	57	3 487	40 715	72 406	108 312	95 000	114 734	123 985
China, Hong Kong SAR	710	3 275	61 938	33 625	59 621	52 394	71 069	83 156
China, Macao SAR	0	0	-1	1 240	2 591	858	2 828	4 365
China, Taiwan Province of	166	1 330	4 928	1 625	5 432	2 805	2 492	-1 962
Korea, Dem. People's Rep. of	0	-61	3	50	44	2	38	55
Korea, Republic of	17	759	9 004	7 055	8 409	7 501	8 511	4 661
Mongolia	0	0	54	188	845	624	1 691	4 715
Southern Asia	*284*	*213*	*4 864*	*14 431*	*52 869*	*42 370*	*31 746*	*38 942*
Afghanistan	9	..	0	271	94	76	211	83
Bangladesh	9	3	579	845	1 086	700	913	1 136
Bhutan	..	2	0	9	7	18	16	14
India	79	237	3 588	7 622	43 406	35 596	24 159	31 554
Iran (Islamic Rep. of)	81	-362	194	3 136	1 909	3 048	3 648	4 150
Maldives	0	6	22	73	174	152	212	282
Nepal	0	6	0	2	1	39	87	95
Pakistan	64	278	309	2 201	5 438	2 338	2 022	1 327
Sri Lanka	43	43	173	272	752	404	478	300

For sources and notes, see end of table.

1980	1990	2000	2005	2008	2009	2010	2011	Régions, pays ou territoires
		Outward flows - Flux sortants / Millions de dollars						
899	301	49 881	44 138	97 013	54 305	119 908	99 653	**Économies en développement : Amérique**
121	-1 718	42 415	24 543	58 650	41 647	72 696	67 507	*Caraïbes*
0	0	0	0	0	0	0	0	Anguilla
0	0	2	0	0	0	0	0	Antigua-et-Barbuda
0	487	3	-9	3	2	3	3	Aruba
115	0	140	143	410	216	149	524	Bahamas
1	1	1	9	-6	-56	-54	-39	Barbade
..	-2 520	34 459	17 755	44 118	35 143	58 717	62 507	Îles Vierges britanniques
5	282	7 649	6 122	13 377	6 311	13 857	4 456	Îles Caïmanes
0	0	0	-2	0	0	0	0	Cuba
							13	Curaçao
–	–	0	–	–	–	–	0	Dominique
0	0	61	21	-19	-32	-23	-25	République dominicaine
0	0	0	0	0	0	0	0	Grenade
0	-8	0	0	0	0	0	0	Haïti
..	37	74	101	76	61	58	62	Jamaïque
0	0	0	0	0	0	0	0	Montserrat
1	2	-3	65	-14	-6	-18	–	Antilles néerlandaises
0	0	0	0	0	0	0	0	Saint-Kitts-et-Nevis
0	0	0	0	0	0	0	0	Sainte-Lucie
0	0	0	0	0	0	0	0	Saint-Vincent-et-les Grenadines
–	–	–	–	–	–	–	-1	Saint-Martin (partie néerlandaise)
0	0	25	341	700	0	0	0	Trinité-et-Tobago
0	0	4	-3	6	9	7	7	Îles Turques et Caïques
358	907	-573	7 747	3 215	9 404	16 012	11 298	*Amérique centrale*
..	2	0	1	3	0	1	1	Belize
5	2	8	-43	6	7	25	56	Costa Rica
0	0	5	-113	-80	0	0	0	El Salvador
2	0	40	38	16	26	24	17	Guatemala
1	-1	7	-1	1	-1	1	-7	Honduras
3	223	363	6 474	1 157	7 019	13 570	8 946	Mexique
0	0	8	18	16	15	14	15	Nicaragua
347								Panama, sans la zone du canal
–	681	-1 004	1 372	2 095	2 336	2 377	2 269	Panama
420	1 112	8 038	11 848	35 149	3 255	31 201	20 848	*Amérique du Sud*
-110	35	901	1 311	1 391	712	965	1 488	Argentine
1	1	3	3	5	-3	-29	0	Bolivie (État plurinational de)
367	625	2 282	2 517	20 457	-10 084	11 588	-1 029	Brésil
44	8	3 987	2 135	9 151	7 233	9 231	11 822	Chili
106	16	325	4 662	2 254	3 088	6 562	8 289	Colombie
1	3	13	10	8	36	12	18	Équateur
0	0	0	0	0	0	0	0	Îles Falkland (Malvinas)
0	0	2	0	0	0	0	0	Guyana
0	0	6	6	8	8	-4	0	Paraguay
0	50	0	0	736	411	266	113	Pérou
0	0	0	0	0	0	0	-12	Suriname
..	..	-1	36	-11	16	-60	-15	Uruguay
12	375	521	1 167	1 150	1 838	2 671	173	Venezuela (Rép. bolivarienne du)
1 179	10 943	83 690	86 425	223 116	210 925	273 033	280 478	**Économies en développement : Asie**
150	9 574	71 229	51 914	133 192	143 639	198 809	180 002	*Asie orientale*
..	830	916	12 261	52 150	56 530	68 811	65 117	Chine
82	2 448	59 374	27 196	50 581	63 991	95 396	81 607	Chine (RAS de Hong Kong)
0	0	0	60	-83	-11	-312	62	Chine (RAS de Macao)
42	5 243	6 701	6 028	10 287	5 877	11 574	12 766	Province chinoise de Taiwan
0	1	6	0	0	0	0	0	Corée, Rép. populaire dém. de
26	1 052	4 233	6 366	20 251	17 197	23 278	20 355	Corée, République de
0	0	0	2	6	54	62	94	Mongolie
11	10	551	3 524	19 756	16 403	13 605	15 234	*Asie méridionale*
0	0	0	0	0	0	0	0	Afghanistan
..	1	2	3	9	29	15	9	Bangladesh
0	0	0	0	0	0	0	0	Bhoutan
4	6	514	2 985	19 257	15 927	13 151	14 752	Inde
7	0	22	452	380	356	346	360	Iran (Rép. islamique d')
0	0	0	0	0	0	0	0	Maldives
0	0	0	0	0	0	0	0	Népal
0	2	11	45	49	71	47	62	Pakistan
..	1	2	38	62	20	46	50	Sri Lanka

Pour les sources et les notes, se reporter à la fin du tableau.

Region, country or territory	Inward flows - Flux entrants Millions of dollars							
	1980	1990	2000	2005	2008	2009	2010	2011
South-Eastern Asia	*2 636*	*12 821*	*22 696*	*43 301*	*50 254*	*47 408*	*92 760*	*116 559*
Brunei Darussalam	-20	7	550	289	330	371	626	1 208
Cambodia	1	0	149	381	815	539	783	892
Indonesia (…2002)	180	1 092	-4 495	–	–	–	–	–
Indonesia	–	–	–	8 336	9 318	4 877	13 771	18 906
Lao People's Dem. Rep.	0	6	34	28	228	319	333	450
Malaysia	934	2 611	3 788	4 065	7 172	1 453	9 103	11 966
Myanmar	0	225	208	236	976	963	450	850
Philippines	114	550	2 240	1 854	1 544	1 963	1 298	1 262
Singapore	1 236	5 575	15 515	18 090	11 798	24 418	48 637	64 003
Thailand	189	2 575	3 410	8 067	8 455	4 854	9 733	9 572
Timor-Leste	–	–	–	1	40	50	27	20
Viet Nam	2	180	1 298	1 954	9 579	7 600	8 000	7 430
Western Asia	*-3 328*	*804*	*3 586*	*44 499*	*91 985*	*66 276*	*58 193*	*48 682*
Bahrain	-418	-183	364	1 049	1 794	257	156	781
Iraq	2	0	-3	515	1 856	1 598	1 396	1 617
Jordan	34	38	913	1 984	2 826	2 413	1 651	1 469
Kuwait	1	6	16	234	-6	1 114	319	399
Lebanon	-12	6	964	3 321	4 333	4 804	4 280	3 200
Occupied Palestinian territory	0	0	62	47	52	301	180	214
Oman	98	142	83	1 540	2 952	1 508	1 142	788
Qatar	11	5	252	2 500	3 779	8 125	4 670	-87
Saudi Arabia	-3 192	312	183	12 097	38 151	32 100	28 105	16 400
Syrian Arab Republic	0	40	270	583	1 467	1 514	1 850	1 059
Turkey	18	684	982	10 031	19 504	8 411	9 038	15 876
United Arab Emirates	98	-116	-506	10 900	13 724	4 003	5 500	7 679
Yemen, Arab Republic	34	–						
Yemen	–	-131	6	-302	1 555	129	-93	-713
Developing economies: Oceania	**120**	**454**	**224**	**265**	**2 298**	**1 940**	**2 075**	**1 602**
Cook Islands	0	4	-28	1	1	1	1	1
Fiji	36	84	3	160	354	137	195	204
French Polynesia	0	22	2	8	14	10	95	40
Kiribati	0	0	1	5	3	3	4	4
Marshall Islands	–	1	125	7	6	8	9	7
Micronesia (Federated States of)	–	0	0	0	6	8	10	8
Nauru	0	0	0	1	1	1	1	1
New Caledonia	2	31	-41	-7	1 746	1 182	1 439	1 415
Niue	0	0	0	-1	0	0	0	0
Northern Mariana Islands	–	124	12	0	0	0	0	0
Pacific Islands (Trust Territory)	-1	–	–	–	–	–	–	–
Palau	–	1	15	1	2	2	2	2
Papua New Guinea	76	155	98	34	-30	423	29	-309
Samoa	0	7	-1	4	49	10	1	12
Solomon Islands	2	10	13	19	95	120	238	146
Tokelau	0	0	0	0	0	0	0	0
Tonga	0	0	5	8	6	0	9	10
Tuvalu	0	0	-1	0	2	2	2	2
Vanuatu	5	13	20	28	44	32	41	58
Wallis and Futuna Islands	0	0	0	0	1	1	1	1
Transition economies	**24**	**75**	**7 038**	**30 854**	**121 041**	**72 386**	**73 755**	**92 163**
Albania	0	0	144	264	974	996	1 051	1 031
Armenia	–	–	104	239	935	778	570	525
Azerbaijan	–	–	130	1 680	14	473	563	1 465
Belarus	–	–	119	305	2 181	1 884	1 403	3 986
Bosnia and Herzegovina	–	–	146	351	1 002	251	230	435
Croatia	–	–	1 051	1 825	6 180	3 355	394	1 494
Georgia	–	–	131	453	1 564	658	814	975
Kazakhstan	–	–	1 283	1 971	14 322	13 243	10 768	12 910
Kyrgyzstan	–	–	-2	43	377	189	438	694
Montenegro	–	–	–	–	960	1 527	760	558
Republic of Moldova	–	–	128	191	711	145	197	274
Russian Federation	–	–	2 714	12 886	75 002	36 500	43 288	52 878
Serbia and Montenegro	–	–	52	2 078	–	–	–	–
Serbia	–	–	–	–	2 955	1 959	1 329	2 709
SFR of Yugoslavia (1)	24	71	–	–	–	–	–	–
Tajikistan	–	–	24	54	376	16	-15	11
TFYR of Macedonia	–	–	215	96	586	201	211	422
Turkmenistan	–	–	131	418	1 277	4 553	3 631	3 186
Ukraine	–	–	595	7 808	10 913	4 816	6 495	7 207

For sources and notes, see next page.

Outward flows - Flux sortants Millions de dollars								Régions, pays ou territoires
1980	1990	2000	2005	2008	2009	2010	2011	
394	*2 328*	*8 978*	*18 534*	*32 255*	*32 997*	*44 171*	*59 890*	**Asie du Sud-Est**
0	0	30	15	16	9	6	10	Brunéi Darussalam
0	0	7	6	20	19	21	24	Cambodge
6	-11	150	–					Indonésie (…2002)
–	–	–	3 065	5 900	2 249	2 664	7 771	Indonésie
0	0	10	0	-75	1	6	7	Rép. dém. populaire lao
201	129	2 026	3 076	14 965	7 784	13 329	15 258	Malaisie
0	0	0	0	0	0	0	0	Myanmar
86	22	125	189	259	359	616	9	Philippines
98	2 034	6 650	11 589	6 812	17 704	21 215	25 227	Singapour
3	154	-20	529	4 057	4 172	5 415	10 634	Thaïlande
–	–	–	0	0	0	0	0	Timor-Leste
0	0	0	65	300	700	900	950	Viet Nam
624	*-969*	*2 931*	*12 453*	*37 913*	*17 886*	*16 448*	*25 353*	**Asie occidentale**
..	25	10	1 135	1 620	-1 791	334	894	Bahreïn
0	0	0	89	34	72	125	77	Iraq
3	-31	9	163	13	72	28	31	Jordanie
407	-239	-303	5 142	9 091	8 582	5 065	8 711	Koweït
2	-16	108	715	987	1 126	487	900	Liban
0	0	213	13	-8	-15	77	-20	Territoire palestinien occupé
1	0	-2	234	585	109	1 012	572	Oman
2	2	18	352	3 658	3 215	1 863	6 027	Qatar
211	-638	1 550	-350	3 498	2 177	3 907	3 442	Arabie saoudite
0	3	44	80	2	-3	0	0	République arabe syrienne
0	-16	870	1 064	2 549	1 553	1 464	2 464	Turquie
-2	-58	424	3 750	15 820	2 723	2 015	2 178	Émirats arabes unis
0	–	–	–	–	–	–	–	Yémen, République arabe du
–	0	-9	65	66	66	70	77	Yémen
18	*11*	*12*	*125*	*96*	*77*	*176*	*110*	**Économies en développement : Océanie**
0	0	0	0	0	0	0	0	Îles Cook
2	3	2	10	-8	3	6	-3	Fidji
0	0	0	16	30	8	89	42	Polynésie française
0	0	0	0	1	0	0	1	Kiribati
–	0	2	54	0	0	0	0	Îles Marshall
–	0	0	0	0	0	0	0	Micronésie (États fédérés de)
0	0	0	0	0	0	0	0	Nauru
0	0	2	31	64	58	76	65	Nouvelle-Calédonie
0	0	5	1	2	0	0	1	Nioué
–	0	0	0	0	0	0	0	Îles Mariannes du Nord
0	–	–	–	–	–	–	–	Îles du Pacifique (Territoire sous tutelle des)
–	0	-1	-2	0	0	0	0	Palaos
16	8	1	7	0	4	0	1	Papouasie-Nouvelle-Guinée
0	0	0	1	0	-1	0	-1	Samoa
0	0	0	2	4	3	2	4	Îles Salomon
0	0	0	0	0	0	0	0	Tokélaou
0	0	0	5	2	0	2	1	Tonga
0	0	0	0	0	0	0	0	Tuvalu
0	0	0	1	1	1	1	1	Vanuatu
0	0	0	0	0	0	0	0	Îles Wallis-et-Futuna
0	*0*	*3 195*	*14 310*	*60 462*	*48 840*	*61 644*	*73 135*	**Économies en transition**
0	0	0	4	81	36	6	42	Albanie
–	–	-1	7	10	53	8	78	Arménie
–	–	1	1 221	556	326	232	533	Azerbaïdjan
–	–	0	3	31	102	50	57	Bélarus
–	–	0	0	17	6	42	20	Bosnie-Herzégovine
–	–	5	239	1 421	1 234	-150	44	Croatie
–	–	3	-89	147	-19	135	146	Géorgie
–	–	4	-146	1 204	3 159	7 837	4 530	Kazakhstan
–	–	5	0	0	0	0	0	Kirghizistan
–	–	–	–	108	46	29	17	Monténégro
–	–	0		16	7	4	21	République de Moldova
–	–	3 177	12 767	55 594	43 665	52 523	67 283	Fédération de Russie
–	–	2	27	–	–	–	–	Serbie-et-Monténégro
–	–	–	–	283	52	189	170	Serbie
0	0	–	–	–	–	–	–	RSF de Yougoslavie (1)
–	–	0	0	0	0	0	0	Tadjikistan
–	–	-1	3	-14	11	2	2	LERY de Macédoine
–	–	0	0	0	0	0	0	Turkménistan
–	–	1	275	1 010	162	736	192	Ukraine

Pour les sources et les notes, se reporter à la page suivante.

7

7.2.1 Foreign direct investment: Inward and outward flows of countries and geographical regions

Region, country or territory	Inward flows - Flux entrants Millions of dollars							
	1980	1990	2000	2005	2008	2009	2010	2011
USSR (2)	..	4	–	–	–	–	–	–
Uzbekistan	–	–	75	192	711	842	1 628	1 403
Developed economies: America	**22 725**	**56 004**	**380 859**	**130 545**	**363 716**	**164 939**	**221 549**	**268 292**
Bermuda	0	0	67	44	173	-70	231	424
Canada	5 807	7 582	66 795	25 692	57 177	21 406	23 413	40 932
United States	16 918	48 422	313 997	104 809	306 366	143 604	197 905	226 937
Developed economies: Asia	**287**	**1 943**	**15 280**	**7 594**	**35 300**	**16 545**	**4 258**	**9 616**
Israel	9	137	6 957	4 818	10 875	4 607	5 510	11 374
Japan	278	1 806	8 323	2 775	24 426	11 938	-1 252	-1 758
Developed economies: Europe	**21 363**	**104 415**	**724 898**	**507 185**	**569 026**	**398 935**	**356 588**	**425 266**
Austria	239	653	8 840	10 784	6 858	9 303	4 265	14 128
Belgium (3)	1 545	8 047	88 739	34 370	193 950	61 744	81 190	89 142
Bulgaria	0	4	1 016	3 920	9 855	3 385	1 601	1 864
Cyprus	85	127	855	1 170	1 415	3 472	766	276
Czechoslovakia	..	165	–	–	–	–	–	–
Czech Republic	–	–	4 985	11 653	6 451	2 927	6 141	5 405
Denmark	104	1 132	33 823	12 871	1 824	3 917	-7 397	14 771
Estonia	–	–	392	2 869	1 729	1 839	1 540	257
Finland	28	787	8 834	4 750	-1 144	398	6 733	54
France	3 328	15 629	43 252	84 949	64 184	24 219	30 638	40 945
Germany, Federal Republic of	342	–	–	–	–	–	–	–
Germany	–	2 962	198 277	47 439	8 109	24 156	46 860	40 402
Gibraltar	2	36	138	122	159	172	165	166
Greece	672	1 005	1 108	623	4 499	2 436	373	1 823
Hungary	0	554	2 764	7 709	6 325	2 048	2 274	4 698
Iceland	22	22	171	3 081	917	86	246	1 013
Ireland	286	622	25 779	-31 689	-16 453	25 960	26 330	13 102
Italy	577	6 345	13 375	23 291	-10 835	20 077	9 178	29 059
Latvia	–	–	413	707	1 261	94	379	1 562
Lithuania	–	–	379	1 028	1 965	66	753	1 217
Luxembourg	..	..	..	6 564	11 216	22 408	9 211	17 530
Malta	27	46	582	676	802	746	1 063	539
Netherlands	2 005	10 516	63 855	39 047	4 549	36 042	-8 966	17 129
Norway	60	1 564	7 090	5 558	10 564	13 403	17 519	3 569
Poland	10	88	9 445	10 293	14 839	12 932	8 858	15 139
Portugal	165	2 902	6 635	3 930	4 665	2 706	2 646	10 344
Romania	..	0	1 057	6 483	13 909	4 844	2 940	2 670
Slovakia	–	–	1 932	2 429	4 687	-6	526	2 143
Slovenia	–	–	137	588	1 947	-653	359	999
Spain	1 493	13 294	39 575	25 020	76 993	10 407	40 761	29 476
Sweden	251	1 971	23 430	11 896	37 153	10 023	-1 347	12 091
Switzerland	..	5 484	19 255	-951	15 144	28 642	20 381	-196
United Kingdom	10 123	30 461	118 764	176 006	91 489	71 140	50 604	53 949
Developed economies: Oceania	**2 200**	**10 164**	**16 959**	**-22 698**	**51 605**	**25 793**	**36 192**	**44 686**
Australia	1 866	8 479	15 612	-24 246	47 218	26 554	35 556	41 317
New Zealand	334	1 685	1 347	1 548	4 388	-761	636	3 369

Source:
UNCTAD, *FDI/TNC database*

Notes:

- Foreign direct investment (FDI) is defined as an investment involving a long-term relationship and reflecting a lasting interest in and control by a resident entity in one economy (foreign direct investor or parent enterprise) of an enterprise resident in a different economy (FDI enterprise or affiliate enterprise or foreign affiliate). Such investment involves both the initial transaction between the two entities and all subsequent transactions between them and among foreign affiliates.

  FDI inflows and outflows comprise capital provided (either directly or through other related enterprises) by a foreign direct investor to a FDI enterprise, or capital received by a foreign direct investor from a FDI enterprise. FDI includes the three following components: equity capital, reinvested earnings and intra-company loans. Data on FDI flows are presented on net bases (capital transactions' credits less debits between direct investors and their foreign affiliates). Net decreases in assets or net increases in liabilities are recorded as credits, while net increases in assets or net decreases in liabilities are recorded as debits. Hence, FDI flows with a negative sign indicate that at least one of the three components of FDI is negative and not offset by positive amounts of the remaining components. These are called reverse investment or disinvestment.

(1) Data from 1988 to 1991 inclusive refer to Slovenia only, except for the FDI inflows that also cover other Republics of the former SFR Yugoslavia.
(2) Partial data; total USSR territory is not covered.
(3) Data from 1970 to 2001 inclusive refer to Belgium-Luxembourg Economic Union; from 2002 onwards data cover Belgium only.

Outward flows - Flux sortants Millions de dollars								Régions, pays ou territoires
1980	1990	2000	2005	2008	2009	2010	2011	
..	0							URSS (2)
–		0	0	0	0	0	0	Ouzbékistan
23 328	**36 219**	**187 318**	**42 939**	**388 492**	**308 641**	**342 951**	**445 915**	**Économies développées : Amérique**
0	0	14	31	403	21	-33	-310	Bermudes
4 098	5 237	44 678	27 538	79 794	41 665	38 585	49 569	Canada
19 230	30 982	142 626	15 369	308 296	266 955	304 399	396 656	États-Unis
2 382	**51 036**	**34 113**	**47 216**	**133 635**	**75 392**	**64 830**	**117 351**	**Économies développées : Asie**
-3	261	2 556	1 435	5 616	693	8 567	2 998	Israël
2 385	50 775	31 557	45 781	128 019	74 699	56 263	114 353	Japon
22 156	**139 342**	**862 059**	**684 247**	**1 024 605**	**458 103**	**568 414**	**651 387**	**Économies développées : Europe**
101	1 701	5 740	11 145	29 452	10 006	7 732	30 451	Autriche
196	6 314	86 362	32 658	221 023	9 205	55 709	70 706	Belgique (3)
0	-3	3	310	765	-95	229	190	Bulgarie
0	5	172	550	2 717	383	679	1 828	Chypre
0	20							Tchécoslovaquie
–	–	43	-19	4 323	949	1 167	1 152	République tchèque
196	1 482	26 549	16 193	13 240	6 305	3 467	23 413	Danemark
–	–	61	691	1 112	1 549	133	-1 458	Estonie
137	2 708	24 030	4 223	9 297	4 917	10 471	5 417	Finlande
3 137	36 233	177 449	114 978	155 047	107 130	76 867	90 146	France
4 699								Allemagne, Rép. fédérale d'
–	24 235	56 557	75 893	72 758	75 391	109 321	54 368	Allemagne
0	0	0	0	0	0	0	0	Gibraltar
..	11	2 137	1 468	2 418	2 055	979	1 788	Grèce
0	0	620	2 179	2 234	1 984	1 307	4 530	Hongrie
..	12	394	7 090	-4 209	2 292	-2 357	-29	Islande
0	364	4 629	14 313	18 949	26 616	17 802	-2 148	Irlande
740	7 614	6 686	39 362	67 000	21 275	32 655	47 210	Italie
–	–	12	128	243	-62	21	93	Lettonie
–	–	4	346	336	217	79	165	Lituanie
..	..	..	9 932	11 759	7 547	15 123	11 741	Luxembourg
0	0	20	-21	291	114	57	21	Malte
3 847	13 660	75 634	123 072	68 334	28 180	55 217	31 867	Pays-Bas
253	1 583	9 505	21 964	25 683	34 400	23 086	19 999	Norvège
21	5	17	3 437	4 414	4 699	5 487	5 860	Pologne
12	163	8 132	2 111	2 741	816	-7 493	12 639	Portugal
..	18	-13	-31	274	-88	-20	32	Roumanie
–	–	29	150	530	904	327	490	Slovaquie
–	–	66	641	1 440	260	-212	112	Slovénie
311	3 349	58 213	41 829	74 717	13 070	38 341	37 256	Espagne
625	14 746	40 964	27 706	31 326	25 908	17 956	26 850	Suède
..	7 176	44 673	51 118	45 333	27 793	64 780	69 612	Suisse
7 881	17 948	233 371	80 833	161 056	44 381	39 502	107 086	Royaume-Uni
531	**2 988**	**4 831**	**-32 658**	**34 020**	**15 656**	**13 381**	**22 854**	**Économies développées : Océanie**
460	624	4 221	-31 137	33 618	16 693	12 791	19 999	Australie
71	2 363	610	-1 521	402	-1 037	591	2 856	Nouvelle-Zélande

Source :
CNUCED, *base de données IED/STN*

Notes :

- L'investissement étranger direct (IED) est un investissement impliquant une relation à long terme et témoignant de l'intérêt durable d'une entité résidant dans un pays (investisseur étranger direct ou société mère) à l'égard d'une entreprise résidant dans un autre pays (entreprise bénéficiaire, entreprise affiliée, ou encore filiale étrangère). Cet investissement englobe à la fois la transaction initiale entre les deux entités et toutes les transactions ultérieures entre elles et entre filiales étrangères.

  Les flux entrants et sortants de l'IED comprennent les capitaux fournis par l'investisseur direct (soit directement, soit par l'intermédiaire d'autres entreprises avec lesquelles il est lié) à l'entreprise d'investissement direct ou les capitaux reçus de cette entreprise par l'investisseur. L'IED est composé des trois catégories suivantes : le capital social, les bénéfices réinvestis et les emprunts intra-compagnie. Les données sur l'IED se présentent sur une base nette (les crédits moins les débits des transactions en capital entre l'investisseur direct et son entreprise apparentée). Les augmentations nettes en passifs et les décroissances nettes en actifs se déclarent comme crédits, tandis que les augmentations nettes en actifs et les décroissances nettes en passifs se déclarent comme débits. Les flux de l'IED précédés d'un signe négatif indiquent qu'au moins une des trois catégories de l'IED est négative et n'est pas contrebalancée par les valeurs positives des autres catégories. Il s'agit alors de désinvestissements ou de réductions d'investissement.

(1) Les données de 1988 à 1991 se réfèrent seulement à la Slovénie, à l'exception des flux entrants qui comprennent aussi d'autres Républiques de l'ex Yougoslavie (RSF).
(2) Données partielles : elles ne couvrent pas la totalité du territoire de l'URSS.
(3) Les données de 1970 à 2001 se réfèrent à l'Union économique belgo-luxembourgeoise ; à partir de 2002 les données couvrent uniquement la Belgique.

7

7.2.2 Foreign direct investment: Inward and outward flows of economic groupings

Economic grouping	Inward flows - Flux entrants Millions of dollars							
	1980	1990	2000	2005	2008	2009	2010	2011
DEVELOPING ECONOMIES	**7 479**	**34 853**	**255 506**	**327 248**	**650 017**	**519 225**	**616 661**	**684 399**
Developing economies excluding China	7 422	31 366	214 791	254 842	541 705	424 225	501 927	560 414
Developing economies excluding LDCs	6 940	34 281	251 373	320 074	631 520	500 883	599 762	669 388
High-income developing economies	2 235	21 363	156 113	154 445	318 728	259 057	317 198	332 983
Middle-income developing economies	4 714	10 036	92 243	139 414	230 795	178 247	222 545	257 223
Low-income developing economies	530	3 455	7 150	33 383	100 493	81 920	76 918	94 193
Heavily indebted poor countries (IMF)	791	831	4 229	9 211	19 295	17 755	23 844	27 320
Landlocked developing countries	384	603	3 954	6 813	25 011	28 017	28 191	34 837
Small island developing States	359	779	2 747	4 003	8 640	4 431	4 231	4 142
Least developed countries	*538*	*573*	*4 133*	*7 173*	*18 497*	*18 342*	*16 899*	*15 011*
Africa and Haiti	478	431	3 122	5 631	13 419	15 314	13 859	11 936
Asia	53	111	975	1 470	4 762	2 783	2 700	2 808
Islands	7	31	36	72	316	246	341	267
Major petroleum and gas exporters	*-4 264*	*1 632*	*7 529*	*39 304*	*79 260*	*65 871*	*53 033*	*42 148*
Africa	-1 442	867	2 609	5 794	15 701	16 911	7 045	5 900
America	80	778	4 701	2 589	1 195	-2 536	1 209	5 302
Asia	-2 902	-13	218	30 921	62 364	51 495	44 779	30 946
Major exporters of manufactured goods	*5 408*	*22 245*	*157 407*	*169 340*	*236 338*	*204 544*	*284 988*	*314 935*
America	2 099	2 633	18 110	24 407	27 140	16 119	20 709	19 554
Asia	3 308	19 612	139 297	144 933	209 198	188 425	264 280	295 381
Emerging economies	*7 469*	*19 010*	*103 622*	*93 317*	*145 631*	*106 434*	*178 574*	*207 229*
America	4 928	6 160	66 977	54 414	104 366	65 403	100 098	118 989
Asia	2 541	12 850	36 645	38 903	41 265	41 031	78 476	88 240
Newly industrialized Asian economies	*3 545*	*17 767*	*96 328*	*82 717*	*111 748*	*100 265*	*164 615*	*191 564*
First tier	2 128	10 939	91 385	60 395	85 259	87 118	130 709	149 858
Second tier	1 417	6 828	4 943	22 322	26 489	13 148	33 905	41 706
Developing economies: Africa	**400**	**2 845**	**9 671**	**30 505**	**57 842**	**52 645**	**43 122**	**42 652**
Northern Africa excluding Sudan	144	1 187	2 858	9 932	20 514	16 408	13 645	5 750
Sub-Saharan Africa	257	1 659	6 813	20 573	37 328	36 237	29 477	36 902
Sub-Saharan Africa excluding South Africa	267	1 737	5 926	13 926	28 321	30 872	28 249	31 094
Developing economies: America	**6 416**	**8 926**	**97 824**	**78 057**	**209 517**	**149 402**	**187 401**	**216 988**
Central America and Greater Caribbean Islands excluding Puerto Rico	2 639	3 372	21 718	30 064	39 235	23 526	29 209	30 799
Central America and Greater Caribbean Islands excluding Mexico and Puerto Rico	539	739	3 608	5 657	12 094	7 407	8 500	11 244
South America and Central America	6 026	8 098	77 349	72 258	127 694	77 080	117 207	149 367
South America excluding Brazil	1 610	4 053	24 277	28 975	47 762	30 374	41 851	54 812
Developing economies: Asia	**543**	**22 628**	**147 787**	**218 420**	**380 360**	**315 238**	**384 063**	**423 157**
Eastern and South-Eastern Asia excluding China	3 529	18 125	98 622	87 084	127 194	111 591	179 390	211 548
Southern Asia excluding India	205	-24	1 276	6 810	9 462	6 774	7 586	7 388

Sources:
For sources and notes, see end of table 7.2.1.

Outward flows - Flux sortants Millions de dollars								Groupements économiques
1980	1990	2000	2005	2008	2009	2010	2011	
3 192	**11 914**	**135 116**	**132 507**	**328 121**	**268 476**	**400 144**	**383 754**	**ÉCONOMIES EN DÉVELOPPEMENT**
3 192	11 084	134 201	120 246	275 971	211 946	331 333	318 637	Économies en développement sans la Chine
2 958	11 917	134 324	131 997	324 739	267 381	397 053	380 484	Économies en développement sans les PMA
1 195	8 968	129 856	102 084	218 070	189 925	282 588	270 763	Économies en développement à revenu élevé
1 740	2 497	3 578	23 637	82 154	60 003	98 385	86 858	Économies en développement à revenu intermédiaire
257	450	1 682	6 787	27 897	18 548	19 172	26 132	Économies en développement à revenu faible
227	13	831	429	768	837	1 618	1 799	Pays pauvres très endettés (FMI)
8	33	49	1 125	1 639	4 008	9 323	6 492	Pays en développement sans littoral
137	53	268	767	1 244	275	299	647	Petits États insulaires en développement
234	*-3*	*792*	*510*	*3 381*	*1 095*	*3 091*	*3 270*	*Pays les moins avancés*
234	-5	782	417	3 354	975	2 975	3 149	Afrique et Haïti
0	1	10	75	21	116	112	116	Asie
0	1	0	18	6	4	4	5	Îles
724	*-32*	*2 510*	*10 958*	*41 932*	*18 916*	*20 363*	*22 784*	*Principaux exportateurs de pétrole et de gaz*
85	525	281	123	7 717	-155	3 360	1 243	Afrique
12	375	521	1 167	1 150	1 838	2 671	173	Amérique
626	-932	1 708	9 669	33 065	17 233	14 333	21 368	Asie
455	*12 113*	*80 244*	*73 520*	*160 260*	*180 274*	*252 588*	*239 910*	*Principaux exportateurs d'articles manufacturés*
3	223	363	6 474	1 157	7 019	13 570	8 946	Amérique
452	11 889	79 880	67 046	159 103	173 255	239 018	230 964	Asie
673	*9 551*	*27 123*	*40 025*	*89 264*	*58 024*	*110 430*	*105 581*	*Économies émergentes*
303	940	7 532	12 437	32 892	5 290	35 619	21 340	Amérique
370	8 611	19 591	27 589	56 372	52 734	74 811	84 240	Asie
544	*11 070*	*79 240*	*58 039*	*113 112*	*119 333*	*173 487*	*173 627*	*Économies nouvellement industrialisées d'Asie*
248	10 776	76 958	51 180	87 931	104 769	151 463	139 955	Première génération
296	294	2 281	6 859	25 181	14 564	22 024	33 672	Deuxième génération
1 097	**659**	**1 534**	**1 820**	**7 896**	**3 169**	**7 027**	**3 512**	**Économies en développement : Afrique**
87	135	223	289	8 654	2 498	4 781	1 668	Afrique septentrionale sans le Soudan
1 009	524	1 311	1 531	-757	670	2 246	1 844	Afrique subsaharienne
254	496	1 041	601	2 376	-481	2 322	2 479	Afrique subsaharienne sans l'Afrique du Sud
899	**301**	**49 881**	**44 138**	**97 013**	**54 305**	**119 908**	**99 653**	**Économies en développement : Amérique**
358	936	-437	7 866	3 271	9 432	16 047	11 335	Amérique centrale et Grandes Antilles sans Porto Rico
354	713	-800	1 392	2 114	2 413	2 477	2 389	Amérique centrale et Grandes Antilles sans le Mexique et Porto Rico
778	2 019	7 466	19 594	38 364	12 658	47 213	32 146	Amérique du Sud et Amérique centrale
54	488	5 756	9 331	14 692	13 339	19 613	21 877	Amérique du Sud sans le Brésil
1 179	**10 943**	**83 690**	**86 425**	**223 116**	**210 925**	**273 033**	**280 478**	**Économies en développement : Asie**
544	11 072	79 292	58 187	113 296	120 106	174 169	174 775	Asie orientale et Asie du Sud-Est sans la Chine
7	4	37	538	500	476	454	482	Asie méridionale sans l'Inde

Sources :
Pour les sources et les notes, se reporter à la fin du tableau 7.2.1.

Trade group	Inward flows - Flux entrants Millions of dollars							
	1980	1990	2000	2005	2008	2009	2010	2011
AFRICA								
CEMAC	206	4	549	2 653	2 267	5 425	6 494	6 720
CEPGL	131	-6	92	15	1 834	783	2 982	1 795
COMESA	-208	1 250	2 992	10 101	21 124	16 266	17 977	8 529
EAC	109	60	593	1 351	2 179	2 030	1 788	2 331
ECCAS	374	-336	1 523	1 380	5 859	8 429	6 274	2 947
ECOWAS	-461	1 547	2 146	6 303	12 274	13 464	11 695	16 055
MRU	148	324	304	583	1 169	810	977	2 112
SADC	372	31	3 126	7 664	17 235	12 934	6 957	9 573
UMA	-378	459	1 663	5 370	11 362	9 693	7 390	6 278
WAEMU	208	239	514	783	1 803	2 538	2 282	2 021
AMERICA								
ANCOM	301	734	3 959	13 036	19 062	14 312	16 155	22 894
CACM	188	268	1 460	2 721	5 368	3 270	3 694	5 457
CARICOM	262	428	2 056	3 701	7 244	3 189	2 515	3 018
FTAA	29 088	64 703	461 160	207 346	501 222	247 262	343 294	422 947
LAIA	5 601	7 745	75 191	68 359	120 038	72 396	111 610	141 556
MERCOSUR	2 907	2 937	43 571	21 214	57 098	31 588	58 079	76 397
NAFTA	24 825	58 638	398 902	154 908	390 683	181 129	242 027	287 423
OAS	29 088	64 704	461 150	207 362	501 246	247 286	343 379	423 057
OECS	51	221	10 208	-8 446	52 705	47 142	49 601	54 208
ASIA								
APTA	204	4 536	54 092	88 228	162 193	139 520	149 128	162 086
ASEAN	2 636	12 821	22 696	43 300	50 214	47 358	92 733	116 539
ECO	172	600	3 124	19 997	44 023	33 188	31 932	41 106
GCC	-3 403	166	391	28 319	60 393	47 107	39 892	25 960
SAARC	203	575	4 671	11 296	50 960	39 323	28 098	34 792
EUROPE								
EFTA	82	7 070	26 517	7 687	26 625	42 131	38 145	4 386
EU	21 279	97 309	698 244	499 376	542 242	356 631	318 277	420 715
Euro area	10 791	62 934	502 167	256 809	357 171	245 255	253 471	307 349
OCEANIA								
MSG	119	263	134	240	463	711	503	100
INTERREGIONAL								
ACP	730	2 487	10 064	25 667	48 030	42 410	34 538	42 564
APEC	31 203	92 906	571 556	314 947	794 097	478 338	632 085	732 638
BSEC	690	1 693	8 110	44 578	140 837	65 402	68 258	89 298
CIS	_	_	5 299	25 787	106 820	63 439	68 966	84 539

Sources:
For sources and notes, see end of table 7.2.1.

Outward flows - Flux sortants Millions de dollars								Groupements commerciaux
1980	1990	2000	2005	2008	2009	2010	2011	
AFRIQUE								
-	51	35	42	49	-54	45	13	CEMAC
0	0	-2	13	55	35	7	91	CEPGL
67	141	185	303	8 051	2 226	5 246	2 308	COMESA
1	0	0	10	44	46	-2	9	CAE
0	52	33	70	2 673	-12	1 393	1 404	CEEAC
238	412	965	416	-402	-971	-425	-285	CEDEAO
236	6	788	429	508	354	399	385	UFM
770	59	311	1 047	-551	1 555	2 558	2 018	SADC
80	123	172	199	6 738	1 932	3 609	1 047	UMA
-3	-10	16	-28	139	200	115	154	UEMOA
AMÉRIQUE								
108	70	341	4 675	3 002	3 532	6 810	8 420	ANCOM
8	1	68	-101	-40	49	63	82	MCAC
116	32	244	595	1 182	222	154	536	CARICOM
24 222	38 268	195 073	63 117	427 613	321 467	390 327	478 893	ZLEA
423	1 335	8 399	18 320	36 306	10 273	44 771	29 806	ALADI
257	660	3 188	3 870	21 845	-9 348	12 489	444	MERCOSUR
23 332	36 442	187 667	49 381	389 247	315 639	356 554	455 171	ALENA
24 222	38 268	195 073	63 115	427 613	321 467	390 327	478 893	OEA
0	-2 520	34 461	17 755	44 118	35 143	58 717	62 507	OECO
ASIE								
-	1 889	5 677	21 654	91 654	89 705	105 307	100 290	ACAP
394	2 328	8 978	18 534	32 255	32 997	44 171	59 890	ANASE
7	-14	912	2 636	4 737	5 465	9 926	7 950	ECO
619	-908	1 696	10 263	34 272	15 014	14 196	21 825	CCG
4	9	529	3 072	19 377	16 047	13 259	14 873	SAARC
EUROPE								
-	8 770	54 572	80 171	66 808	64 485	85 509	89 582	AELE
21 902	130 572	807 487	604 076	957 798	393 618	482 905	561 805	UE
13 181	96 355	505 917	472 995	739 586	309 419	413 709	392 433	Zone euro
OCÉANIE								
18	11	4	20	-3	12	9	3	MSG
INTERRÉGIONAUX								
1 143	567	1 627	2 223	408	870	2 389	2 359	ACP
26 851	102 170	311 405	147 794	782 344	633 879	731 423	911 302	CEAP
0	10	6 177	16 995	63 701	47 708	56 486	72 937	CEMN
–	–	3 186	14 126	58 420	47 474	61 390	72 694	CEI

Sources :
Pour les sources et les notes, se reporter à la fin du tableau 7.2.1.

Region, country or territory	Millions of dollars - Millions de dollars							
	1980	1990	2000	2005	2008	2009	2010	2011
WORLD	**41 691**	**80 814**	**139 268**	**277 542**	**458 161**	**432 896**	**453 863**	**488 791**
DEVELOPING ECONOMIES	18 950	34 653	83 462	177 409	294 998	286 288	305 197	328 527
TRANSITION ECONOMIES	4 102	9 360	6 170	12 262	30 632	27 331	28 185	32 328
DEVELOPED ECONOMIES	18 639	36 801	49 637	87 871	132 531	119 277	120 480	127 935
Developing economies: Africa	**5 819**	**8 996**	**11 484**	**22 704**	**41 604**	**37 700**	**38 463**	**41 796**
Eastern Africa	*116*	*244*	*1 097*	*1 660*	*3 454*	*3 362*	*3 754*	*4 195*
Burundi	..	..	..	0	4	4	4	4
Comoros	2	10	12	12	12	12	12	12
Djibouti	..	..	12	26	30	32	33	35
Ethiopia (...1991)	12	5	–	–	–	–	–	–
Ethiopia	–	–	53	174	387	262	345	242
Kenya	28	139	538	805	1 692	1 686	1 777	2 236
Madagascar	0	8	11	11	13	6	10	13
Malawi	..	..	1	1	1	1	1	-
Mauritius	..	..	177	146	318	297	337	405
Mozambique	53	70	37	59	116	111	132	132
Rwanda	3	3	7	21	68	93	103	97
Seychelles	..	8	3	12	3	16	17	12
Uganda	..	..	238	322	724	778	915	937
United Republic of Tanzania	..	..	8	19	19	23	25	25
Zambia	..	..	..	53	68	41	44	45
Zimbabwe	17	1	..	..	..	..	..	..
Middle Africa	*33*	*29*	*51*	*108*	*207*	*224*	*149*	*243*
Angola	..	..	(e)4	(e)7	(e)8	(e)6	(e)9	(e)10
Cameroon	29	23	30	77	167	192	115	206
Central African Republic	0	0	..	..	..	..	..	..
Chad	..	1	..	..	..	..	..	..
Congo	3	4	10	11	15	15	15	16
Gabon	0	1	6	11	14	9	8	9
Sao Tome and Principe	1	0	0	2	3	2	2	2
Northern Africa	*4 736*	*7 255*	*7 249*	*14 091*	*22 885*	*19 594*	*19 117*	*21 011*
Algeria	406	352	790	2 060	2 202	2 059	2 044	1 942
Egypt	2 696	4 284	2 852	5 017	8 694	7 150	7 150	8 047
Libya	..	..	9	15	16	16	17	19
Morocco	1 054	2 006	2 161	4 590	6 895	6 270	6 423	7 081
Sudan (...2011)	262	62	641	1 016	3 100	2 135	1 420	2 055
Tunisia	319	551	796	1 393	1 977	1 964	2 063	1 867
Southern Africa	*443*	*775*	*914*	*1 506*	*1 637*	*1 742*	*2 090*	*2 189*
Botswana	77	86	26	131	114	110	100	100
Lesotho	263	428	478	604	596	623	746	753
Namibia	..	13	9	18	14	14	16	15
South Africa	67	136	344	658	823	902	1 119	1 212
Swaziland	35	113	57	95	90	93	109	109
Western Africa	*491*	*693*	*2 172*	*5 339*	*13 422*	*12 779*	*13 354*	*14 159*
Benin	77	101	87	173	251	150	248	250
Burkina Faso	150	140	67	57	99	99	95	95
Cape Verde	40	59	87	137	155	138	133	159
Côte d'Ivoire	32	44	119	163	199	185	179	195
Gambia	5	10	14	59	65	80	116	125
Ghana	1	6	32	99	126	114	136	141
Guinea	..	18	1	42	72	64	60	61
Guinea-Bissau	..	1	8	20	49	49	48	51
Liberia	..	..	..	32	58	25	31	28
Mali	59	107	73	177	431	454	436	440
Mauritania	6	14	2	2	2	2	2	2
Niger	11	14	14	66	94	102	88	88
Nigeria	22	10	1 392	3 329	9 980	9 585	10 045	10 681
Senegal	77	142	233	789	1 476	1 350	1 346	1 437
Sierra Leone	0	0	7	2	28	47	58	60
Togo	10	27	34	193	337	335	333	345
Developing economies: America	**1 936**	**5 842**	**21 074**	**50 889**	**65 596**	**58 111**	**58 738**	**63 388**
Caribbean	*416*	*786*	*4 355*	*6 745*	*8 585*	*8 311*	*8 771*	*9 449*
Anguilla	..	6	13	22	25	24	24	-
Antigua and Barbuda	..	13	21	22	26	24	24	25

For sources and notes, see end of table.

As percentage of GDP (1) En pourcentage du PIB (1)				As percentage of exports of goods and services (2) En pourcentage des exportations des biens et services (2)				Régions, pays ou territoires
1990	2000	2010	2011	1990	2000	2010	2011	
0.40	**0.45**	**0.75**	**0.73**	**2.24**	**1.94**	**2.60**	**2.38**	**MONDE**
1.01	1.29	1.56	1.45	5.10	4.09	4.62	4.15	ÉCONOMIES EN DÉVELOPPEMENT
11.77	1.63	1.37	1.29	45.26	3.59	4.01	3.51	ÉCONOMIES EN TRANSITION
0.22	0.21	0.31	0.31	1.27	1.00	1.18	1.09	ÉCONOMIES DÉVELOPPÉES
2.13	**1.99**	**2.31**	**2.28**	**8.63**	**6.49**	**6.74**	**6.52**	**Économies en développement : Afrique**
0.56	*1.96*	*2.36*	*2.40*	*4.10*	*9.46*	*8.36*	*8.01*	*Afrique orientale*
..	..	0.25	0.21	..	..	2.02	1.62	Burundi
4.08	5.94	2.22	1.97	28.55	20.20	14.72	13.01	Comores
..	2.21	2.86	2.82	..	6.36	7.76	7.75	Djibouti
0.04	–	–	–	0.87	–	–	–	Éthiopie (...1991)
–	0.66	1.28	0.80	–	5.36	7.43	4.29	Éthiopie
1.26	4.27	5.47	6.56	6.25	19.38	19.97	23.89	Kenya
0.26	0.29	0.11	0.13	1.67	0.95	0.48	0.49	Madagascar
..	0.03	0.02	-	..	0.17	0.06	-	Malawi
..	3.80	3.47	3.57	..	6.75	6.80	6.64	Maurice
2.37	0.85	1.38	0.99	30.69	5.34	4.42	3.82	Mozambique
0.10	0.37	1.82	1.54	1.84	5.19	16.98	11.04	Rwanda
1.64	0.41	1.75	1.15	3.28	0.66	1.75	1.10	Seychelles
..	3.75	5.37	5.70	..	35.91	25.84	23.27	Ouganda
..	0.08	0.11	0.10	..	0.59	0.39	0.32	République-Unie de Tanzanie
..	..	0.27	0.24	..	..	0.57	0.50	Zambie
0.01	..	..	..	0.04	..	..	..	Zimbabwe
0.12	*0.19*	*0.11*	*0.15*	*0.40*	*0.30*	*0.19*	*0.25*	*Afrique centrale*
..	(e)0.04	(e)0.01	(e)0.01	..	(e)0.05	(e)0.02	(e)0.02	Angola
0.19	0.32	0.49	0.77	0.92	1.13	2.03	3.13	Cameroun
0.01	..	..	..	0.04	..	..	..	République centrafricaine
0.04	..	..	..	0.22	..	..	..	Tchad
0.16	0.32	0.14	0.12	0.29	0.39	0.15	0.14	Congo
0.02	0.11	0.04	0.04	0.03	0.17	0.08	0.06	Gabon
0.26	0.60	0.94	0.82	3.93	2.80	8.32	7.73	Sao Tomé-et-Principe
4.74	*2.78*	*2.89*	*3.10*	*20.55*	*9.99*	*8.58*	*9.79*	*Afrique septentrionale*
0.57	1.44	1.29	1.04	2.62	3.50	3.37	2.48	Algérie
11.92	2.98	3.32	3.47	43.29	16.91	14.64	16.86	Égypte
..	0.02	0.02	0.06	..	0.07	0.04	0.10	Libye
6.95	5.84	7.02	7.07	32.16	20.67	21.32	19.96	Maroc
0.49	4.89	1.79	2.59	12.40	34.94	12.18	16.26	Soudan (...2011)
4.06	3.71	4.66	4.03	10.59	9.25	9.28	8.23	Tunisie
0.65	*0.63*	*0.53*	*0.49*	*2.49*	*2.13*	*1.85*	*1.65*	*Afrique australe*
2.30	0.47	0.67	0.57	4.27	0.87	1.98	1.64	Botswana
78.56	61.99	35.03	31.56	427.60	177.86	82.90	67.21	Lesotho
0.50	0.24	0.14	0.12	1.10	0.64	0.32	0.27	Namibie
0.12	0.26	0.31	0.30	0.50	0.93	1.12	1.03	Afrique du Sud
10.71	3.70	2.78	2.58	17.15	4.59	5.28	4.76	Swaziland
0.84	*2.48*	*4.28*	*3.85*	*2.82*	*6.62*	*11.74*	*9.93*	*Afrique occidentale*
5.48	3.69	3.78	3.43	27.77	16.48	14.96	12.54	Bénin
4.46	2.56	1.11	0.98	40.00	28.41	5.54	4.11	Burkina Faso
19.20	16.12	8.24	8.63	104.05	59.57	20.27	19.78	Cap-Vert
0.37	1.12	0.79	0.81	1.27	2.73	1.69	1.70	Côte d'Ivoire
1.41	1.79	11.56	12.21	5.77	7.41	45.26	39.63	Gambie
0.06	0.41	0.42	0.37	0.61	1.33	1.44	0.94	Ghana
0.62	0.04	1.42	1.22	2.17	0.16	3.94	4.03	Guinée
0.16	2.16	5.89	5.39	3.83	11.92	29.38	18.32	Guinée-Bissau
..	..	3.60	2.74	..	..	7.87	5.68	Libéria
4.26	2.76	4.74	4.25	25.47	11.36	17.88	15.62	Mali
0.84	0.15	0.05	0.04	2.91	0.50	0.09	0.07	Mauritanie
0.53	0.84	1.59	1.43	2.61	4.50	8.37	7.02	Niger
0.03	3.00	5.11	4.50	0.07	6.64	13.08	11.14	Nigéria
2.29	4.99	10.48	9.96	9.78	17.87	42.53	39.34	Sénégal
0.00	0.77	2.79	2.53	0.01	12.96	13.60	12.51	Sierra Leone
1.50	2.65	10.53	9.67	4.05	8.08	27.45	24.04	Togo
0.53	**1.00**	**1.18**	**1.13**	**3.35**	**4.91**	**5.71**	**5.02**	**Économies en développement : Amérique**
1.40	*5.10*	*5.12*	*5.17*	*4.91*	*14.14*	*16.18*	*14.78*	*Caraïbes*
11.56	12.23	11.54	-	15.29	19.04	19.65	-	Anguilla
3.20	3.11	2.14	2.19	3.63	4.17	4.57	4.62	Antigua-et-Barbuda

Pour les sources et les notes, se reporter à la fin du tableau.

Region, country or territory	Millions of dollars - Millions de dollars							
	1980	1990	2000	2005	2008	2009	2010	2011
Aruba	..	..	8	12	15	21	16	16
Barbados	9	38	115	131	131	131	131	131
Cuba	..	(e)16	(e)700	(e)800	(e)855	(e)1 026	(e)1 231	(e)1 601
Dominica	9	14	16	25	26	25	26	26
Dominican Republic	183	315	1 839	2 719	3 667	3 467	3 473	3 593
Grenada	..	18	46	52	55	53	53	58
Haiti	106	61	578	986	1 370	1 376	1 474	1 598
Jamaica	96	229	892	1 784	2 181	1 908	2 044	2 143
Montserrat	..	18	1	1	1	1	1	-
Netherlands Antilles	6	5	12	11	32	37	37	–
Saint Kitts and Nevis	1	19	27	34	44	43	52	44
Saint Lucia	..	16	26	29	31	30	32	31
Saint Vincent and the Grenadines	..	16	22	26	31	33	33	33
Trinidad and Tobago	6	3	38	92	95	109	120	126
Central America	*1 185*	*3 786*	*10 869*	*31 867*	*38 808*	*33 648*	*34 228*	*36 429*
Belize	..	18	26	46	78	80	80	77
Costa Rica	4	12	136	420	605	513	552	585
El Salvador	49	366	1 765	3 030	3 758	3 405	3 449	3 655
Guatemala	26	119	596	3 067	4 460	4 019	4 232	4 508
Honduras	2	63	484	1 818	2 858	2 512	2 640	2 907
Mexico	1 039	3 098	7 525	22 742	26 035	22 014	22 048	23 516
Nicaragua	..	..	320	616	818	768	823	902
Panama, excl. Canal Zone	65	–	–	–	–	–	–	–
Panama	–	110	16	130	196	336	406	279
South America	*336*	*1 269*	*5 850*	*12 276*	*18 202*	*16 153*	*15 739*	*17 509*
Argentina	56	23	86	432	698	621	637	674
Bolivia (Plurinational State of)	1	5	127	346	1 144	1 069	953	1 188
Brazil	111	573	1 649	3 540	5 089	4 234	4 000	4 629
Chile	..	0	13	13	3	4	3	3
Colombia	106	495	1 610	3 346	4 884	4 180	4 058	4 205
Ecuador	3	51	1 322	2 460	2 828	2 502	2 332	2 711
Guyana	..	..	27	201	278	278	308	330
Paraguay	52	34	278	269	588	619	664	785
Peru	..	87	718	1 440	2 444	2 409	2 534	2 731
Suriname	6	1	1	4	2	5	4	5
Uruguay	..	..	..	77	108	101	103	112
Venezuela (Bolivarian Rep. of)	..	1	17	148	137	131	143	138
Developing economies: Asia	**11 157**	**19 708**	**50 762**	**102 357**	**186 107**	**188 854**	**206 326**	**221 369**
Eastern Asia	*1 139*	*2 645*	*10 101*	*31 374*	*60 680*	*59 492*	*63 698*	*70 155*
China	576	196	4 822	23 478	48 407	48 852	53 038	57 282
China, Hong Kong SAR	..	..	136	297	355	348	340	364
China, Macao SAR	..	..	..	588	507	725	835	968
China, Taiwan Province of	..	36	274	323	454	455	500	613
Korea, Republic of	563	2 413	4 858	6 509	10 732	8 913	8 708	10 576
Mongolia	..	..	12	180	225	200	277	353
Southern Asia	*5 295*	*6 771*	*17 742*	*34 956*	*72 753*	*76 135*	*83 390*	*91 829*
Bangladesh	339	779	1 968	4 315	8 941	10 521	10 850	11 989
Bhutan	..	..	..	..	4	5	6	5
India	2 757	2 384	12 884	22 125	49 977	49 468	54 035	57 817
Iran (Islamic Rep. of)	..	(e)1 200	536	1 032	1 115	1 072	1 181	1 330
Maldives	..	2	2	2	3	4	4	4
Nepal	..	..	111	1 212	2 727	2 986	3 469	3 951
Pakistan	2 048	2 006	1 075	4 280	7 039	8 717	9 690	12 190
Sri Lanka	152	401	1 166	1 991	2 947	3 363	4 155	4 542
South-Eastern Asia	*1 050*	*2 806*	*12 415*	*24 771*	*35 928*	*36 977*	*41 979*	*42 811*
Cambodia	..	..	121	200	325	338	321	407
Indonesia (...2002)	..	166	1 190	–	–	–	–	–
Indonesia	–	–	–	5 420	6 794	6 793	6 916	6 924
Lao People's Dem. Rep.	..	11	1	1	18	38	41	44
Malaysia	41	185	342	1 117	1 329	1 131	1 301	1 457
Myanmar	..	6	104	131	116	116	133	137
Philippines	626	1 465	6 961	13 566	18 642	19 765	21 427	23 065
Thailand	383	973	1 697	1 187	1 898	2 776	3 580	2 177
Viet Nam	..	..	(e)2 000	3 150	6 805	6 020	8 260	8 600
Western Asia	*3 673*	*7 485*	*10 504*	*11 255*	*16 745*	*16 250*	*17 260*	*16 573*
Jordan	794	499	1 845	2 500	3 794	3 597	3 641	3 554
Lebanon	..	1 818	1 582	4 924	7 181	7 558	7 619	7 558
Occupied Palestinian territory	..	..	1 010	705	1 228	1 106	1 151	1 198

For sources and notes, see end of table.

As percentage of GDP (1) En pourcentage du PIB (1)				As percentage of exports of goods and services (2) En pourcentage des exportations des biens et services (2)				Régions, pays ou territoires
1990	2000	2010	2011	1990	2000	2010	2011	
..	0.42	0.63	0.56	..	0.22	0.86	0.23	Aruba
1.96	3.95	3.29	3.12	4.34	8.88	6.31	6.41	Barbade
(e)0.06	(e)2.29	(e)1.92	(e)2.29	(e)0.27	(e)16.21	(e)8.00	(e)8.59	Cuba
6.96	5.03	5.52	5.30	15.56	11.28	15.72	15.76	Dominique
3.35	7.77	6.73	6.30	17.19	20.51	29.69	26.68	République dominicaine
8.13	8.92	6.88	7.26	19.31	19.67	31.80	31.74	Grenade
2.33	17.21	24.07	23.57	19.18	114.75	184.36	159.32	Haïti
4.74	9.95	15.22	14.57	10.32	24.85	51.03	49.08	Jamaïque
27.04	2.29	2.11	-	94.94	4.60	9.56	-	Montserrat
0.23	0.44	0.92	_	0.31	0.60	0.88	_	Antilles néerlandaises
12.11	8.23	9.43	7.51	23.41	18.07	21.69	19.26	Saint-Kitts-et-Nevis
3.87	3.78	2.71	2.56	5.72	7.02	5.02	5.61	Sainte-Lucie
6.65	5.66	4.93	4.56	12.01	12.53	18.13	17.50	Saint-Vincent-et-les Grenadines
0.07	0.47	0.59	0.57	0.15	0.79	0.99	0.81	Trinité-et-Tobago
1.19	*1.54*	*2.90*	*2.76*	*6.41*	*5.22*	*9.14*	*8.32*	*Amérique centrale*
4.55	3.18	5.68	5.26	7.54	6.08	9.59	8.18	Belize
0.17	0.85	1.54	1.44	0.61	1.75	3.99	3.80	Costa Rica
7.63	13.44	16.26	16.05	37.64	48.21	62.12	56.44	El Salvador
1.74	3.47	10.20	9.54	7.57	15.44	39.09	35.01	Guatemala
1.73	6.73	17.14	16.73	6.09	12.57	39.03	35.08	Honduras
1.08	1.18	2.14	2.04	6.35	4.18	7.02	6.44	Mexique
..	8.13	12.56	12.43	..	29.04	22.06	19.12	Nicaragua
_	_	_	_	_	_	_	_	Panama, sans la zone du canal
1.81	0.14	1.52	0.90	2.47	0.21	2.16	1.16	Panama
0.17	*0.45*	*0.43*	*0.43*	*1.28*	*3.08*	*2.62*	*2.30*	*Amérique du Sud*
0.02	0.03	0.17	0.15	0.15	0.28	0.78	0.68	Argentine
0.09	1.51	4.85	4.85	0.47	8.63	13.93	13.01	Bolivie (État plurinational de)
0.14	0.26	0.19	0.19	1.63	2.55	1.71	1.57	Brésil
0.00	0.02	0.00	0.00	0.00	0.06	0.00	0.00	Chili
0.87	1.61	1.41	1.26	5.70	10.19	8.96	6.71	Colombie
0.45	8.12	3.96	4.01	1.56	22.39	11.89	11.08	Équateur
..	2.40	13.64	13.18	..	4.06	27.23	26.13	Guyana
0.73	3.92	3.71	3.51	1.34	9.51	6.64	6.38	Paraguay
0.30	1.35	1.61	1.51	2.11	8.43	6.41	5.36	Pérou
0.08	0.13	0.12	0.12	0.06	0.26	0.18	0.18	Suriname
..	..	0.26	0.23	..	..	0.97	0.88	Uruguay
0.00	0.01	0.04	0.04	0.01	0.05	0.21	0.15	Venezuela (Rép. bolivarienne du)
1.04	**1.34**	**1.60**	**1.45**	**4.94**	**3.55**	**4.13**	**3.70**	**Économies en développement : Asie**
0.31	*0.45*	*0.86*	*0.79*	*1.29*	*1.12*	*2.02*	*1.90*	*Asie orientale*
0.05	0.40	0.92	0.81	0.34	1.72	3.03	2.75	Chine
..	0.08	0.15	0.15	..	0.06	0.07	0.07	Chine (RAS de Hong Kong)
..	..	3.07	2.80	..	..	2.81	2.38	Chine (RAS de Macao)
0.02	0.08	0.12	0.13	0.05	0.16	0.16	0.17	Province chinoise de Taiwan
0.89	0.91	0.86	0.95	3.25	2.32	1.59	1.63	Corée, République de
..	1.06	4.47	4.13	..	1.96	8.15	6.49	Mongolie
1.35	*2.49*	*3.40*	*3.27*	*12.53*	*15.34*	*15.83*	*13.47*	*Asie méridionale*
2.77	4.33	10.88	11.05	37.74	27.27	50.09	44.06	Bangladesh
..	..	0.38	0.30	..	..	0.92	0.65	Bhoutan
0.73	2.75	3.14	2.98	10.40	21.50	15.47	12.60	Inde
(e)1.32	0.52	0.31	0.28	(e)6.08	1.77	1.04	0.91	Iran (Rép. islamique d')
0.86	0.35	0.28	0.30	0.95	0.48	0.43	0.37	Maldives
..	1.95	21.65	21.72	..	8.70	220.43	212.16	Népal
4.19	1.51	5.56	5.83	29.35	10.62	34.53	38.90	Pakistan
4.88	6.97	8.39	7.68	17.48	18.28	38.54	33.29	Sri Lanka
0.90	*2.45*	*2.58*	*2.26*	*2.72*	*3.80*	*5.27*	*4.55*	*Asie du Sud-Est*
..	3.29	2.85	3.17	..	6.60	4.66	4.28	Cambodge
0.13	0.72	_	_	0.57	1.69	_	_	Indonésie (…2002)
_	_	0.98	0.82	_	_	3.96	3.12	Indonésie
1.26	0.04	0.63	0.56	10.64	0.13	1.81	1.48	Rép. dém. populaire lao
0.41	0.37	0.55	0.52	0.57	0.30	0.56	0.55	Malaisie
0.12	1.42	0.32	0.25	1.88	4.86	1.62	1.40	Myanmar
2.98	8.59	10.74	10.25	12.82	17.09	33.04	36.80	Philippines
1.14	1.38	1.12	0.63	3.33	2.08	1.57	0.82	Thaïlande
..	(e)6.42	7.95	7.13	..	(e)11.66	10.37	8.13	Viet Nam
3.16	*3.04*	*1.24*	*1.05*	*20.74*	*12.81*	*3.32*	*2.46*	*Asie occidentale*
12.42	21.81	13.24	11.68	19.88	52.14	28.83	27.13	Jordanie
64.66	9.49	19.41	18.31	364.90	35.36	35.53	31.51	Liban
..	24.07	15.66	16.30	..	99.74	76.90	81.95	Territoire palestinien occupé

Pour les sources et les notes, se reporter à la fin du tableau.

Region, country or territory	Millions of dollars - Millions de dollars							
	1980	1990	2000	2005	2008	2009	2010	2011
Oman	35	39	39	39	39	39	39	39
Saudi Arabia	..	..	..	94	217	214	236	239
Syrian Arab Republic	774	385	180	823	1 400	1 550	2 079	1 574
Turkey	2 071	3 246	4 560	887	1 476	1 026	993	1 087
Yemen	–	1 498	1 288	1 283	1 411	1 160	1 502	1 323
Developing economies: Oceania	**38**	**108**	**142**	**1 460**	**1 691**	**1 623**	**1 670**	**1 974**
Fiji	5	22	44	185	123	154	158	205
French Polynesia	..	..	..	557	763	728	700	869
Kiribati	2	5	7	7	9	9	9	-
New Caledonia	..	..	..	512	544	509	552	638
Papua New Guinea	5	5	7	7	15	12	15	15
Samoa	19	43	45	110	135	131	143	151
Solomon Islands	..	..	4	7	2	2	2	2
Tonga	7	24	..	69	94	72	85	78
Vanuatu (3)	..	8	35	5	6	6	6	7
Transition economies	**4 102**	**9 360**	**6 170**	**12 262**	**30 632**	**27 331**	**28 185**	**32 328**
Albania	..	..	598	1 290	1 495	1 318	1 156	1 221
Armenia	–	–	87	498	1 062	769	996	1 295
Azerbaijan	–	–	57	693	1 554	1 274	1 432	1 915
Belarus	–	–	139	255	680	589	589	697
Bosnia and Herzegovina	–	–	1 607	2 043	2 735	2 133	1 824	1 959
Croatia	–	–	641	711	1 292	1 271	1 287	1 262
Georgia	–	–	209	346	732	714	806	1 110
Kazakhstan	–	–	122	178	192	261	291	240
Kyrgyzstan	–	–	9	322	1 232	992	1 275	1 500
Montenegro	–	–	–	–	298	302	301	-
Republic of Moldova	–	–	179	920	1 897	1 211	1 363	1 612
Russian Federation (4)	–	–	1 275	3 012	6 033	5 359	5 264	5 667
Serbia and Montenegro (5)	–	–	1 132	705	–	–	–	–
Serbia	–	–	–	–	2 710	3 936	3 351	3 719
SFR of Yugoslavia	4 102	9 360	–	–	–	–	–	–
Tajikistan	–	–	..	467	2 544	1 748	2 254	2 680
TFYR of Macedonia	–	–	81	227	407	381	388	435
Ukraine	–	–	33	595	5 769	5 073	5 607	6 716
Developed economies: America	**80**	**1 170**	**4 395**	**4 795**	**6 775**	**6 521**	**6 633**	**6 782**
Bermuda	..	..	..	..	1 594	1 345	1 356	1 345
United States	80	1 170	4 395	4 795	5 181	5 176	5 277	5 437
Developed economies: Asia	**561**	**1 225**	**1 774**	**1 930**	**3 351**	**3 043**	**3 214**	**3 646**
Israel	421	812	400	850	1 422	1 267	1 411	1 715
Japan	140	-	1 374	1 080	1 929	1 776	1 802	1 931
Developed economies: Europe	**17 110**	**31 274**	**41 328**	**77 417**	**117 051**	**104 505**	**104 951**	**111 357**
Austria	245	635	1 805	2 608	3 317	3 100	3 042	3 111
Belgium (6)	1 139	3 583	(e)3 426	7 242	10 416	10 448	10 308	10 676
Bulgaria (7)	..	..	58	1 613	1 919	1 592	1 387	1 498
Cyprus	94	79	64	189	279	153	146	152
Czech Republic	–	–	297	1 528	2 168	2 077	2 066	1 849
Denmark	..	..	667	867	1 295	1 214	1 184	1 256
Estonia	–	–	4	264	370	309	322	418
Faeroe Islands	..	..	43	80	137	139	146	..
Finland	106	63	473	693	908	875	848	889
France	1 440	4 035	8 610	11 945	16 597	15 866	15 629	16 705
Germany, Federal Republic of	2 380		–	–	–	–	–	–
Germany	–	4 876	3 644	6 933	11 172	11 453	11 905	13 393
Greece	1 119	1 817	2 194	1 220	2 687	2 020	1 499	1 186
Hungary	..	..	281	1 931	2 509	2 135	2 225	2 402
Iceland	2	62	88	88	35	23	25	27
Ireland	..	286	252	513	633	573	601	691
Italy	4 013	5 075	1 937	2 397	5 555	5 221	6 803	6 962
Latvia	–	–	72	381	601	591	614	695
Lithuania	–	–	50	534	1 566	1 239	1 674	1 956
Luxembourg	..	..	579	1 268	1 621	1 585	1 586	1 756
Malta	35	58	20	34	54	51	48	54
Netherlands	604	709	1 157	2 197	3 300	3 697	3 834	3 958
Norway	102	158	270	505	685	631	680	743
Poland	..	..	1 496	6 482	10 447	8 126	7 575	7 602
Portugal	2 968	4 479	3 495	3 101	4 057	3 585	3 599	3 834
Romania (8)	..	..	96	(b)4 733	9 381	4 952	3 952	3 750

For sources and notes, see end of table.

360

As percentage of GDP (1) En pourcentage du PIB (1)				As percentage of exports of goods and services (2) En pourcentage des exportations des biens et servicés (2)				Régions, pays ou territoires
1990	2000	2010	2011	1990	2000	2010	2011	
0.34	0.20	0.07	0.05	0.71	0.33	0.10	0.08	Oman
..	..	0.05	0.04	..	..	0.09	0.06	Arabie saoudite
3.45	0.92	3.47	2.72	7.65	2.63	10.60	8.50	République arabe syrienne
1.60	1.71	0.14	0.14	15.43	9.06	0.64	0.60	Turquie
32.02	12.83	4.34	3.53	100.57	32.13	16.10	13.35	Yémen
2.10	**2.32**	**5.41**	**5.65**	**4.52**	**3.87**	**14.39**	**14.32**	**Économies en développement : Océanie**
1.62	2.55	5.18	5.60	2.64	4.54	9.40	11.45	Fidji
..	..	10.48	13.01	..	..	62.80	71.54	Polynésie française
12.47	10.48	6.04	-	46.39	55.53	84.75	-	Kiribati
..	..	6.23	7.20	..	..	29.98	30.67	Nouvelle-Calédonie
0.17	0.21	0.15	0.12	0.39	0.31	0.25	0.20	Papouasie-Nouvelle-Guinée
38.26	19.48	23.44	22.17	96.24	61.39	74.00	76.08	Samoa
..	1.28	0.26	0.30	..	3.56	0.50	0.45	Îles Salomon
14.83	..	22.93	17.86	62.59	..	177.82	125.15	Tonga
4.74	12.74	0.91	0.82	11.11	22.08	1.96	1.85	Vanuatu (3)
11.77	**1.63**	**1.37**	**1.29**	**45.26**	**3.59**	**4.01**	**3.51**	**Économies en transition**
..	16.42	9.81	9.53	..	84.98	29.98	27.80	Albanie
–	4.58	10.63	12.49	–	19.58	51.41	53.86	Arménie
–	1.08	2.77	3.02	–	2.70	5.01	5.14	Azerbaïdjan
–	1.34	1.08	1.27	–	1.82	1.97	1.49	Bélarus
–	28.94	10.83	10.74	–	101.74	29.31	26.70	Bosnie-Herzégovine
–	2.98	2.12	1.98	–	7.42	5.52	4.85	Croatie
–	6.85	6.91	7.71	–	24.38	19.85	21.20	Géorgie
–	0.67	0.20	0.13	–	1.18	0.45	0.26	Kazakhstan
–	0.65	27.63	26.32	–	1.54	51.60	43.50	Kirghizistan
–	–	7.32	-	–	–	20.58	-	Monténégro
–	13.86	23.47	23.03	–	27.85	59.50	51.14	République de Moldova
–	0.49	0.36	0.31	–	1.11	1.18	0.98	Fédération de Russie (4)
–	9.90	–	–	–	48.23	–	–	Serbie-et-Monténégro (5)
–	–	7.74	7.29	–	–	23.85	22.07	Serbie
11.77	–	–	–	45.26	–	–	–	RSF de Yougoslavie
–	..	40.17	41.08	–	..	149.11	152.74	Tadjikistan
–	2.26	4.25	4.28	–	4.94	9.21	7.85	LERY de Macédoine
–	0.11	4.06	4.07	–	0.17	8.10	7.56	Ukraine
0.02	**0.04**	**0.05**	**0.04**	**0.22**	**0.41**	**0.36**	**0.32**	**Économies développées : Amérique**
..	..	22.55	22.37	..	..	94.09	91.97	Bermudes
0.02	0.04	0.04	0.04	0.22	0.41	0.29	0.26	États-Unis
0.04	**0.04**	**0.06**	**0.06**	**0.36**	**0.31**	**0.34**	**0.36**	**Économies développées : Asie**
1.41	0.32	0.65	0.71	4.69	0.86	1.76	1.91	Israël
-	0.03	0.03	0.03	-	0.26	0.21	0.21	Japon
0.43	**0.46**	**0.61**	**0.60**	**1.59**	**1.28**	**1.48**	**1.35**	**Économies développées : Europe**
0.39	0.94	0.80	0.74	1.00	2.06	1.50	1.32	Autriche
1.77	(e)1.47	2.20	2.08	2.59	(e)1.60	2.81	2.53	Belgique (6)
..	0.45	2.91	2.80	..	0.83	5.05	4.19	Bulgarie (7)
1.36	0.70	0.63	0.61	2.66	1.28	1.53	1.45	Chypre
–	0.50	1.04	0.86	–	0.83	1.50	1.14	République tchèque
..	0.42	0.38	0.38	..	0.90	0.76	0.71	Danemark
..	0.07	1.70	1.88	..	0.08	1.99	1.88	Estonie
..	..	..	..	..	8.10	14.40	..	Îles Féroé
0.05	0.39	0.36	0.33	0.20	0.88	0.87	0.84	Finlande
0.32	0.65	0.61	0.60	1.46	2.26	2.36	2.21	France
								Allemagne, Rép. fédérale d'
0.28	0.19	0.36	0.37	1.03	0.58	0.77	0.74	Allemagne
1.93	1.73	0.50	0.40	13.96	7.45	2.48	1.79	Grèce
..	0.61	1.73	1.72	..	0.81	2.01	1.86	Hongrie
0.98	1.01	0.20	0.19	2.90	2.97	0.35	0.33	Islande
0.59	0.26	0.29	0.32	1.07	0.27	0.29	0.30	Irlande
0.45	0.18	0.33	0.32	2.31	0.65	1.24	1.10	Italie
–	0.93	2.55	2.46	–	2.24	4.82	4.21	Lettonie
–	0.43	4.59	4.58	–	0.98	6.73	5.87	Lituanie
..	2.85	2.97	2.99	..	6.70	1.90	1.90	Luxembourg
2.29	0.50	0.58	0.61	2.99	0.56	0.66	0.63	Malte
0.24	0.30	0.49	0.47	0.45	0.45	0.64	0.58	Pays-Bas
0.13	0.16	0.16	0.16	0.34	0.35	0.39	0.35	Norvège
..	0.87	1.61	1.48	..	3.23	3.82	3.29	Pologne
5.77	2.99	1.57	1.61	20.78	10.25	4.99	4.47	Portugal
..	0.26	2.45	2.01	..	0.79	6.80	5.14	Roumanie (8)

Pour les sources et les notes, se reporter à la fin du tableau.

7.3.1 Migrants' remittances:
Receipts of countries and geographical regions

Region, country or territory	Millions of dollars - Millions de dollars							
	1980	1990	2000	2005	2008	2009	2010	2011
Slovakia	–	–	18	946	1 973	1 671	1 591	1 792
Slovenia	–	–	205	264	347	277	309	410
Spain	2 188	2 186	4 859	7 961	11 836	10 372	10 538	11 526
Sweden	66	153	438	673	780	652	688	776
Switzerland	609	924	1 119	1 924	2 544	2 626	2 730	3 279
United Kingdom	..	2 099	3 614	6 302	7 862	7 252	7 399	8 011
Developed economies: Oceania	**888**	**3 131**	**2 139**	**3 729**	**5 354**	**5 207**	**5 683**	**6 150**
Australia	632	2 370	1 903	2 990	4 713	4 579	4 840	5 141
New Zealand	256	762	236	739	641	628	843	1 009

Sources:
UNCTAD secretariat calculations, based on:
- IMF, *Balance of Payments Statistics*
- World Bank, *Migration and Remittances*
- Economist Intelligence Unit, *Country Data*
- Other national sources

Notes:
- Migrants' remittances data cover: workers' remittances, compensation of employees and migrants' transfers.

(1) GDP data source: UNCTAD series.
(2) Exports and imports of goods and services data are based on IMF balance-of-payments statistics.
(3) Year 2002: break in series; migrants' transfers data are no longer available starting with 2002.
(4) Workers' remittances and compensation of employees: From 1995 to 2000 (inclusive), data represent compensation of employees only; workers' remittances are available starting from 2001 onwards. Total remittances (including migrants transfers) reflect the same break in series.
(5) Total remittances receipts (credit) figures refer to both Serbia and Montenegro. Other data cover Serbia only.
(6) Data up to 1994 inclusive refer to Belgium-Luxembourg Economic Union. From 1995, the figures cover Belgium only.
(7) Receipts (credits): Year 2001 - break in series.
(8) Year 2005: break in series; change in classification.

As percentage of GDP (1) En pourcentage du PIB (1)				As percentage of exports of goods and services (2) En pourcentage des exportations des biens et services (2)				Régions, pays ou territoires
1990	2000	2010	2011	1990	2000	2010	2011	
–	0.09	1.82	1.86	–	0.13	2.26	2.11	Slovaquie
–	1.03	0.66	0.83	–	1.92	1.01	1.15	Slovénie
0.42	0.84	0.75	0.76	2.61	2.89	2.80	2.56	Espagne
0.06	0.18	0.15	0.15	0.22	0.40	0.30	0.29	Suède
0.39	0.44	0.51	0.51	0.95	0.89	0.80	0.78	Suisse
0.21	0.24	0.33	0.33	0.88	0.89	1.12	1.06	Royaume-Uni
0.84	**0.46**	**0.40**	**0.36**	**5.09**	**2.10**	**1.88**	**1.65**	**Économies développées : Océanie**
0.72	0.46	0.38	0.34	4.75	2.27	1.85	1.59	Australie
1.71	0.44	0.60	0.62	6.52	1.32	2.06	2.08	Nouvelle-Zélande

Sources :
Calculs du secrétariat de la CNUCED, basés sur :
- FMI, *Statistiques de la balance des paiements*
- Banque Mondiale, *Migration and Remittances*
- Economist Intelligence Unit, *Country Data*
- Autres sources nationales

Notes :
- Les envois de fonds des migrants couvrent : les envois de fonds des travailleurs, la rémunération des employés et les transferts des migrants.

(1) Source de données du PIB : série de la CNUCED.
(2) Les données sur les exportations et importations des biens et services se basent sur les statistiques de la balance des paiements du FMI.
(3) Année 2002 : rupture de série ; les données sur les transferts des migrants ne sont plus disponibles à partir de 2002.
(4) L'envoi de fonds des travailleurs et la rémunération des salariés : De 1995 à 2000 (incluses), les données comprennent seulement la rémunération des salariés ; les envois de fonds des travailleurs ne sont disponibles qu'à partir de l'année 2001. Le total des envois de fonds (y compris les transferts des migrants) présentent la même rupture de série.
(5) La série sur les recettes (crédit) de total des envois de fonds des travailleurs se réfère à la Sérbie-Monténégro. Les autres données couvrent uniquement la Serbie.
(6) Jusqu'à l'année 1994 comprise, les données se réfèrent à l'Union économique belgo-luxembourgeoise. A partir de 1995, les chiffres couvrent uniquement la Belgique.
(7) Recettes (crédits) : Année 2001 - rupture de série.
(8) Année 2005 : rupture de série ; changement des méthodes de classification.

7

Economic grouping	Millions of dollars - Millions de dollars							
	1980	1990	2000	2005	2008	2009	2010	2011
DEVELOPING ECONOMIES	**18 950**	**34 653**	**83 462**	**177 409**	**294 998**	**286 288**	**305 197**	**328 527**
Developing economies excluding China	18 374	34 458	78 640	153 931	246 591	237 436	252 159	271 246
Developing economies excluding LDCs	17 492	31 082	77 156	165 217	271 825	262 717	280 581	301 558
High-income developing economies	3 830	10 997	19 842	40 059	51 602	45 484	45 780	49 865
Middle-income developing economies	8 741	15 351	37 767	84 821	136 248	133 350	142 376	151 261
Low-income developing economies	6 379	8 305	25 852	52 529	107 148	107 455	117 041	127 401
Heavily indebted poor countries (IMF)	905	938	3 287	7 940	15 684	13 726	13 790	15 529
Landlocked developing countries	683	945	2 079	7 014	16 269	14 211	16 394	18 914
Small island developing States	200	552	1 628	2 895	3 498	3 212	3 437	3 678
Least developed countries	*1 458*	*3 571*	*6 305*	*12 192*	*23 173*	*23 572*	*24 616*	*26 970*
Africa and Haiti	1 097	1 211	2 610	4 909	9 465	8 247	8 120	8 929
Asia	339	2 294	3 592	7 140	13 541	15 163	16 322	17 857
Islands	23	66	103	143	166	162	174	183
Major petroleum and gas exporters	*462*	*1 602*	*2 787*	*6 724*	*13 714*	*13 122*	*13 715*	*14 398*
Africa	428	362	2 195	5 411	12 206	11 665	12 116	12 652
America	..	1	17	148	137	131	143	138
Asia	35	1 239	575	1 165	1 371	1 325	1 457	1 608
Major exporters of manufactured goods	*2 602*	*6 901*	*19 653*	*55 653*	*89 210*	*84 489*	*89 514*	*95 984*
America	1 039	3 098	7 525	22 742	26 035	22 014	22 048	23 516
Asia	1 563	3 803	12 128	32 911	63 175	62 475	67 467	72 468
Emerging economies	*2 193*	*7 389*	*17 162*	*37 303*	*48 681*	*42 557*	*43 310*	*46 376*
America	1 206	3 781	9 991	28 167	34 268	29 282	29 221	31 553
Asia	987	3 607	7 171	9 136	14 413	13 275	14 089	14 823
Newly industrialized Asian economies	*1 613*	*5 238*	*15 458*	*28 418*	*40 205*	*40 180*	*42 771*	*45 175*
First tier	563	2 449	5 267	7 129	11 541	9 715	9 547	11 553
Second tier	1 050	2 789	10 190	21 290	28 663	30 465	33 224	33 623
Developing economies: Africa	**5 819**	**8 996**	**11 484**	**22 704**	**41 604**	**37 700**	**38 463**	**41 796**
Northern Africa excluding Sudan	4 474	7 193	6 608	13 075	19 784	17 458	17 697	18 956
Sub-Saharan Africa	1 345	1 803	4 876	9 629	21 820	20 242	20 765	22 841
Sub-Saharan Africa excluding South Africa	1 278	1 667	4 532	8 971	20 997	19 340	19 646	21 629
Developing economies: America	**1 936**	**5 842**	**21 074**	**50 889**	**65 596**	**58 111**	**58 738**	**63 388**
Central America and Greater Caribbean Islands excluding Puerto Rico	1 570	4 407	14 877	38 157	46 881	41 425	42 450	45 364
Central America and Greater Caribbean Islands excluding Mexico and Puerto Rico	531	1 309	7 353	15 415	20 846	19 411	20 403	21 848
South America and Central America	1 521	5 055	16 718	44 143	57 011	49 801	49 967	53 938
South America excluding Brazil	225	696	4 200	8 736	13 113	11 918	11 739	12 881
Developing economies: Asia	**11 157**	**19 708**	**50 762**	**102 357**	**186 107**	**188 854**	**206 326**	**221 369**
Eastern and South-Eastern Asia excluding China	1 613	5 255	17 695	32 667	48 201	47 616	52 638	55 685
Southern Asia excluding India	2 538	4 388	4 858	12 831	22 776	26 666	29 355	34 012

For sources and notes, see end of table 7.3.1.

As percentage of GDP (1) En pourcentage du PIB (1)				As percentage of exports of goods and services (2) En pourcentage des exportations des biens et services (2)				Groupements économiques
1990	2000	2010	2011	1990	2000	2010	2011	
1.01	**1.29**	**1.56**	**1.45**	**5.10**	**4.09**	**4.62**	**4.15**	**ÉCONOMIES EN DÉVELOPPEMENT**
1.14	1.49	1.82	1.74	5.54	4.47	5.20	4.66	Économies en développement sans la Chine
0.94	1.22	1.47	1.37	4.66	3.86	4.36	3.91	Économies en développement sans les PMA
0.90	0.76	0.85	0.84	3.57	1.79	1.67	1.55	Économies en développement à revenu élevé
1.02	1.32	1.34	1.20	5.62	5.41	4.85	4.31	Économies en développement à revenu intermédiaire
1.19	2.60	3.25	3.08	8.43	11.03	12.73	10.85	Économies en développement à revenu faible
0.86	2.55	3.47	3.53	5.00	10.10	12.03	11.12	Pays pauvres très endettés (FMI)
1.79	2.33	3.92	3.82	8.67	6.82	10.12	8.75	Pays en développement sans littoral
2.77	4.53	4.75	4.49	5.94	8.68	9.44	8.43	Petits États insulaires en développement
3.45	*3.91*	*4.41*	*4.30*	*28.61*	*16.27*	*15.15*	*13.50*	*Pays les moins avancés*
1.89	3.03	2.36	2.33	14.52	12.22	7.31	6.54	Afrique et Haïti
5.90	4.86	7.71	7.42	57.72	21.17	32.31	28.79	Asie
9.63	8.72	6.09	5.51	38.60	23.49	17.96	15.06	Îles
0.65	*0.72*	*0.77*	*0.73*	*2.22*	*1.98*	*1.91*	*1.56*	*Principaux exportateurs de pétrole et de gaz*
0.37	1.48	2.38	2.27	1.29	3.43	5.09	4.89	Afrique
0.00	0.01	0.04	0.04	0.01	0.05	0.21	0.15	Amérique
1.21	0.47	0.17	0.15	4.91	1.37	0.35	0.28	Asie
0.55	*0.64*	*0.99*	*0.90*	*2.18*	*1.54*	*2.30*	*2.11*	*Principaux exportateurs d'articles manufacturés*
1.08	1.18	2.14	2.04	6.35	4.18	7.02	6.44	Amérique
0.39	0.50	0.85	0.76	1.42	1.10	1.89	1.74	Asie
0.51	*0.62*	*0.74*	*0.70*	*2.29*	*1.94*	*2.09*	*1.90*	*Économies émergentes*
0.42	0.59	0.76	0.71	3.34	3.25	3.89	3.48	Amérique
0.64	0.67	0.70	0.67	1.72	1.25	1.07	0.97	Asie
0.71	*1.04*	*1.37*	*1.28*	*2.09*	*1.66*	*2.07*	*1.90*	*Économies nouvellement industrialisées d'Asie*
0.56	0.51	0.57	0.63	1.65	0.84	0.70	0.74	Première génération
0.91	2.20	2.27	1.98	2.72	3.34	4.75	4.13	Deuxième génération
2.13	**1.99**	**2.31**	**2.28**	**8.63**	**6.49**	**6.74**	**6.52**	**Économies en développement : Afrique**
5.13	2.67	3.04	3.17	20.67	9.35	8.38	9.38	Afrique septentrionale sans le Soudan
0.64	1.48	1.92	1.85	2.60	4.59	5.78	5.21	Afrique subsaharienne
0.98	2.32	2.73	2.62	3.95	6.54	7.57	6.74	Afrique subsaharienne sans l'Afrique du Sud
0.53	**1.00**	**1.18**	**1.13**	**3.35**	**4.91**	**5.71**	**5.02**	**Économies en développement : Amérique**
1.22	1.92	3.23	3.09	6.36	6.59	10.45	9.54	Amérique centrale et Grandes Antilles sans Porto Rico
1.76	5.39	7.18	6.91	6.38	16.03	22.14	19.82	Amérique centrale et Grandes Antilles sans le Mexique et Porto Rico
0.48	0.83	1.04	1.00	3.19	4.20	5.13	4.50	Amérique du Sud et Amérique centrale
0.21	0.63	0.76	0.77	1.08	3.36	3.21	2.76	Amérique du Sud sans le Brésil
1.04	**1.34**	**1.60**	**1.45**	**4.94**	**3.55**	**4.13**	**3.70**	**Économies en développement : Asie**
0.70	1.15	1.58	1.48	2.09	1.86	2.40	2.19	Asie orientale et Asie du Sud-Est sans la Chine
2.50	1.99	4.03	3.92	14.10	8.72	16.55	15.28	Asie méridionale sans l'Inde

Pour les sources et les notes, se reporter à la fin du tableau 7.3.1.

7.4.1 Migrants' remittances:
Payments of countries and geographical regions

Region, country or territory	Millions of dollars - Millions de dollars							
	1980	1990	2000	2005	2007	2008	2009	2010
WORLD	**30 246**	**67 941**	**120 703**	**198 058**	**276 603**	**319 381**	**302 062**	**306 709**
DEVELOPING ECONOMIES	11 607	19 572	36 186	54 792	73 927	87 502	92 188	98 022
TRANSITION ECONOMIES	..	..	1 890	10 249	23 749	31 892	23 606	23 694
DEVELOPED ECONOMIES	18 639	48 369	82 626	133 018	178 927	199 988	186 269	184 994
Developing economies: Africa	**4 660**	**3 407**	**3 078**	**4 396**	**5 387**	**5 953**	**6 428**	**7 002**
Eastern Africa	*317*	*127*	*657*	*510*	*618*	*870*	*934*	*1 100*
Burundi	..	6	2	0	0	0	1	1
Comoros	2	4	..	..	..	..	..	..
Djibouti	..	..	2	5	5	5	6	6
Eritrea			1	..	..	..	..	..
Ethiopia (...1991)	1	1	—	—	—	—	—	—
Ethiopia	—	—	13	16	15	21	27	27
Kenya	13	7	34	56	16	64	61	58
Madagascar	31	18	12	21	21	21	21	21
Malawi	0	0	0	7	10	10	13	..
Mauritius	2	1	1	11	12	14	12	13
Mozambique	25	25	156	24	45	57	66	80
Rwanda	22	21	28	35	68	70	71	76
Seychelles	..	10	10	10	9	12	21	21
Uganda	4	..	353	197	236	381	482	602
United Republic of Tanzania	..	..	20	33	57	74	87	127
Zambia	82	18	24	94	124	139	66	68
Zimbabwe	135	16	..	..	..	..	..	..
Middle Africa	*308*	*539*	*411*	*523*	*981*	*1 019*	*956*	*871*
Angola	..	150	266	215	603	669	716	714
Cameroon	102	111	30	56	90	62	137	54
Central African Republic	20	36	..	..	..	..	..	..
Chad	4	39	..	..	..	..	..	..
Congo	39	55	37	66	102	102	102	102
Gabon	144	147	78	186	186	186	..	..
Sao Tome and Principe	0	0	1	0	1	0	1	1
Northern Africa	*1 370*	*534*	*556*	*1 055*	*1 059*	*1 307*	*1 737*	*2 037*
Algeria	165	31	..	27	48	27	46	46
Egypt	..	27	32	57	180	241	255	305
Libya	1 052	446	463	914	762	964	1 361	1 609
Morocco	77	16	29	40	52	58	61	62
Sudan (...2011)	53	2	4	2	2	2	2	2
Tunisia	22	13	27	16	15	16	13	13
Southern Africa	*1 051*	*1 352*	*873*	*1 218*	*1 338*	*1 332*	*1 296*	*1 517*
Botswana	26	119	147	129	120	145	106	96
Lesotho	..	..	10	6	8	5	5	5
Namibia	..	30	9	19	16	43	16	33
South Africa	1 017	1 199	685	1 055	1 186	1 133	1 158	1 372
Swaziland	9	4	21	8	8	7	11	12
Western Africa	*1 614*	*855*	*582*	*1 088*	*1 392*	*1 423*	*1 504*	*1 477*
Benin	2	21	9	40	115	88	76	88
Burkina Faso	52	81	45	84	93	100	100	100
Cape Verde	..	2	0	5	6	10	12	8
Côte d'Ivoire	786	471	390	597	698	756	754	754
Gambia	2	..	..	1	1	1	1	1
Ghana	9	4	6	6	6	6	6	6
Guinea	..	20	27	48	119	56	45	43
Guinea-Bissau	..	12	5	5	4	17	20	17
Liberia	32	..	..	0	0	0	1	1
Mali	19	45	26	69	83	105	167	167
Mauritania	33	31	..	..	..	..	..	..
Niger	53	66	12	29	18	22	25	22
Nigeria	523	9	1	68	54	58	47	48
Senegal	91	79	55	98	143	144	174	144
Sierra Leone	2	0	..	2	4	3	3	6
Togo	9	13	7	35	47	58	72	72

For sources and notes, see end of table.

As percentage of GDP (1) En pourcentage du PIB (1)				As percentage of imports of goods and services (2) En pourcentage des importations des biens et services (2)				Régions, pays ou territoires
1990	2000	2009	2010	1990	2000	2009	2010	
0.35	0.41	0.56	0.52	1.96	1.74	2.18	1.86	**MONDE**
0.74	0.69	0.62	0.55	3.81	2.29	2.12	1.75	ÉCONOMIES EN DÉVELOPPEMENT
..	0.52	1.36	1.15	..	1.59	4.95	4.10	ÉCONOMIES EN TRANSITION
0.29	0.34	0.50	0.48	1.64	1.58	2.06	1.79	ÉCONOMIES DÉVELOPPÉES
0.72	**0.59**	**0.45**	**0.43**	**2.95**	**2.11**	**1.30**	**1.23**	**Économies en développement : Afrique**
0.23	*1.08*	*0.62*	*0.72*	*0.96*	*3.58*	*1.65*	*1.77*	*Afrique orientale*
0.36	0.25	0.09	0.08	1.83	1.64	0.23	0.20	Burundi
1.82	..	..	..	4.97	..	..	..	Comores
..	0.32	0.55	0.51	..	0.63	1.00	1.20	Djibouti
–	0.19	..	..	–	0.26	..	..	Érythrée
0.01	–	..	..	0.05		..	..	Éthiopie (…1991)
–	0.15	0.09	0.10	–	0.77	0.29	0.27	Éthiopie
0.07	0.27	0.20	0.18	0.27	0.90	0.54	0.43	Kenya
0.57	0.31	0.25	0.24	2.16	0.78	0.54	0.67	Madagascar
0.00	0.02	0.27	..	0.01	0.07	0.63	..	Malawi
0.02	0.01	0.14	0.14	0.03	0.02	0.24	0.22	Maurice
0.86	3.62	0.68	0.84	2.55	10.47	1.46	1.70	Mozambique
0.83	1.58	1.36	1.34	6.05	6.62	4.83	4.64	Rwanda
2.14	1.31	2.69	2.08	3.97	2.01	1.88	1.75	Seychelles
..	5.57	2.86	3.54	..	25.06	9.25	9.80	Ouganda
..	0.19	0.40	0.55	..	0.99	1.16	1.41	République-Unie de Tanzanie
0.47	0.74	0.51	0.42	0.92	1.84	1.59	1.21	Zambie
0.14	..	..	..	0.82	..	..	..	Zimbabwe
1.59	*1.51*	*0.89*	*0.74*	*5.46*	*3.69*	*1.76*	*1.72*	*Afrique centrale*
1.46	2.92	0.95	0.87	4.43	4.64	1.71	2.02	Angola
0.94	0.32	0.59	0.23	4.48	1.20	2.17	0.85	Cameroun
2.50	..	..	..	8.77	..	..	..	République centrafricaine
2.53	..	..	..	7.98	..	..	..	Tchad
1.98	1.13	1.25	0.95	4.33	3.06	1.67	1.15	Congo
2.52	1.41	..	..	8.13	4.69	..	..	Gabon
0.07	0.83	0.28	0.29	0.41	1.67	0.53	0.47	Sao Tomé-et-Principe
0.29	*0.27*	*0.30*	*0.31*	*1.12*	*1.07*	*0.87*	*0.94*	*Afrique septentrionale*
0.05	..	0.03	0.03	0.31	..	0.09	0.09	Algérie
0.07	0.03	0.14	0.14	0.19	0.14	0.47	0.51	Égypte
1.43	1.20	2.32	2.24	4.97	9.22	5.03	5.24	Libye
0.06	0.08	0.07	0.07	0.21	0.23	0.16	0.15	Maroc
0.02	0.03	0.00	0.00	0.24	0.22	0.02	0.01	Soudan (…2011)
0.09	0.13	0.03	0.03	0.21	0.29	0.06	0.05	Tunisie
1.13	*0.60*	*0.42*	*0.38*	*5.33*	*2.21*	*1.36*	*1.30*	*Afrique australe*
3.20	2.62	0.93	0.65	5.98	6.35	2.14	1.69	Botswana
..	1.34	0.29	0.23	..	0.99	0.25	0.20	Lesotho
1.11	0.23	0.17	0.28	1.88	0.55	0.31	0.58	Namibie
1.07	0.52	0.41	0.38	5.71	2.07	1.43	1.37	Afrique du Sud
0.39	1.35	0.35	0.30	0.54	1.44	0.47	0.45	Swaziland
1.05	*0.69*	*0.55*	*0.48*	*4.45*	*2.29*	*1.65*	*1.22*	*Afrique occidentale*
1.12	0.38	1.15	1.34	4.56	1.25	3.40	3.84	Bénin
2.58	1.69	1.20	1.17	10.66	6.77	5.15	3.94	Burkina Faso
0.59	0.09	0.76	0.48	1.23	0.14	1.09	0.70	Cap-Vert
3.96	3.65	3.27	3.31	13.68	10.74	8.57	8.91	Côte d'Ivoire
..	..	0.10	0.09	..	..	0.28	0.31	Gambie
0.04	0.08	0.02	0.02	0.26	0.18	0.05	0.04	Ghana
0.70	0.84	1.01	1.02	2.14	3.09	3.23	2.41	Guinée
1.91	1.30	2.34	2.08	13.18	4.75	6.98	5.69	Guinée-Bissau
..	..	0.12	0.13	..	..	0.06	0.06	Libéria
1.81	0.99	1.86	1.81	5.47	2.84	5.94	4.46	Mali
1.92	..	..	..	6.01	..	..	..	Mauritanie
2.52	0.69	0.47	0.40	9.13	2.61	1.00	0.88	Niger
0.03	0.00	0.03	0.02	0.13	0.01	0.10	0.06	Nigéria
1.28	1.17	1.37	1.12	4.32	3.15	3.31	2.80	Sénégal
0.01	..	0.16	0.29	0.03	..	0.55	0.67	Sierra Leone
0.75	0.52	2.28	2.28	1.59	1.12	4.26	4.23	Togo

Pour les sources et les notes, se reporter à la fin du tableau.

7

Region, country or territory	Millions of dollars - Millions de dollars							
	1980	1990	2000	2005	2007	2008	2009	2010
Developing economies: America	1 083	1 140	2 238	2 524	4 036	4 618	4 159	4 952
Caribbean	209	143	432	845	1 006	917	807	813
Anguilla	..	4	9	9	19	15	11	11
Antigua and Barbuda	..	6	2	2	2	2	2	2
Aruba	..	..	49	70	82	86	77	69
Bahamas	42	46	73	144	171	83	71	92
Barbados	1	6	19	41	55	39	40	40
Dominica	..	2	0	0	0	0	0	0
Dominican Republic	..	..	19	25	28	35	27	33
Grenada	3	1	3	3	4	4	4	3
Haiti	54	..	11	60	96	117	135	167
Jamaica	35	27	179	410	454	419	312	323
Montserrat	..	3	4	5	5	5	5	4
Netherlands Antilles	41	11	47	59	72	94	106	51
Saint Kitts and Nevis	2	7	7	8	6	6	6	6
Saint Lucia	..	4	3	4	4	4	4	5
Saint Vincent and the Grenadines	..	3	6	6	7	7	7	7
Trinidad and Tobago	31	22	..	..	..	..	..	..
Central America	71	45	260	384	493	550	545	598
Belize	..	7	11	20	22	29	23	23
Costa Rica	..	..	142	209	271	269	239	271
El Salvador	9	3	20	24	29	19	21	23
Guatemala	11	14	56	42	17	26	22	21
Honduras	..	..	9	0	2	9	12	12
Mexico	11	..	..	..	..	..	..	..
Nicaragua	2	..	..	..	..	..	..	..
Panama, excl. Canal Zone	37	–	–	–	–	–	–	–
Panama	–	22	22	88	151	198	229	248
South America	804	951	1 547	1 295	2 537	3 151	2 807	3 541
Argentina	36	94	268	314	463	630	767	1 033
Bolivia (Plurinational State of)	2	8	37	67	79	106	103	102
Brazil	152	12	366	498	896	1 191	1 003	1 198
Chile	70	7	16	16	6	6	6	5
Colombia	39	44	219	56	95	88	92	112
Ecuador	67	2	6	54	83	66	81	79
Guyana	..	..	27	55	62	77	77	77
Paraguay	2	..	..	..	..	..	..	..
Peru	..	75	275	129	137	133	85	122
Suriname	18	8	2	10	65	8	5	1
Uruguay	..	..	..	2	4	5	6	7
Venezuela (Bolivarian Rep. of)	418	701	331	95	649	842	581	805
Developing economies: Asia	5 821	14 937	30 742	47 607	64 048	76 393	81 077	85 563
Eastern Asia	58	1 033	6 502	13 348	17 284	18 015	15 699	18 766
China	..	5	790	2 550	4 372	5 737	4 444	4 444
China, Hong Kong SAR	..	..	225	348	388	393	413	483
China, Macao SAR	..	..	..	227	838	960	693	569
China, Taiwan Province of	..	..	1 831	1 413	1 394	1 640	1 417	1 715
Korea, Republic of	58	1 028	3 653	8 769	10 202	9 114	8 648	11 385
Mongolia	..	..	3	40	90	172	83	169
Southern Asia	31	114	575	1 749	2 548	4 412	3 523	4 656
Bangladesh	0	..	4	5	3	14	8	9
Bhutan	..	..	..	..	60	61	54	62
India	29	106	486	1 348	2 059	3 812	2 891	3 888
Maldives	0	8	46	70	106	129	116	110
Nepal	..	..	17	66	4	5	12	32
Pakistan	1	1	2	3	2	5	8	9
Sri Lanka	..	..	20	257	314	385	435	545
South-Eastern Asia	66	434	3 784	7 453	8 726	9 484	9 977	10 166
Brunei Darussalam	..	..	..	376	430	420	445	445
Cambodia	..	..	104	184	186	230	215	258
Indonesia	–	..	–	1 179	1 654	1 971	2 702	2 840
Lao People's Dem. Rep.	..	..	0	1	1	1	1	1
Malaysia (3)	19	230	-	5 679	6 388	6 786	6 529	6 528
Myanmar	..	..	14	19	32	32	32	32
Philippines	12	5	21	15	35	44	54	62
Thailand	35	199	..	..	..	..	..	..

For sources and notes, see end of table.

As percentage of GDP (1) En pourcentage du PIB (1)				As percentage of imports of goods and services (2) En pourcentage des importations des biens et services (2)				Régions, pays ou territoires
1990	2000	2009	2010	1990	2000	2009	2010	
0.15	**0.16**	**0.14**	**0.13**	**1.32**	**0.93**	**0.80**	**0.74**	**Économies en développement : Amérique**
0.74	*0.81*	*0.92*	*0.86*	*1.54*	*1.51*	*2.08*	*1.87*	*Caraïbes*
8.09	8.25	5.07	5.05	10.15	7.18	5.20	5.43	Anguilla
1.61	0.23	0.19	0.18	1.85	0.31	0.30	0.30	Antigua-et-Barbuda
..	2.60	3.07	2.82	..	1.51	2.45	3.38	Aruba
1.25	1.15	0.90	1.19	2.81	2.41	1.89	2.43	Bahamas
0.32	0.66	1.03	1.01	0.71	1.26	1.93	1.79	Barbade
0.81	0.04	0.04	0.04	1.21	0.07	0.06	0.06	Dominique
..	0.08	0.06	0.06	..	0.18	0.19	0.19	République dominicaine
0.58	0.63	0.47	0.43	0.93	1.06	0.99	0.89	Grenade
..	0.33	2.27	2.73	..	0.80	4.81	4.09	Haïti
0.55	2.00	2.53	2.40	1.12	4.05	4.92	5.00	Jamaïque
4.97	11.80	9.43	7.54	6.10	9.85	11.38	9.74	Montserrat
0.54	1.64	2.67	1.26	0.65	2.13	2.99	1.19	Antilles néerlandaises
4.38	2.27	1.10	1.05	5.27	3.01	1.73	1.72	Saint-Kitts-et-Nevis
1.07	0.48	0.41	0.40	1.39	0.75	0.67	0.61	Sainte-Lucie
1.40	1.44	1.06	1.11	2.16	2.86	1.83	1.92	Saint-Vincent-et-les Grenadines
0.43	..	..	..	1.51	..	..	..	Trinité-et-Tobago
0.25	*0.39*	*0.43*	*0.42*	*0.57*	*0.81*	*0.93*	*0.86*	*Amérique centrale*
1.76	1.27	1.69	1.65	2.88	1.75	2.92	2.85	Belize
..	0.89	0.82	0.76	..	1.95	1.94	1.84	Costa Rica
0.06	0.15	0.10	0.11	0.17	0.35	0.26	0.25	El Salvador
0.20	0.32	0.06	0.05	0.75	1.00	0.17	0.14	Guatemala
..	0.13	0.08	0.08	..	0.20	0.14	0.12	Honduras
..	..	..	..	..	..	..	..	Mexique
..	..	..	..	..	..	..	..	Nicaragua
–	–	–	–	–	–	–	–	Panama, sans la zone du canal
0.36	0.19	0.95	0.93	0.52	0.27	1.40	1.25	Panama
0.13	*0.12*	*0.10*	*0.10*	*1.38*	*0.85*	*0.67*	*0.64*	*Amérique du Sud*
0.07	0.09	0.25	0.28	1.37	0.81	1.55	1.52	Argentine
0.16	0.44	0.60	0.52	0.71	1.78	2.01	1.65	Bolivie (État plurinational de)
0.00	0.06	0.06	0.06	0.04	0.51	0.57	0.49	Brésil
0.02	0.02	0.00	0.00	0.08	0.07	0.01	0.01	Chili
0.08	0.22	0.04	0.04	0.64	1.52	0.24	0.24	Colombie
0.02	0.04	0.16	0.13	0.08	0.12	0.48	0.35	Équateur
..	2.41	3.80	3.41	..	3.69	5.62	4.69	Guyana
..	..	..	..	..	..	..	..	Paraguay
0.26	0.52	0.07	0.08	1.84	2.85	0.33	0.35	Pérou
1.37	0.19	0.16	0.03	1.00	0.39	0.32	0.07	Suriname
..	..	0.02	0.02	..	..	0.07	0.07	Uruguay
1.49	0.28	0.18	0.21	7.42	1.55	1.15	1.62	Venezuela (Rép. bolivarienne du)
1.07	**0.93**	**0.78**	**0.70**	**4.84**	**2.58**	**2.45**	**1.96**	**Économies en développement : Asie**
0.15	*0.29*	*0.24*	*0.25*	*0.84*	*0.77*	*0.74*	*0.65*	*Asie orientale*
0.00	0.07	0.09	0.08	0.01	0.31	0.40	0.29	Chine
..	0.13	0.20	0.22	..	0.10	0.11	0.10	Chine (RAS de Hong Kong)
..	..	3.34	2.09	..	..	6.62	4.12	Chine (RAS de Macao)
..	0.56	0.38	0.40	..	1.11	0.70	0.60	Province chinoise de Taiwan
0.38	0.68	1.04	1.12	1.34	1.89	2.16	2.04	Corée, République de
..	0.26	1.82	2.73	..	0.39	3.17	4.37	Mongolie
0.03	*0.09*	*0.21*	*0.23*	*0.29*	*0.55*	*0.87*	*0.87*	*Asie méridionale*
..	0.01	0.01	0.01	..	0.05	0.03	0.03	Bangladesh
..	..	4.27	4.16	..	..	7.92	6.62	Bhoutan
0.03	0.10	0.21	0.23	0.36	0.67	0.88	0.88	Inde
4.16	7.42	8.80	7.45	5.16	10.26	10.20	8.59	Maldives
..	0.29	0.10	0.20	..	0.93	0.24	0.55	Népal
0.00	0.00	0.01	0.01	0.01	0.02	0.02	0.02	Pakistan
..	0.12	1.04	1.10	..	0.24	3.71	3.57	Sri Lanka
0.24	*2.02*	*1.04*	*0.83*	*0.53*	*2.55*	*3.04*	*2.33*	*Asie du Sud-Est*
..	..	4.14	3.42	..	..	11.97	11.26	Brunéi Darussalam
..	2.83	2.07	2.29	..	4.59	3.14	3.28	Cambodge
..	..	0.50	0.40	..	..	2.42	1.85	Indonésie
–	0.03	0.02	0.01	–	0.08	0.05	0.04	Rép. dém. populaire lao
0.50	-	3.38	2.75	0.72	-	4.51	3.44	Malaisie (3)
..	0.19	0.10	0.08	..	0.56	0.69	0.61	Myanmar
0.01	0.03	0.03	0.03	0.04	0.04	0.10	0.08	Philippines
0.23	..	..	..	0.55	..	..	..	Thaïlande

Pour les sources et les notes, se reporter à la fin du tableau.

7

Region, country or territory	Millions of dollars - Millions de dollars							
	1980	1990	2000	2005	2007	2008	2009	2010
Western Asia	*5 667*	*13 356*	*19 881*	*25 057*	*35 489*	*44 482*	*51 878*	*51 976*
Bahrain	330	332	1 013	1 223	1 483	1 774	1 391	1 642
Jordan	154	71	197	349	479	472	502	495
Kuwait	692	770	1 734	2 648	9 764	10 323	11 749	11 770
Lebanon	..	..	..	4 012	2 962	4 366	5 749	4 560
Occupied Palestinian territory	..	..	6	8	9	9	8	9
Oman	397	856	1 451	2 257	3 670	5 181	5 316	5 704
Saudi Arabia	4 094	11 221	15 390	14 315	16 447	21 697	26 470	27 069
Syrian Arab Republic	..	..	29	40	252	212	214	214
Turkey	..	..	..	96	106	111	141	175
Yemen	–	106	61	109	319	337	337	338
Developing economies: Oceania	**42**	**88**	**128**	**265**	**455**	**537**	**524**	**504**
Fiji	10	22	26	34	31	44	22	23
French Polynesia	..	..	..	47	56	69	64	71
Kiribati	3	1	..	..	..	..	..	..
New Caledonia	..	..	..	28	56	68	92	66
Papua New Guinea	28	43	18	128	284	328	323	323
Samoa	..	3	5	11	10	9	8	7
Solomon Islands	..	6	6	2	4	3	3	3
Tonga	1	1	..	12	13	14	9	9
Vanuatu (4)	..	12	73	3	3	3	3	3
Transition economies	..	..	**1 890**	**10 249**	**23 749**	**31 892**	**23 606**	**23 694**
Albania	..	..	..	7	10	16	10	10
Armenia	–	–	5	152	176	185	145	157
Azerbaijan	–	–	101	269	435	593	652	652
Belarus	–	–	58	95	109	141	112	104
Bosnia and Herzegovina	–	–	2	40	65	69	61	54
Croatia	–	–	44	100	163	194	174	167
Georgia	–	–	25	29	28	47	32	50
Kazakhstan	–	–	440	2 000	4 303	3 559	3 058	3 020
Kyrgyzstan	–	–	45	125	220	196	188	297
Montenegro	–	–	–	–	–	27	26	28
Republic of Moldova	–	–	46	68	87	115	104	120
Russian Federation (5)	–	–	1 099	7 008	17 763	26 323	18 779	18 796
Serbia and Montenegro (6)	–	–	..	162	139			
Serbia	–	–	–	–	–	140	91	70
Tajikistan	–	–	..	145	184	199	124	124
TFYR of Macedonia	–	–	14	16	25	33	26	23
Ukraine	–	–	10	34	42	54	25	24
Developed economies: America	**1 360**	**11 850**	**34 397**	**46 293**	**51 833**	**54 581**	**51 825**	**51 799**
Bermuda	..	..	..	..	179	182	187	202
United States	1 360	11 850	34 397	46 293	51 654	54 399	51 639	51 597
Developed economies: Asia	**251**	**2 041**	**6 422**	**3 487**	**6 835**	**8 293**	**7 352**	**8 213**
Israel	31	850	3 255	2 206	2 798	3 550	3 283	3 739
Japan	220	–	3 167	1 281	4 037	4 743	4 069	4 474
Developed economies: Europe	**16 573**	**33 437**	**40 295**	**79 873**	**115 962**	**132 770**	**122 965**	**120 050**
Austria	334	320	1 298	2 567	3 008	3 505	3 279	3 354
Belgium (7)	1 280	2 310	(e)868	2 754	3 202	4 048	4 253	4 142
Bulgaria	..	..	26	35	103	162	101	101
Cyprus	9	12	63	273	370	584	409	404
Czech Republic	–	–	605	1 187	2 100	3 359	2 768	2 304
Denmark	..	..	662	1 488	3 019	3 977	3 359	2 888
Estonia	–	–	3	50	93	98	78	94
Faeroe Islands	..	..	6	18	33	41	31	31
Finland	15	16	100	266	391	457	454	517
France	5 070	6 949	3 769	4 182	5 998	6 452	5 413	5 264
Germany, Federal Republic of	5 819							
Germany	–	6 856	9 042	13 148	14 521	15 702	14 846	14 215
Greece	59	122	545	902	1 460	1 912	1 843	1 932
Hungary	..	..	86	915	1 374	1 536	1 213	1 213
Iceland	6	25	31	65	100	56	34	34
Ireland	..	165	181	1 535	2 625	2 779	1 992	1 751
Italy	428	3 764	2 582	7 622	11 284	13 058	12 868	12 201
Latvia	–	–	7	20	45	58	46	43
Lithuania	–	–	38	47	567	652	680	553
Luxembourg	..	..	2 720	6 573	9 068	10 839	10 563	10 432
Malta	8	25	14	33	53	57	52	50

For sources and notes, see end of table.

As percentage of GDP (1) En pourcentage du PIB (1)				As percentage of imports of goods and services (2) En pourcentage des importations des biens et services (2)				Régions, pays ou territoires
1990	2000	2009	2010	1990	2000	2009	2010	
8.37	*6.72*	*3.97*	*3.37*	*20.83*	*21.25*	*11.41*	*9.85*	*Asie occidentale*
7.74	12.62	7.20	7.16	8.31	19.73	12.25	12.54	Bahreïn
1.75	2.33	2.00	1.80	1.98	3.41	3.05	2.73	Jordanie
4.17	4.60	11.09	9.47	10.74	15.25	37.74	34.59	Koweït
..		16.65	11.62	..		19.20	14.64	Liban
..	0.14	0.13	0.12	..	0.18	0.17	0.16	Territoire palestinien occupé
7.40	7.46	11.34	9.86	25.60	22.85	24.69	23.60	Oman
9.62	8.17	7.10	6.23	25.57	29.08	16.33	15.54	Arabie saoudite
..	0.15	0.40	0.36	..	0.54	1.29	1.10	République arabe syrienne
..	..	0.02	0.02	..		0.09	0.09	Turquie
2.27	0.60	1.22	0.98	4.90	1.84	3.37	3.06	Yémen
1.65	*2.11*	*1.84*	*1.64*	*3.06*	*3.87*	*3.90*	*3.00*	*Économies en développement : Océanie*
1.59	1.48	0.79	0.74	2.40	2.32	1.27	1.07	Fidji
..	..	0.94	1.06	..	..	2.67	2.89	Polynésie française
3.22	..	..	..	2.86	..	..	..	Kiribati
..	..	1.06	0.75	..	..	2.68	1.49	Nouvelle-Calédonie
1.30	0.53	4.00	3.30	2.83	1.04	6.85	5.14	Papouasie-Nouvelle-Guinée
2.72	2.02	1.61	1.18	3.21	3.92	2.96	1.97	Samoa
2.77	1.91	0.43	0.40	3.70	3.92	0.74	0.47	Îles Salomon
0.75	..	2.91	2.52	1.64	..	4.94	4.59	Tonga
7.18	26.71	0.44	0.37	12.05	49.39	0.88	0.63	Vanuatu (4)
..	*0.52*	*1.36*	*1.15*	*..*	*1.59*	*4.95*	*4.10*	*Économies en transition*
..	..	0.08	0.09	..	..	0.15	0.16	Albanie
–	0.25	1.68	1.67	–	0.49	3.94	3.72	Arménie
–	1.91	1.47	1.26	–	4.99	6.58	6.15	Azerbaïdjan
–	0.56	0.23	0.19	–	0.72	0.37	0.28	Bélarus
–	0.04	0.36	0.32	–	0.06	0.64	0.55	Bosnie-Herzégovine
–	0.20	0.27	0.27	–	0.46	0.70	0.71	Croatie
–	0.82	0.29	0.43	–	1.90	0.60	0.82	Géorgie
–	2.41	2.65	2.06	–	4.91	7.84	6.98	Kazakhstan
–	3.31	4.00	6.43	–	6.93	5.10	7.60	Kirghizistan
–	–	0.62	0.67	–	–	0.92	1.04	Monténégro
–	3.57	1.91	2.06	–	4.73	2.61	2.61	République de Moldova
–	0.42	1.54	1.27	–	1.78	7.42	5.83	Fédération de Russie (5)
–	..	–	–	–	..	–	–	Serbie-et-Monténégro (6)
–	–	0.20	0.16	–	–	0.47	0.35	Serbie
–	..	2.48	2.20	–	..	4.04	3.71	Tadjikistan
–	0.40	0.28	0.25	–	0.62	0.46	0.37	LERY de Macédoine
–	0.03	0.02	0.02	–	0.06	0.04	0.03	Ukraine
0.20	*0.35*	*0.37*	*0.36*	*1.92*	*2.37*	*2.64*	*2.21*	*Économies développées : Amérique*
..	..	3.27	3.36	..	..	9.12	10.14	Bermudes
0.20	0.35	0.37	0.35	1.92	2.37	2.63	2.20	États-Unis
0.07	*0.13*	*0.14*	*0.14*	*0.64*	*1.29*	*1.03*	*0.94*	*Économies développées : Asie*
1.47	2.61	1.68	1.72	4.20	6.96	5.20	4.91	Israël
-	0.07	0.08	0.08	-	0.70	0.63	0.56	Japon
0.46	*0.45*	*0.71*	*0.70*	*1.72*	*1.27*	*2.00*	*1.76*	*Économies développées : Europe*
0.19	0.68	0.86	0.88	0.52	1.52	1.87	1.77	Autriche
1.14	(e)0.37	0.90	0.88	1.71	(e)0.43	1.28	1.14	Belgique (7)
..	0.20	0.21	0.21	..	0.34	0.37	0.36	Bulgarie
0.21	0.68	1.75	1.76	0.38	1.22	3.82	3.69	Chypre
–	1.03	1.41	1.17	–	1.61	2.53	1.76	République tchèque
..	0.41	1.09	0.93	..	1.03	2.49	2.08	Danemark
–	0.05	0.41	0.50	–	0.06	0.63	0.64	Estonie
..	..	..	..	..	0.94	2.87	2.80	Îles Féroé
0.01	0.08	0.19	0.22	0.05	0.25	0.53	0.55	Finlande
0.56	0.28	0.21	0.21	2.54	1.03	0.82	0.73	France
–	–	–	–	–	–	–	–	Allemagne, Rép. fédérale d'
0.40	0.48	0.45	0.43	1 60	1.44	1.21	1.05	Allemagne
0.13	0.43	0.57	0.64	0.62	1.31	2.20	2.41	Grèce
..	0.19	0.96	0.94	..	0.24	1.32	1.18	Hongrie
0.39	0.36	0.28	0.27	1.19	0.87	0.64	0.58	Islande
0.34	0.19	0.89	0.85	0.67	0.23	1.19	1.04	Irlande
0.33	0.24	0.61	0.59	1.72	0.90	2.52	2.08	Italie
–	0.08	0.18	0.18	–	0.17	0.40	0.34	Lettonie
–	0.33	1.84	1.52	–	0.65	3.31	2.19	Lituanie
..	13.42	20.33	19.56	..	24.60	19.90	17.76	Luxembourg
0.97	0.35	0.64	0.61	1.09	0.35	0.82	0.72	Malte

Pour les sources et les notes, se reporter à la fin du tableau.

Region, country or territory	Millions of dollars - Millions de dollars							
	1980	1990	2000	2005	2007	2008	2009	2010
Netherlands	970	1 393	3 122	5 928	12 635	14 914	14 237	12 923
Norway	110	295	1 060	2 174	3 577	4 750	4 174	4 045
Poland	..	..	311	756	1 232	1 775	1 388	1 575
Portugal	33	77	455	1 306	1 284	1 410	1 459	1 406
Romania (8)	..	..	6	(b)33	353	664	305	360
Slovakia	–	–	8	39	73	144	138	70
Slovenia	–	–	29	94	250	427	211	158
Spain	11	254	2 486	8 136	15 191	14 826	12 751	12 244
Sweden	83	654	539	537	741	742	787	695
Switzerland	2 339	8 168	7 591	13 311	16 378	19 150	19 834	21 611
United Kingdom	..	2 034	2 044	3 877	4 834	4 637	3 400	3 439
Developed economies: Oceania	**455**	**1 041**	**1 512**	**3 365**	**4 297**	**4 343**	**4 126**	**4 933**
Australia	304	674	1 053	2 375	3 024	3 049	3 173	3 776
New Zealand	151	367	459	991	1 273	1 295	953	1 156

Sources:
UNCTAD secretariat calculations, based on:
- IMF, *Balance of Payments Statistics*
- World Bank, *Migration and Remittances*
- Economist Intelligence Unit, *Country Data*
- Other national sources

Notes:
-   Migrants' remittances data cover: workers' remittances, compensation of employees and migrants' transfers.

(1)   GDP data source: UNCTAD series.
(2)   Exports and imports of goods and services data are based on IMF balance-of-payments statistics.
(3)   Payments (debits), breaks in series: for years 1985-1994 and 1999-2001 inclusive, data include compensation of employees only; workers' remittances were not available. Migrants' transfers are not available after 1994 neither.
(4)   Year 2002: break in series; migrants' transfers data are no longer available starting with 2002.
(5)   Workers' remittances and compensation of employees: From 1995 to 2000 (inclusive), data represent compensation of employees only; workers' remittances are available starting from 2001 onwards. Total remittances (including migrants transfers) reflect the same break in series.
(6)   Covers Serbia only.
(7)   Data up to 1994 inclusive refer to Belgium-Luxembourg Economic Union. From 1995, the figures cover Belgium only.
(8)   Year 2005: break in series; change in classification.

As percentage of GDP (1) En pourcentage du PIB (1)				As percentage of imports of goods and services (2) En pourcentage des importations des biens et services (2)				Régions, pays ou territoires
1990	2000	2009	2010	1990	2000	2009	2010	
0.47	0.81	1.79	1.66	0.94	1.31	2.96	2.42	Pays-Bas
0.25	0.63	1.13	0.98	0.76	2.14	4.02	3.45	Norvège
..	0.18	0.32	0.34	..	0.54	0.80	0.76	Pologne
0.10	0.39	0.62	0.61	0.28	0.96	1.75	1.61	Portugal
..	0.02	0.19	0.22	..	0.04	0.51	0.54	Roumanie (8)
–	0.04	0.16	0.08	–	0.05	0.22	0.10	Slovaquie
–	0.15	0.43	0.34	–	0.26	0.76	0.52	Slovénie
0.05	0.43	0.87	0.87	0.25	1.34	3.41	3.04	Espagne
0.27	0.22	0.19	0.15	0.93	0.56	0.47	0.35	Suède
3.41	3.01	3.99	4.05	8.47	7.07	8.17	7.56	Suisse
0.20	0.14	0.16	0.15	0.77	0.47	0.52	0.47	Royaume-Uni
0.28	**0.33**	**0.37**	**0.35**	**1.61**	**1.44**	**1.77**	**1.72**	**Économies développées : Océanie**
0.21	0.26	0.32	0.30	1.27	1.20	1.58	1.53	Australie
0.83	0.86	0.81	0.82	3.13	2.65	2.97	2.97	Nouvelle-Zélande

Sources:
Calculs du secrétariat de la CNUCED, basés sur :
- FMI, *Statistiques de la balance des paiements*
- Banque Mondiale, *Migration and Remittances*
- Economist Intelligence Unit, *Country Data*
- Autres sources nationales

Notes :
- Les envois de fonds des migrants couvrent : les envois de fonds des travailleurs, la rémunération des employés et les transferts des migrants.

(1) Source de données du PIB : série de la CNUCED.
(2) Les données sur les exportations et importations des biens et services se basent sur les statistiques de la balance des paiements du FMI.
(3) Paiements (débits), ruptures de série : pour les années 1985-1994 et 1999-2001, incluses, les données comprennent seulement la rémunération des salariés ; les envois de fonds des travailleurs ne sont pas disponibles. Les transferts des migrants ne sont également pas disponibles après 1994.
(4) Année 2002 : rupture de série ; les données sur les transferts des migrants ne sont plus disponibles à partir de 2002.
(5) L'envoi de fonds des travailleurs et la rémunération des salariés : De 1995 à 2000 (incluses), les données comprennent seulement la rémunération des salariés ; les envois de fonds des travailleurs ne sont disponibles qu'à partir de l'année 2001. Le total des envois de fonds (y compris les transferts des migrants) présentent la même rupture de série.
(6) Couvre uniquement la Serbie.
(7) Jusqu'à l'année 1994 comprise, les données se réfèrent à l'Union économique belgo-luxembourgeoise. A partir de 1995, les chiffres couvrent uniquement la Belgique.
(8) Année 2005 : rupture de série ; changement des méthodes de classification.

Economic grouping	Millions of dollars - Millions de dollars							
	1980	1990	2000	2005	2007	2008	2009	2010
DEVELOPING ECONOMIES	**11 607**	**19 572**	**36 186**	**54 792**	**73 927**	**87 502**	**92 188**	**98 022**
Developing economies excluding China	11 607	19 567	35 397	52 242	69 554	81 765	87 744	93 577
Developing economies excluding LDCs	11 010	18 754	34 813	53 263	71 388	84 641	89 133	94 719
High-income developing economies	7 293	15 805	30 384	43 339	56 763	65 964	72 419	76 212
Middle-income developing economies	2 089	2 197	3 508	6 400	9 622	11 376	9 636	10 290
Low-income developing economies	2 226	1 570	2 294	5 053	7 541	10 162	10 133	11 520
Heavily indebted poor countries (IMF)	1 534	1 189	1 393	1 875	2 562	2 801	3 036	3 236
Landlocked developing countries	431	460	1 390	3 625	6 447	6 231	5 624	5 934
Small island developing States	159	238	479	905	1 181	1 131	976	998
Least developed countries	*597*	*818*	*1 373*	*1 529*	*2 539*	*2 861*	*3 055*	*3 303*
Africa and Haiti	592	685	1 089	1 128	1 917	2 166	2 382	2 557
Asia	0	106	200	385	604	680	659	733
Islands	4	27	84	16	17	14	14	13
Major petroleum and gas exporters	*7 341*	*14 184*	*19 637*	*20 539*	*31 996*	*39 761*	*46 286*	*47 765*
Africa	1 740	636	730	1 224	1 467	1 719	2 170	2 417
America	418	701	331	95	649	842	581	805
Asia	5 183	12 847	18 576	19 220	29 880	37 200	43 535	44 543
Major exporters of manufactured goods	*123*	*1 462*	*10 143*	*18 759*	*22 744*	*23 669*	*21 452*	*24 556*
America	11	..	..	..	..	..	..	..
Asia	112	1 462	10 143	18 759	22 744	23 669	21 452	24 556
Emerging economies	*381*	*1 645*	*10 053*	*16 818*	*19 485*	*19 499*	*18 455*	*21 986*
America	269	188	925	957	1 501	1 960	1 861	2 358
Asia	112	1 457	9 128	15 861	17 984	17 539	16 594	19 628
Newly industrialized Asian economies	*124*	*1 462*	*9 375*	*17 403*	*20 061*	*19 948*	*19 763*	*23 013*
First tier	58	1 028	5 709	10 530	11 983	11 147	10 479	13 583
Second tier	66	434	3 665	6 873	8 078	8 801	9 284	9 430
Developing economies: Africa	**4 660**	**3 407**	**3 078**	**4 396**	**5 387**	**5 953**	**6 428**	**7 002**
Northern Africa excluding Sudan	1 317	532	551	1 054	1 057	1 306	1 736	2 035
Sub-Saharan Africa	3 344	2 875	2 527	3 342	4 330	4 647	4 692	4 967
Sub-Saharan Africa excluding South Africa	2 327	1 676	1 842	2 287	3 145	3 514	3 534	3 595
Developing economies: America	**1 083**	**1 140**	**2 238**	**2 524**	**4 036**	**4 618**	**4 159**	**4 952**
Central America and Greater Caribbean Islands excluding Puerto Rico	160	72	469	878	1 071	1 121	1 020	1 120
Central America and Greater Caribbean Islands excluding Mexico and Puerto Rico	149	72	469	878	1 071	1 121	1 020	1 120
South America and Central America	875	997	1 807	1 679	3 030	3 701	3 352	4 139
South America excluding Brazil	652	939	1 181	797	1 641	1 960	1 804	2 343
Developing economies: Asia	**5 821**	**14 937**	**30 742**	**47 607**	**64 048**	**76 393**	**81 077**	**85 563**
Eastern and South-Eastern Asia excluding China	124	1 462	9 496	18 251	21 638	21 763	21 232	24 487
Southern Asia excluding India	1	9	89	401	489	599	633	768

For sources and notes, see end of table 7.4.1.

As percentage of GDP (1) En pourcentage du PIB (1)				As percentage of imports of goods and services (2) En pourcentage des importations des biens et services (2)				Groupements économiques
1990	2000	2009	2010	1990	2000	2009	2010	
0.74	**0.69**	**0.62**	**0.55**	**3.81**	**2.29**	**2.12**	**1.75**	**ÉCONOMIES EN DÉVELOPPEMENT**
0.88	0.87	0.89	0.78	4.19	2.66	2.72	2.29	Économies en développement sans la Chine
0.74	0.68	0.62	0.55	3.81	2.27	2.14	1.74	Économies en développement sans les PMA
2.15	1.58	1.91	1.69	7.60	3.52	4.07	3.35	Économies en développement à revenu élevé
0.16	0.14	0.12	0.10	0.98	0.63	0.53	0.43	Économies en développement à revenu intermédiaire
0.28	0.29	0.36	0.33	1.93	1.42	1.37	1.22	Économies en développement à revenu faible
1.08	1.10	0.86	0.85	4.73	3.53	2.46	2.34	Pays pauvres très endettés (FMI)
0.84	1.61	1.64	1.50	3.42	4.15	4.56	4.27	Pays en développement sans littoral
0.90	1.41	1.80	1.69	1.83	2.63	3.15	2.85	Petits États insulaires en développement
0.98	*0.84*	*0.62*	*0.60*	*3.85*	*2.85*	*1.80*	*1.82*	*Pays les moins avancés*
0.88	1.24	0.76	0.76	3.69	3.94	2.04	2.18	Afrique et Haïti
2.27	0.27	0.37	0.35	4.90	1.00	1.27	1.17	Asie
3.02	9.20	0.74	0.60	5.30	17.99	1.38	0.89	Îles
4.27	*4.30*	*3.58*	*3.15*	*15.22*	*17.11*	*10.70*	*10.08*	*Principaux exportateurs de pétrole et de gaz*
0.46	0.78	0.49	0.47	2.17	3.21	1.30	1.26	Afrique
1.49	0.28	0.18	0.21	7.42	1.55	1.15	1.62	Amérique
8.76	7.56	8.29	7.22	23.62	26.29	20.27	19.17	Asie
0.18	*0.44*	*0.32*	*0.32*	*0.77*	*1.08*	*0.95*	*0.81*	*Principaux exportateurs d'articles manufacturés*
..	..	..	..	..	..	..	..	Amérique
0.18	0.44	0.32	0.32	0.77	1.08	0.95	0.81	Asie
0.16	*0.50*	*0.51*	*0.49*	*0.85*	*1.71*	*1.76*	*1.52*	*Économies émergentes*
0.03	0.09	0.08	0.08	0.39	0.67	0.62	0.57	Amérique
0.36	0.96	1.18	1.17	1.01	2.02	2.22	1.90	Asie
0.32	*0.78*	*0.85*	*0.82*	*0.92*	*1.27*	*1.51*	*1.32*	*Économies nouvellement industrialisées d'Asie*
0.38	0.56	0.74	0.81	1.34	0.96	1.05	1.02	Première génération
0.24	2.10	1.03	0.82	0.53	2.56	2.98	2.27	Deuxième génération
0.72	**0.59**	**0.45**	**0.43**	**2.95**	**2.11**	**1.30**	**1.23**	**Économies en développement : Afrique**
0.31	0.29	0.33	0.35	1.13	1.11	0.92	0.99	Afrique septentrionale sans le Soudan
0.95	0.77	0.52	0.47	4.20	2.62	1.52	1.37	Afrique subsaharienne
0.88	0.93	0.57	0.52	3.53	2.91	1.56	1.37	Afrique subsaharienne sans l'Afrique du Sud
0.15	**0.16**	**0.14**	**0.13**	**1.32**	**0.93**	**0.80**	**0.74**	**Économies en développement : Amérique**
0.31	0.46	0.53	0.53	0.70	0.97	1.24	1.15	Amérique centrale et Grandes Antilles sans Porto Rico
0.31	0.46	0.53	0.53	0.70	0.97	1.24	1.15	Amérique centrale et Grandes Antilles sans le Mexique et Porto Rico
0.13	0.13	0.11	0.11	1.30	0.85	0.70	0.67	Amérique du Sud et Amérique centrale
0.29	0.18	0.14	0.15	2.30	1.09	0.73	0.76	Amérique du Sud sans le Brésil
1.07	**0.93**	**0.78**	**0.70**	**4.84**	**2.58**	**2.45**	**1.96**	**Économies en développement : Asie**
0.32	0.78	0.88	0.84	0.92	1.28	1.59	1.37	Asie orientale et Asie du Sud-Est sans la Chine
0.02	0.06	0.21	0.22	0.09	0.28	0.82	0.83	Asie méridionale sans l'Inde

Pour les sources et les notes, se reporter à la fin du tableau 7.4.1.

7

Region, country or territory	Total reserves including gold (1) - Réserves totales, y compris l'or (1) Millions of dollars - Millions de dollars							
	1980	1990	2000	2005	2008	2009	2010	2011
DEVELOPING ECONOMIES	177 117	330 903	1 057 607	2 694 143	5 153 080	5 947 389	6 783 239	7 448 583
Developing economies: Africa	**36 550**	**27 978**	**79 903**	**220 395**	**456 965**	**474 640**	**490 091**	**503 173**
Eastern Africa	*1 788*	*2 326*	*6 017*	*10 735*	*15 914*	*21 590*	*24 082*	*24 630*
Burundi	95	106	34	100	266	322	331	294
Comoros	6	30	43	86	112	150	145	155
Djibouti	-	94	68	89	175	242	249	244
Eritrea			27	28	58	90	114	115
Ethiopia (...1991)	94	25						
Ethiopia			316	1 043	871	1 781	2 766	2 665
Kenya	495	209	898	1 799	2 879	3 849	4 320	4 264
Madagascar	9	92	285	481	982	1 135	1 172	1 279
Malawi	69	138	244	160	243	150	308	198
Mauritius	92	741	900	1 343	1 746	2 186	2 449	2 589
Mozambique	-	232	726	1 059	1 583	2 103	2 163	2 473
Rwanda	196	44	191	406	596	743	813	1 050
Seychelles	18	17	44	56	64	191	236	252
Somalia	26	..	..	..	..	..	..	..
Uganda	3	44	808	1 344	2 301	2 994	2 706	2 617
United Republic of Tanzania	20	193	974	2 049	2 863	3 470	3 905	3 726
Zambia	88	194	245	560	1 096	1 892	2 094	2 324
Zimbabwe	229	168	214	(e)133	(e)80	(e)291	(e)312	(e)383
Middle Africa	*2 344*	*2 401*	*2 187*	*8 176*	*32 793*	*28 321*	*34 084*	*43 894*
Angola	-	-	1 198	3 197	17 869	13 664	19 749	27 401
Cameroon	190	27	213	951	3 088	3 676	3 643	3 199
Central African Republic	55	119	134	140	122	211	181	155
Chad	6	128	111	226	1 346	617	632	968
Congo	86	6	223	732	3 872	3 806	4 447	5 641
Dem. Rep. of the Congo	217	224	83	131	78	1 035	1 300	1 268
Equatorial Guinea	-	1	23	2 102	4 431	3 252	2 346	3 054
Gabon	108	274	191	669	1 924	1 993	1 736	2 157
Sao Tome and Principe	1	0	12	27	61	67	49	51
Northern Africa	*19 482*	*12 721*	*44 993*	*139 591*	*300 856*	*315 712*	*329 711*	*325 694*
Algeria	4 022	981	12 278	56 582	143 544	149 347	162 915	183 122
Egypt	1 155	2 805	13 228	20 731	32 347	32 386	33 743	15 046
Libya	13 228	6 018	12 672	39 739	92 563	98 979	99 895	100 307
Morocco	430	2 102	4 855	16 223	22 142	22 836	22 651	19 564
Sudan (...2011)	49	11	138	1 869	1 399	1 094	1 036	295
Tunisia	598	804	1 821	4 448	8 861	11 069	9 471	7 359
Southern Africa	*1 811*	*4 912*	*13 700*	*26 163*	*42 903*	*48 089*	*49 741*	*54 380*
Botswana	334	3 331	6 318	6 309	9 119	8 704	7 885	8 082
Lesotho	50	72	418	519	940	918	1 012	1 100
Namibia	..	80	260	312	1 293	2 051	1 696	1 787
South Africa	1 268	1 212	6 352	18 779	30 800	35 458	38 392	42 811
Swaziland	159	216	352	244	752	959	756	601
Western Africa	*11 125*	*5 618*	*13 007*	*35 731*	*64 499*	*60 928*	*52 472*	*54 575*
Benin	9	65	459	655	1 263	1 230	1 200	887
Burkina Faso	69	301	243	438	928	1 296	1 068	957
Cape Verde	42	77	28	174	361	398	382	339
Côte d'Ivoire	22	6	674	1 367	2 253	3 267	3 624	4 316
Gambia	6	55	109	98	117	224	202	223
Ghana	192	231	245	1 767	1 785	3 402	4 778	5 498
Guinea	-	-	151	95	98	53	179	642
Guinea-Bissau	-	18	67	80	125	169	156	220
Liberia	5	-	0	25	161	372	377	548
Mali	15	191	382	854	1 072	1 604	1 344	1 379
Mauritania	140	55	47	65	189	226	272	485
Niger	126	223	81	251	705	656	760	673
Nigeria	10 265	3 899	9 942	28 314	53 039	44 800	34 956	35 249
Senegal	9	12	388	1 186	1 602	2 123	2 047	1 946
Sierra Leone	31	5	49	171	220	405	409	439
Togo	78	354	141	192	582	703	715	774
Developing economies: America	**40 316**	**49 202**	**157 762**	**259 016**	**503 260**	**554 611**	**638 805**	**744 656**
Caribbean	*3 445*	*1 712*	*5 471*	*14 564*	*21 936*	*24 394*	*26 368*	*27 837*
Anguilla	..	7	20	40	41	37	40	38
Antigua and Barbuda	8	28	64	127	138	128	137	148
Aruba	..	103	213	279	610	584	574	542
Bahamas	92	158	350	586	568	1 010	1 044	1 070
Barbados	79	118	473	603	739	871	834	813
Cuba	..	(e)198	543	2 747	4 047	4 647	4 847	5 147
Curaçao								(e)1 003
Dominica	5	14	29	49	55	75	76	81
Dominican Republic	208	62	628	1 934	2 683	3 564	3 858	4 090

For sources and notes, see end of table.

Annual change in reserves (millions of dollars) Variations annuelles des réserves (millions de dollars)				Number of months of imports (2) Nombre de mois d'importations (2)								Régions, pays ou territoires
2005	2009	2010	2011	1980	1990	2000	2005	2008	2009	2010	2011	
517 207	794 309	835 850	664 905	4.4	5.0	6.6	9.5	10.8	15.3	13.6	12.3	ÉCONOMIES EN DÉVELOPPEMENT
54 097	17 676	15 450	13 082	4.6	3.6	7.4	10.3	11.7	13.9	12.5	10.8	Économies en développement : Afrique
-458	5 676	2 492	547	2.0	2.2	4.4	4.1	3.3	5.0	4.8	4.1	Afrique orientale
34	56	9	-37	6.8	5.5	2.7	4.5	7.9	9.6	7.8	4.7	Burundi
-18	38	-5	10	2.6	6.9	12.0	10.4	7.7	10.6	9.7	9.8	Comores
-5	66	7	-5	-	5.2	3.9	3.9	3.7	6.4	8.2	7.1	Djibouti
-7	32	24	1	_	_	0.7	0.7	1.2	1.8	2.0	1.5	Érythrée
				1.6	0.3							Éthiopie (...1991)
-454	910	985	-102	_	_	3.0	3.1	1.2	2.7	3.9	3.6	Éthiopie
280	970	471	-56	2.8	1.1	3.5	3.5	3.1	4.5	4.3	3.5	Kenya
-22	153	36	108	0.1	2.0	3.4	3.4	3.1	4.3	5.5	5.3	Madagascar
31	-93	158	-110	1.9	2.9	5.5	1.6	1.3	0.9	1.7	1.0	Malawi
-266	440	263	141	1.8	5.5	4.9	5.1	4.5	7.0	6.7	6.0	Maurice
-76	521	60	310	-	3.2	7.5	5.3	4.7	6.7	5.8	4.7	Mozambique
91	146	70	237	9.0	1.9	10.7	10.3	6.1	6.8	6.8	7.3	Rwanda
22	127	45	17	2.2	1.1	1.5	1.0	0.7	2.8	3.9	3.5	Seychelles
..	..	..	..	0.7	..	..	..	..	..	..	..	Somalie
36	694	-288	-89	0.1	1.8	6.3	7.9	6.1	8.5	6.9	6.8	Ouganda
-247	608	434	-179	0.2	1.7	7.7	7.5	4.9	6.6	5.8	4.0	République-Unie de Tanzanie
223	796	202	230	1.0	1.9	3.3	2.6	2.6	6.0	4.7	3.9	Zambie
(e)-79	(e)212	(e)21	(e)71	2.0	1.1	1.4	(e)0.7	(e)0.3	(e)1.2	(e)1.0	(e)1.0	Zimbabwe
3 834	-4 472	5 763	9 810	4.8	4.1	3.4	5.1	9.3	7.7	10.0	10.3	Afrique centrale
1 823	-4 205	6 085	7 652	-	-	4.7	4.6	10.2	7.2	14.2	15.1	Angola
120	587	-33	-444	1.4	0.2	1.7	4.2	6.9	9.9	8.5	5.9	Cameroun
-9	88	-29	-27	8.2	9.3	13.7	9.7	4.9	9.3	7.1	4.9	République centrafricaine
4	-729	15	336	0.9	3.1	4.2	2.9	8.0	3.7	3.6	5.5	Tchad
612	-66	641	1 194	1.8	0.1	5.6	6.5	15.2	15.8	13.2	13.3	Congo
-105	958	264	-32	1.7	1.5	1.4	0.6	0.2	3.3	3.5	2.9	Rép. dém. du Congo
1 158	-1 179	-906	707	-	0.1	0.5	19.3	14.2	7.5	5.0	6.1	Guinée équatoriale
225	69	-257	421	1.9	3.6	2.4	5.5	8.9	9.6	8.4	6.8	Gabon
7	5	-17	2	0.7	0.0	4.7	6.4	6.4	7.7	5.3	4.8	Sao Tomé-et-Principe
34 035	14 856	13 999	-4 017	7.4	4.1	11.1	19.3	20.8	24.3	23.0	20.3	Afrique septentrionale
13 033	5 803	13 568	20 207	4.6	1.2	16.1	33.4	43.6	45.7	47.7	47.3	Algérie
6 325	39	1 357	-18 697	2.9	3.7	11.4	12.6	8.0	8.6	7.7	3.1	Égypte
13 799	6 416	916	413	23.4	13.5	41.1	78.7	121.8	118.3	114.1	116.9	Libye
-152	694	-185	-3 087	1.2	3.6	5.1	9.4	6.3	8.3	7.7	5.3	Maroc
531	-305	-58	-741	0.4	0.2	1.1	3.3	1.8	1.4	1.2	0.4	Soudan (...2011)
500	2 208	-1 598	-2 112	2.0	1.8	2.6	4.1	4.3	6.9	5.1	3.7	Tunisie
5 973	5 186	1 652	4 639	1.0	2.6	4.6	4.3	4.7	6.5	5.4	4.6	Afrique australe
648	-415	-819	197	5.8	20.5	36.4	23.4	21.0	22.1	16.7	13.3	Botswana
18	-22	95	88	1.4	1.3	6.2	4.4	5.5	5.6	5.5	5.2	Lesotho
-33	758	-355	91	..	0.8	2.0	1.5	3.6	4.9	3.8	3.3	Namibie
5 421	4 658	2 934	4 420	0.8	0.8	2.5	3.5	3.8	5.6	4.8	4.2	Afrique du Sud
-80	207	-203	-156	3.0	3.9	4.0	1.5	5.2	6.4	4.5	3.6	Swaziland
10 711	-3 571	-8 456	2 103	5.2	4.7	7.4	9.4	9.2	10.6	7.4	6.3	Afrique occidentale
20	-34	-30	-313	0.3	3.0	9.0	7.7	6.6	7.1	6.7	3.9	Bénin
-221	368	-228	-111	2.3	6.7	4.8	4.2	5.0	8.3	6.3	4.4	Burkina Faso
34	36	-16	-44	7.5	6.8	1.5	4.8	5.3	6.7	6.2	4.2	Cap-Vert
-313	1 014	358	692	0.1	0.0	3.3	2.8	3.4	5.6	5.5	7.7	Côte d'Ivoire
15	108	-23	22	0.4	3.5	4.0	4.5	4.3	8.9	8.5	7.8	Gambie
125	1 617	1 377	720	2.0	2.3	1.0	4.0	2.1	5.1	5.2	4.3	Ghana
-15	-45	126	463	-	-	3.0	1.4	0.9	0.6	1.5	4.0	Guinée
8	44	-12	64	-	2.6	13.5	7.8	6.6	8.6	8.2	8.1	Guinée-Bissau
7	212	5	171	0.1	-	0.0	0.9	2.3	7.9	6.3	8.1	Libéria
3	533	-260	34	0.4	3.8	5.7	6.6	3.9	7.9	5.8	5.1	Mali
31	37	46	213	5.9	3.0	1.2	0.5	1.2	1.9	1.7	2.4	Mauritanie
1	-50	105	-87	2.6	6.9	2.5	3.2	5.4	3.3	4.0	3.4	Niger
11 321	-8 238	-9 844	292	7.4	8.3	13.7	15.9	15.0	15.9	9.5	7.7	Nigéria
-182	521	-76	-102	0.1	0.1	4.0	3.1	2.9	5.4	5.1	4.0	Sénégal
45	185	4	30	0.9	0.4	4.0	5.9	5.0	9.3	6.4	4.6	Sierra Leone
-166	121	12	59	1.7	7.3	3.0	2.2	4.6	5.6	5.7	5.5	Togo
35 401	51 351	84 194	105 411	4.1	4.7	4.8	5.8	6.5	9.6	8.5	8.2	Économies en développement : Amérique
3 774	2 458	1 974	1 029	2.0	1.1	2.0	4.2	3.9	6.2	6.0	5.3	Caraïbes
5	-4	2	-2	..	..	2.6	3.7	1.8	2.7	3.0	3.1	Anguilla
7	-10	9	11	1.1	1.3	1.9	2.8	2.2	2.9	3.3	3.6	Antigua-et-Barbuda
-22	-27	-10	-32	..	2.1	1.0	1.0	1.7	3.7	5.1	3.2	Aruba
-88	442	34	26	0.1	1.7	2.0	2.7	2.1	4.5	4.4	3.8	Bahamas
24	133	-38	-21	1.8	2.0	4.9	4.5	4.7	7.1	6.4	5.4	Barbade
500	600	200	300	* ..	(e)0.4	1.3	4.1	3.2	5.8	5.1	4.3	Cuba
											(e)5.7	Curaçao
7	20	1	5	1.3	1.5	2.4	3.6	2.7	3.9	4.1	4.2	Dominique
1 135	881	295	232	1.3	0.2	0.8	2.4	2.0	3.5	3.0	2.8	République dominicaine

Pour les sources et les notes, se reporter à la fin du tableau.

Region, country or territory	Total reserves including gold (1) - Réserves totales, y compris l'or (1) Millions of dollars - Millions de dollars							
	1980	1990	2000	2005	2008	2009	2010	2011
Grenada	13	18	58	94	105	129	119	121
Haiti	17	4	182	133	541	789	1 335	1 195
Jamaica	105	(e)168	1 054	2 170	1 773	2 076	2 501	2 282
Montserrat	..	10	10	14	12	14	17	25
Netherlands Antilles	119	242	280	566	842	890	-	
Saint Kitts and Nevis	..	16	45	72	110	136	169	244
Saint Lucia	8	45	79	116	143	175	206	213
Saint Vincent and the Grenadines	7	26	55	70	84	88	113	90
Sint Maarten (Dutch part)								(e)327
Trinidad and Tobago	2 783	495	1 389	4 964	9 446	9 181	9 609	10 409
Central America	*4 116*	*11 728*	*43 037*	*86 124*	*112 070*	*118 431*	*140 539*	*164 126*
Belize	13	70	123	71	166	214	218	237
Costa Rica	149	521	1 318	2 313	3 799	4 066	4 627	4 756
El Salvador	101	438	1 794	1 739	2 456	2 882	2 582	2 165
Guatemala	468	292	1 756	3 675	4 474	4 976	5 649	5 847
Honduras	151	41	1 314	2 328	2 475	2 088	2 672	2 751
Mexico	3 052	9 909	35 520	74 060	95 137	99 604	120 277	144 174
Nicaragua	65	113	489	728	1 141	1 573	1 799	1 892
Panama, excl. Canal Zone	117							
Panama	–	344	723	1 211	2 424	3 028	2 714	2 304
South America	*32 756*	*35 762*	*109 254*	*158 327*	*369 254*	*411 786*	*471 898*	*552 693*
Argentina (3)	6 915	4 803	25 148	27 267	44 950	46 190	49 829	43 333
Bolivia (Plurinational State of)	140	211	969	1 373	6 976	7 634	8 195	9 984
Brazil	5 853	7 668	32 531	53 299	192 902	237 424	287 114	350 415
Chile	3 199	6 161	15 038	16 930	23 073	25 284	27 817	41 932
Colombia	4 955	4 659	8 931	14 803	23 491	24 760	27 778	30 504
Ecuador	1 031	861	985	1 757	3 784	2 920	1 480	1 710
Guyana	13	29	305	252	356	631	782	802
Paraguay	763	663	764	1 297	2 846	3 840	4 138	4 951
Peru	2 042	1 150	8 424	13 655	30 332	32 074	42 708	47 266
Suriname	192	24	75	127	476	662	642	945
Uruguay	537	643	2 528	3 074	6 353	8 029	7 644	10 289
Venezuela (Bolivarian Rep. of)	7 116	8 891	13 555	24 493	33 716	22 339	13 771	10 562
Developing economies: Asia	**99 596**	**252 901**	**818 969**	**2 213 349**	**4 190 175**	**4 914 393**	**5 649 790**	**6 194 779**
Eastern Asia	*13 441*	*143 242*	*483 419*	*1 418 060*	*2 642 887*	*3 312 233*	*3 836 739*	*4 217 244*
China	3 117	30 219	168 857	822 479	1 950 305	2 417 911	2 867 905	3 204 615
China, Hong Kong SAR	(e)5 041	24 579	107 545	124 247	182 473	255 772	268 652	285 299
China, Macao SAR	..	521	3 323	6 689	15 930	18 350	23 726	34 026
China, Taiwan Province of	2 345	73 115	107 360	253 971	292 442	348 946	382 739	386 277
Korea, Republic of	2 938	14 809	96 150	210 340	201 170	269 958	291 515	304 349
Mongolia	..	..	183	333	567	1 296	2 200	2 678
Southern Asia	*19 546*	*9 587*	*56 683*	*197 283*	*366 014*	*381 254*	*391 580*	*391 622*
Afghanistan	414	314	-	-	2 469	3 540	4 212	5 306
Bangladesh	302	633	1 491	2 773	5 695	10 225	10 588	8 533
Bhutan	-	89	318	467	765	891	1 002	790
India	7 327	2 053	38 427	132 500	248 039	266 166	276 243	272 249
Iran (Islamic Rep. of)	10 417	5 351	12 426	45 459	96 559	81 309	75 060	79 860
Maldives	1	24	123	189	244	276	364	349
Nepal	190	303	952	1 505	2 458	2 761	2 925	3 631
Pakistan	577	393	1 609	10 138	7 308	11 434	14 457	14 639
Sri Lanka	248	426	1 054	2 658	2 478	4 653	6 728	6 265
South-Eastern Asia	*21 461*	*60 508*	*187 248*	*297 858*	*488 707*	*548 267*	*670 963*	*741 493*
Brunei Darussalam	..	..	408	492	751	1 357	1 563	(e)1 761
Cambodia	..	..	520	973	2 313	2 873	3 277	3 471
Indonesia (...2002)	5 499	7 614	28 643					
Indonesia	–	–	–	33 296	49 723	63 692	93 035	106 665
Lao People's Dem. Rep.	..	2	139	234	629	609	703	774
Malaysia	4 491	9 871	28 383	69 916	91 212	95 496	104 947	131 843
Myanmar	272	325	234	782	3 730	5 265	5 729	(e)5 985
Philippines	2 932	1 068	13 420	16 174	33 460	39 056	55 630	67 565
Singapore	6 567	27 790	79 961	115 960	173 981	187 591	225 504	237 663
Thailand	1 671	13 428	32 124	50 826	108 807	135 631	167 703	167 653
Timor-Leste	–	–	–	153	210	250	406	462
Viet Nam	-	409	3 417	9 051	23 890	16 447	12 467	17 652
Western Asia	*45 147*	*39 564*	*91 619*	*300 148*	*692 567*	*672 639*	*750 508*	*844 419*
Bahrain	960	1 242	1 571	1 982	3 929	3 853	5 097	4 553
Iraq	-	-	7 882	12 114	49 948	44 138	50 387	60 678
Jordan (4)	1 188	886	3 350	5 271	8 584	11 712	13 079	11 489
Kuwait	4 042	2 078	7 198	8 990	17 250	20 407	21 373	25 932
Lebanon	2 000	1 119	6 364	12 348	20 742	29 609	32 011	34 236
Occupied Palestinian territory	..	..	..	..	510	498	532	498
Oman	591	1 687	2 393	4 358	11 582	12 203	13 024	14 365
Qatar	365	673	1 159	4 543	9 671	18 392	30 642	16 220
Saudi Arabia (5)	23 640	11 897	19 795	(b)155 259	442 809	410 263	445 281	541 235

For sources and notes, see end of table.

Annual change in reserves (millions of dollars) Variations annuelles des réserves (millions de dollars)				Number of months of imports (2) Nombre de mois d'importations (2)								Régions, pays ou territoires
2005	2009	2010	2011	1980	1990	2000	2005	2008	2009	2010	2011	
-27	24	-10	2	3.1	2.0	2.9	3.4	3.5	5.5	4.5	4.6	Grenade
19	247	546	-140	0.5	0.1	2.1	1.1	2.8	4.5	5.1	4.5	Haïti
323	303	425	-219	1.1	(e)1.0	3.8	5.8	2.5	4.9	5.7	4.2	Jamaïque
0	3	3	8	..	2.5	5.8	5.6	3.7	5.8	6.9	10.1	Montserrat
128	49	-	_	0.3	1.4	1.2	3.5	3.3	4.1	-	_	Antilles néerlandaises
-7	26	32	75	..	1.8	2.8	4.1	4.1	5.7	7.6	10.8	Saint-Kitts-et-Nevis
-16	32	31	7	0.8	2.0	2.7	2.9	2.6	3.9	3.8	3.9	Sainte-Lucie
-5	4	25	-23	1.5	2.3	4.1	3.5	2.7	3.2	3.6	3.1	Saint-Vincent-et-les Grenadines
			..								(e)5.3	Saint-Martin (partie néerlandaise)
1 792	-265	428	800	10.5	5.4	5.0	10.5	11.8	15.8	17.8	14.4	Trinité-et-Tobago
11 520	*6 360*	*22 108*	*23 587*	*1.7*	*2.7*	*2.5*	*3.8*	*3.4*	*4.7*	*4.4*	*4.4*	*Amérique centrale*
23	48	4	19	1.0	4.0	2.8	1.4	2.4	3.8	3.7	3.2	Belize
391	268	561	129	1.2	3.1	2.5	2.8	3.0	4.3	4.1	3.5	Costa Rica
-38	426	-299	-417	1.3	4.2	4.4	3.1	3.0	4.7	3.7	2.6	El Salvador
237	502	673	198	3.5	2.1	4.1	4.2	3.7	5.2	4.9	4.2	Guatemala
357	-387	584	79	1.8	0.5	4.0	4.3	2.8	3.4	3.8	3.2	Honduras
9 911	4 467	20 673	23 897	1.7	2.7	2.3	3.8	3.5	4.9	4.6	4.7	Mexique
60	432	226	93	0.9	2.1	3.3	3.4	3.2	5.5	5.1	4.4	Nicaragua
				1.0								Panama, sans la zone du canal
580	604	-314	-411	_	2.7	2.6	3.5	1.8	2.6	1.9	1.3	Panama
20 107	*42 532*	*60 112*	*80 795*	*5.9*	*7.6*	*8.7*	*8.7*	*9.5*	*14.3*	*12.1*	*11.5*	*Amérique du Sud*
8 286	1 240	3 639	-6 495	7.9	14.1	12.0	11.4	9.4	14.2	10.6	7.8	Argentine (3)
451	657	561	1 789	2.5	3.7	6.4	7.0	16.5	20.7	18.3	15.8	Bolivie (État plurinational de)
779	44 522	49 690	63 301	2.8	4.1	6.7	8.2	12.7	21.3	18.0	17.9	Brésil
935	2 211	2 533	14 115	6.6	9.3	9.8	6.2	4.5	7.3	5.7	6.8	Chili
1 392	1 269	3 018	2 726	12.5	10.0	9.3	8.4	7.2	9.0	8.2	6.7	Colombie
641	-864	-1 439	229	5.5	5.5	3.2	2.0	2.4	2.3	0.9	0.8	Équateur
20	275	151	20	0.4	1.2	6.3	3.8	3.3	6.5	6.7	5.5	Guyana
129	994	298	813	14.9	5.9	4.1	4.8	3.8	6.6	4.9	4.8	Paraguay
1 418	1 742	10 634	4 558	9.8	5.2	13.6	13.1	12.2	17.6	17.1	15.1	Pérou
-3	186	-20	302	4.6	0.6	1.7	1.5	4.4	5.7	5.5	7.0	Suriname
566	1 676	-385	2 645	3.8	5.7	8.8	9.5	8.5	14.0	10.6	11.6	Uruguay
5 493	-11 376	-8 569	-3 209	7.2	14.5	9.6	12.2	8.2	6.6	3.9	2.5	Venezuela (Rép. bolivarienne du)
427 784	**724 218**	**735 397**	**544 989**	**4.4**	**5.4**	**7.1**	**10.2**	**11.6**	**16.7**	**14.7**	**13.3**	**Économies en développement : Asie**
231 838	*669 345*	*524 506*	*380 506*	*1.9*	*6.6*	*7.8*	*12.1*	*14.4*	*21.4*	*18.3*	*16.6*	*Asie orientale*
206 931	467 606	449 994	336 710	1.9	6.8	9.0	14.9	20.7	28.9	24.6	22.1	Chine
704	73 299	12 880	16 647	(e)2.7	3.6	6.1	5.0	5.6	8.8	7.4	7.1	Chine (RAS de Hong Kong)
1 253	2 420	5 376	10 300	..	4.1	17.7	20.5	35.6	47.6	51.6	52.6	Chine (RAS de Macao)
11 494	56 504	33 793	3 538	1.4	16.0	9.2	16.7	14.6	24.0	18.3	16.5	Province chinoise de Taiwan
11 319	68 788	21 558	12 833	1.6	2.5	7.2	9.7	5.5	10.0	8.2	7.0	Corée, République de
138	729	904	478	..	..	3.6	3.4	1.9	7.3	8.1	4.9	Mongolie
18 529	*15 240*	*10 326*	*42*	*5.9*	*2.0*	*7.1*	*10.0*	*9.4*	*12.0*	*9.3*	*7.4*	*Asie méridionale*
-	1 071	672	1 094	5.9	4.0	-	-	9.8	12.7	9.8	10.6	Afghanistan
-406	4 530	363	-2 055	1.4	2.1	2.0	2.4	2.9	5.6	4.6	2.8	Bangladesh
69	126	111	-212	-	13.1	21.8	14.5	17.0	20.2	14.1	10.0	Bhoutan
5 281	18 127	10 077	-3 993	5.9	1.0	8.9	11.1	9.3	12.4	9.5	7.2	Inde
12 500	-15 250	-6 249	4 800	9.3	3.5	9.8	13.6	20.2	19.3	14.4	14.1	Iran (Rép. islamique d')
-17	32	89	-16	0.4	2.1	3.8	3.0	2.1	3.4	4.0	2.9	Maldives
35	303	164	706	6.6	5.8	7.3	7.9	8.2	7.6	6.8	7.6	Népal
225	4 126	3 024	182	1.3	0.6	1.8	4.8	2.1	4.3	4.6	4.0	Pakistan
517	2 175	2 075	-463	1.5	1.9	2.0	3.6	2.1	5.6	6.0	3.8	Sri Lanka
12 525	*59 561*	*122 696*	*70 530*	*4.0*	*4.5*	*5.9*	*5.9*	*6.2*	*9.0*	*8.4*	*7.7*	*Asie du Sud-Est*
3	606	206	(e)198	..	..	4.4	4.0	3.5	6.7	7.6	(e)7.6	Brunéi Darussalam
8	560	404	195	..	..	3.2	3.0	4.3	5.9	5.8	4.5	Cambodge
				6.1	4.2	8.0						Indonésie (...2002)
-1 825	13 969	29 342	13 630	_	_	_	5.3	4.7	8.1	8.3	7.3	Indonésie
11	-20	95	70	..	0.1	3.1	3.2	5.4	5.2	4.1	3.5	Rép. dém. populaire lao
3 972	4 284	9 451	26 897	5.0	4.0	4.2	7.3	6.7	9.3	7.6	8.4	Malaisie
98	1 534	465	(e)255	9.1	14.3	1.2	4.9	10.4	14.4	14.3	(e)7.9	Myanmar
2 671	5 597	16 573	11 935	4.2	1.0	4.3	3.9	6.6	10.2	11.5	12.7	Philippines
3 593	13 610	37 912	12 159	3.3	5.5	7.1	7.0	6.5	9.2	8.7	7.8	Singapour
2 015	26 825	32 072	-50	2.2	4.9	6.2	5.2	7.3	12.1	10.9	8.8	Thaïlande
-29	40	156	55	_	_	_	16.4	9.4	10.2	16.4	18.5	Timor-Leste
2 009	-7 443	-3 981	5 186	-	1.8	2.6	3.0	3.6	2.8	1.8	2.0	Viet Nam
164 891	*-19 929*	*77 869*	*93 912*	*6.6*	*5.6*	*6.5*	*9.9*	*11.7*	*14.0*	*13.9*	*13.2*	*Asie occidentale*
34	-75	1 243	-544	3.3	4.0	4.1	2.5	3.3	4.8	5.5	4.5	Bahreïn
4 279	-5 810	6 249	10 291	-	-	7.2	6.2	16.9	13.8	13.7	13.5	Iraq
-18	3 128	1 367	-1 590	5.9	4.1	8.7	6.0	6.1	9.7	10.4	7.5	Jordanie (4)
610	3 157	967	4 558	7.4	6.3	12.1	6.8	8.3	12.0	11.4	12.3	Koweït
113	8 867	2 402	2 225	6.6	5.3	12.3	15.4	14.9	21.4	20.8	19.8	Liban
..	-11	34	-34	..	..	..	..	1.7	1.7	1.6	1.3	Territoire palestinien occupé
761	621	821	1 341	4.1	7.5	5.7	5.9	6.1	8.2	7.9	7.4	Oman
1 145	8 721	12 251	-14 422	3.0	4.8	4.3	5.4	4.2	8.9	16.7	7.5	Qatar
(b)127 718	-32 546	35 018	95 954	9.4	5.9	7.9	(b)31.3	46.2	51.5	50.0	58.1	Arabie saoudite (5)

Pour les sources et les notes, se reporter à la fin du tableau.

7

Region, country or territory	Total reserves including gold (1) - Réserves totales, y compris l'or (1) Millions of dollars - Millions de dollars							
	1980	1990	2000	2005	2008	2009	2010	2011
Syrian Arab Republic (6)	374	1 730	2 805	(b)17 388	17 107	17 443	19 510	14 833
Turkey	1 245	6 253	22 659	50 766	70 629	71 078	80 914	78 660
United Arab Emirates	2 040	4 624	13 541	21 010	31 694	26 104	32 785	37 269
Yemen, Arab Republic	1 283							
Yemen, Democratic	236	–	–	–	–	–	–	–
Yemen	–	425	2 903	6 118	8 114	6 938	5 871	4 452
Developing economies: Oceania	**655**	**823**	**974**	**1 383**	**2 680**	**3 745**	**4 554**	**5 976**
Fiji	168	261	412	321	322	569	719	832
Micronesia (Federated States of)	–	..	113	50	40	56	56	75
Papua New Guinea	426	406	290	721	1 957	2 564	3 037	4 172
Samoa	3	69	64	82	87	166	209	167
Solomon Islands	30	18	32	95	90	146	266	412
Tonga	14	31	25	47	70	96	105	143
Vanuatu	-	38	39	67	115	149	161	174

Sources:

UNCTAD secretariat calculations, based on:
- IMF, *International Financial Statistics*
- World Bank, *Global Development Finance*
- IMF, *World Economic Outlook*
- Economist Intelligence Unit, *Country Data*
- Other national sources

Notes:
(1)   End of year position.
(2)   Reserve stock of the year, divided by the average monthly imports of the current year. Data on imports are based on figures shown in table 1.1.1.

(3)   Year 1985, break in series.
(4)   Year 1993, break in series.
(5)   Year 1996, break in series. Year 2005, break in series: prior to 2005, data exclude Saudi Arabian Monetary Agency investments and deposits abroad.

(6)   Year 2005, break in series.

Annual change in reserves (millions of dollars) Variations annuelles des réserves (millions de dollars)				Number of months of imports (2) Nombre de mois d'importations (2)								Régions, pays ou territoires
2005	2009	2010	2011	1980	1990	2000	2005	2008	2009	2010	2011	
(b)12 425	337	2 067	-4 677	1.1	8.7	8.8	(b)19.2	11.3	13.6	13.3	10.9	République arabe syrienne (6)
14 894	449	9 836	-2 254	1.9	3.4	5.0	5.2	4.2	6.1	5.2	3.9	Turquie
2 480	-5 590	6 681	4 484	2.8	5.0	4.6	3.0	1.9	1.8	2.3	2.2	Émirats arabes unis
–	–	–	–	8.3	–	–	–	–	–	–	–	Yémen, République arabe du
–	–	–	–	1.9	–	–	–	–	–	–	–	Yémen, Démocratique
450	-1 176	-1 067	-1 419	–	3.2	15.0	13.7	9.3	9.1	7.2	6.5	Yémen
-74	**1 065**	**808**	**1 422**	**3.9**	**4.5**	**4.8**	**4.0**	**4.5**	**7.8**	**7.7**	**7.8**	**Économies en développement : Océanie**
-162	248	150	113	3.6	4.2	5.8	2.4	1.7	4.8	4.7	4.3	Fidji
-5	16	0	19	–	..	12.7	4.6	3.1	3.9	3.9	5.3	Micronésie (États fédérés de)
85	607	473	1 135	4.3	4.4	3.0	5.0	6.6	9.6	9.2	9.1	Papouasie-Nouvelle-Guinée
-4	79	44	-43	0.5	10.3	8.5	4.1	3.6	8.6	8.1	5.8	Samoa
15	56	120	146	4.0	2.3	4.2	6.2	3.3	6.5	7.9	10.5	Îles Salomon
-8	26	9	39	4.4	6.1	4.3	4.7	5.0	7.9	7.9	9.4	Tonga
5	33	13	12	-	4.7	5.4	5.4	4.4	6.1	6.8	7.1	Vanuatu

Sources :
Calculs du secrétariat de la CNUCED, basés sur :
- FMI, *Statistiques financières internationales*
- Banque mondiale, *Global Development Finance*
- FMI, *World Economic Outlook*
- Economist Intelligence Unit, *Country Data*
- Autres sources nationales

Notes :
(1)   Position en fin d'année.
(2)   Montant des réserves de l'année, divisé par la moyenne mensuelle des importations de l'année en cours. Les données des importations se basent sur les chiffres présentés dans le tableau 1.1.1.
(3)   Année 1985, rupture de série.
(4)   Année 1993, rupture de série.
(5)   Année 1996, rupture de série. Année 2005, rupture de série : avant 2005 les données ne comprennent pas les investissements et les dépôts en devises de l'Agence monétaire de l'Arabie Saudite à l étranger.
(6)   Année 2005, rupture de série.

Economic grouping	Total reserves including gold (1) - Réserves totales, y compris l'or (1) Millions of dollars - Millions de dollars							
	1980	1990	2000	2005	2008	2009	2010	2011
DEVELOPING ECONOMIES	**177 117**	**330 903**	**1 057 607**	**2 694 143**	**5 153 080**	**5 947 389**	**6 783 239**	**7 448 583**
Developing economies excluding China	174 000	300 685	888 750	1 871 664	3 202 775	3 529 478	3 915 334	4 243 968
Developing economies excluding LDCs	170 672	323 911	1 042 257	2 659 441	5 081 409	5 867 796	6 694 749	7 352 628
High-income developing economies	93 588	218 442	606 580	1 238 275	1 882 997	2 090 340	2 299 735	2 507 181
Middle-income developing economies	44 607	83 068	342 373	1 189 957	2 756 994	3 313 796	3 891 690	4 314 505
Low-income developing economies	38 921	29 393	108 654	265 912	513 089	543 253	591 814	626 898
Heavily indebted poor countries (IMF)	3 104	3 970	11 627	25 615	47 152	58 821	65 543	71 098
Landlocked developing countries	3 166	6 884	20 434	37 492	93 289	105 732	115 596	129 650
Small island developing States	3 917	2 797	5 719	12 263	18 639	21 131	23 392	25 644
Least developed countries	*6 445*	*6 992*	*15 350*	*34 702*	*71 670*	*79 593*	*88 490*	*95 955*
Africa and Haiti	3 624	4 748	8 321	19 745	44 822	45 565	52 945	61 594
Asia	2 766	2 091	6 839	14 447	26 173	33 101	34 308	32 941
Islands	54	154	190	510	676	927	1 238	1 421
Major petroleum and gas exporters	*84 569*	*54 668*	*114 040*	*404 058*	*1 000 243*	*941 945*	*999 840*	*1 132 201*
Africa	29 175	12 518	36 091	127 832	307 015	306 790	317 516	346 079
America	7 116	8 891	13 555	24 493	33 716	22 339	13 771	10 562
Asia	48 279	33 260	64 394	251 733	659 513	612 815	668 554	775 559
Major exporters of manufactured goods	*29 222*	*203 720*	*655 901*	*1 721 800*	*3 095 526*	*3 810 909*	*4 429 243*	*4 861 873*
America	3 052	9 909	35 520	74 060	95 137	99 604	120 277	144 174
Asia	26 170	193 811	620 381	1 647 740	3 000 389	3 711 305	4 308 965	4 717 699
Emerging economies	*39 073*	*168 704*	*460 640*	*886 224*	*1 254 004*	*1 478 197*	*1 700 152*	*1 854 906*
America	21 061	29 691	116 661	185 211	386 393	440 575	527 745	627 120
Asia	18 012	139 013	343 979	701 013	867 611	1 037 622	1 172 408	1 227 785
Newly industrialized Asian economies	*31 483*	*172 275*	*493 587*	*874 731*	*1 133 267*	*1 396 142*	*1 589 724*	*1 687 314*
First tier	16 891	140 293	391 017	704 519	850 066	1 062 267	1 168 410	1 213 588
Second tier	14 593	31 982	102 570	170 212	283 202	333 876	421 314	473 726
Developing economies: Africa	**36 550**	**27 978**	**79 903**	**220 395**	**456 965**	**474 640**	**490 091**	**503 173**
Northern Africa excluding Sudan	19 433	12 710	44 855	137 723	299 457	314 618	328 675	325 399
Sub-Saharan Africa	17 117	15 268	35 048	82 673	157 508	160 023	161 416	177 774
Sub-Saharan Africa excluding South Africa	15 849	14 056	28 696	63 894	126 708	124 565	123 025	134 962
Developing economies: America	**40 316**	**49 202**	**157 762**	**259 016**	**503 260**	**554 611**	**638 805**	**744 656**
Central America and Greater Caribbean Islands excluding Puerto Rico	4 446	12 160	45 443	93 108	121 114	129 506	153 080	176 839
Central America and Greater Caribbean Islands excluding Mexico and Puerto Rico	1 394	2 252	9 923	19 048	25 977	29 901	32 803	32 665
South America and Central America	36 872	47 490	152 291	244 452	481 324	530 217	612 437	716 819
South America excluding Brazil	26 903	28 094	76 724	105 028	176 352	174 362	184 784	202 278
Developing economies: Asia	**99 596**	**252 901**	**818 969**	**2 213 349**	**4 190 175**	**4 914 393**	**5 649 790**	**6 194 779**
Eastern and South-Eastern Asia excluding China	31 785	173 531	501 810	893 439	1 181 289	1 442 589	1 639 797	1 754 122
Southern Asia excluding India	12 219	7 533	18 256	64 783	117 975	115 089	115 337	119 373

Sources:
UNCTAD secretariat calculations, based on:
- IMF, *International Financial Statistics*
- World Bank, *Global Development Finance*
- IMF, *World Economic Outlook*
- Economist Intelligence Unit, *Country Data*
- Other national sources

Notes:
(1) End of year position.
(2) Reserve stock of the year, divided by the average monthly imports of the current year. Data on imports are based on figures shown in table 1.1.1.

Annual change in reserves (millions of dollars) Variations annuelles des réserves (millions de dollars)				Number of months of imports (2) Nombre de mois d'importations (2)								Groupements économiques
2005	2009	2010	2011	1980	1990	2000	2005	2008	2009	2010	2011	
517 207	**794 309**	**835 850**	**664 905**	**4.4**	**5.0**	**6.6**	**9.5**	**10.8**	**15.3**	**13.6**	**12.3**	**ÉCONOMIES EN DÉVELOPPEMENT**
310 276	326 704	385 855	328 195	4.5	4.9	6.3	8.2	8.4	11.6	10.2	9.2	Économies en développement sans la Chine
514 055	786 386	826 954	657 439	4.4	5.1	6.7	9.6	10.9	15.7	13.8	12.5	Économies en développement sans les PMA
222 474	207 343	209 395	207 006	4.7	5.8	6.3	8.6	8.3	11.7	10.3	9.6	Économies en développement à revenu élevé
271 015	556 802	577 894	422 815	3.5	4.2	7.3	11.6	15.5	22.1	19.4	17.5	Économies en développement à revenu intermédiaire
23 718	30 164	48 561	35 084	5.0	3.4	6.5	7.3	7.2	9.1	7.8	6.5	Économies en développement à revenu faible
1 380	11 669	6 722	5 556	1.5	2.0	3.8	4.1	4.2	6.1	5.8	5.3	Pays pauvres très endettés (FMI)
2 216	12 442	9 864	14 054	3.7	5.6	6.7	5.9	7.3	9.7	9.8	8.5	Pays en développement sans littoral
1 668	2 492	2 261	2 252	3.0	3.3	4.0	5.7	5.4	8.2	8.5	7.5	Petits États insulaires en développement
3 152	*7 923*	*8 896*	*7 466*	*3.1*	*3.3*	*4.3*	*4.8*	*5.3*	*6.2*	*6.3*	*5.7*	*Pays les moins avancés*
2 585	743	7 380	8 649	2.6	3.3	4.2	4.4	5.1	5.4	6.1	6.0	Afrique et Haïti
591	6 929	1 206	-1 367	4.4	3.4	4.3	5.6	5.9	7.8	6.6	5.1	Asie
-24	252	310	184	2.4	5.4	6.6	7.3	5.4	8.2	9.3	9.9	Îles
194 961	*-58 298*	*57 895*	*132 361*	*8.6*	*6.7*	*9.1*	*15.0*	*18.6*	*20.0*	*19.9*	*19.5*	*Principaux exportateurs de pétrole et de gaz*
39 975	-224	10 725	28 564	9.9	6.7	17.6	27.4	32.9	34.8	33.9	31.1	Afrique
5 493	-11 376	-8 569	-3 209	7.2	14.5	9.6	12.2	8.2	6.6	3.9	2.5	Amérique
149 493	-46 698	55 738	107 005	8.2	5.8	7.1	12.5	16.4	17.6	17.9	18.1	Asie
249 938	*715 383*	*618 334*	*432 631*	*2.3*	*5.7*	*6.6*	*10.0*	*11.7*	*17.6*	*15.3*	*14.0*	*Principaux exportateurs d'articles manufacturés*
9 911	4 467	20 673	23 897	1.7	2.7	2.3	3.8	3.5	4.9	4.6	4.7	Amérique
240 027	710 915	597 661	408 734	2.4	6.1	7.3	10.8	12.6	18.9	16.3	14.8	Asie
53 722	*224 193*	*221 955*	*154 753*	*3.1*	*6.2*	*6.3*	*8.4*	*7.5*	*12.0*	*10.2*	*9.4*	*Économies émergentes*
21 330	54 182	87 170	99 376	3.8	4.4	4.8	5.8	7.1	11.0	9.7	9.6	Amérique
32 392	170 010	134 786	55 377	2.5	6.7	7.1	9.6	7.8	12.4	10.5	9.3	Asie
33 941	*262 875*	*193 582*	*97 589*	*3.0*	*5.7*	*6.8*	*8.1*	*7.1*	*11.3*	*9.7*	*8.8*	*Économies nouvellement industrialisées d'Asie*
27 109	212 201	106 143	45 178	2.3	6.3	7.2	9.0	7.4	11.7	9.9	8.8	Première génération
6 832	50 674	87 439	52 412	4.5	4.0	5.5	5.7	6.4	10.1	9.3	8.7	Deuxième génération
54 097	**17 676**	**15 450**	**13 082**	**4.6**	**3.6**	**7.4**	**10.3**	**11.7**	**13.9**	**12.5**	**10.8**	**Économies en développement : Afrique**
33 505	15 161	14 057	-3 275	7.8	4.1	11.5	20.6	21.9	25.8	24.3	21.3	Afrique septentrionale sans le Soudan
20 592	2 515	1 393	16 357	3.1	3.2	5.1	5.6	6.2	7.3	6.3	5.7	Afrique subsaharienne
15 171	-2 143	-1 540	11 938	4.2	4.3	6.6	6.9	7.3	8.0	7.0	6.4	Afrique subsaharienne sans l'Afrique du Sud
35 401	**51 351**	**84 194**	**105 411**	**4.1**	**4.7**	**4.8**	**5.8**	**6.5**	**9.6**	**8.5**	**8.2**	**Économies en développement : Amérique**
13 497	8 391	23 575	23 759	1.6	2.3	2.4	3.8	3.3	4.7	4.4	4.3	Amérique centrale et Grandes Antilles sans Porto Rico
3 586	3 924	2 902	-137	1.5	1.3	2.7	3.5	2.8	4.2	3.9	3.2	Amérique centrale et Grandes Antilles sans le Mexique et Porto Rico
31 627	48 892	82 221	104 382	4.6	5.3	5.1	6.0	6.7	9.8	8.6	8.4	Amérique du Sud et Amérique centrale
19 328	-1 989	10 422	17 494	7.8	10.0	10.0	9.0	7.5	9.9	8.0	7.1	Amérique du Sud sans le Brésil
427 784	**724 218**	**735 397**	**544 989**	**4.4**	**5.4**	**7.1**	**10.2**	**11.6**	**16.7**	**14.7**	**13.3**	**Économies en développement : Asie**
37 432	261 301	197 207	114 326	2.9	5.6	6.7	7.9	7.0	11.0	9.5	8.6	Asie orientale et Asie du Sud-Est sans la Chine
13 248	-2 886	249	4 035	5.9	2.7	4.9	8.3	9.7	11.2	9.0	7.9	Asie méridionale sans l'Inde

Sources :
Calculs du secrétariat de la CNUCED, basés sur :
- FMI, *Statistiques financières internationales*
- Banque mondiale, *Global Development Finance*
- FMI, *World Economic Outlook*
- Economist Intelligence Unit, *Country Data*
- Autres sources nationales

Notes :
(1) Position en fin d'année.
(2) Montant des réserves de l'année, divisé par la moyenne mensuelle des importations de l'année en cours. Les données des importations se basent sur les chiffres présentés dans le tableau 1.1.1.

Region, country or territory / Régions, pays ou territoires	Year / Année	Total official net (1) / Total secteur officiel net (1)	Total ODA Net (2) / APD totale nette (2)			Total OOF Net (3) / Flux AASP nets (3)		
			Total donors (4) / Tous donneurs (4)	of which: / dont :		Total donors / Tous donneurs	of which: / dont :	
				DAC bilateral donors / Donneurs bilatéraux du CAD	Multilateral donors / Donneurs multilatéraux		DAC bilateral donors / Donneurs bilatéraux du CAD	Multilateral donors / Donneurs multilatéraux
			Millions of dollars / Millions de dollars					
WORLD - MONDE	1990	76 625.9	58 532.9	38 474.0	12 608.8	18 093.1	7 958.7	10 146.8
	2000	53 530.2	49 776.0	36 195.3	12 679.6	3 754.3	-4 995.0	8 749.2
	2005	112 531.5	108 649.8	82 895.2	22 745.6	3 881.6	2 982.9	504.5
	2010	167 465.9	130 185.7	90 677.4	34 329.3	37 280.2	5 393.8	31 609.5
DEVELOPING ECONOMIES - ÉCONOMIES EN DÉVELOPPEMENT (5)	1990	75 082.2	56 896.9	36 874.1	12 578.6	18 185.2	8 065.1	10 128.2
	2000	48 161.0	45 112.4	33 422.6	10 902.7	3 048.6	-5 196.4	8 245.0
	2005	106 618.2	103 356.7	79 594.6	21 142.3	3 261.6	2 794.9	439.1
	2010	156 447.0	123 552.8	87 554.2	31 312.3	32 894.1	4 736.6	27 852.3
TRANSITION ECONOMIES - ÉCONOMIES EN TRANSITION	1990	72.4	177.9	165.5	12.4	-105.6	-83.7	-17.2
	2000	5 249.7	4 581.5	2 750.9	1 715.8	668.1	203.3	464.8
	2005	5 913.2	5 293.2	3 300.6	1 603.3	620.1	188.0	65.4
	2010	11 018.9	6 632.9	3 123.2	3 017.0	4 386.1	657.2	3 757.2
DEVELOPED ECONOMIES - ÉCONOMIES DÉVELOPPÉES	1990	1 471.4	1 458.1	1 434.3	17.8	13.4	-22.8	35.9
	2000	119.5	82.1	21.9	61.1	37.5	-1.9	39.4
Developing economies: Africa - Économies en développement : Afrique	1990	29 138.0	26 187.1	15 826.4	6 126.3	2 950.9	850.9	1 950.3
	2000	14 191.3	15 466.2	10 396.8	4 708.4	-1 274.8	-343.5	-931.4
	2005	35 513.1	35 833.3	24 628.0	10 741.8	-320.2	-499.0	178.8
	2010	50 364.7	47 976.1	29 345.5	18 252.4	2 388.6	-715.3	3 100.8
Eastern Africa - Afrique orientale	*1990*	*8 379.3*	*8 226.4*	*5 169.2*	*2 708.0*	*152.9*	*137.0*	*11.9*
	2000	*6 587.3*	*6 691.1*	*4 296.4*	*2 326.6*	*-103.9*	*-38.1*	*-65.8*
	2005	*11 189.8*	*11 587.0*	*6 985.1*	*4 546.3*	*-397.2*	*-308.5*	*-88.7*
	2010	*19 322.4*	*18 231.5*	*10 968.5*	*7 129.5*	*1 090.9*	*642.1*	*448.8*
Burundi	1990	259.1	262.6	157.6	104.7	-3.4	1.0	-4.4
	2000	93.1	93.1	40.9	52.2	0.0	0.0	0.0
	2005	364.0	364.0	180.5	183.4	0.0	0.0	0.0
	2010	629.9	629.9	282.6	347.0	0.0	0.0	0.0
Comoros - Comores	1990	45.0	44.9	30.6	14.0	0.1	0.1	0.0
	2000	18.7	18.7	10.8	7.7	0.0	0.0	0.0
	2005	22.8	22.8	15.1	7.7	0.0	0.0	0.0
	2010	69.5	67.2	22.4	28.4	2.3	2.3	0.0
Djibouti	1990	207.0	207.0	88.3	17.3	-0.1	-0.1	0.0
	2000	72.1	72.1	42.2	19.7	0.0	0.0	0.0
	2005	74.1	74.1	53.7	21.4	0.0	0.0	0.0
	2010	155.0	132.2	98.9	25.3	22.8	12.8	10.0
Eritrea - Érythrée	2000	177.1	177.0	112.0	54.7	0.0	0.0	0.0
	2005	349.2	349.2	226.0	127.1	0.0	0.0	0.0
	2010	160.5	160.5	36.2	104.5	0.0	0.0	0.0
Ethiopia (...1991) - Éthiopie (...1991)	1990	1 011.7	1 013.7	509.8	431.7	-1.9	-2.3	0.3
Ethiopia - Éthiopie	2000	668.4	687.2	380.0	291.5	-18.8	-1.0	-17.9
	2005	1 818.1	1 927.8	1 186.8	714.0	-109.7	-69.3	-40.4
	2010	3 689.3	3 525.2	1 927.7	1 562.2	164.1	148.8	15.3
Kenya	1990	1 141.3	1 181.3	735.2	441.6	-40.0	15.4	-55.4
	2000	478.9	512.7	292.4	211.4	-33.8	-4.9	-29.0
	2005	779.4	759.2	520.9	229.7	20.2	16.6	3.6
	2010	1 699.0	1 628.6	1 158.8	464.4	70.4	-23.2	93.6
Madagascar	1990	411.9	397.0	268.2	129.9	14.9	11.2	3.2
	2000	314.7	320.2	138.7	182.6	-5.5	1.4	-6.9
	2005	786.2	913.0	497.7	415.8	-126.9	-126.5	-0.4
	2010	865.5	470.1	214.4	246.5	395.5	383.6	11.9
Malawi	1990	486.3	500.4	216.2	283.6	-14.1	-5.8	-8.3
	2000	443.7	446.1	269.3	170.7	-2.4	-0.1	-2.3
	2005	570.8	573.4	325.4	246.5	-2.6	0.1	-2.6
	2010	1 014.0	1 022.9	517.2	503.7	-8.8	-1.2	-7.7
Mauritius - Maurice	1990	107.2	88.3	75.7	11.9	18.9	16.2	2.7
	2000	-18.1	20.2	12.4	7.2	-38.3	-20.7	-17.5
	2005	18.5	34.6	21.5	10.4	-16.1	-1.8	-14.3
	2010	473.0	125.3	58.2	69.1	347.8	70.3	277.5

For sources and notes, see end of table.

Pour les sources et les notes, se reporter à la fin du tableau.

Region, country or territory / Régions, pays ou territoires	Year / Année	Total official net (1) / Total secteur officiel net (1)	Total ODA Net (2) / APD totale nette (2)			Total OOF Net (3) / Flux AASP nets (3)		
			Total donors (4) / Tous donneurs (4)	of which: / dont :		Total donors / Tous donneurs	of which: / dont :	
				DAC bilateral donors / Donneurs bilatéraux du CAD	Multilateral donors / Donneurs multilatéraux		DAC bilateral donors / Donneurs bilatéraux du CAD	Multilateral donors / Donneurs multilatéraux
		Millions of dollars / Millions de dollars						
Mayotte	1990	60.5	60.5	58.5	2.0	0.0	0.0	0.0
	2000	103.2	103.2	103.0	0.2	0.0	0.0	0.0
	2005	190.2	201.3	201.9	-0.5	-11.1	-11.1	0.0
	2010	605.9	603.9	602.9	1.0	2.0	2.0	0.0
Mozambique	1990	999.4	997.3	750.3	246.9	2.1	3.3	-1.5
	2000	1 072.7	906.2	623.6	282.7	166.5	105.2	61.2
	2005	1 279.4	1 297.2	760.3	535.3	-17.8	-21.1	3.3
	2010	1 999.6	1 951.5	1 357.3	590.2	48.1	58.1	-10.0
Rwanda	1990	286.9	287.9	183.2	94.5	-1.0	-0.1	-0.9
	2000	323.5	321.5	175.4	145.9	2.1	2.2	-0.2
	2005	572.0	577.4	281.4	295.6	-5.4	-5.4	0.0
	2010	1 062.4	1 032.2	547.8	482.4	30.2	18.3	11.9
Seychelles	1990	37.4	35.6	32.7	3.0	1.9	-0.8	-0.4
	2000	19.3	23.1	3.3	8.2	-3.8	-0.7	-3.1
	2005	15.5	16.7	7.9	6.6	-1.3	0.0	-1.3
	2010	88.2	56.0	29.3	9.7	32.1	3.0	29.1
Somalia - Somalie	1990	513.6	514.8	269.6	139.8	-1.2	-0.8	-0.4
	2000	102.2	102.2	56.4	44.4	0.0	0.0	0.0
	2005	240.2	240.2	145.1	91.8	0.0	0.0	0.0
	2010	497.5	497.5	308.3	180.7	0.0	0.0	0.0
Uganda - Ouganda	1990	665.2	663.1	244.4	376.1	2.1	9.4	-7.3
	2000	809.7	853.3	578.2	269.2	-43.6	-46.3	2.8
	2005	1 189.3	1 192.2	690.8	499.3	-2.8	-0.1	-2.7
	2010	1 810.1	1 723.5	1 033.0	685.9	86.6	23.0	63.6
United Republic of Tanzania - République-Unie de Tanzanie	1990	1 163.1	1 163.2	844.1	315.8	-0.1	28.2	-28.2
	2000	1 091.0	1 063.9	779.0	286.6	27.1	32.0	-4.9
	2005	1 491.4	1 499.1	860.7	629.0	-7.7	-7.8	0.1
	2010	2 953.5	2 958.2	1 655.5	1 297.8	-4.6	-18.7	14.0
Zambia - Zambie	1990	540.8	474.8	408.9	65.9	66.0	47.2	18.8
	2000	674.5	794.7	486.3	308.1	-120.1	-104.4	-15.8
	2005	1 067.8	1 172.1	822.6	347.4	-104.3	-79.2	-25.1
	2010	817.6	914.4	593.1	321.2	-96.7	-37.0	-59.7
Zimbabwe	1990	443.0	334.3	295.9	29.3	108.7	14.9	93.8
	2000	142.4	175.6	192.7	-16.3	-33.2	-0.9	-32.3
	2005	361.0	372.7	186.9	185.8	-11.7	-2.9	-8.9
	2010	731.8	732.5	525.0	209.5	-0.7	0.0	-0.6
Middle Africa - Afrique centrale	*1990*	*3 591.1*	*2 628.2*	*1 821.6*	*725.4*	*963.0*	*678.6*	*284.4*
	2000	*969.9*	*1 162.5*	*667.9*	*498.5*	*-192.6*	*-52.5*	*-140.2*
	2005	*4 993.7*	*4 740.1*	*3 214.2*	*1 517.7*	*253.6*	*521.0*	*-267.4*
	2010	*5 547.0*	*6 619.0*	*4 613.0*	*1 993.8*	*-1 072.1*	*-1 110.6*	*38.6*
Angola	1990	343.5	265.8	163.2	100.8	77.7	76.2	1.5
	2000	256.3	302.2	197.7	107.1	-45.9	-23.3	-22.6
	2005	406.7	414.6	247.7	167.4	-7.9	-6.3	-1.6
	2010	292.9	238.2	149.6	85.3	54.6	55.1	-0.4
Cameroon - Cameroun	1990	607.2	444.4	339.1	107.9	162.8	75.1	87.7
	2000	306.1	376.7	213.7	165.9	-70.6	9.4	-80.0
	2005	321.8	413.9	332.1	79.4	-92.2	-35.5	-56.7
	2010	585.7	540.5	266.5	273.7	45.2	11.0	34.3
Central African Republic - République centrafricaine	1990	251.6	248.9	99.9	146.7	2.8	3.9	-1.1
	2000	74.0	75.3	53.1	22.4	-1.3	-1.3	0.0
	2005	88.9	88.9	60.5	28.0	0.0	0.0	0.0
	2010	240.1	261.0	112.8	147.7	-20.9	-20.9	0.0
Chad - Tchad	1990	310.5	310.6	183.3	125.0	-0.1	-0.1	0.0
	2000	130.4	131.3	53.5	76.1	-0.9	-0.9	0.0
	2005	379.9	384.5	161.7	214.0	-4.6	-0.2	-4.4
	2010	521.3	486.0	285.0	201.6	35.2	-3.5	38.7

For sources and notes, see end of table.

Pour les sources et les notes, se reporter à la fin du tableau.

Region, country or territory Régions, pays ou territoires	Year Année	Total official net (1) Total secteur officiel net (1)	Total ODA Net (2) APD totale nette (2)			Total OOF Net (3) Flux AASP nets (3)		
			Total donors (4) Tous donneurs (4)	of which: / dont :		Total donors Tous donneurs	of which: / dont :	
				DAC bilateral donors Donneurs bilatéraux du CAD	Multilateral donors Donneurs multilatéraux		DAC bilateral donors Donneurs bilatéraux du CAD	Multilateral donors Donneurs multilatéraux
						Millions of dollars / Millions de dollars		
Congo	1990	226.3	217.2	202.0	15.2	9.1	13.2	-4.1
	2000	16.4	32.0	23.0	9.0	-15.6	-12.4	-3.2
	2005	1 855.7	1 425.5	1 344.0	81.5	430.2	458.7	-28.5
	2010	338.3	1 312.3	1 215.3	96.1	-974.0	-965.7	-8.3
Dem. Rep. of the Congo - Rép. dém. du Congo	1990	1 419.7	895.8	632.7	185.9	523.9	380.6	143.3
	2000	173.7	177.1	102.7	74.3	-3.4	0.0	-3.4
	2005	1 810.3	1 881.7	990.4	893.5	-71.5	60.2	-131.7
	2010	3 416.9	3 543.0	2 388.3	1 146.8	-126.1	-122.7	-3.4
Equatorial Guinea - Guinée équatoriale	1990	60.8	60.2	43.6	16.5	0.6	0.0	0.6
	2000	20.2	21.3	18.2	3.3	-1.1	-0.7	-0.4
	2005	54.0	38.1	29.8	9.2	15.9	15.9	0.0
	2010	49.5	84.7	78.7	6.3	-35.2	-35.5	0.4
Gabon	1990	317.5	131.2	126.9	4.4	186.3	129.7	56.5
	2000	-42.1	11.7	-11.6	23.3	-53.7	-23.2	-30.5
	2005	44.0	60.4	29.5	30.9	-16.4	28.1	-44.6
	2010	53.0	104.0	83.8	20.2	-51.0	-28.4	-22.6
Sao Tome and Principe - Sao Tomé-et-Principe	1990	54.1	54.1	31.0	23.1	0.0	0.0	0.0
	2000	34.9	34.9	17.7	17.2	0.0	0.0	0.0
	2005	32.4	32.4	18.4	14.0	0.0	0.0	0.0
	2010	49.3	49.3	33.0	16.3	0.0	0.0	0.0
Northern Africa - Afrique septentrionale	*1990*	*9 063.3*	*8 886.4*	*4 501.3*	*653.2*	*176.9*	*-949.7*	*977.3*
	2000	*2 081.0*	*2 451.0*	*1 750.9*	*428.0*	*-370.0*	*91.4*	*-461.4*
	2005	*4 177.0*	*4 325.1*	*2 962.4*	*1 045.0*	*-148.1*	*-786.4*	*638.3*
	2010	*5 682.9*	*4 417.7*	*3 018.8*	*1 256.7*	*1 265.2*	*-95.0*	*1 357.1*
Algeria - Algérie	1990	875.6	331.7	102.2	21.5	543.9	114.2	283.3
	2000	-41.8	199.6	65.7	62.7	-241.4	-143.4	-98.0
	2005	-1 159.9	346.6	266.6	68.5	-1 506.5	-813.4	-693.1
	2010	103.0	198.3	143.0	57.4	-95.4	-94.8	-0.5
Egypt - Égypte	1990	4 793.4	6 064.5	3 163.1	76.2	-1 271.1	-1 234.0	-37.6
	2000	1 410.5	1 370.6	1 139.6	134.2	39.9	220.0	-180.0
	2005	2 101.8	1 034.2	667.2	240.3	1 067.6	131.6	936.0
	2010	1 472.3	592.4	366.0	147.5	879.9	59.4	820.5
Libya - Lybie	1990	8.3	8.3	7.7	0.7	0.0	0.0	0.0
	2005	23.8	23.8	16.8	3.1	0.0	0.0	0.0
	2010	6.5	8.5	17.4	-9.9	-2.0	-2.0	0.0
Morocco - Maroc	1990	1 889.2	1 241.1	595.4	91.5	648.1	164.5	486.2
	2000	291.4	434.4	293.1	129.8	-143.0	-47.3	-95.7
	2005	1 070.7	732.3	288.3	313.3	338.4	-47.2	385.6
	2010	1 123.1	992.5	598.9	382.4	130.6	-10.0	140.6
Sudan (...2011) - Soudan (...2011)	1990	845.7	848.2	420.0	385.2	-2.6	2.7	-5.2
	2000	215.2	224.7	90.3	30.7	-9.5	-9.1	-0.4
	2005	1 852.0	1 825.8	1 455.5	318.7	26.2	0.1	26.2
	2010	2 143.7	2 075.5	1 538.3	487.1	68.2	0.5	64.6
Tunisia - Tunisie	1990	651.1	392.5	212.9	78.1	258.5	2.9	250.7
	2000	205.7	221.7	162.3	70.6	-16.0	71.2	-87.2
	2005	288.6	362.4	268.2	101.2	-73.8	-57.5	-16.3
	2010	834.3	550.4	355.3	192.2	284.0	-48.0	331.9
Southern Africa - Afrique australe	*1990*	*460.8*	*457.6*	*281.9*	*177.8*	*3.2*	*-2.2*	*5.4*
	2000	*842.3*	*719.1*	*500.4*	*219.5*	*123.2*	*-83.6*	*206.8*
	2005	*1 033.9*	*977.5*	*645.0*	*331.3*	*56.4*	*-114.8*	*171.2*
	2010	*2 795.7*	*1 790.8*	*1 264.2*	*520.8*	*1 004.9*	*-26.9*	*1 031.8*
Botswana	1990	167.4	145.2	121.2	25.8	22.2	4.6	17.6
	2000	34.2	30.6	23.5	8.0	3.6	23.1	-19.5
	2005	63.9	48.0	30.0	19.8	15.9	2.0	13.9
	2010	155.1	156.1	106.1	50.5	-1.0	0.0	-1.0

For sources and notes, see end of table.

Pour les sources et les notes, se reporter à la fin du tableau.

7.6.1   Official financial flows from
        bilateral and multilateral sources
        by country and geographical region

7.6.1   Flux financiers publics bilatéraux
        et multilatéraux par pays et régions
        géographiques

Region, country or territory / Régions, pays ou territoires	Year / Année	Total official net (1) / Total secteur officiel net (1)	Total ODA Net (2) / APD totale nette (2)			Total OOF Net (3) / Flux AASP nets (3)		
			Total donors (4) / Tous donneurs (4)	of which: / dont :		Total donors / Tous donneurs	of which: / dont :	
				DAC bilateral donors / Donneurs bilatéraux du CAD	Multilateral donors / Donneurs multilatéraux		DAC bilateral donors / Donneurs bilatéraux du CAD	Multilateral donors / Donneurs multilatéraux
		Millions of dollars / Millions de dollars						
Lesotho	1990	139.7	139.1	85.2	54.3	0.5	-1.5	2.0
	2000	47.1	36.7	21.8	16.1	10.4	-8.2	18.6
	2005	58.7	67.5	39.9	28.6	-8.8	-0.5	-8.3
	2010	258.2	256.2	94.1	159.1	2.0	0.0	2.0
Namibia - Namibie	1990	119.6	119.6	39.4	80.3	0.0	0.0	0.0
	2000	154.0	152.3	96.8	54.5	1.6	-0.5	2.1
	2005	142.0	125.1	88.1	33.0	16.9	-3.1	20.0
	2010	402.7	256.4	211.3	44.2	146.3	46.2	100.1
South Africa - Afrique du Sud	2000	591.2	486.4	355.5	130.8	104.8	-94.5	199.3
	2005	732.3	690.2	466.0	223.5	42.1	-113.2	155.2
	2010	1 903.1	1 030.5	821.6	207.2	872.6	-73.1	945.7
Swaziland	1990	34.1	53.6	36.1	17.4	-19.5	-5.3	-14.2
	2000	15.9	13.1	2.8	10.2	2.8	-3.5	6.2
	2005	37.0	46.7	21.0	26.3	-9.6	0.0	-9.6
	2010	76.5	91.5	31.1	59.7	-14.9	0.0	-14.9
Western Africa - Afrique occidentale	*1990*	*6 724.3*	*5 085.8*	*3 212.0*	*1 808.8*	*1 638.5*	*981.3*	*660.7*
	2000	*2 678.4*	*3 411.0*	*2 333.6*	*1 065.0*	*-732.6*	*-267.6*	*-465.0*
	2005	*11 761.9*	*11 975.5*	*9 022.1*	*2 895.8*	*-213.5*	*104.1*	*-317.7*
	2010	*12 444.9*	*12 649.9*	*6 324.6*	*6 271.3*	*-205.0*	*-256.0*	*51.0*
Benin - Bénin	1990	294.8	266.9	125.7	141.5	27.9	26.2	1.7
	2000	232.5	243.5	190.5	54.0	-11.0	-11.0	0.0
	2005	346.3	346.9	207.7	139.7	-0.7	-0.3	-0.3
	2010	670.7	689.1	339.0	348.9	-18.4	-3.3	-15.1
Burkina Faso	1990	328.0	326.5	238.7	76.5	1.4	1.3	0.1
	2000	174.3	179.8	227.8	-51.8	-5.5	-3.5	-2.0
	2005	694.3	693.4	338.5	346.7	1.0	-0.3	1.2
	2010	1 081.0	1 062.3	458.8	598.2	18.6	0.0	18.6
Cape Verde - Cap-Vert	1990	103.9	105.3	75.9	29.0	-1.4	-0.2	-1.1
	2000	92.2	93.7	69.7	24.4	-1.6	-0.1	-1.4
	2005	168.9	162.2	104.1	55.7	6.6	0.0	6.6
	2010	344.4	327.9	247.9	80.7	16.5	2.7	13.8
Côte d'Ivoire	1990	1 121.9	686.4	530.6	155.8	435.5	134.2	301.3
	2000	275.7	350.6	250.1	99.9	-74.9	17.8	-92.7
	2005	75.1	91.2	129.3	-38.5	-16.1	-10.0	-6.1
	2010	769.1	845.0	437.5	405.8	-75.9	-58.9	-17.0
Gambia - Gambie	1990	105.3	97.3	56.9	39.9	8.0	8.5	-0.5
	2000	49.0	49.6	14.6	32.6	-0.7	0.0	-0.7
	2005	60.5	60.5	14.8	45.4	0.0	0.0	0.0
	2010	123.6	120.2	33.3	85.4	3.4	0.0	3.4
Ghana	1990	716.4	559.7	264.9	293.7	156.6	26.4	130.2
	2000	581.4	598.2	375.6	219.2	-16.8	8.6	-25.3
	2005	1 118.7	1 150.7	615.3	529.2	-32.0	-14.1	-17.9
	2010	1 749.5	1 692.5	899.7	789.2	56.9	27.0	30.0
Guinea - Guinée	1990	300.4	291.6	139.0	148.4	8.8	19.6	-10.8
	2000	141.5	152.9	92.8	57.5	-11.4	-1.4	-10.0
	2005	189.6	198.2	126.0	60.5	-8.6	-0.3	-8.3
	2010	225.6	217.7	91.7	127.6	7.9	0.0	7.9
Guinea-Bissau - Guinée-Bissau	1990	125.0	126.4	75.4	51.0	-1.3	0.0	-1.3
	2000	81.1	81.1	41.6	39.5	0.0	0.1	-0.1
	2005	65.9	66.0	26.8	39.2	-0.1	-0.1	0.0
	2010	138.7	139.3	53.8	84.7	-0.6	-0.6	0.0
Liberia - Libéria	1990	66.5	113.7	42.3	69.2	-47.3	-12.5	-34.8
	2000	69.1	67.4	23.8	43.6	1.6	-1.9	3.5
	2005	221.8	222.5	143.9	78.4	-0.7	0.0	-0.7
	2010	1 348.0	1 419.3	702.5	714.6	-71.2	-74.2	3.0

For sources and notes, see end of table.

Pour les sources et les notes, se reporter à la fin du tableau.

Region, country or territory / Régions, pays ou territoires	Year / Année	Total official net (1) / Total secteur officiel net (1)	Total ODA Net (2) / APD totale nette (2)			Total OOF Net (3) / Flux AASP nets (3)		
			Total donors (4) / Tous donneurs (4)	of which: / dont :		Total donors / Tous donneurs	of which: / dont :	
				DAC bilateral donors / Donneurs bilatéraux du CAD	Multilateral donors / Donneurs multilatéraux		DAC bilateral donors / Donneurs bilatéraux du CAD	Multilateral donors / Donneurs multilatéraux
				Millions of dollars / Millions de dollars				
Mali	1990	480.3	479.2	312.5	151.1	1.1	1.9	-0.8
	2000	271.6	288.0	299.8	-10.6	-16.4	-6.9	-9.5
	2005	716.3	721.3	370.8	326.3	-5.1	-4.1	-1.0
	2010	1 156.2	1 088.6	684.4	403.9	67.6	1.3	66.2
Mauritania - Mauritanie	1990	224.9	236.2	106.4	105.1	-11.3	0.8	-12.1
	2000	219.3	223.5	82.5	138.2	-4.2	6.8	-11.0
	2005	188.1	188.7	105.4	81.3	-0.6	0.0	-0.6
	2010	438.3	374.4	105.6	250.5	63.9	10.4	53.5
Niger	1990	392.9	387.6	254.6	129.4	5.3	6.7	-1.4
	2000	184.8	209.1	105.8	102.6	-24.3	-24.3	0.0
	2005	513.9	522.2	254.4	265.3	-8.2	-5.8	-2.4
	2010	744.2	744.5	380.8	360.6	-0.4	-7.0	6.7
Nigeria - Nigéria	1990	1 307.7	255.1	181.7	73.4	1 052.6	739.4	313.2
	2000	-390.6	173.7	84.4	89.1	-564.3	-260.5	-303.8
	2005	6 308.6	6 408.8	5 930.5	477.4	-100.2	154.8	-255.0
	2010	1 906.2	2 062.0	849.2	1 210.2	-155.8	-16.3	-139.5
Saint Helena - Sainte-Hélène	1990	24.7	24.7	23.3	1.4	0.0	0.0	0.0
	2000	18.7	18.7	18.4	0.3	0.0	0.0	0.0
	2005	22.6	22.6	22.5	0.1	0.0	0.0	0.0
	2010	53.7	53.7	53.7	..	0.0	0.0	..
Senegal - Sénégal	1990	823.8	811.7	589.2	220.1	12.0	31.1	-15.6
	2000	425.2	431.2	288.5	145.6	-6.0	9.2	-15.2
	2005	653.0	698.0	444.1	254.3	-45.0	-15.0	-29.9
	2010	923.7	927.7	534.4	379.5	-4.0	0.7	-4.7
Sierra Leone	1990	55.1	59.3	39.9	19.3	-4.3	-3.4	-0.9
	2000	178.8	180.6	115.6	65.0	-1.8	-0.9	-0.9
	2005	338.7	339.9	129.3	211.3	-1.2	0.0	-1.1
	2010	466.1	466.9	199.5	266.4	-0.8	0.0	-0.8
Togo	1990	252.8	258.2	155.0	103.9	-5.4	1.3	-6.7
	2000	74.0	69.6	52.0	16.2	4.5	0.4	4.1
	2005	79.7	82.5	58.8	23.4	-2.9	-0.6	-2.3
	2010	306.0	418.9	252.8	165.3	-112.9	-137.7	24.8
Developing economies: Africa n.e.s. - Économies en développement : Afrique n.d.a. (6)	*1990*	*(e)919.3*	*(e)902.8*	*(e)840.4*	*(e)53.1*	*16.5*	*5.8*	*10.6*
	2000	*(e)1 032.5*	*(e)1 031.4*	*(e)847.7*	*(e)170.9*	*1.1*	*6.9*	*-5.8*
	2005	*(e)2 356.9*	*(e)2 228.2*	*(e)1 799.2*	*(e)405.8*	*128.8*	*85.6*	*43.1*
	2010	*(e)4 571.8*	*(e)4 267.2*	*(e)3 156.5*	*(e)1 080.3*	*304.7*	*131.1*	*173.6*
Developing economies: America - Économies en développement : Amérique	**1990**	**13 525.1**	**5 189.4**	**4 146.4**	**1 032.0**	**8 335.7**	**3 729.7**	**4 634.3**
	2000	**10 364.7**	**4 837.7**	**3 858.4**	**940.8**	**5 527.0**	**-1 012.2**	**6 539.2**
	2005	**3 452.5**	**6 707.9**	**4 854.9**	**1 827.7**	**-3 255.4**	**-1 589.2**	**-1 666.3**
	2010	**26 355.0**	**10 718.3**	**7 856.0**	**2 830.6**	**15 636.6**	**2 657.9**	**12 978.7**
Caribbean - Caraïbes	*1990*	*1 015.6*	*808.2*	*624.6*	*180.0*	*207.4*	*93.9*	*130.5*
	2000	*570.5*	*418.7*	*279.2*	*121.1*	*151.8*	*-88.9*	*240.6*
	2005	*858.5*	*769.5*	*517.7*	*240.8*	*89.0*	*43.9*	*45.1*
	2010	*5 606.0*	*3 719.7*	*2 550.1*	*1 151.2*	*1 886.3*	*339.7*	*1 546.6*
Anguilla	1990	3.9	3.8	2.4	1.4	0.1	0.0	0.1
	2000	7.7	3.5	3.8	-0.3	4.2	0.0	4.2
	2005	3.7	4.0	4.3	-0.3	-0.3	0.0	-0.3
	2010	61.1	8.3	0.3	8.0	52.9	0.0	52.9
Antigua and Barbuda - Antigua-et-Barbuda	1990	-2.7	4.6	2.9	1.7	-7.3	-7.3	0.0
	2000	9.9	9.8	3.7	1.1	0.1	0.0	0.1
	2005	7.1	7.8	7.0	0.2	-0.7	-0.6	-0.2
	2010	19.0	19.1	7.0	12.0	-0.1	-8.3	8.2
Aruba	1990	30.0	30.0	28.9	1.1	0.0	0.0	0.0
Bahamas	1990	30.6	3.2	0.4	1.8	27.4	-0.6	28.0

For sources and notes, see end of table.

Pour les sources et les notes, se reporter à la fin du tableau.

Region, country or territory / Régions, pays ou territoires	Year / Année	Total official net (1) / Total secteur officiel net (1)	Total ODA Net (2) / APD totale nette (2)			Total OOF Net (3) / Flux AASP nets (3)		
			Total donors (4) / Tous donneurs (4)	of which: / dont :		Total donors / Tous donneurs	of which: / dont :	
				DAC bilateral donors / Donneurs bilatéraux du CAD	Multilateral donors / Donneurs multilatéraux		DAC bilateral donors / Donneurs bilatéraux du CAD	Multilateral donors / Donneurs multilatéraux
				Millions of dollars / Millions de dollars				
Barbados - Barbade	1990	21.4	2.6	1.4	1.2	18.8	10.7	8.1
	2000	13.1	0.2	1.0	-0.8	12.8	3.1	9.7
	2005	-2.8	-1.8	6.1	-7.9	-1.0	5.8	-6.8
	2010	59.9	16.2	2.5	13.8	43.7	-1.1	44.8
British Virgin Islands - Îles Vierges britanniques	1990	9.4	5.6	3.0	2.5	3.9	1.6	2.3
Cayman Islands - Îles Caïmanes	1990	11.9	3.0	2.1	0.9	8.9	2.4	6.5
Cuba	1990	60.1	50.8	33.6	17.2	9.3	8.3	0.0
	2000	47.5	44.0	30.8	12.8	3.5	3.5	0.0
	2005	109.0	88.4	68.0	18.9	20.6	20.6	0.0
	2010	129.1	129.1	87.5	41.4	0.0	0.0	0.0
Dominica - Dominique	1990	19.4	19.6	10.8	8.4	-0.3	-0.4	0.1
	2000	18.5	15.2	5.9	6.4	3.3	-0.1	3.4
	2005	24.2	21.1	4.6	10.8	3.1	0.0	3.1
	2010	31.3	32.5	5.8	25.0	-1.2	0.0	-1.2
Dominican Republic - République dominicaine	1990	136.4	101.7	72.7	27.8	34.7	1.4	33.3
	2000	72.9	56.0	44.7	11.3	16.9	-36.3	53.1
	2005	264.1	80.6	55.8	24.8	183.5	40.5	143.0
	2010	1 227.4	175.2	91.8	83.3	1 052.3	499.6	552.6
Grenada - Grenade	1990	12.9	13.8	5.0	8.7	-0.9	-1.1	0.2
	2000	19.9	16.5	9.9	3.2	3.4	-0.2	3.6
	2005	61.6	52.5	26.1	24.6	9.1	0.0	9.1
	2010	30.3	33.8	6.7	29.1	-3.6	-4.6	1.0
Haiti - Haïti	1990	166.9	167.4	117.1	50.1	-0.5	-0.1	-0.4
	2000	206.7	207.8	153.9	53.9	-1.1	-1.1	0.0
	2005	425.5	425.6	284.0	141.6	-0.1	-0.1	0.0
	2010	3 039.8	3 064.8	2 327.8	714.6	-25.0	-37.2	12.2
Jamaica - Jamaïque	1990	325.3	270.6	251.9	18.9	54.7	55.4	17.3
	2000	128.8	8.6	-26.3	28.5	120.2	-19.9	140.1
	2005	-56.7	39.6	11.4	24.8	-96.3	-5.8	-90.5
	2010	926.0	141.2	-1.9	144.6	784.8	9.0	775.8
Montserrat	1990	8.3	8.4	7.8	0.5	-0.1	0.0	-0.1
	2000	30.9	30.9	30.9	0.1	-0.1	0.0	-0.1
	2005	27.6	27.8	27.0	0.9	-0.2	0.0	-0.2
	2010	25.8	25.8	16.6	9.2	0.0	0.0	0.0
Netherlands Antilles - Antilles néerlandaises	1990	50.1	58.0	53.0	5.0	-7.9	-10.9	3.0
Saint Kitts and Nevis - Saint-Kitts-et-Nevis	1990	8.2	8.1	5.0	2.9	0.1	0.0	0.1
	2000	6.0	3.9	0.1	4.1	2.1	-1.3	3.3
	2005	1.7	2.5	1.8	1.8	-0.8	-2.0	1.2
	2010	11.2	11.4	0.2	12.1	-0.3	-0.2	-0.1
Saint Lucia - Sainte-Lucie	1990	15.8	12.3	6.2	5.8	3.5	-0.4	3.9
	2000	13.5	11.0	7.1	4.4	2.5	0.0	2.5
	2005	11.5	10.5	6.6	4.5	1.0	0.0	1.0
	2010	25.6	41.2	1.5	40.9	-15.6	-0.2	-15.4
Saint Vincent and the Grenadines - Saint-Vincent-et-les Grenadines	1990	15.4	15.4	5.2	9.7	0.0	0.0	0.0
	2000	9.7	6.2	3.8	1.1	3.5	0.0	3.5
	2005	10.5	7.7	5.8	2.4	2.8	0.0	2.8
	2010	57.7	16.9	1.1	16.5	40.8	0.0	40.8
Trinidad and Tobago - Trinité-et-Tobago	1990	80.8	17.8	6.1	11.7	63.0	34.8	28.2
	2000	-21.6	-1.5	4.4	-5.9	-20.1	-36.7	16.5
	2005	-34.3	-2.0	6.1	-8.1	-32.3	-14.7	-17.6
	2010	-38.0	4.3	3.5	0.8	-42.4	-117.3	75.0
Turks and Caicos Islands - Îles Turques et Caïques	1990	11.6	11.6	8.9	2.8	0.0	0.0	0.0
	2000	7.3	6.7	5.6	1.1	0.6	0.0	0.6
	2005	5.8	5.2	3.1	2.1	0.6	0.0	0.6

For sources and notes, see end of table.

Pour les sources et les notes, se reporter à la fin du tableau.

Region, country or territory / Régions, pays ou territoires	Year / Année	Total official net (1) / Total secteur officiel net (1)	Total ODA Net (2) / APD totale nette (2)			Total OOF Net (3) / Flux AASP nets (3)		
			Total donors (4) / Tous donneurs (4)	of which: / dont :		Total donors / Tous donneurs	of which: / dont :	
				DAC bilateral donors / Donneurs bilatéraux du CAD	Multilateral donors / Donneurs multilatéraux		DAC bilateral donors / Donneurs bilatéraux du CAD	Multilateral donors / Donneurs multilatéraux
		Millions of dollars / Millions de dollars						
Central America - Amérique centrale	*1990*	*6 613.6*	*1 839.6*	*1 599.5*	*234.1*	*4 774.0*	*2 028.6*	*2 751.0*
	2000	*1 723.2*	*1 433.3*	*1 011.4*	*414.7*	*289.9*	*-740.0*	*1 029.9*
	2005	*1 389.7*	*2 159.6*	*1 565.3*	*594.9*	*-769.9*	*-423.2*	*-346.7*
	2010	*9 727.3*	*2 591.8*	*1 914.4*	*674.4*	*7 135.5*	*1 189.6*	*5 945.9*
Belize	1990	38.5	30.3	18.8	11.3	8.1	4.1	4.1
	2000	31.8	14.7	2.9	11.2	17.2	3.5	13.7
	2005	10.8	12.2	7.5	5.6	-1.3	-0.1	-1.2
	2010	21.9	24.8	11.9	13.6	-2.9	-1.8	-1.2
Costa Rica	1990	237.7	227.0	206.6	19.1	10.8	21.1	-10.3
	2000	-39.6	9.6	17.4	-8.4	-49.2	-26.9	-22.3
	2005	-102.6	25.8	25.5	0.2	-128.4	7.1	-135.5
	2010	608.8	95.0	90.0	4.9	513.8	-13.1	526.9
El Salvador	1990	308.3	347.3	312.0	34.3	-39.0	-0.9	-38.1
	2000	283.4	179.7	172.4	6.8	103.7	-13.5	117.2
	2005	323.3	204.5	164.6	39.2	118.9	-14.6	133.4
	2010	626.3	283.5	238.6	44.7	342.8	-14.0	356.8
Guatemala	1990	221.5	201.4	149.5	50.5	20.1	6.2	13.9
	2000	321.2	263.1	230.4	32.3	58.0	6.7	51.4
	2005	251.7	256.6	220.5	35.8	-4.9	-5.5	0.6
	2010	1 002.1	393.5	354.2	39.0	608.6	21.7	586.8
Honduras	1990	433.3	448.5	383.5	64.0	-15.2	-0.7	-14.6
	2000	396.1	448.3	310.7	133.1	-52.2	19.5	-71.7
	2005	510.2	690.1	458.0	234.1	-179.9	-82.9	-97.0
	2010	608.2	574.2	280.5	292.9	34.0	1.0	33.0
Mexico - Mexique	1990	5 024.2	156.3	144.8	11.5	4 868.0	2 035.6	2 837.9
	2000	74.1	-57.8	-68.3	10.0	131.9	-710.7	842.6
	2005	-204.2	180.5	161.1	18.7	-384.7	-209.3	-175.4
	2010	5 487.6	471.1	421.1	48.8	5 016.5	918.1	4 098.4
Nicaragua	1990	326.6	329.6	288.5	41.1	-2.9	-1.8	-1.1
	2000	552.1	560.4	326.1	234.1	-8.3	-6.2	-2.0
	2005	636.7	763.4	510.2	252.7	-126.7	-115.0	-11.7
	2010	673.9	620.9	394.5	225.6	53.0	-12.9	65.9
Panama	1990	23.5	99.3	96.0	2.4	-75.8	-35.0	-40.8
	2000	104.0	15.4	19.8	-4.5	88.7	-12.4	101.1
	2005	-36.3	26.7	17.9	8.8	-63.0	-3.1	-59.9
	2010	698.6	128.9	123.8	4.9	569.7	290.4	279.3
South America - Amérique du Sud	*1990*	*5 246.4*	*2 030.9*	*1 569.5*	*460.0*	*3 215.5*	*1 607.5*	*1 613.8*
	2000	*6 917.9*	*1 868.6*	*1 565.0*	*290.6*	*5 049.3*	*-184.8*	*5 234.2*
	2005	*250.2*	*2 756.0*	*2 096.5*	*654.0*	*-2 505.8*	*-1 209.8*	*-1 296.0*
	2010	*9 383.2*	*2 911.9*	*2 224.7*	*677.2*	*6 471.3*	*1 023.0*	*5 448.3*
Argentina - Argentine	1990	903.8	168.7	166.2	2.6	735.1	411.9	323.2
	2000	677.1	52.5	43.5	1.4	624.6	-553.4	1 178.0
	2005	-435.7	96.2	77.9	18.8	-531.9	-106.3	-425.6
	2010	680.6	121.1	107.9	13.9	559.5	-62.5	622.0
Bolivia (Plurinational State of) - Bolivie (État plurinational de)	1990	576.2	545.4	364.7	180.7	30.8	10.4	20.4
	2000	445.9	481.7	336.3	145.4	-35.8	-25.4	-10.4
	2005	618.9	643.1	441.6	201.3	-24.1	-30.1	5.9
	2010	771.5	675.0	457.3	217.5	96.6	128.0	-31.5
Brazil - Brésil	1990	526.5	151.1	142.1	9.0	375.5	715.7	-334.5
	2000	4 097.7	231.4	222.5	7.3	3 866.3	430.9	3 435.4
	2005	175.0	243.1	174.5	67.4	-68.1	-425.9	357.8
	2010	4 574.5	661.3	611.0	48.6	3 913.1	-156.7	4 069.9
Chile - Chili	1990	787.2	103.5	83.4	20.2	683.7	207.9	475.8
	2000	-207.6	48.9	41.0	7.3	-256.5	-175.6	-80.8
	2005	28.6	167.3	91.7	75.1	-138.8	50.7	-189.5
	2010	961.6	197.5	157.3	37.0	764.0	770.1	-6.0

For sources and notes, see end of table.

Pour les sources et les notes, se reporter à la fin du tableau.

Region, country or territory / Régions, pays ou territoires	Year / Année	Total official net (1) / Total secteur officiel net (1)	Total ODA Net (2) / APD totale nette (2)			Total OOF Net (3) / Flux AASP nets (3)		
			Total donors (4) / Tous donneurs (4)	of which: / dont :		Total donors / Tous donneurs	of which: / dont :	
				DAC bilateral donors / Donneurs bilatéraux du CAD	Multilateral donors / Donneurs multilatéraux		DAC bilateral donors / Donneurs bilatéraux du CAD	Multilateral donors / Donneurs multilatéraux
			Millions of dollars / Millions de dollars					
Colombia - Colombie	1990	-1.5	88.5	86.7	1.9	-90.0	-93.2	3.2
	2000	-24.9	185.9	178.5	6.8	-210.9	-276.9	66.0
	2005	-245.6	620.5	572.1	47.7	-866.1	-119.6	-746.5
	2010	2 167.7	901.1	787.0	112.1	1 266.6	13.5	1 253.2
Ecuador - Équateur	1990	352.6	159.3	122.2	36.7	193.3	112.7	80.6
	2000	226.4	146.1	137.9	7.9	80.3	-28.4	108.7
	2005	45.5	225.8	192.2	33.4	-180.3	-68.7	-111.7
	2010	110.2	150.5	136.0	14.0	-40.3	-18.8	-21.5
Falkland Islands (Malvinas) - Îles Falkland (Malvinas)	1990	1.8	1.8	1.8	..	0.0	0.0	..
Guyana	1990	221.5	168.3	35.8	132.5	53.2	72.0	-18.8
	2000	103.9	115.8	51.9	64.0	-11.9	-0.7	-11.2
	2005	152.4	149.9	40.1	109.8	2.5	0.0	2.5
	2010	164.1	153.2	64.2	89.0	10.9	0.0	10.9
Paraguay	1990	29.4	57.2	47.6	8.6	-27.8	1.6	-29.4
	2000	202.0	81.6	73.1	8.2	120.5	8.3	112.2
	2005	45.3	50.7	57.3	-6.8	-5.3	-3.9	-1.4
	2010	257.5	105.0	67.6	37.1	152.5	-3.0	155.5
Peru - Pérou	1990	398.3	397.1	350.4	46.7	1.2	-2.0	3.2
	2000	1 111.9	396.8	374.5	21.7	715.1	513.2	201.9
	2005	229.7	450.5	391.5	57.0	-220.8	-399.6	178.8
	2010	-327.9	-255.9	-314.0	56.8	-72.0	431.8	-503.8
Suriname	1990	64.3	61.1	51.2	10.0	3.1	-0.9	4.0
	2000	36.2	34.3	29.2	5.2	1.8	0.0	1.8
	2005	42.7	44.2	33.6	10.6	-1.5	-0.6	-0.8
	2010	144.6	103.7	79.9	23.8	40.9	9.7	31.2
Uruguay	1990	86.6	52.4	41.7	10.7	34.2	1.1	33.1
	2000	198.7	17.4	15.4	1.3	181.3	2.0	179.2
	2005	62.5	14.4	3.0	11.0	48.1	4.2	43.9
	2010	-431.0	46.7	32.9	13.0	-477.7	51.1	-528.8
Venezuela (Bolivarian Rep. of) - Venezuela (Rép. bolivarienne du)	1990	1 299.5	76.4	75.8	0.6	1 223.2	170.3	1 052.9
	2000	50.6	76.1	61.3	14.1	-25.5	-78.8	53.3
	2005	-469.1	50.3	21.0	28.8	-519.4	-110.0	-409.4
	2010	309.9	52.7	37.5	14.7	257.2	-140.1	397.2
Developing economies: America n.e.s. - Économies en développement : (6) Amérique n.d.a.	*1990*	*(e)649.5*	*(e)510.7*	*(e)352.8*	*(e)157.9*	*138.8*	*-0.2*	*139.1*
	2000	*(e)1 153.2*	*(e)1 117.1*	*(e)1 002.7*	*(e)114.4*	*36.1*	*1.5*	*34.5*
	2005	*(e)954.2*	*(e)1 022.9*	*(e)675.3*	*(e)337.9*	*-68.7*	*0.0*	*-68.7*
	2010	*(e)1 638.5*	*(e)1 495.0*	*(e)1 166.8*	*(e)327.7*	*143.5*	*105.7*	*37.8*
Developing economies: Asia - Économies en développement : Asie	**1990**	**24 710.4**	**18 298.2**	**10 546.2**	**4 600.1**	**6 412.3**	**3 072.7**	**3 481.1**
	2000	**13 501.6**	**15 042.5**	**10 383.9**	**4 146.7**	**-1 541.0**	**-4 175.8**	**2 634.8**
	2005	**51 817.9**	**45 403.9**	**37 242.6**	**6 702.9**	**6 414.0**	**4 514.8**	**1 871.6**
	2010	**48 465.7**	**35 337.5**	**24 325.9**	**7 555.8**	**13 128.3**	**1 775.1**	**11 353.1**
Eastern Asia - Asie orientale	***1990***	***2 881.4***	***2 179.9***	***1 553.4***	***605.2***	***701.6***	***662.3***	***39.3***
	2000	***1 451.7***	***2 002.0***	***1 450.0***	***546.7***	***-550.3***	***-2 189.4***	***1 639.1***
	2005	***2 400.5***	***2 121.5***	***1 855.2***	***175.6***	***279.1***	***-961.1***	***1 240.2***
	2010	***3 468.1***	***1 026.9***	***949.3***	***6.7***	***2 441.2***	***1 047.5***	***1 393.7***
China - Chine	1990	3 296.5	2 032.4	1 465.5	570.1	1 264.1	835.9	428.2
	2000	1 160.6	1 711.8	1 270.8	440.3	-551.2	-2 190.2	1 639.1
	2005	2 092.5	1 814.3	1 684.3	79.9	278.2	-962.0	1 240.2
	2010	2 922.6	646.1	702.8	-109.4	2 276.4	1 044.3	1 232.1
China, Hong Kong SAR - Chine (RAS de Hong Kong)	1990	31.4	38.2	19.5	18.7	-6.8	-6.8	0.0
China, Macao SAR - Chine (RAS de Macao)	1990	0.2	0.2	0.1	0.1	0.0	0.0	0.0
China, Taiwan Province of - Province chinoise de Taiwan	1990	24.6	36.3	6.4	..	-11.7	-3.1	-8.6

For sources and notes, see end of table.

Pour les sources et les notes, se reporter à la fin du tableau.

Region, country or territory / Régions, pays ou territoires	Year / Année	Total official net (1) / Total secteur officiel net (1)	Total ODA Net (2) / APD totale nette (2) — Total donors (4) / Tous donneurs (4)	Total ODA Net (2) of which: / dont : DAC bilateral donors / Donneurs bilatéraux du CAD	Total ODA Net (2) of which: / dont : Multilateral donors / Donneurs multilatéraux	Total OOF Net (3) / Flux AASP nets (3) — Total donors / Tous donneurs	Total OOF Net (3) of which: / dont : DAC bilateral donors / Donneurs bilatéraux du CAD	Total OOF Net (3) of which: / dont : Multilateral donors / Donneurs multilatéraux
					Millions of dollars / Millions de dollars			
Korea, Dem. People's Rep. of - Corée, Rép. populaire dém. de	1990	6.9	7.7	0.9	6.9	-0.9	-0.9	0.0
	2000	74.2	73.3	26.9	46.4	0.9	0.9	0.0
	2005	88.2	87.6	39.5	42.2	0.6	0.6	0.0
	2010	80.0	78.8	27.9	45.6	1.2	1.2	0.0
Korea, Republic of - Corée, République de	1990	-491.2	52.0	54.8	2.7	-543.2	-162.9	-380.3
Mongolia - Mongolie	1990	13.1	13.1	6.4	6.7	0.0	0.0	0.0
	2000	217.0	217.0	152.3	60.1	0.0	0.0	0.0
	2005	219.8	219.6	131.4	53.5	0.2	0.3	0.0
	2010	465.5	302.0	218.7	70.5	163.6	2.0	161.5
Southern Asia - Asie méridionale	*1990*	*7 892.6*	*6 064.8*	*3 318.8*	*2 741.1*	*1 827.9*	*174.5*	*1 654.6*
	2000	*3 371.7*	*4 247.8*	*2 480.3*	*1 744.6*	*-876.1*	*-662.2*	*-213.9*
	2005	*11 837.1*	*9 507.0*	*5 790.7*	*3 467.1*	*2 330.1*	*651.2*	*1 651.3*
	2010	*20 216.3*	*15 421.8*	*12 057.7*	*2 964.1*	*4 794.5*	*-310.7*	*5 105.2*
Afghanistan	1990	121.7	121.7	100.4	22.7	0.0	0.0	0.0
	2000	136.0	136.0	87.5	47.8	0.0	0.0	0.0
	2005	2 892.6	2 837.6	2 175.4	603.9	54.9	12.9	42.0
	2010	6 498.2	6 426.4	5 472.1	782.8	71.8	67.0	4.8
Bangladesh	1990	2 112.4	2 092.8	1 103.3	999.8	19.7	21.9	-2.2
	2000	1 172.1	1 172.8	623.0	519.9	-0.7	-5.3	4.6
	2005	1 459.8	1 318.9	580.3	735.1	140.9	-12.8	153.7
	2010	1 529.5	1 415.0	883.5	534.5	114.6	-41.6	156.2
Bhutan - Bhoutan	1990	46.0	46.0	20.1	26.7	0.0	0.0	0.0
	2000	53.0	53.1	33.8	19.8	-0.1	-0.1	0.0
	2005	94.9	90.1	57.2	33.3	4.8	4.4	0.4
	2010	147.8	131.0	76.1	54.2	16.8	-2.8	19.5
India - Inde	1990	2 900.2	1 398.9	751.9	644.6	1 501.2	252.9	1 248.3
	2000	1 153.4	1 372.8	650.5	734.0	-219.4	51.6	-271.0
	2005	2 964.8	1 875.8	861.8	1 003.3	1 089.0	-166.7	1 255.7
	2010	7 834.7	2 806.4	2 219.2	585.3	5 028.3	442.6	4 585.7
Iran (Islamic Rep. of) - Iran (Rép. islamique d')	1990	-94.4	106.5	34.8	35.7	-200.9	-133.9	-67.0
	2000	-586.5	129.9	112.8	16.9	-716.4	-756.8	40.4
	2005	982.1	109.0	77.4	27.0	873.1	831.4	41.8
	2010	-601.7	121.2	72.7	30.7	-722.9	-755.0	32.1
Maldives	1990	24.9	20.9	11.6	9.9	4.1	4.1	0.0
	2000	16.2	19.2	13.3	7.1	-3.0	-1.8	-1.2
	2005	118.8	75.8	42.8	22.5	43.0	-1.1	44.0
	2010	85.1	110.8	56.6	49.2	-25.6	3.3	-28.9
Nepal - Népal	1990	432.1	422.8	239.0	181.5	9.3	0.0	9.2
	2000	409.1	386.1	233.6	151.3	23.0	2.7	20.2
	2005	416.3	424.1	347.3	77.1	-7.9	-0.6	-7.2
	2010	811.6	818.4	475.8	341.1	-6.7	0.7	-7.5
Pakistan	1990	1 631.4	1 126.9	653.8	492.3	504.5	31.2	474.7
	2000	766.0	702.7	475.5	224.3	63.3	74.7	-11.4
	2005	1 684.9	1 614.6	790.1	685.2	70.3	-22.4	65.1
	2010	3 148.6	3 013.0	2 415.9	395.7	135.5	-39.5	175.0
Sri Lanka	1990	718.3	728.3	404.0	328.0	-10.0	-1.6	-8.5
	2000	252.4	275.2	250.4	23.5	-22.8	-27.2	4.4
	2005	1 223.1	1 161.2	858.6	279.8	61.9	6.2	55.8
	2010	762.6	579.8	385.7	190.6	182.8	14.5	168.3
South-Eastern Asia - Asie du Sud-Est	*1990*	*7 777.3*	*4 782.1*	*4 086.8*	*677.7*	*2 995.1*	*1 561.3*	*1 456.8*
	2000	*4 310.6*	*5 661.7*	*4 767.5*	*894.6*	*-1 351.0*	*-1 685.8*	*334.8*
	2005	*4 722.5*	*6 040.2*	*4 647.7*	*1 315.1*	*-1 317.7*	*-218.3*	*-1 099.5*
	2010	*9 530.2*	*6 648.5*	*4 460.6*	*2 181.8*	*2 881.6*	*1 054.9*	*1 826.7*
Brunei Darussalam - Brunéi Darussalam	1990	-4.5	3.9	3.7	0.1	-8.4	-8.4	0.0

For sources and notes, see end of table.

Pour les sources et les notes, se reporter à la fin du tableau.

Region, country or territory / Régions, pays ou territoires	Year / Année	Total official net (1) / Total secteur officiel net (1)	Total ODA Net (2) / APD totale nette (2)			Total OOF Net (3) / Flux AASP nets (3)		
			Total donors (4) / Tous donneurs (4)	DAC bilateral donors / Donneurs bilatéraux du CAD	Multilateral donors / Donneurs multilatéraux	Total donors / Tous donneurs	DAC bilateral donors / Donneurs bilatéraux du CAD	Multilateral donors / Donneurs multilatéraux
		Millions of dollars / Millions de dollars						
Cambodia - Cambodge	1990	41.3	41.3	28.5	12.8	0.0	0.0	0.0
	2000	395.3	395.7	248.6	147.0	-0.4	-0.4	0.0
	2005	550.9	535.6	364.3	171.2	15.3	2.3	13.0
	2010	732.3	733.7	517.5	213.8	-1.4	3.8	-5.2
Indonesia (...2002) - Indonésie (...2002)	1990	3 255.5	1 716.0	1 520.7	171.4	1 539.6	534.3	1 029.3
	2000	2 965.9	1 884.3	1 760.1	121.4	1 081.6	360.4	721.2
Indonesia - Indonésie	2005	863.7	2 534.0	2 260.4	214.2	-1 670.3	-1 346.9	-323.4
	2010	2 941.8	1 392.5	988.3	407.7	1 549.3	411.3	1 138.0
Lao People's Dem. Rep. - Rép. dém. populaire lao	1990	149.1	148.1	51.2	96.9	1.0	0.0	0.0
	2000	280.3	280.6	195.5	84.9	-0.4	-0.5	0.2
	2005	361.5	301.9	168.6	132.7	59.6	10.2	49.4
	2010	386.7	413.8	285.9	105.5	-27.1	28.2	-55.2
Malaysia - Malaisie	1990	538.5	468.5	458.7	13.3	70.1	-6.3	76.4
	2000	-117.3	45.7	43.5	3.3	-163.0	-89.1	-73.9
	2005	-542.4	26.2	18.5	5.5	-568.5	-423.8	-144.7
	2010	148.3	2.1	-14.9	16.6	146.2	176.7	-30.5
Myanmar	1990	184.0	160.8	83.1	77.7	23.2	23.6	-0.4
	2000	125.8	105.6	68.9	36.6	20.2	20.2	0.0
	2005	116.9	144.8	85.8	59.0	-27.9	-27.9	0.0
	2010	353.4	355.1	248.1	133.2	-1.7	-1.7	0.0
Philippines	1990	2 176.9	1 270.6	1 102.2	167.3	906.3	411.7	494.6
	2000	353.3	571.7	505.1	66.3	-218.4	-20.3	-198.1
	2005	-191.5	567.1	532.3	30.1	-758.6	-574.6	-184.1
	2010	-26.8	531.2	453.1	78.5	-558.0	-392.0	-166.0
Singapore - Singapour	1990	152.1	-3.1	-3.2	0.1	155.2	193.2	-38.1
Thailand - Thaïlande	1990	1 103.8	795.6	734.0	65.7	308.2	413.2	-104.9
	2000	-1 246.6	696.6	683.6	15.8	-1 943.2	-1 783.5	-159.7
	2005	1 340.8	-167.7	-210.5	37.0	1 508.4	2 000.7	-492.3
	2010	202.6	-11.4	-100.2	87.9	214.0	246.1	-32.0
Timor-Leste	2005	185.8	184.8	160.4	24.3	1.1	1.1	0.0
	2010	297.3	291.5	258.2	32.8	5.8	5.8	0.0
Viet Nam	1990	180.6	180.6	107.9	72.5	0.0	0.2	-0.1
	2000	1 553.9	1 681.4	1 262.2	419.1	-127.5	-172.5	45.1
	2005	2 036.7	1 913.5	1 268.1	641.0	123.3	140.7	-17.4
	2010	4 494.5	2 940.1	1 824.5	1 105.7	1 554.4	576.7	977.7
Western Asia - Asie occidentale	*1990*	*5 064.2*	*4 176.5*	*1 349.8*	*203.4*	*887.7*	*674.6*	*330.4*
	2000	*3 734.0*	*2 498.3*	*1 254.6*	*834.1*	*1 235.7*	*352.7*	*883.0*
	2005	*29 856.3*	*24 818.7*	*23 284.6*	*1 295.7*	*5 037.7*	*4 960.5*	*77.1*
	2010	*10 574.9*	*7 918.8*	*5 383.4*	*2 180.1*	*2 656.1*	*-265.2*	*2 921.4*
Bahrain - Bahreïn	1990	136.7	137.5	1.9	2.3	-0.8	-0.8	0.0
	2000	60.2	60.4	1.6	-0.1	-0.2	-0.2	0.0
Iraq	1990	700.0	63.1	-8.6	16.3	636.9	642.3	-5.4
	2000	101.8	101.8	84.1	15.4	0.0	0.0	0.0
	2005	27 256.4	22 057.1	21 972.6	49.3	5 199.3	5 199.3	0.0
	2010	2 470.5	2 191.6	2 006.9	142.5	278.9	28.9	250.0
Jordan - Jordanie	1990	1 145.7	951.7	435.0	25.0	194.1	126.1	75.5
	2000	552.5	552.7	385.0	167.7	-0.2	-21.4	21.2
	2005	787.0	708.5	441.5	138.9	78.6	26.4	52.2
	2010	1 187.4	954.5	414.5	432.9	232.9	125.7	107.2
Kuwait - Koweït	1990	12.9	12.9	2.2	3.5	0.0	0.0	0.0
Lebanon - Liban	1990	263.2	285.7	64.9	39.0	-22.5	-13.6	-8.9
	2000	268.8	200.0	93.7	90.9	68.8	2.8	66.0
	2005	182.8	230.5	129.7	102.7	-47.7	-2.7	-45.0
	2010	389.4	447.9	263.6	127.3	-58.5	-55.3	-3.3

For sources and notes, see end of table. Pour les sources et les notes, se reporter à la fin du tableau.

Region, country or territory / Régions, pays ou territoires	Year / Année	Total official net (1) / Total secteur officiel net (1)	Total ODA Net (2) / APD totale nette (2)			Total OOF Net (3) / Flux AASP nets (3)		
			Total donors (4) / Tous donneurs (4)	of which: / dont :		Total donors / Tous donneurs	of which: / dont :	
				DAC bilateral donors / Donneurs bilatéraux du CAD	Multilateral donors / Donneurs multilatéraux		DAC bilateral donors / Donneurs bilatéraux du CAD	Multilateral donors / Donneurs multilatéraux
		Millions of dollars / Millions de dollars						
Occupied Palestinian territory - Territoire palestinien occupé	2000	729.8	684.5	306.8	226.1	45.3	-0.1	45.4
	2005	1 015.2	1 015.7	570.6	398.4	-0.5	0.2	-0.8
	2010	2 525.1	2 518.7	1 630.0	762.3	6.4	0.5	5.9
Oman	1990	64.7	68.2	11.4	2.2	-3.5	6.0	-9.6
	2000	84.6	79.7	9.2	1.7	5.0	9.7	-4.7
	2005	263.8	19.0	3.7	0.7	244.7	191.0	53.8
	2010	-74.4	-40.3	7.6	-0.6	-34.0	-24.0	-10.1
Qatar	1990	2.9	3.0	1.3	0.2	0.0	0.0	0.0
Saudi Arabia - Arabie saoudite	1990	14.1	14.7	12.8	1.7	-0.6	-0.6	0.0
	2000	48.1	22.0	18.0	2.1	26.1	26.1	0.0
	2005	-34.7	25.1	13.2	1.2	-59.8	-109.5	49.7
Syrian Arab Republic - République arabe syrienne	1990	873.7	882.6	69.4	34.2	-8.9	0.5	-10.3
	2000	486.8	158.9	97.4	38.1	327.9	342.1	-14.2
	2005	101.7	70.2	5.8	65.5	31.4	-17.5	48.9
	2010	101.9	135.0	44.1	123.0	-33.1	-24.8	-8.2
Turkey - Turquie	1990	1 393.9	1 303.9	587.9	-16.2	90.0	-88.5	289.1
	2000	1 082.4	326.9	99.1	190.3	755.5	-6.2	761.6
	2005	-11.1	396.0	-9.4	407.4	-407.1	-326.7	-80.5
	2010	3 427.6	1 047.2	734.6	296.2	2 380.5	-171.7	2 552.2
United Arab Emirates - Émirats arabes unis	1990	3.8	3.5	2.8	0.7	0.3	0.3	0.0
Yemen - Yémen	1990	452.6	449.8	168.8	94.5	2.8	2.8	0.0
	2000	318.9	311.3	159.7	101.9	7.6	0.0	7.7
	2005	295.3	296.5	156.9	131.7	-1.2	0.0	-1.2
	2010	547.3	664.2	282.1	296.5	-116.9	-144.6	27.6
Developing economies: Asia n.e.s. - Économies en développement : Asie n.d.a. (6)	1990	(e)1 094.9	(e)1 094.9	(e)237.5	(e)372.6	0.0	0.0	0.0
	2000	(e)633.6	(e)632.8	(e)431.4	(e)126.7	0.7	8.9	-8.2
	2005	(e)3 001.5	(e)2 916.6	(e)1 664.4	(e)449.4	84.9	82.4	2.5
	2010	(e)4 676.2	(e)4 321.4	(e)1 474.9	(e)223.1	354.8	248.7	106.2
Developing economies: Oceania - Économies en développement : Océanie	**1990**	**1 495.0**	**1 372.5**	**1 215.0**	**154.6**	**122.5**	**60.0**	**62.5**
	2000	**886.8**	**815.9**	**712.5**	**102.2**	**70.9**	**68.4**	**2.4**
	2005	**1 157.7**	**1 160.6**	**974.4**	**184.9**	**-2.8**	**-11.3**	**8.5**
	2010	**2 856.6**	**2 018.2**	**1 766.3**	**251.6**	**838.4**	**789.5**	**48.9**
Cook Islands - Îles Cook	1990	11.4	12.1	10.1	2.0	-0.8	-0.8	0.0
	2000	4.2	4.3	3.4	0.9	-0.2	-0.2	0.0
	2005	7.4	7.8	7.0	0.8	-0.3	-0.3	0.0
	2010	23.1	13.4	13.4	0.0	9.7	-0.4	10.0
Fiji - Fidji	1990	34.9	49.6	43.5	5.6	-14.7	-0.4	-14.3
	2000	22.8	29.1	28.9	0.2	-6.3	-0.1	-6.2
	2005	76.4	66.1	39.2	27.0	10.2	2.2	8.1
	2010	91.2	76.4	62.4	13.4	14.8	5.0	9.9
French Polynesia - Polynésie française	1990	304.0	259.7	258.0	1.7	44.3	44.7	-0.4
Kiribati	1990	20.2	20.2	17.7	2.5	0.0	0.0	0.0
	2000	17.9	17.9	14.8	3.1	0.0	0.0	0.0
	2005	28.2	28.0	21.4	6.6	0.2	0.2	0.0
	2010	23.7	22.8	21.3	1.5	0.8	0.8	0.0
Marshall Islands - Îles Marshall	2000	57.2	57.2	47.1	10.1	0.0	0.0	0.0
	2005	56.7	56.8	55.8	1.0	-0.1	0.0	-0.1
	2010	90.3	90.6	82.4	8.3	-0.3	0.0	-0.3
Micronesia (Federated States of) - Micronésie (États fédérés de)	2000	101.4	101.5	96.6	4.9	-0.1	-0.1	0.0
	2005	106.8	106.6	104.4	2.2	0.3	0.3	0.0
	2010	126.0	125.2	125.0	0.2	0.8	0.8	0.0
Nauru	1990	0.2	0.2	0.2	..	0.0	0.0	..
	2000	4.0	4.0	3.9	0.1	0.0	0.0	0.0
	2005	9.5	9.3	9.0	0.2	0.2	0.2	0.0
	2010	28.1	27.8	26.7	1.1	0.3	0.5	-0.2

For sources and notes, see end of table.

Pour les sources et les notes, se reporter à la fin du tableau.

Region, country or territory / Régions, pays ou territoires	Year / Année	Total official net (1) / Total secteur officiel net (1)	Total ODA Net (2) / APD totale nette (2)			Total OOF Net (3) / Flux AASP nets (3)		
			Total donors (4) / Tous donneurs (4)	of which: / dont :		Total donors / Tous donneurs	of which: / dont :	
				DAC bilateral donors / Donneurs bilatéraux du CAD	Multilateral donors / Donneurs multilatéraux		DAC bilateral donors / Donneurs bilatéraux du CAD	Multilateral donors / Donneurs multilatéraux
		Millions of dollars / Millions de dollars						
New Caledonia - Nouvelle-Calédonie	1990	325.8	302.4	300.2	2.2	23.4	24.0	-0.6
Niue - Nioué	1990	7.2	7.2	7.0	0.2	0.0	0.0	0.0
	2000	3.2	3.2	3.0	0.2	0.0	0.0	0.0
	2005	21.1	21.1	20.1	1.0	0.0	0.0	0.0
	2010	15.2	15.2	14.1	1.1	0.0	0.0	0.0
Northern Mariana Islands - Îles Mariannes du Nord	1990	63.1	63.1	61.9	1.2	0.0	0.0	0.0
Palau - Palaos	2000	37.7	39.1	39.0	0.2	-1.5	-1.5	0.0
	2005	21.6	23.7	23.4	0.3	-2.1	-2.1	0.0
	2010	26.3	26.3	25.6	0.7	0.0	0.0	0.0
Papua New Guinea - Papouasie-Nouvelle-Guinée	1990	474.9	412.4	320.2	90.8	62.5	-15.3	77.8
	2000	357.0	275.2	270.4	4.9	81.9	72.7	9.2
	2005	263.9	266.9	244.9	22.4	-3.0	-3.6	0.6
	2010	1 256.5	511.4	440.7	70.7	745.1	749.3	-4.1
Samoa	1990	47.4	47.6	27.8	19.5	-0.1	-0.1	0.0
	2000	27.5	27.1	18.2	9.0	0.4	0.3	0.1
	2005	44.0	43.6	30.1	13.5	0.4	0.5	-0.1
	2010	147.8	147.5	89.4	58.1	0.3	0.8	-0.5
Solomon Islands - Îles Salomon	1990	46.2	45.7	31.1	14.2	0.5	0.5	0.0
	2000	69.5	68.3	20.8	46.2	1.2	1.2	0.0
	2005	186.8	198.5	172.3	26.1	-11.7	-11.7	0.0
	2010	399.7	340.5	296.4	44.5	59.2	24.2	35.0
Tokelau - Tokélaou	1990	4.8	4.8	4.4	0.4	0.0	0.0	0.0
	2000	3.5	3.5	3.4	0.1	0.0	0.0	0.0
	2005	16.0	16.0	15.9	0.1	0.0	0.0	0.0
	2010	14.6	14.6	14.5	0.1	0.0	0.0	0.0
Tonga	1990	29.6	29.8	24.2	5.4	-0.2	-0.2	0.0
	2000	18.9	18.8	14.9	4.0	0.0	0.0	0.0
	2005	32.4	32.0	24.8	7.2	0.4	0.4	0.0
	2010	70.8	70.5	57.6	12.8	0.3	0.7	-0.3
Tuvalu	1990	5.1	5.1	4.8	0.3	0.0	0.0	0.0
	2000	4.0	4.0	3.8	0.2	0.0	0.0	0.0
	2005	9.2	9.2	5.9	3.3	0.0	0.0	0.0
	2010	13.3	13.3	13.0	0.3	0.0	0.0	0.0
Vanuatu	1990	54.1	49.5	42.1	7.5	4.6	4.6	0.0
	2000	45.2	45.8	28.3	17.5	-0.7	0.0	-0.7
	2005	40.3	39.5	33.4	6.1	0.8	0.8	0.0
	2010	110.4	108.3	107.5	0.8	2.1	2.5	-0.5
Wallis and Futuna Islands - Îles Wallis-et-Futuna	1990	3.9	0.9	0.0	0.9	3.0	3.0	0.0
	2000	53.3	52.1	52.1	0.0	1.2	1.2	0.0
	2005	69.0	72.0	71.7	0.4	-3.0	-3.0	0.0
	2010	126.0	127.4	123.1	4.3	-1.4	-1.4	0.0
Developing economies: Oceania n.e.s. - Économies en développement : Océanie n.d.a. (6)	*1990*	*(e)62.4*	*(e)62.4*	*(e)61.9*	*(e)0.1*	*0.0*	*0.0*	*0.0*
	2000	*(e)59.5*	*(e)64.7*	*(e)64.0*	*(e)0.7*	*-5.2*	*-5.2*	*0.0*
	2005	*(e)168.5*	*(e)163.7*	*(e)95.1*	*(e)66.9*	*4.9*	*4.9*	*0.0*
	2010	*(e)293.7*	*(e)286.9*	*(e)253.2*	*(e)33.7*	*6.8*	*6.8*	*0.0*
Developing economies n.e.s. - Économies en développement n.d.a. (6)	*1990*	*(e)6 213.6*	*(e)5 849.7*	*(e)5 140.0*	*(e)665.6*	*363.9*	*351.9*	*0.0*
	2000	*(e)9 216.6*	*(e)8 950.0*	*(e)8 071.0*	*(e)1 004.5*	*266.6*	*266.6*	*0.0*
	2005	*(e)14 677.0*	*(e)14 251.0*	*(e)11 894.8*	*(e)1 685.0*	*426.0*	*379.5*	*46.5*
	2010	*(e)28 404.9*	*(e)27 502.7*	*(e)24 260.5*	*(e)2 422.0*	*902.2*	*229.3*	*370.8*
Transition economies - ☐ Économies en transition	**1990**	**72.4**	**177.9**	**165.5**	**12.4**	**-105.6**	**-83.7**	**-17.2**
	2000	**5 249.7**	**4 581.5**	**2 750.9**	**1 715.8**	**668.1**	**203.3**	**464.8**
	2005	**5 913.2**	**5 293.2**	**3 300.6**	**1 603.3**	**620.1**	**188.0**	**65.4**
	2010	**11 018.9**	**6 632.9**	**3 123.2**	**3 017.0**	**4 386.1**	**657.2**	**3 757.2**
Albania - Albanie	1990	11.1	11.1	9.0	2.0	0.0	0.0	0.0
	2000	316.4	317.9	141.9	175.0	-1.5	-1.1	-0.4
	2005	426.5	319.1	178.2	131.7	107.3	10.3	74.3
	2010	382.2	340.7	226.7	101.7	41.5	-0.5	43.7

For sources and notes, see end of table.

Pour les sources et les notes, se reporter à la fin du tableau.

Region, country or territory / Régions, pays ou territoires	Year / Année	Total official net (1) / Total secteur officiel net (1)	Total ODA Net (2) / APD totale nette (2)			Total OOF Net (3) / Flux AASP nets (3)		
			Total donors (4) / Tous donneurs (4)	DAC bilateral donors / Donneurs bilatéraux du CAD	Multilateral donors / Donneurs multilatéraux	Total donors / Tous donneurs	DAC bilateral donors / Donneurs bilatéraux du CAD	Multilateral donors / Donneurs multilatéraux
		Millions of dollars / Millions de dollars						
Armenia - Arménie	2000	232.8	215.9	139.4	75.6	16.9	2.5	14.4
	2005	159.8	170.3	126.4	43.1	-10.6	0.0	-10.6
	2010	524.0	342.8	205.8	133.5	181.2	19.9	161.3
Azerbaijan - Azerbaïdjan	2000	204.8	139.1	70.7	60.2	65.7	42.4	23.3
	2005	332.1	216.5	95.6	91.9	115.6	71.6	3.1
	2010	435.7	159.1	60.5	76.3	276.6	-25.1	305.9
Belarus - Bélarus	2005	72.5	57.8	33.8	13.2	14.7	0.2	5.3
	2010	219.3	137.9	80.7	36.8	81.4	12.9	68.4
Bosnia and Herzegovina - Bosnie-Herzégovine	2000	775.9	737.9	.452.6	266.2	37.9	18.5	19.5
	2005	578.2	548.5	265.6	241.1	29.7	-0.7	30.4
	2010	554.9	510.4	243.7	238.5	44.6	-8.4	53.0
Croatia - Croatie	2000	154.9	65.5	42.5	22.7	89.4	-18.1	107.5
	2005	250.9	123.5	62.6	57.6	127.5	-11.7	139.2
	2010	680.0	150.7	36.9	109.2	529.2	22.6	506.6
Georgia - Géorgie	2000	230.9	169.2	120.4	42.9	61.8	2.5	59.3
	2005	378.8	292.1	183.3	99.7	86.7	1.0	23.5
	2010	837.6	625.2	350.0	248.6	212.4	-7.1	225.4
Kazakhstan	2000	277.7	189.2	160.6	14.4	88.5	-12.1	100.6
	2005	-362.4	228.9	149.9	25.4	-591.2	172.7	-860.5
	2010	2 289.4	223.9	95.3	61.2	2 065.5	445.4	1 633.1
Kyrgyzstan - Kirghizistan	2000	211.5	214.7	91.9	111.6	-3.2	0.0	-3.2
	2005	329.3	267.9	125.3	84.1	61.5	-0.4	7.2
	2010	405.3	380.4	158.5	138.2	25.0	-0.4	25.4
Montenegro - Monténégro	2010	107.4	80.3	43.0	25.3	27.2	3.1	24.1
Republic of Moldova - République de Moldova	2000	121.3	122.5	61.6	51.1	-1.2	-2.4	1.2
	2005	138.6	169.1	84.5	76.5	-30.5	0.0	-40.7
	2010	525.3	470.4	90.4	347.9	54.9	5.9	49.8
Serbia and Montenegro - Serbie-et-Monténégro	2000	1 132.5	1 134.3	592.9	540.2	-1.8	-1.8	0.0
	2005	1 371.4	1 070.2	766.5	260.8	301.1	97.3	203.8
Serbia - Serbie	2010	1 119.2	659.9	313.1	335.9	459.3	9.1	450.2
SFR of Yugoslavia - RSF de Yougoslavie	1990	0.0	0.0	..	..	0.0	..	..
Tajikistan - Tadjikistan	2000	124.3	123.5	38.2	84.8	0.7	0.0	0.7
	2005	274.9	251.5	105.0	134.6	23.4	0.0	8.9
	2010	446.9	436.7	164.5	265.3	10.3	0.0	12.8
TFYR of Macedonia - LERY de Macédoine	2000	269.4	250.2	110.9	138.7	19.2	-5.9	25.1
	2005	277.8	227.3	165.4	54.6	50.5	-17.3	67.9
	2010	270.7	187.2	95.0	61.7	83.6	-2.2	85.8
Turkmenistan - Turkménistan	2000	196.9	35.3	9.9	5.7	161.6	138.0	23.6
	2005	26.7	30.4	11.9	7.0	-3.7	-28.5	-12.3
	2010	-22.2	44.7	11.4	16.0	-66.8	-63.5	-3.3
Ukraine	2005	792.2	411.7	236.0	138.3	380.5	-50.0	430.5
	2010	787.9	626.4	392.6	194.8	161.5	84.2	77.4
Uzbekistan - Ouzbékistan	2000	324.2	185.8	152.2	16.9	138.5	40.0	98.4
	2005	187.8	169.8	123.5	32.6	18.0	-58.8	58.3
	2010	279.4	230.9	84.3	107.3	48.6	44.4	4.2
Transition economies n.e.s. - Économies en transition n.d.a. (6)	*1990*	*(e)61.3*	*(e)166.8*	*(e)156.5*	*(e)10.3*	*-105.6*	*-83.7*	*-17.2*
	2000	*(e)676.3*	*(e)680.6*	*(e)565.3*	*(e)110.0*	*-4.4*	*0.8*	*-5.2*
	2005	*(e)678.0*	*(e)738.6*	*(e)587.3*	*(e)111.2*	*-60.6*	*2.3*	*-62.9*
	2010	*(e)1 175.9*	*(e)1 025.5*	*(e)470.7*	*(e)518.9*	*150.4*	*116.8*	*33.6*
Developed economies: America - Économies développées : Amérique	**1990**	**51.0**	**42.2**	**42.1**	**0.1**	**8.8**	**8.8**	**0.0**
Bermuda - Bermudes	1990	51.0	42.2	42.1	0.1	8.8	8.8	0.0
Developed economies: Asia - Économies développées : Asie	**1990**	**1 351.1**	**1 371.9**	**1 370.7**	**1.2**	**-20.8**	**-47.1**	**26.2**
Israel - Israël	1990	1 351.1	1 371.9	1 370.7	1.2	-20.8	-47.1	26.2

For sources and notes, see end of table.

Pour les sources et les notes, se reporter à la fin du tableau.

Region, country or territory / Régions, pays ou territoires	Year / Année	Total official net (1) Total secteur officiel net (1)	Total ODA Net (2) APD totale nette (2)			Total OOF Net (3) Flux AASP nets (3)		
			Total donors (4) Tous donneurs (4)	of which: / dont :		Total donors Tous donneurs	of which: / dont :	
				DAC bilateral donors Donneurs bilatéraux du CAD	Multilateral donors Donneurs multilatéraux		DAC bilateral donors Donneurs bilatéraux du CAD	Multilateral donors Donneurs multilatéraux
		Millions of dollars / Millions de dollars						
Developed economies: Europe - Économies développées : Europe	**1990**	**69.4**	**44.0**	**21.6**	**16.5**	**25.4**	**15.4**	**9.7**
	2000	**119.5**	**82.1**	**21.9**	**61.1**	**37.5**	**-1.9**	**39.4**
Cyprus - Chypre	1990	42.4	38.1	18.5	14.8	4.3	3.1	1.0
Gibraltar	1990	-0.8	0.6	0.6	..	-1.3	-1.3	..
Malta - Malte	1990	27.7	5.3	2.5	1.8	22.4	13.7	8.7
	2000	19.6	21.2	21.2	0.9	-1.6	-0.6	-1.1
Slovenia - Slovénie	2000	99.9	60.8	0.6	60.1	39.1	-1.4	40.5

Source:
OECD, OECD.Stat Extracts

Notes:

(1)   Total Official Flows: The sum of Official Development Assistance (ODA) and Other Official Flows (OOF) represents the total net disbursements by the official sector at large to the recipient country.

(2)   The Total Official Development Assistance (ODA) includes grants or loans to countries and territories on the DAC List of Developing Countries which are:
- undertaken by the official sector;
- with promotion of economic development and welfare as the main objective;
- at concessional financial terms (if a loan, have a grant element of at least 25%).

(3)   The Other Official Flows (OOF) are transactions by the official sector whose main objective is other than development motivated, or, if development motivated, whose grant element is below the 25% threshold which would make them eligible to be recorded as ODA. The main classes of transactions included here are official export credits, official sector equity and portfolio investment, and debt reorganisation undertaken by the official sector at non-concessional terms (irrespective of the nature or the identity of the original creditor).

(4)   Total Donors is the sum of the three following donor types:
- DAC Bilateral Donors: The Development Assistance Committee (DAC) is the Committee of the OECD which deals with development co-operation matters. It consists of 23 Member countries.
- Multilateral Donors (i.e. AfDB, IBRD, IMF, UNDP).
- Other Bilateral Donors: the Non-DAC Bilateral Donors (i.e Hungary, Lithuania, Turkey)

(5)   Developing economies is the sum of:
- Developing economies: Africa
- Developing economies: America
- Developing economies: Asia
- Developing economies: Oceania
- Developing economies n.e.s.

(6)   "n.e.s." refers to Unallocated or Unspecified economies, i.e. a group of recipient economies and not an individual recipient economy.

Source :
OCDE, OECD.Stat Extracts

Notes :

(1)   Apports totaux du secteur public: il s'agit du total de l'aide publique au développement (APD) et des autres apports du secteur public (AASP). Cet agrégat correspond aux versements nets effectués par le secteur public dans son ensemble aux pays bénéficiaires considérés.

(2)   Par aide publique au développement (APD), on entend l'ensemble des apports de ressources qui sont fournis aux pays en développement et aux institutions multilatérales par des organismes officiels, y compris les collectivités locales, ou par leurs agents d'exécution et qui, considérés au niveau de chaque opération, répondent aux critères suivants :
a) être dispensés dans le but essentiel de favoriser le développement économique et l'amélioration du niveau de vie dans les pays en développement ; et
b) revêtir un caractère de faveur et comporter un élément de libéralité d'au moins 25%.

(3)   Autres apports du secteur public (AASP) : il s'agit des opérations du secteur public dont le but essentiel est autre que le développement ou qui, tout en visant à favoriser le développement, sont assorties d'un élément de libéralité inférieur au seuil de 25 pour cent à partir duquel elles auraient pu être notifiées comme de l'APD. Les principales catégories d'opérations couvertes dans les AASP sont les crédits publics à l'exportation, les prises de participation et les investissements de portefeuille du secteur public et le réaménagement de la dette effectué par le secteur public aux conditions du marché (et ce, quelle que soit la nature ou l'identité du créancier initial).

(4)   Tous Donneurs est la somme des 3 types de donneurs suivants :
- Donneurs Bilatéraux du CAD : Le Comité d'aide au développement (CAD) est la principale instance chargée, à l'OCDE, des questions relatives à la coopération avec les pays en développement. Le CAD regroupe 23 pays membres.
- Donneurs Multilatéraux (i.e. BAfD, BIRD, FMI, PNUD).
- Autres Donneurs Biletéraux : les Donneurs Bilatéraux non-membres du CAD (i.e. Hongrie, Lituanie, Turquie).

(5)   Économies en développement est la somme de :
- Économies en développement : Afrique
- Économies en développement : Amérique
- Économies en développement : Asie
- Économies en développement : Océanie
- Économies en développement n.d.a.

(6)   "n.d.a." se réfère à des économies "Non ventilées" ou "Non spécifiées", c-à-d un groupe d' économies bénéficiaires et non pas une économie bénéficiaire individuelle.

7

7.6.2 Official financial flows from bilateral and multilateral sources to developing economies by economic grouping

7.6.2 Flux financiers publics bilatéraux et multilatéraux à destination des économies en développement par groupements économiques

Economic grouping / Groupements économiques	Year / Année	Total official net (1) / Total secteur officiel net (1)	Total ODA Net (2) / APD totale nette (2)			Total OOF Net (3) / Flux AASP nets (3)		
			Total donors (4) / Tous donneurs (4)	of which: / dont :		Total donors / Tous donneurs	of which: / dont :	
				DAC bilateral donors / Donneurs bilatéraux du CAD	Multilateral donors / Donneurs multilatéraux		DAC bilateral donors / Donneurs bilatéraux du CAD	Multilateral donors / Donneurs multilatéraux
		Millions of dollars / Millions de dollars						
DEVELOPING ECONOMIES - ÉCONOMIES EN DÉVELOPPEMENT (5)	1990	75 082.2	56 896.9	36 874.1	12 578.6	18 185.2	8 065.1	10 128.2
	2000	48 161.0	45 112.4	33 422.6	10 902.7	3 048.6	-5 196.4	8 245.0
	2005	106 618.2	103 356.7	79 594.6	21 142.3	3 261.6	2 794.9	439.1
	2010	156 447.0	123 552.8	87 554.2	31 312.3	32 894.1	4 736.6	27 852.3
Developing economies excluding China - Économies en développement sans la Chine	1990	62 846.0	46 444.0	28 776.1	10 759.1	16 402.0	6 871.7	9 550.3
	2000	34 905.1	31 604.5	21 734.9	9 045.2	3 300.5	-3 284.9	6 585.4
	2005	83 367.6	80 960.1	61 781.6	18 117.4	2 407.5	3 204.5	-824.6
	2010	113 939.3	85 033.6	56 539.5	27 335.0	28 905.7	2 970.9	25 931.8
Developing economies excluding LDCs - Économies en développement sans les PMA	1990	48 798.4	31 853.9	20 440.9	5 209.5	16 944.5	7 020.1	9 942.9
	2000	23 890.1	21 068.2	15 332.6	5 151.2	2 821.9	-5 404.3	8 226.1
	2005	59 776.0	56 819.9	47 552.3	8 372.4	2 956.0	2 529.8	398.7
	2010	71 504.4	40 985.2	28 776.8	11 499.9	30 519.2	3 856.6	26 662.6
High-income developing economies - Économies en développement à revenu élevé	1990	11 581.5	4 128.9	2 794.4	199.8	7 452.7	2 853.9	4 711.7
	2000	2 331.3	1 036.8	499.0	330.5	1 294.5	-1 638.1	2 932.6
	2005	-1 098.4	1 416.5	702.7	684.1	-2 515.0	-1 033.3	-1 481.7
	2010	11 881.6	2 771.4	2 047.3	676.4	9 110.2	1 287.4	7 822.8
Middle-income developing economies - Économies en développement à revenu intermédiaire	1990	22 275.8	18 949.3	11 681.5	2 274.8	3 326.5	1 650.3	1 556.3
	2000	12 313.4	10 854.3	8 330.3	2 157.8	1 459.2	-3 916.9	5 376.1
	2005	15 699.5	14 653.6	10 912.8	3 184.3	1 046.0	-203.8	1 249.7
	2010	28 366.6	16 452.8	11 677.5	4 397.1	11 913.8	435.8	11 478.0
Low-income developing economies - Économies en développement à revenu faible	1990	32 224.7	25 337.8	15 707.2	8 852.6	6 887.0	3 203.5	3 710.5
	2000	21 317.7	21 322.0	14 073.4	6 996.9	-4.3	79.9	-84.2
	2005	70 668.9	66 503.0	51 648.5	14 329.4	4 165.9	3 490.6	647.7
	2010	76 007.7	65 851.6	42 914.7	22 151.2	10 156.1	2 290.0	7 863.1
Heavily indebted poor countries (IMF) - Pays pauvres très endettés (FMI)	1990	17 232.1	15 820.3	10 011.9	5 387.8	1 411.8	888.5	525.9
	2000	11 750.4	12 125.8	7 723.6	4 232.9	-375.4	-46.2	-329.2
	2005	26 919.6	27 340.4	17 354.6	9 712.0	-420.8	-92.1	-383.4
	2010	45 166.6	45 321.9	28 663.5	16 160.6	-155.3	-620.8	462.4
Landlocked developing countries - Pays en développement sans littoral	1990	7 165.1	6 981.7	4 176.8	2 635.9	183.4	87.9	94.4
	2000	7 793.7	7 447.6	4 858.1	2 470.5	346.2	11.6	334.6
	2005	14 509.9	15 050.6	9 317.3	5 371.7	-540.7	-33.2	-780.1
	2010	28 481.1	25 074.2	15 598.8	8 909.1	3 406.9	766.5	2 661.1
Small island developing States - Petits États insulaires en développement	1990	1 612.1	1 376.9	1 064.1	307.6	235.2	99.5	150.5
	2000	1 123.9	967.7	723.4	214.3	156.2	-5.8	162.0
	2005	1 461.1	1 547.3	1 210.3	310.1	-86.2	-31.8	-54.4
	2010	4 913.7	2 905.1	2 079.6	793.2	2 008.6	749.2	1 259.4
Least developed countries - Pays les moins avancés	*1990*	*17 344.1*	*16 622.5*	*9 800.7*	*6 119.8*	*721.6*	*687.6*	*35.6*
	2000	*12 175.6*	*12 248.1*	*7 673.1*	*4 334.2*	*-72.5*	*-70.8*	*-1.7*
	2005	*25 684.2*	*25 954.5*	*15 913.6*	*9 824.9*	*-270.3*	*-287.4*	*17.0*
	2010	*45 357.4*	*44 694.5*	*28 465.5*	*15 725.7*	*662.9*	*158.6*	*501.3*
Africa and Haiti - Afrique et Haïti	1990	13 532.9	12 872.2	7 821.2	4 526.1	660.6	634.4	28.9
	2000	9 067.4	9 190.1	5 908.2	3 124.1	-122.7	-88.9	-33.8
	2005	18 946.6	19 446.3	11 521.0	7 779.3	-499.7	-266.8	-232.9
	2010	33 239.6	32 696.6	19 383.2	13 081.3	543.0	213.0	326.9
Asia - Asie	1990	3 539.3	3 483.3	1 794.4	1 512.6	56.0	48.2	6.7
	2000	2 890.5	2 841.3	1 650.6	1 109.2	49.2	16.5	32.7
	2005	6 188.1	5 949.6	3 935.7	1 944.0	238.6	-11.5	250.1
	2010	11 006.9	10 957.5	8 241.2	2 461.7	49.4	-91.0	140.3
Islands - Îles	1990	272.0	267.0	185.1	81.1	5.0	5.0	0.0
	2000	217.6	216.7	114.3	100.9	0.9	1.5	-0.6
	2005	549.5	558.7	457.0	101.6	-9.2	-9.1	-0.1
	2010	1 111.0	1 040.5	841.1	182.7	70.5	36.5	34.0

For sources and notes, see end of table.

Pour les sources et les notes, se reporter à la fin du tableau.

Economic grouping / Groupements économiques	Year / Année	Total official net (1) / Total secteur officiel net (1)	Total ODA Net (2) / APD totale nette (2)			Total OOF Net (3) / Flux AASP nets (3)		
			Total donors (4) / Tous donneurs (4)	DAC bilateral donors / Donneurs bilatéraux du CAD	Multilateral donors / Donneurs multilatéraux	Total donors / Tous donneurs	DAC bilateral donors / Donneurs bilatéraux du CAD	Multilateral donors / Donneurs multilatéraux
			Millions of dollars / Millions de dollars					
Major petroleum and gas exporters - Principaux exportateurs de pétrole et de gaz	*1990*	*4 538.6*	*1 209.0*	*587.2*	*257.2*	*3 329.6*	*1 614.4*	*1 568.9*
	2000	*-477.5*	*1 084.9*	*633.2*	*309.0*	*-1 562.4*	*-1 226.9*	*-335.4*
	2005	*33 577.7*	*29 454.3*	*28 549.5*	*823.3*	*4 123.4*	*5 337.3*	*-1 213.8*
	2010	*4 412.9*	*4 832.3*	*3 283.8*	*1 530.3*	*-419.4*	*-948.2*	*528.8*
Africa - Afrique	1990	2 535.1	860.8	454.8	196.3	1 674.2	929.9	597.9
	2000	-176.1	675.5	347.7	258.8	-851.6	-427.2	-424.4
	2005	5 579.2	7 193.8	6 461.6	716.3	-1 614.5	-664.9	-949.6
	2010	2 308.6	2 507.1	1 159.2	1 343.0	-198.5	-58.1	-140.4
America - Amérique	1990	1 299.5	76.4	75.8	0.6	1 223.2	170.3	1 052.9
	2000	50.6	76.1	61.3	14.1	-25.5	-78.8	53.3
	2005	-469.1	50.3	21.0	28.8	-519.4	-110.0	-409.4
	2010	309.9	52.7	37.5	14.7	257.2	-140.1	397.2
Asia - Asie	1990	704.0	271.8	56.7	60.3	432.2	514.2	-82.0
	2000	-352.0	333.3	224.1	36.1	-685.3	-721.0	35.7
	2005	28 467.6	22 210.2	22 066.9	78.1	6 257.4	6 112.1	145.3
	2010	1 794.4	2 272.5	2 087.2	172.6	-478.1	-750.1	272.0
Major exporters of manufactured goods - Principaux exportateurs d'articles manufacturés	*1990*	*9 679.9*	*3 576.1*	*2 880.3*	*682.1*	*6 103.9*	*3 298.9*	*2 810.5*
	2000	*-129.2*	*2 396.3*	*1 929.6*	*469.4*	*-2 525.5*	*-4 773.5*	*2 248.1*
	2005	*2 686.7*	*1 853.3*	*1 653.4*	*141.1*	*833.5*	*405.6*	*427.9*
	2010	*8 761.0*	*1 107.8*	*1 008.8*	*43.9*	*7 653.2*	*2 385.2*	*5 268.0*
America - Amérique	1990	5 024.2	156.3	144.8	11.5	4 868.0	2 035.6	2 837.9
	2000	74.1	-57.8	-68.3	10.0	131.9	-710.7	842.6
	2005	-204.2	180.5	161.1	18.7	-384.7	-209.3	-175.4
	2010	5 487.6	471.1	421.1	48.8	5 016.5	918.1	4 098.4
Asia - Asie	1990	4 655.7	3 419.8	2 735.5	670.6	1 235.9	1 263.3	-27.4
	2000	-203.3	2 454.1	1 997.9	459.4	-2 657.3	-4 062.8	1 405.5
	2005	2 890.9	1 672.8	1 492.3	122.4	1 218.1	614.8	603.3
	2010	3 273.4	636.8	587.7	-4.9	2 636.7	1 467.1	1 169.6
Emerging economies - Économies émergentes	*1990*	*8 967.9*	*2 326.0*	*2 137.4*	*171.6*	*6 642.0*	*3 803.2*	*2 850.1*
	2000	*4 389.4*	*1 414.1*	*1 340.3*	*66.9*	*2 975.3*	*-2 368.3*	*5 343.6*
	2005	*591.7*	*996.0*	*704.8*	*279.5*	*-404.4*	*486.4*	*-890.8*
	2010	*11 727.2*	*1 185.8*	*868.2*	*309.5*	*10 541.4*	*2 323.4*	*8 218.0*
America - Amérique	1990	7 640.1	976.7	886.8	89.9	6 663.4	3 369.1	3 305.7
	2000	5 753.2	671.8	613.2	47.8	5 081.4	-495.7	5 577.1
	2005	-206.7	1 137.6	896.8	237.0	-1 344.3	-1 090.5	-253.8
	2010	11 376.3	1 195.1	983.3	205.0	10 181.2	1 900.7	8 280.5
Asia - Asie	1990	1 327.8	1 349.3	1 250.6	81.7	-21.5	434.1	-455.6
	2000	-1 363.9	742.3	727.1	19.2	-2 106.2	-1 872.6	-233.6
	2005	798.4	-141.5	-192.0	42.5	939.9	1 576.9	-637.0
	2010	350.9	-9.3	-115.1	104.5	360.2	422.8	-62.5
Newly industrialized Asian economies - Économies nouvellement industrialisées d'Asie	*1990*	*6 791.6*	*4 374.1*	*3 893.0*	*439.1*	*2 417.6*	*1 373.3*	*1 068.3*
	2000	*1 955.3*	*3 198.3*	*2 992.2*	*206.9*	*-1 243.0*	*-1 532.5*	*289.5*
	2005	*1 470.6*	*2 959.6*	*2 600.6*	*286.9*	*-1 489.0*	*-344.6*	*-1 144.4*
	2010	*3 265.9*	*1 914.4*	*1 326.4*	*590.8*	*1 351.6*	*442.1*	*909.5*
First tier - Première génération	1990	-283.1	123.4	77.5	21.5	-406.5	20.5	-427.0
Second tier - Deuxième génération	1990	7 074.8	4 250.7	3 815.5	417.7	2 824.1	1 352.8	1 495.3
	2000	1 955.3	3 198.3	2 992.2	206.9	-1 243.0	-1 532.5	289.5
	2005	1 470.6	2 959.6	2 600.6	286.9	-1 489.0	-344.6	-1 144.4
	2010	3 265.9	1 914.4	1 326.4	590.8	1 351.6	442.1	909.5

For sources and notes, see end of table.

Pour les sources et les notes, se reporter à la fin du tableau.

7

Economic grouping / Groupements économiques	Year / Année	Total official net (1) / Total secteur officiel net (1)	Total ODA Net (2) / APD totale nette (2)			Total OOF Net (3) / Flux AASP nets (3)		
			Total donors (4) / Tous donneurs (4)	of which: / dont : DAC bilateral donors / Donneurs bilatéraux du CAD	Multilateral donors / Donneurs multilatéraux	Total donors / Tous donneurs	of which: / dont : DAC bilateral donors / Donneurs bilatéraux du CAD	Multilateral donors / Donneurs multilatéraux
		Millions of dollars / Millions de dollars						
Developing economies: Africa - Économies en développement : Afrique	1990	29 138.0	26 187.1	15 826.4	6 126.3	2 950.9	850.9	1 950.3
	2000	14 191.3	15 466.2	10 396.8	4 708.4	-1 274.8	-343.5	-931.4
	2005	35 513.1	35 833.3	24 628.0	10 741.8	-320.2	-499.0	178.8
	2010	50 364.7	47 976.1	29 345.5	18 252.4	2 388.6	-715.3	3 100.8
Northern Africa excluding Sudan - Afrique septentrionale sans le Soudan	1990	8 217.6	8 038.1	4 081.3	268.0	179.4	-952.3	982.5
	2000	1 865.8	2 226.3	1 660.6	397.3	-360.5	100.5	-461.0
	2005	2 325.0	2 499.3	1 507.0	726.4	-174.4	-786.5	612.1
	2010	3 539.2	2 342.2	1 480.5	769.6	1 197.0	-95.5	1 292.5
Sub-Saharan Africa - Afrique subsaharienne	1990	20 001.2	17 246.2	10 904.7	5 805.2	2 755.0	1 797.4	957.1
	2000	11 293.1	12 208.4	7 888.5	4 140.2	-915.4	-450.8	-464.6
	2005	30 831.3	31 105.8	21 321.8	9 609.7	-274.6	201.9	-476.4
	2010	42 253.7	41 366.8	24 708.6	16 402.5	887.0	-750.8	1 634.7
Sub-Saharan Africa excluding South Africa - Afrique subsaharienne sans l'Afrique du Sud	1990	20 001.2	17 246.2	10 904.7	5 805.2	2 755.0	1 797.4	957.1
	2000	10 701.9	11 722.1	7 533.0	4 009.4	-1 020.2	-356.2	-663.9
	2005	30 099.0	30 415.6	20 855.8	9 386.2	-316.6	315.0	-631.6
	2010	40 350.6	40 336.2	23 887.0	16 195.3	14.4	-677.7	689.0
Developing economies: America - Économies en développement : Amérique	1990	13 525.1	5 189.4	4 146.4	1 032.0	8 335.7	3 729.7	4 634.3
	2000	10 364.7	4 837.7	3 858.4	940.8	5 527.0	-1 012.2	6 539.2
	2005	3 452.5	6 707.9	4 854.9	1 827.7	-3 255.4	-1 589.2	-1 666.3
	2010	26 355.0	10 718.3	7 856.0	2 830.6	15 636.6	2 657.9	12 978.7
Central America and Greater Caribbean Islands excluding Puerto Rico - Amérique centrale et Grandes Antilles sans Porto Rico	1990	7 302.3	2 430.1	2 074.9	348.1	4 872.2	2 093.5	2 801.2
	2000	2 179.0	1 749.7	1 214.4	521.3	429.4	-793.8	1 223.1
	2005	2 131.7	2 793.8	1 984.6	804.9	-662.2	-367.9	-294.2
	2010	15 049.7	6 102.1	4 419.6	1 658.4	8 947.5	1 661.0	7 286.6
Central America and Greater Caribbean Islands excluding Mexico and Puerto Rico - Amérique centrale et Grandes Antilles sans le Mexique et Porto Rico	1990	2 278.0	2 273.8	1 930.2	336.6	4.2	57.9	-36.7
	2000	2 104.9	1 807.4	1 282.7	511.3	297.5	-83.1	380.5
	2005	2 335.9	2 613.3	1 823.5	786.2	-277.5	-158.6	-118.9
	2010	9 562.1	5 631.1	3 998.5	1 609.6	3 931.0	742.9	3 188.1
South America and Central America - Amérique du Sud et Amérique centrale	1990	11 860.0	3 870.5	3 169.0	694.1	7 989.5	3 636.0	4 364.7
	2000	8 641.1	3 301.9	2 576.4	705.3	5 339.2	-924.9	6 264.1
	2005	1 639.8	4 915.6	3 661.8	1 248.9	-3 275.7	-1 633.1	-1 642.7
	2010	19 110.5	5 503.7	4 139.1	1 351.6	13 606.8	2 212.6	11 394.2
South America excluding Brazil - Amérique du Sud sans le Brésil	1990	4 719.9	1 879.9	1 427.4	451.0	2 840.0	891.8	1 948.2
	2000	2 820.2	1 637.2	1 342.5	283.3	1 183.0	-615.7	1 798.7
	2005	75.2	2 512.9	1 922.0	586.6	-2 437.7	-783.9	-1 653.8
	2010	4 808.7	2 250.6	1 613.7	628.6	2 558.2	1 179.7	1 378.4
Developing economies: Asia - Économies en développement : Asie	1990	24 710.4	18 298.2	10 546.2	4 600.1	6 412.3	3 072.7	3 481.1
	2000	13 501.6	15 042.5	10 383.9	4 146.7	-1 541.0	-4 175.8	2 634.8
	2005	51 817.9	45 403.9	37 242.6	6 702.9	6 414.0	4 514.8	1 871.6
	2010	48 465.7	35 337.5	24 325.9	7 555.8	13 128.3	1 775.1	11 353.1
Eastern and South-Eastern Asia excluding China - Asie orientale et Asie du Sud-Est sans la Chine	1990	7 362.2	4 929.6	4 174.8	712.8	2 432.6	1 387.7	1 067.9
	2000	4 601.8	5 951.9	4 946.7	1 001.0	-1 350.2	-1 684.9	334.8
	2005	5 030.5	6 347.3	4 818.6	1 410.8	-1 316.9	-217.4	-1 099.5
	2010	10 075.7	7 029.4	4 707.2	2 297.9	3 046.4	1 058.1	1 988.3
Southern Asia excluding India - Asie méridionale sans l'Inde	1990	4 992.5	4 665.9	2 566.9	2 096.5	326.6	-78.4	406.3
	2000	2 218.3	2 874.9	1 829.9	1 010.6	-656.7	-713.8	57.1
	2005	8 872.4	7 631.3	4 929.0	2 463.8	1 241.1	817.9	395.6
	2010	12 381.7	12 615.5	9 838.5	2 378.9	-233.8	-753.3	519.5

For sources and notes, see next page.

Pour les sources et les notes, se reporter à la page suivante.

Source:
OECD, *OECD.Stat Extracts*

Notes:
- The groupings presented in this table do not include "n.e.s." recipient countries.

(1) Total Official Flows: The sum of Official Development Assistance (ODA) and Other Official Flows (OOF) represents the total net disbursements by the official sector at large to the recipient country.

(2) The Total Official Development Assistance (ODA) includes grants or loans to countries and territories on the DAC List of Developing Countries which are:
- undertaken by the official sector;
- with promotion of economic development and welfare as the main objective;
- at concessional financial terms (if a loan, have a grant element of at least 25%).

(3) The Other Official Flows (OOF) are transactions by the official sector whose main objective is other than development motivated, or, if development motivated, whose grant element is below the 25% threshold which would make them eligible to be recorded as ODA. The main classes of transactions included here are official export credits, official sector equity and portfolio investment, and debt reorganisation undertaken by the official sector at non-concessional terms (irrespective of the nature or the identity of the original creditor).

(4) Total Donors is the sum of the three following donor types:
- DAC Bilateral Donors: The Development Assistance Committee (DAC) is the Committee of the OECD which deals with development co-operation matters. It consists of 23 Member countries.
- Multilateral Donors (i.e. AfDB, IBRD, IMF, UNDP).
- Other Bilateral Donors: the Non-DAC Bilateral Donors (i.e Hungary, Lithuania, Turkey)

(5) Developing economies is the sum of:
- Developing economies: Africa
- Developing economies: America
- Developing economies: Asia
- Developing economies: Oceania
- Developing economies n.e.s.

Source :
OCDE, *OECD.Stat Extracts*

Notes :
- Les groupements présentés dans ce tableau n'incluent pas les pays bénéficiaires "n.d.a.".

(1) Apports totaux du secteur public: il s'agit du total de l'aide publique au développement (APD) et des autres apports du secteur public (AASP). Cet agrégat correspond aux versements nets effectués par le secteur public dans son ensemble aux pays bénéficiaires considérés.

(2) Par aide publique au développement (APD), on entend l'ensemble des apports de ressources qui sont fournis aux pays en développement et aux institutions multilatérales par des organismes officiels, y compris les collectivités locales, ou par leurs agents d'exécution et qui, considérés au niveau de chaque opération, répondent aux critères suivants :
a) être dispensés dans le but essentiel de favoriser le développement économique et l'amélioration du niveau de vie dans les pays en développement ; et
b) revêtir un caractère de faveur et comporter un élément de libéralité d'au moins 25%.

(3) Autres apports du secteur public (AASP) : il s'agit des opérations du secteur public dont le but essentiel est autre que le développement ou qui, tout en visant à favoriser le développement, sont assorties d'un élément de libéralité inférieur au seuil de 25 pour cent à partir duquel elles auraient pu être notifiées comme de l'APD. Les principales catégories d'opérations couvertes dans les AASP sont les crédits publics à l'exportation, les prises de participation et les investissements de portefeuille du secteur public et le réaménagement de la dette effectué par le secteur public aux conditions du marché (et ce, quelle que soit la nature ou l'identité du créancier initial).

(4) Tous Donneurs est la somme des 3 types de donneurs suivants :
- Donneurs Bilatéraux du CAD : Le Comité d'aide au développement (CAD) est la principale instance chargée, à l'OCDE, des questions relatives à la coopération avec les pays en développement. Le CAD regroupe 23 pays membres.
- Donneurs Multilatéraux (i.e. BAfD, BIRD, FMI, PNUD).
- Autres Donneurs Bilétéraux : les Donneurs Bilatéraux non-membres du CAD (i.e. Hongrie, Lituanie, Turquie).

(5) Économies en développement est la somme de :
- Économies en développement : Afrique
- Économies en développement : Amérique
- Économies en développement : Asie
- Économies en développement : Océanie
- Économies en développement n.d.a.

7

	Total long-term debt (1) / Dette totale à long terme (1)	Public and publicly guaranteed debt (2) / Dette publique et garantie par l'état (2)									Private non-guaranteed debt (5) / Dette privée non garantie (5)
		Total creditors / Total créanciers	Official creditors (3) / Créanciers publics (3)					Private creditors (4) / Créanciers privés (4)			
			Total	Bilateral / Bilatéraux			Multilateral / Multilatéraux	Total	Bonds / Obligations	Commercial banks / Banques commerciales	
				Total	DAC CAD	OPEC OPEP					
	Millions of dollars / Millions de dollars										
1980											
Debt outstanding	366 377	309 125	140 815	96 767	68 531	13 743	44 048	168 310	12 676	109 472	57 252
Disbursments (6)	85 197	67 517	24 024	15 602	10 439	2 479	8 422	43 493	1 573	28 407	17 680
Debt service (7)	62 006	46 475	10 436	6 779	4 946	872	3 657	36 038	1 404	24 897	15 531
Principal repayments	34 609	24 935	5 655	4 184	2 930	525	1 471	19 279	500	12 141	9 675
Interest payments	27 397	21 540	4 781	2 595	2 016	347	2 186	16 759	904	12 756	5 857
Net transfers on debt (8)	23 190	21 042	13 588	8 823	5 493	1 606	4 765	7 454	169	3 510	2 148
1990											
Dette totale	961 787	905 658	505 210	308 920	209 326	18 380	196 290	400 448	97 364	196 392	56 129
Décaissements (6)	95 678	79 625	45 284	19 141	16 306	572	26 143	34 340	3 862	13 507	16 053
Service de la dette (7)	105 496	95 232	39 018	17 759	13 423	1 123	21 259	56 214	8 389	29 113	10 264
Remboursement du principal	60 772	54 704	21 827	10 562	7 544	871	11 265	32 876	4 367	15 145	6 069
Paiement des intérêts	44 724	40 529	17 191	7 197	5 879	253	9 994	23 337	4 022	13 969	4 195
Transfers nets (8)	-9 818	-15 608	6 266	1 382	2 883	-551	4 884	-21 874	-4 527	-15 607	5 789
2000											
Debt outstanding	1 583 318	1 132 781	650 766	346 408	252 367	13 868	304 358	482 015	301 362	120 367	450 537
Disbursments (6)	214 283	130 067	47 930	16 479	13 860	456	31 451	82 137	54 996	16 975	84 215
Debt service (7)	286 092	165 505	67 023	31 730	24 766	791	35 294	98 481	54 163	30 991	120 587
Principal repayments	199 125	107 076	43 339	22 120	16 890	624	21 219	63 736	31 104	22 614	92 050
Interest payments	86 967	58 429	23 684	9 610	7 877	167	14 074	34 745	23 058	8 378	28 537
Net transfers on debt (8)	-71 809	-35 437	-19 093	-15 251	-10 906	-335	-3 843	-16 344	833	-14 017	-36 371
2005											
Dette totale	1 615 183	1 145 277	642 453	298 518	244 194	13 142	343 935	502 825	358 582	107 185	469 906
Décaissements (6)	267 972	124 498	41 869	11 008	7 641	835	30 861	82 629	58 862	20 288	143 474
Service de la dette (7)	292 648	168 139	68 561	35 366	30 623	865	33 196	99 578	64 976	25 719	124 509
Remboursement du principal	222 241	114 653	48 054	24 468	21 014	728	23 586	66 599	37 726	21 281	107 588
Paiement des intérêts	70 407	53 486	20 507	10 897	9 609	137	9 610	32 979	27 251	4 438	16 921
Transfers nets (8)	-24 676	-43 641	-26 692	-24 358	-22 982	-30	-2 334	-16 948	-6 115	-5 431	18 965
2007											
Debt outstanding	1 871 361	1 163 166	613 394	273 855	211 918	14 155	339 539	549 772	407 131	113 182	708 194
Disbursments (6)	433 407	140 709	53 990	13 999	7 475	1 291	39 991	86 720	61 723	21 542	292 698
Debt service (7)	356 882	163 613	66 799	31 561	24 158	849	35 238	96 814	66 057	23 103	193 269
Principal repayments	271 637	110 240	48 561	24 852	18 928	683	23 709	61 679	37 660	17 973	161 397
Interest payments	85 245	53 373	18 238	6 709	5 230	166	11 529	35 135	28 396	5 130	31 872
Net transfers on debt (8)	76 525	-22 904	-12 809	-17 562	-16 684	443	4 753	-10 095	-4 334	-1 561	99 429
2008											
Dette totale	2 005 131	1 208 128	653 360	293 796	223 687	15 518	359 564	554 768	411 891	117 348	797 003
Décaissements (6)	384 855	145 296	61 825	18 802	10 490	2 145	43 023	83 471	59 040	22 104	239 558
Service de la dette (7)	353 212	165 497	62 391	27 416	23 515	841	34 975	103 106	75 322	19 636	187 714
Remboursement du principal	267 181	114 377	45 353	21 369	18 484	664	23 983	69 025	47 438	14 972	152 804
Paiement des intérêts	86 030	51 120	17 039	6 047	5 031	178	10 992	34 081	27 884	4 665	34 911
Transfers nets (8)	31 643	-20 201	-566	-8 615	-13 025	1 304	8 048	-19 635	-16 282	2 468	51 844
2009											
Debt outstanding	2 084 491	1 276 565	705 129	307 381	221 789	16 202	397 748	571 437	430 809	111 810	807 926
Disbursments (6)	357 307	169 920	84 511	24 796	11 004	1 503	59 715	85 409	62 372	16 773	187 387
Debt service (7)	347 590	145 728	57 952	25 760	21 500	923	32 192	87 776	52 189	27 480	201 861
Principal repayments	269 044	98 423	42 552	19 744	16 769	708	22 808	55 871	25 696	23 182	170 621
Interest payments	78 546	47 305	15 400	6 016	4 732	215	9 384	31 905	26 492	4 298	31 241
Net transfers on debt (8)	9 717	9 717	24 192	26 559	-964	-10 497	27 523	-2 367	10 183	-10 706	-14 474
2010											
Dette totale	2 248 729	1 364 364	746 451	313 369	217 024	16 179	433 082	617 912	467 142	122 721	884 365
Décaissements (6)	467 048	212 672	93 719	31 944	12 123	1 903	61 776	118 953	76 920	32 443	254 375
Service de la dette (7)	348 340	146 838	59 354	28 105	21 995	1 317	31 249	87 484	58 381	20 364	201 502
Remboursement du principal	266 926	99 120	44 251	20 980	17 494	1 056	23 272	54 869	30 049	17 168	167 806
Paiement des intérêts	81 414	47 718	15 102	7 125	4 501	261	7 977	32 615	28 332	3 196	33 696
Transfers nets (8)	118 708	65 834	34 366	3 839	-9 872	586	30 527	31 469	18 539	12 079	52 873

For sources and notes, see end of table 7.7.G.

Pour les sources et les notes, se reporter à la fin du tableau 7.7.G.

7.7.B External long-term debt by lending source
Developing economies:
Africa

7.7.B Dette extérieure à long terme par catégories de prêt
Économies en développement :
Afrique

	Total long-term debt (1) — Dette totale à long terme (1)	Public and publicly guaranteed debt (2) — Dette publique et garantie par l'état (2)									Private non-guaranteed debt (5) — Dette privée non garantie (5)
		Total creditors — Total créanciers	Official creditors (3) — Créanciers publics (3)					Private creditors (4) — Créanciers privés (4)			
			Total	Bilateral / Bilatéraux			Multilateral — Multilatéraux	Total	Bonds — Obligations	Commercial banks — Banques commerciales	
				Total	DAC CAD	OPEC OPEP					
1980											
Debt outstanding	90 299	85 137	47 338	35 672	20 855	7 813	11 666	37 799	1 357	16 435	5 162
Disbursments (6)	19 421	17 985	7 888	5 721	4 001	1 265	2 166	10 098	119	3 922	1 436
Debt service (7)	11 561	10 354	2 529	1 773	1 237	276	756	7 826	141	3 922	1 207
Principal repayments	6 512	5 806	1 249	932	627	96	317	4 557	57	1 995	706
Interest payments	5 049	4 548	1 280	841	610	180	439	3 269	84	1 928	501
Net transfers on debt (8)	7 861	7 631	5 359	3 949	2 764	989	1 410	2 272	-22	0	230
1990											
Dette totale	235 385	228 691	157 999	107 383	77 559	11 464	50 616	70 692	1 721	24 622	6 694
Décaissements (6)	21 528	20 809	12 158	5 502	4 701	204	6 656	8 651	0	1 032	719
Service de la dette (7)	23 034	21 957	9 982	5 725	4 755	294	4 257	11 975	231	3 782	1 078
Remboursement du principal	14 680	14 038	5 402	3 013	2 521	210	2 389	8 636	108	2 517	643
Paiement des intérêts	8 354	7 919	4 580	2 712	2 234	84	1 868	3 339	123	1 265	435
Transfers nets (8)	-1 507	-1 148	2 176	-223	-54	-90	2 399	-3 324	-231	-2 750	-359
2000											
Debt outstanding	250 363	235 780	196 061	123 727	78 700	9 352	72 334	39 719	10 630	15 351	14 582
Disbursments (6)	14 550	11 265	6 502	1 724	1 298	271	4 778	4 764	765	2 514	3 284
Debt service (7)	22 271	20 184	11 334	6 224	4 421	340	5 109	8 850	1 580	4 155	2 087
Principal repayments	15 337	13 752	6 957	3 714	2 456	256	3 243	6 795	903	3 425	1 585
Interest payments	6 934	6 432	4 377	2 510	1 965	84	1 867	2 055	677	730	502
Net transfers on debt (8)	-7 721	-8 918	-4 832	-4 500	-3 123	-69	-332	-4 087	-815	-1 641	1 197
2005											
Dette totale	251 394	236 995	192 413	100 799	81 959	8 748	91 615	44 582	14 363	21 927	14 399
Décaissements (6)	23 691	19 041	10 045	2 268	1 067	468	7 777	8 996	1 499	6 872	4 650
Service de la dette (7)	30 770	28 968	20 970	15 032	13 646	488	5 938	7 998	971	5 026	1 802
Remboursement du principal	20 688	19 437	13 130	8 730	7 565	412	4 400	6 307	178	4 455	1 251
Paiement des intérêts	10 082	9 530	7 840	6 301	6 081	76	1 538	1 691	793	571	551
Transfers nets (8)	-7 079	-9 927	-10 925	-12 764	-12 579	-20	1 839	998	528	1 846	2 848
2007											
Debt outstanding	214 109	191 758	147 766	77 704	57 155	9 609	70 062	43 992	18 765	19 252	22 352
Disbursments (6)	33 255	24 223	13 393	4 179	1 369	589	9 214	10 830	4 423	5 979	9 032
Debt service (7)	27 698	22 793	12 919	7 315	5 232	393	5 604	9 874	2 338	5 656	4 905
Principal repayments	21 323	17 176	9 322	5 583	3 860	298	3 739	7 854	1 472	4 757	4 147
Interest payments	6 375	5 617	3 597	1 733	1 372	94	1 865	2 020	866	899	757
Net transfers on debt (8)	5 557	1 430	474	-3 136	-3 863	196	3 610	956	2 084	323	4 128
2008											
Dette totale	216 206	195 864	151 007	78 483	55 231	9 938	72 525	44 856	18 009	21 614	20 342
Décaissements (6)	21 449	18 360	12 778	5 015	2 099	656	7 764	5 582	0	5 120	3 089
Service de la dette (7)	22 294	17 688	11 245	5 457	4 247	408	5 788	6 443	1 649	3 500	4 606
Remboursement du principal	16 293	12 463	7 940	4 006	3 119	313	3 934	4 523	640	2 804	3 830
Paiement des intérêts	6 001	5 225	3 305	1 451	1 129	96	1 854	1 920	1 009	696	776
Transfers nets (8)	-845	672	1 533	-442	-2 149	248	1 975	-861	-1 649	1 619	-1 517
2009											
Debt outstanding	233 092	210 387	163 659	83 606	57 736	9 945	80 053	46 729	19 027	21 960	22 704
Disbursments (6)	28 944	24 785	17 305	5 909	2 018	483	11 396	7 481	2 200	3 961	4 159
Debt service (7)	21 874	17 440	10 289	5 157	3 733	445	5 132	7 151	1 586	4 631	4 435
Principal repayments	16 352	12 718	7 224	3 789	2 773	342	3 434	5 495	608	4 102	3 634
Interest payments	5 522	4 721	3 065	1 367	959	103	1 698	1 656	978	528	801
Net transfers on debt (8)	7 070	7 346	7 016	752	-1 715	39	6 263	330	614	-669	-276
2010											
Dette totale	235 903	211 307	163 816	79 123	46 510	9 808	84 693	47 491	21 552	20 340	24 596
Décaissements (6)	33 402	28 923	20 926	9 680	1 919	755	11 246	7 997	4 827	2 276	4 480
Service de la dette (7)	21 441	16 038	10 103	5 697	4 196	514	4 407	5 935	1 179	3 976	5 403
Remboursement du principal	15 475	11 709	7 324	4 271	3 173	398	3 053	4 385	23	3 685	3 766
Paiement des intérêts	5 966	4 329	2 779	1 426	1 022	115	1 353	1 550	1 157	291	1 637
Transfers nets (8)	11 961	12 885	10 823	3 983	-2 277	242	6 839	2 062	3 647	-1 700	-924

Millions of dollars / Millions de dollars

For sources and notes, see end of table 7.7.G.

Pour les sources et les notes, se reporter à la fin du tableau 7.7.G.

7.7.C External long-term debt by lending source
Developing economies:
America

7.7.C Dette extérieure à long terme par catégories de prêt
Économies en développement :
Amérique

	Total long-term debt (1) Dette totale à long terme (1)	Public and publicly guaranteed debt (2) / Dette publique et garantie par l'état (2)									Private non-guaranteed debt (5) Dette privée non garantie (5)
		Total creditors Total créanciers	Official creditors (3) / Créanciers publics (3)					Private creditors (4) / Créanciers privés (4)			
			Total	Bilateral / Bilatéraux			Multilateral Multilatéraux	Total	Bonds Obligations	Commercial banks Banques commerciales	
				Total	DAC CAD	OPEC OPEP					
	Millions of dollars / Millions de dollars										
1980											
Debt outstanding	172 968	130 521	31 057	16 929	12 991	1 240	14 128	99 464	9 599	76 682	42 447
Disbursements (6)	43 969	31 009	6 423	3 462	2 230	506	2 961	24 586	1 219	19 937	12 960
Debt service (7)	38 537	27 148	3 910	2 196	1 695	111	1 714	23 238	1 128	18 776	11 389
Principal repayments	21 175	14 215	2 134	1 421	1 110	48	713	12 081	401	9 332	6 960
Interest payments	17 362	12 933	1 776	775	585	63	1 001	11 157	727	9 444	4 429
Net transfers on debt (8)	5 432	3 861	2 513	1 266	535	395	1 247	1 348	92	1 161	1 571
1990											
Dette totale	352 866	327 848	121 469	61 499	48 108	1 742	59 970	206 378	75 976	101 883	25 018
Décaissements (6)	27 731	23 033	13 183	4 198	3 245	211	8 986	9 850	1 938	4 803	4 698
Service de la dette (7)	36 600	32 124	11 950	3 075	2 368	182	8 875	20 174	4 406	11 917	4 476
Remboursement du principal	18 470	16 255	6 453	1 702	1 215	133	4 751	9 803	2 008	5 219	2 215
Paiement des intérêts	18 130	15 869	5 498	1 373	1 153	49	4 124	10 371	2 398	6 698	2 261
Transfers nets (8)	-8 869	-9 091	1 233	1 123	876	29	110	-10 324	-2 468	-7 113	222
2000											
Debt outstanding	639 102	397 381	141 183	47 004	36 397	833	94 179	256 198	216 334	31 404	241 722
Disbursments (6)	116 405	58 503	16 250	2 880	2 210	39	13 371	42 252	35 022	6 484	57 903
Debt service (7)	158 123	82 075	25 495	9 209	8 174	114	16 286	56 580	44 517	9 649	76 048
Principal repayments	110 058	52 034	16 920	7 001	6 431	80	9 920	35 114	26 575	6 935	58 024
Interest payments	48 065	30 041	8 575	2 209	1 743	34	6 367	21 466	17 942	2 715	18 024
Net transfers on debt (8)	-41 717	-23 572	-9 245	-6 330	-5 964	-75	-2 915	-14 327	-9 494	-3 166	-18 145
2005											
Dette totale	616 471	419 988	135 100	31 070	25 073	430	104 029	284 889	242 005	38 499	196 483
Décaissements (6)	102 363	57 693	12 878	2 342	1 904	140	10 536	44 815	38 150	6 169	44 670
Service de la dette (7)	118 245	68 607	22 340	6 880	5 900	47	15 460	46 267	36 384	8 901	49 638
Remboursement du principal	84 179	43 749	16 727	5 742	5 103	39	10 986	27 021	18 967	7 272	40 430
Paiement des intérêts	34 066	24 858	5 613	1 139	797	7	4 474	19 246	17 417	1 629	9 208
Transfers nets (8)	-15 882	-10 914	-9 462	-4 538	-3 995	94	-4 924	-1 452	1 767	-2 732	-4 968
2007											
Debt outstanding	702 718	426 750	122 150	26 132	21 006	1 362	96 018	304 600	257 143	43 363	275 968
Disbursments (6)	158 826	54 607	14 776	1 711	1 001	487	13 065	39 830	33 351	6 146	104 220
Debt service (7)	145 188	74 593	21 968	6 036	4 999	75	15 933	52 625	43 321	8 219	70 595
Principal repayments	103 058	47 841	15 951	5 059	4 313	69	10 892	31 891	24 603	6 507	55 217
Interest payments	42 130	26 752	6 017	977	686	6	5 041	20 734	18 718	1 712	15 378
Net transfers on debt (8)	13 638	-19 987	-7 192	-4 324	-3 998	412	-2 867	-12 795	-9 970	-2 073	33 625
2008											
Dette totale	752 753	439 047	131 413	29 382	22 185	2 327	102 031	307 634	261 615	42 650	313 706
Décaissements (6)	158 748	63 507	19 451	3 603	1 207	1 040	15 848	44 056	36 097	7 800	95 242
Service de la dette (7)	145 921	73 504	18 461	3 200	2 612	54	15 261	55 043	46 400	7 754	72 417
Remboursement du principal	103 656	48 353	12 974	2 393	1 991	37	10 581	35 379	28 623	6 125	55 303
Paiement des intérêts	42 265	25 151	5 486	807	621	18	4 680	19 664	17 777	1 630	17 114
Transfers nets (8)	12 827	-9 997	991	404	-1 405	986	587	-10 987	-10 304	45	22 824
2009											
Debt outstanding	777 820	456 316	149 840	34 213	22 683	2 887	115 627	306 476	265 202	37 106	321 503
Disbursements (6)	159 751	73 598	31 159	6 822	2 103	640	24 336	42 439	37 371	4 403	86 153
Debt service (7)	139 117	62 687	18 713	4 678	3 827	159	14 034	43 974	29 785	12 702	76 430
Principal repayments	99 314	39 276	13 656	3 728	3 147	119	9 928	25 620	13 563	10 868	60 039
Interest payments	39 803	23 411	5 057	951	680	40	4 106	18 355	16 222	1 835	16 392
Net transfers on debt (8)	20 634	10 911	12 446	2 144	-1 725	481	10 302	-1 535	7 586	-8 299	9 723
2010											
Dette totale	872 469	502 000	171 390	38 924	22 249	3 202	132 466	330 610	279 996	45 332	370 469
Décaissements (6)	209 204	92 450	35 499	8 539	2 386	789	26 960	56 951	37 790	16 709	116 754
Service de la dette (7)	136 560	65 003	19 189	5 134	3 921	205	14 055	45 814	36 250	7 982	71 557
Remboursement du principal	96 253	41 508	14 484	4 200	3 506	153	10 285	27 024	18 944	6 751	54 745
Paiement des intérêts	40 307	23 496	4 705	935	415	52	3 770	18 791	17 306	1 231	16 811
Transfers nets (8)	72 644	27 447	16 310	3 405	-1 535	584	12 905	11 137	1 539	8 726	45 197

For sources and notes, see end of table 7.7.G.

Pour les sources et les notes, se reporter à la fin du tableau 7.7.G.

7.7.D External long-term debt by lending source
Developing economies:
Asia

7.7.D Dette extérieure à long terme par catégories de prêt
Économies en développement :
Asie

	Total long-term debt (1) Dette totale à long terme (1)	Public and publicly guaranteed debt (2) Dette publique et garantie par l'état (2)									Private non-guaranteed debt (5) Dette privée non garantie (5)
		Total creditors Total créanciers	Official creditors (3) / Créanciers publics (3)					Private creditors (4) Créanciers privés (4)			
			Total	Bilateral / Bilatéraux			Multilateral Multilatéraux	Total	Bonds Obligations	Commercial banks Banques commerciales	
				Total	DAC CAD	OPEC OPEP					
	Millions of dollars / Millions de dollars										
1980											
Debt outstanding	102 144	92 704	62 024	44 030	34 561	4 687	17 993	30 681	1 629	16 101	9 439
Disbursments (6)	21 561	18 293	9 599	6 379	4 170	704	3 219	8 694	235	4 442	3 268
Debt service (7)	11 759	8 886	3 971	2 797	2 002	485	1 174	4 914	118	2 164	2 874
Principal repayments	6 837	4 869	2 261	1 824	1 185	380	437	2 608	33	797	1 968
Interest payments	4 922	4 017	1 710	974	817	105	737	2 307	85	1 367	905
Net transfers on debt (8)	9 802	9 407	5 627	3 582	2 168	219	2 046	3 780	118	2 278	394
1990											
Dette totale	370 418	347 034	224 149	139 592	83 247	5 164	84 557	122 885	19 628	69 557	23 384
Décaissements (6)	45 737	35 458	19 665	9 382	8 304	157	10 282	15 793	1 923	7 651	10 279
Service de la dette (7)	45 197	40 785	16 923	8 913	6 256	646	8 010	23 862	3 749	13 239	4 411
Remboursement du principal	27 149	24 160	9 874	5 822	3 783	527	4 053	14 285	2 251	7 271	2 989
Paiement des intérêts	18 048	16 626	7 049	3 091	2 473	119	3 958	9 577	1 498	5 968	1 422
Transfers nets (8)	540	-5 327	2 742	469	2 048	-490	2 272	-8 069	-1 826	-5 588	5 868
2000											
Debt outstanding	691 049	497 597	311 563	174 980	136 705	3 673	136 583	186 034	74 398	73 558	193 452
Disbursements (6)	83 037	60 043	24 935	11 730	10 218	143	13 205	35 108	19 208	7 963	22 993
Debt service (7)	105 373	63 037	30 010	16 225	12 110	336	13 785	33 027	8 066	17 173	42 336
Principal repayments	73 503	41 146	19 339	11 356	7 959	288	7 983	21 807	3 626	12 244	32 357
Interest payments	31 870	21 891	10 671	4 870	4 151	48	5 801	11 220	4 440	4 929	9 978
Net transfers on debt (8)	-22 336	-2 994	-5 075	-4 495	-1 893	-192	-580	2 081	11 142	-9 210	-19 343
2005											
Dette totale	745 012	486 380	313 078	166 112	136 762	3 957	146 966	173 303	102 213	46 751	258 631
Décaissements (6)	141 549	47 685	18 868	6 395	4 667	227	12 473	28 817	19 212	7 247	93 864
Service de la dette (7)	143 356	70 378	25 091	13 387	11 018	330	11 704	45 287	27 622	11 775	72 978
Remboursement du principal	117 163	51 330	18 083	9 947	8 300	276	8 136	33 247	18 581	9 538	65 833
Paiement des intérêts	26 192	19 048	7 008	3 440	2 717	53	3 568	12 040	9 041	2 237	7 144
Transfers nets (8)	-1 807	-22 693	-6 223	-6 992	-6 351	-102	769	-16 470	-8 410	-4 528	20 887
2007											
Debt outstanding	952 319	542 684	341 696	169 531	133 404	3 179	172 164	200 988	131 073	50 563	409 635
Disbursements (6)	240 648	61 797	25 738	8 096	5 105	216	17 642	36 059	23 950	9 417	178 851
Debt service (7)	182 939	65 963	31 665	18 157	13 885	378	13 508	34 298	20 387	9 227	116 976
Principal repayments	146 277	45 022	23 093	14 173	10 723	314	8 920	21 929	11 584	6 707	101 255
Interest payments	36 662	20 942	8 572	3 985	3 162	64	4 588	12 369	8 802	2 519	15 721
Net transfers on debt (8)	57 708	-4 167	-5 927	-10 061	-8 780	-161	4 134	1 761	3 563	190	61 875
2008											
Dette totale	1 033 852	571 268	369 185	185 439	145 951	3 251	183 746	202 084	132 117	53 081	462 584
Décaissements (6)	203 648	63 346	29 512	10 143	7 184	449	19 369	33 834	22 943	9 184	140 302
Service de la dette (7)	183 969	74 055	32 452	18 641	16 545	377	13 811	41 602	27 263	8 381	109 914
Remboursement du principal	146 270	53 368	24 251	14 868	13 276	313	9 383	29 117	18 175	6 043	92 902
Paiement des intérêts	37 699	20 687	8 201	3 773	3 270	64	4 428	12 486	9 088	2 338	17 012
Transfers nets (8)	19 679	-10 709	-2 940	-8 498	-9 361	72	5 558	-7 769	-4 319	803	30 388
2009											
Debt outstanding	1 071 174	607 893	389 849	189 041	141 074	3 368	200 808	218 044	146 429	52 742	463 281
Disbursements (6)	168 013	71 434	35 946	12 011	6 882	380	23 935	35 488	22 801	8 409	96 579
Debt service (7)	186 005	65 468	28 835	15 887	13 910	319	12 948	36 633	20 807	10 147	120 537
Principal repayments	152 834	46 338	21 589	12 202	10 826	247	9 387	24 749	11 525	8 211	106 496
Interest payments	33 171	19 130	7 246	3 686	3 084	72	3 560	11 884	9 282	1 935	14 041
Net transfers on debt (8)	-17 992	5 966	7 111	-3 876	-7 028	61	10 987	-1 145	1 994	-1 738	-23 958
2010											
Dette totale	1 133 843	648 958	409 330	194 699	147 952	3 168	214 631	239 627	165 444	57 047	484 886
Décaissements (6)	221 099	91 110	37 106	13 639	7 813	359	23 467	54 005	34 303	13 458	129 989
Service de la dette (7)	189 469	65 661	29 944	17 235	13 848	598	12 709	35 717	20 941	8 406	123 808
Remboursement du principal	154 401	45 806	22 353	12 484	10 792	504	9 869	23 453	11 082	6 732	108 595
Paiement des intérêts	35 068	19 855	7 591	4 751	3 056	94	2 839	12 264	9 859	1 674	15 213
Transfers nets (8)	31 630	25 449	7 162	-3 597	-6 035	-239	10 758	18 288	13 363	5 052	6 181

For sources and notes, see end of table 7.7.G.

Pour les sources et les notes, se reporter à la fin du tableau 7.7.G.

7.7.E External long-term debt by lending source
Developing economies: Oceania

7.7.E Dette extérieure à long terme par catégories de prêt
Économies en développement : Océanie

	Total long-term debt (1) / Dette totale à long terme (1)	Public and publicly guaranteed debt (2) / Dette publique et garantie par l'état (2)									Private non-guaranteed debt (5) / Dette privée non garantie (5)
		Total creditors / Total créanciers	Official creditors (3) / Créanciers publics (3)					Private creditors (4) / Créanciers privés (4)			
			Total	Bilateral / Bilatéraux			Multilateral / Multilatéraux	Total	Bonds / Obligations	Commercial banks / Banques commerciales	
				Total	DAC CAD	OPEC OPEP					
				Millions of dollars / Millions de dollars							
1980											
Debt outstanding	966	763	396	136	123	3	261	367	92	254	204
Disbursements (6)	245	230	115	40	37	3	75	115	0	106	15
Debt service (7)	149	87	27	13	12	0	14	61	17	35	62
Principal repayments	86	46	12	7	7	0	4	34	10	17	40
Interest payments	64	42	15	6	5	0	9	27	8	18	22
Net transfers on debt (8)	96	143	89	27	26	3	62	54	-17	71	-47
1990											
Dette totale	3 118	2 085	1 593	447	412	10	1 146	493	39	330	1 033
Décaissements (6)	682	325	279	59	57	0	219	46	0	21	358
Service de la dette (7)	665	366	163	47	44	0	116	203	3	175	299
Remboursement du principal	473	251	99	26	25	0	73	152	0	137	222
Paiement des intérêts	193	115	65	21	19	0	44	50	3	38	77
Transfers nets (8)	17	-42	115	12	13	0	103	-157	-3	-155	59
2000											
Debt outstanding	2 804	2 023	1 959	697	564	10	1 263	64	0	54	781
Disbursements (6)	291	256	243	145	134	2	98	13	0	13	35
Debt service (7)	326	209	184	71	60	1	113	25	0	13	116
Principal repayments	227	144	124	50	43	1	74	20	0	10	84
Interest payments	98	65	61	21	17	0	40	5	0	3	33
Net transfers on debt (8)	-34	47	58	74	74	1	-16	-11	0	0	-81
2005											
Dette totale	2 307	1 913	1 862	537	400	7	1 324	52	0	8	393
Décaissements (6)	369	80	78	3	3	0	75	1	0	0	290
Service de la dette (7)	277	186	160	67	59	1	93	26	0	17	91
Remboursement du principal	210	137	113	50	45	1	64	23	0	15	73
Paiement des intérêts	67	49	47	17	14	0	29	2	0	1	18
Transfers nets (8)	92	-106	-82	-64	-56	-1	-18	-25	0	-17	199
2007											
Debt outstanding	2 214	1 974	1 782	488	353	5	1 295	192	150	4	239
Disbursements (6)	678	83	83	13	0	0	70	0	0	0	595
Debt service (7)	1 057	263	246	52	43	4	194	17	10	1	794
Principal repayments	979	201	195	38	32	2	157	6	0	0	777
Interest payments	78	62	51	14	10	2	37	11	10	0	16
Net transfers on debt (8)	-379	-180	-163	-40	-43	-4	-124	-17	-10	-1	-199
2008											
Dette totale	2 320	1 949	1 754	492	320	3	1 262	195	150	4	371
Décaissements (6)	1 009	83	83	41	0	0	42	0	0	0	926
Service de la dette (7)	1 028	251	233	119	110	2	115	17	10	1	777
Remboursement du principal	963	194	187	103	98	2	85	6	0	0	769
Paiement des intérêts	65	57	46	16	12	0	30	11	10	0	8
Transfers nets (8)	-19	-168	-150	-78	-110	-2	-72	-17	-10	-1	149
2009											
Debt outstanding	2 405	1 968	1 780	521	296	2	1 260	188	150	3	437
Disbursements (6)	599	102	102	53	1	0	49	1	0	0	497
Debt service (7)	593	133	115	38	30	1	78	18	10	0	460
Principal repayments	543	91	84	26	22	1	58	7	0	0	452
Interest payments	50	43	32	12	8	0	20	11	10	0	7
Net transfers on debt (8)	6	-31	-14	15	-29	-1	-29	-17	-10	0	37
2010											
Dette totale	6 514	2 099	1 915	624	313	2	1 291	184	150	3	4 414
Décaissements (6)	3 342	189	189	87	6	0	102	0	0	0	3 153
Service de la dette (7)	870	136	117	39	30	1	79	19	10	0	734
Remboursement du principal	797	97	90	25	22	0	65	8	0	0	699
Paiement des intérêts	73	39	27	14	8	0	14	11	10	0	35
Transfers nets (8)	2 472	53	72	48	-24	-1	24	-18	-10	0	2 419

For sources and notes, see end of table 7.7.G.

Pour les sources et les notes, se reporter à la fin du tableau 7.7.G.

7.7.F External long-term debt by lending source
Developing economies:
Major petroleum and gas exporters

7.7.F Dette extérieure à long terme par catégories de prêt
Économies en développement :
Principaux exportateurs de pétrole et de gaz

	Total long-term debt (1) — Dette totale à long terme (1)	Public and publicly guaranteed debt (2) — Dette publique et garantie par l'état (2)									Private non-guaranteed debt (5) — Dette privée non garantie (5)
		Total creditors — Total créanciers	Official creditors (3) / Créanciers publics (3)					Private creditors (4) / Créanciers privés (4)			
			Total	Bilateral / Bilatéraux			Multilateral — Multilatéraux	Total	Bonds — Obligations	Commercial banks — Banques commerciales	
				Total	DAC CAD	OPEC OPEP					
	Millions of dollars / Millions de dollars										
1980											
Debt outstanding	41 301	37 023	6 340	4 589	3 670	264	1 751	30 683	1 671	17 356	4 278
Disbursments (6)	10 318	7 861	830	683	613	7	147	7 031	305	3 748	2 456
Debt service (7)	10 371	8 611	847	529	448	13	318	7 764	133	4 552	1 760
Principal repayments	6 451	5 039	510	337	271	11	173	4 529	28	2 320	1 412
Interest payments	3 920	3 572	337	193	177	2	145	3 235	106	2 232	348
Net transfers on debt (8)	-54	-750	-18	154	165	-6	-171	-732	172	-804	696
1990											
Dette totale	98 584	94 543	27 197	19 493	16 065	238	7 704	67 346	21 064	14 847	4 041
Décaissements (6)	11 296	11 296	3 814	1 569	1 255	14	2 245	7 482	599	249	0
Service de la dette (7)	17 859	17 267	3 918	2 793	2 265	36	1 125	13 349	509	6 043	592
Remboursement du principal	10 653	10 464	2 188	1 520	1 348	27	669	8 276	269	2 803	188
Paiement des intérêts	7 206	6 803	1 730	1 273	917	9	456	5 073	240	3 240	403
Transfers nets (8)	-6 563	-5 971	-104	-1 224	-1 010	-22	1 120	-5 867	90	-5 794	-592
2000											
Debt outstanding	100 344	93 997	54 634	43 167	16 840	500	11 467	39 363	18 268	9 667	6 347
Disbursments (6)	6 225	6 225	2 246	1 198	619	10	1 049	3 979	462	1 946	0
Debt service (7)	15 827	14 551	6 852	4 786	1 854	81	2 066	7 699	2 545	2 524	1 276
Principal repayments	10 608	9 918	4 636	3 388	989	49	1 248	5 282	1 119	2 027	690
Interest payments	5 219	4 633	2 216	1 398	864	32	819	2 417	1 426	497	586
Net transfers on debt (8)	-9 602	-8 326	-4 606	-3 588	-1 234	-71	-1 017	-3 720	-2 083	-578	-1 276
2005											
Dette totale	91 440	86 872	39 156	30 598	27 632	609	8 558	47 716	24 988	13 351	4 568
Décaissements (6)	15 293	14 830	2 190	1 076	232	25	1 113	12 640	6 143	5 026	463
Service de la dette (7)	24 291	23 001	14 073	11 354	10 619	114	2 719	8 928	2 563	3 807	1 290
Remboursement du principal	15 134	14 218	8 269	6 017	5 395	103	2 253	5 949	646	3 158	916
Paiement des intérêts	9 157	8 783	5 804	5 337	5 224	11	467	2 979	1 917	649	374
Transfers nets (8)	-8 998	-8 171	-11 883	-10 277	-10 387	-89	-1 606	3 712	3 580	1 219	-827
2007											
Debt outstanding	59 668	55 560	14 640	7 954	3 346	575	6 686	40 919	20 675	12 785	4 108
Disbursments (6)	9 997	9 694	2 438	1 499	344	48	939	7 255	1 250	5 388	304
Debt service (7)	14 146	13 013	2 838	1 246	776	80	1 592	10 176	1 960	5 569	1 133
Principal repayments	10 124	9 318	2 177	900	619	63	1 277	7 141	209	4 686	806
Interest payments	4 023	3 696	660	345	157	17	315	3 035	1 751	882	327
Net transfers on debt (8)	-4 149	-3 320	-399	253	-433	-33	-653	-2 920	-710	-181	-829
2008											
Dette totale	63 424	58 670	15 604	8 684	3 131	532	6 920	43 066	23 353	14 142	4 754
Décaissements (6)	12 140	11 082	2 620	1 516	251	47	1 104	8 462	4 000	4 047	1 057
Service de la dette (7)	11 452	10 627	2 395	1 256	547	98	1 139	8 232	3 305	2 832	825
Remboursement du principal	7 403	6 959	1 820	946	428	91	874	5 139	1 299	2 094	444
Paiement des intérêts	4 049	3 668	575	310	119	7	265	3 092	2 005	738	382
Transfers nets (8)	688	456	225	260	-296	-51	-35	231	695	1 215	232
2009											
Debt outstanding	67 918	63 626	17 298	9 338	2 912	509	7 960	46 328	28 360	13 485	4 292
Disbursments (6)	11 098	10 974	2 975	1 520	132	13	1 455	7 999	4 992	2 828	123
Debt service (7)	10 895	10 000	2 084	1 273	501	42	812	7 916	2 024	4 413	895
Principal repayments	7 253	6 731	1 579	972	421	36	607	5 152	0	3 855	522
Interest payments	3 642	3 269	505	301	80	6	205	2 764	2 024	558	373
Net transfers on debt (8)	203	974	891	248	-370	-28	643	83	2 968	-1 586	-771
2010											
Dette totale	70 732	66 704	22 012	11 987	2 499	485	10 025	44 692	29 762	11 076	4 028
Décaissements (6)	10 041	10 039	6 558	3 780	33	16	2 778	3 481	3 000	204	2
Service de la dette (7)	10 646	9 831	1 888	1 168	477	46	720	7 943	4 020	2 936	815
Remboursement du principal	7 101	6 617	1 457	929	418	41	528	5 161	1 609	2 650	484
Paiement des intérêts	3 545	3 214	431	239	59	5	192	2 783	2 411	286	331
Transfers nets (8)	-605	208	4 670	2 612	-444	-30	2 058	-4 462	-1 020	-2 731	-813

For sources and notes, see end of table 7.7.G.

Pour les sources et les notes, se reporter à la fin du tableau 7.7.G.

7.7.G External long-term debt by lending source
Developing economies:
Major manufactured goods exporters

7.7.G Dette extérieure à long terme par catégories de prêt
Économies en développement :
Principaux exportateurs d'articles manufacturés

	Total long-term debt (1) / Dette totale à long terme (1)	Public and publicly guaranteed debt (2) / Dette publique et garantie par l'état (2)									Private non-guaranteed debt (5) / Dette privée non garantie (5)
		Total creditors / Total créanciers	Official creditors (3) / Créanciers publics (3)					Private creditors (4) / Créanciers privés (4)			
			Total	Bilateral / Bilatéraux			Multilateral / Multilatéraux	Total	Bonds / Obligations	Commercial banks / Banques commerciales	
				Total	DAC / CAD	OPEC / OPEP					
Millions of dollars / Millions de dollars											
1980											
Debt outstanding	56 620	46 369	8 539	3 613	3 507	34	4 926	37 830	3 576	29 887	10 251
Disbursments (6)	18 180	14 001	2 159	1 163	1 125	18	996	11 841	330	8 900	4 179
Debt service (7)	12 208	9 638	1 023	440	437	1	583	8 615	417	7 301	2 570
Principal repayments	6 500	4 921	488	278	278	0	211	4 433	134	3 675	1 578
Interest payments	5 708	4 716	535	163	159	1	372	4 181	283	3 626	992
Net transfers on debt (8)	5 972	4 363	1 136	723	688	17	413	3 227	-87	1 599	1 609
1990											
Dette totale	160 518	145 541	49 609	23 667	20 974	305	25 942	95 932	50 354	25 561	14 976
Décaissements (6)	27 963	21 726	9 655	4 315	3 558	8	5 340	12 071	1 252	5 966	6 237
Service de la dette (7)	22 974	20 613	5 873	2 303	2 067	41	3 571	14 740	4 054	6 560	2 360
Remboursement du principal	12 291	11 034	3 290	1 379	1 241	28	1 911	7 744	2 115	2 981	1 257
Paiement des intérêts	10 683	9 580	2 583	924	826	13	1 659	6 996	1 938	3 579	1 103
Transfers nets (8)	4 989	1 113	3 782	2 012	1 491	-33	1 769	-2 669	-2 802	-594	3 877
2000											
Debt outstanding	364 180	225 528	97 037	47 301	41 965	204	49 736	128 491	77 530	23 308	138 652
Disbursments (6)	61 788	29 899	12 247	5 599	4 639	59	6 648	17 651	9 277	2 354	31 889
Debt service (7)	95 454	46 397	15 369	8 008	6 853	102	7 361	31 027	16 283	8 463	49 057
Principal repayments	71 420	31 599	10 162	6 044	5 129	91	4 118	21 436	10 072	6 822	39 821
Interest payments	24 034	14 798	5 207	1 964	1 724	11	3 243	9 591	6 211	1 641	9 236
Net transfers on debt (8)	-33 666	-16 498	-3 122	-2 409	-2 214	-43	-713	-13 376	-7 006	-6 109	-17 168
2005											
Dette totale	356 885	239 205	85 615	40 949	31 553	79	44 666	153 590	110 989	27 329	117 680
Décaissements (6)	80 211	31 823	5 894	1 858	1 601	1	4 036	25 929	19 243	5 177	48 388
Service de la dette (7)	85 377	41 319	10 253	4 838	4 477	6	5 414	31 066	20 329	7 080	44 058
Remboursement du principal	69 783	29 894	7 482	3 620	3 442	3	3 863	22 412	12 747	6 437	39 888
Paiement des intérêts	15 594	11 424	2 770	1 219	1 036	3	1 552	8 654	7 582	643	4 170
Transfers nets (8)	-5 166	-9 496	-4 359	-2 981	-2 876	-6	-1 378	-5 137	-1 086	-1 903	4 330
2007											
Debt outstanding	407 568	243 238	80 016	40 872	25 096	42	39 143	163 222	121 559	30 424	164 330
Disbursments (6)	102 551	33 019	6 049	1 861	873	0	4 188	26 970	22 634	2 158	69 532
Debt service (7)	93 162	37 280	10 025	5 423	4 286	8	4 601	27 255	20 449	3 870	55 882
Principal repayments	72 987	24 520	7 454	4 448	3 644	5	3 006	17 067	11 696	3 112	48 467
Interest payments	20 175	12 760	2 571	976	642	2	1 596	10 188	8 754	759	7 415
Net transfers on debt (8)	9 389	-4 261	-3 976	-3 562	-3 414	-8	-414	-285	2 185	-1 713	13 650
2008											
Dette totale	445 808	258 274	87 887	45 910	26 740	28	41 976	170 387	128 114	31 632	187 535
Décaissements (6)	90 121	33 735	6 826	1 328	303	0	5 498	26 909	18 748	6 536	56 386
Service de la dette (7)	88 192	36 890	8 214	4 009	3 957	16	4 205	28 675	20 364	4 115	51 302
Remboursement du principal	70 008	25 614	6 100	3 327	3 298	14	2 773	19 514	12 576	3 470	44 394
Paiement des intérêts	18 184	11 276	2 114	682	659	2	1 432	9 162	7 788	645	6 908
Transfers nets (8)	1 929	-3 155	-1 388	-2 681	-3 654	-16	1 293	-1 767	-1 616	2 421	5 084
2009											
Debt outstanding	434 429	251 237	100 136	49 179	25 591	17	50 957	151 100	110 852	26 485	183 192
Disbursments (6)	77 872	39 429	12 153	1 904	1 250	0	10 249	27 276	20 235	3 335	38 443
Debt service (7)	91 352	34 252	7 788	3 690	3 619	11	4 098	26 464	14 749	6 917	57 099
Principal repayments	76 471	24 884	5 911	3 025	2 972	10	2 886	18 974	8 624	6 043	51 586
Interest payments	14 881	9 368	1 878	665	647	1	1 212	7 490	6 125	874	5 513
Net transfers on debt (8)	-13 480	5 177	4 365	-1 787	-2 369	-11	6 151	812	5 485	-3 582	-18 657
2010											
Dette totale	482 188	279 681	103 959	46 795	25 091	11	57 164	175 722	131 695	30 249	202 507
Décaissements (6)	122 750	58 847	10 748	3 366	1 641	0	7 381	48 099	29 508	11 456	63 903
Service de la dette (7)	88 756	35 670	9 225	5 593	4 542	7	3 631	26 445	13 851	6 557	53 085
Remboursement du principal	71 231	25 803	6 543	3 977	3 928	6	2 566	19 260	7 699	5 919	45 428
Paiement des intérêts	17 524	9 867	2 682	1 616	614	1	1 065	7 185	6 152	638	7 657
Transfers nets (8)	33 994	23 177	1 523	-2 227	-2 901	-7	3 750	21 654	15 656	4 899	10 817

For sources and notes, see next page.   Pour les sources et les notes, se reporter à la page suivante.

Source:
World Bank, *Global Development Finance*

Source :
Banque mondiale, *Global Development Finance*

Notes:

(1) Long-term debt is defined as debt that has an original or extended maturity of more than one year and that is owed to nonresidents and repayable in foreign currency, goods, or services.
Long-term debt has three components:
-"Public debt";
-"Publicly guaranteed debt";
-"Private nonguaranteed debt".
In this table, "Public debt" and "Publicly guaranteed debt" are aggregated.
Outstanding long-term debt at year end is the sum of long-term debt outstanding and long-term debt disbursed.

(2) "Public debt" is an obligation of a public debtor, including the national government, a political subdivision (or an agency of either), and autonomous public bodies.
"Publicly guaranteed debt" is an external obligation of a private debtor that is guaranteed for repayment by a public entity.
In this table, "Public debt" and "Publicly guaranteed debt" are aggregated.
Data of "Public and publicly guaranteed debt" is shown by type of creditor: official creditors and private creditors.

(3) "Public and publicly guaranteed debt" from official creditors includes loans from governments (referred to as bilateral creditors) and loans from international organizations (referred to as multilateral creditors).
Government loans include loans from governments and their agencies (including central banks), loans from autonomous bodies, and direct loans from official export credit agencies.
Loans from international organizations include loans and credits from the World Bank, regional development banks, and other multilateral and intergovernmental agencies. Excluded are loans from funds administered by an international organization on behalf of a single donor government; these are classified as loans from governments.

(4) "Public and publicly guaranteed debt" from private creditors includes:
- "Bonds" that are either publicly issued or privately placed;
- "Commercial bank loans" from private banks and other private financial institutions;
- "Other private credits" from manufacturers, exporters, and other suppliers of goods, and bank credits covered by a guarantee of an export credit agency.

(5) Private nonguaranteed long-term debt outstanding and disbursed is an obligation of a private debtor that is not guaranteed for repayment by a public entity.

(6) Disbursements on long-term debt are drawings on loan commitments during the year specified.

(7) Long-term debt service payments are the sum of principal repayments and interest payments in the year specified.

(8) Net transfers on long-term debt are "disbursements" minus "debt service payments".

Notes :

(1) La dette à long terme a une durée de remboursement (d'origine ou différée) supérieure à une année, et son amortissement est dû, en monnaies convertibles ou en nature, à des créanciers non-résidents.
La dette à long terme a trois composantes :
- "Dette publique" ;
- "Dette garantie par l'État" ;
- "Dette du secteur privé non garantie".
Dans ce tableau, la "dette publique" et la "dette garantie par l'État" sont agrégées.

(2) La "dette publique" est une dette contractée par le secteur public, y compris le gouvernement, une entité politique et d'autres organismes publics autonomes.
La "dette garantie par l'État" est une dette contractée par le secteur privé, dont l'amortissement est garanti par une entité publique.
Dans ce tableau, "dette publique" et "dette garantie par l'État" sont agrégées.
Les données de la "dette publique et garantie par l'État" sont indiquées par types de créanciers : créanciers publics et créanciers privés.

(3) La "dette publique et garantie par l'État" octroyée par les créanciers publics inclut les prêts des gouvernements (appelés créditeurs bilatéraux) et les prêts des organisations internationales (appelées créditeurs multilatéraux).
Les prêts des gouvernements incluent les prêts des gouvernements et des organismes publics (y compris les banques centrales), les prêts provenant d'entités autonomes et les prêts octroyés directement par des organismes publics de crédits à l'exportation.
Les prêts des organisations internationales incluent les prêts et les crédits de la Banque mondiale, des banques régionales de développement, et d'autres organismes multilatéraux et intergouvernementaux.Ne sont pas compris les prêts provenant des fonds administrés par une organisation internationale, pour le compte d'un gouvernement ; ceux-ci sont classés sous la rubrique des prêts des gouvernements.

(4) La "dette publique et garantie par l'État" octroyée par les créanciers privés comprend :
- "Obligations" qui sont soit des émissions publiques, soit des placements privés ;
- "Prêts des banques commerciales" octroyés par des banques privées et par d'autres entités financières ;
- "Autres crédits privés" provenant du secteur manufacturier, du secteur des exportations, et d'autres fournisseurs de biens, ainsi que des crédits bancaires couverts par un organisme de crédits à l'exportation.

(5) La dette du secteur privé non-garantie encourue et décaissée, est une dette contractée par le secteur privé, dont l'amortissement n'est pas garanti par une entité publique.

(6) Les décaissements de la dette à long terme sont les tirages sur les engagements de la dette effectués au cours de l'année spécifiée.

(7) Les paiements du service de la dette à long terme sont la somme du remboursement du principal et du paiement des intérêts, effectués au cours de l'année spécifiée.

(8) Les transferts nets sont les "décaissements" moins les "paiements du service de la dette".

DEVELOPMENT
INDICATORS

INDICATEURS DU
DÉVELOPPEMENT

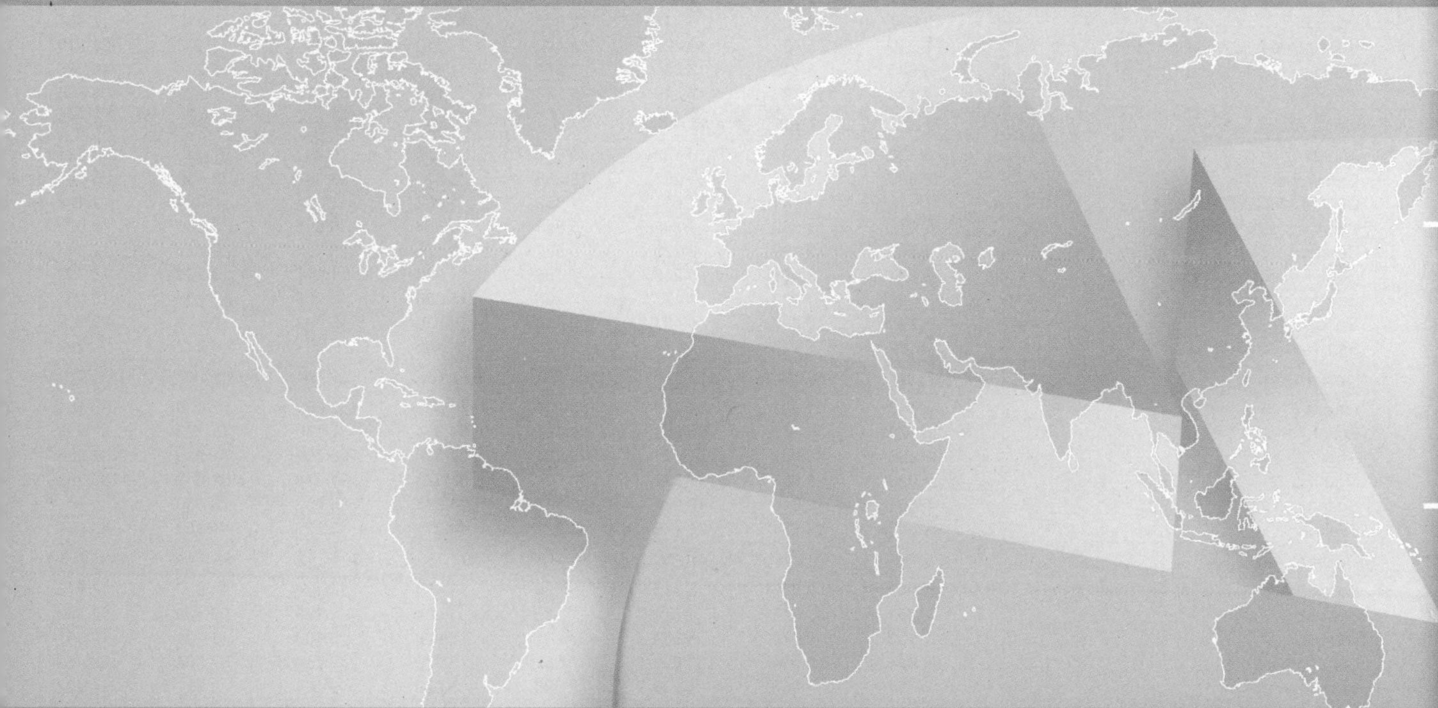

1
2
3
4
5
6
7
8

Region, country or territory	Total gross domestic product / Produit intérieur brut total (1) Millions of dollars / Millions de dollars							
	1980	1990	2000	2005	2008	2009	2010	2011 (e)
World	11 883 110	22 233 768	32 286 779	45 744 751	61 232 771	57 960 080	63 063 973	69 711 938
DEVELOPING ECONOMIES	2 568 673	3 891 832	7 026 938	10 846 202	17 577 186	17 311 604	20 530 256	23 812 034
TRANSITION ECONOMIES	1 012 216	850 055	397 600	1 097 739	2 341 669	1 787 094	2 116 578	2 590 339
DEVELOPED ECONOMIES	8 302 221	17 491 881	24 862 242	33 800 810	41 313 916	38 861 382	40 417 139	43 309 565
Developing economies: Africa	434 164	495 104	599 818	1 006 833	1 570 188	1 484 880	1 710 100	1 874 224
Eastern Africa	*51 361*	*65 109*	*70 573*	*99 048*	*159 841*	*161 193*	*169 453*	*189 351*
Burundi	1 332	1 608	995	1 117	1 312	1 321	1 481	1 721
Comoros	124	244	202	387	530	535	541	608
Djibouti	301	457	557	709	983	1 049	1 140	1 252
Eritrea	–	–	706	1 098	1 380	1 873	2 254	2 778
Ethiopia (...1991)	5 889	11 658	–	–	–	–	–	–
Ethiopia	–	–	8 111	12 286	25 866	28 476	26 928	30 649
Kenya	9 165	11 035	12 604	18 739	30 519	30 580	32 483	34 378
Madagascar	3 265	3 080	3 878	5 039	9 413	8 552	8 739	9 905
Malawi	1 705	2 414	2 402	2 755	4 220	4 897	5 325	5 545
Mauritius	1 160	2 619	4 663	6 489	9 641	8 865	9 729	11 295
Mozambique	4 826	2 969	4 310	6 579	9 891	9 674	9 533	12 919
Rwanda	1 401	2 574	1 772	2 581	4 712	5 262	5 655	6 412
Seychelles	183	459	769	928	921	788	991	1 047
Somalia	571	994	2 052	2 316	2 600	2 012	1 071	-
Uganda	3 097	4 039	6 341	10 040	16 377	16 843	17 015	17 457
United Republic of Tanzania	7 310	5 480	10 424	14 492	21 340	22 034	23 163	24 218
Zambia	3 885	3 742	3 239	7 271	14 641	12 805	16 201	19 225
Zimbabwe	7 148	11 738	7 549	6 223	5 495	5 626	7 204	8 875
Middle Africa	*33 209*	*43 365*	*35 949*	*84 482*	*172 622*	*152 642*	*171 061*	*210 974*
Angola	5 390	10 297	9 133	30 629	84 179	75 493	82 470	104 331
Cameroon	8 869	11 846	9 287	16 588	23 322	23 381	23 649	26 612
Central African Republic	1 112	1 441	914	1 350	1 983	1 981	1 984	2 192
Chad	919	1 542	1 385	5 873	8 354	6 895	8 166	8 929
Congo	1 706	2 799	3 220	6 087	10 176	8 196	10 775	12 944
Dem. Rep. of the Congo	9 837	9 350	5 268	7 166	11 933	11 147	13 230	15 797
Equatorial Guinea	54	133	1 177	7 206	15 668	9 968	11 803	16 067
Gabon	5 240	5 838	5 487	9 459	16 825	15 382	18 771	23 839
Sao Tome and Principe	82	120	77	123	182	198	212	262
Northern Africa	*137 693*	*184 003*	*260 537*	*370 125*	*616 140*	*585 386*	*661 140*	*685 520*
Algeria	42 348	61 891	54 790	103 234	171 392	137 892	158 650	193 161
Egypt	20 120	35 940	95 688	94 461	164 844	187 978	215 272	231 922
Libya	38 186	31 088	38 471	45 451	81 376	58 762	71 945	34 906
Morocco (2)	21 030	28 855	37 022	59 524	88 879	91 374	91 542	100 087
Sudan (...2011)	6 365	12 645	13 092	35 183	64 833	65 852	79 480	-
Tunisia	9 645	13 584	21 473	32 272	44 815	43 528	44 252	45 964
Southern Africa	*85 188*	*120 006*	*144 726*	*268 519*	*302 330*	*308 292*	*396 319*	*445 663*
Botswana	1 047	3 715	5 633	10 256	13 473	11 474	14 857	17 572
Lesotho	351	545	771	1 355	1 601	1 720	2 129	2 433
Namibia	2 532	2 679	3 909	7 261	8 958	9 183	11 701	12 997
South Africa	80 544	112 014	132 878	247 052	275 279	282 754	363 704	408 439
Swaziland	714	1 053	1 536	2 596	3 020	3 161	3 927	4 222
Western Africa	*126 713*	*82 620*	*88 033*	*184 660*	*319 255*	*277 367*	*312 127*	*342 716*
Benin	1 374	1 845	2 359	4 358	6 634	6 585	6 558	7 300
Burkina Faso	1 933	3 133	2 633	5 463	8 398	8 358	8 559	9 881
Cape Verde	142	308	539	972	1 531	1 549	1 609	1 844
Côte d'Ivoire	10 176	11 893	10 682	16 354	23 281	23 043	22 780	23 926
Gambia	504	707	783	630	985	907	1 001	1 022
Ghana	5 205	9 983	7 985	17 198	28 528	25 978	32 520	39 620
Guinea	1 486	2 920	3 192	2 937	3 778	4 441	4 267	4 935
Guinea-Bissau	513	608	371	573	848	862	817	947
Liberia	765	487	528	578	751	832	873	1 044
Mali	1 423	2 510	2 655	5 486	8 738	8 964	9 204	10 351
Mauritania	1 496	1 622	1 294	2 184	3 704	3 083	3 913	4 470
Niger	2 697	2 638	1 727	3 369	5 403	5 319	5 549	6 171
Nigeria	93 181	35 026	46 386	112 248	208 065	169 408	196 410	210 736
Senegal	3 254	6 205	4 680	8 708	13 287	12 756	12 841	14 428
Sierra Leone	1 433	946	926	1 491	2 156	2 118	2 064	2 359
Togo	1 131	1 789	1 294	2 110	3 168	3 162	3 162	3 682

For sources and notes, see end of table.

Per capita gross domestic product / Produit intérieur brut par habitant Dollars								Régions, pays ou territoires
1980	1990	2000	2005	2008	2009	2010	2011 (e)	
2 679	4 207	5 293	7 057	9 119	8 532	9 178	9 998	**Monde**
781	958	1 456	2 092	3 255	3 164	3 703	4 222	ÉCONOMIES EN DÉVELOPPEMENT
3 496	2 697	1 303	3 638	7 752	5 909	6 989	8 543	ÉCONOMIES EN TRANSITION
9 700	19 308	25 705	33 948	40 771	38 138	39 456	42 071	ÉCONOMIES DÉVELOPPÉES
901	780	741	1 107	1 611	1 489	1 676	1 795	**Économies en développement : Afrique**
359	339	282	348	521	512	525	571	*Afrique orientale*
322	287	156	154	165	162	177	201	Burundi
376	557	359	602	761	748	737	806	Comores
885	813	761	877	1 148	1 203	1 283	1 382	Djibouti
–	–	193	245	279	367	429	513	Érythrée
155	226	–	–	–	–	–	–	Éthiopie (…1991)
–	–	124	165	326	351	325	362	Éthiopie
563	471	403	526	794	775	802	826	Kenya
379	273	252	282	482	425	422	465	Madagascar
273	257	214	215	301	339	357	360	Malawi
1 203	2 472	3 899	5 163	7 510	6 864	7 488	8 644	Maurice
397	219	237	317	443	423	408	540	Mozambique
271	362	219	281	471	510	532	586	Rwanda
2 920	6 457	9 775	11 113	10 763	9 155	11 451	12 047	Seychelles
89	151	277	277	291	221	115	-	Somalie
245	228	262	353	523	520	509	506	Ouganda
391	215	306	373	505	506	517	524	République-Unie de Tanzanie
673	476	317	634	1 183	1 006	1 238	1 427	Zambie
981	1 121	603	495	441	451	573	696	Zimbabwe
622	605	374	762	1 435	1 236	1 350	1 623	*Afrique centrale*
706	996	656	1 858	4 667	4 069	4 322	5 318	Angola
974	972	592	945	1 243	1 219	1 207	1 329	Cameroun
489	491	247	336	468	459	451	489	République centrafricaine
202	256	168	600	784	630	727	775	Tchad
949	1 172	1 027	1 723	2 653	2 079	2 665	3 127	Congo
364	257	106	125	191	174	201	233	Rép. dém. du Congo
244	356	2 263	11 856	23 656	14 635	16 852	22 309	Guinée équatoriale
7 677	6 284	4 442	6 901	11 601	10 411	12 469	15 538	Gabon
869	1 036	545	808	1 140	1 218	1 283	1 555	Sao Tomé-et-Principe
1 219	1 261	1 482	1 932	3 052	2 850	3 164	3 227	*Afrique septentrionale*
2 251	2 446	1 794	3 139	4 978	3 945	4 473	5 369	Algérie
448	632	1 414	1 273	2 105	2 358	2 654	2 810	Égypte
12 467	7 172	7 354	7 878	13 233	9 383	11 321	5 435	Libye
1 075	1 164	1 286	1 959	2 838	2 888	2 865	3 101	Maroc (2)
317	477	383	916	1 565	1 550	1 825	-	Soudan (…2011)
1 494	1 653	2 271	3 256	4 373	4 200	4 222	4 339	Tunisie
2 581	2 851	2 813	4 889	5 327	5 381	6 859	7 656	*Afrique australe*
1 051	2 688	3 204	5 468	6 892	5 790	7 403	8 653	Botswana
268	332	393	656	752	800	981	1 109	Lesotho
2 500	1 894	2 062	3 491	4 071	4 096	5 125	5 592	Namibie
2 770	3 044	2 969	5 169	5 582	5 683	7 255	8 094	Afrique du Sud
1 183	1 221	1 444	2 349	2 625	2 706	3 311	3 509	Swaziland
907	453	373	690	1 105	935	1 026	1 098	*Afrique occidentale*
381	387	362	571	794	766	741	802	Bénin
268	336	214	385	541	523	520	582	Burkina Faso
474	885	1 233	2 055	3 142	3 151	3 244	3 683	Cap-Vert
1 197	950	644	907	1 226	1 191	1 154	1 187	Côte d'Ivoire
800	732	604	419	602	539	579	576	Gambie
476	675	417	795	1 226	1 090	1 333	1 587	Ghana
337	507	383	325	395	455	427	483	Guinée
615	598	299	419	583	581	539	612	Guinée-Bissau
398	229	185	182	205	217	219	253	Libéria
196	289	235	416	604	601	599	653	Mali
985	813	490	717	1 124	913	1 131	1 262	Mauritanie
459	339	158	259	374	355	358	384	Niger
1 233	359	375	803	1 381	1 097	1 240	1 297	Nigéria
601	857	492	801	1 127	1 054	1 033	1 130	Sénégal
453	238	223	289	384	369	352	393	Sierra Leone
424	488	270	390	548	536	525	598	Togo

Pour les sources et les notes, se reporter à la fin du tableau.

8

Region, country or territory	Total gross domestic product / Produit intérieur brut total (1) Millions of dollars / Millions de dollars							
	1980	1990	2000	2005	2008	2009	2010	2011 (e)
Developing economies: America	756 475	1 123 109	2 132 984	2 703 564	4 371 076	4 061 746	5 007 431	5 607 505
Caribbean	*43 519*	*61 858*	*95 087*	*132 604*	*182 890*	*175 244*	*184 466*	*194 832*
Anguilla	9	54	108	170	290	216	211	220
Antigua and Barbuda	110	392	664	867	1 203	1 132	1 118	1 104
Aruba	493	828	1 873	2 331	2 745	2 502	2 456	2 791
Bahamas	1 581	3 700	6 328	7 706	8 240	7 807	7 702	7 718
Barbados	971	1 931	2 913	3 685	3 988	3 895	3 963	4 026
British Virgin Islands	28	105	751	870	992	876	909	-
Cayman Islands	173	930	2 277	3 042	3 559	3 353	3 208	-
Cuba	19 913	28 645	30 565	42 644	60 806	62 279	64 220	70 154
Dominica	71	200	324	362	462	480	476	471
Dominican Republic	8 178	9 385	23 655	33 542	45 523	46 598	51 576	56 081
Grenada	75	221	520	697	830	761	776	816
Haiti	1 384	2 614	3 358	3 807	5 872	5 937	6 123	6 779
Jamaica	3 045	4 822	8 958	11 163	13 877	12 327	13 428	14 674
Montserrat	24	67	35	43	50	53	55	-
Netherlands Antilles	943	1 980	2 857	3 277	3 944	3 966	4 078	–
Saint Kitts and Nevis	48	159	329	439	570	545	550	584
Saint Lucia	135	416	700	847	1 083	1 062	1 164	1 184
Saint Vincent and the Grenadines	70	235	397	551	699	672	675	689
Trinidad and Tobago	6 236	5 068	8 154	15 982	27 179	19 623	20 397	21 989
Turks and Caicos Islands	32	106	319	579	975	1 160	1 381	-
Central America	*251 487*	*319 756*	*706 585*	*941 573*	*1 227 000*	*1 012 502*	*1 180 933*	*1 317 461*
Belize	195	405	832	1 115	1 359	1 349	1 401	1 453
Costa Rica	6 139	7 254	15 947	19 965	29 838	29 241	35 891	40 638
El Salvador	1 173	4 801	13 134	17 094	21 431	20 661	21 215	22 777
Guatemala	7 024	6 820	17 196	27 211	39 136	37 683	41 473	47 064
Honduras	3 061	3 637	7 187	9 757	13 882	14 176	15 400	17 447
Mexico	227 664	288 013	636 731	846 095	1 091 981	879 099	1 032 224	1 150 016
Nicaragua	2 176	2 749	3 938	4 872	6 372	6 214	6 551	7 282
Panama, excl. Canal Zone (3)	4 054							
Panama	_	6 077	11 621	15 465	23 002	24 080	26 777	30 785
South America	*461 469*	*741 494*	*1 331 311*	*1 629 387*	*2 961 186*	*2 874 000*	*3 642 032*	*4 095 213*
Argentina	75 516	141 353	284 346	183 196	328 468	308 740	370 263	447 938
Bolivia (Plurinational State of)	3 502	4 868	8 398	9 549	16 674	17 340	19 640	23 937
Brazil	191 125	402 137	644 729	882 044	1 653 353	1 593 018	2 088 966	2 414 170
Chile	29 479	33 507	75 197	118 250	170 741	160 859	203 443	234 047
Colombia	47 204	56 925	99 876	146 566	244 465	234 693	288 086	335 124
Ecuador	12 351	11 248	16 283	36 942	54 209	52 022	58 910	67 545
Guyana	943	632	1 137	1 315	1 923	2 026	2 260	2 578
Paraguay	3 931	4 653	7 095	7 473	16 873	14 240	17 886	23 165
Peru	16 738	29 281	53 336	79 389	129 107	130 355	157 324	180 612
Suriname	891	615	946	1 785	3 065	3 252	3 682	3 903
Uruguay	10 642	9 239	22 823	17 363	31 177	31 322	40 265	47 720
Venezuela (Bolivarian Rep. of)	69 147	47 036	117 146	145 513	311 131	326 133	391 307	314 472
Developing economies: Asia	1 370 761	2 262 148	4 280 375	7 113 846	11 605 092	11 735 434	13 780 830	16 294 337
Eastern Asia	*453 547*	*936 368*	*2 239 551*	*3 698 213*	*6 117 916*	*6 508 695*	*7 454 024*	*8 944 603*
China	306 520	404 494	1 192 836	2 283 671	4 531 831	5 050 543	5 739 358	7 062 848
China, Hong Kong SAR	28 818	76 890	169 121	177 772	215 365	209 285	224 459	243 989
China, Macao SAR	1 053	3 397	6 302	11 502	20 149	20 738	27 177	34 649
China, Taiwan Province of	42 225	164 974	326 162	364 849	400 206	377 450	430 190	466 420
Korea, Dem. People's Rep. of	9 879	14 702	10 608	13 031	13 337	12 035	12 278	-
Korea, Republic of	64 385	270 405	533 385	844 866	931 405	834 060	1 014 369	1 115 670
Mongolia	667	1 507	1 137	2 523	5 623	4 584	6 192	8 749
Southern Asia	*332 364*	*509 988*	*715 635*	*1 250 800*	*1 940 262*	*2 020 193*	*2 467 048*	*2 830 317*
Afghanistan	3 642	3 622	3 532	6 840	10 789	12 490	15 676	18 666
Bangladesh	16 729	28 137	45 470	57 628	79 568	89 050	99 689	107 480
Bhutan	131	279	439	819	1 258	1 265	1 486	1 649
India	184 761	326 796	467 788	837 299	1 283 209	1 353 215	1 722 328	1 944 068
Iran (Islamic Rep. of)	91 928	91 036	104 016	205 586	366 295	352 420	386 670	470 378
Maldives	54	198	624	750	1 260	1 319	1 480	1 442
Nepal	2 089	3 780	5 730	8 259	11 692	12 742	16 020	18 164
Pakistan	28 757	47 937	71 319	109 213	145 478	155 716	174 150	209 315
Sri Lanka	4 273	8 204	16 717	24 406	40 714	41 977	49 549	59 155

For sources and notes, see end of table.

Per capita gross domestic product / Produit intérieur brut par habitant Dollars								Régions, pays ou territoires
1980	1990	2000	2005	2008	2009	2010	2011 (e)	
2 111	**2 561**	**4 129**	**4 897**	**7 641**	**7 020**	**8 558**	**9 481**	**Économies en développement : Amérique**
1 690	*2 074*	*2 821*	*3 741*	*5 031*	*4 783*	*4 996*	*5 265*	*Caraïbes*
1 304	6 536	9 760	12 504	19 709	14 355	13 750	14 046	Anguilla
1 567	6 295	8 553	10 330	13 850	12 890	12 602	12 321	Antigua-et-Barbuda
8 195	13 322	20 754	23 080	26 017	23 467	22 851	25 807	Aruba
7 506	14 447	21 258	24 130	24 696	23 072	22 462	22 230	Bahamas
3 904	7 440	10 890	13 623	14 652	14 280	14 497	14 698	Barbade
2 521	6 362	36 617	39 565	43 575	38 095	39 113	-	Îles Vierges britanniques
10 272	35 699	56 658	58 195	64 373	60 126	57 048	-	Îles Caïmanes
2 029	2 710	2 753	3 789	5 397	5 530	5 704	6 234	Cuba
939	2 821	4 656	5 246	6 780	7 069	7 021	6 962	Dominique
1 411	1 304	2 753	3 621	4 710	4 756	5 195	5 577	République dominicaine
841	2 298	5 120	6 788	8 002	7 311	7 429	7 779	Grenade
243	367	388	407	603	602	613	670	Haïti
1 428	2 039	3 470	4 163	5 101	4 514	4 899	5 333	Jamaïque
2 034	6 265	7 052	7 696	8 519	8 941	9 343	-	Montserrat
5 444	10 393	15 890	17 622	20 227	20 029	20 321	_	Antilles néerlandaises
1 109	3 909	7 144	8 922	11 161	10 530	10 494	11 016	Saint-Kitts-et-Nevis
1 151	3 014	4 455	5 125	6 349	6 160	6 677	6 723	Sainte-Lucie
698	2 187	3 684	5 070	6 404	6 153	6 172	6 298	Saint-Vincent-et-les Grenadines
5 784	4 169	6 311	12 150	20 419	14 684	15 205	16 332	Trinité-et-Tobago
4 276	9 171	16 926	18 953	27 122	31 124	36 000	-	Îles Turques et Caïques
2 740	*2 823*	*5 213*	*6 476*	*8 093*	*6 586*	*7 576*	*8 337*	*Amérique centrale*
1 354	2 131	3 320	3 968	4 541	4 417	4 496	4 571	Belize
2 620	2 363	4 069	4 633	6 598	6 370	7 704	8 598	Costa Rica
252	900	2 211	2 825	3 496	3 354	3 426	3 657	El Salvador
998	764	1 530	2 140	2 859	2 685	2 882	3 189	Guatemala
844	744	1 156	1 418	1 901	1 903	2 026	2 250	Honduras
3 310	3 416	6 370	7 946	9 871	7 847	9 101	10 018	Mexique
671	667	776	898	1 131	1 088	1 132	1 241	Nicaragua
2 076								Panama, sans la zone du canal (3)
	2 515	3 931	4 776	6 752	6 956	7 614	8 620	Panama
1 917	*2 510*	*3 834*	*4 389*	*7 709*	*7 403*	*9 283*	*10 330*	*Amérique du Sud*
2 684	4 330	7 699	4 736	8 271	7 706	9 162	10 988	Argentine
654	731	1 011	1 044	1 734	1 774	1 978	2 373	Bolivie (État plurinational de)
1 570	2 687	3 696	4 743	8 632	8 243	10 716	12 276	Brésil
2 637	2 541	4 877	7 254	10 166	9 487	11 888	13 553	Chili
1 756	1 714	2 512	3 405	5 432	5 141	6 223	7 141	Colombie
1 552	1 096	1 319	2 751	3 856	3 648	4 073	4 606	Équateur
1 214	872	1 550	1 763	2 558	2 690	2 996	3 410	Guyana
1 230	1 096	1 328	1 267	2 708	2 245	2 771	3 527	Paraguay
968	1 350	2 062	2 881	4 536	4 532	5 411	6 143	Pérou
2 435	1 511	2 026	3 574	5 951	6 255	7 018	7 373	Suriname
3 651	2 972	6 876	5 226	9 318	9 329	11 952	14 118	Uruguay
4 599	2 389	4 811	5 457	11 089	11 435	13 503	10 683	Venezuela (Rép. bolivarienne du)
561	**758**	**1 225**	**1 915**	**3 019**	**3 020**	**3 508**	**4 080**	**Économies en développement : Asie**
434	*770*	*1 662*	*2 664*	*4 338*	*4 592*	*5 234*	*6 151*	*Asie orientale*
317	360	957	1 777	3 472	3 850	4 354	5 241	Chine
5 703	13 271	24 932	26 105	31 093	29 949	31 824	34 258	Chine (RAS de Hong Kong)
4 275	9 443	14 592	23 893	38 863	39 040	49 990	62 349	Chine (RAS de Macao)
2 393	8 135	14 702	16 051	17 397	16 352	18 590	20 072	Province chinoise de Taiwan
573	730	463	549	553	497	504	-	Corée, Rép. populaire dém. de
1 719	6 291	11 598	17 959	19 512	17 389	21 052	23 055	Corée, République de
394	687	471	991	2 108	1 690	2 247	3 125	Mongolie
352	*426*	*490*	*789*	*1 171*	*1 202*	*1 448*	*1 637*	*Asie méridionale*
257	278	155	248	362	408	499	577	Afghanistan
207	267	351	410	547	606	670	714	Bangladesh
304	499	769	1 242	1 793	1 772	2 047	2 234	Bhoutan
264	374	444	734	1 078	1 120	1 406	1 566	Inde
2 383	1 659	1 592	2 948	5 067	4 819	5 227	6 289	Iran (Rép. islamique d')
342	901	2 285	2 540	4 097	4 230	4 685	4 504	Maldives
139	198	235	303	404	433	535	596	Népal
357	429	493	688	869	913	1 003	1 184	Pakistan
283	473	892	1 230	1 989	2 031	2 375	2 811	Sri Lanka

Pour les sources et les notes, se reporter à la fin du tableau.

8

Region, country or territory	Total gross domestic product / Produit intérieur brut total (1) Millions of dollars / Millions de dollars							
	1980	1990	2000	2005	2008	2009	2010	2011 (e)
South-Eastern Asia	*200 340*	*362 601*	*606 956*	*912 437*	*1 516 506*	*1 505 060*	*1 863 899*	*2 161 998*
Brunei Darussalam	5 587	3 520	6 001	9 531	14 394	10 733	13 024	17 224
Cambodia	712	1 698	3 667	6 293	10 352	10 402	11 272	12 869
Indonesia (…2002)	79 636	125 866	165 337					
Indonesia	–	–		285 869	510 229	539 356	707 448	846 142
Lao People's Dem. Rep.	321	866	1 653	2 739	5 285	5 585	6 496	7 863
Malaysia	25 429	45 716	93 790	137 954	222 574	192 917	237 797	277 407
Myanmar	5 905	5 172	7 275	11 931	25 859	32 805	42 027	53 950
Philippines	35 954	49 095	81 026	103 072	174 195	168 335	199 591	224 771
Singapore	12 046	38 835	94 308	125 429	189 384	183 332	222 699	254 499
Thailand	32 354	85 361	122 725	176 352	272 578	263 711	318 850	345 610
Timor-Leste	–	–	–	350	562	704	794	997
Viet Nam	2 396	6 472	31 173	52 917	91 094	97 180	103 902	120 667
Western Asia	*384 509*	*453 190*	*718 233*	*1 252 396*	*2 030 408*	*1 701 486*	*1 995 859*	*2 357 419*
Bahrain	3 292	4 293	8 028	13 459	22 151	19 319	22 945	27 620
Iraq	12 458	17 043	16 900	18 164	23 487	25 908	28 141	38 232
Jordan	4 013	4 020	8 461	12 589	22 698	25 092	27 504	30 017
Kuwait	28 691	18 471	37 718	80 798	147 380	105 902	124 331	166 837
Lebanon	4 074	2 812	16 679	21 861	29 933	34 528	39 248	41 271
Occupied Palestinian territory	1 074	1 936	4 195	4 634	6 247	6 764	7 349	-
Oman	6 256	11 556	19 450	30 905	60 567	46 865	57 850	70 988
Qatar	7 838	7 360	17 760	44 530	115 270	97 798	127 333	173 519
Saudi Arabia	164 540	116 622	188 442	315 583	476 305	372 663	434 666	569 251
Syrian Arab Republic	13 146	11 150	19 666	28 397	52 494	54 078	59 834	57 794
Turkey	92 477	202 546	266 560	482 986	730 325	614 570	734 440	778 457
United Arab Emirates	43 599	50 701	104 337	180 617	314 845	270 335	297 648	358 499
Yemen, Arab Republic	2 446							
Yemen, Democratic	606	–	–	–	–	–	–	–
Yemen		4 680	10 039	17 872	28 707	27 663	34 569	37 584
Developing economies: Oceania	**7 274**	**11 472**	**13 760**	**21 959**	**30 829**	**29 545**	**31 895**	**35 968**
Cook Islands	22	59	92	183	233	207	248	-
Fiji	1 215	1 351	1 723	3 006	3 565	2 825	3 052	3 650
French Polynesia	1 381	3 181	3 444	5 463	6 995	6 815	6 679	-
Kiribati	35	41	67	106	136	124	146	172
Marshall Islands	–	79	108	139	166	163	166	-
Micronesia (Federated States of)	–	155	234	250	263	280	297	-
Nauru	36	49	21	26	42	54	63	-
New Caledonia	1 182	2 529	3 412	6 236	9 124	8 754	8 861	-
Pacific Islands (Trust Territory)	116							
Palau	–	77	120	145	187	204	222	–
Papua New Guinea	2 823	3 286	3 499	4 866	8 000	8 060	9 796	12 841
Samoa	112	112	231	435	546	525	612	684
Solomon Islands	144	208	338	429	608	598	642	819
Tonga	79	162	189	259	341	320	369	436
Tuvalu	4	10	12	22	30	27	31	35
Vanuatu	125	173	272	393	593	590	710	795
Transition economies	**1 012 216**	**850 055**	**397 600**	**1 097 739**	**2 341 669**	**1 787 094**	**2 116 578**	**2 590 339**
Albania	2 219	2 222	3 640	8 159	12 970	12 041	11 783	12 938
Armenia			1 912	4 900	11 662	8 648	9 371	10 251
Azerbaijan	–	–	5 273	13 246	48 851	44 292	51 797	63 424
Belarus			10 418	30 210	60 752	49 271	54 713	54 629
Bosnia and Herzegovina	–	–	5 553	10 909	18 512	17 050	16 837	18 312
Croatia	–	–	21 518	44 821	69 911	63 435	60 852	63 951
Georgia	–	–	3 058	6 411	12 795	10 767	11 665	14 400
Kazakhstan	–	–	18 292	57 124	133 442	115 309	146 908	184 766
Kyrgyzstan	–	–	1 370	2 460	5 140	4 690	4 616	5 699
Montenegro					4 520	4 141	4 111	4 565
Republic of Moldova	–	–	1 288	2 988	6 055	5 439	5 809	6 997
Russian Federation	–	–	259 446	764 016	1 660 848	1 221 989	1 479 823	1 841 119
Serbia and Montenegro	–	–	11 431	31 223				
Serbia			–	–	53 402	45 583	43 304	50 796
SFR of Yugoslavia	69 959	79 502						
Tajikistan	–	–	861	2 312	5 161	4 979	5 613	6 524
TFYR of Macedonia	–	–	3 587	5 987	9 834	9 314	9 138	10 240
Turkmenistan	–	–	4 932	12 436	19 098	19 947	23 130	29 306
Ukraine	–	–	31 262	86 142	179 992	117 227	137 936	167 082
USSR	940 038	768 331						
Uzbekistan	–	–	13 759	14 396	28 723	32 971	39 173	45 341

For sources and notes, see end of table.

Per capita gross domestic product / Produit intérieur brut par habitant Dollars								Régions, pays ou territoires
1980	1990	2000	2005	2008	2009	2010	2011 (e)	
558	*814*	*1 159*	*1 630*	*2 614*	*2 565*	*3 141*	*3 603*	**Asie du Sud-Est**
29 513	13 963	18 351	26 249	37 415	27 391	32 648	41 568	Brunéi Darussalam
110	178	295	471	749	744	797	900	Cambodge
526	680	772	—					Indonésie (…2002)
—	—	—	1 258	2 172	2 272	2 949	3 492	Indonésie
99	206	311	476	878	914	1 048	1 250	Rép. dém. populaire lao
1 838	2 511	4 006	5 286	8 093	6 902	8 373	9 612	Malaisie
180	132	162	258	547	689	876	1 116	Myanmar
764	797	1 048	1 205	1 932	1 836	2 140	2 370	Philippines
4 989	12 874	24 063	29 402	39 685	37 069	43 783	49 056	Singapour
681	1 496	1 943	2 644	3 993	3 838	4 613	4 971	Thaïlande
			346	521	640	706	864	Timor-Leste
44	96	396	636	1 060	1 118	1 183	1 359	Viet Nam
4 018	*3 566*	*4 448*	*6 884*	*10 311*	*8 424*	*9 649*	*11 149*	**Asie occidentale**
9 197	8 710	12 579	18 569	21 049	16 518	18 184	20 868	Bahreïn
906	981	708	664	788	843	889	1 170	Iraq
1 746	1 177	1 753	2 357	3 881	4 164	4 445	4 742	Jordanie
20 836	8 848	19 434	35 688	57 834	40 019	45 430	59 203	Koweït
1 458	954	4 457	5 394	7 183	8 227	9 284	9 689	Liban
711	930	1 311	1 303	1 633	1 721	1 820	—	Territoire palestinien occupé
5 296	6 186	8 590	12 721	22 968	17 280	20 791	24 942	Oman
35 371	15 537	30 053	54 240	82 568	61 209	72 398	92 789	Qatar
16 787	7 226	9 401	13 127	18 203	13 901	15 836	20 271	Arabie saoudite
1 476	905	1 230	1 536	2 665	2 697	2 931	2 783	République arabe syrienne
2 097	3 742	4 189	7 088	10 297	8 554	10 095	10 571	Turquie
42 903	28 033	34 395	44 385	50 727	38 960	39 625	45 432	Émirats arabes unis
409	—	—	—	—	—	—	—	Yémen, République arabe du
252	—	—	—	—	—	—	—	Yémen, Démocratique
—	392	566	866	1 269	1 186	1 437	1 515	Yémen
1 467	*1 841*	*1 762*	*2 530*	*3 335*	*3 131*	*3 312*	*3 662*	**Économies en développement : Océanie**
1 276	3 330	5 139	9 409	11 661	10 247	12 212	—	Îles Cook
1 913	1 854	2 122	3 655	4 226	3 314	3 546	4 203	Fidji
9 138	16 282	14 492	21 434	26 440	25 458	24 669		Polynésie française
631	574	795	1 148	1 404	1 266	1 468	1 701	Kiribati
—	1 666	2 067	2 678	3 140	3 060	3 069		Îles Marshall
—	1 613	2 181	2 285	2 387	2 528	2 678	—	Micronésie (États fédérés de)
4 775	5 377	2 099	2 600	4 081	5 312	6 190	—	Nauru
8 302	14 906	16 095	26 987	37 562	35 455	35 319	—	Nouvelle-Calédonie
872								Îles du Pacifique (Territoire sous tutelle des)
—	5 096	6 252	7 267	9 252	10 008	10 822	—	Palaos
878	790	651	798	1 222	1 202	1 428	1 831	Papouasie-Nouvelle-Guinée
723	695	1 308	2 415	3 004	2 876	3 343	3 722	Samoa
626	672	827	914	1 192	1 140	1 193	1 493	Îles Salomon
845	1 697	1 926	2 566	3 309	3 087	3 543	4 169	Tonga
534	1 059	1 302	2 289	3 028	2 716	3 187	3 579	Tuvalu
1 083	1 181	1 470	1 862	2 602	2 525	2 963	3 239	Vanuatu
3 496	*2 697*	*1 303*	*3 638*	*7 752*	*5 909*	*6 989*	*8 543*	**Économies en transition**
831	675	1 185	2 597	4 077	3 771	3 677	4 023	Albanie
		621	1 598	3 787	2 803	3 031	3 307	Arménie
—	—	650	1 542	5 462	4 885	5 638	6 815	Azerbaïdjan
—	—	1 036	3 075	6 276	5 113	5 702	5 715	Bélarus
—	—	1 503	2 885	4 905	4 525	4 478	4 880	Bosnie-Herzégovine
—	—	4 776	10 090	15 823	14 382	13 820	14 549	Croatie
—	—	644	1 432	2 912	2 462	2 680	3 326	Géorgie
—	—	1 223	3 765	8 524	7 279	9 167	11 401	Kazakhstan
—	—	277	488	988	890	865	1 057	Kirghizistan
			—	7 184	6 569	6 510	7 219	Monténégro
—	—	314	793	1 666	1 510	1 626	1 974	République de Moldova
—	—	1 768	5 311	11 601	8 542	10 351	12 890	Fédération de Russie
—	—	1 062	2 978					Serbie-et-Monténégro
		—	—	5 426	4 627	4 394	5 155	Serbie
3 263	3 481							RSF de Yougoslavie
		139	358	771	734	816	935	Tadjikistan
—	—	1 785	2 937	4 791	4 528	4 434	4 962	LERY de Macédoine
—	—	1 096	2 619	3 883	4 006	4 587	5 740	Turkménistan
—	—	639	1 836	3 914	2 564	3 035	3 697	Ukraine
3 542	2 658		—	—	—	—	—	URSS
—	—	555	555	1 071	1 215	1 427	1 633	Ouzbékistan

Pour les sources et les notes, se reporter à la fin du tableau.

8

8.1.1 Nominal gross domestic product: Total and per capita of countries and geographical regions

Region, country or territory	Total gross domestic product / Produit intérieur brut total (1) Millions of dollars / Millions de dollars							
	1980	1990	2000	2005	2008	2009	2010	2011 (e)
Developed economies: America	**3 053 740**	**6 372 838**	**10 697 508**	**13 790 763**	**15 825 486**	**15 305 169**	**16 131 380**	**16 867 707**
Bermuda	919	1 997	3 518	4 846	6 068	5 715	6 015	-
Canada	268 889	582 735	724 914	1 133 757	1 502 678	1 337 577	1 577 040	1 738 953
Greenland	476	1 019	1 068	1 703	2 228	2 016	2 022	-
United States	2 783 456	5 787 087	9 968 008	12 650 457	14 314 511	13 959 861	14 546 302	15 120 717
Developed economies: Asia	**1 094 711**	**3 115 802**	**4 792 343**	**4 686 159**	**5 081 498**	**5 227 848**	**5 676 318**	**6 075 554**
Israel	23 714	57 763	124 894	133 968	201 660	194 865	217 445	243 371
Japan	1 070 997	3 058 038	4 667 448	4 552 191	4 879 838	5 032 983	5 458 873	5 832 184
Developed economies: Europe	**3 955 605**	**7 631 255**	**8 907 997**	**14 446 064**	**19 223 608**	**17 209 065**	**17 196 091**	**18 684 170**
Andorra	546	1 259	1 387	3 179	4 127	3 731	3 491	-
Austria	81 464	164 851	192 071	304 984	414 174	381 775	379 047	417 751
Belgium	125 368	202 958	232 673	377 253	507 020	472 878	469 347	511 681
Bulgaria	10 778	20 726	12 904	28 894	51 824	48 569	47 702	53 502
Cyprus	2 230	5 777	9 174	16 902	25 132	23 413	22 957	24 695
Czechoslovakia	47 822	52 522						
Czech Republic	–	–	58 803	130 066	225 427	196 151	197 674	215 690
Denmark	69 709	135 839	160 082	257 676	341 467	308 925	309 866	329 860
Estonia	–	–	5 680	13 903	23 854	19 235	18 958	22 342
Finland	52 984	138 852	121 715	195 626	271 947	240 701	238 731	265 286
France	691 723	1 246 615	1 328 990	2 140 835	2 838 376	2 630 063	2 565 273	2 775 142
Germany, Federal Republic of (4)	919 651							
Germany	–	1 714 447	1 886 400	2 766 254	3 623 688	3 298 634	3 280 334	3 572 727
Greece	54 702	94 203	127 088	240 076	341 188	321 795	301 065	298 378
Hungary	25 009	36 500	46 386	110 322	154 234	126 632	128 629	139 898
Iceland	3 331	6 373	8 697	16 286	16 851	12 113	12 574	14 023
Ireland	21 435	48 167	97 525	203 280	263 654	223 098	206 600	220 256
Italy	459 811	1 133 465	1 097 343	1 777 694	2 296 498	2 111 157	2 051 290	2 189 887
Latvia	–	–	7 776	15 938	33 453	25 854	24 014	28 261
Lithuania	–	–	11 501	26 100	47 552	37 002	36 478	42 736
Luxembourg	5 969	12 670	20 270	37 659	57 768	51 945	53 330	59 611
Malta	1 250	2 547	3 957	5 981	8 554	8 099	8 163	8 933
Netherlands	180 777	294 869	385 074	638 471	870 812	793 430	779 310	836 176
Norway	63 714	117 624	168 288	302 013	445 193	370 671	413 056	479 701
Poland	57 828	64 550	171 276	303 912	529 391	430 546	469 393	514 128
Portugal	32 421	77 584	117 014	191 176	251 925	234 199	228 859	237 715
Romania	36 432	40 550	37 305	99 173	204 339	164 344	161 629	186 619
San Marino	229	565	774	1 375	1 844	1 531	1 487	1 540
Slovakia	–	–	20 403	47 895	94 395	87 374	87 263	96 165
Slovenia	–	–	19 982	35 718	54 608	49 053	46 906	50 014
Spain	225 984	520 938	580 673	1 130 170	1 593 913	1 464 088	1 407 322	1 497 279
Sweden	132 136	244 545	247 259	370 580	486 159	403 613	458 725	532 042
Switzerland	110 387	239 641	252 396	376 135	508 289	497 058	533 065	639 504
United Kingdom	541 917	1 012 617	1 477 132	2 280 538	2 635 954	2 171 385	2 253 552	2 419 136
Developed economies: Oceania	**198 165**	**371 986**	**464 394**	**877 824**	**1 183 323**	**1 119 300**	**1 413 351**	**1 682 134**
Australia	175 082	327 559	411 009	764 765	1 052 897	1 001 935	1 271 945	1 521 812
New Zealand	23 082	44 426	53 385	113 058	130 426	117 365	141 406	160 322

Source:
UNCTAD secretariat calculations, based on UN DESA Statistics Division, *National Accounts Main Aggregates Database*

Notes:
(1) GDP by expenditure, in current prices and current exchange rates.
(2) Including Western Sahara.
(3) Data refer to Panama from 1970 to 1980.
(4) Data refer to Germany from 1970 to 1989.

Per capita gross domestic product / Produit intérieur brut par habitant Dollars								Régions, pays ou territoires
1980	1990	2000	2005	2008	2009	2010	2011 (e)	
11 848	22 378	33 724	41 399	46 232	44 318	46 304	48 000	Économies développées : Amérique
16 391	33 400	55 995	75 568	93 847	88 197	92 625	-	Bermudes
10 968	21 037	23 638	35 119	45 088	39 720	46 361	50 625	Canada
9 482	18 343	19 005	29 770	38 878	35 181	35 293	-	Groenland
11 940	22 520	34 802	42 068	46 347	44 808	46 290	47 708	États-Unis
9 148	24 582	36 379	35 235	38 025	39 068	42 375	45 320	Économies développées : Asie
6 331	12 836	20 764	20 284	28 434	26 837	29 312	32 183	Israël
9 240	25 014	37 126	36 016	38 562	39 770	43 141	46 105	Japon
8 587	16 103	17 987	28 605	37 578	33 509	33 366	36 144	Économies développées : Europe
14 630	23 856	21 459	40 821	49 981	44 591	41 138	-	Andorre
10 792	21 492	23 995	37 048	49 650	45 614	45 159	49 653	Autriche
12 731	20 400	22 866	36 225	47 822	44 356	43 815	47 580	Belgique
1 216	2 350	1 612	3 734	6 827	6 439	6 365	7 185	Bulgarie
4 384	9 971	13 227	22 298	31 693	29 277	28 364	30 699	Chypre
3 141	3 373	_	_	_	_	_	_	Tchécoslovaquie
		5 741	12 726	21 723	18 789	18 839	20 475	République tchèque
13 607	26 423	29 981	47 546	62 115	55 915	55 830	59 193	Danemark
_	_	4 144	10 330	17 773	14 337	14 135	16 666	Estonie
11 086	27 846	23 527	37 302	51 153	45 062	44 502	49 266	Finlande
12 546	21 414	21 859	34 051	44 323	40 837	39 608	42 613	France
11 747	_	_	_	_	_	_	_	Allemagne, Rép. fédérale d' (4)
_	21 675	22 907	33 514	43 937	40 029	39 857	43 484	Allemagne
5 673	9 271	11 567	21 468	30 216	28 411	26 504	26 196	Grèce
2 338	3 518	4 543	10 937	15 390	12 660	12 884	14 037	Hongrie
14 601	25 012	30 928	54 884	54 241	38 389	39 278	43 233	Islande
6 272	13 640	25 639	48 888	60 570	50 564	46 220	48 667	Irlande
8 179	19 944	19 256	30 299	38 344	35 041	33 877	36 025	Italie
_	_	3 260	6 913	14 729	11 433	10 663	12 599	Lettonie
_	_	3 286	7 641	14 153	11 075	10 975	12 921	Lituanie
16 391	33 236	46 544	82 370	118 673	104 384	105 095	115 538	Luxembourg
3 827	6 931	9 958	14 612	20 665	19 506	19 599	21 378	Malte
12 832	19 801	24 275	39 157	52 766	47 915	46 910	50 176	Pays-Bas
15 595	27 732	37 473	65 324	93 157	76 680	84 589	97 404	Norvège
1 625	1 696	4 472	7 963	13 852	11 256	12 263	13 424	Pologne
3 313	7 817	11 321	18 132	23 689	21 976	21 438	22 238	Portugal
1 641	1 747	1 681	4 555	9 465	7 631	7 522	8 706	Roumanie
10 703	23 392	28 698	45 392	59 113	48 818	47 171	48 522	Saint-Marin
_	_	3 775	8 844	17 348	16 026	15 976	17 576	Slovaquie
_	_	10 064	17 840	27 058	24 235	23 110	24 577	Slovénie
6 027	13 395	14 413	26 044	35 306	32 080	30 543	32 231	Espagne
15 900	28 572	27 907	41 042	52 632	43 347	48 906	56 356	Suède
17 443	35 753	35 051	50 490	66 803	64 916	69 226	82 645	Suisse
9 592	17 634	24 995	37 738	42 858	35 086	36 189	38 611	Royaume-Uni
11 097	18 151	20 171	35 775	45 880	42 681	53 061	62 255	Économies développées : Océanie
11 902	19 160	21 447	37 482	48 941	45 746	57 119	67 320	Australie
7 334	13 074	13 837	27 348	30 489	27 151	32 372	36 317	Nouvelle-Zélande

Source :
Calculs du secrétariat de la CNUCED, basés sur ONU DAES Division de statistique, *National Accounts Main Aggregates Database*

Notes :
(1)   PIB par dépenses, aux prix et taux de change courants.
(2)   Y compris le Sahara occidental.
(3)   Les données se réfèrent au Panama de 1970 à 1980.
(4)   Les données se réfèrent à l'Allemagne de 1970 à 1989.

8

8.1.2 Nominal gross domestic product: Total and per capita of economic groupings

Economic grouping	Total gross domestic product / Produit intérieur brut total (1) Millions of dollars / Millions de dollars							
	1980	1990	2000	2005	2008	2009	2010	2011 (e)
DEVELOPING ECONOMIES	**2 568 673**	**3 891 832**	**7 026 938**	**10 846 202**	**17 577 186**	**17 311 604**	**20 530 256**	**23 812 034**
Developing economies excluding China	2 262 153	3 487 338	5 834 101	8 562 531	13 045 355	12 261 061	14 790 898	16 749 186
Developing economies excluding LDCs	2 458 463	3 739 702	6 845 607	10 534 837	17 035 481	16 765 121	19 916 634	23 113 687
High-income developing economies	1 000 804	1 597 765	3 115 025	4 278 472	6 022 912	5 257 578	6 229 511	6 944 328
Middle-income developing economies	999 715	1 503 855	2 864 946	4 747 000	8 621 445	9 036 344	10 612 187	12 640 644
Low-income developing economies	568 154	790 212	1 046 966	1 820 730	2 932 829	3 017 682	3 688 558	4 227 062
Heavily indebted poor countries (IMF)	110 392	143 950	147 702	248 370	403 377	401 216	439 777	491 246
Landlocked developing countries	48 935	73 922	126 921	232 073	459 754	436 938	513 136	616 375
Small island developing States	18 775	26 794	42 977	62 376	87 238	76 032	81 710	90 927
Least developed countries	*110 211*	*152 130*	*181 331*	*311 365*	*541 705*	*546 483*	*613 622*	*698 346*
Africa and Haiti	77 004	102 990	102 326	196 738	365 007	351 180	382 699	435 749
Asia	32 581	48 232	77 806	112 382	173 511	192 001	227 234	258 225
Islands	626	908	1 199	2 246	3 188	3 301	3 689	4 372
Major petroleum and gas exporters	*603 561*	*498 129*	*754 550*	*1 313 260*	*2 360 290*	*2 039 580*	*2 357 421*	*2 705 310*
Africa	179 104	138 302	148 780	291 563	545 012	441 555	509 475	543 134
America	69 147	47 036	117 146	145 513	311 131	326 133	391 307	314 472
Asia	355 310	312 790	488 624	876 184	1 504 148	1 271 892	1 456 639	1 847 704
Major exporters of manufactured goods	*739 441*	*1 374 688*	*3 169 059*	*4 956 986*	*7 855 323*	*7 990 398*	*9 219 947*	*10 916 457*
America	227 664	288 013	636 731	846 095	1 091 981	879 099	1 032 224	1 150 016
Asia	511 777	1 086 675	2 532 328	4 110 891	6 763 342	7 111 299	8 187 723	9 766 442
Emerging economies	*716 961*	*1 499 583*	*2 864 709*	*3 758 423*	*5 389 797*	*4 923 542*	*6 076 126*	*6 886 388*
America	540 522	894 292	1 694 338	2 108 974	3 373 650	3 072 071	3 852 220	4 426 783
Asia	176 439	605 291	1 170 370	1 649 449	2 016 146	1 851 472	2 223 906	2 459 605
Newly industrialized Asian economies	*320 847*	*857 142*	*1 585 854*	*2 216 161*	*2 915 935*	*2 768 446*	*3 355 404*	*3 774 507*
First tier	147 474	551 104	1 122 976	1 512 915	1 736 359	1 604 127	1 891 718	2 080 577
Second tier	173 373	306 038	462 878	703 246	1 179 576	1 164 319	1 463 686	1 693 930
Developing economies: Africa	434 164	495 104	599 818	1 006 833	1 570 188	1 484 880	1 710 100	1 874 224
Northern Africa excluding Sudan	131 328	171 358	247 445	334 942	551 307	519 534	581 660	606 040
Sub-Saharan Africa	302 836	323 746	352 374	671 891	1 018 881	965 346	1 128 440	1 268 184
Sub-Saharan Africa excluding South Africa	222 293	211 732	219 496	424 839	743 603	682 592	764 736	859 745
Developing economies: America	756 475	1 123 109	2 132 984	2 703 564	4 371 076	4 061 746	5 007 431	5 607 505
Central America and Greater Caribbean Islands excluding Puerto Rico	284 007	365 222	773 122	1 032 729	1 353 078	1 139 642	1 316 281	1 465 148
Central America and Greater Caribbean Islands excluding Mexico and Puerto Rico	56 343	77 209	136 391	186 634	261 098	260 543	284 057	315 133
South America and Central America	712 955	1 061 251	2 037 897	2 570 960	4 188 186	3 886 502	4 822 966	5 412 673
South America excluding Brazil	270 344	339 357	686 582	747 343	1 307 833	1 280 982	1 553 067	1 681 043
Developing economies: Asia	1 370 761	2 262 148	4 280 375	7 113 846	11 605 092	11 735 434	13 780 830	16 294 337
Eastern and South-Eastern Asia excluding China	347 367	894 475	1 653 671	2 326 979	3 102 591	2 963 212	3 578 565	4 043 753
Southern Asia excluding India	147 604	183 193	247 847	413 501	657 054	666 978	744 720	886 249

Source:
UNCTAD secretariat calculations, based on UN DESA Statistics Division, *National Accounts Main Aggregates Database*

Notes:
(1)   GDP by expenditure, in current prices and current exchange rates.

Per capita gross domestic product / Produit intérieur brut par habitant Dollars								Groupements économiques
1980	1990	2000	2005	2008	2009	2010	2011 (e)	
781	**958**	**1 456**	**2 092**	**3 255**	**3 164**	**3 703**	**4 222**	**ÉCONOMIES EN DÉVELOPPEMENT**
973	1 186	1 629	2 195	3 186	2 947	3 500	3 902	Économies en développement sans la Chine
849	1 052	1 643	2 373	3 701	3 600	4 227	4 827	Économies en développement sans les PMA
3 681	4 779	7 954	10 194	13 716	11 800	13 792	15 189	Économies en développement à revenu élevé
680	853	1 429	2 259	4 003	4 162	4 851	5 674	Économies en développement à revenu intermédiaire
367	402	431	683	1 045	1 057	1 270	1 431	Économies en développement à revenu faible
395	395	303	446	671	650	695	757	Pays pauvres très endettés (FMI)
321	373	383	629	1 170	1 088	1 250	1 469	Pays en développement sans littoral
1 752	2 108	2 860	3 615	4 829	4 147	4 391	4 815	Petits États insulaires en développement
280	*299*	*274*	*418*	*680*	*671*	*737*	*821*	*Pays les moins avancés*
333	337	255	427	732	685	727	807	Afrique et Haïti
202	238	302	398	589	643	750	839	Asie
634	725	765	811	1 076	1 091	1 192	1 381	Îles
3 245	*1 978*	*2 397*	*3 727*	*6 237*	*5 266*	*5 950*	*6 681*	*Principaux exportateurs de pétrole et de gaz*
1 705	1 006	858	1 495	2 604	2 061	2 323	2 419	Afrique
4 599	2 389	4 811	5 457	11 089	11 435	13 503	10 683	Amérique
5 390	3 306	4 174	6 703	10 663	8 798	9 850	12 239	Asie
638	*1 013*	*2 095*	*3 167*	*4 928*	*4 983*	*5 717*	*6 637*	*Principaux exportateurs d'articles manufacturés*
3 310	3 416	6 370	7 946	9 871	7 847	9 101	10 018	Amérique
470	854	1 793	2 819	4 559	4 768	5 461	6 384	Asie
1 959	*3 385*	*5 603*	*6 936*	*9 652*	*8 734*	*10 680*	*11 996*	*Économies émergentes*
2 188	2 966	4 805	5 624	8 714	7 856	9 753	11 098	Amérique
1 485	4 276	7 377	9 886	11 771	10 724	12 786	14 039	Asie
995	*2 175*	*3 470*	*4 555*	*5 793*	*5 442*	*6 527*	*7 266*	*Économies nouvellement industrialisées d'Asie*
2 357	7 647	14 237	18 713	21 063	19 331	22 665	24 787	Première génération
667	950	1 224	1 734	2 803	2 735	3 399	3 889	Deuxième génération
901	**780**	**741**	**1 107**	**1 611**	**1 489**	**1 676**	**1 795**	**Économies en développement : Afrique**
1 414	1 434	1 747	2 187	3 436	3 189	3 517	3 612	Afrique septentrionale sans le Soudan
778	629	527	888	1 251	1 157	1 319	1 447	Afrique subsaharienne
617	443	352	599	972	870	950	1 041	Afrique subsaharienne sans l'Afrique du Sud
2 111	**2 561**	**4 129**	**4 897**	**7 641**	**7 020**	**8 558**	**9 481**	**Économies en développement : Amérique**
2 465	2 599	4 644	5 804	7 314	6 081	6 935	7 623	Amérique centrale et Grandes Antilles sans Porto Rico
1 214	1 374	2 050	2 612	3 511	3 457	3 719	4 071	Amérique centrale et Grandes Antilles sans le Mexique et Porto Rico
2 144	2 597	4 221	4 976	7 818	7 171	8 798	9 762	Amérique du Sud et Amérique centrale
2 270	2 327	3 972	4 033	6 792	6 570	7 869	8 414	Amérique du Sud sans le Brésil
561	**758**	**1 225**	**1 915**	**3 019**	**3 020**	**3 508**	**4 080**	**Économies en développement : Asie**
792	1 665	2 648	3 509	4 528	4 280	5 116	5 723	Asie orientale et Asie du Sud-Est sans la Chine
603	569	610	930	1 412	1 412	1 553	1 820	Asie méridionale sans l'Inde

Source :
Calculs du secrétariat de la CNUCED, basés sur ONU DAES Division de statistique, *National Accounts Main Aggregates Database*

Notes :
(1)   PIB par dépenses, aux prix et taux de change courants.

8

8.2.1 Annual average growth rates of total and per capita real gross domestic product of countries and geographical regions

Region, country or territory	Total real gross domestic product (1) / Produit intérieur brut réel total (1) Percentage / En pourcentage										
	80 -89	92 -00	00 -10	05 -08	05 -09	05 -11 (e)	2005	2008	2009	2010	2011 (e)
WORLD	3.3	3.1	2.8	3.3	2.0	1.9	3.5	1.4	-2.3	4.0	2.7
DEVELOPING ECONOMIES	3.5	4.8	6.1	7.0	5.9	5.8	6.8	5.1	2.5	7.5	5.8
TRANSITION ECONOMIES	3.5	-1.8	5.7	7.5	4.4	3.2	6.5	5.2	-6.5	4.2	4.5
DEVELOPED ECONOMIES	3.2	2.9	1.6	1.9	0.5	0.5	2.4	-0.1	-4.0	2.7	1.4
Developing economies: Africa	1.8	3.1	5.1	5.7	4.6	3.7	5.4	4.8	0.9	4.0	0.8
Eastern Africa	2.5	3.4	5.3	6.4	6.1	6.0	6.1	5.8	4.9	6.5	5.8
Burundi	4.3	-2.9	3.5	5.5	5.0	4.5	0.9	4.3	3.4	3.9	4.2
Comoros	3.0	1.1	1.9	0.9	1.0	1.4	4.2	1.0	1.8	2.1	2.2
Djibouti	0.4	1.0	4.6	7.3	6.6	5.8	3.2	5.0	5.5	4.5	4.5
Eritrea	–	5.7	0.2	-2.8	-2.1	-0.1	2.6	-9.8	3.6	1.8	8.7
Ethiopia (...1991)	1.7										
Ethiopia	–	5.3	8.9	11.1	10.6	10.4	11.8	10.8	8.8	12.4	7.5
Kenya	4.3	2.5	4.4	5.1	4.3	4.3	5.9	1.5	2.6	5.6	4.4
Madagascar	0.8	2.8	3.4	6.1	4.1	2.5	4.6	7.1	-4.1	0.5	1.8
Malawi	2.0	3.4	5.7	7.7	8.1	7.6	3.3	8.3	8.9	6.7	4.3
Mauritius	6.2	5.1	4.1	5.4	4.9	4.5	1.5	5.5	3.0	4.0	4.1
Mozambique	-1.5	8.7	7.9	7.6	7.2	7.1	8.4	6.8	6.3	7.0	7.3
Rwanda	2.1	3.0	8.1	9.2	8.8	8.4	9.3	11.5	6.1	7.5	8.6
Seychelles	3.7	4.8	2.7	6.2	4.4	4.7	6.7	-1.3	0.7	9.5	5.1
Somalia	1.7	-1.6	2.9	2.5	2.6	2.7	3.0	2.6	2.6	2.6	4.0
Uganda	3.0	7.6	7.0	8.5	7.8	6.3	10.0	10.4	4.4	2.5	5.1
United Republic of Tanzania	2.4	4.0	7.0	7.1	6.9	6.8	7.3	7.4	6.0	6.8	6.8
Zambia	1.0	0.8	5.6	6.2	6.2	6.4	5.2	6.0	6.1	7.1	6.6
Zimbabwe	3.3	1.7	-2.8	-3.8	-1.8	1.6	-4.1	-4.7	7.3	9.0	5.9
Middle Africa	2.4	2.9	8.1	10.2	8.6	6.7	10.6	8.9	2.4	3.8	4.6
Angola	3.5	5.0	13.0	18.7	14.9	10.2	20.6	13.8	2.4	3.4	3.9
Cameroon	1.5	3.6	3.2	3.1	2.8	2.9	2.3	2.9	1.6	3.0	4.2
Central African Republic	1.1	1.3	1.7	4.3	3.8	3.5	2.4	4.4	1.8	3.3	3.3
Chad	6.7	3.0	8.0	0.2	0.2	1.3	7.9	0.3	0.3	5.1	1.8
Congo	4.0	1.2	4.4	2.9	4.0	5.1	7.6	5.9	7.5	8.7	3.4
Dem. Rep. of the Congo	2.2	-3.6	5.5	6.0	5.4	5.6	7.8	6.1	2.8	7.2	6.9
Equatorial Guinea	2.3	28.5	16.6	15.2	13.3	9.4	8.9	15.2	4.6	-0.8	7.8
Gabon	0.5	2.1	1.8	2.0	1.6	2.7	5.6	1.7	-0.4	5.6	6.6
Sao Tome and Principe	-1.2	1.7	5.6	7.4	6.9	6.1	3.1	9.4	4.8	4.5	4.9
Northern Africa	2.9	3.4	4.9	5.3	4.9	3.5	5.2	4.9	3.7	4.1	-5.7
Algeria	2.9	2.5	3.9	2.5	2.5	2.6	5.1	2.4	2.4	3.3	2.4
Egypt	7.7	4.8	5.1	7.0	6.6	5.6	4.5	7.2	4.7	5.1	1.8
Libya	-3.4	0.8	5.2	4.9	3.5	-6.8	10.3	2.7	-0.7	4.2	-59.7
Morocco (2)	4.2	2.9	4.9	5.1	5.0	4.7	3.0	5.6	4.9	3.3	4.9
Sudan (...2011)	2.2	6.4	7.4	9.0	8.7	6.5	6.1	7.8	8.2	5.1	-4.5
Tunisia	3.2	4.7	4.7	5.5	5.0	3.8	4.0	4.5	3.1	3.7	-1.8
Southern Africa	1.6	2.9	3.9	4.9	3.5	2.8	5.0	3.5	-1.7	3.0	3.2
Botswana	11.0	7.2	4.1	4.3	2.3	2.7	1.7	2.9	-4.9	7.2	5.1
Lesotho	3.7	3.7	3.4	4.6	4.3	3.9	2.4	4.7	3.0	2.4	4.9
Namibia	2.2	2.9	5.0	5.5	4.1	3.7	2.5	4.3	-0.7	4.4	4.9
South Africa	1.4	2.7	3.9	5.0	3.5	2.8	5.3	3.6	-1.7	2.8	3.1
Swaziland	7.5	3.4	2.5	2.7	2.2	1.8	2.3	0.5	1.2	2.0	0.3
Western Africa	-0.3	3.1	5.8	4.8	2.8	2.6	4.0	3.5	-4.1	3.7	6.2
Benin	3.4	4.9	3.8	4.5	4.2	3.7	2.9	5.0	2.7	2.6	3.5
Burkina Faso	2.6	6.0	5.8	5.4	5.0	4.9	8.7	6.4	3.2	5.8	4.2
Cape Verde	5.6	7.9	6.3	8.4	7.2	6.2	6.5	6.2	3.6	5.4	5.0
Côte d'Ivoire	3.3	4.1	1.1	2.4	2.1	1.3	1.8	3.8	0.0	2.6	-4.7
Gambia	3.4	3.0	3.8	4.0	4.6	5.0	-0.9	5.6	6.3	6.1	3.3
Ghana	2.6	4.3	5.7	6.5	6.2	7.2	6.2	8.4	4.0	7.7	14.4
Guinea	3.0	4.6	2.4	2.5	2.1	2.2	3.0	4.9	-0.3	1.9	3.9
Guinea-Bissau	2.8	-0.5	2.9	3.7	4.6	4.4	4.0	4.0	7.9	1.6	5.3
Liberia	-0.4	16.7	0.9	8.2	7.4	6.8	5.3	7.1	4.6	5.1	8.2
Mali	3.8	4.4	5.2	4.8	4.7	4.4	6.1	5.0	4.5	4.5	2.7
Mauritania	1.4	2.9	5.8	6.3	4.6	4.0	9.0	0.8	1.6	4.7	4.0
Niger	-1.9	3.6	4.5	5.8	4.7	4.6	7.4	9.6	-0.9	7.5	2.3
Nigeria	-2.3	2.3	7.3	5.0	1.9	1.6	3.4	2.3	-8.3	2.8	7.4
Senegal	3.2	4.1	4.2	3.7	3.4	3.3	5.6	3.2	2.2	4.2	2.6
Sierra Leone	2.5	-9.5	8.2	5.0	4.9	5.0	7.5	4.7	4.9	4.9	6.0
Togo	1.3	3.1	2.4	2.7	2.8	3.2	1.2	2.4	3.6	3.7	4.9

For sources and notes, see end of table.

Per capita real gross domestic product (1) / Produit intérieur brut réel par habitant (1) Percentage / En pourcentage											Régions, pays ou territoires
80-89	92-00	00-10	05-08	05-09	05-11 (e)	2005	2008	2009	2010	2011 (e)	
1.5	**1.7**	**1.5**	**2.0**	**0.8**	**0.7**	**2.3**	**0.2**	**-3.5**	**2.9**	**1.2**	**MONDE**
1.4	3.0	4.6	5.5	4.5	4.3	5.3	3.7	1.2	6.1	4.0	ÉCONOMIES EN DÉVELOPPEMENT
2.5	-1.7	5.8	7.5	4.3	3.1	6.6	5.1	-6.6	4.1	4.4	ÉCONOMIES EN TRANSITION
2.6	2.3	1.0	1.3	-0.1	-0.1	1.8	-0.7	-4.5	2.1	0.9	ÉCONOMIES DÉVELOPPÉES
-0.9	**0.7**	**2.7**	**3.2**	**2.2**	**1.4**	**3.0**	**2.4**	**-1.4**	**1.6**	**-1.5**	**Économies en développement : Afrique**
-0.5	*0.7*	*2.7*	*3.8*	*3.4*	*3.3*	*3.4*	*3.2*	*2.3*	*3.8*	*3.1*	*Afrique orientale*
1.0	-3.8	0.6	2.3	1.9	1.6	-2.0	1.2	0.5	1.3	1.9	Burundi
0.1	-1.5	-0.8	-1.8	-1.6	-1.2	1.5	-1.7	-0.9	-0.5	-0.4	Comores
-4.5	-1.7	2.6	5.2	4.6	3.8	1.3	3.0	3.5	2.6	2.5	Djibouti
‾	3.8	-3.4	-5.9	-5.2	-3.1	-1.3	-12.5	0.5	-1.2	5.5	Érythrée
-1.4											Éthiopie (...1991)
‾	2.2	6.4	8.6	8.2	8.0	9.2	8.4	6.5	10.0	5.2	Éthiopie
0.5	-0.3	1.7	2.5	1.7	1.6	3.2	-1.1	0.0	2.8	1.6	Kenya
-1.8	-0.4	0.3	3.0	1.1	-0.5	1.5	4.0	-6.9	-2.3	-1.1	Madagascar
-2.2	1.4	2.8	4.6	4.9	4.3	0.5	5.1	5.6	3.4	1.1	Malawi
5.3	3.9	3.2	4.6	4.2	3.9	0.6	4.8	2.4	3.4	3.6	Maurice
-2.5	5.5	5.2	5.0	4.7	4.6	5.7	4.3	3.9	4.6	4.9	Mozambique
-1.6	-0.7	5.4	6.2	5.7	5.2	7.0	8.3	2.9	4.3	5.4	Rwanda
2.4	3.7	1.7	5.3	3.6	4.1	5.6	-1.9	0.1	9.0	4.7	Seychelles
1.8	-3.2	0.5	0.3	0.4	0.5	0.7	0.4	0.4	0.3	1.5	Somalie
-0.4	4.3	3.6	5.0	4.4	3.0	6.5	6.9	1.1	-0.7	1.8	Ouganda
-0.7	1.2	4.1	4.1	3.9	3.8	4.4	4.3	3.0	3.7	3.6	République-Unie de Tanzanie
-2.1	-1.8	3.0	3.5	3.4	3.5	2.7	3.2	3.2	4.1	3.5	Zambie
-0.5	0.1	-2.8	-3.5	-1.6	1.5	-3.9	-4.5	7.1	8.2	4.4	Zimbabwe
-0.5	*0.1*	*5.2*	*7.3*	*5.7*	*3.9*	*7.5*	*6.1*	*-0.2*	*1.2*	*2.0*	*Afrique centrale*
0.4	2.0	9.4	15.2	11.5	7.1	16.7	10.6	-0.5	0.6	1.1	Angola
-1.4	1.1	0.9	0.9	0.5	0.6	0.0	0.6	-0.7	0.8	2.0	Cameroun
-1.5	-1.0	0.0	2.5	2.0	1.6	0.7	2.5	-0.1	1.4	1.3	République centrafricaine
3.8	-0.2	4.7	-2.6	-2.5	-1.5	4.5	-2.3	-2.3	2.3	-0.9	Tchad
1.0	-1.6	1.8	0.2	1.2	2.4	5.0	3.0	4.6	6.0	1.0	Congo
-0.8	-6.3	2.5	3.1	2.5	2.8	4.7	3.2	0.0	4.3	4.1	Rép. dém. du Congo
-3.4	24.4	13.2	12.0	10.1	6.3	5.7	12.0	1.7	-3.5	4.8	Guinée équatoriale
-2.6	-0.7	-0.2	0.1	-0.3	0.8	3.6	-0.1	-2.2	3.6	4.6	Gabon
-3.2	-0.2	3.9	5.7	5.2	4.4	1.5	7.7	3.1	2.7	3.0	Sao Tomé-et-Principe
0.2	*1.5*	*3.1*	*3.5*	*3.1*	*1.7*	*3.4*	*3.1*	*1.9*	*2.4*	*-7.3*	*Afrique septentrionale*
-0.1	0.7	2.3	1.0	1.0	1.1	3.5	0.8	0.9	1.8	0.9	Algérie
5.2	3.0	3.2	5.1	4.7	3.8	2.6	5.3	2.9	3.3	0.0	Égypte
-6.9	-1.0	3.1	2.6	1.4	-8.5	8.1	0.6	-2.5	2.6	-60.1	Libye
1.7	1.4	3.8	4.0	4.0	3.6	1.9	4.5	3.9	2.3	3.8	Maroc (2)
-0.6	3.7	4.8	6.3	6.0	3.8	3.6	5.1	5.5	2.5	-6.8	Soudan (...2011)
0.7	3.3	3.7	4.4	3.8	2.6	3.0	3.3	2.0	2.5	-2.8	Tunisie
-0.9	*1.0*	*2.7*	*3.8*	*2.4*	*1.8*	*3.8*	*2.5*	*-2.7*	*2.2*	*2.5*	*Afrique australe*
7.4	4.7	2.7	2.9	0.9	1.3	0.5	1.4	-6.2	5.8	3.9	Botswana
1.4	1.8	2.4	3.6	3.3	2.9	1.5	3.6	2.0	1.4	3.9	Lesotho
-1.2	0.1	3.1	3.6	2.2	1.8	0.7	2.3	-2.6	2.5	3.0	Namibie
-1.0	0.9	2.7	3.9	2.5	1.9	4.0	2.6	-2.5	2.1	2.5	Afrique du Sud
3.6	1.3	1.4	1.3	0.8	0.3	1.4	-1.1	-0.4	0.5	-1.2	Swaziland
-2.9	*0.5*	*3.2*	*2.2*	*0.2*	*0.0*	*1.4*	*0.9*	*-6.6*	*1.0*	*3.5*	*Afrique occidentale*
0.6	1.8	0.7	1.4	1.1	0.7	-0.3	2.0	-0.3	-0.3	0.7	Bénin
0.0	3.1	2.8	2.4	2.0	1.9	5.5	3.3	0.2	2.7	1.1	Burkina Faso
4.0	5.5	5.0	7.3	6.1	5.2	5.1	5.3	2.7	4.5	4.1	Cap-Vert
-0.6	1.4	-0.6	0.6	0.3	-0.6	0.2	1.9	-1.9	0.6	-6.7	Côte d'Ivoire
-1.0	0.1	0.8	1.1	1.8	2.1	-3.7	2.7	3.4	3.2	0.5	Gambie
-0.5	1.7	3.2	3.9	3.6	4.7	3.6	5.9	1.5	5.2	11.8	Ghana
0.5	1.5	0.6	0.6	0.2	0.1	1.3	2.9	-2.4	-0.3	1.5	Guinée
0.9	-2.4	0.8	1.6	2.4	2.3	2.0	1.9	5.7	-0.5	3.2	Guinée-Bissau
-1.7	11.5	-2.5	3.3	2.5	2.1	2.3	1.8	-0.2	1.0	4.6	Libéria
2.0	1.6	2.0	1.6	1.5	1.3	2.9	1.8	1.3	1.3	-0.3	Mali
-1.4	0.0	3.0	3.5	1.9	1.4	6.0	-1.7	-0.9	2.2	1.6	Mauritanie
-4.6	0.1	0.9	2.2	1.1	0.9	3.7	5.8	-4.4	3.7	-1.3	Niger
-4.8	-0.1	4.7	2.4	-0.6	-0.9	0.9	-0.2	-10.5	0.2	4.7	Nigéria
0.2	1.4	1.4	0.9	0.6	0.6	2.8	0.5	-0.5	1.5	-0.1	Sénégal
0.0	-9.9	4.4	2.1	2.2	2.4	3.3	2.2	2.5	2.6	3.7	Sierra Leone
-2.0	0.2	0.1	0.5	0.6	1.0	-1.0	0.2	1.4	1.5	2.7	Togo

Pour les sources et les notes, se reporter à la fin du tableau.

8

Region, country or territory	Total real gross domestic product (1) / Produit intérieur brut réel total (1) Percentage / En pourcentage										
	80 -89	92 -00	00 -10	05 -08	05 -09	05 -11 (e)	2005	2008	2009	2010	2011 (e)
Developing economies: America	1.8	3.1	3.6	5.1	3.5	3.5	4.6	3.9	-2.2	6.0	4.3
Caribbean	2.6	3.7	4.6	6.0	4.5	3.5	7.6	3.1	0.0	2.9	2.7
Anguilla	7.7	5.2	7.0	15.2	4.3	-1.4	8.3	1.3	-25.5	-3.8	-2.0
Antigua and Barbuda	6.8	3.6	4.3	7.5	3.4	-0.3	4.2	0.2	-8.5	-4.1	-5.0
Aruba	11.0	4.7	-0.1	-0.4	-2.2	-2.0	1.0	-2.5	-8.1	-3.7	8.9
Bahamas	4.5	4.6	0.7	0.9	-0.6	-0.6	3.4	-1.4	-5.4	0.9	1.6
Barbados	1.7	3.0	1.7	2.5	0.6	-0.2	3.9	-0.2	-5.5	-0.5	0.6
British Virgin Islands	5.9	17.4	1.8	1.1	1.8	2.7	14.3	1.5	4.3	4.5	3.5
Cayman Islands	8.9	8.1	1.4	2.4	-0.1	-1.5	6.5	-0.8	-7.9	-4.0	1.1
Cuba	4.0	2.2	6.1	7.7	6.1	4.4	11.2	4.1	1.4	2.1	2.7
Dominica	5.2	2.0	3.2	6.0	4.7	3.3	-0.5	7.7	-0.9	2.1	-0.3
Dominican Republic	3.0	6.3	5.6	8.1	6.9	6.4	9.3	5.3	3.5	7.8	4.5
Grenada	5.4	8.4	1.3	1.5	-0.5	-0.9	12.0	0.9	-8.3	0.4	1.0
Haiti	0.1	1.1	0.6	2.3	2.3	1.3	1.8	0.8	2.9	-5.1	5.6
Jamaica	1.5	0.3	0.9	1.1	0.1	-0.3	1.4	-0.5	-3.0	-1.1	1.3
Montserrat	2.8	-11.2	1.2	0.7	1.9	2.1	0.4	6.7	3.6	1.3	1.2
Netherlands Antilles	-0.9	0.8	1.5	2.6	2.0	_	1.1	2.4	-0.5	0.0	_
Saint Kitts and Nevis	6.3	4.7	2.7	3.7	1.3	-0.4	5.6	4.3	-7.7	-1.5	-2.0
Saint Lucia	7.7	2.7	2.4	2.2	0.8	0.3	8.5	0.8	-3.8	0.4	1.3
Saint Vincent and the Grenadines	6.2	3.2	3.3	4.6	2.9	0.9	2.0	1.4	-2.2	-2.8	0.1
Trinidad and Tobago	-3.7	5.9	6.6	6.5	3.9	2.2	6.2	2.4	-3.5	2.5	-1.4
Turks and Caicos Islands	10.7	9.2	11.8	13.7	13.5	11.8	14.4	12.8	13.5	13.9	-1.0
Central America	0.8	3.3	2.4	3.5	1.4	1.7	3.4	1.5	-5.6	5.6	4.0
Belize	3.8	4.6	4.0	2.9	2.3	2.2	3.1	3.8	0.0	2.7	2.5
Costa Rica	2.8	5.0	4.9	6.6	4.6	3.8	5.9	2.7	-1.3	4.2	4.2
El Salvador	0.3	4.2	2.2	3.1	1.7	1.1	3.6	1.3	-3.1	1.4	1.5
Guatemala	0.4	4.1	3.6	5.1	4.0	3.4	3.3	3.3	0.5	2.6	3.9
Honduras	2.7	2.9	4.6	5.7	4.0	3.1	6.1	4.2	-2.1	2.8	3.6
Mexico	0.8	3.3	2.1	3.2	1.1	1.4	3.3	1.2	-6.3	5.8	3.9
Nicaragua	-1.7	4.6	3.1	3.5	2.4	2.7	4.3	2.8	-1.5	4.5	5.1
Panama	_	4.2	7.0	10.6	9.0	8.4	7.2	10.7	2.6	7.5	10.6
South America	2.2	2.9	4.2	5.9	4.6	4.4	5.0	5.3	-0.4	6.4	4.5
Argentina	-0.2	3.0	5.6	8.0	6.4	6.6	9.2	6.8	0.9	9.2	8.9
Bolivia (Plurinational State of)	-0.7	4.0	4.1	5.1	4.8	4.7	4.4	6.1	3.4	4.1	5.2
Brazil	3.1	2.9	3.7	5.2	4.0	4.1	3.2	5.2	-0.6	7.5	2.7
Chile	2.5	5.7	4.0	4.3	3.0	3.3	5.6	3.7	-1.7	5.2	6.0
Colombia	3.5	2.4	4.5	5.8	4.7	4.4	4.7	3.5	1.5	4.3	5.9
Ecuador	1.9	1.9	4.6	4.4	3.8	3.9	5.7	7.2	0.4	3.2	7.8
Guyana	-3.2	4.6	2.4	4.9	4.4	4.1	-2.0	2.0	3.3	3.6	5.4
Paraguay	2.5	1.7	3.8	5.7	3.8	5.1	2.9	5.8	-3.8	15.3	4.4
Peru	0.4	4.8	6.1	8.8	7.3	6.9	6.8	9.8	0.9	8.8	6.9
Suriname	1.0	1.4	5.0	5.1	4.7	4.5	3.9	5.1	3.1	4.4	4.5
Uruguay	0.7	2.8	3.9	6.8	6.1	6.3	7.5	8.6	2.6	8.5	5.7
Venezuela (Bolivarian Rep. of)	0.6	0.9	4.6	7.7	5.1	2.9	10.3	4.2	-3.3	-1.4	4.2
Developing economies: Asia	5.4	5.9	7.2	7.9	7.0	6.9	7.9	5.5	4.4	8.4	6.9
Eastern Asia	9.7	7.6	8.3	9.5	8.5	8.3	8.6	6.9	5.9	9.5	7.7
China	10.8	9.9	10.8	12.4	11.5	10.8	11.3	9.6	9.2	10.4	9.2
China, Hong Kong SAR	7.3	2.8	4.6	5.3	3.4	3.5	7.1	2.3	-2.7	7.0	5.0
China, Macao SAR	7.4	0.6	12.0	10.9	8.3	11.6	8.3	2.8	1.5	26.2	20.7
China, Taiwan Province of	7.8	5.7	4.1	4.2	2.7	3.7	4.7	0.7	-1.9	10.9	4.0
Korea, Dem. People's Rep. of	2.7	-2.3	1.2	0.1	0.2	0.5	3.8	3.1	-0.9	0.7	1.9
Korea, Republic of	10.1	5.8	4.1	4.3	3.3	3.5	4.0	2.3	0.3	6.2	3.6
Mongolia	3.8	3.0	7.2	9.3	7.1	7.3	7.3	8.9	-1.3	6.4	17.5
Southern Asia	4.6	5.3	7.1	7.3	7.0	6.7	8.2	4.1	6.9	7.1	5.9
Afghanistan	-1.0	-2.2	13.1	10.4	7.7	6.7	14.5	2.3	0.6	8.2	5.8
Bangladesh	3.7	4.9	5.9	6.4	6.3	6.2	6.0	6.2	5.7	6.1	6.5
Bhutan	10.4	6.1	8.3	10.5	9.4	8.0	7.1	4.7	6.7	6.7	5.3
India	5.7	6.3	8.0	8.2	8.1	8.0	9.3	4.9	9.1	8.8	6.8
Iran (Islamic Rep. of)	1.5	3.3	5.0	5.4	4.0	2.7	5.3	1.0	0.1	1.0	2.0
Maldives	11.9	8.2	6.1	9.9	5.1	4.6	-5.0	3.4	-8.9	11.6	5.8
Nepal	4.6	4.9	3.9	4.3	4.5	4.5	3.1	6.1	4.4	4.6	3.9
Pakistan	6.4	3.4	5.1	4.6	4.1	3.8	7.7	1.6	3.6	4.1	3.0
Sri Lanka	4.1	5.3	5.7	6.8	6.1	6.4	6.2	6.0	3.5	8.0	8.3
South-Eastern Asia	4.7	4.2	5.4	5.9	4.8	4.9	5.8	4.0	1.3	8.0	4.5
Brunei Darussalam	-2.5	1.7	1.3	0.8	0.0	0.6	0.4	-1.9	-1.8	4.1	2.2
Cambodia	6.6	6.5	8.7	9.3	7.2	6.2	13.3	6.7	0.1	6.0	7.1

For sources and notes, see end of table.

Per capita real gross domestic product (1) / Produit intérieur brut réel par habitant (1) Percentage / En pourcentage											Régions, pays ou territoires
80 -89	92 -00	00 -10	05 -08	05 -09	05 -11 (e)	2005	2008	2009	2010	2011 (e)	
-0.3	1.4	2.3	3.8	2.3	2.3	3.3	2.7	-3.3	4.8	3.1	**Économies en développement : Amérique**
1.1	*2.4*	*3.6*	*5.1*	*3.6*	*2.7*	*6.6*	*2.2*	*-0.7*	*2.1*	*2.0*	*Caraïbes*
5.7	2.6	3.5	12.0	1.7	-3.7	4.4	-1.0	-27.1	-5.7	-3.8	Anguilla
8.4	1.0	2.9	6.3	2.3	-1.4	2.8	-0.9	-9.5	-5.1	-6.0	Antigua-et-Barbuda
10.8	1.3	-1.9	-1.8	-3.5	-3.1	-1.0	-3.7	-9.1	-4.5	8.2	Aruba
2.4	3.1	-0.7	-0.5	-2.0	-2.0	1.9	-2.9	-6.7	-0.4	0.4	Bahamas
1.3	2.7	1.5	2.3	0.4	-0.4	3.7	-0.4	-5.7	-0.7	0.4	Barbade
1.5	14.9	0.5	0.0	0.7	1.6	12.9	0.4	3.2	3.4	2.4	Îles Vierges britanniques
4.4	3.7	-1.9	0.5	-1.6	-2.7	2.4	-1.9	-8.7	-4.8	0.2	Îles Caïmanes
3.3	1.8	6.0	7.7	6.0	4.4	11.0	4.1	1.5	2.1	2.7	Cuba
5.9	2.3	3.5	6.4	5.1	3.6	-0.2	8.1	-0.6	2.3	-0.2	Dominique
0.8	4.5	4.1	6.6	5.4	4.9	7.7	3.8	2.1	6.3	3.1	République dominicaine
4.2	7.8	1.0	1.1	-0.9	-1.2	11.7	0.6	-8.7	0.0	0.6	Grenade
-2.2	-0.8	-0.9	0.9	0.9	-0.1	0.3	-0.5	1.6	-6.3	4.2	Haïti
0.4	-0.7	0.3	0.7	-0.3	-0.8	0.8	-1.0	-3.4	-1.5	0.9	Jamaïque
4.0	-1.5	-1.6	-0.9	0.6	1.1	-4.5	6.1	3.3	0.6	0.3	Montserrat
-1.9	1.7	0.3	1.0	0.4	_	-0.2	0.7	-2.0	-1.3		Antilles néerlandaises
7.0	3.3	1.3	2.4	0.0	-1.6	4.3	2.9	-8.9	-2.7	-3.2	Saint-Kitts-et-Nevis
6.0	1.3	1.4	1.1	-0.3	-0.8	7.4	-0.2	-4.9	-0.6	0.3	Sainte-Lucie
5.5	3.2	3.1	4.5	2.7	0.8	1.8	1.3	-2.3	-2.8	0.1	Saint-Vincent-et-les Grenadines
-5.0	5.3	6.2	6.1	3.5	1.8	5.8	2.0	-3.9	2.1	-1.7	Trinité-et-Tobago
6.0	4.7	4.0	7.6	8.0	7.3	5.6	7.9	9.5	10.7	-3.1	Îles Turques et Caïques
-1.3	*1.5*	*0.9*	*2.1*	*0.0*	*0.3*	*2.0*	*0.1*	*-7.0*	*4.1*	*2.6*	*Amérique centrale*
0.9	1.8	1.7	0.8	0.2	0.1	0.8	1.7	-2.0	0.7	0.5	Belize
0.0	2.5	3.1	4.9	3.0	2.2	4.1	1.1	-2.8	2.6	2.7	Costa Rica
-1.0	3.3	1.8	2.6	1.2	0.6	3.2	0.8	-3.6	0.9	0.9	El Salvador
-2.0	1.8	1.1	2.6	1.5	0.9	0.7	0.8	-1.9	0.1	1.3	Guatemala
-0.4	0.5	2.5	3.6	1.9	1.1	4.0	2.2	-4.1	0.7	1.6	Honduras
-1.2	1.5	0.9	1.9	-0.2	0.2	2.0	-0.1	-7.5	4.5	2.7	Mexique
-4.0	2.5	1.8	2.2	1.1	1.3	3.0	1.4	-2.8	3.1	3.6	Nicaragua
_	2.1	5.1	8.8	7.2	6.6	5.3	8.9	1.0	5.8	8.9	Panama
0.1	*1.3*	*3.0*	*4.7*	*3.4*	*3.3*	*3.7*	*4.2*	*-1.5*	*5.3*	*3.4*	*Amérique du Sud*
-1.7	1.7	4.6	7.1	5.5	5.7	8.2	5.8	0.0	8.2	7.9	Argentine
-2.9	1.8	2.2	3.4	3.1	3.0	2.6	4.4	1.7	2.5	3.5	Bolivie (État plurinational de)
0.9	1.3	2.6	4.1	3.0	3.1	2.0	4.2	-1.5	6.6	1.8	Brésil
0.9	4.1	2.9	3.3	2.0	2.3	4.5	2.7	-2.6	4.2	5.0	Chili
1.3	0.6	2.9	4.3	3.2	2.9	3.1	2.0	0.0	2.9	4.5	Colombie
-0.7	0.2	3.0	2.8	2.2	2.4	4.0	5.7	-1.1	1.8	6.3	Équateur
-2.4	4.4	2.1	4.7	4.1	3.9	-2.3	1.8	3.1	3.4	5.2	Guyana
-0.4	-0.6	1.9	3.8	1.9	3.3	0.9	3.9	-5.5	13.3	2.6	Paraguay
-1.9	3.0	4.9	7.6	6.1	5.8	5.6	8.6	-0.2	7.6	5.7	Pérou
0.0	0.0	3.7	4.0	3.6	3.5	2.7	4.1	2.1	3.5	3.6	Suriname
0.1	2.1	3.7	6.5	5.9	6.0	7.4	8.3	2.2	8.1	5.3	Uruguay
-2.1	-1.2	2.7	5.9	3.3	1.2	8.4	2.5	-4.9	-2.9	2.6	Venezuela (Rép. bolivarienne du)
3.3	4.3	5.9	6.6	5.8	5.7	6.6	4.4	3.2	7.3	5.2	**Économies en développement : Asie**
8.0	*6.6*	*7.7*	*8.9*	*8.0*	*7.6*	*8.0*	*6.4*	*5.4*	*9.0*	*5.5*	*Asie orientale*
9.2	8.9	10.2	11.8	10.9	10.0	10.7	9.0	8.7	9.9	6.9	Chine
5.9	1.0	4.3	4.7	2.7	2.7	7.0	1.5	-3.5	6.0	4.0	Chine (RAS de Hong Kong)
3.2	-1.0	9.4	8.2	5.6	9.0	5.8	0.3	-0.9	23.3	18.1	Chine (RAS de Macao)
6.3	4.8	3.6	3.8	2.3	3.3	4.3	0.3	-2.3	10.6	3.6	Province chinoise de Taiwan
1.1	-3.5	0.6	-0.4	-0.3	0.0	3.1	2.6	-1.4	0.3	1.5	Corée, Rép. populaire dém. de
8.6	5.1	3.6	3.8	2.8	3.0	3.5	1.8	-0.2	5.7	3.2	Corée, République de
1.0	2.2	5.8	7.7	5.4	5.6	5.9	7.2	-2.9	4.7	15.7	Mongolie
2.2	*3.3*	*5.5*	*5.7*	*5.4*	*5.2*	*6.6*	*2.6*	*5.4*	*5.6*	*4.4*	*Asie méridionale*
0.9	-6.6	9.5	7.6	5.0	3.9	10.7	-0.1	-1.8	5.4	2.7	Afghanistan
1.0	2.8	4.5	5.2	5.1	5.0	4.5	5.1	4.6	4.9	5.2	Bangladesh
7.3	5.4	5.7	8.2	7.2	6.1	4.4	2.8	4.9	4.9	3.5	Bhoutan
3.3	4.4	6.4	6.6	6.5	6.5	7.7	3.4	7.6	7.3	5.4	Inde
-2.1	1.6	3.7	4.1	2.7	1.5	4.0	-0.2	-1.1	-0.1	0.9	Iran (Rép. islamique d')
8.1	6.0	4.5	8.4	3.7	3.2	-6.4	2.1	-10.1	10.1	4.5	Maldives
2.1	2.3	1.8	2.3	2.5	2.6	1.0	4.2	2.5	2.7	2.1	Népal
2.9	0.7	3.2	2.7	2.3	2.0	5.8	-0.2	1.7	2.3	1.2	Pakistan
2.6	4.6	4.5	5.7	5.0	5.3	5.0	4.9	2.6	7.0	7.3	Sri Lanka
2.5	*2.5*	*4.1*	*4.6*	*3.6*	*3.7*	*4.5*	*2.8*	*0.1*	*6.8*	*3.4*	*Asie du Sud-Est*
-5.3	-0.8	-0.7	-1.2	-1.9	-1.4	-1.6	-3.8	-3.6	2.2	-1.6	Brunéi Darussalam
2.4	3.9	7.3	8.1	6.0	5.0	11.9	5.5	-1.0	4.8	5.8	Cambodge

Pour les sources et les notes, se reporter à la fin du tableau.

8

Region, country or territory	Total real gross domestic product (1) / Produit intérieur brut réel total (1) Percentage / En pourcentage										
	80 -89	92 -00	00 -10	05 -08	05 -09	05 -11 (e)	2005	2008	2009	2010	2011 (e)
Indonesia (...2002)	5.7	2.9	–	–	–	–	–	–	–	–	–
Indonesia			–	6.1	5.7	5.7	5.7	4.9	4.6	6.1	6.5
Lao People's Dem. Rep.	5.0	6.5	8.5	12.0	10.9	9.6	7.3	7.8	7.5	7.7	8.0
Malaysia	4.9	6.1	5.0	5.8	4.2	4.2	5.3	4.8	-1.6	7.2	5.1
Myanmar	0.9	7.2	12.3	11.8	11.4	10.4	13.6	10.2	10.4	10.4	5.5
Philippines	0.5	3.7	4.9	5.5	4.5	4.6	4.8	4.2	1.1	7.6	3.9
Singapore	6.7	6.7	6.0	6.5	4.6	5.6	7.4	1.5	-0.8	14.5	4.9
Thailand	7.0	2.8	4.5	4.3	2.8	2.8	4.6	2.5	-2.3	7.8	0.1
Timor-Leste	–	–	–	4.9	7.2	8.2	6.2	11.0	12.9	6.1	10.6
Viet Nam	5.6	7.8	7.5	7.7	7.1	6.7	8.4	6.3	5.3	6.8	5.9
Western Asia	*1.1*	*3.9*	*5.0*	*5.0*	*3.6*	*4.0*	*6.9*	*3.8*	*-1.1*	*6.4*	*7.2*
Bahrain	-0.7	3.7	6.3	7.2	6.3	5.2	7.9	6.3	3.1	4.5	2.1
Iraq	0.9	16.8	4.6	5.5	6.2	7.0	4.4	6.6	9.3	7.3	8.9
Jordan	2.0	3.8	6.7	8.1	6.9	5.3	8.1	7.6	2.3	3.1	2.6
Kuwait	1.1	3.8	6.2	4.8	2.7	2.4	10.6	5.0	-5.2	2.0	8.2
Lebanon	1.6	3.4	4.9	6.0	6.8	6.6	0.9	9.3	8.0	7.5	1.5
Occupied Palestinian territory	2.8	8.1	4.1	2.6	4.1	5.7	8.6	7.1	7.4	6.5	10.7
Oman	8.2	3.7	4.7	8.2	7.1	6.0	4.0	12.8	1.1	4.2	5.4
Qatar	1.4	8.9	14.2	20.3	18.2	17.3	7.5	17.7	12.0	19.4	14.1
Saudi Arabia	-2.2	1.8	3.6	3.0	2.5	3.0	5.6	4.2	0.2	3.8	7.1
Syrian Arab Republic	0.9	5.3	5.1	5.1	5.3	4.0	6.2	4.5	6.0	3.2	-3.4
Turkey	5.3	3.8	4.7	4.1	1.9	3.1	8.4	0.7	-4.8	9.0	8.5
United Arab Emirates	-2.9	6.3	5.1	5.2	3.5	2.8	4.9	3.3	-1.6	1.4	5.2
Yemen, Arab Republic	5.1	–	–	–	–	–	–	–	–	–	–
Yemen, Democratic	2.4	–	–	–	–	–	–	–	–	–	–
Yemen	–	8.9	4.8	4.3	4.4	3.4	5.9	4.7	4.7	8.0	-10.5
Developing economies: Oceania	**3.8**	**1.9**	**2.8**	**3.1**	**2.8**	**2.9**	**3.4**	**2.6**	**1.9**	**3.4**	**3.8**
Cook Islands	4.9	0.7	0.9	0.3	-0.9	-1.7	-1.1	-3.5	-3.6	-2.4	-2.4
Fiji	1.3	3.1	1.2	0.3	-0.4	-0.3	5.4	-0.1	-3.0	0.1	2.1
French Polynesia	5.9	1.8	1.9	1.7	1.7	1.7	1.3	1.8	1.6	1.6	1.6
Kiribati	0.8	4.2	1.2	1.8	1.0	0.6	0.0	3.4	-2.3	-0.4	1.8
Marshall Islands	–	-1.0	2.2	1.2	0.6	0.8	2.0	1.4	-2.1	0.5	5.0
Micronesia (Federated States of)	–	0.6	-0.2	-1.5	-1.2	0.0	2.1	-2.4	0.7	3.1	1.4
Nauru	-1.0	-9.6	-1.9	9.1	8.5	4.9	-9.8	95.6	-18.2	0.0	-7.8
New Caledonia	4.6	1.4	3.6	3.8	3.3	3.0	3.6	1.4	2.4	3.5	1.9
Palau	–	3.2	1.9	1.4	1.5	2.2	5.5	-1.0	2.9	2.5	5.8
Papua New Guinea	2.3	2.0	3.9	5.5	5.7	6.3	3.9	6.6	5.5	7.1	8.9
Samoa	1.1	3.5	3.0	1.7	0.7	0.6	5.3	-3.4	-1.7	1.5	2.0
Solomon Islands	1.8	1.7	4.8	5.9	3.8	4.4	12.8	7.1	-4.7	7.1	10.7
Tonga	4.6	2.1	0.9	0.4	0.3	0.4	-0.8	2.6	-1.0	0.3	1.5
Tuvalu	6.6	4.1	1.9	4.3	3.4	2.6	-4.1	1.3	1.5	1.6	1.1
Vanuatu	6.0	2.9	4.1	6.7	6.0	5.2	5.2	6.2	3.5	5.0	2.5
Transition economies	**3.5**	**-1.8**	**5.7**	**7.5**	**4.4**	**3.2**	**6.5**	**5.2**	**-6.5**	**4.2**	**4.5**
Albania	1.9	6.3	5.6	6.3	5.8	4.9	5.8	7.7	3.3	3.5	3.0
Armenia	–	4.4	9.2	11.5	5.5	2.7	13.9	6.9	-14.1	2.1	4.6
Azerbaijan	–	-2.1	17.1	23.2	19.1	12.9	26.4	10.8	9.3	5.0	0.1
Belarus	–	0.6	8.0	9.5	7.6	6.7	9.4	10.2	0.2	7.6	5.3
Bosnia and Herzegovina	–	22.2	4.3	6.0	4.1	2.6	3.9	5.7	-2.9	0.8	1.3
Croatia	–	3.6	3.2	4.1	1.9	0.3	4.3	2.2	-6.0	-1.2	0.0
Georgia	–	1.2	6.9	8.4	5.3	4.6	9.6	2.3	-3.8	6.4	7.0
Kazakhstan	–	-2.5	8.3	7.6	5.9	5.7	9.7	3.3	1.2	7.0	7.5
Kyrgyzstan	–	-0.8	4.4	6.8	6.2	4.6	-0.2	8.4	2.9	-1.4	5.7
Montenegro	–								-5.7	2.5	3.2
Republic of Moldova	–	-6.4	5.2	5.0	2.9	3.2	7.5	7.8	-6.0	6.9	6.4
Russian Federation	–	-1.8	5.4	7.4	4.0	2.9	6.4	5.2	-7.8	4.0	4.3
Serbia and Montenegro	–	-0.2	–	–	–	–	5.3	–	–	–	–
Serbia	–	–	–	–	–	–	–	–	-2.3	2.1	2.1
SFR of Yugoslavia	1.0	–	–	–	–	–	–	–	–	–	–
Tajikistan	–	-6.8	8.1	7.4	6.7	6.5	6.7	7.6	4.0	6.5	7.4
TFYR of Macedonia	–	1.3	3.3	5.5	4.1	3.1	4.4	5.0	-0.9	1.8	3.0
Turkmenistan	–	-1.0	8.3	12.1	11.1	10.8	13.0	14.7	6.1	9.2	14.7
Ukraine	–	-7.9	4.8	6.0	1.2	0.5	2.7	2.3	-14.8	4.2	5.2
USSR	3.8	–	–	–	–	–	–	–	–	–	–
Uzbekistan	–	1.6	7.2	8.7	8.6	8.5	7.0	9.0	8.1	8.5	8.3
Developed economies: America	**3.6**	**3.9**	**1.7**	**1.5**	**0.3**	**0.5**	**3.1**	**-0.3**	**-3.5**	**3.0**	**1.8**
Bermuda	1.6	4.1	2.7	3.5	0.7	-0.4	5.2	-0.3	-8.1	1.5	-2.0
Canada	3.3	3.7	2.0	1.9	0.9	1.1	3.0	0.7	-2.8	3.2	2.4
Greenland	2.4	3.2	0.5	0.8	-0.6	-0.4	2.0	-1.1	-5.2	1.7	1.7
United States	3.7	3.9	1.7	1.4	0.3	0.5	3.1	-0.4	-3.5	3.0	1.8

For sources and notes, see end of table.

Per capita real gross domestic product (1) / Produit intérieur brut réel par habitant (1) Percentage / En pourcentage											Régions, pays ou territoires
80-89	92-00	00-10	05-08	05-09	05-11 (e)	2005	2008	2009	2010	2011 (e)	
3.5	1.4	–									Indonésie (…2002)
		–	4.9	4.6	4.6	4.4	3.8	3.5	5.0	5.4	Indonésie
2.3	4.2	6.8	10.3	9.2	8.0	5.7	6.2	5.9	6.2	6.5	Rép. dém. populaire lao
2.0	3.5	3.0	4.0	2.4	2.5	3.3	3.1	-3.2	5.5	3.4	Malaisie
-0.9	5.8	11.6	11.1	10.6	9.6	13.0	9.5	9.6	9.6	4.6	Myanmar
-2.2	1.4	3.0	3.6	2.7	2.9	2.8	2.4	-0.5	5.8	2.2	Philippines
4.3	4.0	3.1	2.6	0.7	2.1	4.7	-2.5	-4.2	11.3	2.8	Singapour
5.0	1.7	3.5	3.5	2.0	2.1	3.6	1.8	-3.0	7.2	-0.5	Thaïlande
–	–	–	2.7	5.0	5.9	2.4	9.0	10.8	3.8	7.8	Timor-Leste
3.3	6.2	6.3	6.6	6.0	5.6	7.3	5.1	4.2	5.6	4.8	Viet Nam
-1.8	*1.5*	*2.4*	*2.2*	*0.9*	*1.4*	*4.2*	*1.1*	*-3.6*	*3.9*	*4.8*	*Asie occidentale*
-3.7	1.0	-1.3	-5.4	-5.8	-5.2	0.0	-6.5	-7.2	-3.1	-2.7	Bahreïn
-1.4	13.1	1.7	2.5	3.2	3.8	1.6	3.5	6.1	4.1	5.5	Iraq
-1.9	0.9	4.0	4.8	3.7	2.3	5.5	4.3	-0.7	0.4	0.3	Jordanie
-3.6	3.3	2.6	0.7	-1.2	-1.3	7.0	0.8	-8.7	-1.4	5.0	Koweït
1.2	1.1	3.6	5.0	5.8	5.7	-0.5	8.5	7.2	6.7	0.7	Liban
-0.3	3.5	1.8	0.1	1.5	3.0	6.4	4.4	4.6	3.6	7.7	Territoire palestinien occupé
3.3	2.5	2.5	5.2	4.2	3.2	1.8	9.6	-1.7	1.6	3.1	Oman
-6.6	6.2	1.2	0.7	-0.1	1.8	-6.4	-0.7	-2.2	8.5	7.3	Qatar
-7.2	0.0	0.3	0.2	-0.2	0.4	1.9	1.6	-2.2	1.3	4.6	Arabie saoudite
-2.4	2.7	2.6	2.9	3.1	2.0	3.5	2.5	4.1	1.4	-5.1	République arabe syrienne
3.1	2.2	3.3	2.7	0.6	1.7	7.0	-0.7	-6.0	7.6	7.2	Turquie
-8.2	0.9	-4.7	-8.7	-9.6	-8.3	-5.7	-10.0	-12.0	-6.3	0.1	Émirats arabes unis
2.2	–	–	–	–	–	–	–	–	–	–	Yémen, République arabe du
-3.5	–	–	–	–	–	–	–	–	–	–	Yémen, Démocratique
	5.0	1.6	1.2	1.3	0.3	2.7	1.5	1.6	4.8	-13.2	Yémen
1.4	*-0.4*	*0.7*	*1.0*	*0.7*	*0.8*	*1.2*	*0.5*	*-0.2*	*1.3*	*1.8*	*Économies en développement : Océanie*
4.8	0.8	-0.5	-0.7	-1.8	-2.6	-2.8	-4.3	-4.2	-3.1	-3.0	Îles Cook
-0.2	2.0	0.6	-0.5	-1.3	-1.2	5.0	-1.1	-4.0	-0.9	1.2	Fidji
3.2	-0.1	0.6	0.5	0.5	0.5	0.0	0.5	0.4	0.4	0.5	Polynésie française
-2.0	2.6	-0.5	0.2	-0.6	-1.0	-1.7	1.8	-3.8	-2.0	0.2	Kiribati
	-1.7	1.9	0.7	-0.1	-0.1	1.9	0.7	-3.0	-0.7	3.5	Îles Marshall
	0.0	-0.5	-1.8	-1.5	-0.4	1.6	-2.6	0.4	2.8	1.0	Micronésie (États fédérés de)
-3.0	-10.2	-2.1	8.9	8.2	4.5	-10.0	95.1	-18.4	-0.4	-8.3	Nauru
2.9	-0.9	1.9	2.1	1.6	1.3	1.9	-0.3	0.7	1.8	0.3	Nouvelle-Calédonie
	0.8	1.3	0.9	0.9	1.6	5.0	-1.5	2.3	1.9	5.1	Palaos
-0.4	-0.6	1.4	3.0	3.2	3.9	1.4	4.1	3.1	4.6	6.5	Papouasie-Nouvelle-Guinée
0.8	2.5	2.6	1.5	0.4	0.2	5.0	-3.7	-2.1	1.1	1.6	Samoa
-1.2	-1.1	2.0	3.0	1.0	1.7	9.8	4.2	-7.3	4.3	8.7	Îles Salomon
4.4	1.8	0.2	-0.2	-0.3	-0.2	-1.4	1.9	-1.6	-0.2	1.0	Tonga
5.3	3.7	1.4	4.0	3.1	2.3	-4.6	1.0	1.3	1.4	0.9	Tuvalu
3.6	0.7	1.4	4.0	3.3	2.6	2.5	3.5	0.9	2.4	0.0	Vanuatu
2.5	*-1.7*	*5.8*	*7.5*	*4.3*	*3.1*	*6.6*	*5.1*	*-6.6*	*4.1*	*4.4*	*Économies en transition*
-0.4	7.2	5.1	5.8	5.4	4.5	5.2	7.3	3.0	3.1	2.6	Albanie
	5.9	9.1	11.3	5.3	2.5	13.7	6.8	-14.3	1.9	4.3	Arménie
	-3.1	15.6	21.6	17.5	11.4	24.9	9.2	7.8	3.6	-1.2	Azerbaïdjan
	0.9	8.5	10.0	8.1	7.2	10.0	10.8	0.6	8.0	5.7	Bélarus
	22.8	4.2	6.0	4.2	2.7	3.9	5.8	-2.8	1.0	1.5	Bosnie-Herzégovine
	3.9	3.4	4.3	2.0	0.5	4.5	2.3	-5.8	-1.0	0.2	Croatie
	2.7	7.8	9.0	5.9	5.2	10.6	2.8	-3.3	6.9	7.5	Géorgie
	-1.2	7.4	6.5	4.7	4.5	8.8	2.1	0.0	5.8	6.3	Kazakhstan
	-2.1	3.7	5.7	5.1	3.4	-0.7	7.0	1.6	-2.5	4.5	Kirghizistan
								-5.8	2.3	3.1	Monténégro
	-5.6	6.8	6.2	4.0	4.3	9.2	8.9	-5.1	7.8	7.3	République de Moldova
	-1.6	5.7	7.6	4.1	3.0	6.7	5.3	-7.8	4.1	4.4	Fédération de Russie
	-0.5	–	–	–	–	5.7	–	–	–	–	Serbie-et-Monténégro
	–	–	–	–	–	–	–	-2.4	2.0	2.1	Serbie
0.4											RSF de Yougoslavie
	-8.1	6.9	6.1	5.4	5.1	5.7	6.2	2.6	5.0	5.9	Tadjikistan
	0.8	3.1	5.2	3.9	2.9	4.1	4.7	-1.1	1.6	2.8	LERY de Macédoine
	-2.8	7.1	10.8	9.8	9.4	11.8	13.4	4.8	7.9	13.2	Turkménistan
	-7.2	5.6	6.8	1.9	1.1	3.5	3.0	-14.2	4.8	5.8	Ukraine
2.8	–	–	–	–	–	–	–	–	–	–	URSS
	-0.2	6.1	7.5	7.4	7.3	6.0	7.7	6.8	7.2	7.1	Ouzbékistan
2.6	*2.8*	*0.8*	*0.5*	*-0.6*	*-0.4*	*2.1*	*-1.2*	*-4.3*	*2.1*	*1.0*	*Économies développées : Amérique*
0.9	3.6	2.3	3.2	0.4	-0.7	4.9	-0.6	-8.3	1.3	-2.2	Bermudes
2.1	2.7	0.9	0.9	-0.2	0.0	1.9	-0.4	-3.8	2.2	1.4	Canada
1.2	3.1	0.3	0.8	-0.6	-0.5	1.7	-1.1	-5.2	1.8	1.7	Groenland
2.7	2.8	0.8	0.5	-0.6	-0.4	2.1	-1.2	-4.4	2.1	0.9	États-Unis

Pour les sources et les notes, se reporter à la fin du tableau.

8

Region, country or territory	Total real gross domestic product (1) / Produit intérieur brut réel total (1) Percentage / En pourcentage										
	80 -89	92 -00	00 -10	05 -08	05 -09	05 -11 (e)	2005	2008	2009	2010	2011 (e)
Developed economies: Asia	**4.4**	**1.0**	**1.0**	**1.3**	**-0.4**	**-0.3**	**2.0**	**-1.0**	**-6.1**	**4.0**	**-0.6**
Israel	3.4	5.2	3.6	5.1	4.1	4.0	4.9	4.0	0.8	4.8	4.6
Japan	4.5	0.9	0.9	1.2	-0.5	-0.4	1.9	-1.2	-6.3	4.0	-0.8
Developed economies: Europe	**2.4**	**2.6**	**1.6**	**2.4**	**0.8**	**0.6**	**2.0**	**0.3**	**-4.2**	**1.9**	**1.5**
Andorra	2.9	3.9	3.4	0.2	-1.2	-2.3	6.6	-4.1	-4.7	-3.4	-3.4
Austria	1.9	2.7	1.8	3.0	1.5	1.2	2.4	1.4	-3.8	2.3	2.7
Belgium	1.9	2.5	1.6	2.3	1.1	1.0	1.7	1.0	-2.8	2.3	1.8
Bulgaria	4.1	-0.8	4.8	6.4	3.9	2.1	6.4	6.2	-5.5	0.2	1.7
Cyprus	6.1	4.5	3.1	4.4	3.0	1.9	3.9	3.6	-1.9	1.1	0.5
Czechoslovakia	2.1	–	–	–	–	–	–	–	–	–	–
Czech Republic	–	–	4.0	5.3	3.0	2.1	6.8	3.1	-4.7	2.7	1.9
Denmark	2.6	3.0	0.9	1.3	-0.3	-0.4	2.4	-1.1	-5.2	1.7	0.8
Estonia	–	4.5	4.3	4.8	-0.1	-0.5	8.9	-3.7	-14.3	2.3	8.3
Finland	3.3	4.1	2.2	3.8	1.0	0.7	2.9	1.0	-8.2	3.6	2.7
France	2.2	2.2	1.3	1.6	0.6	0.5	1.8	-0.1	-2.7	1.5	1.7
Germany, Federal Republic of (3)	2.0	–	–	–	–	–	–	–	–	–	–
Germany	–	1.6	1.0	2.7	1.0	1.0	0.7	1.1	-5.1	3.7	3.0
Greece	0.7	2.6	2.6	2.8	1.3	-1.1	2.3	-0.2	-3.3	-3.5	-7.1
Hungary	1.6	2.5	2.2	1.5	-0.3	-0.5	4.0	0.9	-6.8	1.3	1.6
Iceland	3.2	3.8	3.2	4.2	1.7	-0.1	7.2	1.3	-6.7	-4.0	2.6
Ireland	2.1	8.3	2.8	2.7	0.2	-0.7	5.3	-3.0	-7.0	-0.4	1.4
Italy	2.5	1.7	0.3	0.8	-0.6	-0.7	0.7	-1.3	-5.2	1.3	0.4
Latvia	–	3.0	4.8	6.0	0.0	-1.6	10.1	-3.3	-17.7	-0.3	5.5
Lithuania	–	1.2	5.2	7.1	2.0	0.5	7.8	2.9	-14.8	1.4	5.9
Luxembourg	5.0	4.7	3.2	4.3	2.1	1.3	5.4	0.8	-5.3	2.7	1.7
Malta	3.2	5.2	1.8	3.7	2.5	2.0	3.7	4.4	-2.7	2.7	1.9
Netherlands	2.2	3.6	1.6	3.1	1.7	1.1	2.0	1.8	-3.5	1.7	1.0
Norway	3.1	4.0	1.8	2.0	1.1	0.7	2.7	0.3	-1.7	0.3	1.4
Poland	2.3	5.7	4.3	6.1	5.1	4.5	3.6	5.1	1.6	3.9	4.3
Portugal	2.9	3.4	0.7	1.4	0.5	0.1	0.8	0.0	-2.5	1.4	-1.7
Romania	2.0	1.1	4.9	7.1	4.2	1.9	4.2	7.3	-6.6	-1.9	2.5
San Marino	2.5	6.3	1.3	2.2	-1.3	-2.2	2.3	-1.1	-13.0	1.3	-2.6
Slovakia	–	–	5.4	8.5	5.5	4.0	6.7	5.9	-4.9	4.2	3.3
Slovenia	–	4.3	3.3	5.6	2.6	1.1	4.0	3.6	-8.0	1.4	0.6
Spain	2.9	3.2	2.4	2.9	1.3	0.4	3.6	0.9	-3.7	-0.1	0.4
Sweden	2.6	3.1	2.2	2.4	0.5	1.1	3.2	-0.6	-5.3	5.7	3.9
Switzerland	2.0	1.5	1.9	3.2	2.1	1.8	2.7	2.0	-1.9	2.7	1.9
United Kingdom	3.3	3.5	1.8	1.8	0.3	0.1	2.1	-1.1	-4.4	1.8	0.9
Developed economies: Oceania	**3.4**	**4.1**	**3.1**	**2.8**	**2.5**	**2.4**	**3.1**	**1.1**	**2.1**	**2.5**	**2.0**
Australia	3.6	4.1	3.1	3.0	2.7	2.5	3.1	1.4	2.3	2.5	2.1
New Zealand	2.3	3.6	2.6	1.5	1.1	1.2	3.2	-1.1	0.8	2.3	1.3

Source:
UNCTAD secretariat calculations, based on UN DESA Statistics Division, *National Accounts Main Aggregates Database*

Notes:
(1)   Growth rates are based on gross domestic product at constant 2005 US dollars.
(2)   Including Western Sahara.
(3)   Data refer to Germany from 1970 to 1989.

8.2.1 Taux de croissance annuels moyens du produit intérieur brut réel total et par habitant des pays et des régions géographiques

80 -89	92 -00	00 -10	05 -08	05 -09	05 -11 (e)	2005	2008	2009	2010	2011 (e)	Régions, pays ou territoires
3.8	**0.7**	**0.8**	**1.1**	**-0.6**	**-0.4**	**1.8**	**-1.2**	**-6.2**	**3.9**	**-0.7**	**Économies développées : Asie**
1.7	2.3	1.4	2.6	1.7	1.6	2.8	1.5	-1.5	2.6	2.6	Israël
3.9	0.7	0.8	1.2	-0.6	-0.4	1.9	-1.2	-6.3	4.0	-0.8	Japon
2.1	**2.4**	**1.2**	**1.9**	**0.4**	**0.2**	**1.5**	**-0.1**	**-4.5**	**1.6**	**1.2**	**Économies développées : Europe**
-0.7	2.8	0.5	-1.7	-2.9	-3.9	3.0	-5.4	-5.9	-4.7	-4.8	Andorre
1.8	2.4	1.3	2.5	1.0	0.8	1.8	1.0	-4.1	2.0	2.5	Autriche
1.8	2.3	1.0	1.6	0.5	0.4	1.2	0.4	-3.4	1.8	1.4	Belgique
4.0	0.1	5.5	7.1	4.6	2.8	7.0	6.9	-4.9	0.8	2.4	Bulgarie
4.9	2.9	1.4	2.8	1.6	0.9	1.0	2.6	-2.7	-0.1	1.1	Chypre
1.9	–										Tchécoslovaquie
		3.7	4.8	2.5	1.5	6.6	2.5	-5.3	2.2	1.5	République tchèque
2.6	2.5	0.5	0.8	-0.8	-0.8	2.1	-1.6	-5.7	1.3	0.4	Danemark
–	5.9	4.5	4.9	0.0	-0.5	9.1	-3.6	-14.2	2.3	8.3	Estonie
2.9	3.8	1.8	3.3	0.6	0.3	2.6	0.5	-8.7	3.2	2.3	Finlande
1.6	1.8	0.6	1.0	0.0	-0.1	1.1	-0.7	-3.3	0.9	1.1	France
2.0	–	–	–	–	–	–	–	–	–	–	Allemagne, Rép. fédérale d' (3)
	1.3	1.0	2.8	1.0	1.1	0.7	1.1	-5.0	3.8	3.2	Allemagne
0.3	1.9	2.3	2.5	0.9	-1.4	2.0	-0.5	-3.5	-3.8	-7.4	Grèce
2.0	2.7	2.4	1.7	-0.1	-0.3	4.2	1.1	-6.6	1.4	1.8	Hongrie
2.1	2.8	1.8	2.6	0.1	-1.6	5.9	-0.3	-8.1	-5.4	1.3	Islande
1.7	7.4	1.2	1.1	-1.3	-2.1	3.5	-4.3	-8.2	-1.7	0.1	Irlande
2.4	1.7	-0.3	0.1	-1.3	-1.3	0.0	-2.0	-5.8	0.8	0.0	Italie
–	4.1	5.4	6.5	0.4	-1.2	10.8	-2.8	-17.4	0.1	5.9	Lettonie
–	1.9	5.8	7.7	2.5	1.1	8.3	3.5	-14.4	2.0	6.4	Lituanie
4.7	3.2	1.6	2.2	-0.1	-0.8	4.0	-1.5	-7.4	0.7	0.0	Luxembourg
1.9	4.5	1.3	3.3	2.1	1.7	3.1	4.0	-3.0	2.4	1.6	Malte
1.6	2.9	1.2	2.7	1.3	0.7	1.5	1.4	-3.9	1.4	0.7	Pays-Bas
2.7	3.4	0.9	0.9	0.0	-0.4	1.9	-0.9	-2.8	-0.7	0.5	Norvège
1.5	5.7	4.3	6.1	5.1	4.4	3.6	5.0	1.5	3.9	4.2	Pologne
2.7	3.0	0.4	1.1	0.2	-0.1	0.4	-0.3	-2.7	1.2	-1.8	Portugal
1.6	1.6	5.2	7.4	4.5	2.2	4.5	7.6	-6.3	-1.7	2.7	Roumanie
1.3	5.3	-0.3	1.2	-2.1	-2.9	0.4	-1.7	-13.5	0.7	-3.2	Saint-Marin
–	5.3	8.3	5.3	3.8	6.6	5.7	-5.1	4.0	3.1	Slovaquie
–	4.0	3.0	5.3	2.3	0.8	3.8	3.3	-8.3	1.1	0.3	Slovénie
2.5	2.9	1.0	1.5	0.1	-0.7	2.0	-0.4	-4.8	-1.1	-0.4	Espagne
2.3	2.9	1.6	1.6	-0.2	0.4	2.6	-1.4	-6.1	4.9	3.2	Suède
1.4	0.8	1.2	2.5	1.4	1.1	1.9	1.3	-2.5	2.1	1.4	Suisse
3.1	3.2	1.2	1.2	-0.3	-0.5	1.6	-1.7	-5.0	1.1	0.3	Royaume-Uni
2.0	**2.9**	**1.5**	**1.1**	**0.8**	**0.7**	**1.6**	**-0.6**	**0.4**	**0.9**	**0.6**	**Économies développées : Océanie**
2.1	3.0	1.6	1.2	0.9	0.8	1.6	-0.4	0.5	0.8	0.6	Australie
1.5	2.4	1.3	0.3	0.0	0.1	1.9	-2.1	-0.3	1.3	0.3	Nouvelle-Zélande

Per capita real gross domestic product (1) / Produit intérieur brut réel par habitant (1)
Percentage / En pourcentage

Source :
Calculs du secrétariat de la CNUCED, basés sur ONU DAES Division de statistique, *National Accounts Main Aggregates Database*

Notes :
(1) Les taux de croissance sont basés sur le produit intérieur brut aux prix constants en dollars des États-Unis de 2005.
(2) Y compris le Sahara occidental.
(3) Les données se réfèrent à l'Allemagne de 1970 à 1989.

8

Region, country or territory	Total real gross domestic product (1) / Produit intérieur brut réel total (1) Percentage / En pourcentage										
	80 - 89	92 - 00	00 - 10	05 - 08	05 - 09	05 - 11 (e)	2005	2008	2009	2010	2011 (e)
DEVELOPING ECONOMIES	3.5	4.8	6.1	7.0	5.9	5.8	6.8	5.1	2.5	7.5	5.8
Developing economies excluding China	2.9	3.9	4.8	5.4	4.3	4.3	5.7	3.7	0.4	6.5	4.5
Developing economies excluding LDCs	3.6	4.8	6.0	6.9	5.9	5.8	6.8	5.0	2.4	7.5	5.9
High-income developing economies	2.7	4.1	4.2	4.7	3.2	3.4	5.5	2.7	-2.1	6.7	4.7
Middle-income developing economies	4.3	5.5	7.4	8.8	7.9	7.5	7.6	7.1	5.0	8.2	6.5
Low-income developing economies	4.0	4.8	6.8	7.2	6.7	6.5	7.7	5.0	5.9	7.1	5.9
Heavily indebted poor countries (IMF)	1.7	3.5	5.4	6.1	5.6	5.2	5.9	6.0	3.9	5.3	3.7
Landlocked developing countries	2.4	1.1	7.1	8.2	7.0	6.5	8.3	6.4	3.1	6.8	6.2
Small island developing States	1.4	3.4	3.4	3.9	2.5	1.9	3.9	1.9	-2.1	2.2	1.9
Least developed countries	*2.5*	*4.5*	*7.2*	*8.4*	*7.6*	*6.5*	*8.2*	*7.6*	*4.9*	*5.6*	*3.5*
Africa and Haiti	2.1	4.0	7.4	9.1	8.1	6.7	8.7	8.4	4.6	4.8	3.3
Asia	3.2	5.4	6.8	7.1	6.7	6.3	7.4	6.2	5.4	7.0	3.7
Islands	2.4	2.3	5.6	4.1	3.7	3.9	6.1	4.4	1.9	4.2	5.5
Major petroleum and gas exporters	*-0.4*	*3.0*	*5.3*	*5.8*	*4.3*	*3.5*	*6.5*	*4.4*	*-0.6*	*3.2*	*3.6*
Africa	0.0	2.3	6.3	5.7	4.0	2.2	6.7	4.0	-2.1	3.3	-5.3
America	0.6	0.9	4.6	7.7	5.1	2.9	10.3	4.2	-3.3	-1.4	4.2
Asia	-0.8	3.7	5.2	5.4	4.3	4.1	5.8	4.6	0.4	3.9	6.3
Major exporters of manufactured goods	*6.1*	*6.4*	*7.0*	*8.1*	*7.0*	*6.9*	*7.4*	*5.7*	*3.5*	*9.0*	*6.8*
America	0.8	3.3	2.1	3.2	1.1	1.4	3.3	1.2	-6.3	5.8	3.9
Asia	9.3	7.3	8.0	9.1	8.1	7.9	8.3	6.5	5.2	9.5	7.2
Emerging economies	*3.5*	*4.1*	*3.8*	*4.7*	*3.2*	*3.5*	*4.2*	*3.1*	*-1.8*	*7.5*	*3.9*
America	1.7	3.2	3.4	4.7	3.1	3.4	4.0	3.9	-2.7	7.0	4.1
Asia	8.5	5.5	4.3	4.6	3.3	3.7	4.6	2.1	-0.7	8.1	3.6
Newly industrialized Asian economies	*7.2*	*4.8*	*4.5*	*4.9*	*3.7*	*4.0*	*4.9*	*2.6*	*-0.1*	*7.7*	*4.1*
First tier	8.8	5.5	4.3	4.6	3.3	3.7	4.8	1.9	-0.7	8.1	4.0
Second tier	4.7	3.5	5.0	5.5	4.5	4.6	5.2	4.2	1.2	6.9	4.3
Developing economies: Africa	1.8	3.1	5.1	5.7	4.6	3.7	5.4	4.8	0.9	4.0	0.8
Northern Africa excluding Sudan	2.9	3.1	4.7	4.9	4.5	3.1	5.1	4.6	3.2	4.0	-5.9
Sub-Saharan Africa	1.4	3.2	5.3	6.0	4.7	4.0	5.6	4.8	-0.2	4.0	4.1
Sub-Saharan Africa excluding South Africa	1.4	3.5	6.2	6.6	5.3	4.6	5.8	5.6	0.6	4.6	4.7
Developing economies: America	1.8	3.1	3.6	5.1	3.5	3.5	4.6	3.9	-2.2	6.0	4.3
Central America and Greater Caribbean Islands excluding Puerto Rico	1.0	3.3	2.6	3.8	1.8	2.0	3.9	1.8	-4.9	5.4	4.0
Central America and Greater Caribbean Islands excluding Mexico and Puerto Rico	2.2	3.7	4.7	6.4	5.0	4.2	6.7	4.1	0.7	3.7	4.1
South America and Central America	1.7	3.1	3.5	5.0	3.4	3.5	4.4	4.0	-2.3	6.1	4.4
South America excluding Brazil	1.1	2.9	4.8	6.8	5.2	4.8	7.3	5.5	-0.2	5.2	6.6
Developing economies: Asia	5.4	5.9	7.2	7.9	7.0	6.9	7.9	5.5	4.4	8.4	6.9
Eastern and South-Eastern Asia excluding China	7.0	4.8	4.7	5.0	3.8	4.1	5.0	2.7	0.1	7.8	4.3
Southern Asia excluding India	3.1	3.6	5.3	5.5	4.6	3.9	6.1	2.3	2.1	3.3	3.5

Source:
UNCTAD secretariat calculations, based on UN DESA Statistics Division, *National Accounts Main Aggregates Database*

Notes:
(1) Growth rates are based on gross domestic product at constant 2005 U.S. dollars.

80 - 89	92 - 00	00 - 10	05 - 08	05 - 09	05 - 11 (e)	2005	2008	2009	2010	2011 (e)	Régions, pays ou territoires
				Per capita real gross domestic product (1) / Produit intérieur brut réel par habitant (1) Percentage / En pourcentage							
1.4	**3.0**	**4.6**	**5.5**	**4.5**	**4.3**	**5.3**	**3.7**	**1.2**	**6.1**	**4.0**	**ÉCONOMIES EN DÉVELOPPEMENT**
0.5	1.9	3.0	3.7	2.6	2.6	3.9	2.1	-1.2	4.8	2.9	Économies en développement sans la Chine
1.5	3.2	4.7	5.6	4.6	4.5	5.5	3.8	1.3	6.3	4.2	Économies en développement sans les PMA
0.5	2.5	2.7	3.2	1.6	1.9	4.0	1.2	-3.5	5.3	3.4	Économies en développement à revenu élevé
2.4	4.2	6.5	7.9	7.0	6.5	6.7	6.2	4.2	7.4	4.6	Économies en développement à revenu intermédiaire
1.5	2.6	5.0	5.3	4.9	4.7	5.8	3.2	4.1	5.2	4.1	Économies en développement à revenu faible
-0.9	0.7	2.7	3.4	3.0	2.5	3.2	3.4	1.3	2.6	1.1	Pays pauvres très endettés (FMI)
-0.3	-1.2	4.9	5.9	4.8	4.2	6.1	4.2	0.9	4.5	3.9	Pays en développement sans littoral
-0.3	1.6	1.1	2.4	1.0	0.4	2.2	0.4	-3.5	0.7	0.4	Petits États insulaires en développement
-0.1	*1.8*	*4.8*	*6.0*	*5.2*	*4.2*	*5.7*	*5.3*	*2.6*	*3.3*	*1.2*	*Pays les moins avancés*
-0.7	1.2	4.6	6.2	5.3	3.9	5.8	5.5	1.8	2.1	0.6	Afrique et Haïti
0.9	3.0	5.1	5.6	5.2	4.8	5.7	4.8	4.0	5.4	2.1	Asie
-0.1	0.1	-1.8	1.8	1.5	1.6	3.2	2.2	-0.2	1.9	3.2	Îles
-3.4	*0.8*	*2.9*	*3.3*	*1.9*	*1.2*	*4.0*	*1.9*	*-2.9*	*0.9*	*1.3*	*Principaux exportateurs de pétrole et de gaz*
-2.7	0.0	3.9	3.3	1.5	-0.2	4.2	1.5	-4.4	0.9	-7.5	Afrique
-2.1	-1.2	2.7	5.9	3.3	1.2	8.4	2.5	-4.9	-2.9	2.6	Amérique
-4.4	1.5	2.7	2.8	1.7	1.6	3.3	1.9	-2.0	1.6	4.1	Asie
4.4	*5.3*	*6.3*	*7.4*	*6.3*	*6.1*	*6.7*	*5.1*	*2.9*	*8.4*	*4.7*	*Principaux exportateurs d'articles manufacturés*
-1.2	1.5	0.9	1.9	-0.2	0.2	2.0	-0.1	-7.5	4.5	2.7	Amérique
7.6	6.3	7.3	8.4	7.5	7.1	7.7	6.0	4.7	8.9	5.1	Asie
1.5	*2.7*	*2.7*	*3.6*	*2.2*	*2.5*	*3.1*	*2.1*	*-2.7*	*6.5*	*3.0*	*Économies émergentes*
-0.3	1.7	2.2	3.6	2.1	2.3	2.8	2.8	-3.6	5.9	3.1	Amérique
6.5	4.3	3.4	3.7	2.4	2.9	3.6	1.3	-1.5	7.3	2.8	Asie
5.1	*3.3*	*3.3*	*3.7*	*2.5*	*2.9*	*3.6*	*1.5*	*-1.1*	*6.6*	*3.0*	*Économies nouvellement industrialisées d'Asie*
7.2	4.5	3.7	3.9	2.6	3.1	4.2	1.1	-1.3	7.5	3.4	Première génération
2.4	1.9	3.6	4.2	3.3	3.3	3.8	3.0	0.0	5.7	3.1	Deuxième génération
-0.9	**0.7**	**2.7**	**3.2**	**2.2**	**1.4**	**3.0**	**2.4**	**-1.4**	**1.6**	**-1.5**	**Économies en développement : Afrique**
0.3	1.5	3.1	3.3	2.9	1.6	3.5	3.0	1.6	2.5	-7.2	Afrique septentrionale sans le Soudan
-1.4	0.5	2.8	3.5	2.1	1.5	3.0	2.3	-2.6	1.5	1.6	Afrique subsaharienne
-1.4	0.8	3.6	4.0	2.7	2.0	3.1	2.9	-1.9	1.9	2.0	Afrique subsaharienne sans l'Afrique du Sud
-0.3	**1.4**	**2.3**	**3.8**	**2.3**	**2.3**	**3.3**	**2.7**	**-3.3**	**4.8**	**3.1**	**Économies en développement : Amérique**
-0.9	1.6	1.3	2.5	0.5	0.6	2.5	0.4	-6.1	4.1	2.7	Amérique centrale et Grandes Antilles sans Porto Rico
0.3	2.0	3.2	5.0	3.6	2.8	5.3	2.7	-0.7	2.4	2.8	Amérique centrale et Grandes Antilles sans le Mexique et Porto Rico
-0.4	1.4	2.2	3.8	2.2	2.2	3.1	2.7	-3.4	4.9	3.2	Amérique du Sud et Amérique centrale
-0.9	1.2	3.5	5.4	3.9	3.5	5.9	4.2	-1.5	4.0	5.3	Amérique du Sud sans le Brésil
3.3	**4.3**	**5.9**	**6.6**	**5.8**	**5.7**	**6.6**	**4.4**	**3.2**	**7.3**	**5.2**	**Économies en développement : Asie**
4.8	3.3	3.5	3.9	2.7	3.0	3.9	1.7	-0.9	6.7	3.2	Asie orientale et Asie du Sud-Est sans la Chine
0.3	1.3	3.6	3.9	3.0	2.3	4.4	0.8	0.6	1.7	1.9	Asie méridionale sans l'Inde

Source :
Calculs du secrétariat de la CNUCED, basés sur ONU DAES Division de statistique, *National Accounts Main Aggregates Database*

Notes :
(1) Les taux de croissance sont basés sur le produit intérieur brut aux prix constants en dollars des États-Unis de 2005.

8

8.3.1 Nominal gross domestic product by type of expenditure and by kind of economic activity of countries and geographical regions

8.3.1 Produit intérieur brut nominal par catégories de dépenses et par branches d'activité économique des pays et des régions géographiques

Region, country or territory / Régions, pays ou territoires	Year / Année	Total GDP / PIB total	GDP by type of expenditure (1) / PIB par catégories de dépenses (1)					GDP by kind of economic activity (2) / PIB par branches d'activité économique (2)			
			Final consumption / Consommation finale		Gross capital formation / Formation brute de capital	Exports / Exportations	Less imports / Moins les importations	Agriculture (3) / Agriculture (3)	Industry (4) / Industrie (4)		Services (5)
			Government / Administration publique	Household / Ménages	Formation brute de capital	Of goods and services / Des biens et services			Total	Manufacturing / Activités de fabrication	
			Percentage / En pourcentage								
WORLD - MONDE	1990	100.0	17.3	59.2	23.5	19.6	19.9	5.5	32.9	21.8	61.7
	2000	100.0	16.3	61.2	22.4	24.9	24.7	3.6	28.9	19.0	67.5
	2005	100.0	17.1	60.2	22.4	28.4	28.1	3.5	28.8	17.9	67.7
	2010	100.0	17.9	58.7	22.7	29.6	28.9	4.3	29.4	17.0	66.3
DEVELOPING ECONOMIES - ÉCONOMIES EN DÉVELOPPEMENT	1990	100.0	13.8	59.3	25.2	25.9	24.8	15.0	36.3	22.0	48.7
	2000	100.0	14.0	58.4	24.8	34.9	32.3	10.1	36.3	22.5	53.5
	2005	100.0	13.4	54.6	27.1	40.8	36.1	9.4	39.0	23.2	51.6
	2010	100.0	14.0	51.9	31.8	35.6	32.9	9.6	39.0	21.4	51.4
TRANSITION ECONOMIES - ÉCONOMIES EN TRANSITION	1990	100.0	20.9	49.0	28.1	22.8	24.8	17.7	38.0	28.7	44.3
	2000	100.0	16.3	52.6	19.4	45.0	32.9	10.3	37.3	21.3	52.3
	2005	100.0	16.9	52.7	22.2	38.9	30.3	6.9	37.1	18.4	56.0
	2010	100.0	18.4	54.0	23.0	34.8	28.5	5.6	36.6	16.4	57.8
DEVELOPED ECONOMIES - ÉCONOMIES DÉVELOPPÉES	1990	100.0	17.9	59.7	22.9	18.0	18.6	2.8	31.9	21.4	65.4
	2000	100.0	16.9	62.1	21.8	21.7	22.5	1.7	26.7	18.0	71.6
	2005	100.0	18.3	62.2	20.8	24.0	25.4	1.5	25.3	16.1	73.2
	2010	100.0	19.9	62.5	18.1	26.4	26.8	1.5	24.1	14.8	74.4
Developing economies: Africa - Économies en développement : Afrique	1990	100.0	16.7	63.8	20.4	25.6	25.3	18.3	34.6	14.9	47.1
	2000	100.0	15.1	63.3	17.5	31.3	27.0	15.2	35.5	12.8	49.2
	2005	100.0	14.6	61.6	18.9	35.9	31.0	15.3	39.0	11.3	45.7
	2010	100.0	16.0	59.7	22.1	35.3	33.7	16.0	38.4	10.0	45.6
Eastern Africa - Afrique orientale	1990	100.0	18.8	69.9	19.0	17.4	24.3	31.1	23.6	15.7	45.4
	2000	100.0	14.8	75.1	19.0	22.1	30.7	31.0	18.8	10.6	50.2
	2005	100.0	15.6	76.3	20.4	25.2	37.7	28.4	21.8	9.8	49.7
	2010	100.0	12.8	77.1	21.9	27.1	38.8	27.8	21.8	9.5	50.4
Burundi	1990	100.0	13.5	82.6	19.3	3.2	16.8	62.4	19.5	13.5	18.0
	2000	100.0	8.1	89.1	13.1	4.2	15.1	49.1	21.4	14.7	29.5
	2005	100.0	14.5	90.0	18.3	6.2	28.9	51.2	22.0	15.4	26.8
	2010	100.0	19.3	84.7	13.9	5.9	23.3	40.1	24.4	13.3	35.5
Comoros - Comores	1990	100.0	25.7	79.7	20.2	11.7	37.3	40.4	8.1	4.1	51.5
	2000	100.0	11.7	94.0	10.1	16.7	32.5	47.7	11.3	4.5	41.0
	2005	100.0	13.5	98.7	9.3	14.3	35.8	48.5	10.5	4.1	41.0
	2010	100.0	14.7	104.6	16.5	13.2	50.8	48.2	10.4	4.1	41.3
Djibouti	1990	100.0	33.6	67.2	27.1	81.4	109.3	3.1	22.0	3.6	74.9
	2000	100.0	25.6	81.0	12.2	43.7	63.2	3.5	15.4	2.6	81.1
	2005	100.0	25.1	72.1	16.5	44.4	64.1	3.5	16.2	2.6	80.2
	2010	100.0	18.6	77.4	17.3	32.8	54.0	3.9	19.6	2.3	76.5
Eritrea - Érythrée	2000	100.0	54.8	71.7	22.0	9.7	58.2	15.1	23.0	11.2	61.9
	2005	100.0	35.2	93.2	20.3	6.2	54.9	22.6	20.5	6.8	56.9
	2010	100.0	21.6	80.6	12.3	4.4	18.9	17.7	21.3	5.6	61.1
Ethiopia (...1991) - Éthiopie (...1991)	1990	100.0	19.2	72.9	12.5	7.7	12.2	41.1	16.4	11.1	42.5
Ethiopia - Éthiopie	2000	100.0	17.9	73.1	20.3	12.0	23.9	49.4	12.2	5.5	38.4
	2005	100.0	12.4	81.7	23.8	15.1	35.5	46.4	12.9	4.7	40.8
	2010	100.0	8.3	86.1	22.3	13.6	33.0	46.3	10.4	4.0	43.3
Kenya	1990	100.0	18.3	68.8	18.0	20.2	24.7	29.9	20.9	13.9	49.2
	2000	100.0	15.3	78.1	17.6	22.3	30.5	32.8	17.3	11.5	49.9
	2005	100.0	17.4	75.4	16.9	27.9	37.0	27.0	18.9	11.7	54.1
	2010	100.0	16.6	77.8	19.3	27.5	37.9	25.0	19.6	11.3	55.4
Madagascar	1990	100.0	8.0	86.0	17.0	15.9	26.9	31.8	14.0	12.2	54.1
	2000	100.0	7.9	83.5	16.2	31.1	38.7	28.9	15.9	12.2	55.2
	2005	100.0	9.0	86.2	22.2	28.2	45.6	28.1	18.6	14.4	53.3
	2010	100.0	9.4	86.3	18.8	26.5	41.0	27.6	19.6	14.3	52.8

For sources and notes, see end of table.

Pour les sources et les notes, se reporter à la fin du tableau.

8.3.1 Nominal gross domestic product by type of expenditure and by kind of economic activity of countries and geographical regions

8.3.1 Produit intérieur brut nominal par catégories de dépenses et par branches d'activité économique des pays et des régions géographiques

Region, country or territory / Régions, pays ou territoires	Year / Année	Total GDP / PIB total	GDP by type of expenditure (1) / PIB par catégories de dépenses (1)					GDP by kind of economic activity (2) / PIB par branches d'activité économique (2)			
			Final consumption / Consommation finale		Gross capital formation / Formation brute de capital	Exports / Exportations	Less imports / Moins les importations	Agriculture (3)	Industry (4) / Industrie (4)		Services (5)
			Government / Administration publique	Household / Ménages		Of goods and services / Des biens et services			Total	Manufacturing / Activités de fabrication	
			Percentage / En pourcentage								
Malawi	1990	100.0	9.4	75.1	23.7	22.0	29.5	40.7	31.0	17.5	28.4
	2000	100.0	8.5	78.6	20.0	21.8	28.8	35.5	18.4	11.5	46.0
	2005	100.0	10.8	94.6	22.7	24.0	52.2	31.1	16.2	8.7	52.7
	2010	100.0	10.0	86.6	24.8	23.3	44.9	29.9	16.6	10.6	53.5
Mauritius - Maurice	1990	100.0	12.6	64.3	30.2	66.6	73.7	11.9	34.3	26.4	53.8
	2000	100.0	14.3	59.9	26.0	61.1	61.2	6.5	29.6	22.5	63.9
	2005	100.0	14.5	68.0	22.7	59.0	64.2	5.7	26.6	19.2	67.8
	2010	100.0	13.7	73.6	25.1	49.9	62.2	3.6	27.5	18.5	68.9
Mozambique	1990	100.0	11.0	104.9	17.2	6.4	37.2	37.1	18.4	12.7	44.5
	2000	100.0	11.5	80.1	33.5	12.7	37.8	23.6	24.1	12.0	52.3
	2005	100.0	13.0	83.3	17.9	30.5	44.4	26.4	24.8	15.1	48.9
	2010	100.0	12.9	83.9	21.9	30.6	49.2	28.1	24.0	14.6	47.9
Rwanda	1990	100.0	20.0	77.8	10.9	5.5	13.2	43.1	18.6	12.1	38.3
	2000	100.0	17.6	83.1	14.2	6.1	21.8	39.2	15.2	7.4	45.6
	2005	100.0	18.2	79.8	15.8	11.4	25.2	40.9	15.0	7.5	44.1
	2010	100.0	15.4	83.3	21.0	10.8	30.6	34.3	15.9	7.1	49.8
Seychelles	1990	100.0	26.1	54.1	24.2	62.5	66.7	5.7	8.3	5.0	86.0
	2000	100.0	6.7	68.3	27.6	75.5	78.0	4.3	18.9	12.5	76.8
	2005	100.0	35.7	52.5	32.7	77.5	95.3	3.7	19.4	10.4	76.9
	2010	100.0	27.3	60.2	52.4	89.4	132.2	2.7	15.8	8.8	81.5
Somalia - Somalie	1990	100.0	10.3	71.0	23.6	0.9	5.7	69.3	6.0	2.0	24.7
	2000	100.0	8.6	72.3	20.5	0.3	1.7	60.2	7.3	2.5	32.5
	2005	100.0	8.7	72.4	20.3	0.3	1.7	60.1	7.3	2.5	32.6
	2010	100.0	8.7	72.7	19.9	0.3	1.7	60.2	7.4	2.5	32.5
Uganda - Ouganda	1990	100.0	9.9	80.1	14.1	6.2	16.1	42.5	14.2	5.3	43.3
	2000	100.0	14.0	79.2	18.1	9.7	21.6	28.9	22.5	7.5	48.6
	2005	100.0	13.7	74.9	21.6	15.2	25.3	25.5	24.4	7.3	50.1
	2010	100.0	9.9	75.7	21.4	23.4	30.7	23.1	25.2	7.7	51.7
United Republic of Tanzania - République-Unie de Tanzanie	1990	100.0	29.1	53.7	41.4	10.2	27.5	30.9	18.1	11.2	51.0
	2000	100.0	11.7	78.3	16.7	13.4	20.1	33.0	18.9	9.2	48.1
	2005	100.0	17.6	66.3	24.9	20.8	29.7	31.3	22.3	8.5	46.3
	2010	100.0	17.5	65.1	28.3	23.6	34.8	29.4	23.1	8.7	47.6
Zambia - Zambie	1990	100.0	19.0	63.2	17.3	35.9	36.6	20.6	51.3	36.1	28.1
	2000	100.0	9.5	82.1	18.7	21.1	31.4	21.0	23.8	10.8	55.2
	2005	100.0	20.2	63.3	28.3	23.4	35.3	21.4	29.0	10.9	49.7
	2010	100.0	10.1	53.2	23.8	47.7	34.9	19.7	35.9	8.8	44.5
Zimbabwe	1990	100.0	25.5	58.0	16.3	18.7	17.3	15.3	33.0	22.7	51.7
	2000	100.0	24.3	59.9	13.6	38.6	36.4	23.1	19.2	13.6	57.8
	2005	100.0	15.7	92.0	1.6	34.6	43.8	12.3	41.9	6.5	45.9
	2010	100.0	6.6	106.6	8.9	36.9	58.9	21.6	32.9	11.8	45.5
Middle Africa - Afrique centrale	*1990*	*100.0*	*19.2*	*60.6*	*14.3*	*32.1*	*26.2*	*21.4*	*34.0*	*11.0*	*44.6*
	2000	*100.0*	*17.4*	*54.0*	*15.5*	*48.3*	*35.0*	*19.0*	*50.3*	*8.2*	*30.7*
	2005	*100.0*	*16.3*	*44.1*	*15.7*	*60.4*	*36.5*	*13.6*	*60.3*	*6.6*	*26.1*
	2010	*100.0*	*20.2*	*45.3*	*21.2*	*57.2*	*47.8*	*13.6*	*58.3*	*6.6*	*28.1*
Angola	1990	100.0	28.5	44.7	11.7	38.9	23.8	18.0	41.0	5.0	41.0
	2000	100.0	34.1	39.5	11.7	67.5	52.8	5.8	72.8	3.0	21.4
	2005	100.0	25.7	36.4	8.1	79.3	49.4	7.5	73.0	3.5	19.4
	2010	100.0	30.2	45.4	10.3	60.3	54.7	10.1	61.5	6.3	28.5
Cameroon - Cameroun	1990	100.0	12.8	68.9	17.9	20.5	20.1	21.7	30.5	19.8	47.8
	2000	100.0	9.5	70.2	16.7	23.3	19.7	22.0	35.8	20.7	42.3
	2005	100.0	10.0	72.0	19.1	20.5	21.5	20.4	31.8	18.5	47.8
	2010	100.0	11.5	74.7	18.3	17.5	22.3	24.9	31.6	16.4	43.5

For sources and notes, see end of table.

Pour les sources et les notes, se reporter à la fin du tableau.

8.3.1 Nominal gross domestic product by type of expenditure and by kind of economic activity of countries and geographical regions

8.3.1 Produit intérieur brut nominal par catégories de dépenses et par branches d'activité économique des pays et des régions géographiques

Region, country or territory / Régions, pays ou territoires	Year / Année	Total GDP / PIB total	GDP by type of expenditure (1) / PIB par catégories de dépenses (1)					GDP by kind of economic activity (2) / PIB par branches d'activité économique (2)			
			Final consumption / Consommation finale		Gross capital formation / Formation brute de capital	Exports / Exportations	Less imports / Moins les importations	Agriculture (3)	Industry (4) / Industrie (4)		Services (5)
			Government / Administration publique	Household / Ménages		Of goods and services / Des biens et services			Total	Manufacturing / Activités de fabrication	
			Percentage / En pourcentage								
Central African Republic - République centrafricaine	1990	100.0	15.4	80.7	12.7	17.1	25.9	47.6	19.7	11.3	32.7
	2000	100.0	16.3	77.6	11.1	20.4	25.3	49.6	17.1	8.7	33.3
	2005	100.0	10.4	88.1	9.8	13.2	21.5	53.1	16.1	8.3	30.8
	2010	100.0	8.1	91.2	11.4	11.0	21.7	53.4	14.7	7.7	31.8
Chad - Tchad	1990	100.0	47.3	51.7	7.2	19.0	24.8	39.2	17.0	14.6	43.8
	2000	100.0	39.4	65.8	17.5	20.0	42.7	42.3	11.3	9.1	46.4
	2005	100.0	21.0	24.9	25.1	54.5	25.5	21.3	53.8	5.8	24.9
	2010	100.0	24.3	25.8	23.5	49.1	24.1	19.1	51.5	5.3	29.3
Congo	1990	100.0	20.4	52.7	15.9	50.2	39.1	12.9	40.6	8.3	46.5
	2000	100.0	11.1	27.7	19.7	81.8	40.3	5.4	73.9	3.6	20.7
	2005	100.0	10.1	27.3	24.5	79.2	41.2	4.6	73.4	4.1	22.0
	2010	100.0	9.1	29.2	44.9	78.4	61.6	4.2	75.0	4.1	20.8
Dem. Rep. of the Congo - Rép. dém. du Congo	1990	100.0	11.5	79.1	9.0	29.5	29.2	31.0	29.0	11.3	40.0
	2000	100.0	6.5	88.3	3.5	22.4	20.7	50.0	20.3	4.8	29.7
	2005	100.0	11.4	87.2	14.0	33.7	45.3	44.7	28.2	6.2	27.1
	2010	100.0	9.7	71.9	26.4	68.1	76.7	41.7	26.5	5.6	31.8
Equatorial Guinea - Guinée équatoriale	1990	100.0	11.4	69.2	54.4	31.8	66.8	61.9	10.6	1.6	27.6
	2000	100.0	4.9	19.0	61.9	105.2	90.9	8.3	88.1	0.2	3.7
	2005	100.0	3.1	7.6	21.7	98.5	31.0	1.9	95.6	0.1	2.5
	2010	100.0	4.3	7.4	70.6	89.5	68.9	2.0	95.1	0.3	2.8
Gabon	1990	100.0	20.7	42.3	20.6	46.8	30.0	4.8	41.4	5.2	53.9
	2000	100.0	14.3	33.1	19.0	63.6	28.8	4.3	59.7	3.7	36.0
	2005	100.0	12.7	31.5	20.7	59.1	24.0	3.8	63.0	4.9	33.2
	2010	100.0	10.4	24.7	24.4	62.3	21.1	2.6	71.1	3.7	26.3
Sao Tome and Principe - Sao Tomé-et-Principe	1990	100.0	27.6	100.8	29.5	14.5	72.5	27.6	17.9	7.8	54.5
	2000	100.0	31.6	92.4	35.8	35.1	95.0	20.0	17.3	7.7	62.6
	2005	100.0	13.0	94.9	21.8	13.0	42.8	18.4	16.4	7.0	65.2
	2010	100.0	14.3	115.3	21.1	9.4	60.0	17.6	18.9	7.1	63.5
Northern Africa - Afrique septentrionale	*1990*	*100.0*	*15.9*	*61.0*	*26.6*	*26.1*	*29.3*	*15.7*	*36.4*	*13.0*	*47.9*
	2000	*100.0*	*14.2*	*61.9*	*19.7*	*29.0*	*24.9*	*12.5*	*38.4*	*12.6*	*49.2*
	2005	*100.0*	*13.0*	*53.9*	*23.3*	*40.5*	*30.6*	*12.2*	*44.9*	*10.8*	*42.9*
	2010	*100.0*	*13.2*	*57.4*	*26.2*	*33.7*	*30.4*	*12.9*	*44.2*	*11.0*	*42.9*
Algeria - Algérie	1990	100.0	16.2	56.6	28.9	23.4	25.1	11.9	48.3	11.6	39.8
	2000	100.0	13.6	41.6	23.5	42.1	20.7	8.8	56.7	6.0	34.5
	2005	100.0	11.4	33.7	31.7	47.2	24.1	7.9	59.8	4.5	32.3
	2010	100.0	15.4	35.2	41.1	40.6	32.1	7.9	56.6	4.2	35.4
Egypt - Égypte	1990	100.0	11.0	71.7	31.2	22.0	35.8	19.5	29.6	18.0	50.9
	2000	100.0	11.1	76.8	17.7	19.1	24.7	13.5	32.4	17.5	54.1
	2005	100.0	11.1	72.9	17.6	31.3	32.9	14.1	36.1	17.0	49.8
	2010	100.0	11.2	74.7	18.9	21.3	26.1	14.0	37.5	16.9	48.5
Libya - Libye	1990	100.0	24.4	48.4	18.6	39.7	31.1	6.6	39.7	6.6	53.7
	2000	100.0	20.6	46.4	13.0	35.2	15.3	6.5	47.6	5.4	45.9
	2005	100.0	12.0	32.4	8.9	72.5	25.8	2.2	75.7	4.7	22.2
	2010	100.0	12.5	36.1	9.6	68.7	26.9	2.2	75.9	4.9	21.9
Morocco - Maroc (6)	1990	100.0	14.4	61.1	29.6	26.5	30.9	20.0	28.6	18.6	51.4
	2000	100.0	18.4	61.4	25.5	28.0	33.4	14.2	27.7	17.5	58.1
	2005	100.0	19.4	57.5	28.8	32.3	37.9	14.0	26.9	15.8	59.1
	2010	100.0	17.7	57.7	34.0	33.1	42.6	14.1	27.2	14.4	58.6
Sudan (...2011) - Soudan (...2011)	1990	100.0	8.7	78.7	16.1	3.0	6.5	41.4	12.1	6.0	46.5
	2000	100.0	5.5	86.0	11.5	14.6	17.6	37.1	17.3	5.7	45.6
	2005	100.0	9.2	76.5	24.7	14.0	24.5	34.5	21.7	7.8	43.7
	2010	100.0	7.8	70.8	22.4	13.6	14.6	33.4	27.3	7.8	39.3

For sources and notes, see end of table.

Pour les sources et les notes, se reporter à la fin du tableau.

8.3.1 Nominal gross domestic product by type of expenditure and by kind of economic activity of countries and geographical regions

8.3.1 Produit intérieur brut nominal par catégories de dépenses et par branches d'activité économique des pays et des régions géographiques

Region, country or territory / Régions, pays ou territoires	Year / Année	Total GDP / PIB total	GDP by type of expenditure (1) / PIB par catégories de dépenses (1)					GDP by kind of economic activity (2) / PIB par branches d'activité économique (2)			
			Final consumption / Consommation finale		Gross capital formation / Formation brute de capital	Exports / Exportations	Less imports / Moins les importations	Agriculture (3)	Industry (4) / Industrie (4)		Services (5)
			Government / Administration publique	Household / Ménages		Of goods and services / Des biens et services			Total	Manufacturing / Activités de fabrication	
			Percentage / En pourcentage								
Tunisia - Tunisie	1990	100.0	17.1	64.3	25.3	38.9	45.1	14.2	30.0	18.7	55.8
	2000	100.0	16.7	60.6	25.9	39.7	42.9	11.1	29.8	18.1	59.1
	2005	100.0	16.9	61.8	21.7	44.9	45.3	10.0	28.8	17.0	61.3
	2010	100.0	16.6	62.7	26.1	48.7	54.0	7.9	31.7	17.7	60.4
Southern Africa - Afrique australe	*1990*	*100.0*	*19.9*	*60.5*	*18.7*	*25.9*	*21.6*	*4.9*	*40.6*	*23.0*	*54.4*
	2000	*100.0*	*18.7*	*62.6*	*16.5*	*29.7*	*27.3*	*3.6*	*32.6*	*18.4*	*63.8*
	2005	*100.0*	*19.6*	*62.2*	*18.3*	*29.3*	*29.5*	*3.0*	*32.0*	*17.9*	*65.0*
	2010	*100.0*	*21.8*	*58.8*	*19.8*	*28.4*	*29.4*	*2.8*	*31.6*	*14.5*	*65.6*
Botswana	1990	100.0	24.4	36.1	37.0	53.5	51.9	4.3	59.5	5.2	36.2
	2000	100.0	25.4	33.4	31.8	53.3	41.2	2.7	52.6	4.5	44.7
	2005	100.0	22.4	36.6	26.3	51.2	34.5	1.8	50.6	3.7	47.6
	2010	100.0	20.9	42.3	27.9	32.6	39.7	2.4	45.3	4.0	52.3
Lesotho	1990	100.0	14.1	139.1	52.9	16.9	123.0	18.6	19.0	9.6	62.4
	2000	100.0	35.4	123.0	43.5	34.8	134.7	11.9	30.4	13.6	57.7
	2005	100.0	37.1	107.0	24.6	49.3	122.0	8.9	32.8	19.2	58.2
	2010	100.0	39.8	94.8	31.2	44.3	112.5	8.0	34.1	18.6	57.9
Namibia - Namibie	1990	100.0	25.1	50.5	29.6	46.7	59.0	13.3	39.5	16.8	47.1
	2000	100.0	23.5	60.8	17.1	40.9	44.5	11.6	27.5	12.6	60.9
	2005	100.0	19.3	57.9	19.7	40.4	40.3	11.2	28.8	13.4	60.0
	2010	100.0	25.4	54.5	26.3	43.5	48.2	9.9	33.5	14.7	56.7
South Africa - Afrique du Sud	1990	100.0	19.7	61.0	17.7	24.2	18.8	4.6	40.1	23.6	55.3
	2000	100.0	18.1	63.4	15.7	27.9	24.9	3.3	31.8	19.0	64.9
	2005	100.0	19.5	63.1	18.0	27.4	27.9	2.7	31.2	18.5	66.2
	2010	100.0	21.5	59.2	19.3	27.4	27.5	2.5	30.8	14.6	66.7
Swaziland	1990	100.0	15.3	84.4	16.2	59.5	72.8	9.8	43.4	36.7	46.8
	2000	100.0	18.3	77.3	18.1	74.4	88.1	11.9	43.3	37.6	44.8
	2005	100.0	15.2	73.9	15.0	86.9	91.1	8.5	43.8	37.8	47.6
	2010	100.0	25.0	81.5	8.9	50.3	65.6	7.7	45.4	41.1	46.9
Western Africa - Afrique occidentale	*1990*	*100.0*	*10.9*	*71.7*	*13.3*	*27.1*	*22.3*	*31.4*	*30.9*	*9.7*	*37.7*
	2000	*100.0*	*11.1*	*63.0*	*11.9*	*40.9*	*26.8*	*27.9*	*38.6*	*7.9*	*33.5*
	2005	*100.0*	*9.4*	*76.0*	*11.3*	*30.9*	*27.5*	*32.1*	*35.6*	*6.2*	*32.4*
	2010	*100.0*	*14.3*	*64.3*	*16.7*	*40.1*	*35.8*	*33.7*	*31.8*	*4.8*	*34.5*
Benin - Bénin	1990	100.0	13.2	80.4	14.2	20.4	28.2	35.4	12.7	7.5	51.9
	2000	100.0	12.6	73.1	18.7	25.4	29.7	37.8	14.0	8.9	48.2
	2005	100.0	12.0	76.8	18.2	21.6	28.5	35.2	14.5	8.6	50.2
	2010	100.0	11.9	76.6	21.0	15.1	24.6	35.4	14.4	8.4	50.2
Burkina Faso	1990	100.0	21.1	73.5	18.9	11.0	24.5	28.8	21.0	14.3	50.3
	2000	100.0	20.7	74.7	20.1	9.5	25.0	32.4	21.3	13.0	46.3
	2005	100.0	19.8	72.2	24.1	9.7	25.8	38.4	17.7	11.5	43.9
	2010	100.0	21.2	65.2	29.5	16.7	30.5	37.6	16.6	9.2	45.8
Cape Verde - Cap-Vert	1990	100.0	18.9	88.9	43.6	17.1	68.6	15.2	22.6	7.9	62.3
	2000	100.0	18.9	82.8	30.7	24.8	57.3	14.0	16.3	5.4	69.7
	2005	100.0	21.5	81.3	36.0	18.8	57.6	9.9	17.1	4.0	73.0
	2010	100.0	18.9	60.0	69.0	24.7	71.6	7.8	18.6	3.2	73.7
Côte d'Ivoire	1990	100.0	20.7	69.1	6.1	28.8	24.6	29.7	24.0	19.8	46.3
	2000	100.0	15.5	67.2	11.3	39.8	33.8	24.8	27.4	22.5	47.8
	2005	100.0	12.6	69.2	11.2	52.1	45.1	25.3	28.7	18.6	46.0
	2010	100.0	15.0	65.8	9.0	49.2	38.7	27.4	27.6	16.5	45.0
Gambia - Gambie	1990	100.0	13.7	82.9	18.0	44.3	59.0	17.8	13.8	8.2	68.4
	2000	100.0	11.2	89.9	4.6	31.0	36.6	23.8	14.4	6.6	61.7
	2005	100.0	7.0	82.5	32.8	6.8	35.4	28.7	13.6	7.1	57.7
	2010	100.0	7.7	73.2	30.2	10.0	24.6	32.1	11.3	4.9	56.6

For sources and notes, see end of table.

Pour les sources et les notes, se reporter à la fin du tableau.

8

8.3.1 Nominal gross domestic product by type of expenditure and by kind of economic activity of countries and geographical regions

8.3.1 Produit intérieur brut nominal par catégories de dépenses et par branches d'activité économique des pays et des régions géographiques

Region, country or territory / Régions, pays ou territoires	Year / Année	Total GDP / PIB total	GDP by type of expenditure (1) / PIB par catégories de dépenses (1)					GDP by kind of economic activity (2) / PIB par branches d'activité économique (2)			
			Final consumption / Consommation finale		Gross capital formation / Formation brute de capital	Exports / Exportations	Less imports / Moins les importations	Agri-culture (3)	Industry (4) / Industrie (4)		Services (5)
			Government / Administration publique	Household / Ménages		Of goods and services / Des biens et services			Total	Manu-facturing / Activités de fabrication	
			Percentage / En pourcentage								
Ghana	1990	100.0	7.0	92.3	8.2	9.8	15.0	34.5	14.4	10.6	51.1
	2000	100.0	10.9	83.8	16.0	31.1	42.3	30.7	21.2	11.1	48.1
	2005	100.0	9.9	87.7	19.4	22.9	38.6	31.8	20.3	10.4	47.9
	2010	100.0	9.5	77.6	19.7	29.3	41.1	29.9	18.6	6.8	51.4
Guinea - Guinée	1990	100.0	14.0	57.0	34.9	26.9	24.8	19.5	33.3	3.0	47.1
	2000	100.0	10.2	59.1	36.7	17.9	18.6	22.7	32.7	3.0	44.6
	2005	100.0	8.1	65.4	29.6	32.1	35.2	24.3	34.8	6.4	40.9
	2010	100.0	12.3	76.1	18.0	32.8	39.2	22.5	44.5	7.0	33.1
Guinea-Bissau - Guinée-Bissau	1990	100.0	11.4	100.9	14.7	12.0	39.0	44.6	18.2	7.4	37.2
	2000	100.0	14.0	94.6	11.3	31.8	51.6	58.1	12.5	9.7	29.4
	2005	100.0	15.3	90.4	6.6	15.8	28.1	44.5	14.2	12.6	41.3
	2010	100.0	9.5	88.5	7.3	18.1	29.3	45.3	13.3	12.5	41.4
Liberia - Libéria	1990	100.0	13.0	69.8	10.8	34.2	27.8	53.4	16.5	11.2	30.0
	2000	100.0	13.5	80.6	7.5	26.5	28.1	72.6	0.7	0.3	26.8
	2005	100.0	11.1	86.4	16.4	37.9	51.9	72.7	10.2	5.9	17.2
	2010	100.0	16.3	204.9	20.0	29.6	170.8	72.0	11.1	6.7	16.9
Mali	1990	100.0	15.2	79.0	22.2	17.3	33.7	47.8	13.5	8.1	38.8
	2000	100.0	16.4	73.4	20.2	22.8	32.7	36.3	20.9	7.2	42.9
	2005	100.0	16.9	68.9	22.0	25.0	32.9	37.5	24.0	9.8	38.5
	2010	100.0	17.3	61.7	22.5	22.7	24.2	40.1	19.9	5.6	40.0
Mauritania - Mauritanie	1990	100.0	15.0	85.3	14.8	25.9	35.9	45.8	23.1	7.7	31.1
	2000	100.0	20.2	74.5	20.6	30.0	45.3	35.9	27.4	11.1	36.7
	2005	100.0	25.2	65.1	61.5	30.7	82.5	29.8	32.4	9.0	37.8
	2010	100.0	23.6	60.4	23.4	56.7	65.5	23.6	38.0	6.7	38.5
Niger	1990	100.0	19.4	72.6	15.2	20.1	27.4	34.0	17.4	6.4	48.6
	2000	100.0	18.3	73.9	15.6	18.6	26.4	41.1	12.7	6.4	46.1
	2005	100.0	15.8	73.5	23.1	18.7	31.1	45.5	11.8	5.9	42.7
	2010	100.0	15.0	69.3	41.1	18.8	44.2	44.2	16.1	5.2	39.7
Nigeria - Nigéria	1990	100.0	5.0	62.9	14.4	35.3	17.7	31.5	45.3	5.5	23.2
	2000	100.0	8.3	52.5	7.0	51.7	19.7	26.0	52.2	3.7	21.8
	2005	100.0	6.8	75.2	5.5	31.7	19.1	32.8	43.5	2.8	23.7
	2010	100.0	14.5	59.5	13.6	45.6	33.1	35.2	37.3	2.2	27.5
Senegal - Sénégal	1990	100.0	16.7	77.8	8.8	22.4	24.8	19.1	23.4	17.3	57.5
	2000	100.0	12.6	76.2	20.5	27.9	37.2	19.1	23.2	14.7	57.6
	2005	100.0	13.0	77.9	24.5	27.0	42.4	16.8	23.6	15.1	59.6
	2010	100.0	14.6	75.2	29.8	24.5	44.1	15.4	23.4	14.2	61.2
Sierra Leone	1990	100.0	7.8	84.0	10.0	22.4	23.8	46.9	19.2	4.6	33.9
	2000	100.0	14.3	98.9	6.9	18.1	39.3	58.4	28.4	3.5	13.3
	2005	100.0	15.1	96.6	11.0	18.9	41.6	51.4	10.1	2.3	38.5
	2010	100.0	16.3	71.3	52.3	17.7	46.1	58.5	5.1	1.8	36.4
Togo	1990	100.0	12.9	89.4	15.7	28.6	46.6	37.9	25.3	10.5	36.9
	2000	100.0	14.5	83.5	15.8	32.7	46.5	37.8	19.7	9.2	42.4
	2005	100.0	13.5	98.7	16.9	39.7	68.8	43.3	19.0	9.5	37.6
	2010	100.0	12.0	85.2	18.6	38.9	54.7	46.6	18.2	8.4	35.2
Developing economies: America - Économies en développement : Amérique	**1990**	**100.0**	**13.8**	**64.2**	**20.3**	**16.2**	**14.5**	**9.3**	**35.7**	**21.9**	**55.0**
	2000	**100.0**	**14.4**	**65.6**	**21.1**	**20.5**	**21.5**	**5.7**	**31.7**	**18.5**	**62.6**
	2005	**100.0**	**14.5**	**63.0**	**20.4**	**25.0**	**22.8**	**5.5**	**33.6**	**17.9**	**60.9**
	2010	**100.0**	**16.5**	**61.8**	**21.6**	**21.4**	**21.3**	**5.7**	**32.6**	**16.1**	**61.7**
Caribbean - Caraïbes	*1990*	*100.0*	*20.3*	*61.5*	*22.2*	*40.6*	*45.3*	*11.0*	*24.6*	*11.8*	*64.4*
	2000	*100.0*	*17.5*	*67.2*	*19.7*	*35.3*	*39.6*	*6.4*	*28.4*	*15.7*	*65.2*
	2005	*100.0*	*18.2*	*63.5*	*19.3*	*36.5*	*37.3*	*5.1*	*27.5*	*13.3*	*67.4*
	2010	*100.0*	*21.1*	*68.3*	*16.2*	*30.4*	*35.9*	*4.9*	*27.2*	*14.1*	*67.9*

For sources and notes, see end of table.

Pour les sources et les notes, se reporter à la fin du tableau.

8.3.1 Nominal gross domestic product by type of expenditure and by kind of economic activity of countries and geographical regions

8.3.1 Produit intérieur brut nominal par catégories de dépenses et par branches d'activité économique des pays et des régions géographiques

Region, country or territory / Régions, pays ou territoires	Year / Année	Total GDP / PIB total	GDP by type of expenditure (1) / PIB par catégories de dépenses (1)					GDP by kind of economic activity (2) / PIB par branches d'activité économique (2)			
			Final consumption / Consommation finale		Gross capital formation / Formation brute de capital	Exports / Exportations	Less imports / Moins les importations	Agriculture (3)	Industry (4) / Industrie (4)		Services (5)
			Government / Administration publique	Household / Ménages		Of goods and services / Des biens et services			Total	Manufacturing / Activités de fabrication	
			Percentage / En pourcentage								
Anguilla	1990	100.0	13.4	51.6	40.8	75.6	79.7	4.9	21.0	0.7	74.1
	2000	100.0	17.1	90.2	43.4	64.2	114.9	2.4	19.0	1.2	78.5
	2005	100.0	18.6	80.7	34.0	67.2	100.6	2.0	21.4	2.0	76.6
	2010	100.0	15.7	88.3	52.8	49.1	105.9	1.5	29.3	1.8	69.1
Antigua and Barbuda - Antigua-et-Barbuda	1990	100.0	18.0	47.6	32.4	89.0	87.0	4.0	19.0	3.2	77.0
	2000	100.0	22.3	34.4	48.1	70.2	74.8	3.6	18.3	2.1	78.1
	2005	100.0	19.0	41.9	59.2	57.4	77.5	3.3	21.1	1.9	75.6
	2010	100.0	17.4	22.9	72.0	49.7	60.2	3.0	25.9	1.7	71.1
Aruba	1990	100.0	18.6	50.2	30.0	83.2	81.9	0.5	15.9	2.1	83.6
	2000	100.0	21.4	49.4	25.5	74.4	70.7	0.4	16.3	4.0	83.3
	2005	100.0	23.1	52.7	33.6	68.5	77.9	0.4	19.6	3.8	80.0
	2010	100.0	24.9	58.7	28.7	61.7	74.0	0.4	19.6	4.0	80.0
Bahamas	1990	100.0	11.0	65.8	23.2	54.5	49.5	2.9	13.0	3.6	84.1
	2000	100.0	10.8	63.8	27.9	44.4	46.8	2.7	16.7	5.3	80.5
	2005	100.0	11.3	66.2	25.3	45.2	48.0	2.1	14.6	4.3	83.4
	2010	100.0	14.9	72.6	21.7	42.0	51.2	2.1	14.1	4.2	83.8
Barbados - Barbade	1990	100.0	14.9	69.1	15.6	45.2	45.5	4.4	20.9	11.4	74.7
	2000	100.0	14.2	72.5	19.0	45.4	49.7	3.1	19.1	9.5	77.9
	2005	100.0	13.0	76.9	19.4	46.5	54.7	2.2	18.5	8.8	79.3
	2010	100.0	16.4	73.8	18.0	45.6	53.7	2.4	16.3	8.0	81.3
British Virgin Islands - Îles Vierges britanniques	1990	100.0	14.0	45.4	25.7	101.0	86.2	3.2	10.6	2.5	86.1
	2000	100.0	10.5	40.4	23.2	104.5	78.7	1.2	11.9	3.5	86.8
	2005	100.0	9.2	37.2	22.4	108.9	77.7	1.1	11.9	3.1	87.1
	2010	100.0	9.0	36.5	22.3	109.7	77.5	1.0	12.1	2.8	86.9
Cayman Islands - Îles Caïmanes	1990	100.0	14.2	62.5	21.4	64.1	58.5	0.3	9.7	0.8	90.1
	2000	100.0	14.6	63.3	22.4	61.9	61.1	0.2	9.2	0.8	90.5
	2005	100.0	14.6	63.4	22.4	61.9	61.3	0.2	9.1	0.8	90.7
	2010	100.0	14.6	63.4	22.4	61.9	61.3	0.3	8.6	0.8	91.1
Cuba	1990	100.0	31.0	53.9	24.8	30.2	40.9	14.0	18.6	7.7	67.4
	2000	100.0	29.6	60.7	12.5	14.1	16.9	8.4	27.9	17.7	63.7
	2005	100.0	33.6	52.9	10.8	21.0	18.3	5.6	19.4	9.5	75.0
	2010	100.0	37.9	49.6	11.8	19.6	19.0	5.0	20.5	10.6	74.5
Dominica - Dominique	1990	100.0	17.0	73.0	29.8	41.8	62.9	19.1	13.8	6.1	67.1
	2000	100.0	18.8	72.6	20.5	44.5	56.4	13.3	17.5	7.6	69.3
	2005	100.0	15.6	82.7	20.2	35.8	54.2	13.2	15.0	4.6	71.9
	2010	100.0	17.6	81.9	24.7	32.8	54.1	13.0	15.0	3.4	72.0
Dominican Republic - République dominicaine	1990	100.0	2.8	80.0	20.3	42.6	45.6	12.9	36.9	28.3	50.2
	2000	100.0	7.8	77.8	23.3	37.0	45.9	7.0	34.6	25.2	58.4
	2005	100.0	6.7	82.3	16.5	30.0	35.5	7.2	31.1	22.2	61.7
	2010	100.0	7.7	87.6	16.5	22.3	34.0	6.0	31.0	23.3	63.0
Grenada - Grenade	1990	100.0	20.5	64.9	42.0	44.4	71.8	12.6	17.0	6.2	70.4
	2000	100.0	11.7	68.1	34.5	45.4	59.7	5.9	20.6	5.2	73.6
	2005	100.0	13.0	82.4	40.0	21.3	56.8	3.4	26.1	3.3	70.5
	2010	100.0	16.2	97.7	16.7	21.8	51.1	5.3	13.9	4.5	80.7
Haiti - Haïti	1990	100.0	8.0	81.3	14.3	18.1	21.7	30.9	24.0	14.2	45.2
	2000	100.0	9.0	99.6	14.3	13.8	35.9	23.5	32.0	10.0	44.6
	2005	100.0	8.3	109.7	14.3	15.3	46.1	22.4	32.9	10.1	44.8
	2010	100.0	13.1	126.7	13.1	13.2	61.5	20.9	33.6	8.6	45.5
Jamaica - Jamaïque	1990	100.0	12.5	64.7	24.4	49.5	51.4	6.2	33.7	15.3	60.1
	2000	100.0	14.0	74.4	23.6	39.0	51.0	6.7	24.4	10.1	68.9
	2005	100.0	13.8	77.4	26.8	35.4	53.5	5.7	24.1	8.5	70.2
	2010	100.0	15.1	82.8	18.1	29.9	45.6	5.8	21.3	8.4	72.9

For sources and notes, see end of table.

Pour les sources et les notes, se reporter à la fin du tableau.

8.3.1 Nominal gross domestic product by type of expenditure and by kind of economic activity of countries and geographical regions

8.3.1 Produit intérieur brut nominal par catégories de dépenses et par branches d'activité économique des pays et des régions géographiques

Region, country or territory / Régions, pays ou territoires	Year / Année	Total GDP / PIB total	GDP by type of expenditure (1) / PIB par catégories de dépenses (1)					GDP by kind of economic activity (2) / PIB par branches d'activité économique (2)			
			Final consumption / Consommation finale		Gross capital formation / Formation brute de capital	Exports / Exportations	Less imports / Moins les importations	Agriculture / Agriculture (3)	Industry (4) / Industrie (4)		Services (5)
			Government / Administration publique	Household / Ménages		Of goods and services / Des biens et services			Total	Manufacturing / Activités de fabrication	
			Percentage / En pourcentage								
Montserrat	1990	100.0	17.7	61.6	73.4	28.6	81.4	2.4	37.6	2.3	60.0
	2000	100.0	49.6	73.8	46.6	49.8	119.8	1.3	20.6	0.7	78.0
	2005	100.0	52.0	94.2	36.6	37.8	120.5	1.0	20.4	0.8	78.7
	2010	100.0	55.3	85.5	29.8	35.7	106.4	1.2	17.2	0.7	81.7
Netherlands Antilles - Antilles néerlandaises	1990	100.0	23.9	56.9	29.8	82.8	92.8	0.8	17.1	7.5	82.1
	2000	100.0	22.8	53.6	27.2	73.2	76.8	0.7	16.2	6.8	83.1
	2005	100.0	16.6	60.4	29.9	75.8	82.6	0.8	15.6	5.2	83.7
	2010	100.0	17.0	64.6	35.4	78.0	95.0	0.6	15.7	6.3	83.7
Saint Kitts and Nevis - Saint-Kitts-et-Nevis	1990	100.0	18.0	57.9	55.4	51.7	83.1	6.1	27.4	12.1	66.5
	2000	100.0	21.1	59.3	49.6	45.6	75.6	2.6	27.1	9.8	70.3
	2005	100.0	19.6	50.3	42.3	51.7	63.8	2.8	23.8	8.8	73.4
	2010	100.0	19.6	67.4	38.0	35.4	62.6	2.5	22.7	7.9	74.9
Saint Lucia - Sainte-Lucie	1990	100.0	15.2	69.8	24.6	68.5	78.1	13.7	16.8	7.7	69.5
	2000	100.0	18.7	61.4	29.8	53.8	63.7	6.9	18.8	4.6	74.2
	2005	100.0	19.1	57.3	31.9	62.0	70.2	3.7	20.4	5.6	76.0
	2010	100.0	16.5	60.2	34.5	51.0	62.2	3.2	16.2	3.8	80.6
Saint Vincent and the Grenadines - Saint-Vincent-et-les Grenadines	1990	100.0	17.6	75.5	26.5	55.4	64.8	16.7	19.1	8.2	64.2
	2000	100.0	16.4	65.4	23.3	45.1	50.3	8.4	19.4	5.7	72.1
	2005	100.0	15.7	74.1	26.6	36.4	52.8	6.2	18.6	5.8	75.2
	2010	100.0	16.2	88.8	25.5	27.2	57.7	7.1	19.2	5.6	73.7
Trinidad and Tobago - Trinité-et-Tobago	1990	100.0	16.2	54.8	13.8	49.1	33.5	2.6	46.4	13.8	51.0
	2000	100.0	12.0	57.4	16.8	59.2	45.3	1.2	44.8	16.9	53.9
	2005	100.0	11.6	31.4	30.2	65.8	39.0	0.5	56.7	21.3	42.8
	2010	100.0	14.8	53.6	12.7	56.6	39.7	0.6	52.7	19.3	46.7
Turks and Caicos Islands - Îles Turques et Caïques	1990	100.0	27.6	51.0	30.8	62.2	71.9	1.3	16.4	4.4	82.3
	2000	100.0	15.2	30.8	26.3	78.5	50.8	1.5	15.6	3.5	82.9
	2005	100.0	17.2	50.3	38.7	56.6	62.7	1.2	19.7	2.2	79.1
	2010	100.0	17.8	54.0	45.9	62.0	79.7	1.0	22.1	1.8	76.8
Central America - Amérique centrale	*1990*	*100.0*	*8.6*	*68.6*	*25.0*	*19.1*	*20.4*	*8.3*	*35.0*	*20.2*	*56.7*
	2000	*100.0*	*10.8*	*66.0*	*26.0*	*29.7*	*32.1*	*5.0*	*34.2*	*21.0*	*60.7*
	2005	*100.0*	*10.8*	*67.8*	*23.8*	*28.7*	*31.2*	*4.1*	*33.4*	*18.6*	*62.6*
	2010	*100.0*	*11.9*	*66.2*	*24.5*	*31.7*	*34.1*	*4.4*	*33.0*	*17.6*	*62.7*
Belize	1990	100.0	14.4	60.4	26.1	60.3	61.3	20.7	25.4	14.9	53.8
	2000	100.0	12.9	74.0	31.7	53.0	73.7	16.4	20.7	10.6	63.0
	2005	100.0	14.5	71.6	19.5	54.6	62.7	14.5	16.5	8.6	69.0
	2010	100.0	16.6	63.1	17.8	57.8	55.7	11.8	20.9	12.9	67.3
Costa Rica	1990	100.0	15.0	74.5	19.6	29.9	39.0	12.1	29.3	22.0	58.6
	2000	100.0	13.3	67.0	16.9	48.6	45.8	9.1	31.0	24.5	59.9
	2005	100.0	13.8	67.3	24.3	48.5	54.0	8.6	27.8	20.7	63.6
	2010	100.0	17.8	64.8	20.0	38.2	40.7	7.3	27.1	18.9	65.6
El Salvador	1990	100.0	9.9	88.9	13.9	18.6	31.2	17.1	26.8	21.8	56.1
	2000	100.0	10.2	87.9	16.9	27.4	42.4	10.0	30.3	23.6	59.7
	2005	100.0	9.6	92.8	16.1	25.6	44.2	10.2	28.7	22.2	61.1
	2010	100.0	10.9	93.3	13.3	26.2	43.6	12.2	25.9	19.8	61.9
Guatemala	1990	100.0	9.0	81.6	15.0	29.6	33.9	25.9	19.8	15.1	54.3
	2000	100.0	9.3	81.9	19.7	30.3	41.3	22.8	19.8	13.2	57.4
	2005	100.0	8.5	87.7	19.7	25.1	41.0	13.1	28.6	19.7	58.3
	2010	100.0	10.0	84.5	15.8	25.1	35.7	11.9	28.6	19.3	59.5
Honduras	1990	100.0	13.8	67.0	21.2	48.6	48.1	21.2	26.4	18.2	52.5
	2000	100.0	13.4	70.8	28.3	54.0	66.4	15.2	31.1	21.7	53.7
	2005	100.0	15.5	75.3	27.6	59.0	77.5	13.1	27.6	20.1	59.3
	2010	100.0	18.2	79.6	23.0	43.9	64.6	11.8	25.1	17.4	63.1

For sources and notes, see end of table.

Pour les sources et les notes, se reporter à la fin du tableau.

8.3.1 Nominal gross domestic product by type of expenditure and by kind of economic activity of countries and geographical regions

8.3.1 Produit intérieur brut nominal par catégories de dépenses et par branches d'activité économique des pays et des régions géographiques

Region, country or territory / Régions, pays ou territoires	Year / Année	Total GDP / PIB total	GDP by type of expenditure (1) / PIB par catégories de dépenses (1)					GDP by kind of economic activity (2) / PIB par branches d'activité économique (2)			
			Final consumption / Consommation finale		Gross capital formation / Formation brute de capital	Exports / Exportations	Less imports / Moins les importations	Agriculture (3)	Industry (4) / Industrie (4)		Services (5)
			Government / Administration publique	Household / Ménages		Of goods and services / Des biens et services			Total	Manufacturing / Activités de fabrication	
			Percentage / En pourcentage								
Mexico - Mexique	1990	100.0	8.0	68.0	25.8	17.0	17.9	7.4	36.1	20.4	56.4
	2000	100.0	10.6	65.1	26.6	28.2	30.0	4.1	35.2	21.3	60.7
	2005	100.0	10.7	66.6	24.1	27.2	28.6	3.3	34.1	18.7	62.5
	2010	100.0	11.7	64.8	25.2	30.4	31.8	3.5	34.1	17.7	62.4
Nicaragua	1990	100.0	30.3	60.6	18.3	15.9	27.7	20.3	26.4	18.5	53.3
	2000	100.0	17.2	79.0	31.0	23.9	51.1	20.1	27.2	16.4	52.7
	2005	100.0	18.8	80.8	30.1	29.0	58.6	18.2	28.1	17.7	53.8
	2010	100.0	16.8	84.0	27.5	41.3	69.6	20.3	28.3	18.8	51.4
Panama	1990	100.0	15.7	63.3	14.7	77.9	70.5	9.0	17.7	13.2	73.3
	2000	100.0	13.2	59.9	24.1	72.6	69.8	7.0	18.5	9.7	74.5
	2005	100.0	13.2	62.1	18.4	75.5	69.1	6.8	16.3	7.2	76.9
	2010	100.0	11.3	58.1	27.5	76.0	72.8	5.6	16.8	6.4	77.6
South America - Amérique du Sud	*1990*	*100.0*	*15.4*	*62.6*	*18.1*	*13.0*	*9.4*	*9.7*	*37.0*	*23.8*	*53.3*
	2000	*100.0*	*16.2*	*65.2*	*18.7*	*14.5*	*14.6*	*5.9*	*30.5*	*17.3*	*63.6*
	2005	*100.0*	*16.3*	*60.2*	*18.5*	*21.9*	*16.8*	*6.4*	*34.3*	*17.8*	*59.3*
	2010	*100.0*	*17.7*	*60.1*	*20.9*	*17.7*	*16.4*	*6.2*	*32.7*	*15.7*	*61.1*
Argentina - Argentine	1990	100.0	12.9	66.8	14.6	10.3	4.6	8.0	35.6	26.5	56.4
	2000	100.0	13.8	69.3	17.5	11.0	11.6	5.0	27.6	17.5	67.4
	2005	100.0	11.9	61.3	20.9	25.1	19.2	9.4	35.6	23.2	55.0
	2010	100.0	14.9	57.3	24.5	21.7	18.4	10.0	30.9	20.5	59.1
Bolivia (Plurinational State of) - Bolivie (État plurinational de)	1990	100.0	11.8	76.9	12.5	22.8	23.9	16.4	34.2	18.2	49.4
	2000	100.0	14.5	76.4	18.1	18.3	27.3	14.3	28.3	14.6	57.4
	2005	100.0	16.0	66.3	14.3	35.5	32.1	13.9	30.9	13.7	55.2
	2010	100.0	13.8	62.3	17.0	41.2	34.3	12.4	35.8	13.4	51.8
Brazil - Brésil	1990	100.0	18.1	60.9	18.5	7.4	5.6	10.6	35.9	24.4	53.6
	2000	100.0	19.2	64.3	18.3	10.0	11.7	5.6	27.7	17.2	66.7
	2005	100.0	19.9	60.3	16.2	15.1	11.5	5.7	29.3	18.1	65.0
	2010	100.0	21.2	60.6	19.2	11.2	12.1	5.8	26.9	15.8	67.4
Chile - Chili	1990	100.0	10.4	60.2	25.6	33.1	29.4	7.1	41.2	18.0	51.7
	2000	100.0	12.5	63.8	21.9	31.6	29.7	5.9	37.0	18.7	57.1
	2005	100.0	11.1	58.2	22.2	41.3	32.8	4.4	42.0	15.8	53.5
	2010	100.0	13.1	57.3	22.4	40.5	33.3	3.2	42.9	11.5	53.9
Colombia - Colombie	1990	100.0	8.9	70.3	24.1	13.7	13.8	12.0	32.6	17.5	55.4
	2000	100.0	16.5	69.5	14.9	15.9	16.8	8.9	29.4	15.0	61.6
	2005	100.0	15.7	66.0	20.2	16.8	18.8	8.4	32.8	15.4	58.8
	2010	100.0	16.2	62.8	23.2	15.8	17.9	7.1	36.4	15.1	56.5
Ecuador - Équateur	1990	100.0	13.1	67.4	17.0	31.4	28.6	13.9	39.5	20.1	46.6
	2000	100.0	9.6	63.6	21.3	36.2	30.8	10.8	40.9	18.8	48.3
	2005	100.0	11.2	66.3	23.6	30.9	32.0	6.9	36.6	11.4	56.5
	2010	100.0	12.5	68.3	25.2	32.3	38.4	6.8	39.1	11.7	54.2
Guyana	1990	100.0	8.5	75.8	26.5	34.5	49.2	31.5	26.7	10.1	41.8
	2000	100.0	17.3	62.0	24.1	40.0	51.5	28.1	31.5	6.7	40.4
	2005	100.0	16.9	91.4	20.3	53.7	75.8	26.2	27.3	7.5	46.6
	2010	100.0	15.3	86.7	25.8	50.9	78.8	17.4	34.2	6.6	48.4
Paraguay	1990	100.0	9.2	66.0	27.1	52.4	50.4	26.4	25.9	19.3	47.7
	2000	100.0	12.7	79.2	18.8	38.1	48.8	18.5	24.8	17.2	56.7
	2005	100.0	10.9	74.1	19.8	52.1	55.6	23.2	22.7	15.2	54.1
	2010	100.0	12.2	74.9	16.9	53.1	57.1	23.9	22.6	14.1	53.5
Peru - Pérou	1990	100.0	11.5	71.2	18.1	15.1	14.5	7.7	30.4	19.4	61.9
	2000	100.0	10.6	71.2	20.2	16.0	18.0	8.5	29.9	15.8	61.6
	2005	100.0	10.1	66.1	17.9	25.1	19.2	7.2	34.3	16.4	58.5
	2010	100.0	9.5	60.7	26.4	25.4	22.0	7.2	35.8	15.3	57.1

For sources and notes, see end of table.

Pour les sources et les notes, se reporter à la fin du tableau.

8

8.3.1 Nominal gross domestic product by type of expenditure and by kind of economic activity of countries and geographical regions

8.3.1 Produit intérieur brut nominal par catégories de dépenses et par branches d'activité économique des pays et des régions géographiques

Region, country or territory / Régions, pays ou territoires	Year / Année	Total GDP / PIB total	GDP by type of expenditure (1) / PIB par catégories de dépenses (1)					GDP by kind of economic activity (2) / PIB par branches d'activité économique (2)			
			Final consumption / Consommation finale		Gross capital formation / Formation brute de capital	Exports / Exportations / Of goods and services / Des biens et services	Less imports / Moins les importations	Agriculture (3)	Industry (4) / Industrie (4)		Services (5)
			Government / Administration publique	Household / Ménages					Total	Manufacturing / Activités de fabrication	
			Percentage / En pourcentage								
Suriname	1990	100.0	20.0	44.0	17.0	22.4	21.7	9.9	27.6	11.7	62.4
	2000	100.0	4.6	16.0	56.2	51.2	46.2	11.9	30.9	17.7	57.2
	2005	100.0	5.7	19.9	87.9	57.4	70.9	6.1	42.2	20.9	51.6
	2010	100.0	4.3	15.0	68.3	58.7	51.9	5.7	44.4	22.5	49.8
Uruguay	1990	100.0	12.4	71.5	12.1	22.2	19.8	10.7	28.3	22.5	61.0
	2000	100.0	12.4	76.5	14.5	16.7	20.0	6.4	23.6	13.4	70.0
	2005	100.0	10.9	69.4	17.7	30.4	28.5	9.8	26.6	16.6	63.6
	2010	100.0	12.7	68.6	17.9	25.9	25.0	9.2	26.5	14.6	64.3
Venezuela (Bolivarian Rep. of) - Venezuela (Rép. bolivarienne du)	1990	100.0	16.8	46.6	13.4	40.6	20.4	5.9	57.3	27.1	36.8
	2000	100.0	12.4	51.7	24.2	29.7	18.1	4.1	48.4	19.3	47.5
	2005	100.0	11.1	46.8	23.0	39.7	20.5	4.0	56.9	16.2	39.2
	2010	100.0	10.8	56.8	20.8	28.7	17.2	4.0	53.6	14.6	42.4
Developing economies: Asia - Économies en développement : Asie	**1990**	**100.0**	**13.1**	**55.8**	**28.7**	**30.7**	**29.6**	**17.0**	**37.1**	**23.6**	**46.0**
	2000	**100.0**	**13.6**	**54.1**	**27.7**	**42.6**	**38.4**	**11.6**	**38.6**	**25.9**	**49.8**
	2005	**100.0**	**12.8**	**50.4**	**30.9**	**47.5**	**41.9**	**10.0**	**40.9**	**26.8**	**49.1**
	2010	**100.0**	**12.8**	**47.2**	**36.7**	**40.7**	**37.0**	**10.1**	**41.3**	**24.6**	**48.6**
Eastern Asia - Asie orientale	*1990*	*100.0*	*13.0*	*50.2*	*32.7*	*33.9*	*31.5*	*15.5*	*39.2*	*31.1*	*45.3*
	2000	*100.0*	*14.0*	*51.0*	*31.9*	*40.5*	*37.8*	*9.8*	*39.5*	*32.7*	*50.7*
	2005	*100.0*	*13.6*	*45.2*	*35.8*	*47.7*	*42.6*	*8.7*	*41.8*	*35.2*	*49.5*
	2010	*100.0*	*13.2*	*39.5*	*44.1*	*39.3*	*35.1*	*8.4*	*43.8*	*30.9*	*47.8*
China - Chine	1990	100.0	13.6	48.8	34.9	15.5	12.9	26.7	40.9	36.5	32.4
	2000	100.0	15.9	46.4	35.3	23.4	21.0	15.1	45.9	40.4	39.0
	2005	100.0	14.1	38.8	41.6	36.6	31.2	12.1	47.4	41.8	40.5
	2010	100.0	13.1	35.0	49.3	27.0	23.0	10.1	46.8	32.4	43.1
China, Hong Kong SAR - Chine (RAS de Hong Kong)	1990	100.0	7.2	57.1	27.0	130.6	122.0	0.2	22.7	15.0	77.1
	2000	100.0	9.1	59.0	27.5	143.3	138.8	0.1	12.7	4.8	87.2
	2005	100.0	8.8	58.2	20.6	198.7	186.3	0.1	8.8	2.9	91.2
	2010	100.0	8.4	62.2	23.7	223.0	217.3	0.1	7.3	1.9	92.6
China, Macao SAR - Chine (RAS de Macao)	1990	100.0	9.3	42.8	23.7	92.5	69.6	..	23.8	16.5	76.2
	2000	100.0	13.1	46.2	11.1	97.4	67.8	..	14.7	9.6	85.3
	2005	100.0	10.0	31.9	27.1	94.2	63.3	..	15.2	4.3	84.8
	2010	100.0	8.1	23.3	12.7	107.0	51.1	..	15.9	2.2	84.1
China, Taiwan Province of - Province chinoise de Taiwan	1990	100.0	17.4	53.9	24.4	45.7	41.4	4.2	40.7	32.2	55.0
	2000	100.0	13.4	58.8	25.7	52.9	50.8	2.1	31.5	25.4	66.4
	2005	100.0	12.5	60.4	22.7	62.5	58.1	1.7	32.2	27.3	66.1
	2010	100.0	12.2	58.0	22.6	73.7	66.5	1.6	32.3	27.1	66.1
Korea, Dem. People's Rep. of - Corée, Rép. populaire dém. de	1990	100.0	..	..	..	7.5	11.8	27.4	54.6	31.8	18.0
	2000	100.0	..	..	..	4.2	10.0	30.4	37.1	17.7	32.4
	2005	100.0	..	..	..	6.0	11.1	25.0	42.8	19.0	32.2
	2010	100.0	..	..	..	5.9	11.1	21.2	46.0	21.5	32.8
Korea, Republic of - Corée, République de	1990	100.0	11.8	50.7	38.1	27.6	28.3	8.7	39.9	26.6	51.5
	2000	100.0	12.0	54.8	30.6	38.6	35.7	4.6	38.1	28.3	57.3
	2005	100.0	13.9	53.8	29.7	39.3	36.6	3.3	37.7	27.5	59.0
	2010	100.0	15.4	52.5	29.2	52.4	49.6	2.6	39.3	30.5	58.1
Mongolia - Mongolie	1990	100.0	21.9	65.5	33.0	15.8	33.4	14.3	34.8	15.4	50.9
	2000	100.0	14.7	75.7	29.0	54.0	67.9	30.9	23.7	7.6	45.4
	2005	100.0	11.3	56.0	37.5	58.8	63.6	22.1	35.3	6.5	42.6
	2010	100.0	13.5	54.5	41.4	47.1	59.4	16.2	37.5	7.3	46.3
Southern Asia - Asie méridionale	*1990*	*100.0*	*11.4*	*66.4*	*27.4*	*9.4*	*13.6*	*27.5*	*27.0*	*15.6*	*45.5*
	2000	*100.0*	*11.9*	*63.8*	*24.7*	*15.4*	*16.3*	*22.3*	*27.5*	*15.3*	*50.2*
	2005	*100.0*	*11.0*	*58.7*	*31.6*	*21.4*	*22.9*	*17.4*	*31.0*	*15.2*	*51.6*
	2010	*100.0*	*11.1*	*59.2*	*32.5*	*21.4*	*24.1*	*17.6*	*29.3*	*14.1*	*53.1*

For sources and notes, see end of table.

Pour les sources et les notes, se reporter à la fin du tableau.

8.3.1 Nominal gross domestic product by type of expenditure and by kind of economic activity of countries and geographical regions

8.3.1 Produit intérieur brut nominal par catégories de dépenses et par branches d'activité économique des pays et des régions géographiques

Region, country or territory / Régions, pays ou territoires	Year / Année	Total GDP / PIB total	GDP by type of expenditure (1) / PIB par catégories de dépenses (1)					GDP by kind of economic activity (2) / PIB par branches d'activité économique (2)			
			Final consumption / Consommation finale		Gross capital formation / Formation brute de capital	Exports / Exportations	Less imports / Moins les importations	Agriculture (3)	Industry (4) / Industrie (4)		Services (5)
			Government / Administration publique	Household / Ménages		Of goods and services / Des biens et services			Total	Manufacturing / Activités de fabrication	
			Percentage / En pourcentage								
Afghanistan	1990	100.0	6.2	83.3	13.4	11.5	14.4	35.7	23.7	20.2	40.6
	2000	100.0	8.8	117.7	14.3	35.6	76.4	57.0	23.2	16.8	19.8
	2005	100.0	9.7	105.1	31.3	25.2	71.3	40.9	26.2	16.3	32.9
	2010	100.0	35.9	81.5	26.5	19.8	63.8	35.0	25.2	15.6	39.8
Bangladesh	1990	100.0	4.5	84.6	18.3	6.3	14.0	31.5	21.4	13.4	47.2
	2000	100.0	4.6	77.5	23.0	14.0	19.2	25.5	25.3	15.2	49.2
	2005	100.0	5.5	74.4	24.5	16.6	23.0	20.1	27.2	16.5	52.6
	2010	100.0	5.4	75.4	24.9	18.5	24.9	18.6	28.5	17.9	53.0
Bhutan - Bhoutan	1990	100.0	17.5	54.2	36.3	28.9	33.0	39.0	28.0	8.4	33.0
	2000	100.0	21.9	47.7	48.2	29.0	53.5	27.4	36.0	8.4	36.6
	2005	100.0	21.9	40.4	49.9	39.1	62.8	23.2	37.3	7.4	39.5
	2010	100.0	19.5	37.6	47.9	65.1	75.1	19.0	44.3	8.5	36.7
India - Inde	1990	100.0	11.8	65.9	27.8	7.1	8.5	30.0	27.6	17.2	42.4
	2000	100.0	12.6	63.7	24.2	13.2	14.2	23.2	26.4	15.8	50.4
	2005	100.0	10.9	58.3	34.3	19.3	22.0	18.7	28.3	15.6	53.0
	2010	100.0	11.5	57.2	34.8	21.5	24.8	19.0	26.3	14.2	54.7
Iran (Islamic Rep. of) - Iran (Rép. islamique d')	1990	100.0	12.1	57.5	34.2	14.7	27.2	17.8	28.0	10.5	54.1
	2000	100.0	13.8	46.4	33.4	22.1	17.0	13.4	36.2	13.2	50.5
	2005	100.0	14.3	42.7	30.2	33.3	23.9	9.0	44.5	11.3	46.5
	2010	100.0	10.7	51.0	32.6	25.1	19.3	9.2	44.1	11.2	46.7
Maldives	1990	100.0	17.2	35.9	31.5	92.0	76.5	14.3	12.3	6.9	73.4
	2000	100.0	22.9	32.9	26.3	89.5	71.6	8.4	14.5	7.7	77.1
	2005	100.0	41.6	30.4	61.1	67.0	100.1	7.1	15.5	6.4	77.4
	2010	100.0	38.9	26.2	56.7	76.5	98.3	5.0	12.2	5.0	82.8
Nepal - Népal	1990	100.0	7.2	87.8	17.1	10.6	22.3	48.4	12.3	6.0	39.3
	2000	100.0	7.4	79.8	22.5	23.5	34.3	37.7	17.3	9.2	45.0
	2005	100.0	8.9	79.5	26.5	14.6	29.5	35.2	17.1	7.9	47.7
	2010	100.0	10.6	82.0	35.0	9.8	37.4	35.0	15.0	6.4	50.1
Pakistan	1990	100.0	11.7	72.3	20.4	12.2	16.6	25.2	25.3	16.7	49.4
	2000	100.0	8.6	75.4	17.2	13.4	14.7	25.9	23.3	14.7	50.7
	2005	100.0	7.8	76.9	19.1	15.7	19.6	21.5	27.1	18.6	51.4
	2010	100.0	7.9	82.5	15.4	13.6	19.4	21.2	25.4	17.7	53.4
Sri Lanka	1990	100.0	12.7	75.3	20.6	29.5	37.3	26.0	29.9	18.9	44.1
	2000	100.0	13.7	70.9	25.6	38.2	48.4	17.6	29.9	19.5	52.5
	2005	100.0	13.1	69.0	26.1	32.3	41.3	13.5	32.2	20.5	54.3
	2010	100.0	15.6	65.8	27.4	21.7	30.8	14.1	30.1	18.0	55.8
South-Eastern Asia - Asie du Sud-Est	*1990*	*100.0*	*9.7*	*56.3*	*31.6*	*48.8*	*49.3*	*16.0*	*36.7*	*23.4*	*47.3*
	2000	*100.0*	*9.6*	*56.4*	*24.4*	*83.8*	*74.4*	*11.6*	*41.1*	*27.7*	*47.2*
	2005	*100.0*	*9.8*	*57.9*	*24.7*	*84.8*	*76.8*	*11.0*	*42.3*	*27.8*	*46.7*
	2010	*100.0*	*10.3*	*55.1*	*27.6*	*68.1*	*61.3*	*13.0*	*41.6*	*25.5*	*45.4*
Brunei Darussalam - Brunéi Darussalam	1990	100.0	22.0	26.5	18.7	61.8	37.3	2.3	53.6	8.8	44.1
	2000	100.0	25.8	24.8	13.1	67.3	35.8	1.0	63.7	15.4	35.3
	2005	100.0	18.4	22.5	11.4	70.2	27.3	0.9	71.6	12.3	27.5
	2010	100.0	21.0	20.7	14.7	73.0	30.4	0.7	70.3	12.7	29.0
Cambodia - Cambodge	1990	100.0	7.2	90.4	8.3	2.4	8.4	50.1	11.7	7.3	38.2
	2000	100.0	5.2	88.8	17.5	49.8	61.8	37.8	23.0	16.9	39.1
	2005	100.0	5.8	84.3	18.5	64.1	72.7	32.4	26.4	18.8	41.2
	2010	100.0	8.4	75.2	17.2	66.1	66.4	36.1	23.1	15.7	40.8
Indonesia (...2002) - Indonésie (...2002)	1990	100.0	8.1	53.0	27.9	24.1	21.6	17.6	39.0	23.0	43.5
	2000	100.0	6.6	61.7	22.3	41.0	30.5	15.6	45.9	27.7	38.5
Indonesia - Indonésie	2005	100.0	8.1	64.4	25.1	34.1	29.9	13.1	46.5	27.4	40.3
	2010	100.0	9.1	56.7	32.5	24.6	23.0	15.3	47.0	24.8	37.6

For sources and notes, see end of table.

Pour les sources et les notes, se reporter à la fin du tableau.

8

8.3.1 Nominal gross domestic product by type of expenditure and by kind of economic activity of countries and geographical regions

8.3.1 Produit intérieur brut nominal par catégories de dépenses et par branches d'activité économique des pays et des régions géographiques

Region, country or territory / Régions, pays ou territoires	Year / Année	Total GDP / PIB total	GDP by type of expenditure (1) / PIB par catégories de dépenses (1)					GDP by kind of economic activity (2) / PIB par branches d'activité économique (2)			
			Final consumption / Consommation finale		Gross capital formation / Formation brute de capital	Exports / Exportations	Less imports / Moins les importations	Agriculture (3)	Industry (4) / Industrie (4)		Services (5)
			Government / Administration publique	Household / Ménages		Of goods and services / Des biens et services			Total	Manufacturing / Activités de fabrication	
			Percentage / En pourcentage								
Lao People's Dem. Rep. - Rép. dém. populaire lao	1990	100.0	9.5	92.3	11.3	11.3	24.5	48.7	9.6	4.3	41.7
	2000	100.0	8.1	77.7	28.3	30.0	44.1	44.4	16.1	7.8	39.5
	2005	100.0	7.7	73.5	34.5	33.1	48.8	36.5	24.5	9.1	39.0
	2010	100.0	9.2	54.8	37.1	28.3	32.9	32.0	26.8	9.5	41.2
Malaysia - Malaisie	1990	100.0	13.5	53.5	31.8	71.7	69.7	14.7	39.9	22.7	45.3
	2000	100.0	10.2	43.8	26.9	119.8	100.6	8.3	46.8	29.9	44.9
	2005	100.0	12.3	44.8	20.0	117.5	94.6	8.2	48.7	29.0	43.1
	2010	100.0	12.7	48.0	21.4	97.3	79.5	10.4	43.6	25.6	46.0
Myanmar	1990	100.0	13.6	74.7	13.4	1.9	3.6	55.8	10.3	7.6	34.0
	2000	100.0	9.4	78.3	12.4	0.5	0.6	57.2	9.7	7.2	33.1
	2005	100.0	3.6	83.4	13.2	0.2	0.1	46.7	17.5	12.8	35.8
	2010	100.0	3.9	69.4	23.0	0.1	0.1	36.4	25.8	19.6	37.7
Philippines	1990	100.0	10.1	69.5	27.8	23.6	30.5	19.2	37.7	26.8	43.1
	2000	100.0	11.4	72.2	18.4	51.4	53.4	14.0	34.5	24.5	51.6
	2005	100.0	9.0	75.0	21.6	46.1	51.7	12.7	33.8	24.1	53.5
	2010	100.0	9.7	71.6	20.5	34.8	36.6	12.3	32.6	21.4	55.1
Singapore - Singapour	1990	100.0	9.5	45.4	35.1	177.4	167.4	0.3	31.9	25.1	67.8
	2000	100.0	10.9	41.9	33.2	192.4	179.6	0.1	34.5	26.9	65.4
	2005	100.0	10.5	40.1	20.0	230.0	200.6	0.1	31.6	26.8	68.3
	2010	100.0	10.7	37.9	23.8	211.1	183.0	0.0	28.3	22.2	71.7
Thailand - Thaïlande	1990	100.0	9.4	56.5	41.3	34.1	41.6	14.4	35.9	24.9	49.7
	2000	100.0	11.3	56.1	22.8	66.8	58.1	9.0	42.0	33.6	49.0
	2005	100.0	11.9	57.2	31.4	73.6	74.7	10.3	44.0	34.7	45.8
	2010	100.0	12.9	53.7	26.0	71.3	63.9	12.4	44.7	35.6	42.9
Timor-Leste	2005	100.0	51.7	109.4	29.4	12.0	102.5	31.8	15.2	3.4	53.0
	2010	100.0	49.2	103.9	21.9	11.7	86.7	29.6	13.8	2.5	56.6
Viet Nam	1990	100.0	7.5	89.6	14.4	26.4	35.7	38.7	22.7	12.3	38.6
	2000	100.0	6.4	66.5	29.6	55.0	57.5	24.5	36.7	18.6	38.7
	2005	100.0	6.2	63.5	35.6	69.0	73.2	21.0	41.0	20.6	38.0
	2010	100.0	6.5	66.5	38.9	74.4	88.2	20.6	41.1	19.7	38.3
Western Asia - Asie occidentale	*1990*	*100.0*	*17.8*	*55.2*	*19.4*	*33.5*	*27.9*	*9.6*	*43.6*	*17.1*	*46.8*
	2000	*100.0*	*17.5*	*52.6*	*20.1*	*41.4*	*31.6*	*6.8*	*44.6*	*13.5*	*48.7*
	2005	*100.0*	*14.6*	*52.4*	*20.2*	*46.0*	*33.3*	*5.8*	*46.9*	*12.7*	*47.3*
	2010	*100.0*	*15.7*	*53.9*	*23.0*	*44.5*	*37.5*	*5.0*	*45.3*	*11.9*	*49.7*
Bahrain - Bahreïn	1990	100.0	23.6	55.6	16.9	91.9	90.3	0.8	36.7	11.1	62.5
	2000	100.0	17.4	44.5	12.6	89.5	63.9	0.7	40.0	10.5	59.3
	2005	100.0	15.7	36.7	24.5	99.5	76.4	0.4	39.1	11.0	60.5
	2010	100.0	12.4	35.0	29.4	81.2	59.3	0.4	43.8	16.0	55.8
Iraq	1990	100.0	12.1	21.3	17.1	118.6	69.1	18.9	30.0	8.4	51.1
	2000	100.0	14.7	16.8	36.2	93.9	61.6	4.6	84.6	0.9	10.8
	2005	100.0	27.5	51.7	30.5	74.9	84.6	6.9	63.3	1.3	29.9
	2010	100.0	42.8	34.6	24.3	65.0	66.7	5.0	49.8	2.3	45.1
Jordan - Jordanie	1990	100.0	24.9	74.1	31.9	61.9	92.7	7.5	30.9	17.0	61.7
	2000	100.0	23.7	80.6	22.4	41.8	68.5	2.3	24.4	14.8	73.3
	2005	100.0	19.5	87.8	34.1	52.7	94.2	3.0	26.9	16.6	70.1
	2010	100.0	17.4	76.1	26.6	44.3	65.1	2.6	29.6	18.8	67.8
Kuwait - Koweït	1990	100.0	38.6	58.6	15.9	44.8	57.8	0.9	51.7	11.5	47.4
	2000	100.0	21.5	41.5	10.7	56.5	30.1	0.3	57.2	6.7	42.5
	2005	100.0	15.7	32.2	16.4	64.0	28.3	0.3	60.2	7.0	39.5
	2010	100.0	16.7	30.4	19.1	60.1	26.3	0.2	57.5	5.1	42.4
Lebanon - Liban	1990	100.0	25.1	123.3	28.7	22.2	99.2	8.8	21.2	12.6	70.0
	2000	100.0	17.6	85.6	20.3	13.6	37.1	6.4	20.9	12.0	72.7
	2005	100.0	15.1	84.2	21.9	21.4	42.6	5.3	17.9	10.7	76.8
	2010	100.0	15.9	78.6	30.8	21.4	46.5	5.6	17.9	8.8	76.5

For sources and notes, see end of table.

Pour les sources et les notes, se reporter à la fin du tableau.

8.3.1 Nominal gross domestic product by type of expenditure and by kind of economic activity of countries and geographical regions

8.3.1 Produit intérieur brut nominal par catégories de dépenses et par branches d'activité économique des pays et des régions géographiques

Region, country or territory / Régions, pays ou territoires	Year / Année	Total GDP / PIB total	GDP by type of expenditure (1) / PIB par catégories de dépenses (1)					GDP by kind of economic activity (2) / PIB par branches d'activité économique (2)			
			Final consumption / Consommation finale		Gross capital formation / Formation brute de capital	Exports / Exportations	Less imports / Moins les importations	Agriculture (3)	Industry (4) / Industrie (4)		Services (5)
			Government / Administration publique	Household / Ménages		Of goods and services / Des biens et services			Total	Manufacturing / Activités de fabrication	
			Percentage / En pourcentage								
Occupied Palestinian territory - Territoire palestinien occupé	1990	100.0	22.2	102.0	36.8	14.6	72.0	13.5	30.9	18.5	55.6
	2000	100.0	26.5	94.5	33.8	16.6	71.4	11.3	25.7	13.1	63.0
	2005	100.0	18.0	103.1	27.5	13.2	61.8	6.5	27.4	15.3	66.1
	2010	100.0	21.8	113.6	26.1	13.7	75.2	6.6	24.3	13.9	69.0
Oman	1990	100.0	27.4	33.6	17.6	37.4	22.8	2.7	56.9	2.9	40.5
	2000	100.0	21.5	35.2	15.4	53.9	26.0	2.0	58.5	5.7	39.4
	2005	100.0	20.9	30.6	21.1	58.6	31.2	1.5	62.3	8.3	36.2
	2010	100.0	17.6	35.3	24.2	55.3	37.7	1.2	62.1	9.7	36.7
Qatar	1990	100.0	32.9	27.8	18.0	53.5	32.1	0.8	55.7	12.7	43.6
	2000	100.0	19.7	15.2	20.2	67.3	22.3	0.4	69.5	5.3	30.1
	2005	100.0	11.0	17.4	33.8	65.1	31.9	0.1	73.8	9.8	26.0
	2010	100.0	13.5	22.0	34.7	52.0	28.6	0.1	67.0	10.5	32.9
Saudi Arabia - Arabie saoudite	1990	100.0	29.2	46.7	15.1	40.6	31.6	5.7	48.6	8.6	45.7
	2000	100.0	26.0	36.5	18.7	43.7	24.9	4.9	53.6	9.6	41.5
	2005	100.0	22.2	26.5	18.2	60.9	27.8	3.2	62.9	9.3	33.9
	2010	100.0	22.5	34.1	22.0	56.8	35.4	2.6	61.8	10.1	35.7
Syrian Arab Republic - République arabe syrienne	1990	100.0	14.3	68.7	16.5	28.3	28.0	28.3	24.2	5.5	47.6
	2000	100.0	12.4	63.4	17.3	36.1	29.2	24.7	33.3	1.5	41.9
	2005	100.0	13.7	65.9	18.4	41.0	39.1	20.3	31.2	2.5	48.5
	2010	100.0	10.0	59.0	33.1	35.1	35.6	20.2	31.8	4.5	48.0
Turkey - Turquie	1990	100.0	8.8	65.9	22.3	11.6	12.7	13.4	38.9	29.1	47.6
	2000	100.0	11.7	70.5	20.8	20.1	23.1	10.8	30.0	21.4	59.2
	2005	100.0	11.8	71.7	20.0	21.9	25.4	10.6	28.0	19.6	61.3
	2010	100.0	14.3	71.3	19.9	21.1	26.6	9.4	26.1	17.3	64.5
United Arab Emirates - Émirats arabes unis	1990	100.0	16.3	38.6	20.4	65.4	40.8	1.0	58.1	7.3	40.9
	2000	100.0	15.4	43.5	23.2	73.7	55.8	2.2	51.4	12.8	46.4
	2005	100.0	6.9	58.3	19.2	67.6	52.0	1.4	53.8	10.3	44.8
	2010	100.0	8.2	59.4	25.3	75.3	68.2	0.8	53.2	9.3	46.0
Yemen - Yémen	1990	100.0	16.2	84.3	8.2	13.2	18.5	23.7	24.3	7.8	52.0
	2000	100.0	13.0	64.3	15.8	39.7	32.8	12.9	44.5	5.6	42.6
	2005	100.0	11.5	60.2	23.6	38.3	33.6	10.1	46.6	7.3	43.3
	2010	100.0	10.5	81.0	15.8	25.7	29.0	10.1	41.8	7.5	48.1
Developing economies: Oceania - Économies en développement : Océanie	**1990**	**100.0**	**23.1**	**67.6**	**22.7**	**31.1**	**44.5**	**14.5**	**22.6**	**8.3**	**62.9**
	2000	**100.0**	**19.0**	**66.9**	**20.5**	**38.2**	**45.8**	**15.3**	**25.1**	**10.2**	**59.7**
	2005	**100.0**	**18.0**	**72.2**	**21.5**	**36.5**	**50.2**	**12.9**	**25.3**	**10.2**	**61.8**
	2010	**100.0**	**18.6**	**76.4**	**23.7**	**35.9**	**56.0**	**14.1**	**28.9**	**9.8**	**57.0**
Cook Islands - Îles Cook	1990	100.0	55.5	52.5	17.1	81.2	106.3	11.3	8.2	4.2	80.5
	2000	100.0	34.2	42.4	13.8	83.8	74.2	10.3	8.3	3.5	81.4
	2005	100.0	35.0	40.3	13.1	73.8	62.3	6.9	9.6	3.9	83.5
	2010	100.0	31.8	47.3	15.4	82.8	77.4	5.1	9.2	3.5	85.6
Fiji - Fidji	1990	100.0	17.8	65.1	19.7	63.5	66.1	19.1	20.0	10.9	60.9
	2000	100.0	17.3	69.6	18.3	58.3	63.5	16.3	19.2	14.7	64.5
	2005	100.0	16.1	81.0	17.1	51.2	65.3	14.1	19.2	14.2	66.8
	2010	100.0	18.0	79.7	17.6	47.6	61.4	12.6	21.7	16.7	65.7
French Polynesia - Polynésie française	1990	100.0	9.9	89.5	18.7	11.1	29.2	3.8	16.6	8.9	79.7
	2000	100.0	8.2	87.0	15.5	17.6	32.8	3.8	15.9	8.1	80.3
	2005	100.0	6.2	96.2	17.2	12.0	39.3	2.5	14.4	7.1	83.1
	2010	100.0	7.3	94.7	17.3	12.3	38.9	2.4	14.2	7.0	83.3
Kiribati	1990	100.0	49.8	129.6	56.2	11.6	147.2	28.0	14.0	9.6	58.0
	2000	100.0	29.6	76.9	33.4	6.9	46.8	22.0	11.6	4.9	66.4
	2005	100.0	54.0	140.5	61.0	18.3	173.8	24.2	6.7	4.5	69.2
	2010	100.0	52.2	135.8	58.9	18.2	165.1	26.3	8.6	5.4	65.1

For sources and notes, see end of table.

Pour les sources et les notes, se reporter à la fin du tableau.

443

8

8.3.1 Nominal gross domestic product by type of expenditure and by kind of economic activity of countries and geographical regions

8.3.1 Produit intérieur brut nominal par catégories de dépenses et par branches d'activité économique des pays et des régions géographiques

Region, country or territory / Régions, pays ou territoires	Year / Année	Total GDP / PIB total	GDP by type of expenditure (1) / PIB par catégories de dépenses (1)					GDP by kind of economic activity (2) / PIB par branches d'activité économique (2)			
			Final consumption / Consommation finale		Gross capital formation / Formation brute de capital	Exports / Exportations	Less imports / Moins les importations	Agriculture / Agriculture (3)	Industry (4) / Industrie (4)		Services (5)
			Government / Administration publique	Household / Ménages		Of goods and services / Des biens et services			Total	Manufacturing / Activités de fabrication	
			Percentage / En pourcentage								
Marshall Islands - Îles Marshall	1990	100.0	50.2	97.6	88.4	11.0	147.2	13.9	12.9	1.0	73.2
	2000	100.0	54.1	91.1	56.8	12.4	114.5	10.0	19.2	4.6	70.9
	2005	100.0	54.1	91.1	56.8	12.4	114.5	10.0	19.1	4.4	70.9
	2010	100.0	54.1	91.1	56.8	12.4	114.5	10.0	19.2	4.4	70.8
Micronesia (Federated States of) - Micronésie (États fédérés de)	1990	100.0	52.2	75.1	33.8	17.3	78.3	24.6	7.5	1.4	67.9
	2000	100.0	50.1	72.1	32.4	16.4	71.0	25.5	8.7	1.7	65.8
	2005	100.0	51.2	73.7	33.2	14.7	72.8	24.1	5.7	0.6	70.2
	2010	100.0	51.0	73.4	33.0	17.0	74.3	26.0	8.0	0.5	66.0
Nauru	1990	100.0	49.8	129.6	56.2	11.6	147.2	7.5	4.4	4.5	88.1
	2000	100.0	29.6	76.9	33.4	6.9	46.8	7.1	7.7	4.5	85.2
	2005	100.0	54.0	140.5	61.0	18.3	173.8	7.8	-6.5	3.5	98.7
	2010	100.0	52.2	135.8	58.9	18.2	165.1	6.2	35.6	13.3	58.2
New Caledonia - Nouvelle-Calédonie	1990	100.0	32.6	57.3	23.3	22.0	35.4	2.0	25.2	6.4	72.8
	2000	100.0	26.8	65.1	22.9	22.8	37.6	2.4	26.0	14.9	71.6
	2005	100.0	25.6	63.6	29.8	21.5	40.4	1.7	26.6	16.0	71.7
	2010	100.0	24.6	60.6	39.2	20.5	44.9	1.6	29.4	16.3	69.0
Palau - Palaos	1990	100.0	33.2	44.2	38.3	35.8	47.5	25.9	15.5	0.7	58.6
	2000	100.0	41.9	125.5	29.0	9.6	106.1	3.9	15.3	1.4	80.8
	2005	100.0	34.6	52.5	16.5	77.6	81.2	3.2	19.2	0.4	77.6
	2010	100.0	34.6	49.5	21.3	71.1	76.5	3.2	20.9	0.4	75.9
Papua New Guinea - Papouasie-Nouvelle-Guinée	1990	100.0	26.3	51.8	24.0	43.0	45.4	29.7	31.2	9.2	39.0
	2000	100.0	16.6	44.6	21.9	66.2	49.2	35.2	40.7	7.4	24.1
	2005	100.0	16.1	48.0	17.5	74.5	56.1	34.0	44.3	6.3	21.7
	2010	100.0	16.5	76.7	15.1	61.4	69.7	31.9	44.7	5.9	23.4
Samoa	1990	100.0	27.7	82.6	22.9	28.0	61.2	20.5	28.8	19.2	50.6
	2000	100.0	24.0	85.2	14.2	30.6	53.9	16.7	26.8	15.0	56.6
	2005	100.0	22.4	91.6	10.4	29.9	54.3	12.3	30.5	15.5	57.2
	2010	100.0	20.3	92.9	9.0	30.8	53.0	9.6	27.7	9.8	62.7
Solomon Islands - Îles Salomon	1990	100.0	31.1	57.4	20.1	46.5	56.8	45.5	7.9	3.7	46.6
	2000	100.0	31.8	48.5	19.6	59.1	59.1	34.7	12.7	8.0	52.6
	2005	100.0	38.4	64.5	17.2	32.9	52.0	30.4	7.5	5.2	62.1
	2010	100.0	40.1	70.1	20.3	44.0	74.5	28.3	10.0	5.9	61.6
Tonga	1990	100.0	18.7	93.7	18.1	33.2	63.8	34.7	13.6	6.0	51.7
	2000	100.0	18.2	90.5	21.7	15.4	46.9	22.2	20.7	10.2	57.0
	2005	100.0	15.5	101.7	22.1	18.0	57.9	21.4	18.7	9.0	59.9
	2010	100.0	19.1	99.0	29.4	13.4	60.0	19.9	17.4	7.4	62.6
Tuvalu	1990	100.0	55.2	28.5	68.6	2.8	55.1	25.6	14.5	1.5	59.8
	2000	100.0	147.1	5.6	11.7	2.1	66.5	17.3	13.1	1.4	69.7
	2005	100.0	73.3	33.6	73.4	1.7	82.0	21.2	8.4	0.9	70.4
	2010	100.0	70.7	35.4	77.4	1.7	85.2	21.6	9.4	0.9	69.0
Vanuatu	1990	100.0	30.1	75.2	31.4	48.1	78.3	23.6	10.0	5.5	66.4
	2000	100.0	15.5	66.4	25.8	39.5	47.7	25.2	12.3	5.0	62.5
	2005	100.0	13.3	70.4	20.4	52.4	57.2	23.8	8.5	4.3	67.7
	2010	100.0	15.7	62.9	28.8	50.1	57.0	19.5	10.4	3.9	70.1
Transition economies - Économies en transition	**1990**	**100.0**	**20.9**	**49.0**	**28.1**	**22.8**	**24.8**	**17.7**	**38.0**	**28.7**	**44.3**
	2000	**100.0**	**16.3**	**52.6**	**19.4**	**45.0**	**32.9**	**10.3**	**37.3**	**21.3**	**52.3**
	2005	**100.0**	**16.9**	**52.7**	**22.2**	**38.9**	**30.3**	**6.9**	**37.1**	**18.4**	**56.0**
	2010	**100.0**	**18.4**	**54.0**	**23.0**	**34.8**	**28.5**	**5.6**	**36.6**	**16.4**	**57.8**
Albania - Albanie	1990	100.0	10.2	72.7	24.4	14.9	22.2	40.2	43.8	21.5	16.0
	2000	100.0	9.5	76.6	34.2	17.9	38.1	25.5	16.1	4.8	58.5
	2005	100.0	10.9	78.0	35.8	22.8	47.5	20.6	24.4	6.6	55.0
	2010	100.0	9.5	86.5	25.1	35.6	56.6	18.8	24.2	7.9	57.0

For sources and notes, see end of table.

Pour les sources et les notes, se reporter à la fin du tableau.

444

8.3.1 **Nominal gross domestic product by type of expenditure and by kind of economic activity of countries and geographical regions**

8.3.1 **Produit intérieur brut nominal par catégories de dépenses et par branches d'activité économique des pays et des régions géographiques**

Region, country or territory / Régions, pays ou territoires	Year / Année	Total GDP / PIB total	GDP by type of expenditure (1) / PIB par catégories de dépenses (1)					GDP by kind of economic activity (2) / PIB par branches d'activité économique (2)			
			Final consumption / Consommation finale		Gross capital formation / Formation brute de capital	Exports / Exportations	Less imports / Moins les importations	Agriculture (3)	Industry (4) / Industrie (4)		Services (5)
			Government / Administration publique	Household / Ménages		Of goods and services / Des biens et services			Total	Manufacturing / Activités de fabrication	
			Percentage / En pourcentage								
Armenia - Arménie	2000	100.0	11.8	97.1	18.6	23.4	50.5	25.1	38.3	18.2	36.5
	2005	100.0	10.6	75.5	30.5	28.8	43.2	20.6	44.7	14.6	34.6
	2010	100.0	13.1	80.9	33.4	19.8	45.2	19.2	35.4	10.5	45.4
Azerbaijan - Azerbaïdjan	2000	100.0	15.2	64.4	20.7	40.2	38.4	17.0	45.1	5.6	37.9
	2005	100.0	10.4	42.1	41.5	62.9	52.9	9.8	63.2	7.0	27.0
	2010	100.0	9.6	43.9	17.0	55.1	21.1	5.7	64.0	5.8	30.4
Belarus - Bélarus	2000	100.0	19.5	56.9	25.4	64.7	68.2	13.9	40.4	31.0	45.8
	2005	100.0	20.8	52.0	28.5	59.8	59.1	9.6	43.2	33.3	47.2
	2010	100.0	16.1	55.6	40.6	54.6	68.3	8.9	44.1	30.3	47.0
Bosnia and Herzegovina - Bosnie-Herzégovine	2000	100.0	20.3	98.3	26.8	27.8	73.2	10.9	27.0	12.0	62.1
	2005	100.0	22.2	97.2	28.0	32.5	73.7	10.1	25.6	12.2	64.2
	2010	100.0	20.7	80.6	20.3	36.7	58.3	9.1	26.7	13.3	64.2
Croatia - Croatie	2000	100.0	22.4	61.8	19.1	41.7	45.0	6.5	28.5	20.3	65.0
	2005	100.0	19.0	60.2	27.3	42.3	48.7	5.0	28.5	17.5	66.4
	2010	100.0	20.5	56.7	23.4	38.3	38.8	5.5	25.7	16.2	68.8
Georgia - Géorgie	2000	100.0	8.5	90.5	26.6	23.0	39.7	21.7	22.1	12.9	56.1
	2005	100.0	17.3	66.9	33.5	33.7	51.6	16.5	26.5	13.5	57.0
	2010	100.0	21.0	76.0	19.5	34.8	52.3	8.3	22.9	12.7	68.8
Kazakhstan	2000	100.0	12.1	61.9	18.1	56.6	49.1	8.6	40.1	17.5	51.3
	2005	100.0	11.2	49.9	31.0	53.5	44.7	6.6	39.2	12.5	54.2
	2010	100.0	10.9	45.2	25.3	44.3	29.4	4.5	41.9	11.8	53.6
Kyrgyzstan - Kirghizistan	2000	100.0	20.0	65.7	20.0	41.8	47.6	36.6	31.3	19.4	32.1
	2005	100.0	17.5	84.5	16.4	38.3	56.8	31.3	22.0	14.1	46.7
	2010	100.0	19.0	83.9	28.4	57.7	89.2	20.0	26.9	17.2	53.1
Montenegro - Monténégro	2010	100.0	23.4	82.2	22.8	34.7	63.1	9.5	20.7	6.5	69.8
Republic of Moldova - République de Moldova	2000	100.0	14.7	88.4	23.9	49.6	76.6	28.3	21.2	15.8	50.6
	2005	100.0	16.4	93.4	30.8	51.2	91.9	19.1	22.2	15.5	58.7
	2010	100.0	21.8	93.2	23.7	39.6	78.2	14.0	19.3	12.4	66.8
Russian Federation - Fédération de Russie	2000	100.0	15.5	46.1	18.7	44.1	24.1	6.8	39.3	22.2	53.9
	2005	100.0	17.0	49.5	20.1	35.2	21.5	5.0	38.1	18.3	57.0
	2010	100.0	19.5	51.9	22.8	30.0	21.7	4.0	36.7	16.4	59.3
Serbia and Montenegro - Serbie-et-Monténégro	2000	100.0	22.0	81.2	12.1	14.5	29.8	22.3	30.3	21.8	47.4
	2005	100.0	20.2	77.9	23.3	27.3	48.8	12.2	27.4	16.8	60.4
Serbia - Serbie	2010	100.0	19.1	81.7	19.0	33.1	52.8	12.0	21.8	13.9	66.2
SFR of Yugoslavia - RSF de Yougoslavie	1990	100.0	17.6	66.1	22.1	23.7	29.4	12.9	43.3	31.2	43.9
Tajikistan - Tadjikistan	2000	100.0	11.6	87.7	9.4	92.4	100.2	27.3	38.4	36.1	34.3
	2005	100.0	14.6	81.1	11.6	54.3	72.8	23.8	30.7	25.6	45.6
	2010	100.0	9.7	111.2	18.4	15.2	54.5	21.7	28.3	17.6	50.1
TFYR of Macedonia - LERY de Macédoine	2000	100.0	18.2	74.4	22.3	48.6	63.5	11.7	32.9	20.2	55.4
	2005	100.0	18.4	77.3	21.3	44.1	61.1	12.3	28.2	17.4	59.5
	2010	100.0	18.7	76.7	23.3	47.6	66.3	12.1	27.3	16.8	60.6
Turkmenistan - Turkménistan	2000	100.0	14.2	36.5	34.7	95.5	80.9	22.9	41.8	35.0	35.2
	2005	100.0	13.2	46.6	22.9	65.0	47.8	18.8	37.6	31.1	43.6
	2010	100.0	9.1	45.5	14.4	74.5	43.4	14.5	48.4	40.3	37.0
Ukraine	2000	100.0	18.6	56.6	19.7	62.4	57.4	16.8	37.6	21.3	45.5
	2005	100.0	18.2	58.3	22.6	51.5	50.6	10.3	34.4	21.9	55.3
	2010	100.0	20.1	63.3	19.3	50.2	53.0	7.8	29.5	16.5	62.7
USSR - URSS	1990	100.0	21.2	47.1	28.7	22.7	24.3	18.1	37.5	28.5	44.4

For sources and notes, see end of table.

Pour les sources et les notes, se reporter à la fin du tableau.

8.3.1 Nominal gross domestic product by type of expenditure and by kind of economic activity of countries and geographical regions

8.3.1 Produit intérieur brut nominal par catégories de dépenses et par branches d'activité économique des pays et des régions géographiques

Region, country or territory / Régions, pays ou territoires	Year / Année	Total GDP / PIB total	GDP by type of expenditure (1) / PIB par catégories de dépenses (1)					GDP by kind of economic activity (2) / PIB par branches d'activité économique (2)			
			Final consumption / Consommation finale		Gross capital formation / Formation brute de capital	Exports / Exportations	Less imports / Moins les importations	Agriculture (3) / Agriculture (3)	Industry (4) / Industrie (4)		Services (5)
			Government / Administration publique	Household / Ménages	Formation brute de capital	Of goods and services / Des biens et services			Total	Manufacturing / Activités de fabrication	
			Percentage / En pourcentage								
Uzbekistan - Ouzbékistan	2000	100.0	18.7	61.9	19.6	24.6	21.5	34.9	22.8	13.2	42.3
	2005	100.0	17.6	46.7	26.5	37.9	28.7	29.5	29.1	19.8	41.4
	2010	100.0	17.3	56.1	23.9	39.5	37.6	23.0	34.8	23.5	42.1
Developed economies: America - Économies développées : Amérique	**1990**	**100.0**	**17.5**	**65.7**	**17.9**	**11.4**	**12.6**	**2.0**	**27.8**	**18.2**	**70.2**
	2000	**100.0**	**14.6**	**68.0**	**20.5**	**13.8**	**16.9**	**1.0**	**23.7**	**15.7**	**75.3**
	2005	**100.0**	**16.0**	**68.8**	**20.1**	**13.1**	**17.9**	**1.1**	**22.7**	**13.9**	**76.3**
	2010	**100.0**	**17.9**	**69.6**	**15.9**	**14.8**	**18.1**	**1.1**	**21.6**	**12.8**	**77.3**
Bermuda - Bermudes	1990	100.0	12.5	69.1	16.4	47.5	43.7	0.8	10.3	2.4	88.9
	2000	100.0	10.9	51.5	20.1	47.4	41.1	0.7	11.0	2.4	88.4
	2005	100.0	20.4	74.8	20.1	37.1	52.5	0.8	9.7	1.6	89.5
	2010	100.0	20.0	74.9	20.0	41.0	55.9	0.8	8.4	1.5	90.8
Canada	1990	100.0	22.3	56.7	20.9	25.8	25.7	2.9	31.3	16.9	65.8
	2000	100.0	18.6	55.4	20.2	45.6	39.8	2.3	33.2	19.2	64.5
	2005	100.0	18.9	55.2	22.1	37.8	34.1	1.8	32.4	15.0	65.8
	2010	100.0	21.8	57.9	22.2	29.4	31.3	1.6	29.0	11.4	69.4
Greenland - Groenland	1990	100.0	53.4	27.0	19.0	44.3	43.7	8.6	24.0	13.7	67.4
	2000	100.0	52.4	32.9	23.2	25.5	34.1	8.0	23.1	12.3	68.9
	2005	100.0	51.1	31.8	28.3	23.9	35.1	5.6	21.5	9.3	72.9
	2010	100.0	53.0	31.3	30.5	18.9	39.8	5.9	21.3	10.0	72.8
United States - États-Unis	1990	100.0	17.0	66.6	17.7	10.0	11.3	1.9	27.5	18.3	70.6
	2000	100.0	14.3	68.9	20.6	11.5	15.2	1.0	23.1	15.5	76.0
	2005	100.0	15.7	70.0	19.9	10.9	16.5	1.0	21.9	13.9	77.1
	2010	100.0	17.4	70.8	15.2	13.2	16.6	1.0	20.9	12.9	78.1
Developed economies: Asia - Économies développées : Asie	**1990**	**100.0**	**13.6**	**53.1**	**32.5**	**10.7**	**9.9**	**2.5**	**38.2**	**25.9**	**59.3**
	2000	**100.0**	**17.1**	**56.2**	**25.3**	**11.7**	**10.3**	**1.7**	**31.0**	**21.2**	**67.3**
	2005	**100.0**	**18.3**	**57.0**	**23.4**	**15.1**	**13.8**	**1.5**	**29.0**	**20.5**	**69.6**
	2010	**100.0**	**20.2**	**59.1**	**20.0**	**16.0**	**14.9**	**1.4**	**27.2**	**19.2**	**71.4**
Israel - Israël	1990	100.0	28.1	55.4	19.7	30.5	34.4	3.0	25.6	18.5	71.5
	2000	100.0	25.8	53.9	20.5	37.3	37.5	1.7	25.0	17.5	73.3
	2005	100.0	25.7	55.8	18.9	42.7	43.1	2.0	21.4	15.0	76.6
	2010	100.0	23.9	58.2	16.0	36.9	34.9	1.9	21.7	15.1	76.4
Japan - Japon	1990	100.0	13.3	53.0	32.7	10.4	9.4	2.5	38.4	26.0	59.1
	2000	100.0	16.9	56.2	25.4	11.0	9.5	1.7	31.1	21.3	67.2
	2005	100.0	18.1	57.0	23.6	14.3	12.9	1.5	29.1	20.6	69.4
	2010	100.0	20.0	59.1	20.2	15.2	14.1	1.4	27.3	19.4	71.3
Developed economies: Europe - Économies développées : Europe	**1990**	**100.0**	**19.9**	**57.5**	**23.0**	**26.5**	**27.2**	**3.5**	**32.8**	**22.7**	**63.7**
	2000	**100.0**	**19.5**	**58.4**	**21.4**	**36.4**	**35.7**	**2.4**	**28.2**	**19.3**	**69.4**
	2005	**100.0**	**20.6**	**58.0**	**20.3**	**37.6**	**36.5**	**1.9**	**26.6**	**17.1**	**71.5**
	2010	**100.0**	**21.9**	**57.7**	**18.9**	**41.0**	**39.6**	**1.7**	**25.4**	**15.6**	**72.9**
Andorra - Andorre	1990	100.0	16.7	60.4	26.1	16.1	19.4	0.4	19.9	4.8	79.6
	2000	100.0	17.2	59.7	26.3	29.0	32.2	0.5	17.8	4.5	81.7
	2005	100.0	18.0	57.8	29.5	25.7	31.0	0.4	17.7	3.8	81.9
	2010	100.0	20.8	58.4	23.0	26.3	28.4	0.4	14.8	4.1	84.7
Austria - Autriche	1990	100.0	18.8	56.4	25.1	37.1	36.9	3.7	32.2	21.7	64.1
	2000	100.0	19.0	54.9	24.5	46.2	44.5	2.0	30.8	20.6	67.2
	2005	100.0	18.4	55.0	22.7	53.8	49.9	1.6	29.5	19.6	68.9
	2010	100.0	19.4	54.5	21.6	54.0	49.7	1.5	29.2	19.2	69.3
Belgium - Belgique	1990	100.0	19.7	55.3	22.4	69.4	67.4	2.3	30.9	22.5	66.8
	2000	100.0	21.3	53.2	22.6	78.1	75.2	1.4	27.0	19.3	71.6
	2005	100.0	22.8	51.4	21.9	78.7	74.8	0.8	24.1	17.1	75.1
	2010	100.0	24.2	52.9	20.2	80.0	77.3	0.7	21.9	14.6	77.4

For sources and notes, see end of table.

Pour les sources et les notes, se reporter à la fin du tableau.

446

8.3.1 Nominal gross domestic product by type of expenditure and by kind of economic activity of countries and geographical regions

8.3.1 Produit intérieur brut nominal par catégories de dépenses et par branches d'activité économique des pays et des régions géographiques

Region, country or territory / Régions, pays ou territoires	Year / Année	Total GDP / PIB total	GDP by type of expenditure (1) / PIB par catégories de dépenses (1)					GDP by kind of economic activity (2) / PIB par branches d'activité économique (2)			
			Final consumption / Consommation finale		Gross capital formation / Formation brute de capital	Exports / Exportations	Less imports / Moins les importations	Agri-culture (3)	Industry (4) / Industrie (4)		Services (5)
			Government / Administration publique	Household / Ménages		Of goods and services / Des biens et services			Total	Manu-facturing / Activités de fabrication	
			Percentage / En pourcentage								
Bulgaria - Bulgarie	1990	100.0	7.2	66.8	30.4	42.5	46.9	18.7	46.2	28.1	35.1
	2000	100.0	19.0	68.4	18.0	50.5	55.8	13.6	25.9	14.2	60.6
	2005	100.0	18.3	69.2	27.6	40.5	55.6	9.1	29.0	16.7	61.9
	2010	100.0	15.8	61.2	24.9	57.8	59.7	5.3	31.2	16.4	63.5
Cyprus - Chypre	1990	100.0	14.7	60.6	26.6	55.7	57.7	6.8	27.0	13.5	66.1
	2000	100.0	16.2	65.1	17.8	56.1	55.2	3.8	20.9	9.7	75.3
	2005	100.0	18.0	64.8	19.8	48.6	51.2	2.9	22.2	8.4	74.9
	2010	100.0	19.4	67.3	18.8	43.0	48.5	2.4	18.8	6.4	78.8
Czechoslovakia - Tchécoslovaquie	1990	100.0	23.9	50.4	26.0	-2.9	38.4	7.6	44.0	34.9	48.4
Czech Republic - République tchèque	2000	100.0	20.3	51.9	29.9	60.9	63.1	3.9	38.1	26.8	58.0
	2005	100.0	21.4	49.3	26.5	64.4	61.7	3.0	37.9	26.3	59.1
	2010	100.0	21.4	50.3	25.1	67.9	64.7	2.4	37.6	24.5	60.0
Denmark - Danemark	1990	100.0	25.1	50.3	19.9	37.2	32.6	4.0	25.6	17.4	70.4
	2000	100.0	25.1	47.7	21.2	46.6	40.5	2.6	26.8	16.2	70.6
	2005	100.0	26.0	48.2	20.8	49.0	44.1	1.4	25.5	14.2	73.1
	2010	100.0	29.4	49.0	16.4	50.6	45.0	1.2	22.1	12.3	76.7
Estonia - Estonie	2000	100.0	19.8	55.5	28.4	84.6	88.2	4.8	27.6	17.0	67.7
	2005	100.0	17.2	55.5	33.8	77.7	84.2	3.5	29.7	16.5	66.8
	2010	100.0	20.9	52.1	19.5	79.4	72.5	3.3	28.5	16.4	68.2
Finland - Finlande	1990	100.0	21.7	51.0	28.5	22.5	24.1	6.3	33.6	22.7	60.1
	2000	100.0	20.5	49.4	20.9	43.6	34.5	3.5	34.7	26.5	61.8
	2005	100.0	22.5	51.6	21.9	41.8	37.7	2.8	32.5	23.4	64.8
	2010	100.0	24.6	54.6	18.6	40.3	39.0	2.9	29.0	18.8	68.1
France	1990	100.0	21.7	57.5	21.7	21.5	22.4	3.8	26.6	17.9	69.6
	2000	100.0	22.9	56.2	19.9	28.8	27.8	2.8	22.9	16.0	74.3
	2005	100.0	23.8	56.9	20.0	26.4	27.0	2.3	20.7	13.2	77.1
	2010	100.0	24.8	58.2	19.4	25.5	27.8	2.0	19.8	11.6	78.2
Germany - Allemagne	1990	100.0	19.3	57.8	23.2	24.8	24.9	1.5	37.3	28.1	61.2
	2000	100.0	19.0	58.4	22.3	33.4	33.1	1.3	30.3	22.9	68.5
	2005	100.0	18.8	58.8	17.3	41.3	36.1	0.9	29.1	22.7	70.0
	2010	100.0	19.7	57.5	17.3	46.8	41.4	0.9	27.9	20.7	71.3
Greece - Grèce	1990	100.0	15.2	75.2	22.6	17.5	29.6	9.3	25.9	14.5	64.8
	2000	100.0	17.8	72.4	23.3	24.9	38.4	6.6	21.0	11.1	72.5
	2005	100.0	18.1	69.8	21.4	23.2	32.5	4.8	19.2	9.7	76.0
	2010	100.0	18.2	74.5	16.2	21.5	30.4	3.3	17.9	10.8	78.8
Hungary - Hongrie	1990	100.0	21.8	49.2	24.1	28.6	24.8	12.5	34.0	20.4	53.5
	2000	100.0	21.5	54.9	27.1	74.6	78.1	5.4	31.7	23.0	62.9
	2005	100.0	22.6	55.0	24.5	65.9	68.1	4.2	30.1	22.3	65.7
	2010	100.0	21.8	53.3	18.4	86.5	80.0	3.6	31.1	23.7	65.3
Iceland - Islande	1990	100.0	19.9	59.8	19.0	33.6	32.3	11.7	30.8	16.9	57.4
	2000	100.0	23.4	60.6	23.2	33.6	40.9	9.1	26.1	13.9	64.8
	2005	100.0	24.6	59.4	28.2	31.7	44.0	6.3	24.4	10.5	69.3
	2010	100.0	26.0	51.3	12.8	56.0	46.0	6.4	26.1	13.0	67.5
Ireland - Irlande	1990	100.0	17.0	58.5	19.3	56.3	51.5	9.0	34.6	27.6	56.4
	2000	100.0	14.2	48.6	23.9	97.3	84.0	3.7	41.0	32.2	55.3
	2005	100.0	15.8	46.2	27.1	81.1	69.4	2.7	34.2	22.9	63.1
	2010	100.0	18.9	50.8	11.0	101.1	82.0	2.5	30.9	25.5	66.6
Italy - Italie	1990	100.0	20.1	57.3	22.3	19.2	19.0	3.5	32.1	23.3	64.4
	2000	100.0	18.4	59.9	20.7	27.1	26.1	2.8	28.4	21.0	68.8
	2005	100.0	20.3	59.0	20.7	25.9	26.0	2.2	26.9	18.5	70.9
	2010	100.0	21.2	60.4	20.2	26.8	28.5	1.9	25.3	16.8	72.8

For sources and notes, see end of table.

Pour les sources et les notes, se reporter à la fin du tableau.

8

8.3.1 Nominal gross domestic product by type of expenditure and by kind of economic activity of countries and geographical regions

8.3.1 Produit intérieur brut nominal par catégories de dépenses et par branches d'activité économique des pays et des régions géographiques

Region, country or territory / Régions, pays ou territoires	Year / Année	Total GDP / PIB total	GDP by type of expenditure (1) / PIB par catégories de dépenses (1)					GDP by kind of economic activity (2) / PIB par branches d'activité économique (2)			
			Final consumption / Consommation finale		Gross capital formation / Formation brute de capital	Exports / Exportations	Less imports / Moins les importations	Agri-culture (3)	Industry (4) / Industrie (4)		Services (5)
			Government / Administration publique	Household / Ménages		Of goods and services / Des biens et services			Total	Manu-facturing / Activités de fabrication	
			Percentage / En pourcentage								
Latvia - Lettonie	2000	100.0	20.9	63.0	23.1	41.9	49.0	4.5	25.4	14.4	70.0
	2005	100.0	17.8	63.1	33.6	48.2	62.6	3.9	23.1	12.9	72.9
	2010	100.0	17.5	63.0	20.9	53.8	55.2	4.5	24.7	13.4	70.9
Lithuania - Lituanie	2000	100.0	22.6	65.2	18.5	44.5	50.8	6.3	29.8	19.3	63.9
	2005	100.0	18.6	64.9	23.6	57.3	64.4	4.8	32.9	20.8	62.3
	2010	100.0	20.5	64.4	16.4	68.3	69.5	3.4	27.9	18.2	68.7
Luxembourg	1990	100.0	15.8	47.0	23.7	101.5	88.2	1.5	29.3	20.4	69.2
	2000	100.0	15.1	40.7	23.2	150.0	129.0	0.7	18.4	11.3	81.0
	2005	100.0	16.5	35.5	22.5	155.8	130.3	0.4	16.6	9.2	82.9
	2010	100.0	16.6	33.5	18.7	165.0	133.8	0.3	12.8	6.1	86.9
Malta - Malte	1990	100.0	16.2	67.2	30.6	75.8	88.7	3.5	31.8	24.1	64.8
	2000	100.0	18.2	64.4	25.3	90.6	98.4	2.3	28.5	22.4	69.2
	2005	100.0	19.5	65.5	18.1	76.8	79.9	2.6	21.8	16.1	75.6
	2010	100.0	21.0	61.7	13.9	88.2	84.8	1.9	19.3	13.4	78.8
Netherlands - Pays-Bas	1990	100.0	23.0	49.7	23.5	56.5	52.6	4.4	29.4	18.6	66.2
	2000	100.0	22.0	50.4	22.0	70.1	64.5	2.6	24.9	15.6	72.4
	2005	100.0	23.7	48.8	19.0	69.6	61.1	2.1	24.2	14.3	73.7
	2010	100.0	28.5	45.4	18.7	78.0	70.6	1.9	23.7	13.2	74.3
Norway - Norvège	1990	100.0	21.2	49.8	22.7	40.1	33.8	3.4	34.0	12.3	62.6
	2000	100.0	19.3	43.2	20.4	46.5	29.4	2.1	42.0	10.6	56.0
	2005	100.0	19.9	42.5	21.2	44.6	28.2	1.5	42.9	9.8	55.6
	2010	100.0	22.4	43.0	21.3	41.9	28.6	1.6	40.6	9.3	57.8
Poland - Pologne	1990	100.0	20.8	48.0	24.3	26.2	19.7	10.4	52.2	33.2	37.4
	2000	100.0	17.4	64.1	24.8	27.1	33.5	5.0	31.7	18.5	63.3
	2005	100.0	18.1	63.4	19.3	37.1	37.8	4.5	30.7	18.5	64.8
	2010	100.0	18.9	61.4	21.0	42.3	43.5	3.5	31.6	18.5	64.8
Portugal	1990	100.0	15.1	64.4	27.5	29.6	36.7	8.6	28.6	18.7	62.8
	2000	100.0	18.8	63.8	28.5	29.0	40.0	3.6	28.5	17.1	67.8
	2005	100.0	20.9	64.9	23.6	27.8	37.2	2.8	25.6	14.6	71.7
	2010	100.0	21.4	66.7	19.0	30.9	38.1	2.4	23.5	13.0	74.2
Romania - Roumanie	1990	100.0	12.7	67.0	28.9	15.4	24.0	22.0	46.5	36.9	31.6
	2000	100.0	17.5	68.5	19.4	32.8	38.1	12.1	34.4	23.4	53.6
	2005	100.0	17.4	69.5	23.3	33.1	43.2	9.5	35.5	24.0	55.0
	2010	100.0	16.4	62.5	26.5	35.8	41.2	6.7	39.7	25.6	53.6
San Marino - Saint-Marin	1990	100.0	20.1	57.3	22.3	19.2	19.0	3.5	32.1	23.3	64.4
	2000	100.0	4.3	42.9	50.4	193.7	199.4	2.8	28.4	21.0	68.8
	2005	100.0	3.4	38.0	55.5	184.0	187.7	2.2	26.9	18.5	70.9
	2010	100.0	3.5	39.1	36.1	213.2	198.9	1.9	25.3	16.8	72.8
Slovakia - Slovaquie	2000	100.0	20.1	56.5	26.0	70.4	73.0	4.5	36.2	24.7	59.3
	2005	100.0	18.3	57.5	28.9	76.3	80.9	3.7	36.5	24.1	59.8
	2010	100.0	19.6	58.3	23.4	81.1	82.4	3.8	34.8	20.6	61.4
Slovenia - Slovénie	2000	100.0	18.7	57.3	27.4	53.7	57.2	3.4	34.7	24.4	61.9
	2005	100.0	19.0	54.3	27.2	62.2	62.6	2.6	33.7	23.0	63.6
	2010	100.0	20.8	56.0	22.6	65.4	64.9	2.5	29.9	19.4	67.6
Spain - Espagne	1990	100.0	16.7	60.4	26.1	16.1	19.4	5.5	33.0	20.7	61.5
	2000	100.0	17.2	59.7	26.3	29.0	32.2	4.4	29.2	18.6	66.4
	2005	100.0	18.0	57.8	29.5	25.7	31.0	3.2	29.7	15.8	67.1
	2010	100.0	20.8	58.4	23.0	26.3	28.4	2.7	25.7	13.2	71.7
Sweden - Suède	1990	100.0	26.9	49.3	23.5	30.4	29.8	4.1	31.1	20.8	64.8
	2000	100.0	25.8	49.2	18.6	46.5	40.2	2.1	28.8	22.0	69.1
	2005	100.0	26.2	48.2	17.7	48.4	40.6	1.2	28.1	19.9	70.6
	2010	100.0	27.2	48.4	18.5	50.0	44.1	1.9	26.6	16.4	71.5

For sources and notes, see next page.

Pour les sources et les notes, se reporter à la page suivante.

8.3.1 Nominal gross domestic product by type of expenditure and by kind of economic activity of countries and geographical regions

8.3.1 Produit intérieur brut nominal par catégories de dépenses et par branches d'activité économique des pays et des régions géographiques

Region, country or territory / Régions, pays ou territoires	Year / Année	Total GDP / PIB total	GDP by type of expenditure (1) / PIB par catégories de dépenses (1)					GDP by kind of economic activity (2) / PIB par branches d'activité économique (2)			
			Final consumption / Consommation finale		Gross capital formation / Formation brute de capital	Exports / Exportations	Less imports / Moins les importations	Agri-culture (3)	Industry (4) / Industrie (4)		Services (5)
			Government / Administration publique	Household / Ménages		Of goods and services / Des biens et services			Total	Manu-facturing / Activités de fabrication	
			Percentage / En pourcentage								
Switzerland - Suisse	1990	100.0	11.2	56.9	30.2	36.4	34.7	2.9	31.9	21.2	65.1
	2000	100.0	11.1	59.9	23.2	46.5	40.7	1.6	27.3	19.0	71.1
	2005	100.0	11.7	60.0	21.6	49.0	42.3	1.3	27.2	19.3	71.6
	2010	100.0	11.5	57.9	19.2	53.6	42.2	1.1	27.1	19.2	71.8
United Kingdom - Royaume-Uni	1990	100.0	19.7	62.2	20.2	24.0	26.1	1.8	34.1	22.5	64.1
	2000	100.0	18.6	65.6	17.7	27.6	29.5	1.0	27.3	17.4	71.7
	2005	100.0	21.4	65.0	17.0	26.4	29.8	0.7	23.5	13.3	75.9
	2010	100.0	23.2	64.3	15.4	29.9	32.7	0.7	21.8	11.5	77.5
Developed economies: Oceania - Économies développées : Océanie	1990	100.0	17.9	58.5	23.3	17.1	17.3	3.8	29.7	14.4	66.5
	2000	100.0	17.5	59.2	23.0	23.5	23.1	4.4	25.7	12.7	69.9
	2005	100.0	17.2	56.9	27.5	20.5	22.2	3.3	27.3	11.3	69.5
	2010	100.0	18.5	53.3	26.8	21.6	20.5	2.8	27.6	10.5	69.6
Australia - Australie	1990	100.0	17.8	58.1	23.8	15.8	16.1	3.4	30.1	13.9	66.5
	2000	100.0	17.5	59.1	23.2	22.0	21.8	3.9	25.9	12.2	70.2
	2005	100.0	17.1	56.5	27.9	19.5	21.1	3.0	27.7	10.8	69.3
	2010	100.0	18.3	52.7	27.6	20.9	19.8	2.5	28.0	10.0	69.5
New Zealand - Nouvelle-Zélande	1990	100.0	18.9	61.1	19.8	26.5	26.3	6.7	26.8	18.0	66.6
	2000	100.0	17.3	59.7	21.3	35.0	33.4	8.6	24.4	16.3	66.9
	2005	100.0	18.0	59.5	24.7	27.4	29.6	5.2	24.2	14.7	70.6
	2010	100.0	20.4	58.2	19.6	28.3	26.8	5.5	24.1	14.7	70.5

Source:
UNCTAD secretariat calculations, based on UN DESA Statistics Division, *National Accounts Main Aggregates Database*

Source :
Calculs du secrétariat de la CNUCED, basés sur ONU DAES Division de statistique, *National Accounts Main Aggregates Database*

Notes:

- Data in this table are shown as percentage of GDP / Value added at current prices in US Dollars.

- For countries' notes on GDP / Value added breakdown, see:
  http://unstats.un.org/unsd/snaama/downloads/Download-GDPcurrent-USD-countries.xls

(1) The breakdown in shares by type of expenditure is shown as percentage of GDP. The breakdown in shares of GDP might not add-up to 100 percent due to statistical discrepancies.

(2) The breakdown in shares by kind of economic activity is shown as percentage of total value added.

(3) Includes agriculture, hunting, forestry and fishing (ISIC Revision 3 divisions 01-05).

(4) Includes mining and quarrying, manufacturing, electricity, gas and water supply, and construction (ISIC Revision 3 divisions 10-45).

(5) Include all other economic activities (ISIC Revision 3 divisions 50-99).

(6) Including Western Sahara.

Notes :

- Les données de ce tableau sont indiquées en pourcentage du PIB / Valeur Ajoutée aux prix courants en dollars des États-Unis.

- Pour les notes des pays sur la ventilation du PIB / Valeur Ajoutée, se référer à:
  http://unstats.un.org/unsd/snaama/downloads/Download-GDPcurrent-USD-countries.xls

(1) La ventilation par catégories de dépense est calculée en pourcentage du PIB. La somme des pourcentages du PIB ventilé peut ne pas être égale à 100 à cause des écarts statistiques.

(2) La ventilation par branches d'activité économique est calculée en pourcentage de la valeur ajoutée totale.

(3) Inclut l'agriculture, la chasse, la sylviculture et la pêche (CITI Révision 3 divisions 01-05).

(4) Inclut les activités extractives, les activités de fabrication, la production et distribution d'électricité, de gaz et d'eau et la construction (CITI Révision 3 divisions 10-45).

(5) Incluent toutes les autres activités économiques (CITI Révision 3 divisions 50-99).

(6) Y compris le Sahara occidental.

8.3.2 Nominal gross domestic product by type of expenditure and by kind of economic activity of economic groupings

8.3.2 Produit intérieur brut nominal par catégories de dépenses et par branches d'activité économique des groupements économiques

Economic grouping / Groupements économiques	Year / Année	Total GDP / PIB total	GDP by type of expenditure (1) / PIB par catégories de dépenses (1)					GDP by kind of economic activity (2) / PIB par branches d'activité économique (2)			
			Final consumption / Consommation finale		Gross capital formation / Formation brute de capital	Exports / Exportations — Of goods and services / Des biens et services	Less imports / Moins les importations — Of goods and services / Des biens et services	Agriculture (3)	Industry (4) / Industrie (4)		Services (5)
			Government / Administration publique	Household / Ménages					Total	Manufacturing / Activités de fabrication	
			Percentage / En pourcentage								
DEVELOPING ECONOMIES - ÉCONOMIES EN DÉVELOPPEMENT	1990	100.0	13.8	59.3	25.2	25.9	24.8	15.0	36.3	22.0	48.7
	2000	100.0	14.0	58.4	24.8	34.9	32.3	10.1	36.3	22.5	53.5
	2005	100.0	13.4	54.6	27.1	40.8	36.1	9.4	39.0	23.2	51.6
	2010	100.0	14.0	51.9	31.8	35.6	32.9	9.6	39.0	21.4	51.4
Developing economies excluding China - Économies en développement sans la Chine	1990	100.0	13.8	60.5	24.1	27.1	26.1	13.5	35.8	20.2	50.7
	2000	100.0	13.6	60.9	22.7	37.3	34.6	9.1	34.2	18.7	56.7
	2005	100.0	13.2	58.9	23.3	41.9	37.5	8.6	36.6	18.0	54.8
	2010	100.0	14.3	58.4	25.0	38.9	36.8	9.4	35.7	16.8	54.9
Developing economies excluding LDCs - Économies en développement sans les PMA	1990	100.0	13.8	58.6	25.6	26.3	24.9	14.2	36.9	22.4	48.9
	2000	100.0	14.1	57.9	25.0	35.3	32.4	9.6	36.6	22.9	53.8
	2005	100.0	13.5	54.2	27.3	41.1	36.2	8.9	39.2	23.6	52.0
	2010	100.0	14.0	51.3	32.0	35.8	32.9	9.1	39.2	21.8	51.7
High-income developing economies - Économies en développement à revenu élevé	1990	100.0	13.6	57.5	24.9	37.8	34.3	7.2	39.5	22.1	53.3
	2000	100.0	13.2	57.9	24.5	48.3	43.8	4.4	36.1	20.0	59.5
	2005	100.0	12.6	55.7	23.1	55.7	47.1	4.0	39.2	19.2	56.8
	2010	100.0	13.6	55.3	24.0	58.1	51.1	3.9	39.5	18.0	56.6
Middle-income developing economies - Économies en développement à revenu intermédiaire	1990	100.0	15.1	58.6	26.9	18.1	18.9	16.8	36.5	24.9	46.7
	2000	100.0	16.0	56.6	26.3	24.3	23.4	11.5	38.1	27.8	50.4
	2005	100.0	15.3	50.1	30.8	33.0	29.4	10.0	40.9	29.6	49.2
	2010	100.0	15.0	46.6	37.1	25.6	23.6	9.1	41.0	25.5	49.9
Low-income developing economies - Économies en développement à revenu faible	1990	100.0	11.5	64.4	22.6	16.5	16.6	27.8	29.4	16.4	42.7
	2000	100.0	10.8	65.1	21.4	24.2	22.6	23.6	31.9	15.9	44.5
	2005	100.0	10.4	64.2	27.0	26.1	27.9	20.5	33.5	15.9	46.0
	2010	100.0	11.5	61.2	29.5	26.2	28.9	20.5	32.6	15.2	46.9
Heavily indebted poor countries (IMF) - Pays pauvres très endettés (FMI)	1990	100.0	14.9	75.2	15.2	18.3	23.1	32.2	22.5	13.3	45.3
	2000	100.0	12.6	77.4	17.8	24.1	31.9	30.9	23.9	11.6	45.2
	2005	100.0	13.1	75.4	21.9	27.2	37.6	29.6	25.6	11.0	44.9
	2010	100.0	13.1	72.6	22.7	28.5	37.3	29.0	26.4	9.8	44.6
Landlocked developing countries - Pays en développement sans littoral	1990	100.0	17.5	70.7	17.8	20.0	25.6	30.4	26.6	15.4	42.9
	2000	100.0	15.8	69.9	20.2	35.3	40.7	25.7	28.1	13.7	46.2
	2005	100.0	14.1	62.3	26.1	41.1	43.3	20.2	33.6	12.5	46.2
	2010	100.0	13.3	59.3	23.5	39.5	37.0	16.8	36.5	12.5	46.6
Small island developing States - Petits États insulaires en développement	1990	100.0	16.9	62.4	23.0	51.2	52.7	10.6	28.7	11.8	60.6
	2000	100.0	14.6	63.7	23.6	51.2	52.9	8.4	27.7	11.4	63.9
	2005	100.0	15.1	59.8	26.6	52.3	53.7	7.3	32.2	12.2	60.5
	2010	100.0	16.9	69.7	21.2	47.1	55.3	8.2	31.5	11.3	60.3
Least developed countries - Pays les moins avancés	*1990*	*100.0*	*13.7*	*76.6*	*16.3*	*14.8*	*20.9*	*34.5*	*21.6*	*10.9*	*43.9*
	2000	*100.0*	*11.2*	*76.8*	*18.9*	*21.6*	*28.5*	*31.3*	*25.2*	*9.8*	*43.5*
	2005	*100.0*	*12.3*	*70.4*	*21.8*	*29.0*	*34.1*	*26.6*	*31.9*	*9.8*	*41.5*
	2010	*100.0*	*13.2*	*69.1*	*22.9*	*28.1*	*34.7*	*25.4*	*32.5*	*10.3*	*42.1*
Africa and Haiti - Afrique et Haïti	1990	100.0	16.6	73.2	16.4	18.1	23.7	33.8	22.8	10.5	43.4
	2000	100.0	14.4	75.8	17.5	22.7	30.4	32.1	25.2	7.6	42.7
	2005	100.0	15.2	67.3	20.6	33.2	36.5	27.6	34.1	7.5	38.3
	2010	100.0	15.7	65.3	22.2	33.7	38.8	26.2	35.0	7.4	38.9
Asia - Asie	1990	100.0	7.2	83.9	15.9	7.3	14.1	36.1	19.4	11.7	44.5
	2000	100.0	6.7	78.3	20.7	19.8	25.7	30.2	25.4	12.7	44.4
	2005	100.0	7.0	75.6	23.8	21.9	29.4	24.8	28.5	13.8	46.7
	2010	100.0	8.7	75.2	24.1	18.6	27.1	24.0	28.8	15.2	47.2
Islands - Îles	1990	100.0	29.7	78.6	26.0	28.9	62.4	33.3	12.7	6.9	54.0
	2000	100.0	24.3	71.2	20.1	37.0	52.7	29.5	15.5	7.9	55.0
	2005	100.0	28.4	88.6	19.8	27.2	64.0	28.2	14.4	6.6	57.3
	2010	100.0	29.6	89.7	21.9	28.1	69.6	26.1	14.5	5.2	59.4

For sources and notes, see end of table.

Pour les sources et les notes, se reporter à la fin du tableau.

8.3.2 Nominal gross domestic product by type of expenditure and by kind of economic activity of economic groupings

8.3.2 Produit intérieur brut nominal par catégories de dépenses et par branches d'activité économique des groupements économiques

Economic grouping / Groupements économiques	Year / Année	Total GDP / PIB total	GDP by type of expenditure (1) / PIB par catégories de dépenses (1)					GDP by kind of economic activity (2) / PIB par branches d'activité économique (2)			
			Final consumption / Consommation finale		Gross capital formation / Formation brute de capital	Exports / Exportations / Of goods and services / Des biens et services	Less imports / Moins les importations	Agriculture (3)	Industry (4) / Industrie (4)		Services (5)
			Government / Administration publique	Household / Ménages					Total	Manufacturing / Activités de fabrication	
			Percentage / En pourcentage								
Major petroleum and gas exporters - Principaux exportateurs de pétrole et de gaz	*1990*	*100.0*	*19.8*	*49.3*	*21.0*	*38.7*	*30.8*	*10.5*	*45.2*	*10.5*	*44.4*
	2000	*100.0*	*17.8*	*42.4*	*21.4*	*45.5*	*27.3*	*6.8*	*51.8*	*10.5*	*41.5*
	2005	*100.0*	*14.4*	*41.3*	*20.8*	*52.9*	*30.1*	*6.6*	*57.2*	*8.9*	*36.3*
	2010	*100.0*	*15.0*	*45.7*	*24.4*	*47.7*	*33.5*	*6.7*	*54.5*	*9.1*	*38.9*
Africa - Afrique	1990	100.0	16.1	55.5	21.6	31.2	24.5	15.8	44.8	8.4	39.4
	2000	100.0	15.0	46.1	14.9	44.9	21.0	13.2	53.8	5.0	33.0
	2005	100.0	11.2	49.8	15.6	48.5	25.1	16.3	57.8	3.8	25.9
	2010	100.0	17.0	46.3	21.1	49.7	35.4	17.7	53.3	3.9	29.1
America - Amérique	1990	100.0	16.8	46.6	13.4	40.6	20.4	5.9	57.3	27.1	36.8
	2000	100.0	12.4	51.7	24.2	29.7	18.1	4.1	48.4	19.3	47.5
	2005	100.0	11.1	46.8	23.0	39.7	20.5	4.0	56.9	16.2	39.2
	2010	100.0	10.8	56.8	20.8	28.7	17.2	4.0	53.6	14.6	42.4
Asia - Asie	1990	100.0	21.8	46.9	21.8	41.8	35.1	8.9	43.5	9.0	47.6
	2000	100.0	20.0	39.0	22.7	49.5	31.4	5.4	51.9	10.1	42.7
	2005	100.0	16.1	37.6	22.2	56.5	33.4	3.8	57.0	9.5	39.2
	2010	100.0	15.4	42.4	26.5	52.1	37.2	3.5	55.1	9.6	41.3
Major exporters of manufactured goods - Principaux exportateurs d'articles manufacturés	*1990*	*100.0*	*11.8*	*54.8*	*32.2*	*35.9*	*34.5*	*13.1*	*38.0*	*27.9*	*48.9*
	2000	*100.0*	*13.0*	*53.7*	*30.5*	*45.9*	*43.2*	*8.2*	*38.9*	*30.3*	*52.9*
	2005	*100.0*	*13.0*	*49.3*	*32.9*	*51.6*	*46.8*	*7.5*	*40.6*	*32.1*	*51.9*
	2010	*100.0*	*12.9*	*43.1*	*40.4*	*44.9*	*40.4*	*7.9*	*42.5*	*29.4*	*49.6*
America - Amérique	1990	100.0	8.0	68.0	25.8	17.0	17.9	7.4	36.1	20.4	56.4
	2000	100.0	10.6	65.1	26.6	28.2	30.0	4.1	35.2	21.3	60.7
	2005	100.0	10.7	66.6	24.1	27.2	28.6	3.3	34.1	18.7	62.5
	2010	100.0	11.7	64.8	25.2	30.4	31.8	3.5	34.1	17.7	62.4
Asia - Asie	1990	100.0	12.8	51.3	33.9	40.9	38.9	14.7	38.6	30.1	46.7
	2000	100.0	13.7	50.8	31.5	50.4	46.5	9.3	39.8	32.5	50.9
	2005	100.0	13.4	45.7	34.7	56.7	50.5	8.4	41.9	34.8	49.7
	2010	100.0	13.1	40.3	42.3	46.7	41.5	8.4	43.5	30.8	48.1
Emerging economies - Économies émergentes	*1990*	*100.0*	*13.3*	*59.5*	*26.0*	*26.0*	*24.8*	*8.5*	*37.2*	*24.8*	*54.3*
	2000	*100.0*	*13.5*	*60.9*	*24.3*	*37.1*	*35.7*	*4.7*	*33.6*	*22.7*	*61.7*
	2005	*100.0*	*13.9*	*59.0*	*23.1*	*43.1*	*39.1*	*4.5*	*35.0*	*23.0*	*60.5*
	2010	*100.0*	*15.8*	*57.8*	*23.4*	*41.6*	*38.5*	*5.1*	*33.5*	*21.3*	*61.4*
America - Amérique	1990	100.0	13.5	64.4	20.5	12.1	10.6	8.7	35.9	22.9	55.3
	2000	100.0	14.5	65.7	21.5	18.2	19.6	5.0	31.2	18.9	63.8
	2005	100.0	14.7	63.0	20.2	22.7	20.5	5.0	32.8	18.6	62.2
	2010	100.0	17.1	61.2	21.8	19.5	19.5	5.5	30.7	16.6	63.9
Asia - Asie	1990	100.0	12.9	52.3	34.1	46.4	45.8	8.1	39.1	27.5	52.8
	2000	100.0	12.1	54.1	28.3	64.4	59.0	4.4	37.1	28.1	58.5
	2005	100.0	13.0	53.8	26.8	69.1	62.7	3.9	37.7	28.4	58.4
	2010	100.0	13.6	51.8	26.1	79.9	71.5	4.5	38.1	29.2	57.3
Newly industrialized Asian economies - Économies nouvellement industrialisées d'Asie	*1990*	*100.0*	*11.5*	*53.8*	*32.2*	*49.4*	*48.2*	*9.5*	*37.5*	*25.6*	*53.0*
	2000	*100.0*	*11.1*	*56.3*	*27.1*	*69.7*	*64.3*	*5.6*	*35.3*	*25.3*	*59.1*
	2005	*100.0*	*11.8*	*56.5*	*25.8*	*73.9*	*67.9*	*5.3*	*36.3*	*25.9*	*58.4*
	2010	*100.0*	*12.1*	*54.7*	*26.9*	*75.1*	*68.9*	*7.1*	*37.7*	*26.0*	*55.2*
First tier - Première génération	1990	100.0	12.7	52.2	32.2	58.0	55.1	5.5	37.1	26.5	57.4
	2000	100.0	11.9	55.5	28.9	71.4	67.7	2.8	31.8	23.6	65.4
	2005	100.0	12.7	54.8	26.1	79.4	73.0	2.2	32.2	24.4	65.6
	2010	100.0	13.3	53.2	26.4	96.1	89.0	1.7	32.4	25.2	65.9
Second tier - Deuxième génération	1990	100.0	9.6	56.7	32.2	33.9	35.8	16.6	38.1	24.0	45.3
	2000	100.0	9.4	58.4	22.7	65.6	56.0	12.1	43.1	29.1	44.9
	2005	100.0	10.0	60.3	25.2	62.1	57.0	11.4	44.5	29.1	44.2
	2010	100.0	10.6	56.7	27.6	48.0	42.9	13.5	44.0	26.8	42.5

For sources and notes, see end of table.

Pour les sources et les notes, se reporter à la fin du tableau.

8

8.3.2 Nominal gross domestic product by type of expenditure and by kind of economic activity of economic groupings

8.3.2 Produit intérieur brut nominal par catégories de dépenses et par branches d'activité économique des groupements économiques

Economic grouping / Groupements économiques	Year / Année	Total GDP / PIB total	GDP by type of expenditure (1) / PIB par catégories de dépenses (1)					GDP by kind of economic activity (2) / PIB par branches d'activité économique (2)			
			Final consumption / Consommation finale		Gross capital formation / Formation brute de capital	Exports / Exportations	Less imports / Moins les importations	Agriculture (3)	Industry (4) / Industrie (4)		Services (5)
			Government / Administration publique	Household / Ménages		Of goods and services / Des biens et services			Total	Manufacturing / Activités de fabrication	
			Percentage / En pourcentage								
Developing economies: Africa - Économies en développement : Afrique	**1990**	**100.0**	**16.7**	**63.8**	**20.4**	**25.6**	**25.3**	**18.3**	**34.6**	**14.9**	**47.1**
	2000	**100.0**	**15.1**	**63.3**	**17.5**	**31.3**	**27.0**	**15.2**	**35.5**	**12.8**	**49.2**
	2005	**100.0**	**14.6**	**61.6**	**18.9**	**35.9**	**31.0**	**15.3**	**39.0**	**11.3**	**45.7**
	2010	**100.0**	**16.0**	**59.7**	**22.1**	**35.3**	**33.7**	**16.0**	**38.4**	**10.0**	**45.6**
Northern Africa excluding Sudan - Afrique septentrionale sans le Soudan	1990	100.0	16.4	59.6	27.3	27.8	31.0	13.8	38.2	13.5	48.0
	2000	100.0	14.7	60.6	20.2	29.8	25.2	11.2	39.5	13.0	49.4
	2005	100.0	13.4	51.5	23.1	43.3	31.3	10.0	47.2	11.1	42.8
	2010	100.0	13.9	55.6	26.7	36.4	32.6	10.2	46.4	11.4	43.4
Sub-Saharan Africa - Afrique subsaharienne	1990	100.0	16.8	66.0	16.7	24.4	22.3	20.8	32.7	15.7	46.6
	2000	100.0	15.4	65.2	15.6	32.3	28.3	18.2	32.7	12.6	49.2
	2005	100.0	15.3	66.6	16.7	32.3	30.8	18.1	34.7	11.4	47.2
	2010	100.0	17.1	61.9	19.7	34.7	34.4	19.2	34.0	9.3	46.8
Sub-Saharan Africa excluding South Africa - Afrique subsaharienne sans l'Afrique du Sud	1990	100.0	15.3	68.6	16.2	24.5	24.2	29.0	28.9	11.6	42.1
	2000	100.0	13.7	66.3	15.5	35.0	30.4	26.9	33.2	8.9	39.9
	2005	100.0	12.8	68.6	16.0	35.1	32.5	26.4	36.7	7.5	36.9
	2010	100.0	15.0	63.2	19.8	38.2	37.6	26.7	35.5	6.9	37.8
Developing economies: America - Économies en développement : Amérique	**1990**	**100.0**	**13.8**	**64.2**	**20.3**	**16.2**	**14.5**	**9.3**	**35.7**	**21.9**	**55.0**
	2000	**100.0**	**14.4**	**65.6**	**21.1**	**20.5**	**21.5**	**5.7**	**31.7**	**18.5**	**62.6**
	2005	**100.0**	**14.5**	**63.0**	**20.4**	**25.0**	**22.8**	**5.5**	**33.6**	**17.9**	**60.9**
	2010	**100.0**	**16.5**	**61.8**	**21.6**	**21.4**	**21.3**	**5.7**	**32.6**	**16.1**	**61.7**
Central America and Greater Caribbean Islands excluding Puerto Rico - Amérique centrale et Grandes Antilles sans Porto Rico	1990	100.0	10.3	67.7	24.7	21.0	23.1	9.0	33.8	19.4	57.2
	2000	100.0	11.4	66.4	25.3	29.4	32.1	5.3	33.9	20.8	60.8
	2005	100.0	11.7	67.9	23.0	28.5	31.1	4.3	32.7	18.3	63.0
	2010	100.0	13.0	66.7	23.5	30.6	33.6	4.5	32.3	17.4	63.2
Central America and Greater Caribbean Islands excluding Mexico and Puerto Rico - Amérique centrale et Grandes Antilles sans le Mexique et Porto Rico	1990	100.0	18.8	66.9	20.7	36.0	42.4	15.2	24.2	15.1	60.6
	2000	100.0	15.2	72.6	19.5	34.7	42.0	11.3	27.7	18.5	61.0
	2005	100.0	16.0	73.9	18.1	34.2	42.2	9.1	25.7	16.4	65.2
	2010	100.0	18.0	73.3	17.2	31.4	39.8	8.3	25.4	16.1	66.3
South America and Central America - Amérique du Sud et Amérique centrale	1990	100.0	13.4	64.4	20.2	14.8	12.7	9.2	36.3	22.5	54.4
	2000	100.0	14.3	65.5	21.2	19.8	20.7	5.6	31.9	18.6	62.5
	2005	100.0	14.3	63.0	20.4	24.4	22.1	5.5	33.9	18.1	60.5
	2010	100.0	16.3	61.6	21.8	21.1	20.7	5.7	32.8	16.2	61.5
South America excluding Brazil - Amérique du Sud sans le Brésil	1990	100.0	12.3	64.6	17.6	19.6	13.9	8.9	38.1	23.2	53.0
	2000	100.0	13.4	66.1	19.0	18.8	17.4	6.2	32.9	17.3	60.9
	2005	100.0	12.1	60.0	21.2	29.8	23.1	7.2	39.8	17.4	53.0
	2010	100.0	13.1	59.5	23.0	26.4	22.1	6.8	40.0	15.6	53.2
Developing economies: Asia - Économies en développement : Asie	**1990**	**100.0**	**13.1**	**55.8**	**28.7**	**30.7**	**29.6**	**17.0**	**37.1**	**23.6**	**46.0**
	2000	**100.0**	**13.6**	**54.1**	**27.7**	**42.6**	**38.4**	**11.6**	**38.6**	**25.9**	**49.8**
	2005	**100.0**	**12.8**	**50.4**	**30.9**	**47.5**	**41.9**	**10.0**	**40.9**	**26.8**	**49.1**
	2010	**100.0**	**12.8**	**47.2**	**36.7**	**40.7**	**37.0**	**10.1**	**41.3**	**24.6**	**48.6**
Eastern and South-Eastern Asia excluding China - Asie orientale et Asie du Sud-Est sans la Chine	1990	100.0	11.4	53.3	31.3	48.3	47.2	10.4	37.4	25.3	52.2
	2000	100.0	11.0	56.2	26.8	68.7	63.4	6.5	35.2	24.9	58.3
	2005	100.0	11.6	56.4	25.8	73.0	67.2	6.1	36.4	25.5	57.5
	2010	100.0	11.8	54.7	27.0	74.1	68.1	8.0	37.6	25.4	54.4
Southern Asia excluding India - Asie méridionale sans l'Inde	1990	100.0	10.7	67.4	26.7	13.4	22.5	23.2	25.9	12.9	50.9
	2000	100.0	10.4	63.9	25.8	19.6	20.3	20.6	29.5	14.3	49.9
	2005	100.0	11.2	59.5	26.3	25.8	24.8	15.0	36.2	14.3	48.9
	2010	100.0	10.2	63.8	27.2	21.0	22.4	14.5	35.9	14.0	49.6

For sources and notes, see next page.   Pour les sources et les notes, se reporter à la page suivante.

8.3.2 Nominal gross domestic product by type of expenditure and by kind of economic activity of economic groupings

8.3.2 Produit intérieur brut nominal par catégories de dépenses et par branches d'activité économique des groupements économiques

Source:
UNCTAD secretariat calculations, based on UN DESA Statistics Division, *National Accounts Main Aggregates Database*

Notes:

- Data in this table are shown as percentage of GDP / Value Added at current prices in US dollars.

(1) The breakdown in shares by type of expenditure is shown as percentage of GDP. The breakdown in shares might not add-up to 100 percent due to statistical discrepancies.

(2) The breakdown in shares by kind of economic activity is shown as percentage of total value added.

(3) Includes agriculture, hunting, forestry and fishing (ISIC Revision 3 divisions 01-05).

(4) Includes mining and quarrying, manufacturing, electricity, gas and water supply, and construction (ISIC Revision 3 divisions 10-45).

(5) Include all other economic activities (ISIC Revision 3 divisions 50-99).

Source :
Calculs du secrétariat de la CNUCED, basés sur ONU DAES Division de statistique, *National Accounts Main Aggregates Database*

Notes :

- Les données de ce tableau sont indiquées en pourcentage du PIB /Valeur Ajoutée aux prix courants en dollars des États-Unis.

(1) La ventilation par catégories de dépense est calculée en pourcentage du PIB. La somme des pourcentages du PIB peut ne pas être égale à 100 à cause des écarts statistiques.

(2) La ventilation par branches d'activité économique est calculée en pourcentage de la valeur ajoutée totale.

(3) Inclut l'agriculture, la chasse, la sylviculture et la pêche (CITI Révision 3, divisions 01-05).

(4) Inclut les activités extractives, les activités de fabrication, la production et distribution d'électricité, de gaz et d'eau et la construction (CITI Révision 3, divisions 10-45).

(5) Incluent toutes les autres activités économiques (CITI Révision 3, divisions 50-99).

8

Region, country or territory Régions, pays ou territoires	Year Année	Population		Total labour force Main-d'œuvre totale		Agriculture labour force Main-d'œuvre dans l'agriculture	
		Total (thousands) Total (milliers)	Urban population (% of total population) Population urbaine (en % de la population totale)	Total (thousands) Total (milliers)	Female labour (% of total labour force) Main-d'œuvre féminine (en % de la main-d'œuvre totale)	Total (thousands) Total (milliers)	Female labour (% of total agriculture labour force) Main-d'œuvre féminine (en % de la main-d'œuvre totale dans l'agriculture)
		(1)	(2)	(3)	(4)	(5)	(6)
WORLD - MONDE	**1990**	**5 306 425**	**42.9**	**2 375 048**	**39.3**	**1 146 816**	**41.6**
	2000	**6 122 770**	**46.8**	**2 796 254**	**39.9**	**1 236 175**	**42.1**
	2010	**6 895 889**	**50.9**	**3 276 145**	**40.6**	**1 307 071**	**42.6**
	2011	**6 974 036**	**51.3**	**3 321 820**	**40.7**	**1 312 010**	**42.7**
DEVELOPING ECONOMIES - ÉCONOMIES EN DÉVELOPPEMENT	1990	4 064 787	34.5	1 768 280	37.9	1 086 867	41.7
	2000	4 828 134	39.9	2 159 799	38.5	1 192 669	42.3
	2010	5 545 091	45.2	2 566 384	38.4	1 272 876	42.9
	2011	5 640 963	45.5	2 609 521	38.4	1 278 647	42.9
TRANSITION ECONOMIES - ÉCONOMIES EN TRANSITION	1990	315 195	64.0	153 486	47.4	29 389	40.2
	2000	305 154	63.4	144 092	47.5	21 316	35.8
	2010	302 849	62.9	151 578	47.5	18 235	33.2
	2011	303 221	62.9	152 214	47.5	17 918	32.9
DEVELOPED ECONOMIES - ÉCONOMIES DÉVELOPPÉES	1990	906 022	71.8	437 127	42.5	30 560	38.8
	2000	967 297	74.3	476 930	44.1	22 190	37.5
	2010	1 024 439	76.8	510 467	45.2	15 960	36.3
	2011	1 029 520	77.1	512 807	45.2	15 445	36.3
Developing economies: Africa - Économies en développement : Afrique	**1990**	**634 675**	**32.3**	**227 627**	**39.9**	**144 596**	**45.9**
	2000	**810 362**	**36.3**	**302 119**	**41.5**	**177 263**	**47.1**
	2010	**1 021 388**	**40.4**	**397 233**	**42.5**	**214 508**	**48.4**
	2011	**1 045 067**	**40.8**	**408 355**	**42.5**	**218 682**	**48.5**
Eastern Africa - Afrique orientale	*1990*	*192 189*	*17.8*	*83 428*	*47.9*	*68 513*	*50.2*
	2000	*250 845*	*20.7*	*110 102*	*48.0*	*88 608*	*51.0*
	2010	*323 198*	*23.6*	*148 140*	*48.5*	*112 616*	*51.3*
	2011	*331 681*	*24.0*	*152 612*	*48.5*	*115 366*	*51.3*
Burundi	1990	5 602	6.4	2 809	52.5	2 546	55.7
	2000	6 374	8.4	2 915	53.2	2 754	56.5
	2010	8 383	11.2	4 314	52.1	3 741	56.0
	2011	8 575	11.5	4 433	52.0	3 804	56.0
Comoros - Comores	1990	438	27.9	126	25.6	135	50.4
	2000	562	27.6	179	28.0	171	50.9
	2010	735	26.5	243	30.2	222	51.8
	2011	754	26.6	250	30.4	228	51.8
Djibouti	1990	562	75.4	147	29.5	182	46.2
	2000	732	75.8	209	32.4	233	46.4
	2010	889	75.4	292	34.9	285	46.3
	2011	906	75.3	301	35.1	291	46.4
Eritrea - Érythrée	2000	3 668	17.7	1 661	47.3	1 090	44.0
	2010	5 254	21.5	2 596	48.6	1 547	43.6
	2011	5 415	21.9	2 680	48.6	1 590	43.5
Ethiopia (...1991) - Éthiopie (...1991)	1990	51 492	12.8	22 957	45.2	18 086	42.3
Ethiopia - Éthiopie	2000	65 578	14.9	28 972	45.2	24 049	44.3
	2010	82 950	17.1	40 787	47.2	31 657	45.5
	2011	84 734	17.3	42 134	47.2	32 403	45.5
Kenya	1990	23 447	18.2	8 997	47.2	7 846	49.4
	2000	31 254	19.8	11 857	46.8	10 757	49.4
	2010	40 513	22.4	15 461	46.5	13 220	48.7
	2011	41 610	22.7	15 952	46.4	13 487	48.6
Madagascar	1990	11 281	23.5	5 373	48.4	4 029	54.2
	2000	15 364	27.0	7 299	48.7	5 243	53.7
	2010	20 714	29.4	10 147	48.9	7 255	53.5
	2011	21 315	29.7	10 490	48.9	7 492	53.4
Malawi	1990	9 381	11.6	3 945	50.7	3 377	55.7
	2000	11 229	16.0	4 816	49.7	3 907	57.1
	2010	14 901	20.8	6 710	51.5	4 909	58.9
	2011	15 381	21.3	6 914	51.4	5 060	59.1

For sources and notes, see end of table.   Pour les sources et les notes, se reporter à la fin du tableau.

Region, country or territory / Régions, pays ou territoires	Year / Année	Population		Total labour force / Main-d'œuvre totale		Agriculture labour force / Main-d'œuvre dans l'agriculture	
		Total (thousands) / Total (milliers)	Urban population (% of total population) / Population urbaine (en % de la population totale)	Total (thousands) / Total (milliers)	Female labour (% of total labour force) / Main-d'œuvre féminine (en % de la main-d'œuvre totale)	Total (thousands) / Total (milliers)	Female labour (% of total agriculture labour force) / Main-d'œuvre féminine (en % de la main-d'œuvre totale dans l'agriculture)
		(1)	(2)	(3)	(4)	(5)	(6)
Mauritius - Maurice	1990	1 060	43.8	444	31.8	75	28.0
	2000	1 196	42.6	532	34.5	63	25.4
	2010	1 299	41.8	603	37.7	48	25.0
	2011	1 307	41.8	612	37.9	47	25.5
Mayotte	1990	92	36.0	..	..	..	..
	2000	149	47.7	..	..	..	..
	2010	204	48.8	..	..	..	..
	2011	211	48.5	..	..	..	..
Mozambique	1990	13 547	21.1	6 019	55.5	5 209	62.2
	2000	18 201	30.8	8 726	55.1	7 092	64.3
	2010	23 391	38.5	11 078	53.5	8 674	65.2
	2011	23 930	39.2	11 349	53.4	8 856	65.2
Rwanda	1990	7 110	5.4	3 222	51.1	2 824	53.9
	2000	8 098	13.5	3 799	52.3	3 242	55.9
	2010	10 624	18.2	5 228	51.8	4 360	56.4
	2011	10 943	18.5	5 372	51.7	4 488	56.4
Seychelles	1990	71	50.0	..	..	25	52.0
	2000	79	52.6	..	..	28	50.0
	2010	87	54.1	..	..	30	50.0
	2011	87	54.6	..	..	30	50.0
Somalia - Somalie	1990	6 599	29.6	2 060	31.9	1 875	44.4
	2000	7 399	33.2	2 348	32.8	2 048	45.3
	2010	9 331	37.6	2 926	33.6	2 440	45.9
	2011	9 557	38.1	2 993	33.7	2 490	45.9
Uganda - Ouganda	1990	17 700	11.1	7 550	50.8	6 665	49.6
	2000	24 213	12.2	10 133	50.0	8 420	50.1
	2010	33 425	13.4	13 419	49.3	11 016	49.6
	2011	34 509	13.6	13 851	49.2	11 317	49.6
United Republic of Tanzania - République-Unie de Tanzanie	1990	25 479	18.9	12 246	49.8	10 554	54.0
	2000	34 038	22.4	16 709	49.7	13 557	54.3
	2010	44 841	26.5	22 137	49.8	16 879	54.9
	2011	46 218	27.0	22 764	49.8	17 329	55.0
Zambia - Zambie	1990	7 860	39.7	3 402	46.8	2 215	47.5
	2000	10 202	35.7	4 475	47.2	2 685	47.1
	2010	13 089	36.2	5 579	46.1	3 215	46.3
	2011	13 475	36.2	5 719	46.1	3 299	46.2
Zimbabwe	1990	10 469	29.0	4 131	46.3	2 870	54.8
	2000	12 509	33.6	5 470	46.4	3 269	54.4
	2010	12 571	38.5	6 620	49.3	3 118	52.4
	2011	12 754	39.0	6 797	49.3	3 155	52.3
Middle Africa - Afrique centrale	*1990*	*71 676*	*33.1*	*27 167*	*46.8*	*19 582*	*50.4*
	2000	*96 187*	*37.9*	*36 817*	*48.3*	*23 998*	*49.7*
	2010	*126 689*	*43.9*	*49 787*	*47.9*	*28 772*	*50.7*
	2011	*129 981*	*44.5*	*51 325*	*47.9*	*29 233*	*50.8*
Angola	1990	10 335	38.3	3 844	47.6	3 323	53.3
	2000	13 926	50.2	5 199	48.4	4 337	53.1
	2010	19 082	58.2	7 109	45.9	5 878	54.8
	2011	19 618	59.0	7 363	45.9	6 036	55.0
Cameroon - Cameroun	1990	12 181	40.9	4 493	41.8	3 086	48.1
	2000	15 678	50.5	6 199	45.1	3 482	48.1
	2010	19 599	59.5	8 211	45.6	3 569	47.4
	2011	20 030	60.3	8 433	45.7	3 573	47.2
Central African Republic - République centrafricaine	1990	2 935	36.7	1 301	45.7	1 038	50.0
	2000	3 702	38.1	1 679	46.4	1 189	50.4
	2010	4 401	39.9	2 064	47.1	1 254	49.8
	2011	4 487	40.1	2 114	47.1	1 265	49.7

For sources and notes, see end of table.   Pour les sources et les notes, se reporter à la fin du tableau.

8

Region, country or territory / Régions, pays ou territoires	Year / Année	Population		Total labour force / Main-d'œuvre totale		Agriculture labour force / Main-d'œuvre dans l'agriculture	
		Total (thousands) / Total (milliers)	Urban population (% of total population) / Population urbaine (en % de la population totale)	Total (thousands) / Total (milliers)	Female labour (% of total labour force) / Main-d'œuvre féminine (en % de la main-d'œuvre totale)	Total (thousands) / Total (milliers)	Female labour (% of total agriculture labour force) / Main-d'œuvre féminine (en % de la main-d'œuvre totale dans l'agriculture)
		(1)	(2)	(3)	(4)	(5)	(6)
Chad - Tchad	1990	6 011	21.1	2 363	45.3	1 889	45.5
	2000	8 222	23.9	3 215	45.5	2 418	51.6
	2010	11 227	28.3	4 425	45.2	2 962	56.9
	2011	11 525	28.9	4 550	45.2	2 997	57.2
Congo	1990	2 389	55.6	891	45.5	447	59.1
	2000	3 136	56.5	1 251	48.0	501	58.7
	2010	4 043	57.8	1 693	48.6	524	56.3
	2011	4 140	58.0	1 737	48.6	526	56.1
Dem. Rep. of the Congo - Rép. dém. du Congo	1990	36 406	28.3	13 694	48.7	9 460	50.9
	2000	49 626	30.6	18 525	50.1	11 694	48.2
	2010	65 966	36.2	25 270	49.9	14 194	48.6
	2011	67 758	36.9	26 083	49.8	14 439	48.7
Equatorial Guinea - Guinée équatoriale	1990	374	35.2	201	45.1	108	38.9
	2000	520	39.4	260	44.3	142	41.5
	2010	700	39.3	369	44.7	176	42.0
	2011	720	39.4	380	44.8	180	42.2
Gabon	1990	929	68.9	344	45.1	207	50.2
	2000	1 235	80.0	444	45.6	207	48.3
	2010	1 505	85.8	587	46.4	183	45.4
	2011	1 534	86.1	605	46.4	184	46.2
Sao Tome and Principe - Sao Tomé-et-Principe	1990	116	43.6	35	33.4	24	41.7
	2000	141	53.1	45	35.2	28	42.9
	2010	165	62.2	59	37.2	32	50.0
	2011	169	62.8	61	37.4	33	48.5
Northern Africa - Afrique septentrionale	*1990*	*146 188*	*45.0*	*42 285*	*23.5*	*17 638*	*35.8*
	2000	*176 166*	*48.6*	*54 479*	*22.9*	*19 564*	*39.5*
	2010	*209 459*	*52.0*	*70 050*	*24.7*	*20 886*	*42.9*
	2011	*212 988*	*52.4*	*71 688*	*24.8*	*20 950*	*43.1*
Algeria - Algérie	1990	25 299	52.1	6 032	11.8	1 907	49.8
	2000	30 534	59.8	8 802	13.7	2 718	51.6
	2010	35 468	66.4	11 207	16.9	3 175	52.7
	2011	35 980	67.0	11 474	17.1	3 188	52.7
Egypt - Égypte	1990	56 843	44.2	16 842	26.5	6 495	37.5
	2000	67 648	44.4	20 085	21.4	6 339	36.2
	2010	81 121	45.2	27 076	24.2	6 620	40.4
	2011	82 537	45.3	27 738	24.4	6 599	40.5
Libya - Libye	1990	4 334	76.2	1 166	17.7	127	41.7
	2000	5 231	78.1	1 801	26.1	103	60.2
	2010	6 355	80.2	2 381	28.0	71	70.4
	2011	6 423	81.1	2 378	28.2	67	73.1
Morocco - Maroc	1990	24 781	48.4	7 867	25.3	3 264	35.6
	2000	28 793	53.4	10 206	27.9	3 372	43.2
	2010	31 951	59.0	11 375	27.1	3 009	47.7
	2011	32 273	59.7	11 562	27.4	2 972	48.4
Sudan (...2011) - Soudan (...2011)	1990	26 494	27.2	7 863	26.0	5 151	28.7
	2000	34 188	34.1	10 326	27.8	6 223	35.8
	2010	43 552	39.8	13 991	28.7	7 124	39.5
	2011	44 632	40.4	14 437	28.8	7 232	39.8
Tunisia - Tunisie	1990	8 215	57.9	2 448	21.6	652	34.2
	2000	9 456	63.4	3 151	24.9	756	34.7
	2010	10 481	66.6	3 801	26.9	805	33.0
	2011	10 594	66.9	3 871	27.0	808	32.9
Western Sahara - Sahara occidental	1990	221	86.1	68	14.6	42	47.6
	2000	315	83.9	109	17.8	53	50.9
	2010	531	81.8	219	23.3	82	53.7
	2011	548	82.1	228	23.5	84	54.8

For sources and notes, see end of table.

Pour les sources et les notes, se reporter à la fin du tableau.

Region, country or territory Régions, pays ou territoires	Year Année	Population		Total labour force Main-d'œuvre totale		Agriculture labour force Main-d'œuvre dans l'agriculture	
		Total (thousands) Total (milliers) (1)	Urban population (% of total population) Population urbaine (en % de la population totale) (2)	Total (thousands) Total (milliers) (3)	Female labour (% of total labour force) Main-d'œuvre féminine (en % de la main-d'œuvre totale) (4)	Total (thousands) Total (milliers) (5)	Female labour (% of total agriculture labour force) Main-d'œuvre féminine (en % de la main-d'œuvre totale dans l'agriculture) (6)
Southern Africa - *Afrique australe*	*1990* *2000* *2010* *2011*	*42 093* *51 442* *57 780* *58 212*	*48.7* *53.8* *58.9* *59.3*	*12 816* *18 132* *21 481* *21 841*	*36.7* *43.6* *43.2* *43.1*	*2 479* *2 512* *2 272* *2 247*	*40.5* *41.4* *42.2* *42.3*
Botswana	1990 2000 2010 2011	1 382 1 758 2 007 2 031	41.0 52.1 60.2 61.0	561 817 1 036 1 054	46.6 46.9 46.3 46.3	206 281 317 322	45.6 53.0 56.5 56.5
Lesotho	1990 2000 2010 2011	1 639 1 964 2 171 2 194	13.7 19.2 25.8 26.5	682 848 894 912	49.6 49.1 46.0 45.9	301 348 362 365	67.1 67.0 65.7 65.5
Namibia - Namibie	1990 2000 2010 2011	1 415 1 896 2 283 2 324	27.7 31.1 36.8 37.4	444 639 929 955	44.5 44.4 46.3 46.3	219 253 267 269	48.9 45.5 43.8 43.5
South Africa - Afrique du Sud	1990 2000 2010 2011	36 794 44 760 50 133 50 460	52.0 57.0 62.1 62.6	10 878 15 497 18 208 18 496	35.0 43.1 42.8 42.7	1 614 1 482 1 188 1 154	31.7 30.7 29.4 29.3
Swaziland	1990 2000 2010 2011	863 1 064 1 186 1 203	22.9 23.0 21.7 21.6	251 331 414 425	41.7 40.3 39.6 39.5	139 148 138 137	64.0 58.8 54.3 54.0
Western Africa - *Afrique occidentale*	*1990* *2000* *2010* *2011*	*182 529* *235 722* *304 261* *312 205*	*33.2* *39.1* *45.1* *45.7*	*61 930* *82 588* *107 773* *110 890*	*37.9* *41.6* *43.0* *43.0*	*36 384* *42 581* *49 962* *50 886*	*40.5* *41.3* *43.2* *43.4*
Benin - Bénin	1990 2000 2010 2011	4 773 6 518 8 850 9 100	34.6 39.2 43.8 44.3	1 850 2 559 3 616 3 728	42.5 46.5 47.6 47.7	1 095 1 384 1 601 1 616	41.1 42.2 40.7 40.7
Burkina Faso	1990 2000 2010 2011	9 324 12 294 16 469 16 968	13.1 16.9 25.4 26.3	4 084 5 500 7 548 7 775	48.5 48.2 47.6 47.5	3 742 4 982 6 909 7 146	48.5 48.2 48.1 48.1
Cape Verde - Cap-Vert	1990 2000 2010 2011	348 437 496 501	44.9 53.6 63.1 64.1	117 163 224 231	36.9 38.1 38.4 38.5	34 35 32 32	38.2 37.1 40.6 40.6
Côte d'Ivoire	1990 2000 2010 2011	12 518 16 582 19 738 20 153	40.0 45.4 55.3 56.2	4 607 6 384 7 792 8 007	30.1 35.1 37.4 37.6	2 686 2 946 2 814 2 812	35.6 36.5 36.1 36.0
Gambia - Gambie	1990 2000 2010 2011	966 1 297 1 728 1 776	35.5 49.3 58.9 59.6	399 544 752 776	44.8 47.0 47.9 47.9	351 461 605 622	50.7 51.6 53.6 53.7
Ghana	1990 2000 2010 2011	14 793 19 165 24 392 24 966	36.9 44.8 51.3 51.9	5 899 8 426 10 372 10 666	48.4 48.1 47.6 47.6	3 585 4 785 6 075 6 233	45.2 43.9 44.1 44.1
Guinea - Guinée	1990 2000 2010 2011	5 759 8 344 9 982 10 222	29.9 31.2 36.6 37.2	2 282 3 294 4 090 4 204	45.1 44.6 45.2 45.3	2 372 3 320 3 832 3 912	49.6 49.6 49.7 49.7

For sources and notes, see end of table.

Pour les sources et les notes, se reporter à la fin du tableau.

8

457

Region, country or territory / Régions, pays ou territoires	Year / Année	Population		Total labour force / Main-d'œuvre totale		Agriculture labour force / Main-d'œuvre dans l'agriculture	
		Total (thousands) / Total (milliers)	Urban population (% of total population) / Population urbaine (en % de la population totale)	Total (thousands) / Total (milliers)	Female labour (% of total labour force) / Main-d'œuvre féminine (en % de la main-d'œuvre totale)	Total (thousands) / Total (milliers)	Female labour (% of total agriculture labour force) / Main-d'œuvre féminine (en % de la main-d'œuvre totale dans l'agriculture)
		(1)	(2)	(3)	(4)	(5)	(6)
Guinea-Bissau - Guinée-Bissau	1990	1 017	28.3	396	44.5	338	45.3
	2000	1 241	31.2	498	45.5	391	45.5
	2010	1 515	32.6	649	47.3	447	45.4
	2011	1 547	32.9	665	47.3	455	45.5
Liberia - Libéria	1990	2 127	41.7	694	47.2	568	45.6
	2000	2 847	44.0	963	49.1	712	44.9
	2010	3 994	49.1	1 375	47.7	913	44.0
	2011	4 129	49.4	1 426	47.6	935	43.9
Mali	1990	8 673	23.3	2 328	38.8	1 953	36.2
	2000	11 295	26.4	3 058	37.5	2 376	36.3
	2010	15 370	31.1	4 296	35.4	3 049	37.2
	2011	15 840	31.6	4 440	35.3	3 122	37.0
Mauritania - Mauritanie	1990	1 996	39.5	521	19.9	435	48.3
	2000	2 643	39.4	761	23.3	570	50.9
	2010	3 460	40.3	1 116	26.6	745	54.2
	2011	3 542	40.5	1 150	26.7	763	54.8
Niger	1990	7 788	15.6	2 285	22.6	2 247	36.5
	2000	10 922	16.3	3 526	30.9	3 099	35.4
	2010	15 512	17.5	5 114	31.2	4 237	36.4
	2011	16 069	17.7	5 301	31.2	4 378	36.5
Nigeria - Nigéria	1990	97 552	35.2	30 564	34.5	12 689	34.2
	2000	123 689	42.9	39 254	40.1	12 443	35.2
	2010	158 423	49.8	50 245	42.9	12 267	39.2
	2011	162 471	50.3	51 637	42.8	12 277	39.8
Saint Helena - Sainte-Hélène	1990	6	41.6	..	..	1	..
	2000	5	39.8	..	..	1	..
	2010	4	42.5	..	..	1	..
	2011	4	42.8	..	..	1	..
Senegal - Sénégal	1990	7 242	40.5	2 897	41.5	2 296	45.6
	2000	9 506	42.0	3 948	43.0	2 929	46.1
	2010	12 434	43.8	5 384	43.9	3 821	47.4
	2011	12 768	44.1	5 547	43.9	3 932	47.6
Sierra Leone	1990	3 982	33.8	1 516	50.3	1 083	59.2
	2000	4 143	36.2	1 560	53.2	1 041	57.7
	2010	5 868	38.2	2 262	50.7	1 326	61.6
	2011	5 997	38.6	2 315	50.6	1 343	61.9
Togo	1990	3 666	32.2	1 490	45.1	909	38.1
	2000	4 794	40.0	2 150	49.0	1 106	39.4
	2010	6 028	48.9	2 938	50.5	1 288	41.2
	2011	6 155	49.8	3 021	50.5	1 307	41.5
Developing economies: America - Économies en développement : Amérique	1990	438 537	70.1	170 320	33.7	42 460	16.8
	2000	516 529	75.3	225 581	38.3	43 453	19.5
	2010	585 126	79.2	279 453	41.2	41 502	20.9
	2011	591 667	79.5	284 773	41.3	41 159	20.9
Caribbean - Caraïbes	1990	29 827	53.2	11 955	37.4	3 653	24.0
	2000	33 706	57.0	13 747	39.6	3 657	24.0
	2010	36 922	63.4	16 408	41.8	3 667	24.4
	2011	37 205	63.5	16 638	41.9	3 664	24.4
Anguilla	1990	8	100.0	..	..	1	..
	2000	11	100.0	..	..	1	..
	2010	15	100.0	..	..	1	..
	2011	16	100.0	..	..	1	..
Antigua and Barbuda - Antigua-et-Barbuda	1990	62	35.3	..	..	7	28.6
	2000	78	31.9	..	..	7	28.6
	2010	89	30.3	..	..	8	25.0
	2011	90	30.3	..	..	8	25.0

For sources and notes, see end of table.

Pour les sources et les notes, se reporter à la fin du tableau.

Region, country or territory Régions, pays ou territoires	Year Année	Population		Total labour force Main-d'œuvre totale		Agriculture labour force Main-d'œuvre dans l'agriculture	
		Total (thousands) Total (milliers)	Urban population (% of total population) Population urbaine (en % de la population totale)	Total (thousands) Total (milliers)	Female labour (% of total labour force) Main-d'œuvre féminine (en % de la main-d'œuvre totale)	Total (thousands) Total (milliers)	Female labour (% of total agriculture labour force) Main-d'œuvre féminine (en % de la main-d'œuvre totale dans l'agriculture)
		(1)	(2)	(3)	(4)	(5)	(6)
Aruba	1990	62	51.2	..	..	7	28.6
	2000	90	46.9	..	..	9	22.2
	2010	107	46.8	..	..	9	22.2
	2011	108	46.9	..	..	9	22.2
Bahamas	1990	256	79.7	125	45.9	6	16.7
	2000	298	84.0	148	48.8	5	20.0
	2010	343	84.8	197	48.3	5	..
	2011	347	84.9	200	48.3	4	
Barbados - Barbade	1990	260	32.7	136	46.8	9	44.4
	2000	268	36.1	145	46.5	7	42.9
	2010	273	41.7	159	46.7	4	50.0
	2011	274	42.4	160	46.7	4	50.0
Bonaire, Sint Eustatius and Saba - Bonaire, Saint-Eustache et Saba	2011	(e)21	..	10	49.7	..	..
British Virgin Islands - Îles Vierges britanniques	1990	16	..	..	..	2	..
	2000	20	..	..	..	2	..
	2010	23	..	..	..	2	50.0
	2011	24	..	..	..	2	50.0
Cayman Islands - Îles Caïmanes	1990	26	100.0	..	..	3	33.3
	2000	40	100.0	..	..	4	25.0
	2010	56	100.0	..	..	5	20.0
	2011	57	100.0	..	..	5	20.0
Cuba	1990	10 570	73.5	4 363	32.6	833	14.9
	2000	11 104	75.5	4 697	35.0	733	17.6
	2010	11 258	74.9	5 270	38.0	586	17.7
	2011	11 254	74.9	5 299	38.2	574	18.1
Curaçao	2011	(e)144	..	72	49.7	..	..
Dominica - Dominique	1990	71	65.7	..	..	8	25.0
	2000	70	65.6	..	..	7	28.6
	2010	68	66.0	..	..	6	16.7
	2011	68	66.2	..	..	6	16.7
Dominican Republic - République dominicaine	1990	7 195	56.6	2 848	34.0	621	8.9
	2000	8 592	63.5	3 537	36.6	547	19.7
	2010	9 927	71.3	4 432	39.4	457	31.3
	2011	10 056	71.9	4 515	39.5	447	32.2
Grenada - Grenade	1990	96	33.4	..	..	10	30.0
	2000	102	36.0	..	..	10	20.0
	2010	104	39.2	..	..	9	22.2
	2011	105	39.7	..	..	9	22.2
Haiti - Haïti	1990	7 125	28.4	2 713	44.0	1 787	33.0
	2000	8 645	35.6	3 242	46.5	1 994	27.1
	2010	9 993	53.1	4 163	47.0	2 277	24.6
	2011	10 124	54.7	4 258	47.0	2 300	24.4
Jamaica - Jamaïque	1990	2 365	49.4	1 133	46.3	275	27.3
	2000	2 582	51.5	1 187	44.3	248	27.4
	2010	2 741	51.8	1 240	45.1	214	27.6
	2011	2 751	51.9	1 251	45.1	212	27.4
Montserrat	1990	11	12.6		..	1	..
	2000	5	11.1	..	..	..	..
	2010	6	14.3	..	..	1	..
	2011	6	14.5	..	..	1	..
Netherlands Antilles - Antilles néerlandaises	1990	191	85.6	83	43.8	1	..
	2000	180	90.6	83	48.4	..	..
	2010	201	93.2	100	49.7	..	..

For sources and notes, see end of table.

Pour les sources et les notes, se reporter à la fin du tableau.

8

Region, country or territory / Régions, pays ou territoires	Year / Année	Population		Total labour force Main-d'œuvre totale		Agriculture labour force Main-d'œuvre dans l'agriculture	
		Total (thousands) Total (milliers)	Urban population (% of total population) Population urbaine (en % de la population totale)	Total (thousands) Total (milliers)	Female labour (% of total labour force) Main-d'œuvre féminine (en % de la main-d'œuvre totale)	Total (thousands) Total (milliers)	Female labour (% of total agriculture labour force) Main-d'œuvre féminine (en % de la main-d'œuvre totale dans l'agriculture)
		(1)	(2)	(3)	(4)	(5)	(6)
Saint Kitts and Nevis - Saint-Kitts-et-Nevis	1990	41	34.6	..	..	4	25.0
	2000	46	32.8	..	..	4	25.0
	2010	52	32.4	..	..	5	20.0
	2011	53	32.5	..	..	5	20.0
Saint Lucia - Sainte-Lucie	1990	138	29.4	58	45.0	15	26.7
	2000	157	28.0	73	47.0	16	25.0
	2010	174	27.9	91	47.2	17	23.5
	2011	176	28.1	92	47.3	17	23.5
Saint Vincent and the Grenadines - Saint-Vincent-et-les Grenadines	1990	107	41.4	42	36.0	12	25.0
	2000	108	45.2	48	38.4	11	27.3
	2010	109	49.3	54	41.0	11	27.3
	2011	109	49.8	54	41.1	11	27.3
Sint Maarten (Dutch part) - Saint-Martin (partie néerlandaise)	2011	(e)38	..	19	49.7	..	..
Trinidad and Tobago - Trinité-et-Tobago	1990	1 215	8.6	455	35.2	50	18.0
	2000	1 292	10.9	586	39.9	50	18.0
	2010	1 341	13.9	701	43.3	47	17.0
	2011	1 346	14.3	707	43.3	46	17.4
Turks and Caicos Islands - Îles Turques et Caïques	1990	12	74.3	..	..	1	..
	2000	19	84.5	..	..	2	..
	2010	38	80.2	..	..	3	33.3
	2011	39	79.7	..	..	3	33.3
Central America - Amérique centrale	*1990*	*113 249*	*64.4*	*40 464*	*30.2*	*12 217*	*11.5*
	2000	*135 555*	*68.6*	*53 574*	*33.4*	*12 545*	*11.6*
	2010	*155 881*	*70.7*	*67 215*	*36.8*	*12 173*	*11.9*
	2011	*158 018*	*70.9*	*68 778*	*37.0*	*12 099*	*11.9*
Belize	1990	190	47.4	63	31.2	18	5.6
	2000	251	48.0	91	32.6	25	4.0
	2010	312	52.5	131	37.5	31	3.2
	2011	318	52.9	135	37.6	31	3.2
Costa Rica	1990	3 070	50.8	1 158	27.6	307	7.2
	2000	3 919	59.2	1 600	30.8	326	9.8
	2010	4 659	64.2	2 192	36.3	322	12.7
	2011	4 727	64.6	2 247	36.5	319	13.2
El Salvador	1990	5 333	49.2	1 890	35.4	655	9.0
	2000	5 940	59.0	2 218	39.6	661	8.3
	2010	6 193	64.3	2 594	41.5	590	9.3
	2011	6 227	64.8	2 638	41.7	583	9.4
Guatemala	1990	8 923	41.1	3 133	31.6	1 488	7.3
	2000	11 237	45.1	3 969	34.6	1 492	7.2
	2010	14 389	49.4	5 680	38.1	2 061	9.9
	2011	14 757	49.9	5 876	38.2	2 103	9.9
Honduras	1990	4 889	40.6	1 590	28.1	672	18.2
	2000	6 218	45.5	2 363	34.2	735	21.6
	2010	7 601	51.7	2 988	34.1	665	20.8
	2011	7 755	52.3	3 084	34.3	663	20.8
Mexico - Mexique	1990	84 307	70.7	30 395	29.9	8 439	12.4
	2000	99 960	74.4	40 256	33.0	8 658	12.3
	2010	113 423	75.9	49 605	36.5	7 905	12.3
	2011	114 793	76.0	50 673	36.7	7 807	12.3
Nicaragua	1990	4 121	52.6	1 308	30.3	391	10.0
	2000	5 074	55.0	1 797	32.5	390	7.7
	2010	5 788	57.7	2 376	37.9	351	7.7
	2011	5 870	58.0	2 441	38.1	347	7.8

For sources and notes, see end of table.

Pour les sources et les notes, se reporter à la fin du tableau.

Region, country or territory / Régions, pays ou territoires	Year / Année	Population		Total labour force / Main-d'œuvre totale		Agriculture labour force / Main-d'œuvre dans l'agriculture	
		Total (thousands) / Total (milliers)	Urban population (% of total population) / Population urbaine (en % de la population totale)	Total (thousands) / Total (milliers)	Female labour (% of total labour force) / Main-d'œuvre féminine (en % de la main-d'œuvre totale)	Total (thousands) / Total (milliers)	Female labour (% of total agriculture labour force) / Main-d'œuvre féminine (en % de la main-d'œuvre totale dans l'agriculture)
		(1)	(2)	(3)	(4)	(5)	(6)
Panama	1990	2 416	53.8	926	32.6	247	3.6
	2000	2 956	65.7	1 281	35.4	258	3.9
	2010	3 517	74.6	1 649	37.3	248	3.6
	2011	3 571	75.3	1 684	37.4	246	3.3
South America - Amérique du Sud	*1990*	*295 460*	*74.1*	*117 901*	*34.5*	*26 590*	*18.2*
	2000	*347 268*	*79.7*	*158 259*	*39.9*	*27 251*	*22.5*
	2010	*392 324*	*84.1*	*195 830*	*42.6*	*25 662*	*24.6*
	2011	*396 444*	*84.4*	*199 356*	*42.8*	*25 396*	*24.7*
Argentina - Argentine	1990	32 642	86.6	13 304	36.1	1 458	6.7
	2000	36 931	90.1	15 408	38.1	1 458	9.9
	2010	40 412	93.0	18 366	40.2	1 405	10.7
	2011	40 765	93.2	18 629	40.4	1 396	10.7
Bolivia (Plurinational State of) - Bolivie (État plurinational de)	1990	6 658	55.7	2 600	39.0	1 190	34.8
	2000	8 307	61.9	3 529	43.2	1 560	40.7
	2010	9 930	67.2	4 585	44.8	1 973	41.9
	2011	10 088	67.7	4 703	44.9	2 014	41.9
Brazil - Brésil	1990	149 650	73.9	62 657	35.1	14 062	18.5
	2000	174 425	81.1	83 762	41.2	13 325	23.4
	2010	194 946	86.7	101 601	43.6	11 049	24.5
	2011	196 655	87.1	103 222	43.8	10 763	24.5
Chile - Chili	1990	13 188	83.3	4 999	30.5	934	9.7
	2000	15 420	85.9	6 087	33.1	962	11.5
	2010	17 114	89.1	8 032	39.6	964	14.2
	2011	17 270	89.4	8 161	39.7	961	14.5
Colombia - Colombie	1990	33 203	68.3	11 362	30.0	3 342	18.6
	2000	39 764	72.1	17 269	38.7	3 584	22.6
	2010	46 295	75.1	22 143	42.4	3 529	24.8
	2011	46 927	75.4	22 637	42.7	3 509	24.9
Ecuador - Équateur	1990	10 261	55.2	3 862	31.9	1 117	14.7
	2000	12 345	60.1	5 391	37.4	1 210	20.2
	2010	14 465	63.8	6 857	39.7	1 228	24.8
	2011	14 666	64.2	7 026	40.0	1 224	25.2
Falkland Islands (Malvinas) - Îles Falkland (Malvinas)	1990	2	75.3	..	..	..	..
	2000	3	68.1	..	..	..	..
	2010	3	74.1	..	..	..	..
	2011	3	74.7	..	..	..	..
Guyana	1990	725	30.6	281	31.4	58	12.1
	2000	733	29.6	285	32.6	55	10.9
	2010	754	28.9	302	34.7	50	8.0
	2011	756	28.9	308	35.1	49	8.2
Paraguay	1990	4 244	48.8	1 802	36.7	576	8.3
	2000	5 344	55.4	2 281	36.7	715	8.1
	2010	6 455	61.5	3 088	39.7	831	7.7
	2011	6 568	62.1	3 168	40.0	841	7.6
Peru - Pérou	1990	21 686	69.2	8 273	37.4	2 773	26.1
	2000	25 862	73.4	11 968	41.2	3 344	28.2
	2010	29 077	78.0	15 481	44.5	3 692	31.3
	2011	29 400	78.4	15 777	44.7	3 711	31.5
Suriname	1990	407	60.0	157	37.3	29	27.6
	2000	467	64.9	166	35.1	30	26.7
	2010	525	69.3	204	37.1	33	24.2
	2011	529	69.8	207	37.3	33	24.2
Uruguay	1990	3 109	89.0	1 392	39.0	184	10.9
	2000	3 319	91.4	1 586	43.1	197	12.7
	2010	3 369	92.6	1 708	44.5	186	14.0
	2011	3 380	92.7	1 722	44.6	185	14.1

For sources and notes, see end of table.

Pour les sources et les notes, se reporter à la fin du tableau.

8

Region, country or territory Régions, pays ou territoires	Year Année	Population		Total labour force Main-d'œuvre totale		Agriculture labour force Main-d'œuvre dans l'agriculture	
		Total (thousands) Total (milliers)	Urban population (% of total population) Population urbaine (en % de la population totale)	Total (thousands) Total (milliers)	Female labour (% of total labour force) Main-d'œuvre féminine (en % de la main-d'œuvre totale)	Total (thousands) Total (milliers)	Female labour (% of total agriculture labour force) Main-d'œuvre féminine (en % de la main-d'œuvre totale dans l'agriculture)
		(1)	(2)	(3)	(4)	(5)	(6)
Venezuela (Bolivarian Rep. of) - Venezuela (Rép. bolivarienne du)	1990	19 685	84.5	7 213	31.5	867	4.2
	2000	24 348	90.1	10 527	37.2	811	5.4
	2010	28 980	93.6	13 463	39.4	722	6.4
	2011	29 437	93.8	13 795	39.6	710	6.3
Developing economies: Asia - Économies en développement : Asie	**1990**	**2 985 103**	**29.8**	**1 367 866**	**38.1**	**898 011**	**42.2**
	2000	**3 493 136**	**35.5**	**1 628 874**	**37.9**	**969 780**	**42.4**
	2010	**3 928 620**	**41.5**	**1 885 572**	**37.1**	**1 014 276**	**42.6**
	2011	**3 994 078**	**41.8**	**1 912 165**	**37.0**	**1 016 166**	**42.6**
Eastern Asia - Asie orientale	*1990*	*1 216 665*	*29.0*	*687 487*	*44.4*	*489 840*	*47.2*
	2000	*1 347 625*	*38.0*	*773 268*	*44.7*	*510 620*	*47.8*
	2010	*1 424 218*	*49.1*	*851 089*	*44.4*	*505 536*	*47.9*
	2011	*1 454 123*	*49.2*	*857 159*	*44.3*	*503 218*	*47.9*
China - Chine (7)(8)	1990	1 124 916	26.8	649 073	44.6	482 507	47.2
	2000	1 246 932	36.3	728 129	45.0	504 849	47.9
	2010	1 318 194	48.2	801 588	44.6	500 977	48.0
	2011	1 347 565	48.3	807 141	44.6	498 770	47.9
China, Hong Kong SAR - Chine (RAS de Hong Kong)	1990	5 794	98.0	2 892	36.5	..	..
	2000	6 783	98.3	3 410	41.9	..	..
	2010	7 053	100.0	3 689	46.0	..	..
	2011	7 122	100.0	3 729	46.1	..	..
China, Macao SAR - Chine (RAS de Macao)	1990	360	100.0	155	40.5	..	..
	2000	432	100.0	217	45.3	..	..
	2010	544	100.0	337	48.8	..	..
	2011	556	99.8	347	48.8	..	..
China, Taiwan Province of - Province chinoise de Taiwan (9)	1990	20 279	..	3 220	18.4	..	..
	2000	22 185	..	4 825	20.2	..	..
	2010	23 141	..	5 452	15.2	..	..
	2011	23 238	..	5 623	15.4	..	..
Korea, Dem. People's Rep. of - Corée, Rép. populaire dém. de	1990	20 143	58.4	12 192	48.1	3 618	45.2
	2000	22 894	59.3	13 565	47.5	3 328	45.3
	2010	24 346	59.3	14 575	47.7	3 065	46.4
	2011	24 451	59.4	14 684	47.7	3 029	46.4
Korea, Republic of - Corée, République de	1990	42 980	73.8	19 207	39.7	3 470	44.1
	2000	45 988	80.4	22 175	40.5	2 206	44.0
	2010	48 184	83.5	24 265	41.3	1 274	43.4
	2011	48 391	83.7	24 427	41.4	1 201	43.3
Mongolia - Mongolie	1990	2 193	57.6	748	46.6	245	44.1
	2000	2 411	56.3	946	46.8	237	45.1
	2010	2 756	60.8	1 183	46.4	220	47.7
	2011	2 800	61.0	1 209	46.4	218	48.2
Southern Asia - Asie méridionale	*1990*	*1 195 985*	*26.6*	*441 093*	*27.5*	*274 258*	*33.0*
	2000	*1 460 201*	*29.1*	*554 268*	*27.9*	*313 156*	*33.5*
	2010	*1 704 146*	*32.0*	*663 247*	*26.8*	*355 387*	*34.8*
	2011	*1 728 477*	*32.4*	*676 608*	*26.8*	*359 276*	*34.9*
Afghanistan	1990	13 032	17.5	3 459	14.9	2 804	28.6
	2000	22 856	18.1	5 745	13.3	4 485	29.0
	2010	31 412	20.9	8 270	15.2	6 046	32.1
	2011	32 358	21.3	8 575	15.4	6 218	32.5
Bangladesh	1990	105 256	21.8	45 675	39.4	30 773	44.9
	2000	129 592	25.6	57 288	37.5	31 757	45.0
	2010	148 692	31.0	72 274	39.9	32 100	50.9
	2011	150 494	31.6	73 948	40.1	31 976	51.4
Bhutan - Bhoutan	1990	559	16.1	206	37.1	166	22.9
	2000	571	25.0	228	39.5	169	23.1
	2010	726	33.9	365	42.5	311	34.4
	2011	738	34.6	376	42.4	320	34.7

For sources and notes, see end of table.   Pour les sources et les notes, se reporter à la fin du tableau.

Region, country or territory / Régions, pays ou territoires	Year / Année	Population — Total (thousands) / Total (milliers) (1)	Population — Urban population (% of total population) / Population urbaine (en % de la population totale) (2)	Total labour force / Main-d'œuvre totale — Total (thousands) / Total (milliers) (3)	Total labour force — Female labour (% of total labour force) / Main-d'œuvre féminine (en % de la main-d'œuvre totale) (4)	Agriculture labour force / Main-d'œuvre dans l'agriculture — Total (thousands) / Total (milliers) (5)	Agriculture labour force — Female labour (% of total agriculture labour force) / Main-d'œuvre féminine (en % de la main-d'œuvre totale dans l'agriculture) (6)
India - Inde	1990	873 785	25.2	330 509	27.4	210 181	32.4
	2000	1 053 898	27.4	409 206	27.9	239 959	32.4
	2010	1 224 614	29.8	472 580	25.3	269 740	32.4
	2011	1 241 492	30.1	481 098	25.3	272 706	32.5
Iran (Islamic Rep. of) - Iran (Rép. islamique d')	1990	54 871	58.2	13 329	10.8	5 040	27.2
	2000	65 342	65.7	18 491	16.0	5 761	39.2
	2010	73 974	71.8	25 226	17.9	6 553	46.5
	2011	74 799	72.4	25 855	18.1	6 562	47.3
Maldives	1990	219	25.4	58	19.4	20	15.0
	2000	273	27.6	89	33.8	21	28.6
	2010	316	39.9	153	41.8	23	39.1
	2011	320	41.1	157	42.0	22	40.9
Nepal - Népal	1990	19 081	8.9	9 379	46.9	6 653	39.4
	2000	24 401	13.4	12 352	49.0	8 677	44.1
	2010	29 959	18.6	16 034	49.2	12 066	48.1
	2011	30 486	19.1	16 507	49.2	12 411	48.3
Pakistan	1990	111 845	31.7	31 717	12.8	15 044	16.3
	2000	144 522	34.0	43 036	15.3	18 712	22.9
	2010	173 593	38.2	59 739	20.7	24 520	30.1
	2011	176 745	38.7	61 394	20.9	25 022	30.7
Sri Lanka	1990	17 337	18.6	6 761	31.5	3 577	38.0
	2000	18 745	15.8	7 833	33.1	3 615	34.1
	2010	20 860	14.0	8 607	32.2	4 028	37.2
	2011	21 045	14.0	8 697	32.3	4 039	37.3
South-Eastern Asia - Asie du Sud-Est	*1990*	*445 361*	*31.2*	*200 255*	*42.8*	*119 013*	*43.2*
	2000	*523 831*	*37.7*	*251 831*	*42.0*	*131 986*	*42.5*
	2010	*593 415*	*41.6*	*302 270*	*42.4*	*139 939*	*42.4*
	2011	*600 033*	*42.0*	*307 408*	*42.4*	*140 360*	*42.4*
Brunei Darussalam - Brunéi Darussalam	1990	252	67.1	105	31.7	2	50.0
	2000	327	72.5	154	40.7	1	..
	2010	399	78.6	195	42.0	1	..
	2011	414	77.5	199	42.0	1	..
Cambodia - Cambodge	1990	9 532	12.8	4 321	52.6	3 138	55.7
	2000	12 447	17.3	5 773	51.2	4 028	53.5
	2010	14 138	21.4	7 973	49.8	4 966	51.3
	2011	14 305	21.8	8 142	49.7	5 031	51.2
Indonesia (…2002) - Indonésie (…2002)	1990	185 089	29.4	76 784	38.6	43 171	39.4
	2000	214 226	40.3	99 691	37.6	48 669	39.1
Indonesia - Indonésie	2010	239 871	42.9	118 023	38.2	49 513	39.4
	2011	242 326	43.2	119 909	38.3	49 489	39.5
Lao People's Dem. Rep. - Rép. dém. populaire lao	1990	4 192	15.5	1 924	49.7	1 486	51.3
	2000	5 317	22.3	2 459	49.9	1 865	52.0
	2010	6 201	34.4	3 169	49.8	2 368	52.3
	2011	6 288	35.8	3 250	49.7	2 424	52.2
Malaysia - Malaisie	1990	18 209	49.5	7 124	34.3	1 933	32.1
	2000	23 415	61.6	9 890	34.7	1 849	26.3
	2010	28 401	70.9	11 977	35.8	1 612	21.0
	2011	28 859	71.7	12 233	35.9	1 585	20.6
Myanmar	1990	39 268	25.7	19 003	48.4	14 482	47.3
	2000	44 958	28.8	24 151	48.3	17 125	47.3
	2010	47 963	35.4	27 971	48.9	18 788	47.8
	2011	48 337	36.2	28 352	48.9	18 965	47.8

For sources and notes, see end of table. Pour les sources et les notes, se reporter à la fin du tableau.

8

Region, country or territory Régions, pays ou territoires	Year Année	Population		Total labour force Main-d'œuvre totale		Agriculture labour force Main-d'œuvre dans l'agriculture	
		Total (thousands) Total (milliers)	Urban population (% of total population) Population urbaine (en % de la population totale)	Total (thousands) Total (milliers)	Female labour (% of total labour force) Main-d'œuvre féminine (en % de la main-d'œuvre totale)	Total (thousands) Total (milliers)	Female labour (% of total agriculture labour force) Main-d'œuvre féminine (en % de la main-d'œuvre totale dans l'agriculture)
		(1)	(2)	(3)	(4)	(5)	(6)
Philippines	1990	61 629	49.2	23 724	36.6	10 844	24.4
	2000	77 310	48.2	30 971	37.4	12 405	24.1
	2010	93 261	49.1	38 719	38.8	13 404	24.2
	2011	94 852	49.4	39 716	38.9	13 472	24.2
Singapore - Singapour	1990	3 017	100.0	1 539	39.1	6	16.7
	2000	3 919	100.0	2 012	40.7	3	..
	2010	5 086	95.1	2 809	42.3	2	..
	2011	5 188	94.6	2 872	42.3	2	..
Thailand - Thaïlande	1990	57 072	29.2	32 486	47.4	21 272	48.0
	2000	63 155	30.7	34 824	46.1	20 089	46.4
	2010	69 122	33.5	39 404	45.7	19 302	45.1
	2011	69 519	33.9	39 783	45.8	19 096	44.9
Timor-Leste	2010	1 124	29.3	343	33.3	352	44.9
	2011	1 154	30.0	353	33.4	362	45.0
Viet Nam	1990	67 102	20.0	33 244	49.6	22 679	50.7
	2000	78 758	24.5	41 906	49.1	25 952	50.1
	2010	87 848	30.8	51 687	48.5	29 631	49.1
	2011	88 792	31.4	52 599	48.5	29 933	49.0
Western Asia - Asie occidentale	*1990*	*127 092*	*62.2*	*39 031*	*22.7*	*14 900*	*41.4*
	2000	*161 478*	*66.1*	*49 508*	*22.0*	*14 018*	*43.5*
	2010	*206 841*	*67.0*	*68 966*	*22.1*	*13 414*	*47.9*
	2011	*211 444*	*67.1*	*70 989*	*22.2*	*13 312*	*48.3*
Bahrain - Bahreïn	1990	493	88.2	214	17.0	4	..
	2000	638	90.0	302	21.4	3	..
	2010	1 262	56.7	711	19.3	4	..
	2011	1 324	55.1	746	19.3	4	..
Iraq	1990	17 374	72.5	3 712	14.2	626	34.8
	2000	23 857	70.1	5 437	15.9	535	42.8
	2010	31 672	65.7	7 452	17.6	436	50.7
	2011	32 665	65.3	7 746	17.8	430	51.4
Jordan - Jordanie	1990	3 416	68.8	708	10.7	102	37.3
	2000	4 827	78.7	1 212	14.3	118	50.0
	2010	6 187	82.1	1 589	18.1	114	61.4
	2011	6 330	81.9	1 659	18.2	112	62.5
Kuwait - Koweït	1990	2 088	100.0	786	26.9	9	..
	2000	1 941	100.0	962	25.1	11	..
	2010	2 737	100.0	1 357	23.9	14	..
	2011	2 818	100.0	1 399	24.0	14	..
Lebanon - Liban	1990	2 948	83.9	786	21.1	69	31.9
	2000	3 742	86.7	1 140	22.9	48	33.3
	2010	4 228	87.8	1 454	25.5	28	32.1
	2011	4 259	88.0	1 478	25.6	27	33.3
Occupied Palestinian territory - Territoire palestinien occupé	1990	2 081	70.2	425	12.5	128	61.7
	2000	3 199	70.9	656	13.4	125	66.4
	2010	4 039	80.9	947	17.9	110	72.7
	2011	4 152	81.4	987	18.2	109	73.4
Oman	1990	1 868	65.2	558	12.9	256	6.6
	2000	2 264	75.9	787	17.1	293	6.8
	2010	2 782	76.3	1 216	17.9	318	6.9
	2011	2 846	76.3	1 271	17.7	321	6.9
Qatar	1990	474	91.0	274	14.4	7	..
	2000	591	99.1	332	15.6	4	..
	2010	1 759	82.2	1 315	12.4	8	..
	2011	1 870	80.6	1 391	12.2	8	..

For sources and notes, see end of table.

Pour les sources et les notes, se reporter à la fin du tableau.

Region, country or territory Régions, pays ou territoires	Year Année	Population		Total labour force Main-d'œuvre totale		Agriculture labour force Main-d'œuvre dans l'agriculture	
		Total (thousands) Total (milliers)	Urban population (% of total population) Population urbaine (en % de la population totale)	Total (thousands) Total (milliers)	Female labour (% of total labour force) Main-d'œuvre féminine (en % de la main-d'œuvre totale)	Total (thousands) Total (milliers)	Female labour (% of total agriculture labour force) Main-d'œuvre féminine (en % de la main-d'œuvre totale dans l'agriculture)
		(1)	(2)	(3)	(4)	(5)	(6)
Saudi Arabia - Arabie saoudite	1990	16 139	77.2	4 998	10.7	966	6.9
	2000	20 045	82.9	5 963	14.8	659	6.5
	2010	27 448	78.5	9 557	14.8	515	5.6
	2011	28 083	78.5	9 800	15.2	492	5.5
Syrian Arab Republic - République arabe syrienne	1990	12 324	50.5	3 220	18.4	954	41.7
	2000	15 989	53.6	4 825	20.2	1 116	49.1
	2010	20 411	61.5	5 452	15.2	1 337	60.7
	2011	20 766	62.2	5 627	15.4	1 342	61.6
Turkey - Turquie	1990	54 130	61.3	19 951	30.0	10 355	47.8
	2000	63 628	67.6	21 960	26.9	9 131	48.7
	2010	72 752	72.5	26 531	28.7	8 067	52.6
	2011	73 640	72.9	26 964	28.7	7 962	53.1
United Arab Emirates - Émirats arabes unis	1990	1 809	81.6	905	9.7	73	..
	2000	3 033	85.7	1 718	12.0	87	..
	2010	7 512	52.7	4 927	14.8	148	..
	2011	7 891	51.4	5 189	14.8	148	..
Yemen - Yémen	1990	11 948	21.6	2 497	18.9	1 351	27.8
	2000	17 723	26.9	4 212	24.0	1 888	34.3
	2010	24 053	32.1	6 459	25.9	2 315	40.3
	2011	24 800	32.6	6 735	26.1	2 343	40.5
Developing economies: Oceania - **Économies en développement : Océanie**	**1990**	**6 473**	**24.3**	**2 468**	**43.8**	**1 800**	**48.1**
	2000	**8 107**	**23.5**	**3 225**	**45.3**	**2 173**	**50.3**
	2010	**9 956**	**23.0**	**4 127**	**45.4**	**2 590**	**51.9**
	2011	**10 151**	**23.0**	**4 228**	**45.4**	**2 640**	**51.9**
American Samoa - Samoa américaines	1990	47	81.0	..	..	7	28.6
	2000	58	88.9	..	..	8	37.5
	2010	68	93.1	..	..	8	37.5
	2011	70	93.4	..	..	8	37.5
Cook Islands - Îles Cook	1990	18	58.2	..	..	3	33.3
	2000	18	64.2	..	..	2	50.0
	2010	20	74.0	..	..	2	50.0
	2011	20	74.7	..	..	2	50.0
Fiji - Fidji	1990	728	41.3	253	25.5	116	16.4
	2000	812	47.3	311	32.9	125	20.8
	2010	861	51.5	365	32.4	126	21.4
	2011	868	51.7	369	32.4	127	21.3
French Polynesia - Polynésie française	1990	195	55.9	78	37.4	33	36.4
	2000	238	52.0	94	39.4	34	35.3
	2010	271	51.8	117	40.5	33	36.4
	2011	274	51.8	118	40.6	32	37.5
Guam	1990	134	90.8	61	35.4	20	25.0
	2000	155	93.1	68	38.5	19	26.3
	2010	180	93.2	79	38.6	20	25.0
	2011	182	93.2	81	38.7	20	25.0
Kiribati	1990	72	35.0	..	..	10	30.0
	2000	84	43.0	..	..	10	30.0
	2010	100	43.9	..	..	11	27.3
	2011	101	44.0	..	..	11	27.3
Marshall Islands - Îles Marshall	1990	47	65.1	..	..	..	..
	2000	52	68.4	..	..	6	33.3
	2010	54	84.2	..	..	6	33.3
	2011	55	85.1	..	..	6	33.3
Micronesia (Federated States of) - Micronésie (États fédérés de)	1990	96	25.8	..	..	..	..
	2000	107	22.3	..	..	13	23.1
	2010	111	22.7	..	..	12	25.0
	2011	112	22.8	..	..	12	25.0

For sources and notes, see end of table.

Pour les sources et les notes, se reporter à la fin du tableau.

8

Region, country or territory Régions, pays ou territoires	Year Année	Population		Total labour force Main-d'œuvre totale		Agriculture labour force Main-d'œuvre dans l'agriculture	
		Total (thousands) Total (milliers)	Urban population (% of total population) Population urbaine (en % de la population totale)	Total (thousands) Total (milliers)	Female labour (% of total labour force) Main-d'œuvre féminine (en % de la main-d'œuvre totale)	Total (thousands) Total (milliers)	Female labour (% of total agriculture labour force) Main-d'œuvre féminine (en % de la main-d'œuvre totale dans l'agriculture)
		(1)	(2)	(3)	(4)	(5)	(6)
Nauru	1990	9	99.9	..	..	1	..
	2000	10	100.0	..	..	1	..
	2010	10	100.0	..	..	1	..
	2011	10	100.0	..	..	1	..
New Caledonia - Nouvelle-Calédonie	1990	170	60.0	68	37.6	30	40.0
	2000	212	60.1	90	40.1	32	40.6
	2010	251	58.0	108	40.9	32	40.6
	2011	255	57.9	110	41.0	32	37.5
Niue - Nioué	1990	2	30.5	..	..	..	..
	2000	2	32.8	..	..	..	..
	2010	1	36.8	..	..	..	..
	2011	1	37.3	..	..	..	..
Northern Mariana Islands - Îles Mariannes du Nord	1990	44	89.3	..	..	..	..
	2000	68	90.9	..	..	8	25.0
	2010	61	100.0	..	..	7	28.6
	2011	61	100.0	..	..	7	28.6
Palau - Palaos	1990	15	68.9	..	..	..	50.0
	2000	19	70.3	..	..	2	50.0
	2010	20	83.6	..	..	2	50.0
	2011	21	84.3	..	..	2	50.0
Papua New Guinea - Papouasie-Nouvelle-Guinée	1990	4 158	14.9	1 740	48.1	1 421	52.4
	2000	5 379	13.2	2 319	48.5	1 725	54.4
	2010	6 858	12.6	3 025	48.3	2 110	55.5
	2011	7 014	12.6	3 107	48.3	2 155	55.6
Samoa	1990	161	21.2	56	31.9	24	29.2
	2000	177	22.0	65	33.0	22	31.8
	2010	183	19.8	69	34.3	18	33.3
	2011	184	19.6	70	34.3	18	33.3
Solomon Islands - Îles Salomon	1990	310	13.9	110	39.2	90	45.6
	2000	409	16.0	158	38.9	118	45.8
	2010	538	18.3	217	38.5	151	46.4
	2011	548	18.7	224	38.5	155	46.5
Tokelau - Tokélaou	1990	2	..	..	..	..	..
	2000	2	..	..	..	..	..
	2010	1	..	..	..	..	..
	2011	1	..	..	..	..	..
Tonga	1990	95	22.6	32	32.3	12	25.0
	2000	98	23.2	37	40.1	12	41.7
	2010	104	23.5	42	42.7	11	45.5
	2011	105	23.5	42	42.7	11	36.4
Tuvalu	1990	9	40.2	..	..	1	..
	2000	9	46.6	..	..	1	..
	2010	10	51.1	..	..	1	..
	2011	10	51.7	..	..	1	..
Vanuatu	1990	147	19.1	69	46.2	30	50.0
	2000	185	22.2	83	44.7	33	48.5
	2010	240	26.2	105	42.9	38	47.4
	2011	246	26.7	108	42.9	39	46.2
Wallis and Futuna Islands - Îles Wallis-et-Futuna	1990	14	..	..	..	2	50.0
	2000	14	..	..	..	2	50.0
	2010	14	..	..	..	1	100.0
	2011	13	..	..	..	1	100.0

For sources and notes, see end of table.

Pour les sources et les notes, se reporter à la fin du tableau.

Region, country or territory Régions, pays ou territoires	Year Année	Population		Total labour force Main-d'œuvre totale		Agriculture labour force Main-d'œuvre dans l'agriculture	
		Total (thousands) Total (milliers)	Urban population (% of total population) Population urbaine (en % de la population totale)	Total (thousands) Total (milliers)	Female labour (% of total labour force) Main-d'œuvre féminine (en % de la main-d'œuvre totale)	Total (thousands) Total (milliers)	Female labour (% of total agriculture labour force) Main-d'œuvre féminine (en % de la main-d'œuvre totale dans l'agriculture)
		(1)	(2)	(3)	(4)	(5)	(6)
Transition economies - Economies en transition	1990	315 195	64.0	153 486	47.4	29 389	40.2
	2000	305 154	63.4	144 092	47.5	21 316	35.8
	2010	302 849	62.9	151 578	47.5	18 235	33.2
	2011	303 221	62.9	152 214	47.5	17 918	32.9
Albania - Albanie	1990	3 289	36.4	1 415	40.4	921	47.6
	2000	3 072	41.7	1 331	41.7	620	44.4
	2010	3 204	51.3	1 496	41.6	614	42.5
	2011	3 216	52.4	1 512	41.5	609	42.2
Armenia - Arménie	2000	3 076	64.7	1 472	48.8	174	23.0
	2010	3 092	64.2	1 438	46.5	148	16.2
	2011	3 100	64.2	1 453	46.5	145	15.9
Azerbaijan - Azerbaïdjan	2000	8 111	51.3	3 573	47.0	972	54.4
	2010	9 188	50.5	4 676	49.0	1 085	53.4
	2011	9 306	50.5	4 764	48.9	1 089	53.2
Belarus - Bélarus	2000	10 058	69.9	4 768	48.9	636	25.3
	2010	9 595	74.6	4 530	48.9	434	18.7
	2011	9 559	75.1	4 535	48.9	417	18.2
Bosnia and Herzegovina - Bosnie-Herzégovine	2000	3 694	43.2	1 332	39.0	100	60.0
	2010	3 760	48.6	1 478	40.0	44	59.1
	2011	3 752	49.2	1 481	40.0	41	58.5
Croatia - Croatie	2000	4 506	55.6	2 005	44.2	170	35.3
	2010	4 403	57.8	1 964	46.0	84	29.8
	2011	4 396	58.1	1 963	45.9	79	29.1
Georgia - Géorgie	2000	4 746	52.6	2 357	46.2	472	39.6
	2010	4 352	51.1	2 322	47.0	354	36.2
	2011	4 329	51.1	2 323	47.0	345	35.7
Kazakhstan	2000	14 957	56.3	7 585	49.1	1 321	29.1
	2010	16 026	57.5	8 625	49.4	1 192	24.2
	2011	16 207	57.6	8 701	49.4	1 181	23.6
Kyrgyzstan - Kirghizistan	2000	4 955	35.2	2 090	44.7	543	35.2
	2010	5 334	35.9	2 476	42.7	510	29.8
	2011	5 393	36.0	2 518	42.7	507	29.4
Montenegro - Monténégro	2010	631	60.9	..	..	39	38.5
	2011	632	60.9	..	..	38	36.8
Republic of Moldova - République de Moldova	2000	4 107	44.5	1 857	49.7	390	34.4
	2010	3 573	47.0	1 221	49.2	200	30.0
	2011	3 545	47.8	1 226	49.3	190	29.5
Russian Federation - Fédération de Russie	2000	146 758	73.3	73 524	48.6	7 648	28.9
	2010	142 958	71.8	76 185	48.8	6 251	24.6
	2011	142 836	71.7	76 213	48.9	6 101	24.1
Serbia and Montenegro - Serbie-et-Monténégro	2000	10 766	53.5	4 758	45.0	1 007	44.0
Serbia - Serbie	2010	9 856	56.1	4 433	43.2	617	38.1
	2011	9 854	56.4	4 456	43.3	590	37.5
SFR of Yugoslavia - RSF de Yougoslavie	1990	22 839	49.5	10 231	43.9	911	49.0
Tajikistan - Tadjikistan	2000	6 173	26.5	2 374	44.1	610	52.8
	2010	6 879	27.1	2 847	45.2	773	53.2
	2011	6 977	27.2	2 917	45.2	779	53.1
TFYR of Macedonia - LERY de Macédoine	2000	2 009	59.4	831	38.8	107	36.4
	2010	2 061	58.8	946	38.5	68	32.4
	2011	2 064	58.9	953	38.6	65	30.8
Turkmenistan - Turkménistan	2000	4 501	45.8	1 735	40.6	627	52.2
	2010	5 042	50.8	2 164	39.3	705	53.2
	2011	5 105	51.3	2 212	39.2	713	53.3

For sources and notes, see end of table.

Pour les sources et les notes, se reporter à la fin du tableau.

Region, country or territory Régions, pays ou territoires	Year Année	Population		Total labour force Main-d'œuvre totale		Agriculture labour force Main-d'œuvre dans l'agriculture	
		Total (thousands) Total (milliers)	Urban population (% of total population) Population urbaine (en % de la population totale)	Total (thousands) Total (milliers)	Female labour (% of total labour force) Main-d'œuvre féminine (en % de la main-d'œuvre totale)	Total (thousands) Total (milliers)	Female labour (% of total agriculture labour force) Main-d'œuvre féminine (en % de la main-d'œuvre totale dans l'agriculture)
		(1)	(2)	(3)	(4)	(5)	(6)
Ukraine	2000	48 892	67.1	23 259	49.2	3 295	33.0
	2010	45 448	68.8	22 999	49.3	2 412	27.4
	2011	45 190	69.0	22 946	49.4	2 334	26.9
USSR - URSS	1990	289 067	65.4	141 840	47.8	27 557	39.6
Uzbekistan - Ouzbékistan	2000	24 776	37.4	9 243	40.6	2 624	45.5
	2010	27 445	36.7	11 780	39.8	2 705	43.5
	2011	27 760	36.7	12 041	39.7	2 695	43.2
Developed economies: America - Économies développées : Amérique	**1990**	**284 794**	**75.8**	**144 627**	**44.6**	**4 263**	**22.6**
	2000	**317 212**	**80.7**	**163 523**	**45.8**	**3 515**	**25.8**
	2010	**348 387**	**84.1**	**176 863**	**46.2**	**2 867**	**28.9**
	2011	**351 418**	**84.4**	**178 381**	**46.2**	**2 806**	**29.2**
Bermuda - Bermudes	1990	60	100.0	..	..	1	..
	2000	63	100.0	..	..	1	..
	2010	65	100.0	..	..	1	..
	2011	65	100.0	..	..	1	..
Canada	1990	27 701	76.6	14 669	44.1	495	32.1
	2000	30 667	79.5	16 206	45.7	382	41.9
	2010	34 017	80.3	18 930	47.1	332	52.4
	2011	34 350	80.4	19 122	47.1	326	53.7
Greenland - Groenland	1990	56	79.7	..	..	1	..
	2000	56	81.6	..	..	1	..
	2010	57	84.2	..	..	..	..
	2011	57	84.5	..	..	..	..
Saint Pierre and Miquelon - Saint-Pierre-et-Miquelon	1990	6	89.0	..	..	..	..
	2000	6	89.2	..	..	..	..
	2010	6	90.5	..	..	..	..
	2011	6	90.6	..	..	..	..
United States - États-Unis	1990	256 971	75.7	129 958	44.7	3 766	21.3
	2000	286 419	80.8	147 317	45.8	3 131	23.9
	2010	314 242	84.5	157 933	46.1	2 534	25.8
	2011	316 940	84.8	159 259	46.1	2 479	26.0
Developed economies: Asia - Économies développées : Asie	**1990**	**126 751**	**64.5**	**64 860**	**40.7**	**4 678**	**46.2**
	2000	**131 735**	**66.9**	**69 349**	**40.8**	**2 773**	**42.3**
	2010	**133 954**	**68.4**	**69 284**	**42.6**	**1 469**	**39.7**
	2011	**134 059**	**68.5**	**69 102**	**42.6**	**1 375**	**39.5**
Israel - Israël	1990	4 500	90.6	1 603	40.4	65	21.5
	2000	6 015	92.5	2 343	45.8	61	23.0
	2010	7 418	90.2	3 094	47.1	51	21.6
	2011	7 562	89.9	3 150	47.1	50	22.0
Japan - Japon	1990	122 251	63.6	63 257	40.7	4 613	46.5
	2000	125 720	65.7	67 006	40.6	2 712	42.7
	2010	126 536	67.1	66 190	42.4	1 418	40.3
	2011	126 497	67.2	65 952	42.4	1 325	40.2
Developed economies: Europe - Économies développées : Europe	**1990**	**473 983**	**70.7**	**217 474**	**41.6**	**20 978**	**40.8**
	2000	**495 327**	**71.7**	**232 496**	**43.8**	**15 285**	**39.3**
	2010	**515 461**	**73.7**	**250 149**	**45.1**	**10 981**	**37.5**
	2011	**517 023**	**73.9**	**250 960**	**45.2**	**10 619**	**37.4**
Andorra - Andorre	1990	53	94.7	..	..	3	33.3
	2000	65	94.9	..	..	2	50.0
	2010	85	89.9	..	..	2	50.0
	2011	86	89.4	..	..	2	50.0
Austria - Autriche	1990	7 671	65.8	3 524	40.9	274	47.1
	2000	8 005	65.8	3 860	43.5	199	46.7
	2010	8 394	67.5	4 337	45.9	144	45.8
	2011	8 413	67.7	4 352	45.9	139	46.0

For sources and notes, see end of table.

Pour les sources et les notes, se reporter à la fin du tableau.

Region, country or territory / Régions, pays ou territoires	Year / Année	Population		Total labour force / Main-d'œuvre totale		Agriculture labour force / Main-d'œuvre dans l'agriculture	
		Total (thousands) / Total (milliers)	Urban population (% of total population) / Population urbaine (en % de la population totale)	Total (thousands) / Total (milliers)	Female labour (% of total labour force) / Main-d'œuvre féminine (en % de la main-d'œuvre totale)	Total (thousands) / Total (milliers)	Female labour (% of total agriculture labour force) / Main-d'œuvre féminine (en % de la main-d'œuvre totale dans l'agriculture)
		(1)	(2)	(3)	(4)	(5)	(6)
Belgium - Belgique	1990	9 949	96.2	3 924	39.0	..	..
	2000	10 176	97.3	4 402	43.0	79	29.1
	2010	10 712	97.3	4 810	45.3	59	32.2
	2011	10 754	97.3	4 824	45.4	57	31.6
Bulgaria - Bulgarie	1990	8 819	66.4	4 128	47.9	572	47.0
	2000	8 006	68.9	3 535	47.1	228	37.7
	2010	7 494	71.5	3 491	46.8	124	30.6
	2011	7 446	71.8	3 474	46.8	115	30.4
Cyprus - Chypre (10)	1990	579	78.4	344	38.1	50	42.0
	2000	694	77.9	445	40.7	38	42.1
	2010	809	76.4	584	43.6	30	36.7
	2011	804	77.9	594	43.5	29	37.9
Czechoslovakia - Tchécoslovaquie	1990	15 573	68.8	7 467	45.2	985	36.8
Czech Republic - République tchèque	2000	10 243	73.9	5 155	44.4	431	29.0
	2010	10 493	73.0	5 277	43.3	327	23.2
	2011	10 534	73.0	5 303	43.4	318	22.6
Denmark - Danemark	1990	5 141	84.8	2 912	46.1	162	24.1
	2000	5 340	85.0	2 863	46.6	108	24.1
	2010	5 550	85.8	2 941	47.1	75	24.0
	2011	5 573	85.8	2 946	47.1	72	25.0
Estonia - Estonie	2000	1 371	69.4	657	48.7	76	30.3
	2010	1 341	69.4	699	50.4	61	26.2
	2011	1 341	69.5	700	50.3	60	26.7
Faeroe Islands - Îles Féroé	1990	48	30.5	..	..	1	..
	2000	46	36.2	..	..	1	..
	2010	49	41.5	..	..	1	..
	2011	49	41.7	..	..	1	..
Finland - Finlande	1990	4 986	79.4	2 615	47.1	218	35.3
	2000	5 173	82.2	2 613	47.4	143	35.0
	2010	5 365	84.8	2 696	47.8	98	35.7
	2011	5 385	85.0	2 696	47.8	94	35.1
France	1990	58 214	74.5	25 094	43.3	1 414	34.8
	2000	60 799	77.4	26 474	45.5	913	34.2
	2010	64 767	85.3	28 918	47.1	598	32.9
	2011	65 124	85.8	29 003	47.1	570	32.8
Germany - Allemagne	1990	79 098	73.4	37 155	40.7	1 557	41.7
	2000	82 349	72.8	40 445	43.7	1 016	39.7
	2010	82 302	73.6	42 465	45.6	661	36.9
	2011	82 163	73.8	42 390	45.6	632	36.6
Gibraltar	1990	27	100.0	..	..	2	50.0
	2000	27	100.0	..	..	1	..
	2010	29	100.0	..	..	1	..
	2011	29	100.0	..	..	1	..
Greece - Grèce	1990	10 161	58.8	4 185	36.1	963	45.4
	2000	10 987	59.5	4 897	39.2	826	49.6
	2010	11 359	60.5	5 293	41.5	637	52.7
	2011	11 390	60.7	5 320	41.7	617	52.8
Holy See - Saint-Siège	1990	1	100.0	..	..	..	..
	2000	1	100.0	..	..	..	..
	2010	0	100.0	..	..	..	..
	2011	0	100.0	..	..	..	..
Hungary - Hongrie	1990	10 376	65.8	4 540	44.5	701	31.0
	2000	10 211	64.6	4 178	44.7	452	26.3
	2010	9 984	68.0	4 312	46.0	322	22.7
	2011	9 966	68.4	4 308	46.0	310	22.3

For sources and notes, see end of table.

Pour les sources et les notes, se reporter à la fin du tableau.

8

Region, country or territory / Régions, pays ou territoires	Year / Année	Population		Total labour force Main-d'œuvre totale		Agriculture labour force Main-d'œuvre dans l'agriculture	
		Total (thousands) Total (milliers)	Urban population (% of total population) Population urbaine (en % de la population totale)	Total (thousands) Total (milliers)	Female labour (% of total labour force) Main-d'œuvre féminine (en % de la main-d'œuvre totale)	Total (thousands) Total (milliers)	Female labour (% of total agriculture labour force) Main-d'œuvre féminine (en % de la main-d'œuvre totale dans l'agriculture)
		(1)	(2)	(3)	(4)	(5)	(6)
Iceland - Islande	1990	255	90.8	143	45.4	15	20.0
	2000	281	92.3	166	46.8	13	15.4
	2010	320	96.1	189	47.3	12	16.7
	2011	324	96.6	192	47.3	11	18.2
Ireland - Irlande	1990	3 531	56.6	1 360	34.2	186	8.1
	2000	3 804	59.1	1 757	40.6	166	8.4
	2010	4 470	63.6	2 124	43.7	149	7.4
	2011	4 526	64.1	2 151	43.7	146	7.5
Italy - Italie	1990	56 832	66.9	23 830	36.4	2 068	38.9
	2000	56 986	67.4	23 312	38.6	1 250	40.9
	2010	60 551	67.8	25 151	40.3	845	45.0
	2011	60 789	68.0	25 282	40.3	809	45.5
Latvia - Lettonie	2000	2 385	67.7	1 095	48.1	132	31.8
	2010	2 252	67.4	1 163	50.0	113	25.7
	2011	2 243	67.3	1 169	49.9	111	24.3
Lithuania - Lituanie	2000	3 500	67.0	1 685	49.5	204	28.9
	2010	3 324	65.6	1 648	50.3	126	23.0
	2011	3 307	65.5	1 651	50.2	121	22.3
Luxembourg	1990	381	81.1	160	34.7	..	..
	2000	435	84.0	189	39.7	4	25.0
	2010	507	82.6	238	43.4	3	33.3
	2011	516	82.3	243	43.6	3	33.3
Malta - Malte	1990	368	88.6	143	26.7	3	..
	2000	397	90.4	159	30.4	3	..
	2010	417	93.2	181	34.7	2	..
	2011	418	93.4	182	34.9	2	..
Netherlands - Pays-Bas	1990	14 892	69.0	6 860	38.9	314	28.7
	2000	15 863	77.1	8 131	43.1	269	33.1
	2010	16 613	83.1	8 860	45.7	213	36.6
	2011	16 665	83.5	8 894	45.7	208	36.5
Norway - Norvège	1990	4 241	72.0	2 169	44.6	139	27.3
	2000	4 491	76.0	2 376	46.4	110	33.6
	2010	4 883	79.0	2 613	46.9	88	39.8
	2011	4 925	79.3	2 640	47.0	87	40.2
Poland - Pologne	1990	38 056	61.4	18 069	45.5	4 956	45.5
	2000	38 302	61.9	17 302	45.8	3 763	41.3
	2010	38 277	60.6	18 230	45.1	2 960	36.2
	2011	38 299	60.4	18 237	45.1	2 884	35.7
Portugal	1990	9 925	48.2	4 782	42.8	857	50.6
	2000	10 336	53.8	5 277	45.4	678	58.0
	2010	10 676	61.0	5 614	47.4	515	63.7
	2011	10 690	61.7	5 637	47.4	507	64.9
Romania - Roumanie	1990	23 207	53.2	10 529	44.7	2 603	53.7
	2000	22 192	52.9	11 704	46.6	1 739	48.8
	2010	21 486	56.7	10 208	44.7	868	43.3
	2011	21 436	57.1	10 256	44.8	821	42.8
San Marino - Saint-Marin	1990	24	90.5	..	..	1	100.0
	2000	27	93.4	..	..	1	..
	2010	32	94.1	..	..	1	..
	2011	32	94.1	..	..	1	..
Slovakia - Slovaquie	2000	5 405	56.0	2 598	45.6	240	28.3
	2010	5 462	54.5	2 742	44.6	197	21.8
	2011	5 472	54.4	2 759	44.7	193	21.2

For sources and notes, see end of table.

Pour les sources et les notes, se reporter à la fin du tableau.

Region, country or territory / Régions, pays ou territoires	Year / Année	Population		Total labour force / Main-d'œuvre totale		Agriculture labour force / Main-d'œuvre dans l'agriculture	
		Total (thousands) Total (milliers) (1)	Urban population (% of total population) Population urbaine (en % de la population totale) (2)	Total (thousands) Total (milliers) (3)	Female labour (% of total labour force) Main-d'œuvre féminine (en % de la main-d'œuvre totale) (4)	Total (thousands) Total (milliers) (5)	Female labour (% of total agriculture labour force) Main-d'œuvre féminine (en % de la main-d'œuvre totale dans l'agriculture) (6)
Slovenia - Slovénie	2000	1 985	50.8	960	46.3	19	47.4
	2010	2 030	49.4	1 031	46.4	7	42.9
	2011	2 035	49.3	1 031	46.4	6	50.0
Spain - Espagne	1990	38 889	75.3	15 825	34.4	1 890	30.3
	2000	40 288	76.2	18 209	39.5	1 339	34.8
	2010	46 077	76.1	23 235	44.3	1 015	37.6
	2011	46 455	76.3	23 395	44.3	975	37.8
Sweden - Suède	1990	8 559	83.1	4 687	47.7	209	28.7
	2000	8 860	84.0	4 545	47.1	146	31.5
	2010	9 380	83.9	4 990	47.0	115	35.7
	2011	9 441	83.8	5 019	47.0	112	36.6
Switzerland - Suisse	1990	6 703	73.4	3 756	42.8	196	31.1
	2000	7 201	73.2	3 990	44.3	167	38.3
	2010	7 700	72.7	4 404	45.8	137	43.1
	2011	7 738	72.7	4 419	45.9	136	44.1
United Kingdom - Royaume-Uni	1990	57 425	78.0	29 273	43.3	639	20.3
	2000	59 096	78.5	29 517	45.0	529	22.9
	2010	62 272	79.3	31 707	45.9	475	24.8
	2011	62 655	79.4	31 889	46.0	469	25.2
Developed economies: Oceania - Économies développées : Océanie	**1990**	**20 494**	**85.2**	**10 166**	**41.6**	**641**	**29.3**
	2000	**23 022**	**87.0**	**11 562**	**44.0**	**617**	**35.7**
	2010	**26 637**	**85.9**	**14 172**	**45.5**	**643**	**41.8**
	2011	**27 020**	**85.7**	**14 364**	**45.6**	**645**	**42.5**
Australia - Australie	1990	17 096	85.4	8 505	41.3	470	28.9
	2000	19 164	87.2	9 631	43.8	442	36.7
	2010	22 268	86.1	11 822	45.3	457	44.6
	2011	22 606	85.8	11 987	45.4	458	45.4
New Zealand - Nouvelle-Zélande	1990	3 398	84.4	1 660	43.2	171	30.4
	2000	3 858	85.9	1 932	45.2	175	33.1
	2010	4 368	84.9	2 350	46.8	186	34.9
	2011	4 415	84.8	2 376	46.8	187	35.3

Sources:
- UN DESA Population Division, *World Population Prospects: The 2010 Revision*
- UN DESA Population Division, *World Urbanisation Prospects: The 2009 Revision*
- ILO, *LABORSTA*
- FAO, *FAOSTAT*
- Other national sources

Notes:
- Labour force data are derived from activity rates that were based on population estimates and projections of *World Population Prospects: The 2010 Revision*

(1) Total population: de facto population in a country, area or region as of 1 July of the year indicated. Figures are presented in thousands.
(2) Urban population as percentage of total population: population living in areas classified as urban according to the criteria used by each area or country. Data refer to 1st July of the year indicated.
(3) Total labour force: comprises all persons (both sexes) of age 15 and above.
(4) Female labour force as percentage of total labour force: comprises all persons of feminine sex of age 15 and above.
(5) Total labour force in agriculture: is that part (male and female) of the total labour force engaged in or seeking work agriculture, hunting, fishing or forestry.
(6) Female labour force as percentage of total agriculture labour force: is that part (female) of the total labour force engaged or seeking work in agriculture, hunting, fishing or forestry.
(7) Agriculture labour force: includes Hong Kong, Macao and Taiwan; Total labour force: includes Taiwan only.
(8) From 1961, excluding Taiwan.
(9) National source.
(10) Population data refer to Republic of Cyprus and labour data refer to Cyprus Island.

Sources :
- ONU DAES Division de la population, *Perspectives de la population mondiale : La révision de 2010*
- ONU DAES Division de la population, *Perspectives de l'urbanisation mondiale : La révision de 2009*
- BIT, *LABORSTA*
- FAO, *FAOSTAT*
- Autres sources nationales

Notes :
- Les données de la main-d'œuvre sont dérivées des taux d'activité qui sont basés sur des estimations et projections du *Perspectives de la population mondiale : La révision de 2010*

(1) Population totale : de facto la population dans un pays ou région au 1er juillet de l'année indiquée. Les chiffres sont présentés en milliers.
(2) Population urbaine en pourcentage de la population totale : la population au 1er juillet vivant dans une région classée comme urbaine selon les critères définis par une région ou un pays.
(3) Main-d'œuvre totale : toutes les personnes (hommes et femmes) de 15 ans et plus.
(4) Main-d'œuvre féminine en pourcentage de la main d'œuvre totale : toutes les personnes de sexe féminin de 15 ans et plus.
(5) Main-d'œuvre totale dans l'agriculture : la part (hommes et femmes) du total de la main-d'œuvre qui travaille ou cherche du travail dans l'agriculture, la chasse, la pêche ou la sylviculture.
(6) Main-d'œuvre totale féminine en pourcentage du total de la main-d'œuvre dans l'agriculture : la part (femmes) du total de la main-d'œuvre qui travaille ou cherche du travail dans l'agriculture, la chasse, la pêche ou la sylviculture.
(7) La main-d'œuvre agricole inclut Hong Kong, Macao et Taiwan. La main-d'œuvre totale inclut uniquement Taiwan.
(8) Taiwan est exclu à partir de 1961.
(9) Source nationale.
(10) Les données de la population se réfèrent à la République de Chypre et les données de la main-d'œuvre se réfèrent à l'île de Chypre.

8

Economic grouping Groupements économiques	Year Année	Population		Total labour force Main-d'œuvre totale		Agriculture labour force Main-d'œuvre agricole	
		Total (thousands) Total (milliers) (1)	Urban population (% of total population) Population urbaine (en % de la population totale) (2)	Total (thousands) Total (milliers) (3)	Female labour (% of total labour force) Main-d'œuvre féminine (en % de la main-d'œuvre totale) (4)	Total (thousands) Total (milliers) (5)	Female labour (% of total agriculture labour force) Main-d'œuvre féminine (en % de la main-d'œuvre agricole totale) (6)
DEVELOPING ECONOMIES - **ÉCONOMIES EN DÉVELOPPEMENT**	**1990**	**4 064 787**	**34.5**	**1 768 280**	**37.9**	**1 086 867**	**41.7**
	2000	**4 828 134**	**39.9**	**2 159 799**	**38.5**	**1 192 669**	**42.3**
	2010	**5 545 091**	**45.2**	**2 566 384**	**38.4**	**1 272 876**	**42.9**
	2011	**5 640 963**	**45.5**	**2 609 521**	**38.4**	**1 278 647**	**42.9**
Developing economies excluding China - Économies en développement sans la Chine	1990	2 939 871	37.4	1 119 207	34.0	604 360	37.3
	2000	3 581 201	41.1	1 431 670	35.1	687 820	38.2
	2010	4 226 897	44.3	1 764 796	35.5	771 899	39.5
	2011	4 293 397	44.6	1 802 380	35.6	779 877	39.7
Developing economies excluding LDCs - Économies en développement sans les PMA	1990	3 555 424	36.4	1 558 285	37.1	927 692	40.9
	2000	4 166 967	42.2	1 883 339	37.7	997 256	41.3
	2010	4 712 762	48.0	2 200 196	37.3	1 034 113	41.4
	2011	4 789 863	48.2	2 233 125	37.3	1 035 348	41.4
High-income developing economies - Économies en développement à revenu élevé	1990	334 545	68.2	123 601	31.4	29 799	29.2
	2000	391 935	73.3	154 660	32.9	27 192	28.0
	2010	451 983	75.6	193 460	34.3	23 983	28.2
	2011	457 724	75.7	197 222	34.4	23 628	28.3
Middle-income developing economies - Économies en développement à revenu intermédiaire	1990	1 763 763	37.2	884 015	41.6	567 818	44.9
	2000	2 004 830	45.1	1 033 202	42.3	592 965	45.7
	2010	2 187 840	54.3	1 177 417	42.3	589 582	46.1
	2011	2 227 645	54.5	1 190 246	42.3	586 959	46.1
Low-income developing economies - Économies en développement à revenu faible	1990	1 966 167	26.4	760 595	34.7	489 208	38.8
	2000	2 430 904	30.1	971 828	35.2	572 459	39.4
	2010	2 904 534	33.7	1 195 288	35.1	659 229	40.5
	2011	2 954 835	34.1	1 221 825	35.2	667 976	40.6
Heavily indebted poor countries (IMF) - Pays pauvres très endettés (FMI)	1990	364 193	24.9	143 551	43.8	109 172	46.4
	2000	487 999	28.5	195 498	44.5	139 657	47.0
	2010	632 739	32.8	263 341	44.9	175 108	47.9
	2011	649 121	33.3	271 274	44.9	179 095	48.0
Landlocked developing countries - Pays en développement sans littoral	1990	198 187	18.2	81 990	44.6	63 218	44.8
	2000	331 296	26.0	137 856	44.6	88 243	45.6
	2010	410 363	28.0	181 313	45.0	112 445	46.6
	2011	419 472	28.2	186 365	45.0	115 068	46.6
Small island developing States - Petits États insulaires en développement	1990	12 711	29.9	4 989	41.9	2 414	44.1
	2000	15 028	30.0	6 169	43.0	2 779	46.7
	2010	18 607	30.0	7 890	43.5	3 552	48.6
	2011	18 882	30.1	8 047	43.6	3 614	48.8
Least developed countries - *Pays les moins avancés*	*1990*	*509 364*	*21.6*	*209 995*	*43.9*	*159 175*	*46.6*
	2000	*661 166*	*25.2*	*276 460*	*43.8*	*195 413*	*47.3*
	2010	*832 330*	*29.9*	*366 188*	*44.4*	*238 763*	*49.0*
	2011	*851 099*	*30.4*	*376 396*	*44.5*	*243 299*	*49.1*
Africa and Haiti - Afrique et Haïti	1990	305 243	22.3	123 134	45.6	98 008	47.9
	2000	401 734	26.0	163 721	46.2	125 036	48.7
	2010	526 091	30.4	222 638	46.4	158 978	49.5
	2011	540 128	30.8	229 446	46.4	162 764	49.6
Asia - Asie	1990	202 869	20.5	86 464	41.5	60 853	44.4
	2000	257 865	24.0	112 209	40.3	69 994	44.8
	2010	303 144	29.2	142 514	41.4	78 960	48.0
	2011	307 806	29.7	145 885	41.5	79 688	48.2
Islands - Îles (7)	1990	1 252	24.5	397	34.5	314	45.9
	2000	1 567	26.5	530	35.1	383	46.7
	2010	3 095	28.2	1 035	34.9	825	46.8
	2011	3 165	28.6	1 065	35.0	847	46.8

For sources and notes, see end of table.
Pour les sources et les notes, se reporter à la fin du tableau.